W9-CRE-165

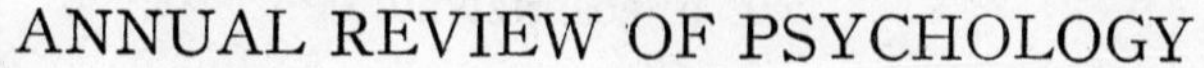

ANNUAL REVIEW OF PSYCHOLOGY

ANNUAL REVIEW OF PSYCHOLOGY

PAUL H. MUSSEN, *Editor*
University of California, Berkeley

MARK R. ROSENZWEIG, *Editor*
University of California, Berkeley

VOLUME 21

1970

ANNUAL REVIEWS, INC.
PALO ALTO, CALIFORNIA

ANNUAL REVIEWS, INC.
PALO ALTO, CALIFORNIA, U.S.A.

Standard Book Number 8243–0221–4

Library of Congress Catalog Card Number: 50–13143

FOREIGN AGENCY

Maruzen Company, Limited
6, Tori-Nichome Nihonbashi
Tokyo

PRINTED AND BOUND IN THE UNITED STATES OF AMERICA BY
GEORGE BANTA COMPANY, INC.

PREFACE

The authors of the 16 chapters included in the present volume have faced even greater problems of review and selection of literature than have authors of chapters in past years. The annual increase in the number and variety of articles in each major area of psychology is enormous. The master plan of the *Annual Review of Psychology* still calls for yearly representation of relatively broad fields of psychology—e.g., learning, developmental, personality, psychotherapeutic processes, vision—as well as less frequent treatment of some more specialized fields. The editors and the editorial committee feel that their most important task is to choose highly competent authorities in each area and then give them considerable latitude (but a limited number of pages) in handling their review.

More and more frequently, however, authors assigned a broad area feel that they can cover only a particular subarea within it. Such restrictions are reflected in the titles of certain chapters in the present volume. For example, instead of attempting to cover the general area of animal learning, Bitterman and Schoel chose to focus on instrumental learning and especially on parameters of reinforcement. Analogously, Shapiro and Schwartz restricted their review of social psychology to interesting new work in the psychophysiological aspects of social behavior. In other cases a broad title is used, but the author makes clear at the outset the specialized nature of his chapter. For example, Rosner devotes his chapter on brain functions to a review of the variables that affect restoration of function after damage to the central nervous system.

Annual Review authors must not only cover the literature in the area but also make wise judgments about which aspects of the field are of greatest current importance and advancement. In a real sense, they are not only reporting but also evaluating major trends and progress in their fields. A reader may feel that in any one volume a field is only partially represented, or is represented in a somewhat one-sided manner. But our goal is to reflect all major fields, trends, and points of view over a period of years. The editorial committee and editors are always happy to have comments from readers on coverage and treatment, and such communications are considered at our annual meetings.

In view of the problems facing *Annual Review* authors, it is understandable that there are occasional deferrals and defaults of chapters. Some of the chapters in the present volume had originally been scheduled for earlier publication. The chapter on audition, originally planned for this volume, has been deferred to the next. Unfortunately, the following chapters, announced for this volume, will not appear: cognitive functions, engineering psychology, industrial relations, and mathematical models of learning.

With the close of 1969, Dr. Marvin Dunnette completed his five-year term of membership on the editorial committee. Throughout this period he has given us wise counsel over a wide range of topics and fields. Professor Lyman Porter has accepted the board's invitation to fill this position for the next term. Miss Jean Heavener, as assistant editor, continues to be a full collaborator in all aspects of organizing and producing this series. We also wish to thank Mrs. Dorothy Read for preparing the accurate and detailed subject index.

P.H.M.
M.R.R.

CONTENTS

ERRATA

Volume 20

P. 165, line 31, beginning "Thus Bryden ......" *should read:*
Thus Bryden (62) reported an increase in accuracy of report as tachistoscopic exposure duration increased from 20 to 120 msec, while Raymond & Glanzer (308) found an increase in the number of stimuli reported as a function of increasing exposure times from 15 to 1500 msec.

P. 181, Ref. 62 *should read:*
Bryden, M. P. Accuracy and order of report in tachistoscopic recognition. *Can. J. Psychol.*, **20,** 262–72 (1966)

P. 199, line 16, beginning "Spectral sensitivity ......" *should read:*
Spectral sensitivity measurements on a variety of ganglion-cell types revealed only red-sensitive ($\lambda_{max} \approx 625$ nm) and green-sensitive ($\lambda_{max} \approx 525$ nm) units: the absence of blue-sensitive units is attributed to paucity of blue-sensitive cones in the goldfish retina (149).

P. 207, line 38, beginning "Jameson & Hurvich ......" *should read:*
Jameson & Hurvich (114) stress that the apparent colors of foveal test fields are affected by the color of the relatively minute fixation dots.

P. 447, line 14: *for* consist *read* consists.

P. 461, line 10: *for* independent variable *read* dependent variable.

P. 461, line 31; *for* Supples & Zinnes *read* Suppes & Zinnes.

A WORD ABOUT REPRINTS

The reader may be puzzled by the conspicuous number (144 to 159) aligned in the margin with the title of each review in this volume. The number is a key for use in the ordering of reprints. These are priced uniformly at $0.95 each, postpaid. Payment must accompany the order if the purchase totals less than $10.00. All payments are to be made to Annual Reviews, Inc. in U.S. dollars. California orders are subject to 5 per cent sales tax. Delivery in the U.S.A. will require approximately two to six weeks.

Reprints at $0.95 each are available from the *Annual Review of Biochemistry* as well as the *Annual Review of Psychology* (since 1961 for both Reviews) and from the *Annual Review of Microbiology* and the *Annual Review of Physiology* starting with the 1968 volumes.

The sale of reprints of articles published in the *Reviews* has been initiated in the belief that reprints as individual copies, as sets covering stated topics, and in quantity for classroom use will have a special appeal to students and teachers.

Annual Reviews, Inc., and the Editors of its publications assume no responsibility for the statements expressed by the contributors to this *Review*.

TOPICS AND AUTHORS
ANNUAL REVIEW OF PSYCHOLOGY
VOLUME 22 (1971)

AUDITION, *David H. Raab*

BASIC DRIVES, *Frank Finger*

BEHAVIOR GENETICS, *Gardner Lindzey*

CLASSIFICATION OF BEHAVIOR DISORDERS, *Leslie Phillips and Juris Draguns*

DEVELOPMENTAL PSYCHOLOGY, *Willard Hartup and Albert Yonas*

MASS COMMUNICATION, *Walter Weiss*

MOTOR LEARNING, *E. R. F. W. Crossman*

PERCEPTION, *Herbert L. Pick, Jr. and Sarah M. Ryan*

PERSONALITY, *Irwin G. Sarason and Ronald E. Smith*

PERSONNEL DEVELOPMENT AND TRAINING, *John P. Campbell*

PHARMACOLOGY OF LEARNING AND MEMORY, *Murray E. Jarvik and Larry Squire*

PSYCHOLINGUISTICS, *Samuel Fillenbaum*

PSYCHOTHERAPY: BEHAVIOR THERAPY, *Leonard Krasner*

SPATIAL VISION, *P. O. Bishop and G. H. Henry*

STATISTICAL THEORY (BEHAVIORAL SCIENCE APPLICATION), *Murray A. Aitkin*

STUDENT DEVELOPMENT AND COUNSELING, *Wilbur L. Layton*

TEST THEORY, *R. Darrell Bock*

PERSONALITY

BY W. GRANT DAHLSTROM
University of North Carolina, Chapel Hill, North Carolina

INTRODUCTION

Busy and productive as psychologists have been this year, the interval is too short to expect much change in the characteristics of their endeavors in the field of personality described vividly by Adelson (2) in this series last year: abundance, diffuseness, and diversity. While applauding the abundance, Adelson felt that the pay-off from this volume of effort was inexcusably low, seemingly lacking any clear focus or steady convergence of effort. Our research was seen to be centrifugal, rapidly expanding into ever-new regions of empirical exploration with new technology outrunning theory, and theory failing to articulate with accumulating empirical data. In addition, in Adelson's view, personological research showed over-inclusiveness, paying too little attention to the enduring dispositions that are the proper domain of personologists while attending unduly to transient states in the subjects under study. After delineating the major symptoms of this disorder that he discerned in the field, Adelson offered both a diagnostic appraisal and a prescription. He felt that we were in the midst of a methodological crisis arising from the poor habits of inquiry and inference pandemic among personologists. In choice of tools and in sampling of subjects, we have been controlled more by pragmatic considerations of availability and expediency than by appropriateness for the problem, more by the need for quick publication and rapid professional advancement than by the desire for deep and penetrating understanding of the phenomena, more by the convenience of the laboratory than by the challenge of the naturalistic field study. In so doing, Adelson also feels we have been naive, stifled, and often even unethical in the way we have conducted our personality investigations. Warnings from Rosenthal (289) and from Orne (271) about experimenter biases or situational constraints upon the behavior of our subjects in the laboratory have largely been ignored, as he sees it, further vitiating the meaning of experimental findings already weakened by unrepresentative sampling unduly restricted to college undergraduate populations. We must cure these habits or be doomed to triviality and must move from the laboratory to fields of real human interactions. We must tackle these problems with innovative methods and instruments better suited to these tasks. While the present reviewer cannot refute the impression of "sprawl and diversity" [Sanford (296)] generated by reading through another year of personological research, it will be clear from what follows that he does not concur in the conclusions drawn by Adelson about the extent of pathology, his formulation of the etiology, or our prognosis under the various suggested remedies.

CENTRAL CONCEPTS

Some large part of the sprawl and diversity in our field of which Adelson and Sanford complain, but by no means the major component of this variance, can be attributed to fundamental differences in the definition of personality. Rather than methodological ineptitude or negligence, the central problem for personologists at this stage in the development of our field seems to be lack of any consensus in conceptualization. Perhaps as a result of bullying and ragging by hard-headed psychonomists, personologists all too often have accepted the dictum that if you cannot directly see and point to your variables you have no legitimate field of study. The many recent volumes on personality which serve as introductory texts (4, 34, 66, 147, 164, 173, 196, 208, 214, 219, 241, 252, 258, 277, 282, 298, 299, 313), which provide resumes of present theories of personality (232, 234, 248, 259, 266, 293, 294), or which focus upon methodological problems in personality research (250, 280, 310, 352) show a startling diversity in definitions of personality, each with its characteristic variables and methods of study. With great good fortune, however, this seems to be the year of the handbooks (39, 56, 140, 205) devoted exclusively or in large part to personological theories, methodological issues, and research findings. Undoubtedly, these volumes are appearing now as a partial solution to the problem facing anyone who conscientiously tries to read and digest the staggering outpouring of research reports in the area of personality stemming from the high level of research support and from the growth of the journals covering these topics. Nevertheless, they also provide a timely summing up and thinking through of the pervasive implications linked inextricably to these various formulations of human personality. The organization of this chapter will focus upon these different formulations. No extensive exegesis on the way the term "personality" is currently being construed [cf. Hallett (151)] in our theoretical and research literature has been attempted, but some of the implications of these various broad definitions may be made clearer in the following presentation.

A few definitions of personality have logical or conceptual flaws in them. For example, some side-step the issue, apparently to satisfy a demand for ostensive definitions. Thus, Sarason (298) states, "We shall consider personality as an area of investigation rather than as an entity, real or hypothetical" (298, p. 15). While such a definition makes it easy to point to the definienda ("I am studying what the personologist over there is doing"), it obviously leaves the central definition itself unformulated. It is little help to shift the emphasis to the investigator and to the fact that he must make abstractions and introduce constructs to account for the phenomena in his domain; the abstractions and constructs themselves are derived from and bear upon phenomena which constitute the legitimate basis for the definienda of this area of study. Similar logical problems seem to plague the definitions which equate personality with social stimulus value or with a person's total response repertoire.

Personality as social stimulus value.—Burnham (47), in an excellent historical reconstruction of the conceptual antecedents of our present-day definitions and concepts of personality, deals explicitly with the limitations in those approaches to personality based upon the impact one individual (A) has upon another (B). There is an infinite regress built into this form of definition in trying to explain the impact. Logically, pursuit of personality characteristics of person A leads more to a determination of why person B reacts to A in the particular way; suddenly the question enters all over again—why does B behave in these characteristic ways—except we have the personality of B under scrutiny rather than A. The fallacy lies in examining the reactions of B, C, or D to discern basic personological features of A. Taken to its logical extreme, the social stimulus value definitions of personality require endless catalogs of all possible aspects of person A to which some aspect of the behavior of persons B, C, etc. could become attached. The diffuseness that is inherent in such a listing, for example, is clearly demonstrated in the material included in a lengthy review of this research by Marlowe & Gergen (239). Despite gallant efforts to impose some order on this array of research, these reviewers labor in a lost cause.

Further insight into the inherent difficulties in trying to discern lawfulness within a domain of personality based upon a social stimulus value formulation comes this year from a study by Rosenberg, Nelson & Vivekanathan (288). Carrying out various multidimensional scaling efforts on the co-occurrences that they found among sets of descriptors which people employed in describing their acquaintances, these investigators appear to have found once again the pervasive dimensions of Osgood: evaluation, potency, and activity. In their impact upon others, of course, people have meaning; the dimensionality of this meaning structure can be decomposed into the Osgood framework. Does this signify, then, that any given individual can simply be characterized as active to x extent, powerful to y extent, and bad to z extent, and have this serve as an adequate reconstruction of his personality? It seems unlikely. A similar difficulty enters the approach used by Triandis, Vassiliou & Nassiakou (329) to study differences in "subjective culture." They found dimensions of affect, intimacy, dominance, and hostility which were generated factor analytically from sets of perceptions of roles, of specific behaviors, and of significant figures recorded by American and Greek subjects. As an approach to "national character" or "modal personality" of particular cultures, this method seems too inextricably bound to folk psychological structures and person perceptions to provide a satisfactory way of schematizing how people raised in different cultures develop personological processes to resolve universal psychological problems. In sharp contrast, résumés by Child (60), Clausen (64), De Vos & Hippler (94), Inkeles & Levinson (168), Izard (169), and Kramer (192) all seem to give more insightful presentations of the processes of mutuality in interaction that generate modal personality systems. It is also noteworthy in the chapter of Marlowe & Gergen (239) that when they take up material relating to mutual interaction effects and the phenomena generated by dyadic or higher order social nexuses, orderliness can be readily discerned. They are by then dealing with social psychological phenomena rather than primarily personological issues and thus a whole new order of laws.

It is precisely at this juncture that another important divergence in personality conceptions occurs. For some personologists, the essence of personality is in the interplay of person and social environment. McCurdy states this position well: "I find it convenient to separate 'person' from 'personality.' A human person is that psychophysical compound which is capable of establishing emotional relations with objects, sensed, imagined, and conceived. Personality is the actual existence of these relations" (219, p. 580). This definition considers personality to be a product of particular interactions and not a phenomenon discernible in the absence of these components in active transaction [cf. Marlowe & Gergen (239)]. This year, Carson (53) has presented this position with clarity, force, and cogency. He has skillfully integrated research findings from the general personolgical literature and from relevant psychopathological and psychotherapeutic studies into his sociopsychological formulations.

Personality as the total response repertoire.—By polemics, by fiat, or by prestidigitation, many writers are also attempting to define away personality. By such maneuvers, for example, this chapter on personality research would become either co-extensive with all of the remaining content of this review series or totally irrelevant to any of the traditional areas of psychological theory and research. Among the other efforts of this sort, perhaps Peterson's ploy is the most dramatic:

> An ostensive definition of the relevant theory (for a useful personality framework) can be given very simply. With one hand pick up a good introductory textbook in general psychology. With the other hand pick up a good introductory textbook in general sociology. Hold both books aloft and say, 'Here are the concepts we need.' (280, p. 67).

Several features of this approach to personality study are captured in this epitome: First, pressures for an ostensive definition are often paramount; since all behavior is personality, one can directly point to personality. Second, no special constructs, no special methods, and no special theories are needed since personality is merely the subset of a person's repertoire that happens to show temporal endurance. Third, this approach carries the implication that close examination of these enduring aspects of any person's behavior will reveal them to be the behavioral reflections of stable patterns of environmental reinforcements. Thus, personality is a will-o'-the-wisp; proper attention, in concept and in "personality assessment" [cf. Mischel (252)] alike, must be shifted to the sources of stimulus configurations and reinforcement patterns in the individual's life situation. Langer (194) calls this formulation the "mechanical mirror theory."

Such definitions of human personality seem particularly attractive to sociologists [cf. Moore (253)] and to psychologists who have concentrated upon children in their own research programs [e.g., Bandura (13), Mischel (252), or Peterson (280)]. Similar treatment of personality can be found in the publications of behavior modification or behavior therapy advocates. For example, Ayllon & Azrin (10), through careful paring of the data being gathered and a narrowing of their observational framework, effectively dispense with individual differences appearing in the impact of token economy programs upon wards of diverse psychiatric patients. That is, data on such variables as choice of work detail or number of hours worked are plotted and shown to be virtually independent of psychiatric status, but we are given little or no glimmering [illegible]equency of stealing of tokens from other patients, different patter[illegible]ger and resentment to the deprivation manipulations, or the way that [illegible]ent aspects of the ward economy system become incorporated into these patients' long-standing delusional systems. While traditional psychiatric status variables may not be helpful in predicting such individual differences, it seems misleading to report the data in such ways as to suggest that such differences do not in fact emerge.

This move to equate personality with all behavior is well suited to the research style and ecological formulations of Barker (19, 20) and his associates (352). His method has been most readily adapted to work with children, but even with a child in the course of one ordinary day, the hemerographic transcription of "total behavior" generates an astounding data base. The thought of such detailed tallies from hundreds of subjects over sizable stretches of their biographical spans would give pause to even the most dedicated behavioral atomist. Records of behavioral runs of this sort call for conceptualizations to impose some economy and theories to impose some order.

The formulations of personality based upon dimensionalized traits (discussed in the next section) have been the particular targets of these polemics from the total repertoire positions, but the strong implication in these arguments is that there is no personal stability to behavior, no matter how it is conceptualized or depicted. As Craik (78) has noted, the large body of empirically established correlates of our personality scales seems to be consistently ignored in these arguments. As will be discussed later in considering Langer's *Theories of Development* (194), even the highly touted malleability of children's behavior has probably been greatly exaggerated and misconstrued by exponents of the social behavior view of personality. It is no help in this difficult problem of how to conceptualize personality structure simply to eliminate structural manifestations by verbal legerdemain.

An important consequence of this negativistic approach to personological constructs is that in their place one must substitute identifiable aspects of the sociopsychological culture. Take, for example, an individual's birth order, sibling rank, or ordinal position in his sibship. Many studies this year (6, 61, 67, 87, 138, 156, 157, 216, 262, 283, 285, 286, 300, 311, 319, 322, 327, 361, 365) have been devoted to elucidating the various correlates of a person's position within his family context and its associated stimulus patterns and reinforcement contingencies. That is, in many of these reports, sibling rank has been advanced as a personological variable. For this use, sibling status has serious drawbacks, lacking as it does any univocal personological implications [cf. Datta (87)]. In fact, Meehl (245) has described a complex nexus of interconnections which he and Lykken found among "congeries of 45 miscellaneous variables such as sex, birth order, religious preference, number of siblings, vocational choice, club membership, college choice, mother's education, dancing, interest in woodworking, liking for school and the like." (245, p. 109). Such data were available to them on a sample of over 50,000 high school seniors. Taking the associations among these variables a pair at a time, they found 91 per cent of these correlations were stable and different from zero at a significant level, statistically. Meehl then points out at length the methodological implications which such findings have for personologists. Over a period of time, individual subjects come to bind the effects of these cultural variables into different configurations. Accordingly, our research designs cannot simply be based upon these psychosocial classifications (by levels or treatments) which can only be extricated one from the other conceptually, but by classifications of subjects meaningfully homogeneous in personality configuration.

Although it was not included in the list from Meehl's paper, it is also to be hoped that racial or ethnic classification (27, 30, 33, 44, 52, 93, 96, 119, 120, 144, 153, 159, 184, 188, 287, 312, 332, 334, 344) can soon be decomposed in our personological studies of the future into directly relevant personality variables like self-esteem, particular values of motivations or attitudes, identifications, or affiliations. While a constellation of personological variables are associated with ethnic status [cf. Baughman & Dahlstrom (27); Deutsch, Katz & Jensen (93); Dreger & Miller (96)], little in the way of dependable personality meaning is conveyed by any socioethnic designation per se. A similar resolution of the role of such variables as family structure [cf. Toman (327)] [e.g., father absence (27, 33, 257)], socioeconomic status, religious affiliation, geographic region, or cultural membership may be anticipated. Even age (141) and sex membership [cf. Garai & Scheinfeld (124)] may also be decomposable into the relevant personological variables. If so, then these diverse membership designations can be dropped from personality depictions and so may, along with other sociopsychological variables, serve in their rightful place as descriptors of the situation within which the personality system is found to be interacting. As Block (36) has pointed out, these situational variations help greatly to clarify apparent inconsistencies in personality manifestations. They should not, however, be confused with the variables in the personality domain itself.

Differential approach to personality.—The unidimensional, homogeneous psychological trait has come to serve as the core concept in the definition of personality that rests upon salient individual differences. Guilford put it succinctly a decade ago: "It is in individual differences . . . that we find the logical key to personality. . . . An individual's personality . . . is his unique pattern of traits. . . . A trait is any distinguishable, relatively enduring way in which one individual differs from others" (147, pp. 5–6). This approach has been extended and developed in great detail by many investigators [cf. Horst (164)], but particularly by Cattell and his associates. This year this large body of research has been organized and synthesized into a coherent and considerably more manageable presentation in several chapters included by Cattell (56). Originally derived from a descriptive framework, the resulting dimensions of differences have by now been given construct status and are utilized to summarize large numbers of observations and, in combination with situational specifications, to predict specific acts or behavioral sequences. In the present form of Cattell's (56) framework, this reconstruction of the intrapsychic structure includes role specifications, state levels, and setting factors, in addition to a set of fixed traits. While these adumbrations may serve to offset somewhat the most telling criticisms of trait formulation raised by writers this year [e.g., Peterson (280); Mischel (252)], these additional constructs are also employed within a basically linear and additive formulation of their mode of combination. However, as Goldberg (132, 134) has convincingly demonstrated, with the limits of precision of present-day measuring instruments and criterion specifications, it is nearly impossible to discern any pragmatic differences between simple linear approximations and the more elegant systems of data combination. He also voices strong pessimism of the likelihood that future theories or instruments will change this circumstance appreciably.

Emmerich (105), in a thoughtful and searching comparison of three different personality formulations and the ways in which they each treat development of personality structure, contrasts the differential approach (such as Guilford's or Cattell's) with classical views of development of personality organization through fixed stages (such as Freud's or Piaget's) and with the ipsative constructions based upon intra-individual scaling of attributes and unique configurations of these characteristics (as represented by Allport or Murphy). In Emmerich's view, these different formulations have taken as their point of departure rather different personological issues, usually employing different kinds of research subjects as well, but they carry important implications for a common set of developmental problems. In the area of personality structure, for example, one central concern in the differential approach is the question of equivalence of a trait identified at a given age level with designations of that trait in younger or older research subjects. In Cattell's research program, two monographs this year have been directed to this question and to the related issues, arising from the necessary shift in composition of the test battery, of instrument-bound factors and errors. Hundleby & Cattell (166) studied sixth-graders with a battery made up primarily of objective performance tests of both ability and personality rather than the usual verbal scales upon which Cattell's factor framework was originally developed. They felt that they were able to equate 8 of the 17 sources of variance found among their 69 variables with adult counterparts, plus 4 more tagged tentatively. At the preschool level, studying children from nurseries, kindergartens, and summer camps, Damarin & Cattell (86) found 18 first-order factors among their 93 variables of which 5 met their criteria for equivalence to adult dimensions. Four additional ones were identified with some reservations. They drew encouragement for the worth of this approach from the fact that, among the factors identified at both age levels, there were four in common: will, anxiety, superego, and neurotic debility. Nevertheless, specific characteristics of the test administration and the testing instruments required by the age levels of these subjects entered into these analyses to an important extent. Cattell's solutions to these plaguing problems have been to seek order at the level of second-order, or higher, factors and to carry out cross-cultural comparisons (56).

These studies actually deal only with the issue of invariance of the structural variables over age levels as raised by Emmerich (105); other important issues that he discussed are the patterning among these variables, the sequences appearing in changes of these patterns, and the way in which individuality is to be represented within each conceptual framework. Emmerich felt that the differential model has not yet dealt satisfactorily with these challenges from developmental investigations.

As Goldberg (133) has pointed out, in general, our personological research efforts based upon dimensional analyses have not been tied into the organized framework of Guilford, Eysenck (109), or Cattell. We do not yet have data gathered systematically enough to permit an adequate appraisal of the full potentiality of these trait taxonomies. Only recently have even the studies of the empirical relations among Cattell's batteries, MMPI-based indices, Eysenck's scales, or Guilford's measures been initiated [Cattell & Bolton (57); Cattell & Gibbons (59); Hundleby & Connor (167)]. Instead, most personality research is devoted to the elucidation of rather separate, often individually developed and scaled, measures of personality dimensions. Nor are these scales typically tied into coherent formulations or particular theories. Thus, this year we have studies based upon Byrne's repression-sensitization measure (31, 65, 98, 100, 114, 182, 281, 335, 346), Rotter's locus of control of reinforcements scale (165, 172, 179, 180, 203, 206, 221, 243, 278, 306), Witkin's (357) field-independence indices (primarily the rod-frame and embedded figures measures) (100, 146, 276, 305, 315, 337, 356). Personality research based upon Taylor's manifest anxiety scale and its derivatives (141, 162, 174–176, 183, 213, 307, 314, 315, 345) also continues to grow, along with studies of traditional level of aspiration measures (83, 89, 181, 237), dogmatism (88, 261, 328, 334), and need for approval measures (80, 95, 101, 184, 203, 309, 333). Imagine how much more powerful the convergence would be if, through all of this flow of research reports, some one common battery of personality measures, no matter how badly conceived or executed, had always been included and reported upon in addition to the chosen criterion instruments! Instead, there continue to appear new, autonomous efforts to measure and evaluate dimensions like Machiavellianism (39, 62, 362), future time perspective (49, 74, 110, 198, 236, 283, 316), or impulsivity (1, 88, 89, 185, 186). Even when the measures are derived from some common instrument, such as the MMPI-based Taylor or Byrne scales mentioned above, the tendency is to take the items of the scales from their original item pools and administer them separately, thus vitiating even that chance to collate and integrate findings from different investigators.

There is by now a predictable pattern to this kind of research development. The usual sequence that these single-dimensional research approaches follow goes something like this: subjects high and low are contrasted on some index or indices of behavior resulting in stable separations but with great overlap; subjects showing exceptions to the general trend are examined and found either to be misplaced by measurement errors from the crudeness of the scale or to be demonstrating criterion contaminations from other sources of variance; further efforts then turn backward upon the instrument or diverge to introduce new dimensions in a growing lattice of intersecting dimensions, hopefully orthogonal. In either of the latter eventualities, a multitrait, multimethod matrix, as suggested by Campbell & Fiske (51) may then be constructed to hone the scale or disentangle the growing number of dimensions. In contrast to this round of research effort, Cattell's general personological framework is offered as a ready-made solution, with its multidimensional batteries of scales (not necessarily orthogonal) already on hand to serve personality investigators. There is another strategy altogether, of course, in which one moves to a parallel development of some theory about the personality processes under study along with the scale development. This approach is described below in a discussion of recent work on achievement motivation and need scales in general. The difference between these research strategies is primarily in the concern that the latter approach gives to the interconnections and resulting interactions among the variables that are abstracted in contrast to the latticework of "dimensions" with which the former concludes.

As this reviewer has pointed out (85), an approach to personality starting from the behavioral phenomena that are uniformly characteristic of individuals and that clearly differentiate such individuals from others (the individual difference approach) is unlikely to end up with dynamic personality processes. Rather, it is destined to center upon control and stabilizing features of an individual's personality. It is a challenge to any personality formulation to account for such stable individual differences as represented in the factors or dimensions in the schemata of Cattell, Guilford, or Horst, but these traits are actually more like parameter settings in a complex, dynamic system than they are component variables in such a system.

PERSONALITY AS A DYNAMIC SYSTEM

Baughman & Welsh (28) give a succinct definition of personality that conceives of it as a separate entity with component parts in interaction:

> Thus, we arrive at the conclusion that personality is a complex hypothetical construct. It is a hypothetical construct because we develop it—from behavioral observations, of course. It is complex because we assume that it is composed of lesser units—traits, or needs, or id, ego, and superego, and so on. A major task for personality science is to determine those constructs that are most useful in explaining and predicting observable behavior (28, p. 31).

This year, several contributions have appeared which elaborate upon this common formulation of personality as a relatively autonomous, increasingly differentiated system of variables [Allport (4, 5); Gochman (131); Loehlin (208); Milsum (251); Murray (256)]. In the material in Milsum's (251) collection of papers, the special characteristics of complex systems with both negative and positive feedback interconnections become clear; not only is stability in the face of widely varying environmental inputs typical, but growth, alteration, and increased internal complexity is possible and likely. In view of this last feature, it is natural to look to developmental studies of personality to gain insight into the nature of these systems as they evolve.

Development of personality systems.—Unfortunately, these research endeavors are still plagued by methodological and conceptual problems. Escalona (108) presents a detailed and insightful discussion of these difficulties in her report this year of efforts to trace the development of individuality during the first 8 months of life in normal infants. After a great deal of work, she has tentatively identified recurring configurations of developmental "structures" appearing in infants' reactivity to various kinds of stimulation, typical levels of arousal, and kinds of balance they achieve amongst competing sources of stimulation—constellations which she terms stable patterns of experience (SPE). Her data help correct and extend the notions of ego functions as a stimulus barrier that were carefully integrated by Martin (240) this year. Escalona has also shown that these different SPE's reflect important differences in capability of managing environmental inputs at very early age levels; some of these differences are likely to have important implications for later adaptational success or failure [see also Bronson (45); Flynn (118); Thomas, Chess & Birch (325)].

A careful effort to delineate and then integrate the major current theories of behavioral development by Langer (194) this year may help clarify the conceptual difficulties with which Escalona and other investigators of early personality manifestations have had to struggle. In Langer's view there are three fundamentally different formulations of development, each with its different concepts and explanatory hypotheses. The first one that he treats is the "mechanical mirror" model alluded to above. This theory posits in the biological equipment of a person only the requisite reflexes needed to "ensure that he will acquire and reflect the content inherent in the environmental agents that stimulate and shape his behavior. Change occurs only in the quantity of behavioral content (impressions, associations, and responses) that the person acquires in the course of life . . ." (194, p. 159). Langer concludes that as a complete model of behavioral development the mechanical mirror formulation is inadequate; while accounting for the content, it does little to explain the organization of an individual's experience.

A second formulation that he takes up is the psychoanalytic model of development. Langer sees this model as positing "biologically rooted functions (that) are the organizing forces that differentiate and relate inborn structures into increasingly complex organizations, subject to the nature of the individual's particular history of interaction with his environment" (194, p. 161). Thus, from the very beginning organization is present and, through the predicted changes in instinctual energies and their attachments, is destined to follow a particular maturational sequence. In this sequence, motivational variations are controlling. Langer sees drawbacks to this model in that rational processes are presumed to evolve somehow from irrational processes (id) only under environmental pressures.

A third general model that Langer takes up, which he terms the "organic lamp theory," places a special emphasis upon an individual's own actions as the determiner of development and differentiation.

> Man develops many ways of acting in his lifetime, however. The most primitive ways are the child's sensorimotor acts, which range from purely pragmatic movements to symbolic gestures and images. But these acts already include more than the unconditioned and conditioned behaviors that mechanical mirror theory usually assumes to constitute the totality of psychological acts. The most advanced means of psychological acting are mental operations, which range from egocentric intuitions to self-conscious thinking about one's own actions, thoughts, feelings, attitudes, and so forth, in relationship to those of others (194, p. 160).

The emphasis in the organic lamp model is upon the distinction between form and content in an individual's experience. The form is seen as a resultant of the person's own actions, while the specific content is influenced by his interactions with his environment. The forms are to be understood in terms of the stage of development a person has reached. Many experiences with the environment may not be integrated or incorporated if at the time he has not reached the required stage of organization of his perceptual and cognitive processes. The most important limitation of this organic lamp model in Langer's view seems to be its lack of specification of the generative "rules" whereby the direction of development can be determined from characteristics of a person at some earlier stage: what new forms will emerge? What transformations will take place?

Langer ends with a synthesis of these various theories of development in which the forms of behavioral organization are viewed as a joint product of maturational processes and self-shaping efforts by the person himself; within these evolving forms, the content of experience is shaped through the individual's interactions with his specific environment; and changes in the person's development can be conceived of as involving pathologically retrogressive alterations as well as the generally progressive developmental ones. Thus, Langer opens up the developmental model for the elaboration of psychogenetic processes underlying maturation [cf. Loehlin (209); Thoday & Parkes (324)]; the elaboration of perceptual and cognitive processes into stable systems [Witkin (356); Gardner & Moriarty (125); Gough (142, 143); Goldschmid (136); Kohlberg (190); Marks (238)]; the evolution and impact of self-perceiving and self-evaluative processes [Aronfreed (7); Bannister & Mair (14); Coopersmith (68); deCharms (92); Erikson (107); Fisher (117); Gorsuch & Cattell (139); Rousey & Holzman (292); Winter et al. (355); Wylie (358)]; and the growth of styles of expression like sex-roles [Mussen (257)] or adaptational patterns [Lazarus (196); Phillips (282)] or creativity [Barron (22); Stein (317)].

All of these subsystems serve to stabilize the personality system internally as well as in relation to the environment. Among personologists who concur on the level of abstraction represented by this definitional approach, there is yet little agreement about the most economical and workable set of constructs to be employed to delineate the dynamic variables. An adequate construct set [Dahlstrom (85] will likely include a specification of the dynamic state variables in the system, the nature of the mechanisms exerting control over these state variables, the parametric settings by means of which the control processes come into play and operate, as well as the consequences of any defects in the operation of these controls. Personological theories differ greatly in the best way to conceive of the basic variables making up personality processes. In addition, we are still quite primitive and clumsy in our efforts to trace out the basic connections among any subset of these variables through testing of the step-functions linking them. Our methods of studying the full system in its elaborate interconnection in any one social setting also are limited. Yet each kind of procedure in this analysis of personality systems has been vigorously pursued this year.

Our fundamental dynamic variables in a personality system are generally characterized as motivations, but except for the common term covering these conceptions, there appears to be little consensus yet about these variables. Madsen (234) has provided a real service for the field by bringing together in brief, manageable epitomes the different ways in which motivations are formulated and articulated in most of the major behavioral and personological theories currently under active investigation. As a result of his efforts, it is easier to compare and contrast alternative interpretations of common sets of observations and experiments. It is also easier to discern where and when operational definitions enter this variable-abstracting and theory-building endeavor to maximize clarity and minimize ambiguities. Such defining operations, however, are only one kind of definitional maneuver. Within the context of the individual theories, many other procedures are equally necessary and equally powerful [cf. Madsen (235); Rychlak (293)].

Characteristics of individual personality systems.—In the section above, conceptualizations of what can be appropriately included in a description of the components of a personality system were discussed as they have been considered in the personological literature this year. Even if this endeavor were much more fully developed and work was much advanced, these analytic approaches would still not deal adequately with the problem posed by Emmerich (105) about how best to delineate a particular individual within this kind of framework. The solution to this problem still eludes us. For example, Allport (4) advanced such notions as "generic formations" or "complex integrative generic attitudes" by means of which the life pattern of a particular person could be epitomized. The key concept seems to be generic, focussing upon the concept of class membership. What seems called for is some schema of taxonomy or typology [Dahlstrom (85); Tiryakian (326)]. The traditional types have been virtually abandoned with few conceptualizations appearing as yet to take their place in providing a basis for research systematization, sampling delineations, or individual specifications.

Some taxonomic efforts are now being pursued along two related lines: (*a*) developmental stages or sequences by means of which a person is typified as showing a personality organization characteristic of some stage or other; and (*b*) mature personological configurations which summarize the recognizable ways that personalities can differ in basic organization. Advances along both lines appeared this year which can materially accelerate the elaboration of the requisite taxonomy for both personological systematics and individual typifications.

Smith (313) has elaborated the stage-sequential formulation of ego development presented by Loevinger (210) into his framework for systematic personality description. Although unaccountably leaving out one of Loevinger's stages, he has utilized this set of stages to conceptualize the findings from MacKinnon's classic studies (223, 224) of creativity demonstrated by practicing architects; to articulate both Erikson's (107) and Maslow's (241) formulations; to integrate various defense mechanisms into the characterological features of each stage; and even to tie in several forms of psychopathology and therapy that relate to personality organization at these different levels. Smith documents the fact that personality styles appearing at various stages in Loevinger's schema can be used as means of describing individuals when they reach or remain at these various stages.

Several thoughtful writers have speculated upon such long-range patterns of personality development, usually focussing on crucial developmental challenges or environmental demands which the person must inevitably encounter in his development [Bühler & Massarik (46); Erikson (107); Frankenstein (119); Lidz (204); Maslow (241); Otto (272); and Perlman (277)]. Few of these writers have had access to the necessary empirical data to try out their projected formulations on the same subjects from childhood well into adulthood. It is noteworthy, however, that personology is now starting to get the benefits from the pioneering work of Jones (177),

Macfarlane (220), Bayley (29), and Terman (269). Thanks to their industry, insights, and imagination, as well as to the dedication of their followers and proteges, hard data about the patterns of personality elaboration which men and women in general actually manifest over these crucial years are being published.

Some of the most penetrating analyses of these personality data come from the work of Block (37) based upon two of the three growth study populations that were studied over the last 35 years in the San Francisco Bay Area: the Oakland study of Jones (177) and the Guidance study of Macfarlane (220). Organizing the data from tests, ratings, and measurements in these longitudinal files by means of independent sets of Q-sort judgments at the junior high school, senior high school, and adult age periods, Block carried out cluster searches for recurring personality configurations. One result of this person-oriented rather than variable-oriented approach was the emergence of five identifiable developmental routes to mature personality status for men, and six, generally different, routes for women. Not all of these routes of personality development uniformly diverge; some individuals who come to resemble each other to an appreciable extent arrive at this adult personality status by remarkably different stages. In other words, there is sufficient evidence within Block's elaborate delineations of these patterns to question whether a single universal sequence of personality maturational stages can be discerned in the diversity of human nature. If not, perhaps the best taxonomic system for personality structures will eventually be a combination of different developmental sequences, each further qualified by indicating the stage reached along that pathway.

Not all of Block's subjects were assignable to these different "developmental ways"; some had to be assigned to a residual group. The schema is then an open one, awaiting further elaboration and clarification. Hopefully, other longitudinal files around the country at Stanford, Fels, Harvard, Merrill-Palmer, and elsewhere will soon be explored in the same imaginative manner to help fill the long-felt gap in our knowledge and terminology of personality development and organization. It is to be hoped that additional instances of Block's *ego resilients, cognitive copers,* or *nonintraceptors* will be located to strengthen the already strong case that he makes for these patterns, and that the identification of new patterns will rescue some of his other cases from the limbo of assignment to residual categories. A taxonomy of clearly differentiated personality patterns along the lines which Block has been working on will offer a high pay-off for future research efforts in personology. How many patterns will suffice? We have reason to believe their number is larger than the first power of 10; will it exceed the second? the third?

The investigations by Block are only part of the research dividends that our field is getting from the Bay Area growth studies. Adding this year to her husband's earlier work is the set of analyses Mary Cover Jones (178) has made of the antecedents of different drinking patterns appearing in these men and women [cf. also Gomberg 137); Sanford (297)]. Occupational patterns and social mobility have been reported by Elder (104) within these sets of data. These individuals seem destined to become some of psychology's best-known subjects, along with Terman's bright youngsters (269), less intelligent perhaps but more modal and more easily recognized in their resemblance to our friends and neighbors.

In this work, Block has also demonstrated again for us the utility of the Q-sort for comparisons across time. This method has been further developed for even younger ages by Schachter, Cooper & Gordet (301), based upon a common set of items to be used at younger levels and retained at higher age levels, with new items to be added as they become relevant to the age and population under investigation. With these features, the Q-sort methods offer a distinct advantage over conventional rating procedures for developmental work [cf. Barnard, Zimbardo & Sarason (21); Baughman & Dahlstrom (27)].

The method of type-finding exemplified by Block, however, is in sharp contrast to the methods advanced by workers using more conventional multivariate analytic techniques. The psychometric strategy usually involves the identification of basic dimensions [Horst (164)] or scalable attributes [Norman (267)], generating sets of intercorrelations among these attributes or dimensions on some reference population, and searching for some underlying order in the resulting factor structure or scaled common dimensions. The resulting multidimensional grid is considered to be the taxonomic lattice which one requires for personological systematizing. Recent innovations by Cattell (55), McQuitty (230), Norman (268), and Lorr (212) have shifted the emphasis, however, to similarities among sets of attributes manifested by individuals rather than sets of covariations among attributes. In addition, Meehl (246) has elaborated this year upon a method that he advanced (244) for searching for latent taxa through a procedure he and Dawes (90) called "mixed group validation." Although it employs correlational or covariance values, the observed attributes are expected to be uncorrelated within classes, and the observed correlational values themselves serve as indices of the heterogeneity resulting from the successive groupings being tried. The new, simpler procedure, based upon single attributes rather than correlations of pairs of attributes, offers considerable promise (247) in this type-search problem.

THE STUDY OF PERSONALITY SYSTEMS

For some personologists, the careful delineation of a functional relationship between gradations of manipulation A and alterations in observed values of variable X constitutes the primary objective of personality research. For others, the covariations between changes in A and X are viewed as the concern of basic research workers, and the only personological issues are those that arise from the complications in the relation of A and X introduced by other variables or parameters, Y or Z, k or l. In the combinatorial laws and the new phenomena generated by their patterned contributions to basic processes, personological problems are presumably introduced. If personality is conceived to be a complex, dynamically interactive system, then both views are correct. Polemics aside, both of these kinds of interest and investigation are necessary variations on step-function analysis and testing of the system under study. From this point of view, neither of these research strategies is sufficient by itself, nor sufficient even in combination. Step-function testing must be augmented by studies of the fully integrated and functioning system in connection with environmental variables, both input and output. Study of the operation of the fully connected system may be profitably investigated in environments where the situational variations are drastically restricted, or in environments where the impacts of the separate actions and reactions are allowed to accumulate and divergent processes set in. For many personologists, only in this last research context do they find the phenomena which for them constitute human personality processes. In other words, the preferences of particular investigators seem to dictate not only the degree of abstraction of their variables, the form of the conceptualization of their basic observations, but the level at which they prefer to intercede with manipulations or the mode of observation of these processes that they consider to be most enlightening. The field is fortunate, perhaps, to have an abundance of personologists of all persuasions whose joint efforts and cumulative findings will eventually give us the full understanding at all levels that we seek.

Step-function testing of connections.—It is a constant challenge to the skill and insightfulness of personality experimenters to devise ways of testing the lower order relationships obtaining between basic variables in a system when the whole system is in operation. Yet, as indicated earlier, such manipulative operations are seen by many experimentally oriented investigators as a crucial part of the basic steps in defining their variables. At the present stage of our knowledge, and within the limitations of manipulations permitted by the ethics of humane research on human subjects, the problems of carrying out simple step-functional studies of these relationships in human personality systems are almost insurmountable. Some of these general problems have received attention in the literature this year. A discussion of these issues will be followed by an examination of some current developments in this kind of research.

One of the central problems in step-function testing is circumvention of the regulatory controls over variables in the system or over behavioral output. These controls involve different forms of negative feedback, serving to maintain system stability within limits [Milsum (251)]. In efforts to manipulate the level of some variable under such control, one of the most frequently encountered phenomena is the Law of Initial Value. That is, under feedback control, any manipulation A directed toward raising values of variable X may have the anticipated effect only if the initial value of X is below some critical value, say k. At any initial value of k, the value of X

will not further increase under manipulation *A* but will show a paradoxical decrease. This year, Wilder (351) has summarized findings from many different fields demonstrating this phenomenon. Only if the control mechanism can in some way be disconnected can the full range of the effect of manipulation *A* upon variable *X* be plotted.

A second general problem in conducting step-function analyses with human subjects is that the manipulations of the experimenter may lose their effectiveness or undergo alterations in their impact through adaptation over successive exposures. As the frequency range is increased in any of these studies of habituation or adaptation, the point at which specific training enters as a complication of the response measure is also a persistent concern. The phenomena both of temporal adaptation and of longer-range learning seem to be general properties of systems with positive feedback connections [cf. Milsum (251)].

Zajonc (359), employing such stimuli as nonsense syllables, Chinese-like characters, or photographs of human faces, has concluded that exposure of stimuli to research subjects generates increasingly positive affective reactions to them merely as a function of increasing frequency of encounter. Maddi (231) and Jacobovits (171) have both critically evaluated the evidence for both the accuracy and the generality of such an effect of "mere exposure" over wider ranges of exposure frequency and an array of different stimulus objects. Hare (152) plotted habituation to novel stimuli observed in autonomic recordings from groups of psychopathic and nonpsychopathic prisoners. Although he found differences between these groups in initial reactivity for the stimuli that he employed, they followed similar habituation curves over successive exposures. Katkin & McCubbin (183) contrasted high and low anxious subjects selected on Taylor MAS (Manifest Anxiety Scale) and high and low autonomically labile subjects chosen on the basis of spontaneous GSR's (galvanic skin responses) during rest on habituation to auditory stimuli. Differences on MAS were not predictive of habituation course, but autonomically stabile and labile subjects differed consistently to moderate level auditory signals. The role of defensive and orienting reactions were invoked to account for these differences.

Verinis, Brandsma & Cofer (336) explored an additional complication that is introduced by unexpected departures, positive or negative in direction, from an adaptation level once established. Trying to test the motivational properties of such shifts, these investigators found relatively little support for the "butterfly function" that was posited by McClelland (218) and associates. According to their view, a generally positive emotional reaction may be expected from research subjects to small discrepancies from a given level of adaptation, no matter which direction this shift from the adaptational level may take. Large discrepancies, however, are expected to yield negatively toned reactions. Verinis, Brandsma & Cofer found the resulting affective changes to be a complicated function of the shift from adaptational level and the subject's expectations, results more in line with recent formulations of Atkinson [cf. Atkinson & Feather (9)].

A third general problem arising in step-function studies in human personality stems from the lack of precision in impact of the manipulations we employ. A given effort to raise anxiety level, for example, may simultaneously induce frustrations, so the resulting behavior is a manifestation of anxiety and some expression of the resulting aggressive impulses as well. Many of our interventions can have even more pervasive or general repercussions. These ramifications are a growing concern in all experimental studies of humans, but have been particularly a matter of empirical research by experimental social psychologists [Brehm (42); deCharms (92); Freedman & Doob (120); Korman (191); Petersen & Hergenhahn (279); Zimbardo (362)].

Probably the most widely discussed at this time is the experimenter bias effect written up systematically by Rosenthal (289). This year, Barber and his associates (18) and Wessler & Strauss (349) have published the results they obtained from a series of studies attempting to duplicate and document the magnitude of unconscious experimenter determination of experimental outcomes originally reported by Rosenthal in one situational context (student experimenters running other students in a rating study). Their negative findings raise doubts about the pervasiveness of this biasing effect. In a series of exchanges in the journals (15–17, 290, 291), perhaps some additional focus has been achieved: are such biases more likely to arise from poor management of the experimental session by naive experimenters who thereby inadvertently convey special cues affecting outcomes, or from prestigious experimenters with high stakes in particular experimental outcomes who influence behaviors by imposing various constraints? If the experimenter bias effect does turn out to be primarily a variation on the demand characteristics of the situation [Orne (271)], one contributed by the personal needs of the experimenter himself, the phenomenon can perhaps be better accommodated within the growing body of evidence on suggestion and hypnotic effects.

A further complication in human experimentation has been highlighted by Freedman & Doob (120) in their efforts to appraise the consequences of a subject's perception of the fact that he is deviant. To the extent to which a particular manipulation by the experimenter serves to generate such a perception in his subjects, the various reactions they noted—such as affiliative movement, aggression, concern over mistreatment, or other attitude changes—must be taken into account in the analysis of results. Also, deCharms (92) has spelled out the importance in such settings of the subject's perception of whether he is the originator of some of the crucial changes himself or whether he feels that he is merely a pawn among all these various forces.

It should also be noted in any discussion of the general problems arising from experimental manipulations of human behavior in a highly controlled setting—those conditions necessary from the standpoint of meticulous step-function testing—that the seeming importance of habituation, adaptation, reactance, originship, or demand characteristics may be more of an index of the weakness of our manipulations than a real gauge of the role such processes will play in the research efforts of the future. To anticipate a little the discussion below on anxiety arousal procedures, note how ineffectual the manipulations of anxiety level by stressors available to investigators in the psychological laboratory appear to be, compared to the alterations in anxiety levels studied by Epstein (106) in parachute-jumping activities; by Radloff & Helmreich (284) in divers in deep sea submergence in Sealab II; by Drew, Moriarty & Shapiro (97) or by Tsushima (331) in patients facing surgery; or by Zucker, Manosevitz & Lanyon (365), who capitalized upon the stress-inducing effects of a natural disaster—the New York power blackout—to trace reactions to levels of induced anxiety. Do these various effects of being a research subject in a psychology laboratory essentially wash out when the manipulation is actually an effective and important one? Certainly the results reported by Masters & Johnson (242) on the effects of various sexually arousing stimuli upon the physiological and behavioral variables that they included in their laboratory-based investigations of the human sexual response would suggest that this is the case [cf. Brecher & Brecher (41)]. Their systematic research could serve as a prototype of step-function testing. The results of these studies do not constitute anything like a full delineation of spontaneous sexual behavior in a natural psychosexual context [cf. Farber (111)], but these investigators have shown that their methods of study can overcome a number of constraints included in any laboratory situation—instrumentation, inhibitions from being observed and recorded, loss of intimacy, and, for some subjects, even the absence of meaningful interpersonal context. Undoubtedly, some of this effectiveness can be attributed to the power of the stimuli employed and the strength of the drive under study.

These investigators also dealt explicitly with the possible limitations in generality of their results arising from the selection of research subjects for the pioneering phase of this controversial research. It is likely, for example, that these subjects were freer of sexual inhibitions and sexual guilt reactions than would be true in the general population. Is this the reason that none of the women studied were able to bring about orgasm solely by imaginative processes, contrary to expectations from experiences women reported in the Kinsey studies?

Our experimentation to carry out step-function testing could profit from a careful theoretical development of the psychological processes invoked in experimentation upon humans which was called for by Levy (202) in a thoughtful and insightful commentary upon the exchanges between Barber and Rosenthal alluded to above. In his remarks, Levy was concerned with the problems of getting clean replications in our experimental studies and the way we often seem to waste our research efforts in replications which fail to cumulate into a general understanding of the psychology of the experimental situation. Our difficulties in gaining reproducibility reflect not only the lack of comprehension of what such transactions may involve but also the fact that we cannot readily communicate from one worker to another the crucial attributes of the personality systems that we had under study in particular experiments. Greater consistency in findings could be assured by selecting subjects more homogeneous in personality organization, in modes of defense or susceptability to various influences, and in reactivity to experimental apparatus and procedures [cf. Moos (254)].

One of Adelson's (2) contentions about current personological laboratory studies was that we tended to stick too exclusively to college sophomore samples for this kind of work. A similar concern was voiced by Lockard (207) this year about the traditional reliance in basic psychological research upon the albino rat. Contrary to the interpretation of both Adelson and Lockard, it seems quite likely that this kind of concentration has not been blind restriction to some sterile cul-de-sac on the part of personologists or psychonomists but the only rational way to proceed to try to get reproduceable results in an enterprise as complex as we have all undertaken. Lacking either genetic controls or even a schema for describing crucial subject attributes, the relative uniformity of personality status and organization appearing among college undergraduates has been vital to our efforts to get some degree of replication in our exploratory work. As the college population becomes increasingly heterogeneous in succeeding generations of students, the precision of our typifications will have to increase severalfold if we are going to be able to convey our results from one research context to another.

One last point in this discussion of step-function testing: the ubiquity of control mechanisms and compensatory processes in human reactions puts investigators in this area on their mettle. Research workers are constantly on the alert for ways in which these feedback systems can be disconnected or circumvented. Sometimes this result can be accomplished by innocuous means [reversible drug effects (353); suggestion or hypnosis (211); or dissociations under prolonged sensory isolation (363, 364)], or they can capitalize upon naturally occurring and normal states, like sleep (54), or conditions produced by pathological processes, such as a congenital absence of pain or various special states (320). The more that we are able to integrate findings from various pathological phenomena into our basic formulations of personological processes, the more we will be in a position to take advantage of variations in retardation conditions, psychotic reactions, or other adaptational deviations to study the processes that these alterations leave undefended.

The findings from the literature in which step-function analyses were attempted in experimental studies of personality indicate that to be effective in modifying the state variables the manipulations must be tailored to the subjects under study. Thus, even stressors that have been taken over from standard physiological procedures, such as electric shock, are considerably enhanced when labeled in terms of discomfort rather than specifically pain

[Blitz & Dinnerstein (35)], or when perceived as beyond the subject's own control [Bowers (40)]. Similar increases could be gained by proper introductions of other standard stressors like heat (211) or extreme cold (115).

Standard stress films have also been employed in laboratories to induce desired anxiety states [cf. Lazarus (196)]. Two experimental versions of one of these films depicting three bad sawmill accidents were monitored in a study by Nomikos and his associates (265) to determine whether the shock value of the accident scene would be enhanced by signaling ahead of time in the film that such an eventuality was coming. The other film introduced the first two accidents as surprises without warning. As it turned out, the physiological effects demonstrated by the subjects during the showings were almost all attributable to the anticipation; the effects of the accident scenes seemed less distressing. Suspense and build-up rather than traumatic impacts seem to be the more effective manipulations. Perhaps this enhancement is attributable to vicarious, self-engendered anxiety arousal [Craig (73); Grossberg & Wilson (145)]. Such self-arousing processes apparently produce appreciable psychophysiological alterations and are now a mainstay in desensitization efforts carried out by behavior therapists [cf. Bandura & Menlove (12)]. A complication of the opposite sort that may enter studies of anxiety induction that are monitored psychophysiologically was pointed up by an intriguing study by Dean, Martin & Streiner (91). They were able to train subjects in their laboratory to control their own GSR reactivity. That is, after training they could inhibit the appearance of a GSR but seemed unable to produce them upon demand. This finding has important implications for standard lie detection practices as well.

Further evidence on the desirability of tailoring the procedures to the subjects being used comes from the work of Weiss, Katkin & Rubin (347), which was also based upon a film presentation to induce anxiety. After carrying out a factor analysis upon the items in a general fear survey developed by Geer (127), they chose a subset of items that reflected a homogeneous array of fears of death and illness. Subjects who scored high and low on this special scale were then shown a film that depicted either the course of a fatal illness or neutral fine art scenes; all subjects were then re-examined on the Digit Symbol subtest of the Wechsler-Bellevue. A performance decrement on this task was observed only in high fear subjects who were shown the death and illness film; the other three groups were unaffected by the films they were shown.

Not all of the induction procedures for anxiety involve pain, physical damage, or injury, of course, but more psychologically based techniques require even more careful introduction. Thus, both the presence of a parent or parental figure [Cox (71)] and the absence of parent [Cox & Campbell (72)] can be stress-inducing given the proper context. In addition, Heilbrun (155) has shown that procedures that simulate maternal censuring are effective in altering a boy's cognitive proficiency only in those subjects who have a particular kind of mothering history and who lack an adequate means of coping with this kind of stress. He found that the differences in coping capacity for this kind of problem were identifiable by means of selected MMPI configurations.

Deprivations of various sorts have been used to induce anxiety states, but the effectiveness of these manipulations also depends to an appreciable extent upon the expectations engendered in the experimental subjects. Thus, situations involving activity reduction [Zubek (363, 364)], sensory reduction [Suedfeld (319)], or social isolation [Taylor, Wheeler & Altman (321); Zuckerman et al. (366)] have all proved to be effective in eliciting severe anxiety levels in some subjects. Such effectiveness has been shown to be a joint function of trait anxiety, commitment to the study, and expectations about the length of the period of confinement.

Many studies of anxiety in the laboratory have employed tests of anxiety level to select subjects high or low in this variable rather than deliberately attempting to modify levels by direct manipulations [Dustin (99)]. The equivalence of these two general approaches has been under considerable discussion and investigation in recent years. This year, Spielberger (314) has brought together a wide variety of findings bearing upon a distinction that he has been emphasizing between trait anxiety (the average or general level of anxiety that a given subject shows over relatively long periods of time) and state anxiety (momentary or transitory shifts away from his average level that may be brought about by special circumstances). He has used this distinction to try to account for discrepancies in the experimental findings between these two general research strategies mentioned above. He also has advanced verbal test scales to evaluate both trait and state anxiety levels. Johnson & Spielberger (176) have employed these measures to study the important parameters of dissipation rates after given anxiety arousals.

Johnson (174, 175) and Hodges (162) have explored another aspect of anxiety induction, namely, the possibility that trait anxiety differences in Spielberger's formulation (314) can be interpreted as differences in predisposition to anxiety state shifts under stress. Both Johnson and Hodges found support for interpreting Spielberger's trait anxiety measure as susceptibility to anxiety induction, but apparently only for threats to self-esteem and not for threats of painful shock (162). In line with a formulation by Palmer (273), perhaps the trait anxiety variable in Spielberger's paradigm indicates a generalized vigilance on the part of the subject in contrast to a defensive pattern, an orientation which would be likely to enhance any relevant threat or stressor that an experimenter might introduce. Katkin & McCubbin (183) invoke individual differences in autonomic lability to account for such differences in orientation, rather than a variable akin to trait anxiety.

Current studies of anxiety and anxiety control have tended to concentrate upon the generally negative implications [Dustin (99)] of these variables, and Bakan (11) and Stotland (318) have both devoted attention to broader aspects of anxiety, pain, and suffering as well as the means men use to keep these miseries within acceptable limits of endurance. It is important to note that the way in which some individuals react to anxiety-inducing stressors is contrary to our general views [Kish & Busse (187); Klausner (189); Nisbett (262)]; some people seek these situations and enhance these experiences.

As noted earlier in the discussion of the kinds of subjects serving in the sexual studies of Masters and Johnson, the operation of guilt mechanisms in such studies of highly emotionally charged behaviors is a vital research issue. Does guilt over sexual activities operate prior to impulse expression as an inhibitor, or is its role primarily a self-excoriative process once the act has occurred? Although the manipulations of sexual arousal employed are probably quite weak compared to those in the St. Louis studies of Masters and Johnson, studies this year have shed some light in this area on the role of guilt reactions in covering up the effects of sexual arousal [Galbraith (121); Galbraith & Mosher (122)]. Manipulation of sexual arousal level was by means of a task [modeled after the early work of Clark (63)] in which male subjects judged various attributes of photographs of nude females. A guilt scale over sexual expression developed by Mosher (255) was also administered and, in one study (122), a separate manipulation of experimental atmosphere—permissive or suppressive—was introduced. The effects of exposure to the sexual stimuli were evaluated by means of associations to a specially devised word list that included a number of explicitly sexual terms as stimuli. Subjects high and low on the guilt scale were found to differ in the number of sexually related responses after the arousal experience, the difference being particularly clearcut in the situation calculated to enhance disapproval (an experimenter who expressed negative reactions to men who got vicarious sexual pleasures from nude pictures). Thus, when the situational cues are appropriate, sexual guilt as measured by the Mosher scale seems to lead to both response inhibition and self-condemnation [cf. Galbraith, Hahn & Leiberman (123)].

Similar arousal manipulations employing pictures of nudes were used by Lamb (193) to study the impact on such drive changes upon the appreciation of humor of different kinds. He found that subjects were more appreciative of humor of widely diverse content after sexual arousal by this means than those without prior sexual stimulation. This result is in some contrast to the greater specificity of appreciation and tension reduction by means of humor recorded by Singer (312) in Negro subjects after arousal of high levels of hostility in them by means of passages that were played to them on tape from a bitterly anti-Negro speech made by a segregationist. Only those humorous excerpts from Negro comedians which focussed directly upon the targets of this aroused hostility (anti-integrationist whites) were effective in altering their measured hostility level or in gaining their appreciation as humor. Subjects exposed to less effective passages with lower levels of induced hostility, however, showed the generality of humor response reported by Lamb and, in addition, showed a drop in their rated hostility after listening to any of the passages, even the more diffusely directed humor.

One final comment on the use of pictures of females to arouse sexual responses in male subjects pertains to the matching of stimuli to subjects. Wiggins, Wiggins & Conger (350) offer evidence that such pictorial stimuli probably can be better selected to fit the particular personological attributes of the male subjects being sampled. Even in silhouette presentation, they found that there were stable differences in preference among various salient features in the anatomy of the nude figures that they used. These preferences in turn were found to be related both to the general personality and background characteristics, as well as to the heterosexual orientation of these men.

Hess (160) brought together the various kinds of evidence available that measurements of changes in the size of the pupil of a person's eye give a direct measure of interest and arousal by sexual stimuli. Moreover, he reports that his pupillometric procedures can be used not only to evaluate the effectiveness of pictorial stimuli that have direct and obvious sexual reference but also to measure the impact of pictures of other people's eyes. Using photos that show pupillary states of (presumably) sexually aroused subjects, Hess finds corresponding changes in the pupillary size in the eyes of the viewers. If these techniques prove trustworthy, some of the controls over more explicit but well-defended sexual expression may be circumvented, and this form of indirect measure may prove useful in step-function research. Some of the studies on voluntary control over autonomic functions (91) may foreshadow some difficulties in this kind of procedure, though.

In the same way that Hess has explored the use of indirect response measures to evaluate the effectiveness of various sexual stimuli in the hope of finding a way around various personological defenses, efforts to devise stimulus features that will be equally indirect in their impact on the research subject are constantly being tried. This year, Lessler & Erickson (199) found some limitations in the use of less obviously sexually relevant cues to evoke sexually pertinent responses. Various potential sexual symbols were given to school children to be sorted on the basis of their relationship to a particular sex-role. They found that cultural stereotypes were more controlling in these subjects than psychoanalytic symbolism, unless the stimuli were very ambiguous.

For a variety of reasons, women have not been used as subjects in experimental studies of sexual arousal and defense as often as men have. Part of this reliance upon male samples is attributable to the relatively uniform drive level which they show. The fluctuations of sexual interest and arousability are not well understood, and few dependable indices of momentary drive level are available for them. Some findings of Shader, DiMascio & Harmaty (307) suggest a way that better plots of these fluctuations can be achieved. Changes in sexual interest and desire were studied in a group of normal women who reported at regular intervals during various phases of their menstrual cycles. In their sample, middle-class women with high Taylor Manifest Anxiety Scale scores reported closer correspondence between libidinal level and menstrual phase than low scorers. These latter women experienced more uniform levels of sexual interest, and few experienced marked changes in libido before the onset of menstruation.

Since expression of aggression in its various forms is also heavily defended against in most psychosocial contexts [cf. Berkowitz (32); Okel & Mosher (270)], step-function testing of the effectiveness of various means of provoking aggression is also fraught with procedural difficulties. Using a film showing violent scenes, as well as prior training in giving electric shocks, Geen (126) demonstrated that the level of a punishing shock employed by his experimental subjects increased progressively from a task-based failure, through failure apparently induced by the victim of the subsequent aggression, to the highest values for a condition in which the aggressors had been directly insulted by their victims. That is, frustrations involving loss of self-esteem for Geen's subjects appeared to give rise to greater aggression than task-related frustrations.

Several features of this kind of investigation of the step-function testing of frustrative manipulations and resulting aggressive behaviors have been under scrutiny this year. The response measure employed is derived from a task that was modeled after the Buss Aggression Machine (48) or the comparable device developed by Milgram (249). It requires the experimental subject to give another person different intensities of shock. It is crucial that the subject believe that the shocks are in fact being delivered to the other person, usually a stooge. Leibowitz (197) found that this kind of aggressive expression was virtually independent of verbally mediated aggressive actions. Is this specificity a result of stylistic differences in the subjects, or some product of the manipulations used to induce frustrative motivation to various aggressive acts?

Geen's study also employed a film presentation of other individuals engaged in aggressive kinds of behavior. This mode of manipulating aggressive behavior has been employed in several studies (32, 161, 233, 341), either to provide a model for the kind of response under investigation or to disinhibit the behavior by signaling the permissiveness for aggressive acts that is in effect. There is reason to question the generality of such effects of lowering inhibitions or altering the perceived sanctions against aggression that may result from the modeling of aggressive behavior. This limitation is suggested by results from a study by Hicks (161), in which he found that children who were exposed to modeling of aggression showed the expected disinhibition of their own aggressive acts only in situations in which the model was also present. A series of papers collected by Zimbardo (43, 116, 129, 362) on the expression of aggression under various conditions of provocation, and under different kinds of involvement with the task and with the potential victim, serve to highlight the complexity of interaction of motivation, array of behavioral choices, and attitudes involved in the experimental manipulation of this powerful motivational variable.

Individual differences in susceptibility to the influence from an aggressive model have also been given some attention this year. One general concept that implies reduced effectiveness in modulation or inhibition of socially disapproved behaviors in general, namely impulsivity, was explored in the context of aggressive behavior. Kipnis (185) found that subjects high in impulsivity as reflected in scores on his Insolence Scale [Kipnis & Wagner (186)] showed more aggression in criticizing an individual with extremely deviant opinions than did other Navy enlisted men who were middle or low on impulsivity. This difference was greatly enhanced, however, when their performance was preceded by hearing another man, apparently like themselves, give a strongly aggressive and hostile evaluation. Thus, even the most impulsive individuals were found to be sensitive to situational constraints and sanctions, or to their suspension.

Another personological variable shown to be related to degree of aggressive display in recent research is the adequacy of a person's sex-role fulfillment. Leventhal, Shemberg & Van Schoelandt (200) found that those men who were more masculine and those women who were more feminine than their like-sex comparison groups were consistently more extreme in their shock administrations in a simulated training situation.

Full-functioning of the total system.—In the same way that our basic step-function analyses can be seen to weave back and forth between the testing of first-order relationships between pairs of variables and the examination of the way combinatorial patterns of interrelationship among these basic variables operate, there is a movement from laboratory context to free field conditions and back again in studies of the way that individuals with particular personological characteristics actually behave in particular contexts. The emphasis in step-function testing is upon obtaining an undistorted view of the relationship actually holding between variables. The emphasis in testing the fully interconnected system is upon the mutual, interactive consequences of starting with a particular set of circumstances and letting the processes run their course. In so doing, some investigators concentrate upon the inner processes and experiential events reported by the subject, while others focus primarily upon the observable behavioral events and their impact upon the situation or the social group. A complete study of these interactions requires that we be able to record and plot all phase sequences with fidelity and reliability.

The basic procedure is simple in essence; the difficulty lies in the execution. The investigator brings the system to some initial state—with the values of the variables in the system all known at time T_0, and the parameter settings also specified—and then releases the system, plotting the sequence of values assumed by each of the variables over the period of observation, and noting the final state of the system at T_n, some arbitrary end of the period of study. Obviously, only very crude approximations to this idealized set of operations are now possible in our studies of behavioral systems in human subjects.

In the drama of the divergent processes set in motion by this kind of investigation, we have generated the phenomena which many personologists feel are the only true bases for personality study [cf. Bühler & Massarik (46); Lidz (204); Otto (272); Perlman (277)]. Also, in the research approaches included in Willems & Raush (352) are many naturalistic styles of psychological research that all have in common the aim of capturing in action the essential events of personalities in meaningful and nonartificial interaction with different environments. They highlight the problems in this kind of study: the fact of observation of the processes may *ab initio* spoil their naturalness; our best measuring techniques are still reactive rather than unobtrusive [Webb et al. (343)]; and our comprehension of many of these processes is still primitive, stemming from limitations in our concept and in our factual knowledge. Nevertheless, this kind of understanding is the goal of the whole enterprise. Several attempts at this kind of research in personality processes are particularly noteworthy this year: Schachter's studies of the effects of food deprivation on obese subjects, studies of motivational interactions in various kinds of achievement striving, and the attempts to analyze the psychological processes involved in creative behavior.

In 1967, Schachter (302) formulated a fundamental difference between obese and normal-weight adult subjects in the role that internally generated cues (arising from stomach contents, stomach contractions, blood sugar levels, and the like) play for each in determining their eating behavior. In a series of studies published this year, the implications of this formulation were tested in actual eating behavior (263, 303, 304) and in observations upon presumably related behaviors such as willingness to undergo religious fasts (135), degree of eating disruption and personal discomfort experienced after drastic time shifts (135), and impulse buying in a food market (264). The initial differences in internal cue patterns were manipulated by having subjects begin a period of cracker eating with or without full stomachs and either anxious or nonanxious about forthcoming electric shocks (304). The obese subjects, in fact, ate quite steadily in spite of these different internal conditions, while normal-sized subjects were found to eat appreciably less when anxious or when their stomachs were already full. In a related study, using ice cream of two sorts—undoctored high quality versus low quality that was flavored with quinine sulphate—Nisbett (263) tested the role of external cues in combination with internal cues from a full versus empty stomach. He plotted the amount of ice cream consumed by obese, normal, and underweight subjects. He found that obese subjects ate considerably more than the others when the taste was acceptable, but their consumption was equal to that of the normal-sized individuals when it was distasteful. Underweight subjects seemed quite unresponsive to taste differences, relatively, consuming more of the doctored ice cream than the others did but appreciably less of the well-liked ice cream. Instead, their eating behavior was more affected by their prior deprivation and the fullness of their stomachs—the sets of internal cues operating in this situation. A third attempt to plot the impact of external cues on eating behavior employed a clock that registered the wrong time. It indicated either that the time that the subject normally ate supper was already past or was still some way in the future. The obese subjects in general matched their eating behavior to the external cue, the altered time on the clock, while the normal-size subjects either ignored the time or used the manipulated cue as a basis for deciding not to eat very much at all in order not to spoil their own suppers (303).

Obese subjects were also observed to undergo more willingly a fast (Yom Kippur) that was dictated as part of their usual Jewish religious practice (135), experienced less discomfort from arriving in New York in mid-afternoon from Paris by air flight at a time that they would normally have had supper (135), and were less sensitive to hours of food deprivation and the subsequent rise in impulse-buying in a supermarket (264) than were normal-size subjects in these various circumstances. Although, in some of these studies, the definition of obesity was strained (subjects being included who were more likely well developed mesomorphs than the sought-after endomorphs), the results were quite consistent and convergent. The personological basis, however, for the differential roles of internal and external cues in modifying these naturally occurring behaviors has not been well explicated.

This year, Feather (113) reported a study in which he followed up some special implications in a more general theory of achievement motivation that he and Atkinson and their associates (9) published in 1966. Using a task that has often proved to be the proper context for eliciting stable differences in achievement striving—solving anagrams problems—he deliberately had some subjects encounter a series of five successes by means of easy items, while others encountered a series of five failures on insolvable ones. One-half of the subjects so treated were also characterized as believing strongly in their own ability to control various outcomes for themselves [low on Rotter's internal-external control of reinforcement (I-E) scale]; the other subjects were characterized as believing in fate control (high on the I-E scale). Since they also expressed repeatedly their confidence of success for each of the items of the anagrams task, Feather was able to plot successive shifts in expectations and performance over the series. He also obtained reports of changes in their fear of failure or disappointments over these outcomes. By correlational means but not by initial selection of subjects, Feather was also able to study the role of achievement motivation (n Ach) and fear of failure to their actual performances on this task. In this situation, the initial run of successes or failures made a difference upon the actual success achieved by these subjects: those with an initial success series gave a higher performance on the anagrams than those encountering failures. The subjects who had the strongest belief in their own control over fate consistently demonstrated that they were affected by the initial runs; they showed shifts in their confidence and corresponding shifts in their actual anagram-solving behaviors. The magnitude of their average shift was not larger than for the believers in external control, however, and the actual amount of shift in rated confidence in the task was a better gauge of their subsequent proficiency on this task than was measured I-E scale level, need achievement scores, or fear of failure indices. If a subject showed a marked shift in confidence, either up or down, after encountering the easy items or trying to cope with the insoluble ones, he was likely to do well on the remaining 10 items.

Zander & Forward (360) explored another implication of the Atkinson & Feather (9) theory of achievement motivation in a special social setting. The context was a group problem-solving task. For part of the time, the subject was primarily responsible for a group's goal setting and that group's actual goal attainment; but at other times he was only peripherally involved in these activities. These investigators expected that subjects who were more characterized by need for achievement and less by fear of failure would seek expression on this need in the group's attainments, even when in a peripheral capacity; subjects with the reverse pattern in which fear of failure was predominant and need for achievement low would not manifest this pattern when in a peripheral position. They expected that the high fear-low need individuals would not behave appreciably differently from the low fear-high need subjects when placed in the central role of the group's activities. These patterns were confirmed. In this study, the crucial role of the social setting and the subject's role in that context was clearly documented. Only in special circumstances, then, can we expect that the important differences between these two kinds of motivation toward success will appear in an individual's behavior.

The Zander & Forward study above involved an ipsative measurement issue—which is stronger in the given subject, his need for achievement or his fear of failure?—but the special scaling problems involved were not tackled directly in that study. For their purpose, the subjects were merely chosen from among the students who showed the widest separations on the two score distributions. In a study by Terhune (323), an ipsative problem involving three variables (need achievement, need affiliation, and need power) was selected. Terhune handled this intra-individual scaling issue by resorting to separate *T* scores for the three fantasy measures that he employed, and by picking subjects above the middle of the total group on one need scale and below the middle on both of the other measures. He then ran his subjects in a game situation (the prisoner's dilemma) in which a subject can either cooperate with a partner to their mutual advantage or defect with the chance of gaining appreciably or spoiling the chance for either to gain. In such a situation, the investigator expected subjects differing in predominant need would behave in characteristic ways: affiliators (Naffs) should cooperate, achievers (Naches) should work for maximal gains, and power-oriented (Nepos) subjects should engender the most conflicts. He ran the subjects on both a short run, with only a single game completed, and on a long series, with and without communications between subjects over 30 consecutive games.

On the short runs in which experience with the task was minimal, Terhune found important differences in behavior related to need status. Subjects high on need achievement turned out to be the most cooperative, while Naffs proved to be defensive, and Nepos were highly exploitative. This last finding was not anticipated but seems quite consistent with a reformulation of need power advanced by Winter (354), in which he raises questions about the arousal procedures and theoretical implications of this variable advanced by the Michigan group. Dominance seems to be a consistent manifestation of need power in Winter's conceptualization [cf. McClelland & Winter (217)].

When Terhune examined the subsequent behavior of his subjects in the prisoner's dilemma game on the long runs, he found that measured need status had a great deal less bearing upon their performance (although still quite relevant to their reported experiences during these runs) than the actual outcomes of their initial game and the way that the series then progressed. Task characteristics such as pay-off matrices and the opportunity to communicate were more controlling over the long series than were personological differences. In fact, even in the one-game series, if the pay-off matrix were severe enough (a very low cooperation index where defection was highly expected), the need differences were also obliterated.

McKeachie et al. (222) have made a serious effort to disentangle some of the complexities of relationship between measured need achievement and grades earned in college. They reviewed the literature covering these questions which is filled with contradictory findings. There is no clear basis for anticipating what the field performance of subjects high and low on need achievement will be in a particular college setting. McKeachie and his associates expected that some of the differences among the various reports could be attributed to important variations from one specific course to another. They speculated that each course presented different arrays of cues calculated to elicit achievement striving in the students enrolled. Only those courses which contain the appropriate achievement-related cues would generate the expected differences between the students who show high or low motivation for achievement. Striving for grades as a means of gratifying need for achievement would be found only in selected courses. In a context of high standards for achievement, challenging work, and strong competition, subjects high in n Ach were expected to work particularly hard and perform best. In line with McClelland's interpretation (218), middle-level scorers on n Ach were expected to do appreciably poorer because these scores reflect more fear of failure than genuine need for achievement. In this study, little support was found for any context and need interaction effects either way. Need achievement as measured did not bear dependably upon grades earned in French, mathematics, or psychology, nor on achievement test performances in these various sections, nor under instructors differing in achievement-arousing characteristics [cf. Glass et al. (130)].

A college setting was also used by Wallach to make an extension of his formulation of creative processes from elementary school children (339) to college students (340). Wallach & Wing (340) chose two groups of highly selected undergraduates at a private university: high and low scorers on tests of divergent thinking who were comparable on the Educational Testing Service's Scholastic Aptitude Tests. The former tasks, which include both verbal items and visual-geometric designs to which the subject is asked to give unusual interpretations and associations, are considered as measures of the subjects' modes of cognitive functioning and hence his creativity. The SAT measures are interpreted as typical intelligence measures. Wallach accepts the distinction advanced by Guilford (148, 149) that creativity involves divergent cognitive processes and intelligence convergent processes. Wallach & Wing (340) then followed their two groups of undergraduates as they evolved their academic and extracurricular patterns of achievement in the university context. As indices of creative expression, they plotted a variety of "nonacademic talented accomplishments," such as leadership in campus organizations, talented products in the visual arts, special prizes and awards, science projects, and talented performances in musical activities. They found that the students who scored high on the divergent thinking tasks [termed Guilford-like measures by Stein (317)] were dependably separated from their equally "intelligent" classmates on most of these extracurricular activity measures. Musical performances, however, seemed unrelated to either the number of unusual ideas or the uniqueness of the ideas given by their students. Creative writing was predictable from these tasks only among the women in their sample. The groups did not earn different grade-point records however, so the SAT measures appear to be equally predictive of academic college success in these two groups.

As clear and straightforward as this field-testing venture of Wallach & Wing was, it is an interesting commentary on the present status of creativity research that unanimity on any one aspect of their work—criteria, hypothesized processes, measures, or context—is unlikely in any substantial majority of the investigators. The present state of this research domain has been admirably depicted by Stein (317), along with his synthesis of the personological framework within which future research can most profitably be pursued.

For many investigators, creativity can only be represented by genuine contributions to mankind and unique artistic products or compositions. Winning a prize for creative writing in a local campus competition, therefore, cannot be considered to be in the same domain as writing *Jean-Cristophe;* world success is the *sine qua non.* By so severely restricting the definition of creative behavior, investigations of creativity by necessity become long-term, expensive, and high risk projects, such as Terman's classic follow-up studies of his "gifted" children [cf. Oden (269)] or highly speculative reconstructive efforts from biographical material and particular theoretical assumptions, as represented this year by the scholarly synthesis of psychoanalytic formulations of the creative process by Havelka (154). Otherwise, this definition of creativity renders the phenomenon uncapturable and places it outside the reach of scientific investigation. At the other end of the range of phenomena covered by the concept of creative behavior lies the incidental mastery of verbal concepts which was considered in the study of Laughlin, Doherty & Dunn (195). They contrasted this proficiency with learning carried out under instructions to solve the verbal problem. Their results show many of the features common to the intelligence-creativity distinction: intellective variations were more predictive of performance in tasks requiring deliberate learning effort, and creativity variations (on a Guildford-like measure of remote associates) were more related to the incidental learning behavior.

One of the persistent difficulties in research on creative activity is the lack of agreement on a proper definition. Realistic definitions will have to be formulated, together with measures that can be used in large-scale field studies, before these research projects can be expected to show effective convergence. The sustained efforts of the investigators at the Institute of Personality Assessment and Research (IPAR) at the University of California, Berkeley, have led to a number of practical instruments for assessment of various aspects of creativity and creative productivity [Barron (25); Tryk (330)]. Adoption of these instruments for wide use in creativity research could accelerate this needed convergence.

The same kind of dissension is evident in the choice that investigators make of the means to select subjects expected to differ in creative behavior. Studies of these potential predictors at IPAR [MacKinnon (228); Tryk (330)] and elsewhere [Stein (317)] have shown that only a few show the requisite validity for field studies. They also differ greatly in their psychological rationales. For example, Wallach calls his selection criterion for high and low creative subjects a measure of their "mode of cognitive functioning." Does this mean some special talent, over and above general intellective competence; some characteristic style of expression of the intellective capacities; or some more pervasive temperamental characteristic reflecting itself in interests, activities, and patterns of eager involvement in a variety of different pursuits, as well as the way they tackle the Guilford-like tasks posed for them by the psychologist? Here, too, there is little agreement. From their general presentation, it seems that Wallach & Wing (340) conceptualize their measures as another, and as yet rather neglected, aspect of a person's basic capacity. For Guilford (149), the creative processes appear to be those kinds of information that are available and ready for functional application to any new situation. Proper training can presumably enhance the functional utility of such information, making it fully available for use in divergent problem-solving processes.

If this view of creative processes is accepted, of course, the discussion of this kind of research should be placed in a chapter on cognitive functions. The fact is that there is a great deal of divergence in opinions about the proper formulation of these processes and the implications of differences found on measures like those employed by Wallach & Wing. Findings from studies like those of Cropley (81) or Ginsburg & Whittemore (128) suggest that the separation between intelligence and creativity which Wallach and his associates [cf. Ward (342); Pankove & Kogan (274)] are attempting to draw may be a function of sampling biases or restrictions in range on their test measures. Another possible source of this difference is suggested by Boersma & O'Bryan (38), who found shifts in level of measured proficiency on divergent thinking tasks, and a drop in correlation with intellective measures, with a change from test-like to game-like administration of the Guilford-like tasks. For purposes of distinguishing between capacity-interpretations and stylistic interpretations of these measures, it would be useful to know which administrative approach generates scores of divergent thinking that are most predictive of full-field functioning. Are these measures merely eliciting some capacity like Thurstone's ideational fluency, or showing some important personality style which may be dampened out in the usual manner of test administration? For example, Levy (201) raises the possibility that some of the creativity measures may be reflecting some self-imposed role of either a conforming or a deviating sort based upon judgments of what is appropriate. His subjects were found to differ in originality when such roles were imposed from without by explicit instruction and training, strengthening the belief that such roles, were they to be imposed from within, could be quite influential in both tests and free field situations.

A somewhat different view of the intelligence-creativity distinction would seem to follow from some findings of Faucheux & Moscovici (112) on cognitive activities of groups of teenage subjects. When simple variations on designs were all that was required, the processes observed were quite comparable to those sampled by the divergent thinking tasks employed by Wallach and his associates. When additional classifications were introduced in the task requirement, these subjects had first to master the construction rules before they could distinguish among the general classifications. This mastery seemed to require different cognitive processes, more akin to intellective processes of the convergent sort. Creative effort in this altered circumstance, therefore, required that both kinds of cognitive activity be brought to bear upon the tasks. Deliberate efforts to modify the way that children apply different task-solving techniques this year by Allen & Levine (3) and by Lundsteen (215) have met with only partial success. General discussions of these efforts have also appeared by Covington (70), by Crutchfield (84), and by MacKinnon (227) covering programs, motivational problems, and evaluations of their effectiveness.

In addition to the interpretations offered above along the lines of capacity differences, selective sets, or products of educative programs, the characteristics of subjects on measures of divergent thinking are also interpreted in explicitly personological terms. A whole style of creative orientation to the world and to the various challenges posed, be they career choice or specific task, is often formulated [Stein (317)]. Helson (157, 158) has continued her studies at IPAR of the different styles of creative expression as manifested by each of the sexes and the ways they develop out of particular home situations [cf. MacKinnon (225)]. Helson relates the stylistic differences between men and women to their sex-role patterns and ways in which they have resolved various conflicts with siblings and parents. Creative styles may be reflected in stable preferences for various designs as was originally demonstrated by Welsh & Barron [cf. Barron (23)]. Eisenman (102, 103, 322) has found that the simplicity-complexity distinction advanced by Welsh & Barron to account for these differences stands up well on a different set of test items. Further insight into the personality characteristics of subjects high and low on such measures is also provided by a series of studies by Welsh (348) on talented high school students. Picking subjects who scored high or low on preference for complex figures on the Art scale of the Welsh Figure Preference Test and high or low on a measure of general intelligence, the Terman Concept Mastery Test, he was able to generate stable personality scales reflecting primarily brightness or dullness in intelligence or high promise or low promise in originality on three different item pools: Strong Vocational Interest Blank, Gough's ACL, and the MMPI. He calls the personality measures relating to intellective differences "scales of intellectence" and the creativity measures "scales of origence." Both general personological correlates and specific creativity indices have been found in the records and observations on groups of these teenagers during special summer school programs devoted to promoting their creative endeavors that relate dependably to differences in origence and intellectence.

At the present time, therefore, available evidence suggests [Barron (22, 24, 26); Cattell & Butcher (58); Covington (69); Hall & MacKinnon (150); Jackson & Messick (170); MacKinnon (223, 224, 226, 228, 229); Parloff et al. (275); Stein (317); Walberg (338)] that the creative process involves a variety of enhancing variables: interest, involvement, sensitivity, and self-confidence; and a variety of inhibiting variables: fears, self-doubts, and disabling sets and misperceptions acting jointly to determine the degree of expression of whatever the level of skill and proficiency of the individual for that situational demand will permit.

Little headway can be made in full functional analyses of behavioral sequences characterized by creativity, originality, or inventiveness until the initial states of the individuals under study can be properly conceptualized, specified, and measured. Better understanding of the way these variables interrelate in contributing to the final creative resolutions will also await means of appraising the values they take in different phases of the sequence from start to terminal state. At that time we will be more able to take into account the role of different situational parameters. Some of the differences in the way personological characteristics enter into creative efforts at adolescence and in adulthood [Parloff et al. (275); Walberg (338)]; the different situations facing men and women in expressing creative needs [Helson (158); Walberg (338); Wallach & Wing (340)]; or the differences within a college setting of creative production in fine arts versus musical performance [Wallach & Wing (340)] make it clear that context of field observation will be crucial in predictive efforts of this kind. Even more challenging will be the longer range observations of selected individuals in situations in which the subjects will also select their own environments as they evolve career patterns [Astin (8); Sandeen (295)] and make work choices [Campbell et al. (50); Holland (163); Neff (260); Shaw (308)]. Some attention to these situational constraints within a large industrial complex has been paid by Crosby (82) in Great Britain. However, most of the empirical studies [Elder (104); Oden (269)] have had to be efforts to reconstruct the important variables and crucial events even though the data for their studies were gathered in ambitious longitudinal programs.

A rather different and exciting method of depicting and studying the nature of an individual's reactions to general features of his environment and their impact upon him has been elaborated this year by Craik (75–77, 79). A variety of important features and configurations of the environment have been identified and models of interactive effects delineated. The feasibility of studying in sequence different individuals' reactions to the landscape in the course of tours has been demonstrated as well as the possibility of studying comparable processes in the laboratory with mock-up displays. In addition to their relevance to personological research, such findings have great potential pay-off in architectural and city planning programs.

LITERATURE CITED

1. Achenbach, T. M. Cue-learning, associative responding, and impulsivity in children. *Proc. 76th Ann. Conv. APA,* **3,** 365–66 (1968)
2. Adelson, J. Personality. *Ann. Rev. Psychol.,* **20,** 217–52 (1969)
3. Allen, V. L., Levine, J. M. Creativity and conformity. *J. Pers.,* **36,** 405–19 (1968)
4. Allport, G. W. *The Person in Psychology: Selected Essays* (Beacon, Boston, 1968)
5. Allport, G. W. Personality: Contemporary viewpoints. I. A unique and open system. *International Encyclopedia of the Social Sciences,* **12,** 1–12 (Macmillan, New York, 1968)
6. Amir, Y., Sharan, S., Kovarsky, Y. Birth order, family structure, and avoidance behavior. *J. Pers. Soc. Psychol.,* **10,** 271–78 (1968)
7. Aronfreed, J. *Conduct and Conscience: The Socialization of Internalized Control over Behavior* (Academic Press, New York, 1968)
8. Astin, H. S. Stability and change in the career plans of ninth grade girls. *Personnel & Guid. J.,* **46,** 961–66 (1968)
9. Atkinson, J. W., Feather, N. T., Eds. *A Theory of Achievement Motivation* (Wiley, New York, 1966)
10. Ayllon, T., Azrin, N. *The Token Economy: A Motivational System for Therapy and Rehabilitation* (Appleton-Century-Crofts, New York, 288 pp., 1968)
11. Bakan, D. *Disease, Pain, and Sacrifice: Toward a Psychology of Suffering* (Univ. Chicago Press, Chicago, Ill., 1968)

12. Bandura, A., Menlove, F. L. Factors determining vicarious extinction of avoidance behavior through symbolic modeling. *J. Pers. Soc. Psychol.*, **8**, 99–108 (1968)
13. Bandura, A., Walters, R. H. *Social Learning and Personality Development* (Holt, Rinehart & Winston, New York, 1963)
14. Bannister, D., Mair, J. M. M. *The Evaluation of Personal Constructs* (Academic Press, New York, 232 pp., 1968)
15. Barber, T. X. Invalid arguments, postmortem analyses, and the experimeter bias effect. *J. Consult. Clin. Psychol.*, **33**, 11–14 (1969)
16. Barber, T. X., Silver, M. J. Fact, fiction, and the experimenter bias effect. *Psychol. Bull. Monogr.*, **70**, No. 6, Part 2, 1–29 (1968)
17. Barber, T. X., Silver, M. J. Pitfalls in data analysis and interpretation: A reply to Rosenthal. *Ibid.*, 48–62 (1968)
18. Barber, T. X., Calverley, D. S., Forgione, A., McPeake, J. D., Chaves, J. F., Bowen, B. Five attempts to replicate the experimenter bias effect. *J. Consult. Clin. Psychol.*, **33**, 1–6 (1969)
19. Barker, R. *Ecological Psychology* (Stanford Univ. Press, Stanford, Calif., 346 pp., 1968)
20. Barker, R. *The Stream of Behavior: Explorations of its Structure and Content* (Appleton-Century-Crofts, New York, 1968)
21. Barnard, J. W., Zimbardo, P. G., Sarason, S. Teachers' ratings of student personality traits as they relate to IQ and social desirability. *J. Educ. Psychol.*, **59**, 128–32 (1968)
22. Barron, F. *Creative Person and Creative Process* (Holt, Rinehart & Winston, New York, 1969)
23. Barron, F. *Creativity and Personal Freedom* (Van Nostrand, Princeton, N.J., 1968)
24. Barron, F. The dream of art and poetry. *Psychology Today*, **2**, 19–23, 65–66 (1968)
25. Barron, F. The measurement of creativity. In *Handbook of Measurement in Psychology and Education*, Chap. 10, 348–66 (Whitla, D., Ed., Addison-Wesley, Reading, Mass., 1968)
26. Barron, F., Mordkoff, A. M. An attempt to relate creativity to possible extrasensory empathy as measured by physiological arousal in identical twins. *J. Am. Soc. Psych. Res.*, **62**, 73–79 (1968)
27. Baughman, E. E., Dahlstrom, W. G. *Negro and White Children: A Psychological Study in the Rural South* (Academic Press, New York, 1968)
28. Baughman, E. E., Welsh, G. S. *Personality: A Behavioral Science* (Prentice-Hall, Englewood Cliffs, N. J., 1962)
29. Bayley, N. Behavioral correlates of mental growth: Birth to 36 years. *Am. Psychologist*, **23**, 1–17 (1968)
30. Bayton, J. A., Muldrow, T. W. Interacting variables in the perception of racial personality traits. *J. Exptl. Res. Pers.*, **3**, 39–44 (1968)
31. Bergquist, W. H., Lewinsohn, P. M., Sue, D. W., Flippo, J. R. Short and long term memory for various types of stimuli as a function of repression-sensitization. *J. Exptl. Res. Pers.*, **3**, 28–38 (1968)
32. Berkowitz, L., Ed. *Roots of Aggression* (Atherton, New York, 1968)
33. Biller, H. B. A note on father absence and masculine development in lower-class Negro and white boys. *Child Develpm.*, **39**, 1003–6 (1968)
34. Bischof, L. J. *Adult Psychology* (Harper & Row, New York, 310 pp., 1969)
35. Blitz, B., Dinnerstein, A. J. Effects of different types of instructions on pain parameters. *J. Abnorm. Psychol.*, **73**, 276–80 (1968)
36. Block, J. Some reasons for the apparent inconsistency of personality. *Psychol. Bull.*, **70**, 210–12 (1968)
37. Block, J. *Ways of Personality Development* (Appleton-Century-Crofts, New York, 1970)
38. Boersma, F. J., O'Bryan, K. An investigation of the relationship between creativity and intelligence under two conditions of testing. *J. Pers.*, **36**, 341–48 (1968)
39. Borgatta, E. F., Lambert, W. W., Eds. *Handbook of Personality Theory and Research* (Rand McNally, Chicago, 1232 pp., 1969)
40. Bowers, K. S. Pain, anxiety, and perceived control. *J. Consult. Clin. Psychol.*, **32**, 596–602 (1968)
41. Brecher, R., Brecher, E., Eds. *An Analysis of Human Sexual Response* (New American Library,

New York, 1966)
42. Brehm, J. W. *A Theory of Psychological Reactance* (Academic Press, New York, 1966)
43. Brock, T. C., Pallak, M. S. The consequence of choosing to be aggressive: An analysis of the dissonance model and review of relevant research. In *Cognitive Control of Motivation: The Consesequences of Choice and Dissonance* (Zimbardo, P. G., Ed., Scott, Foresman, Glenview, Ill., 1969)
44. Brody, E. B., Ed. *Minority Group Adolescents in the United States* (Williams & Wilkins, Baltimore, 243 pp., 1968)
45. Bronson, G. W. The development of fear in man and other animals. *Child Develpm.,* **39,** 409–31 (1968)
46. Bühler, C., Massarik, F., Eds. *The Course of Human Life: A Study of Goals in Humanistic Perspective* (Springer, New York, 1969)
47. Burnham, J. C. Historical background for the study of personality. In *Handbook of Personality Theory and Research,* Chap. 1, 3–81 (See Ref. 39)
48. Buss, A. *The Psychology of Aggression* (Wiley, New York, 1961)
49. Calabresi, R., Cohen, J. Personality and time attitudes. *J. Abnorm. Psychol.,* **73,** 431–39 (1968)
50. Campbell, D. P., Borgen, F. H., Eastes, S. H., Johansson, C. B., Peterson, R. A. A set of basic interest scales for the Strong Vocational Interest Blank for Men. *J. Appl. Psychol. Monogr.,* **52,** No. 6, Part 2 (1968)
51. Campbell, D. T., Fiske, D. W. Convergent and discriminant validation by the multitrait-multimethod matrix. *Psychol. Bull.,* **56,** 81–105 (1959)
52. Carpenter, P. Teen-age rioter in Detroit: A clinical portrait. *Proc. 76th Ann. Conv. APA,* **3,** 373–74 (1968)
53. Carson, R. C. *Interaction Concepts of Personality* (Aldine, Chicago, 1969)
54. Castaldo, V., Holzman, P. S. The effects of hearing one's own voice on dream content: a replication. *J. Nerv. Ment. Dis.,* **148,** 74–82 (1969)
55. Cattell, R. B. Taxonomic principles for locating and using types (and the derived Taxonome program). In *Formal Representation of Human Judgment,* Chap. 5, 99–148 (Kleinmuntz, B., Ed., Wiley, New York, 1968)
56. Cattell, R. B., Ed. *Handbook of Modern Personality Theory* (Aldine, Chicago, 1970)
57. Cattell, R. B., Bolton, L. S. What pathological dimensions lie beyond the normal dimensions of the 16PF? A comparison of MMPI and 16PF factor domains. *J. Consult. Clin. Psychol.,* **33,** 18–29 (1969)
58. Cattell, R. B., Butcher, H. J. *The Prediction of Achievement and Creativity* (Bobbs-Merrill, Indianapolis, 1968)
59. Cattell, R. B., Gibbons, B. D. Personality factor structure of the combined Guilford and Cattell personality questionnaires. *J. Pers. Soc. Psychol.,* **9,** 107–20 (1968)
60. Child, I. L. Personality in culture. In *Handbook of Personality Theory and Research,* Chap. 2, 82–145 (See Ref. 39)
61. Chittenden, E. A., Foan, M. W., Zweil, D. M., Smith, J. R. School achievement of first- and second-born siblings. *Child Develpm.,* **39,** 1223–28 (1968)
62. Christie, R., Geis, F., Eds. *Studies in Machiavellianism* (Academic Press, New York, in press)
63. Clark, R. A. The projective measurement of experimentally induced levels of sexual stimulation. *J. Exptl. Psychol.,* **44,** 391–99 (1952)
64. Clausen, J. A., Ed. *Socialization and Society* (Little, Brown, Boston, 1968)
65. Cohen, A. M., Foerst, J. R. Organizational behaviors and adaptations to organizational change of sensitizer and represser problem-solving groups. *J. Pers. Soc. Psychol.,* **8,** 209–16 (1968)
66. Cohen, J. *Personality Dynamics* (Rand McNally, Chicago, 64 pp., 1969)
67. Collard, R. R. Social and play responses of first-born and later-born infants in an unfamiliar situation. *Child Develpm.,* **39,** 325–34 (1968)
68. Coopersmith, S. *The Antecendents of Self-Esteem* (Freeman, San Francisco, 283 pp., 1967)

69. Covington, M. V. A childhood attitude inventory for problem solving: Technical report. *Bulletin for Psychologists* (Australian Council for Educational Research, No. 9, 1968)
70. Covington, M. V. Promoting creative thinking in the classroom. In *Research and Development toward the Improvement of Education,* 22–30 (Klausmeier, H. J., O'Hearn, G. T., Eds., Dembar Educ. Res. Serv., Madison, Wis., 1968)
71. Cox, F. N. Some relationships between test anxiety, presence or absence of male persons, and boys' performance on a repetitive motor task. *J. Exptl. Child Psychol.,* **6,** 1–12 (1968)
72. Cox, F. N., Campbell, D. Young children in a new situation with and without their mothers. *Child Develpm.,* **39,** 123–31 (1968)
73. Craig, K. D. Physiological arousal as a function of imagined, vicarious, and direct stress experiences. *J. Abnorm. Psychol.,* **73,** 513–20 (1968)
74. Craik, K. H. Of time and personality. *Am. Psychologist,* **20,** 591 (1965)
75. Craik, K. H. The prospects for an environmental psychology. *Research Bulletin* (Inst. of Pers. Assess. Res., Univ. California, Berkeley, 1966)
76. Craik, K. H. The comprehension of the everyday physical environment. *J. Am. Inst. Planners,* **34,** 29–37 (1968)
77. Craik, K. H. Human responsiveness to landscape: An environmental psychological perspective. *Student Publication of the School of Design* (North Carolina State Univ., Raleigh, 1968)
78. Craik, K. H. Personality unvanquished: A review of *Personality and Assessment* by Walter Mischel. *Contemp. Psychol.,* **14,** 147–48 (1969)
79. Craik, K. H. Transportation and the person. *High Speed Ground Transport. J.,* **3,** 86–91 (1969)
80. Crandall, J. E. Effects of need for approval and intolerance of ambiguity upon stimulus preference. *J. Pers.,* **36,** 67–83 (1968)
81. Cropley, A. J. A note on the Wallach-Kogan test of creativity. *Brit. J. Educ. Psychol.,* **38,** 197–201 (1968)
82. Crosby, A. *Creativity and Performance in Industrial Organization* (Travistock, London, 1968)
83. Crowne, D. P., Conn, L. K., Marlowe, D., Edwards, C. N. Some developmental antecedents of level of aspiration. *J. Pers.,* **37,** 73–92 (1969)
84. Crutchfield, R. S. Nurturing the cognitive skills of productive thinking. In *Life Skills in School and Society, 1969 ASCD Yearbook,* 53–71 (Rubin, L. J., Ed., Natl. Educ. Assoc., Assoc. for Supervision and Curriculum Development, Washington, D.C., 1969)
85. Dahlstrom, W. G. The structure of types and some exemplifications in psychopathology. In *Handbook of Modern Personality Theory,* Chap. 12 (See Ref. 56)
86. Damarin, F. L., Cattell, R. B. Personality factors in early childhood and their relation to intelligence. *Monogr. Soc. Res. Child Develpm.,* **33,** No. 6 (1968)
87. Datta, L-E. Birth order and potential scientific creativity. *Sociometry,* **31,** 76–88 (1968)
88. Davids, A. Cognitive styles in potential scientists and underachieving high school students. *J. Special Educ.,* **2,** 197–201 (1968)
89. Davids, A. Ego functions in disturbed and normal children: Aspiration, inhibition, time estimation, and delayed gratification. *J. Consult. Clin. Psychol.,* **33,** 61–70 (1969)
90. Dawes, R. M., Meehl, P. E. Mixed group validation: A method for determining the validity of diagnostic signs without using criterion groups. *Psychol. Bull.,* **66,** 63–67 (1966)
91. Dean, S. J., Martin, R. B., Streiner, D. Mediational control of the GSR. *J. Exptl. Res. Pers.,* **3,** 71–76 (1968)
92. deCharms, R. *Personal Causation: The Internal Affective Determinants of Behavior* (Academic Press, New York, 1968)
93. Deutsch, M., Katz, I., Jensen, A. R., Eds. *Social Class, Race, and Psychological Development* (Holt, Rinehart & Winston, New York, 1968)
94. De Vos, G. A., Hippler, A. A. Cultural psychology: Comparative studies of human behavior. In *The Handbook of Social Psychol-*

ogy, 2nd ed., Chap. 33 (Lindzey, G., Aronson, E., Eds., Addison-Wesley, Reading, Mass., 1969)

95. Dodge, M., Muench, G. A. Relationship of conformity and the need for approval in children. *Develpm. Psychol.*, **1**, 67–68 (1969)
96. Dreger, R. M., Miller, K. S. Comparative psychological studies of Negroes and whites in the United States: 1959–1965. *Psychol. Bull. Monogr.*, **70**, Part 2 (1968)
97. Drew, F. I., Moriarty, R. W., Shapiro, A. P. An approach to the measurement of the pain and anxiety responses of surgical patients. *Psychosom. Med.*, **30**, 826–36 (1968)
98. Dublin, J. E. Perception of and reaction to ambiguity by repressors and sensitizers: A construct-validity study. *J. Consult. Clin. Psychol.*, **32**, 198–205 (1968)
99. Dustin, D. S. *How Psychologists Do Research: The Example of Anxiety* (Prentice-Hall, Englewood Cliffs, N.J., 108 pp., 1969)
100. Duvall, N. *Field articulation and the repression-sensitization dimension in perception and memory* (Doctoral dissertation, Univ. North Carolina, Chapel Hill, 1969)
101. Efran, J. S. Looking for approval: Effects on visual behavior of approbation from persons differing in importance. *J. Pers. Soc. Psychol.*, **10**, 21–25 (1968)
102. Eisenman, R. Personality and demography in complexity-simplicity. *J. Consult. Clin. Psychol.*, **32**, 140–43 (1968)
103. Eisenman, R., Gellens, H. K. Preferences for complexity-simplicity and symmetry-asymmetry. *Proc. 76th Ann. Conv. APA*, **3**, 443–44 (1968)
104. Elder, G. H. Occupational level, achievement motivation, and social mobility: A longitudinal analysis. *J. Counsel. Psychol.*, **15**, 1–7 (1968)
105. Emmerich, W. Personality development and concepts of structure. *Child Develpm.*, **39**, 671–90 (1968)
106. Epstein, S. Toward a unified theory of anxiety. In *Progress in Experimental Personality Research*, **4** (Maher, B. A., Ed., Academic Press, New York, 1967)
107. Erikson, E. H. *Identity, Youth and Crisis* (Norton, New York, 1968)
108. Escalona, S. K. *The Roots of Individuality: Normal Patterns of Development in Infancy* (Aldine, Chicago, 547 pp., 1968)
109. Eysenck, H. J. *The Biological Basis of Personality* (Thomas, Springfield, Ill., 1967)
110. Ezekiel, R. S. The personal future and Peace Corps competence. *J. Pers. Soc. Psychol. Monogr. Suppl.*, **8**, No. 2, Part 2 (1968)
111. Farber, L. H. "I'm sorry, dear.": A critique of the Masters and Johnson research. In *An Analysis of Human Sexual Response* (See Ref. 41)
112. Faucheux, C., Moscovici, S. Studies on group creativity: III. Noise and complexity in the inferential processes. *Human Relations*, **21**, 40 (1968)
113. Feather, N. T. Change in confidence following success or failure as a predictor of subsequent performance. *J. Pers. Soc. Psychol.*, **9**, 38–46 (1968)
114. Feder, C. Z. Relationship between self-acceptance and adjustment, repression-sensitization and social competence. *J. Abnorm. Psychol.*, **73**, 317–22 (1968)
115. Fine, B. J., Sweeney, D. R. Personality traits, and situational factors, and catecholamine excretion. *J. Exptl. Res. Pers.*, **3**, 15–27 (1968)
116. Firestone, I. J. Insulted and provoked: The effects of choice and provocation on hostility and aggression. In *The Cognitive Control of Motivation: The Consequences of Choice and Dissonance* (See Ref. 43)
117. Fisher, S. Body boundary and perceptual vividness. *J. Abnorm. Psychol.*, **73**, 392–96 (1968)
118. Flynn, J. T. *Identification and Individuality: Instincts Fundamental to Human Behavior* (Beekman, New York, 82 pp., 1968)
119. Frankenstein, C. *Psychodynamics of Externalism: Life from Without* (Williams & Wilkins, Baltimore, 1968)
120. Freedman, J. L., Doob, A. N. *Deviancy: The Psychology of Being Different* (Academic Press, New York, 1968)
121. Galbraith, G. G. Effects of sexual arousal and guilt upon free associative sexual responses. *J. Consult. Clin. Psychol.*, **32**, 707–11 (1968)

122. Galbraith, G. G., Mosher, D. L. Associative sexual responses in relation to sexual arousal, guilt, and external approval contingencies. *J. Pers. Soc. Psychol.,* **10,** 142–47 (1968)
123. Galbraith, G. G., Hahn, K., Leiberman, H. Personality correlates of free-associative sex responses to double-entendre words. *J. Consult. Clin. Psychol.,* **32,** 193–97 (1968)
124. Garai, J. E., Scheinfeld, A. Sex differences in mental and behavioral traits. *Genet. Psychol. Monogr.,* **77,** 169–299 (1968)
125. Gardner, R. W., Moriarty, A. *Personality Development at Preadolescence: Explorations of Structure Formation* (Univ. Washington Press, Seattle, 344 pp., 1968)
126. Geen, R. G. Effects of frustration, attack, and prior training in aggressiveness upon aggressive behavior. *J. Pers. Soc. Psychol.,* **9,** 316–21 (1968)
127. Geer, J. H. The development of a scale to measure fear. *Behav. Res. Ther.,* **3,** 45–53 (1965)
128. Ginsburg, G. P., Whittemore, R. G. Creativity and verbal ability: A direct examination of their relationship. *Brit. J. Educ. Psychol.,* **38,** 133–39 (1968)
129. Glass, D. C., Wood, J. D. The control of aggression by self-esteem and dissonance. In *The Cognitive Control of Motivation: The Consequences of Choice and Dissonance* (See Ref. 43)
130. Glass, D. C., Canavan, D., Schiavo, S. Achievement motivation, dissonance, and defensiveness. *J. Pers.,* **36,** 474–92 (1968)
131. Gochman, D. S. Systems analysis. V. Psychological systems. In *Intern. Encycl. Soc. Sci.,* **15,** 486–95 (See Ref. 5)
132. Goldberg, L. R. *The diagnosis of psychosis vs. neurosis from the MMPI* (Invited address, 3rd Ann. Symp. "Recent Developments in the Use of the MMPI," Univ. Minnesota, April 5, 1968)
133. Goldberg, L. R. Explorer on the run: A review of *Objective Personality and Motivation Tests: A Theoretical Introduction and Practical Compendium* by R. B. Cattell and F. W. Warburton. *Contemp. Psychol.,* **13,** 617–19 (1968)
134. Goldberg, L. R. Simple models or simple processes: Some research on clinical judgments. *Am. Psychologist,* **23,** 483–96 (1968)
135. Goldman, R., Jaffa, M., Schachter, S. Yom Kippur, Air France, dormitory food, and the eating behavior of obese and normal persons. *J. Pers. Soc. Psychol.,* **10,** 117–23 (1968)
136. Goldschmid, M. L. The relation of conservation to emotional and environmental aspects of development. *Child Develpm.,* **39,** 579–89 (1968)
137. Gomberg, E. S. L. Etiology of alcoholism. *J. Consult. Clin. Psychol.,* **32,** 18–20 (1968)
138. Gormly, R. Birth order, family size, and psychological masculinity-femininity. *Proc. 76th Ann. Conv. APA,* **3,** 165–66 (1968)
139. Gorsuch, R. L., Cattell, R. B. Personality and socio-ethical values: The structure of self and superego. In *Handbook of Modern Personality Theory,* Chap. 30 (See Ref. 56)
140. Goslin, D. A., Ed. *Handbook of Socialization Theory and Research* (Rand McNally, Chicago, 1969)
141. Gotts, E. E. A note on cross-cultural by age-group comparisons of anxiety scores. *Child Develpm.,* **39,** 945–47 (1968)
142. Gough, H. G., McGurk, E. A group test of perceptual acuity. *Percept. Motor Skills,* **24,** 1107–15 (1967)
143. Gough, H. G., Delcourt, M-J. Developmental increments in perceptual acuity among Swiss and American school children. *Develpm. Psychol.,* **I,** 260–64 (1969)
144. Greenwald, H. J., Oppenheim, D. B. Reported magnitude of self-misidentification among Negro children—artifact? *J. Pers. Soc. Psychol.,* **8,** 49–52 (1968)
145. Grossberg, J. M., Wilson, H. K. Physiological changes accompanying the visualization of fearful and neutral situations. *J. Pers. Soc. Psychol.,* **10,** 124–33 (1968)
146. Gruenfeld, L., Arbuthnot, J. Field independence, achievement values, and the evaluation of a competency related dimension on the Least Preferred Co-worker (LPC) measure. *Percept. Motor Skills,* **27,** 991–1002 (1968)
147. Guilford, J. P. *Personality* (McGraw-Hill, New York, 1959)

148. Guilford, J. P. *The Nature of Human Intelligence* (McGraw-Hill, New York, 1967)
149. Guilford, J. P. *Intelligence, Creativity, and Their Educational Implications* (Knapp, San Diego, Calif., 1968)
150. Hall, W. B., MacKinnon, D. W. Personality inventory correlates of creativity among architects. *J. Appl. Psychol.*, **53** (In press)
151. Hallett, G. *Wittgenstein's Definition of Meaning As Use* (Fordham Univ. Press, New York, 1967)
152. Hare, R. D. Psychopathy, autonomic functioning, and the orienting response. *J. Abnorm. Psychol. Monogr. Suppl.*, **73**, No. 3, Part 2 (1968)
153. Harrison, R. H., Kass, E. H. MMPI correlates of Negro acculturation in a northern city. *J. Pers. Soc. Psychol.*, **10**, 262–70 (1968)
154. Havelka, J. *The Nature of the Creative Process in Art: A Psychological Study* (Martinus Nijhoff, The Hague, 1968)
155. Heilbrun, A. B. Cognitive sensitivity to aversive maternal stimulation in late-adolescent males. *J. Consult. Clin. Psychol.*, **32**, 326–32 (1968)
156. Helmreich, R., Kuiken, D., Collins, B. Effects of stress and birth order on attitude change. *J. Pers.*, **36**, 466–73 (1968)
157. Helson, R. Effects of sibling characteristics and parental values on creative interest and achievement. *J. Pers.*, **36**, 589–607 (1968)
158. Helson, R. Generality of sex differences in creative style. *Ibid.*, 33–48
159. Hertzig, M. E., Birch, H. G., Thomas, A., Mendez, O. A. Class and ethnic differences in the responsiveness of preschool children to cognitive demands. *Monogr. Soc. Res. Child Developm.*, **33**, No. 1 (1968)
160. Hess, E. H. Pupillometric assessment. In *Research in Psychotherapy*, Vol. III (Shlien, J. M., Ed., Am. Psychol. Assoc., Washington, D.C., 1968)
161. Hicks, D. J. Effects of co-observer's sanctions and adult presence on imitative aggression. *Child Develpm.*, **39**, 303–9 (1968)
162. Hodges, W. F. Effects of ego threat and threat of pain on state anxiety. *J. Pers. Soc. Psychol.*, **8**, 364–72 (1968)
163. Holland, J. L. *The Psychology of Vocational Choice: A Theory of Personality Types and Model Environments* (Blaisdell, Waltham, Mass., 130 pp., 1966)
164. Horst, P. *Personality: Measurement of Dimensions* (Jossey-Bass, San Francisco, 1968)
165. Hsieh, T. T., Shybut, J., Lotsof, E. J. Internal versus external control and ethnic group membership: A cross-cultural comparison. *J. Consult. Clin. Psychol.*, **33**, 122–24 (1969)
166. Hundleby, J. D., Cattell, R. B. Personality structure in middle childhood and the prediction of school achievement and adjustment. *Monogr. Soc. Res. Child Develpm.*, **33**, No. 5 (1968)
167. Hundleby, J. D., Connor, W. H. Interrelationships between personality inventories: The 16PF, MMPI, and the MPI. *J. Consult. Clin. Psychol.*, **32**, 152–57 (1968)
168. Inkeles, A., Levinson, D. J. National character: The study of modal personality and sociocultural systems. In *The Handbook of Social Psychology*, 2nd ed., **IV**, Chap. 34 (See Ref. 94)
169. Izard, C. E. The emotions and emotion concepts in personality and culture research. In *Handbook of Modern Personality Theory*, Chap. 21 (See Ref. 56)
170. Jackson, P. W., Messick, S. Creativity. In *Foundations of Abnormal Psychology*, 226–50 (London, P., Rosenhan, D., Eds., Holt, Rinehart & Winston, New York, 1968)
171. Jakobovits, L. A. Effects of mere exposure: A comment. *J. Pers. Soc. Psychol. Monogr. Suppl.*, **9**, 30–32 (1968)
172. James, W. H., Steele, B. J. *Internal control of reinforcement and resistance to extinction in operant learning* (Presented at Midwestern Psychol. Assoc. meetings, Chicago, May 1968)
173. Janis, I. L., Mahl, G. F., Kagan, J., Holt, R. R. *Personality: Dynamics, Development and Assessment* (Harcourt, Brace & World, New York, 1969)
174. Johnson, D. T. Effects of interview stress on measures of state and trait anxiety. *J. Abnorm. Psychol.*, **73**, 245–51 (1968)

175. Johnson, D. T. Trait anxiety, state anxiety, and the estimation of elapsed time. *J. Consult. Clin. Psychol.*, **32**, 654–58 (1968)

176. Johnson, D. T., Spielberger, C. D. The effects of relaxation training and the passage of time on measures of state- and trait-anxiety. *J. Clin. Psychol.*, **24**, 20–23 (1968)

177. Jones, H. E. *Development in Adolescence: Approaches to the Study of the Individual* (Appleton-Century-Crofts, New York, 1943)

178. Jones, M. C. Personality correlates and antecedents of drinking patterns in adult males. *J. Consult. Clin. Psychol.*, **32**, 2–12 (1968)

179. Jones, S. C., Shrauger, J. S. Locus of control and interpersonal evaluations. *J. Consult. Clin. Psychol.*, **32**, 664–68 (1968)

180. Julian, J. W., Katz, S. B. Internal versus external control and the value of reinforcement. *J. Pers. Soc. Psychol.*, **8**, 89–94 (1968)

181. Kahan, J. P. Effects of level of aspiration in an experimental bargaining situation. *J. Pers. Soc. Psychol.*, **8**, 154–59 (1968)

182. Kaplan, M. F. Elicitation of information and response biases of repressors, sensitizers, and neutrals in behavior prediction. *J. Pers.*, **36**, 84–91 (1968)

183. Katkin, E. S., McCubbin, R. J. Habituation of the orienting response as a function of individual differences in anxiety and autonomic lability. *J. Abnorm. Psychol.*, **74**, 54–60 (1969)

184. Katz, I., Henchy, T., Allen, H. Effects of race of tester, approval-disapproval, and need on Negro children's learning. *J. Pers. Soc. Psychol.*, **8**, 38–42 (1968)

185. Kipnis, D. Studies in character structure. *J. Pers. Soc. Psychol.*, **8**, 217–27 (1968)

186. Kipnis, D., Wagner, S. Character structure and response to leadership power. *J. Exptl. Res. Pers.*, **2**, 16–24 (1967)

187. Kish, G. B., Busse, W. Correlates of stimulus-seeking: Age, education, intelligence, and aptitudes. *J. Consult. Clin. Psychol.*, **32**, 633–37 (1968)

188. Klaus, R. A., Gray, S. W. The early training project for disadvantaged children: A report after five years. *Monogr. Soc. Res. Child Develpm.*, **33**, No. 4 (1968)

189. Klausner, S. Z., Ed. *Why Men Take Chances: Studies in Stress Seeking.* (Doubleday, New York, 1968)

190. Kohlberg, L. Stage and sequence: The cognitive-developmental approach to socialization. In *Handbook of Socialization Theory and Research* (See Ref. 140)

191. Korman, A. K. Self-esteem, social influence, and task performance: Some tests of a theory. *Proc. 76th Ann. Conv. APA*, **3**, 567–68 (1968)

192. Kramer, E. Man's behavior patterns. In *Positive Feedback: A General Systems Approach to Positive/Negative Feedback and Mutual Causality* (See Ref. 251)

193. Lamb, C. W. Personality correlates of humor enjoyment following motivational arousal. *J. Pers. Soc. Psychol.*, **9**, 237–41 (1968)

194. Langer, J. *Theories of Development* (Holt, Rinehart & Winston, New York, 1969)

195. Laughlin, P. R., Doherty, M. A., Dunn, R. F. Intentional and incidental concept formation as a function of motivation, creativity, intelligence, and sex. *J. Pers. Soc. Psychol.*, **8**, 401–9 (1968)

196. Lazarus, R. S. *Patterns of Adjustment and Human Effectiveness* (McGraw-Hill, New York, 1969)

197. Leibowitz, G. Comparison of self-report and behavioral techniques of assessing aggression. *J. Consult. Clin. Psychol.*, **32**, 21–25 (1968)

198. Lessing, E. E. Demographic, developmental, and personality correlates of length of future time perspective (FTP). *J. Pers.*, **36**, 183–201 (1968)

199. Lessler, K., Erickson, M. T. Response to sexual symbols by elementary school children. *J. Consult. Clin. Psychol.*, **32**, 473–77 (1968)

200. Leventhal, D. B., Shemberg, K. M., Van Schoelandt, S. K. Effects of sex-role adjustment upon the expression of aggression. *J. Pers. Soc. Psychol.*, **8**, 393–96 (1968)

201. Levy, L. H. Originality as role-defined behavior. *J. Pers. Soc. Psychol.*, **9**, 72–78 (1968)

202. Levy, L. H. Reflections on replications and the experimenter bias effect. *J. Consult. Clin. Psychol.*, **33**, 15–17 (1969)

203. Lewit, D. W., Virolainen, K. Conformity and independence in ad-

olescents' motivation for orthodontic treatment. *Child Develpm.*, **39,** 1189–1200 (1968)

204. Lidz, T. *The Person: His Development Throughout the Life Cycle* (Basic Books, New York, 1968)
205. Lindzey, G., Aronson, E., Eds. *Handbook of Social Psychology* (See Ref. 94)
206. Lipp, L., Kolstoe, R., James, W., Randall, H. Denial of disability and internal control of reinforcement: A study using a perceptual defense paradigm. *J. Consult. Clin. Psychol.*, **32,** 72–75 (1968)
207. Lockard, R. B. The albino rat: A defensible choice or a bad habit. *Am. Psychologist,* **23,** 734–42 (1968)
208. Loehlin, J. C. *Computer Models of Personality* (Random House, New York, 1968)
209. Loehlin, J. C. Psychological genetics from the study of human behavior. In *Handbook of Modern Personality Theory,* Chap. 14 (See Ref. 56)
210. Loevinger, J. The meaning and measurement of ego development. *Am. Psychologist,* **21,** 195–206 (1966)
211. London, P., Ogle, M. E., Unikel, I. P. Effects of hypnosis and motivation on resistance to heat stress. *J. Abnorm. Psychol.,* **73,** 532–41 (1968)
212. Lorr, M. A typology for functional psychotics. In *The Role and Methodology of Classification in Psychiatry and Psychopathology* (Katz, M. M., Cole, J. O., Barton, W. E., Eds., Natl. Inst. Ment. Health, Chevy Chase, Md., 1968)
213. Lott, B. E., Lott, A. J. The relation of manifest anxiety in children to learning task performance and other variables. *Child Develpm.*, **39,** 207–20 (1968)
214. Lundin, R. W. *Personality: A Behavioral Analysis* (Macmillan, New York, 455 pp., 1969)
215. Lundsteen, S. W. Improving the abstract quality in creative problem solving. *J. Special Educ.,* **2,** 177–183 (1968)
216. Lunneborg, P. W. Birth order, aptitude, and achievement. *J. Consult. Clin. Psychol.,* **32,** 101 (1968)
217. McClelland, D. C., Winter, D. G. *Motivating Economic Achievement* (The Free Press, New York, 1969)
218. McClelland, D. C., Atkinson, J. W., Clark, R. A., Lowell, E. L. *The Achievement Motive* (Appleton-Century-Crofts, New York, 1953)
219. McCurdy, H. G. *The Personal World: An Introduction to the Study of Personality* (Harcourt, Brace, & World, New York, 1961)
220. Macfarlane, J. W., Allen, L., Honzik, M. P. *A Developmental Study of the Behavior Problems of Normal Children between Twenty-one Months and Fourteen Years* (Univ. California Press, Berkeley, 1954)
221. McGhee, P. E., Crandall, V. C. Beliefs in internal-external control of reinforcements and academic performance. *Child Develpm.*, **39,** 91–102 (1968)
222. McKeachie, W. J., Isaacson, R. L., Milholland, J. E., Lin, Y. Student achievement motives, achievement cues, and academic achievement. *J. Consult. Clin. Psychol.,* **32,** 26–29 (1968)
223. MacKinnon, D. W. The characteristics of creative architects. In *The Teaching of Architecture* (Am. Inst. Architects, 1963)
224. MacKinnon, D. W. Creativity and images of the self. In *The Study of Lives* (White, R. W., Ed., Atherton, New York, 1963)
225. MacKinnon, D. W. Childhood variables and adult personality in two professional samples: Architects and research scientists. In *Creativity at Home and in School: A Report of the Conference on Child Rearing Practices for Developing Creativity,* 125–60 (Williams, F. E., Ed., Macalester College Creativity Project, St. Paul, Minn., 1968)
226. MacKinnon, D. W. Creativity: I. Psychological aspects. In *Intern. Encycl. Soc. Sci.,* **3,** 435–42 (See Ref. 5)
227. MacKinnon, D. W. Educating for creativity: A modern myth? In *The Creative College Student: An Unmet Challenge,* 147–60 (Heist, P., Ed., Jossey-Bass, San Francisco, 1968)
228. MacKinnon, D. W. Selecting students with creative potential. *Ibid.,* 101–16
229. MacKinnon, D. W. The courage to be: Realizing creative potential. In *Life Skills in School and Society, 1969 ASCD Yearbook,* 95–

110 (See Ref. 84)

230. McQuitty, L. L. Group based pattern analysis of the single individual. *Multivar. Behav. Res.*, **2**, 529–36 (1967)

231. Maddi, S. R. Meaning, novelty, and affect: Comments on Zajonc's paper. *J. Pers. Soc. Psychol. Monogr. Suppl.*, **9**, 28–29 (1968)

232. Maddi, S. R. *Personality Theories: A Comparative Analysis* (Dorsey, Homewood, Ill., 1968)

233. Madsen, C., Jr. Nurturance and modeling in preschoolers. *Child Developm.*, **39**, 221–36 (1968)

234. Madsen, K. B. *Theories of Motivation: A Comparative Study of Modern Theories of Motivation* (Kent State Univ. Press, Kent, Ohio, 1968)

235. Madsen, K. B. Formal properties of Cattellian personality theory. In *Handbook of Modern Personality Theory*, Chap. 32 (See Ref. 56)

236. Mann, H., Siegler, M., Osmond, H. The many worlds of time. *J. Anal. Psychol.*, **13**, 33–56 (1968)

237. Marks, E. Feelings of environmental mastery, attainment discrepancy, and credibility as related to level of aspiration behavior. *Proc. 76th Ann. Conv. APA*, **3**, 427–28 (1968)

238. Marks, E. Personality factors in the performance of a perceptual recognition task under competing incentives. *J. Pers. Soc. Psychol.*, **8**, 69–74 (1968)

239. Marlowe, D., Gergen, K. J. Personality and social interaction. In *Handbook of Social Psychology*, 2nd ed., **III** (See Ref. 94)

240. Martin, R. M. The stimulus barrier and the autonomy of the ego. *Psychol. Rev.*, **75**, 478–93 (1968)

241. Maslow, A. H. *Toward a Psychology of Being*, 2nd ed. (Van Nostrand, Princeton, N.J., 1968)

242. Masters, W. H., Johnson, V. E. *Human Sexual Response* (Little, Brown, Boston, 1966)

243. Mathis, R. W., Hippe, D. L., James, W. H. *Effects of internal control and expectancy upon operant learning rates* (Presented at Midwestern Psychol. Assoc., Chicago, May 1968)

244. Meehl, P. E. Detecting latent clinical taxa by fallible quantitative indicators lacking an acceptable criterion. *Res. Lab. Rept. No. PR-65-2*, Dept. of Psychiatry, Univ. Minnesota, Minneapolis, 1965

245. Meehl, P. E. Theory-testing in psychology and physics: A methodological paradox. *Phil. Sci.*, **34**, 103–15 (1967)

246. Meehl, P. E. Detecting latent clinical taxa. II: A simplified procedure, some additional hitmax cut locators, a single-indicator method, and miscellaneous theorems. *Res. Lab. Rept. No. PR-68-4* (See Ref. 244)

247. Meehl, P. E., Lykken, D. T., Burdick, M. R., Schoener, G. R. Identifying latent clinical taxa. III: An empirical trial of the normal single-indicator method, using MMPI scale 5 to identify the sexes. *Res. Lab. Rept. No. PR–69–1* (See Ref. 244)

248. Mehrabian, A. *An Analysis of Personality Theories* (Prentice-Hall, Englewood Cliffs, N.J., 1968)

249. Milgram, S. Behavioral study of obedience. *J. Abnorm. Soc. Psychol.*, **67**, 371–78 (1963)

250. Millon, T., Ed. *Approaches to Personality* (Pitman, New York, 1968)

251. Milsum, J. H., Ed. *Positive Feedback: A General Systems Approach to Positive/Negative Feedback and Mutual Causality* (Pergamon, Oxford, 1968)

252. Mischel, W. *Personality and Assessment* (Wiley, New York, 1968)

253. Moore, W. E. Social structure and behavior. In *The Handbook of Social Psychology*, 2nd ed., **IV**, 283–322 (See Ref. 94)

254. Moos, R. H. Behavioral effects of being observed: Reaction to a wireless radio transmitter. *J. Consult. Clin. Psychol.*, **32**, 383–88 (1968)

255. Mosher, D. L. The development and multitrait-multimethod matrix analysis of three measures of three aspects of guilt. *J. Consult. Psychol.*, **30**, 25–29 (1966)

256. Murray, H. A. Personality: Contemporary viewpoints. II. Components of an evolving personological system. *Intern. Encycl. Soc. Sci.*, **12**, 5–13 (See Ref. 5)

257. Mussen, P. H. Early sex-role development. In *Handbook of Socialization Theory and Research* (See Ref. 140)

258. Mussen, P. H., Conger, J. J., Kagan,

J. *Child Development and Personality* (Harper, Row, New York, 1968)

259. Nash, P. *Models of Man* (Wiley, New York, 1968)
260. Neff, W. S. *Work and Human Behavior* (Atherton, New York, 296 pp., 1968)
261. Nidorf, L. J., Argabrite, A. H. Dogmatism, sex of the subject, and cognitive complexity. *J. Project. Tech. Pers. Assess.*, **32**, 585–88 (1968)
262. Nisbett, R. E. Birth order and participation in dangerous sports. *J. Pers. Soc. Psychol.*, **8**, 351–53 (1968)
263. Nisbett, R. E. Taste, deprivation, and weight determinants of eating behavior. *Ibid.*, **10**, 107–16 (1968)
264. Nisbett, R. E., Kanouse, D. E. Obesity, hunger, and supermarket shopping behavior. *Proc. 76th Ann. Conv. APA*, **3**, 683–84 (1968)
265. Nomikos, M. S., Opton, E., Jr., Averill, J. R., Lazarus, R. S. Surprise versus suspense in the production of stress reaction. *J. Pers. Soc. Psychol.*, **8**, 204–8 (1968)
266. Norbeck, E., Price-Williams, D., McCord, W. M., Eds. *The Study of Personality: An Interdisciplinary Appraisal* (Holt, Rinehart & Winston, New York, 1968)
267. Norman, W. T. 2800 personality trait descriptors: Normative operating characteristics for a university population. (*Res. Rept. 08310-1-T,* Univ. Michigan, Ann Arbor, 1967)
268. Norman, W. T. Cluster analysis: A diametric rationale and procedure (Mimeographed materials, 1968)
269. Oden, M. H. The fulfillment of promise: 40-year follow-up of the Terman gifted group. *Genet. Psychol. Monogr.*, **77**, 3–93 (1968)
270. Okel, E., Mosher, D. L. Changes in affective states as a function of guilt over aggressive behavior. *J. Consult. Clin. Psychol.*, **32**, 265–70 (1968)
271. Orne, M. T. On the social psychology of the psychological experiment. *Am. Psychologist,* **17**, 776–83 (1962)
272. Otto, H. A., Ed. *Human Potentialities: The Challenge and the Promise* (Green, St. Louis, 1968)
273. Palmer, R. D. Patterns of defensive response to threatening stimuli: Antecedents and consistency. *J. Abnorm. Psychol.*, **73**, 30–36 (1968)
274. Pankove, E., Kogan, N. Creative ability and risk-taking in elementary school children. *J. Pers.*, **36**, 420–39 (1968)
275. Parloff, M. B., Datta, L-E, Kleman, M., Handlon, J. H. Personality characteristics which differentiate creative male adolescents and adults. *J. Pers.*, **36**, 528–52 (1968)
276. Pedersen, F. A., Wender, P. H. Early social correlates of cognitive functioning in six-year-old boys. *Child Develpm.*, **39**, 185–93 (1968)
277. Perlman, H. H. *Persona: Social Role and Personality* (Univ. Chicago Press, Chicago, 1968)
278. Pesce, C. T. A note on the reliability of the Children's Locus of Control scale. *Train. Sch. Bull.*, **65**, 84–86 (1968)
279. Petersen, R. C., Hergenhahn, B. R. Test of cognitive dissonance theory in an elementary school setting. *Psychol. Rept.*, **22**, 199–202 (1968)
280. Peterson, D. R. *The Clinical Study of Social Behavior* (Appleton-Century-Crofts, New York, 1968)
281. Petzel, T. P., Gynther, M. D. Task performance of repressors and sensitizers under ego-oriented versus task-oriented instructions. *J. Consult. Clin. Psychol.*, **32**, 486–87 (1968)
282. Phillips, L. *Human Adaptation and Its Failures* (Academic Press, New York, 1968)
283. Platt, J. J., Eisenman, R., DeGross, E. Birth order and sex differences in future time perspective. *Develpm. Psychol.*, **1**, 70 (1969)
284. Radloff, R., Helmreich, R. *Groups under Stress: Psychological Research in Sealab II* (Appleton-Century-Crofts, New York, 1968)
285. Rhine, W. R. Birth order differences in conformity and level of achievement arousal. *Child Develpm.*, **39**, 987–96 (1968)
286. Rhine, W. R. Motivational and situational determinants of birth order differences in conformity among preadolescent girls. *Proc. 76th Ann. Conv. APA*, **3**, 351–52 (1968)
287. Richardson, S. A., Royce, J. Race and physical handicap in children's preference for other children. *Child Develpm.*, **39**, 467–80 (1968)
288. Rosenberg, S., Nelson, C., Viveka-

nanthan, P. S. A multidimensional approach to the structure of personality impressions. *J. Pers. Soc. Psychol.*, **9**, 283–94 (1968)

289. Rosenthal, R. *Experimenter Effects in Behavioral Research* (Appleton-Century-Crofts, New York, 1966)
290. Rosenthal, R. Experimenter expectancy and the reassuring nature of the null hypothesis decision procedure. *Psychol. Bull. Monogr.*, **70,** No. 6, Part 2, 30–47 (1968)
291. Rosenthal, R. On not so replicated experiments and not so null results. *J. Consult. Clin. Psychol.*, **33,** 7–10 (1969)
292. Rousey, C., Holzman, P. S. Some effects of listening to one's own voice systematically distorted. *Percept. Motor Skills,* **27,** 1303–13 (1968)
293. Rychlak, J. F. *A Philosophy of Science for Personality Theory* (Houghton Mifflin, Boston, 1968)
294. Sahakian, W. S. *Psychology of Personality: Readings in Theory* (Rand McNally, Chicago, 1968)
295. Sandeen, C. A. Aspirations for college. *Personnel Guid. J.*, **46,** 462–65 (1968)
296. Sanford, N. Personality: I. The field. *Intern. Encycl. Soc. Sci.*, **11,** 587–606 (See Ref. 5)
297. Sanford, N. Personality and patterns of alcohol consumption. *J. Consult. Clin. Psychol.*, **32,** 13–17 (1968)
298. Sarason, I. G. *Personality: An Objective Approach* (Wiley, New York, 1966)
299. Sarason, I. G. *Contemporary Research in Personality: A Reader* (Van Nostrand, Princeton, N.J., 1968)
300. Sarason, I. G. Birth order, test anxiety, and learning. *J. Pers.*, **37,** 171–77 (1969)
301. Schachter, F. F., Cooper, A., Gordet, R. A method for assessing personality development for follow-up evaluations of the preschool child. *Monogr. Soc. Res. Child Develpm.*, **33,** No. 3 (1968)
302. Schachter, S. Cognitive effects on bodily functioning: Studies of obesity and eating. In *Neurophysiology and Emotion* (Glass, D., Ed., Rockefeller Univ. Press, New York, 1967)
303. Schachter, S., Gross, L. P. Manipulated time and eating behavior. *J. Pers. Soc. Psychol.*, **10,** 98–106 (1968)
304. Schachter, S., Goldman, R., Gordon, A. Effects of fear, food deprivation, and obesity on eating. *J. Pers. Soc. Psychol.*, **10,** 91–97 (1968)
305. Schimek, J. G. Cognitive style and defenses: A longitudinal study of intellectualization and field independence. *J. Abnorm. Psychol.*, **73,** 575–80 (1968)
306. Schneider, J. M. Skill versus chance activity preference and locus of control. *J. Consult. Clin. Psychol.*, **32,** 333–37 (1968)
307. Shader, R. I., DiMascio, A., Harmatz, J. Characterological anxiety levels and premenstrual libido changes. *Psychosomatics,* **9,** 197–98 (1968)
308. Shaw, L. C. *The Bonds of Work* (Jossey-Bass, San Francisco, 1968)
309. Shemberg, K. M., Leventhal, D. B. Masculinity-femininity and need for social approval. *J. Project. Tech. & Pers. Assess.*, **32,** 575–77 (1968)
310. Shontz, F. C. *Research Methods in Personality* (Appleton-Century-Crofts, New York, 1965)
311. Shrader, W. K., Leventhal, T. Birth order of children and parental report of problems. *Child Develpm.*, **39,** 1165–75 (1968)
312. Singer, D. L. Aggression arousal, hostile humor, catharsis. *J. Pers. Soc. Psychol. Monogr. Suppl.*, **8,** No. 1, Part 2, 1–14 (1968)
313. Smith, H. C. *Personality Development* (McGraw-Hill, New York, 1968)
314. Spielberger, C. D., Lushene, R. E., McAdoo, W. G. Theory and measurement of anxiety states. In *Handbook of Modern Personality Theory,* Chap. 10 (See Ref. 56)
315. Steele, J. The hysteria and psychasthenia constructs as an alternative to manifest anxiety and conflict-free ego functions. *J. Abnorm. Psychol.*, **74,** 79–85 (1969)
316. Stein, K. B., Sarbin, T. R., Kulik, J. A. Future time perspective: Its relation to the socialization process and the delinquent role. *J. Consult. Clin. Psychol.*, **32,** 257–64 (1968)
317. Stein, M. I. Creativity. In *Handbook of Personality Theory and*

Research, Chap. 16, 900–42 (See Ref. 39)
318. Stotland, E. *The Psychology of Hope* (Jossey-Bass, San Francisco, 284 pp., 1969)
319. Suedfeld, P. Sensory deprivation stress: Birth order and instructional set as interacting variables. *J. Pers. Soc. Psychol.,* **11,** 70–74 (1969)
320. Tart, C., Ed. *Altered States of Consciousness* (Wiley, New York, 1969)
321. Taylor, D. A., Wheeler, L., Altman, I. Stress relations in socially isolated groups. *J. Pers. Soc. Psychol.,* **9,** 369–76 (1968)
322. Taylor, R. E., Eisenman, R. Birth order and sex difference in complexity-simplicity, color-form preference and personality. *J. Project. Tech. & Pers. Assess.,* **32,** 383–87 (1968)
323. Terhune, K. W. Motives, situation, and interpersonal conflict within prisoner's dilemma. *J. Pers. Soc. Psychol. Monogr. Suppl.,* **8,** No. 3, Part 2 (1968)
324. Thoday, J. M., Parkes, A., Eds., *Genetic and Environmental Influences on Behavior* (Plenum, New York, 1968)
325. Thomas, A., Chess, S., Birch, H. G. *Temperament and Behavior Disorders in Children* (New York Univ. Press, New York, 1968)
326. Tiryakian, E. A. Typologies. *Intern. Encycl. Soc. Sci.,* **16,** 177–86 (See Ref. 5)
327. Toman, W. *Family Constellation: Its Effects on Personality and Social Behavior,* 2nd ed. (Springer, New York, 1969)
328. Torcivia, J. M., Laughlin, P. R. Dogmatism and concept-attainment strategies. *J. Pers. Soc. Psychol.,* **8,** 397–400 (1968)
329. Triandis, H. C., Vassiliou, V., Nassiakou, M. Three cross-cultural studies of subjective culture. *J. Pers. Soc. Psychol. Monogr. Suppl.,* **8,** No. 4, Part 2 (1968)
330. Tryk, H. E. Assessment in the study of creativity. In *Advances in Psychological Assessment,* **I,** 34–54 (McReynolds, P., Ed., Science & Behavior Books, Palo Alto, Calif., 1968)
331. Tsushima, W. T. Responses of Irish and Italian patients of two social classes under preoperative stress. *J. Pers. Soc. Psychol.,* **8,** 43–48 (1968)
332. Tulkin, S. R. Race, class, family, and school achievement. *J. Pers. Soc. Psychol.,* **9,** 31–37 (1968)
333. Tulkin, S. R., Muller, J. P., Conn, L. K. Need for approval and popularity: Sex differences in elementary school students. *J. Consult. Clin. Psychol.,* **33,** 35–39 (1969)
334. Vacchiano, R. B., Strauss, P. S., Schiffman, D. C. Personality correlates of dogmatism. *J. Consult. Clin. Psychol.,* **32,** 83–85 (1968)
335. Van Egeren, L. Repression and sensitization: Sensitivity and recognition criteria. *J. Exptl. Res. Pers.,* **3,** 1–8 (1968)
336. Verinis, J. S., Brandsma, J. M., Cofer, C. N. Discrepancy from expectation in relation to affect and motivation: Tests of McClelland's hypothesis. *J. Pers. Soc. Psychol.,* **9,** 47–58 (1968)
337. Wachtel, P. L. Style and capacity in analytic functioning. *J. Pers.,* **36,** 202–12 (1968)
338. Walberg, H. I. Physics, femininity, and creativity. *Develpm. Psychol.,* **1,** 47–54 (1969)
339. Wallach, M. A., Kogan, N. *Modes of Thinking in Young Children: A Study of the Creativity-Intelligence Distinction* (Holt, Rinehart & Winston, New York, 1965)
340. Wallach, M. A., Wing, C. W. *The Talented Student: A Validation of the Creativity-Intelligence Distinction* (Holt, Rinehart & Winston, New York, 1969)
341. Walters, R. H., Willows, D. C. Imitative behavior of disturbed and nondisturbed children following exposure to aggressive and nonaggressive models. *Child Develpm.,* **39,** 79–89 (1968)
342. Ward, W. C. Creativity in young children. *Child Develpm.,* **39,** 737–54 (1968)
343. Webb, E. J., Campbell, D. T., Schwartz, R. D., Sechrest, L. *Unobtrusive Measures: Nonreactive Research in the Social Sciences* (Rand McNally, Chicago, 1966)
344. Weinberg, M. *Desegregation Research: An Appraisal* (Phi Delta Kappa, Bloomington, Ind., 1968)
345. Weinstein, L. The mother-child schema, anxiety, and academic

achievement in elementary school boys. *Child Develpm.*, **39**, 257–64 (1968)

346. Weinstein, M. S., Lewinsohn, P. M. Optional stopping and decision latency as a function of repression-sensitization. *J. Exptl. Res. Pers.*, **3**, 60–64 (1968)
347. Weiss, B. W., Katkin, E. S., Rubin, B. M. Relationship between a factor analytically derived measure of a specific fear and performance after related fear induction. *J. Abnorm. Psychol.*, **73**, 461–63 (1968)
348. Welsh, G. S. *Personality Dimensions of Creativity* (Jossey-Bass, San Francisco, in press)
349. Wessler, R. L., Strauss, M. E. Experimenter expectancy: A failure to replicate. *Psychol. Rept.*, **22**, 687–88 (1968)
350. Wiggins, J. S., Wiggins, N., Conger, J. C. Correlates of heterosexual somatic preference. *J. Pers. Soc. Psychol.*, **10**, 82–90 (1968)
351. Wilder, J. *Stimulus and Response: The Law of Initial Value* (Williams & Wilkens, Baltimore, 1968)
352. Willems, E. P., Raush, H. L., Eds. *Naturalistic Viewpoints in Psychological Research* (Holt, Rinehart & Winston, New York, 294 pp., 1969)
353. Williams, A. F. Psychological needs and social drinking among college students. *Quart. J. Stud. Alcohol,* **29**, 355–63 (1968)
354. Winter, D. G. Need for power in thought and action. *Proc. 76th Ann. Conv. APA,* **3**, 429–30 (1968)
355. Winter, S. K., Griffith, J. C., Kolb, D. A. Capacity for self-direction. *J. Consult. Clin. Psychol.*, **32**, 35–41 (1968)
356. Witkin, H. A. Social influences in the development of cognitive style. In *Handbook of Socialization Theory and Research* (See Ref. 140)
357. Witkin, H. A., Dyk, R. B., Faterson, H. F., Goodenough, D. R., Karp, S. A. *Psychological Differentiation: Studies of Development* (Wiley, New York, 1962)
358. Wylie, R. C. The present status of self theory. In *Handbook of Personality Theory and Research,* Chap. 12, 728–87 (See Ref. 39)
359. Zajonc, R. B. Attitudinal effects of mere exposure. *J. Pers. Soc. Psychol. Monogr. Suppl.*, **9**, 1–27 (1968)
360. Zander, A., Forward, J. Position in group, achievement motivation, and group aspirations. *J. Pers. Soc. Psychol.*, **8**, 282–88 (1968)
361. Zeller, W., Zeller, L., Thomas, K. *Begabung und Charakter: Der Älteste und der Jungste* (Hografe, Göttingen, 1968)
362. Zimbardo, P. G., Ed. *The Cognitive Control of Motivation: The Consequences of Choice and Dissonance* (See Ref. 43)
363. Zubek, J. P. Urinary excretion of adrenaline and noradrenaline during prolonged immobilization. *J. Abnorm. Psychol.*, **73**, 223–25 (1968)
364. Zubek, J. P., Ed. *Sensory Deprivation: Fifteen Years of Research* (Appleton-Century-Crofts, New York, 1969)
365. Zucker, R. A., Manosevitz, M., Lanyon, R. I. Birth order, anxiety, and affiliation during a crisis. *J. Pers. Soc. Psychol.*, **8**, 354–59 (1968)
366. Zuckerman, M., Persky, H., Link, K. E., Basu, G. K. Experimental and subject factors determining responses to sensory deprivation, social isolation, and confinement. *J. Abnorm. Psychol.*, **73**, 183–94 (1968)

THEORY AND TECHNIQUES OF PERSONALITY MEASUREMENT[1] 145

By Donald W. Fiske and Pamela H. Pearson[2]

University of Chicago, Chicago, Illinois

This chapter is one of the intermittent series which has had "assessment" in its title. The authors have dropped that term because of its imprecision and its connotations. Assessment has often been used to refer to the combining of measures, usually by human judgment, to predict a criterion. But personality measurement as a whole involves the combination or reduction of observations to obtain an index and is concerned with much more than the prediction of criteria. Additionally, the terms assessment and criteria have an evaluative flavor; while adequacy of functioning is involved in much of personality, a science of personality must not be limited to normative considerations. Finally, assessment has the connotation of dealing with the whole person. It seems quite clear that we cannot have a science of the whole person, or even of substantial segments of personality, until we understand the components.

Most concepts in the personality field are so broad and heterogeneous in their referents that when one concept is used to describe different persons, it is very doubtful that the identical attribute is applied to each. The task facing personality today is the identification and delineation of attributes which can be uniformly applied to persons, the objects of this science, with the specific applications of each attribute differing only in quantity, not quality. Coordinate with that task is the work of developing operations for measuring each of these attributes. Such procedures must be standardized so that the measurements can, in principle, be replicated for the same persons and, particularly critical in this area, so that the measurements are getting at the same attribute in the different persons measured, without any sizable person-instrument interaction. This chapter is concerned with the extent to which these standards are being approximated in personality measurement today.

A science develops by an interactive or cyclical process, observations leading to concepts, and concepts guiding the next set of observations. In personality, an infinity of observations has been conceptualized in a variety of sets of terms with general statements about them. These literary or even

[1] The preparation of this paper was supported by a PHS Biomedical Science Support Grant from the University of Chicago and Grant No. GS-1998 from the National Science Foundation. We are also indebted to Arondelle L. Schreiber for her assistance in the bibliographic work.

[2] Now at the University of Illinois College of Medicine.

lay concepts have often been linked uncritically with measurement operations, even though it is quite apparent that the operations at best represent only a portion of each concept, and typically yield measurements confounded by other variables. The empiricist who prefers to start with such relatively objective observations as test responses finds that his analytically derived variables partake of similar confounding. So the student of personality measurement finds himself with no solid rock on which to build: personality constructs are too vague to serve as blueprints for test construction, while observed responses vary with the stimuli, the setting, and subject's perceptions of them, i.e., with the method or the class of observations which are utilized.

Coverage.—To make this review manageable, we have paid little or no attention to several topics which fall within a broad definition of personality measurement, such as psychodiagnostics, the measurement of ability, and personnel selection. We have also neglected some topics which have clear relevance, such as test theory. All these topics are well covered by other chapters in the *Annual Reviews.* This paper will focus on the measurement of personality variables for purposes of basic research, with particular attention to coordination between concepts and operations, to method variance, and to the measuring process. Many contributions which could not be included here are cited in recent chapters on personality [see especially (1)], personality structure, personality dynamics, and projective techniques.

Conceptual-Operational Coordination and Validation of Measures

The lack of specification and insufficient delineation of target concepts to be measured, in combination with the nonsystematic coordination of measures with constructs, has led to the present state of chaos in personality measurement today. Adelson (1) speaks of a crisis in methodology, concluding that there is only occasional and erratic coordination between theory and data.

Although the coordination between a target construct and a measuring instrument is rarely systematic, it usually emphasizes one of three strategies: Global-Rational; Separated-Rational, or Empirical. The two Rational strategies derive their measures from a priori notions concerning the target concept, although they may use empirical techniques to refine their measures. In contrast, the Empirical strategists derive their measuring instruments by operational techniques (e.g., factor analysis), then proceed to conceptualize or, more typically, label their variables by induction. By and large, the Global-Rational and Empirical strategists make the untenable assumption that their measure covers the total domain of the target concept, while the Separated-Rational adherents more wisely consider their measure(s) as covering only a part of the target construct. Rationally derived measures do have the advantage of being integrated into a nomological net which permits construct validation operations, while empirically derived procedures are typically validated by common-sense predictions. Factors can, of course, be considered as constructs, as Royce (182) has suggested, but substantial conceptual work must be done to integrate the measures into the network of scientific theory. Coan (42) has dealt cogently with some of these issues.

Many investigators have recognized the lack of conceptual specification (3, 70, 76), and some attempts to remedy it have been made. In a major advance in the conceptualization of creativity, Jackson & Messick (104) define response properties, judgmental standards, and subjective responses associated with creativity, relating these properties to cognitive styles and personal qualities. Noting that other disciplines have their own special views of creativity which have been adopted by various psychologists, Tryk (216) classifies procedures for assessing creativity under four orientations: creativity as a product, as a capacity, as a process, and as an aspect of the total person. These diverse approaches naturally lead to somewhat separate bodies of empirical investigation. Others have tackled the conceptualization of different constructs: aggression (111), ego development (134), social influence (208), nonconformity (242), and attention (225).

But the problem of coordinating the measures with the concepts has not been solved. Fiske (70) suggests that constructs should be divided into facets, each with its set of elements, so that, e.g., each situation is paired with each mode of response. Support for this Separated-Rational approach is given by various studies which indicate that variance in test scores is a function of the situation, the person, and the type of response (23, 25, 64). Additional support for this strategy was given in a recent paper (27) which compared four strategies for measuring dominance. The rational facet approach seemed most promising for theoretical work, while the factorial facet approach yielded more relationships with outside variables. The authors concluded that different purposes (such as prediction vs. theory testing) would seem to require different strategies.

For the purposes of basic research and the testing of theoretical propositions, however, the fact that a single measure typically can be considered as measuring several constructs is undesirable. For example, Dana (48) has proposed six constructs to define the Rorschach human movement score. In effect he has suggested that several constructs can contribute jointly to the variance on this score, rendering it uninterpretable. Confounding of conceptually different variables in a measure precludes an adequate interpretation of that score, the result being that coordination of that measure with a term in a nomological net is at best tenuous, and at worst erroneous.

Studies of the validity of personality measures aimed at single concepts are organized here by the type of strategy, in the hope that useful contrasts and comparisons of results can be made. Discussion of the validity of some tests designed to assess personality adjustment and functioning will then be considered.

Validity of Global-Rational measures: Self-report inventories.—Considerable attention has been given to the Internal versus External Control (I–E) scale, and in terms of construct validation, the results look quite promising. In a major contribution, Rotter (181) reviewed the research on this 29-item scale. Adequate internal consistency and stability were reported, as well as absence of large covariation with the control variables of intelligence and social desirability (Marlowe-Crowne SDS). He further reported that high Internals took steps to improve their environmental condition, placed greater value on skill, were more concerned with their ability, particularily their failures, and were more resistant to attempts to influence them. Internal control was also positively related to scores on an insight test, while external control was related to overt death anxiety (212). Other studies (123, 192) provided results which were generally consistent with theory.

Although the I-E scale looks quite promising from a construct validation point of view, there are several suggestions for further validation. The first suggestion, stemming from the finding of Hersch & Scheibe (93) that Internals were more homogeneous as a group than were Externals, is for greater specification of the types of controls. They suggest that it may be profitable to distinguish the perceived benevolence vs. malevolence of environmental forces, and these could be further classified as realistically vs. unrealistically controlling subjects. The second suggestion is to measure the construct by other methods (e.g., peer ratings) to provide evidence concerning convergent validity.

In order to measure the global concept of optimal level of activation, the Sensation Seeking Scale (SSS) was developed (245). Validation studies have shown positive relationships with extraversion (66); positive relationships with educational attainment, intellectual level, perceptual, spatial and numerical abilities, but negative relationships with age (116); positive relationships with autonomy, change, and exhibition, but negative relationships with deference, nurturance, orderliness, and affiliation on two self-report measures of Murray's needs; negative relationships with two usual measures of field dependence (246). These results seem generally consistent with theoretical expectations.

That the SSS is composed of several different aspects of sensation seeking was shown in a factor analysis of the total pool of items. Zuckerman & Link (246) reported four interpretable factors for males: thrill-seeking, general (social, work), visual, and antisocial. For females, the first two factors were similar to the ones for males. Pursuing these distinctions might yield research that could be more precisely interpreted. Evidence of convergent and discriminant validity would also be desirable.

In a major study clarifying the constructs of authoritarianism and dogmatism, Kerlinger & Rokeach (115) factor analyzed the F and D item intercorrelations obtained from administering the two scales to over a thousand subjects in three different states. Factor analyzing 10 oblique, first-order factors, they found three second-order factors which were interpreted as dogmatism, fascistic authoritarianism, and authoritarian aggression and submission. They conclude that the two scales are factorially discriminable, even though both are measuring aspects of authoritarianism. Again, aspects or parts of a unitary global construct emerge empirically separated.

Among several analyses of test anxiety measures, one by Sassenrath (187) is of particular interest. The several factors he found in the Test Anxiety Questionnaire are associated with both situational and mode of response aspects (cf. 64). Thus this questionnaire, in spite of its high reliability, is composed of distinct reactions to specific situations. For many purposes, it would seem that one or more subscores would provide more fruitful findings than the usual total composite score.

Essentially negative evidence for the validity of some other standard measures was found. Results pertinent to the Taylor Manifest Anxiety Scale (MAS) were reviewed by Adelson (1), who dealt extensively with the measurement of the anxiety concept. His major point was that test scores from the MAS can hardly be construed to measure "anxiety," as separated from either general emotionality or defensiveness. Of course, such confounding implies the lack of discriminant validity, which seriously impairs the interpretation of test scores. Essentially negative evidence of convergent validity across different methods of measurement was reported for the Edwards Personal Preference Schedule (EPPS) (32). Using Jackson's multimethod factor analysis, which analyzes only variance common to more than one method, Jackson & Guthrie (101) found that common variance on Murray's needs, as measured by self-report (Personality Research Form), self-ratings, and peer-ratings, could be accounted for by 13 specific concept factors with each of the three methods loading on them, two factors with pairs of psychologically related concepts, and only three somewhat mixed factors.

Although some newer scales (I-E, SSS), measured by self-report and a Global-Rational approach, have shown initial promise as measures of their intended constructs, subsequent evidence on these two scales has suggested that further conceptual and operational separation might well be in order. Older scales in general fail to meet the requirements of convergent and discriminant validation, and in some cases are so confounded with sources of construct-irrelevant variance that test scores are in effect conceptually uninterpretable.

Validity of Global-Rational measures: Projective methodologies.—In a major study, Skolnick (202) reported data on motivational imagery and behavior over 20 years. TAT scores for achievement, affiliation, power, and aggression were correlated wth behavioral measures. While the predominant trend was a direct relationship between fantasy and behavior, no one statement held for all motives, ages, and both sexes. Results were clearest for achievement (adults) and for power (males), indicating the complexity of situation. Commenting on that study, McClelland (149) conceptualizes fantasy and behavior as related but separate types of behavior, while Lazarus

(122) argues that substantial correlations will not be found until such moderating variables as conditions are taken into account. Several studies supported Lazarus' contention (e.g., 67, 197, 223).

Validity of Global-Rational measures: Performance measures.—Many of the same trends found in self-report and projective measures of unitary constructs also held true for cognitive style variables. Wachtel (226) suggested that it would be profitable to differentiate persons who can function in a field-independent way from those who must. Several studies questioned the dimensionality of different cognitive styles. In a factor analytic study, Messick & Fritzky (156) reported two relatively independent modes of stimulus analysis, element articulation and highlighting of large figural forms against the background. Element articulation was linked to Witkin's field-independent dimension by virtue of a large factor loading of the Embedded Figures Test. Another factor analytic study concluded that cognitive complexity-simplicity was multidimensional, consisting of a number of distinct, possibly independent tendencies (220). A paper (211) examining the concept of equivalence range calls for more specification and suggests that moderator variables affect consistencies. Two studies showed that adjustment variables (e.g., ego strength, neuroticism) can in fact be used fruitfully as moderators (210, 221).

Two major trends can be noted which are similar for all constructs measured by a Global-Rational strategy. First, and most importantly, investigators are calling for greater conceptual specificity along with examination of the effects of possible moderator variables. Empirical studies have shown that most constructs are multidimensional in nature. An alternative approach, to divide the construct rationally, has been taken by some other investigators.

Validity of Separated-Rational measures.—Mosher (159, 160) has divided the concept of guilt into three types: sex guilt, hostility guilt, and morality-conscience guilt, and has evaluated the convergent and discriminant validity of his measures. In a study with females, convergent validity was excellent; the validity diagonals comparing self-report and sentence completion varied from 0.52 to 0.90. Measures of these three aspects of guilt were not related to two social desirability measures. The results look promising, and Mosher's distinctions appear fruitful.

In an excellent paper, emphasizing the importance of conceptual distinctions, Kasl, Sampson & French (109) conceptualized independence and dependence as separate constructs (rather than polar opposites), then further specified each dimension motivationally. Four dimensions were proposed: approach need independence; avoidance need independence; approach need dependence; avoidance need dependence. Four separate measures were derived by scoring thematic apperceptions, the scoring procedure based on that of McClelland and Atkinson. Results indicated adequate scorer and internal consistency reliabilities. The four needs were relatively independent of each other and of self-report factors of emotional dependence, task dependence, and independence. The most promising evidence of construct validity was for approach need independence; there was limited evidence for avoidance need dependence, and no evidence for either avoidance need independence or approach need dependence. It would be important to measure these constructs by other methods to obtain data concerning convergent and discriminant validity.

Maddi and his associates have carried out a series of studies (139–141) which have rationally divided the need for variety into three forms: active-interoceptive; active-exteroceptive; and passive, all measured by thematic apperception. Promising evidence of construct validity has been established for the two active forms. In addition, moderate convergent and discriminant validity was found with a structured self-report measure of the active-interoceptive form (172). Additional evidence of convergent validity for the other two forms would be desirable, as well as evidence of construct validity for the passive form.

The concept of n Affiliation has been divided into approach and avoidant motives in two studies. Byrne, McDonald & Mikawa (30) suggested that on the typical thematic apperception measure of n Affiliation, high scores represented approach motivation, medium scores represent ambivalent affiliation tendencies, and low scores represented avoidant motivation. To measure approach and avoidant motivation separately, they used an affect scoring system, derived from thematic apperception protocols. Results were in accordance with their prediction for the typical n Affiliation scoring. Some further validation evidence was obtained. The affect index of approach motivation correlated positively with Murray's affiliation questionnaire, which was designed to measure approach motivation, while the affect index of avoidance motivation did not.

The fruitfulness of distinguishing approach and avoidant n Affiliation was also shown in a second study (33). It was suggested that the approach n Affiliation is a more general trait, associated with adjustment, while avoidance of affiliation is a more specific trait, associated with the lack of social effectiveness.

In general, the results for the Separated-Rational strategy appear promising. While on logical grounds alone, definitions are improved by separating constructs into parts and measuring the parts separately, empirical evidence of validity is available on only a few constructs, compared to the many formulated in the more traditional Global-Rational and Empirical approaches. It will be a formidable task to establish validity for Separated-Rational measures, not just because of the inevitable increase in the number of measuring instruments, but also because most theories of personality conceptualize at the global level. Increased specificity in theory must accompany increased specificity in operationalization. When nomological networks are viewed as consisting of constructs formulated and measured by Separated-Rational approach, the task of reformulating theory looms large.

Validity of empirical measures.—Various scales derived from the MMPI continue to enjoy considerable attention. Most of the recent research has concentrated on a measure of ego defensiveness, the Repression-Sensitization (R-S) scale developed by Byrne (28). In reviewing construct validation studies, he reported that most suggest a linear relationship between sensitizing defenses and maladjustment, rather than a U-shaped curve. This finding was supported by a later correlational study (29) with the California Psychological Inventory (CPI). Questioning whether repressors are really better adjusted, Petzel & Gynther (174) compared the task performance of repressors and sensitizers under ego-oriented vs. task-oriented instructions. They found that sensitizers performed better than repressors under ego-oriented instructions, while the reverse was true under task-oriented instructions. Consistent with their finding, Hare (90) found repressors to exhibit greater disturbance at the physiological level, but a stronger tendency to avoid thinking about an impending shock. The results of another study (65) provided data suggesting that repressors are more prone to defend against anxiety at a perceptual level, while sensitizers defend more at a nonperceptual level of response. Supporting this view, Lomont (135) suggested that repressors are more vulnerable to being threatened by the stimuli they actually encounter. The issue of whether repressors or sensitizers are better adjusted, of course, depends upon the criteria used to measure adjustment. It seems that repressors report themselves as better adjusted, but one should not forget that ego-defense theory would predict that repression is the most successful defense, functioning to keep the conscious awareness of ego-alien material at a minimum.

Although many studies have reported interesting findings with the R-S scale, important criticisms have been made. Dublin (53) found results inconsistent with the notion of the R-S scale as a continuum from repression to sensitization. More important, however, is the criticism that R-S is measuring both defensiveness and anxiety in undeterminable proportions. The MAS and the R-S were found to be correlated 0.87 (82) and R-S correlated 0.76 with another self-report anxiety measure (135). Given the size of these correlations when corrected for attentuation, the scales can be considered to be measuring the same thing, whatever that is. A similar case can be made for many of the MMPI-derived measures.

Some convergent and discriminant validity was demonstrated for five CPI scales, but only two showed evidence of discriminant validation (50). Gough (83) developed an equation for social maturity from four CPI scales, and showed that it differentiated between several pairs of criterion groups. He has also discussed the rationale for the CPI and research on it (84).

The importance of the type of task used in validity studies was suggested by the results obtained by Weiss, Katkin & Rubin (234), who found that subjects scoring high on a factor-analytically derived measure of fear showed more signs of behavior disruption on a motor, but not on a perceptual task, than those scoring low. In another interesting paper, subjects classified on the basis of repeating vs. not-repeating conforming behavior in a laboratory situation showed different personality correlates (204). The authors suggest that failure to determine the stability of conforming behavior may explain the inconsistent findings in this substantive area.

In a major factor analytic study, Comrey & Duffy (43) compared Cattell's, Eysenck's, and Comrey's personality factors, finding some matching factors: e.g., Eysenck's neuroticism, Comrey's neuroticism, and Cattell's second-order anxiety; Eysenck's introversion and Comrey's shyness. Ten first-order Cattell factors overlapped those of Comrey, but did not match. Four loaded highly on Comrey's socialization factor; five loaded highly on an empathy-hostility factor.

Although many of the results found with empirically based measures are interesting and the tests can be shown to be adequately reliable, there is always the problem of interpretation. When defensiveness is equated with anxiety and anxiety is equated with neuroticism, and all may be equated with social desirability, conceptual distinctions no longer exist in any meaningful sense. Theory testing when using a test that can be equated with four separate interpretations seems impossible. In such cases, research should seek evidence for discriminant validity.

Validity of projective scoring categories.—The measures included in this section are projective, were constructed as measures of adjustment or of its aspects, and were not intended to measure unitary constructs. The Rorschach is still a favorite subject for study. Scoring systems derived to measure psychological health predicted external criteria in two studies. The Rorschach Prognostic Rating Scale correlated with improvement (ratings) in both a treated and an untreated group (63). Proposing two types of adjustment scores, function and structure, Gaylin (75) found that the function change score differentiated success in therapy, while the more traditional structure change scores did not. Holt's primary-process scoring index was found to be higher in subjects with nonintegrated as opposed to integrated or moralistic-repressive types of consciences (14). All studies provide positive validation support for the measures.

Human movement, interpreted as a measure of the capacity for delayed need satisfaction, was inversely related to the level of motivation for the rapid passage of time (120). When viewed as an active energy system, human movement was reported to be related to creative expressions in a variety of measures (54). Subjects engaged in a response-inhibition task produced more movement than subjects engaged in a noninhibition task (49). As scored by Klopfer's technique, human movement, animal movement, and inanimate movement increased after sensory isolation, but only human and animal movement increased after motor inhibition (13). The results are difficult to interpret conceptually, as Dana (48) has proposed six constructs for the human movement response alone, but it is apparent that movement is related to other behaviors.

In an interesting study (2), it was shown that good whole responses, as measured by Friedman's qualitative scoring, were positively related to intelligence (WAIS)[3] when the index was the proportion of good wholes (among all responses). In contrast, total wholes over total responses were unrelated to intelligence. This study shows the utility of differentiating the quality of the wholes in estimating intelligence. Some support was given for the interpretation of the shading determinant as an index of resignation and inhibition in a study by Elstein (60). In a study of the personality correlates of the Rorschach color response, Cerbus & Nichols (38) note that the only established relationship between color and personality is that of the reduced use of color by depressives. Research does not show that color is associated either with impulsivity or with suggestibility.

The Holtzman Inkblot Technique (HIT) also received considerable attention. Human movement was related to social interests and differentiated high from low pathology (69). In a study of therapists and clients, therapists' general movement, human movement, and hostility were related negatively to clients' hostile competing and positively to their support seeking. But therapists' HIT scores had only chance correlations with therapists' behavior (161). Another study (177) investigated the HIT correlates of creative potential, as measured by the Myer-Briggs Type Indicator in female students. Lows on both intuition and perception tended to have less color, movement, definite form, human content, integration of blot elements, pathognomic verbalizations, hostility, and abstract content than high-scoring subjects. It should also be pointed out, however, that only a little over half the hypotheses were confirmed, and only one of seven exploratory hypotheses.

Sappenfield (186) tested a Szondi assumption and interpreted his findings to indicate that any positive validity findings with this test are likely to be based on stereotyped perceptions of the pictures themselves, rather than upon the correct perception of personality characteristics represented in them. The research on sentence completions is seen by Goldberg (78) as generally favorable, although it is unclear why or how the technique works. Adding to the puzzle is the empirical evidence that subjects can exercise conscious control over their responses. Other work on projective techniques includes a number of reviews of single projective techniques: the Blacky Pictures (18), the Bender-Gestalt (213), human figure drawings (178, 209), and the Rorschach (52, 79, 89, 119).

An extensive critical review of projective techniques, centering on the Rorschach and the TAT, has been made by Zubin, Eron & Schumer (244). In their "attempt at returning projective techniques to the scientific fold," they stress the relevance of general psychology's knowledge of perception. They propose that we return to Rorschach's own view and treat these major projective techniques as experiments, the responses to be scored psychometrically by a very detailed scheme. While their objectives are commendable, one wonders how popular their approach will become. It may be more prac-

[3] Wechsler Adult Intelligence Scale.

tical to take a more radical step and look for other procedures which can be applied more systematically and objectively, and which may yield more dependable observations on each of the many variables of interest to those now employing these techniques.

In free-response procedures, general attributes of the protocol can affect both specific scoring categories and overall impressions leading to global ratings. In drawings of human figures, artistic merit (127) and judged distortion (231) appear to intrude into and bias the diagnostic interpretations. There is consensus between naive judges and experienced clinicians about the drawing characteristics associated with symptoms, even when in fact no such association exists in the protocols (40, 190). Such a test is clearly a wide-band technique providing diverse hints with limited reliability and very uncertain fidelity, in terms of the classification and decision theory developed by Cronbach & Gleser (45).

Low interscorer and intrascorer consistency on Rorschach scoring is still a problem (224). While such unreliability can almost always be reduced to a negligible level by intensive training, it makes such a free-response technique highly expensive. Furthermore, the training of one set of judges to the point where they are essentially interchangeable does not provide a total measuring procedure which can be replicated by other sets of judges who have not undergone the identical intensive training. Some limited data on stability over time has been provided by Schimek (191). Scores at age 24 correlated with scores at 17, and even 14, but scores at 10 have little relationship with later scores. These findings are presumably attenuated by scorer inconsistency and by the limited consistency of many such scores.

Overview.—From a survey of the theoretically oriented research, most studies indicate that both concepts and measures are multidimensional, vitiating the assumption of the unitary nature of constructs. To be able to have measures which can be interpreted unequivocally, constructs must be dissected and measuring instruments coordinated with each subconstruct. Although the data gathered so far indicate that this particular strategy of conceptual-operational coordination is promising, it is no panacea. Rational distinctions will vary in their degree of fruitfulness, and it will be no easy task to coordinate the constructs and the operations. Perhaps in the construction of instruments coordinated with specified content, it would be helpful to borrow the model of a blueprint which cross-classifies types of content and different modes of response, as in the construction of achievement tests.

The validational evidence on the projective methodologies yielded conflicting results. Some procedures (e.g., Szondi, human-drawing) appear to be so contaminated by extraneous sources of variance that their clinical or scientific usefulness is doubtful. Other procedures (e.g., sentence-completion) appear more promising. The great attention to specification in scoring procedures for the Rorschach has yielded more promising results, as have configural scoring procedures.

Method Variance or Methods at Variance with Each Other?

Many validity studies involve correlations between scores for the same variable obtained by instruments using different methods. When such correlations are low, method variance is blamed. Yet method variance has never had a conclusive and definitive interpretation. Cattell (36) proposes a trait-view theory in which he argues that any view of any trait of a subject is a function of the subject's other traits in interaction with the subject-observer situation and is also a function of the observer's traits interacting with that situation. Under the rubric of perturbations inescapable in the method, he distinguishes components associated with observer view and those associated with instrument (test and conditions). An observer component is also specified in his Basic Data Relations Matrix (35). Method components appear to be proportionate or multiplicative, rather than additive to trait variances, in data presented by Campbell & O'Connell (31).

Comparisons of methods often yield mixed findings like those of Zuckerman et al. (247). When assessed by clinician ratings and two forms of self report, anxiety and depression showed good convergent but poor discriminant validity, while two projective procedures distinguished hostility from the other two variables but had poor convergent validity. Correlations between therapist and diagnostician descriptions were analyzed by Groves & Petersen (85). The mean *r* (correlation coefficient) closely approached the modest mean *r*s between diagnosticians using different projective tests and between judgments of the same therapist at different times. Two questions remain: Why is a single judge so unreliable? Did the use of Pearson *r* over dichotomous items affect the findings? Moderate convergent and good discriminant validity was obtained by Peterson (173) for two broad factors, equaling or exceeding the patterns typically found for the usual trait variables assessed by questionnaires and ratings. Yet Butt & Fiske (27) were able to get some discrimination between a priori subscores for dominance, together with appropriately differentiated patterns of association with outside variables. No generality of behavioral ratings was found in two studies (142, 143) when both the task and subjects' teammates changed; in the first paper, agreement between these observations and ratings by interviews was limited, even though interrater agreement was satisfactory. Barker (11) asserts that the data when the psychologist is only a transducer yield findings different from those when the psychologist is also an operator.

The dependence of spontaneous flexibility measures on task, set, and scoring system was shown by May & Metcalf (148). Two paper-and-pencil measures of aggression correlated with each other but not with performance on the Buss Aggression Machine, a more direct behavioral measure (125). The patterns of significant relationships with other methods differed for interview and questionnaire measures of mothers' attitudes (195).

Sometimes the relationship between two methods varies with the level of a moderating variable (210, 211, 221). Repression-sensitization moderated the pattern relating self-report and physiological indices of stress (233). The direction of correlation between TAT and self-report hostility varied with level of guilt (184). Relationships can also vary with the way a score is obtained: the correlation between projectives and behavior varied with type of Rorschach index (214) and with card pull on the TAT (e.g., 105). With all these sources of potential attenutation, it is surprising that significant positive relationships are obtained more than rarely. The observed levels of correlation, however, are generally modest at best.

The use of a common trait label for the variables produced by totally distinct procedures is bound to lead to frustrated researchers and confused scholars. In personality measurement as in psychology generally, behavior varies with situation, stimulus, and set. Indices vary with observer and operation for data reduction. For example, five kinds of attitude measures are identified by Cook & Selltiz (44). The problem has been solved for intelligence by defining it as capacity under optimal conditions and by using as the observer only the expert who scores by consensus. Within this highly restricted context, Guilford (86) has provided an epoch-making classification of mental activities based on three aspects: the operation used on the input to effect the product. The considerable specificity of the resulting ability scores, even though obtained under common conditions from a fixed criterial viewpoint, may provide an object lesson for personality measurement.

At this stage of development, the field of personality measurement needs a realistic analysis. Perhaps we should not assume that every construct can, or should, be measurable by any procedure. First, after having formulated the construct more precisely, appropriate methods for measurement should be determined on a rational basis, along with their vulnerabilities to certain kinds of biasing effects which could in principle be controlled. Perhaps for a particular method, or perspective, there would be certain groups of subjects who could not be considered as producers of accurate data (e.g., psychotic groups on a self-ideal sort). Given that at least two independent approaches could be found, then each should be identified with its own separate but equal subconstruct, i.e., with a subvariable that itself varies with the situation encompassing the observations, with the stimuli impinging on subject, and with the task given the data producer. Each such subconstruct would be indexed by its own set of procedures. Hopefully, they would show some convergence, although each instrument in the set would have some specificity associated with context, task, and stimuli. Only later would attention be directed to hypothetical constructs indexed by any obtained convergence between separate approaches. [Cf. the analysis of dreaming as indirectly indexed by rapid eye movement and self-report (206).] Progress in the methodology of personality measurement will be blocked until some fruitful analysis of methods has been developed.

A somewhat similar viewpoint has been developed by Emmerich (62) who argues for "personality assessments conceptualized as perspectives." He localizes personality not in the observer nor in the observed but in their transactional relation, from which it would seem to follow that there are several distinct personalities which can be differentiated (even though they may show some degree of substantive convergence). Emmerich believes that similar processes are involved in inferences about personality, whether the observed is self or another. He adapts Hammond's extension of the Brunswik Lens Model as a framework for analyzing the appraisal within each perspective. The process starts with cues utilized by a perspective, cues which may be specific to the perspective and which can be identified only in terms of their participation in the assessing process. His illustrative application may be misleading in its simplicity: it remains to be shown that the same scheme can be applied profitably to assessment from all perspectives.

A good illustration of the need to give separate consideration to observations from different perspectives is found in some reanalyses of stress studies (233). Distress measured physiologically was uncorrelated with self-reported distress. The discrepancies between the self-report and the autonomic indices were shown to stem from the influence of defensive style on self-reports: repressors showed relatively but not absolutely greater autonomic reactions than sensitizers, a difference which would be predicted by ego-defense theory.

Programmatic Strategies for Personality Measurement

Assessment.—Personality as an immature science seems to face a blooming, buzzing confusion and lacks consensus on how to analyze it. The framework of perspectives, considered above, is a strategy needing further development. Another strategy is the assessment program introduced in the 1940's. It uses standard methods, such as tests and interviews, as well as such uncommon ones as situational tests. Its special quality is the integration of diverse observations and data by an assessor.

The oldest offspring of World War II assessment, the Institute of Personality Assessment and Research, is strong and healthy. It continues to study top-rated, creative people as contrasted with more typical members of particular fields. Somewhat surprisingly, its reports often emphasize scores on paper-and-pencil tests (e.g., 137). Other papers (e.g., 92) consider specific, criterion-oriented tests but also employ structured interviews, data from parents, and assessment staff ratings and Q-sorts based on observations during a variety of procedures. The objective is to understand the background, development, and current characteristics of people with actualized or potential creativity (138), comparisons between various fields of specialization throwing light on the generality or specificity of the findings.

Assessment procedures are used once in a while in personnel work, the results sometimes indicating the value of situational methods and of assessors' ratings (22). In predicting the performance of Peace Corps teachers from mock autobiographies and other data, differential predictivity by subgroup and varied manifestations of competence complicated the applicability of the findings, though perhaps not their conceptual fertility (203).

Assessment research has shown the value of using multiple methods—where one kind of procedure does not work, another may. It has demonstrated the utility of behavioral samples involving interactions with peers, and of judgments by peers as well as by trained observers. What has not been established is the human capacity to integrate the rich data from these varied sources. Where feasible, actuarial or statistical methods provide the most consistently valid weighting of separate data for purposes of prediction. What the researcher can contribute from his assessment experiences is insight into hypotheses to guide intensive and controlled experimentation.

The assessment technique relies almost wholly on behavior and other responses occurring during the assessment period. Hence it shares with specific measuring procedures the problem of effects from reactions to each evaluation procedure and to the total assessment situation. It assumes a stable personality with stable traits.

Although all of us pay lip-service to the obvious fact that personality manifestations are complexly determined, many of us seem intuitively and implicitly to accept, as the object to be understood, some ideal of a simplistic, relatively stable personality underlying the diverse appearances. Block (16) suggests that we have been unable to demonstrate empirically this dogma of personality consistency for several reasons, such as the ignoring of contextual and environmental factors, the equating of behaviors mediated by different underlying variables, and the assumption that a given behavior has the same significance for all subjects.

States and traits.—One constructive way to avoid this handicapping assumption of consistency is to distinguish between measures of enduring dispositions and measures of momentary states, a distinction which has been most studied for anxiety (107). Support for Spielberger's trait-state anxiety theory was found in two studies (95, 106), especially when both trait and state were measured by self-report. After reviewing studies using 88 procedures for measuring anxiety, McReynolds (151) conceptualizes eight possible types of anxiety scores, formed by combinations of three dichotomies: current state vs. characteristic trait, existent anxiety vs. proneness to anxiety, and specific vs. overall or general anxiety. He is careful to note that this analysis does not mean that there must be eight qualitatively different kinds of anxiety corresponding to these scores. Of course, the specific anxiety category can be subdivided with one classification for problems or stimuli associated with anxiety and a cross-classification for mode of reaction, as exemplified by the instrument of Endler & Hunt (64). The trait-state distinction has been extended to other domains by Zuckerman, Persky & Link (248); a similar differentiation has been made in psychophysiological measurement (9).

Clinical versus statistical prediction.—For some years, there has been a controversy over the relative merits of clinical judgments and statistical methods for predicting specified criteria. Sawyer (189) has reviewed the evidence in an extended framework emphasizing the diversity of procedures for obtaining measurements before predictions are made. He decides in favor of mechanical modes of collecting and integrating data, and other studies support the same trend. A Bayesian synthesis of clinical and statistical prediction, a promising approach for clinical investigators willing to record and analyze actual outcomes, has been proposed (168). The studies of clinical judgment considered in a later section of this paper contribute to understanding its poor comparative standing.

Empirical strategies.—Some writers advocate primarily empirical orientations, based on analytic methodologies rather than substantive considerations. Their strategy is to analyze covariations in order to build taxonomies or to delineate structures of attributes. Horst (97) would have us start with personality test data seen as combinations of single items and the respondent. These are certainly the phenomena most readily available, but are they the phenomena we seek to understand? Sines (200) criticizes the design of validation studies in which one starts with a behavior pattern and then looks for an associated test pattern. Since there may be several such test patterns, he would have us classify persons initially on the basis of test pattern, and then seek behavioral correlates. Left unanswered is the question whether such patterns should be isolated from populations which are homogeneous with respect to age, sex, and other demographic or even psychological variables (cf. 167) or from populations which are truly random, the latter strategy obviously permitting the patterns to be associated with quite diverse kinds of variables. Sines' strategy presumes adequate measurements of the behavioral characteristics among which correlates are sought. It requires great persistence, given the almost infinite number of test patterns which can be isolated from the plethora of personality tests. Lieberman (132) asserts that Sines' approach is equivalent to the usual one since, in practice, subjects showing the pattern must be compared to subjects not showing it. He also reminds us that cross-validation is essential in such analyses.

The actuarial taxonomic approach has been pursued by Sines himself (201) and by others. For example, Marks & Seeman (144) have identified 16 configurations for the MMPI which cover about 80 per cent of adults seen in psychiatric settings. Then, from other psychological data, they obtained Q-sorts and looked for Q-statements with extreme average placements by judges, such statements being used to describe the type. The resulting descriptions may be of some use in trying to understand an individual case: a clinician may look up the description associated with the pattern shown by his case and use it as a guide for dispositions he should look for in the other protocols from that case. It is difficult to see how this actuarial approach will contribute to theory or to hypothesis testing in basic research.

A major dilemma in following this approach is the choice between maximizing the homogeneity of each group and minimizing the number of separate groups formed: the fewer the groups, the greater the heterogeneity within each. While the classification rules must be explicit, their selection seems to be largely arbitrary, in the absence of relevant theory. In addition, with all the problems about the determination of MMPI responses by response styles, one wonders whether the extensive use of the MMPI makes it the most suitable instrument for this purpose. An extended critique of actuarial approaches is offered by Sines (201). The issue of applicability of isolated types to samples from a somewhat different population is illustrated by Gynther & Brilliant (87).

Adapted theories.—Various proposals have been made to adapt, for clinical and other personality measurement, such approaches from general psychology as decision theory and information theory. These adaptations should be thoroughly studied to determine their potential fruitfulness. For example, Goldstone & Goldfarb (81) urge a laboratory-based Adaptation Level theory of personality; its merit would seem to depend on its generalizability beyond the laboratory. An alternative method is to treat observations in the laboratory as meaningful phenomena in their own right, coordinate in significance with sets of observations from the testing room, from the clinic, and from the outside environment.

Others urge an approach with conceptual foundations, even in considering the criterion problem in industrial psychology (229). J. Wallace (227, 228) proposes a new abilities conception of personality, with emphasis on response capabilities. Rather than trying to study a man as he typically is, we should determine his capacities. In this view, response performance is seen as a function of three situational factors: formal attributes of situations, reinforcement conditions, and subject's situation-specific hypothesis—his expectancies, etc. The orientation toward capability removes the ambiguity regarding subject's task in the usual personality test. But is the example of ability testing the one to be followed in measuring all personality constructs? His approach might prove particularly fruitful in the area of adjustment (cf. 226). Wallace notes that low scores on measures of capacity (indicating response incapacity) may stem from response inhibition or from a learning deficit. This differential basis for poor performance, if conceptually and operationally separated, could provide a useful distinction in the normative area.

A provocative volume by Mischel (158) epitomizes the current state of personality measurement. Many traditional theories of personality, he argues, assume the existence of highly generalized dispositions or traits which are internal determinants of behavior more or less independent of stimulus constellations and of situations. Reviewing a considerable body of empirical literature, he concludes that "With the possible exception of intelligence, highly generalized behavioral consistencies have not been demonstrated, and the concept of personality traits as broad response predispositions is thus untenable." While he has rendered a service by emphasizing the incontrovertible evidence that behavior is largely specific to the particular situations and the specific types of stimuli encountered, he has not ruled out the possibility of considerable consistency and stability in the individual's responses under well-defined conditions.

Mischel urges the study of behavior change from the perspective of social learning theory. In the context of behavior therapy, he proposes the assessment of the individual's problematic behaviors in terms of the conditions that evoke and support them. He recognizes the problem of transfer of change from the treatment situation to "real life," of generalizing beyond the highly specific conditions utilized for observation and treatment. "Most traditional clinical assessments have ignored the individual's actual behavior in real-life situations," he asserts. And yet, a few lines later, he talks of behavior assessments using "verbal, symbolic, and direct sampling techniques." Applied in his treatment room, these have much the same problems of representativeness of real life as the diagnostic procedures used in the conventional clinic. With all his emphasis on situational determinants of behavior and test responses, he fails to see the role of such determinants in his own assessments. Moreover, he neglects to examine the adequacy of the methods of his choice, with respect to internal consistency and to stability where it is appropriate. His volume emphasizes important questions but fails to indicate the road to their answers.

In a similar vein, Weiss (235) makes several arguments for the value of operant conditioning techniques in assessment. While we should not reject these proposals arbitrarily on the ground that such laboratory techniques do not have obvious pertinence to the personality phenomena that interest us, we may appropriately reserve judgment until clearer demonstrations of relevance are available.

These several programmatic strategies range from the position that suitable methods are now available and all we need to do is integrate their findings to the view that we should start with regularities in test data and see where they lead us. In between are views that an adapted theory is sufficient to interpret the phenomena of personality. None of these strategies is directed toward the delineation and refinement of constructs, the building blocks of any science; none deal adequately with the basic problem of representing these constructs by operations yielding indices relatively free of impurities. Further work with these strategies may reveal the one or two most fruitful ones. Hopefully, the field can make some small advances pending the arrival of its Einstein or Mendeleyev.

The Measuring Process

The situation.—As already noted in earlier sections, the situation contributes to the determination of both personality phenomena and personality measurements. It may contribute both as a main effect and in interaction with other factors. Within data from a self-report questionnaire, Endler & Hunt (64) find that mode of response accounts for a large portion of the variance, with simple interactions between such modes, persons, and situations accounting for other large portions, and with a smaller portion contributed by situations alone. In their Anxiousness Inventory, subjects contribute only a small portion; in their Hostility Inventory, subjects contribute a very large portion—the share for mode of responses being less, but still sizable. They suggest "that personality descriptions might be improved by emphasizing what kinds of responses individuals make with what intensity in various kinds of situations."

Murphy (163) states that half of what is determining personality at any given time is situationally defined while half is tied up with almost invisible inner processes. The consistency of adjustment ratings as a function of setting, rater, and scale is examined in one longitudinal study (59); although the data are not conclusive, the contribution of setting appears sizable.

While the important effects of the situation or environment are generally accepted, very little has been done on measuring the environment. The most systematic work is that of Stern (205), who has developed and applied an instrument for determining the press provided by the college environment. A more individualized approach has been taken by Bloom (17) and his students (e.g., 243). They have assessed the extent to which the home environment fosters the development of intelligence, academic achievement, and some personality characteristics. These are important and promising programs. What is also needed is a procedure for determining the meaning of the temporary environment of the testing situation for each subject. Such an objective involves a difficult methodological problem: just as we want to know how a subject perceives the primary testing instrument, so we should also wonder how he will perceive an instrument seeking a report of that original perception. For example, a highly defensive subject might be difficult to detect.

Testing conditions.—Too obvious to need documentation is the proposition that test responses can be and often are influenced by preceding experiences, the context (explicit or implicit), the mode of administration, and such experimental manipulations as stress. A review of fantasy n Ach indicates that effects of instructions can sometimes be demonstrated (118). This concept has been delineated substantively and formally by Atkinson & Feather (8) in terms which have definite implications for measuring procedures: the tendency is seen as a function of a relatively enduring characteristic and two situational influences. They offer no satisfactory cures for the limited reliability and almost negligible convergent validity of the TAT index for their concept. Creativity measures, if they are to be discriminated from measures of intelligence, must be administered under supportive and nonevaluative conditions. This finding of Wallach & Kogan (230) has been generalized by the work of Boersma & O'Bryan (20).

The observer.—The observers, judges, or clinicians also contribute unwanted variance to personality measurements. It is quite unclear whether experience, training, feedback, and additional information increase predictive accuracy. A disturbing lead toward understanding some limitations of diagnostic judgment has been contributed by Chapman & Chapman (40), who report several studies in which naive subjects agree on the symptoms attributed to alleged patients from their drawings of human figures. Since the data were arranged so that no relationship existed between the protocol characteristics and the symptoms, the correlates were "illusory." The disturbing feature is the marked similarity between these erroneous associations and those in the clinical reports of practicing clinicians using such protocols. Illusory correlation was also found in judgments about observed co-occurrence of words as a consequence of their associative connections (39).

Reviewing work on clinical judgments, Goldberg (77) notes the shift toward studying the process. Since the judges may use either linear or configural models of combining data (241), both kinds of models have been developed and applied by these authors and others. Another review concludes that there is no "fully satisfactory and validated test or procedure for measuring judging accuracy" (41). In the area of person perception, Shrauger & Altrocchi (198) propose a framework emphasizing the personality of the perceived and the phases in the judging process.

The factor structure in ratings based on adequate information recurs in ratings based on inadequate information (169) and in ratings based on stereotypes (162). Criteria for judging the degree of ratee relevance in personality ratings have been proposed (165). Whether raters' implicit personality structures correspond to nature remains to be established; such structures may be idiosyncratic to this perspective on personality phenomena.

Examiner effects.—Although a critical review of the evidence for Rosenthal's experimenter bias effect (10) concludes that such effects are less pervasive than has been claimed, it seems quite clear that examiners can unwittingly influence the responses of their subjects (147) and that assessment research must be designed to prevent contamination from examiner expectancies. Although the empirical findings are not consistent, the presence of some positive results (108, 145, 146) should serve as a warning. Expectancies can also affect interpretations (207). Examiner effects appear to be more likely on free-response tests but are not limited to them (164), and can occur in individual testing of intelligence (188).

The subjects' reactions to tests.—Another component of the measuring process which may introduce unwanted variance is the reaction of subjects to tests and testing. Questions about the heterogeneity of reactions to personality tests (73) led to a survey of reactions to simulated tests (71). Subjects perceive the general domain of a test rather accurately. Subjects vary in the degree and quality of their negative affect towards tests. Some "concern with evaluation of oneself, whether by oneself or by others" is thought to be universal (94); the content of reactions by high anxious subjects is further detailed by Meisels (155). Different personality types use different ways of avoiding the task when taking a sentence completion test (236). Like other reactions, reactions to tests and to test tasks have their personality correlates.

The disturbing possibility that subjects' perceptions of a test vary with their scores is raised by Lefcourt's finding (124) that repressors see the R-S scale as measuring mental illness and sensitizers disagree. He views repressors as interpreting the admission of emotionality on this scale as a sign of instability, while sensitizers see such admissions as revealing honesty with one's self and as not fearing self-disclosure. It seems reasonable to assume that subjects are more or less aware of the content of a scale and of such personal reactions when marking their responses to it. Do such reactions contribute to or detract from the adequacy of the measurements? Perhaps we should be more candid with subjects and give them some idea of what each instrument is intended to assess. Perhaps we should use our ingenuity to develop tests and administrative procedures which rely on a subject's positive motivations and evoke his cooperation [adapting Kelman's recommendation (113) for social psychological experiments].

A rare paper by Lovell (136) notes the potential conflict of interest between the assessor and the respondent when testing serves a personnel function. He sketches three test contracts and eliminates two which are pertinent to the use of tests for personnel or institutional purposes. He urges the use of the client contract, applicable when the testing has the function of providing service to the client and also applicable in research testing. Here, the key phrase is an agreement: "You don't try to fool us and we don't try to fool you." A subject is given the option of accepting or rejecting this agreement. Lovell sees this contract as most likely in the long run to lead to valid measurement. While there is a need for empirical work to determine the best way to present these matters to subjects who are to be tested, the proposal for explicit presentation of the agreement between experimenter and subject is a promising contribution to testing methodology.

Testing and public concerns.—During the period under review, there has been a major upswing in concern about testing from the viewpoints of public acceptance, professional ethics, and legal rights. Also at issue are guidelines for human experimentation and behavioral research as a whole. Four numbers of the *American Psychologist* have focussed on these problems (4–7). While the profession has been concerned with ethical matters for many years, psychologists have previously seemed almost unaware of the need to understand how the testee and the public at large view testing, and of the necessity for helping the public to understand the orientation of testers and their basically good intentions. It is quite possible that this oversight has contributed to the limited validity of personality measurements.

Response Sets, Styles, and Biases

Response sets, another aspect of subjects' reactions to tests, form a particular class of variables which has long been of concern to the psychometrist, since variance from these variables intrudes as a source of error into the scores obtained from his measuring instruments. The basic problem that has yet to be solved is how to separate the content from the bias. Related issues in this area concern the definition, the pervasiveness, and the stability of the bias. Although there have been attempts at more precise definitions of the concepts of set, style, and bias, reports continue to employ the terms interchangeably in spite of their diverse connotations. Pervasiveness or generality within and over different types of methods and content is still an empirical issue to which numerous studies have addressed themselves. Finally, the problem of control remains of central interest to investigators.

In a provocative contribution considering the problem of content-set confounding and the generality of styles, Rorer (179) argues that response styles (preference for a response category, e.g., yea-saying) alone contribute little variance to inventories. He points to studies (e.g., 180) using reversed scales, which showed that only a trivial proportion of response variance was found to be attributable to acquiescence. Replying to and disagreeing with Rorer (179), Rundquist (183) contends that the responses to personality items are a result of content, social desirability of content, form in which content is stated, desire to dissimulate, and response style. He points out that reversed items, as compared to the original items, tend to have different correlations and other characteristics, a situation resulting in inadequate control, confounding, and confusion. He sees the need for external validational studies regarding the factors influencing response.

Block (15) challenged the interpretation that response sets play a dominant role in personality inventories, such as the MMPI. Although he recognizes that the first two factors emerging from factor analysis of the MMPI could be interpreted as social desirability (SD) and acquiescence, Block contends that (*a*) the SD hypothesis advocated by Edwards (55) is a failure in other behavior domains; (*b*) the first two factors of the MMPI have correlates in independent ratings of personality; and (*c*) since "pure" acquiescence measures are difficult to construct, set and content are almost inevitably confounded. In a review of Block's book, Jackson (100) presents several strong criticisms concerning Block's interpretation of data, reasoning, and statement of the issue, arguing that debates concerning style vs. content interpretations are irrelevant. For Jackson, the main point seems to be that the MMPI was constructed for differential diagnosis, a task for which it has been shown to be unqualified.

While armchair debates about factor labeling do seem fruitless and circular, it is of considerable importance for personality measurement to be concerned with logical validity, or the congruence of a measure with a content domain. Therefore, the presence of any construct-irrelevant variance is undesirable. Like any other variable, however, a response set has to be conceptualized more fully so that measuring instruments can be devised to measure it. Like other constructs in personality, each response set seems to be multidimensional, with different measures of it tapping different portions.

Different strategies of measuring response sets: SD and acquiescence.—Investigators in the area of response sets have either taken a Global-Rational approach or an Empirical approach to the conceptualization and measurement of response sets. In general, conceptual-operational coordination is very weak in this area. Using a Global-Rational strategy, Crowne & Marlowe (46) developed the Marlowe-Crowne Social Desirability Scale (MC-SDS) as a measure of SD rationally free of psychopathological content. At the same time, however, MC-SDS is considered a measure of the approval motive, and linked to social learning theory. A number of studies have demonstrated the scale's usefulness in this latter theoretical context. Although the MC-SDS is rationally free of psychopathological content, some correlations with MMPI scales has been found. These correlations were generally lower than those found with Edwards' SD measure, however. Katkin (110) reported much higher correlations with MMPI scales for females than for males. These results underscore the importance of considering sex differences in both conceptual and empirical study of this construct. Such findings are consistent with interpreting MC-SDS as a measure either of the need for approval or of defensive denial. A more specific interpretation of the MC-SDS was proposed by Miller et al. (157), who suggest that high scores reflect the habit of adjusting social responses to unique environmental demands, rather than a gross general tendency toward favorable self description. Further conceptual distinctions need to be made, however, and the interrelationships of the conceptually discrete constructs of approval motive, defensive denial, and social desirability should be specified in the theory.

Social desirability as measured by an empirical strategy has been reviewed by Edwards (57, 58). Such SD, considered as a general personality trait, has generally not been highly correlated with SD as measured by the MC-SDS (e.g., 196), even though both are self-report measures. The two scales appear to be measuring somewhat different constructs. Edwards' SD scale has been construed in many ways: ego strength, adjustment vs. psychopathology, social desirability. Megargee (154) considers the scores on Edwards' SD to be measuring both good adjustment and dissimulation. It has also been considered operationally as a short form of the MMPI (61). Edwards' SD was not related to a SD scale for rating Picture-Frustration responses (238), and another study (199) found that response sets, including Edwards' SD, MC-SDS, the Couch-Keniston scale, and acquiescence measured by an adjective check list, were mostly idiosyncratic to the measure used. Evidence to date suggests limited generality of SD across different methods of measurement.

Measures of acquiescence have been derived either by Empirical or Rational (number of true responses) approaches. As in the area of social desirability, chaos prevails. Measures of SD and acquiescence typically are uncorrelated (47, 68) and usually emerge as separate factors in factor analyses (e.g., 130).

Cruse (47) found that minimal content scales were highly internally consistent and intercorrelated, lending some support to the notion that acquiescence is an internally consistent trait, at least over nonsense material. Its generality, however, is a separate issue, as is the extent to which it intrudes upon other personality measures. Most studies (74, 128, 180, 193) have suggested that while acquiescence may be an internally consistent disposition, it is not a generalized disposition, and occurs more readily when items are weak in content (215), or when subjects are uncertain (171). Wiggins (239) suggests that acquiescence means different things in different contexts.

Methods of control.—For investigators interested in measuring other personality dimensions, it is important to have methods of estimating the influence of these response sets on their measures. If persons agree upon their conceptions of the desirable, as has been concluded in two studies (19, 56), then SD can be controlled by pairing items with equal SD ratings. Scott (194), however, strongly argues and demonstrates with data that there are wide differences among individuals' conceptions of the desirable, with the implication that social desirability has little common meaning. He notes that in a large proportion of college students, there is a strong tendency for a person to believe that his own notions of desirable personal characteristcs are absolute and should be recognized as desirable by others. Wiggins (240) supported Scott's position, finding at least six viewpoints in social desirability judgments of MMPI items. She concluded that forced choice is inadequate as a control for social desirability at the individual level. In projective methodology, judges who evaluated the titles of 60 frequently occurring TAT themes showed little agreement in their ratings for degree of social desirability (176). It would seem that pairing items for mean SD values is a questionable means of control.

Item reversal, the popular technique for the control of acquiescence, has been severely criticized on methodological grounds (129). It is often argued on logical grounds that if responses to a scale are determined largely by acquiescence, then that scale should correlate negatively with a scale of the same items in a reverse form. This position assumes that the reversals of items are valid psychologically. Using this approach for the MMPI, Lichtenstein & Bryan (131) constructed reverse forms for 12 scales and administered them in counterbalanced order to both patients and normals. Correlations between reverse forms tended to approximate the test-retest reliability of these scales. They interpret the results to indicate that factor analytic techniques have exaggerated the role of acquiescence in the MMPI. Surprisingly, it is necessary to point out that the number of items in the two scales should be controlled, as should item endorsement values and variations in item location (185).

The key assumption of psychological equivalence for items which are reversed is a central issue, however, as Klein (117) has pointed out for the F scale. Logical or rational opposition may or may not be equivalent to psychological opposition. Studies of the meaning of item reversals appear to be a fruitful direction for research. Given that such psychological reversals can be established, then the use of psychometric models (e.g., 170) might provide more useful results. Jackson (99) prefers balanced scales to statistical formulas for control procedures. The minimal content scales devised by

Cruse (47) might well be used as control measures in studies of construct validity.

The majority view concerning the role of social desirability and acquiescence tends to be that such sets do in fact exist, but do not appear to be as pervasive as once supposed. Moreover, Dicken (51) used measures of good impression, social desirability, and acquiescence as suppressor variables, and rarely found increased validity (CPI vs. behavior ratings). In an exemplary study, Jackson & Lay (102) chose items from five scales of the Personality Research Form on the basis of high content saturation, freedom from desirability bias, and moderate endorsement frequencies. They then wrote items in four types, true or false keyed and positively or negatively worded. Factor analysis yielded clear content dimensions orthogonal to response style marker variables for both acquiescence and SD. Perhaps for current test construction, this study illustrates the best solution to the problem of controlling these sets.

New Methodological Contributions

The respondent's reaction to being measured is but one of the sources of invalidity identified in a recent thought-provoking methodological treatise by Webb et al. (232). Within this class of error from the respondent, they include subject's awareness of being tested, the role chosen by subject as appropriate to the particular measurement situation, real changes in subject produced by the measurement itself, and response sets. A second class of error is investigator effects, especially in interviewing. The final class includes various imperfections of sampling. While the authors are examining social science generally, their discussion should be studied by scientists measuring personality. The major thesis of the book is that the possibilities of using unobtrusive measures to which subjects cannot react have been seriously neglected. The need for such nonreactive measures in assessing the outcome of psychotherapy has been noted (80).

Recurring dilemmas in personality assessment are formulated by Holtzman (96): How can one separate personality variance from method variance? Can we ever develop a personality theory that is systematic, comprehensive, and closely linked with empirical data? One dilemma poses the fundamental question: What do we mean by personality assessment? When we have resolutions to these probing questions, personality will be well on the road to becoming a mature science.

A major contribution has been the publication by Cattell & Warburton (37) of their compendium with more than 600 objective tests for personality and motivation. For Cattell, "objective" means not only perfect inter-scorer agreement, but also means that "the test stimulus situation, and the whole mode of response, should be such that the subject himself could not fake the response, or distort it to fit his subjective self-concept or his desire for a particular kind of 'good or bad' score." The first part of the volume discusses the classification of tests, design problems, pyschometric concepts, etc. In the compendium itself, considerable information is given about each test, including variables derived from it, theory, rationale, design, sample items, and scoring. The reader will be impressed by the tremendous ingenuity involved in the creation of these diverse instruments. He is likely, however, to feel that many of the tests may not be as subtle as the authors hope. It is also hard to believe that a subject's personal interpretation of the testing situation and his response styles will not introduce unwanted variance into some of the test scores.

The extensive research on such objective tests has been pulled together (98). The emphasis is on the discovery, replication, and matching of factors, these being interpreted in relation to external life criteria. Convergent validity is evaluated, but not discriminant. For each of the 21 factors identified, various data are systematically presented. This tremendous body of work should provide a major opportunity to determine the contribution to prsonality which can be made by a basically empirical, inductive approach.

Analytic techniques.—A method for analyzing multimethod matrices has been proposed by Jackson and its effectiveness demonstrated (101, 121). This approach analyzes only the variance common to two or more methods, the within-method matrices having 1.00 in the diagonals and .00 off the diagonals. While some may feel that the elimination of the coefficients involving common method variance seriously distorts the data, it is certainly true that the factorial structure obtained by this approach is likely to be clearer than that obtained from data dominated by variance associated with each of the common methods. This type of analysis is probably quite sufficient for a multimethod matrix when the investigator's major concern is the adequacy of each method for getting at the several traits. In one published illustration (121), the potential value of judgmental methods for personality assessment was explored, with favorable findings. Two other papers have considered ways of handling method specificity (152, 166).

Considerable progress has been made on the measurement of change. Various models and approaches are considered in a highly competent and technically sophisticated volume edited by Harris (91). A "base-free measure of change" has been developed in a paper (218) which indicates the critical importance of the unreliability of the basic data. The authors also note that each of the various measures of change, including theirs, has its own area of special appropriateness.

Tucker's development of three-mode factor analysis is a major advance (126, 217). The third mode may be occasions, situations, or some other important classification. The method yields factor patterns for each mode: e.g., for the Semantic Differential, there would be scale factors and concepts factors; for the S-R Inventories of Anxiousness and Hostility (cf. 64), there are factors for situations and factors for modes of responses, the classifications used in building the items. In addition, the technique yields a core matrix of idealized types, formed from interactions among these sets of factors.

Going beyond the simple person-item interaction, this rigorous and elegant innovation should prove to have considerable value in multivariate studies of personality.

Items.—Test stimuli themselves are beginning to receive the attention they deserve, with increasing emphasis on the process leading to the subject's response. In a thoughtful review of stimulus functions in projective techniques, Kenny (114) states a series of postulates and cites research relevant to each, indicating how contributions from general psychology can be pertinent.

Stimuli have different meanings for different subjects. Loehlin (133) has reminded us once again that this is true for adjectives used in self-descriptions. In addition, any common word for frequency (often, frequently, rarely, etc.) is seen by subjects as referring to quite diverse relative frequencies (88). One way to handle this problem may be to ask whether a subject has had a particular experience ever, or at any time during a specified interval (cf. 21). Wide individual differences in extent of objections to MMPI items are reported by Butcher & Tellegen (26). They suggest that negative reactions might be reduced by appropriately preparing subjects for the content of the test. While omission and objection rates have low positive correlations over items, omitted items are more likely to be seen as ambiguous than as intrusive (159). Although interpretive ambiguity was significantly related to response ambiguity, items high on interpretive ambiguity but low on response ambiguity were found to be keyed more frequently on 157 different MMPI scales (12). Items also differ in the extent to which they elicit in subjects the response processes intended by the test constructor, these differences being related to item-test homogeneity (219). The formal interchange of persons and items in analyzing a data matrix brings out their quite different psychological roles and throws a little light on the person-item interaction (72).

General contributions.—A series on *Advances in Psychological Assessment* has been initiated by McReynolds (150), who introduces the first volume with a perceptive overview of the area. Human judgments about personality are emphasized in two general treatises (112, 222). Buros (24) continues to keep up to date his standard reference on tests. Handbooks with useful new material have been compiled by several editors (34, 175, 237), and comprehensive volumes of important published papers have been compiled (103, 153). These provide the scholar with convenient reference sources and the student with original papers for supplementary readings.

Overview

The quality of research on personality measurement is improving. We prefer to attribute this gain to the competence of the researchers and not to the necessary enforcement of higher standards by journal editors. Experimenters are becoming more judicious in interpreting their findings. The simultaneous use of samples from different populations is more frequent. The importance of determining how subjects perceived the test or experiment is increasingly recognized. More generally, the multiple determination of each test response is being accepted and studied.

Personality and its measurement are increasingly seen as part of the community of psychology. The relevance of behavior theory and of social learning theory is being asserted. Possible implications of decision theory, information theory, and adaptation level theory are being noted. More general techniques for psychological experimentation are being utilized to study personality, often with personality characteristics as the independent variables, or with attention to subject variance as well as to group differences.

The measuring process has its perceptual and motivational aspects. Almost universally, it introduces something which is unfamiliar to the subject, a condition which, along with subject's natural concern with being evaluated, tends to generate apprehensiveness. It becomes increasingly obvious that we must learn to make the testing situation and our instruments less threatening and more acceptable to subjects, even if such a course rules out the possibility of measuring certain value-laden variables by conventional means.

While some progress is being made, it is apparent that the gains are small relative to the levels of technical adequacy to which we aspire. Obtained correlations are typically low, especially between distinctly different approaches to the same concept. Even if the instruments are similar, the correlations are still low if the occasions, settings, or instructions differ. With all these factors constant for two methods, the relationships are still well below the internal consistencies of the instruments, particularly when the instruments have different authors possessing their personal views of the labeled variable. Specificity is rampant.

Personality phenomena, both within and outside the measurement situation, are multiply determined. At the present stage of methodological sophistication, it does not seem possible to isolate and measure precisely all the several kinds of irrelevant variance in our measurements. The task for personality researchers is to identify and delineate each theoretically significant class of behaviors, to determine which classes seem most amenable to sound methodological investigation, and for these latter, to invent ways of measuring them which are minimally confounded by extraneous factors. First steps should be directed toward simple and accessible variables, to see what degree of success can be attained.

One possibility is to start by differentiating the several types of observations and conceptualizing within each such area. Any phenomenon in personality is observed and processed by an observer who has a particular role or perspective. Perhaps each such perspective should be conceived as a distinct domain, to be studied with procedures congruent with its viewpoint, their data to be conceptualized in terms of a separate theoretical system. Just as a physicist and a musicologist perceive and describe a musical phrase in their own special terms, so perhaps personality does not exist except as a loose collective. Instead, several personalities may be construed: that conceived by the self, that observed by lay associates, that based on adequacy of performance, that inferred by experts from a psychodynamic viewpoint, that derived from psychophysiological indices, etc. Such a reorientation of personality study would make possible a close coordination between conceptualization and measurement operations within each domain. The relationships among the conceptualizations of the several domains could be determined at a later stage in the development of the science of personality.

We seem to be approaching the limits of what can be achieved by measuring operations derived from current assumptions and orientations. The time is ripe for giant steps, for bold reorganizations of our thinking, for creative innovations in the construing of personality and its measurement.

LITERATURE CITED

1. Adelson, J. Personality. *Ann. Rev. Psychol.*, **20**, 217–52 (1969)
2. Allison, J., Blatt, S. J. The relationship of Rorschach whole responses to intelligence. *J. Proj. Tech.*, **28**, 255–60 (1964)
3. Allport, G. W. Traits revisited. *Am. Psychologist*, **21**, 1–10 (1966)
4. *Am. Psychologist*, **20**, No. 2, 123–46 (1965)
5. *Am. Psychologist*, **20**, No. 11, 857–989 (1965)
6. *Am. Psychologist*, **21**, No. 5, 401–78 (1966)
7. *Am. Psychologist*, **22**, No. 5, 345–99 (1967)
8. Atkinson, J. W., Feather, N. T., Eds. *A Theory of Achievement Motivation* (Wiley, New York, 392 pp., 1966)
9. Averill, J. R., Opton, E. M., Jr. Psychophysiological assessment: Rationale and problems. In *Advances in Psychological Assessment*, **1**, Chap. 14, 265–88 (McReynolds, P., Ed., Science and Behavior Books, Palo Alto, 336 pp., 1968)
10. Barber, T. X., Silver, M. J. Fact, fiction, and the experimenter bias effect. *Psychol. Bull. Monogr. Suppl.*, **70**, No. 6, Part 2, 1–29 (1968)
11. Barker, R. G. Explorations in ecological psychology. *Am. Psychologist*, **20**, 1–14 (1965)
12. Baxter, J. C., Morris, K. Item ambiguity and item discrimination in the MMPI. *J. Consult. Clin. Psychol.*, **32**, 309–13 (1968)
13. Bendick, M. R., Klopfer, W. G. The effects of sensory deprivation and motor inhibition on Rorschach movement responses. *J. Proj. Tech.*, **28**, 261–64 (1964)
14. Benfari, R. C., Calogeras, R. C. Levels of cognition and conscience typologies. *J. Proj. Tech.*, **32**, 466–74 (1968)
15. Block, J. *The Challenge of Response Sets* (Appleton-Century-Crofts, New York, 142 pp., 1965)
16. Block, J. Some reasons for the apparent inconsistency of personality. *Psychol. Bull.*, **70**, 210–12 (1968)
17. Bloom, B. S. *Stability and Change in Human Characteristics* (Wiley, New York, 237 pp., 1964)
18. Blum, G. S. Assessment of psychodynamic variables by the Blacky Pictures. In *Advances in Psychological Assessment*, Vol. 1, Chap. 8, 150–68 (See Ref. 9)
19. Boe, E. E., Gocka, E. F., Kogan, W. S. Factor analysis of individual social desirability scale values: Second-order analysis. *Multivar. Behav. Res.*, **2**, 239–40 (1967)
20. Boersma, F. J., O'Bryan, K. An investigation of the relationship between creativity and intelligence under two conditions of testing. *J. Pers.*, **36**, 341–48 (1968)
21. Bradburn, N., Caplovitz, D. *Reports on Happiness* (Aldine, Chicago, 195 pp., 1966)
22. Bray, D. W., Grant, D. L. The assessment center in the measurement of potential for business management. *Psychol. Monogr.*, **80** (17), 27 pp. (1966)

23. Burke, W. W. Leadership behavior as a function of the leader, the follower, and the situation. *J. Pers.*, **33**, 60–81 (1965)
24. Buros, O. K., Ed. *Sixth Mental Measurements Yearbook* (Gryphon Press, Highland Park, N.J., 1752 pp., 1967)
25. Burton, R. V. Generality of honesty reconsidered. *Psychol. Rev.*, **70**, 481–99 (1963)
26. Butcher, J. N., Tellegen, A. Objections to MMPI items. *J. Consult. Psychol.*, **30**, 527–34 (1966)
27. Butt, D. S., Fiske, D. W. Comparison of strategies in developing scales for dominance. *Psychol. Bull.*, **70**, 505–19 (1968)
28. Byrne, D. Repression-sensitization as a dimension of personality. In *Progress in Experimental Personality Research*, **1**, 169–220 (Maher, B. A., Ed., Academic Press, New York, 368 pp., 1964)
29. Byrne, D., Golightly, C., Sheffield, J. The repression-sensitization scale as a measure of adjustment: Relationship with the CPI. *J. Consult. Psychol.*, **29**, 586–89 (1965)
30. Byrne, D., McDonald, R. D., Mikawa, J. Approach and avoidance affiliation motives. *J. Pers.*, **31**, 21–37 (1963)
31. Campbell, D. T., O'Connell, E. J. Methods factors in multitrait-multimethod matrices: Multiplicative rather than additive? *Multivar. Behav. Res.*, **2**, 409–26 (1967)
32. Caputo, D. V., Plapp, J. M., Hanf, L., Anzel, A. S. The validity of the Edwards Personal Preference Schedule (EPPS) employing projective and behavioral criteria. *Educ. Psychol. Measmt.*, **25**, 829–48 (1965)
33. Carrera, R. N. Need for affiliation: Approach and avoidant aspects. *J. Clin. Psychol.*, **20**, 429–32 (1964)
34. Cattell, R. B., Ed. *Handbook of Multivariate Experimental Psychology* (Rand McNally, Chicago, 959 pp., 1966)
35. Cattell, R. B. The data-box: Its ordering of total resources in terms of possible relational systems. *Ibid.*, Chap. 3, 67–128
36. Cattell, R. B. Trait-view theory of perturbations in ratings and self-ratings [L(BR)- and Q data]: Its application to obtaining pure trait score estimates in questionnaires. *Psychol. Rev.*, **75**, 96–113 (1968)
37. Cattell, R. B., Warburton, F. W. *Objective Personality and Motivation Tests: A Theoretical Introduction and Practical Compendium* (Univ. Illinois Press, Urbana, 687 pp., 1967)
38. Cerbus, G., Nichols, R. C. Personality variables and response to color. *Psychol. Bull.*, **60**, 566–75 (1963)
39. Chapman, L. J. Illusory correlation in observational report. *J. Verbal Learn. Verbal Behav.*, **6**, 151–55 (1967)
40. Chapman, L. J., Chapman, J. P. Genesis of popular but erroneous psychodiagnostic observations. *J. Abnorm. Psychol.*, **72**, 193–204 (1967)
41. Cline, V. B. Interpersonal perception. In *Progress in Experimental Personality Research*, **1**, 221–84 (See Ref. 28)
42. Coan, R. W. Facts, factors, and artifacts: The quest for psychological meaning. *Psychol. Rev.*, **71**, 123–40 (1964)
43. Comrey, A. L., Duffy, K. E. Cattell and Eysenck factor scores related to Comrey personality factors. *Multivar. Behav. Res.*, **3**, 379–92 (1968)
44. Cook, S. W., Selltiz, C. A multiple-indicator approach to attitude measurement. *Psychol. Bull.*, **62**, 36–55 (1964)
45. Cronbach, L. J., Gleser, G. C. *Psychological Tests and Personnel Decisions*, 2nd ed. (Univ. Illinois Press, Urbana, 347 pp., 1965)
46. Crowne, D. P., Marlowe, D. *The Approval Motive: Studies in Evaluative Dependence* (Wiley, New York, 233 pp., 1964)
47. Cruse, D. B. Some relations between minimal content, acquiescent-dissentient, and social desirability scales. *J. Pers. Soc. Psychol.*, **3**, 112–19 (1966)
48. Dana, R. H. Six constructs to define Rorschach *M*. *J. Proj. Tech.*, **32**, 138–45 (1968)
49. Darby, J., Hofman, K., Melnick, B. Response inhibition and the Rorschach *M* response. *J. Proj. Tech.*, **31**, 5, 29–30 (1967)
50. Dicken, C. F. Convergent and discriminant validity of the California

Psychological Inventory. *Educ. Psychol. Measmt.,* **23,** 449–59 (1963)

51. Dicken, C. F. Good impression, social desirability, and acquiescence as suppressor variables. *Ibid.,* 699–720
52. Draguns, J. G., Haley, E. M., Phillips, L. Studies of Rorschach content: A review of the research literature. Part 1: Traditional content categories. *J. Proj. Tech.,* **31,** 1, 3–32 (1967)
53. Dublin, J. E. Perception of and reaction to ambiguity by repressors and sensitizers: A construct-validity study. *J. Consult. Clin. Psychol.,* **32,** 198–205 (1968)
54. Dudek, S. Z. *M* an active energy system correlating Rorschach *M* with ease of creative expression. *J. Proj. Tech.,* **32,** 453–61 (1968)
55. Edwards, A. L. The assessment of human motives by means of personality scales. In *Nebraska Symposium on Motivation, 1964,* 135–62 (Levine, D., Ed., Univ. Nebraska Press, Lincoln, 284 pp., 1964)
56. Edwards, A. L. Measurement of individual differences in ratings of social desirability and in the tendency to give socially desirable responses. *J. Exptl. Res. Pers.,* **1,** 91–98 (1965)
57. Edwards, A. L. The social desirability variable: A broad statement. In *Response Set in Personality Assessment,* Chap. 2, 32–47 (Berg, I. A., Ed., Aldine, Chicago, 244 pp., 1967)
58. Edwards, A. L. The social desirability variable: A review of the evidence, *Ibid.,* Chap. 3, 48–70
59. Ellsworth, R. B., Foster, L., Childers, B., Arthur, G., Kroeker, D. Hospital and community adjustment as perceived by psychiatric patients, their families, and staff. *J. Consult. Clin. Psychol., Monogr. Suppl.* **32,** No. 5, Part 2, 1–41 (1968)
60. Elstein, A. S. Behavioral correlates of the Rorschach shading determinant. *J. Consult. Psychol.,* **29,** 231–36 (1965)
61. Elvekrog, M. O., Vestre, N. D. The Edwards Social Desirability Scale as a short form of the MMPI. *J. Consult. Psychol.,* **27,** 503–7 (1963)
62. Emmerich, W. Personality assessments conceptualized as perspectives. *J. Proj. Tech.,* **30,** 307–18 (1966)
63. Endicott, N. A., Endicott, J. Prediction of improvement in treated and untreated patients using the Rorschach Prognostic Rating Scale. *J. Consult. Psychol.,* **28,** 342–48 (1964)
64. Endler, N. S., Hunt, J. McV. S–R Inventories of Hostility and comparisons of the proportions of variance from persons, responses and situations for hostility and anxiousness. *J. Pers. Soc. Psychol.,* **9,** 309–15 (1968)
65. Epstein, S., Fenz, W. D. The detection of areas of emotional stress through variations in perceptual threshold and physiological arousal. *J. Exptl. Res. Pers.,* **2,** 191–99 (1967)
66. Farley, F., Farley, S. V. Extroversion and stimulus-seeking motivation. *J. Consult. Psychol.,* **31,** 215–16 (1967)
67. Feather, N. T. Performance at a difficult task in relation to initial expectation of success, test anxiety, and need achievement. *J. Pers.,* **33,** 200–17 (1965)
68. Feder, C. Z. Relationship of repression-sensitization to adjustment status, social desirability, and acquiescence response set. *J. Consult. Psychol.,* **31,** 401–6 (1967)
69. Fernald, P. S., Linden, J. D. The human content response in the Holtzman Inkblot Technique. *J. Proj. Tech.,* **30,** 441–46 (1966)
70. Fiske, D. W. On the coordination of personality constructs and their measurement. *Hum. Develpm.,* **9,** 74–83 (1966)
71. Fiske, D. W. The subject reacts to tests. *Am. Psychologist,* **22,** 287–96 (1967)
72. Fiske, D. W. Items and persons: Formal duals and psychological differences. *Multivar. Behav. Res.,* **3,** 393–402 (1968)
73. Fiske, D. W., Butler, J. The experimental conditions for measuring individual differences. *Educ. Psychol. Measmt.,* **23,** 249–66 (1963)
74. Foster, R. J., Grigg, A. E. Acquiescent response set as a measure of acquiescence: Further evidence. *J. Abnorm. Soc. Psychol.,* **67,** 304–5

(1963)

75. Gaylin, N. L. Psychotherapy and psychological health: A Rorschach function and structure analysis. *J. Consult. Psychol.,* **30,** 494–500 (1966)
76. Golann, S. E. Psychological study of creativity. *Psychol. Bull.,* **60,** 548–65 (1963)
77. Goldberg, L. R. Simple models or simple processes? Some research on clinical judgments. *Am. Psychologist,* **23,** 483–96 (1968)
78. Goldberg, P. A. A review of sentence completion methods in personality assessment. *J. Proj. Tech.,* **29,** 12–45 (1965)
79. Goldfried, M. R. The assessment of anxiety by means of the Rorschach. *J. Proj. Tech.,* **30,** 364–80 (1966)
80. Goldstein, A. P., Heller, K., Sechrest, L. B. *Psychotherapy and the Psychology of Behavior Change* (Wiley, New York, 472 pp., 1966)
81. Goldstone, S., Goldfarb, J. L. Adaptation level, personality theory, and psychopathology. *Psychol. Bull.,* **61,** 176–87 (1964)
82. Golin, S., Herron, E. W., Lakota, R., Reineck, L. Factor analytic study of the Manifest Anxiety, Extraversion, and Repression-Sensitization Scales. *J. Consult. Psychol.,* **31,** 564–69 (1967)
83. Gough, H. G. Appraisal of social maturity by means of the CPI. *J. Abnorm. Psychol.,* **71,** 189–95 (1966)
84. Gough, H. G. An interpreter's syllabus for the California Psychological Inventory. In *Advances in Psychological Assessment,* **1,** Chap. 4, 55–79 (See Ref. 9)
85. Groves, M. H., Petersen, P. A. Effectiveness of projective techniques as established by the objective agreement of therapists with diagnosticians. *Proc. Am. Psychol. Assoc.,* 1968, 459–60
86. Guilford, J. P. *The Nature of Human Intelligence* (McGraw-Hill, New York, 538 pp., 1967)
87. Gynther, M. D., Brilliant, J. P. The MMPI K+ profile: A re-examination. *J. Consult. Clin. Psychol.,* **32,** 616–17 (1968)
88. Hakel, M. D. How often is often? *Am. Psychologist,* **23,** 533–34 (1968)
89. Haley, E. M., Draguns, J. G., Phillips, L. Studies of Rorschach content: A review of research literature. Part II: Non-traditional uses of content indicators. *J. Proj. Tech.,* **31,** 2, 3–38 (1967)
90. Hare, R. D. Denial of threat and emotional response to impending painful stimulation. *J. Consult. Psychol.,* **30,** 359–61 (1966)
91. Harris, C. W., Ed. *Problems in Measuring Change* (Univ. Wisconsin Press, Madison, 259 pp., 1963)
92. Helson, R. Personality characteristics and developmental history of creative college women. *Genet. Psychol. Monogr.,* **76,** 205–56 (1967)
93. Hersch, P. D., Scheibe, K. E. Reliability and validity of internal-external control as a personality dimension. *J. Consult. Psychol.,* **31,** 609–13 (1967)
94. Hill, W. F. Sources of evaluative reinforcement. *Psychol. Bull.,* **69,** 132–46 (1968)
95. Hodges, W. F. Effects of ego threat and threat of pain on state anxiety. *J. Pers. Soc. Psychol.,* **8,** 364–72 (1968)
96. Holtzman, W. H. Recurring dilemmas in personality assessment. *J. Proj. Tech.,* **28,** 144–50 (1964)
97. Horst, P. *Personality: Measurement of Dimensions* (Jossey-Bass, San Francisco, 244 pp., 1968)
98. Hundleby, J. D., Pawlik, K., Cattell, R. B. *Personality Factors in Objective Test Devices: A Critical Integration of a Quarter Century's Research* (Knapp, San Diego, 542 pp., 1965)
99. Jackson, D. N. Acquiescence response styles: Problems of identification and control. In *Response Set in Personality Assessment,* Chap. 4, 71–114 (See Ref. 57)
100. Jackson, D. N. Review of Block's "The Challenge of Response Sets." *Educ. Psychol. Measmt.,* **27,** 207–19 (1967)
101. Jackson, D. N., Guthrie, G. M. Multitrait-multimethod evaluation of the Personality Research Form. *Proc. Am. Psychol. Assoc.,* 1968, 177–78
102. Jackson, D. N., Lay, C. H. Homogeneous dimensions of personality scale content. *Multivar. Behav. Res.,* **3,** 321–37 (1968)
103. Jackson, D. N., Messick, S., Eds.

Problems in Human Assessment (McGraw-Hill, New York, 873 pp., 1967)

104. Jackson, P. W., Messick, S. The person, the product and the response: Conceptual problems in the assessment of creativity. *J. Pers.,* **33,** 309–29 (1965)
105. James, P. B., Mosher, D. L. Thematic aggression, hostility-guilt and aggressive behavior. *J. Proj. Tech.,* **31,** 1, 61–67 (1967)
106. Johnson, D. T. Effects of interview stress on measures of state and trait anxiety. *J. Abnorm. Psychol.,* **73,** 245–51 (1968)
107. Johnson, D. T., Spielberger, C. D. The effects of relaxation training and the passage of time on measures of state- and trait-anxiety. *J. Clin. Psychol.,* **24,** 20–23 (1968)
108. Kaplan, M. F. Interview interaction of repressors and sensitizers. *J. Consult. Psychol.,* **31,** 513–16 (1967)
109. Kasl, S. V., Sampson, E. E., French, J. R. P. The development of a projective measure of the need for independence: A theoretical statement and some preliminary evidence. *J. Pers.,* **32,** 566–86 (1964)
110. Katkin, E. S. Sex differences and the relationship between the Marlowe-Crowne Social Desirability Scale and MMPI indices of psychopathology. *J. Consult. Psychol.,* **30,** 564 (1966)
111. Kaufmann, H. Definitions and methodology in the study of aggression. *Psychol. Bull.,* **64,** 351–64 (1965)
112. Kelly, E. L. *Assessment of Human Characteristics* (Brooks/Cole, Belmont, Calif., 114 pp., 1967)
113. Kelman, H. C. Human use of human subjects: The problem of deception in social psychological experiments. *Psychol. Bull.,* **67,** 1–11 (1967)
114. Kenny, D. T. Stimulus functions in projective techniques. In *Progress in Experimental Personality Research,* **1,** 285–354 (See Ref. 28)
115. Kerlinger, F., Rokeach, M. The factorial nature of the F and D scales. *J. Pers. Soc. Psychol.,* **4,** 391–99 (1966)
116. Kish, G. B., Busse, W. Correlates of stimulus-seeking: Age, education, intelligence, and aptitudes. *J. Consult. Clin. Psychol.,* **32,** 633–37 (1968)
117. Klein, E. B. Stylistic components of response as related to attitude change. *J. Pers.,* **31,** 38–51 (1963)
118. Klinger, E. Fantasy need achievement as a motivational construct. *Psychol. Bull.,* **66,** 291–308 (1966)
119. Klopfer, W. G. Current status of the Rorschach test. In *Advances in Psychological Assessment,* **1,** Chap. 7, 131–49 (See Ref. 9)
120. Kurz, R. B. Relationship between time imagery and Rorschach human movement responses. *J. Consult. Psychol.,* **27,** 273–76 (1963)
121. Kusyszyn, I., Jackson, D. N. A multimethod factor analytic appraisal of endorsement and judgment methods in personality assessment. *Educ. Psychol. Measmt.,* **28,** 1047–61 (1968)
122. Lazarus, R. S. Story telling and the measurement of motivation: The direct vs. substitutive controversy. *J. Consult. Psychol.,* **30,** 483–87 (1966)
123. Lefcourt, H. M. Internal vs. external control of reinforcement: A review. *Psychol. Bull.,* **65,** 206–20 (1966)
124. Lefcourt, H. M. Repression-sensitization: A measure of the evaluation of emotional expression. *J. Consult. Psychol.,* **30,** 444–49 (1966)
125. Leibowitz, G. Comparison of self-report and behavioral techniques of assessing aggression. *J. Consult. Clin. Psychol.,* **32,** 21–25 (1968)
126. Levin, J. Three-mode factor analysis. *Psychol. Bull.,* **64,** 442–52 (1965)
127. Levy, B. I., Lomax, J. V., Jr., Minsky, R. An underlying variable in the clinical evaluation of drawings of human figures. *J. Consult. Psychol.,* **27,** 508–12 (1963)
128. Lewis, L. H. Acquiescence response set: Construct or artifact. *J. Proj. Tech.,* **32,** 578–84 (1968)
129. Liberty, P. G., Jr. Methodological considerations in the assessment of acquiescence in the *MA* and *SD* Scale. *J. Consult. Psychol.,* **29,** 37–42 (1965)
130. Liberty, P. G., Jr., Lunneborg, C. E., Atkinson, G. C. Perceptual defense, dissimulation, and response styles. *J. Consult. Psychol.,* **28,** 529–37 (1964)

131. Lichtenstein, E., Bryan, J. H. Acquiescence and the MMPI: An item reversal approach. *J. Abnorm. Psychol.*, **70,** 290–93 (1965)
132. Lieberman, L. R. On "Actuarial methods as appropriate strategy for the validation of diagnostic tests." *Psychol. Rev.*, **73,** 262–64 (1966)
133. Loehlin, J. C. Word meanings and self-descriptions: A replication and extension. *J. Pers. Soc. Psychol.*, **5,** 107–9 (1967)
134. Loevinger, J. The meaning and measurement of ego development. *Am. Psychologist,* **21,** 195–206 (1966)
135. Lomont, J. F. The repression-sensitization dimension in relation to anxiety responses. *J. Consult. Psychol.*, **29,** 84–86 (1965)
136. Lovell, V. R. The human use of personality tests: A dissenting view. *Am. Psychologist,* **22,** 383–93 (1967)
137. MacKinnon, D. W. The creativity of architects. In *Widening Horizons in Creativity,* 359–78 (Taylor, C. W., Ed., Wiley, New York, 466 pp., 1964)
138. MacKinnon, D. W. Personality and the realization of creative potential. *Am. Psychologist,* **20,** 273–81 (1965)
139. Maddi, S. R., Andrews, S. L. The need for variety in fantasy and self-description. *J. Pers.*, **34,** 610–25 (1966)
140. Maddi, S. R., Berne, N. Novelty of productions and desire for novelty as active and passive forms of the need for variety. *J. Pers.*, **32,** 270–77 (1964)
141. Maddi, S. R., Propst, B. S., Feldinger, I. Three expressions of the need for variety. *J. Pers.*, **33,** 82–98 (1965)
142. Magnusson, D., Gerzen, M., Nyman, B. The generality of behavioral data I: Generalization from observations on one occasion. *Multivar. Behav. Res.*, **3,** 295–320 (1968)
143. Magnusson, D. Heffler, B., Nyman, B. The generality of behavioral data II: Replication of an experiment on generalization from observations on one occasion. *Multivar. Behav. Res.*, **3,** 415–21 (1968)
144. Marks, P. A., Seeman, W. *The Actuarial Description of Abnormal Personality: An Atlas for Use with the MMPI* (Williams & Wilkins, Baltimore, 331 pp., 1963)
145. Marwit, S. J., Marcia, J. E. Tester bias and response to projective instruments. *J. Consult. Psychol.*, **31,** 253–58 (1967)
146. Masling, J. Differential indoctrination of examiners and Rorschach responses. *J. Consult. Psychol.*, **29,** 198–201 (1965)
147. Masling, J. Role-related behavior of the subject and psychologist and its effect upon psychological data. In *Nebraska Symposium on Motivation, 1966,* 67–103 (Levine, D., Ed., Univ. Nebraska Press, Lincoln, 209 pp., 1966)
148. May, F. B., Metcalf, A. W. A factor-analytic study of spontaneous-flexibility measures. *Educ. Psychol. Measmt.*, **25,** 1039–50 (1965)
149. McClelland, D. C. Longitudinal trends in the relation of thought to action. *J. Consult. Psychol.*, **30,** 479–83 (1966)
150. McReynolds, P., Ed. *Advances in Psychological Assessment,* **1** (Science and Behavior Books, Palo Alto, 336 pp., 1968)
151. McReynolds, P. The assessment of anxiety: A survey of available techniques. *Ibid.*, Chap. 13, 244–64
152. Mefferd, R. B., Jr. Technique for minimizing the instrumental factor. *Multivar. Behav. Res.*, **3,** 339–54 (1968)
153. Megargee, E. I., Ed. *Research in Clinical Assessment* (Harper & Row, New York, 702 pp., 1966)
154. Megargee, E. I. The Edwards SD Scale: A measure of adjustment or dissimulation? *J. Consult. Psychol.*, **30,** 566 (1966)
155. Meisels, M. Test anxiety, stress, and verbal behavior. *J. Consult. Psychol.*, **31,** 577–82 (1967)
156. Messick, S., Fritzky, F. J. Dimensions of analytic attitude in cognition and personality. *J. Pers.*, **31,** 346–70 (1963)
157. Miller, N., Doob, A. N., Butler, D. C., Marlowe, D. The tendency to agree: Situational determinants and social desirability. *J. Exptl. Res. Pers.*, **1,** 78–83 (1965)
158. Mischel, W. *Personality and Assessment* (Wiley, New York, 365 pp., 1968)
159. Mosher, D. L. The development and multitrait-multimethod matrix analysis of three measures of three

aspects of guilt. *J. Consult. Psychol.*, **30,** 25–29 (1966)
160. Mosher, D. L. Measurement of guilt in females by self-report inventories. *J. Consult. Clin. Psychol.*, **32,** 690–95 (1968)
161. Mueller, W. J., Dilling, C. A. Therapist-client interview behavior and personality characteristics of therapists. *J. Proj. Tech.*, **32,** 281–88 (1968)
162. Mulaik, S. A. Are personality factors raters' conceptual factors? *J. Consult. Psychol.*, **28,** 506–11 (1964)
163. Murphy, G. Shall we ever really understand personality? *J. Proj. Tech.*, **28,** 140–43 (1964)
164. Newberry, L. A. Defensiveness and need for approval. *J. Consult. Psychol.*, **31,** 396–400 (1967)
165. Norman, W. T., Goldberg, L. R. Raters, ratees, and randomness in personality structure. *J. Pers. Soc. Psychol.*, **4,** 681–91 (1966)
166. Norman, W. T., Harshbarger, T. R. Matching components of self-report and peer-nomination personality measures. *Psychometrika*, **30,** 481–90 (1965)
167. Owens, W. A. Toward one discipline of scientific psychology. *Am. Psychologist*, **23,** 782–85 (1968)
168. Pankoff, L. D., Roberts, H. V. Bayesian synthesis of clinical and statistical prediction. *Psychol. Bull.*, **70,** 762–73 (1968)
169. Passini, F. L., Norman, W. T. A universal conception of personality structure? *J. Pers. Soc. Psychol.*, **4,** 44–49 (1966)
170. Peabody, D. Models for estimating content and set components in attitude and personality scales. *Educ. Psychol. Measmt.*, **24,** 255–69 (1964)
171. Peabody, D. Authoritarianism scales and response bias. *Psychol. Bull.*, **65,** 11–23 (1966)
172. Pearson, P. H., Maddi, S. R. The Similes Preference Inventory: Development of a structured measure of the tendency toward variety. *J. Consult. Psychol.*, **30,** 301–8 (1966)
173. Peterson, D. R. Scope and generality of verbally defined personality factors. *Psychol. Rev.*, **72,** 48–59 (1965)
174. Petzel, T. P., Gynther, M. D. Task performance of repressors and sensitizers under ego-oriented versus task-oriented instructions. *J. Consult. Clin. Psychol.*, **32,** 486–87 (1968)
175. Rabin, A. I., Ed. *Projective Techniques in Personality Assessment: A Modern Introduction* (Springer, New York, 638 pp., 1968)
176. Reynolds, D. Social desirability in the TAT: A replication and extension of Reznikoff's study. *J. Proj. Tech.*, **28,** 78–80 (1964)
177. Richter, R. H., Winter, W. D. Holtzman Inkblot correlates of creative potential. *J. Proj. Tech.*, **30,** 62–67 (1966)
178. Roback, H. B. Human figure drawings: Their utility in the clinical psychologist's armamentarium for personality assessment. *Psychol. Bull.*, **70,** 1–19 (1968)
179. Rorer, L. G. The great response-style myth. *Psychol. Bull.*, **63,** 129–56 (1965)
180. Rorer, L. G., Goldberg, L. R. Acquiescence in the MMPI? *Educ. Psychol. Measmt.*, **25,** 801–17 (1965)
181. Rotter, J. B. Generalized expectancies for internal vs. external control of reinforcement. *Psychol. Monogr.*, **80,** (1), 28 pp. (1966)
182. Royce, J. R. Factors as theoretical constructs. *Am. Psychologist*, **18,** 522–28 (1963)
183. Rundquist, E. A. Item and response characteristics in attitude and personality assessment: A reaction to L. G. Rorer's "The great response-style myth." *Psychol. Bull.*, **66,** 166–77 (1966)
184. Saltz, G., Epstein, S. Thematic hostility and guilt responses as related to self-reported hostility, guilt and conflict. *J. Abnorm. Soc. Psychol.*, **67,** 469–79 (1963)
185. Samelson, F. Agreement set and anticontent attitudes in the F scale: A reinterpretation. *J. Abnorm. Soc. Psychol.*, **68,** 338–42 (1964)
186. Sappenfield, B. R. Test of a Szondi assumption by means of M-F photographs. *J. Pers.*, **33,** 409–17 (1965)
187. Sassenrath, J. M. A factor analysis of rating-scale items on the Test Anxiety Questionnaire. *J. Consult. Psychol.*, **28,** 371–77 (1964)
188. Sattler, J. M., Theye, F. Procedural, situational, and interpersonal variables in individual intelligence

testing. *Psychol. Bull.,* **68,** 347–60 (1967)

189. Sawyer, J. Measurement *and* prediction, clinical *and* statistical. *Psychol. Bull.,* **66,** 178–200 (1966)
190. Schaeffer, R. W. Clinical psychologists' ability to use the Draw-A-Person Test as an indicator of personality adjustment. *J. Consult. Psychol.,* **28,** 383 (1964)
191. Schimek, J. G. A note on the long-range stability of selected Rorschach scores. *J. Proj. Tech.,* **32,** 63–65 (1968)
192. Schneider, J. M. Skill versus chance activity preference and locus of control. *J. Consult. Clin. Psychol.,* **32,** 333–37 (1968)
193. Schutz, R. E., Foster, R. J. A factor analytic study of acquiescent and extreme response set. *Educ. Psychol. Measmt.,* **23,** 435–47 (1963)
194. Scott, W. A. Social desirability and individual conceptions of the desirable. *J. Abnorm. Soc. Psychol.,* **67,** 574–85 (1963)
195. Sears, R. R. Comparison of interviews with questionnaires for measuring mothers' attitudes toward sex and aggression. *J. Pers. Soc. Psychol.,* **2,** 37–44 (1965)
196. Shemberg, K. M., Leventhal, D. B. Masculinity-femininity and need for social approval. *J. Proj. Tech.,* **32,** 575–77 (1968)
197. Sherwood, J. J. Self-report and projective measures of achievement and affiliation. *J. Consult. Psychol.,* **30,** 329–37 (1966)
198. Shrauger, S., Altrocchi, J. The personality of the perceiver as a factor in person perception. *Psychol. Bull.,* **62,** 289–308 (1964)
199. Siller, J., Chipman, A. Response set paralysis: Implications for measurement and control. *J. Consult. Psychol.,* **27,** 432–38 (1963)
200. Sines, J. O. Actuarial methods as appropriate strategy for the validation of diagnostic tests. *Psychol. Rev.,* **71,** 517–23 (1964)
201. Sines, J. O. Actuarial methods in personality assessment. In *Progress in Experimental Personality Research,* **3,** 133–93 (Maher, B. A., Ed., Academic Press, New York, 319 pp., 1966)
202. Skolnick, A. Motivational imagery and behavior over twenty years. *J. Consult. Psychol.,* **30,** 463–78 (1966)
203. Smith, M. B. Explorations in competence: A study of Peace Corps teachers in Ghana. *Am. Psychologist,* **21,** 555–66 (1966)
204. Steiner, I. D., Vannoy, J. S. Personality correlates of two types of conformity behavior. *J. Pers. Soc. Psychol.,* **4,** 307–15 (1966)
205. Stern, G. G. The measurement of psychological characteristics of students and learning environments. In *Measurement in Personality and Cognition,* Chap. 3, 27–68 (Messick, S., Ross, J., Eds., Wiley, New York, 334 pp., 1962)
206. Stoyva, J., Kamiya, J. Electrophysiological studies of dreaming, as the prototype of a new strategy in the study of consciousness. *Psychol. Rev.,* **75,** 192–205 (1968)
207. Strauss, M. E. The influence of pretesting information on Rorschach based personality reports. *J. Proj. Tech.,* **32,** 323–25 (1968)
208. Stricker, L. J., Messick, S., Jackson, D. N. Dimensionality of social influence. *Proc. Am. Psychol. Assoc.,* 1968, 189–90
209. Swensen, C. H. Empirical evaluations of human figure drawings: 1957–1966. *Psychol. Bull.,* **70,** 20–44 (1968)
210. Taft, R. Extraversion, neuroticism, and expressive behavior: An application of Wallach's moderator effect to handwriting analysis. *J. Pers.,* **35,** 570–84 (1967)
211. Tajfel, H., Richardson, A., Everstine, L. Individual consistencies in categorizing: A study of judgment behavior. *J. Pers.,* **32,** 90–108 (1964)
212. Tolor, A., Reznikoff, M. Relation between insight, repression-sensitization, internal-external control, and death anxiety. *J. Abnorm. Psychol.,* **72,** 426–30 (1967)
213. Tolor, A., Schulberg, H. C. *An Evaluation of the Bender-Gestalt Test* (C. C. Thomas, Springfield, Ill., 229 pp., 1963)
214. Townsend, J. K. The relation between Rorschach signs of aggression and behavioral aggression in emotionally disturbed boys. *J. Proj. Tech.,* **31,** 6, 13–21 (1967)
215. Trott, D. M., Jackson, D. N. An experimental analysis of acquiescence. *J. Exptl. Res. Pers.,* **2,** 278–88 (1967)
216. Tryk, H. E. Assessment in the study

of creativity. In *Advances in Psychological Assessment,* **1,** Chap. 3, 34–54 (See Ref. 9)

217. Tucker, L. R. Some mathematical notes on three-mode factor analysis. *Psychometrika,* **31,** 279–311 (1966)
218. Tucker, L. R., Damarin, F., Messick, S. A base-free measure of change. *Psychometrika,* **31,** 457–73 (1966)
219. Turner, C. B., Fiske, D. W. Item quality and appropriateness of response processes. *Educ. Psychol. Measmt.,* **28,** 297–315 (1968)
220. Vannoy, J. S. Generality of cognitive complexity-simplicity as a personality construct. *J. Pers. Soc. Psychol.,* **2,** 385–96 (1965)
221. Vaught, G. M. The relationship of role identification and ego-strength to sex differences in the rod-and-frame test. *J. Pers.,* **33,** 271–83 (1965)
222. Vernon, P. E. *Personality Assessment: A Critical Survey* (Wiley, New York, 333 pp., 1964)
223. Veroff, J., Feld, S., Crockett, H. Explorations into the effects of picture cues of thematic apperception expression of achievement motivation. *J. Pers. Soc. Psychol.,* **3,** 171–81 (1966)
224. Voigt, W. H., Dana, R. H. Inter- and intra-scorer Rorschach reliability. *J. Proj. Tech.,* **28,** 92–95 (1964)
225. Wachtel, P. L. Conceptions of broad and narrow attention. *Psychol. Bull.,* **68,** 417–29 (1967)
226. Wachtel, P. L. Style and capacity in analytic functioning. *J. Pers.,* **36,** 202–12 (1968)
227. Wallace, J. An abilities conception of personality: Some implications for personality measurement. *Am. Psychologist,* **21,** 132–38 (1966)
228. Wallace, J. What units shall we employ? Allport's question revisited. *J. Consult. Psychol.,* **31,** 56–64 (1967)
229. Wallace, S. R. Criteria for what? *Am. Psychologist,* **20,** 411–17 (1965)
230. Wallach, M. A., Kogan, N. A new look at the creativity-intelligence distinction. *J. Pers.,* **33,** 348–69 (1965)
231. Watson, C. G. Relation of distortion to DAP diagnostic accuracy among psychologists at three levels of sophistication. *J. Consult. Psychol.,* **31,** 142–46 (1967)
232. Webb, E. J., Campbell, D. T., Schwartz, R. D., Sechrest, L. *Unobtrusive Measures: Nonreactive Research in the Social Sciences* (Rand McNally, Chicago, 225 pp., 1966)
233. Weinstein, J., Averill, J. R., Opton, E. M., Jr., Lazarus, R. S. Defensive style and discrepancy between self-report and physiological indexes of stress. *J. Pers. Soc. Psychol.,* **10,** 406–13 (1968)
234. Weiss, B. W., Katkin, E. S., Rubin, B. M. Relationship between a factor analytically derived measure of a specific fear and performance after related fear induction. *J. Abnorm. Psychol.,* **73,** 461–63 (1968)
235. Weiss, R. L. Operant conditioning techniques in psychological assessment. In *Advances in Psychological Assessment,* **1,** Chap. 9, 169–90 (See Ref. 9)
236. Weitman, M. Forms of failure to respond and varieties of authoritarianism. *J. Pers.,* **32,** 109–18 (1964)
237. Whitla, D. K., Ed. *Handbook of Measurement and Assessment in Behavioral Sciences* (Addison-Wesley, Reading, Mass., 508 pp., 1968)
238. Whitman, J. R., Schwartz, A. N. The relationship between two measures of the tendency to give socially desirable responses. *J. Proj. Tech.,* **31,** 5, 72–75 (1967)
239. Wiggins, J. S. Convergences among stylistic response measures from objective personality tests. *Educ. Psychol. Measmt.,* **24,** 551–62 (1964)
240. Wiggins, N. Individual viewpoints of social desirability. *Psychol. Bull.,* **66,** 68–77 (1966)
241. Wiggins, N., Hoffman, P. J. Three models of clinical judgment. *J. Abnorm. Psychol.,* **73,** 70–77 (1968)
242. Willis, R. H. The phenomenology of shifting agreement and disagreement in dyads. *J. Pers.,* **33,** 188–99 (1965)
243. Wolf, R. The measurement of environments. In *Proceedings of the 1964 Invitational Conference on Testing Problems,* 93–106 (Harris, C. W., Chairman, Educ. Testing Serv., Princeton, N.J., 140 pp.,

1965)

244. Zubin, J., Eron, L. D., Schumer, F. *An Experimental Approach to Projective Techniques* (Wiley, New York, 645 pp., 1965)

245. Zuckerman, M., Kolin, E. A., Price, L., Zoob, I. Development of a Sensation-Seeking Scale. *J. Consult. Psychol.*, **28**, 477–82 (1964)

246. Zuckerman, M., Link, K. Construct validity for the Sensation-Seeking Scale. *J. Consult. Clin. Psychol.*, **32**, 420–26 (1968)

247. Zuckerman, M., Persky, H., Eckman, K. M., Hopkins, T. R. A multitrait multimethod measurement approach to the traits (or states) of anxiety, depression, and hostility. *J. Proj. Tech.*, **31**, 2, 39–48 (1967)

248. Zuckerman, M., Persky, H., Link, K. Relation of mood and hypnotizability: An illustration of the importance of the state versus trait distinction. *J. Consult. Psychol.*, **31**, 464–70 (1967)

PSYCHOPHYSIOLOGICAL CONTRIBUTIONS TO SOCIAL PSYCHOLOGY

146

BY DAVID SHAPIRO[1]
Harvard Medical School, Boston, Massachusetts
AND GARY E. SCHWARTZ
Harvard University, Cambridge, Massachusetts

INTRODUCTION

It is often said that science progresses as new means are found to observe, measure, and quantify the phenomena of interest. The history of research on learning is largely told by such devices as the memory drum, problem box, Pavlovian method, T-maze, and Skinner box. The Binet test served as a model for much research on educational achievement and potential. In current work on sensation and perception, the methodology of signal detection has stimulated new thinking and data.

In psychophysiological research, it is the multichannel physiological recorder or polygraph that has given impetus to new approaches in the study of autonomic and peripheral somatic nervous functions in the intact organism. This basic instrument provides a means of obtaining simultaneous measures of a wide range of human bodily reactions: heart rate, respiration, eye movements, blood pressure, electrodermal activity, muscle tension, to mention only a few. Not only are the measures obtained with the polygraph of some direct physiological or medical significance (e.g., the electrocardiogram), but they are of interest as objective indices of human reaction. Social psychology, concerned with human behavior in a social context, is one of several disciplines (e.g., child development, clinical psychology) that has been turning to psychophysiology as a way of augmenting its tools of investigation.

In a broad sense, social psychology can be defined as both a social and a biological discipline. In the main, there has been little cooperation between biological sciences and social psychology, and physiological phenomena have been relatively neglected [Means (85)]. Hamburg (47) discusses the importance of expanding lines of inquiry cutting across social and biological disciplines and suggests a possibly important role for social organization in the biological adaptation and evolution of man. Although many writers have considered physiological substrates of social behavior, it is only in the past decade that more explicit recognition has been given to the potential advantages of bringing together social and physiological methods in experimental

[1] Supported by NIMH Research Grant MH-08853-06, Research Scientist Award K3-MH-20,476-06, Research Fellowship Award MH-36213-02; also by Office of Naval Research Contract Nonr-1866(43), Group Psychology and Physiological Psychology Branches.

studies of social behavior. [See Kaplan & Bloom (64); Leiderman & Shapiro (78); Shapiro & Crider (101)].

One explanation for this new alliance is the emergence of psychophysiology as a field in its own right, spurred on by the development of the polygraph. Improvements in instrumentation have occurred at a rapid pace so that recording systems are now readily available and are easily put to work. More important, basic research in the field has moved rapidly in the past two decades. It is now represented by a special journal, *Psychophysiology*, published by the Society for Psychophysiological Research. This society, established in 1961, has grown to a current membership of about 600. Articles in the field may be found throughout the major psychological journals as well as in journals in medicine, physiology, and psychiatry. An elementary textbook has appeared [Sternbach (111)] as well as handbooks on research and techniques in the field [Brown (13); Greenfield & Sternbach (45); Venables & Martin (118)].

Concepts in psychophysiology are changing rapidly. The polygraph has provided data challenging traditional views on the role of peripheral nervous processes in behavior. Basic notions of generalized autonomic arousal serving emergency or regulatory functions [Cannon (17)] have had to be modified by new knowledge of autonomic functioning. Current research in the field emphasizes the sensitivity of different physiological responses to the stimulus and behavioral demands placed on the individual. There is growing evidence that autonomic responses are patterned in different emotional and behavioral states [e.g., Ax (5); Davis (28)] and vary according to the specific requirements of simple experimental tasks [e.g., Lacey and associates (70, 71)].

A number of theories have been proposed concerning the specific adaptive or behavioral significance of some of these response patterns. For example, Sokolov (108) has identified several broad categories of patterned response, the orienting and defensive reactions, specifiable in terms of directional changes in neural effectors, that appear to be directly implicated in attentional and adaptive processes. Lacey (70) has argued that changes in blood pressure feed back into the central nervous system through pressure sensitive receptors in the aortic arch and carotid sinus and lead to certain modulations in cortical excitability, sensory-motor integration, and sensory acuity. He finds, for example, that an individual's heart rate typically slows down while he is preparing to respond to the signal in a reaction time task. This is contrary to what might be predicted using a more traditional physiological activation notion, and may be accounted for by the proposed feedback mechanism. These theoretical developments have excited the interest of many social researchers.

At the very simplest methodological level, the attraction of social psychologists to physiological techniques is not hard to understand. The techniques provide nonverbal, objective, relatively bias-free indices of human reaction that have some of the same appeal as gestural, postural, and other indicators of overt response. Much social behavior is probably immediate and automatic, and physiological measures may be able to capture these changes as they occur. Thus, physiological reactions may well anticipate and predict overt decisions, for example, or indicate persistent reactions even where the individual no longer admits to the concern. Finally, as equipment is becoming more sophisticated, it is readily adapted to augment the tools we employ in gauging overt behaviors. Examples are eye movements, fidgeting, implicit motor acts, muscle tension, and subvocal speech.

In this review, we summarize several areas of social psychology that have been stimulated by the methodology of psychophysiology. The material emphasizes those topics and specific studies not covered in detail in the last review by Shapiro & Crider (101).

SOCIAL STIMULI

One of the simplest experimental procedures in psychophysiology is to present simple stimuli to the individual and examine the amplitude, frequency, and rate of habituation of the elicited autonomic responses. [see Woodworth & Schlosberg (123)]. It is known, for example, that the louder the sound the larger the galvanic skin response it produces. This methodology has also been employed in evaluating stimuli with socially relevant or personally relevant content. The study of "emotional" words and word associational processes has had a long tradition dating back to work on "emotional complexes" in psychiatric patients [Peterson & Jung (90)]. The social psychologist has readily adapted similar techniques. For example, Cooper (19) used the galvanic skin response to different ethnic names ("Mexicans," "Swedes") or to statements coupled with these names as a way of assessing racial prejudice and social stereotypes. The methods of semantic conditioning offer additional means of studying physiological reactions to verbal material and associational processes [see Creelman (24); Cole & Williams (18)].

At a very simple level is a recent study by Wilson (121) on the arousal properties of red versus green in the form of colored slides. He found red to be more arousing in its effects on the galvanic skin response, presumably reflecting a common cultural evaluation of these colors. The same author (122) reported that such responsiveness may also be a function of the subject's own appraisal of the stimulus. Thus, personally fear-related stimuli were found to elicit larger galvanic skin responses.

Attempts have been made to categorize responses according to the interest value of stimuli, research largely stimulated by Hess & Polt (50), who reported that pupil dilation to pictures varies with degree of interest. For example, women compared to men show larger dilation of the pupil when viewing pictures of babies, mothers, and nude males. Other measures, aside from pupil response, have also been studied. Bergum & Lehr (10) found that the level of interest of words (presented visually and aurally) was functionally related to capillary pulse pressure but not to pulse rate. Using the average evoked cortical response as a response measure, Lifshitz (79) observed that pictorial material elicited different responses than defocused or blank slides. There were differences depending on whether the projected pictures were indifferent scenes, repulsive medical photographs, or pictures of nude females. Recognition threshold has been used as an objective index of response to words having emotional connotation [Hutt & Anderson (57)]. Using taboo, pleasant, and unpleasant words, a significant negative correlation was obtained between pupil diameter and recognition threshold. These results were thought to support the notion that the pupil response to emotional stimuli is related to the mechanism of perceptual defense.

An intriguing approach to meaningful auditory material is the study of reactions to human voices. Significantly different physiological responses were observed when subjects listened to their own voices as compared to voices of other people [Olivos (88)]. Gaviria (40) reported on the habituation of electrodermal, plethysmographic, and heart rate in response to noise, the subject's own voice, voice of the spouse, and an unknown voice. Habituation occurred sooner to unknown voices, and plethysmographic responses were greater and more frequent to known voices. Magnitude of heart rate and electrodermal responses did not vary systematically.

It is apparent that psychophysiological studies of social stimuli are neither extensive nor systematic. Having objective indices of comparative reaction, however, is of considerable importance. In research on child development, for example, many behavioral and verbal indices are either difficult or impossible to obtain. Physiological techniques have come into their own in assessing how infants respond to social stimuli and cognitive tasks and in evaluating changes in these responses during the course of growth and socialization [see Kagan (61)].

SOCIAL DIMENSIONS OF PERSONALITY

In view of the history of theory and research in personality, it is not surprising that the coupling of psychophysiology with personality has led to a number of interesting, suggestive, yet inconsistent findings. Harris & Bereiter (48), in their chapter on individual differences in this journal, reviewed the "generally disappointing results from attempts to relate specific physiological measures to psychological variables." With advances in physiological recording, data reduction, experimental design, and theoretical formulation, the situation has improved somewhat in the past few years.

One of the basic theoretical procedural issues in personality research has revolved around the nomothetic-idiographic distinction [Allport (3)]. Traditionally, experimental personality has used the nomothetic approach, for example, exposing groups differing on some personality variable to some experimental treatment [e.g., Lazarus & Alfert (76)]. Alfert (2) has theoretically argued and empirically demonstrated the superiority of an idiographic approach in studying personality differences in response to different stressors. Using data derived from an earlier study [Alfert (1)] in which each of 48 subjects was exposed to a direct threat (anticipation of electric shock) and to a vicariously experienced threat (anticipation of machine shop accidents in a film), Alfert (2) looked at heart rate, skin resistance, and self-report anxiety measures in both a nomothetic and an idiographic manner to determine which subjects reacted to direct threat and which to vicariously experienced threat.

> In the nomothetic comparison, an individual's designation as high reactor to either stimulus was based on the group, in the idiographic analysis an individual was considered a high reactor to the film situation if he responded more to the film than to the threat of shock, and he was considered a high reactor to the threat of shock if he reacted to it more than to the film (2, p. 201).

Both approaches were used to perform item analyses of paper and pencil personality inventory data collected prior to the experiment. Alfert found that only the idiographic analysis yielded a number of significant personality factors. People who respond to vicarious threat tended to be extroverted, self-confident, dominant, and at ease in social interpersonal relationships, compared to people who react to direct threat. Assuming that cross validation is needed to substantiate these findings, Alfert's use of an idiographic method is an excellent example of innovative research in this area. Similar theoretical and statistical analyses of these data are provided by Opton & Lazarus (89).

A number of studies have examined psychophysiological correlates of achievement. Lakie (73) related skin resistance of 39 subjects performing a hand dynamometer task to Need Achievement and to the Neuroticism scale of the Maudsley Personality Inventory. Although Need Achievement and the Neuroticism measures alone showed no significant relation to skin resistance, subjects high on Need Achievement and low on Neuroticism had higher mean skin resistance scores than subjects low on Need Achievement and high on Neuroticism. Lakie did not report the relation of these findings to dynamometer performance. The author suggests that skin resistance is part of the subject's preparation for action and an index of the subject's attitude toward overcoming difficulty. Interestingly, Bry & Daniel (15) have reported that college underachievers have "unresponsive EEGs." They studied the 10 most extreme underachievers at an arts college and compared them to achieving students. Using advanced computer averaging techniques [Daniel (26, 27)], they found that underachievers evidenced EEG patterns indicative of lower arousal under conditions of opening eyes and mental arithmetic. Furthermore, underachievers had significantly more alpha wave activity throughout the experiment. The authors suggest that a fundamental biological or firmly habituated pattern of nonresponsivity exists for underachievers. This result is in accordance with data observed by Lakie (73).

Ax & Bamford (6) have recently reported a pioneering study on a psychophysiological test of aptitude for learning social motives. They suggest that varying widely in the population is an aptitude related to learning a "hierarchy of motives." This aptitude was measured using a discrimination learning task requiring the acquisition of differential autonomic responding. Sixty-three Negro subjects were classified into high and low motivation groups as indicated by the history of employment or by teachers' ratings in vocational training school. Ax & Bamford (6) found that of 27 physiological and 24 psychological variables, 10 physiological and 8 psychological variables significantly differentiated the two groups. Ax & Bamford subjected these 18 variables to a discriminant function analysis, and the resulting equation correctly placed 92 per cent of the subjects into their appropriate groups, a diagnostic efficiency about as high as the reliability of the original selection procedures would allow. This research indicates the potential for effectively studying the development of social motives and accurately assessing social motivation using psychophysiological procedures. Again, cross validation is needed.

Other psychophysiological research on social motives which has used paradigms common to experimental psychology is a study by Hill (52), who was interested in the effects of instructions on the conditioned galvanic skin response in relation to the Need for Approval. Although Need for Approval was not related to Hill's instructional treatment per se, high Need for Approval subjects consistently responded with larger galvanic skin responses than the low subjects. Hill suggested that drive or associative factors may be involved.

A number of studies have shown that autonomic responses are sensitive to individual differences in specific social attitudes such as religious beliefs. Brown (14) reported no differences in galvanic skin responses to secular words between groups of high and low believers in Christianity. Dickson & McGinnies (29) find a similar result in that, over-all, galvanic skin responses to religious statements do not differ between pro-church, neutral church, or anti-church subjects. However, the kind of statement (pro, neutral, or anti-church) does affect the galvanic skin response, and this depends on whether the subject is a believer or not (see Fig. 1). Pro-church subjects show the largest galvanic skin response to anti-church statements, while anti-church subjects show the largest galvanic skin response to pro-church statements. Dickson & McGinnies (29) suggest that on a religious attitudinal continuum, both extremes have an affective component, and that larger autonomic responses occur when an attitude is challenged than when it is reinforced. The experimental sensitivity of using both a between (different groups of subjects) and within (different stimulus conditions to the same subject) subject design is indicated by this study.

Individual differences in prejudice also affect autonomic responses. In a series of studies, Cooper and associates (19-22) found that prejudiced subjects show greater galvanic skin responses to statements which compliment groups they dislike than statements which compliment groups they are not prejudiced against [a finding similar to Dickson & McGinnies (29) for religious attitudes]. Consistent with these findings are data by Westie & De-

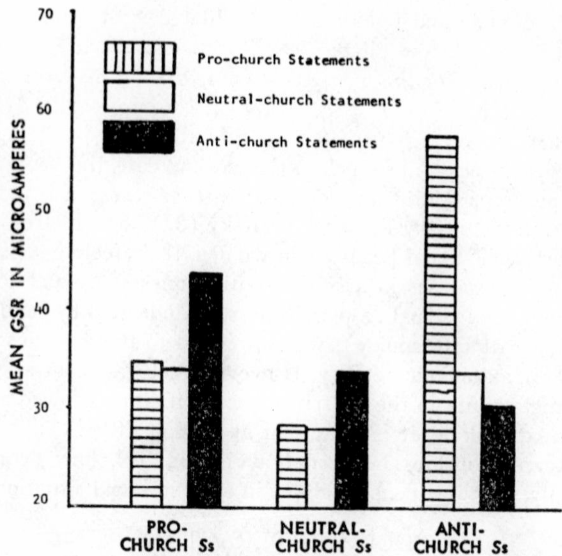

FIG. 1. Mean galvanic skin response for each group for each statement category. (From Dickson & McGinnies, 29)

Fleur (120), indicating that prejudiced white subjects produce larger galvanic skin responses to colored slides of Negroes in various social situations than white subjects who are not prejudiced. Recently, Porier & Lott (93) tried to replicate an earlier study by Rankin & Campbell (94) in which white and Negro experimenters were used. Porier & Lott reported that skin resistance showed a significant correlation with a paper and pencil measure of prejudice, but they did not obtain significantly greater skin resistance response to Negro than to white experimenters. The authors suggest that their sample may have been relatively low in racial prejudice, which would explain the failure to replicate Rankin & Campbell. Had Porier & Lott separated their subjects into high and low prejudice groups as measured by the personality scales, they might have obtained the Rankin & Campbell findings for high prejudice subjects.

Turning now to questions of sex and sex differences, Simms (105) used the pupil response to measure the interest of married males and females in pictures of males and females. This approach is based on work initiated by Hess & Polt (50), who found that pupil dilation was influenced by the interest value of visual stimuli. For example, Hess, Seltzer & Shlien (51) reported that heterosexual males show larger dilations to pictures of females than of males, and that this is reversed for homosexual men. Simms presented 12 couples with pictures of males and females; half of the male and female pictures had small pupils, the other half had large pupils. Simms found that both male and female subjects dilated most to opposite sex pictures with large pupils and dilated least to like sex pictures with large pupils. The explanation for this intriguing finding is not elaborated. It may be that pupil dilation in others is a signal for or a sign of sexual arousal or interest and that the average person finds this attractive in the opposite sex, but not in the same sex. Like much of the work to date, this research tends to raise more questions than it answers, and further research is indicated.

An interesting study by Fisher & Osofsky (37) has explored the interrelationships between sexual behavior in women, their feelings about sex, and their autonomic responses in a setting with numerous sexual connotations. By and large, actual sexual responsiveness, as indicated by sexual behavior (e.g., frequency of intercourse), was unrelated to the women's feelings as well as to their autonomic activity. However, feelings about sexual matters and autonomic activity in the contrived social situation showed a number of significant relationships. It is clear that at present little is known about the complex interrelationships between how people feel, how people respond physiologically, and how people behave in specific social situations.

SOCIAL INTERACTION

Psychophysiological studies in which the responses of more than one person are monitored simultaneously have not been extensive, although the possibility of observing mutual reactions has attracted interest for many years. A landmark study was carried out by Riddle (95) in 1925. She related indices of breathing to aggressive behavior in an experimental poker game. The results of the study, not unlike many that followed, revealed physiological changes during the interaction, but the effects were relatively nonspecific and uncorrelated with the behaviors observed. Psychophysiological research on the psychotherapeutic interview situation [see Lacey's review (69)], while producing few results bearing on therapeutic outcome, suggested that physiological data might well be an important means of making finer evaluations of interpersonal interaction. Several research teams have published work in this field largely concerned with role bahaviors, interpersonal rapport, and conformity [see Leiderman & Shapiro (78)].

The same kinds of criticism levelled by Lacey (69) at the psychotherapy studies are of relevance to the group research. To the extent that group studies are poorly designed and controlled, the physiological data remain difficult to evaluate. The interpretation of evidence, whether physiological or behavioral, naturally depends on the experimental procedures and design used to generate the evidence. Nonetheless, there has been a steady progression toward research on interpersonal interaction in which variables are more exactly specified and experiments more tightly controlled. Shapiro & Crider (101, pp. 14–18) describe some recent advances in psychophysiological group research and discuss its feasibility and potential significance for social psychology.

More indirect approaches to the study of interpersonal interaction, not depending entirely on small group methodology, will be emphasized first. Gottlieb, Gleser & Gottschalk (43) used the technique of suggesting certain specific attitudes to people under hypnosis and observing their physiological and verbal responses. Inasmuch as the content of these attitudes involves specific dispositions to behave toward other persons, this work has implications for research on social interaction. Gottlieb, Gleser & Gottschalk selected particular attitudes on the basis of previous work by Graham, Kabler & Graham (44), who derived the proposition that any one psychosomatic disorder embodies a given constellation of attitudes and that there is a link between these attitudes and physiological symptoms characteristic of the disorder. Graham, Kabler & Graham were able to show that hypnotized subjects, given the suggestion that they had attitudes like those found in different psychosomatic conditions, responded appropriately. That is, the physiological correlates of the induced attitude seem to mimic salient features of the disorder.

Gottlieb, Gleser & Gottschalk chose two attitudes, one related to hives and the other to Raynaud's disease. The hives attitude is a feeling of being mistreated without doing anything but ruminating about it. The Raynaud's attitude is a similar one of feeling mistreated but with a desire to strike back at the aggressor. The autonomic symptom in hives is an increase in skin temperature. In Raynaud's disease, the symptom is a decrease in skin temperature. The subjects were 16- to 17-year-old boys. Replicating the findings of Graham, Kabler & Graham (44), the induced attitude of hives resulted in a rise in skin temperature, compared to no such change in Raynaud's disease (see Fig. 2). In the latter, there were also significant increases in heart rate and systolic blood pressure.

It is known that specific patterns of overt emotional expression associated with fear and anger in an interpersonal situation are correlated with different patterns of physiological change [Ax (5); Funkenstein, King & Drolette (39); Schachter (97)]. That different implicit tendencies or disposi-

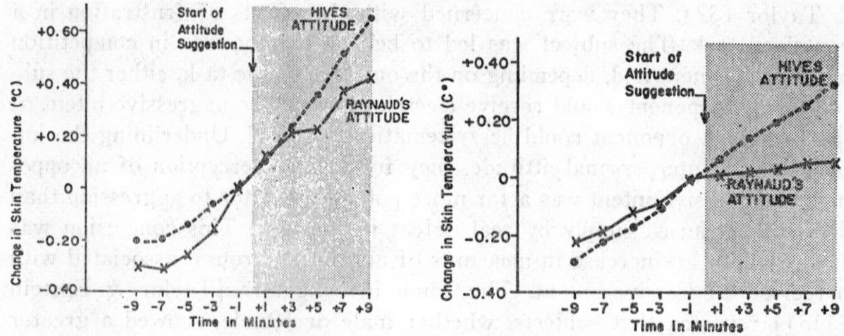

FIG. 2. The graph on the left shows the results of inducing attitudes toward the hypnotist. In the right graph, the attitude is induced toward the assistant. (From Gottlieb et al., 43)

tions to respond toward others may also be reflected in differential autonomic patterns is indicated in the study by Gottlieb, Gleser & Gottschalk. Evidence supporting this speculation is still limited, however, and additional data are needed on the induction of other kinds of interpersonal attitudes.

Such attitudes may be induced by hypnosis or by simple suggestion in the normal waking state. Damaser, Shor & Orne (25) found that "suggested" emotions lead to consistent autonomic patterns in subjects who are either hypnotized, simulating hypnosis, or in a waking state. Hepps & Brady (49) were able to induce tachycardia, an increase in heart rate, in real as well as simulating hypnotic subjects. There is also related evidence on the physiological effects of specific instructions, explicit and implicit sets, and the like [see Shapiro & Crider (101, pp. 18–23); Sternbach (111, Ch. 8 and 9)].

Of considerable significance was another result in the study by Gottlieb, Gleser & Gottschalk. The physiological effects were found to be significant only when the induced attitudes are directed toward a research assistant but not toward the hypnotist, the person obviously in control of the experimental situation (see Fig. 2). The possibility of retaliating against the source of mistreatment must have had an influence on the degree of induced autonomic change. That is, the real interpersonal context of the experimental situation proved to be a significant variable. Had the subjects been adults rather than teenagers, other results might have been forthcoming.

In a series of related studies, Hokanson and associates (54–56) had reported that the status of the experimenter made a similar difference. Typically in these studies, subjects are harassed and insulted while performing a simple mental task. The resulting frustration leads to a rise in systolic blood pressure. When subjects are given the opportunity to retaliate against the aggressor (experimenter), there is a drop in pressure but only if the counter-aggression is directed toward someone who is in reality of equal or lower status than the subject. The effect occurred when the experiment was run by a graduate student but not when run by a higher-status researcher.

The interpersonal context of aggression has also been studied by Epstein & Taylor (32). They were concerned with the effects of frustration in a contrived task. The subject was led to believe that he was in competition with an opponent and, depending on the outcome of the task, either the subject or his opponent would receive electric shocks. The aggressive intent of the presumed opponent could be systematically varied. Underlining the importance of interpersonal attitude, they found that perception of an opponent's aggressive intent was a far more potent instigator to aggression than frustration caused simply by real defeat in the task. This conclusion was supported by an increase in measures of autonomic arousal associated with perceived aggressive intent. The same investigators [Taylor & Epstein (113)] reported that subjects, whether male or female, showed a greater rise in skin conductance when competing with female rather than male opponents, again underscoring the significance of interpersonal context.

In the above studies, interpersonal effects were investigated largely by inducing attitudes and dispositions to respond toward some target or the experimenter. More global affective attitudes have also been used as an independent variable by Kaplan (63), who put together groups of people who either liked or disliked one another as determined by sociometric questionnaires. Kaplan concluded from the evidence that different affective groups generate functional roles resulting in a variable association between role behavior and the galvanic skin response. The processes whereby generalized affective attitudes of this kind influence physiological responses are difficult to specify precisely.

Current research on social interaction has also continued along the lines of more traditional group methodology. Some investigators have been concerned with social variables as a source of stress for the individual. A long-range aim of this research is an evaluation of the social origins or causes of physiological and psychological dysfunction. Social pressure toward conformity is one such variable. Costell & Leiderman (23) used an experimental situation based on a contrived manipulation of group opinion [Asch (4)]. They found that individuals who are independent and manage to fend off the majority opinion of four other people in a group exhibit higher arousal levels as measured by skin potential level (see Fig. 3). In conforming to

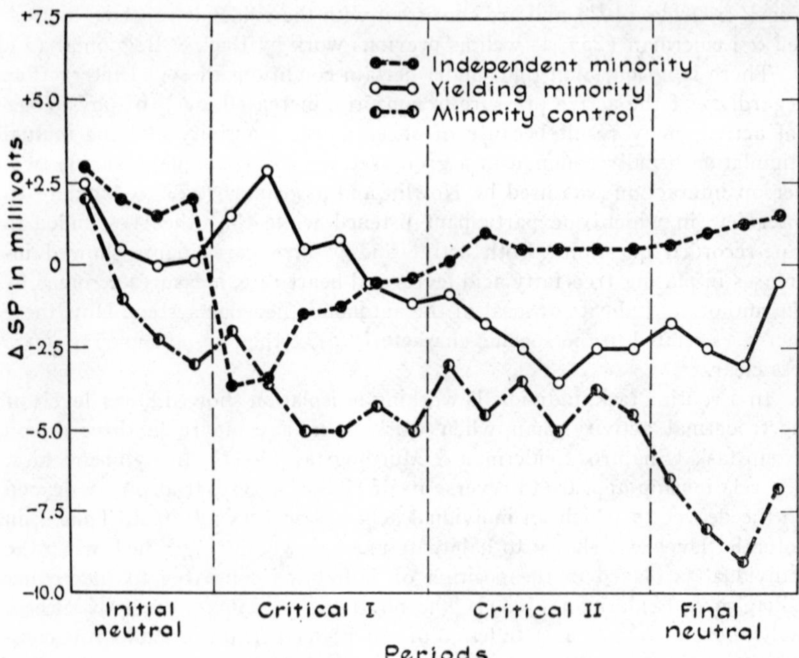

FIG. 3. Skin potential level in minority subjects (difference from initial rest period level). (From Costell & Leiderman, 23)

group opinion, the nonindependent subject shows a reduction in skin potential level. This reduction, the authors suggest, may serve to reinforce conformity. The relation between physiological arousal reduction and reinforcement is still uncertain [Berlyne (11)].

In related work, Buckhout (16) observed that attitude change is accompanied by a decline in heart rate. Anticonformers who are lower on heart rate measures tend to maintain their initial levels of physiological activity during the attempt to influence their opinions with certain counter-communications. This is consistent with the findings of Costell & Leiderman (23). Walters & Amoroso (119), however, concluded that heart rate was a relatively unimportant determinant of conforming. The conformity in this case consisted of imitating a model who had been looking at certain slides containing sexual material.

In a slightly different context, mention should be made of the earlier work by Smith (106) on the autonomic effects of announced standards on attitudes and opinions. Smith found that holding a position contrary to the group's opinion yielded more electrodermal activity than being in agreement with the majority. Changing one's opinions toward independence of group standards was associated with higher autonomic response levels. These results have since been followed up and confirmed by Gerard (41) and by Snoek & Dobbs (107) and are consistent with the evidence reported by Costell & Leiderman (23), as well as previous work by Back & Bogdonoff (7).

There is no question that, under certain conditions of social interaction, regardless of the active pressure to conform, increased levels of physiological activity may result because of sheer physical activity and the mutual stimulation usually common in a group setting. For example, a simple two-person interaction was used by Nowlin and associates (87) to simulate an interview in which one participant listened while the other responded to tape-recorded questions. Both active and passive participants showed increases in plasma free-fatty acid levels and heart rate, measures assumed by the authors to indicate arousal of the autonomic nervous system. How these increases related to the specific characteristics of the two-person situation is less clear.

In a routine task, individuals working in isolation showed lower levels of electrodermal activity than when working in a comparable three-person group task [Shapiro, Leiderman & Morningstar (104)]. In a difficult task, this relationship appears to reverse itself [Kissel (65)]. It also may depend on the degree to which an individual achieves success in a task. Thus, skin potential level was shown to habituate more slowly during a task when the individual is placed in the position of failing, as compared to succeeding [Shapiro & Leiderman (103)]. The physiological consequences of success and failure also vary as a function of other social factors such as role composition. Skin potential level was shown to decline at a faster rate when the individual was the only one in the group to succeed or to fail. Roles in which the individual shared the same fate as another person showed slower habituation rates [Shapiro & Leiderman (103)].

While the above studies of induced social stress have not as yet isolated specific patterns of physiological responses, they suggest that responses vary according to the social demands placed on the individual. Autonomic response levels and their time course provide a means of assessing different conditions of social interaction. It is possible to gauge reaction on a continuous basis in this manner, even where overt behavior may be completely undifferentiated. In a study by Shapiro & Leiderman (103), all subjects behaved overtly in identical fashion, yet the consequences of their behavior and the role constellations present in the group had differential effects on an autonomic variable. Physiological data also provide a means of evaluating differences in expectation brought about through prior experiences of success and failure in groups [Shapiro & Leiderman (102)].

A further example is derived from an unpublished study (D. Shapiro) in which individuals were waiting for an experiment to begin, either alone or in groups of three, without overt activity or talking. Under these conditions, skin potential level showed a faster decline or habituation for the individuals who were grouped in threes than for those in isolation. These were student nurses who knew each other and worked together. Comparable physiological variations for groups of "strangers" versus groups of "friends" have been noted by Back & Bogdonoff (7).

Rate of habituation of a physiological variable may be an index of choice in evaluating certain kinds of interaction; for example, while subjects are waiting either before or after some experimental manipulation, as discussed above. An illuminating discussion of the role of continuous physiological measures in supplementing basic experimental data may be found in Back and associates (8). These authors were able to show how physiological data obtained during "in-between" times, such as periods of rest, could provide a more complete assessment of the effects of experimental stress.

It should be apparent from the above account that the research on social interaction has progressed along a number of different but related lines. Meaningful data have been obtained showing that interpersonal contexts, whether at an overt or attitudinal level, generate predictable behavioral and physiological consequences. By and large, the physiological data continue to be dealt with as indicants of general autonomic arousal. While such an assumption may not be completely warranted [see Lacey (70); Shapiro & Crider (101)], social situations possess varying properties to arouse the individual in different degrees, and these may be usefully looked at on the physiological level. To the extent that these data allow certain kinds of individual predictability—for example, conforming or anticonforming behaviors or ongoing reactions to success, failure, or stress—than they add greatly to the tools of interpersonal research. The approach of inducing interpersonal attitudes and observing consequent specific patterns of autonomic response is promising both for the study of interaction and the assessment of individual personality.

SOCIO-CULTURAL DIFFERENCES

Since socio-cultural factors play an important role in determining human behavior, it is not surprising that these variables should have an effect on physiological behaviors as well. It is possible to study socio-cultural effects both to better understand the multideterminants of autonomic behavior as well as to study the socio-cultural phenomena themselves.

Data presented by Lazarus (74, 75), including a published round-table discussion of the work (75), serves to illustrate some of the complexities and concerns in this growing area of research. Lazarus studied 80 Japanese students and 64 Japanese adults in an experimental situation similar to the one used in the United States [Speisman et al. (110)]. Lazarus (74) found that self-reported distress ratings of both Japanese groups were similar to comparison American groups [Mordkoff (86)]. However, he found that Japanese subjects (students in particular) evidenced higher skin conductance, not only during the subincision (stress) film but during the rice farming (control) film as well (see Fig. 4).

Lazarus favors a psychological interpretation of the results, suggesting that the Japanese subjects were more stressed by the whole experimental situation than were the American sample, and that skin conductance is differentially sensitive to this over-all stress factor. He suggests that the skin conductance differences are not a function of racial differences in basal sweat gland activity or skin characteristics between Orientals and Caucasians per se. Further discussion of the Japanese data which also evaluates instructional experimental treatments can be found in Lazarus and associates (77).

The general question of autonomic level (basal) versus autonomic reactivity is important when different groups of subjects are studied. Kugelmass (66) and Kugelmass & Lieblich (67) have found differences in skin resistance reactivity in a card detection experiment between Jewish subjects of different ethnic backgrounds. Generally, Jewish subjects of Near Eastern origin show less skin resistance reactivity than Jewish subjects born in America, Europe, or Israel. Using data of three Jewish and one Bedouin samples, Kugelmass & Lieblich (68) recently reported that subjects of Near Eastern origin tend also to show higher basal skin conductance and lower pulse rate. They suggest that (*a*) the lower skin resistance reactivity is not simply a function of higher basal skin conductance, and (*b*) the higher basal skin conductance, in conjunction with the lower pulse rate, indicates socio-cultural autonomic patterning.

Racial differences between Negroes and whites have also been observed in basal skin conductance and skin resistance reactivity [Johnson & Corah (59); Johnson & Landon (60); Bernstein (12)]. Negroes tend to show lower basal skin conductance and initially lower skin resistance reactivity.

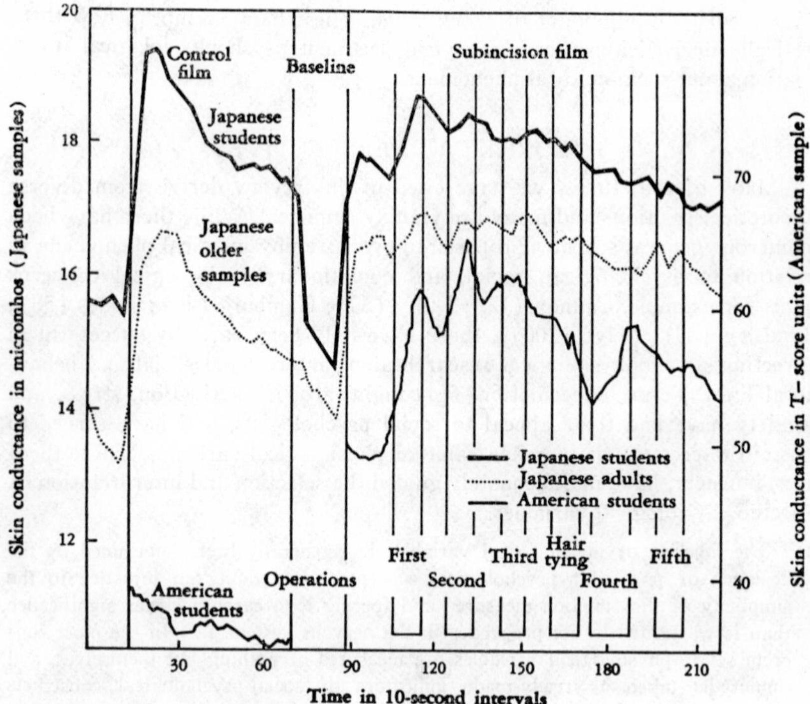

FIG. 4. Japanese and American skin conductance curves during the subincision and control movies (74). (From *Psychological Stress and the Coping Process* by R. S. Lazarus. Used with permission of McGraw Hill Book Company, copyright 1966.)

Johnson & Landon (60) suggest that the Negro-white reactivity differences are simply a function of the different levels of skin conductance. As yet, the reasons for these are not clear, although it appears likely that both psychological (socio-cultural) and local (e.g., epidermal) factors may be involved.

Socio-cultural differences in attitude toward pain, as reflected in standardized interviews, have been shown to have psychophysical and psychophysiological correlates [Sternbach & Tursky (112)]. Using shock apparatus developed by Tursky & Watson (115), Sternbach & Tursky found that Yankee, Irish, Jewish, and Italian housewives differ in the amount of shock they will take, as well as in their autonomic reactivity to the noxious stimuli. As predicted from earlier research on pain [Zborowski (124)], Yankee women took the most shock and Italian women the least. Furthermore, the Yankees showed the most rapid habituation of biphasic skin potential responses to the electric shocks and the Italians the least. Tursky & Sternbach (114), in a further evaluation of the physiological data, found group differences in resting skin resistance, heart rate, and facial temperature. They also found that the ethnic groups differed as to which autonomic measure best predicted the amount of shock taken. These data exemplify how theoretically derived hypotheses can yield pertinent psychophysiological information about socio-cultural phenomena.

THEORETICAL PERSPECTIVES

Many of the studies we have cited in this review derive from diverse theoretical positions and many are frankly empirical. While there have been numerous general schemes proposed to organize physiological phenomena in relation to psychological, social, and evolutionary or biological concerns [see, for example, Cannon (17); Duffy (30); Hamburg (46); James (58); Lindsley (80); Selye (100)], these have only been partially successful in directing psychophysiological research along interrelated social and behavioral lines. Terms like emotion, fight-flight, arousal, activation, stress, and anxiety have had their appeal to social psychologists, and have served to sustain interest in the possible value of physiological variables. These theories, however, have not adequately guided the selection and interpretation of specific physiological variables.

> The labeling of physiological variables has generally been determined by the demands of particular psychological concepts, often doing an injustice to the simplicity of the function measured and forcing it to carry a larger significance than is warranted by its properties in the nervous system. . . . In the most concrete sense, physiological variables are measures of nothing but themselves, and cannot be taken as ready-made indicators of social-psychological constructs [Shapiro & Crider (101, pp. 2–3)].

There have been some developments of smaller, circumscribed theories such as those in Lazarus' work (74) on coping or those by Fenz and Epstein on conflict and anxiety (33, 34) which have been found effective for the study of specific problems of behavioral and psychological adaptation. Shapiro & Crider (101) discuss other theoretical contributions deriving from psychophysiological research on response patterning and autonomic feedback.

Following the traditions of James and Cannon, a broad formulation has been recently put forth by Stanley Schachter (98). As a combined social and psychophysiological theory, it is worthy of discussion here. The formulation may be called a social-cognitive-activation theory of emotional states. It is a modified version of the visceral theory of emotion put forth by William James (58), stating that emotional experience depends on the perception of bodily changes following upon the exciting circumstances.

Schachter (98) begins with the assumption that a general (undifferentiated) pattern of sympathetic discharge is characteristic of emotional states.

> Given such a state of arousal, it is suggested that one labels, interprets, and identifies this state in terms of the characteristics of the precipitating situation and one's apperceptive mass. This suggests, then, that an emotional state may be considered a function of a state of physiological arousal and a cognition

> appropriate to this state of arousal. The cognition, in a sense, exerts a steering function. Cognitions arising from the immediate situation as interpreted by past experience provide the framework within which one understands and labels one's feelings. It is the cognition that determines whether the state of physiological arousal will be labeled 'anger,' 'joy,' or whatever [Schachter (98, p. 139)].

In effect, a state of autonomic arousal leads to a need to label, or an "evaluative need" in Festinger's terms (35). The individual, then, relates his own bodily functioning, as well as other perceptions and behavior, to socially defined or group norms. According to Schachter, a state of autonomic arousal for which an individual has an appropriate explanation (for example, it could be attributed to a drug or to the weather) will not result in a socially defined emotional experience. The same social circumstance without the physiological substrate will likewise not lead to evaluative or emotional processes.

While Schachter's formulation has in it a number of theoretical difficulties, and while his empirical interpretations tend to lean too heavily on *post hoc* internal analyses, it has nonetheless contributed experimental work unique to social psychology and worthy of continued attention. It has also stimulated important applications to the study of anxiety and emotionality [Valins (116, 117)] and obesity [Schachter (99)]. It has opened to inquiry an exciting problem for psychology—the question of internal versus external regulations of behavior. For a critique of Schachter's work on theoretical and empirical grounds, see Lykken (81), Plutchik & Ax (92), and Shapiro & Crider (101, pp. 28–31).

The major theoretical questions in Schachter's formulation should be mentioned briefly. First is the assumption that the individual becomes aware of changes in autonomic excitation and can label or identify them verbally. This equation of visceral activity and subjective emotionality is in much need of empirical verification. Studies in the area have tended to yield inconsistent results [Baron (9); Fisher (36); Flocks & Stunkard (38); Hohmann (53); Lykken (81); Mandler & Kahn (83); Mandler & Kremen (84)]. There is little support for the view that we can identify autonomic activity or that this activity is correlated to a significant degree with subjective emotional experience. Second is the assumption that the same continuum of physiological activation exists in different emotional states. While this position is generally held and is perhaps still justified, evidence in the past decade on the patterning of physiological responses under varying environmental demands [Shapiro & Crider (101)] limits its applicability.

As the specific empirical research of Schachter and associates has been widely summarized and reviewed, there is no need to recapitulate the major findings here. Whether the interactions of cognition and bodily activation follow the foundation laid out by Schachter is perhaps less important than the fact that his work supports the view that feelings, physiological functions, and behaviors are readily modified by the social environment and its vicissitudes. Continuous monitoring of physiological variables before, during, and after the manipulation of cognitive and social stimuli may provide the kinds of data needed to lend additional support to theoretical formulations of this kind.

Our theoretical position, briefly stated, is that physiological, overt behavioral, verbal, and subjective responses are most simply considered multiple concurrent responses functionally related to environmental conditions but not necessarily to each other [see Elliott (31)]. There may be varying degrees of integration or differentiation of the different responses depending upon prior experience and learning and possibly constitutional factors. The fact that overt and covert reaction, for example, may differ widely suggests a greater independence of nervous function than we are accustomed to believe. It is perhaps in the analysis of discontinuities, inconsistencies, or the general patterning among these different sources of individual reactions that we shall find new sources of worthwhile information regarding social-psychophysiological interaction. Informative analyses of some differential patterns of behavioral and physiological response in social psychological contexts have been provided by Shapiro & Leiderman (102), Fenz & Epstein (34), and Epstein & Taylor (32).

CONCLUSION

From the social psychological and psychophysiological research to date, it is clear that there is no one major theory or formulation which manages to integrate the two disciplines into something more complete than either alone. One reason for this is the relative infancy of this scientific merger. Another reason is that neither approach brings a truly unifying theoretical framework along to encompass the other. A final reason is the sheer complexity which is inherent in the very nature of the interrelationships between social, psychological, and physiological phenomena. Yet, a foundation of scientific knowledge and technique is being developed on which a more solid superstructure will likely be established.

Our enthusiasm for social psychological-psychophysiological research stems in part from the observation that each approach simultaneously extends and increases the understanding of the other. As Shapiro & Crider comment,

> a growing understanding of the social psychology of the psychophysiological experiment points up sources of variation in physiological measures and, conversely, the remarkable sensitivity of these measures to social attributes such as race, sex, and status leads to a fuller appreciation of the impact of social factors on individual behavior (101, pp. 37–38).

Potential candidates for mutual integration presently include these: Sokolov's (108) orienting and defensive reaction; Lacey's (69, 70, 72) concepts of individual and situational stereotypy and cardiovascular changes accompanying various forms of attention; Germana's (42) concept of activation peaking in a learning situation; Lazarus' (74) concepts of cognitive influences on stress; Schachter's (98) concept of social, cognitive, and physiological bases of emotion; Rosenthal's (96) concepts of experimenter effects and expectancies; and Festinger's (35) concept of social comparison. It is our opinion that carefully planned social-psychophysiological experimentation will lead to a fruitful merger, resulting extension, and final creation of new unifying concepts.

As illustrated in the research reviewed to date, a number of methodological procedures appear promising and are worth noting. Exposing each subject to two or more conditions consistently results in more powerful differentiation of experimental effects, whether it be different words, different statements, different classes of pictures, different films, different stressors, different experimenters, and so forth. Because of large inter-subject differences in levels of physiological functioning (e.g., resting heart rates can often vary from 50 to 100 beats per minute) and relatively small effects across treatments (e.g., heart rate changes of 2 to 5 beats per minute), it is advisable that within-subject designs be used whenever possible in social-psychophysiological research, with appropriate controls for or evaluation of possible order effects. Another important consideration is the use of idiographic analyses when individual differences are of concern. At least a comparison of idiographic and nomothetic approaches is warranted. With the development of easy, reliable means of continuously recording physiological responses, it is suggested that more than one physiological measure be monitored during an experiment. The autonomic patterning data [see Shapiro & Crider (101, pp. 23–28)] suggest that some measures may be more sensitive to certain social psychological phenomena than others, and it may well turn out that patterns of physiological activity will prove to be a sensitive, complex dependent variable. If polygraph facilities are not available, it is possible, for example, to obtain single readings of sweat gland activity using sweat print techniques [Malmo (82); Pillard et al. (91)], or even to train subjects at various points in the experiment to reliably take their own pulse [Southard & Katahn (109)]. Of course, such techniques may result in less reliable, time consuming, interfering, and intermittent data sampling. It should be mentioned that subjects need not be confined to a chair. Telemetry equipment [Brown (14); Venables & Martin (118)] has been developed to the point that continuous measures of physiological functioning can easily be obtained in the freely moving subject.

One methodological innovation not yet discussed which we feel may serve to magnify social-psychological effects is the use of paced, time-locked procedures. In a mental effort task, Kahneman and associates (62) have demonstrated that pupil dilation, heart rate, and skin resistance sensitively track phases of a mental task and line up according to the difficulty of the task when a sequential pacing procedure is employed (see Fig. 5). The subject receives an initial ready signal followed by a series of clicks presented one per second. The task is announced, information is given, and the subject responds, all in synchrony with specific clicks. For example, in

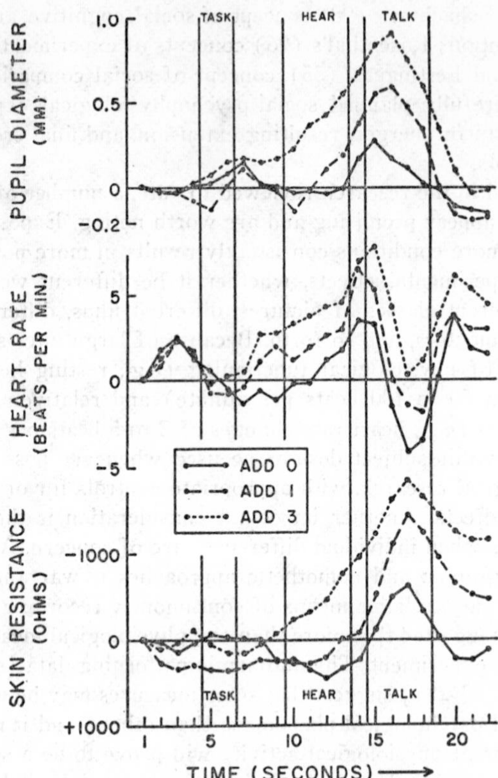

FIG. 5. Second-by-second autonomic changes during digit transformation task. (From Kahneman et al., 62)

this experiment, the subject gave a four-digit answer, one digit per click, on seconds 15 to 18. This makes it possible to obtain second by second evoked autonomic responses throughout the various phases of the task, and with the aid of averaging devices to obtain a mean curve per subject per condition. It is our opinion that the paced, time-locked procedure may well be adapted to tasks in research areas such as decision making, attitudes, and attitude change. In studying conformity, for example, pressure to conform can be augmented or diminished in a step-wise fashion so as to examine the time course of reaction to this form of social stress. Similarly, the degree of conflict in a particular choice or decision process may be sequentially varied. Clearly, effects of such variables as status, race, and sex can be investigated in relation to the particular paced tasks. Group variables can be investigated, for subjects can do time-locked tasks simultaneously, or in pairs, and so on. Finally, socio-cultural differences using time-locked tasks can be evaluated.

In closing, it is apparent that psychologists are becoming increasingly aware of the major influence of social psychological variables on overt behavior. The present research indicates that covert, physiological behavior is similarly affected, in ways as yet sometimes confusing, but often intriguing. We feel that this present state of affairs should be expected, not only because of the relative infancy of social-psychophysiology, but because of the frequent counter-common sense characteristic of psychophysiological data per se. For example, in classical conditioning, while we might expect the heart to accelerate to a conditioned stimulus prior to the onset of electric shock, it decelerates, or while we might expect the heart to accelerate when males attend to arousing stimuli like slides of nude females, it decelerates [see Shapiro & Crider (101)]. It seems safe to predict that social-psychophysiology will uncover new, counter-intuitive phenomena which will bring us closer to more fully understanding social behavior. It is our opinion, in view of the data so far available, that social-psychophysiology is a natural scientific merger, one which at the present stage of theory may be premature, but for which there is now a technology for studying the inherent social-biological nature of man.

LITERATURE CITED

1. Alfert, E. Comparison of response to a vicarious and direct threat. *J. Exptl. Res. Pers.*, **1**, 179–86 (1966)
2. Alfert, E. An idiographic analysis of personality differences between reactors to a vicariously experienced threat and reactors to a direct threat. *Ibid.*, **2**, 200–7 (1967)
3. Allport, G. W. The general and the unique in psychological science. *J. Pers.*, **30**, 405–22 (1962)
4. Asch, S. Studies of independence and conformity. I. A minority of one against a unanimous majority. *Psychol. Monogr.*, **70** (9) (1956)
5. Ax, A. F. The physiological differentiation between fear and anger in humans. *Psychosomat. Med.*, **15**, 433–42 (1953)
6. Ax, A. F., Bamford, J. L. Validation of a psychophysiological test of aptitude for learning social motives. *Psychophysiology*, **5**, 316–32 (1968)
7. Back, K. W., Bogdonoff, M. D. Plasma lipid responses to leadership, conformity, and deviation. In *Psychobiological Approaches to Social Behavior*, 24–42 (Leiderman, P. H., Shapiro, D., Eds., Stanford Univ. Press, Stanford, Calif., 203 pp., 1964)
8. Back, K. W., Wilson, S. R., Bogdonoff, M. D., Troyer, W. G. In-between times and experimental stress. *J. Pers.*, **35**, 456–73 (1967)
9. Baron, J. An EEG correlate of autonomic discrimination. *Psychon. Sci.*, **4**, 255–56 (1966)
10. Bergum, B. O., Lehr, D. J. Affect level, capillary pulse pressure, and response latency. *J. Appl. Psychol.*, **51**, 316–19 (1967)
11. Berlyne, D. E. *Conflict, Arousal, and Curiosity* (McGraw-Hill, New York, 350 pp., 1960)
12. Bernstein, A. S. Race and examiner as significant influences on basal skin impedance. *J. Pers. Soc. Psychol.*, **1**, 346–49 (1965)
13. Brown, C. C., Ed. *Methods in Psychophysiology* (Williams & Wilkins, Baltimore, 502 pp., 1967)
14. Brown, L. B. Religious belief and skin conductance. *Percept. Mot. Skills*, **23**, 477–78 (1966)
15. Bry, B. H., Daniel, R. S. The unresponsive EEGs of college underachievers. *Psychon. Sci.*, **9**, 103–4 (1967)
16. Buckhout, R. Changes in heart rate accompanying attitude change. *J. Pers. Soc. Psychol.*, **4**, 695–99 (1966)
17. Cannon, W. B. *Bodily Changes in Pain, Hunger, Fear, and Rage*, 2nd ed. (Appleton-Century-Crofts, New York, 404 pp., 1929)
18. Cole, S., Williams, R. L. Semantic generalization as a function of associative value of stimuli. *Psychon. Sci.*, **6**, 173–74 (1966)
19. Cooper, J. B. Emotion in prejudice. *Science*, **130**, 314–18 (1959)
20. Cooper, J. B., Pollock, D. A. Identification of prejudicial attitudes by the GSR. *J. Soc. Psychol.*, **50**, 241–45 (1959)
21. Cooper, J. B., Siegel, H. E. The GSR as a measure of emotion in prejudice. *J. Psychol.*, **42**, 149–55 (1956)
22. Cooper, J. B., Singer, D. N. The role of emotion in prejudice. *J. Soc. Psychol.*, **44**, 241–47 (1956)
23. Costell, R. M., Leiderman, P. H. Psychophysiological concomitants of social stress: The effects of conformity pressure. *Psychosomat. Med.*, **30**, 298–310 (1968)
24. Creelman, M. B. *The Experimental Investigation of Meaning* (Springer, New York, 228 pp., 1966)
25. Damaser, E. C., Shor, R. E., Orne, M. T. Physiological effects during hypnotically requested emotions. *Psychosomat. Med.*, **25**, 334–43 (1963)
26. Daniel, R. S. Electroencephalographic correlogram ratios and their stability. *Science*, **145**, 721–23 (1964)
27. Daniel, R. S. Electroencephalographic pattern quantification and the arousal continuum. *Psychophysiology*, **2**, 146–60 (1965)
28. Davis, R. C. Response patterns. *Trans. N.Y. Acad. Sci. 19* (Series II), 731–39 (1957)
29. Dickson, H. W., McGinnies, E. Affectivity in the arousal of attitudes as measured by galvanic skin response. *Am. J. Psychol.*, **79**, 584–87 (1966)
30. Duffy, E. *Activation and Behavior* (Wiley, New York, 384 pp., 1962)
31. Elliott, R. Physiological activity and

performance: A comparison of kindergarten children with young adults. *Psychol. Monogr.,* **78** (10, Whole No. 287) (1964)

32. Epstein, S., Taylor, S. P. Instigation to aggression as a function of degree of defeat and perceived aggressive intent of the opponent. *J. Pers.,* **35,** 265–89 (1967)
33. Fenz, W. D. Conflict and stress as related to physiological activation and sensory, perceptual, and cognitive functioning. *Psychol. Monogr.,* **78** (8, Whole No. 585) (1964)
34. Fenz, W. D., Epstein, S. Gradients of physiological arousal in parachutists as a function of an approaching jump. *Psychosomat. Med.,* **29,** 33–51 (1967)
35. Festinger, L., A theory of social comparison processes. *Hum. Relat.,* **7,** 114–40 (1954)
36. Fisher, S. Organ awareness and organ activation. *Psychomat. Med.,* **29,** 643–47 (1967)
37. Fisher, S., Osofsky, H. Sexual responsiveness in women: Physiological correlates. *Psychol. Rept.,* **22,** 215–26 (1968)
38. Flocks, J., Stunkard, A. The perception of gastric events. *Cond. Reflex,* **2,** 162 (1967)
39. Funkenstein, D. H., King, S. H., Drolette, M. E. *Mastery of Stress* (Harvard Univ. Press, Cambridge, Mass., 329 pp., 1957)
40. Gaviria, B. Autonomic reaction magnitude and habituation to different voices. *Psychosomat. Med.,* **29,** 598–605 (1967)
41. Gerard, H. B. Disagreement with others, their credibility, and experienced stress. *J. Abnorm. Soc. Psychol.,* **62,** 559–64 (1961)
42. Germana, J. The psychophysiological correlates of conditioned response formation. *Psychol. Bull.,* **70,** 105–14 (1968)
43. Gottlieb, A. A. Gleser, G. C., Gottschalk, L. A. Verbal and physiological responses to hypnotic suggestion of attitudes. *Psychosomat. Med.,* **29,** 172–83 (1967)
44. Graham, D. T., Kabler, J. D., Graham, F. K. Physiological response to the suggestion of attitudes specific for hives and hypertension. *Psychosomat. Med.,* **24,** 159–69 (1962)
45. Greenfield, N. S., Sternbach, R. A., Eds. *Handbook of Psychophysiology* (Holt, Rinehart & Winston, New York, in press)
46. Hamburg, D. Emotions in the perspective of human evoluation. In *Expression of the Emotions in Man,* 300–17 (Knapp, P. J., Ed., Intern. Univ. Press, New York, 354 pp., 1963)
47. Hamburg, D. Foreword. In *Psychobiological Approaches to Social Behavior* (See Ref. 7)
48. Harris, C. W., Bereiter, C. E. Individual differences. In *Ann. Rev. Psychol.,* **10,** 89–108 (1959)
49. Hepps, R. B., Brady, J. P. Hypnotically induced tachycardia: An experiment with simulating controls. *J. Nerv. Ment. Dis.,* **145,** 131–37 (1967)
50. Hess, E. H., Polt, J. M. Pupil size as related to interest value of visual stimuli. *Science,* **132,** 349–50 (1960)
51. Hess, E. H., Seltzer, A. L., Shlien, J. M. Pupil response of hetero- and homosexual males to pictures of men and women: A pilot study. *J. Abnorm. Psychol.,* **70,** 165–68 (1965)
52. Hill, F. A. Effects of instructions and subject's need for approval on the conditioned galvanic skin response. *J. Exptl. Psychol.,* **73,** 461–67 (1967)
53. Hohmann, G. W. Some effects of spinal cord lesions on experienced emotional feelings. *Psychophysiology,* **3,** 143–56 (1966)
54. Hokanson, J. E., Burgess, M. The effects of status, type of frustration, and aggression on vascular processes. *J. Abnorm. Soc. Psychol.,* **65,** 232–37 (1962)
55. Hokanson, J. E., Burgess, M., Cohen, M. F. Effect of displaced aggression on systolic blood pressure. *J. Abnorm. Soc. Psychol.,* **67,** 214–18 (1963)
56. Hokanson, J. E., Shetler, S. The effect of overt aggression on physiological arousal. *J. Abnorm. Soc. Psychol.,* **63,** 446–48 (1961)
57. Hutt, L. D., Anderson, J. P. The relationship between pupil size and recognition threshold. *Psychon. Sci.,* **9,** 477–78 (1967)
58. James, W. *The Principles of Psychology,* **II** (Holt, New York, 704 pp., 1890)
59. Johnson, L. C., Corah, N. L. Racial differences in skin resistance.

Science, **139,** 766–67 (1963)

60. Johnson, L. C., Landon, M. M. Eccrine sweat gland activity and racial differences in resting skin conductance. *Psychophysiology,* **1,** 322–29 (1965)
61. Kagan, J. On cultural deprivation. In *Biology and Behavior: Environmental Influences,* 211–50 (Glass, D. C., Ed., Rockefeller Press, New York, 234 pp., 1968)
62. Kahneman, D., Tursky, B., Shapiro, D., Crider, A. Pupillary, heart rate, and skin resistance changes during a mental task. *J. Exptl. Psychol.,* **79,** 164–67 (1969)
63. Kaplan, H. B. Physiological correlates (GSR) of affect in small groups. *J. Psychosomat. Res.,* **11,** 173–79 (1967)
64. Kaplan, H. B., Bloom, S. W. The use of sociological and social-psychological concepts in physiological research: A review of selected experimental studies. *J. Nerv. Ment. Dis.,* **131,** 128–34 (1960)
65. Kissel, S. Stress reducing properties of social stimuli. *J. Pers. Soc. Psychol.,* **2,** 378–84 (1965)
66. Kugelmass, S. Effects of three levels of realistic stress on differential physiological reactivity. *Air Force Off. Sci. Res.,* Washington, D.C. AFEOAR Grant 63–61 (1963)
67. Kugelmass, S., Lieblich, I. Effects of realistic stress and procedural interference in experimental lie detection. *J. Appl. Psychol.,* **50,** 211–16 (1966)
68. Kugelmass, S., Lieblich, I. Relation between ethnic origin and GSR reactivity in psychophysiological detection. *Ibid.,* **52,** 158–62 (1968)
69. Lacey, J. I. Psychophysiological approaches to the evaluation of psychotherapeutic process and outcome. In *Research in Psychotherapy,* 160–208 (Rubinstein, E. A., Parloff, M. B., Eds., Am. Psychol. Assoc., Washington, D.C., 293 pp., 1959)
70. Lacey, J. I. Somatic response patterning and stress: Some revisions of activation theory. In *Psychological Stress,* 14–42 (Appley, M. H., Trumbull, R., Eds., Appleton-Century-Crofts, New York, 472 pp., 1967)
71. Lacey, J. I., Kagan, J., Lacey, B. C., Moss, H. A. The visceral level: Situational determinants and behavioral correlates of autonomic response patterns. In *Expression of the Emotions in Man,* 161–96 (See Ref. 46)
72. Lacey, J. I., Lacey, B. C. The relationship of resting autonomic activity to motor impulsivity. *Res. Publ., Assoc. Res. Nerv. Ment. Dis.,* **36,** 144–209 (1958)
73. Lakie, W. L. Relationship of galvanic skin response to task difficulty, personality traits, and motivation. *Res. Quart.,* **38,** 58–63 (1967)
74. Lazarus, R. S. *Psychological Stress and the Coping Process* (McGraw-Hill, New York, 466 pp., 1966)
75. Lazarus, R. S. Cognitive and personality factors underlying threat and coping. In *Psychological Stress,* 151–81 (See Ref. 70)
76. Lazarus, R. S., Alfert, E. Short-circuiting of threat by experimentally altering cognitive appraisal. *J. Abnorm. Soc. Psychol.,* **69,** 195–205 (1964)
77. Lazarus, R. S., Tomita, M., Opton, E. M., Jr., Kodama, M. A cross-cultural study of stress-reaction patterns in Japan. *J. Pers. Soc. Psychol.,* **4,** 622–33 (1966)
78. Leiderman, P. H., Shapiro, D., Eds. *Psychobiological Approaches to Social Behavior* (See Ref. 7)
79. Lifshitz, K. The averaged evoked cortical response to complex visual stimuli. *Psychophysiology,* **3,** 55–68 (1966)
80. Lindsley, D. B. Emotion. In *Handbook of Experimental Psychology,* 473–516 (Stevens, S. S., Ed., Wiley, New York, 1436 pp., 1951)
81. Lykken, D. T. Valins' "Emotionality and autonomic reactivity": An appraisal. *J. Exptl. Res. Pers.,* **2,** 46–55 (1967)
82. Malmo, R. B. Finger-sweat prints in the differentiation of low and high incentive. *Psychophysiology,* **1,** 231–40 (1965)
83. Mandler, G., Kahn, M. Discrimination of changes in heart rate: Two unsuccessful attempts. *J. Exptl. Anal. Behav.,* **3,** 21–25 (1960)
84. Mandler, G., Kremen, I. Autonomic feedback: A correlational study.

J. Pers., **26**, 388–99 (1958)

85. Means, R. L. Sociology, biology, and the analysis of social problems. *Soc. Probl.*, **15**, 200–12 (1967)
86. Mordkoff, A. M. The relationship between psychological and physiological response to stress. *Psychosomat. Med.*, **26**, 135–49 (1964)
87. Nowlin, J. B., Eisdorfer, C., Bogdonoff, M. D., Nichols, C. B. Physiologic response to active and passive participation in a two-person interaction situation. *Psychosomat. Med.*, **30**, 87–94 (1968)
88. Olivos, G. Response delay, psychophysiologic activation, and recognition of one's own voice. *Psychosomat. Med.*, **29**, 433–40 (1967)
89. Opton, E. M., Jr., Lazarus, R. S. Personality determinants of psychophysiological response to stress: A theoretical analysis and an experiment. *J. Pers. Soc. Psychol.*, **6**, 291–303 (1967)
90. Peterson, F., Jung, C. Psychophysiological investigations with the galvanometer and pneumograph in normal and insane individuals. *Brain*, **30**, 153–218 (1907)
91. Pillard, R. C., Carpenter, J., Atkinson, K. W., Fisher, S. Palmar sweat prints and self-ratings as measures of film-induced anxiety. *Percept. Mot. Skills*, **23**, 771–77 (1966)
92. Plutchik, R., Ax, A. F. A critique of "determinants of emotional state" by Schachter & Singer (1962). *Psychophysiology*, **4**, 79–82 (1967)
93. Porier, G. W., Lott, A. J. Galvanic skin responses and prejudice. *J. Pers. Soc. Psychol.*, **5**, 253–59 (1967)
94. Rankin, R. E., Campbell, D. T. Galvanic skin responses to Negro and white experimenters. *J. Abnorm. Soc. Psychol.*, **51**, 30–33 (1955)
95. Riddle, E. M. Aggressive behavior in a small social group. *Arch. Psychol.*, No. 78 (1925)
96. Rosenthal, R. *Experimenter Effects in Behavioral Research* (Appleton-Century-Crofts, New York, 464 pp., 1966)
97. Schachter, J. Pain, fear, and anger in hypertensives and normotensives: A psychophysiological study. *Psychosomat. Med.*, **19**, 17–29 (1957)
98. Schachter, S. The interaction of cognitive and physiological determinants of emotional state. In *Psychobiological Approaches to Social Behavior*, 138–73 (See Ref. 7)
99. Schachter, S. Obesity and eating. *Science*, **161**, 751–56 (1968)
100. Selye, H. *The Stress of Life* (McGraw-Hill, New York, 324 pp., 1956)
101. Shapiro, D., Crider, A. Psychophysiological approaches in social psychology. In *The Handbook of Social Psychology*, 2nd ed., **III**, 1–49 (Lindzey, G., Aronson, E., Eds., Addison-Wesley, Reading, Mass., 978 pp., 1969)
102. Shapiro, D., Leiderman, P. H. Acts and Activation: A psychophysiological study of social interaction. In *Psychobiological Approaches to Social Behavior*, 110–26 (See Ref. 7)
103. Shapiro, D., Leiderman, P. H. Arousal correlates of task role and group setting. *J. Pers. Soc. Psychol.*, **5**, 103–7 (1967)
104. Shapiro, D., Leiderman, P. H., Morningstar, M. E. Social isolation and social interaction: A behavioral and physiological comparison. In *Recent Advances in Biological Psychiatry*, **6**, 129–38 (Wortis, J., Ed., Plenum Press, New York, 278 pp., 1964)
105. Simms, T. M. Pupillary response of male and female subjects to pupillary difference in male and female picture stimuli. *Percept. Psychophys.*, **2**, 553–55 (1967)
106. Smith, C. A study of the autonomic excitation resulting from the interaction of individual opinion and group opinion. *J. Abnorm. Soc. Psychol.*, **31**, 138–64 (1936)
107. Snoek, J. D., Dobbs, M. F. Galvanic skin responses to agreement and disagreement in relation to dogmatism. *Psychol. Rept.*, **20**, 195–98 (1967)
108. Sokolov, Ye. N. *Perception and the Conditioned Reflex* (Pergamon, Oxford, England, 309 pp., 1963)
109. Southard, L. D., Katahn, M. The correlation between self-reported and mechanically-recorded pulse rates. *Psychon. Sci.*, **8**, 343–44 (1967)
110. Speisman, J. C., Lazarus, R. S.,

Mordkoff, A. M., Davison, L. A. Experimental reduction of stress based on ego-defense theory. *J. Abnorm. Soc. Psychol.,* **68,** 367–80 (1964)

111. Sternbach, R. A. *Principles of Psychophysiology* (Academic Press, New York, 297 pp., 1966)
112. Sternbach, R. A., Tursky, B. Ethnic differences among housewives in psychophysical and skin potential responses to electric shock. *Psychophysiology,* **1,** 241–46 (1965)
113. Taylor, S. P., Epstein, S. Aggression as a function of the interaction of the sex of the aggressor and the sex of the victim. *J. Pers.,* **35,** 474–86 (1967)
114. Tursky, B., Sternbach, R. A. Further physiological correlates of ethnic differences in response to shock. *Psychophysiology,* **4,** 67–74 (1967)
115. Tursky, B., Watson, P. D. Controlled physical and subjective intensities of electric shock. *Psychophysiology,* **1,** 151–62 (1964)
116. Valins, S. Emotionality and autonomic reactivity. *J. Exptl. Res. Pers.,* **2,** 41–48 (1967)
117. Valins, S. Emotionality and information concerning internal reactions. *J. Pers. Soc. Psychol.,* **6,** 458–63 (1967)
118. Venables, P. H., Martin, I. *Manual of Psychophysiological Methods* (Wiley, New York, 557 pp., 1967)
119. Walters, R. H., Amoroso, D. M. Cognitive and emotional determinants of the occurrence of imitative behaviour. *Brit. J. Soc. Clin. Psychol.,* **6,** 174–85 (1967)
120. Westie, F. R., DeFleur, M. L. Autonomic responses and their relationship to race attitudes. *J. Abnorm. Soc. Psychol.,* **58,** 340–47 (1959)
121. Wilson, G. D. Arousal properties of red versus green. *Percept. Mot. Skills,* **23,** 947–49 (1966)
122. Wilson, G. D. GSR responses to fear-related stimuli. *Ibid.,* **24,** 401–2 (1967)
123. Woodworth, R. S., Schlosberg, H. *Experimental Psychology* (Holt, Rinehart & Winston, New York, 948 pp., 1954)
124. Zborowski, M. Cultural components in responses to pain. *J. Soc. Issues,* **8,** 16–30 (1952)

PSYCHOLOGICAL DEFICIT IN SCHIZOPHRENIA AND BRAIN DAMAGE[1] 147

BY CARL N. ZIMET
AND DANIEL B. FISHMAN
University of Colorado School of Medicine
Denver, Colorado

As Hunt & Cofer (68) pointed out 25 years ago, some loss of perceptual, cognitive, or psychomotor capacity is one of the most common manifestations of psychiatric disorder and cerebral injury. Because the words current at that time to refer to this loss (e.g., "dementia," "deterioration," and "regression") had become associated with various theories about the nature of the loss, Hunt & Cofer coined the more neutral term, "psychological deficit." Reitan (130) and Yates (184) have pointed out in previous issues of the *Annual Review* that articles on psychological deficit encompass such a voluminous literature that it is necessary to delimit the scope of a review of this area. We have largely restricted this paper to quantitative studies of perceptual, cognitive, or psychomotor deficit in adult schizophrenics and brain-damaged children and adults. The last review of psychological deficit by Yates (184) covered the literature through December 1964. Thus, we began our review with the 1965 literature and carried it through December 1968.

In order to orient the reader to the specific material to follow, we shall begin with some comments about the overall logic of deficit studies. Basically, the researcher is interested in showing that a certain kind of perceptual, cognitive, or psychomotor deficit is intrinsically associated with a particular psychopathological condition. For example, suppose that the researcher is interested in showing, by use of a reaction-time (RT) experimental task, that schizophrenics have more of a problem in maintaining a mental set than do individuals with no significant psychopathology. In order to accomplish this rigorously, the researcher's experiment must satisfy the following criteria: (*a*) *Adequate subject selection.* The researcher must demonstrate that his two groups of subjects have been reliably and validly assigned to the categories of schizophrenic and normal. (*b*) *Significant group differences.* The researcher must demonstrate that the schizophrenic

[1] The following abbreviations will be used in this chapter: BG (Bender Gestalt Test); CFFT (critical flicker fusion threshold); MBD (minimal brain dysfunction); MMPI (Minnesota Multiphasic Personality Inventory); RT (reaction time); SVAT (Spiral Visual Aftereffect Test); WAIS (Wechsler Adult Intelligence Scale); WISC (Wechsler Intelligence Scale for Children).

group has a significantly longer RT than the normal group. (*c*) *Specific meaning of group differences.* The researcher must demonstrate that the longer RTs of the schizophrenics are due to their poorer ability to maintain a mental set per se than to such other factors as lower verbal intelligence (making it harder to understand the experimental directions), less motivation to do one's best in an experimental situation, and slower physical reflexes.

Demonstration of the specific meaning of group differences can be accomplished in two sorts of ways. The first way is to demonstrate that on independent measures of verbal intelligence, motivation to do one's best, and physical reflexes, there are no differences between the schizophrenics and the normals. The second way is to demonstrate that the amount of deficit that schizophrenics show relative to normals can be experimentally manipulated. This can be accomplished by varying the experimental task along a dimension that is relevant to the ability to maintain a mental set, but independent of verbal intelligence, motivation to do one's best, and physical reflexes. In past RT studies, such experimental manipulation has been successfully shown in terms of varying the "preparatory interval" (the interval between the onset of the preparatory stimulus and the onset of the stimulus to be responded to). Specifically, these studies have shown that the RTs of schizophrenics increase relative to normals as the preparatory interval increases in length or increases in variability.[2]

While the above three criteria might appear fairly straightforward, it is sadly true that a majority of the published studies we reviewed were deficient in at least one criterion, usually *a* or *c*. These deficiencies will be discussed further at various points below.

Before closing this section, we would like to mention a study by Price (118) which further illustrates criterion *c* above. Price points out that researchers in the psychological deficit area frequently employ complex experimental tasks but simplistically assume that deficit on these tasks involves a single underlying deficiency. Using a typical concept identification task, Price argues that such an assumption is fallacious:

> Formal conceptual tasks are complex and should be analyzed in terms of the behavioral requirements they make on the subject. A formal concept identification task, for example, not only measures the subject's ability to form or identify a particular concept; it also requires at least the following of the subject: (*a*) experimentally demonstrable understanding of task instructions, (*b*) discrimination of the dimensional properties of concept stimuli, (*c*) the ability to use symbolic information relevant to the concept, and (*d*) retention of information relevant to the concept. A failure of the subject to meet any one of these

[2] In order to facilitate readability, throughout this chapter we shall refer to statistically insignificant differences as simply no differences, and to statistically significant differences as simply differences. Thus, this sentence has the identical meaning as the following one: "Specifically, these studies have shown that the RTs of schizophrenics significantly increase relative to normals . . ."

task requirements will result in a gross but unspecifiable performance deficit (118, p. 285).

Price designed a study in line with the above conceptual analysis. After demonstrating that his subjects understood the instructions for the concept identification task that he employed, Price showed that each of the three other task requirements that he conceptually differentiated (*b, c,* and *d* above) made meaningful and independent contributions to schizophrenic deficit in concept identification performance. He thus concludes that "there is little justification for attributing an obtained schizophrenic performance decrement to any single behavioral source" (118, p. 292).

PSYCHOLOGICAL DEFICIT IN ADULT SCHIZOPHRENICS

Before discussing specific studies, we shall make a few comments about general methodological issues. The problem of subject selection, mentioned above as criterion *a,* has been referred to again and again in articles reviewing schizophrenic studies. However, as a paper by Shearn & Whitaker (149) reveals, experimenters continue to deal inadequately with this issue. These authors reviewed 41 articles which were a sample of every fifth article on schizophrenia appearing in 12 major journals during a recent 5-year period. Subject selection procedures in each article were evaluated in terms of: (*a*) whether the author discussed the reliability of the subject selection process and the representativeness of the subjects selected, and (*b*) whether the author discussed the subject selection process in sufficient detail so as to permit investigators at other institutions to replicate the subject selection process. Of the 41 articles Shearn & Whitaker reviewed, only nine gave evidence of reliability; only one gave some indication of the representativeness of the procedure; and only two gave evidence of replicability.

In a discussion of research with the reactive versus process schizophrenia distinction, Kantor & Herron (76) point out an additional problem with respect to replicability. This problem arises:

> because different investigators use different methods to distinguish the process vs. reactive syndromes. Thus, the results of their experiments are hard to compare. For example, the Phillips Scale emphasizes sexual adjustment, whereas the criteria of Kantor et al. include a broader range of factors. Moreover, even when workers use the same rating scale, they frequently assign different values to the scores of process and reactive patients, so that the score on the Phillips Scale required to be rated as good (reactive) or poor (process) varies among researchers (76, p. 23).

Ralph & McCarthy (123) explored the problem of the representativeness of subject selection. They examined the selection procedures in a study carried out by Ralph (122) in order to see how extensive a reduction in sample size occurred as a result of the introduction of experimental controls. This was a study of stimulus generalization among male schizophrenic patients at a veterans' psychiatric hospital. The study accepted as subjects only chronic, poor-premorbid schizophrenics who also had the following characteristics: age between 25 and 50; IQ between 80 and 124; ability to reach criterion on a simple discrimination task; a lack of organic, neurological, or alcoholic secondary diagnoses; and no ECT (electroconvulsive therapy) within a year prior to the study. Out of a total of 455 diagnosed schizophrenics on the male psychiatric wards, only 207 (46 per cent) met the requirements of age and length of hospitalization, and only 52 (11 per cent) met all the conditions for acceptance in the study. Ralph & McCarthy conclude:

> The small size and high selectivity of the tested group raise serious questions concerning generalization of the findings not only to the total population of schizophrenics but even to the subgroup of "chronic" schizophrenics. The dilemma which this raises is that results of carefully controlled studies using schizophrenic subjects cannot be generalized beyond the tested sample. More detailed reporting of methods of sample selection and the degree of sample shrinkage due to the use of experimental controls together with more restraint in generalizing the findings seem essential in studies dealing with schizophrenics (123, p. 964).

Schwartz (145) points out that:

> while the literature on cognitive deficit and psychopathology leaves little doubt that the symptoms of psychosis are associated with relatively poor cognitive functioning, . . . most literature in the area deals with schizophrenics as the exclusive psychopathological group and seems to assume implicitly that schizophrenics have special kinds of cognitive deficits compared with other diagnostic groups (145, p. 446).

In the context of this issue, Schwartz administered a wide range of cognitive tasks typical of the schizophrenic deficit literature to three groups of subjects who were matched on age, education, and occupational level: normals, nonschizophrenic psychiatric patients, and schizophrenics. The latter two groups were chosen so as to be comparable in manifesting relatively little overt, disruptive symptomatology. Schwartz found no difference between the two patient groups on cognitive performance but did find both these groups inferior to the normals. Schwartz thus concluded that cognitive deficit is more a function of amount of current overt symptomatology than of psychiatric diagnosis per se. Unfortunately, there are very few other studies in the literature which in their design discriminate between the independent variables of psychiatric diagnosis and degree of manifest psychopathology.

Schooler & Feldman (143) have prepared a very useful book of abstracts of 995 quantitative empirical studies on schizophrenia published between 1950 and early 1966. In their introduction to the abstracts, the authors mention two general problems with the schizophrenia studies they reviewed. The first major difficulty they list is the one we have been discussing: the lack of reliable, representative, and replicable subject selection procedures. A second major difficulty they describe involves the nature of journal publication policies and their effect on authors:

> Purely negative results are rarely published. Furthermore, since the average study tests considerably more than one hypothesis, authors have free reign to

pick and choose from among possibly chance findings those which conform to their perceptions of current editorial policy. Under such conditions, one can only speculate on the true level of significance represented by reported rejections of the null hypothesis at the .05 level (143, p. iii).

As we reviewed the voluminous literature from 1965 through 1968 on psychological deficit in schizophrenia, we were struck by the depressing fact that there are so few careful and precise replications. Instead, there is a dazzling but dismaying proliferation of different kinds of experimental tasks, experimental procedures, and techniques of statistical analysis, such that precise comparison of results from among different studies is impossible. One must wonder if editors place a strong emphasis upon newness and innovation, rejecting out of hand replication studies. There is, of course, the alternative possibility that researchers do not consider undertaking replications in the first place because they consider them as lacking in creativity.

If one plunges directly into the relevant empirical studies on psychological deficit in schizophrenia, these studies can appear quite fragmented and confusing. However, armed with a theoretical framework, the literature appears more cohesive and articulated; for many of the studies are designed for and focused upon confirming or disconfirming a particular theory concerning the nature and cause of schizophrenic deficit. Buss & Lang (16, 83) have performed a very important service by setting forth, comparing, and critically contrasting many of these theories and reviewing some of the empirical literature prior to March 1964 that bears upon them. A further discussion and technical critical analysis of these theories is beyond the scope of this paper. However, we have used the various theories as a heuristic way of organizing the studies we have reviewed. A list of the theories, adapted from Buss & Lang, is presented in Table I.

The remaining part of this section will consider the relevant articles[3] (those associated with each of the theories listed in Table I) which have been published during the period 1965 through 1968. In reviewing these studies, only those aspects that are relevant to the theory being considered will be discussed. This is unlike Schooler & Feldman's (143) book which presents an exhaustive collection of abstracts. Other previous reviews of schizophrenic deficit which have been published during the period 1965 through 1968 are oriented towards presenting and documenting a particular theoretical approach to schizophrenic deficit (e.g., 13, 64, 75, 150, 169). In contrast, the present review is not oriented toward arguing for a particular theoretical point of view. Rather its purpose is to collate the empirical findings which have been published during 1965 through 1968 and to organize them in terms of their relevance to some of the main theoretical positions existent in the field of schizophrenic deficit. In line with this goal, on the

[3] There are a small number of articles which were relevant to the theories but which were deleted from this review because of either gross methodological inadequacies or very unclear, often confusing presentation of results.

TABLE I

THEORIES OF SCHIZOPHRENIC DEFICIT

Theory	Reference number of studies in text below with results that are, with respect to this theory:		
	Confirmatory	Disconfirmatory	Inconclusive
I. *Socioemotional Motivation Theories*			
A. *General Social Censure:* This theory holds that schizophrenics are abnormally sensitive to and disrupted by social censure and stimuli connoting censure. Research has employed censure in terms of censurious content being depicted in task stimuli and in terms of experimenter-administered verbal criticism or physical punishment.	96 50 57 88	146 140 137 12	34
B. *Specific Social Censure* [Rodnick & Garmezy (135)]: This theory differentiates between schizophrenics with good vs. poor premorbid adjustment histories [usually assessed by the Phillips (115)] scale. The theory holds that good-premorbids are more disturbed by paternal censure, while poor-premorbids are more disturbed by maternal censure.	91 176 36 85 84	20 84 86	
C. *Affective Sensitivity:* This theory resembles social censure theory, but it is broader in that it hypothesizes that schizophrenics are especially sensitive to, and disrupted by all "affective stimuli." The term "affective stimuli" is very broad and refers to aspects of both task conditions and task content.	57 6 48 116 182	11 177 167 120	
II. ***Hullian-Drive Theory*** [Mednick (95)]: According to this theory, acute schizophrenics have abnormally high anxiety. This is equated with high drive in Hull's sense of the term of drive as an energizer of response hierarchies. This high drive leads to: (*a*) excessive generalization of anxiety-arousing stimuli and associations, so that more and more stimuli and	156 30 179 157 162 63	172 15 100 35	134

TABLE I—(*Continued*)

Theory	Reference number of studies in text below with results that are, with respect to this theory: Confirmatory	Disconfirmatory	Inconclusive
thoughts become anxiety-arousing; and (*b*) the occurrence of unusual and "remote" associative responses above the threshold of awareness. These remote associations sometimes result in the removal from awareness of anxiety-arousing stimuli and thoughts. Thus the remote associations tend to be followed by anxiety reduction, and this increases the probability of such associations recurring. In line with this, it is hypothesized that over time, the movement from acute to chronic schizophrenia involves movement from a state of high anxiety and relatively few remote associations to a state of relatively low anxiety and pervasive remote associations.			
III. ***Perceptual and Cognitive Capacity Theories***	72	159	
A. *Perceptual Deficit:* Yates (184) points out that an individual's response to a situation can be construed as involving at least four different sequential stages: (*a*) sensory receipt of stimuli; (*b*) initial organization of the information in stage *a*; (*c*) central processing of the information in stage *b*; and (*d*) motor response on the basis of the information in stage *c*. Perceptual Deficit Theory contends that schizophrenic deficit is a result of malfunctioning at the two "perceptual" stages, *a* and *b*. In contrast, theories B, C, and D below all hold that schizophrenic deficit is a result of malfunctioning at the central processing stage, *c*.	97 107 119 103 11 138 8 17 94 71 177 104 105 167	21 7 73	
B. *Loss of Abstractness* [Goldstein (52, 53)]: This theory holds that the psychological deficit in schizophrenia is mainly due to the fact that schizophrenics have lost "the abstract attitude" and can function in thought and language only	74 129 56 54 59 164	141 10 60 154	

TABLE I—(*Continued*)

Theory	Reference number of studies in text below with results that are, with respect to this theory:		
	Confirmatory	Disconfirmatory	Inconclusive
at the concrete level. Generally, by "abstract attitude" is meant the ability to abstract common properties and to form concepts.	1 166 44 5		
C. *Loss of Communication* [Sullivan (165); Cameron (18)]: This theory holds that the problem in schizophrenia is a basic lack of communication. The schizophrenic's concepts are bizarre because he is withdrawn and asocial, because appropriate communication skills have been crowded out by autistic fantasy.	87 121 56 24	47 69	
D. *Interference* [Buss & Lang (16, 83)]: This theory assumes that when a schizophrenic is faced with a task, he cannot attend properly or in a sustained fashion, maintain a set, or change the set quickly when necessary. His ongoing response tendencies suffer interference from irrelevant, external cues and from "internal" stimuli which consist of deviant thoughts and associations. These irrelevant, distracting stimuli prevent him from maintaining a clear focus on the task at hand, and the result is psychological deficit.	161 125 126 185 160 109	160	79

right-hand side of Table I, each study to be reviewed below is listed by reference number and categorized in terms of whether its results are confirmatory, disconfirmatory, or inconclusive with respect to the theory that it was testing. It is important to note that theoretically oriented reviews (such as the ones listed above) and empirically oriented reviews (such as the present one) are both necessary and in fact complementary if one is to obtain a balanced understanding of a particular area of research.

Finally, before starting the literature review proper, it is important to note that because of space limitations, it has been necessary to work with a fairly narrow definition of what is encompassed by "psychological deficit in adult schizophrenics." Excluded from this definition are such areas of research (and their associated theories) as the nature of interaction within schizophrenic families, the effects of drugs or institutionalization or both upon schizophrenic thought and perception, and the nature of "physiological arousal" in schizophrenics [which is discussed in Mirsky's recent *Annual Review* article (99)]. Also excluded from the present review are studies which are primarily oriented to the development of new assessment techniques per se rather than to the investigation of the nature of schizophrenic deficit.

General Social Censure

Censure has been employed as a variable both in terms of censurious content being depicted in task stimuli and in terms of verbal criticism or physical punishment (frequently shock) which is administered to a subject by the experimenter. The latter, experimenter-administered censure is frequently contrasted with reward, which includes verbal praise or material rewards (e.g., candy and cigarettes) given to a subject by the experimenter. The studies in the area of General Social Censure to be reviewed below have investigated whether ongoing experimenter-induced censure for incorrect responses inhibits or facilitates learning on a task in comparison to ongoing reward for correct responses.[4] General censure theory would, of course, predict that censure generally inhibits learning. The opposite prediction is made on the basis of learning or arousal theory, as put forth by Buss & Lang (16). They point out that certain tasks like paired-word learning are such that a correct response to one stimulus word is wrong for other stimuli. Thus, one might well predict that censure would facilitate learning more than reward on such tasks. The former would tend to break up maladaptive perseverative tendencies (i.e., tendencies to maintain a previously correct response that is wrong on subsequent trials). Buss & Lang also suggest that physical punishment such as shock might facilitate learning via serving an attention-focusing or arousal function.

Two studies have found reward to be more facilitative of learning than censure. Meichenbaum (96) studied the effect of different kinds of verbal reward and censure upon the ability of schizophrenics to learn to give abstract interpretations of proverbs. There were four different reinforcement conditions: verbal reward contingent upon the giving of abstract responses; verbal reward not so contingent; verbal censure contingent upon the giving of nonabstract responses; and verbal censure not so contingent. Meichenbaum's main finding was that contingent verbal reward increased abstract performance on the proverbs task while the other three conditions did not. Goldman (50) studied schizophrenic learning of paired-words under three different conditions: contingent verbal reward, contingent verbal censure, and "nonevaluation" (involving neither reward nor censure). These three

[4] In the area of General Social Censure Theory, none of the studies that we reviewed from 1965 through 1968 employed the variable of censurious content depicted in task stimuli (although there were a number of examples of this type of study prior to 1965). However, as is discussed below, in the area of Specific Censure Theory there were a number of studies between 1965 and 1968 which did employ this type of variable.

conditions were introduced after an initial period of nonevaluation for all subjects. Goldman found that while both the introduction of verbal reward and verbal censure disrupted learning relative to continuation of nonevaluation, a comparison of the former two conditions revealed that verbal reward was less disrupting than verbal censure.

In contrast to the above two studies, three investigations have found censure to be more facilitative of learning than reward. Sermat & Greenglass (146) employed various kinds of contingent feedback with a probability learning task, i.e., a task requiring the subject to learn to predict which of two lights would go on. They found that for schizophrenics, verbal censure and shock censure facilitated learning more than verbal reward or "information-only" feedback. Moreover, this finding appeared specific to schizophrenia since normals showed no learning differences between the shock censure and information-only feedback. Salzberg & Williams (140) employed various kinds of contingent feedback with a concept formation task. They found that for schizophrenics, verbal censure was most effective, white noise censure the next, and material reward the least effective in facilitating performance. Finally, Rosenbaum (137) studied the effect of three conditions upon a reaction-time task in which schizophrenic and normal subjects were required to release a key in response to a buzzer. He found that schizophrenics showed greater reaction times than normals when exposed to social encouragement and noncontingent shock censure, but that these differences disappeared in a contingent shock censure condition.

With regard to the issue of the contingency or reward and censure, it should be noted that the above two studies (96, 137) which compared contingent vs. noncontingent reward and censure both found that contingent evaluation facilitated task performance more than did noncontingent evaluation.

The results of the above studies taken as a whole would seem to strongly disconfirm the notion that either reward or censure is consistently related to increased learning. It would seem, rather, that to predict the direction of such a relationship, it is necessary to take into account other factors, such as the type of task involved and the particular conditions under which it is administered.

The above-discussed studies primarily employed censure or reward that was directly related to the experimental task, being contingent upon the ongoing correctness of task responses. In contrast, four studies employed censure or reward that was relatively independent of the experimental task, with two yielding results consistent with General Social Censure Theory, one yielding results inconsistent with the theory, and one yielding inconclusive results. Guller (57) studied the relationship between the experience of failure (on the Stroop Color Word Interference Test) and the stability (consistency over time) of self-concept. Guller found that while the experience of failure did not affect self-concept stability in normals, it did decrease self-concept stability in schizophrenics. Between administrations of parallel forms of a proverb scale, Little (88) subjected schizophrenics to one of three conditions: a structured interview in which the interviewer was positive, warm, and interested; the same interview in which the interviewer was negative, businesslike, and sarcastic; and no interview at all. The author found that, relative to their performance before the different interpersonal conditions, the schizophrenic subjects manifested the highest level of abstract proverb interpretation in the positive condition and the lowest level in the negative condition. In an experiment with a design very similar to Little's, Brenner (12) found just the opposite result in terms of schizophrenics' performance on a word association test: relative to their performance before the interpersonal conditions, subjects in the negative condition gave the most common associations (i.e., most like normals), and subjects in the positive condition, the fewest common associations. Finally, De Luca (34) investigated the manner in which schizophrenic concept formation was affected by noncontingent verbal praise or censure and by ongoing information on how to improve task performance. The findings revealed that schizophrenic concept formation was enhanced by the presence of information on how to improve, while it was not affected by the presence or absence of noncontingent verbal praise or verbal censure.

Taking the results of the above four studies as a whole, we come to the same conclusion for noncontingent censure vs. reward that we did above for contingent censure vs. reward, namely, that no clear-cut relationship has been demonstrated between censure vs. reward on the one hand, and psychological deficit on the other.

Throughout our discussion of the General Social Censure Theory literature, the reader has probably noted that most of the studies only employed schizophrenic subjects. Thus, these studies are guilty of violating criterion *c* discussed above (cf. p. 113). In other words, because these studies only involved schizophrenic subjects, it cannot be ascertained as to whether the behavior recorded in the studies was at all distinctive of schizophrenia per se.

Specific Social Censure

While General Social Censure Theory is concerned with characteristics which are common to all schizophrenics, Specific Social Censure Theory is concerned with the differential reactions of two types of schizophrenics: those with good premorbid histories ("good-premorbids") and those with poor premorbid histories ("poor-premorbids"). One of the classical studies often cited in support of this theory is that of Dunham (37). This researcher found that compared to normals, good-premorbids showed difficulty in making accurate size-estimations only for stimuli depicting paternal censure, while poor-premorbids showed such difficulties only for stimuli depicting maternal censure. Three researchers have utilized this type of task to further investigate Specific Social Censure Theory, with two of the studies being confirmatory and one being disconfirmatory. Magaro (91) replicated Dunham's experiment using both lower-class and middle-class good-premorbids and poor-premorbids. He found that the relative ability to accurately discriminate the maternal censure vs. the paternal censure pictures was related to the premorbid-adjustment dimension, but not to the social-class dimension. Webb, Davis & Cromwell (176) and Cicchetti et al. (20) also attempted to replicate Dunham's original results. The former group was successful and the latter group unsuccessful in this attempt.

The studies mentioned so far have explored Specific Social Censure Theory in terms of schizophrenics' reactions to pictorial representations of censurious parents. Another group of studies has focused upon the interaction of schizophrenic patients with actual male and female persons. The reasoning behind these studies has been that: (*a*) a schizophrenic has had more negative experiences with one parent than the other; (*b*) via generalization he should anticipate a greater likelihood of negative reinforcement when interacting with a person of the same sex as the more censurious parent; and (*c*) this in turn should lead to avoidance or deficit behavior. Three studies are confirmatory and two are disconfirmatory of this differential-sensitivity-to-sex formulation. Donovan & Webb (36) found that poor-premorbids exhibited higher thresholds for the recognition of words recorded by female vs. male voices, while good-premorbids did not show this effect. Lefcourt and his co-workers (84, 85) found that poor-premorbids were less cooperative towards and manifested less frequent eye contact with a female experimenter than a male experimenter, while good-premorbids tended to show the opposite type of pattern. In contrast, Lefcourt's group also reported that a female examiner facilitated digit span performance for poor-premorbids (84) while a male examiner facilitated finger-tapping performance for good-premorbids (86).

Affective Sensitivity

Task content.—The studies in this area have presented schizophrenics and normals with a particular perceptual or cognitive task which involves both affective and neutral content. Affective Sensitivity Theory has been investigated by assessing whether, compared with normals, schizophrenics' performance with the affective stimuli is poor relative to their performance with the neutral stimuli. Four studies obtained data confirmatory of Affective Sensitivity Theory. In these studies, the affective vs. neutral task content involved rating one's self concept vs. rating one's food preferences (57); rating people on such adjectives as "kind" and "stupid" vs. rating objects (e.g., a bowler hat) on such adjective dimensions as "large to small" and "heavy to light" (6); making inferences from visual cues involving faces vs. geometric designs (48); and making size estimations of a figure dressed as oneself vs. dressed as another person (116). In contrast, three studies obtained data disconfirmatory of Affective Sensitivity Theory, i.e., schizophrenic performance was not differentially affected by affectivity of task content. In these studies, the affective vs. neutral task content involved estimating distances between pairs of cutout figures representing hostile vs. neutral relationships (11); perceiving the vertical for pictures of a human female, bottle, and cat as opposed to a simple rod (177); and estimating degree of distortion for one's own body vs. that for a simple rectangular frame (167).

Task conditions.—The studies in this area have investigated how schizophrenics deal with the same task content when working with other people (affective task condition) vs. working alone (neutral task condition). Wolfgang, Pishkin & Rosenbluh (182) presented subjects with concept identification problems which they had to solve either alone or in free interaction with a partner. Consistent with Affective Sensitivity Theory, in the alone condition, schizophrenic females performed better, schizophrenic males performed the same, and normal males performed worse than in the free interaction condition. Query, Moore & Lerner (120) had schizophrenics construct poppies either alone (where a subject was paid for the number of poppies he himself assembled) or with others (where the subject was paid one fifth of the money earned by the entire group). In contrast to Affective Sensitivity Theory, the findings revealed that the schizophrenics in the social condition were more productive than those in the alone condition.

Hullian-Drive Theory

Eyelid conditioning.—Hullian-Drive Theory's assumption that schizophrenics have a higher level of Hullian drive than normals theoretically implies that schizophrenics should acquire classically conditioned responses faster than normals. Spain (156), using eyelid conditioning, obtained results confirmatory of this hypothesis. In addition, she found that schizophrenics had higher arousal, as reflected by skin potential level; and when this difference in arousal was controlled for, the eyelid conditioning difference between schizophrenics and normals disappeared.

Overgeneralization.—Hullian-Drive Theory postulates that schizophrenics manifest more overgeneralization than do normals. Three relevant studies have been reported, one confirmatory and two disconfirmatory of this hypothesis. Craig (30) developed a Breadth of Association Test, in which the subject is presented with a "concept word" and is then asked to select from among a group of "response words" all those that are essential to the concept word. In comparing a group of neurotics and schizophrenics matched on age, education, and IQ, Craig found that while the schizophrenics selected the same number of essential words as the neurotics, the former chose more unessential words than the latter. In contrast, Watson (172) administered the Epstein Overinclusion Test, which is similar to Craig's Breadth of Association Test, to a heterogeneous group of psychiatric inpatients. He found no relationship between performance deficit on the overinclusion test and psychiatric ratings of psychoticism, the MMPI Paranoia Scale, or the MMPI Schizophrenia Scale. Finally, Buss & Daniell (15) found no difference between schizophrenics and normals on the tendency to overgeneralize in a size-estimation task.

Associational disturbance.—Hullian-Drive Theory postulates that schizophrenics are disturbed in their association processes. Three studies have yielded data confirmatory of this hypothesis. Whitaker (179) developed an Index of Schizophrenic Thinking which assesses the ability to think in a logical manner and to resist distracting, irrelevant associations. The test has two forms: Form A involves items with anxiety-inducing stimuli (e.g., "CRY ______: a. baby, b. fry, c. hurt me, d. sklerp, e. make tears"), and Form B involves items with non-anxiety-inducing stimuli (e.g., "CAR ______: a. jar, b. automobile, c. smickle, d. tires, e. my transportation"). Acute and chronic schizophrenics did worse on both forms of this test than did normals, even when vocabulary ability was statistically partialed out. Spence & Lair (157) employed a paired-work task, i.e., a task on which the subject is presented with a series of "stimulus words" and is required to learn what particular "response word" is paired with it. There were two lists of paired-words which differed in their amount of intralist interference." This was defined as the extent to which there was a low "associative connection"[5] between a particular stimulus word and its paired response word, while at the same time there was a high associative connection between that stimulus word and other response words in the same list. "Associative interference" was defined as the extent to which a subject had more difficulty learning the paired-word list with high intralist interference as compared with his learning the list with low intralist interference. Spence & Lair found that schizophrenics manifested more associative interference than did normals. Storms, Broen & Levin (162) employed a word association task which was administered on two separate occasions. They found that acute schizophrenics manifested more associational disturbance than normals both in terms of: (*a*) less "stable" word associations (i.e., word associations that involved fewer similarities over the two separate test administrations); and (*b*) less "common" word associations (i.e., word associations that were less like those given by a representative sample of normals).

A study which is very relevant to the interpretation of results obtained by Spence & Lair and Storm et al. was conducted by Moon et al. (100). These researchers employed a word association task with schizophrenics and matched normals. Two word lists were employed. One list had instructions to repeat each word as rapidly as possible; a response was scored as mis-

[5] "Associative connection" refers to a situation in which a word X is presented as a stimulus word in a word association task to a representative sample of normals. If, in this situation, the normals show a high tendency to respond to X with Y, X and Y are described as having "a high associative connection"; if, in this situation, the normals show a low tendency to respond to X with Y, X and Y are described as having "a low associative connection."

heard if the subject repeated a word other than the stimulus word. The other list had instructions to give the first word that came to mind; a response here was scored as misheard if it was both unrelated in content to the stimulus and also formed a meaningful association with a word that rhymed with the stimulus (e.g., the response of "groom" to the stimulus word "ride," which rhymes with "bride"). While it was found that schizophrenics generally gave less common associations, it was also found that they misheard more stimulus words on both lists than did normals. Moreover, when the effect of mishearing was partialed out of the "common association" results, the difference between schizophrenics and normals disappeared. These results suggest that studies reporting findings of more associational disturbance in schizophrenics (such as is reported by Storms et al. and Spence & Lair, mentioned above) might well be due to a problem in mishearing words rather than to deviantly associating to them. Such mishearing could be caused by a problem of poor perception per se (cf. Perceptual Deficit Theory below) or by a problem of inattention to task-relevant stimuli (cf. Interference Theory below).

Differences among schizophrenics.—Hullian-Drive Theory postulates that acute schizophrenics have abnormally high anxiety and thus abnormally high drive, which leads to the occurrence of "remote" associations above the threshold of awareness. It follows from this postulate that acute schizophrenics should manifest even more associational disturbance when dealing with anxiety-inducing stimuli than with non-anxiety-inducing stimuli. On the other hand, chronic schizophrenics should not manifest such a difference because they are seen as having relatively low anxiety. In order to collect data relevant to these implications of Hullian-Drive Theory, two of the studies mentioned above (162, 179) employed task stimuli with both anxiety-inducing and non-anxiety-inducing content. The results of both these studies were consistent with Hullian-Drive Theory.

It follows from Hullian-Drive Theory that associative disturbance should be related to chronicity per se independent of pre-illness level of adjustment. Three studies relevant to this hypothesis have been reported. All three employed a word association task, with one finding results confirmatory of the hypothesis (63), one finding results disconfirmatory of the hypothesis (35), and one finding results inconclusive with respect to the hypothesis (134).

Perceptual Deficit

Six studies found schizophrenics to be deficient in time-estimation or size-estimation (11, 72, 97, 103, 107, 119), while one did not find such a deficiency (159).

In perceptual areas other than time estimation and size estimation, nine studies obtained results confirmatory of Perceptual Deficit Theory. Rosenbaum, Flenning & Rosen (138) studied weight discrimination thresholds using a heavy, easier-to-distinguish series of weights and a light, harder-to-distinguish series of weights. On the lighter weights, normals performed much better than schizophrenics. However, the schizophrenics improved more than the normals when dealing with the heavier weights, approaching the performance of the normals with these weights. The authors interpret these findings as supporting the hypothesis of a schizophrenic deficit in proprioceptive acuity. They reason that if the poor performance of the schizophrenics on the light weights had instead been due to an attentional or motivational deficit, these subjects would not have improved more than the normals on the heavier weights. Bemporad (8) found pronounced perceptual fragmentation in schizophrenics. He employed three stimulus cards from the Pseudo-Isochromatic Plates for Testing Color Perception. These cards can be perceived in terms of either whole organization (numerals) or part fragmentation (dots). The data revealed that fragmented responses were given by 2 per cent of the normals, 65 per cent of the "recovered" schizophrenics, 78 per cent of the chronic schizophrenics, and 97 per cent of the acute schizophrenics. Another finding was that while the recovered and chronic schizophrenics gave more whole responses than the acutes, many of these whole responses were incorrect, suggesting an attempt to restructure fragmented percepts by bizarre and individualistic processes. Callaway, Jones & Layne (17) employed an EEG method for investigating sensory reactions. They found that in reaction to a 600 cps tone and a 1000 cps tone, the EEG patterns of normals were more similar than the EEG patterns of schizophrenics. They interpret this finding as suggesting that schizophrenics are preoccupied with trivial distinctions.

In the final six confirmatory studies to be mentioned, schizophrenics were found to manifest perceptual deficit in the ability to interpret projective tests (71, 94); in the ability to perceive the vertical (177); in the ability to perceive designs (104, 105); and in the ability to differentiate extent of visual distortion in a mirror (167).

Three further disconfirmatory studies remain to be mentioned. Clark, Brown & Rutschmann (21) assessed critical flicker fusion threshold (CFFT) by two different psychophysiological methods. They found that the schizophrenic "method-of-limits CFFT" was higher than that of normals, while the "forced-choice CFFT" of these same subjects did not differ. Since the method-of-limits CFFT is a function of both a subject's sensory sensitivity and his response bias, while the forced-choice CFFT is purely a function of sensory sensitivity, the authors conclude that schizophrenics and normals differed only with respect to response bias. Bauman & Murray (7) employed a verbal memory task and found that schizophrenics were poorer than normals in recall, but not in recognition. These findings suggest that schizophrenics do not manifest deficit in their perception of verbal material, but do manifest deficit in their ability to organize information for self-initiated retrieval. Finally, Johannsen & Testin (73) found no differences between schizophrenics and normals on a simple visual recognition task.

In sum, then, there were 15 studies confirmatory and only four disconfirmatory of Perceptual Deficit Theory. However, an important qualification of this tally must be kept in mind; for all but one of the confirmatory studies are methodologically unsatisfactory from the point of view of criterion *c* (cf. above, p. 3). That is, while these studies found that schizophrenics performed more poorly than normals on a perceptual task, none of them demonstrated that this poorer performance was due to perceptual deficit per se. Thus, for example, the deficit manifested in these studies could have been due to an initial misunderstanding of the task at hand, to an inability to maintain attention upon the task during the experiment, or to a reduced motivation to perform well in the experiment. The one exception to this problem is the study by Rosenbaum, Flenning & Rosen (138). These authors satisfied criterion *c* by showing that, with all other factors held constant, the amount of weight-discrimination deficit manifested by schizophrenics was a direct function of the amount of proprioceptive acuity demanded by the experimental task.

Loss of Abstractness

Four studies (54, 56, 74, 129) found schizophrenic deficit in the ability to make abstract interpretations of proverbs, while one (141) did not.

Two studies found schizophrenic deficit in the ability to give abstract, objective (vs. concrete, personalistic) explanations of natural events while one did not. Hamilton (59) employed a series of Piaget's tests which assessed cognitive skills that are usually developed in children by 12 years of age (conservation of quantity and volume, the skill of seriation, and the knowledge of parameters entering into perspective). He found that schizophrenic men performed worse on these tasks than 12-year-old boys who were matched on IQ. Strauss (164) employed tasks that were similar to Hamilton's and found that chronic schizophrenics (but not acute schizophrenics) performed more poorly than normals who were equated on age and occupational status. In contrast to these two positive studies, Biles & Heckel (10) compared chronic schizophrenics and normals with respect to their explanations of everyday news events (e.g., "Recently a satellite called the Early Bird was launched into orbit. What is the purpose of this satellite?"). Chronic schizophrenics manifested no more primitive or precausal thought processes than did a group of normals who were matched on education, age, sex, and awareness of everyday news events.

Four other studies yielded data confirmatory of the Loss of Abstractness Theory. Al-Issa (1) employed a vocabulary test of words known to the subject. He found that schizophrenics gave fewer abstract definitions than did a group of normals who were matched for education and occupation. True (166) administered a word-association test and verbally reinforced abstract (as opposed to concrete) responses. He found that while reactive schizophrenics gave as many abstract responses as normals, process schizophrenics gave significantly fewer than the other two groups. Furth & Youniss (44) were interested in determining whether schizophrenics manifest problems in abstraction independent of linguistic difficulties. They developed a conceptual abstraction battery of tests which were entirely nonverbal—that is, while the tests required no linguistic instructions or responses, they were composed of tasks which entailed logical rules of classification, disjunction, and conjunction. Even on these nonverbal abstraction tasks, schizophrenics showed deficit as compared with normals matched on age and education. Bannister & Fransella (5) developed an objective measure of concept formation adequacy in which subjects were shown photographs of people and asked to rank order them on various adjectives, such as "kind," "stupid," and "selfish." This procedure was done twice and two scores were derived from the resulting data: Intensity (vs. Looseness), which reflects the extent to which the adjectives were intercorrelated across photographs; and Consistency, which reflects the correlation between the initial and second rankings. While these two scores were not correlated with vocabulary ability, they were lower in schizophrenics than in normals, depressives, neurotics, and organics.

Two other studies have yielded data disconfirmatory of the Loss of Abstraction Theory. Hamlin, Haywood & Folsom (60) employed an experimental task requiring the abstract interpretations of both single proverbs and proverb sets of three, which were viewed as involving "enriched" input relative to the single proverbs. It was found that schizophrenics with mild and medium degrees of psychosis showed improvement in abstract responses with enriched input, while nonschizophrenic subjects did not. In fact, with enriched input, deficit in abstract responses disappeared entirely for the mildly schizophrenic subjects. Since the multiple proverbs procedure does not make the abstracting task easier, the authors conclude that the schizophrenic deficit they found was not due to inability to abstract per se. Snelbecker et al. (154) administered a programmed series of inductive reasoning tasks to schizophrenics and matched normals. Although the schizophrenics were found to be slower in completing the experimental task, their responses were as correct as those of the normals. These results, as those of the Hamlin et al. study just discussed, suggest that schizophrenic deficit is due to factors other than the ability to reason abstractly per se.

Loss of Communication

Some researchers have investigated schizophrenic communication in terms of the linguistic variable of "contextual constraint." This variable is a measure of the degree to which any one word in a verbal passage is determined by the semantic and syntactic context of the words which precede it. Contextual constraint is at its highest in a passage of English text and at its lowest in a passage of unrelated words selected at random. Miller & Selfridge (98) showed that in normal subjects, recall of verbal material improves as the degree of contextual constraint within the verbal material increases. Three studies have employed modifications of Miller & Selfridge's task to investigate the extent to which schizophrenics manifest a deficit in the ability to use contextual constraint to facilitate recall. Levy & Maxwell (87) and Raeburn & Tong (121) both found that schizophrenics were less able to use contextual constraint than nonpsychotic patients matched on age and vocabulary ability. However, Levy & Maxwell found no difference between schizophrenics and severely depressed patients, suggesting that the inability to use contextual constraint is not specific to schizophrenia. Moreover, in another study, Gerver (47) found that schizophrenics were more able than matched nonpsychotic patients to use contextual constraint to facilitate recall.

Three other studies are relevant to Loss of Communication Theory. Gregg & Frank (56) found that schizophrenics manifested more autistic verbalization on a test of proverb interpretation than psychiatric controls. Cohen & Camhi (24) employed a task in which a "speaker" was told which of two words was correct and was asked to generate a one-word clue to another person (the "listener") to communicate to this person which one of the two words was correct. Provided with the clue word, the listener then guessed the correct word. The research design included an equal number of schizophrenic and normal listeners and speakers, and all four groups were equated on age and education. There was no difference in the performance of schizophrenic and normal listeners, but the schizophrenic speakers were significantly poorer than the normal speakers. The authors conclude that these findings indicate a specific kind of communication difficulty in schizophrenics which is not simply a deficiency in association, since if the latter were true, the schizophrenic listeners should have been inferior to the normal listeners.

In contrast to the above two studies, which are consistent with Loss of Communication Theory, Hunt & Walker (69) found that schizophrenics are as accurate as normals in judging the extent of disorganization manifested in the vocabulary test responses of psychiatric patients.

Interference

Research relevant to this theory has generally attempted to demonstrate that schizophrenics manifest psychological deficit in three empirically distinct, but theoretically related areas. Each of these will be discussed separately.

Inability to focus attention on task-relevant sensory information and to ignore competing, irrelevant sensory information.—Stilson et al. (161) studied visual thresholds for various geometric shapes under conditions of the absence vs. presence of visual noise (similar to "snow" on TV). They found that while the visual recognition performance of schizophrenics was not different from that of nonschizophrenic psychiatric patients or hospital employees when noise was absent, the schizophrenics had higher thresholds than the other two groups when noise was present. Thus, it would appear that the schizophrenics manifested poorer thresholds in the presence of noise because the noise distracted them from focusing upon the task-relevant stimuli. Similar findings have been obtained for the area of auditory recognition in the absence vs. presence of auditory noise (125, 126, 161).

One study failed to find schizophrenic deficit in the ability to focus sensory attention. Steinmeyer (160) employed a reaction time task in which subjects pressed a button and waited for a green light, which signaled them to release this button as quickly as possible. The green light occurred at any of seven points along a visual angle of 120 degrees. Each subject was run under a condition in which a red light predicted where the green light would come on, and a condition in which no red light occurred. The author found that in their reaction time performance, schizophrenics were as able to benefit from the red light condition as were nonschizophrenic psychiatric patients, thus indicating no deficit in the ability to constructively attend to task-relevant sensory information.

Inability to adopt and maintain a preparatory mental set.—This type of deficit has been studied primarily in terms of reaction-time (RT) experiments. Zahn & Rosenthal (185) studied the performance of acute schizophrenics and nonschizophrenic psychiatric patients on an RT task in which length of preparatory interval and type of preparatory interval (variable vs. constant) were varied. On the "set index," an overall measure of RT performance developed by Rodnick & Shakow (136) over 25 years ago, the acute schizophrenics were poorer than the nonschizophrenics, but better than a group of previously tested chronic schizophrenics. Moreover, relative to their overall performance, the acute schizophrenics gave disproportionately slower RT's to the longer preparatory intervals—that is, as the preparatory intervals got longer, the acute schizophrenics become slower and slower in their RT's. This finding is interpreted as indicating that as preparatory intervals become longer, acute schizophrenics have more and more time in which to become distracted by internal and external task-irrelevant stimuli. In a related study, findings similar to Zahn & Rosenthal's were obtained by Steinmeyer (160).

King (79) employed a typical RT task in which a subject, in response to an auditory signal, had to lift his right-hand index finger from a rest position, move it across a short distance to a target key, and depress the target key. Two different measures were obtained: the time it took a subject initially to lift his finger, and the time it took him to move his lifted finger over to depress the target key. It was found that schizophrenics had longer times on both measures. The author concludes that elevation of RT in schizophrenia is not only due to a deficit in "readiness to respond" (because of disturbance in the ability to maintain a set), but also to a psychomotor deficit in speed of finger movement. However, it is important to note that King's psychomotor-deficit interpretation of RT does not explain Zahn &

Rosenthal's (185) and Steinmeyer's (160) finding that schizophrenic RT becomes progressively worse as preparatory interval is increased.

In a study closely related to the RT literature, Orzack & Kornetsky (109) found that schizophrenics manifested impairment relative to age- and education-matched normals and alcoholics on a Continuous Performance Test, which assesses the ability to maintain a mental set. In contrast, no schizophrenic impairment was found on the Wechsler Digit Symbol Substitution Test, which assesses the ability to manipulate symbols relatively independent of the ability to maintain a mental set.

Inability to screen out deviant, distracting associations.—With respect to this deficit, Interference Theory makes the same predictions as Hullian-Drive Theory. Thus, the section on "Associational Disturbance" above under Hullian-Drive Theory is directly applicable to the present discussion of Interference Theory.

PSYCHOLOGICAL DEFICIT IN ORGANIC BRAIN PATHOLOGY

Reitan (132) divides the investigation of the psychological deficit accompanying brain damage into two broad categories: experimental or problem-oriented and clinical or patient-oriented. In the experimental area, the focus is upon the molecular study of particular neurological functions in "animal analogues" or upon the relationship between extent and localization of damage on the one hand and degree and type of psychological deficit on the other. In contrast, clinical studies generally veiw brain damage as a unitary phenomenon. The focus in the clinical area is upon how such undifferentiated damage impairs various types of psychological functioning (perception, learning and memory, attention, etc.), and how these impairments can be used to make a differential diagnosis of the presence vs. absence of organic brain pathology.

In this section of the review we shall proceed differently than we did in our discussion of the schizophrenia literature. Theoretical groupings so helpful for understanding studies of schizophrenia are not useful for studies of CNS pathology. Theories (e.g., Goldstein, Shapiro, Kardiner) lack clarity. Moreover, they are appropriate to all kinds of mental disorders and thus are not uniquely applicable to brain damage.

Before discussing specific studies, some general comments about problems encountered in this area need to be made.

We have been impressed in our review with how concerned and careful some investigators are about their procedures, the scoring reliability of their dependent variables, and the appropriateness and detail of their statistical methods. Yet, these very same researchers are naively willing to accept the determination of "organic brain pathology" from almost any medical source, without checking the reliability and validity of the diagnostic process upon which this determination is based.

Not only are experimental groups lacking in clear definition, but also control or comparison groups suffer from meaningful categorization and description. The use of a "psychiatric sample" as a control group, frequently without further definition, is a common occurrence. Whether these patients are schizophrenic, hypomanic, depressed or character disorders, or an admixture of all of them, is far too often left to the reader's imagination.

Group matching on age, educational achievement, and IQ (if appropriate) has become almost standard. However, the use of "normal" controls continues in the literature. We find it hard to comprehend how hospitalized patients with cerebral lesions can be meaningfully compared to a nonhospitalized, effectively functioning group of people.

Since the focus of a large number of studies is on the ability of psychological tests to differentiate brain-damaged from nonbrain-damaged patients, a better definition of the brain-damaged patient is needed in most studies. If, for instance, the patients used to validate a test are those with severe damage so that a diagnosis of CNS lesion can be made with certainty in a 5-min neurological examination, the test results, though highly predictive for this group, may be useless. If someone is so evidently damaged that a brief physical examination can establish this diagnosis without a doubt, there is no need for testing. The high "hit" rate reported in a study may then simply exist for severe neurological conditions and be of no consequence for those patients whose diagnosis is questionable.

Even with the best tests (i.e., those which effectively differentiate experimental and control groups), we run into difficulty in applying the findings to an individual patient. Reitan (131) states that in formal research efforts there is a selective consideration of limited sets of variables, whereas the individual person represents a host of complex and interacting factors which can never be reproduced or fully stated in a published study. The psychological effects of cerebral damage on an individual are influenced by innumerable factors, a few of which are (not necessarily in order of importance): age, localization and degree of damage, acute vs. chronic, general physical status, premorbid personality, and family support and encouragement.

The final determination regarding the existence of a cerebral lesion (or its exact nature and location) often cannot be made until autopsy. Even then, we are left in a quandary if we try to validate the inferences made by psychological testing at an earlier time since neurological and other changes may have occurred.

As we have already mentioned, the central question in the clinical brain damage literature has been that of differential diagnosis and the effect of undifferentiated cerebral pathology on the whole gamut of psychological processes.

By far the largest segment of the clinical brain damage literature deals with adult deficit. "Organic brain syndrome" implies that the individual has achieved full psychological development before deterioration in cerebral functioning took place. This condition is characteristically found when adults sustain CNS damage. When such a lesion occurs in children, it is likely that development is considerably retarded. Thus, since we are excluding the retardation literature, the studies on deficit as a result of brain damage are largely limited to adults (excluding cerebral deterioration caused by aging or such conditions as presenile dementia) and to a syndrome in children generally known as "minimal brain dysfunction." In the subsequent review we have separated the literature into that dealing with adults and that dealing with children.

Brain Damage in Adults

New tests.—Gaddes (45) compared the performance of normal and brain damaged subjects, ages 9 to adult, on a new Visual Retention Test. Because organics have difficulty in perceiving the phi phenomenon and have few *M* (movement) responses on the Rorschach, Gaddes designed his test so as to assess both visual retention and motion perception. His results differentiated normals from brain-damaged patients with 75 to 90 per cent accuracy, depending on the age group.

Another new test, still very much an experimental instrument, is the Williams Memory Scale (180). Williams points out that there are only two scales available that measure more than one aspect of memory: the 1923 Wells-Martin Scale and the Wechsler Memory Scale. The former is not suitable because of its length; the latter does not lend itself to a breakdown of specific memory functions. The new test contains five subtests on which the scores can be compared with each other. The subtests are: Immediate Recall, Nonverbal Learning, Verbal Learning, Retention for Recent Events, and Memory for Past Events.

Satz's Block Rotation Task (142) is a visual-motor test in which eight designs are presented in a horizontal or vertical position or both, and seven at various angles *vis-á-vis* the subject. The test was standardized on 59 organics and 63 schizophrenics, neurotics, and normals. The predictive power of the test was high, with almost all the false negatives limited to convulsive disorders and neoplastic lesions outside of the cerebral cortex.

The Design Reproduction Test devised by Wagner & Schaff (171) produces constantly changing geometric patterns by moving a slide. The patient is presented with a series of 12 photographs of designs, and he is required to move the slide to the point where the matching design appears. This procedure allows for a separation of the motor and the perceptual functions considered so crucial by Garron & Cheifetz (46). Wagner & Schaff found a clear-cut continuum of scores ranging from organic brain damage to retardation to psychiatric condition to normal.

It is unlikely that any of these new tests, though interesting, will improve to any extent the evaluative or discriminative power of psychological tests for brain pathology.

Batteries of tests.—As stated earlier, a major interest among clinicians is in differential diagnosis. Spreen & Benton (158) compared the differential diagnostic power of a number of tests employed singly and in combination. They found that the former procedure yielded a mean hit rate of 71 per cent, and the latter revealed a mean hit rate of 80 per cent.

Shaw (147) re-evaluated the Halstead Test Battery. He found it to be not only a good discriminator between groups of subjects with and without brain damage, but also to be a reasonably adequate indicator of severity of damage.

Age of onset of cerebral lesion and length of hospitalization are variables that have come under scrutiny. Fitzhugh & Fitzhugh (42) studied the effects of early vs. later onset of brain damage on 22 measures that included the Halstead and Wechsler-Bellevue (WB) tests. Matched pairs of organics differing only as to age at which the damage occurred (prior to age 10 and after age 12) were employed. The advantage of a longer period of normal development was demonstrated by the finding that the later onset individuals performed better than the early onset individuals.

Reed & Fitzhugh (127) administered the Wechsler-Bellevue, the Trail-making, and several tests from the Halstead Battery to a group of children and a group of adults, each with two degrees of severity of cerebral damage. Control subjects consisted of normally functioning children and adults and psychiatrically hospitalized adults. The control groups performed at a higher level than the brain-damaged groups, and the mildly impaired group gave a consistently higher performance than the moderately impaired groups. The findings also suggest that brain damage that occurs in adulthood has quite different effects than such damage occurring in childhood. In brain-damaged adults there was greater impairment on tests involving stored memory than on tests of problem solving ability; in children the opposite pattern was in evidence.

In a series of studies, Watson (173–175) investigated whether the ability of tests to differentiate organics and schizophrenics varies as a function of length of hospitalization. He found (174) that WAIS (Wechsler Adult Intelligence Scale) profiles distinguish organics from schizophrenics when patients have been hospitalized for a long period. They are ineffective differentiators in short hospitalizations. In looking at the types of WAIS errors that occurred, Watson (173) obtained data consistent with the clinical hypothesis that organics show greater psychological impotence (higher number of inadequate attempts at problem solution), and schizophrenics are more negativistic (higher number of "no attempts" at problem solutions). This finding applied only to the briefly hospitalized group. Using Reitan's six sensory-perceptual tests, Watson et al. (175) found that only one of the six, the Auditory Inception Test, distinguished organics from schizophrenics. This measure, however, was more strongly associated with chronicity than diagnosis.

Fogel (43) compared several subtests of the WAIS with the Multiple

Choice Proverbs Test for effectiveness in discriminating brain-damaged patients from normal controls. He found that the most successful WAIS subtest, Picture Arrangement, screened out 68.5 per cent of the organics, while the Proverbs screened out 63 per cent.

Perceptual motor tests.—Within the area of perceptual-motor tests, the Bender-Gestalt (BG) has received the most attention. Several studies have attempted to improve the diagnosticability of the test through new variations in administration and scoring (19, 28, 29, 102, 155). In the area of new variations in BG administration, Canter (19) compared subjects' BG performance on both plain paper and "background interference paper." He found that brain-damaged patients performed poorer on the interference paper, while psychiatric control groups performed equally on both types of paper. Snortum (155) required brain-damaged, neurotic, and alcoholic patients to take the BG under standard conditions and by tachistoscopic exposure. While the tachistoscopic procedure discriminated the organic group from others, the standard administration did not.

Cooper & Barnes (28) and Cooper, Dwarshuis & Blechman (29) reported that their scoring systems of the BG differentiated brain damaged from psychiatric and normal subjects. On the other hand, Mosher & Smith (102), using the Peek-Quast and Hain scoring systems for the BG, concluded that diagnostic errors were so frequent as to preclude the BG from being useful for individual diagnosis.

The BG, as usually administered, involves two phases: (*a*) the subject copies directly from the design cards, and (*b*) the subject reproduces the designs from memory. Armstrong (4) found that the "memory phase" was more effective in differentiating organics from nonorganics than the "copying phase." Since the two phases differ only in the factor of dependence upon memory, Armstrong's results strongly suggest that organics are characterized in part by a memory deficit per se. Garron & Cheifetz (46), however, warn that an adequate memory reproduction on the BG does not necessarily rule out CNS disease.

Employing the BG memory phase and knowledge of the year, Orme (108) contrasted brain-damaged patients with depressives, two diagnostic types that are often difficult to tell apart. He found that among patients who had poor BG performances and did not know the year, there was a much better than chance possibility that they were brain damaged. Among the other patients, it was not possible to make a differential diagnosis accurately. Kendrick & Post (78), also using brain-damaged and depressed patients, obtained similar results.

The final two BG studies to be mentioned involved comparing the test's differential diagnostic power with that of other tests. The two comparisons both found the BG to be less discriminating than either the Graham-Kendall Memory for Designs Test (3) or Reitan's two graphomotor tests, the "Greek Cross" and Aphasia Screening (170).

The Graham-Kendall Memory for Designs Test was revised by one of its originators. Kendall (77), using brain-damaged and control groups of over 200 and 300 subjects respectively, found that certain types of "rotations" and "reversals" on the test differentiate those with cerebral damage from those without such damage, while other signs lack this power. Horizontal and 90° rotations were the best discriminators between presence and absence of brain pathology. "Orientation errors" were less powerful predictors, particularly in older and less educated subjects. "Vertical errors" were not useful in separating the groups, while 45° errors were of partial value.

Goldstein & Neuringer (51) administered the Trail Making Test to schizophrenic and brain-damaged patients to find qualitative differences between them. Schizophrenics either completed the task without error, abandoned it, or made illogical patterns. Brain-damaged patients, on the other hand, had a tendency to lose track of the alternation pattern and developed a number or letter sequence. Taking a score-oriented approach to the Trail Making Test, Orgel & McDonald (106) found no differences between organic, "neuropsychiatric" and hospitalized, normal control patients.

Huse & Parsons (70) found large differences in level of performance and rate of improvement between brain-damaged and control patients on the Pursuit Rotor. The poorer performance of the brain-damaged was due to sensory-motor dysfunction and impairment in new learning, and it was not associated with disturbances of inhibition. Fernald et al. (41) conducted a study with the Purdue Pegboard. They found that this test could differentiate organics from nonpsychotic controls, but not organics from psychotic controls.

Haydu & Rutsky (62) employed a task requiring chronic brain-damaged patients, chronic schizophrenic patients, and a group of normal subjects to draw the reversal of a clear, unambiguous figure. Schizophrenics, as well as normals, were able to reverse the figure, while most of those with cerebral impairment could not.

Perceptual tests.—Two studies have employed the Archimedes Spiral Visual Aftereffect Test (SVAT). Smith (151) evaluated differences between patients with brain damage, patients with chronic physical illness but no brain damage, and individuals with neither physical illness nor brain damage. While the brain-damaged performed no differently on the SVAT than the chronically ill controls, the brain-damaged did perform more poorly than the physically healthy controls. In contrast, Morant & Efstathiou (101) found no SVAT differences between brain-damaged and normal individuals. These authors question previous SVAT findings separating organics from nonorganics, arguing that these findings are due to a factor not necessarily related to the SVAT task, namely, the inability of organics to maintain fixation at the center of the spiral. They support this argument by citing an unpublished study they conducted. In this study, organic deficit in SVAT appeared when fixation was not controlled and disappeared when fixation was controlled.

Three other perceptual test studies have obtained negative results with respect to differentiating organics. Currie, Anderson & Price (32) found no differences between individuals with and without CNS impairment on Timed Block Counting, a subtest of the Army General Classification Test. Rosenberg (139) compared elderly individuals on a task involving visual discrimination of newly appearing stimuli from stimuli which had formerly appeared in the experiment. While nonhospitalized controls performed better than patients with brain pathology, there was no difference between the latter group and a group of nonbrain-damaged patients hospitalized for lower limb amputations. Finally, Knehr (80) found that Progressive Matrices did not differentiate patients with an organic diagnosis from those with a psychiatric one. However, it should be noted that, independent of diagnosis, this test was an excellent indicator of extent of impairment.

An initially surprising finding was reported by Daston (33), who employed a test of spatial incongruity. The stimulus was a photograph of a three-sided building, which was taken so that only the front was visible, yielding the impression of a two-dimensional facade. Sensitivity to the incongruity was evaluated individually. Daston's data revealed that brain-damaged patients performed much better than schizophrenics. However, the schizophrenic group consisted of chronically hospitalized patients, whereas the brain-damaged group consisted of recent admissions to a general hospital. These can hardly be considered comparable samples.

In the single function tests we have been reviewing, it is striking that, over all, those in the perceptual-motor category discriminated brain damage quite effectively, while the purely perceptual tests were quite ineffective. [Two exceptions, both of them discussed in the "New Tests" section above, must be noted: Gaddes' (3) Visual Retention Test and Wagner & Schaff's (171) Design Reproduction Test.] This would strongly suggest that adequacy of motor functioning, at least when it is integrated with perceptual functioning, is a better discriminator of brain damage than adequacy of perception per se.

Personality tests.—Projective tests were once very prominent in the brain damage literature. For the period of our review, only one study is in evidence. Kunce & Worley (82) evaluated the House-Tree-Person drawings of three groups: patients with organic brain damage, patients with physical disability (but no CNS involvement), and university students. Using seven objective items such as location of window and relative size of door, the brain-injured group obtained significantly higher error scores than the physically disabled, who in turn had higher error scores than the normal controls.

As an alternative to projective tests, the MMPI has been employed. Hovey (66) was able to select five MMPI items that discriminated between neurology service patients with and without CNS damage across two different samples. All the items involved physical symptoms and were scored so that admission of these symptoms was associated with brain damage. Zimmerman (186) cross-validated these five items and found them effective in discriminating patients with very severe brain damage, but ineffective in discriminating patients with moderate, mild, or minimal cerebral pathology.

Shaw & Matthews (148) studied MMPI differences between brain-damaged and "pseudo-neurologic" patients. These latter individuals were initially admitted to a neurological ward because of symptomatology suggestive of organic brain damage. After undergoing an extensive battery of tests, brain damage was subsequently ruled out. The authors found 17 MMPI items that differentiated the two groups. There was no overlap with the Hovey items. In fact, although 12 of Shaw & Matthews' items involved physical symptoms, as did all the Hovey items, the Shaw & Matthews items were scored in the opposite direction from Hovey's items so that admission of physical symptoms was associated with not being in the brain-damaged group.

Matthews, Shaw & Klove (92), using the same population as Shaw & Matthews, administered several other tests in addition to the MMPI to determine "pseudo-neurologic" symptomatology. Several Performance Subtests of the WAIS, many tests of the Halstead Battery, and some others of varying types discriminated neurological from pseudo-neurological patients. Since all patients were initially suspected of having CNS impairment, these results have a unique pragmatic value.

Parsons & Stewart (112) set out to test Goldstein's hypothesis that brain injury results in the impairment of the abstract attitude, leading to a greater dependence upon external cues. Experimenter attitude was varied. Brain-damaged patients performed more poorly with an impersonal experimenter than with a warm, supportive experimenter. No variation occurred in a control group of neurotics. Similar results were obtained by Elliott (39), who employed the SVAT. This investigator found that compared to their performance in a socially neutral experimental atmosphere, brain-damaged subjects manifested more deficit in a socially stressful atmosphere and less deficit in a socially supportive atmosphere. Unfortunately, no control group was employed.

In contrast to the above two studies, Lodge (89) found that on the flicker fusion, SVAT, and reversible figure tests, suggestive facilitating instructions improved the performance of the brain-damaged patients. On the other hand, inhibiting instructions (suggestion against the perceptual effect) tended to impair the performance of the normal controls but not the organics.

Brain Damage in Children

The literature on brain damage in children focuses to a large extent on the areas of minimal brain dysfunction, psychological testing for CNS disorders, and therapeutic efforts, both drug and psychological, to modify behavior. In our review, we shall limit ourselves to these three main topics, excluding mental deficiency, cerebral palsy, and epilepsy.

Minimal Brain Dysfunction.—There is a dearth of experimental investigation, but no shortage of clinical-impressionistic articles in the area of minimal brain dysfunction (MBD). This serves as a commentary on the state of evaluative procedures where any dependable signs of cerebral damage are missing. Thus, instead of a diagnosis made on "hard" neurological signs, this syndrome is usually diagnosed on the existence of one or several psychological behavioral factors. These include abnormal activity level of a hypokinetic or hyperkinetic nature, perceptual-motor deficits, specific learning disabilities, short attention span, impulsivity and lability, and a generalized developmental lag. In spite of the term "brain dysfunction," the question of whether or not damage has been sustained at all remains. There are no well-established data that demonstrate damage to the underlying cerebral structure. The frustration that neurologists experience is evident in a number of papers (22, 23, 67, 90 144). Paine (111), a pediatric neurologist, states:

> . . . unless we borrow from the psychologist or from that area that overlaps both neurology and psychology, we come up with nothing. I am afraid that the average neurologist, even more than the average pediatrician, has usually examined children like this on referrals from school and sent them back to school with the statement that nothing was wrong . . . (111, p. 22).

Gomez (55) found the term "MBD" thoroughly objectionable because of its lack of definition. As a result, he sent questionnaires to pediatricians. The responses indicated that MBD had become a wastebasket diagnosis applied to "all children who were not quite normal" (55, p. 589).

Werry (178), objecting to a priori classification of MBD, suggested the empirical approach of a factor analysis. Using 103 chronically hyperactive children of normal intelligence and in good physical health, the investigator found a very low degree of interrelatedness among neurological, medical-historical, behavioral, cognitive, and EEG dysfunctions. A factor analysis of these data revealed 10 basically unrelated dysfunctions, each of which tends to be comprised largely of measures from one source (neurologist, psychologist, or psychiatrist). These disparate factors do not lead to a holistic dimension of MBD.

The International Study Group on Child Neurology proposed several years ago that the term "MBD" be discarded in favor of a more meaningful classification of disturbances of cerebral function subclassified as: motor disorders, hyperkinetic behavior, disorders of communication, dominance problems, perceptual disorders, mental deficiency, and convulsive disorders (90). From the continued outpouring of papers dealing with MBD, it is clear that no one has heeded the call for a revision of the nomenclature. But then, no change of names is going to bring about a better understanding of this elusive syndrome that may be caused by genetic variations, prenatal or perinatal brain injuries, biochemical irregularities, or unknown causes possibly having to do with the maturation of the central nervous system (26, 49, 61).

Pollack (117) has pointed out that the relationship of MBD in children to psychiatric disorders at a later age is quite unclear. In an effort to shed some light on this issue, he studied 13 patients between the ages of 15 and 25 who had been admitted to a psychiatric hospital because of severe psychiatric disturbance. These patients were found to have evidence of MBD in childhood and severe psychopathology in adolescence. All had histories of learning defects and behavior disorders in childhood, and in nine of them pre- or peri-natal abnormalities had been present. The neurological examination was normal for all; however, equivocal signs were in evidence.

It is obvious that MBD refers to behavior and not to brain damage as such, since we have no knowledge of etiology. We would agree with Conners (26) that the term "MBD" ". . . should be a descriptive label and a prescription for action, not a statement of etiology" (p. 749). Thus, while the effort to understand the neurological basis continues, the difficulties that these children experience need to be described in psychoeducational rather than in neurological terms.

Strauss & Lehtinen (163) first introduced the hypothesis that distractibility is a major behavioral consequence of presumed cerebral injury in children. This concept has been widely accepted and further corroborated by clinical evidence (2, 9, 31, 38).

In reviewing the literature, Browning (14) found an absence of controlled experimental studies relating irrelevant visual stimuli and learning in children with MBD. He carried out a series of three experiments using brain-damaged and nonbrain-damaged children of like mean mental age and chronological age. In one of the experiments, he set out to determine if distracting stimulus conditions interfered in discrimination learning in children without brain damage. In two others, he compared the performance of MBD children with that of nonbrain-damaged children in the presence vs. the absence of distracting stimulus conditions (flashing, multicolored lights). None of the experiments supported the hypothesis that the task-irrelevant visual stimuli interfere with learning in MBD children to a greater degree than in nonbrain-damaged children. The author pointed out that the distracting stimuli were in the subjects' visual periphery and were not background stimuli incorporated within the discrimination task as discussed by Strauss & Lehtinen. Despite Browning's own caveat, the findings cannot be easily dismissed. They do raise important questions about long standing and accepted concepts which have been vigorously applied to classroom situations for such children.

Ozer (110) discussed the fact that children from low income groups have a higher incidence of prematurity and that this, plus other factors (e.g., poorer prenatal care), may lead to a higher incidence of MBD. The identification of such children is further complicated by the fact that they frequently come from relatively disorganized and nonverbal environments. As a result, an attempt was made to devise measures of level of functioning which were not affected by the background of the children. The use of the Face-Hand Test with eyes open and closed has been found useful as has the Sound-Touch Test, which also involves the ability to "tune out" meaningless stimuli. The author found that middle-class and Headstart children performed equally on the Face-Hand Test; however, the former received better scores on the Sound-Touch Test. It seems likely that with the extension of Headstart and poverty programs the diagnosis of MBD will become more frequent as we become more aware of such disturbances in children from other than middle-class backgrounds.

Psychological tests.—The literature on the use of psychological tests for CNS disorders in children is far less extensive than for adults. This is not surprising as most of the brain damage in children occurs before, at, or shortly after birth. In many cases these children become quite retarded. We are thus left with testing for MBD, for consequences of early damage to a specific area, or for a lesion that occurred during childhood and did not hinder, in large measure, normal development. Yates' (184) comments on formal tests of brain damage in children are quite appropriate here. He stated that besides the problems of unreliability of tests and the absence of adequate independent criteria of brain damage, test construction has been extremely complicated because of the difficulty in distinguishing the brain-injured child from the autistic or retarded one.

Almost all of the tests used in studies with children are of the perceptual-motor type. Two investigations used the Koppitz (81) developmental scoring system for the BG. McConnell (93) divided each of 120 children with a mean IQ of 66 according to three levels of organicity (substantial, minimal, and nonorganic) and four levels of emotional disturbance (situational, neurotic, borderline psychotic, and psychotic). The Koppitz developmental scores related to organic but not emotional problems, indicating their usefulness for assessing brain pathology in emotionally disturbed children. Holroyd (65) compared the Koppitz and the Quast scoring systems for the BG as to their respective accuracy in identifying children with CNS disorders. Out of 38 children with varying diagnoses, both scoring systems correctly predicted 10 out of 25 children who had been classified as brain damaged, at the cost of one false negative each. Despite their equal predictive power, each system identified some different cases as brain damaged. When combined, they yielded 13 "hits" out of 25.

Rapin, Tourk & Costa (124) used the Purdue Pegboard as a screening instrument. No discrimination among brain damage, severe emotional disturbance, and mental retardation was possible. Similar negative findings were reported by Colman (25) when he used the Marble Board and the Ellis Visual Designs Tests. Reed & Reed (128) also found that they could not differentiate 50 brain-damaged children from 50 controls on the WISC and the Halstead Category Test.

It is curious that while the more formal tests were generally ineffectual in separating brain-damaged children from other comparison groups, psychometrically less sophisticated tests have been reported to be highly discriminating. Conners & Barta (27) could differentiate brain-injured children from those with severe emotional disturbance on the basis of tactual learning and visual recognition performance. Rennick & Halstead (133) found that children with diffuse cerebral dysfunction made more errors in naming colors and required more time than normals. Brain-damaged children took more time on tasks requiring the reproduction of geometric figures with sticks and made almost twice as many errors as did the non-damaged children (181).

Some attention, though not nearly enough, has been paid to personality factors in brain-damaged children. Two studies reported on personality and social aspects of children with CNS disturbance compared with those with psychoses. Yaker, Goldberg & Benson (183) compared brain-damaged and functionally psychotic children on the Vineland Social Maturity Scale and on a psychiatric checklist. They found, as might be expected, that psychotic children have poorer object relations leading to marked deficiencies in socialization behavior. An unexpected result was that the psychotic group showed a better communication ability.

Farnham-Diggory (40) carried out an interesting study on self-image in brain-damaged, psychotic, and normal children. Compared with normals, psychotic children underestimated and brain-damaged children overestimated their ability to arouse affection in others. Following this up with correlations of IQ and Self-Evaluation for each of the three groups, Farnham-Diggory found negative and positive correlations for the brain-damaged and normal groups respectively and a zero correlation for the psychotics. He hypothesizes that brain-damaged children must learn to arouse affection in other people in order to survive. Turnure & Zigler (168) found outer directedness to be the predominant characteristic of retarded children, which in a certain sense supports Farnham-Diggory's results that brain-damaged children overestimate their ability to arouse affection in others.

Therapy.—The therapeutic possibilities for brain-injured children have been limited almost exclusively to the pharmacological approach. Only recently have behavior modification techniques been introduced.

Insofar as drugs are concerned, we shall not discuss here the usual psychoactive agents as amphetamines and phenothiazines. However, we do want to bring to the attention of the reader a new drug, the claims for which are impressive. Smith & Weyl (153) and Smith, Philippus & Guard

(152) have studied the effects of a new drug "ethosuximide" (an anticonvulsive medication under the trade name of "Zarontin," Parke-Davis) on intellectual functions in children with learning deficits and cortical brain dysfunctions. In a double-blind study, they found that children (ages 8 to 14), with a 14–6 positive spike EEG pattern, showed increases in Full and Verbal WISC IQs while on Zarontin. No such increases occurred with a placebo. Zarontin did not affect performance on the Rorschach, the Ravens Progressive Matrices, or the Wechsler Performance IQ. The researchers speculate that Zarontin has an effect on the verbal functions of the left hemisphere and that the presence of a 14–6 positive spike EEG pattern is associated with MBD. It is quite clear that further research using Zarontin will be most important in anchoring these findings.

The use of behavior therapy with brain-injured children is in its very beginning stages, but it promises to be effective in the management of those children whose behavior tends to make their school and social participation particularly problematic. Hall & Broden (58) taught parents and teachers to carry out operant conditioning techniques. Observations of behavior were made during recess periods of a special public school class. Problem behaviors of three children were modified through this method. There was no indication that brain-damaged children conform to a different set of conditioning principles than do other children or adults. The three children were followed over a three-month period during which the positive changes were maintained. Patterson et al. (114) describe the conditioning procedure for one 10-year-old, brain-injured, hyperactive boy. A child of the same age and with similar behavior served as the control. Both were observed in the classroom, and a seven category checklist of nonattending behavior was used. Conditioning trials took place in the classroom setting. During each time interval in which one of the subject's high rate responses did not occur, he received an auditory stimulus which had previously been paired with getting candy. Over a three-month period the experimental subject showed a significant decrease in nonattending behavior. No change occurred in the control subject. A similar procedure with a 9-year-old, hyperactive boy produced the same results (113). It is obvious that these are exploratory studies and so limited in scope that they can hardly be considered as documenting a new treatment modality for this population. Yet this approach deserves much attention since hyperactivity is one of the most frequent problems for which children are referred to clinics.

Conclusions

It is clear that the difficult diagnostic problems of separating the patient with a cerebral lesion from the one with schizophrenia or other psychopathology has not been solved either in adults or children. That there is a good deal of research activity in this area is clear, and some of the reports are quite hopeful. Yet the problems mentioned earlier continue to plague this area of research, and without a more precise definition of the brain-damaged population, we are likely to continue to get inconclusive or contradictory results. But the most critical need is for an adequate theory of brain functioning upon which tests of brain damage can be based.

Acknowledgments

Thanks are extended to Miss Ruth Hartman for her assistance, and to Miss Patricia Pannier of the Denison Memorial Library of the University of Colorado School of Medicine for her help in conducting the MEDLARS search of the literature.

LITERATURE CITED

1. Al-Issa, I. Effects of literacy and schizophrenia on verbal abstraction in Iraq. *J. Soc. Psychol.*, **71**, 39–43 (1967)
2. Anderson, W. W. Hyperkinetic child: Neurological appraisal. *Neurology*, **13**, 968 (1963)
3. Anglin, R., Pullen, M., Games, P. Comparison of two tests of brain damage. *Percept. Mot. Skills*, **20**, 977–80 (1965)
4. Armstrong, R. G. A re-evaluation of copied and recalled Bender-Gestalt reproductions. *J. Project. Tech.*, **29**, 134–39 (1965)
5. Bannister, D., Fransella, F. A grid test of schizophrenic thought disorder. *Brit. J. Soc. Clin. Psychol.*, **5**, 95–102 (1966)
6. Bannister, D., Salmon, P. Schizophrenic thought disorder: specific or diffuse. *Brit. J. Med. Psychol.*, **39**, 215–19 (1966)
7. Bauman, E., Murray, D. J. Recognition versus recall in schizophrenia. *Can. J. Psychol.*, **22**, 18–25 (1968)
8. Bemporad, J. R. Perceptual disorders in schizophrenia. *Am. J. Psychiat.*, **123**, 971–76 (1967)
9. Benton, A. L. Behavioral indices of brain injury in school children. *Child Develpm.*, **33**, 199–208 (1962)
10. Biles, P. E., Heckel, R. V. "Awareness" in chronic schizophrenics. II. Awareness of causal factors in recent events. *Psychol. Rept.*, **22**, 255–58 (1968)
11. Blumenthal, R., Meltzoff, J. Social schemas and perceptual accuracy in schizophrenia. *Brit. J. Soc. Clin. Psychol.*, **6**, 119–28 (1967)
12. Brenner, A. R. Effects of prior experimenter-subject relationships on responses to the Kent-Rosanoff word-association list in schizophrenics. *J. Abnorm. Psychol.*, **72**, 273–76 (1967)
13. Broen, W. E., Jr., Storms, L. H. Lawful disorganization: The process underlying a schizophrenic syndrome. *Psychol. Rev.*, **73**, 265–79 (1966)
14. Browning, R. M. Effect of irrelevant peripheral visual stimuli on discrimination learning in minimally brain-damaged children. *J. Consult. Psychol.*, **31**, 371–76 (1967)
15. Buss, A. H., Daniell, E. F. Stimulus generalization and schizophrenia. *J. Abnorm. Psychol.*, **72**, 50–53 (1967)
16. Buss, A. H., Lang, P. J. Psychological deficit in schizophrenia: I. affect, reinforcement, and concept attainment. *J. Abnorm. Psychol.*, **70**, 2–24 (1965)
17. Callaway, E., III, Jones, R. T., Layne, R. S. Evoked responses and segmental set of schizophrenia. *Arch. Gen. Psychiat. (Chicago)*, **12**, 83–89 (1965)
18. Cameron, N. S. Experimental analysis of schizophrenic thinking. In *Language and Thought in Schizophrenia*, 50–64 (Kasanin, J. S., Ed., Univ. Calif. Press, Berkeley, 1946)
19. Canter, A. A background interference procedure to increase sensitivity of the Bender-Gestalt test to organic brain disorder. *J. Consult. Psychol.*, **30**, 91–97 (1966)
20. Cicchetti, D. V., Klein, E. B., Fontana, A. F., Spohn, H. E. A test of the censure-deficit model in schizophrenia, employing the Rodnick-Garmezy visual-discrimination task. *J. Abnorm. Psychol.*, **72**, 326–34 (1967)
21. Clark, W. C., Brown, J. C., Rutschmann, J. Flicker sensitivity and response bias in psychiatric patients and normal subjects. *J. Abnorm. Psychol.*, **72**, 35–42 (1967)
22. Clements, S. D. The child with minimal brain dysfunction. A multidisciplinary catalyst. *J. Lancet*, **86**, 121–23 (1966)
23. Clemmens, R. L., Glaser, K. Specific learning disabilities. I. medical aspects. *Clin. Pediat. (Phila.)*, **6**, 481–86 (1967)
24. Cohen, B. D., Camhi, J. Schizophrenic performance in a word-communication task. *J. Abnorm. Psychol.*, **72**, 240–46 (1967)
25. Colman, P. G. A comparative study of the test performances of brain-injured. Emotionally disturbed and normal children. *S. Afr. Med. J.*, **40**, 945–50 (1966)
26. Conners, C. K. The syndrome of minimal brain dysfunction: psychological aspects. *Pediat. Clin. N. Am.*, **14**, 749–66 (1967)
27. Conners, C. K., Barta, F., Jr. Trans-

fer of information from touch to vision in brain-injured and emotionally disturbed children. *J. Nerv. Ment. Dis.*. **145,** 138–41 (1967)

28. Cooper, J. R., Barnes, E. J. Technique for measuring reproductions of visual stimuli. II. Adult reproductions of the Bender-Gestalt. *Percept. Mot. Skills,* **23,** 1135–38 (1966)
29. Cooper, J. R., Dwarshuis, L., Blechman, G. Technique for measuring reproductions of visual stimuli. 3. Bender-Gestalt and severity of neurological deficit. *Percept. Mot. Skills,* **25,** 506–8 (1967)
30. Craig, W. J. Breadth of association in psychiatric patients. *J. Clin. Psychol.,* **23,** 11–15 (1967)
31. Cruickshank, W. M., Bentzen, F. A., Ratzeburg, F. H., Taunenhauser, M. T. *A Teaching Method for Brain Injured and Hyperactive Children* (Syracuse Univ. Press, Syracuse, 1961)
32. Currie, J. S., Anderson, R. J., Price, A. C. Timed block counting as a test for organic brain impairment. *J. Geront.,* **20,** 372–73 (1965)
33. Daston, P. G. Space perception in chronic schizophrenia and brain damage. *Percept. Mot. Skills,* **18,** 183–90 (1964)
34. De Luca, J. N. Motivation and performance in chronic schizophrenia. *Psychol. Rept.,* **22,** 1261–69 (1968)
35. Dokecki, P. R., Cromwell, R. L., Polidoro, L. G. The premorbid adjustment and chronicity dimensions as they relate to commonality and stability of word associations in schizophrenics. *J. Nerv. Ment. Dis.,* **146,** 310–11 (1968)
36. Donovan, M. J., Webb, W. W. Meaning dimensions and male-female voice perception in schizophrenics with good and poor premorbid adjustment. *J. Abnorm. Psychol.,* **70,** 426–31 (1965)
37. Dunham, R. M. *Sensitivity of Schizophrenics to Parental Censure* (Unpublished doctoral dissertation, Duke Univ., 1959)
38. Eisenberg, L. Behavioral manifestations of cerebral damage in childhood. *Brain-Damage in Children: Biological and Social Aspects,* 61–76 (Birch, H. G., Ed., Williams & Wilkins, Baltimore, 1964)
39. Elliott, J. J., III. Response bias in SAET responses of persons with organic brain damage. *Percept. Mot. Skills,* **21,** 647–52 (1965)
40. Farnham-Diggory, S. Self, future, and time: a developmental study of the concepts of psychotic, brain-damaged, and normal children. *Monogr. Soc. Res. Child Develpm.,* **31,** 1–63 (1966)
41. Fernald, L. D., Jr., Fernald, P. S., Rines, W. B. Purdue Pegboard and differential diagnosis. *J. Consult. Psychol.,* **30,** 279 (1966)
42. Fitzhugh, K. B., Fitzhugh, L. C. Effects of early and later onset of cerebral dysfunction upon psychological test performance. *Percept. Mot. Skills,* **20,** 1099–1100 (1965)
43. Fogel, M. L. The proverbs test in the appraisal of cerebral disease. *J. Gen. Psychol.,* **72,** 269–75 (1965)
44. Furth, H. G., Youniss, J. Schizophrenic thinking on nonverbal conceptual, discovery, and transfer tasks. *J. Nerv. Ment. Dis.,* **146,** 376–83 (1968)
45. Gaddes, W. H. A new test of dynamic visual retention. *Percept. Mot. Skills,* **25,** 393–96 (1967)
46. Garron, D. C., Cheifetz, D. Comment on "Bender-Gestalt discernment of organic pathology." *Psychol. Bull.,* **63,** 197–200 (1965)
47. Gerver, D. Linguistic rules and the perception and recall of speech by schizophrenic patients. *Brit. J. Soc. Clin. Psychol.,* **6,** 204–11 (1967)
48. Gillis, J. S. *Schizophrenic Thinking in a Probabilistic Situation* (Presented at meeting of the Western Psychol. Assoc., Honolulu, June 1965)
49. Glaser, K., Clemmens, R. L. School failure. *Pediatrics,* **35,** 128–41 (1965)
50. Goldman, A. R. Differential effects of social reward and punishment on dependent and dependency-anxious schizophrenics. *J. Abnorm. Psychol.,* **70,** 412–18 (1965)
51. Goldstein, G., Neuringer, C. Schizophrenic and organic signs on the Trail Making Test. *Percept. Mot. Skills,* **22,** 347–50 (1966)
52. Goldstein, K. Methodological approach to the study of schizophrenic thought disorder. *Language and Thought in Schizophrenia,* 17–40 (See Ref. 18)
53. Goldstein, K. Concerning the con-

creteness in schizophrenia. *J. Abnorm. Soc. Psychol.,* **59,** 146–48 (1959)

54. Goldstein, R. H., Salzman, L. F. Cognitive functioning in acute and remitted psychiatric patients. *Psychol. Rept.,* **21,** 24–26 (1967)
55. Gomez, M. R. Minimal cerebral dysfunction (Maximal neurologic confusion). *Clin. Pediat. (Phila.),* **6,** 589–91 (1967)
56. Gregg, A., Frank, G. H. An exploration of the thought disorder in schizophrenia through the use of proverbs. *J. Gen. Psychol.,* **77,** 177–82 (1967)
57. Guller, I. B. Stability of self-concept in schizophrenia. *J. Abnorm. Psychol.,* **71,** 275–79 (1966)
58. Hall, R. V., Broden, M. Behavior changes in brain-injured children through social reinforcement. *J. Exptl. Child Psychol.,* **5,** 463–79 (1967)
59. Hamilton, V. Deficits in primitive perceptual and thinking skills in schizophrenia. *Nature (London),* **211,** 389–92 (1966)
60. Hamlin, R. M., Haywood, H. C., Folsom, A. T. Effect of enriched input on schizophrenic abstraction. *J. Abnorm. Psychol.,* **70,** 390–94 (1965)
61. Hartocollis, P. The syndrome of minimal brain dysfunction in young adult patients. *Bull. Menninger Clin.,* **32,** 102–14 (1968)
62. Haydu, G. G., Rutsky, A. Figure-reversing ability in chronic brain syndrome and controls. *J. Nerv. Ment. Dis.,* **142,** 168–71 (1966)
63. Higgins, J. Commonality of word association responses in schizophrenia as a function of chronicity and adjustment. *J. Nerv. Ment. Dis.,* **146,** 312–13 (1968)
64. Hoffer, A., Osmond, H. Some psychological consequences of perceptual disorder and schizophrenia. *Intern. J. Neuropsychiat.,* **2,** 1–19 (1966)
65. Holroyd, J. Cross validation of the Quast and Koppitz Bender-Gestalt signs of cerebral dysfunction. *J. Clin. Psychol.,* **22,** 200 (1966)
66. Hovey, H. B. Brain lesions and five MMPI items. *J. Consult. Psychol.,* **28,** 78–79 (1964)
67. Huessy, H. R. Study of the prevalence and therapy of the choreatiform syndrome or hyperkinesis in rural Vermont. *Acta Paedopsychiat. (Basel),* **34,** 130–35 (1967)
68. Hunt, J. McV., Cofer, C. N. Psychological deficit. In *Personality and the Behavior Disorders,* Chap. 32, 971–1032 (Hunt, J. McV., Ed., Ronald Press, New York, 1242 pp., 1944)
69. Hunt, W. A., Walker, R. E. Schizophrenics' judgments of schizophrenic test responses. *J. Clin. Psychol.,* **22,** 118–20 (1966)
70. Huse, M. M., Parsons, O. A. Pursuit-rotor performance in the brain damaged. *J. Abnorm. Psychol.,* **70,** 350–59 (1965)
71. Husni-Palacios, M., Palacios, J. R., Gibeau, P. J. Auditory perceptual patterns of process and reactive schizophrenics. *J. Project. Tech.,* **31,** 86–91 (1967)
72. Jenkins, S. B., Winkelman, A. C. Inverted perception of time sequence in mental disorders. *Intern. J. Neuropsychiat.,* **2,** 122–28 (1966)
73. Johannsen, W. J., Testin, R. F. Assimilation of visual information. A function of chronicity in schizophrenia. *Arch. Gen. Psychiat. (Chicago),* **15,** 492–98 (1966)
74. Johnson, M. H. Verbal abstracting ability and schizophrenia. *J. Consult. Psychol.,* **30,** 275–77 (1966)
75. Kantor, R. E., Herron, W. G. Perceptual learning in the reactive-process schizophrenias. *J. Project. Tech.,* **29,** 58–70 (1965)
76. Kantor, R. E., Herron, W. G. *Reactive and Process Schizophrenia* (Science & Behavior Books, Palo Alto, 184 pp., 1966)
77. Kendall, B. S. Orientation errors in the Memory-for-Designs Test: tentative findings and recommendations. *Percept. Mot. Skills,* **22,** 335–45 (1966)
78. Kendrick, D. C., Post, F. Differences in cognitive status between healthy, psychiatrically ill, and diffusely brain-damaged elderly subjects. *Brit. J. Psychiat.,* **113,** 75–81 (1967)
79. King, H. E. Reaction time and speed of voluntary movement by normal and psychotic subjects. *J. Psychol.,* **59,** 219–27 (1965)
80. Knehr, C. A. Revised approach to detection of cerebral damage: Progressive matrices revisited. *Psychol. Rept.,* **17,** 71–77 (1965)

81. Koppitz, E. *The Bender Test for Young Children* (Grune & Stratton, N. Y., 1964)
82. Kunce, J. T., Worley, B. Projective drawings of brain-injured subjects. *Percept. Mot. Skills,* **22,** 163–68 (1966)
83. Lang, P. J., Buss, A. H. Psychological deficit in schizophrenia: II. Interference and activation. *J. Abnorm. Psychol.,* **70,** 77–106 (1965)
84. Lefcourt, H. M., Rotenberg, F., Buckspan, B., Steffy, R. A. *Visual Interaction and Performance of Process and Reactive Schizophrenics as a Function of Examiner's Sex* (Presented at Eastern Psychol. Assoc., Boston, Mass., 1967)
85. Lefcourt, H. M., Steffy, R. A. Sex-linked censure expectancies in process and reactive schizophrenics. *J. Pers.,* **34,** 366–80 (1966)
86. Lefcourt, H. M., Steffy, R. A., Buckspan, B., Rotenberg, F. Avoidance of censure by process and reactive schizophrenics as a function of examiner's sex and type of task. *J. Gen. Psychol.,* **79,** 87–96 (1968)
87. Levy, R., Maxwell, A. E. The effect of verbal context on the recall of schizophrenics and other psychiatric patients. *Brit. J. Psychiat.,* **114,** 311–16 (1968)
88. Little, L. K. Effects of the interpersonal interaction on abstract thinking performance in schizophrenics. *J. Consult. Psychol.,* **30,** 158–64 (1966)
89. Lodge, A. Effects of facilitating, neutral and inhibiting instructions on perceptual tasks following brain damage. *Acta Psychol. (Amst.),* **25,** 173–98 (1966)
90. MacKeith, R. C., Bax, M. C. O. Foreward: Minimal brain damage—a concept discarded. In *Minimal Cerebral Dysfunction* (Little Club Clinics in Develpm. Med. No. 10, Nat. Spastics Soc. Med. Educ., London, 1963)
91. Magaro, P. A. Perceptual discrimination performance of schizophrenics as a function of censure, social class, and premorbid adjustment. *J. Abnorm. Psychol.,* **72,** 415–20 (1967)
92. Matthews, C. G., Shaw, D. J., Klove, H. Psychological test performances in neurologic and "pseudo-neurologic" subjects. *Cortex,* **2,** 244–53 (1966)
93. McConnell, O. L. Koppitz's Bender-Gestalt scores in relation to organic and emotional problems in children. *J. Clin. Psychol.,* **23,** 370–74 (1967)
94. McReynolds, P. A comparison of normals and schizophrenics on a new scale of the Rorschach CET. *J. Project. Tech.,* **30,** 262–64 (1966)
95. Mednick, S. A. A learning theory approach to research in schizophrenia. *Psychol. Bull.,* **55,** 316–27 (1958)
96. Meichenbaum, D. H. Effects of social reinforcement on the level of abstraction in schizophrenics. *J. Abnorm. Psychol.,* **71,** 354–62 (1966)
97. Melges, F. T., Fougerousse, C. E., Jr. Time sense, emotions, and acute mental illness. *J. Psychiat. Res.,* **4,** 127–39 (1966)
98. Miller, G. A., Selfridge, J. A. Verbal context and the recall of meaningful material. *Am. J. Psychol.,* **63,** 176–85 (1950)
99. Mirsky, A. F. Neuropsychological bases of schizophrenia. *Ann. Rev. Psychol.,* **20,** 321–48 (1969)
100. Moon, A. F., Mefferd, R. B., Jr., Wieland, B. A., Porkorny, A. D., Falconer, G. A. Perceptual dysfunction as a determinant of schizophrenic word associations. *J. Nerv. Ment. Dis.,* **146,** 80–84 (1968)
101. Morant, R. B., Efstathiou, A. The Archimedes spiral and diagnosis of brain damage. *Percept. Mot. Skills,* **22,** 391–97 (1966)
102. Mosher, D. L., Smith, J. P. The usefulness of two scoring systems for the Bender-Gestalt Test for identifying brain damage. *J. Consult. Psychol.,* **29,** 530–36 (1965)
103. Neale, J. M., Cromwell, R. L. Size estimation in schizophrenics as a function of stimulus-presentation time. *J. Abnorm. Psychol.,* **73,** 44–48 (1968)
104. Nickols, J. Schizophrenic deficit as a function of the test materials. *J. Clin. Psychol.,* **22,** 77–79 (1966)
105. Nickols, J., Nickols, M. A brief Arthur's Stencils Test, Form I. *J. Clin. Psychol.,* **22,** 436–38 (1966)
106. Orgel, S. A., McDonald, R. D. An

evaluation of the Trail Making Test. *J. Consult. Psychol.*, **31**, 77–79 (1967)

107. Orme, J. E., Time estimation and the nosology of schizophrenia. *Brit. J. Psychiat.*, **112**, 37–39 (1966)
108. Orme, J. E., Knowledge of the year, brain damage and memory for designs. *Dis. Nerv. Syst.*, **27**, 202–3 (1966)
109. Orzack, M. H., Kornetsky, C. Attention dysfunction in chronic schizophrenia. *Arch. Gen. Psychiat.* (Chicago) **14**, 323–26 (1966)
110. Ozer, M. N. Symposium: the role of sensory experience in the maturation of sensorimotor function in early infancy. 3. Clinical applications. *Clin. Proc. Child. Hosp.* (Wash), **22**, 279-82 (1966)
111. Paine, R. S. Neurological grand rounds: minimal chronic brain syndromes. *Clin. Proc. Child Hosp. (Wash.)*, **22**, 21–40 (1966)
112. Parsons, O. A., Stewart, K. D. Effects of supportive versus disinterested interviews on perceptual-motor performance in brain-damaged and neurotic patients. *J. Consult. Psychol.*, **30**, 260–66 (1966)
113. Patterson, G. R. An application of conditioning techniques to the control of a hyperactive child. *Case Studies in Behavior Modification* (Ullman, L. P., Krasner, L., Eds., Holt, Rinehart & Winston, New York, 1964)
114. Patterson, G. R., Jones, R., Whittier, J. A behaviour modification technique for the hyperactive child. *Behav. Res. Ther.*, **2**, 217–26 (1965)
115. Phillips, L. Case history data and prognosis in schizophrenia. *J. Nerv. Ment. Dis.*, **117**, 515–25 (1953)
116. Pishkin, V. Perceptual judgment of schizophrenics and normals as a function of social cues and symbolic stimuli. *J. Clin. Psychol.*, **22**, 3–10 (1966)
117. Pollack, M. Early "minimal brain damage" and the development of severe psychopathology in adolescence. *Am. J. Orthopsychiat.*, **37**, 213–14 (1967)
118. Price, R. H. Analysis of task requirements in schizophrenic concept-identification performance. *J. Abnorm. Psychol.*, **73**, 285–93 (1968)
119. Price, R. H., Eriksen, C. W. Size constancy in schizophrenia: a reanalysis. *J. Abnorm. Psychol.*, **71**, 155–60 (1966)
120. Query, W. T., Moore, K. B., Lerner, M. J. Social factors and chronic schizophrenia. The effect on performance and group cohesiveness. *Psychiat. Quart.*, **40**, 504–14 (1966)
121. Raeburn, J. M., Tong, J. E. Experiments on contextual constraint in schizophrenia. *Brit. J. Psychiat.*, **114**, 43–52 (1968)
122. Ralph, D. E. Social reinforcement and stimulus generalization in schizophrenic and normal subjects. *Proc. 74th Ann. Conv. Am. Psychol. Assoc.* (Abstr. 2, 175–76, 1966)
123. Ralph, D. E., McCarthy, J. F. Experimental control, subject selection, and problems of generalization in research with schizophrenic Ss. *Psychol. Rept.*, **21**, 963–64 (1967)
124. Rapin, I., Tourk, L. M., Costa, L. D. Evaluation of the Purdue Pegboard as a screening test for brain damage. *Develpm. Med. Child Neurol.*, **8**, 45–54 (1966)
125. Rappaport, M. Competing voice messages. Effects of message load and drugs on the ability of acute schizophrenics to attend. *Arch. Gen. Psychiat. (Chicago)*, **17**, 97–103 (1967)
126. Rappaport, M., Rogers, N., Reynolds, S., Weinmann, R. Comparative ability of normal and chronic schizophrenic subjects to attend to competing voice messages: Effects of method of presentation, message load and drugs. *J. Nerv. Ment. Dis.*, **143**, 16–27 (1966)
127. Reed, H. B., Jr., Fitzhugh, K. B. Patterns of deficits in relation to severity of cerebral dysfunction in children and adults. *J. Consult. Psychol.*, **30**, 98–102 (1966)
128. Reed, J. C., Reed, H. C. Concept formation ability and nonverbal abstract thinking among older children with chronic cerebral dysfunction. *J. Spec. Educ.*, **1**, 157–61 (1967)
129. Reed, J. L. The Proverbs Test in schizophrenia. *Brit. J. Psychiat.*, **114**, 317–21 (1968)
130. Reitan, R. M. Psychological deficit. *Ann. Rev. Psychol.*, **13**, 415–44 (1962)

131. Reitan, R. M. Diagnostic inferences of brain lesions based on psychological test results. *Can. J. Psychol.*, **7**, 368–83 (1966)

132. Reitan, R. M. Problems and prospects in studying the psychological correlates of brain lesions. *Cortex*, **2**, 127–54 (1966)

133. Rennick, P. M., Halstead, W. C. Color-naming, delayed speech feedback and cerebral dysfunction. *J. Clin. Psychol.*, **24**, 155–61 (1968)

134. Ries, H. A., Johnson, M. H. Commonality of word associations and good and poor premorbid schizophrenia. *J. Abnorm. Psychol.*, **72**, 487–88 (1967)

135. Rodnick, E. H., Garmezy, N. An experimental approach to the study of motivation in schizophrenia. In *Nebraska Symposium on Motivation* 109–84 (Jones, M. R., Ed., Univ. Nebraska Press, Lincoln, 1957)

136. Rodnick, E. H., Shakow, D. Set in the schizophrenic as measured by a composite reaction time index. *Am. J. Psychiat.*, **97**, 214–25 (1940)

137. Rosenbaum, G. Reaction time indices of schizophrenic motivation: A cross-cultural replication. *Brit. J. Psychiat.*, **113**, 537–41 (1967)

138. Rosenbaum, G., Flenning, F., Rosen, H. Effects of weight intensity on discrimination thresholds of normals and schizophrenics. *J. Abnorm. Psychol.*, **70**, 446–50 (1965)

139. Rosenberg, D. N. Performance of brain-damaged Ss with a "New-Old" discrimination task. *Percept. Mot. Skills*, **26** 387–90 (1968)

140. Salzberg, H. C., Williams, J. T., Jr. Effect of three types of feedback on concept formation in chronic schizophrenics. *Psychol. Rept.*, **18**, 831–37 (1966)

141. Salzman, L. F., Goldstein, R. H., Atkins, R., Barbigian, H. Conceptual thinking in psychiatric patients. *Arch. Gen. Psychiat. (Chicago)*, **14**, 55–59 (1966)

142. Satz, P. A Block Rotation Task: The application of multivariate and decision theory analysis for the prediction of organic brain disorder. *Psychol. Monogr.*, **80**, 1–29 (1966)

143. Schooler, C., Feldman, S. E. *Experimental Studies of Schizophrenia* (Psychonomic Press, Goleta, Calif., 260 pp., 1967)

144. Schwalb, E. Clinical considerations of cerebral dysfunction in children. *N.Y. J. Med.*, **67**, 2320–24 (1967)

145. Schwartz, S. Diagnosis, level of social adjustment, and cognitive deficits. *J. Abnorm. Psychol.*, **72**, 446–50 (1967)

146. Sermat, V., Greenglass, E. R. Effect of punishment on probability learning in schizophrenia. *Brit. J. Soc. Clin. Psychol.*, **4**, 52–62 (1965)

147. Shaw, D. J. The reliability and validity of the Halstead Category Test. *J. Clin. Psychol.*, **22**, 176–80 (1966)

148. Shaw, D. J., Matthews, C. G. Differential MMPI performance of brain-damaged vs. pseudo-neurologic groups. *J. Clin. Psychol.*, **21**, 405–8 (1965)

149. Shearn, C. R., Whitaker, L. C. Selecting subjects in studies of schizophrenia. *Schizophrenia*, **1**, 4–8 (1969)

150. Silverman, J. Variations in cognitive control and psychophysiological defense in the schizophrenias. *Psychosomat. Med.*, **29**, 225–51 (1967)

151. Smith, J. P. The spiral visual aftereffect in organic and chronically ill patients with control for response set and communication. *J. Clin. Psychol.*, **21**, 13–15 (1965)

152. Smith, W. L., Philippus, M. J., Guard, H. L. Psychometric study of children with learning problems and 14–6 positive spike EEG patterns treated with ethosuximide (Zarontin) and placebo. *Arch. Dis. Child.*, **43**, 616–19 (1968)

153. Smith, W. L., Weyl, T. C. The effects of ethosuximide (Zarontin) on intellectual functions of children with learning deficits and cortical brain dysfunction. *Current Therap. Res.*, **10**, 265–69 (1968)

154. Snelbecker, G. E., Sherman, L. J., Rothstein, E., Downes, R. C. Schizophrenic and normal behavior on programmed inductive reasoning problems. *J. Clin. Psychol.*, **22**, 415–17 (1966)

155. Snortum, J. R. Performance of different diagnostic groups on the tachistoscopic and copy phases of the Bender-Gestalt. *J. Consult.*

Psychol., **29**, 345–51 (1965)
156. Spain, B. Eyelid conditioning and arousal in schizophrenic and normal subjects. *J. Abnorm. Psychol.*, **71**, 260–66 (1966)
157. Spence, J. T., Lair, C. V. Associative interference in the paired-associate learning of remitted and nonremitted schizophrenics. *J. Abnorm. Psychol.*, **70**, 119–22 (1965)
158. Spreen, O., Benton, A. L. Comparative studies of some psychological tests for cerebral damage. *J. Nerv. Ment. Dis.*, **140**, 323–33 (1965)
159. Starr, B. J., Leibowitz, H. W., Lundy, R. M. Size constancy in catatonia. *Percept. Mot. Skills*, **26**, 747–52 (1968)
160. Steinmeyer, C. H. *The Relationship Between Schizophrenia and Attention in the Visual Field* (Doctoral dissertation, Univ. Indiana, Bloomington, 1968)
161. Stilson, D. W., Kopell, B. S., Vandenbergh, R., Downs, M. P. Perceptual recognition in the presence of noise by psychiatric patients. *J. Nerv. Ment. Dis.*, **142**, 235–47 (1966)
162. Storms, L. H., Broen, W. E., Jr., Levin, I. P. Verbal associative stability and commonality as a function of stress in schizophrenics, neurotics, and normals. *J. Consult. Psychol.*, **31**, 181–87 (1967)
163. Strauss, A. A., Lehtinen, L. E. *Psychopathology and Education of the Brain-Injured Child* (Grune & Stratton, N. Y., 1947)
164. Strauss, J. The clarification of schizophrenic concreteness by Piaget's tests. *Psychiatry*, **30**, 294–301 (1967)
165. Sullivan, H. S. The language of schizophrenia. *Language and Thought in Schizophrenia*, 4–16 (See Ref. 18)
166. True, J. E. Learning of abstract responses by process and reactive schizophrenic patients. *Psychol. Rept.*, **18**, 51–55 (1966)
167. Traub, A. C., Olson, R., Orbach, J., Cardone, S. S. Psychophysical studies of body-image. 3. Initial studies of disturbances in a chronic schizophrenic group. *Arch. Gen. Psychiat. (Chicago)*, **17**, 664–70 (1967)
168. Turnure, J., Zigler, E. Outer-directedness in the problem solving of normal and retarded children. *J. Abnorm. Soc. Psychol.*, **69**, 427–36 (1964)
169. Wachtel, P. L. Conceptions of broad and narrow attention. *Psychol. Bull.*, **68**, 417–29 (1967)
170. Wagner, E. E., Evans, K. A. A brief note on the comparison of two graphomotor techniques in diagnosing brain damage. *J. Project. Tech.*, **30**, 54 (1965)
171. Wagner, E. E., Schaff, J. E. Design reproduction with motor performance held constant. *J. Project. Tech.*, **32**, 395–96 (1968)
172. Watson, C. G. Relationships between certain personality variables and overinclusion. *J. Clin. Psychol.*, **23**, 327–30 (1967)
173. Watson, C. G. WAIS error types in schizophrenics and organics. *Psychol. Rept.*, **16**, 527–30 (1965)
174. Watson, C. G. WAIS profile patterns of hospitalized brain-damaged and schizophrenic patients. *J. Clin. Psychol.*, **21**, 294–95 (1965)
175. Watson, C. G., Thomas, R. W., Felling, J., Anderson, D. Differentiation of organics from schizophrenics with Reitan's sensory-perceptual disturbances tests. *Percept. Mot. Skills*, **26**, Suppl:1191–98 (1968)
176. Webb, W. W., Davis, D., Cromwell, R. L. Size estimation in schizophrenics as a function of thematic content of stimuli. *J. Nerv. Ment. Dis.*, **143**, 252–55 (1966)
177. Wells, J. O., Caldwell, W. E. Perception of the vertical as a function of affective stimuli and extraneous stimulation in schizophrenic and normal subjects. *Genet. Psychol. Monogr.*, **75**, 209–34 (1967)
178. Werry, J. S. Studies on the hyperactive child. IV. An empirical analysis of the minimal brain dysfunction syndrome. *Arch. Gen. Psychiat. (Chicago)*, **19**, 9–16 (1968)
179. Whitaker, L. C. An introduction to the Whitaker Index of Schizophrenic Thinking. *Dynamic Psychiatry (A Bilingual Journal)* (In press)
180. Williams, M. The measurement of memory in clinical practice. *Brit. J. Soc. Clin. Psychol.*, **7**, 19–34

(1968)

181. Wise, J. H. Performance of neurologically impaired children copying geometric designs with sticks. *Percept. Mot. Skills,* **26,** 763–72 (1968)

182. Wolfgang, A., Pishkin, V., Rosenbluh, E. S. Concept identification of schizophrenics as a function of social interaction, sex and task complexity. *J. Abnorm. Psychol.,* **73,** 336–42 (1968)

183. Yaker, H. M., Goldberg, B. R., Benson, H. A., Jr. Differential features of the brain injured and psychotic child. *Penn. Psychiat. Quart.,* **5,** 3–12 (1966)

184. Yates, A. J. Psychological deficit. *Ann. Rev. Psychol.,* **17,** 111–44 (1966)

185. Zahn, T. P., Rosenthal, D. Preparatory set in acute schizophrenia. *J. Nerv. Ment. Dis.,* **141,** 352–58 (1965)

186. Zimmerman, I. L. Residual effects of brain damage and five MMPI items. *J. Consult. Psychol.,* **29,** 394 (1965)

PSYCHOTHERAPEUTIC PROCESSES[1] 148

BY EUGENE T. GENDLIN
The University of Chicago, Chicago, Illinois

AND JOSEPH F. RYCHLAK
Purdue University, Lafayette, Indiana

Rather than imposing a prearranged order, we attempted to find the natural groupings of 1968, the very drift of 1968, reflecting its mood and preoccupations. But in some ways our effort resembles that of other years. For example, we wanted to welcome theoretical publications, yet we found very few of these. In the order of their relative frequency, it would be possible to organize the publications of this year under the following five rubrics: Techniques of Therapy; Patient or Therapist Variables; Methodological Research Studies; Outcome Studies; and Theoretical Topics. The chapter will be organized according to this rough rank-ordering of 1968 publication topics.

Before starting, it might be of interest to give the reader some indication of just what impression the year made on us, the "feel" of 1968 in psychotherapy so to speak. Both in practice and in research, several trends which at first seem unrelated do go to make up a distinct picture.

It seemed clear that the behavior therapies were again the dominant preoccupation of the psychotherapeutic profession, and (as in the last 2 or 3 years) these techniques are now clearly the primary stimulus for publications in our area.

Secondly, 1968 also continues the broad cross-orientational emphasis on interaction, relationship therapy, family therapy, groups, and community viewpoints. The place of intrapsychic concepts is largely taken by interactional concepts such as roles, games, interpersonal attitudes, family systems, community and institutional structures, and other interactional approaches to the human individual.

Both behavior therapies and interactional therapies showed great internal variety. The number of supposedly different approaches to therapy continues to increase. Along with this great number of "methods" there is also an increasing tendency to combine them. It is as though each specific little innovation is called a new method, but because of greater specificity such a new method is also more combinable with other "methods."

The reported therapy techniques appear to share three trends: (1) There is a giving up on intricate explanatory concepts in favor of a spirit that might be characterized as: "Never mind why the patient is as he is, let

[1] The authors would like to extend their appreciation to Paul J. Handal for his help in the literature coverage.

us change him." Hopefully, new theory will also result from this outlook, but perhaps it will come later and based on an accumulation of effective procedures. (2) The therapies written about tend to reject the older conception of maladjustment as a long-term illness needing long-term treatment and substitute instead a much briefer intervention which much less implies that the patient is seriously ill. Instead of deep dynamics, the therapies now tend to make the difficulty a mode of interaction, "game," or "behavior pattern" which is to be knocked out, not by years of treatment, but simply by taking up some other mode of interaction, game or behavior pattern. The given family is an instance of interaction type *X*. We invite or push them into doing type *Y* instead. Behavior therapy similarly says: "Never mind the complexities of why you do *X*. Do *Y* which is new to you." Thus these therapies all view maladjustment as abruptly changeable by new patterns of behavior and interaction, new patterns of actually functioning in new ways. (3) There were many methods in which the patient is given instructions in specific steps. Such specific instructions are only natural, of course, if methods tend to consist of abruptly imposed new modes of acting. One can and wants to reduce them to specific steps in order to get people to do them at a time when they cannot yet grasp them as more holistic attitudes or approaches to life and other people. (Once there are such specific steps, it is also natural that some can become "do-it-yourself kits" for the patient to use on his own.)

The combination of different "methods" is made more possible by the format of specific steps of instruction. Relaxation instructions, guided imagery, changing the consequence, these can be used by anyone in the context of any other aspects of therapy and interaction.

On the research side there appears to be a closely related trend toward questions such as: "Are the therapeutic effects different if procedure *X* is omitted than if it is included?" The trend, in practice, toward more specific procedures seems to lead to research on such more specific procedures.

At first, surveying the research studies, we were only dismayed at the rarity of good studies (although, in this respect, 1968 is not different from previous years). We were struck by the lack of control groups and properly blind ratings. We were also surprised by the rarity of straightforward outcome studies. Does it mean only that research is still poor? It means at least that. Gradually we came to think also that authors and editors have become less rigid about what a research must look like. We would welcome that side of current change as a trend toward a freedom to study exactly what one wants to study, without devoting most of one's economy of effort for the sake of the finished look. In our field, none of the needed research steps can at the same time also constitute truly finished research. Hence honesty regarding the limitation on conclusions is better than sacrificing significance for the sake of form. But finally we thought we saw more than just a group of studies in which the experimenters felt free to go after their own specific interests without providing the elaborate trappings of controlled outcome research. The largest groups of studies were those concerning specific procedures in therapy. They asked the question: "Does procedural aspect *X* make a difference or not?"

Perhaps we are seeing a trend toward greater specificity in research variables and objectives, related to what is occurring on the practice side of the field. If so, a second main group of studies also fits. These were the methodological studies. They did not set about answering a question, but rather attacked the problem: "How good or valid is a given sort of data for the purpose of answering a given sort of question?"

We will now consider studies under each of our five headings: techniques, patient-therapist variables, methodological issues, outcome, and theoretical matters. We will mention the trends just discussed wherever we perceive them. But, of course, we will mention many reports which do not fit these trends, thus enabling the reader to form his own impression of what is happening in the field.

TECHNIQUES OF THERAPY

Under the "technique" designation we shall include all those reports which have as their main emphasis the testing, presentation, further description, etc. of some approach to psychotherapy. There is often an element of improvement or outcome in these publications, but their main emphasis is on furthering our understanding of a given approach to therapy, and especially its parts, steps, or subprocesses.

An interesting group of studies in this subdivision dealt with the nature of desensitization therapy. What are its essential ingredients? Kahn & Baker (61) have put together a "do-it-yourself" kit with which the potential patient can arrange a hierarchy and practice relaxation with the help of a manual and Jacobson-like training records. Based on follow-up telephone contacts, it was found that subjects who used these kits with minimal therapist contact improved as much in managing their subclinical phobias as did those subjects who were put through desensitization by a therapist in the usual manner.

Using female college students with snake fears, Davison (33) investigated whether or not systematic desensitization required both a hierarchy of aversive stimuli and relaxation. He found that either alone is insufficient. Relaxation to irrelevant stimuli, and ascending a hierarchy of feared snake situations without relaxation, failed to result in subject improvement as compared to a "no treatment" control. When aversion and relaxation are properly used in combination, as called for in the original Wolpian technique, significant improvement in snake phobia reduction was demonstrated.

On the other hand, Zeisset (137) has shown that when psychotics are given muscle relaxation training and simply encouraged to use this technique in real life situations at their own discretion, there is as much improvement in self and rater reports of anxiety level as when an actual hierarchy is used. The difference in findings on the necessity of a hierarchy may be explained as a function of the degree of disturbance. Davison's subjects, who were not so pervasively anxious, had a very specific fear stimulus (snake); whereas Zeisset's subjects, who were far more disturbed, suffered from what might be termed a free-floating level of anxiety. But the difference may also be explained by the fact that Davison used either hierarchically arranged aversive stimuli or irrelevant ones. He did not test the need for a hierarchy if stimuli were relevant. The self-administering patients of Zeisset used relaxation in the presence of aversive situational stimuli.

If research studies of this specific nature can build on each other, the next step might be a test of the need for a hierarchical arrangement as such. Zeisset has shown that relaxation as such, regardless of when used, is not effective. As we know, Wolpe (136) does advocate relaxation periods during the regular daily routine, which would be tantamount to what Zeisset's patients were doing, but with the specification that it be done in the presence of aversive stimulus situations. Cooke (26) found that desensitization without relaxation was as effective in reducing fears of laboratory rats among female college students as was desensitization with relaxation. Wilson & Smith (134) have also shown that relaxation of a given hierarchy of situations is unnecessary for effective outcome in counterconditioning therapy. Their clients simply relaxed while discussing preoccupations whch occurred to them under instructions to "free associate" (in one case, under slight hypnosis).

The question of whether improvement in free-floating anxiety is really due to the muscle relaxation received a very balanced review from Gelder (44). He concludes that formal relaxation instruction is not nearly so important as the general reduction of arousal level and the repetition of imagined stimuli induced by the procedure. He notes that recent desensitization findings on the extremely anxious individual have been unrewarding, which would be contrary to Wolpe's (136) original hypothesis. Again, Zeisset's (137) study may explain the difference by the use of situational aversive stimuli. It is still an open question as to precisely how the desensitization technique actually works. When it does work, it would seem to be most effective in cases of specific phobia (44, 58).

One has to admire the scalpel-like efficiency with which the behavior therapist not only treats his patient's symptoms, but often succinctly puts his finger on the order of events which brings about the problem. These authors have a great capacity for translating their sensitivities into operational procedures. For example, Lazarus (68) tells us that the depressed individual learns to be chronically "blue" because this pattern has resulted in positive reinforcement by way of those friends who always sought to "cheer him up." Lazarus also uses an interesting variation on the "time heals all wounds" truism by taking his depressed patient forward in time under hypnosis. By hypnotically providing them with a broader time perspective into the future and back again to the painful present, he claims moderate to excellent success in eight of eleven depressed patients, even though only one session was necessary.

The self-control exerted by the patient in counter-conditioning technique is amusingly footnoted by Davison (32). After having a sadistic fantasy (torturing women) supposedly extinguished to the point where it could no longer excite the male patient, Davison learned much later that the patient purposively decided to return to his masturbatory fantasy 6 months after treatment had ended initially. He apparently did so, enjoyed the sadistic interlude for a predetermined length of time, and then used the therapist's aversive tactic (imagining drinking a hot urine and fecal-matter soup while viewing a woman being tortured) as well as his positive tactic (masturbating to *Playboy* pictures) to successfully re-extinguish the more aberrant obsession. As demonstrated in this case history, the use of aversive techniques seems to be most effective when used in conjunction with other, positive procedures. Marks (78), in his work with tranvestites, found that shock applied to deviant fantasy behavior repressed this aberrant pattern, but it did not in itself encourage the more appropriate, heterosexual alternative to emerge in all cases. One must build on the positive side as he represses or extinguishes on the negative.

Occasionally one wonders if the hierarchy is properly named. For example, in one instance Lazarus (67) used relaxation to a hierarchy of "shame at being seen with an erection" in a male who used pseudonecrophiliac fantasies in masturbation. A hierarchy of more (that is, dead) to less (unconscious, then distracted, etc.) potentially accepting females was constructed in order to desensitize the feeling of shame this young men had in approaching the opposite sex with an erection. After five sessions he succeeded in having sexual relations with his girl friend. Even though some case history material is presented to convince the reader—as it presumably had the patient—that this young man did indeed fear being shamed by women over having an erection, one could also have viewed this in another light. That is, since the patient lacked shame in fantasying sexual relations with a dead woman, an unconscious woman, a drunken woman, and a distracted prostitute, could not the actual hierarchy have been "sexual contact with women of varying levels of consciousness, willingness, or vulnerability" rather than "sex along an array of shameful situations?" The fact that the patient was "cured," just as he is in psychoanalytical case histories, is not proof of the clinical insight settled upon. Since operational procedures on bodily felt anxiety and relaxation are used, the issue of naming or conceptualizing may be moot. In forming a hierarchy, however, that question does enter and brings along the ills of supposedly discarded unexamined theory and conceptual categories.

In two well-done studies on the effectiveness of contingent reinforcement to alter a subject's response, Ince (59) manipulated the number of first-person references made by female undergraduates, and Atthowe &

Krasner (5) present preliminary data on a token economy established in a chronic psychiatric ward. Both investigations used a "base rate and variation" tactic to make their point and once again convince us that people surely do respond to verbal and/or material reinforcements. The more subtle issue which grows out of the line of research followed by Dulany (35) and DeNike & Spielberger (34) these days is: "How much of this is a matter of conditioning or control, and how much of this is a matter of problem solution and cooperation on the part of a subject?" [see Holmes (56)]. We are back to the issue of what is happening and unfortunately not too much is being done to resolve some of these more thorny questions. For those readers who would like an extensive literature review of behavioral modification techniques with children, 1968 was a good year. Ryan & Watson (104) focused specifically on frustrative nonreward; Gelfand & Hartman (45) evaluated the research methodologies in such studies; and Leff (70) confined his review to behavior modification in childhood psychoses. The need for clearer understanding of subject change is emphasized in these reviews. One of the persistent problems (or advantages) stems from the fact that unrewarded behaviors change concomitantly with rewarded behaviors, and, according to Leff (70), this is not precisely a "generalization" of behavior. His discussion is well worth reading. We will return to this question several times in this review.

Whatever the shortcomings in theoretical explanations may be, no sensible person can argue with the fact that behavior therapies are clinically effective, and the old bugaboo about a symptom substitution is probably greatly overstated. No well-documented research has been presented to date which would support a symptom substitution hypothesis (44, 94). Cahoon (19) takes up the problem of symptom substitution in detail, and traces the difficulty between the behavioral and dynamic camps on this matter to their conflicting terminology and consequent theoretical outlooks.

The role of verbal behavior, or what used to be called "awareness" continues to remain a question mark for the critical reader of behavioral studies. For example, although it was not a specific goal of theirs, Wahler & Pollio (129) found that along with behavioral changes in an 8-year-old patient seen for about two dozen 20-min sessions, there were significant changes in the semantic values of words used by the boy as therapy progressed. Both the parents and the therapist reinforced "independent" behaviors and not specific verbal contents, yet the contents changed values in the direction one would expect if the child were "aware" of the changes taking place in his behavior. The authors admit that if the behavior had changed without the verbal changes, this would be a clear victory for the behaviorist position.

Using a sophisticated design which included random assignment of schizophrenic subjects to either a "reinforcement" or a "relationship" therapy condition, as well as a switchover phenomenon over time, Marks, Sonoda & Schalock (79) found virtually no difference between conditions. Considered from the angle of finances, however, the reinforcement approach proved the more economical approach.

One is impressed by the number of reports of what used to be called the case history variety, with one or more "subjects" (the term sometimes used to describe a patient) under special laboratory-like investigation. There is almost a "déjà vu" experience in reading these accounts, for they seem a rephrase of the more classical case histories of the psychoanalysts. It would be impossible to include every one of these individual case presentations in a review of this nature.

The analysts, in turn, seem to be writing fewer of these case history reports for publication, but this impression may simply be due to the great influx of reading matter in general for psychotherapists these days. There is a kind of role-reversal in all of this, with the difference being that earlier one came away with a—skeptical or satisfied—reaction of "aha," whereas now he has a more practical "how to" feeling, which in some ways is not so intellectually gratifying, although the remarkable variations on the behavioral technique do acquire a fascination akin to our earlier satisfaction with the clinical insight.

Behavior therapy reports show a trend toward combining specific procedures which could occur in the context of various approaches. Following are some examples, both of such case reports and of discussions of combinations.

Lazarus (69) asks: "Is relaxation necessarily the best antidote for anxiety? Would therapy not be expedited by combining relaxation with other anti-anxiety responses? Can 'cognitive variables' play a specific role in desensitization therapy? Does verbal communication (despite its disrupting effect on deep relaxation) have advantages over finger signals for anxiety?" Finding that "certain individuals find relaxation ineffective in combating anxiety," Lazarus specifies muscular activity and emotive imagery as two other specific procedures. He had the patient select a "personal relaxing image" (a sunny beach, a warm bath) and add it to the usual relaxation instructions. Three patients using this addition showed fewer avoidance responses and relaxed in a third of the time needed by three other patients not using the additional image in their relaxation.

Lazarus (69) next compared two patients using only relaxation to combat "fears of criticism and rejection" with two patients who "were instructed to imagine handling the situation assertively while deeply relaxed." He reported the latter two patients more rapidly improved.

In another of these illuminating rapid-fire clinical studies, Lazarus (69) found that "five out of six individuals reported a newfound capacity to handle critical onslaughts" when they used his "advice" to ask the critic to define his terms and to identify the situations he means to refer to. Lazarus had first thought of this as a "fatuous placebo procedure," but he now views the three cited techniques as "other anxiety-inhibiting responses" to be added to relaxation. In addition, he reports "cognitive desensitization" (having "cardiac neurotics" read about benign conditions which can cause chest pains).

During desensitization, Lazarus now uses verbal communication. He used to have patients give finger signals when they felt anxious, but he finds these disruptive and not sufficiently informative.

> The patient may not be picturing the scenes . . . it is wasteful to be told after 20 or 30 min that the patient was unable to visualize the scenes clearly that day, or that he had experienced no anxiety (or too much anxiety) because he was picturing the scenes incorrectly. For these reasons, immediate dialogue after each scene is recommended.

He found the level of relaxation impaired by talking, but capable of being reinstated easily. By this procedure, "the therapist has immediate information about the efficacy of the procedure and can modify each scene according to the patient's successive requirements."

It is clear in these "studies" that specific procedural aspects are being dealt with, and that many aspects of psychotherapy are re-entering behavior therapy as specific additions. The resulting method may not be too different a combination of procedures than one might find where behavior therapy and guided imagery has been added to some psychotherapy.

D'Alessio (29) reports a case combining behavior therapy and psychotherapy techniques in a way that might exemplify a great many case reports which do something of the sort. After eight interviews of psychotherapy on past and present difficulties, he began using systematic desensitization in the latter part of each session, using an orthodox hierarchy. Reports of insight and conflict resolution between sessions and successful working through of "resistance" during sessions continues as a result of the concurrent use of the two methods. Evidently, one way of combining these methods is simply to use them both, side by side.

In an excellent, careful study using one patient, Levin et al. (71) graphed MMPI, Sentence Completion, Rorschach, and TAT scores at pre-therapy, post-therapy, and follow-up. The authors form no conclusions about which therapeutic technique made for the positive finding of change. In addition to behavioral methods, they also used a psychotherapeutic one. Their combining of techniques was in the interest of "a flexible orientation to behavior therapy in order to deal with problems unique to the individual patient." A systematic desensitization hierarchy was used simultaneously with avoidance conditioning. Desensitization was used on the patient's anxiety toward women, while avoidance was used on homosexual tendencies. Thus old patterns were avoidance conditioned while the anxiety in the path of new patterns was desensitized. In addition, the patient was instructed to practice outside the sessions, once a given hierarchy was finished. Whatever anxiety-arousing incidents he reported were then included in the next week's hierarchy. Similarly, the avoidance-conditioning procedure was guided by the patient's reports, as his reported fantasies were used to make pictures presented as slides, with an electric shock the patient could avoid if he rang a bell and said "no" within 10 sec of the first appearance of a slide. (Delay and nonreinforcement trials were also used.) In addition, when the patient showed an "uncharacteristically emotional manner" in one session, he was given three sessions of traditional psychotherapy. Again we note the trend toward combining specific procedures from various orientations. A striking advantage that this study shows clearly for such combinations can be the greater realism and humaneness with which the patient is treated when various methods, and the details in each, are guided by and adjusted to his responses. (This is in sharp contrast to single methods, especially those in which the therapist cannot know what is happening in the patient.) As Lazarus also pointed out, such constant attuning of method to immediate events in a session is likely to improve the efficacy of any procedure.

Widening of theoretical views appears to occur simultaneously with the combination of techniques. Carlin & Armstrong (23), using money tokens as rewards and penalties in a group play technique, comment that the rewards "stimulated behaviors in the first place. But the children genuinely enjoyed the . . . experiences which ensued and . . . these interpersonal gratifications came to outweigh the benefits of monetary reward." The authors see this as an answer to the criticism that token systems breed conformity and psychopathy. The authors urge "respect for the intrinsic value of and potential gratifications inherent in interpersonal relationships."

Colligan & Bellamy (25), a male-female team, successfully obtained and measured language development, eye contact, attention span, and peer interaction in an autistic child. Using both methods, they report that during the second year "the importance of relationship therapy increased although operant techniques were continued." Again, here "individually tailored contingencies" were necessary, and operant techniques succeeded only where the authors were able to apply them "to a specific behavior in a controlled setting." Lack of transfer was a problem until milieu and parental participation were worked on, and "individual therapy sessions" were used to "shape cognitive and verbal behaviors which would be important for . . . adaption to the regular public school."

Bank (7) used operant behavior modification with a boy who had never walked. He also discusses "intrinsic reinforcement." He means "the feedback provided to the patient through the mere performance of the response for its own sake. . . . Anyone who has observed a toddler learning to walk has been impressed with the new sense of autonomy, joy, and mastery that the infant receives from the simple performance of the walking response." Bank's discussion also illustrates the problem we mentioned earlier: when behavior therapists call a given problem by some name, do they need—and do they unintentionally make contact with—the wider concepts of the field of personality and interpersonal relations which they otherwise ignore? Bank, writing about his child patient, asks:

> What did Billy learn? . . . He learned a set of neuromuscular coordinations (responses) leading to walking. But he had to learn much more than responses . . . he had to learn . . . that he was not as helpless as he and others had believed . . . that he could have more choice and control over what happened to him . . . walking had to become an internalized and general strategy that could

be applied in a variety of situations. The question of response learning versus internalization of strategies deserves more attention from behavior therapists because we are not interested in the mere acquisition of discrete responses.

This problem of developing broad and complex learnings rather than single behaviors is receiving considerable attention and seems to be leading to exciting results. Bear (9) reports new advances on programming "similarity" as a reinforcer. This work, in which retarded children learn to imitate—i.e., learn to learn large classes of behavior—has been going on since 1964. Salzinger (108) offers an excellent analysis of six different aspects of complexity in shaped behaviors. If a response such as "I am happy" is reinforced, there is "an increase in frequency of occurrence of other members of that class of self-referred effect, like 'I am sad,' 'I am angry.' " Reinforcing a given word may increase the frequency of a whole sentence, not just that word. Conditioning a child " to play next to other children places him in a situation where he can make a large group of new responses which will be positively reinforced by the other children."

Lovaas (73) concentrates "on facilitating the schizophrenic child's acquisition of social reinforcers, rather than on building behaviors." The eleven children began with "a virtual absence of response to social stimuli . . . and behaved as if they were blind and deaf." Neither affection nor pairing personal response with food delivery had any effect, because

> the child . . . did not attend to, or otherwise respond to our behavior. These . . . children fail to attend to social (or almost any external) stimuli to a profound degree. In . . . the procedure which we developed . . . the child was 'forced' to respond (hence, to attend) to the social stimulus. That is, the social stimulus was first established as discriminative for primary reinforcement . . . we electrified the floor on which the children stood, and terminated the painful shock contingent upon their seeking the company of the attending adults. We . . . observed not only a change in a particular response which was shaped, but change in a larger class . . . the increase in the children's physical contact with attending adults. (During shock avoidance) the children appear happy and . . . this was the first time these children had given social smiles.

Lovaas also reports teaching play behavior and then using opportunities for this behavior as a reinforcer in itself. Here again is the theme that some behaviors "maintain themselves without apparent extrinsic reinforcement," as Lovaas puts it. He relies "very heavily on play behavior as reinforcement for other behaviors." The considerable success of this program is impressive.

We may summarize the wider meaning of the developments in behavior therapy. It used to be a common criticism of behavior therapy that it ignored the interpersonal relationship, both its inevitable existence in any therapy and its possible major usefulness. As the preceding examples show, this is no longer true. Not only are behavior therapists increasingly using relationship therapy of one kind or another, but also in other ways they are altering that aspect of their procedures which used to seem less than human to their critics. As we saw, the method can be adjusted to the patient moment by moment. Goldiamond & Dyrud (50) have discarded the usual differential reinforcement in favor of giving positive reinforcement all the time for all behavior, only giving distinctly more for desired behavior. In a study of psychoanalytic interviews, they found that "there is very little direct use of reinforcement . . . for shaping purposes." Comparing the implicit "program" of psychotherapy to programmed instruction, they say:

> The differential reinforcement does not teach Russian. It is the sequence of Russian frames and behavior required which do. The reinforcement does maintain the behavior through the program, however . . . Accordingly, much of the verbal conditioning research with nods and 'uh-huhs' may be beside the point when it assumes that such reinforcers change behavior therapeutically. They merely keep the patient talking and maintain the behavior of going through the implicit program . . . borne by the content of the transactions.

Finally, much is being done about the problem of values, which for so long behavior therapists wanted to ignore: who determines what shall be changed in whom and toward what?

Let us now look at other variants, not called behavior therapy, but which are similar techniques for engendering a more than verbal process in the individual, and, like desensitization, are done in the office and in silence.

Relaxation is not usually called "hypnosis," nor are instructions called "suggestions," but again, if the vocabulary is translated, hypnotherapy belongs to this family of techniques. Ritchie (97) reports such a case. Using the orthodox psychoanalytic theory of exhibitionism, he successfully instructed a patient to touch his penis and reassure himself of its existence whenever he felt the urge to exhibit himself. The practice of hypnotherapy is also reviewed and carefully delineated by Klemperer (64).

Horowitz (57) discusses various clinically observed maneuvers by the patient to use visual imagery as a defense. For example, as a compromise between resistance and compliance to the analyst's instruction, the patient may report highly immature, regressive images, or there may be punitive fantasies forthcoming as if in response to a superego prompting. Often the psychological import of a preverbal though highly meaningful image is lost to the patient in his attempt to translate the sensory impression into lexical units (words).

Although called "behavior therapy," the reports reviewed (and the large number of reports they represent here) include different varieties: desensitization has little but theory in common with operant conditioning and shaping, and there are many further differences in each. Desensitization itself appears quite similar to Jungian "guided daydream" techniques, "implosive therapy," and many others which we might call instruction methods which instruct the patient in the office, in silence, to engage in a nonverbal therapeutic process.

A somewhat different variant of this group is Gendlin's (49) "experiential focusing." The patient is asked to stop talking or thinking "at himself."

Five steps of instruction lead the patient first to physically sense "all of the problem" (the whole thing comes to him physically, like a dull thud, when he lets it) and then to "let a specific feeling come up." (The patient then pays attention to this specific feeling and is told to "let it do whatever it does.") Words and images are supposed to be ignored, unless as they form there is some "experiential effect" which is bodily experienced, leading to physically felt relief and a shift in the way the problem is felt and verbalized. Galvanic skin response (GSR) shows relaxation even when (reportedly) threatening material is focused upon. A questionnaire given afterwards showed "focusing ability" correlating with some of Cattell's factors. The procedure for deepening therapy was devised because earlier research showed that failure was predictable from early interviews of patients whose "experiential level" is low (when measured with the Experiencing Scale from tape-recorded interviews). The focusing procedure and its experiential effects resemble desensitization and its intensification, content flow, and subsequent extinction of anxiety.

The variety of instruction methods for a more than verbal therapeutic process (a bodily process) might lead one to establish instruction procedures as one major dimension of the therapies being reported.

Another, perhaps the other, major dimension is interaction and interactive feedback, already cited above in the discussion of a number of behavior therapies. Here is one more: In addition to teaching a mother the principles of behavior modification, Bernal et al. (14) had the woman observe on video tape her interactions with a "brat" son. It was found that this third person objectivity aided significantly in providing the mother with an objective approach to the behavioral modification of the boy's abusive behavior, which changed dramatically after a few weeks of therapy. We surmise that before the age of television, grandmothers served this function. Video feedback was also reported upon by Stoller (120) and by Rogers (99) , both of whom emphasize the patient's greater ability to change behavior patterns once he has observed himself in them on television. Danet (30) reviews a number of studies of videotape playback as a therapeutic tool. Thus, again, here is a technique used in the context of a variety of approaches.

Another innovation is "symptom scheduling" (86), doing a symptom on purpose at preselected junctures of situations during the day. Again, this is reported to develop control and the capacity not to engage in it.

A few family therapy and interactional therapy reports may here represent the gamut of this type. Zweben & Miller (140) formulated Virginia Satir's method in terms of four roles one may play: concerned only with self, only with other, with neither, or finally, optimally, with both. By this simple scheme (and simple schemes are much in vogue for their workability in action) patients can be made to role-play exaggeratedly their own usual mode and try out other modes. In answer to "Let's go to the beach" we get: (concerned with self only) "You are just the type of person who would want to go to the beach when I have such a splitting headache"; (concerned with others only) "Anything you would like to do, dear"; (neither) "I wonder if mother has gotten away this year." The good version is to commit oneself and include the other person. "Playing" at these roles reportedly induces much experiencing of affects usually had helplessly in real situations, as well as much laughter. Again here is the attempt to work concretely with "both experience and intellect" instead of only with the latter.

For those readers who would like a rather workmanlike job of presenting "how to do" family therapy, we would recommend a paper by Ackerman & Behrens (1). This seems to be a development related to the fact that psychotherapy—especially group—is being extended to all levels of the social strata [Scheidlinger (109)]. Family therapy as a form of group therapy seems well suited to work with the lower social classes because of their very practical and thorough approach to problems. It is therefore not surprising to find this tactic being adapted to work with lower-class groups. Sadock, Newman & Normand (106) and Sager et al. (107) give some rules of thumb on how they engage lower-class groups in both family therapy and other group therapies. The lower-class patient wants immediate help, and a rather effective tactic has been the use of a walk-in clinic, where a commitment for no more than 10 contacts is made. Roughly 75 per cent of the lower-class patients approached eventually accepted family therapy out of a walk-in referral, just as long as they were not made to feel "pushed" into it (107). Very often a patient from this lower (deprived) stratum will not complete 10 sessions of group therapy, particularly if some of his most pressing problems quickly improve (106). One is impressed by these attempts to modify therapeutic techniques to meet the needs of the patient, rather than vice versa; it has taken some time for this attitude to develop and we welcome it.

A family therapy case report by Zuk (139) zeroes in on the specific problem of when the family therapist should take sides. The pattern of playing "court" by appealing to the therapist is usually eschewed, and taking sides is thought to engender it. Nevertheless, in this case, Zuk interceded, but specifically to "relabel" the behavior of the 9-year-old son, thereby forcing into the light both the way it functioned in an implicit agreement between mother and son, and enabling the boy to carry that behavior further in a more developed and healthy way. The case and method are another example of interrupting extant patterns of family interaction and engendering a new pattern. The "identified patient" is only the one in whom the family system disturbance manifests itself most visibly (138).

Family therapy and the interactional view generally poses some mysteries, or resolves them, as one may view it. Beebe (11) reports spontaneous remissions of acute psychosis in a number of instances when the patient was made to call home long distance. (His patients are returned seamen who became psychotic on the voyage, the assumption being that the phone call alters the relationship situation in which the psychosis developed.) Fagan (38) reports inversely that an individual patient may find a puzzling setback traceable to a long distance call from mother several days ago. Either way, the lesson is that in working with individual pathology, one must take account of the invisible significant other parties with whom pathology develops. The pathology is "at them," so to speak, and some of these therapies bring them literally into the treatment.

Normal and abnormal four-member families were compared by Ferreira & Winter (40). During decision-making, abnormal families had significantly fewer immediate agreements, longer average discussion times than those of normal families, and more often had members whose first choice was not the one arrived at by the family. The study gives something of the quality of family systems.

These trends are well illustrated in the following: Langsley, et al. (65) studied 75 families who came requesting hospitalization of a family member. The families were seen at once; the request for hospitalization was refused; immediate help was promised; absent family members were called in from home, work, or school; history of the crisis was obtained; interactional aspects of the crisis were stressed; scapegoating of one member by labeling him "mentally ill" was blocked; and regression was discouraged. Tensions were reduced by specific advice and support. Drugs were used for symptom relief in any of the family members. Tasks were assigned for resolving the crisis and returning each member to functioning. With this approach, symptom relief occurred within hours or days. Conflicts in role assignments could then be negotiated (as is usual in family therapy). Hospitalization was avoided in 81 per cent of the cases. (A 6-month follow-up period has been covered so far.) The short-term nature of the treatment was stressed, as was the service team's continuing availability for any subsequent crisis.

Group therapy and the explosion of encounter groups, marathons, sensitivity groups, T Groups, or brainstorming groups cannot be discussed here. Again there are "do-it-yourself" kits (48) and an emphasis on the fact that past and intrapsychic material is at least not the only or preferred focus, though quite often replaced with perhaps too exclusive a focus on present interaction in the group and on present situational problems.

The community emphasis similarly alters and rearranges treatment to be briefer (10 interviews, often less) and more immediately responsive (walk-in clinic), instead of the heavy long-term commitment to therapy and the sick role.

The professional is altering his service pattern (crisis, walk-in) as he is also becoming less essential, as college students (17, 76) and other nonprofessionals do therapy. Perhaps the future of the fully trained professional will be in training, supervising, and trouble-shooting very large numbers of nonprofessionals and community-oriented new service personnel. There is a marked trend toward including new populations, both as servers and as served.

The need to bring mental health services to the lower-class population was emphasized by Myers & Bean (84) in a follow-up study on the original group of patients studied by Hollingshead and Redlich 10 years ago. Myers

& Bean found most of these patients still in the hospital, but this was most true of the lower-class patients. Those patients who received psychotherapy were five times as likely to have been discharged as those who did not. But the finding is hardly an index of the effectiveness of psychotherapy, since it was more often given to middle-class patients, and these were more likely to be discharged anyway, at least intermittently. There are not the resources necessary to keep lower-class patients out of the hospital.

In a related study, Schmidt, Smart & Moss (111) found treatment for alcoholics differing according to economic class, but the descriptive delineation of the cases also differed according to class. Psychotherapy in communist countries seems to share the same trends, with community psychology and emphasis on personal relationships somewhat older there than here (63).

The broad literature on community psychology cannot be discussed here, but should be viewed akin to the trend toward therapeutic methods in which patients are helped to function in new ways, rather than being treated for their intrapsychic, old ways. Crisis and suicide prevention patterns (39) also illustrate the trend toward briefer intervention, with an accent on current functioning (and the changes abruptly brought about in these cases). There was an effort at rapprochement between psychotherapy, group, and community emphases (47, 95) and an explosion of reports on sub- or nonprofessionals. In one of the few research studies in this area, Stollak (119) trained 16 college undergraduates in client-centered play therapy. He found "reflection of content" and "clarification of feeling" responses increased in the first five sessions. On the part of the children, "expression of negative feeling" and "leadership" behaviors increased.

In what was probably the most stimulating group of papers on professional and/or training issues, Carkhuff, Kratochvil & Friel (22) reported on the graduate clinical programs of two APA approved northeastern universities heavily dominated by behavioristic and psychoanalytic faculties. Thirty-two clinical and nonclinical students in the first and fourth graduate years were studied cross-sectionally (university A), and then a first and second graduate year longitudinal study (test-retest) of 14 clinical students was undertaken (university B).

All subjects were asked to role-play a counselor in a 45-min interview, using well-trained "counselees" as coparticipants. Following this interview, all subjects listened to a tape which contained 16 segments of patient-counselor interactions (rated independently by trained raters for empathy and genuineness). Subjects were asked to rate these excerpts on these variables, and in turn expert raters were given excerpts to score from the subject's own role-playing situation. Nine professors in one of the universities also were put through this procedure.

These authors found that although first-year clinical students functioned at higher levels on these variables than nonclinical students, the difference in the fourth year was insignificant. In other words, graduate education could not even sustain the advantage which clinical students brought with them to graduate school, much less improve on it. In the longitudinal study (university B), by the second graduate year their scores on retest were actually lower than initially. The levels on these variables for the nine professors was below average.

Carkhuff (21) went on to review the literature on the entire problem of lay versus professional counselors. In the tradition of Carl Rogers' (100, 101) 20-year-old polemic, Carkhuff argues from a number of studies that the patients of lay counselors do as well or better than the patients of professional counselors. He feels that probably the reason so many of the "untreated" control groups in our studies improve is because these patients seek out talented nonprofessional counselors with whom to relate and work through problems. Carkhuff summarizes: ". . . the direct implication is that the main effects of graduate training are related to the development of discriminators, rather than communicators." Schmidt's (110) rebuttal to Carkhuff calls for research on outcome. One might fault Carkhuff's argument as being based on the views and variables of merely one approach to this thing called psychotherapy. That is, if discriminators can in fact "manipulate" people to health and happiness without tender interpersonal relations of empathy and genuineness, then no amount of downgrading because of a lack of these characteristics in role played or real interviews can counter the modern trend of graduate education. But we do applaud such efforts to show us what sort of professional person we are now selecting and turning out.

Continuing on the theme of the abilities of nonprofessionals, Ellsworth et al. (36) report finding that ratings of hospitalized patients by family members are of equal reliability and validity with those of a professional staff member. The data were used in assessing treatment outcomes for 178 male veterans diagnosed as schizophrenics. Five rating scales were scored on 20 dimensions of adjustment at four different points over a 3-year period. Ratings were made by the patients, relatives, psychiatric aides, and professional staff of the hospital. Split-half and 10-day test-retest reliabilities from .70 through .90 were comparable across all raters, so that patients and relatives were just as reliable in their ratings as the professional group. Validity correlations between adjustment and subsequent length of stay for hospitalized residents did not turn out quite so positively, with reliability falling in the .20 to .40 range. Here again, relatives' ratings of community adjustment predicted subsequent hospital adjustment as well as staff ratings made at the time of first admission. Patients' ratings of their symptoms and adjustment upon admission had little demonstrative validity in predicting the length of hospitalization. Interesting side findings in this study were that independent and socially assertive patients in the community tend to make a poor hospital adjustment.

Many other studies also report descriptively, or by today's crude criteria, that undergraduates, mothers, and others practice and evaluate as well as highly trained psychologists. Are subprofessionals and new "mental health professionals" a "threat" to the status of fully educated psychotherapists? We think not. Supervisory and intellectual leadership will be needed more than ever, and in more places and programs.

Graduate psychology departments cannot, of course, aim to meet the gigantic need for practitioners. Should they give up the attempt to train their students in practice? In any case, the need for practitioners is one that will be filled in other ways. Many types of subprofessionals and new "mental health professionals" are now being created. If extant federal plans are realized, these will very greatly increase in numbers, and there will be a new professionalized "mental health" field of its own. Hopefully, psychologists will not be excluded from this new mental health profession now in formation. Psychologists are now excluded, for example, from the already formed professions of social work and education. Although psychologists once could and did work in these fields, today they cannot. These fields now have educational and professional requirements of their own. Without the genuine experience of practice, psychologists cannot formulate significant concepts and hypotheses relevant to practice. (Perhaps this accounts for the paucity of research and thought relevant to these practical fields already closed off, and the corresponding absence of many important questions in the psychology of the last five decades.) If psychologists again work themselves out of a role in still another practice profession, the new mental health field will lack just those who could eventually advance a science that would be relevant to it. The growth of new types of professionals can therefore be viewed as an urgent opportunity for psychologists, if some of them can be trained to take a leading part. Rather than viewing practice as something enough others will do, we might view these others as at last making possible the ideal of a clinically experienced psychologist who can have a properly psychological and intellectual role in a bigger context. This is possible if he is genuinely trained in, and can continue to be permitted to practice in therapeutic processes.

The findings which imply that people do as well or better at practice after a short training period as university trained psychologists could be read to mean that it is eminently possible and economical to give future researchers and thinkers on human behavior the necessary practice training which would enable them to be part of the new field of mental health practice.

We turn now to other research studies which are relevant to settings outside the consulting room, such as hospitals, communities, etc., and relevant to populations other than office patients, such as the aged, lower-class people, adolescents, and others. Again, these studies usually exemplify briefer and more interactionally and situationally oriented therapy methods.

Speer et al. (118) find that lower-class families attending a child guidance clinic are less likely to meet individual appointments than are middle-class families, but this is primarily due to the fathers and siblings who do not participate as well as mothers. The lower-class father seemed a particular problem in this study, for he was not only much older than his wife and comparably older than his middle-class counterpart, but he was also very low in educational level. In light of this, it is interesting to note that middle-class families were more likely to bring their oldest (or only) child as patient, whereas in the lower-class sample it was the youngest child who was most likely to appear as the patient referred.

Pittman, Langsley & DeYoung (96) clinically examined 11 cases of work phobia. Basing their conclusion on case history material informally gathered, the authors suggest that work phobia is essentially a "grown-up" school phobia now manifesting itself on a mother surrogate. Childhood school phobia was found in the history of 9 of these 11 cases. The majority of these men were said to be highly dependent upon wives who in turn had great maternal needs. The wives entered into the disturbance by unconsciously encouraging the panic reactions regarding work. These authors apparently achieved successful results by encouraging the wife to insist that her husband go back to the job and stay there. Again, the preferred mode of "treatment" is brief crisis intervention, encouraging the women to facilitate separating for the day, and the man's "rapid return" to work. It is an emphasis on return to functioning, not treatment without functioning.

Blanco & Akabas (15) not only want to meet their lower class client's needs, they advocate going out to the factory site and there recruiting potential cases for physical/psychological (familial or personal) therapy. It was found that these Italian, Puerto Rican, and related Spanish speaking lower-class patients were little concerned about confidentiality, and many of them discussed their difficulties openly right on the plant floor. Turner (127) describes a psychoanalytically oriented psychiatric child guidance procedure which is typified by an environmental manipulation of the child's life circumstances after an initial study of the family stressing analytical theoretical insights. Slivkin & Bernstein (117) report on an approach to group therapy with mental retardates (IQs of 40 to 70), who spoke remarkably openly about their preoccupations and seemed most intent on stressing the fact that they were "slow, but not crazy." The main aim of this therapy is to encourage verbalization rather than acting out, and a modicum of (unmeasured) success is claimed.

Cowen, Leibowitz & Leibowitz (27) report on an experimental therapy approach in which six elderly men and women recruited for modest pay from a "golden age club" served as mental health aides with primary grade children. After brief training, each aide worked for 3 half-days a week in a nearby public school. First through third grade teachers were invited to refer children whom they felt might profit from an individualized contact with an interested adult. Consultation with graduate students in clinical psychology and other professionals was provided the aides. In all, 25 children were seen with anywhere from 4 to 15 hours of contact per child. Subsequent teacher ratings suggested that the children as a group (there were no controls) did benefit from this subprofessional contact.

Turning now to some technique variations with hospitalized patients, Ludwig (74) describes a remarkably thorough milieu therapy, which reads like a grand analogue to all of those social forces which have moved men down through history. Drawing on the tactic of shaman or faith healer, this global approach includes group meetings in which patients are stirred up emotionally. Patients are rated regularly, based on their performance in ward duties, and a "class system" of prerogatives is worked out. If a patient reaches the top class (seventh), he has the added privilege of rating his peers, which is a source of personal status and achievement. Moral suasion is adapted to the hospital milieu, so that certain rule infractions (elopement, sexual activities) are designated "mortal sins" while others (breaking a privilege restriction) are termed "venial sins." Using a slightly questionable "subject as his own control" research tactic—rather than, e.g., a double blind rating procedure—Ludwig finds that significant improvement in ward behavior (via ratings and ward incidents over 10 weeks) results when this regime is followed. Finally, Grinspoon, Ewalt & Shader (51) find that individual (analytically oriented) psychotherapy with institutionalized male schizophrenics over a 2-year period was not effective in reducing symptoms unless this insight therapy was accompanied by regular doses of the drug phenothiazine.

Müller-Hegeman (83) describes a rational approach to therapy stressing the setting of time limits and the use of hypnotic measures. An interesting approach to the handling of a hospitalized suicidal patient is presented by Stone & Shein (121). Essentially, the tactic is a reality oriented one in which the therapist begins with the assumption that a patient has considered the possibility of suicide. The therapist informs the patient that this is not unusual, that it is part of being ill, and he then tries to get the patient to accept his aggressive impulses, expressing them outwardly rather than inwardly in self-destructive fashion.

Harter & Zigler (53) report that mentally retarded children in an institution will respond more readily to the verbal reinforcements of an adult, and continue to put marbles in holes, than they will respond to the verbal reinforcements of a peer-aged child. However, exactly the opposite is found for noninstitutionalized mental retardates. Parsons & Parker (93) used role-play tape recordings of a depressed, hostile, and neutral patient, and then had psychiatrists, medical students, and college undergraduates respond as therapist in the Struppian manner of "what would you say next?" Multiple choice alternatives were given to all subjects, who also made ratings on prognosis and patient likeability. It was found that everyone rated the patient they liked best as having the best prognosis. Everyone also proved least directive with the neutral case and most directive with the hostile patient. The psychiatrists were less directive than the other two groups of subjects, who did not differ from one another on this dimension. Although Ludwig

(75) found a significant correlation between therapists' initial ratings of patient likeability and prognosis estimates, he failed to find that this actually did influence the eventual outcome in subsequent therapy.

PATIENT AND THERAPIST VARIABLES

We turn now to a series of researches which do not concern specified techniques but study variables of the patient, or the therapists, which are of potential importance to psychotherapy. These may be demographic variables, test measures, attitudes manifested during psychotherapy, or other variables. The focus is on the "independent" rather than "dependent" variables of an experimental investigation.

For example, what are the demographic characteristics of psychoanalytic patients? Due to a lack of cooperation from the Baltimore Psychoanalytic Institute, Weintraub & Aronson (3, 131) found it necessary to abandon earlier hopes to sample the Baltimore area and instead called on a number of their psychoanalyst friends practicing in several east coast communities, most of whom were members of the American Psychoanalytic Association. Hence, we have here a self-selected sample of 30 psychoanalysts who reported questionnaire data on 144 patients seen during the year September 1, 1962, to August 31, 1963. Even so, the findings are important and meet the expectations of many concerning the type of person who goes into psychoanalysis.

Roughly 63 per cent of the 144 patients were male, all were white, and over 50 per cent were in their fourth decade of life; there were only 4 per cent under age 20, and but 3 per cent had reached the age of 50. Marital status was as follows: 60 per cent married, 33 per cent single, and 7 per cent divorced, separated, or widowed. Only four of the married patients were in their second marriage, so it can be seen that the percentage of divorced patients in this (admittedly biased) sample is remarkably low. The mean number of offspring for these patients was also low: 1.87. Religious affiliation broke down as follows: 40 per cent were Jewish, 33 per cent were Protestant, and only 13 per cent were Catholic, despite the fact that these eastern cities were in a Catholic belt; 12 per cent said they had no religious affiliation at all, and 2 per cent said they had "other" affiliations. A surprising facet of this sample is that fully 30 per cent (43 patients) were engaged in mental health professions such as psychiatry, psychology, and psychiatric nursing or social work. If we now include all of the nonpsychiatric physicians and social workers and add the clergy as well as the mates of such career professions, we find that a full 51 per cent of the sample can be said to be connected in some way with the "helping" professions.

Only 9 per cent of the Weintraub-Aronson sample reported occupations involving business or physical (skilled or unskilled) labor. Naturally, educational level was high with 50 per cent of the patients having completed postgraduate training; only 7 per cent lacked instruction beyond the high school diploma. Using Hollingshead's (55) two-factor index of social position, it was found that these patients were very high in social status. Thus, 72.8 per cent fell into the highest social level, 21.6 per cent in the second, 4.8 per cent in the third, and less than 1 per cent fell into the fourth classification. Median income fell between $10,000 and $14,999 per year; 22 per cent had yearly incomes of $20,000 or more, and only 2 per cent had incomes of less than $5,000 per year. Almost one-third of the sample had some inherited wealth. Although 95 per cent of these patients were native Americans, only 26 per cent were still living in the general area of their birthplace. So, all in all, we have here a highly educated, well-to-do, non-Catholic sample of very mobile people working primarily in the helping professions of our culture.

Friedman & Simon (43), in a survey and interview of 200 new admissions to a state hospital, found only a small number for whom psychotherapy "was considered suitable" and who stayed for more than two sessions. Age (over 60), brain pathology, alcoholism, retardation, inability to speak English, physical illness, and rapid discharge accounted for all but 66. Of these, 34 were considered suitable (leaving 32 whose psychological condition was not considered "suitable"). Ten refused when therapy was offered.

Witkin, Lewis & Weil (135) have extended the use of the rod and frame test to a study of eight neurotics who were divided into a group of four found to be field-dependent and four who were field-independent; all patients were seen in individual therapy for roughly 20 sessions. Four therapists (two in each designation of field dependence) saw one of each type of patient. Therapy sessions were recorded and later scored for guilt and shame reactions, as well as for other factors. It was found that field-dependent patients express more shame than guilt reactions; field-independent patients report more guilt than shame reactions. Field-independent types direct hostility outward more than do the field-dependent types. A field-dependent patient is more likely to talk to his therapist than a field-independent patient, especially when that therapist also happens to be field-dependent. Field-independent therapists intervene less in sessions than do their counterparts.

Thelan & Harris (124) first identified a number of underachievers and then invited these college students into a counseling center for group therapy. An experimental (given therapy) and control (delayed) group were formed from those who responded, and after roughly eight sessions of group therapy, spread over two quarters of work, it was found that the grade-point average of the therapized group increased significantly in comparison to the controls (.07, one-tailed test). What is more interesting, however, is that the rise in the grade-point average was correlated with the "healthy" factors of the Cattell 16-factor test (24) in the experimental group, whereas for the delayed group the "unhealthy" factors were positively correlated with a rise in grade-point average. It was as if those denied therapy had found a defensive adjustment in their studies, leading to increasing grades but for reasons other than the rise in the therapized group.

Another set of nontechnique variables of individuals in therapy is provided by the self-descriptive measure called the "Q sort." Butler (18) finds increased correlation between self-sort and ideal-sort (with the change occurring in the self-sort) as a result of psychotherapy. Comparing six groups, including a control group, Butler finds clients having a largely common self-ideal but little in common in their self-sorts before therapy, while one factor after therapy accounts for many of the self-descriptions they now share and also is the stable ideal factor.

There were a series of studies around Q-sort ratings of psychotics, neurotics, and delinquents, all of whom were engaged in group psychotherapy. Schuldt & Truax (112) report that the ideal-sort of these clients is more highly correlated with Lewis' (72) "expert sort," which defines an optimal self concept, than is the self-sort of these clients. The move to ideal- and self-sort congruence in the Q sort of these patients was correlated with other adjustment measures, such as the MMPI, and this positive movement resulted from a change in the self-sort to conform to the ideal-sort [Truax and co-workers (125, 126)]. This, of course, supports the view that the individual sees himself as changing to conform to his own image of what he wants to be, rather than adjusting his ideal downward to suit his changed self-image.

Turning now to therapist variables, Berenson, Mitchell & Moravec (13) demonstrate that a "high functioning" therapist, in his initial contact with a client, is likely to stress communications between himself and the client, possible sources of misunderstanding between them, and also focuses on the client's potential strengths. "Low functioning" therapists, on the other hand, fail to clarify on the "me-you" sense of initial contact, and they appear to be more prone to fix on a client's weaknesses and symptoms. The high functioning therapist strikes one as a sensitizer, an opener of channels who is not fearful of confronting his client and investing himself in the relationship [Berenson, Mitchell & Laney (12)]. The characteristics of high-functioning (positive regard, empathy, etc.) can be experimentally manipulated over a 45-min interview and shown to have its positive (or lack of) effects on the client [Cannon & Pierce (20)].

Using paper-pencil measures in an analytically oriented psychotherapy program, Frayn (42) could find virtually no difference among 25 MD residents who had been rated by their supervisors for proficiency in the therapeutic relationship. It seems that the better therapists scored significantly higher on a measure of psychopathic deviancy (MMPI) and lower on a measure of compulsivity. Does that meet one's stereotype of the psychoanalyst?

Using Strupp-like movies, with a modification allowing the therapist subject to stop a movie at any time in order to respond to the bizarre verbalizations of a psychotic patient, Ornston et al. (90) found that experienced therapists asked fewer questions, talked a bit more over-all, made more interpretations, and were more confident in the role-play relationship than were inexperienced therapists.

In a questionnaire survey, Arthur & Birnbaum (4) find that psychiatrists (almost all male in this sample) are more prestige oriented, pragmatic, and authority-prone than psychologists (mostly female in this sample), who are more idealistic and less concerned about status. We are left wondering whether this is a professional or a sex difference. Larson (66) finds that clergymen and psychiatrists fail to agree on the degree of disturbance in a mailed case-history report of the hallucinator, the paranoid schizophrenic, the erotomanic, and the homosexual individual. By and large, it appeared that education determined the extent of agreement between the clergyman and the psychiatrists. The greatest agreement occurred between Catholic priests and the psychiatrists, and the least agreement over how sick a "case history" subject was, who should be seeing the individual, etc., occurred between the fundamentalists and the psychiatrists. All clergymen were more ready to accept hallucinatory behavior as within a normal realm than were the psychiatrists. This in itself is reassuring to the traditional reader, for when the clergy think that hearing voices is prima facie evidence of abnormality, the day of miracles is surely past. Rosenberg, Rubin & Finzi (102) present a "participation-supervision" approach to the teaching of psychotherapy, in which the instructor works as coparticipant with the student and his patient, and then later goes over the shared session in post mortem with the student. Instead of using closed circuit TV, or role-plays after the fact, instructors can now try the "you are there" approach for real.

METHODOLOGICAL ISSUES

By methodological issues we refer to studies which concern the mechanics of answering a given kind of question. Among British researchers especially, there was considerable discussion of how properly to assess outcome in psychotherapy. We could not help but note that George Kelly's Rep test (62) was given major prominence as a tool for assessing such changes or the lack of them [Crown (28); Walton & McPherson (130)]. In one of the more interesting treatments of this problem, Mair & Crisp (77) discuss a modification introduced by one of Kelly's co-workers, Dennis Hinkle (54). Hinkle has devised methods for eliciting more superordinate constructs (laddering procedure) in the Rep test, as well as what he terms an Implications Grid and a Resistance to Change Grid procedure [also discussed in Bannister & Mair (8)]. The essential idea here is to predict the likelihood of personality change based on the extent of construct alternation demanded. If a construct is superordinate to many others, and hence has implications far beyond itself, then the patient may be less likely to revise such a construct dimension because this would necessitate (in his view) many other revisions in his construct hierarchy—leading to extensive threat and hence resistance to any change. The procedure is very interesting and nicely ties together personality and psychotherapy interests.

Analogue studies demand that raters attempt to capture changes of one sort or another in what sometimes are called process studies. Since much of this work is done using subprofessional raters, the question naturally arises of whether or not a minimally trained person can rate therapists or patient responses as well as a more expertly prepared rater. Using the Rogers type ratings of empathy, genuineness, etc., Shapiro (113, 114) and Shapiro, Foster & Powell (115) have confirmed the report in the Rogers book that if asked to rate along a seven-point semantic differential scale, neophyte raters (college undergraduates) can do about as well as a highly trained rater, both in reliability and validity. There are only slight advantages discernible for the experts. A therapist's facial cues are more important for warmth and empathy ratings than are his bodily cues (judged via still pictures), especially for the neophyte raters. Amble et al. (2), using several hundred raters, report in cross-validation that a therapist's rating of his patient's improvement correlates highly (.70 to .80) with ratings made by staff and reassessment therapist. The therapists in this study were psychiatrists, social workers, and psychologists, including trainees and interns, in a child guidance center; patients were children and parents. This finding lends support to those studies which must rely upon nothing but a therapist's rating of his patient's improvement.

For the reader who would like a sophisticated overview and discussion of methodological problems in recent American psychotherapy research, Frank (41) has provided a fine example. He seemed especially drawn to the possibility of researcher bias being transmitted to patients or other subjects by way of the "Rosenthal effect" (103). In this way, the subject might act like the experimenter wanted him to act via nonverbal communication. In a study that was particularly hurt by lack of an adequate control group, Newton (87) was unsuccessful in finding differences between a group of moderately disturbed individuals who were told they were entering psychotherapy and a comparable group who were told they were being "studied" for psychiatric symptoms. Symptom scheduling was used in both groups, and, if anything, what evidence there is suggests that the group merely under study over 10 sessions became more flexible than the group supposedly attending actual psychotherapy.

Orlinsky & Howard (89) find that therapist post-interview ratings on "communication rapport" is a more reliable predictor of patients' sense of progress than the therapist's reflective judgment of progress. A test of growth through reconciliation of dilemmas, based on the work of Frank Shaw, was validated by O'Donovan & Crown (88) as measuring open-closed, warm-cold, rigid-flexible, unaware-aware aspects of an individual's manner of relating to others.

Jourard (60) presents findings to support the importance of interpersonal disclosing, and of "body accessibility" as measured on a questionnaire. In a sample of 100 young unmarried adults, he finds he can measure such facts as that daughters permit more of 24 areas of their bodies to be touched by parents than do sons. Similar findings are given for relations to same sex friends, other sex friends, and other relationships.

Nathan, Bull & Rossi (85) have gone to great lengths to establish control over the interpersonal variables between patient and therapist. They have used TRACCOM (Televised Reciprocal Analysis of Conjugate Communication), in which therapist and patient have to press buttons in order to see and hear one another on closed circuit TV. In the study reported, it was found that a psychiatric resident who saw two patients over several weeks pressed his button more times for the patient he emotively and cognitively preferred (determined independently via ratings made of the therapist's resumé notes on his case). Nathan's TRACCOM is considered an "operant" measure, and it is touted as highly sensitive to rapport characteristics. Only time will tell how much it can teach us about the therapeutic relationship. Finally, through a highly complex system of self-ratings made by patients and staff members across various ward situations (being alone, lunch with a nurse, etc.), Moos (82) demonstrates by way of factor analysis that it is easier to guess staff reactions by knowing the social situation in which they find themselves than it is to predict patient reactions in this way. Is it that patients are less predictable or that staff members are more stereotyped in behavior?

OUTCOME

By outcome study we mean any attempt to identify the longer term adjustment of individuals who had at one time been seen in psychotherapy, the possible characteristics of those who have been fortunate enough to stay healthy, or the factors involved in their possible success or lack of it. These studies are designed with a longer term view in mind, or they are adjunct activities, carried on in order to assess a program which has already been accepted and introduced by professional staff. This type of research study has been heavily criticized in the past, presumably for not making clear just what factors are involved in the successful follow-up adjustment, much less the therapy practiced initially. Possibly that is the reason we have not seen very much of this type study in 1968. With all of the psychotherapy being conducted these days, it does seem a shame that there is such a paucity of really well-done outcome and follow-up research.

In probably the best effort of this kind of the year, Paul (94) presents findings on a 2-year follow-up of an all male college sample which had been put through a group form of desensitization therapy for speech anxiety in other areas of life. There were 66 subjects followed up, and 68 per cent of his original control group was also seen after 2 years. The design was actually a two-step follow-up in which patients were interviewed 6 weeks after termination, contacted after 2 years through the mails, and then given a test battery. There were desensitization and insight oriented therapy subgroups, an "attention" oriented control (where patients were given non-therapy forms of attention), and an untreated control. Paul found that the desensitization groups continued to improve over the 2 years, particularly on measures of speech-related activities. Group desensitization procedures led to better long-term outcome (via patient self-ratings) than did group insight, attention, or control procedures. As already noted above, symptom substitution was simply not found in the reports of ex-patients helped through group administered desensitization.

In an interesting type of "reverse follow-up," Ugelstad & Astrup (128) studied a group of 40 patients with schizophrenic or schizoid diagnoses who had been receiving individual psychotherapy prior to a psychiatric hospitalization. This number represented about 2 per cent of all cases admitted to one hospital during the years 1934 to 1960. What sort of people were these highly unsuccessful individual therapy patients? Several of them had manifested neurotic symptoms earlier, like erythrophobia, character neurosis, hysterical or hypochondriacal symptoms. Sexual conflicts were coded as precipitating factors in 55 per cent of these cases, and roughly the same number had a predominant emotional symptom of anxiety. Clinical factors indicating risks of psychotic development in this group were said to include genetic loading of psychoses and suicides or a schizoid premorbid personality. The forms of therapy used with these patients varied from classical analysis (2 patients) through modified insight (12 patients) and ambulatory supportive (11 patients), on to narcoanalysis (4 patients) and even "wild" analysis (3 patients). In only one instance did the therapist feel he was working with a schizophrenic; all others assumed they were dealing with neurotic and severe nonpsychotic disturbances.

Straker (122) presents data on 107 patients who had been followed up (sans control group) 2 years after contact with a psychiatric outpatient clinic of a university hospital. These were primarily neurotic diagnoses, with depressive reactions accounting for over one-third of the sample. Forty-four patients had been given a brief individual psychotherapy contact of 10 to 12 half-hour sessions. Treatment objectives included the control and reduction of unpleasant symptoms and an attempt to restore more effective functioning. After 2 years, only eight patients (3.6 per cent) had been committed to an institution; 32 patients (30 per cent) were still receiving medical or psychiatric assistance; and the remaining 69 patients (66 per cent) had no further therapy of any kind. Fifty-one patients (47 per cent) expressed complete satisfaction with their health. Those patients receiving brief psychotherapy did particularly well, with 84 per cent placed in the full remission category on follow-up.

Davids, Ryan & Salvatore (31) located 27 male children who had been patients at one time or another over a decade in a children's hospital. They broke this group down into 10 "schizophrenic" and 17 " passive-aggressive" types and then sent questionnaires to the children's parents or legal guardians. Roughly half of these children had received subsequent psychiatric help, and only one-third were making a satisfactory post-hospital adjustment. If anything, it appeared that a child with phobic symptoms, or one who gets upset easily, or who is considered "stubborn" at intake, has a slightly better long-term adjustment after discharge from the hospital than children diagnosed in other terms.

Beckett, Lennox & Grisell (10) followed up a group of delinquents who had been given a special form of institutional treatment stressing inmate self-government, immediate rewards and/or punishments for rule infractions, and concomitant family meetings. Though personality changes and psychiatric symptoms did not differentiate between a group treated under this regime and another group treated under a more traditional philosophy, there were significantly fewer (.01 level) court involvements for assault and other hostile acting-out behaviors in the experimental program group at a 3-year follow-up. We recall that some studies already cited [notably Butler's (18) controlled study] include outcome measures but were included under other headings for the sake of highlighting between them and other studies.

THEORETICAL PAPERS

The last section of this chapter deals with theoretical papers whose main import is that they do not make an attempt to amass controlled data in the research sense, but rather take up some aspect of the general area of psychotherapy in a discursive manner, or with minimal incidents of "case history" material. We do not think that such literature should be ignored in a review of this nature, for it is from such beginnings that subsequent professional and research benefits accrue.

In what seemed to us a further development of Freud's mourning-melancholia dynamic, with a heavy Rankian flavor, Sugar (123) takes up the reaction of "normal" adolescent mourning. The basic depression stems from a separation-protest phase, in which the growing individual loses his tie to infantile objects. Sugar does not favor interpreting such loss, but rather the therapist should fix on some aspect of the adolescent's feelings of deprivation. In time, if he accepts the futility of reunion with his infantile object (clinging to a parent, for example) the adolescent is likely to experience a period of disorganization which can appear very abnormal but is merely a prelude to the normal reorganization of his self-definition and a normal outcome.

Apart from research studies, something must be said concerning the older orientations which are continuing their work. For example, psychoanalytic authors are moving in somewhat the same trends as discussed in the review so far. Family and community aspects loom large [Marmor (80)], and there is a breaking away from orthodoxy toward a freer use of concepts generally. Psychoanalytic and many other orientations can be seen in current form, for example, in Hammer's (52) edited volume, with frequent emphasis on changes in outlook.

Psychoanalytic authors often seem freer than they once were to let their concepts refer directly to describable patient experience, whatever violence this may do to earlier conceptions. For example, Robertiello & Shadmi (98) specify: "With women who are 'bitchy' and castrating to men . . . it is important to distinguish between surface sadism" which defends against a need or expectation to be hurt by the man and "the primary sadism" against the mother. "What needs to be done is for the patient to transfer onto the analyst the bad mother first."

Boyd (16) interprets much of neurosis as an inability to overcome unconscious narcissism and needs for "fusion-incorporation" relationships. Psychoanalytic concepts are used freely to get more directly than usual at the painful nonrelating manifest in this form of needing relationships. An interesting instance is a fear of death, in which death is "not simply cessation of existence," but involves "an unconscious phantasy of complete isolation and helplessness. Death then becomes the epitome of helpless loneliness . . . like being locked in an empty, black room forever" (16).

Something of theoretical value is given in the following: Erikson's (37) work on adolescence concerns the identification process. Maslow, Rand & Newman (81) apply findings from primates to psychotherapy. The same hormones make for sexuality and dominance in men, sexuality and submission in females. Another way to put it: males cannot be afraid and sexual simultaneously; females cannot be aggressive and sexual simultaneously. "The problem is then transformed into understanding how they become separated, independent, e.g., how position in the sexual act becomes detached from dominance-subordination meaning, . . . so either man or woman can be, without . . . degradation, either weak or strong."

Balint (6) finds the "basic fault" in seriously disturbed patients to be a lack of development of an adult interpersonal level, which treatment must gently develop. As in the just-mentioned views, treatment is a differentiation of what is there, not an elimination of it as pathological.

Ovesey & Meyers (91) analyzed 10 men who suffered from retarded ejaculation. Erection was achieved normally, but culmination in sexual release was unattainable. The dynamic suggested for these cases is one of paranoid rage and competition with other males, but also a great fear of retaliation if they better other males (father image?) in the symbolic act of ejaculation. Although this seems like a clinical disturbance well suited to behavior therapy, the authors argue that insight is needed. Yet one case took almost 6 years before the symptoms were fully overcome! One wonders if a behavior therapist as consultant might not have helped things along in this single instance. The other papers seemed to be getting at somewhat the same phenomenon. Gelfman (46) took up narcissism as a central factor in all neuroses. Sounding very much like Adler's overcompensation or Horney's "tyranny of the should," Gelfman nevertheless took the Freud-Fenichel-Masserman line of infantile oceanic feelings. The neurotic does not simply want equality with others when he complains of others' advantages in life, he wants to be put on a pedestal. Shave (116) makes the case that a common feature of all neuroses is continuing orality due to fixation, and, of course, one wonders how much overlap there is between such constructs as narcissism, oceanic feeling, and orality. The point of interest for our review seems to be that theorists in 1968 are looking for a common substrate of some sort which presumably cuts across all the conventionally designated neurotic symptoms. In a sense, Freud had to settle for this as well with the Oedipal complex, for surely he was never fully satisfied with the suggestions he proffered as to why differential disturbances arose in the first place. Narcissism and its lack of further differentiation appears as the prime current common dimension.

Turning to the papers on the nature of therapy, Pande (92) gives us some observations of an Eastern man looking at Western psychotherapy and the need for it. Western man expects his offspring to "grow up" and to cut themselves off from childhood preoccupations and concerns too early; hence, the analytic situation affords an acceptable return to these earlier times. The values of democracy are nourished in America, and we like to think that in therapy as patients we are free to be as we want to be, yet the truth is we are under manipulation by way of a skillful professional who accomplishes this control discretely, without upsetting our delusion of self-determination. Independence and individualism are stressed in Western civilization, hence there is more need for the sensitive intimacy of a therapeutic relationship here than in Eastern countries, where mutual support is more the case among the populace. Both sickness as well as sin in the West is met by rejection and isolation, and that may explain the need for a therapist in an anomic society. Pande feels that in the West we have moved from "you are sinner" to "you are sick," and though this may in fact be defensible, have we gained anything in the terminological transition?

Continuing in this vein, Weisskopf-Joelson (132, 133) unknowingly picked up on the Carkhuff polemic (see p. 170) and suggested that one possible explanation of why male graduate students resist the helping role is that it is feminizing. Putting oneself into the therapy relationship in a personal way is a threat which the masculine power structure foregoes under the guise of scientific detachment and objectivity. The general strategy of acting as an agent rather than simply "being a person" is also countered by graduate education, steeped as it is in rules of experimental manipulation. Psychotherapists must come to see that mental health is not something gained by way of manipulation of past behaviors, but rather achieved through a kind of future orientation of purposiveness and intentionality. Further, Weisskopf-Joelson suggests that trying to achieve mental health directly, rather than viewing it as a consequence of religious, political, or philosophical goals in life, is self-defeating. Medical models must be, if not forsaken entirely, then at least greatly reduced in importance to a secondary role of explanation—giving way to the more fundamental theories of striving for various moral, and socio-political goals of humanity.

Drawing on various philosophical precedents, and in particular the Aristotelian theory of causality, Rychlak (105) argues for reconceptualization of human behavior—including mental illness—in terms of all four explanatory dimensions including formal and final causes. The evolution of modern natural science has prejudiced man's image, making him merely a more complex assemblage of the mechanistic laws which go to make up any other "natural" phenomena. Rychlak argues that this limited conceptualization relying upon only material and efficient causes as theoretical constructs is unable to capture the genuine human condition, as when we speak of mental illness. The modern trend toward viewing mental illness as involved with values, rules of the game infractions, or social "sins" of various types is shown to be a reflection of the need to add final causality to theories being advanced in the healing professions. A unique aspect of this theoretical presentation is the claim that modern science views man in "demonstrative" (fixed and unchangeable input) terms, whereas actually he has the capacity for "dialectical" reasoning (moving from the input to its implied opposite, hence generating an alternative).

The challenge for modern "social" science is to retain the rigor and precision engendered by demonstrative reasoning while adding "dialectical" strategies to psychological science.

LITERATURE CITED

1. Ackerman, N. W., Behrens, M. L. The family approach and levels of interaction. *Am. J. Psychother.*, **22,** 5–14 (1968)
2. Amble, B. R., Kelly, F. J., Fredericks, M., Dingman, P. Assessment of patients by psychotherapists. *Am. J. Orthopsychiat.*, **38,** 476–81 (1968)
3. Aronson, H., Weintraub, W. Social background of the patient in classical psychoanalysis. *J. Nerv. Ment. Dis.*, **146,** 91–97 (1968)
4. Arthur, B., Birnbaum, J. L. Professional identity as a determinant of the response to emotionally disturbed children. *Psychiatry,* **31,** 138–49 (1968)
5. Atthowe, J. M., Jr., Krasner, L. Preliminary report on the application of contingent reinforcement procedures (token economy) on a "chronic" psychiatric ward. *J. Abnorm. Psychol.*, **73,** 37–43 (1968)
6. Balint, M. *The Basic Fault: Therapeutic Aspects of Regression* (Tavistock, London, 205 pp., 1968)
7. Bank, P. Behavior therapy with a boy who had never learned to walk. *Psychotherapy,* **5,** 150–53 (1968)
8. Bannister, D., Mair, J. M. M. *The Evaluation of Personal Constructs* (Academic Press, New York, 1968)
9. Bear, D. M. Some remedial uses of the reinforcement contingency. In *Research in Psychotherapy, Vol. III,* 3–20 (Shlien, J. M., Ed., Am. Psychol. Assoc., Washington, D.C., 618 pp., 1968)
10. Beckett, P. G. S., Lennox, K., Grisell, J. L. Responsibility and rewards in treatment. *J. Nerv. Ment. Dis.*, **146,** 257–63 (1968)
11. Beebe, J. M., III, Allowing the patient to call home: A therapy of acute schizophrenia. *Psychotherapy,* **5,** 18–20 (1968)
12. Berenson, B. G., Mitchell, K. M., Laney, R. C. Level of therapist functioning, types of confrontation and type of patient. *J. Clin. Psychol.*, **24,** 111–13 (1968)
13. Berenson, B. G., Mitchell, K. M., Moravec, J. A. Level of therapist functioning, patient depth of self-exploration, and type of confrontation. *J. Counsel. Psychol.*, **15,** 136–39 (1968)
14. Bernal, M. E., Duryee, J. S., Pruett, H. L., Burns, B. J. Behavior modification and the brat syndrome. *J. Consult. Clin. Psychol.*, **32,** 447–55 (1968)
15. Blanco, A., Akabas, S. H. The factory: Site for community mental health practice. *Am. J. Orthopsychiat.*, **38,** 543–52 (1968)
16. Boyd, H. Love versus omnipotence: The narcissistic dilemma, *Psychotherapy,* **5,** 272–77 (1968)
17. Brown, B. S., Ishiyama, T. Some reflections on the role of students in the mental hospital. *Comm. Ment. Health J.*, **4,** 509–18 (1968)
18. Butler, J. M. Self-ideal congruence in psychotherapy. *Psychotherapy,* **5,** 13–17 (1968)
19. Cahoon, D. D. Sympton substitution and the behavior therapies: A reappraisal. *Psychol. Bull.*, **69,** 149–56 (1968)
20. Cannon, J. R., Pierce, R. M. Order effects in the experimental manipulation of therapeutic conditions. *J. Clin. Psychol.*, **24,** 242–44 (1968)
21. Carkhuff, R. R. Differential functioning of lay and professional helpers. *J. Counsel. Psychol.*, **15,** 117–26 (1968)
22. Carkhuff, R. R., Kratochvil, D., Friel, T. Effects of professional training: Communication and discrimination of facilitative conditions. *J. Counsel. Psychol.*, **15,** 68–74 (1968)
23. Carlin, S., Armstrong, E. Rewarding social responsibility in disturbed children: A group play technique. *Psychotherapy,* **5,** 169–74 (1968)
24. Cattell, R. B. *The Sixteen Personality Factor Questionnaire* (Inst. Pers. Ability Testing, Champaign, Ill., 1957)
25. Colligan, C., Bellamy, C. M. Effects of a two year treatment program for a young autistic child. *Psychotherapy,* **5,** 214–19 (1968)
26. Cooke, G. Evaluation of the efficacy of the component of reciprocal inhibition psychotherapy. *J. Ab-*

norm. Psychol., **73,** 464–67 (1968)

27. Cowen, E. L., Leibowitz, E., Leibowitz, G. Utilization of retired people as mental health aids with children. *Am. J. Orthopsychiat.*, **38,** 900–9 (1968)
28. Crown, S. Criteria for the measurement of outcome in psychotherapy. *Brit. J. Med. Psychol.*, **41,** 31–38 (1968)
29. D'Alessio, G. R. The concurrent use of behavior modification and psychotherapy. *Psychotherapy,* **5,** 154–59 (1968)
30. Danet, B. N. Self-confrontation in psychotherapy reviews. *Am. J. Psychother.*, **22,** 245–57 (1968)
31. Davids, A., Ryan, R., Salvatore, P. D. Effectiveness of residential treatment for psychotic and other disturbed children. *Am. J. Orthopsychiat.*, **38,** 469–75 (1968)
32. Davison, G. C. Elimination of a sadistic fantasy by a client-controlled counterconditioning technique. *J. Abnorm. Psychol.*, **73,** 84–90 (1968)
33. Davison, G. C. Systematic desensitization as a counter-conditioning process. *Ibid.*, 91–99
34. DeNike, L., Spielberger, C. Induced mediating states in verbal conditioning. *J. Verbal Learn. Verbal Behav.*, **1,** 339–45 (1963)
35. Dulany, D. E., Jr. Hypotheses and habits in verbal "operant conditioning." *J. Abnorm. Soc. Psychol.*, **63,** 251–63 (1961)
36. Ellsworth, R. B., Foster, L., Childers, B., Arthur, G., Kroeker, D. Hospital and community adjustment as perceived by psychiatric patients, their families, and staff. *J. Consult. Clin. Psychol. Monogr. 32,* No. 5, 41 pp. (1968)
37. Erikson, E. H. *Identity: Youth and Crisis* (Norton, New York, 336 pp., 1968)
38. Fagan, J. Message from mother. *Psychotherapy,* **5,** 21–23 (1968)
39. Farberow, N. L. Suicide prevention: A view from the bridge. *Comm. Ment. Health J.*, **4,** 469–74 (1968)
40. Ferreira, A. J., Winter, W. D. Decision-making in normal and abnormal two-child families. *Family Process,* **7,** 17–36 (1968)
41. Frank, J. D. Recent American research in psychotherapy. *Brit. J. Med. Psychol.*, **41,** 5–13 (1968)
42. Frayn, D. H. A relationship between rated ability and personality traits in psychotherapists. *Am. J. Psychiat.*, **124,** 118–23 (1968)
43. Friedman, M., Simon, W. B. How many public mental health inmates can benefit from psychotherapy? *Psychotherapy,* **5,** 142–45 (1968)
44. Gelder, M. G. Desensitization and psychotherapy research. *Brit. J. Med. Psychol.*, **41,** 39–46 (1968)
45. Gelfand, D. M., Hartman, D. P. Behavior therapy with children: A review and evaluation of research methodolgy. *Psychol. Bull.*, **69,** 204–15 (1968)
46. Gelfman, M. Narcissism. *Am. J. Psychother.*, **22,** 296–303 (1968)
47. Gendlin, E. T. Psychotherapy and community psychology. *Psychotherapy,* **5,** 67–72 (1968)
48. Gendlin, E. T., Beebe, J. Experiential groups: Instructions for Groups. In *Basic Innovations in Group Psychotherapy and Counseling* (Gazda, G. M., Ed., Thomas, Springfield, Ill., 1968)
49. Gendlin, E. T., Beebe, J., Cassens, J., Klein, M., Oberlander, M. Focusing ability in psychotherapy, personality, and creativity. In *Research in Psychotherapy, Vol. III,* 217–41 (See Ref. 9)
50. Goldiamond, I., Dyrud, J. E. Some applications and implications of behavior analysis for psychotherapy. In *Research in Psychotherapy, Vol. III,* 54–89 (See Ref. 9)
51. Grinspoon, L., Ewalt, J. R., Shader, R. Psychotherapy and pharmacotherapy in chronic schizophrenia. *Am. J. Psychiat.*, **124,** 67–74 (1968)
52. Hammer, E. F., Ed. *Use of Interpretation in Treatment* (Grune & Stratton, New York, 379 pp., 1968)
53. Harter, S., Zigler, E. Effectiveness of adult and peer reinforcement on the performance of institutionalized and non-institutionalized retardates. *J. Abnorm. Psychol.*, **73,** 144–49 (1968)
54. Hinkle, D. N. The Change of Personal Constructs from the Viewpoint of a Theory of Implication (Doctoral thesis, Ohio State Univ.,

1965)

55. Hollingshead, A. B. *Two Factor Index of Social Position* (Available from author: Yale University, New Haven, Conn. 06511, 1957)
56. Holmes, D. S. Verbal conditioning, or problem solving and cooperation? *J. Exptl. Res. Pers.*, **2**, 289–94 (1967)
57. Horowitz, M. J. Visual thought images in psychotherapy. *Am. J. Psychother.*, **22**, 55–59 (1968)
58. Ince, L. P. Densensitization with an aphasic patient. *Behav. Res. Ther.*, **6**, 235–37 (1968)
59. Ince, L. P. Effects of fixed-interval reinforcement on the frequency of a verbal response class in a quasi-counseling situation. *J. Counsel. Psychol.*, **15**, 140–46 (1968)
60. Jourard, S. M. *Disclosing Man to Himself* (Van Nostrand, Princeton, New Jersey, 245 pp., 1968)
61. Kahn, M., Baker, B. Desensitization with minimal therapist contact. *J. Abnorm. Psychol.*, **73**, 198–200 (1968)
62. Kelly, G. A. *The Psychology of Personal Constructs, Vol. I.* (Norton, New York, 556 pp., 1955)
63. Kiev, A., Ed. *Psychiatry in the Communist World* (Science House, New York, 276 pp., 1968)
64. Klemperer, E. *Past Ego States Emerging in Hypnoanalysis* (Thomas, Springfield, Ill., 270 pp., 1968)
65. Langsley, D. G., Pitman, F. S., Machotka, P., Flomenhaft, K. Family crisis therapy—Results and implications. *Family Process*, **7**, 145–58 (1968)
66. Larson, R. F. The clergyman's role in the therapeutic process: Disagreement between clergymen and psychiatrists. *Psychiatry*, **31**, 250–63 (1968)
67. Lazarus, A. A. A case of pseudonecrophilia treated by behavior therapy. *J. Clin. Psychol.*, **24**, 113–15 (1968)
68. Lazarus, A. A. Learning theory and the treatment of depression. *Behav. Res. Ther.*, **6**, 83–89 (1968)
69. Lazarus, A. A. Variations in desensitization therapy. *Psychotherapy*, **5**, 50–53 (1968)
70. Leff, R. Behavior modification and the psychoses of childhood: A review. *Psychol. Bull.*, **69**, 396–409 (1968)
71. Levin, S. M., Hirsch, I. S., Shugar, G., Kapche, R. Treatment of homosexuality and heterosexual anxiety with avoidance conditioning and systematic desensitization: Data and case report. *Psychotherapy*, **5**, 160–68 (1968)
72. Lewis, M. K. Counselor Prediction and Projection in Client-centered Psychotherapy (Doctoral thesis, Univ. Chicago, 1959)
73. Lovaas, O. I. Some studies in childhood schizophrenia. In *Research in Psychotherapy, Vol. III*, 103–21 (See Ref. 9)
74. Ludwig, A. M. The influence of nonspecific healing techniques with chronic schizophenics. *Am. J. Psychother.*, **22**, 382–404 (1968)
75. Ludwig, A. M. Studies in alcoholism and LSD (1): Influence of therapist attitudes on treatment outcome. *Am. J. Orthopsychiat.*, **38**, 733–37 (1968)
76. Lynch, M., Gardner, E. A., Felzer, S. B. The role of indigenous personnel as clinical therapists. *Arch. Gen. Psychiat.*, **19**, 428–34 (1968)
77. Mair, J. M. M., Crisp, A. H. Estimating psychological organization, meaning and change in relation to clinical practice. *Brit. J. Med. Psychol.*, **41**, 15–29 (1968)
78. Marks, I. M. Aversion therapy. *Brit. J. Med. Psychol.*, **41**, 47–52 (1968)
79. Marks, J., Sonoda, B., Schalock, R. Reinforcement versus relationship therapy for schizophrenia. *J. Abnorm. Psychol.*, **73**, 397–402 (1968)
80. Marmor, J., Ed. *Modern Psychoanalysis: New Directions and Perspectives* (Basic Books, New York, 700 pp., 1968)
81. Maslow, A. H., Rand, H., Newman, S. Some parallels between sexual and dominance behavior in infrahuman primates and the fantasies of patients in psychotherapy. In *Interpersonal Dynamics, Essays and Readings on Human Interaction*, 105–20 (Bennis, W. G., Schein, E. H., Steele, F. I., Berlew, D. E., Eds., Dorsey Press, Homewood, Ill., 761 pp., 1968)
82. Moos, R. H. Situational analysis of a therapeutic community milieu.

J. Abnorm. Psychol., **73,** 49–61 (1968)

83. Müller-Hegeman, D. The problem of prolonged psychotherapy. *Am. J. Psychother.,* **22,** 233–44 (1968)
84. Myers, J. K., Bean, L. L. *A Decade Later: A Follow-Up of Social Class and Mental Illness* (Wiley, New York, 250 pp. 1968)
85. Nathan, P. E., Bull, T. A., Rossi, A. M. Operant range and variability during psychotherapy: Description of possible communication signatures. *J. Nerv. Ment. Dis.,* **146,** 41–49 (1968)
86. Newton, J. R. Consideration for the psychotherapeutic technique of symptom scheduling. *Psychotherapy,* **5,** 95–103 (1968)
87. Newton, J. R. Therapeutic paradoxes, paradoxical intentions, and negative practice. *Am. J. Psychother.,* **22,** 68–81 (1968)
88. O'Donovan, D., Crown, B. Construct validity of the Ebner-Shaw test of reconciliation. *J. Indiv. Psychol.,* **24,** 177–80 (1968)
89. Orlinsky, D. E., Howard, K. I. Communication rapport and patient progress. *Psychotherapy,* **5,** 131–36 (1968)
90. Ornston, P. S., Cicchetti, D. V., Levine, J., Fierman, L. B. Some parameters of verbal behavior that reliably differentiate novice from experienced psychotherapists. *J. Abnorm. Psychol.,* **73,** 240–44 (1968)
91. Ovesey, L., Meyers, H. Retarded ejaculation. *Am. J. Psychother.,* **22,** 185–201 (1968)
92. Pande, S. K. The mystique of "western" psychotherapy: An eastern interpretation. *J. Nerv. Ment. Dis.,* **146,** 425–32 (1968)
93. Parsons, L. B., Parker, G. V. C. Personal attitudes, clinical appraisal, and verbal behavior of trained and untrained therapists. *J. Consult. Clin. Psychol.,* **32,** 64–71 (1968)
94. Paul, G. L. Two-year follow-up of systematic desensitization in therapy groups. *J. Abnorm. Psychol.,* **73,** 119–30 (1968)
95. Peck, H. B. The small group: Core of the community mental health center. *Comm. Ment. Health J.,* **4,** 191–200 (1968)
96. Pittman, F. S., Langsley, D. G., DeYoung, C. D. Work and school phobias: A family approach to treatment. *Am. J. Psychiat.,* **124,** 93–99 (1968)
97. Ritchie, G. G., Jr. The use of hypnosis in a case of exhibitionism. *Psychotherapy,* **5,** 40–43 (1968)
98. Robertiello, R. C., Shadmi, R. M. An important set of dynamics in female sexual problems. *J. Contemp. Psychother.,* **1,** 19–25 (1968)
99. Rogers, A. H. Videotape feedback in group psychotherapy. *Psychotherapy,* **5,** 37–39 (1968)
100. Rogers, C. R. *Client-Centered Therapy* (Houghton Mifflin, Boston, Mass., 560 pp., 1951)
101. Rogers, C. R. *On Becoming a Person* (Houghton Mifflin, Boston, Mass., 420 pp. 1968)
102. Rosenberg, L. M., Rubin, S. S., Finzi, H. Participant-supervision in the teaching of psychotherapy. *Am. J. Psychother.,* **22,** 280–95 (1968)
103. Rosenthal, R. On the social psychology of the psychological experiment: The experimenter's hypothesis as unintended determinant of experiment results. *Am. Sci.,* **51,** 268–83 (1963)
104. Ryan, T. J., Watson, P. Frustrative nonreward theory applied to children's behavior. *Psychol. Bull.,* **69,** 111–25 (1968)
105. Rychlak, J. F. *A Philosophy of Science for Personality Theory* (Houghton Mifflin, Boston, Mass., 508 pp., 1968)
106. Sadock, B., Newman, L., Normand, W. C. Short-term group psychotherapy in a psychiatric walk-in clinic. *Am. J. Orthopsychiat.,* **38,** 724–32 (1968)
107. Sager, C. J., Masters, Y. J., Ronall, R. E., Normand, W. C. Selection and engagement of patients in family therapy. *Am. J. Orthopsychiat.,* **38,** 715–23 (1968)
108. Salzinger, K. On the operant conditioning of complex behaviors. In *Research in Psychotherapy, Vol. III,* 122–29 (See Ref. 9)
109. Scheidlinger, S. Group psychotherapy in the sixties. *Am. J. Psychother.,* **22,** 170–84 (1968)
110. Schmidt, L. D. Comment on "differential functioning of lay and professional helpers." *J. Counsel.*

Psychol., **15**, 127–29 (1968)

111. Schmidt, W., Smart, R. C., Moss, M. K. *Social Class and the Treatment of Alcoholism: An Investigation of Social Class as a Determinant of Diagnosis, Prognosis, and Therapy* (Univ. Toronto Press, Toronto, Canada, 111 pp., 1968)
112. Schuldt, W. J., Truax, C. B. Client awareness of adjustment in self- and ideal-self-concepts. *J. Counsel. Psychol.*, **15**, 158–59 (1968)
113. Shapiro, J. G. Relationships between expert and neophyte ratings of therapeutic conditions. *J. Consult. Clin. Psychol.*, **32**, 87–89 (1968)
114. Shapiro, J. G. Relationships between visual and auditory cues of therapeutic effectiveness. *J. Clin. Psychol.*, **24**, 236–38 (1968)
115. Shapiro, J. G., Foster, C. P., Powell, T. Facial and bodily cues of genuineness, empathy, and warmth. *J. Clin. Psychol.*, **24**, 233–36 (1968)
116. Shave, D. W. Problems of orality. *Am. J. Psychother.*, **22**, 82–95 (1968)
117. Slivkin, S. E., Bernstein, N. R. Goal-directed group psychotherapy for retarded adolescents. *Am. J. Psychother.*, **22**, 35–45 (1968)
118. Speer, D. C., Fossum, M., Lippman, H. S., Schwartz, R., Slocum, B. A comparison of middle- and lower-class families in treatment at a child guidance clinic. *Am. J. Orthopsychiat.*, **38**, 814–22 (1968)
119. Stollak, G. E. The experimental effects of training college students as play therapists. *Psychotherapy*, **5**, 77–80 (1968)
120. Stoller, F. Focused feedback with videotape: Extending the group's function. In *Basic Innovations in Group Psychotherapy and Counseling* (See Ref. 48)
121. Stone, A. A., Shein, H. M. Psychotherapy of the hospitalized suicidal patient. *Am. J. Psychother.*, **22**, 15–25 (1968)
122. Straker, M. Brief psychotherapy in an outpatient clinic: Evolution and evaluation. *Am. J. Psychiat.*, **124**, 105–12 (1968)
123. Sugar, M. Normal adolescent mourning. *Am. J. Psychother.*, **22**, 258–69 (1968)
124. Thelan, M. H., Harris, C. S. Personality of college under-achievers who improve with group therapy. *Personnel Guid. J.*, **46**, 561–66 (1968)
125. Truax, C. B., Schuldt, W. J., Wargo, D. G. Self-ideal concept congruence and improvement in group psychotherapy. *J. Consult. Clin. Psychol.*, **32**, 47–53 (1968)
126. Truax, C. B., Shapiro, J. G., Wargo, D. G. The effects of alternate sessions and vicarious therapy pretraining on group psychotherapy. *Intern. J. Group Psychother.*, **18**, 186–98 (1968)
127. Turner, C. H. Psychoanalytically-oriented guidance. *Psychiat. Quart.*, **42**, 62–80 (1968)
128. Ugelstad, E., Astrup, C. A study of psychotic patients treated with individual psychotherapy prior to admission in a mental hospital. *Brit. J. Med. Psychol.*, **41**, 117–24 (1968)
129. Wahler, R. G., Pollio, H. R. Behavior and insight: A case study in behavior therapy. *J. Exptl. Res. Pers.*, **3**, 45–56 (1968)
130. Walton, H. J., McPherson, F. M. Phenomena in a closed psychotherapeutic group. *Brit. J. Med. Psychol.*, **41**, 61–72 (1968)
131. Weintraub, W., Aronson, H. A survey of patients in classical psychoanalysis: Some vital statistics. *J. Nerv. Ment. Dis.*, **146**, 98–102 (1968)
132. Weisskopf-Joelson, E. The present crisis in psychotherapy. *J. Psychol.*, **69**, 107–15 (1968)
133. Weisskopf-Joelson, E. Mental health and intention. *Ibid.*, 101–6
134. Wilson, A., Smith, F. J. Counter-conditioning therapy using free association: A pilot study. *J. Abnorm. Psychol.*, **73**, 474–78 (1968)
135. Witkin, H. A., Lewis, H. B., Weil, E. Affective reactions and patient-therapist interactions among more differentiated and less differentiated patients early in therapy. *J. Nerv. Ment. Dis.*, **146**, 193–208 (1968)
136. Wolpe, J. *Psychotherapy by Reciprocal Inhibition* (Stanford Univ. Press, Stanford, Cal., 239 pp., 1958)
137. Zeisset, R. M. Desensitization and

relaxation in the modification of psychiatric patients' interview behavior. *J. Abnorm. Psychol.*, **73**, 18–24 (1968)

138. Zuk, G. H. Prompting change in family therapy. *Arch. Gen. Psychiat.*, **19**, 727–36 (1968)

139. Zuk, G. H. When the family therapist takes sides: A case report. *Psychotherapy*, **5**, 24–28 (1968)

140. Zweben, J. E., Miller, R. L. The systems game: Teaching, training, psychotherapy. *Psychotherapy*, **5**, 73–76 (1968)

DEVELOPMENTAL PSYCHOLOGY

By David Elkind
and Arnold Sameroff[1]
University of Rochester, Rochester, New York

An *Annual Review* chapter is, of necessity, a servant of many masters, no one of whom it serves particularly well. Space limitations prevent the kind of "in depth" treatment demanded by the expert, while the same limitations make impossible the introductory discussions required for the interested reader from another discipline. Furthermore, the literature in the field is so voluminous that it cannot be surveyed in its entirety, and not every worker who deserves mention will be given recognition here. All that we hope to do is to bring some organization into a part of the work that has been done over the past year and to highlight the directions in which research and theory seem to be moving. In this connection, we chose to group the studies according to the age levels of the subjects employed in the investigations. This was done for heuristic purposes only (the most successful texts in the field use this strategy) and not as an attempt to impose stagewise thinking upon those who reject such delineations. Accordingly, we will divide the chapter into four sections dealing with infancy, early childhood, middle to late childhood, and adolescence, respectively.

INFANCY

It is perhaps fair to say that research on infant behavior is the most rapidly expanding field of investigation in child psychology today. The reasons for this great interest in infants are bound to be multiple and diverse, and it would be rash to speculate concerning them. Whatever the reasons, however, we can be thankful for the results. For beyond the sheer accumulation of new knowledge is the more, or at least equally, important message that this information conveys. The message is that infant behavior is enormously complex and thus provides a warning against overly simplistic interpretations of behavior at later age levels.

The studies of infancy reported during the last year fell more or less readily into five groups that were concerned primarily with vision, audition, learning, intelligence, and emotion. We will take them up in that order.

[1] Preparation of this chapter was supported, in part, by training grant HD-00259 and research grant HD-03454 from the National Institute for Child Health and Human Development, United States Public Health Service. The authors are indebted to Loretta Schafer and Sharon Cerny for their assistance in the preparation of this chapter.

Vision

Investigations of vision in infants dealt primarily with their attention to or tracking of visual stimuli of various degrees of complexity. An elaborate analysis of newborn visual behaviors was made by Salapatek (196). In his investigation, Salapatek used 24 figures derived from all possible combinations of black and white, solid and outline, circles and triangles, and three sizes of stimuli. The response measured was the corneal reflection of the stimulus which was continuously photographed and then analyzed to determine the infant's gaze direction and eye movements. The results supported earlier findings of Salapatek & Kessen (197) in the sense that there was a greater horizontal than vertical dispersion of gaze shifts. In addition, the introduction of a visual figure narrowed the horizontal dispersion and reduced the difference between horizontal and vertical scanning. Although no one pattern was preferred over any other, the mode of looking at each pattern was different. The author hypothesized that accommodation to the contour of the stimulus by infants might lay the groundwork for future discriminations and could play a role in the genesis of form perception. Charlesworth (40) proposes that cognitive development might proceed through perceptual activity to instrumental behavior.

A novel study of visual attention in the newborn was reported by Anderson & Rosenblith (5). These workers found that when a shiny bicycle bell was drawn across their field of vision, a number of infants sneezed! Anderson & Rosenblith call this the "photic sneeze reflex." In another investigation with newborns, Ottinger, Blatchley & Denenberg (174) increased the visual attentiveness of infants by giving them special experiences during the first day of life. When a test of attentiveness to visual stimuli was given on the fourth day, the group of infants that was trained with visual and other stimuli fixated significantly more often than a control group that had not had the additional experience.

Among somewhat older infants, studies that employed more complex stimuli were reported. Fantz's (74) finding that infants prefer intact over scrambled faces in the third month continues to attract critical attention. Koopman & Ames (123) were unable to replicate the Fantz findings and argue that it is the complexity of the stimuli rather than its configurational quality that attracts the infant's attention. In a related study, Fitzgerald (80) used the pupillary reflex as an index of the ability to differentiate visual stimuli in 1-, 2-, and 4-month-old infants. Five stimuli were used in the study; mother's face, stranger's face, triangle, a four-square and a 144-square checkerboard. Results showed that infants responded more vigorously to the faces than to the geometric forms at 1 and 4 months of age. At 4 months, moreover, infants discriminated between the mother's and the stranger's face and made a greater response to the stranger's face. Again, a more complex-less complex stimulus dichotomy seems more parsimonious and adequate than a social-nonsocial stimulus dichotomy.

An added dimension to the intact-scrambled stimulus paradigm was employed by Wilcox & Clayton (247). They presented moving vs. nonmoving colored pictures of a woman's face smiling, frowning, and with a neutral expression. Among 5-month-old infants, the face elicited more attention than a white light control, and the moving faces received more attention than the nonmoving. There were, however, no consistent differences in fixation time to the various facial expressions. This study did not support the notion that infants in the first 6 months of life can discriminate figurative patterns when the complexity of the patterns in question is controlled.

Several other studies dealing with infant vision should be reported. Caron & Caron (37) repeatedly presented various simple and complex visual stimuli to infants 3 to 4 months old and found habituation of fixation to a repeated stimulus and some dishabituation when the stimulus was changed. The amount of habituation and dishabituation was related to the complexity of the stimulus. In another investigation, Nelson (165) studied tracking behavior in infants 2 to 4 months old. What had to be tracked was a left to right sequence of six lights. In an interrupted sequence, two lights were left out. Infants, however, continued to track to the right even in the interrupted sequence. Watson (240) found that infants' fixations were more operantly controlled than tropistically controlled. Finally, Walk (236) reported another in his series of investigations of depth perception in infants. He found that some infants under 9 months showed some difficulty in judging the "deep side" of the apparatus when one eye was covered with a patch.

Audition

Studies using auditory stimulation have tended to focus more on response parameters than on the stimulus parameters, as opposed to studies of vision where the opposite is generally true. In this regard, physiological reactions such as heart rate, respiration, and sucking have received the most attention. Clifton and her colleagues conducted a series of studies relating auditory stimulation to heart-rate response. Clifton & Meyers (48) tested the hypothesis that the decelerative heart-rate response to visual stimuli in infants 4 to 6 months old would also hold for auditory stimuli. They did find the deceleration response to stimulus onset, but the offset response only occurred to the cessation of a constant stimulus. When a pulsed tone was turned off, there was no offset effect. Additionally, there was some indication that the series of onsets and offsets found in a pulsed tone habituated the offset response to the total stimulus configuration.

Clifton, Graham & Hatton (47) and Graham, Clifton & Hatton (99) studied the heart-rate response in newborns and found support for previous studies which had also reported heart-rate acceleration to auditory stimulation. Little habituation was found across the first 5 days of life. The greatest response was to a stimulus of 10-sec duration, while stimulus durations of 2 sec and of 30 sec produced less response. Clifton & Meyers (48) contrasted the heart-rate deceleration found in older infants and the heart-rate acceleration found to the same stimuli in newborns. They discussed the role of heart-rate deceleration in the "orienting reflex" and concluded that the neural mechanisms of the newborn might be too immature to accompany the orienting reflex. Resolution of the maturity or immaturity of the heart-rate component of the orienting reaction must wait until a study is done which tests newborns with visual stimuli that have caused both obvious eye fixations and heart-rate deceleration in infants 4 to 6 months old [Kagan & Lewis (112)].

Change in respiratory response appears to be a more fruitful method of getting at the orienting reaction in newborns. Steinschneider (216) stimulated newborns with a range of intensities of white noise from 55 to 100 db. He found that the major response to the white noise was increase in respiratory rate and that this rate was positively correlated with an increase in sound intensity. If only the first respiratory cycle after stimulus onset was measured, however, then the cycle length increased to low intensity stimuli and decreased to high intensity stimuli. Steinschneider related these findings to the monophasic heart-rate acceleration response to sound stimuli in newborn infants. He cautioned that if the respiratory deceleration in the first cycle following stimulus onset reflects orientation, then one must be careful in generalizing from one response system to another in the newborn period when the coordination of physiological response systems may be at a minimum.

The effect of auditory stimulation on crying in the newborn was investigated in a pair of studies. O'Doherty (170) spoke into the ears of crying babies and found that this quieted them. He suggested that quieting to auditory stimulation might be utilized as a hearing test. Cullen et al. (57) gave crying babies delayed auditory feedback of their own crying and also found that the infants cried less. They concluded that crying was under closed-loop auditory feedback control. However, since there was no control for other forms of auditory stimulation, nor any masking to prevent the infant from hearing his own crying, their conclusion requires more support. Weitzman & Graziani (242) studied auditory evoked potentials in prematures. Latencies of evoked response were longer during "intermittent" than during "continuous" EEG patterns. The responses of infants between the ages of 4 and 15 months were studied with a variety of auditory stimuli by Friedlander (84) and Mendel (151).

While visual and auditory modalities in infants receive considerable research attention, this is not the case for the other sensory modalities. Taste and smell are rarely, if ever, studied. Tactile stimuli have been investigated but mostly in relation to oral sensitivity [Dubignon & Campbell (66)]. A study of evoked potentials to proprioceptive stimulation, the elicitation of a tendon jerk, found that the evoked response in the newborn differed only in time-course and duration from the evoked response in adults. The proprioceptive evoked response in the newborn, moreover, appeared more mature than the visual evoked response at the same age level [Hrbek et al. (108)].

It is to be hoped that some of the new workers with infants will begin to explore these neglected sense modalities.

Sucking.—Sucking is another response frequently employed in the study of auditory stimuli in infants. Semb & Lipsitt (204) investigated the effects of auditory stimulation on nonnutritive sucking in newborns. They found two seemingly dichotomous responses to a 1-sec 90 db tone. When the infant was sucking, stimulation led to sucking cessation, but when the infant was not sucking, stimulation led to sucking initiation. These results contrast with those of Sameroff (199), who found that when stimulated with a 60-sec 60 db tone, infants who had been sucking sucked longer, and infants who had not been sucking suppressed longer. The two studies indicate that auditory stimulation has an effect upon the sucking pattern, but whether that effect is acceleration or deceleration of the sucking pattern will depend upon the intensity or the temporal characteristics of the stimulation, or both.

Although not directly related to auditory stimulation, other studies of sucking might be mentioned here. Dubignon & Campbell (66, 67) found that the sucking pattern was different in nutritive and nonnutritive sucking and that a nipple was a better stimulus for eliciting sucking than a rubber tube. Wolff (252), in another of his studies on sucking, reported differences in nonnutritive sucking rate between groups of normals and infants with diffuse disorders. Although no relation was found between specific disorders and a specific sucking pattern, the diffusely disordered groups showed a slower sucking rate and more variability than a normal control group. An interesting sidelight reported by Wolff was that infants with cortical abnormalities, e.g., anencephaly, could not be differentiated from normals with respect to sucking pattern. Wolff hypothesized the existence of species-specific microrhythms of which sucking is an example.

Learning

Studies of learning in infants seem to have gone in two directions: the study of operant learning in newborns and the exploration of effective reinforcers for learning in older infants. In the area of learning, a notable event was the demonstration of operant learning in the newborn. Siqueland (213) successfully "shaped" head turning in newborns. Milk was used as the reinforcer, and its receipt was made contingent on the infant's moving his head a certain number of degrees. This procedure enabled Siqueland to increase the rate of head-turning. In a second group of infants, a ratio-schedule was used, and the results indicated that this group gave more responses during extinction than did the constant reinforcement group. A possible explanation for the data was that the milk reinforcement excited the infant to move his head more. The crucial control was a third group of subjects who were given milk for not moving their heads. In this control group, head-turning was significantly reduced.

Sameroff (200) also found evidence of operant learning in the sucking behavior of newborns. He designed an apparatus which separately measured "expression," squeezing the nipple between tongue and palate, and "suction," generating negative pressure in the mouth by dropping the floor of the mouth. The apparatus could then be adjusted to give milk contingent on either the suction or expression component, and also on the amplitude of either component. The results indicated that when the infants were reinforced for expression, they suppressed the suction component of sucking. In addition, when different amplitudes of expression were required, the infants adjusted their sucking pressure to match the required levels of response. The results of the Siqueland (213) and Sameroff (200) studies suggest that operant procedures may be very useful in the study of learning parameters in newborns.

Other studies have explored the relative efficiency of different reinforcers. Koch (119, 120) dealt with the learning of a head-turning response in infants 2 to 5 months of age. Four reinforcers were used: mother's face, stranger's face, a single toy presented visually, and a different toy on each trial presented visually. The most rapid learning occurred in the many-toy condition. The least effective reinforcer was the mother's face. Indeed, for many of the children the mother's face caused disruption of the learning process. Koch hypothesized that this disruption might have been due to the strangeness of the context in which the familiar face was seen. In another investigation, Koch (120) used the head-turning paradigm to investigate the effect of organismic variables (biorhythms) on the conditioning process. He found that the infants learned most rapidly when the session occurred 40 min after waking and 150 min after a feeding. Sleep and feeding cycles which produced the above coincidence in schedules produced the most rapid learning.

A fruitful direction in which a number of investigators have been moving is the analysis of the "responsive" stimuli in the environment which will produce change in the infant's behavior. Leuba & Friedlander (132) reported that infants 7 to 11 months old played with a toy that provided audio-visual feedback more than with one that did not. In a related study, Todd & Palmer (230) separated the effects of visual and auditory human stimulation on babbling in 3-month-olds. In one condition, babbling was reinforced with voice alone, while in the second condition, voice and the visual presence of an adult were the reinforcers. Infants increased their rate of babbling for both types of reinforcement, but voice plus visually present adult was relatively more effective as reinforcement than was the human voice alone.

Intelligence

The "test intelligence" of infants continues to be assessed, especially in its relationship to later mental ability scores. Werner, Honzik & Smith (243) found significant correlations between psychological and pediatric evaluations at 20 months and academic achievement test scores at age 10. A score of below 80 on the Cattell, to illustrate, was highly related to serious school achievement problems at age 10. A somewhat contradictory conclusion was drawn by Moore (156). This worker studied general and linguistic ability among English children from 6 months to 8 years of age. Moore concluded that the quality of the home, during the period of language acquisition, together with social class and ordinal position in the family, were better predictors of later ability than was performance on scales of development in the first 2 years. The ambiguities in this area were highlighted by the findings of Golden & Birns (94). These workers studied Negro infants from three social classes: welfare families, families in which the parents had no high school education, and families in which the parents had better than high school educations. Examinations at 12 months, 18 months, and 24 months with the Cattell and a Piaget object permanence scale revealed no differences in test performance between the children from these three socioeconomic strata.

Emotion

The research on emotional development and social stimulation during infancy is still very much in the developmental descriptive stage of enquiry. Researchers have not been clear in defining what makes a stimulus social or a response emotional. A case in point was Moss & Robson's (157) study which related time spent looking at geometric vs. social two-dimensional stimuli to a variety of other measures in 13-week-old infants. The geometric stimuli were checkerboards and the social stimuli were a schematic face, a photograph of a face, and a photograph of a scrambled face. Differences were found between fixation time to the social vs. geometric stimuli. These differences were then related to the amount of time the mother and child looked at each other. The authors, however, did not report that the infants looked more at the intact photograph of a face than at the schematic or scrambled face. Here again, as in the studies of Fantz (74) and Fitzgerald (80), the "social" or figurative characteristics of the stimuli are confounded with its complexity so that the authors may be premature in attributing their results to social learning.

Equally difficult to interpret were studies that purported to deal with temperamental differences among newborns. Evidence for "constitutional" factors in temperament independent of environment were reported by McGrade (148), who found some relation between stress reactions to removal of a nipple at 3 and 4 days and stress reactions during developmental testing at 8 months. Some of the difficulties in the "constitutional" interpretation of individual differences in infancy were indicated by Korner, Chuck & Dontchos (124), who explored some aspects of "temperamental" differences in newborns as they were related to oral behaviors. These workers were able to distinguish and assess finger-sucking, hand-face contacts, hand-mouth contacts, and mouthing behaviors. While all the measures were related to arousal, only mouthing was related to hunger. These investigators concluded that the use of different measures of orality would give different indices of temperament for the same infant. While genetic factors must play a role in individual differences in temperament, much more work needs to be done before the way in which such factors play their part becomes fully known and understood.

One of the major longitudinal studies of individual variation and stability in temperament has resulted in another book-length report [Thomas, Chess & Birch (227)]. These investigators found that modes of behavior, including general activity level and adaptability to new situations, were consistent for particular children across the first 5 years of life. More significantly, these temperamental differences were found to have far-reaching effects upon parental behavior and the quality of parent-child interactions.

Although studies of smiling were missing this year, investigations of fear were prominent. Bronson (31) has proposed a developmental theory of fear, while Collard (51) and Cox & Campbell (55) placed children in situations where elicited fear could be studied. Collard found that when infants 9 to 13 months old were confronted with a stranger or a novel toy, first-borns and infants whose next sibling was 6 or more years older had a stronger negative response than infants with a sibling less than 5 years older. These findings led Collard to conclude that infants exposed to many different people in their everyday environment show weaker fear responses than infants exposed to a limited number of adults. Cox & Campbell (55) had infants playing in a strange room with their mothers absent or present. Mother absence inhibited play behavior. Not surprisingly, the effect of mother absence was more pronounced for the 13- to 15-month-old youngsters than it was for toddlers 20 to 37 months old.

EARLY CHILDHOOD

Studies of children of preschool age have received an added impetus as a result of such programs as Head Start and the National Laboratories for Early Childhood Education and the renewed interest in preschool education. This new focus of attention on young children has had both positive and negative consequences. On the negative side is the increasing pressure being put upon middle-class children for academic achievements prior to kindergarten. Inasmuch as children in Europe often do not begin school until the age of 6 or 7, yet end up better educated when they finish high school, it is questionable whether early academic attainments will solve the problems of elementary and secondary education in this country. On the positive side, the increasing cooperation between educators and psychologists both in the conducting of research and in teaching programs is very much to be welcomed.

The studies dealing with preschool children were many and varied. Some carried on the tradition of similar studies begun when almost every university and college had its own nursery school. Other studies reflected the psychologist's entrance into ghetto areas and his access to preschool populations from other than college or university environs. We have grouped the studies according to whether their major emphasis was learning, cognition, perception, language, intelligence, or personality.

Learning

Preschool children were used as subjects in a number of studies dealing with some aspect of the learning process. In a study of delay of reward, Sheikh (208) found that the delay affected response speed independent of the incentive value of the reinforcement. Lang & Adair (128) reported that 5-year-olds expressed greater preferences for a delayed-large as opposed to an immediate-small reward. Those children who chose the delayed reward, however, took longer to make their decisions. It would be interesting to know whether performance on this task was related to Kagan's impulsive-reflective dimension. Leckart, Briggs & Kirk (129) had preschool children choose between two pictures. One picture was always the same while the other was different on each trial. The frequency with which the novel picture was picked increased as familiarity with the recurring picture increased.

The effects of ratio of reinforcement upon the discrimination learning of children 3 to 5 years old were studied by Endsley (72). This investigator found that the number of correct responses were directly related to the ratio of nonrewarded to rewarded trials. Finally, Osler & Scholnick (173) studied transfer effects in the learning of 5-year-old disadvantaged children. Results showed that children given practice in either stimulus differentiation alone or inference alone did no better than the controls. When, however, the children received both kinds of training, positive transfer was observed.

Cognition

The cognitive development of the preschool child is receiving considerable practical as well as theoretical attention these days. Not unexpectedly, Piaget's work has been a rallying point in this area. To begin on the research level, Mehler & Bever (150) touched off a controversy when they reported that they found conservation of number in 2-year-old children. This conservation, moreover, was not found among children 3 to 4 years old. To account for their results, Mehler & Bever suggested that the inability to conserve was a temporary lapse due to a period (presumably at ages 3 to 5) in which there is an overdependency on perceptual cues. Beilin (18) and Rothenberg & Courtney (194) also studied conservation of number of young children but argued that their results did not support the findings of Mehler & Bever (150). Bever, Mehler & Epstein (20) did not, however, concur with this critique.

Piaget (176) also entered the discussion and reported some results of his own. He indicated that while the child is by nature "a conserver," the presence of conservation in a particular domain depends upon the developmental level of the subject and the structure of the knowledge or concept to be conserved. The issue is extraordinarily complex and involves at the very minimum some agreement as to what is a valid test of conservation, what are valid controls for linguistic understanding, and what constitutes evidence for a "true" concept of number. Without such prior agreements regarding the domain of discourse, controversies such as this one will continue without successful resolution. Indeed, our impression is that some of the disagreement in the domain of conservation rests upon a failure of the various parties to find a definition of conservation which they can all accept.

In a related area of preschool cognition, Kohlberg, Yaeger & Hjertholm (122) dealt with Piaget's early work on egocentric speech. These investigators reported a series of studies that were undertaken to evaluate the views on private speech held by Piaget, Vygotsky, C. H. Mead, and J. H. Flavell. Results seemed to favor Vygostsky's view that private speech manifests a curvilinear course with respect to age. These findings are opposed to Piaget's view that egocentric speech declines directly with cognitive and social maturity. As in all such discussions, however, questions arise because different workers use the expression "egocentric speech" in different senses. Genuine confrontations of theoretical positions can only take place when there is a prior agreement as to the definition of terms.

A scholarly paper by Furth (85) reviewed some of the philosophical history of the concepts of representation and interiorization as a starting point for an explication of these terms as they are used by Piaget. Furth suggested that representation has both a narrow meaning (the making of absent objects or events present) and a broad meaning which is equivalent to thinking as a whole. He argues that in many current theories of cognition in America these two meanings are not differentiated. Piaget, in contrast, does not equate the two and holds that representation in the narrow sense of mental images or symbols should not be confused with thought or mental operations. On the contrary, the task is to discover the modes of interaction between representation in the narrow sense and thinking in general. This is an important point, particularly as studies of mental imagery are coming into fashion again, and we are indebted to Furth (85) for making it.

Perception

Some of the most imaginative studies with preschoolers were reported in the area of perception. Most of these studies were developmental descriptive in the sense of attempting to assess aspects of children's perceptual capacities. Some of the studies dealt with perceptual abilities in a particular domain, while others explored intersensory perception.

Within modality studies.—Clifton & Bogartz (46) found that preschool children taught to attend to messages presented in one ear were less able to report messages presented to the other ear. This suggested that preschool children might have more difficulty in deploying attention to incoming stimuli than is true for older children and adults. A similar conclusion might be drawn from the work of Vurpillot (235). In her study she utilized eye movement photography to study preschool children's judgments of similarity and difference with respect to visual stimuli (pairs of houses which varied in the extent to which they were identical). Vurpillot found that children below the age of 6 failed to scan the configurations systematically and made many errors. Scanning of the entire configuration increased with age (as indicated by the eye movement data) and was correlated with a decrease in the number of errors made by the children in judging the stimuli as same or different. Nickel (166) reported results which suggested that scanning was improved in preschool children when they were given cognitive structuring in the form of a story about the stimulus to be detected. Finally, Jeffrey (110) underscored the importance of studying the orienting reflex and attention for a better understanding of cognitive development.

Intersensory perception studies.—The general consensus of the studies on intersensory perception is that it tends to improve with age. To illustrate, Falk (73) presented 4- and 6-year-old children with a three-choice discrimination task involving stereometric, planometric, and patterned stimuli. Four-year-old children did better than chance only when they were able to use both the visual and the tactual clues provided by stereometric stimuli. In contrast, the 6-year-old children did as well with the visual cues alone as with the visual and tactual cues in combination. Similar results were reported by Abravanel (1), who required 3- to 6-year-old children to make same-different judgments between haptic and visual stimuli which differed in spatial position. The young children (3 to 4) had little success, whereas the older children (5 to 6) demonstrated better than chance accuracy.

The role of intersensory functioning in more complex learning tasks has also been explored. Blank, Altman & Bridger (25), for example, had preschool youngsters learn a discrimination in either the haptic or visual domain and then required them to transfer the discrimination to the other modality. Transfer from touch to vision was much poorer than the reverse. Interestingly, however, Blank & Altman (24) reported that discriminations and reversal learning were more rapid for tactual than for visual stimuli. Performance on the visual material was, however, improved when the children were encouraged to attend to the stimuli separately or to draw them. To complicate these results further were the findings reported by Litvinyuk (137). This worker had children explore real mazes. When his subjects were shown a map or model of the maze, they solved the actual maze more quickly than without such representation. When, however, the children were asked to trace a path on the diagram or model after they had explored the maze they had little success. It seems safe to say that the role of intersensory perception in learning will depend very much upon the nature of the task under investigation, as well as upon the age of the child.

Language

Studies of language in young children seem to have clustered about two problems. One of these has to do with the growth of language in the child from a developmental descriptive perspective, and the other has to do with the role which language plays in the learning and problem solving of young children.

Language development.—In this problem area, another report from the ongoing longitudinal study of Brown & Bellugi (33) is of particular interest. Using data from this study, Brown (32) discussed the grammatical structures that underlie Wh (who, whom, what, where, why, and how) questions in young children. He found that the grammatical structures that appeared to underpin these questions did in fact resemble the structures described in currently popular transformational grammars. While Brown conceded it would be hard to demonstrate how such grammars could be learned, he did not exclude learning and even suggested a possible mechanism for the acquisition of grammatical structures. In a related study, Cazden (39) used the Brown & Bellugi data to discover that plurals occurred before possessives and that the present progressive appeared before past tense and present indicative constructions. On the receptive side of language growth, Carrow (38) found, not unexpectedly, that older children were better able to comprehend oral language than were younger children.

Language development in children from varied ethnic and socioeconomic backgrounds has received considerable impetus from the new programs for disadvantaged children. Alexander, Stoyle & Kirk (3) studied the vocabularies of inner city 3-year-old children in a Head Start program. They found that boys had better vocabularies than girls and that this remained the case after the children had spent a year in the preschool setting. A book edited by Deutsch, Katz & Jensen (62) contains several chapters relevant to language growth among disadvantaged children.

Language in learning and problem solving.—In a partial replication of the Luria studies, Joynt & Cambourne (111) explored the relation between psycholinguistic development and the verbal control of behavior in Australian children. They found that the Australian youngsters passed through stages similar to those reported by Luria. In contrast to Luria's hypothesis, however, they also found that the stages were more closely related to linguistic prowess (as measured by the Illinois Test of Psycholinguistic Ability) than to chronological age. The importance of language development for the use of certain kinds of linguistic cues in learning was demonstrated by Potts (181). This investigator used a transposition task in which the stimuli were either labeled with a distinctive word or with a morphological cue or were not labeled at all. Results showed that the older children utilized the morphological cue more effectively than did the younger children.

Paired-associate learning in young children has also been investigated. Dilley & Paivio (64) employed pictures and words in a paired-associate learning task in which the stimulus-response combinations were either picture-picture, picture-word, word-picture, or word-word. They found that the pictures facilitated learning as stimulus items but impaired learning as response items. These findings suggested that young children have more trouble in decoding memory images into verbal responses than do older children and adults. In a more traditional paired-associate paradigm, Boat & Clifton (27) showed that 4-year-old children could use verbal mediators. The experimental group learned a three-stage chaining sequence (A-B, B-C, A-C) while the controls had no chaining (A-B, D-C, A-C). In this study, the experimental children learned more efficiently than did the controls.

At least one writer [Caron (36)] has suggested that language facilitates associative learning because it enhances attention rather than because it serves as a mediator of response. Presumptive evidence for such a view came from a study of Potter & Levy (180), who found a relation between attentional span and age with 2½- to 4-year old subjects. Some of the difficulties inherent in interpreting the verbal responses of young children were suggested by Donaldson & Balfour (65). Among their 4-year-old subjects, they found only one who used "less" and "more" in the adult sense. Indeed, for young children these two terms appeared to be undifferentiated and the "more" term tended to be preferred. This observation obtained support from a study by Tedford & Kempler (225), who reported that their subjects tended to prefer the large stimulus on a size transposition task.

Intelligence

Some psychological issues appear neither to die nor to fade away but rather to be as perennial as weeds and taxes. The modifiability of the IQ appears to be such an issue. It has received added potency this year as the evaluation returns from the government's crash compensatory education programs began to come in. Often—perhaps too often—IQ gains have been used to assess the effectiveness and value of such programs as Head Start. As Kohlberg (121) suggests in a careful review of preschool education studies, there is little evidence for the efficacy of preschool programs in raising the IQ. Even the gains that have been made might possibly be attributable to factors other than increments in intellectual growth. Zigler & Butterfield (255), to illustrate, found that IQ performance of preschool children could be enhanced by testing them under "optimal" conditions (social interaction with the examiner and considerable success experience with easy items).

A major point of the Zigler & Butterfield study and of the Kohlberg (121) critique was not, it must be emphasized, to downgrade the efficacy or importance of preschool education. On the contrary, what these writers have argued—and in this we very much concur—is that IQ measures are perhaps not appropriate for assessing the very real and important effects of preschool education. As Kohlberg (121) makes clear, intellectual development is but a part of the broader phalanx of social, emotional, and language skills the preschool child is in the process of mastering. To single out the IQ as the index of progress during the preschool years is to distort the nature of the growth that actually is taking place.

The problem of the modifiability of the IQ, however, remains an issue, arguments such as Kohlberg's notwithstanding. Unfortunately, the issue goes beyond the empirical data and touches upon everything from epistemological convictions to racial prejudice. Once again, meaningful discussion on the issue can only begin when the various parties to the controversy start from commonly shared definitions of intelligence, genetics, experience, learning, and so on. Without such a common universe of discourse, the optimism of the IQ modification people will never be reconciled with the pessimism of the developmentalists regarding permanent alterations in test intelligence.

Despite the difficulties with the IQ as a measure of gains made in the preschool, it continues to be employed. Blank & Solomon (26) reported a more responsible use of the IQ for evaluating the effects of a special language program upon disadvantaged preschool children. The experiences of the experimental group with an individualized responsive environment raised their IQ's significantly above those children who had received equal individual attention but no tutoring, and those who had received only classroom experience. Similar results were obtained by Karnes et al. (114) with their program of tutoring the mothers of preschool children. The mothers were seen twice a week and were taught ways of instructing their offspring. After the training period, the experimental group gained in IQ in comparison with an untrained control group. Both of these studies avoid some of the major objections to the use of the IQ as a measure of the efficacy of educational intervention, but more specific measures of particular abilities might have shown even greater effects. We in child psychology are, it seems, only beginning to appreciate some of the difficulties and problems of evaluating educational achievement.

Personality and Socialization

Studies of personality in preschool children seem to have clustered in two areas: sex differences and cognitive styles. Studies of socialization dealt with personality and parent perception and the effects on performance of parent's presence. A mixed bag to be sure, but it provides needed additions to our meager store of information about such matters in preschool children.

With respect to sex differences, Reed & Asbjornsen (185) used the IT scale with preschoolers and found that girls chose opposite sex stimulus figures more often than did boys. Does this mean, however, that girls are more confused about sex roles or that they are sensitive to societal values in this regard? Evidence for the sensitivity hypothesis was provided by Madsen (143), who used modeling of aggressive behavior as a measure. He found that while boys were high in imitative aggression, girls exhibited more nonimitative aggression, i.e., transformed the content of the aggressive act to one more appropriate for girls. Other data on sex role differentiation came from Vroegh (234). In another of her investigations of masculinity and femininity, she found that "most masculine" boys tended to be more extroverted than "least masculine" boys, while "most feminine" girls tended to be more introverted than "least feminine" girls. Both "most" groups were more competent and socially adjusted than the corresponding "least" groups. Finally, Lewis et al. (134) made a case for *not* pooling data in studies of cognitive tasks where both sexes are used. They reported that on impulsivity-reflectivity tasks, boys' errors correlated only with their response speed, while girls' errors correlated only with their intelligence.

If we turn now to cognitive styles, reflectivity-impulsivity appears to be a reliable dimension of behavior among preschoolers. Ward (239) used a variety of tasks to measure the reflectivity-impulsivity dimension and found reliable individual differences. He reported that anxiety over failure played a greater role in the performance of reflective children than it did in the performance of impulsive ones. In a different style domain, Pedersen & Wender (175) rated 2½-year-old boys on autonomy and dependency. When the boys were 6½ they were tested with a battery of cognitive measures. Nonverbal performance was positively related to a cluster of autonomy measures. This correlation was not true for verbal performance.

In the realm of socialization studies, the relation of generosity to parent perception and personality variables in nursery school boys was investigated by Rutherford & Mussen (195). Generosity was related to a pattern of moral characteristics including altruism, kindness, and cooperation. The more generous boys tended to perceive their fathers as warmer and more sympathetic. However, do such ratings mean that the child identifies with the father or merely that the child's generosity extends to parental perceptions as well?

Studies which directly investigated the effect of adults on preschooler performance suggest that the mere presence of an adult has a significant inhibiting or interfering influence. Schwartz (203) presented a "gorilla" fear stimulus to 3½ to 5½-year-old children in the presence of their mother or of a stranger. Surprisingly, the children showed more fear responses and behavior disruption when the mother was present. Perhaps the stranger inhibited motility and emotional communication. Perhaps, too, fear reactions are "put on" to gain parental attention. This might in part explain the results of Harris (106), who had 3 to 5-year-olds make toy choices in the presence of an adult. The younger children spent more time looking at the adult than did the older children. The author interpreted this finding as a reflection of the increases in emotional independence with age.

MIDDLE TO LATE CHILDHOOD

By far the greatest amount of research during the past year, as in previous years, involved elementary school children as subjects. It is an age about which we know a great deal in certain limited domains and about which we know little in others. Topics about which we have considerable information are learning, cognitive development, perceptual and motor development, language, and personality-socialization. An aspect of childhood about which we know little, but where our knowledge is rapidly increasing, is the domain of race, ethnic, and social class differences. These categories will form the headings for the major sections in our review of research on children of elementary school age.

Learning in Children

This section on learning has five main subsections: discrimination learning, verbal learning, concept learning, reinforcement effects in learning, and learning in exceptional children. A closing subsection will deal with some theoretical articles that have appeared during the year. Of interest to those readers concerned with trends is the large number of studies in verbal learning in children which appear, along with infant studies, to be one of the newest growth areas in the field. Straightforward discrimination learning studies, in contrast, seemed to be much less in evidence except in the area of behavior modification, which is another research area experiencing rapid growth. Although we believe that behavior modification work with children deserves mention in the discussion of learning in children, we will not review much of the literature here since it is so vast and because it overlaps with clinical, educational, and abnormal psychology.

Discrimination learning.—A long-standing problem of learning is the stimulus resolving power of the individual and the stimulus and situational factors that affect this power. Generalization studies are often aimed at providing more information about what makes a stimulus distinguishable. In a study by Tempone (226) in which the subjects were 6-year-old children, he observed that stimulus generalization gradients were obtained only for those stimuli which had definite forms and contours and not for stimuli deficient in form and contour. One interpretation of this finding is that discrimination and generalization involve, at least in older children, the identification of a stimulus dimension or category. This also appears to be the conclusion drawn in several studies involving: the extinction of a response to a preferred dimension [Galloway & Petre (87)]; preservation errors in discrimination learning of familiar and unfamiliar material [Brackbill (30)]; the learning of single and double alternation problems with the aid of color cues [Norman & Rieber (167)]; and the ability, or at least readiness, to make a reversal shift response [White & Johnson (245)].

Stimuli can, however, also be made more distinct by the contexts in which they are imbedded. Viney et al. (233) found that resistance to extinction of a discrimination response was positively related to the number of stimuli common to the acquisition and to the extinction trials. One well-established way of making the stimulus distinct is predifferentiation training

[Schroth (202)]. Another way is the use of verbal labels to identify the stimuli. Stephens (217) found that although noun, verb, and adjective labels were more effective than no labels in discriminating geometric shapes, there was no difference in the relative efficacy among these three grammatical types.

Verbal learning.—One of the problems explored in studies of verbal learning is the role of the context of presentation. To illustrate, Levin & Rohwer (133) observed that serial learning in fourth and fifth-grade children was enhanced when the words were presented in phrases and in sentences rather than in isolation. In a related and novel investigation, Reynolds (187) found that when nonsense words were presented as labels on a pictorial map, this facilitated later sentence learning with these words. The effect was found to be greater when the map was intact than when it was presented as fragments. Additionally, the effect appeared to be relatively hardy with respect to age groups, materials, and testing methods. In some situations, then, rote learning of verbal material apparently can be enhanced by embedding the material in meaningful verbal or pictorial contexts.

Another problem in this area has to do with verbal mediation in a paired-associate learning and transfer. Shapiro & Palermo (207) reported that associative strength of words, as assessed by word association norms, had significant effects upon performance in forward and stimulus-equivalence, mediation paradigms. Similar findings were provided by Barsness & Jenkins (13). These investigators examined the relation to response transfer to verbal association strength in fifth-grade children. Results showed response transfer was positively related to the associative strengths of the stimulus words employed. The higher the associative strength, the greater the transfer. Transfer in verbal learning can, however, be impeded by first task practice and by stimulus similarity, as shown by Price, Cobb & Morin (182).

Other investigators have continued to explore the role of verbal mediation in other learning tasks. To illustrate, Hall & Ware (102) presented a word list to elementary school children that had several critical words with strong word associates. In recognition trials, children were more likely to (falsely) assert that the strong associates had been on the original list than they were to make such assertions about control words. When verbal mediators were provided by the experimenter, however, they were found to facilitate the mastery of a simultaneous discrimination problem but to impede the solution of a successive problem [Miller (155)]. In addition, in an investigation by Cole et al. (50), it was reported that pictorial stimuli were more helpful to younger children (third grade) on a paired-associate task than they were for older children (fifth grade). The availability of categories for grouping the verbal stimuli, however, reduced the relative efficacy of the pictorial materials. Finally, the view that verbal mediation may be more prominent in older than in younger children was given support by

Garber & Ross (89). These investigators found significant differences between preschool and second-grade children in shifting within and between dimensions in a reversal shift task.

Reinforcement effects.—Studies of reinforcement effects over the past year seem to have focused upon the efficacy of social reinforcement, upon the cognitive evaluation of reinforcing agents, and upon the effects of reinforcement schedules when considered in the context of other variables. In the area of social reinforcers, Wright (253) found that social reinforcement (verbal praise or disapproval) was more effective in promoting learning on a stylus maze than was nonsocial reinforcement. Moreover, a combination of positive and negative social reinforcement seemed to work best of all. Contrasting results were, however, presented by Barnhart (12) who used a somewhat different design. In the Barnhart study, light signals or experimenter behaviors provided clues to a discrimination task. Under these circumstances, the lights provided more information than the nonverbal social cues. Barnhart, quite rightly in our opinion, interprets these results in terms of selective attention.

A somewhat different approach to the study of reinforcement effects concerns their cognitive evaluation. Nunnally & Faw (168) reported that cues associated with rewards were evaluated as more positive, led to greater expectancies of reward, and were looked at to a greater extent than were cues that had been associated with loss of reward. Findings that might also be interpreted from the perspective of changed cognitive evaluation are those of Early (68). This investigator found that children who were ranked as unpopular, but whose names were paired with high-valued words in a note learning task, were approached more by trained classmates than were control unpopular children. Sociometric ratings of the experimental children, nonetheless, did not change. Similar changes in social ranking as a consequence of social reinforcement and interaction were reported by Blain & Ramirez (23). A final approach to reinforcement contingencies concerned the effects of varied reinforcement schedules in larger contexts. Chertkoff (41) explored the effects of freedom to leave the experimental situation when children were trained to press a lever under 50 per cent or 100 per cent reinforcement conditions. Results showed that subjects who were free to quit the experiment left the room sooner during extinction trials if they were trained under the 50 per cent rather than the 100 per cent reinforcement condition. In a study which also employed 50 per cent and 100 per cent reinforcement, Semler & Pederson (205) reported faster lever movement speed among 6-year-old children given 50 per cent reinforcement than among youngsters given 100 per cent reward.

Before this section on learning is closed, a few of the more theoretical articles that appeared during the year need to be mentioned. Gagné (86) presented an informative discussion of the growth gradient (G. S. Hall, Gesell), cognitive adaptation (Piaget), and cumulative learning models of human intelligence. In an equally thoughtful paper, White (246) reviewed some of the many issues that surround the concepts of maturation and learning. White argued that the long-standing preference for learning studies derives, in part at least, from the simple fact that learning is easier to study experimentally than is maturation. Unfortunately, this has often led to a too ready dismissal of maturational factors in the study and interpretation of the acquisition process. In a more technical piece, Goulet (98) reviewed research on verbal learning with an eye to its implications for developmental research and suggested incorporating age as a treatment variable in such investigations.

Cognitive Development

Studies of cognitive development in children again appeared in quantity this year, and many workers took the Piagetian conservation or other cognitive tasks as starting points. We will begin with the Piagetian-related studies and then, in turn, consider some more traditional concept attainment and problem solving investigations; following this, we report a few experiments in creativity and imagination. The closing paragraphs will review some cross-cultural studies in cognitive development.

Piagetian tasks.—Studies dealing with conservation continue to approach this problem from several different points. Replication and validation studies continue to appear. Bittner and Shinedling's monograph (22) dealt with conservation of substance and revealed that the sequence of substages in the attainment of substance conservation were as Piaget reported, but that for younger (first grade) children, both instructional and task variations affected performance. In an interesting variant of the conservation of continuous quality problem, Halford (101) tested conservers and nonconservers on containers which varied in one or two dimensions from the standard. Conservers were better able to judge equality and inequality even without the standard than were the controls. This finding corresponds with the Piagetian view that conservation presupposes both the ability to coordinate dimensions and the ability to make logical deductions. Finally, Goldschmid & Bentler (96) devised a "conservation scale" which showed high internal consistency and homogeneity. Additionally, scores on the scale correlated highly with school grades and with other nonconservation variables.

A more critical approach to the conservation problems has been taken by other investigators. Hall & Simpson (103) claimed not to have found the resistance to extinction on the part of spontaneous conservers previously reported by Smedslund. In reply, Smedslund (214) noted that the obtained percentages were not far different from those reported by him, and that differences in depth of interrogation could account for the disparity. A somewhat different approach was taken by Farnham-Diggory & Bermon (76), who found that conserving children used verbal compensation descriptions to a significantly greater extent than did nonconservers. Conservers also combined logographs (symbols for whole words) significantly better than did nonconservers. The authors seemed to interpret this finding as favoring linguistic determination of cognitive development.

Training studies aimed at exploring the experimental determinants of conservation were also reported. Smith (215) tried Smedslund's method of addition-subtraction and Beilin's method of verbal rule instruction in weight conservation. Rule instruction was much more effective than addition-subtraction. Smith, like Hall & Simpson, found that both spontaneous conservers and those who acquired it via training were not very resistant to extinction procedures. In contrast, Mackay & Kilkenny (142) found that the conservation responses induced by screening in 4½- to 7-year-old children were retained on the delayed (two-week) post test. Finally, Lefrancois (130) used a Gagné type series of ordered training experiences to induce conservation of mass in 25 of his subjects.

If we may editorialize for a moment, the conservation problems present many and vexing issues. In the first place, the developmental descriptive data are so uniform across nations and social classes that the phenomena of conservation cannot be denied. That there may be a maturational component to these tasks is, moreover, no more nativistic than the assumption that there is a maturational component to subtests of the WISC and the Stanford Binet. One can, of course, quarrel with Piaget's interpretation of conservation. While testing alternate hypotheses to explain conservation is a worthwhile activity, attempts to explain away conservation seem less than a constructive enterprise.

In a sense, the conservation problems present children with an illusion which is then overcome with the aid of reason. Accordingly, the ability to overcome illusions, given the appropriate information, should appear at about the age that concrete operations are established. In several related studies, Murray (160-162) demonstrated that this was indeed the case. Murray used the Mueller-Lyer illusion to assess conservation of length. In one study he found that children who conserved length on the Mueller-Lyer did not show conservation when they had to use the sticks in a problem-solving task. In a second study, Murray found that while ability to make phenomenal-real discriminations is related to conservation, it appears as a necessary but not as a sufficient condition. In still a third experiment, Murray reported that nonconservers trained under reversibility and cognitive procedures did significantly better than nontrained subjects on the Mueller-Lyer test of length conservation. Whereas there was transfer to another length conservation problem, there was no transfer to a problem of area conservation.

The remaining studies dealing with Piagetian tasks are less closely related. Coon & Odom (53) used the transitivity of length task in a simulated Asch type conformity situation. They found that conformity diminished with age (i.e., from age 7 to 11 and 11 to 15) and interpreted their findings with regard to the effects of task irrelevant cues on performance of Piagetian tasks. Murray & Youniss (163), among other findings, reported a clear relation between the ability to make transitive inferences and success on a seriation task (such a relation is postulated by Piaget's theory). In still another training study, Winer (250) did not have much more success than previous investigators in inducing number conservation with addition-subtraction training procedure.

Some interesting findings regarding the class inclusion problem with children 5 to 7 were reported by Wohlwill (251). One consistent result was that verbally presented class inclusion problems were easier for children than pictorially presented items. A second finding was that while practice in counting and in adding elements was beneficial to performance, such training did not override the contribution of the child's level of cognitive development. Finally, a rather interesting take-off on the Piagetian concepts was reported by Saltz & Hamilton (198). These investigators had children use an ingenious motoric index of their affective evaluations of verbal transforms of familiar concepts. "Father studies and becomes a doctor. Is he still a father?" Among 8-year-old subjects, "positively" evaluated transforms were more likely to be accepted than "negatively" evaluated transforms.

In closing this section on Piagetian-related research in children, a further comment might be made. Piaget is often criticized for his nonexperimental methodology. Yet the phenomena which he uncovered by this diagnostic method has provided the starting point for a wealth of experimental research. Science also develops, and while the experimental method may be the ideal, a fledgling science should not ignore its natural history stage of inquiry. It seems possible that the recent transformation of biology into a experimental science was—in part at least—because of, rather than in spite of, the centuries of classificatory work that preceded this explosion into experimentation.

Concept attainment studies.—There is, unfortunately, no common unifying thread which unites the concept attainment studies reported this year. Although it is a highly arbitrary distinction, we will report concept attainment studies first, rule learning studies second, and problem solving investigations last.

Two studies tried somewhat new variations on the traditional concept attainment and assessment paradigms. Suppes & Rosenthal-Hill (222) had children sort cards to samples of positive and positive and negative instances. One finding was that concepts involving geometric forms were attained more readily than concepts involving people and their activities or attire. Starting from the verbal definition method of concept assessment, Clark & McDonald (45) found that the common property selected by the subject was, on the average, that property which had previously been shown to have the highest associative tie to the concept in question. We would suspect, however, that any interpretation of these results would rapidly lead to the old chicken or the egg quandary.

Three studies dealt with size and form concepts. Tsai and Ghien (232) found that the concept of middleness depends not only upon the developmental level of the child but also upon the particular stimulus dimensions employed in the investigations. In a study that may have relevance for conservation problems, Barbara et al. (10) reported that for 5- and 6-year-old children the solid having the greater vertical dimension is the one which was regarded as "bigger." Finally, in a variation of color versus form preference study, Bearison & Sigel (16) reported that form was the most preferred dimension among both boys and girls at all age levels from 7 to 11. When representation was introduced as a third choice, it was preferred over both color and form. Not surprisingly, meaningful stimuli are more interesting than nonmeaningful stimuli.

In two other studies, right-left discrimination was the focus of investigation. Wapner & Cirillo (237) employed an adaptation of Head's hand-and-ear test to subjects from 8 to 18 years of age. Success on this test, which required the subject to imitate the examiner on progressively more difficult items, showed a regular increase with age across all groups tested. Body relations were easiest to imitate, whereas relations utilizing an object shared by the examiner and subject were most difficult to discriminate and copy. In a related study, Boone & Prescott (28) reported normative data for children from 5 through 10 on a test of right-left discrimination. As in the Wapner & Cirillo study, there was a linear increase with age with regard to success on the left-right discrimination items.

To close this section, several developmental descriptive studies dealing with problem solving and rule learning need to be acknowledged. In an investigation by Stevenson et al. (219), it was found that the ability to solve anagrams increased regularly between the ages of 8 and 14. Moreover, girls performed consistently better than boys on these tasks. Neimark & Lewis (164) did a one-year follow-up of children previously tested on a small battery of Piagetian measures and concluded that: "Individual developmental patterns were compatible with the interpretation of the development of cognitive structures as progression through a hierarchy of relatively discrete stages." Finally, King (118) reported that children as young as 6 years of age learned bidimensional classification rules by generating and testing hypotheses rather than by more elementary associative processes.

These various studies reflect the growing acceptance of the role of cognitive processes in a variety of learning situations where they were previously, if not denied, then at least neglected. A caution is in order, however, since there is a danger of cognizing every task. It would be heartening if some investigators reported the deviant as well as the model solution processes used by children in their investigations. The fact that the same problem can be solved by several different kinds of processes cannot be reiterated too often. What we need to know is what processes are used by which children on what tasks under what circumstances. A blind devotion to cognitive processes can produce as narrow an outlook as an equally narrow devotion to processes of association.

Creativity and giftedness.—Surprisingly few studies have appeared this year dealing with creativity. Ward (238) used some of the Kogan and Wallach procedures and controls for setting and found that a creativity dimension could be distinguished in kindergarten children and that this dimension was unrelated to the "reflection-impulsivity" response style. Sutton-Smith (223) revealed some of the subtleties in this area by showing that boys gave more unique responses to "male" toys such as toy trucks and blocks, whereas girls gave more unique responses to "female" toys such as dolls and dishes. Not surprisingly, then, interest, familiarity, and motivation affect performance on "creativity" measures. The term "creativity" has, moreover, become so value laden that it might better, as Cronbach (56) suggests, to drop the term in favor of the neutral labels for the various tasks used in such investigations. A monograph by Oden (169) reporting a recent follow-up on Terman's gifted (i.e., high intelligence) children suggests that high intelligence is, after all, no handicap. This latest evidence again attests to the fact that the highly intelligent child becomes the highly successful adult. Mortality rates are lower and educational and vocational success is much higher, while mental illness, divorce, etc. are much less frequent in the gifted than they are in those of average endowment.

Cross-cultural studies.—Although it doesn't get much publicity, we have more cross-cultural data on cognitive development in children than we have for any other subject area in psychology. The value of this data for assessing such factors as the role of experience in cognitive development has yet to be fully realized and exploited. A few of the more recent studies of this kind are noted below. A preliminary study by Prince (183), undertaken in the territory of Papua and New Guinea, suggested that school grade rather than calendar age was the most significant determinant in the attainment of substance and weight concepts among primary school children and a teacher's college group.

Using an adaptation of King's Piaget-type tests, Poole (178) explored the effect of urbanization upon scientific concept attainment among the Hausa children of Northern Nigeria. School children as well as children living in isolated rural communities were tested. Results supported the findings of previous studies of this kind in that the urban children were more successful than the rural children. A somewhat different approach to studying cognitive development in Nepalese children was employed by Sundberg & Ballinger (221). These investigators used the draw-a-person test and scored it according to the Goodenough criteria. Compared to American norms, Nepalese children averaged IQ's of 100 at age 6, but these scores dropped to 75 by age 13. Sex and caste differences were not significant. The authors provide a good example of how to exploit the richness of cross-cultural data and yet avoid the trap of oversimplistic interpretation of findings.

A very promising type of cross-cultural study was undertaken by Davey (59) with Tristan da Cunha children who had just moved to Great Britain. Davey tested these youngsters soon after their arrival and again about 12 months later. To assess concepts of equivalence, Davey utilized a free-sorting task. The stages of conceptual development observed were comparable to those obtained with British children. The youngest subjects grouped according to sensory attributes, somewhat older children grouped according to function, and the oldest subjects used abstract categories. The effect of a year's stay in Great Britain was merely to move children ahead in this sequence.

Language

Studies dealing with language seemed to fall into two more or less distinct groups. In the first group were studies of a developmental descriptive nature in the sense that they compared language skills of subjects at different age levels. These studies, however, differed from the developmental descriptive studies of even a decade ago. Current studies of this sort emphasize the changes in structures and grammar that occur with age rather than size of vocabulary or the order of appearance of "parts of speech." The second group of studies also stressed the structural and grammatical features of language but approached these features in an experimental rather than in a descriptive way.

Developmental descriptive studies.—By far the greatest number of studies of this kind dealt with developmental changes in the meanings attributed to words. Starting at the most simple level—letter sequence habits—Amster & Keppel (4) found that in comparison to adults, children gave more alphabetical responses to letters and fewer meaningful associations (such as words or initials of institutions). At a somewhat more complex level, Bashaw & Anderson (14) explored age changes in adverbial modifiers (e.g., rather, quite, decidedly). Primary school children identified three adverb groups, whereas adults identified six groups. Some words shifted in meaning across the school grades (i.e., 1, 2, 3, 4, 5, 6; 8, 10, 12 and college).

A comparison of associations given to verbal stimuli by subjects of different age levels continues to amplify the data provided by word association norms. Clark (44) compared the adjective responses given by children and adults to noun stimuli. He found a moderately high degree of similarity between adults and fifth-grade children's responses. Children, however, gave more varied responses than did the older subjects. In a related study, Riegel et al. (191) reported that the "restricted" associations to 22 nouns of third and sixth graders resembled free associations to a greater extent than did the associations of college students. A novel approach to the problem of age differences in understanding was provided by Basit (15), who employed artificial proverbs for his subjects to interpret. Although his small samples (12 children, 12 adults) make generalization risky, he found that children selected long and complex sentences to explain the proverbs, while adults selected sentences with the same number of syllables as the artificial (nonsense) proverb. The method seems to have potential for exploring developmental strategies in interpreting meaningful utterances.

A final study might have been grouped in the next section except that it deals with a prominent developmental phenomenon, the "paradigmatic shift." This "shift" has to do with the well-established observation that the associations of young children tend to be syntactic (go-away), whereas those of older children and adults tend to relate to the same form class (go-come). Anderson & Beh (6) presented some experimental evidence that they feel support NcNeil's hypothesis that the paradigmatic shift represents the acquisition of a tendency to match some sort of semantic markers in recall. It would be interesting, too, to see whether the paradigmatic shift was related to the appearance of Piaget's concrete operations as well as to the acquisition of a lexical marking system.

Learning studies.—Some of the studies reported here might have been grouped under the verbal learning studies reported earlier. They are placed here because they seemed to be concerned with language more as a system than was true for the other studies, but the difference is relative at best. Again we will start at the simplest level. Menyuk (153) explored the role of different types of distinctive features in the acquisition and correct usage of consonants by Japanese and American children. She found that the behavior she observed could be described with regard to a system of distinctive features (gravity, diffuseness, stridency, nasality, continuancy, and voicing). "It was found that these features played a hierarchical role in the acquisition and proportion of correct usage of consonant sounds and in terms of resistance to perceptual and productive confusion."

Several studies dealt with the comprehension and learning of grammatical and ungrammatical constructions. Herriot (107) gave children a comprehension task that required them to match pictures to active and passive affirmative sentences. Semantic content was altered by putting nonsense words in place of some sentence components. Older children were able to use even the sentences with the nonsense words to select the appropriate picture. Herriot concluded that the grammatical construction had referential meaning. In this connection, Menyuk (152) found that it was much more difficult for young children (preschool through second grade) to reproduce nongrammatical sentences than grammatical sentences. Likewise, Lezotte & Byers (135) reported that "syntactical violation" in the presentation of verbal stimuli significantly inhibited recall under some conditions. Finally, Odom, Liebert & Hill (171) found that while children could imitate ungrammatical phrases, they did not generate new ones but rather tended to make such utterances grammatically correct.

In the area of communication, Cohen & Klein (49) observed third, fifth, and seventh-grade children in a word communication task. In this task, the speaker provided clue words to enable the listener to select the correct object. Results showed that communication accuracy—frequency of correct listeners' choices of speakers' referents—increased significantly with age level. Choice of referent words by the speakers at the different grade levels apparently played some part in communication accuracy. A large number of ingenious studies dealing with role taking and communication skills in children and adolescents were reported in a volume by Flavell (83).

Perceptual and Motor Development

Under the above heading we will review three types of investigation. The first group of studies involve form of visual discrimination and attention. The second group of studies is concerned with the preference for visual materials. The third group of studies reviewed under this heading, has to do with motor as well as visual behavior.

Visual discrimination.—Pollack, Ptashne & Carter (177) reported another of their investigations which adduced evidence for Pollack's view that physiological aging of the visual receptor system begins in childhood. In this particular study, 6- to 10-year-old children were tested for their dark interval threshold. Results showed that the threshold decreased with increasing chronological age—a finding that Pollack interprets as supporting his position. A more culturally oriented approach to visual discrimination was taken by Kilbride, Robbins & Freeman (117), who tested the pictorial depth perception of Baganda children. These investigators observed, among other things, that pictorial depth perception among rural Baganda children was directly related to the amount of formal education which they had received. In the area of figurative perception, Westcott & Tolchin (244) found additional evidence for an age-related increase in the ability of school age subjects to recognize incomplete pictures.

Two studies dealt with the responses of subjects to random shapes that varied in complexity. Siegel (212) tested third and sixth-grade children and college students on random shapes that varied in complexity. She found that while systematic training produced significant improvement in college students' judgments of complexity, such training did not have this effect upon children. In a related study, Munsinger (158), one of the early workers in this field, tested children and adults for their responsiveness to the correlation of colors with random shapes differing in complexity. Adults but not children were able to use the color cues to estimate the correlated shapes.

Other studies in this group dealt with stimulus familiarization effects. Cantor & Fenson (35) found that the "stimulus familiarization effect"—faster reaction speeds to nonfamiliarized than to the familiarized stimulus—obtained only for children who were given the maximum number (18) of familiarization trials. Cantor (34) also found that nonfamiliarized stimuli were rated as "liked" significantly more often than familiarized stimuli. In a related study, Manley & Miller (145) explored the effect of familiarization on stimulus preference. They reported that while the nonfamiliar stimulus was chosen more frequently as a consequence of familiarization with its alternate, this effect was not related to the amount of familiarization. Perhaps the discrepancy in these two studies regarding the effects of amount of familiarization has something to do with the criterion behaviors employed. In a more complex exploration of familiarization, Murphy et al. (159) tested the effects of reinforcing responses to animal figures. One of their findings was that the previously reinforced figures were more easily identified in a search task than figures that had not been so reinforced.

Stimulus preference studies.—A number of studies dealt with stimulus preference. An investigation by Child, Hansen & Hornbeck (42) explored age and sex differences in color preferences. They concluded (in part)as follows "consistent preference for cool hues and high saturation; female preference for lighter colors; and with increasing age, a decreasing preference for high saturation, an increasing consistency of hue choices compared with consistency of saturation choices." Preference for complex (5- to 8-sided) figures over less complex (4-sided) figures was found in 5, 9, and 19-year-old subjects by Willis & Dornbush (249).

In a somewhat different vein, Baltes, Schmidt & Boesch (9) presented 8, 10, 12, 14, 17, and 20-year-old subjects with different numbers of light flashes within a 10-sec interval. With increasing age, subjects preferred the slower (less frequent) visual flashes. This result apparently conforms to what has been found with auditory sequences. Finally, Faw & Nunnally (78) took motion pictures of a subject's eye while he viewed pairs of stimuli that varied in complexity, novelty, or affective value. One finding was that the fixations of children were dominated by the more complex or novel figures when these were compared with less complex or banal figures.

Motor performance.—Studies of motor behavior were of two kinds: those concerned with the development of motor skills per se and those in which motor skills were the medium for assessing other aspects of behavior and experience. Connolly, Brown & Bassett (52) studied the performance of 6, 8 and 10-year-old children on a target task. At all ages, girls performed faster than boys, but there was a general increase in speed with age for both sexes. No reliable age or sex differences were found in the accuracy dimension. There was, however, a systematic change in the scatter of shots around the target that the authors attribute to different strategies employed by the different age groups. On a pinball-type motor task, Rieber (190) found that 5, 7, and 9-year-old children's success was related to the availability and utilization of cues in the apparatus.

Geometric form reproduction and its relation to chronological and mental age was investigated by Beery (17). He reported that form reproduction was related primarily to mental age rather than chronological age within his age groups (i.e., first, fourth, and sixth grade children). In a different type of study, Gellert (90) found no support for the hypothesis that, measured by the detail of their figure drawings, elementary school children have more differentiated like-sex than opposite-sex body images.

Personality and Socialization

Trying to classify diverse studies in a meaningful way is always difficult, and the hardships are compounded when we come to studies dealing with personality and socialization. Under the heading of personality studies, we will describe those investigations in which some aspect of personality, such as anxiety, was treated as the independent variable. Contrariwise, when some facet of personality, such as moral behavior, was treated as the dependent variable in relation to social or experimental manipulations, we will describe them under the rubric of socialization. It is an arbitrary distinction at best, but may have some heuristic values. Studies of personality will be presented first, and these will be followed by investigations dealing with socialization.

Personality.—By far the largest number of studies to be reported in this section dealt with anxiety and its effects upon performance. The other studies to be reviewed have to do either with other types of motivation or with self concept. We will begin with the anxiety data. Studies using the Children's Manifest Anxiety Scale (CMAS) were reported by Lott & Lott (140) and by Tryon (231). In the Lott & Lott study, black 9- and 10-year-old youngsters attained higher CMAS scores than white children. Correlations of CMAS scores and sociometric standing were, however, generally low, and there was no evidence of a relation between manifest anxiety and learning task performance. Likewise, Tryon (231) found no relation between CMAS scores and thumb sucking.

Studies employing the Test Anxiety Scale also met with mixed success. Barnard, Zimbardo & Sarason (11) found no relationship between teacher's ratings of children on 24 personality characteristics and the children's test anxiety status. A more complicated design was employed by Cox (54). This investigator was concerned with the effects of test anxiety and the presence or absence of fathers, male teachers, peers, and strange male adults on the marble-dropping behavior of third and fourth grade boys. Results suggested that

> low test-anxious boys showed response increments when any of these persons entered and stayed in the experimental room, while the presence of fathers or male teachers resulted in response decrements in high test-anxious boys. Conversely, when only experimenter and subject were present, low test-anxious subjects showed response decrements while high test-anxious subjects showed response increments under these conditions.

In a study by Weinstein (241), test anxiety was found to be related to the mother-child "schema" (as measured by the figure placement procedure), but partialing out this correlation did not affect the significant correlations between the schema and academic achievement. Apparently, the relation between the mother-child schema and achievement is not mediated by test anxiety.

In addition to these anxiety studies, two attitudinal investigations were of interest. Flanders, Morrison & Brode (82) found a significant loss in positive attitude of pupils towards their teachers and towards school work during the school year. Results were not related to IQ but were related to Rotter's ubiquitous externality and internality (I.E. Scale) dimensions and to teachers' verbal classroom behavior. Children high in externality showed more erosion of positive attitudes than children high on internality. The erosion of positive attitudes was also greater for pupils of teachers who used relatively little verbal praise or encouragement. A related study by Laderne (127) reported that there was no relationship between children's attitudes toward school and measures of attention. Performance on the attention measures was, in contrast, positively related to intelligence and achievement tests.

Attitudes towards the self were explored in several studies. Long, Henderson & Ziller (139) utilized the self-ratings of elementary school children on two scales of the semantic differential. These authors pointed out that their most striking finding was a high negative correlation between mental age and extremity of response set. Of this finding they wrote "it suggests that one characteristic of the immature mind is that judgments tend to be absolute. The thinking of young children appears to be rather dogmatic, with few qualifications and little indecision." One implication of this finding would appear to be that children tend to see themselves as less "all bad" or "all good" as they grow up. A somewhat different approach to the self-concept problem was taken by Boshier (29), who found very high correlations (around .80) between the self-esteem scores of elementary school children and their expressions of liking or disliking of their own first names. Taking still another tack, Goldschmid (95), among other findings, reported that children with a relatively high level of conservation for their age group were more objective in their self evaluations than were youngsters relatively low on conservation. Not surprisingly the self concept appears to be closely related to cognitive development.

Before concluding this section, a couple of theoretical papers should be mentioned. Emmerich (71) suggested that many concepts of personality structure derive from one of three orientations which he calls "classical," "differential," and "ipsative." He compared and contrasted these positions and pointed out some of their research implications. Gewirtz & Stingle (91) attempted to encompass data regarding generalized imitation within instrumental conditioning and stimulus-response chaining concepts. Evaluation of their success in this regard will probably vary with one's own theoretical orientation.

Socialization.—Studies done on socialization over the past year seem to fall into four, less rather than more, distinct groups. Studies in the first group dealt with parent-child relations, attitudes, and so on. A second group of studies concerned itself primarily with the processes of social learning. The third group reflected the growing interest in what has come to be called "prosocial" behavior, the positive rather than the negative interpersonal behaviors. A final set of studies dealt with social forces within the classroom situation.

Parent-child relations.—A number of studies reflected the current interest in birth order differences. Such studies are included here because, presumably, the differences which do occur are mediated, at least in part, by parental behaviors and socialization practices. A study by Chittenden et al. (43) found still more evidence for the superiority of first-born children on measures of school achievement. These writers suggested that the effect may be greater for siblings close in age and for first-born girls. Some of the cautions in interpreting the birth order effects were suggested by Rhine (188). He found that first-born preadolescent girls were more conforming than later-born children under a low achievement arousal condition. The relation was, however, completely reversed under the high achievement arousal condition. In another domain, Shrader & Leventhal (209) reported that first-born children are regarded by their parents as having more emotional problems than later-born children.

The effects of father absence in families with different sibling composition was explored by Sutton-Smith, Rosenberg & Landy (224). Results indicated, in general, that father absence almost always had a depressive effect upon the children. This depressive effect was most prominent during the preschool and elementary school years, especially for boys without brothers and for girls with younger brothers. Surprisingly, father absence also appeared to have more negative effects for only girls than it did for only boys. In a more direct study of parental attitudes and children's behavior, Gibson (92) found that parents' failure to return the completed inventories (regarding the upbringing of their children) was as much related to bad conduct and delinquency as the attitude scales themselves!

Social learning.—One question that has engaged workers in this area has to do with the conditions under which children will violate rules. Liebert & Ora (136) reported, among other things, that high incentive was more conducive to rule violation when the child was alone than was low incentive. Rosenhan, Frederick & Burrowes (193) studied the effects of different socialization paradigms upon the child's adherence to strict and lenient norms. Results indicated that adherence to the strict norm was greatest among children who were taught the norm and who also observed a model practice the norm. Children exposed to a self-indulgent model were the most ambivalent and the least likely to violate both strict and lenient norms. Those youngsters exposed to a child-indulgent model violated the lenient norms least of all.

Other studies have attempted to explore the mediating mechanisms in social learning more directly. To illustrate, O'Leary (172), reported that first-grade boys told to instruct themselves as to whether a game response was "right" or "wrong" appeared to "cheat" less than youngsters who were not told to label their responses. In a related study, Kanfer & Duerfeldt (113) used undeserved self-rewards as "cheating" responses. They reported that "cheating" of this sort was determined by several interacting situational and individual difference factors. To illustrate, the higher the child's standing in class (teacher's rating) and his age (second to fifth grade) the less frequent were his undeserved self-rewards. In still another study in this vein, Stephenson & White (218) observed "cheating" as a function of unjust, poor treatment. As expected, cheating was directly related to the degree of injustice meted out.

Prosocial behavior.—It might be well to start off with an interesting developmental descriptive study by Shure (210). Both adults and elementary school children were presented with story situations to assess their concepts of fairness, generosity, and selfishness in specific situations. Results showed that there was most agreement with respect to fairness and least with respect to selfishness among adults. "In general, the concepts for which there was the highest agreement in adults were the earliest (to be grasped) in children." A more experimental approach was taken by Feshbach & Roe (79). These investigators found support among 6- to 7-year-old boys and girls for the hypothesis that similarity between sex of the subject and of the object facilitates emphatic behavior (defined as a vicarious affective response). Feshbach & Roe also made a useful distinction between recognizing the affective state of another person and making an affective response to that perception. While studies in this domain are just beginning, a review paper by Midlarsky (154) has already appeared. She reviewed the methodology of studies of prosocial behavior and the results of some of the recent investigations in this area. She argued that some of the contradictory results obtained so far derive from a lack of methodological and theoretical sophistication.

Classroom behavior.—This is not the place to review the many educationally oriented studies of classroom behavior, but studies with primarily psychological relevance should be noted. Operant conditioning has appeared to have really caught on in this area. Hall, Lund & Jackson (104) reported that when teachers attended to children's study behaviors and ignored nonstudy behavior, rates of study increased (for one first-grade child and five third-grade children). The increased rates were maintained after the formal program terminated. Likewise, Madsen, Becker & Thomas (144) also found that when teachers ignored inappropriate behavior but rewarded appropriate actions, better classroom behavior was achieved on the part of the three experimental children involved.

Similar results for the entire classroom were reported by Thomas, Becker & Armstrong (228). They reported that approving responses on the part of the teacher served to maintain class order, but that disruption occurred when such approval was withdrawn. Not only teacher approval but also teacher "tempo" may affect the children in her classroom, as demonstrated by Yando & Kagan (254). These investigators found that "children taught by experienced reflective teachers showed a greater increase in response time over the course of the academic year than all other children."

Theoretical articles.—In a careful review, Bell (19) summarized studies which suggested that traditional models of socialization—the action of a parent on a child—are simply too limited to account adequately for data coming from recent studies with human and animal subjects. Bell offered a set of propositions that dealt with the effects of congenital features in children on parent behavior. A useful summary of literature dealing with imitation in dyadic relations was provided by Flanders (81), who evaluated the theoretical viewpoints implicit or explicit in such investigations.

Race and Social Class

Among the positive aspects of the social ferment in America today is the increased recognition among psychologists of the relevance of ethnic and social class differences in behavior and experience. It is probably fair to say that child psychology, as it is taught and presented in textbooks, is largely the psychology of the middle-class child. While this is not necessarily bad, it does emphasize the need to recognize that while "children are children," it is also true that there are black and white as well as rich and poor chidren. Put differently, while all youngsters share features in common by virtue of being children, they may also differ in significant respects because of the ethnic and social class subcultures to which they belong.

The studies presented in this section might easily have been placed in the preceding pigeonholes. Such a procedure would not have provided the impact which we believe such research should produce, however. So, at the risk of being redundant, we will again present studies of learning, cognition, perception and motor skills, language, personality and socialization, wherein the independent variable in whole or part involved racial and social class differences.

Learning.—It is becoming increasingly clear that any racial or social class differences which do appear may be highly task or skill specific and that overall generalizations regarding racial and/or socioeconomic differences in mental or learning ability are probably not warranted. This judgment was highlighted by the findings of Dietz & Johnson (63) that there were no differences between middle and lower-class whites and blacks on a discrimination reversal learning task. In a like manner, Rohwer et al. (192) failed to find differences in paired-associate learning between children in "high" and "low" strata. Disadvantaged school children may nonetheless benefit from a more structured classroom setting than advantaged children as shown by Avila, Gordon & Curran (8). The efficacy of the more structured classroom for the disadvantaged may result from a contrast effect. Middle-class children receive sufficient structure at home to benefit from freedom at school, whereas the reverse may hold true for disadvantaged children.

Cognition.—The specificity regarding social class and ethnic differences mentioned earlier has to be reiterated with respect to cognition. Where such differences do exist, they are likely to be task or process specific rather than general. Scholnick, Osler & Katzenellenbogen (201) compared 5 and 8-

year-old middle and lower-class children at two IQ levels on a discrimination training and on a concept identification task. Social class differences, in the expected direction, were found for the discrimination but not for the concept identification task. Similarly, Katz (116) found the expected developmental progressions and correlations with IQ in a concept attainment study with black elementary school children. Differences between lower and middle-class subjects were, however, observed by London & Robinson (138). These workers used an identification learning task with groups instructed to use verbal labels, mental images, or no instruction. Of relevance here is the finding that while the instructions did not differentially affect the performance of lower social class children, they did significantly affect the learning of middle-class young people.

Perceptual and motor skills.—A novel study of ethnic differences was reported by Goss (97), who explored the differences between estimated and actual physical strength in three ethnic groups (Negro, Latin American, and Anglo-American). One interesting finding was a decrease with age in the overestimation of hand grip strength which held true for all ethnic groups. One ethnic group factor of interest was that blacks were significantly stronger on the dynameter ratings than the other groups and that this was particularly true for black females. Goss offered an interesting cultural explanation for this finding, based upon the role of the woman in black families.

Language.—Language has been one of the most active and fruitful areas for the study of social class and ethnic differences. To illustrate, McNeil (149) found that middle and lower-class white, Mexican-American, and black children differed with respect to their ratings of particular concepts on the semantic differential. McNeil argued that semantic space is neither qualitatively nor quantitatively constant across subcultures. In another domain, Krauss & Rotter (125) had lower-class (black) and middle-class (white) speakers, aged 7 and 12, name novel graphic designs. Middle-class children at both age levels tended to be superior both in providing relevant labels and in identifying the labels provided by other children for identification of the designs. Finally, Eisenberg et al. (69) reported, as one of their findings, that "Negro children showed generally poorer listening scores than whites, and Negro speakers generated slightly poorer intelligibility scores than whites." A book by Deutsch, Katz & Jensen (62) reviews a good deal of the work in this area.

Personality and socialization.—Studies in this group are quite varied and difficult to categorize. This reflects, perhaps, the newness of the field. Greenwald & Oppenheim (100) challenged previous racial doll studies that suggested black children are more given to misidentification than white youngsters. These investigators found that the inclusion of a third (mulatto) alternative in the task significantly reduced the misidentifications of black children. They concluded that "there is nothing unusual about Negro children's misidentifications." A similar conclusion was arrived at by Richardson & Royce (189) who found that the most salient fact determining children's preference for other children was not skin color but rather absence of a physical handicap. This was equally true for children from lower-income black, white, and Puerto Rican families and from upper-income white, Jewish families.

Differences were found in other studies. Katz, Henchy & Allen (115) observed that black children performed better on a verbal learning task when the tester was black rather than white. In a somewhat different type of study, Biller (21) explored the effect of father absence upon the masculinity of lower-class black and white children. Results suggested that white father-present boys were the most masculine and black father-absent boys were the least masculine. There was no significant difference in masculinity ratings between white father-absent boys and black father-present boys.

ADOLESCENCE

Adolescence, as a field for systematic exploration, continues to attract fewer investigators than the earlier age periods. In this respect the pattern of research in child development this year very much resembles the pattern that has been set since the beginning of this century, when Hall complained about the lack of attention paid to the 13 to 18-year-old age group. Accordingly, some of the categories used to organize research in children will be condensed or omitted in our discussion of studies of adolescents. The first section will deal with learning and cognitive growth, the second with personality and social development, while the third and final section will cover studies dealing with sex and socio-cultural differences.

Learning and Cognition

The studies in this category are a somewhat heterogeneous lot. Some of these are most concerned with developmental changes in performance and others with the learning process per se. In a study by Inglis, Ankus & Sykes (109), age-related changes in learning and short-term memory were reported. Subjects ranged in age from 5 to 70, and the expected inverted-U distribution was obtained both for serial learning and some aspects of sequential recall. In contrast, no age differences in long-term memory for apparent movement were found by Raskin (184) for 6 to 19-year-old subjects.

At a somewhat more complex level, Glick & Wapner (93) reported that there was an increase with age (in 8 to 18-year-old subjects) in their subjects' success with verbal and concrete transitivity problems. Developmental progression in another domain was reported by Kugelmass & Breznitz (126). These investigations found that intentionality as a criterion in moral judgment increased during the later years of adolescence. Likewise, Lovell (141) reported several studies with adolescents which suggested that formal operational thought as described by Piaget manifests itself later or earlier depending upon the subject matter under consideration. In history, for example, formal operational thought was not fully in evidence until about the age of 16. Not all tests, however, reveal age differences. To illustrate, Day (61) found no increase in specific curiosity among young people 13 to 16 years of age, nor was specific curiosity related to academic achievement.

A couple of learning studies employed adolescents as subjects. Le Furgy & Sisserson (131) had 13-year-old girls learn concepts under three conditions: preresponse prompting, postresponse confirmation, and a third condition in which subjects chose prompting or confirmation. Free-choice subjects were significantly better able to verbalize the rule and to generalize it than were girls under the other two conditions. An unusual problem-solving task was employed by Faucheux & Moscovici (77), who had children create designs by attaching seven sticks together in as many ways as possible. Among 14 and 17-year-old subjects, success was related to whether the subjects could use memory or had to construct the rules themselves. In another problem-solving study, Elkind, Barocas & Rosenthal (70) found that slow reading adolescents were more concrete on a combinatorial reasoning task than were matched controls (IQ, sex, and age) who were reading at grade level.

Personality and Social Behavior

The studies within this group fell roughly under three headings; those that dealt with personality and school achievement, those that dealt with the effects of various determinants upon personality and, finally, those which dealt with interpersonal or group phenomena.

Personality and academic achievement.—Starting from the Rotter dimension of belief in internal-external control of success and failure, McGhee & Crandall (147) studied the effect of this dimension on course grades and achievement test scores in children and adolescents. They concluded that, "while prediction of girls' performance scores was equally consistent from beliefs in their instrumentality for successes and for failures, boys' performance scores were consistently related to beliefs in responsibility for failure." A somewhat different approach was taken by Williams & Cole (248), who found that among sixth-grade pupils, positive self-concept scores were related to intelligence and to mathematical and reading achievement. A novel investigation in the personality and achievement domain was undertaken by Davids (60). This investigator assessed the rigidity-flexibility and intolerance of ambiguity dimension in underachieving and successful boys of high intelligence. In general, the successful boys showed greater flexibility and tolerance for ambiguity than did the underachievers. A related study dealing with the career aspirations of adolescent girls was offered by Astin (7). Using longitudinal data from Project Talent, she found that as girls matured (from ninth grade to one year after high school), bright girls were more likely to upgrade their career aspirations, whereas the reverse was true for less capable girls.

Determinants of personality.—The studies to be reported here are again quite diverse. Farley (75) did not find evidence for the relation reported in earlier investigations between season of birth, intelligence, and personality. Poppleton (179), in contrast, found that for girls between the ages of 11½ and 15½, family size as well as age at puberty had to be taken into account in relating maturation to educational achievement. (Studies like the two foregoing, by the way, are much more common in England, Europe, and Israel than they are in America.) The relation of achievement aspirations to parents' education was explored by Sewell & Shaw (206). Utilizing questionaire data from 9000 senior high students who were followed for 7 years thereafter, they reported, among other things, that father's education had a slightly stronger effect than did the mother's upon: (*a*) perceived parental encouragement; (*b*) college plans; (*c*) college attendance; and (*d*) college graduation. This was, however, only true for males. For girls, father's and mother's education had an equal effect. Finally, Renson, Schaefer & Levy (186) reported validity data for the "Child's Report of Parent Behavior Inventory" with Walloon high school students. The three obtained factors—Acceptance versus Rejection, Psychological Control, and Lax Control versus Form Control—were "similar for boys and girls, for reports of mothers and fathers, and for American and Walloon subjects."

Interpersonal and social behavior.—Here again we have several heterogeneous studies which took as their starting points rather different conceptual approaches. In a straightforward sociometric investigation, Harper (105) found that among 12-year-old boys rejection as a dimension was considerably more reliable than was the measure of acceptance. Harper offered the entirely reasonable hypothesis that the attributes which lead to social rejection "are more clearly defined than those that lead to acceptance." A more complex study of social attraction was reported by Thornatzky & Gerwitz (229). These workers used the prisoner's dilemma game with male high school students who could send threat and penalty messages. One finding was that subjects who were in the high mutual attraction condition showed more cooperative behavior than subjects in the low mutual attraction condition. Likewise, Alexander & Campbell (2), who also employed the Heider balance model, found that, among other things, sociometric choices of adolescent males could be predicted from a knowledge of their behavioral similarities, including the degree of alcohol use. Results of Sibley, Senn & Epanchin (211) showed that, in the prisoner's dilemma game, girls were more cooperative than boys and that pairs of the same race were more cooperative than mixed racial pairs.

To close this section, we want to summarize an interesting point on male, teenage peer groups. Sugarman (220) studied English secondary school boys and their peer group affiliations as well as their attitudes towards school achievement and conduct. What Sugarman found was that the peer group attitudes were also present in the home backgrounds of the peer group members. As Sugarman rightly points out, "Thus a problem arose as to whether the behaviors and attitudes emanated from the home but were supported by the peer group, or originated in the peer group but were reinforced by the home." This is an interesting and potentially significant point which deserves further investigation. To what extent is the much touted "peer group influence" due to the fact that it reinforces values and attitudes held in the home?

Sex differences.—While sex differences on psychological dimensions are present at all age levels, they are particularly prominent in adolescence. Some of these differences have been reported in the context of other studies. A few additional studies will be reported here which, as it happens, deal with disadvantaged young people. In one study, Mason (146) reported California Psychological Inventory data on disadvantaged junior high school students from American Indian, Mexican, and European ethnic backgrounds. Results suggested that females, regardless of ethnic background, were more poorly motivated and nonconforming than were their male counterparts. Teacher's descriptions, however, give a somewhat different picture. Datta, Schaefer & Davis (58) reported that both ethnic group and sex were significantly related to teacher's descriptions of the classroom behavior of seventh-grade students. Some of the results were: (*a*) girls were described more favorably than boys or Negroes; and (*b*) "higher IQ Negro subjects were described as favorably as were higher IQ Other (than Negro) adolescents, but the lower IQ Negro pupil was more likely than the lower IQ Other child to be described as maladadjusted, verbally aggressive, and low in task orientation."

Before closing this discussion of sex differences, a monograph by Garai & Scheinfeld (88), summarizing many of the studies pertaining to this variable, should be mentioned. These writers provided a comprehensive (474 references) review of sex differences in a variety of domains from sensory discrimination to intellectual performance. While it is not possible to summarize all of their conclusions, the following remarks may convey some of the spirit of the review: "Research has shown that men and women utilize different skills and abilities even when they learn similar subjects, and that the conditions under which males achieve their optimum level of performance differ from those under which women function optimumly."

CONCLUSION

In reviewing the work done in the field of child and developmental psychology over the past year, we found a great deal to applaud and some things to bemoan. On the positive side is the increasing sophistication of research and the increasing refinement and analysis of basic conceptions and assumptions. The interest in disadvantaged children, moreover, promises to broaden our child psychology beyond the narrow confines of the middle-class child. Equally important is the growing cooperation between psychologists and educational researchers and practitioners. Such cooperation is mutually beneficial. For the psychologist, education presents a whole new panorama of research problems which can only enrich his theories and experimental designs. Education, in turn, benefits from the rigor which research psychologists bring to educational problems.

We found other things to applaud as well. The interest in prosocial behavior is a very good omen. For too long we have focused upon the negative emotions such as anxiety, fear, and aggression. It is time we learned more about the positive motives and emotions. We know that frustration leads to aggression; would that we knew the precursors of love. Equally promising is the research on behavior modification with normal, retarded, and disturbed children which, while we could not review much of it, we want very much to acknowledge. Finally, the "new look" in language studies prompted by Skinner on the one hand and by Chomsky on the other has greatly expanded our conceptual and experimental outlooks on this particular area.

Despite these positive features, some of the negative trends in the field persist and should be noted. With a few notable exceptions, little systematic theoretical work in child development seems to be going on. Such theoretical work is essential if we are to begin to integrate the ever-increasing flow of research data. Secondly, there appears to be little interest in the phenomena of children's groups and the culture of childhood. The social psychology of the classroom, for example, has been explored by educators but is ripe for psychological investigation. Finally, we would like to emphasize the need for more work with adolescents. In the context of what is occurring on our campuses today, the importance of learning more about young people hardly needs to be underscored.

An *Annual Review* chapter, we said at the outset, is a servant of many masters, none of whom can be served particularly well. We feel the truth of that statement even more now that we have concluded our labors. Perhaps there is some truth after all to the old saying that "a servant like a mistress should be kept but a year."

LITERATURE CITED

1. Abravanel, E. Intersensory integration of spatial position during early childhood. *Percept. Mot. Skills,* **26,** 251–56 (1968)
2. Alexander, N. C., Jr., Campbell, E. Q. Balance forces and environmental effects: Factors influencing the cohesiveness of adolescent drinking groups. *Soc. Forces,* **46,** 367–74 (1968)
3. Alexander, T., Stoyle, J., Kirk, C. The language of children in the "Inner City." *J. Psychol.,* **68,** 215–21 (1968)
4. Amster, H., Keppel, G. Letter sequence habits in children. *J. Verbal Learn. Verbal Behav.,* **7,** 326–32 (1968)
5. Anderson, R. B., Rosenblith, J. F. The photic sneeze reflex in the human newborn: A preliminary report. *Develpm. Psychobiol.,* **1,** 65–66 (1968)
6. Anderson, S., Beh, W. The reorganization of verbal memory in childhood. *J. Verbal Learn. Verbal Behav.,* **7,** 1049–53 (1968)
7. Astin, H. S. Stability and change in the career plans of ninth grade girls. *Personnel Guid. J.,* **46,** 961–66 (1968)
8. Avila, D., Gordon, I. J., Curran, R. Behavioral changes in culturally disadvantaged children as the result of tutoring. *Psychol. Rept.,* 389–90 (1968)
9. Baltes, P., Schmidt, L. R., Boesch, E. E. Preference for different visual stimulus sequences in children, adolescents, and young adults. *Psychon. Sci.,* **12,** 271–72 (1968)
10. Barbara, W. S., Huisebus, P., Robert, C. The vertical dimension: A significant cue in the preschool child's concept of "bigger." *Psychon. Sci.,* **12,** 369–70 (1968)
11. Barnard, J. W., Zimbardo, P. G., Sarason, S. Teachers' ratings of student personality traits as they relate to IQ and social desirability. *J. Educ. Psychol.,* **59,** 128–32 (1968)
12. Barnhart, J. E. The acquisition of cue properties by social and nonsocial events. *Child Develpm.,* **39,** 1237–46 (1968)
13. Barsness, W. D., Jenkins, J. J. Verbal association strength and response transfer. *Child Develpm.,* **39,** 1201–12 (1968)
14. Bashaw, W. L., Anderson, H. E. Developmental study of the meaning of adverbial modifiers. *J. Educ. Psychol.,* **59,** 111–18 (1968)
15. Basit, A. A comparative study of verbal understanding in children and adults. *J. Verbal Learn. Verbal Behav.,* **7,** 1121–22 (1968)
16. Bearison, D. J., Sigel, I. E. Hierarchical attributes for categorization. *Percept. Mot. Skills,* **27,** 147–53 (1968)
17. Beery, K. E. Geometric form reproduction: Relationship to chronological and mental age. *Percept. Mot. Skills,* **26,** 247–50 (1968)
18. Beilin, H. Cognitive capacities of young children: A replication. *Science,* **162,** 920–21 (1968)
19. Bell, R. Q. A reinterpretation of the direction of effects in studies of socialization. *Psychol. Rev.,* **75,** 81–95 (1968)
20. Bever, T. G., Mehler, J., Epstein, J. What children do in spite of what they know. *Science,* **162,** 921–24 (1968)
21. Biller, H. B. A note on father absence and masculine development in lower-class Negro and white boys. *Child Develpm.,* **39,** 1003–6 (1968)
22. Bittner, A. C., Shinedling, M. M. A methodological investigation of Piaget's concept of conservation of substance. *Genet. Psychol. Monogr.,* **77,** 135–65 (1968)
23. Blain, M. J., Ramirez, M., III. Increasing sociometric rank meaningfulness and discriminability of children's names through reinforcement and interaction. *Child Develpm.,* **39,** 949–55 (1968)
24. Blank, M., Altman, L. D. Effect of stimulus modality and task complexity on discrimination and reversal learning in preschool children. *J. Exptl. Child Psychol.,* **6,** 598–606 (1968)
25. Blank, M. L., Altman, L. D., Bridger, W. H. Crossmodal transfer of form discrimination in preschool children. *Psychon. Sci.,* **10,** 51–52 (1968)
26. Blank, M., Solomon, F. A tutorial

language program to develop abstract thinking in socially disadvantaged preschool children. *Child Developm.*, **39,** 379–90 (1968)

27. Boat, B. M., Clifton, C., Jr. Verbal mediation in four-year-old children. *Child Develpm.*, **39,** 505–14 (1968)
28. Boone, D., Prescott, T. Development of left-right discrimination in normal children. *Percept. Mot. Skills,* **26,** 267–74 (1968)
29. Boshier, R. Self esteem and first names in children. *Psychol. Rept.*, **22,** 762 (1968)
30. Brackbill, Y. Stimulus perserveration errors in children's discrimination learning. *Percept. Mot. Skills,* **27,** 179–84 (1968)
31. Bronson, G. W. The development of fear in man and other animals. *Child Develpm.*, **39,** 409–32 (1968)
32. Brown, R. The development of Wh. questions in child speech. *J. Verbal Learn. Verbal Behav.*, **7,** 279–90 (1968)
33. Brown, R., Bellugi, U. Three processes in the child's acquisition of snytax. *Harv. Educ. Rev.*, **34,** 133–51 (1964)
34. Cantor, G. N. Children's "like-dislike" ratings of familiarized and nonfamiliarized visual stimuli. *J. Exptl. Child Psychol.*, **6,** 651–57 (1968)
35. Cantor, G. N., Fenson, L. New data regarding the relationship of amount of familiarization to the stimulus familiarization effect (SFE). *J. Exptl. Child Psychol.*, **6,** 167–73 (1968)
36. Caron, A. J. Conceptual transfer in preverbal children as a consequence of dimensional training. *J. Exptl. Child Psychol.*, **6,** 522–42 (1968)
37. Caron, R. F., Caron, A. J. The effects of repeated exposure and stimulus complexity on visual fixation in infants. *Psychon. Sci.*, **10,** 207–8 (1968)
38. Carrow, Sister M. A. The development of auditory comprehension of language structure in children. *J. Speech Hearing Dis.*, **33,** 99–111 (1968)
39. Cazden, C. B. The acquisition of noun and verb inflections. *Child Develpm.*, **39,** 433–48 (1968)
40. Charlesworth, W. R. Cognition in infancy: Where do we stand in the mid-sixties. *Merrill-Palmer Quart.*, **14,** 25–46 (1968)
41. Chertkoff, J. M. Response speed under voluntary and involuntary conditions as a function of percentage of reinforcement. *Child. Develpm.*, **39,** 167–76 (1968)
42. Child, I. L., Hansen, J. A., Hornbeck, F. W. Age and sex differences in children's color preferences. *Child Develpm.*, **39,** 237–48 (1968)
43. Chittenden, E. A., Foan, M. W., Zweil, D. M. School achievement of first- and second-born siblings. *Child Develpm.*, **39,**1223–28 (1968)
44. Clark, C. D. Similarity between children's and adults' adjective responses to noun stimuli. *J. Verbal Learn. Verbal Behav.*, **7,** 705–6 (1968)
45. Clark, C. D., McDonald, F. J. Selection of defining properties in concept attainment. *J. Educ. Psychol.*, **59,** 328–33 (1968)
46. Clifton, C., Jr., Bogartz, R. S. Selective attention during dichotic listening by pre-school children. *J. Exptl. Child Psychol.*, **6,** 483–91 (1968)
47. Clifton, R. K., Graham, F. K., Hatton, H. M. Newborn heart-rate response and response habituation as a function of stimulus duration. *J. Exptl. Child Psychol.*, **6,** 265–78 (1968)
48. Clifton, R. K., Meyers, W. J. Heart-rate response of four-month-old infants to auditory stimuli. *Proc. 76th Ann. Conv. Am. Psychol. Assoc.*, **3,** 357–58 (1968)
49. Cohen, B. D., Klein, J. F. Referent communication in school age children. *Child Develpm.*, **39,** 597–610 (1968)
50. Cole, M., Sharp, D. W., Glick, J., Kessen, W. Conceptual and mnemonic factors in paired-associate learning. *J. Exptl. Child Psychol.*, **6,** 120–30 (1968)
51. Collard, R. R. Social and play responses of first-born and later-born infants in an unfamiliar situation. *Child Develpm.*, **39,** 325–34 (1968)
52. Connolly, K., Brown, K., Bassett, E. Developmental changes in some components of a motor skill. *Brit. J. Psychol.*, **59,** 305–14 (1968)
53. Coon, R. C., Odom, R. D. Transi-

tivity and length judgments as a function of age and social influence. *Child Develpm.*, **39,** 1133–44 (1968)

54. Cox, F. N. Some relationships between test anxiety presence or absence of male persons, and boys' performance on a repetitive motor task. *J. Exptl. Child Psychol.*, **6,** 1–12 (1968)
55. Cox, F. N., Campbell, D. Young children in a new situation with and without their mothers. *Child Develpm.*, **39,** 123–32 (1968)
56. Cronbach, L. J. Intelligence, creativity? A parsimonious reinterpretation of the Wallach-Kogan data. *Am. Educ. Res. J.*, **5,** 491–511 (1968)
57. Cullen, J. K., Fargo, N., Chase, R., Baker, P. The development of auditory feedback monitoring: Delayed auditory feedback studies in infant cry. *J. Speech Hearing Res.*, **11,** 85–93 (1968)
58. Datta, L. E., Schaefer, E., Davis, M. Sex and scholastic aptitude as variables in teachers' ratings of the adjustment and classroom behavior of Negro and other seventh-grade students. *J. Educ. Psychol.*, **59,** 94–101 (1968)
59. Davey, A. G. The Tristan Da Cunhan children's concepts of equivalence. *Brit. J. Educ. Psychol.*, **38,** 162–70 (1968)
60. Davids, D. Cognitive styles in potential scientists and underachieving high school students. *J. Spec. Educ.*, **2,** 197–201 (1968)
61. Day, H. Role of specific curiosity in school achievement. *J. Educ. Psychol.*, **59,** 37–43 (1968)
62. Deutsch, M., Katz, I., Jensen, A. R. *Social Class Race, and Psychological Development* (Holt, Rinehart & Winston, 1968)
63. Dietz, S., Johnson, J. W. Performance of lower- and middle-class children on a discrimination reversal task. *Psychon. Sci.*, **11,** 191–92 (1968)
64. Dilley, M. G., Paivio, A. Pictures and words as stimulus and response items in paired-associate learning of young children. *J. Exptl. Child Psychol.*, **6,** 231–40 (1968)
65. Donaldson, M., Balfour, G. Less is more: A study of language comprehension in children. *Brit. J. Psychol.*, **59,** 461–71 (1968)
66. Dubignon, J., Campbell, D. Intraoral stimulation and sucking in the newborn. *J. Exptl. Child Psychol.*, **6,** 154–66 (1968)
67. Dubignon, J., Campbell, D. Sucking in the newborn in three conditions: non-nutritive, nutritive and a feed. *Ibid.*, 335–50
68. Early, J. C. Attitude learning in children. *J. Educ. Psychol.*, **59,** 176–80 (1968)
69. Eisenberg, L., Berlin, C. I., Dill, A., Frank, S. Class and race effects on the intelligibility of monosyllables. *Child Develpm.*, **39,** 1078–90 (1968)
70. Elkind, D., Barocas, R., Rosenthal, B. Combinatorial thinking in adolescents from graded and ungraded classrooms. *Percept. Mot. Skills*, **27,** 1015–18 (1968)
71. Emmerich, W. Personality development and concepts of structure. *Child Develpm.*, **39,** 671–90 (1968)
72. Endsley, R. C. Effects of forced reward-nonreward ratios on children's performance in a discrimination task. *J. Exptl. Child. Psychol.*, **6,** 563–70 (1968)
73. Falk, C. T. Object and pattern discrimination learning by young children as a function of availability of cues. *Child Develpm.*, **39,** 923–31 (1968)
74. Fantz, R. L. Pattern discrimination and selective attention as determinants of perceptual development from birth. In *Perceptual Development in Children* (Kidd, A. H., Rivoire, J. L., Eds., Intern. Univ. Press, New York, 1966)
75. Farley, F. H. Season of birth, intelligence and personality. *Brit. J. Psychol.*, **59,** 281–83 (1968)
76. Farnham-Diggory, S., Bermon, M. Verbal compensation, cognitive synthesis, and conservation. *Merrill-Palmer Quart.*, **14,** 215–27 (1968)
77. Faucheux, C., Moscovici, S. Studies on group creativity: III. Noise and complexity in the inferential processes. *Hum. Relat.*, **21,** 40 (1968)
78. Faw, T. T., Nunnally, J. C. The influence of stimulus complexity, novelty, and affective value on children's visual fixations. *J. Exptl. Child Psychol.*, **6,** 141–53 (1968)

79. Feshbach, N. D., Roe, K. Empathy in six- and seven-year-olds. *Child Develpm.*, **39**, 133–46 (1968)

80. Fitzgerald, H. E. Autonomic pupillary reflex activity during early infancy and its relation to social and nonsocial visual stimuli. *J. Exptl. Child Psychol.*, **6**, 470–82 (1968)

81. Flanders, J. P. A review of research on imitative behavior. *Psychol. Bull.*, **69**, 316–37 (1968)

82. Flanders, N. A., Morrison, B. M., Brode, E. L. Changes in pupil attitudes during the school year. *J. Educ. Psychol.*, **59**, 334–38 (1968)

83. Flavell, J. H. *The Development of Role-Taking and Communication Skills in Children* (Wiley, New York, 1968)

84. Friedlander, B. Z. The effect of speaker identity, voice inflection, vocabulary, and message redundancy on infants' selection of vocal reinforcement. *J. Exptl. Child Psychol.*, **6**, 443–59 (1968)

85. Furth, H. G. Piaget's theory of knowledge: The nature of representation and interiorization. *Psychol. Rev.*, **75**, 143–54 (1968)

86. Gagne, R. M. Contributions of learning to human development. *Psychol. Rev.*, **75**, 177–91 (1968)

87. Galloway, C., Pětre, R. D. An analysis of the functional equivalence of stimulus class members. *J. Exptl. Child Psychol.*, **6**, 384–90 (1968)

88. Garai, J. E., Scheinfeld, A. Sex differences in mental and behavioral traits. *Genet. Psychol. Monogr.*, **77**, 169–299 (1968)

89. Garber, H. L., Ross, L. E. Intradimensional and extradimensional shift performance of children in a differential conditioning task. *Psychon. Sci.*, **10**, 69–70 (1968)

90. Gellert, E. Comparison of children's self-drawings with their drawings of other persons. *Percept. Mot. Skills*, **28**, 123–38 (1968)

91. Gewirtz, J. L., Stingle, K. G. Learning of generalized imitation as the basis for identification. *Psychol. Rev.*, **75**, 374–97 (1968)

92. Gibson, H. B. The measurement of parental attitudes and their relation to boys' behaviour. *Brit. J. Educ. Psychol.*, **38**, 233–39 (1968)

93. Glick, J., Wapner, S. Development of transitivity: Some findings and problems of analysis. *Child Develpm.*, **39**, 621–38 (1968)

94. Golden, M., Birns, B. Social class and cognitive development in infancy. *Merrill-Palmer Quart.*, **14**, 139–49 (1968)

95. Goldschmid, M. L. The relation of conservation to emotional and environmental aspects of development. *Child Develpm.*, **39**, 579–90 (1968)

96. Goldschmid, M. L., Bentler, P. M. The dimensions and measurement of conservation. *Child Develpm.*, **39**, 787–802 (1968)

97. Goss, A. M. Estimated versus actual physical strength in three ethnic groups. *Child Develpm.*, **39**, 283–90 (1968)

98. Goulet, L. R. Verbal learning in children: Implications for developmental research. *Psychol. Bull.*, **69**, 359–73 (1968)

99. Graham, F. K., Clifton, R. K., Hatton, H. M. Habituation of heart rate response to repeated auditory stimulation during the first five days of life. *Child Develpm.*, **39**, 35–52 (1968)

100. Greenwald, H. J., Oppenheim, D. B. Reported magnitude of self-misidentification among Negro children—artifact? *J. Pers. Soc. Psychol.*, **8**, 49–52 (1968)

101. Halford, G. S. An experimental test of Piaget's notions concerning the conservation of quantity in children. *J. Exptl. Child Psychol.*, **6**, 33–43 (1968)

102. Hall, J. W., Ware, W. B. Implicit associative responses and false recognition by young children. *J. Exptl. Child Psychol.*, **6**, 52–60 (1968)

103. Hall, V. C., Simpson, G. J. Factors influencing extinction of weight conservation. *Merrill-Palmer Quart.*, **14**, 197–210 (1968)

104. Hall, V. R., Lund, D., Jackson, D. Effects of teacher attention on study behavior. *J. Appl. Behav. Anal.*, **1**, 1–12 (1968)

105. Harper, D. G. The reliability of measures of sociometric acceptance and rejection. *Sociometry*, **31**, 219–27 (1968)

106. Harris, L. Looks by preschoolers at the experimenter in a choice-of-toys game: Effects of experimenter

and age of child. *J. Exptl. Child Psychol.*, **6**, 493–500 (1968)

107. Herriot, P. The comprehension of syntax. *Child Develpm.*, **39**, 273–82 (1968)
108. Hrbek, A., Prechtl, H. F. R., Hrbkova, M., Lenard, H. G., Kerr Grant, D. Proprioceptive evoked potentials in newborn infants and adults. *Develpm. Med. Child Neurol.*, **10**, 164–67 (1968)
109. Inglis, J., Ankus, M. N., Sykes, D. H. Age-related differences in learning and short-term-memory from childhood to the senium. *Human Develpm.*, **11**, 42–52 (1968)
110. Jeffrey, W. E. The orienting reflex and attention in cognitive development. *Psychol. Rev.*, **75**, 323–34 (1968)
111. Joynt, D., Cambourne, B. Psycholinguistic development and the control of behavior. *Brit. J. Educ. Psychol.*, **38**, 249–60 (1968)
112. Kagan, J., Lewis, M. Studies of attention in the human infant. *Merrill-Palmer Quart.*, **11**, 95–127 (1965)
113. Kanfer, F. H., Duerfeldt, P. H. Age, class standing, and commitment as determinants of cheating in children. *Child Develpm.*, **39**, 545–58 (1968)
114. Karnes, M. B., Studley, W. M., Wright, W. R., Hodgins, A. S. An approach for working with mothers of disadvantaged school children. *Merrill-Palmer Quart.*, **14**, 174–84 (1968)
115. Katz, I., Henchy, T., Allen, H. Effects of race of tester, approval-disapproval, and need on Negro children's learning. *J. Pers. Soc. Psychol.*, **8**, 38–42 (1968)
116. Katz, P. A. Role of irrelevant cues in the formation of concepts by lower-class children. *J. Educ. Psychol.*, **59**, 233–38 (1968)
117. Kilbride, P. L., Robbins, M. C., Freeman, R. B., Jr. Pictorial depth perception and education among Baganda school children. *Percept. Mot. Skills*, **26**, 1116–18 (1968)
118. King, W. L. Rule learning and transfer as a function of age and stimulus structure. *Child Develpm.*, **39**, 311–24 (1968)
119. Koch, J. Conditioned orienting reactions to persons and things in 2–5 month old infants. *Hum. Develpm.*, **11**, 81–91 (1968)
120. Koch, J. The change of conditioned orienting reactions in 5 month old infants through phase shift of partial biorhythms. *Ibid.*, 124–37
121. Kohlberg, L. Early education: A cognitive-developmental view. *Child Develpm.*, **39**, 1013–62 (1968)
122. Kohlberg, L., Yaeger, J., Hjertholm, E. Private speech: Four studies and a review of theories. *Child Devolpm.*, **39**, 691–736 (1968)
123. Koopman, P. R., Ames, E. W. Infant's preferences for facial arrangements: A failure to replicate. *Child Develpm.*, **39**, 481–88 (1968)
124. Korner, A. F., Chuck, B., Dontchos, S. Organismic determinants of spontaneous oral behavior in neonates. *Child Develpm.*, **39**, 1145–58 (1968)
125. Krauss, R. M., Rotter, G. S. Communication abilities of children as a function of status and age. *Merrill-Palmer Quart.*, **14**, 161–73 (1968)
126. Kugelmass, S., Breznitz, S. Intentionality in moral judgment: Adolescent development. *Child Develpm.*, **39**, 249–56 (1968)
127. Lahaderne, H. M. Attitudinal and intellectual correlates of attention: A study of four sixth-grade classrooms. *J. Educ. Psychol.*, **59**, 320–24 (1968)
128. Lang, S., Adair, J. G. Preference for delayed reward as a function of age and personality. *Psychol. Rept.*, **22**, 805–8 (1968)
129. Leckart, B. T., Briggs, B., Kirk, J. Effect of novelty on stimulus selection in children. *Psychon. Sci.*, **10**, 139–40 (1968)
130. Lefrancois, G. A treatment hierarchy for the acceleration of conservation of substance. *Can. J. Psychol.*, **22**, 227–84 (1968)
131. Le Furgy, W., Sisserson, J. A. Effects of prompting, confirmation, and free choice upon children's acquisition, verbalization and generalization of concept. *Psychon. Sci.*, **12**, 277–78 (1968)
132. Leuba, C., Friedlander, B. Z. Effects of controlled audio-visual reinforcement on infants' manipulative play in the home. *J. Exptl. Child Psychol.*, **6**, 87–99 (1968)

133. Levin, J. R., Rohwer, W. D., Jr. Verbal organization and the facilitation of serial learning. *J. Educ. Psychol.*, **59,** 186–90 (1968)
134. Lewis, M., Rausch, M., Goldberg, S., Dodd, C. Error response time and IQ: Sex differences in cognitive style of preschool children. *Percept. Mot. Skills,* **26,** 563–68 (1968)
135. Lezotte, L. W., Byers, J. L. The effects of syntactical violation and practice on the free recall of verbal materials in children. *Psychon. Sci.,* **11,** 285–86 (1968)
136. Liebert, R. M., Ora, J. P., Jr. Children's adoption of self-reward patterns: Incentive level and method of transmission. *Child Develpm.,* **39,** 537–44 (1968)
137. Litvinyuk, A. A. Comparative analysis of the activity of the preschool child with real objects and with their schematic representatives. *Soviet Psychol.,* **6,** 7–16 (1967–68)
138. London, P., Robinson, J. P. Imagination in learning and retention. *Child Develpm.,* **39,** 803–16 (1968)
139. Long, B. H., Henderson, F. H., Ziller, R. C. Self-ratings on the semantic differential: Content versus response set. *Child Develpm.,* **39,** 647–56 (1968)
140. Lott, B. E., Lott, A. J. The relation of manifest anxiety in children to learning task performance and other variables. *Child Develpm.,* **39,** 207–20 (1968)
141. Lovell, K. Some recent studies in cognitive and language development. *Merrill-Palmer Quart.,* **14,** 123–38 (1968)
142. Mackay, C. W., Kilkenny, T. M. A note on the stability of induced conservation. *Brit. J. Educ. Psychol.,* **38,** 313–15 (1968)
143. Madsen, C., Jr. Nurturance and modeling in preschoolers. *Child Develpm.,* **39,** 221–36 (1968)
144. Madsen, C. H., Jr., Becker, W. C., Thomas, D. R. Rules, praise, and ignoring: Elements of elementary classroom control. *J. Appl. Behav. Anal.,* **1,** 139–50 (1968)
145. Manley, S., Miller, F. D. Factors affecting children's alternation and choice behaviors. *Psychon. Sci.,* **13,** 65–66 (1968)
146. Mason, E. P. Sex difference in personality characteristics of deprived adolescents. *Percept. Mot. Skills,* **27,** 934 (1968)
147. McGhee, P. E., Crandall, V. C. Beliefs in internal-external control of reinforcements and academic performance. *Child Develpm.,* **39,** 91–102 (1968)
148. McGrade, B. J. Newborn activity and emotional response at eight months. *Child Developm.,* **39,** 1247–52 (1968)
149. McNeil, K. A. Semantic space as an indicator of socialization. *J. Educ. Psychol.,* **59,** 325–27 (1968)
150. Mehler, J., Bever, T. G. Cognitive capacity of very young children. *Science,* **158,** 141–42 (1967)
151. Mendel, M. S. Infant responses to recorded sounds. *J. Speech Hearing Res.,* **11,** 811–16 (1968)
152. Menyuk, P. Children's learning and reproduction of grammatical and non-grammatical phonological sequences. *Child Develpm.,* **39,** 847–60 (1968)
153. Menyuk, P. The role of distinctive features in children's acquisition of phonology. *J. Speech Hearing Res.,* **11,** 138–46 (1968)
154. Midlarsky, E. Aiding responses: An analysis and review. *Merrill-Palmer Quart.,* **14,** 229–60 (1968)
155. Miller, F. T. Verbal mediation in the successive and simultaneous discrimination learning of children. *J. Exptl. Child Psychol.,* **6,** 510–21 (1968)
156. Moore, T. Language and intelligence: A longitudinal study of the first eight years. *Hum. Develpm.,* **11,** 1–24 (1968)
157. Moss, H. A., Robson, K. S. Maternal influences in early social visual behavior. *Child Develpm.,* **39,** 401–8 (1968)
158. Munsinger, H. Developing sensitivity to correlated cues. *Psychon. Sci.,* **10,** 149–50 (1968)
159. Murphy, G., Santos, J. F., Dolley, C. M. Development and transfer of attentional habits. *Percept. Mot. Skills,* **26,** 515–19 (1968)
160. Murray, F. B. Cognitive conflict and reversibility training in the acquisition of length conservation. *J. Educ. Psychol.,* **59,** 82–87 (1968)
161. Murray, F. B. Operational conservation of illusion-distorted length. *Brit. J. Educ. Psychol.,* **38,** 189–93 (1968)

162. Murray, F. B. Phenomenal-real discrimination and the conservation of illusion-distorted length. *Can. J. Psychol.*, **22,** 114–21 (1968)

163. Murray, J. P., Youniss, J. Achievement of inferential transitivity and its relation to serial ordering. *Child Develpm.*, **39,** 1260–68 (1968)

164. Neimark, E. D., Lewis, N. Development of logical problem solving: A one-year retest. *Child Develpm.*, **39,** 527–36 (1968)

165. Nelson, K. E. Organization of visual-tracking responses in human infants. *J. Exptl. Child Psychol.*, **6,** 194–201 (1968)

166. Nickel, H. Untersuchungen zur Bedeutung einer erhoelten Motivation fuer eine eingelheitliche Auffassurg in der visuellen Wahrnehmung vierjaehriger Kinder. *Psychol. Rundschau,* **19,** 9–17 (1968)

167. Norman, C., Rieber, M. Facilitation of concept formation in children by the use of color cues. *J. Exptl. Psychol.*, **76,** 460–63 (1968)

168. Nunnally, J. C., Faw, T. T. The acquisition of conditioned reward value in discrimination learning. *Child Develpm.*, **39,** 159–66 (1968)

169. Oden, M. H. The fulfillment of promise: 40 year old follow up of the Terman gifted group. *Genet. Psychol. Monogr.*, **77,** 3–94 (1968)

170. O'Doherty, N. A hearing test applicable to the crying newborn infant. *Develpm. Med. Child Neurol.*, **10,** 380–83 (1968)

171. Odom, R. D., Liebert, R. M., Hill, J. H. The effects of modeling cues, reward, and attentional set on the production of grammatical and ungrammatical syntactic constructions. *J. Exptl. Child Psychol.*, **6,** 131–40 (1968)

172. O'Leary, K. D. The effects of self-instruction on immoral behavior. *J. Exptl. Child Psychol.*, **6,** 297–301 (1968)

173. Osler, S. F., Scholnick, E. K. The effect of stimulus differentiation and inferential experience on concept attainment in disadvantaged children. *J. Exptl. Child Psychol.*, **6,** 658–66 (1968)

174. Ottinger, D. R., Blatchley, M. E., Denenberg, V. H. Stimulation of human neonates and visual attentiveness. *Proc. 76th Ann. Conv. Am. Psychol. Assoc.*, **3,** 355–56 (1968)

175. Pedersen, F. A., Wender, P. H. Early social correlates of cognitive functioning in six-year-old boys. *Child. Develpm.*, **39,** 185–94 (1968)

176. Piaget, J. Quantification, conservation, and nativism. *Science,* **162,** 976–79 (1968)

177. Pollack, R. H., Ptashne, R. I., Carter, D. J. The dark-interval threshold as a function of age. *Psychon. Sci.*, **12,** 237–38 (1968)

178. Poole, H. E. The effect of urbanization upon scientific concept attainment among Hausa children of Northern Nigeria. *Brit. J. Educ. Psychol.*, **38,** 64–74 (1968)

179. Poppleton, P. K. Puberty, family size and the educational progress of girls. *Brit. J. Educ. Psychol.*, **38,** 286–92 (1968)

180. Potter, M. C., Levy, E. I. Spatial enumeration without counting. *Child Develpm.*, **39,** 265–72 (1968)

181. Potts, M. The effects of a morphological cue and of distinctive verbal labels on the transposition responses of three-, four-, and five-year olds. *J. Exptl. Child Psychol.*, **6,** 75–86 (1968)

182. Price, L. E., Cobb, N. J., Morin, N. J. Associative interference as a function of amount of first-task practice and stimulus similarity. *J. Exptl. Child Psychol.*, **6,** 202–11 (1968)

183. Prince, J. R. The effect of western education on science conceptualisation in New Guinea. *Brit. J. Educ. Psychol.*, **38,** 57–63 (1968)

184. Raskin, L. M. A developmental study of long-term memory in the perception of apparent movement. *Psychon. Sci.*, **10,** 397–98 (1968)

185. Reed, M. R., Asbjornsen, W. Experimental alteration of the IT scale in the study of sex-role preference. *Percept. Mot. Skills,* **26,** 15–24, (1968)

186. Renson, G. J., Schaefer, E. S., Levy, B. I. Cross-national validity of a spherical conceptual model for parent behavior. *Child Develpm.*, **39,** 1229–35 (1968)

187. Reynolds, J. H. Cognitive transfer in verbal learning: II. Transfer effects after prefamiliarization with integrated versus partially inte-

grated verbal-perceptual structures. *J. Educ. Psychol.*, **59**, 133–38 (1968)

188. Rhine, W. R. Birth order differences in conformity and level of achievement arousal. *Child Develpm.*, **39**, 987–96 (1968)
189. Richardson, S. A., Royce, J. Race and physical handicap in children's preference for other children. *Child Develpm.*, **39**, 467–80 (1968)
190. Rieber, M. Mediational aids and motor skill learning in children. *Child Develpm.*, **39**, 559–68 (1968)
191. Riegel, K. F., Riegel, R. M., Quarterman, C. J., Smith, H. E. Developmental differences in word meaning and semantic structure. *Hum. Develpm.*, **11**, 92–106 (1968)
192. Rohwer, W. D., Jr., Lynch, S., Levin, J. R., Suzuki, N. Grade level, school strata, and learning efficiency. *J. Educ. Psychol.*, **59**, 26–31 (1968)
193. Rosenhan, D., Frederick, F., Burrowes, A. Preaching and practicing: Effects of channel discrepancy on norm internalization. *Child Develpm.*, **39**, 291–302 (1968)
194. Rothenberg, B. B., Courtney, R. G. Conservation of number in very young children: A replication of and comparison with Mehler and Bever's study. *J. Psychol.*, **70**, 205–12 (1968)
195. Rutherford, E., Mussen, P. Generosity in nursery school boys. *Child Develpm.*, **39**, 755–66 (1968)
196. Salapatek, P. Visual scanning of geometric figures by the human newborn. *J. Comp. Physiol. Psychol.*, **66**, 247–48 (1968)
197. Salapatek, P., Kessen, W. Visual scanning of triangles by the human newborn. *J. Exptl. Child Psychol.*, **3**, 155–67 (1966)
198. Saltz, E., Hamilton, H. Concept conservation under positively and negatively evaluated transformations. *J. Exptl. Child Psychol.*, **6**, 44–51 (1968)
199. Sameroff, A. J. Non-nutritive sucking in newborns under visual and auditory stimulation. *Child Develpm.*, **38**, 443–52 (1967)
200. Sameroff, A. J. The components of sucking in the human newborn. *J. Exptl. Child Psychol.*, **6**, 607–23 (1968)
201. Scholnick, E. K., Osler, S. F., Katzenellenbogen, R. Discrimination learning and concept identification in disadvantaged and middle-class children. *Child Developm.*, **39**, 15–26 (1968)
202. Schroth, M. The function of stimulus pre-differentiation pretraining in complex problem solving. *Psychon. Sci.*, **10**, 123–24 (1968)
203. Schwartz, J. C. Fear and attachment in young children. *Merrill-Palmer Quart.*, **14**, 313–22 (1968)
204. Semb, G., Lipsitt, L. P. The effects of acoustic stimulation on cessation and initiation of non-nutritive sucking in neonates. *J. Exptl. Child Psychol.*, **6**, 585–97 (1968)
205. Semler, I. J., Pederson, D. R. Children's reactions to nonreward: Partial versus continuous reinforcement using a within-subjects design. *Psychon. Sci.*, **10**, 285–86 (1968)
206. Sewell, W. H., Shaw, V. P. Parent's education and children's educational aspirations and achievements. *Am. Sociol. Rev.*, **33**, 191–209 (1968)
207. Shapiro, S. I., Palermo, D. S. Mediation in children's aural paired-associate learning. *Child Develpm.*, **39**, 569–78 (1968)
208. Sheikh, A. A. Children's response speed as a function of delay of reward at different distances from the goal and incentive value. *Psychon. Sci.*, **11**, 201 (1968)
209. Shrader, W. K., Leventhal, T. Birth order of children and parental report of problems. *Child Develpm.*, **39**, 1165–76 (1968)
210. Shure, M. B. Fairness, generosity, and selfishness: The naive psychology of children and young adults. *Child Develpm.*, **39**, 875–86 (1968)
211. Sibley, S. A., Senn, S. K., Epanchin, A. Race and sex of adolescents and cooperation in a mixed motive game. *Psychon. Sci.*, **13**, 123–24 (1968)
212. Siegel, L. The role of experience in judgments of complexity of random shapes. *Can. J. Psychol.*, **22**, 474–83 (1968)
213. Siqueland, E. R. Reinforcement patterns and extinction in human newborns. *J. Exptl. Child Psychol.*, **6**, 431–42 (1968)
214. Smedslund, J. Conservation and resistance to extinction: A comment on Hall and Simpson's article.

Merrill-Palmer Quart., **14,** 211–14 (1968)

215. Smith, I. D. The effects of training procedures upon the acquisition of conservation of weight. *Child Develpm.,* **39,** 515–26 (1968)
216. Steinschneider, A. Sound intensity and respiratory responses in the neonate. *Psychosomat. Med.,* **30,** 534–41 (1968)
217. Stephens, W. E. Concept training with three types of verbal labels. *Psychon. Sci.,* **10,** 225–26 (1968)
218. Stephenson, G. M., White, J. H. An experimental study of some effects of injustice on children's moral behavior. *J. Exptl. Soc. Psychol.,* **4,** 460–69 (1968)
219. Stevenson, H. W., Klein, R. E., Hale, G. A., Miller, L. K. Solution of anagrams: A developmental study. *Child Develpm.,* **39,** 905–12 (1968)
220. Sugarman, B. Social norms in teenage boys' peer groups. *Hum. Relat.,* **21,** 41–58 (1968)
221. Sundberg, N., Ballinger, T. Nepalese children's cognitive development as revealed by drawings of man, woman, and self. *Child Develpm.,* **39,** 969–86 (1968)
222. Suppes, P., Rosenthal-Hill, I. Concept formation by kindergarten children in a card-sorting task. *J. Exptl. Child Psychol.,* **6,** 212–30 (1968)
223. Sutton-Smith, B. Novel responses to toys. *Merrill-Palmer Quart.,* **14,** 151–58 (1968)
224. Sutton-Smith, B., Rosenberg, B. G., Landy, F. Father-absence effects in families of different sibling compositions. *Child Develpm.,* **39,** 1213–21 (1968)
225. Tedford, W. H., Jr., Kempler, B. Directional effects on size transposition in preschool children. *J. Exptl. Child Psychol.,* **6,** 394–401 (1968)
226. Tempone, V. J. The nature of the stimulus in primary stimulus generalization. *Can. J. Psychol.,* **22,** 244–51 (1968)
227. Thomas, A., Chess, S., Birch, H. G. *Temperament and Behavior Disorders in Children* (New York Univ. Press, New York, 1968)
228. Thomas, D. R., Becker, W. C., Armstrong, M. Production and elimination of disruptive classroom behavior by systematically varying teacher's behavior. *J. Appl. Behav. Anal.,* **1,** 35–45 (1968)
229. Thornatzky, L., Gerwitz, J. P. The effect of threat and attraction on interpersonal bargaining. *Psychon. Sci.,* **13,** 125–26 (1968)
230. Todd, G. A., Palmer, B. Social reinforcement of infant babbling. *Child Develpm.,* **39,** 591–96 (1968)
231. Tryon, A. F. Thumb-sucking and manifest anxiety: A note. *Child Develpm.,* **39,** 1159–64 (1968)
232. Tsai, L. S., Ghien, C. S. Concept discovery by school children: Six concepts of middleness. *Percept. Mot. Skills,* **26,** 107–14 (1968)
233. Viney, W., Hulicka, I., Bitner, J., Raley, C. L., Brewster, P. Effect of stimulus variation upon resistance to extinction in kindergarten children. *J. Comp. Physiol. Psychol.,* **65,** 539–41 (1968)
234. Vroegh, K. Masculinity and femininity in the preschool years. *Child Develpm.,* **39,** 1253–58 (1968)
235. Vurpillot, E. The development of scanning strategies and their relation to visual differentiation. *J. Exptl. Child Psychol.,* **6,** 632–50 (1968)
236. Walk, R. D. Monocular compared to binocular depth perception in human infants. *Science,* **162,** 473–75 (1968)
237. Wapner, S., Cirillo, L. Imitation of a model's hand movements: Age changes in transposition of left-right relations. *Child Develpm.,* **39,** 887–94 (1968)
238. Ward, W. C. Creativity in young children. *Child Develpm.,* **39,** 737–54 (1968)
239. Ward, W. C. Reflection-impulsivity in kindergarten children. *Ibid.,* 867–74
240. Watson, J. S. Operant fixation in visual preference behavior of infants. *Psychon. Sci.,* **12,** 241–42 (1968)
241. Weinstein, L. The mother-child schema, anxiety, and academic achievement in elementary school boys. *Child Develpm.,* **39,** 257–64 (1968)
242. Weitzman, E. D., Graziani, L. J. Maturation and topography of the auditory evoked response of the prematurely born infant. *Develpm. Psychobiol.,* **1,** 79–89 (1968)
243. Werner, E. E., Honzik, M. P., Smith, R. S. Prediction of intelligence

and achievement at ten years from twenty months pediatric and psychologic examinations. *Child Develpm.*, **39,** 1063–75 (1968)

244. Westcott, M., Tolchin, M. Individual and age-related differences in perceptual inference behavior. *Percept. Mot. Skills,* **26,** 683–97 (1968)

245. White, R. M., Jr., Johnson, P. J. Concept of dimensionality and optional shift performance in nursery school children. *J. Exptl. Child Psychol.,* **6,** 113–19 (1968)

246. White, S. H. The learning maturation controversy. *Merrill-Palmer Quart.,* **14,** 187–95 (1968)

247. Wilcox, B. M., Clayton, F. L. Infant visual fixation on motion pictures of the human face. *J. Exptl. Child Psychol.,* **6,** 22–32 (1968)

248. Williams, R. L., Cole, S. Self concept and school adjustment. *Personnel Guid. J.,* **46,** 478–81 (1968)

249. Willis, E. J., Dornbush, R. L. Preference for visual complexity. *Child Develpm.,* **39,** 639–46 (1968)

250. Winer, G. A. Induced set and acquisition of number conservation. *Child Develpm.,* **39,** 195–206 (1968)

251. Wohlwill, J. F. Responses to class-inclusion questions for verbally and pictorially presented items. *Child Develpm.,* **39,** 449–66 (1968)

252. Wolff, P. H. Organization of sucking in young infant. *Pediatrics,* **42,** 943–56 (1968)

253. Wright, D. Social reinforcement and maze learning in children. *Child Develpm.,* **39,** 177–84 (1968)

254. Yando, R. M., Kagan, J. The effect of teacher tempo on the child. *Child Develpm.,* **39,** 27–34 (1968)

255. Zigler, E., Butterfield, E. C. Motivational aspects of changes in IQ test performance of culturally deprived nursery school children. *Child Develpm.,* **39,** 1–14 (1968)

GEROPSYCHOLOGY[1] 150

By Jack Botwinick

Department of Psychology

Washington University, St. Louis, Missouri

Three related developments seem to characterize the literature on adult aging during the period of this review, the middle of 1963 to the end of 1968. First, the growth rate of the number of publications in the psychology of aging has been nothing short of amazing. Second, probably because of the need to integrate what has been done, more books and chapters on the topic have appeared than at any time previously. And third, all this activity has been an object of concern, if not criticism, as seen by an increased attention to and sophistication regarding issues of methodology.

The growth rate may be evidenced by the fact that 15 to 20 years ago it was possible to know almost all the psychological research on aging published in this country. This is no longer possible. For the five-year period of this report, bibliographic search disclosed nearly 2000 references which could be classed as psychological.[2] Had the goal of this review been simply comprehensiveness, half to two-thirds of these references could have been cited here with some benefit. If this rate of research activity increases or even continues, it will be necessary to specialize in a subarea of geropsychology, rather than in all of it.

BOOKS

The books in which attempts were made to integrate all this material may be categorized into four groups: (*a*) authored books either summarizing portions of the field (26, 32, 47) or reporting investigations of large scope (67, 78, 169, 239, 289); (*b*) edited books with chapters authored by different writers (217, 243, 263, 264, 343); (*c*) published proceedings of symposia which, as books, are sometimes difficult to distinguish from ordinary edited volumes (25, 197, 200, 222, 232, 307, 315, 376, 393); and (*d*) books which are merely compilations of papers presented at colloquia and symposia (15, 75, 161, 191).

As may be expected, the authored, as opposed to edited, books seem to be the most useful. Birren's *The Psychology of Aging* (26), as the title suggests, covers most of the field and is directed to students and researchers.

[1] This report was supported in part by a NICHD research grant, HD-01325.

[2] This extensive bibliographic research was carried out by Mrs. Joanna Morris, who became a well-informed gerontological psychologist in the process. I am very grateful to her.

Bromley's *The Psychology of Human Ageing* (47) is also comprehensive but is directed more to a lay readership. Less extensive, but more intensive, is Botwinick's *Cognitive Processes in Maturity and Old Age* (32). A book promising to be most useful for courses in social gerontology was edited by Neugarten (263). This book, *Middle Age and Aging,* is a selected compilation of previously published reports. Another worthwhile book, appropriate for students more interested in experimental than in social psychology, was edited by Talland (343). Kushner & Bunch (217) directed their efforts to a study of curricula on aging leading to the doctoral degree.

The books mentioned above do not constitute all the attempts which have been made recently to integrate the abundant data. There are at least as many additional references as cited here which are less technical or nontechnical in nature or which consist of one or more chapters on the psychology of aging in books covering all aspects of gerontology.

METHOD

By far the greatest number of studies have been carried out using the method of cross-sectional age comparisons. There is general dissatisfaction with this method because when differences between age groups are found, it is uncertain whether they are due to age as such or to the different cultural influences under which the groups were reared. Another basis for dissatisfaction with the cross-sectional method involves problems of sampling. The general belief exists that cross-sectional studies show deficit with age and longitudinal studies do not. For example, Damon (93) reported that declines in height, handgrip and vital capacity have been found only in cross-sectional studies, not longitudinal ones. He attributed this to the selective survival of small persons as well as to the cultural trend toward increasing height.

The problems of subject selection in gerontological research are not different in kind from those seen in other areas of psychological investigation, but are, perhaps, more difficult. There are the problems, for example, of lack of cooperativeness of aged subjects (29) and of selection on the basis of geographic stability (297). Donahue (108) questioned whether the age of the investigator affected the results of testing people of different ages. She made a plea for "examining and controlling the E (experimenter) effect." Rosenfelt, Kastenbaum & Kempler (298) emphasized the point that elderly subjects tend to be uneven in their functioning, i.e., one set of abilities may decline while others may not. The measured extent of deficit or even lack of deficit is thus a function of the specific abilities assessed.

The whole question of representativeness of an aged sample is in urgent need of investigation. Are volunteer subjects in aging research truly representative (296)? Are instititionalized and community-residing citizens part of the same subject pool? The issue of health always enters into considerations regarding selecting a representative sample.

Many of the problems involved in achieving representativeness are seen in retest or longitudinal research. Riegel and his associates (e.g., 291) have demonstrated clearly that the composition of samples of elderly subjects changes systematically between test and retest. The initially less able tend to drop out and be unavailable for the retest sessions; the more able are thus overrepresented in the higher age brackets. The extent of this type of drop-out is unknown in cross-sectional studies, but it may be assumed to be present to at least a comparable extent.

In light of the foregoing, it must be clear that, from a sampling point of view, the proclaimed desirability of longitudinal as opposed to cross-sectional investigations is of unknown degree if, in fact, there is an advantage at all. In a clever solution to the problem, Schaie (305) proposed a general research model which is of great value in the consideration of all developmental issues. He latter presented a simplified version specific to the problem of investigating old age (306). Schaie's model involves an analysis of three types of comparisons: cross-sectional (which confounds age and cohort or cultural effects), longitudinal (which confounds age and time of testing effects)[3], and tests at different times, all with subjects of the same age (which confounds cohort and time of testing effects). This three-stage analysis permits an evaluation of the relative contribution of each to the three confounded effects. Unfortunately, the model is so difficult to carry out that it becomes impractical; however, it does provide a methodological goal which is the best yet in coping with the complexities of developmental research.

SUBSTANTIVE AREAS

In reading the following, it must be kept in mind that the methodologies used in these investigations were for the most part cross-sectional and, therefore, far from perfect. However, the available data are the best we have and are important in representing approximate truths.

Cognition

Much of the earlier literature on cognition simply described the rise and fall of abilities. While this type of investigation still occupies much attention, there is an increasing concern with correlates of age changes and with the mechanisms underlying them.

Verbal learning.—The older literature which emphasized increasing deficit with age in verbal learning has been challenged on the basis that the observed deficit may have been one of performance rather than learning itself. The general technique used to test this challenge consists of varying stimulus presentation speeds and comparing subjects under differently paced conditions, the idea being that the commonly used rates of stimulus presentation unfairly impose performance limitations on the elderly. With at least one

[3] Kuhlen (216) pointed out that longitudinal comparisons also confound the effects of age and the effects of culture.

exception (182), the quicker the stimulus pacing, the greater the learning-performance deficit of the elderly (8–10, 64, 116, 118, 346).

Arenberg (8) presented elderly and young adult subjects with a paired-associate learning task: one subgroup of each age experienced fast stimulus pacing trials alternated with self-pacing trials, and a second subgroup of each age experienced slow-pacing trials alternated with self-pacing trials. Arenberg found that the older group was disproportionately poorer than the younger group during self-pacing following fast-pacing, indicating that learning as well as performance had been poorer during the fast-pacing. Related similar studies by other investigators tended to place greater emphasis upon the performance (speed) deficit than the learning deficit, but regardless of emphasis, age decrements in verbal learning have been reported even when the stimulus schedules were self-paced (e.g., 64).

Efforts were made to find other methodological factors which would maximize or minimize age decrement in verbal learning. For example, supportive instructions were found to be superior to challenging ones in minimizing age decrement (299), as was a method of "discovery" as compared to rote learning (74). However, variations in instructions or methods of learning did not always have positive effects (346); they were sometimes of minimal influence (203), or even detrimental to the aged (180). In general, the more difficult the task (299) and the lower the associative strength of paired associates (204, 391, 392), the greater the age decrement. Good health (179) and high IQ (120), on the other hand, were seen to minimize age decrement.

Memory.—It is impossible to separate learning from memory in any but the most arbitrary way. For example, paired-associate learning of the type just discussed is often investigated in the framework of short-term memory or immediate recall. The relationship between learning and memory has been studied by Hulicka & Weiss (183), Hulicka & Rust (181), and Davis & Obrist (100). In the first study (183), elderly and young adults learned paired associates under three conditions: equal number of training trials, learning to criterion, and overlearning. Elderly subjects learned less on equal exposures and required more trials to criterion, but once having learned the material, they retained it as well as did the young subjects. In another study (181) using a task different from that in the first study, and a criterion of one perfect repetition, the results were otherwise. Age differences in recall were seen after both one day and one week of delay.

Directing themselves to a similar problem, Davis & Obrist (100) compared elderly and young subjects in paired-associate learning and measured retention and speed of relearning 48 hours later. The elderly were poorer than the young in learning, relearning, and retention, but when a covariance analysis was carried out controlling for age differences in initial learning and immediate recall, the age difference in speed of relearning became statistically nonsignificant.

Desroches (103) was concerned with measuring memory loss in later life as it may be related to delay or "storage" time. He equated elderly and young adults in original learning to a criterion and then compared them on recall 15 minutes, one hour, one day, and one week later. This study failed to demonstrate either significant memory loss with age or significant interaction between such loss and interval of recall. Perhaps equating subjects by criterion, rather than using a constant number of trials, was the basis for the results. If so, learning and immediate recall, rather than longer term memory, may be the primary functions which decline with age. This is suggested also by the results of the Davis & Obrist study (100).

The relationship between memory and acquisition in rats was investigated in a series of studies by Doty and her associates (109–111). These studies involved the administration of chemical agents which either facilitated or hindered acquisition. The agents were administered at different time intervals following acquisition trials in order to determine how long their effects were maximal. The general finding was that the duration of time during which the agents were effective was longer for the old rats than for the young, indicating that the time required for the consolidation of traces was longer for the old than for the young. Much of what may hinder memory performance, therefore, may very well be *interference* with consolidation during the acquisition process. Many studies suggest that elderly adults are especially vulnerable to interference effects (90, 170, 178, 347, 349), although there are exceptions (66). Regardless of mechanisms, there is no doubt that most tests of memory show decline with age (e.g., 79, 81, 177, 273), although there are exceptions here too (214). Recall performance has even been seen to decline with age when recognition performance did not (309). The decline in memory ability may not continue after age 80 (210), and it may diminish in measured extent with repeated testing (273).

There is uncertainty as to the role the nature of the task plays in influencing retention. Contrary to popular belief, meaningful as compared to meaningless materials were not found to be disproportionately easier to remember for older subjects than for younger ones. In fact, just the reverse was the case (90, 170). However, another study reported (192) that older adults were disproportionately benefited to the extent that the task was meaningful and not of a rote nature. Memory loss in old age seems to be exacerbated by increased task difficulty (135, 219, 348), decreased stimulus exposure time (123), and increased stimulus presentation rate (345).

There is a group of studies which involve variables having in common the potential for minimizing the memory deficit in later life. Arenberg (12) measured recall, comparing the effects of visual stimuli alone, visual and active auditory stimuli (subject read stimulus digit aloud), and visual and passive auditory stimuli (experimenter read stimulus digit aloud). Both conditions in which auditory input augmented visual input decreased the extent of age decrement in memory function. The largest age difference was seen in the visual-only condition. Two other studies showed that visual input was disproportionately more difficult for the elderly than was auditory input

(221, 252). When alternation between sense modalities was frequent, the elderly were particularly disadvantaged (46); when cues were available at the time of recall, elderly subjects were benefited (220). Talland (341) reported that memory in later life suffered disproportionately when two simultaneous operations were involved.

There is a series of studies which is difficult to classify, as they are unique in procedure and purpose, and as they involve perceptual processes to as great an extent as memory. This series used Broadbent's technique of dichotic aural stimulation, in which information is delivered by earphones such that the two ears receive different inputs simultaneously. The subject reports all the digits which were presented to one ear first, and then all the digits which were presented to the other ear. He keeps the second set in memory while reporting the first set. The first set is thought to involve perception only; the second set involves memory. Studies using this technique have typically demonstrated age decrements in the second set of information, but not in the first set (e.g., 55, 56, 187–190, 245). While the data from these studies were clear, their interpretation has been challenged. Craik (89), for example, suggested that perceptual or attentional factors might be more important in producing these results than heretofore considered; Inglis (186) did not agree.

Intelligence.—The growth and decline of intelligence test performance with age have continued to interest many investigators. While decline is not always seen before middle age (355), a variety of cross-sectional examinations have left little doubt that it occurs in the terminal decades of life. Decline with age has been reported using the Wechsler Adult Intelligence Scale (e.g., 267), Progressive Matrices (270, 380), aptitude and ability tests (113, 174, 176, 357), and a variety of other measuring instruments (95, 360, 386). It is seen in other cultures as well as our own (368). However, retest studies have shown less conclusive results than cross-sectional studies. While in one study a retest interval of 8.65 years showed decline in Wechsler-Bellevue test scores in an elderly population (22, 23), in another study a retest after 12 years (from age 49 to 61) using the Army Alpha reflected little change in a highly educated sample (271).

More interesting than growth and decline scores is the pattern of intellectual age change. It is well known that performance on verbal intelligence subtests tends to remain relatively intact, while that on psychomotor subtests tends to fall with advancing adult age (113, 159, 206, 267). The actual pattern of age change is much more complicated than this; so complicated, in fact, that many investigators have seen the need to subject their data to factor analysis or principal component analysis (85, 129, 152, 153, 235, 286, 373). Among the generalizations which seem to be possible from such analyses is the fact that increasingly with advancing age the structure of intelligence is affected by the memory deficit (20, 24, 304).

A more hypothesis-oriented analysis of the pattern of age decrement was seen in an interesting study by Reed & Reitan (288). Rather than simply giving tests and describing age changes, they developed a battery of 29 tests which included 11 of the Wechsler-Bellevue subtests. They hypothesized that differences between age groups would be minimal on tests of stored information (e.g., vocabulary) and maximal on tests of problem solving which are relatively independent of experience. The 29 tests were ranked on a dimension from stored information to problem solving, and given to young and elderly adults. Sizable correlations were found between the rankings and the extent of differences between age groups; their hypothesis was upheld. Similar findings were obtained using subjects with known brain damage (130, 131). When the classification of intellectual functions was described as crystallized versus fluid (176) or static versus flexible (368), the results were conceptually compatible with the above. It is of great potential significance that these age deficits may be reversible to some extent; it was reported that changes in serum cholesterol levels could alter some of these age patterns (290). Slight changes in procedure in repeated testing may also minimize or negate the age decrement in performance seen during initial testing (154).

The contribution of age to intellectual functioning takes place in conjunction with other factors which are often as important, or even more important, in their contribution. For example, poor physical health in the elderly has been found to be related to lower IQ (86, 381), but not always (44). The presence of psychosis tends to be associated with a lower IQ in later life (149), as does low social class (44, 206). Educational level is also important (86, 381); the age decrement has been seen to be greatly reduced when level of education was controlled (150). Even without the control for education, however, not all studies showed significant decline with age (175).

Concept attainment and creativity.—Age decrements in performance have been reported with tests and laboratory procedures which assess concept attainment and other aspects of thinking (e.g., 48, 303, 382). Of greater interest are studies designed to determine the exact nature of the age decrement and possible mechanisms that may account for it. For example, Wetherick (378) found that elderly adults, as contrasted with young adults, did not tend to take advantage of negative information and were less willing to change concepts that were no longer adequate. Arenberg (11), however, emphasized general decrement, not finding the negative instance problem to be disproportionately more difficult for the elderly. He reported that the old committed more errors than young when redundant positive information was provided.

Young (390) carried out a study in logical thinking and reported that the performances of the aged were characterized by a high degree of redundancy, difficulty in dealing with new concepts as problems became more complicated, and an inability to apply a solution strategy which was repeatedly demonstrated. In general, the elderly did not tend to take advantage of efficient strategies in solving problems (283), as for example the use of mnemonic devices (91, 181). In another type of data, Gallup poll surveys, Gergen & Back (142) found that elderly respondents tended not to make fine conceptual differentiations with regard to social situations which were peripheral to their lives; in more relevant situations, the authors suggested, age groups might not differ nearly as much.

Concept attainment seems to be related to nonverbal intelligence (that aspect of intelligence which declines most with age). When age groups were matched on the basis of nonverbal intelligence, age decrement in problem solving ability was not detected (377). When age groups were not matched on this basis, the elderly were found to be deficient (11).

To the extent that with advancing adult age there is a decline in learning ability, memory, intelligence, concept attainment, and problem solving, it may be expected that creativity will suffer. Lehman has been unequivocal in pointing out that creative output does decline with age. He reported this for psychologists (227), engineers (226), physicists and chemists (224), medical workers (223), and those in many fields who created masterworks (225). Elo (122) indicated that peak ability among master chess players occurred in the mid-thirties, with slow decline thereafter.

Acceptance of this type of decline is not universal. Lehman's underlying method of data collection was criticized by Dennis (102), and somewhat contradictory results were found by Stewart & Sparks (327); everyone, including Lehman, emphasized that individual differences in the aging pattern are great. Pressey & Pressey (278) referred to the histories of 10 outstanding men who continued important careers when past 80 years. These men had in common a sense of significant purpose in life, "mellowed wisdom," and a role nurturing such career continuance.

Perception and Psychophysiology

The literature reviewed in this section is related to the literature on cognition just discussed. Before information can be learned, remembered, and dealt with intelligently, it must be sensed and processed, and then the necessary responses must be made. These sensorimotor processes and their psychophysiological correlates are discussed next.

Sensation and illusion.—The general psychological literature deals more with the senses of vision and audition than with the others, and it is thus not surprising that this is also true in studies of adult aging. It has long been known, and is continually being replicated, that auditory thresholds are increased with age (87, 107, 255, 308). Hearing loss with age is most severe at the higher frequencies, especially in men (308). This has widespread implications, as evidenced, for example, by a study which reported that voice recognition and the reporting of messages conveyed by the stimulus voice decreased with age (268).

Decline in visual function is also well documented. Burg (52) reported that after age 35 to 40 the visual field constricts progressively, with women consistently showing slightly larger fields than men. Men were found superior, however, in the ability to see visual details in moving objects, although decline with age was evident for both sexes (125). Ability to recover from glare has also been seen to decrease with age in both sexes (51). Recognition ability has been found to deteriorate with age (51); increasing the size of word recognition stimuli improved the performance of elderly subjects (350).

Other modalities also become less sensitive. Olfaction thresholds were found to increase with age (209), as were taste thresholds (145, 146, 168). However, in one study the increase in taste threshold (in subjects aged 16 to 55) was apparent only in smokers (198). For nonsmokers, age differences in taste sensitivity for quinine and for the chemical agent PROP were not found.

Older adults not only have more difficulty in sensing than young adults, but they also tend to fuse inputs more readily. Critical flicker fusion (CFF) thresholds are lowered in later life (36, 184, 194, 195, 321, 384, 385), although the actual correlation between CFF and age may be small (246). The reduction in CFF with age may be due to a reduced blood flow to the brain (77). Temporal thresholds for the resolution of successively presented somesthetic stimuli are similarly fused more readily in old age (14). It is as if stimulus inputs were not processed as quickly by older people as by younger people, and as a result the traces interact with newer inputs to produce fusion.

Perhaps in contradiction to this lingering trace hypothesis is the observation that the elderly are less susceptible to after-effects than are young adults (117, 144, 194, 195). This may possibly be explained on the basis of a stimulus-boundedness hypothesis, i.e., the behavior of the elderly may be more determined by the immediate environment than is that of younger adults. For example, in the perception of verticality, the elderly tend to be more field dependent than the young (199, 312).

The data on perception of visual illusions are somewhat ambiguous. Some studies indicated that elderly people were not as susceptible to illusions as young people (83, 165, 230, 231, 372), some indicated greater susceptibility (83, 137), and at least one study indicated no age change (229).

Vigilance and reaction time set.—While the elderly are disadvantaged by low intensity inputs, stimulation well above threshold level may minimize and even obliterate this disadvantage. More often than not, however, the major factor is not stimulus intensity but the ability to attend alertly, to search for the stimulus and to make the proper response, i.e., vigilance and detection.

In general, vigilance efficiency has been found to decline with age (342, 351, 353, 364, 365), but not always (96, 155, 262, 337). It seems in part to be a function of stimulus pacing. Thompson, Opton & Cohen (353) varied the speed of stimulus presentation in both an auditory and a visual vigilance task and reported that, at the fastest speed in both sense modalities, vigilance performance was poor in old age. At two slower speeds, old and young subjects were similar in their performances. Essentially the same result was reported in a visual task by Talland (342). It has again been seen, therefore, that pacing or rate of environmental change is a key factor in determining the adequacy of functioning in older people.

Efforts have been made to explain age differences in vigilance performance by reference to measures of psychophysiological function. Opton (269) demonstrated a relationship between vigilance performance and moment-to-moment EEG amplitude, and Surwillo inferred a relationship between vigilance and skin temperature (334), and between vigilance and number of spontaneous skin potential responses (337). Latency of the galvanic skin response during vigilance performance was found to increase with age (336). When vigilance was found to be related to measures of psychophysiological function, however, the contribution of age to these relationships remained ambiguous. When the vigilance task consisted of searching and matching in unchanging displays as in, for example, the digit symbol subtest of the Wechsler intelligence tests (310) or card sorting (35), the age decrement could be accounted for, at least in part, by poor memory ability in the older subjects.

A most frequent finding in aging research is that late life is associated with slow responding. This is seen cross-sectionally as well as longitudinally (124), although individual differences are especially large in later life (42). Spieth (326) found that presence of cardiovascular disease was related to slow reaction time (RT). The observed slowing in later life is usually attributed not to decreased vigilance, but to factors which are conceptually similar; i.e., expectancy, anticipation, or the ability to form and maintain set. This is not to say that all of the ageslowing in RT can be explained on this basis. Sensory acuity was seen to account for some RT loss (127), and sensory and motor nerve conduction velocities have been shown to slow with age (218). The motor time components of RT was found to be slower in later life (38, 375), as was movement time itself (106). However, it was the premotor component of RT which was found to account for most of the slowing. This premotor component constituted 84 per cent of total RT, and was a function of set or expectancy (38). Set in RT is similar to vigilance processes in that both are said to be optimum when the subject maintains alertness and monitors the environment for the appearance of the stimulus calling for response. Surwillo & Quilter (335) may have had this concept in mind when they attempted to explain slowing with age by examining the relationship between vigilance and RT. While they did find some relationship between these two variables, age differences in vigilance were not associated with age differences in RT.

In young adulthood, speed of RT is often enhanced by a warning signal preceding the stimulus to respond, but this does not appear always to be the case in old age (340). The warning signal gives the subject an opportunity to prepare and be set to respond to the oncoming stimulus. The duration of time between the warning signal and the stimulus, i.e., foreperiod or preparatory interval (PI), influences the extent of age differences in RT (38). It would be reasonable to expect heightened alertness during the PI, as reflected by psychophysiological indices. An EEG arousal index was found to vary with PI duration (352), but, paradoxically, this functional relation was different for old and young adults. The arousal index and RT were not correlated, leaving the slowing with age unexplained (352). In a series of aging studies (18, 331–333) in which EEG period was examined in relation to RT, it was found that EEG period, RT, and RT variability were related to age. When, however, the EEG period was held constant, the relations of RT and RT variability with age vanished (332, 333). This suggested to Surwillo (332) that the brain wave cycle is the basic unit of time in the organization of simple behavior.

It is clear that RT is not to be understood in terms of reflexology. This becomes even more apparent when RT is investigated in choice or discrimination situations: factors such as stimulus-response correspondence (319), task complexity (338, 359), information during the warning signal (284), interruption (285), and practice (265) were found to be important in determining the extent of age differences in RT. While rate of improvement with practice in choice RT was found to be more rapid in young than in old adults (265), just the opposite was seen (in some PI conditions) in simple RT (40). As may be expected, not all factors were found to be significant: symbolic versus directional cues do not seem to have disproportionate age effects (320).

Before leaving the problem of RT in later life, it is well to emphasize that there is some doubt as to whether it is age per se which slows the responder, or whether it is the lack of exercise, a concomitant of old age, which in part affects the slowing (41). Participation in physical activity over a period of time has been shown to improve speed of response in the elderly to some extent (17, 80).

Motivation, responsivity, and sleep.—Decline in ability with age is often attributed to lowered motivation and to lowered responsivity or alertness. Data on motivation in later life tend to be meager, but one recent study was informative. Ganzler (138) divided a group of elderly and a group of young adults into subgroups such that one subgroup of each age was given two tests with highly motivating instructions, and one subgroup of each age was given these tests under less highly motivating instructions. On only one of the tests, the Hooper Visual Organization Test, was superiority in performance seen with the highly motivating instructions; the extent of superiority, however, was not greater for the older group than for the young. The inference was drawn that the relative decrements in the performances of the elderly subjects were probably not attributable to age differences in motivation.

Psychophysiological responsivity has been regarded by some as an aspect of motivation. The literature on psychophysiological responsivity in later life is often contradictory, probably because the tasks and specific measures of responsivity employed vary from study to study. Two recent studies demonstrate this. During the course of a serial learning task, Powell, Eisdorfer & Bogdonoff (277) measured free fatty acids (FFA) as an aspect of autonomic nervous system activity related to degree of arousal. Both old and young adults showed elevated FFA levels during the course of learning, but of greater interest was the finding that, when the learning task was terminated, the FFA levels dropped in the younger subjects and continued to rise in the older ones. This was interpreted as reflecting greater involvement in the task on the part of the elderly (277). When a fast-paced learning task resulted in more errors and lower FFA levels on the part of elderly subjects than did a slower-paced task, it was interpreted as indicating subjective withdrawal from the more difficult task (362). A more conventional index of responsivity, EEG arousal, was found to be positively associated with learning ability in later life (354).

Some of the changes in responsivity in later life may be seen as changes in the tendency to habituate to repeated stimulation. Kimble & Pennypacker (208) clearly demonstrated that the decreased rate of eyeblink conditioned responses seen in elderly subjects was attributable to their increased tendencies to habituate to the unconditioned stimuli. Lowered rates of conditioned responses during conditioning are frequently seen in old age (94, 196, 208, 324), and conditioned response rates are even lower in senile psychotics (324). Perhaps habituation and, in this sense, lowered responsivity underlie many of the results found in the aging literature on conditioning.

If low responsiveness and high habituation are generally characteristic of old age, it would follow that older people would be less active in their daily lives and, possibly, sleep more than young people. Tune (366) studied sleep charts for an eight-week period and reported that sleep duration decreased from the twenties to the fifties, after which there was an increase. Most of the sleep studies involved EEG monitoring, and the results of these studies were somewhat different from those of Tune (366). Typical findings were that the amount of time spent in the deepest stage of sleep (Stage IV) was reduced in later life and that there were more periods of wakefulness during the night (4, 126). Older people slept more in the course of the whole day (366) but slept less or more fitfully during the usual period of sleep.

Personality and Social Behavior

The world changes for the older person because on the one hand he has changed; on the other hand, people often respond differently to him than they did when he was young.

Personality.—Disengagement is a very important concept in the aging literature; so important, in fact, that it has probably generated more controversy and research than any other single concept. The theory states that with increasing age there is an increasing tendency to dissociate oneself from people and activities. Few investigators have denied the basic observation of withdrawal, but in the recent literature, the mechanisms underlying the withdrawal have been vehemently debated (19, 70–72, 164, 236, 294, 313, 314, 388, 389). As originally propounded, disengagement was presumed to be a natural or normal attribute of old age, and by implication, at least, a desirable one. The strength of the ego has been said to decline in old age (59), and this may lead to a diminution of involvement with the social forces of life. Lending support to these considerations are studies which show that increased age tends to be associated with increased introversion (58, 60, 156, 371). And, as if in corroboration on a psychobiological level, there seems to be a diminution of involvement or interest in sexual behavior in later life (43, 61, 76) with an apparent devaluation of sex-specific body parts (374). The sexes were seen to resemble each other more on a masculinity-femininity dimension as age increased (62).

Most investigators have rejected the idea that disengagement is normal or natural, suggesting instead that cultural patterns are rejecting of the older person and push dissociation upon him. In support of this view is a study in which older men were found to have as high a baseline level of aspiration as younger men and to be equally responsive to perceived failure (99). In old age, possession of a negative self concept is common, especially in those who are ill (311). This may well produce a fear of failure in social involvement and lead to further disengagement. Such a notion was supported in a study by Strauss (330), in which it was concluded that those elderly who perceive the environment as rejecting or devaluing them tend to withdraw from involvement in their surroundings. When self concept was seen to improve with age, it was suggested that denial of faults could account for the results (151).

Depressive affect has often been reported in later life (39, 394), and may be a factor in disengagement. Perhaps the most extreme expression of disengagement is the desire for death: suicide is more frequent in the aged than in the young, and in the aged especially it seems to stem largely from depressive illness (166, 370). If, as Zung (394) believed, feelings of inferiority and loss of self-esteem are among the major causes of depression in the elderly, then it may well turn out that the problem is best studied as a triad: (*a*) feelings of inferiority with loss of self-esteem, (*b*) depression, and (*c*) disengagement.

People who see the environment as rejecting and threatening may be expected to be cautious. The literature has often emphasized cautiousness in the elderly (31, 84, 316), although Tune (365) interpreted his vigilance data as reflecting lessened cautiousness in later life. The concept of cautiousness is not as simple as it may appear. A very recent study indicated that what may at first appear to be cautiousness may in actuality be an interest in avoiding the need to make decisions in the first place (34). The need to avoid making decisions may, of course, be conceptualized as an aspect of disengagement.

In both community-residing (379) and institutionalized (82) aged, the literature also emphasizes rigidity. For example, in later life there seems to be an increased susceptibility both to the effects of set (65) and to the perseveration of incorrect responses (205), although increasing Einstellung effects are not always seen (323). The concept of behavioral rigidity in old age has even been put to test with rat subjects (37) and used as an explanation of their performances (147). Rigidity in later life is a complex phenomenon in that it may be a consequence of intellectual inability, rather than a primary factor in and of itself. When a solution to a problem is not at hand, the rigid repetition of the incorrect response may be the alternative most available to the subject.

Impulsivity has been reported to decrease in old age (322). Older people were found to shy away from responses of anger (132) and, until the mid-fifties at least, were found to be more agreeable and cooperative (358). In national surveys, they tended to prefer solutions that end international conflicts as soon as possible (141). There is evidence that the aged are submissive, avoid hardships, and accept limitations (49). Recent studies suggest that fears (300) and anxieties (367) do not change with age.

The MMPI appears to be the personality test most frequently used in the study of later life. Sizable age differences in MMPI scores have not been seen before age 45 (356), but have been found in older groups. There are five scales which in different studies show change. Depressive affect (D) is seen both in normal aged (e.g., 39, 45) and in elderly psychiatric subjects (158, 276). Somatic complaints (Hs) and tendencies toward hysteria (Hy) have been reported to be frequent in later life (162, 276), as have lowered energy level (Ma) and a tendency to admit less that which is antisocial (F) (162). F-scale score decreases have also been reported in older psychiatric patients (157). Taken together, the data based upon community and institutionalized aged suggest a general neuroticism in old age (1, 162, 276). However, a detailed item analysis of the MMPI revealed a most interesting result which seems to be at variance with these conclusions (274). Items reflecting contentedness, happiness, and related affect states showed the greatest frequency of negative responses at about age 40. Greater amounts of satisfaction were indicated both earlier and later in life.

More Rorschach test data have been reported in years past by Ames, perhaps, than anyone else. In a recent study (6), she found that age changes seen in Rorschach retests were larger in later adulthood than in earlier adulthood. Not all studies have shown age differences in personality, however (143). Eisdorfer (115), who did not find important age differences in Rorschach test performance with subjects having IQs of 116 or over, charged that many previous studies which had shown age changes had done so with institutionalized subjects who were intellectually deteriorated. This created the impression that grave changes occur in the normal aging process, when this may not be so at all.

It is sometimes difficult to separate normal aging from that which involves pathology and institutionalization, and many aging studies have been done using pathological groups of subjects. In an institutional population, disability was found to increase with age more for women than for men, and to be greater for patients with organic mental problems than for those with functional ones (254). Psychopathology was found to be related to failure in adjusting to the changes in ego identity necessitated by the aging process (167), and to failure in accomplishing developmental tasks in earlier life (242). This latter factor was credited as more important in adaptation in old age than were age-linked social traumas such as widowhood and retirement (242). In a community-residing sample also, bereavement was seen as less significant in adjustment than had been expected, and loneliness was found to be more related to personality traits than to actual life situation (140). Attitudes toward aging and death may be predictable from lifelong adjustment patterns (387).

Activities, interests, and morale.—It seems to be generally believed that disengagement is not a satisfactory state of affairs; the general hypothesis is that it is desirable to keep busy in thought and in activity, and that this will make for contentment and better adjustment. Much of the literature in social gerontology involves the investigation of this hypothesis and examination of the factors related to it. For example, Maddox (247) found a positive relationship between activity and morale, although the relationship was modified by health, attitude, and "type of activity" factors. However, Craik (88) found a relationship between emotional adjustment and sociability only in a young group, not in an old one, and Poorkaj (275) found no difference in morale between active and disengaged elderly. While Carp (68) found that the aged were benefited by a new housing facility geared to their needs, Poorkaj (275) found that elderly people living in the general community had better morale than elderly people living in a senior citizen's community in which activity was emphasized. Moreover, people living in relative isolation their whole lives were found to be no more emotionally impaired than their more social aged counterparts (240, 241). Thus, it seems, the activity-morale relationship is not all that clearly a positive one.

This is not to say that feelings of loneliness may not often stem from a reduction in the number of social contacts (260), or that the reduced level of activity seen in older people (50, 92, 105, 329) is what they really want. Aged as well as young adults seem to value an active life shared with other people (212). In fact, it seems that the longer the aged remain in institutions where opportunity for friendship exists, the more friends they tend to have (134); they tend to form friendships with those residing in closest proximity to them (133). In the final analysis, interests and values may not change very much during the adult lifetime, although this may be more true for some types of people than for others. For example, in one study bankers were not seen to change in their interests much over the course of 30 years (63), but in another study values of farmers were said to become less youth-oriented in older age (244). In this latter study, it was suggested that this age change might best be understood as partly generation-determined, but also partly age-determined.

In assessing interests, values, and contentment of older people it is necessary to keep continuously in mind differences in individual circumstances. Elderly people who are still in the working force have been reported to experience less job-related strain than their younger counterparts (185), and to be generally more satisfied or happy (185, 256–258). However, not all studies showed this; one, at least, reported that job satisfaction increased up to age 60, but decreased between ages 60 and 65 (302).

Attitudes toward aging and the self.—A self-perception scale was given to subjects aged over 65; the results showed differences related to social class, with the indigent aged reporting significantly more negative statements than middle- and upper-class aged. The overall results were interpreted as indicating that very positive self-reports may have been a manifestation of denial, while very negative reports may have reflected depression (282). The mechanism of denial is reported often in the aging literature, even in studies which are not basically personality studies (30, 287). However, what may appear to be denial may in fact be a deficit in some ability, e.g., perception (30, 287, 318).

Positive attitudes toward aging may be expected to involve positive and realistic perceptions of health status. While one study reported that two out of three old people residing in the community tended to rate their own health status in a way compatible with that of a physician (248), another study reported that old people rated their health as more negative than did the attending physician (136). The number of symptoms reported by patients was not found to be related to age (101, 104), but to habitual patterns of describing illness (101). Moreover, the number of reported physical and psychiatric complaints was related to poor mental health but not to physical health (104).

In general, aging is not positively regarded by younger people. Young men were seen to hold less favorable attitudes toward old people than young women (317), although both sexes had negative attitudes (363). On the other hand, aged men were more positively disposed toward the future than aged women (228). A factor analysis of an adjective rating scale showed that old people were seen by younger ones to be relatively constricted and socially unable (2). Even doctoral candidates in clinical psychology, young adults presumably interested in deficit problems, showed a strong preference for working with young adults as compared to aged ones (383). One study found that young children regarded old people somewhat favorably, but as they grew older they became less favorable (172, 173). Hospital personnel who had positive attitudes toward geriatric patients also tended to have positive attitudes toward minority groups generally, and toward socially devalued and disabled groups (250).

Retirement.—Retirement constitutes stress for many people and brings about problems of adjustment. Those who intrinsically value work tended to have the most difficulty in adjusting to retirement (160). However, as if to bridge the gap from work to retirement, extrinsic factors such as salary were seen to become generally more important to the workers than intrinsic ones as retirement neared (301). White collar workers, possibly because they posses more of an intrinsic valuation of work, were found to be less satisfied in the initial years of retirement than were blue collar workers, although it was suggested that in the long run, adjustment may favor the white collar worker (328). Nevertheless, in a group of lower and lower-middle class retirees, the older ones were found to have stronger interests in social interactional activities than did the younger ones (369).

Workers on the threshold of retirement were reported to be essentially similar to the newly retired: pre- and post-retirees were found similar in endorsement of traits (279), in reporting potential satisfactions or frustrations (280), and in reporting illnesses or incapacities (281). There seems to be a drop in the incidence of serious illness within the first two years of retirement with a gradual increase thereafter (249). Pre-retired husbands as well as retired ones were more positively oriented toward retirement than were their wives (207). Wives who were glad their husbands retired tended to be younger than those who were not glad, tended to be in better health, and were happier in their marriages (171). Retired husbands tended to do more household tasks than working husbands, but did not tend to engage more in joint work activities with their wives (16). It was seen that being paid to work in retirement can have a powerful positive impact on happiness, self-esteem, and relationships with other people (69).

Relocation.—The progression for a minority of people is from work to retirement and, after some years, relocation in a home or other institution for the aged. What are some of the effects of such relocation? Comparisons between people awaiting institutionalization and people residing in institutions have uncovered similarities and differences. For example, depression was more common in those awaiting institutionalization in a home for the aged than in those already in a home, but time orientation and emotional reactivity were better (234). Self-esteem was found similar in the two groups (7). While level of cognitive functioning remained unchanged following psychiatric institutionalization in a state hospital, self-maintenance and sociability improved (361). As may be expected, however, aged people requiring custodial care were poorer in cognitive functioning than those residing in the community (211).

Relocation seems to have an effect even when it is from one institution to another, for reasons independent of the needs of the residents. Miller &

Lieberman (259) examined elderly women residing in a home for the aged two weeks prior to an enforced move to another home, and again at six and at 18 weeks after the move. Half the women were judged to show negative change. Apparently, the greater the depressive affect prior to the move, the greater the negative change. Havens (163) reported that level of adjustment after moving into a public housing facility was related to how closely the residents' activities resembled those carried out previously: the more similar the activities the better the adjustment. When the activities were stopped and not replaced with others, adjustment declined. Level of adjustment within an institution is not fixed; it can be improved by appropriate methods (128).

Factors in Survival

It has already been indicated that a higher percentage of old people than young people take their own lives; this tends to stem from loneliness (251), illness (139), and very often from depression (139, 166, 215, 370). Older people are more often successful in their suicide attempts than are younger people (121, 215), indicating that greater despair must underlie their efforts.

Depression may also play a role in more natural deaths. For example, it has been found that reminiscing is often seen in old age, and when it is infrequent, there tends to be greater depression and a lower survival rate (253). The question of depression, however, is complicated. Myler (261) investigated survival rates in an aged sample in relation to many different indices of depression. Only one, a psychiatrist's rating, discriminated those who lived from those who died. Other personality factors seem to be related to survival also. Riegel, Riegel & Meyer (292) found rigidity, dogmatism, and negative attitude toward life associated with earlier death.

The opinion is held by some that death frequently follows relocation (27). Kastenbaum (201) accepts as general knowledge the thesis that death occurs with substantial frequency within one month after admission to an institution. One study reported that relocation from one institution to another resulted in an increased death rate, especially of people who were neurotic, depressed, and compulsive. Those who tended to express hostility tended to survive (5).

Some other social factors which are important in survival are high occupational and social status membership and maintenance of occupational and marital roles (53, 295). High intelligence also appears to be related to survival (295); when IQ drops, it has been reported that the potential for survival diminishes (21). Such results are compatible with a study done in the Soviet Union (73) in which it was also found that good health, continued interest and activity, and maintained family life were related to survival. Unlike Rose (295), who found that having a small number of children was a positive factor in survival, the Soviets saw having "many descendants" as a good sign.

Lieberman (233) studied institutionalized aged people every three to four weeks over two and a half years to determine systematic psychological changes prior to death. He reported that "changes preceding death are seen as diminution of the capacity to cope adequately with environmental demands, particularly because of a lowered ability to organize and integrate stimuli in the environment. The primary subjective experience is one of chaos" (233, p. 190). Lieberman suggested that the often-reported lack of correlation between chronological age and psychological functioning may be explained, partially, by individual differences in "distance from death." Unlike Lieberman, however, Kastenbaum (202) was unimpressed with the psychological changes that occur in the course of dying.

Butler (53) indicated that if an aged person has a sense of continued usefulness, this may keep him living, especially if factors such as arteriosclerosis and cigarette smoking are minimal. Factors more subtle than general health are often predictive of death. For example, one study showed that patients with abnormal EEGs were less likely to remain alive than those with normal ones (54).

One theory of longevity is that the potential length of a life is genetically programmed such that rate of biological development is associated with rate of biological decline. To the extent that rate of biological development is rapid, death comes sooner. Evidence for this theory was not found in an analysis involving age at menarche, menopause, and death (33).

Aging Analogues and the Maintenance of Function

There was hope that RNA would be helpful in the maintenance of cognitive ability in later life. Some studies showed improvement in aged samples following administration of RNA (57, 325) and some did not (213, 266, 344); in general, the hope seems to have been raised on a very limited base. Similarly, sex hormones (193, 293) and a "memory drug," magnesium pemoline (119), have been tried—again with limited or no success. For a while, procaine treatments were regarded as useful in improving general level of functioning (3, 237) and even life itself (13), but, once again, negative results were not uncommon (148).

In old rats, negatively ionized air has been found to improve performance (114) and to be preferred to non-ionized air (112), giving some support to the theory that ionization acts to normalize processes under stress (112). Stress was seen to hasten some aspects of aging in the rat (272). Irradiation seems to produce effects similar to those seen in aging (e.g., 97, 339). In fact, irradiation has been accepted by some as an analogue of aging. Not all data, however, support this contention (28, 98, 238).

Investigations attempting to reverse aging patterns and discover analogues of aging processes have not been popular with psychologists, although the potential benefit from such research is self-evident. In this era when we are called upon to be "relevant," there are few areas of investigation which are more necessary.

LITERATURE CITED

1. Aaronson, B. S. Aging, personality change and psychiatric diagnosis. *J. Gerontol.,* **19,** 144–48 (1964)
2. Aaronson, B. S. Personality stereotypes of aging. *Ibid.,* **21,** 458–62 (1966)
3. Abrams, A., Tobin, S. S., Gordon, P., Pechtel, C., Hilkevitch, A. The effects of a European procaine preparation in an aged population: I. Psychological effects. *J. Gerontol.,* **20,** 139–43 (1965)
4. Agnew, H. W., Jr., Webb, W. W., Williams, R. L. Sleep patterns in late middle age males: An EEG study. *Electroenceph. Clin. Neurophysiol.,* **23,** 168–71 (1967)
5. Aldrich, C. K., Mendkoff, E. Relocation of the aged and disabled: A mortality study. *J. Amer. Geriat. Soc.,* **11,** 185–94 (1963)
6. Ames, L. B. Changes in Rorschach response throughout the human life span. *Genet. Psychol. Monogr.,* **74,** 89–125 (1966)
7. Anderson, N. N. Effects of institutionalization on self-esteem. *J. Gerontol.,* **22,** 313–17 (1967)
8. Arenberg, D. Anticipation interval and age differences in verbal learning. *J. Abnorm. Psychol.,* **70,** 419–25 (1965)
9. Arenberg, D. Age differences in retroaction. *J. Gerontol.,* **22,** 88–91 (1967)
10. Arenberg, D. Regression analyses of verbal learning on adult age at two anticipation intervals. *Ibid.,* 411–14
11. Arenberg, D. Concept problem solving in young and old adults. *Ibid.,* **23,** 279–82 (1968)
12. Arenberg, D. Input modality in short-term retention of old and young adults. *Ibid.,* 462–65
13. Aslan, A., Vrabiescu, A., Domilescu, C., Campeanu, L., Costiniu, M., Stanescu, S. Long-term treatment with procaine (Gerovital H_3) in albino rats. *J. Gerontol.,* **20,** 1–8 (1965)
14. Axelrod, S., Thompson, L. W., Cohen, L. D. Effects of senescence on the temporal resolution of somesthetic stimuli presented to one hand or both. *J. Gerontol.,* **23,** 191–95 (1968)
15. Balazs, A., Ed. *International Conference on Gerontology* (Akademiai Kiado, Budapest, 939 pp., 1965)
16. Ballweg, J. A. Resolution of conjugal role adjustment after retirement. *J. Marr. Fam.,* **29,** 277–81 (1967)
17. Barry, A. J., Steinmetz, J. R., Page, H. F., Rodahl, K. The effects of physical conditioning on older individuals. II. Motor performance and cognitive function. *J. Gerontol.,* **21,** 192–99 (1966)
18. Bauer, H. G., Hoch, H., Apfeldorf, M. Alpha wave frequency and auditory reaction time as related to aging in 137 subjects with normal electroencephalograms: A preliminary report. *Activ. Nerv. Sup.,* **9,** 125–29 (1967)
19. Bell, T. The relationship between social involvement and feeling old among residents in homes for the aged. *J. Gerontol.,* **22,** 17–22 (1967)
20. Berger, L., Bernstein, A., Klein, E., Cohen, J., Lucas, G. Effects of aging and pathology on the factorial structure of intelligence. *J. Consult. Psychol.,* **28,** 199–207 (1964)
21. Berkowitz, B. Changes in intellect with age: IV. Changes in achievement and survival in older people. *J. Genet. Psychol.,* **107,** 3–14 (1965)
22. Berkowitz, B., Green, R. F. Changes in intellect with age: I. Longitudinal study of Wechsler-Bellevue scores. *J. Genet. Psychol.,* **103,** 3–21 (1963)
23. Berkowitz, B., Green, R. F. Changes in intellect with age: V. Differential change as functions of time interval and original score. *Ibid.,* **107,** 179–92 (1965)
24. Beverfelt, E., Nygard, M., Nordvik. H. Factor analysis of Wechsler Adult Intelligence Scale performance of elderly Norwegians. *J. Gerontol.,* **19,** 49–53 (1964)
25. Birren, J. E., Ed. *Relations of Development and Aging* (C. C. Thomas, Springfield, Ill., 296 pp., 1964)
26. Birren, J. E. *The Psychology of Aging* (Prentice-Hall, Inc., Englewood Cliffs, N.J., 303 pp., 1964)

27. Blenkner, M. Environmental change and the aging individual. *Gerontologist,* **7,** 101–5 (1967)
28. Boer, A. P., Davis, R. T. Age changes in the behavior of monkeys induced by ionizing radiation. *J. Gerontol.,* **23,** 337–42 (1968)
29. Bortner, R. W. Research cooperation in older institutionalized males. *Percept. Mot. Skills,* **16,** 611–12 (1963)
30. Botwinick, J. Perceptual organization in relation to age and sex. *J. Gerontol.,* **20,** 224–27 (1965)
31. Botwinick, J. Cautiousness in advanced age. *Ibid.,* **21,** 347–53 (1966)
32. Botwinick, J. *Cognitive Processes in Maturity and Old Age* (Springer, New York, 212 pp., 1967)
33. Botwinick, J. A crude test of a hypothesis relating rate of growth to length of life. *Gerontologist,* **8,** 196–97 (1968)
34. Botwinick, J. Disinclination to venture response versus cautiousness in responding: Age differences. *J. Genet. Psychol.* (In press, 1969)
35. Botwinick, J., Birren, J. E. A follow-up study of card-sorting performance in elderly men. *J. Gerontol.,* **20,** 208–10 (1965)
36. Botwinick, J., Brinley, J. F. Age differences in relations between CFF and apparent motion. *J. Genet. Psychol.,* **102,** 189–94 (1963)
37. Botwinick, J., Brinley, J. F., Robbin, J. S. Learning and reversing a four-choice multiple Y-maze by rats of three ages. *J. Gerontol.,* **18,** 279–82 (1963)
38. Botwinick, J., Thompson, L. W. Components of reaction time in relation to age and sex. *J. Genet. Psychol.,* **108,** 175–83 (1966)
39. Botwinick, J., Thompson, L. W. Depressive affect, speed of response, and age. *J. Consult. Psychol.,* **31,** 106 (1967)
40. Botwinick, J., Thompson, L. W. Practice of speeded response in relation to age, sex, and set. *J. Gerontol.,* **22,** 72–76 (1967)
41. Botwinick, J., Thompson, L. W. Age difference in reaction time: An artifact? *Gerontologist,* **8,** 25–28 (1968)
42. Botwinick, J., Thompson, L. W. A research note on individual differences in reaction time in relation to age. *J. Genet. Psychol.,* **112,** 73–75 (1968)
43. Bowers, L. M., Cross, R. R., Lloyd, F. A. Sexual function and urologic disease in the elderly male. *J. Amer. Geriat. Soc.,* **11,** 647–52 (1963)
44. Britton, P. G., Bergmann, K., Kay, D. W. K., Savage, R. D. Mental state, cognitive functioning, physical health, and social class in the community aged. *J. Gerontol.,* **22,** 517–21 (1967)
45. Britton, P. G., Savage, R. D. The MMPI and the aged: Some normative data from a community sample. *Brit. J. Psychiat.,* **112,** 941–43 (1966)
46. Broadbent, D. E., Gregory, M. Some confirmatory results on age differences in memory for simultaneous stimulation. *Brit. J. Psychol.,* **56,** 77–80 (1965)
47. Bromley, D. B. *The Psychology of Human Ageing* (Penguin Books, Baltimore, 366 pp., 1966)
48. Bromley, D. B. Age and sex differences in the serial production of creative conceptual responses. *J. Gerontol.,* **22,** 32–42 (1967)
49. Buhler, C., Brind, A., Horner, A. Old age as a phase of human life: Questionnaire study. *Hum. Develpm.,* **11,** 53–63 (1968)
50. Bultena, G. L. Age-grading in the social interaction of an elderly male population. *J. Gerontol.,* **23,** 539–43 (1968)
51. Burg, A. Light sensitivity as related to age and sex. *Percept. Mot. Skills,* **24,** 1279–88 (1967)
52. Burg, A. Lateral visual field as related to age and sex. *J. Appl. Psychol.,* **52,** 10–15 (1968)
53. Butler, R. N. Aspects of survival and adaptation in human aging. *Amer. J. Psychiat.,* **123,** 1233–43 (1967)
54. Cahan, R. B., Yeager, C. L. Admission EEG as a predictor of mortality and discharge for aged state hospital patients. *J. Gerontol.,* **21,** 248–56 (1966)
55. Caird, W. K. Memory disorder and psychological test performance in aged psychiatric patients. *Dis. Nerv. Syst.,* **26,** 499–505 (1965)
56. Caird, W. K. Aging and short-term

memory. *J. Gerontol.*, **21**, 295–99 (1966)

57. Cameron, D. E., Sved, S., Solyom, L., Wainrib, B., Barik, H. C. Effects of ribonucleic acid on memory defect in the aged. *Amer. J. Psychiat.*, **120**, 320–25 (1963)
58. Cameron, P. Age as a determinant of differences in non-intellective psychological dimensions. *Dissert. Abstr.*, **28B**, 1157 (1967)
59. Cameron, P. Ego strength and happiness of the aged. *J. Gerontol.*, **22**, 199–202 (1967)
60. Cameron, P. Introversion and egocentricity among the aged. *Ibid.*, 465–68
61. Cameron, P. Note on time spent thinking about sex. *Psychol. Rept.*, **20**, 741–42 (1967)
62. Cameron, P. Masculinity-femininity in the aged. *J. Gerontol.*, **23**, 63–65 (1968)
63. Campbell, D. P. Stability of interests within an occupation over thirty years. *J. Appl. Psychol.*, **50**, 51–56 (1966)
64. Canestrari, R. E., Jr. Paced and self-paced learning in young and elderly adults. *J. Gerontol.*, **18**, 165–68 (1963)
65. Canestrari, R. E., Jr. Age differences in spatial stimulus generalization. *J. Genet. Psychol.*, **106**, 129–35 (1965)
66. Canestrari, R. E., Jr. The effects of commonality on paired associate learning in two age groups. *Ibid.*, **108**, 3–7 (1966)
67. Carp, F. M. *A Future for the Aged: Victoria Plaza and Its Residents* (Univ. Texas Press, Austin, 287 pp., 1966)
68. Carp, F. M. The impact of environment on old people. *Gerontologist*, **7**, 106–8; 135 (1967)
69. Carp, F. M. Differences among older workers, volunteers, and persons who are neither. *J. Gerontol.*, **23**, 497–501 (1968)
70. Carp, F. M. Person-situation congruence in engagement. *Gerontologist*, **8**, 184–88 (1968)
71. Carp, F. M. Some components of disengagement. *J. Gerontol.*, **23**, 382–86 (1968)
72. Cassata, M. B. A study of the mass communications behavior and the social disengagement behavior of 177 members of the Age Center of New England. *Dissert. Abstr.*, **28A**, 3765–66 (1968)
73. Chebotaryov, D. F., Sachuk, N. N. Sociomedical examination of longevous people in the U.S.S.R. *J. Gerontol.*, **19**, 435–39 (1964)
74. Chown, S., Belbin, E., Downs, S. Programmed instruction as a method of teaching paired associates to older learners. *J. Gerontol.*, **22**, 212–19 (1967)
75. Chown, S., Riegel, K. F., Eds. *Interdisciplinary Topics in Gerontology* (S. Karger, Basel, 153 pp., 1968)
76. Christenson, C. V., Gagnon, J. H. Sexual behavior in a group of older women. *J. Gerontol.*, **20**, 351–56 (1965)
77. Chyatte, C. Brain blood-shift theory: A preliminary test through correlations of age with alpha EEG and CFF. *J. Psychol.*, **61**, 27–32 (1965)
78. Clark, M., Anderson, B. G. *Culture and Aging: An Anthropological Study of Older Americans* (C. C. Thomas, Springfield, Ill., 478 pp., 1967)
79. Clement, F. Analyse de l'echelle de memoire de Wechsler: Facteurs qui influent sur ses resultats. (Analysis of the Wechsler Memory Scale: Factors influencing results.) *Rev. Psychol. Appl.*, **16**, 197–244 (1966)
80. Clement, F. Effect of physical activity on the maintenance of intellectual capacities. *Gerontologist*, **6**, 91–92; 126 (1966)
81. Clement, F., Poitrenaud, J. La test de retention visuelle de Benton: Evolution des resultats avec l'age en fonction de sexe et du niveau intellectuel. (The Benton test of visual retention: Results as a function of age, sex, and intellectual level.) *Rev. Psychol. Appl.*, **14**, 243–77 (1964)
82. Coleman, K. K. The modification of rigidity in geriatric patients through operant conditioning. *Dissert. Abstr.*, **24**, 2560–61 (1963)
83. Comalli, P. E. Cognitive functioning in a group of 80-90 year old men. *J. Gerontol.*, **20**, 14–17 (1965)
84. Coppinger, N. W., Anthony, N. The

effect of instructions and response demands on the perception of line differences in adults. *J. Gerontol.*, **23**, 50–52 (1968)

85. Coppinger, N. W., Bortner, R. W., Saucer, R. T. A factor analysis of psychological deficit. *J. Genet. Psychol.*, **103**, 23–43 (1963)
86. Correll, R. E., Rokosz, S., Blanchard, B. M. Some correlates of WAIS performance in the elderly. *J. Gerontol.*, **21**, 544–49 (1966)
87. Corso, J. F. Aging and auditory threshold in men and women. *Arch. Environ. Hlth.*, **6**, 350–56 (1963)
88. Craik, F. I. M. An observed age difference in responses to a personality inventory. *Brit. J. Psychol.*, **55**, 453–62 (1964)
89. Craik, F. I. M. The nature of the age decrement in performance on dichotic listening tasks. *Quart. J. Exptl. Psychol.*, **17**, 227–40 (1965)
90. Craik, F. I. M., Masani, P. A. Age differences in the temporal integration of language. *Brit. J. Psychol.*, **58**, 291–99 (1967)
91. Crovitz, E. Reversing a learning deficit in the aged. *J. Gerontol.*, **21**, 236–38 (1966)
92. Cunningham, D. A., Montoye, H. J., Metzner, H. L., Keller, J. B. Active leisure time activities as related to age among males in a total population. *J. Gerontol.*, **23**, 551–56 (1968)
93. Damon, A. Discrepancies between findings of longitudinal and cross-sectional studies in adult life: Physique and physiology. *Hum. Develpm.*, **8**, 16–22 (1965)
94. Davidson, P. O., Payne, R. W., Sloane, R. B. Conditionability and age in human adults. *Psychol. Rept.*, **17**, 351–54 (1965)
95. Davies, A. D. M. The perceptual maze test in a normal population. *Percept. Mot. Skills*, **20**, 287–93 (1965)
96. Davies, D. R., Griew, S. A further note on the effect of aging on auditory vigilance performance; the effect of low signal frequency. *J. Gerontol.*, **18**, 370–71 (1963)
97. Davis, R. T. Chronic effects of ionizing radiations and the hypothesis that irradiation produces aging-like changes in behavior. *J. Genet. Psychol.*, **102**, 311–24 (1963)
98. Davis, R. T., Lovelace, W. E., McKenna, V. V. Size constancy as a function of aging and X-ray irradiation in rhesus monkeys. *Anim. Behav.*, **12**, 16–24 (1964)
99. Davis, R. W. Social influences on the aspiration tendency of older people. *J. Gerontol.*, **22**, 510–16 (1967)
100. Davis, S. H., Obrist, W. D. Age differences in learning and retention of verbal material. *Cornell J. Soc. Relat.*, **1**, 95–103 (1966)
101. Denney, D., Kole, D. M., Matarazzo, R. G. The relationship between age and the number of symptoms reported by patients. *J. Gerontol.*, **20**, 50–53 (1965)
102. Dennis, W. Creative productivity between the ages of 20 and 80 years. *J. Gerontol.*, **21**, 1–8 (1966)
103. Desroches, H. F., Kaiman, B. D., Ballard, H. T. Relationship between age and recall of meaningful material. *Psychol. Rept.*, **18**, 920–22 (1966)
104. Desroches, H. F., Kaiman, B. D., Ballard, H. T. Factors influencing reporting of physical symptoms by the aged patient. *Geriatrics*, **22**, 169–75 (1967)
105. Desroches, H. F., Kaiman, B. D., Larsen, E. R., Carman, P. M. Age and leisure-time activities in a V.A. domiciliary. *Geriatrics*, **20**, 1065–69 (1965)
106. Deupree, R. H., Simon, J. R. Reaction time and movement time as a function of age, stimulus duration, and task difficulty. *Ergonomics*, **6**, 403–11 (1963)
107. Dittrich, F., Fumeaux, J. A generalized expression of auditory sensitivity. *Ergonomics*, **8**, 143–49 (1965)
108. Donahue, W. Relationship of age of perceivers to their social perceptions. *Gerontologists*, **5**, 241–45; 276–77 (1965)
109. Doty, B. A., Doty, L. A. Effect of age and chlorpromazine on memory consolidation. *J. Comp. Physiol. Psychol.*, **57**, 331–34 (1964)
110. Doty, B. A., Doty, L. A. Facilitative effects of amphetamine on avoidance conditioning in relation to

age and problem difficulty. *Psychopharmacologia,* **9,** 234–41 (1966)

111. Doty, B. A., Johnston, M. M. Effects of post-trial eserine administration, age and task difficulty on avoidance conditioning in rats. *Psychon. Sci.,* **6,** 101–2 (1966)
112. Driessen, G. H., Maier, R. A., Macchitelli, F. J. Negative ion preference in "old" rats. *Psychol. Rept.,* **12,** 439–40 (1963)
113. Droege, R. C., Crambert, A. C., Henkin, J. B. Relationship between G.A.T.B. aptitude scores and age for adults. *Personnel Guid. J.,* **41,** 502–8 (1963)
114. Duffee, R. A., Koontz, R. H. Behavioral effect of ionized air on rats. *Psychophysiology,* **1,** 347–59 (1965)
115. Eisdorfer, C. Rorschach performance and intellectual functioning in the aged. *J. Gerontol.,* **18,** 358–63 (1963)
116. Eisdorfer, C. Verbal learning and response time in the aged. *J. Genet. Psychol.,* **107,** 15–22 (1965)
117. Eisdorfer, C., Axelrod, S. Senescence and figural aftereffects in two modalities: A correction. *J. Genet. Psychol.,* **104,** 193–97 (1964)
118. Eisdorfer, C., Axelrod, S., Wilkie, F. L. Stimulus exposure time as a factor in serial learning in an aged sample. *J. Abnorm. Soc. Psychol.,* **67,** 594–600 (1963)
119. Eisdorfer, C., Conner, J. F., Wilkie, F. L. The effect of magnesium pemoline on cognition and behavior. *J. Gerontol.,* **23,** 283–88 (1968)
120. Eisdorfer, C., Service, C. Verbal rote learning and superior intelligence in the aged. *J. Gerontol.,* **22,** 158–61 (1967)
121. Eisenthal, S., Farberow, N. L., Shneidmann, E. S. Followup of neuropsychiatric patients in suicide observation status. *Publ. Hlth. Rept. (Wash.),* **81,** 977–90 (1966)
122. Elo, A. E. Age changes in master chess performance. *J. Gerontol.,* **20,** 289–99 (1965)
123. Eriksen, C. W., Steffy, R. A. Short-term memory and retroactive interference in visual perception. *J. Exptl. Psychol.,* **68,** 423–34 (1964)
124. Evans, R. B. Age and the simple reaction: A longitudinal study over 50 years. *Dissert. Abstr.,* **28B,** 2156–57 (1967)
125. Farrimond, T. Visual and auditory performance variations with age: Some implications. *Australian J. Psychol.,* **19,** 193–201 (1967)
126. Feinberg, I., Carlson, V. R. Sleep variables as a function of age in man. *Arch. Gen. Psychiat.,* **18,** 239–50 (1968)
127. Feldman, R. M., Reger, S. N. Relations among hearing, reaction time, and age. *J. Speech Hearing Res.,* **10,** 479–95 (1967)
128. Filer, R. N., O'Connell, D. D. Motivation of aging persons in an institutional setting. *J. Gerontol.,* **19,** 15–22 (1964)
129. Fisher, J., Pierce, R. C. Dimensions of intellectual functioning in the aged. *J. Gerontol.,* **22,** 166–73 (1967)
130. Fitzhugh, K. B., Fitzhugh, L. C. Patterns of abilities in relation to abstraction ability and age in subjects with long-standing cerebral dysfunction. *J. Gerontol.,* **19,** 479–84 (1964)
131. Fitzhugh, K. B., Fitzhugh, L. C., Reitan, R. M. Influence of age upon measures of problem solving and experiential background in subjects with long-standing cerebral dysfunction. *Ibid.,* 132–34
132. Friedman, A. S., Granick, S. A note on anger and aggression in old age. *J. Gerontol.,* **18,** 283–85 (1963)
133. Friedman, E. P. Spatial proximity and social interaction in a home for the aged. *J. Gerontol.,* **21,** 566–70 (1966)
134. Friedman, E. P. Age, length of institutionalization, and social status in a home for the aged. *Ibid.,* **22,** 474–77 (1967)
135. Friedman, H. Memory organization in the aged. *J. Genet. Psychol.,* **109,** 3–8 (1966)
136. Friedsam, H. J., Martin, H. W. A. comparison of self and physician's health ratings in an older population. *J. Hlth. Hum. Behav.,* **4,** 179–83 (1963)
137. Gajo, F. D. Adult age differences in the perception of visual illusions. *Dissert. Abstr.,* **27B,** 4573 (1967)
138. Ganzler, H. Motivation as a factor

in the psychological deficit of aging. *J. Gerontol.*, **19,** 425–29 (1964)

139. Gardner, E. A., Bahn, A. K., Mack, M. Suicide and psychiatric care in the aging. *Arch. Gen. Psychiat.*, **10,** 547–53 (1964)

140. Garside, R. F., Kay, D. W., Roth, M. Old age mental disorders in Newcastle-upon-Tyne: III. A factorial study of medical, psychiatric and social characteristics. *Brit. J. Psychiat.*, **111,** 939–46 (1965)

141. Gergen, K. J., Back, K. W. Aging, time perspective, and preferred solutions to international conflicts. *J. Confl. Resol.*, **9,** 177–86 (1965)

142. Gergen, K. J., Back, K. W. Communication in the interview and the disengaged respondent. *Publ. Opin. Quart.*, **30,** 385–98 (1966)

143. Gilbert, J. G., Levee, R. F. A comparison of the personality structures of a group of young, married and a group of middle aged, married women. *Percept. Mot. Skills*, **16,** 773–77 (1963)

144. Gilbert, J. G., Levee, R. F. Age differences on the Bender Visual-Motor Gestalt Test and the Archimedes Spiral Test. *J. Gerontol.*, **20,** 196–200 (1965)

145. Glanville, E. V., Kaplan, A. R., Fischer, R. Age, sex, and taste sensitivity. *J. Gerontol.*, **19,** 474–78 (1964)

146. Goodrick, C. L. Alcohol preference of the male Sprague-Dawley albino rat as a function of age. *J. Gerontol.*, **22,** 369–71 (1967)

147. Goodrick, C. L. Learning, retention, and extinction of a complex maze habit for mature-young and senescent Wistar albino rats. *Ibid.*, **23,** 298–304 (1968)

148. Gordon, P., Fudema, J. L., Snider, G. L., Abrams, A., Tobin, S. S., Kraus, J. D. The effects of a European procaine preparation in an aged population. II. Physiological effects. *J. Gerontol.*, **20,** 144–50 (1965)

149. Granick, S. Comparative analysis of psychotic depressives with matched normals on some untimed verbal intelligence tests. *J. Consult. Psychol.*, **27,** 439–43 (1963)

150. Granick, S., Friedman, A. S. The effect of education on the decline of psychometric test performance with age. *J. Gerontol.*, **22,** 191–95 (1967)

151. Grant, C. R. H. Age differences in self concept from early adulthood through old age. *Dissert. Abstr.*, **28B,** 1160–61 (1967)

152. Green, R. F., Berkowitz, B. Changes in intellect with age: II. Factorial analysis of Wechsler-Bellevue scores. *J. Genet. Psychol.*, **104,** 3–18 (1964)

153. Green, R. F., Berkowitz, B. Changes in intellect with age: III. The relationship of heterogeneous brain damage to achievement in older people. *Ibid.*, **106,** 349–59 (1965)

154. Greenwood, D. I., Taylor, C. Adaptive testing in an older population. *J. Psychol.*, **60,** 193–98 (1965)

155. Griew, S. Age, information transmission and the positional relationship between signals and responses in the performance of a choice task. *Ergonomics*, **7,** 267–77 (1964)

156. Gutman, G. M. A note on the MMPI: Age and sex differences in extraversion and neuroticism in a Canadian sample. *Brit. J. Soc. Clin. Psychol.*, **5,** 128–29 (1966)

157. Gynther, M. D., Shimkunas, A. M. Age, intelligence, and MMPI F scores. *J. Consult. Psychol.*, **29,** 383–88 (1965)

158. Gynther, M. D., Shimkunas, A. M. Age and MMPI performance. *Ibid.*, **30,** 118–21 (1966)

159. Hallenbeck, C. E. Evidence for a multiple process view of mental deterioration. *J. Gerontol.*, **19,** 357–63 (1964)

160. Halpern, D. The relationship of work values to satisfaction with retirement and future time perspective. *Dissert. Abstr.*, **28B,** 2125–26 (1967)

161. Hansen, P. F., Ed. *Age With a Future* (F. A. Davis Co., Philadelphia, 662 pp., 1964)

162. Hardyck, C. D. Sex differences in personality changes with age. *J. Gerontol.*, **19,** 78–82 (1964)

163. Havens, B. J. An investigation of activity patterns and adjustment in an aging population. *Gerontologist*, **8,** 201–6 (1968)

164. Havighurst, R. J. Personality and

patterns of aging. *Gerontologist,* **8,** 20–23 (1968)

165. Heath, H. A., Orbach, J. Reversibility of the Necker cube: IV. Responses of elderly people. *Percept. Mot. Skills,* **17,** 625–26 (1963)
166. Hedri, A. (Suicide in advanced ages.) *Schweiz. Arch. Neurol. Psychiat.,* **100,** 179–202 (1967)
167. Heilbrun, A. B., Lair, C. V. Decreased role consistency in the aged: Implications for behavioral pathology. *J. Gerontol.,* **19,** 325–29 (1964)
168. Hempenius, W. L. Investigation of factors affecting perception and preference of flavor levels in sour cream. *Dissert. Abstr.,* **28B,** 731 (1967)
169. Heron, A., Chown, S. *Age and Function* (Little, Brown & Co., Boston, 182 pp., 1967)
170. Heron, A., Craik, F. I. M. Age differences in cumulative learning of meaningful and meaningless material. *Scand. J. Psychol.,* **5,** 209–17 (1964)
171. Heyman, D. K., Jeffers, F. C. Wives and retirement: A pilot study. *J. Gerontol.,* **23,** 488–96 (1968)
172. Hickey, T., Hickey, L. A., Kalish, R. A. Children's perceptions of the elderly. *J. Genet. Psychol.,* **112,** 227–35 (1968)
173. Hickey, T., Kalish, R. A. Young people's perceptions of adults. *J. Gerontol.,* **23,** 1215–19 (1968)
174. Hirt, M. L. Aptitude changes as a function of age. *Personnel Guid. J.,* **43,** 174–76 (1964)
175. Holmes, J. S. Acute psychiatric patient performance on the WAIS. *J. Clin. Psychol.,* **24,** 87–91 (1968)
176. Horn, J. L., Cattell, R. B. Age differences in primary mental ability factors. *J. Gerontol.,* **21,** 210–20 (1966)
177. Hulicka, I. M. Age differences in Wechsler Memory Scale scores. *J. Genet. Psychol.,* **109,** 135–45 (1966)
178. Hulicka, I. M. Age differences in retention as a function of interference. *J. Gerontol.,* **22,** 180–84 (1967)
179. Hulicka, I. M. Short-term learning and memory efficiency as a function of age and health. *J. Amer. Geriat. Soc.,* **15,** 285–94 (1967)
180. Hulicka, I. M., Grossman, J. L. Age-group comparisons for the use of mediators in paired-associate learning. *J. Gerontol.,* **22,** 46–51 (1967)
181. Hulicka, I. M., Rust, L. D. Age related retention deficit as a function of learning. *J. Amer. Geriat. Soc.,* **12,** 1061–65 (1964)
182. Hulicka, I. M., Sterns, H., Grossman, J. Age-group comparisons of paired-associate learning as a function of paced and self-paced association and response times. *J. Gerontol.,* **22,** 274–80 (1967)
183. Hulicka, I. M., Weiss, R. L. Age differences in retention as a function of learning. *J. Consult. Psychol.,* **29,** 125–29 (1965)
184. Huntington, J. M., Simonson, E. Critical flicker fusion frequency as a function of exposure time in two different age groups. *J. Gerontol.,* **20,** 527–29 (1965)
185. Indik, B., Seashore, S. E., Slesinger, J. Demographic correlates of psychological strain. *J. Abnorm. Soc. Psychol.,* **69,** 26–38 (1964)
186. Inglis, J. Influence of motivation, perception and attention on age-related changes in short-term memory. *Nature,* **204,** 103–4 (1964)
187. Inglis, J., Ankus, M. N. Effects of age on short-term storage and serial rote learning. *Brit. J. Psychol.,* **56,** 183–95 (1965)
188. Inglis, J., Ankus, M. N., Sykes, D. H. Age-related differences in learning and short-term memory from childhood to the senium. *Hum. Develpm.,* **11,** 42–52 (1968)
189. Inglis, J., Caird, W. K. Modified digit spans and memory disorder. *Dis Nerv. Syst.,* **24,** 46–50 (1963)
190. Inglis, J., Tansey, C. L. Age differences and scoring differences in dichotic listening performance. *J. Psychol.,* **66,** 325–32 (1967)
191. International Association of Gerontology. *Proceedings of the 7th International Congress of Gerontology,* Vol. 1–8 (Wien Med. Akad., Wien, 3548 pp., 1966)
192. Istomina, Z. M., Samokhvalova, V. I., Preobrazhenskaya, I. N. Kharakteristiki pamyati u lits

vysokointellekual'nogo truda v pozihilom vozraste. (Memory characteristics of elderly individuals engaged in high-level intellectual work.) *Vop. Psikhol.*, **13**, 55–64 (1967)

193. Jakubczak, L. F. Effects of testosterone propionate on age differences in mating behavior. *J. Gerontol.*, **19**, 458–61 (1964)
194. Jalavisto, E. The phenomenon of retinal rivalry in the aged. *Gerontologia*, **9**, 1–8 (1964)
195. Jalavisto, E. On the interdependence of circulatory-respiratory and neural-mental variables. *Ibid.*, **10**, 31–37 (1965)
196. Jawanda, J. S. Age and verbal conditioning. *Psychol. Rept.*, **22**, 815–16 (1968)
197. Jeffers, F. C., Ed. *Duke University Council on Gerontology: Proceedings of Seminars 1961–65* (Duke Univ., Durham, N.C., 344 pp., 1965)
198. Kaplan, A. R., Glanville, E. V., Fischer, R. Cumulative effect of age and smoking on taste sensitivity in males and females. *J. Gerontol.*, **20**, 334–37 (1965)
199. Karp, S. A. Field dependence and occupational activity in the aged. *Percept. Mot. Skills*, **24**, 603–9 (1967)
200. Kastenbaum, R., Ed. *Contributions to the Psychobiology of Aging* (Springer, New York, 115 pp., 1965)
201. Kastenbaum, R. The realm of death: An emerging area in psychological research. *J. Hum. Relat.*, **13**, 538–52 (1965)
202. Kastenbaum, R. The mental life of dying geriatric patients. *Gerontologist*, **7**, 97–100 (1967)
203. Kausler, D. H. Comparison of anticipation and recall methods for geriatric subjects. *Psychol. Rept.*, **13**, 702 (1963)
204. Kausler, D. H., Lair, C. V. Associative strength and paired-associate learning in elderly subjects. *J. Gerontol.*, **21**, 278–80 (1966)
205. Kausler, D. H., Lair, C. V. Informative feedback conditions and verbal-discrimination learning in elderly subjects. *Psychon. Sci.*, **10**, 193–94 (1968)
206. Kelley, P. R. Age changes in mental abilities and their life history antecedents. *Dissert. Abstr.*, **26**, 1765 (1965)
207. Kerckhoff, A. C. Husband-wife expectations and reactions to retirement. *J. Gerontol.*, **19**, 510–16 (1964)
208. Kimble, G. A., Pennypacker, H. S. Eyelid conditioning in young and aged subjects. *J. Genet. Psychol.*, **103**, 283–89 (1963)
209. Kimbrell, G. McA., Furchtgott, E. The effect of aging on olfactory threshold. *J. Gerontol.*, **18**, 364–65 (1963)
210. Klonoff, H., Kennedy, M. Memory and perceptual functioning in octogenarians and nonagenarians in the community. *J. Gerontol.*, **20**, 328–33 (1965)
211. Klonoff, H., Kennedy, M. A comparative study of cognitive functioning in old age. *Ibid.*, **21**, 239–43 (1966)
212. Kowal, K. A., Kemp, D. E., Lakin, M., Wilson, S. Perception of the helping relationship as a function of age. *J. Gerontol.*, **19**, 405–13 (1964)
213. Kral, V. A., Solyom, L., Enesco, H. E. Effect of short-term oral RNA therapy on the serum uric acid level and memory function in senile versus senescent subjects. *J. Amer. Geriat. Soc.*, **15**, 364–72 (1967)
214. Kriauciunas, R. The relationship of age and retention-interval activity in short-term memory. *J. Gerontol.*, **23**, 169–73 (1968)
215. Krupinski, J., Stoller, A., Polke, P. Attempted suicides admitted to the Mental Health Department, Victoria, Australia: A socioepidemiological study. *Intern. J. Soc. Psychiat.*, **13**, 5–13 (1967)
216. Kuhlen, R. G. Age and intelligence: The significance of cultural change in longitudinal versus cross-sectional findings. *Vita Hum.*, **6**, 113–24 (1963)
217. Kushner, R. E., Bunch, M. E., Eds. *Graduate Education in Aging Within the Social Sciences* (Div. Gerontol., Univ. Michigan, Ann Arbor, 118 pp., 1967)
218. LaFratta, C. W., Canestrari, R. E. A comparison of sensory and motor nerve conduction velocities

as related to age. *Arch. Phys. Med. Rehabilit.*, **47**, 286–90 (1966)

219. Laurence, M. W. A developmental look at the usefulness of list categorization as an aid to free recall. *Can. J. Psychol.*, **21**, 153–65 (1967)

220. Laurence, M. W. Memory loss with age: A test of two strategies for its retardation. *Psychon. Sci.*, **9**, 209–10 (1967)

221. Lawson, J. S. Changes in immediate memory with age. *Brit. J. Psychol.*, **56**, 69–75 (1965)

222. Lawton, M. P., Lawton, F. G., Eds. *Mental Impairment in the Aged* (Philadelphia Geriatric Center, Philadelphia, 176 pp., 1965)

223. Lehman, H. C. Chronological age versus present-day contributions to medical progress. *Gerontologist*, **3**, 71–75 (1963)

224. Lehman, H. C. The relationship between chronological age and high level research output in physics and chemistry. *J. Gerontol.*, **19**, 157–64 (1964)

225. Lehman, H. C. The production of masterworks prior to age 30. *Gerontologist*, **5**, 24–30 (1965)

226. Lehman, H. C. The most creative years of engineers and other technologists. *J. Genet. Psychol.*, **108**, 263–77 (1966)

227. Lehman, H. C. The psychologist's most creative years. *Amer. Psychol.*, **21**, 363–69 (1966)

228. Lehr, U. Attitudes towards the future in old age. *Hum. Develpm.*, **10**, 230–38 (1967)

229. Leibowitz, H. W., Gwozdecki, J. The magnitude of the Poggendorff illusion as a function of age. *Child Develpm.*, **38**, 573–80 (1967)

230. Leibowitz, H. W., Judisch, J. M. Size-constancy in other persons: A function of distance. *Amer. J. Psychol.*, **80**, 294–96 (1967)

231. Leibowitz, H. W., Judisch, J. M. The relation between age and the magnitude of the Ponzo Illusion. *Ibid.*, 105–9

232. Levin, S., Kahana, R. J., Eds. *Psychodynamic Studies on Aging: Creativity, Reminiscing, and Dying* (Intern. Univ. Press, New York, 345 pp., 1967)

233. Lieberman, M. A. Psychological correlates of impending death: Some preliminary observations. *J. Gerontol.*, **20**, 181–90 (1965)

234. Lieberman, M. A., Prock, V. N., Tobin, S. S. Psychological effects of institutionalization. *J. Gerontol.*, **23**, 343–53 (1968)

235. Lienert, G. A., Crott, H. W. Studies on the factor structure of intelligence in children, adolescents, and adults. *Vita Hum.*, **7**, 147–63 (1964)

236. Lipman, A., Smith, K. J. Functionality of disengagement in old age. *J. Gerontol.*, **23**, 517–21 (1968)

237. Long, R. F., Gislason, S. S. The effect of procaine on orientation, attention, memory and weight of aged psychiatric patients. *J. Neuropsychiat.*, **5**, 186–96 (1964)

238. Lovelace, W. E., Davis, R. T. Minimum-separable visual acuity of rhesus monkeys as a function of aging and whole-body radiation with X-rays. *J. Genet. Psychol.*, **103**, 251–57 (1963)

239. Lowenthal, M. F. *Lives in Distress* (Basic Books, New York, 266 pp., 1964)

240. Lowenthal, M. F. Social isolation and mental illness in old age. *Amer. Sociol. Rev.*, **20**, 54–70 (1964)

241. Lowenthal, M. F. Antecedents of isolation and mental illness in old age. *Arch. Gen. Psychiat.*, **12**, 245–54 (1965)

242. Lowenthal, M. F. The relationship between social factors and mental health in the aged. *Psychiat. Res. Rept.*, **23**, 187–97 (1968)

243. Lowenthal, M. F., Berkman, P. L., Associates. *Aging and Mental Disorder in San Francisco* (Jossey-Bass, San Francisco, 341 pp., 1967)

244. Ludwig, E. G., Eichhorn, R. L. Age and disillusionment: A study of value changes associated with aging. *J. Gerontol.*, **22**, 59–65 (1967)

245. Mackay, H. A., Inglis, J. The effect of age on a short-term auditory storage process. *Gerontologia*, **8**, 193–200 (1963)

246. Mackie, J. B., Beck, E. C. Relations among age, intelligence, and critical flicker fusion. *Percept. Mot. Skills*, **21**, 875–78 (1965)

247. Maddox, G. L. Activity and morale: A longitudinal study of selected

elderly subjects. *Soc. Forces,* **42,** 195–204 (1963)

248. Maddox, G. L. Self-assessment of health status: A longitudinal study of selected elderly subjects. *J. Chronic Dis.,* **17,** 449–60 (1964)
249. Martin, J., Doran, A. Evidence concerning the relationship between health and retirement. *Sociol. Rev.,* **14,** 329–43 (1966)
250. McCourt, J. F. A study of acceptance of the geriatric patient among selected groups of hospital personnel. *Dissert. Abstr.,* **24,** 4833–34 (1964)
251. McCulloch, J. W., Philip, A. E., Carstairs, G. M. The ecology of suicidal behavior. *Brit. J. Psychiat.,* **113,** 313–19 (1967)
252. McGhie, A., Chapman, J., Lawson, J. S. Changes in immediate memory with age. *Brit. J. Psychol.,* **56,** 69–75 (1965)
253. McMahon, A. W., Rhudick, P. J. Reminiscing, adaptational significance in the aged. *Arch. Gen. Psychiat.,* **10,** 292–98 (1964)
254. Meer, B., Krag, C. L. Correlates of disability in a population of hospitalized geriatric patients. *J. Gerontol.,* **19,** 440–46 (1964)
255. Melrose, J., Welsh, O. L., Luterman, D. M. Auditory responses in selected elderly men. *J. Gerontol.,* **18,** 267–70 (1963)
256. Meltzer, H. Age differences in happiness and life adjustment of workers. *J. Gerontol.,* **18,** 66–70 (1963)
257. Meltzer, H. Age and sex differences in workers' perceptions of happiness for self and others. *J. Genet. Psychol.,* **105,** 1–11 (1964)
258. Meltzer, H. Attitudes of workers before and after age 40. *Geriatrics,* **20,** 425–43 (1965)
259. Miller, D., Lieberman, M. A. The relationship of affect state and adaptive capacity to reactions to stress. *J. Gerontol.,* **20,** 492–97 (1965)
260. Munnichs, J. Loneliness, isolation and social relations in old age: A pilot survey. *Vita Hum.,* **7,** 228–38 (1964)
261. Myler, B. B. Depression and death in the aged. *Dissert. Abstr.,* **28B,** 2146 (1967)
262. Neal, G. L., Pearson, R. G. Comparative effects of age, sex, and drugs upon two tasks of auditory vigilance. *Percept. Mot. Skills,* **23,** 967–74 (1966)
263. Neugarten, B. L., Ed. *Middle Age and Aging: A Reader in Social Psychology* (Univ. Chicago Press, Chicago, 596 pp., 1968)
264. Neugarten, B. L., Associates. *Personality in Middle and Late Life* (Atherton Press, New York, 231 pp., 1964)
265. Noble, C. E., Baker, B. L., Jones, T. A. Age and sex parameters in psychomotor learning. *Percept. Mot. Skills,* **19,** 935–45 (1964)
266. Nodine, J. H., Shulkin, M. W., Slap, J. W., Levine, M., Freiberg, K. A double-blind study of the effect of ribonucleic acid in senile brain disease. *Amer. J. Psychiat.,* **123,** 1257–59 (1967)
267. Norman, R. D. A revised deterioration formula for the Wechsler Adult Intelligence Scale. *J. Clin. Psychol.,* **22,** 287–94 (1966)
268. Olsen, I. A. Discrimination of auditory information as related to aging. *J. Gerontol.,* **20,** 394–97 (1965)
269. Opton, E. M., Jr. Electroencephalographic correlates of performance lapses on an attention task in young and old men. *Dissert. Abstr.,* **25,** 3115–16 (1964)
270. Orme, J. E. Hypothetically true norms for the Progressive Matrices tests. *Hum. Develpm.,* **9,** 222–30 (1966)
271. Owens, W. A. Age and mental abilities: A second adult follow-up. *J. Educ. Psychol.,* **57,** 311–25 (1966)
272. Pare, W. P. The effect of chronic environmental stress on premature aging in the rat. *J. Gerontol.,* **20,** 78–84 (1965)
273. Peak, D. T. Changes in short-term memory in a group of aging community residents. *J. Gerontol.,* **23,** 9–16 (1968)
274. Pearson, J. S., Swenson, W. M., Rome, H. P. Age and sex differences related to MMPI response frequency in 25,000 medical patients. *Amer. J. Psychiat.,* **121,** 988–95 (1965)
275. Poorkaj, H. Social psychological factors and "successful aging."

Dissert. Abstr., **28A,** 306 (1967)

276. Postema, L. J., Schell, R. E. Aging and psychopathology: Some MMPI evidence for seemingly greater neurotic behavior among older people. *J. Clin. Psychol.,* **23,** 140–43 (1967)

277. Powell, A. H., Jr., Eisdorfer, C., Bogdonoff, M. D. Physiologic response patterns observed in a learning task. *Arch. Gen. Psychiat.,* **10,** 192–95 (1964)

278. Pressey, S. L., Pressey, A. D. Genius at 80: And other oldsters. *Gerontologist,* **7,** 183–87 (1967)

279. Preston, C. E. Traits endorsed by older non-retired and retired subjects. *J. Gerontol.,* **21,** 261–64 (1966)

280. Preston, C. E. Self-reporting among older retired and non-retired subjects. *Ibid.,* **22,** 415–20 (1967)

281. Preston, C. E. Subjectively perceived agedness and retirement. *Ibid.,* **23,** 201–4 (1968)

282. Preston, C. E., Gudiksen, K. S. A measure of self-perception among older people. *J. Gerontol.,* **21,** 63–71 (1966)

283. Rabbitt, P. M. A. Grouping of stimuli in pattern recognition as a function of age. *Quart. J. Exptl. Psychol.,* **16,** 172–76 (1964)

284. Rabbitt, P. M. A. Set and age in a choice-response task. *J. Gerontol.,* **19,** 301–6 (1964)

285. Rabbitt, P. M. A., Birren, J. E. Age and responses to sequences of repetitive and interruptive signals. *J. Gerontol.,* **22,** 143–50 (1967)

286. Radcliffe, J. A. WAIS factorial structure and factor scores for ages 18 to 54. *Australian J. Psychol.,* **18,** 228–38 (1966)

287. Ramamurthi, P. V., Parameswaran, E. G. A study of figure reversals in the old and the young. *J. Psychol. Res.,* **8,** 16–18 (1964)

288. Reed, H. B., Jr., Reitan, R. M. Changes in psychological test performance associated with the normal aging process. *J. Gerontol.,* **18,** 271–74 (1963)

289. Reichard, S., Livson, F., Petersen, P. G. *Aging and Personality: A Study of Eighty-Seven Older Men* (Wiley, New York, 237 pp., 1963)

290. Reitan, R. M., Shipley, R. E. The relationship of serum cholesterol changes to psychological abilities. *J. Gerontol.,* **18,** 350–57 (1963)

291. Riegel, K. F., Riegel, R. M., Meyer, G. A study of the dropout rates in longitudinal research on aging and the prediction of death. *J. Pers. Soc. Psychol.,* **5,** 342–48 (1967)

292. Riegel, K. F., Riegel, R. M., Meyer, G. Socio-psychological factors of aging: A cohort-sequential analysis. *Hum. Develpm.,* **10,** 27–56 (1967)

293. Rigby, M. K., Soule, S. D., Barber, W., Rothman, D. Sex hormone replacement in the aged. *J. Gerontol.,* **19,** 313–16 (1964)

294. Roman, P., Taietz, P. Organizational structure and disengagement: The emeritus professor. *Gerontologist,* **7,** 147–52 (1967)

295. Rose, C. L. Social factors in longevity. *Gerontologist,* **4,** 27–37 (1964)

296. Rose, C. L. Representativeness of volunteer subjects in a longitudinal aging study. *Hum. Develpm.,* **8,** 152–56 (1965)

297. Rose, C. L., Bell, B. Selection of geographically stable subjects in longitudinal studies of aging. *J. Amer. Geriat. Soc.,* **13,** 143–51 (1965)

298. Rosenfelt, R. H., Kastenbaum, R., Kempler, B. "The untestables": Methodological problems in drug research with the aged. *Gerontologist,* **4,** 72–74 (1964)

299. Ross, E. Effects of challenging and supportive instructions on verbal learning in older persons. *J. Educ. Psychol.,* **59,** 261–66 (1968)

300. Russell, G. W. Human fears: A factor analytic study of three age levels. *Genet. Psychol. Monogr.,* **76,** 141–62 (1967)

301. Saleh, S. D. A study of attitude change in the preretirement period. *J. Appl. Psychol.,* **40,** 310–12 (1964)

302. Saleh, S. D., Otis, J. L. Age and level of job satisfaction. *Personnel Psychol.,* **17,** 425–30 (1964)

303. Sanders, S., Laurendeau, M., Bergeron, J. Aging and the concept of space: The conservation of surfaces. *J. Gerontol.,* **21,** 281–86 (1966)

304. Savage, R. D., Britton, P. G. The factorial structure of the WAIS

in an aged sample. *J. Gerontol.*, **23,** 183–86 (1968)

305. Schaie, K. W. A general model for the study of developmental problems. *Psychol. Bull.*, **64,** 92–107 (1965)
306. Schaie, K. W. Age changes and age differences. *Gerontologist,* **7,** 128–32 (1967)
307. Schaie, K. W., Ed. *Theory and Methods of Research on Aging: Current Topics in the Psychology of Aging: Perception, Learning, Cognition and Personality* (West Virginia Univ., Morgantown, 197 pp., 1968)
308. Schaie, K. W., Baltes, P., Strother, C. R. A study of auditory sensitivity in advanced age. *J. Gerontol.*, **19,** 453–57 (1964)
309. Schonfield, D., Robertson, E. A. Memory storage and aging. *Can. J. Psychol.*, **20,** 228–36 (1966)
310. Schonfield, D., Robertson, E. A. The coding and sorting of digits and symbols by an elderly sample. *J. Gerontol.*, **23,** 318–23 (1968)
311. Schwartz, A. N., Kleemeier, R. W. The effects of illness and age upon some aspects of personaltiy. *J. Gerontol.*, **20,** 85–91 (1965)
312. Schwartz, D. W., Karp, S. A. Field dependence in a geriatric population. *Percept. Mot. Skills,* **24,** 495–504 (1967)
313. Shanan, J., Sharon, M. Personality and functioning of Israeli males during the middle years. *Hum. Develpm.*, **8,** 2–15 (1965)
314. Shanas, E. A note on restriction of life space: Attitudes of age cohorts. *J. Hlth. Soc. Behav.*, **9,** 86–90 (1968)
315. Shanas, E., Streib, G. F., Eds. *Social Structure and the Family: Generational Relations* (Prentice-Hall, Englewood Cliffs, N.J., 394 pp., 1965)
316. Silverman, I. Age and the tendency to withhold response. *J. Gerontol.*, **18,** 372–75 (1963)
317. Silverman, I. Response-set bias and predictive validity associated with Kogan's "Attitudes toward old people scale." *Ibid.*, **21,** 86–88 (1966)
318. Silverman, I., Reimanis, G. A test of two interpretations of age deficit in the ability to reverse an ambiguous figure. *J. Gerontol.*, **21,** 89–92 (1966)
319. Simon, J. R. Choice reaction time as a function of auditory S-R correspondence, age and sex. *Ergonomics,* **10,** 659–64 (1967)
320. Simon, J. R. Translation processes and aging. *Psychon. Sci.*, **9,** 553–54 (1967)
321. Simonson, E., Anderson, D., Keiper, C. Effect of stimulus movement on critical flicker fusion in young and older men. *J. Gerontol.*, **22,** 353–56 (1967)
322. Slater, P. E., Scarr, H. A. Personality in old age. *Genet. Psychol. Monogr.*, **70,** 229–69 (1964)
323. Smith, D. K. The Einstellung effect in relation to the variables of age and training. *Dissert. Abstr.*, **27B,** 4115 (1967)
324. Solyom, L., Barik, H. C. Conditioning in senescence and senility. *J. Gerontol.*, **20,** 483–88 (1965)
325. Solyom, L., Enesco, H. E., Beaulieu, C. The effect of RNA on learning and activity in old and young rats. *J. Gerontol.*, **22,** 1–7 (1967)
326. Spieth, W. Cardiovascular health status, age, and psychological performance. *J. Gerontol.*, **19,** 277–84 (1964)
327. Stewart, N., Sparks, W. J. Patent productivity of research chemists as related to age and experience. *Personnel Guid. J.*, **45,** 28–36 (1966)
328. Stokes, R. G., Maddox, G. L. Some social factors on retirement adaptation. *J. Gerontol.*, **22,** 329–33 (1967)
329. Stone, J. L., Norris, A. H. Activities and attitudes of participants in the Baltimore Longitudinal Study. *J. Gerontol.*, **21,** 575–80 (1966)
330. Strauss, D. The relationship between perception of the environment and the retrenchment syndrome in a geriatric population. *Dissert. Abstr.*, **24,** 1275–76 (1963)
331. Surwillo, W. W. The relation of simple response time to brainwave frequency and the effects of age. *Electroenceph. Clin. Neurophysiol.*, **15,** 105–14 (1963)
332. Surwillo, W. W. The relation of response-time variability to age and the influence of brain wave frequency. *Ibid.*, 1029–32

333. Surwillo, W. W. The relation of decision time to brain wave frequency and to age. *Ibid.*, **16**, 510–14 (1964)
334. Surwillo, W. W. The relation of autonomic activity to age differences in vigilance. *J. Gerontol.*, **21**, 257–60 (1966)
335. Surwillo, W. W., Quilter, R. Vigilance, age and response-time. *Amer. J. Psychol.*, **77**, 614–20 (1964)
336. Surwillo, W. W., Quilter, R. The influence of age on latency time of involuntary (Galvanic Skin Reflex) and voluntary responses. *J. Gerontol.*, **20**, 173–76 (1965)
337. Surwillo, W. W., Quilter, R. The relation of frequency of spontaneous skin potential responses to vigilance and to age. *Psychophysiology*, **1**, 272–76 (1965)
338. Szafran, J. Age differences in the rate of gain of information, signal detection strategy and cardiovascular status among pilots. *Gerontologia*, **12**, 6–17 (1966)
339. Tacker, R. S., Furchtgott, E. Adjustment to food deprivation cycles as a function of age and prenatal X-irradiation. *J. Genet. Psychol.*, **102**, 257–60 (1963)
340. Talland, G. A. The effect of warning signals on reaction time in youth and old age. *J. Gerontol.*, **19**, 31–38 (1964)
341. Talland, G. A. Three estimates of the word span and their stability over the adult years. *Quart. J. Exptl. Psychol.*, **17**, 301–7 (1965)
342. Talland, G. A. Visual signal detection, as a function of age, input rate, and signal frequency. *J. Psychol.*, **63**, 105–15 (1966)
343. Talland, G. A., Ed. *Human Aging and Behavior* (Academic Press, New York, 322 pp., 1968)
344. Talland, G. A., Mendelson, J. H., Koz, G., Aaron, R. Experimental studies of the effects of tricyanoaminopropene on the memory and learning capacities of geriatric patients. *J. Psychiat. Res.*, **3**, 171–79 (1965)
345. Taub, H. A. Visual short-term memory as a function of age, rate of presentation, and schedule of presentation. *J. Gerontol.*, **21**, 388–91 (1966)
346. Taub, H. A. Paired associates learning as a function of age, rate, and instructions. *J. Genet. Psychol.*, **111**, 41–46 (1967)
347. Taub, H. A. Age differences in memory as a function of rate of presentation, order of report, and stimulus organization. *J. Gerontol.*, **23**, 159–64 (1968)
348. Taub, H. A. Aging and free recall. *Ibid.*, 466–68
349. Taub, H. A., Greiff, S. Effects of age on organization and recall of two sets of stimuli. *Psychon. Sci.*, **7**, 53–54 (1967)
350. Thomas, J. M., Charles, D. C. Effects of age and stimulus size on perception. *J. Gerontol.*, **19**, 447–50 (1964)
351. Thompson, L. W., Axelrod, S., Cohen, L. D. Senescence and visual identification of tactual-kinesthetic forms. *J. Gerontol.*, **20**, 244–49 (1965)
352. Thompson, L. W., Botwinick, J. Age differences in the relationship between EEG arousal and reaction time. *J. Psychol.*, **68**, 167–72 (1968)
353. Thompson, L. W., Opton, E., Jr., Cohen, L. D. Effects of age, presentation speed and sensory modality on performance of a "vigilance" task. *J. Gerontol.*, **18**, 366–69 (1963)
354. Thompson, L. W., Wilson, S. Electrocortical reactivity and learning in the elderly. *J. Gerontol.*, **21**, 45–51 (1966)
355. Thumin, F. J. Ability scores as related to age among male job applicants. *J. Gerontol.*, **23**, 390–92 (1968)
356. Thumin, F. J. MMPI profiles as a function of chronological age. *Psychol. Rept.*, **22**, 479–82 (1968)
357. Thumin, F. J., Boernke, C. Ability scores as related to age among female job applicants. *J. Gerontol.*, **21**, 369–71 (1966)
358. Thumin, F. J., Wittenberg, A. Personality as related to age and mental ability in female job applicants. *J. Gerontol.*, **20**, 105–7 (1965)
359. Tolin, P., Simon, J. R. Effect of task complexity and stimulus duration on perceptual-motor performance of two disparate age groups. *Ergonomics*, **11**, 283–90 (1968)

360. Trembly, D., O'Connor, J. Growth and decline of natural and acquired intellectual characteristics. *J. Gerontol.*, **21**, 9–12 (1966)

361. Trier, T. R. A study of change among elderly psychiatric inpatients during their first year of hospitalization. *J. Gerontol.*, **23**, 354–62 (1968)

362. Troyer, W. G., Eisdorfer, C., Wilkie, F., Bogdonoff, M. D. Free fatty acid responses in the aged individual during performance of learning tasks. *J. Gerontol.*, **21**, 415–19 (1966)

363. Tuckman, J. College students' judgment of the passage of time over the life span. *J. Genet. Psychol.*, **107**, 43–48 (1965)

364. Tune, G. S. Age differences in errors of commission. *Brit. J. Psychol.*, **57**, 391–92 (1966)

365. Tune, G. S. Errors of commission as a function of age and temperament in a type of vigilance task. *Quart. J. Exptl. Psychol.*, **18**, 358–61 (1966)

366. Tune, G. S. Sleep and wakefulness in normal human adults. *Brit. Med. J.*, **2**, (5600), 269–71 (1968)

367. Vassiliou, V., Georgas, J. G., Vassiliou, G. Variations in manifest anxiety due to sex, age, and education. *J. Pers. Soc. Psychol.*, **6**, 194–97 (1967)

368. Verhage, F. Intelligence and age in a Dutch sample. *Hum. Develpm.*, **8**, 238–45 (1965)

369. Vogel, B. S., Schell, R. E. Vocational interest patterns in late maturity and retirement. *J. Gerontol.*, **23**, 66–70 (1968)

370. Walsh, D., McCarthy, P. D. Suicide in Dublin's elderly. *Acta Psychiat. Scand.*, **41**, 227–35 (1965)

371. Walton, H. J., Hope, K. The effect of age and personality on doctor's clinical preferences. *Brit. J. Soc. Clin. Psychol.*, **6**, 43–51 (1967)

372. Warren, R. M., Warren, R. P. A comparison of speech perception in childhood, maturity, and old age by means of the verbal transformation effect. *J. Verbal Learn. Verbal Behav.*, **5**, 142–46 (1966)

373. Weiner, M. Organization of mental abilities from ages 14 to 54. *Educ. Psychol. Measmt.*, **24**, 573–87 (1964)

374. Weinstein, S., Sersen, E. A., Fisher, L., Vetter, R. J. Preferences for bodily parts as a function of sex, age, and socio-economic status. *Amer. J. Psychol.*, **77**, 291–94 (1964)

375. Weiss, A. D. The locus of reaction time change with set, motivation, and age. *J. Gerontol.*, **20**, 60–64 (1965)

376. Welford, A. T., Birren, J. E., Eds. *Behavior, Aging, and the Nervous System* (C. C. Thomas, Springfield, Ill., 637 pp., 1965)

377. Wetherick, N. E. A comparison of the problem-solving ability of young, mididle-aged, and old subjects. *Gerontologia*, **9**, 164–78 (1964)

378. Wetherick, N. E. Changing an established concept: A comparison of the ability of young, middle-aged, and old subjects. *Ibid.*, **11**, 82–95 (1965)

379. Wetherick, N. E. The inferential basis of concept attainment. *Brit. J. Psychol.*, **57**, 61–69 (1966)

380. Wetherick, N. E. The responses of normal adult subjects to the matrices test. *Ibid.*, 297–300

381. White, J. G., Patten, M. P. Intellectual performance, activity level and physical health in old age. *Geront. Clin.*, **10**, 157–70 (1968)

382. Wiersma, W., Klausmeier, H. The effect of age upon speed of concept attainment. *J. Gerontol.*, **20**, 398–400 (1965)

383. Wilensky, H., Barmack, J. E. Interests of doctoral students in clinical psychology in work with older adults. *J. Gerontol.*, **21**, 410–14 (1966)

384. Wilson, T. R. Flicker fusion frequency, age and intelligence. *Gerontologia*, **7**, 200–8 (1963)

385. Wolf, E., Schraffa, A. M. Relationship between critical flicker frequency and age in flicker perimetry. *Arch. Ophthal.*, **72**, 832–45 (1964)

386. Wolfe, R. N., Davis, J. A. Use of the oral directions test in a domiciliary setting. *J. Gerontol.*, **19**, 349–51 (1964)

387. Wolff, K. Personality type and reaction toward aging and death: A clinical study. *Geriatrics*, **21**, 189–92 (1966)

388. Youmans, E. G. Objective and subjective economic disengagement among older rural and urban men. *J. Gerontol.,* **21,** 439–41 (1966)

389. Youmans, E. G. Family disengagement among older urban and rural women. *Ibid.,* **22,** 209–11 (1967)

390. Young, M. L. Problem-solving performance in two age groups. *J. Gerontol.,* **21,** 505–9 (1966)

391. Zaretsky, H. H., Halberstam, J. L. Age differences in paired-associate learning. *J. Gerontol.,* **23,** 165–68 (1968)

392. Zaretsky, H. H., Halberstam, J. L. Effects of aging, brain-damage, and associative strength on paired-associate learning and relearning. *J. Genet. Psychol.,* **112,** 149–63 (1968)

393. Zinberg, N. E., Kaufman, I., Eds. *Normal Psychology of the Aging Process* (Intern. Univ. Press, New York, 182 pp., 1963)

394. Zung, W. W. K. Depression in the normal aged. *Psychosomatics,* **8,** 287–92 (1967)

THE VESTIBULAR SYSTEM[1,2]

By Brant Clark

San Jose State College, San Jose, California

INTRODUCTION

This is the first review in the Annual Review of Psychology devoted exclusively to the vestibular system. In the past this complex sensory modality has been treated as an adjunct to the somesthetic senses, which were most recently reviewed by Sherrick in 1966 (147). Current work on the vestibular system is voluminous, but only a small part of it has been conducted by psychologists. In this connection it is interesting to note that a book on the neuropsychology of spatially oriented behavior has been written without a single direct reference to the vestibular system (73). Nevertheless, psychologists have been interested in the field for a century, and the subject has a long history (18, 78, 166, 167).

Military aviation posed problems of vestibular function to investigators in both World Wars, and now the exploration of space has heightened interest in this field. There was a temporary concern among psychologists with the vestibular system some 50 years ago stemming from the proposed use of vestibular tests as selection devices for airplane pilots. Twenty-five years later a few aviation psychologists undertook investigations in the field because of the importance of the vestibular system in contributing to spatial disorientation in flight (9, 94). Interest in the vestibular system by psychologists and others has increased in the last decade because of the development of manned space flight with attendant zero gravity and the possibility that man may live on rotating space platforms for relatively long periods of time (150).

These new situations have raised both practical and theoretical questions about the function of the vestibular system in man's orientation in space and his efficiency when he is in motion. These two problems are the concern of this review.

Implicit in the discussion will be the notion developed by Gibson (80) that information from the vestibular receptors is actively integrated with information from other perceptual systems. Consequently, throughout the re-

[1] The time span for this review is arbitrarily limited to about 3 years, from mid-1965 to mid-1968.

[2] This review was supported by National Aeronautics and Space Administration Grant NGL 05-046-002 to San Jose State College. Additional support through computer literature searches was also supplied by the Life Sciences Library, NASA, Ames Research Center, Moffett Field, California.

view there will be repeated reference to a variety of perceptual systems as they interact with vestibular effects. Indeed, it is difficult to discuss the vestibular system without considering interactions with other sources of information.

Several arbitrary limitations have been placed on the review. First, in spite of the fact that much important work has been published in languages other than English, for the most part the works cited are in English. A second serious limitation is to be found in the exclusion of a large number of publications of restricted circulation made by universities, governmental agencies, and private organizations. Many of these studies do eventually reach the general literature, but by no means all of them. Third, the review will place emphasis on investigations of material of primary interest to psychology. It will be concerned with the anatomy, physiology, and pathology of the system only insofar as they are related to specific psychological problems pertaining to man's vestibular system. Finally, motion sickness and the effects of drugs on vestibular processes will receive only perfunctory treatment with an emphasis on studies using rotating devices.

RECENT REVIEWS OF THE LITERATURE

During the review period, several useful summaries of research on the vestibular system have been prepared. About one-third of Howard & Templeton's book, *Human Spatial Orientation* (100), comprises an excellent, highly comprehensive, critical review of work on vestibular functions including both early and more recent work. Roberts' *Neurophysiology of Postural Mechanisms* (141) presents a systematic consideration of the anatomy, physiology, and neurology of the vestibular mechanisms rather than a description of current research. Spector's book, *Dizziness and Vertigo* (149), emphasizes some clinical and neurophysiological topics.

Several reviews that emphasize the special interest of the reviewer have also appeared. Of particular interest to psychologists is Guedry's (92) excellent review of his and other extensive psychological investigations of vestibular functions at the Naval Aerospace Medical Institute. The emphasis is on psychophysiological studies, and individual sections are concerned with such varied topics as predictive equations for the semicircular canals, vestibular nystagmus, judgments of subjective velocity, adaptation, and habituation. The review presents a considerable range of materials, only some of which are available in the open literature. Gibson, in his book, *The Senses Considered as Perceptual Systems* (80), gives a detailed analysis of the vestibular system in terms of what he calls the basic orienting system and relates this to his theoretical position on space orientation. Other summaries of the literature in specialized areas include: nomenclature for physiological accelerations (99), thresholds for the perception of rotation (38), drugs used in motion sickness (22), anatomy of the vestibular organs (169), and disorientation in flight (9, 94, 111).

The most extensive consideration of current research on vestibular functions, however, is to be found in the proceedings of three symposia on the *Role of the Vestibular Organs in the Exploration of Space* (82–84). The title of the three symposia is somewhat misleading. Although the symposia were sponsored by the National Aeronautics and Space Administration, and there was indeed a central interest in space exploration, the participants represented many fields of investigation. The subject matter of the individual papers was equally varied, including a consideration of such topics as: artificial gravity in orbiting space stations, the physical and chemical characteristics of the endolymph fluid, electron microscopy of the vestibular mechanisms, mathematical models for the function of the semicircular canals, and—of particular interest to psychologists—adaptation, habituation, intersensory effects, spatial orientation, work efficiency in rotating rooms, and tests of vestibular functions. A fourth symposium was held in September 1968, and the proceedings should be available by the time the current review is published. The present review will refer to only a very limited number of these excellent reports.

METHODS OF INVESTIGATION

A perpetual problem in the psychology of perception is the adequate control of the stimulus, and there are special problems of stimulus control in studies of the vestibular system. First, the semicircular canals and otolith organs are extremely sensitive, so that the application and measurement of the angular or linear acceleration requires highly sophisticated equipment. Second, since the adequate stimulus for the semicircular canals is an angular acceleration and for the otoliths a linear acceleration of the head, the observer's whole body must be tilted, displaced, or rotated. It should be emphasized that direction and velocity of rotation, for example, are irrelevant except as they are produced by a specific angular acceleration. Thus, if an observer is rotating at 20 rpm to the right and is slowed quickly to 10 rpm, the acceleration is left, and his report is that he is turning left. Third, when the whole body is moved, the vestibular organs are affected, but other sensory systems are also stimulated, and consequently stimulus control becomes highly complex (80, 92, 100, 126). The observer's task is, however, quite simple. He merely reports on the direction and perhaps the magnitude of the perceived velocity, and for short durations of angular acceleration, the semicircular canals operate as efficient velocity transducers.

Stimulation by angular acceleration.—In studying rotation, the need for control of angular acceleration has been pointed out repeatedly by students of the problem, and the Bárány test with its unmeasured angular acceleration, short constant velocity, and jarring stop, has been largely discarded. Nevertheless, studies using hand-rotated chairs (102) and other very gross methods of controlling angular acceleration (148) continue to appear in the literature. With these methods only qualitative results can be expected.

In the last decade, several devices have been designed that effectively reduce vibration to a negligible amount, and they also control and measure the angular acceleration to approximately 0.01°/sec² (31, 45, 55, 92). Indeed, one vestibulometric seat (115) has been developed that is purported to rotate an observer about various body axes with accelerations as low as 0.001°/sec². How accurately this chair will produce such low accelerations is open to question since the design would require a high degree of stiffness in the device which appears to be very difficult to obtain. Furthermore, angular accelerometers which would measure angular accelerations accurately at this level are very difficult to construct. Nevertheless, these current devices make it possible to present an observer with angular accelerations of known amounts for rigidly specified durations and consequently make it possible to conduct experiments which can be easily replicated by a similar device.

The semicircular canals can also be stimulated by Coriolis acceleration (92, 127) which is an added acceleration produced when an observer, seated on a rotating device, turns his head about an axis orthogonal to the axis of rotation of the platform. These accelerations may be measured by angular accelerometers and are a function of the velocity of the rotating platform and the direction and velocity of the head motion (88, 92, 127).

Several rotating rooms for humans have been developed in the past decade and have been used in experimental studies as well as in the simulation of the effects to be found on rotating space platforms (77, 88, 128). Animals have been studied sporadically in such rotating environments for some 40 years, and monkeys (151) and rats (137–139) have been studied in detail recently. All of such studies have a serious limitation with regard to stimulus control since, if the animal or human is living in a rotating room, he can completely avoid a Coriolis stimulation by merely holding his head in a fixed position. This is precisely what some subjects do, and techniques to produce standardized head motions have been developed (2, 3, 77, 88, 127).

Although angular acceleration is the normal stimulus to the semicircular canals, the canals may also be stimulated by caloric irrigation of the ears, and this has been a standard test method used in clinical practice and experimental work for many years (36, 48, 66, 108, 117, 166). This procedure has the advantage of making it possible to test one ear at a time. Kellogg & Graybiel (108) have shown that there is no nystagmus response to caloric stimulation in zero gravity; this supports the notion that caloric stimulation is effective because of the convection currents resulting from changes in the specific gravity of the endolymph. Electrical stimulation has also been used (46, 159, 175), but because of its general effects on the whole vestibular mechanism, it has been much less widely utilized in the past 3 years.

The indicators most commonly employed to study the effects of vestibular stimulation are electronystagmograms and two subjective indicators, i.e., the perception of rotation in darkness and the perception of the oculogyral illusion. Electronystagmograms are widely used in both clinical and experimental work and present an objective record of a response to vestibular stimulation (15, 26, 28, 53, 96). In the past an enormous amount of work has been required for a detailed analysis of these records (15, 92, 94), but more recently new techniques of computer analysis have simplified this problem tremendously (98, 104). One significant difficulty in studying nystagmus is the adequate control of arousal during the test (28, 32, 48, 166, 167). If the alertness of the subject is allowed to vary, gross changes in the electronystagmograms occur. Some attempts have been made to control the arousal level in man by mental tasks such as mental arithmetic and in animals by the use of drugs (32, 48, 53).

Stimulation by linear acceleration.—The otolith organs produce information regarding orientation in space as well as static and dynamic reflexes to position the head and body (80, 100, 141). They may be stimulated by changes in the magnitude and/or direction of linear acceleration including the acceleration of gravity. Such changes may be produced experimentally by tilting chairs or platforms (79, 126), linear accelerators (174), parallel swings (92, 144), and by rotating platforms (23–25, 39, 40). The tilting chair is the simplest method to produce these changes since it merely changes the direction of the acceleration of gravity on the observer. Parallel swings change both the magnitude and direction of resultant force in a sinusoidal fashion and are therefore limited to a constantly changing stimulus. Linear accelerators (174) are satisfactory from the point of view of stimulus control, but they have serious limitations regarding stimulus duration due to the restricted lengths of track. Consequently, the rotating platform with the observer seated at some distance from the center of rotation has been widely used to study the effects of various levels of linear acceleration on perceptual processes.

Rotating platforms have the advantage of a wide range of accurate stimulus control, flexibility in positioning and testing the observer, and the possibility of stimulating the individual with a constant or variable acceleration for essentially unlimited periods of time (40). A limiting factor is that there is a change both in the direction and magnitude of the linear acceleration vector as is found on the parallel swing since the force acting on the observer is the resultant of the centripetal force and gravity (100, 127, 128). During the period of acceleration to some angular velocity, the observer is also stimulated by angular acceleration, and he must not move his head or Coriolis acceleration will further complicate the results. The use of the rotating platform has been severely criticized by Howard & Templeton (100), but several authors have emphasized the advantages of the centrifuge (24, 161).

Another method, which has been used for 150 years in studying the vestibular system, is the elimination of the nonacoustic labyrinth (and frequently also the acoustic labyrinth) to study space orientation in animals (101, 151). Such techniques have been used with a variety of animals. Humans who are deaf and labyrinthine-defective as a sequela of such diseases as meningitis also fulfill the requirements of reduction in function or elimination of the vestibular end organs. The study of such persons makes it possible to investigate the loss of canal and otolith function on orientation and reaction to motion (39, 40, 90). The selection of such persons is a complex task and must include a number of tests of vestibular function since deafness alone does not by any means insure loss of labyrinthine function (19, 74, 75, 86). However, tests that will unequivocally establish the complete loss of vestibular function have yet to be developed.

RESPONSE TO LINEAR ACCELERATION

All animals must orient themselves in many ways to the various aspects of their environment. However, for terrestrial man, the primary and perpetual orientation is to the acceleration of gravity, i.e., to the earth (80, 100). The otolith organs are the primary and probably the most accurate sensors for supplying information regarding linear motion and inclination of the body (85, 144, 146). Linear acceleration has been accepted as the adequate stimulus for the otolith organs since the latter part of the nineteenth century. However, several recent studies have attempted to determine whether the model of traction, pressure, or a shearing force is the most adequate description of their action (143, 144).

Schöne and his associates (143) believe that the perception of the visual horizontal can be predicted as a direct linear function of a shearing force on the statolith organs expressed as a function of acceleration times the sine of the angle of the direction of the force. Correia, Hixson & Niven (56) believe, on the other hand, that their findings are more accurately expressed as a function of the tangent of the angle of the acceleration. Young & Miery (174) developed a dynamic otolith model based on the application of control theory to the analysis of vestibular functions which successfully describes much of the experimental data. All of these formulations are based on experiments involving such effects as ocular counterrolling and the perception of the vertical or horizontal.

Orientation to the postural vertical.—It has long been known that man is extremely sensitive to variations of head position from the gravitational vertical (18, 100). Gescheider & Wright (79) investigated the effects of seated, prone, and supine positions of the body on the ability of the observer to set himself to the postural vertical in darkness. They reported that mean constant errors varied between 2° and 5° with the prone and supine conditions essentially the same, providing consistently smaller errors than the seated position. Several studies have shown that practice reduces the errors in setting to the postural vertical, and they confirmed this for their three conditions.

When a subject sets himself to the postural vertical, it is obvious that he will use all of the available information to minimize his errors, including tactual and various other proprioceptive information. Nelson (126) attempted to minimize nonotolithic information and estimate otolith sensitivity itself by total immersion in water. This experiment gives an excellent illustration of the complexity of completely controlling nonvestibular information in such a situation. Nelson included such controls as broad distribution of tactual cues by buoyancy techniques, temperature controls, control of light and sound, and the elimination of bubbles as cues to the vertical. It is probably fair to say that Nelson went about as far as it is possible to go in controlling these experimental conditions. The observer's task was to position himself to one of six standard target positions with respect to the gravitational vertical in each case using two separate planes of adjustment. Nelson reported substantial constant and variable errors which differed for six cardinal target positions. As predicted, the target position, head up, had smaller errors than the head down position for settings in both pitch and roll, but interestingly enough the smallest errors were found for the target position, right ear up, with the adjustment for the head up-head down plane. Thus, Nelson showed that not only the target position but also the direction of the setting had an important influence on the observer's ability to set himself with respect to the gravitational vertical.

Bauermeister, Wapner & Werner (8) have also shown that apparent body position under lateral body tilt is significantly influenced by the procedure used. The number of variables affecting such a task is further shown by a recent study (76) of nonvestibular contributions to postural equilibrium which showed that such factors as abdominal circumference, age, and cigarette smoking have some limited effect on such activities. Finally, it has been found that observers' estimates of the cockpit position in a rotating flight simulator are not significantly different for two clearly different head positions (43). These studies are convincing in indicating that the perceptual processes in postural orientation are highly complex.

The visual vertical during body tilt.—A much more widely used method to determine an observer's orientation to the gravitational horizontal and vertical is to ask him to set a luminous line to the vertical or the horizon in an otherwise dark room. Several recent studies (41, 119, 120) have confirmed earlier work which showed that the average error under these conditions is of the order of 1° or 2° when the observer is seated erect. On the other hand, if the head and body are tilted passively from the gravitational vertical, constant errors are present; these are the A-phenomenon and the E-phenomenon.

The A-phenomenon is the apparent tilt of a physically vertical, luminous line in darkness during lateral head and body tilts greater than about 60°; the apparent displacement is opposite to the direction of body tilt. The E-phenomenon is the apparent tilt of a physically vertical, luminous line in darkness during lateral head and body tilts less than about 60°; the apparent displacement of the line is in the same direction as the body tilt. The perceived vertical is, of course, displaced in the opposite direction in each case, and the amount of the effect is determined by asking the observer to set the luminous line to the perceived vertical.

Miller, Fregly & Graybiel (118) studied the errors in setting to the visual horizontal with normal and labyrinthine-defective men seated in a chair tilted to 19 positions within ±90° of the gravitational vertical. The errors tended to be the same for both groups, but the labyrinthine-defective group was substantially more variable. Both groups demonstrated the A-phenomenon and the E-phenomenon. In another study, Miller & Graybiel (119) showed similar results for head upright, recumbent, and inverted. These data are further evidence that the otoliths appear to be of considerable importance in the perception of the visual horizontal, but in the absence of the otoliths, other sensory systems produce similar though somewhat more variable results. In a related study using a reaction latency method, Attneave & Olson (7) have shown that in discrimination reaction time tests for the perception of lines, the gravitational rather than retinal horizontal determines superior performance.

The importance of nonotolith cues in the perception of the visual horizontal has been further demonstrated in a study of five normal and five labyrinthine-defective observers who made settings while standing rather than being seated and tilted passively (41). The observers stood with their feet on a horizontal floor and actively tilted their heads and bodies 20° from the gravitational vertical, using five separate combinations of head and body position. No significant, constant errors were found for either group in contrast with observations of seated observers (58), and it was concluded that contact cues from the feet interact with kinesthetic information to make veridical judgments. This finding is in accord with the belief of Mygind (125) that the tactual receptors from the feet associated with kinesthetic information from the legs act in a fashion similar to that of the otolith organs.

Some 10 years ago it was reported that observers could set a luminous line to an arbitrarily defined visual vertical while an aircraft was flying a parabolic trajectory to produce zero gravity for short periods of time. Similar experiments involving prolonged zero gravity have been conducted recently in spacecraft during the flights of Gemini 5 and 7 (89). Four astronauts set a luminous line to the perceived visual horizontal in darkness, the horizontal being defined as the position of a horizontal structure in the spacecraft. The astronauts reported that the task was very easy in the complete absence of gravitational information. Three of them made the settings with very small errors which were comparable to those found during tests on the ground, while a fourth showed a consistent, marked deviation from the visual horizontal as defined above. The reason for this individual deviation was not clear to the experimenters, but it may well have been related to the field conditions of testing. It should be noted that in spite of the fact that there was no gravitational force affecting the otolith organs, the astronauts had much information of a tactual nature to orient themselves within the spacecraft cabin. This constituted a complex of tactual information from the harness and the seat in which they made the settings. In any event, these results show that in normal men, as well as labyrinthine-defective men, there is no disorganization of visual space perception of the horizontal with zero otolith stimulation or what might be termed otolith deafferentation.

Although it has been known for many years that the perception of the visual horizontal and vertical in darkness is influenced by passive body tilt, only recently have aftereffects of body tilt on the visual horizontal and vertical been demonstrated (58, 114, 160, 163). The aftereffect was found to be of the order of 2° in the direction opposite to the previous bodily tilt. The amount of the aftereffect was a function of the amount of body tilt (58), and the effect decayed exponentially (162). These studies supply added evidence that kinesthetic information from the neck and trunk operates with otolith information in the perception of the visual horizontal and vertical and that prolonged stimulation by any of these systems leads to changes in visual orientation (114, 163).

Operant conditioning procedures have been used to study the visual perception of the vertical with pigeons (113, 140, 152–154). The birds were trained on a variable interval schedule, with food reinforcement, to peck at a vertical white line, with various amounts of box and floor tilt using a stimulus generalization procedure. These studies demonstrated that with full visual reference in the box, the birds like humans are visual field dependent (113, 140, 153). On the other hand, when the birds were tested in darkness, they responded to floor tilt. The consistency of these findings is somewhat surprising in light of the fact that, unlike human experiments in which head and body position are controlled, these animals had head, body, and feet moving about in a variety of positions during all of the experimental and training trials. This would suggest that animals as well as man (41, 42) are able to use the complex sensory information to make veridical perceptual judgments of the vertical.

The visual vertical during centripetal acceleration.—The spatial orientation of a visual object is influenced by changes in the magnitude and direction of linear acceleration on an observer. These changes in an observer's force field may be brought about by a linear accelerator or by seating the observer on a centrifuge some distance from the center of rotation. The latter method has been by far the most widely used in recent experiments, and two types of spatial displacements have been studied, depending upon whether the observer faced the center or the direction of rotation (24, 40, 41, 56, 144, 145).

Correia, Hixson & Niven (56) seated observers on a centrifuge facing the center of rotation. The observers viewed a horizontal visual target which was at all times fixed directly before them in the darkened compartment. As the centrifuge increased in velocity, the observer reported that he was being tilted backwards and that the visual target moved and was displaced upward. After a constant angular velocity had been obtained, and following a substantial lag effect, the displacement remained relatively constant until the velocity of the centrifuge was changed. If the observer faced the direction of rotation, he felt himself tilting outboard, and a luminous line viewed in darkness appeared to rotate about a center point in the direction of tilt. These two types of visual motion and displacement have been termed the oculogravic illusion, and measurements of the effect are made by simply having the observer set the visual target to the horizon. This involves vertical displacement in the first case and rotation of the object in the second (24, 25, 40, 56). It should be noted that the term "'illusion" applies only if the frame of reference is the gravitational vertical, whereas the perception is essentially veridical with respect to moderate amounts of change in resultant force.

For observers with normal labyrinthine functioning and moderate amounts of change in direction of resultant force, the oculogravic illusion closely approximates the change in resultant force. It has been shown recently, however, that the apparent target displacement is a function of changes in both the magnitude and direction of resultant force (56, 113, 133, 145, 146), although there is some disagreement as to the actual form of the function. Labyrinthine-defective observers show smaller amounts of the oculogravic illusion, and their settings are much more variable. Furthermore, for them the dynamic aspects of the illusion are less clear (40, 85).

A clearly defined lag in the development of the oculogravic illusion occurs in both normals and labyrinthine-defective observers. In normals it requires some 60 sec for the maximum displacement of the target, and this lag effect is prolonged if the visual target is not present for the initial period of constant velocity (39). The apparent displacement is relatively constant for normals for prolonged periods. Labyrinthine-defective observers exhibit about one-half of the apparent displacement found in normals after one minute of constant angular velocity. However, the apparent displacement continues to increase, and after one hour of constant velocity, the amount of the illusion for labyrinthine-defectives is not significantly different from normals (40).

Tests of the oculogravic illusion with the observers immersed in water indicate that both normals and labyrinthine-defectives exhibit a smaller illusion under these conditions (90). The differences between the normals and labryinthine-defectives suggest that these characteristics of the oculogravic illusion make it possible to use it as a measure of otolith function (85). This test and the test of counterrolling constitute two effective procedures to test the otolith organs (89, 121, 122).

Brandt & Fluur (23–25) have performed similar experiments with the observers facing the direction of rotation and setting a target to horizon. Simultaneous records of ocular torsion were made with infrared photography. They found that ocular counterrolling was far less than the subjective displacement of the target reported during the same trials and that there were marked discrepancies between the pattern of the reflex counterrolling and the oculogravic illusion.

It has been generally accepted for many years that angular acceleration is the adequate stimulus for ocular nystagmus. However, in a carefully controlled study, Niven, Hixson & Correia (131) were able to produce a clearly defined nystagmus with sinusoidal linear accelerations. The observer was moved along a track which ran from one side of the room to the other through the center of rotation at three sinusoidal frequencies. Thus with a changing linear acceleration along the observer's left-right axis, horizontal nystagmus similar to horizontal rotational nystagmus was recorded. They were unable, however, to produce vertical nystagmus. The nystagmus demonstrated a clear phase lag from the change in linear acceleration. Subjective effects were also reported. When the observers viewed a luminous line in darkness as they moved right and left, the effect was similar to the oculogyral illusion. The visual target had an apparent velocity, but little or no displacement, while the observers were reporting a lateral movement along the direction of the track. There was no apparent tilt of the line as is uniformly reported in the oculogravic illusion while the observer faces in the direction of rotation with a constant change in the direction of resultant force. The authors suggest that the perception of body tilt is frequency dependent, while the direction of change in resultant force is constant or changes very slowly. The perception of tilt, on the other hand, occurs when the change in linear acceleration is relatively rapid.

There has been recent speculation in the literature regarding the mediating sensory systems in the perception of tilt and the perception of lateral motion, both of which are dependent upon linear acceleration (92). A study by Schöne & Mortag (144), using a parallel swing to produce sinusoidal linear acceleration, reported combinations of lateral motion and tilt of a line contrary to the findings of Niven, Hixson & Correia (131). These differences may well be related to the very different methods used. Schöne & Mortag's (144) parallel swing procedure was much simpler, i.e., it produced simple changes in the magnitude and direction of linear acceleration in the plane of the motion. Although the frequencies involved in the two studies were within the same range, the study by Niven, Hixson & Correia produced centripetal forces at considerably higher levels than the accelerations used by Schöne & Mortag.

In this complicated stimulus field, it is not easy to identify the specific factors leading to these differences in results. Schöne & de Haes (143) used the centrifuge technique to study the perception of the visual vertical as a function of lateral tilt position of the head and trunk. Varying the head position from 0° to 90°, they found head position was a major influence for small head tilts, but with increasing lateral tilt the statolith became less effective in determining the apparent vertical while other somatoreceptors became more important. All of these results appear to add yet another dimension of complexity to the effects of linear acceleration on the perception of a visual object.

RESPONSE TO ANGULAR ACCELERATION

The vestibular system, as a whole, functions in some respects like an inertial guidance system, while the semicircular canals are the primary receptors for rotary accelerations (92, 166, 167). The cupula-endolymph system behaves in many ways like a heavily damped torsion pendulum, and some psychophysiological effects are predictable from the differential equation describing its behavior. The torsion pendulum theory of semicircular canal function has been very useful in understanding the vestibular system, and many experiments have been designed to test the theory which was developed over 20 years ago (92). Recently Cappel (35), Valentinuzzi (157), Fernandez & Valentinuzzi (66), and Weaver (164) have made analyses of the forces involved in the semicircular canals. Several areas of inquiry have been of interest to investigators of vestibular function in the past 3 years: sensitivity to angular acceleration, prolonged effects of vestibular stimulation, deviation from predictive equations of such effects as the response decline following prolonged or repetitive stimulation, effects of Coriolis accelerations, and finally the influence of stimulation by linear acceleration on the effects of simultaneous stimulation by angular acceleration.

Sensitivity of the semicircular canals to angular acceleration.—One of the fascinating characteristics of all sensory systems is their extreme sensitivity to stimulation by certain limited physical stimuli, and the semicircular canals have long been known for their high sensitivity to angular acceleration (38). There have been relatively few recent studies of sensitivity using subjective indicators to determine thresholds, and indeed, the total data reported in the literature during the past 50 years is based on less than 200 observers. Furthermore, most of these experiments describe the rotation of an observer about his cephalocaudal axis. Consequently, there is a very limited amount of information describing the sensitivity to rotary accelerations about other axes.

One study compared three psychophysical methods: the constant method, the staircase method, and a method employing a constantly increasing angular acceleration for use in determining thresholds for the perception of rotation (45). The method using the constantly increasing angular acceleration was found to be completely inadequate because of adaptation effects which resulted in a waxing and waning of the perception of rotation as the acceleration increased. The constant method and the staircase method, on the other hand, produced comparable results, and the staircase method was found to have the advantage of greater efficiency in producing thresholds.

The oculogyral illusion is another subjective indicator of the perception of rotation. The oculogyral illusion is the apparent motion of a visual target in darkness in the direction of an angular acceleration. It is observed when a subject views a target which is fixed with respect to himself. Thresholds for the perception of rotation and the oculogyral illusion for 10-sec accelerations have been compared with the subject rotating about his vertical axis (44). The mean threshold for the perception of rotation was found to be 0.29°/sec,^{2} while that for the oculogyral illusion was 0.10°/sec^2. Thus, presenting the observer with a visual target which rotates with him in darkness reduces the threshold to about one-third of the value found when the observations were made in total darkness. Furthermore the correlation between these two subjective measures is not significantly different from zero. This lack of a correlation between the two indicators of vestibular stimulation and the marked differences between the two thresholds suggest that they involve distinct (although possibly overlapping) psychophysiological mechanisms.

Using the oculogyral illusion as the indicator of the threshold, Doty (61) found an inverse relationship between stimulus duration and the threshold between 0.5 and 6.0 sec. More importantly, he tested the notion that the product of acceleration times time is constant at threshold as in Bloch's law for vision. He found that the threshold expressed as a product of acceleration times time was a linearly increasing function rather than constant within the limits of his conditions, which is contrary to predictions from the torsion-pendulum theory.

Data on the thresholds for nystagmus, in contrast to the subjective measures, are very extensive, and one study a decade ago reported electronystagmographic thresholds for 2000 individuals. Measurements using electronystagmography have the advantage of producing an objective measure of sensitivity; furthermore, the time required for the test is short enough to make these measures useful not only in experimental situations requiring rapid measures but also clinically. They have the disadvantage, however, that vestibular nystagmus is influenced by a wide variety of variables (48, 92, 166, 167). Notable among these is the arousal level of the individual which has been studied by many investigators. Response decline associated with repeated stimulation by angular acceleration may merely reflect a reduction in arousal rather than an effect of repetition per se. Some investigators have suggested that this may be partially controlled in experimental animals by the use of *d*-amphetamine (32, 53, 96).

Various drugs have wide and rather prolonged effects upon vestibular nystagmus (6, 12, 124). Tibbling & Henriksson (155) report that cigarette smoking produces measurable changes in electronystagmograms, while Haas & Eidebenz (97) found that the thresholds in the morning are lower than those in the afternoon. They suggest that this may be a function of repetitive stimulation during the day, but an equally valid, alternative explanation is that it results from a reduction in arousal in the evening when their second measurement was made. A number of studies of sensitivity to angular acceleration using nystagmus as the indicator show that the thresholds for nystagmus are higher than for subjective indicators (60, 100, 156). The comparisons may not be justified, however, because the psychophysical methods were different. Some attempts have been made to measure nystagmus thresholds in infants, and one study by Silverstein (148) did demonstrate vestibular nystagmus in infants from 1 to 12 months of age. Recent data on latency of the nystagmus response are also available (52, 68–70).

Duration of the primary effects of angular acceleration—cupulometry.—The method of cupulometry was introduced some 20 years ago as a test of semicircular canal function following severe criticism of the old Bárány test developed in 1907. The Bárány test used a hand-rotated chair, high accelerations, and inadequate time between accelerations (6, 100). Cupulometry involves the presentation of four or five suprathreshold levels of impulsive stimuli by quickly stopping a rotating chair from moderate angular velocities. The observer's task is simply to report on the duration of the oculogyral illusion, the perception of rotation, or in the case of the electronystagmogram, the duration of the nystagmus is determined from the record. The duration of the effect is plotted against the log of the velocity of the chair before the stop. There is some question regarding the nature of the function, but the resulting straight line constitutes the cupulogram. The slopes and the intercepts have been reported to differ for the three common measures of vestibular stimulation, i.e., perception of rotation, oculogyral illusion, and duration of nystagmus, and the various slopes and intercepts have been related to motion sickness (100). The intercept with the velocity axis which is expressed in terms of the velocity prior to the impulsive deceleration has also been used as a "threshold" measure (9, 12, 13). Although this threshold is of the same order of magnitude as that determined by other methods, it is certainly not directly comparable to thresholds established by standard psychophysical procedures.

It is well known that a number of extra-labyrinthine factors other than angular acceleration influence the duration of these vestibular effects. The most notable effect is on nystagmus which is widely affected by arousal level (12, 48, 92, 166, 167). Aschan (6) and many others (31) have also shown that the perception of rotation and nystagmus decline after repeated stimulation by rotary acceleration and caloric irrigation of the ears, and they attribute the habituation to central factors. Aschan also found that a response decline for nystagmus disappeared in the case of a pilot when his blood alcohol concentration was raised to 0.79 percent. Yuganov (175) found that the duration of nystagmus and the perception of rotation are shorter in zero *g*, whereas Jackson & Sears (102) reported that there was little difference between the nystagmic reaction at 0, 1, and 2 *g* and that the subjective reaction was intensified at 2 *g*. Such results must be accepted with caution because of the brief periods of zero *g* and the crude methods used.

An additional nonvestibular factor in cupulometry is concerned with the fact that it is difficult for an observer to make a consistent response for the end point during an exponentially decaying stimulus in any perceptual situation (13, 130, 136). Nilsson & Henriksson (130) demonstrated that some common extrasensory effect appears to determine the duration of the oculogyral illusion and several other similar effects. They found that the duration of the oculogyral illusion for impulsive stimuli showed a high correlation with the duration of the spiral aftereffect. This finding was confirmed by Reason & Benson (136) for three types of visually perceived aftereffects and the duration of the perception of rotation. They also found positive correlations between the duration of the perception of rotation and visual and auditory signal persistence, whereas nystagmus time showed a positive correlation with perception of rotation but not with the other nonvestibular measures.

These results suggest some general factor in judgment of persistence of an exponentially decaying perception. Further support for the existence of such a factor comes from Anderson's (4) finding of a positive correlation between visual and auditory autokinesis. In another study, Benson, Goorney & Reason (13) found that the duration of the perception of rotation was significantly longer when the instructions were "strong," i.e., supporting of long effects, as compared with "weak" instructions. These studies make it clear that the duration of aftereffects does not provide a pure indicator of the action of the cupula-endolymph system.

Response decline in the vestibular system.—Everyday activities involve repetitive stimulation of the vestibular mechanism with various durations of angular acceleration. These stimuli may result in response declines if they are repeated or if the activities are of unusual patterns (27, 28, 49, 50, 92, 166, 167). The term "response decline" has been used as a convenient general description of the nature of the effects without implications regarding the mechanisms involved. However, the phenomena of response decline may be conveniently classified into two categories: (*a*) response decline associated with prolonged stimulation by angular acceleration which leads to adaptation effects; and (*b*) repetitive stimulation by angular acceleration which leads to habituation. The experimental operations of these two are different although some authors do not make a distinction between them (100, 166, 167). These effects have been of special interest to many students of the vestibular system for 50 years because of their importance in piloting aircraft. Furthermore, they are theoretically interesting because they have proved to be exceptions to the torsion-pendulum theory and thus require additional explanatory formulations. Let us first consider adaptation and then habituation.

Prolonged stimulation-adaptation.—The nature of adaptation of any given sensory modality reveals much regarding the basic mode of action of the system. Consequently, such studies are important in studying the vestibular system, even though the prolonged duration of stimulation used would rarely occur in ordinary life activities. The most detailed studies of adaptation have been conducted by Guedry and his co-workers (53, 92, 96). The subjective experience that accompanies angular acceleration has a direction, right or left, and a magnitude, and consequently a vector notation is appropriate to describe the effect. To obtain estimates of the perceived velocity during prolonged acceleration, Guedry (92) used a displacement estimation procedure in which the observer signaled each time he perceived that he had passed through 45° of rotary displacement. He found that during constant accelerations, subjective velocity increased for some 30 sec and then declined showing a clear adaptation of the subjective effect although Guedry did not trace the adaptation to its zero point. The slow phase velocity of the vestibular nystagmus showed a similar gradual increase for some 30 sec, but unlike the subjective effect, the nystagmus did not show a response decline up to 60 sec of constant acceleration if the observer was maintained at a high level of alertness.

Guedry also gave a detailed analysis of possible factors contributing to the response decline for subjective effects and favored central nervous system mechanisms over peripheral mechanisms. An important consideration in this connection was the failure to find a response decline in nystagmus, although some sense organ adaptation appears possible (167).

In two carefully controlled studies, Collins & Guedry (53, 96) studied the response decline in slow phase nystagmus during prolonged constant accelerations varying between 8.4 and 54 sec. They reported data using the same stimuli for cats and men for rotation about horizontal (y) and vertical (z) body axes. The vertical nystagmus output was smaller than the horizontal output, and the response decline was clearly present during constant acceleration for cats, particularly during vertical nystagmus. The results for the human subjects confirmed the earlier finding that nystagmus did not decline in alert humans. Thus nystagmus response of cats resembled the subjective response of humans for prolonged constant angular acceleration. This difference may well have been, in part, a function of a change in alertness, although Collins & Guedry reported that a control group of cats treated with *d*-amphetamine in an attempt to produce a stable, high level of alertness also produced a response decline in nystagmus. They believe that this response decline may be attributed to inhibitory processes in the central nervous system which suppress nystagmus in cats, whereas similar processes suppress subjective effects but not nystagmus in man. These very different results in cat and man are significant with regard to the generalization of results of vestibular studies from cat to man, particularly since cats have been widely used in physiological studies of the vestibular mechanism and generalizations have commonly been made from cat to man.

Brown (29, 30) has studied the effects of prolonged constant acceleration on the perception of rotation using a magnitude estimation procedure. He employed a large range of constant accelerations and stimulus durations from 10 to 80 sec, the larger accelerations having the shorter durations to keep the testing within certain velocity limits of the equipment. Brown reported response increases and then declines at all levels, but his durations of constant angular acceleration, like those of Guedry & Collins (53, 96), were not long enough to establish the full course of adaptation.

Parsons (134) used a similar procedure to study the effects of suprathreshold levels of angular acceleration on the oculogyral illusion with stimulus durations from 1 to 9 sec. His observers reported magnitude estimates for 160 sec, and thus he was able to describe the full course of the first effect of apparent motion in the direction of the acceleration and an aftereffect in the opposite direction. Part of his results support the torsion-pendulum theory in that equal products of acceleration and time produced similar results for the first effect. The aftereffects, of course, are contrary to the concept of a heavily damped system. More complex adaptation effects, including a waxing and waning of the perceived velocity, have also been reported for a constantly increasing acceleration during threshold determinations (45). Such results are difficult to fit into mathematical models of the cupula-endolymph system and may be caused by transient effects in the central nervous system.

Brown (29) also analyzed his data in an attempt to test Stevens' power law for the vestibular system. He used changes in magnitude estimates during prolonged stimuli rather than magnitude estimates for different levels of impulsive acceleration, and derived an exponent of 1.00 for the power function. He confirmed the exponent that he had found in a previous study (30) using cross-modality matching of the perception of rotation with an auditory signal. It should be noted that his correction for the threshold measure in the first study was quite arbitrary for a best fit for his data and was much higher than the thresholds obtained for most individuals in another experiment (38).

Repetitive stimulation-habituation.—One of the most controversial issues in the history of studies of the vestibular system has been the effects of repetitive stimulation on various vestibular functions (26, 31, 49, 92, 100, 166, 167). The occurrence of habituation under a variety of conditions and the many factors which influence it have no doubt contributed to the confusion. Habituation to motion is so well known in fliers, sailors, dancers, acrobats, and ice skaters that little comment on the general phenomenon is necessary, but the experimental work during the past 3 years has added much to the fund of knowledge on the matter. Habituation has been studied in cats (26, 32, 36, 48, 50, 67, 117), pigeons (154), rats (65, 137–139), rabbits (16), and monkeys (151, 166) as well as man (27, 28, 59, 75, 92, 116, 135), but it should be noted that generalizations from one species to another are hazardous (53, 54, 96).

In the past 10 years there has been a resurgence of interest in human studies of habituation to rotation and the associated effects of Coriolis accelerations which result from head movements as the observer moves about in a rotating room (75, 88, 92, 127–129). These studies of habituation will be considered in the section on applications of vestibular studies. Response decline associated with repetitive stimulation occurs under a wide variety of situations, but it is by no means universal (31, 92, 166, 167). For example, Pfaltz (135) has shown that habituation achieved by angular acceleration can neither be removed nor modified by subsequent caloric stimulation.

Probably the most important single variable influencing the response decline following repetitive stimulation by angular or caloric stimulation is the arousal level of the subjects. In most experiments there is an attempt to hold arousal at some constant high level by giving the observer a continuous task during nystagmus recording. This is not always effective, however, since such operations as changing stimuli, changing tasks, a chance remark, or various other factors will affect arousal level and result in a modification of nystagmus output (28, 48, 92). Some studies have used arousal level as the independent variable. For example, Brown & Marshall (32) found significantly greater nystagmus output in cats with injections of *d*-amphetamine sulfate (high arousal) as compared with cats which had been injected with pentobarbital.

Early students of habituation believed that some visual stimulation was necessary for vestibular habituation to occur, but there is much evidence that response decline may occur in complete darkness (33, 92). It should be noted that in studies of nystagmus, any visual target will inhibit nystagmus, and the response decline may turn out to be an artifact. It has been demonstrated that nystagmus does not have to run its full course on each trial, however, for habituation to occur (27).

Brown & Crampton (31) studied four groups of 20 men each under four conditions of visual stimulation ranging from total darkness to full room illumination with the capsule cover removed. Records of nystagmus, perception of rotation, and the oculogyral illusion were obtained following an acceleration of $24°/sec^2$ for 10 sec. Alertness was controlled by having the observers report on subjective estimates of motion throughout the trials. Brown & Crampton found substantial variability of response for all three indicators using logarithmic transformations of the response for the analysis. There was significant habituation for the four conditions of visual stimulation and for all three of the measures used. Using the same angular acceleration, Marshall & Brown (116) compared two groups, one group which had habituation trials in the illuminated capsule while the second had habituation trials in total darkness. Substantial habituation of nystagmus was found when both the habituation and the criterion trials involved visual stimulation, whereas with the same criterion trials and habituation in darkness, significant habituation was not present. In fact, there was actually an increase in nystagmus output following the habituation trials in darkness.

Figure skaters showed adequate habituation following high angular accelerations (impulsive stops from 235 to 278 rpm), according to Collins (49, 52). They could walk, skate, and keep their balance as long as their eyes were open with a full frame of reference. On the other hand, when visual fixation was not permitted, there was a loss of equilibrium and orientation leading to falling. Collins also noted brisk nystagmus and clear sensations of turning in these figure skaters during laboratory tests in darkness. Consequently, it appears there is no complete vestibular suppression of the nystagmic response during repetitive stimulation, but rather there is some change in the form of the response. This notion is further supported in another study of skaters and nonskaters in which Collins (52) compared subjective response and nystagmic output for three levels of angular acceleration. The tests were made in darkness with a 3-sec period of room illumination following the acceleration. The skaters produced significantly less primary nystagmus and shorter durations of sensation of turning than the nonskaters, but there was no difference in the number of eye movements nor in the duration of nystagmus. The 3-sec period of light decreased nystagmus output and subjective effects for both groups as would be expected.

The notion that habituation changes the form of the vestibular response is further supported by Aschan's (6) investigation which showed a greater response decline for the perception of rotation than for the nystagmus. The direction and magnitude of acceleration are also of considerable importance in determining the nature of the response decline. Although some studies do not completely define the stimulus in detail, the evidence is quite clear that habituation is fairly specific to a particular set of conditions (63, 92, 93, 117, 135). The magnitude of the angular acceleration is of some importance also, and typical habituation studies use very high angular accelerations. Some sort of response decline has been reported in cats, dogs, and man for angular accelerations of $7°/sec^2$ and above when the stimulus lasted for several seconds (31, 51, 52, 54, 116). On the other hand, minimal or no response decline associated with repetitive stimulation at threshold levels has been reported (6, 45).

Current students of vestibular habituation are inclined to consider it to be a learning phenomenon (36, 100), and similarities between vestibular habituation and learning have been noted for many years (92, 100, 166). Early studies reported vestibular conditioning, although Wendt (166) has noted possible artifacts resulting from loss of arousal and from visual stimulation in early investigations. Current studies use a limited number of habituation trials, but have carefully controlled both of these effects and still report some response declines; however, conflicting data have been reported (31, 36, 49, 92).

Studies of repetitive stimulation show characteristic acquisition curves involving a rapid, initial response decline (6, 26, 31, 36). Brown (26), however, found that nystagmus response decline in cats was not influenced by different distributions of angular acceleration experience, thus confirming earlier studies. Capps and Collins (36) showed that for cats the response decline occurred for the slow phase displacement and number of beats per second but not for the duration of the nystagmus. Retention of the habituated response was substantially greater for the distributed accelerations, although there was substantial recovery, from one testing session to the next, of the response decline that occurred during a particular session. Nevertheless, retention does continue for some days or weeks (36, 92, 117, 135), and some transfer has been reported (36, 63), but habituation tends to be directionally specific (92).

Wolfe (171) states that the neural elements underlying habituation are unknown but suggests that there are interactions between brain stem and cortical levels. Aschan (6), on the basis of his studies of alcohol on habituation, suggested that habituation is primarily cortical, and there is ample neurological evidence for substantial vestibular-cortical projections and interaction with deep somatic afferents (71, 72, 100). Neurological studies indicate that the vestibular efferent system may produce direct inhibitory effects upon the sensory elements of the receptor mechanisms, thus leading to response declines (142, 168).

Effects of linear acceleration on response to angular acceleration.—During the past 5 years there has been an increasing interest in the influence of linear acceleration on the stimulation of the semicircular canals by angular acceleration. It has also been shown that changes in linear acceleration modify optokinetic nystagmus (107, 158). The results of these experiments make it apparent that perceptual processes resulting from stimulation of the semicircular canals, as well as the otoliths, are widely influenced by concomitant stimulation of other sensory systems.

Perception of rotation in a changing linear force field.—It has been known for many years that the subjective and nystagmus response to an impulsive angular acceleration about the cephalocaudal axis of an observer seated erect in a chair produces effects that persist for some 20 to 30 sec. It has been shown only recently, however, that rotation about the same body axis with the observer's cephalocaudal axis horizontal, as on a barbecue spit, produces prolonged nystagmus and prolonged perception of rotation (10, 11, 14, 55, 103). The more recent studies have been concerned with the nature of the phenomenon on the one hand and a consideration of whether the prolonged effects of horizontal rotation have a direct effect on the canals. The question is whether rotating about an earth horizontal axis produces systematic changes in the cupula-endolymph system, or whether the results are due to a change in other sensory mechanisms including the otoliths.

Benson & Bodin (10) studied the duration of nystagmus and subjective response in 10 normal observers who were strapped on a horizontal stretcher which was rotated at various constant angular velocities from 10 to 60°/sec. The subjective experiences were very different from those experienced by observers seated erect and rotated at these same velocities. In the first place several observers became severely motion sick as a result of the rotating g vector and were unable to continue with the experiment. Following acceleration about an earth-vertical axis, the perception of rotation and nystagmus would continue for 20 to 30 sec, whereas following acceleration about an earth-horizontal axis, the perception of rotation continued throughout the duration of rotation. The surprising finding to Benson & Bodin, however, was the almost complete lack of continued perception of rotation when the rotation of the stretcher was stopped suddenly. Similarly, constant velocity of rotation about the cephalocaudal axis led to compensatory nystagmus for as long as the rotation continued up to about 40 revolutions of the stretcher. Postrotational nystagmus leading in the opposite direction occurred for all observers at the two higher angular velocities, but only two produced nystagmus following deceleration from 10°/sec. Furthermore, the time constant for the 60°/sec. velocity in horizontal rotation was about one half that with rotation about a vertical axis.

Benson & Bodin explain the effect during rotation on the basis of physical changes in the cupula-endolymph system involving a traveling deformation of the membranous canals resulting from the continuously changing gravitational vector during rotation, rather than to neural mechanisms of a higher order than the reflex arc. The rotating vector in Niven, Hixson & Correia's (131) study in the rotating room produces similar effects.

In another carefully conducted experiment, Benson & Bodin (11) rotated observers about the three major body axes by appropriate positioning of the observers with respect to a device which rotated about an earth vertical axis. Following 60 sec of constant velocity, the chair was stopped abruptly, and immediately the observer was rotated 90° to a new position. In control trials, the observers remained in the same position. For all three body axes, reorientation of the observer led to a decrease in postrotational response, the effect being greater in the yaw axis than in the pitch and roll axes. Both of these experiments show the importance of change in gravitational vector in the perception of rotation and nystagmus, but they still leave open the question of the precise mechanism of the effect.

Correia & Guedry (55) extended the earlier experimental work on the evoked response to horizontal axis rotation to higher velocities in order to test further the hypothesis of changes in semicircular canals as factors leading to nystagmus and perception of rotation. They rotated their observers at 10 and 30 rpm about a horizontal axis, and under these two conditions 12 of 20 observers became sick. Consequently, their results, like those of earlier studies, are based only upon those observers who did not get sick. It is worth noting that the motion sickness was related to the observers' task during rotation. The 12 observers who could not complete the sequences reported verbal and pictorial descriptions of the pattern of their body motion, while the 8 observers who completed the test series used key press to indicate their body position or did mental arithmetic during each trial. Yuganov (175) also reported motion sickness in his observers during zero gravity which produced a deviation from normal otolith stimulation. Correia & Geudry's observers reported their apparent body position, and nystagmus was also recorded.

The results at 10 rpm confirmed earlier studies in that the observers gave veridical reports of body position, and a sustained unidirectional nystagmus continued throughout rotation up to 5 min. The results at 30 rpm were remarkably different, particularly after about 30 sec of rotation. The subjective reports were highly variable, and the subjects became disoriented with regard to their position in space and gave responses similar to labyrinthine-defective observers. A reversing horizontal nystagmus was observed at 30 rpm, and the subjective disorientation began at the same time that the reversing nystagmus occurred. Slow phase nystagmus velocity for both conditions exhibited a cyclic modulation which was related to the observers' orientation to gravity. These unique subjective and nystagmus patterns imply several modes of response of semicircular canals and otolith organs. Correia & Geudry suggest that their data obtained during rotation, together with those reported by Niven, Hixson & Correia (131) showing nystagmus associated with sinusoidal linear accelerations, indicate that the two transducers may have different response ranges, and that there may be a response shift at different frequencies of rotation. This is in accord with mathematical models of the response ranges of the semicircular canals and otolith organs (92, 174). A study by Lansberg, Guedry & Graybiel (110) also supports the notion of semicircular canal stimulation being modulated by linear acceleration. These effects during horizontal rotation are unquestionably complex, but the determination of the specific mechanisms involved awaits the results of experiments involving selective ablation of individual components of the labyrinth.

EFFECTS OF VESTIBULAR STIMULATION ON THE EFFICIENCY OF MAN IN MOTION

Terrestrial man uses vestibular information in conjunction with information from other sources in the perception of motion and in a group of acceleratory, positional, and righting reflexes as he moves about and orients himself in space (80, 100, 141). At the same time, as long as there is adequate visual information available, he may be completely unaware of the importance of the vestibular system. Indeed, deaf, labyrinthine-defective individuals can function quite adequately in most orienting tasks not requiring auditory information as long as they have adequate vision.

On the other hand, when a normal man moves about in vehicles which expose him to unusual accelerative forces, he may find himself working with reduced efficiency or even becoming acutely ill (75, 88, 90, 127–129). Motion sickness has been known throughout the ages, but it is interesting to note that the oculogravic illusion was first observed by Mach in the nineteenth century on a railroad train while it was going around a curve. Modern high speed vehicles can expose man to angular and linear accelerations for prolonged periods of time. In contrast, ordinary body movements are of relatively short duration, and, consequently, in the case of angular acceleration, one stimulus nullifies the effects of the preceding one. In aircraft and spacecraft, however, accelerations may lead to high level effects which may be prolonged and lead to gross degradation in performance (1, 5, 9, 87, 89, 91, 94).

Orientation and disorientation in flight.—Disorientation in flight is a continuing problem for pilots, and reports of accidents or near accidents associated with disorientation are commonplace in aviation studies (1, 5, 9, 17, 37, 87, 94, 112). An analysis of the literature in this field is convincing in showing the complexity of the problem in spatial orientation, especially under the conditions of instrument flight where the pilot has meager, if any, visual information outside of his instruments. Under these conditions, vestibular information may play a significant role.

It is important to note that the vestibular information may be veridical part of the time, as in the initial part of a turn or recovery to straight and level flight, whereas much of the time the information is nonveridical because of the prolonged effects of rotation (57). Thus, Young (173) reported that tracking efficiency may be improved by vestibular information in a flight simulator, whereas others have shown that disorientation may result under such varied conditions as changes in atmospheric pressure in the ears leading to what has been called pressure vertigo (9, 112), increased *g* (9, 170), zero gravity (5, 87, 111), spins in aircraft (105), and normal turns (9). Such disorientation occurs in various types of vehicles, and data are available from safety reports on helicopters (37), transport aircraft (9), fighter aircraft (105–107), and spacecraft (5, 17, 89, 91, 175). The evidence from all of these studies supports the notion that interaction of various sensory mechanisms is important in these situations and that interactions between otolith and semicircular canal information are of particular importance (9, 95).

Vestibular-visual interaction.—During everyday activities on the ground or in aircraft in straight and level flight, vestibular and visual information act synergistically to maintain efficient vision. Normal head and body movements produce interacting accelerations of opposite sign with short intervals between. Consequently, compensatory nystagmus is temporary and leads to stabilized retinal images, and the semicircular canals operate as velocity transducers stimulated by angular acceleration (123).

In flight, on the other hand, during or following prolonged constant velocity turns, the nystagmus following angular acceleration may be prolonged and thus drive the eyes in anticompensatory movements which may lead to lower visual acuity (9, 91, 95, 105, 106). The problem for the observer is quite comparable to that of dynamic visual acuity (34), which involves a target moving with respect to the observer. Guedry (95) has called such visual acuity "dynamic visual acuity-vestibular," and he studied it in 18 flight candidates with normal static acuity. Relatively large, prolonged angular accelerations were used and other conditions were arranged to maximize nystagmus. Guedry found that there was a reduction in acuity which was related to the magnitude of the angular acceleration and the amount of resulting nystagmus. There were wide individual differences in "dynamic visual acuity-vestibular," and practice improved acuity substantially, as has also been shown in regular dynamic visual acuity studies (34). Guedry noted that the effect was essentially transient and was related to the observers' ability to control nystagmus.

Jones (105), in a related investigation, studied vestibular nystagmus in five pilots during eight-turn spins in an aircraft. Electronystagmograms were obtained in pitch, roll, and yaw while the pilots looked at the instrument panel or outside of the cockpit. Jones reported that compensatory eye movements in this highly complex stimulus situation failed to stabilize the retinal image as normally occurs on the ground, the greatest discrepancies in eye movements occurring in the roll plane. He believes that his results as a whole suggest that at times the man-machine combination may lead to insurmountable visual difficulties in attempting to recover from a spin in an aircraft. Serious difficulties were also encountered in the Gemini 8 space flight during which unscheduled, high velocity rotary motions occurred. Under these strenuous conditions, the astronauts reported marked visual impairment (91).

Vestibular-visual interactions may also occur in many other situations, e.g., in the haunted-swing illusion, and many laboratory studies have pitted visual and postural information against each other. An earthquake in Niigate, Japan, which tilted some buildings 1° to 9° from the gravitational vertical, made it possible for Kitahara & Uno (109) to study 66 persons who were obliged to live in these tilted buildings. Some of these individuals spent much time in the buildings while others spent the day elsewhere. The residents of the buildings reported various symptoms such as sickness, fatigue, and insomnia. The symptoms appeared to be related to the amount of tilt of the building and the amount of time spent in the tilted situation. At the time of the investigation, five months after the earthquake, "the subjects still could not distinguish the true horizontal and vertical lines in the tilted room." For example, there were problems of spilling water from a cup. The vertigo tended to diminish with time, but difficulties with orientation remained even after five months. These findings appear to be similar to those of Collins (49, 52) in suggesting that response declines in such conditions are complex and selective rather than simple and general.

Effects of Coriolis acceleration during rotation.—Coriolis acceleration is an added acceleration due to physical forces that occur when the head is moved about an axis other than the axis of rotation in a rotating device. After some 30 sec of rotation at a constant velocity, the semicircular canals are in effect not stimulated as long as the head is held fixed. But if an observer moves his head, the semicircular canals are stimulated by the Coriolis acceleration which can be measured with an accelerometer. The effects on the semicircular canals are essentially the same as those produced by simple angular acceleration (20, 92, 127–129). The magnitude of the Coriolis acceleration is a function of the velocity of rotation of the device and the velocity and duration of the head movement.

Coriolis accelerations are of importance in aircraft (9, 94) and spacecraft (17, 91) flights since these vehicles expose pilots to long-term constant angular velocity. Their effects on aircraft pilots have been known for many years, and flight instruments have been arranged to minimize their effects. Their importance in space flight is also a result of the possibility that it may be necessary to rotate space platforms in order to produce a simulated gravity for man's comfort and well being (150). From an engineering point of view this is quite feasible in frictionless space, but the consequences of living in a constantly rotating environment have not been studied in detail until the past decade. Thus the question of man's ability to become habituated to an unusual force environment raised by psychologists in World War I is again of practical and theoretical importance.

Several slow rotation rooms have been developed to investigate the effects of prolonged constant rotation on man (77, 88, 127, 131). Like all simulators, these devices do not reproduce space flight conditions precisely either in terms of the probable g levels nor in the plane in which the man is rotated. Some use horizontal platforms, which suffer from a variable resultant force as the observer walks to the periphery of the room and from the fact that the resultant force is not directly in the individual's cephalocaudal axis. One device (127) overcomes this difficulty by having the platform swing out so that the resultant gravitational force is aligned with the vertical axis of the subject, but the device has the limitation of an increased resultant force acting on the observer.

Several problems have been of concern to investigators in studying man in rotating rooms: the effects on man's physiological functions, his ability to move about and perform various tasks, the stress imposed due to conflicting stimulus information, and particularly man's ability to habituate to the situation. An important consideration in these rooms is that the Coriolis acceleration is completely under the control of the subject, and if he chooses to sit quietly without moving, there is no Coriolis acceleration. Consequently, it is sometimes necessary to use standard tasks requiring head motions to insure that the stimulation does occur (2, 3, 51, 77, 88, 127). The technique is in many respects similar to various sensory rearrangement experiments. The study of Coriolis effects has also been used as a standardized laboratory method to investigate the effects of drugs on motion sickness (172).

Ambler & Guedry (2, 3) have shown that ratings of the signs of motion sickness following controlled head movements of flight trainees during rotation are related to success in flight training. Trainees with very high motion sickness ratings are unlikely to complete flight training. Galle & Emel'ianov (77) have reported similar results.

General effects of rotation.—The initial effects of working in a rotating environment on naive, normal observers involve complex symptoms which have been called "canal sickness." A better term would be "slow rotation room sickness" since the force environment of a man moving about in a constantly rotating room is incredibly complex. In general, the condition can be considered one involving stress with wide individual differences (47, 77, 88, 128, 129). Some observers must be eliminated from such studies because of acute motion sickness including dizziness, headache, difficulty in walking, inactivity designed to avoid the noxious stimulation, drowsiness, fatigue, and loss of appetite or even vomiting. Countermeasures, such as the use of drugs, limitation of head movements, and habituation, may relieve the symptoms in some observers at low velocities.

Factors contributing to Coriolis effects.—Many psychological and physiological factors have been studied in the last decade while observers lived or worked in a rotating room, e.g., chemical or physiological changes, the oculogyral illusion, critical flicker frequency, walking, miscellaneous psychomotor tests, reaction time, tracking, solving mathematical problems, and reading. Collins (51) conducted an experimental study that was designed to compare the effects of Coriolis acceleration with different types of rapid, 30° lateral head movements during rotation at 12 rpm. He used three different visual frameworks, and the observers reported varying estimates of "diving" or "climbing" maneuvers ranging from 34° to 87° and lasting as long as 30 sec during lateral head movements. The maximum apparent motion occurred when the observers viewed isolated lights in darkness. Some observers appeared to enjoy these illusory movements, while others found that they were unpleasant or even made them sick. Collins showed that the effects are highly predictable, and Gillingham (81) has suggested that a trained observer can use this information to identify his direction of rotation even at very low velocities of rotation.

Differences between pilots and nonpilots in these effects have been shown in studies by Dowd, Moore & Cramer (64) and De Francesco (59). O'Laughlin, Brady & Newsom (132) found that well-motivated and trained observers can perform reaching movements in a slow rotation room at 12.2 rpm with no significant decrement over comparable static tests.

The effects of slow rotation on the rat have also been investigated (65, 137–139, 165). In general, the data from these studies support human studies, but since rats cannot vomit, the activity level of the rat was used as a measure of the effect using an operant conditioning procedure. These studies indicated that, for the normal rat, rotation is certainly an aversive stimulus and that activity level may be used as an indicator of motion sickness. Weissman (165) also showed that rats may be trained to respond differentially to speed of rotation of the test chamber.

Habituation to rotation.—Habituation to rotation has been studied in animals and man for nearly 50 years (100, 166), and current studies continue to be concerned with the topic. Many recent studies involve work on rotating platforms with the limitations noted above. The primary problems of interest to the investigators have been: physiological changes including motion sickness during rotation, psychological changes in performance, maximum rotation velocity during which habituation is possible, and postrotational effects. All of these studies show initial subjective effects followed by some habituation. Studies have been made showing habituation of physiological effects (47, 62, 64, 75, 88), walking (20, 75, 128, 129), reaching movements (127, 132), oculogyral illusion (88), and various other measures (21, 88). On the other hand, certain types of effects do not appear to show very significant changes during prolonged periods of rotation. In general, balancing and walking with eyes closed habituate relatively little (20, 129), and certain types of head movements cause less difficulty than others (127). Aftereffects of rotation occur (75, 88, 92, 127) and may last for 48 hours, but prolonged, incapacitating aftereffects have not been reported.

Early studies suggested that habituation to constant velocities greater than about 4 rpm would be difficult (88, 92), but more recent studies in the United States and abroad have shown that well-motivated observers can habituate at velocities of 6 or 7 rpm (20, 21, 77, 127–129). It would appear, however, that for velocities above 10 rpm, habituation is dependent upon countermeasures such as the use of drugs and restriction of head movements. More rapid habituation has been found in pilots than in nonpilots (64), and habituation is facilitated by gradually increasing the velocity of rotation in prearranged steps (47). These studies and various others have suggested that the use of Coriolis stimulation may have some value in training (62, 81, 128, 132) as well as in selection of pilots (2, 3, 77).

LITERATURE CITED

1. Alyakrinskiy, B. S., Stepanova, S. I. The mechanisms of spatial orientation in flight and certain causes of its disruption. *Space Biol. Med.*, **2**, 91–98 (1968)
2. Ambler, R. K., Guedry, F. E., Jr. Validity of a brief vestibular disorientation test in screening pilot trainees. *Aerospace Med.*, **37**, 124–26 (1966)
3. Ambler, R. K., Guedry, F. E., Jr. Cross-validation of a brief vestibular disorientation test administered by a variety of personnel. *Ibid.*, **39**, 603–5 (1968)
4. Anderson, T. I. Correlations of auditory and visual autokinetic effects. *Percept. Mot. Skills*, **20**, 697–707 (1965)
5. Apanasenko, Z. E. Effect of the space-flight factors on the functional state of the vestibular analyzer. Review of literature. In *Nekotorye Voprosy Kosmicheskog Neyrofiziologii* (*Certain problems of Space Neurophysiology*) (Nauka Press, Moscow, 1967, NASA. Technical Translation: NASA TT-II, 503, 1968)
6. Aschan, G. Habituation to repeated rotatory stimuli (cupulometry) and the effect of antinausea drugs and alcohol on the results. *Acta Otolaryng.*, **64**, 95–106 (1967)
7. Attneave, F., Olson, R. K. Discriminability of stimuli varying in physical and retinal orientation. *J. Exptl. Psychol.*, **74**, 149–57 (1967)
8. Bauermeister, M., Wapner, S., Werner, H. Method of stimulus presentation and apparent body position under lateral body tilt. *Percept. Mot. Skills*, **24**, 43–50 (1967)
9. Benson, A. J. Spatial disorientation in flight. In *A Textbook of Aviation Physiology*, 1086–1129 (Gillies, J. A., Ed., Pergamon Press, New York, 1226 pp., 1965)

10. Benson, A. J., Bodin, M. A. Interaction of linear and angular accelerations on vestibular receptors in man. *Aerospace Med.*, **37**, 144–54 (1966)
11. Benson, A. J., Bodin, M. A. Comparison of the effect of the direction of the gravitational acceleration on post-rotational responses in yaw, pitch, and roll. *Ibid.*, 889–97
12. Benson, A. J., Brand, J. J. Some effects of l-hyoscine hydrobromide on post-rotatory sensation and nystagmus in man. *Quart. J. Exptl. Physiol.*, **53**, 296–311 (1968)
13. Benson, A. J., Goorney, A. B., Reason, J. T. The effect of instructions upon post-rotational sensations and nystagmus. *Acta Otolaryng.*, **62**, 442–52 (1966)
14. Benson, A. J., Guedry, F. E., Jones, G. M. Response of lateral semicircular canal units in brain stem to a rotating linear acceleration vector. *J. Physiol. (London)*, **191**, 26p–27p (1967)
15. Benson, A. J., Stuart, H. F. A trace reader for the direct measurement of the slope of graphical records. *Proc. Physiol. Soc.*, **189**, 1–2p (1966)
16. Bergman, F., Costin, A., Chaimovitz, M., Gutman, J., Zelig, S. Asymmetric inhibitory effect of light on labyrinthine nystagmus in the rabbit. *Confin. Neurol.*, **25**, 413–23 (1965)
17. Billingham, J. Russian experience of problems in vestibular physiology related to the space environment. In *Second Symposium on the Role of the Vestibular Organs in Space Exploration*, NASA SP-115, 5–13 (Graybiel, A., Ed., U.S. Govt. Printing Office, Washington, D.C., 312 pp., 1966)
18. Boring, E. G. *Sensation and Perception in the History of Experimental Psychology* (Appleton-Century, New York, 644 pp., 1942)
19. Boyd, J. Comparison of motor behavior in deaf and hearing boys. *Am. Ann. Deaf*, **112**, 598–605 (1967)
20. Brady, J. F., Goble, G. J., Newsom, B. D. Equilibrium and walking changes observed at 5, 7½, 10 and 12 RPM in the revolving space station simulator. *Aerospace Med.*, **36**, 322–26 (1965)
21. Brady, J. F., Newsom, B. D. Large excursion rotary tracking of target and target light in a space station simulator revolving at 7.5, 10.0 and 12.0 RPM. *Aerospace Med.*, **36**, 332–43 (1965)
22. Brand, J. J., Perry, W. L. M. Drugs used in motion sickness. *Pharmacol. Rev.*, **18**, 895–924 (1966)
23. Brandt, U., Fluur, E. Postural perceptions and compensatory displacements of the eye in respect to a presented force field. Synchronous three-orthogonal registrations. *Acta Oto-laryng.*, **62**, 252–64 (1966)
24. Brandt, U., Fluur, E. Postural perceptions and eye displacements produced by a resultant vector acting in the medial sagittal plane of the head. I. Responses along three axes by stepwise increasing phi with the subject heading centripetally in an erect and tilted position. *Ibid.*, **63**, 489–502 (1967)
25. Brandt, U., Fluur, E. Postural perceptions and eye displacements produced by a resultant vector acting in the median sagittal plane of the head: II. Continuous responses along the Y axis with the subject in a vertical position, heading centripetally and centrifugally. *Ibid.*, 564–78
26. Brown, J. H. Acquisition and retention of nystagmic habituation in cats with distributed acceleration experience. *J. Comp. Physiol. Psychol.*, **60**, 340–43 (1965)
27. Brown, J. H. Interacting vestibular stimuli and nystagmic habituation. *Acta Otolaryng.*, **62**, 341–50 (1966)
28. Brown, J. H. Modification of vestibular nystagmus by change of task during stimulation. *Percept. Mot. Skills*, **22**, 603–11 (1966)
29. Brown, J. H. Magnitude estimation of angular velocity during passive rotation. *J. Exptl. Psychol.*, **72**, 169–72 (1966)
30. Brown, J. H. Cross-modal estimation of angular velocity. *Percept. Psychophys.*, **3**, 115–17 (1968)
31. Brown, J. H., Crampton, G. H. Concomitant visual stimulation does not alter habituation of nystagmic, oculogyral or psychophysical responses to angular acceleration. *Acta Oto-laryng.*, **61**, 80–91 (1966)
32. Brown, J. H., Marshall, J. E. Drug control of arousal and nystagmic

habituation in the cat. *Acta Oto-laryng.*, **64**, 345–52 (1967)

33. Brown, J. H., Marshall, J. E. Visual-arousal interaction and specificity of nystagmic habituation. *Aerospace Med.*, **38**, 597–99 (1967)
34. Burg, A. Visual acuity as measured by dynamic and static tests. *J. Appl. Psychol.*, **50**, 460–66 (1966)
35. Cappel, K. L. Determination of physical constants of the semicircular canals from the measurement of single neural unit activity under constant angular acceleration. In *Second Symposium on the Role of the Vestibular Organs in Space Exploration*, 229–36 (See Ref. 17)
36. Capps, M. J., Collins, W. E. Effects of bilateral caloric habituation on vestibular nystagmus in the cat. *Acta Oto-laryng.*, **59**, 511–30 (1965)
37. Chappell, H. R., Jones, Q. W., Ogden, F. W. Disorientation experiences of army helicopter pilots. *Aerospace Med.*, **37**, 140–43 (1966)
38. Clark, B. Thresholds for the perception of angular acceleration in man. *Aerospace Med.*, **38**, 443–50 (1967)
39. Clark, B., Graybiel, A. Factors contributing to the delay in the perception of the oculogravic illusion. *Am. J. Psychol.*, **79**, 377–88 (1966)
40. Clark, B., Graybiel, A. Perception of the visual horizontal in normal and labyrinthine defective subjects during prolonged rotation. *Ibid.*, 608–12
41. Clark, B., Graybiel, A. Egocentric localization of the visual horizontal in normal and labyrinthine-defective observers as a function of head and body tilt. *Percept. Psychophys.*, **2**, 609–11 (1967)
42. Clark, B., Graybiel, A. Influence of contact cues on the perception of the oculogravic illusion. *Acta Oto-laryng.*, **65**, 373–80 (1968)
43. Clark, B., Stewart, J. D. Vestibular and non-vestibular information in judgments of attitude and Coriolis motion in a piloted flight simulator. *Aerospace Med.*, **38**, 936–40 (1967)
44. Clark, B., Stewart, J. D. Comparison of sensitivity for the perception of bodily rotation and the oculogyral illusion. *Percept. Psychophys.*, **3**, 253–56 (1968)
45. Clark, B., Stewart, J. D. Comparison of three methods to determine thresholds for perception of angular acceleration. *Am. J. Psychol.*, **81**, 207–16 (1968)
46. Cohen, B., Tokumasu, K., Goto, K. Semicircular canal nerve eye and head movements. *Arch. Ophthalmol.*, **76**, 523–31 (1966)
47. Colehour, J. K., Graybiel, A. Biochemical changes occurring with adaptation to accelerative forces during rotation. *Aerospace Med.*, **37**, 1205–7 (1966)
48. Collins, W. E. Subjective responses and nystagmus following repeated unilateral caloric stimulation. *Ann. Otol. Rhinol. Laryng.*, **74**, 1034–54 (1965)
49. Collins, W. E. Vestibular responses from figure skaters. *Aerospace Med.*, **37**, 1098–1104 (1966)
50. Collins, W. E. Effects on vestibular habituation of interrupting nystagmic responses with opposing stimuli. *J. Comp. Physiol. Psychol.*, **64**, 308–12 (1967)
51. Collins, W. E. Coriolis vestibular stimulation and the influence of different visual surrounds. *Aerospace Med.*, **39**, 125–30 (1968)
52. Collins, W. E. Special effects of brief periods of visual fixation on nystagmus and sensations of turning. *Ibid.*, 257–66
53. Collins, W. E., Guedry, F. E., Jr. Duration of angular acceleration and ocular nystagmus from cat and man. I. Responses from the lateral and the vertical canals to two stimulus durations. *Acta Oto-laryng.*, **64**, 373–87 (1967)
54. Collins, W. E., Updegraff, B. P. A comparison of nystagmus habituation in the cat and dog. *Acta Oto-laryng.*, **62**, 19–26 (1966)
55. Correia, M. J., Guedry, F. E., Jr. Modification of vestibular response as a function of rate of rotation about an earth-horizontal axis. *Acta Oto-laryng.*, **62**, 297–308 (1967)
56. Correia, M. J., Hixson, W. C., Niven, J. I. On predictive equations for subjective judgments of vertical and horizon in a force field. *Acta Oto-laryng.* Suppl. 230, 1–20 (1968)
57. Cramer, R. L. Subjective responses to oscillation in yaw. *Aerospace Med.*, **38**, 457–58 (1967)

58. Day, R. H., Wade, N. J. Visual spatial aftereffect from prolonged head-tilt. *Science,* **154,** 1201–2 (1966)
59. De Francesco, E. Sull' adattamento vastibolare nei piloti di aviogetto. *Riv. Med. Aero.,* **29,** 333–60 (1966)
60. Dittrich, F. L., Wilmot, T. J. Threshold testing of vestibular function. *J. Laryng.,* **79,** 888–92 (1965)
61. Doty, R. L. *The Effect of Duration of Stimulus Presentation upon the Angular Acceleration Threshold of Man* (Master's thesis, San Jose State College, San Jose, Calif., 1968)
62. Dowd, P. J. Factors affecting vestibular nystagmus in Coriolis stimulation. *Acta Oto-laryng.,* **61,** 228–36 (1966)
63. Dowd, P. J., Cramer, R. L. Habituation transference in Coriolis acceleration. *Aerospace Med.,* **38,** 1103–7 (1967)
64. Dowd, P. J., Moore, E. W., Cramer, R. L. Effects of flying experience on the vestibular system: A comparison between pilots and nonpilots to Coriolis stimulation. *Aerospace Med.,* **37,** 45–47 (1966)
65. Eskin, A., Riccio, D. C. The effects of vestibular stimulation on spontaneous activity in the rat. *Psychol. Rec.,* **16,** 523–27 (1966)
66. Fernandez, C., Valentinuzzi, M. Nystagmic Coriolis reaction in the cat. I. Preliminary report. *Acta Oto-laryng.,* **65,** 186–99 (1968)
67. Fernandez, C., Valentinuzzi, M. A study of the biophysical characteristics of the cat labyrinth. *Ibid.,* 293–310
68. Fluur, E., Mendel, L. Relation between strength of stimulus and duration of latency time in vestibular rotary nystagmus. *Acta Oto-laryng.,* **61,** 463–74 (1966)
69. Fluur, E., Mendel, L., Lagerstrom, L. Reproducibility of duration of latency time in unidirectional perrotatory nystagmus. *Acta Oto-laryng.,* **62,** 118–25 (1966)
70. Fluur, E., Mendel, L., Lagerstrom, L. Latency time of vestibular nystagmus in repeated bidirectional rotatory stimulation. *Ibid.,* **64,** 125–35 (1967)
71. Fredrickson, J. M. Vestibular nerve projection to the cerebral cortex of the rhesus monkey. *Exptl. Brain Res.,* **2,** 318–27 (1966)
72. Fredrickson, J. M., Schuwary, D., Kornhuber, H. H. Convergence and interaction of vestibular and deep somatic afferents upon neurons in the vestibular nuclei of the cat. *Acta Oto-Laryng.,* **61,** 168–88 (1966)
73. Freedman, S. J. *The Neuropsychology of Spatially Oriented Behavior* (Dorsey Press, Homewood, Illinois, 290 pp., 1968)
74. Fregly, A. R., Graybiel, A. An ataxia test battery not requiring rails. *Aerospace Med.,* **39,** 277–82 (1968)
75. Fregly, A. R., Kennedy, R. S. Comparative effects of prolonged rotation at 10 RPM on postural equilibrium in vestibular normal and vestibular defective human subjects. *Aerospace Med.,* **36,** 1160–67 (1965)
76. Fregly, A. R., Oberman, A., Graybiel, A., Mitchell, R. E. Thousand aviator study: Nonvestibular contributions to postural equilibrium functions. *Aerospace Med.,* **39,** 33–37 (1968)
77. Galle, R. R., Emel'ianov, M. D. Results of physiological studies performed in a slow rotation chamber. *Space Biol. Med.,* **1,** 108–18 (1967)
78. Gernandt, B. E. Vestibular mechanisms. In *Handbook of Physiology, Vol. I, Section 1, Neurophysiology,* 549–64 (Field, J., Magoun, H. W., Hall, V. E., Eds., Am. Physiol. Soc., Washington, D.C., 779 pp., 1959)
79. Gescheider, G. A., Wright, J. H. Effects of body position on judgment of the postural vertical. *Percept. Mot. Skills,* **21,** 783–86 (1965)
80. Gibson, J. J. *The Senses Considered as Perceptual Systems* (Houghton Mifflin, Boston, 335 pp., 1966)
81. Gillingham, K. Training the vestibule for aerospace operations using Coriolis effect to assess rotation. *Aerospace Med.,* **37,** 47–51 (1966)
82. Graybiel, A., Ed. *The Role of the Vestibular Organs in the Exploration of Space,* NASA SP-77 (U.S. Govt. Printing Office, Washington, D.C., 391 pp., 1965)

83. Graybiel, A., Ed. *Second Symposium on the Role of the Vestibular Organs in Space Exploration* (See Ref. 17)
84. Graybiel, A., Ed. *Third Symposium on the Role of the Vestibular Organs in Space Exploration* NASA SP-152 (U.S. Govt. Printing Office, Washington, D.C., 437 pp., 1968)
85. Graybiel, A., Clark, B. The validity of the oculogravic illusion as a specific indicator of otolith function. *Aerospace Med.*, **36**, 1173–81 (1965)
86. Graybiel, A., Fregly, A. R. A new quantitative ataxia test battery. *Acta Oto-laryng.*, **61**, 292–312 (1966)
87. Graybiel, A., Kellogg, R. S. The inversion illusion in parabolic flight: Its probable dependence on otolith function. *Aerospace Med.*, **38**, 1099–1102 (1967)
88. Graybiel, A., Kennedy, R. S., Knoblock, E. C., Guedry, F. E., Jr., Mertz, W., McLeod, M. E., Colehour, J. K., Miller, E. F., II, Fregly, A. R. The effects of exposure to a rotating environment (10 rpm) on four aviators for a period of twelve days. *Aerospace Med.*, **36**, 733–54 (1965)
89. Graybiel, A., Miller, E. F., II, Billingham, J., Waite, R., Berry, C. A., Dietlein, L. F. Vestibular experiments in Gemini flights V and VII. *Aerospace Med.*, **38**, 360–70 (1967)
90. Graybiel, A., Miller, E. F., II, Newsom, B. D., Kennedy, R. S. The effect of water immersion on perception of the oculogravic illusion in normal and labyrinthine-defective subjects. *Acta Otolaryng.*, **65**, 599–610 (1968)
91. Grose, V. L. Deleterious effect on astronaut capability of vestibulo-ocular disturbance during spacecraft roll acceleration. *Aerospace Med.*, **38**, 1138–44 (1967)
92. Guedry, F. E., Jr. Psychophysiological studies of vestibular function. In *Contributions to Sensory Physiology,* 63–135 (Neff, W. D., Ed., Academic Press, New York, 274 pp., 1965)
93. Guedry, F. E., Jr. Habituation to complex visual stimulation in man: Transfer and retention of effects from twelve days of rotation at 10 RPM. *Percept. Mot. Skills,* **21**, 459–81 (1965)
94. Guedry, F. E., Jr. Some vestibular problems related to orientation in space. *Acta Oto-laryng.*, **65**, 174–85 (1968)
95. Guedry, F. E., Jr. Relations between vestibular nystagmus and visual performance. *Aerospace Med.*, **39**, 570–79 (1968)
96. Guedry, F. E., Jr., Collins, W. E. Duration of angular acceleration and ocular nystagmus from cat and man. II. Responses from the lateral canals to varied stimulus durations. *Acta Oto-laryng.*, **65**, 257–69 (1968)
97. Haas, E., Eidebenz, H. Untersuchungen zur tageszeitlich bedingten Variabilität der Dredreigschwelle. *Z. Laryng. Rhinol. Otol.*, **46**, 96–100 (1967)
98. Herberts, G., Abrahamsson, S., Einarsson, S., Hoffmann, H., Linder, H. Computer analysis of electronystagmographic data. *Acta Oto-laryng.*, **65**, 200–8 (1968)
99. Hixson, W. C., Niven, J. E., Correia, M. *Kinematics nomenclature for physiological accelerations. Monogr. 14, U.S. Aerospace Med. Inst.*, Pensacola, Fla., 81 pp. (1966)
100. Howard, I. P., Templeton, W. B. *Human Spatial Orientation* (Wiley, New York, 533 pp., 1966)
101. Igarashi, M., McLeod, M. E., Graybiel, A. Clinical pathological correlations in squirrel monkeys after suppression of semicircular canal function by streptomycin sulfate. *Acta Oto-laryng.* Suppl. 214, 1–28 (1966)
102. Jackson, M. M., Sears, C. W. Effect of weightlessness upon the normal nystagmic reaction. *Aerospace Med.*, **37**, 719–21 (1966)
103. Janeke, J. B., Jongkees, L. B. Barbecue rotation in combination with sinusoidal rotation about a vertical axis. *Acta Oto-laryng.*, **65**, 244–50 (1968)
104. Johnson, W. H., Smith, J. B., Sullivan, J. A. Assessment of vestibular sensitivity. *Ann. Otol. Rhinol. Laryng.*, **76**, 709–15 (1967)
105. Jones, G. M. Vestibulo-ocular disorganization in the aerodynamic spin. *Aerospace Med.*, **36**, 976–83 (1965)

106. Jones, G. M. Disturbance of oculomotor control in flight. *Ibid.*, 461–65

107. Jones, G. M. Interactions between optokinetic and vestibulo-ocular responses during head rotation in various planes. *Ibid.*, **37**, 172–77 (1966)

108. Kellogg, R. S., Graybiel, A. Lack of response to thermal stimulation of the semicircular canals in the weightless phase of parabolic flight. *Aerospace Med.*, **38**, 487–90 (1967)

109. Kitahara, M., Uno, R. Equilibrium and vertigo in a tilting environment. *Ann. Otol. Rhinol. Laryng.*, **76**, 166–78 (1967)

110. Lansberg, M. P., Guedry, F. E., Jr., Graybiel, A. Effect of changing resultant linear acceleration relative to the subject on nystagmus generated by angular acceleration. *Aerospace Med.*, **36**, 456–60 (1965)

111. Lebedev, V. I., Chekirda, I. F. Role of the vestibular analyzer in man's spatial orientation during weightlessness in aircraft flights. *Space Biol. Med.*, **2**, 112–16 (1968)

112. Lundgren, E. G., Malm, L. U. Alternobaric vertigo among pilots. *Aerospace Med.*, **37**, 178–80 (1966)

113. Lyons, J., Thomas, D. R. Influence of postural distortion on the perception of the visual vertical in pigeons. *J. Exptl. Psychol.*, **76**, 120–24 (1968)

114. McFarland, J. H., Clarkson, F. Perception of orientation: adaptation to lateral body tilt. *Am. J. Psychol.*, **79**, 265–71 (1966)

115. Markaryan, S. S., Matveyev, A. A., Pavlov, I. V. Universal vestibulometric seat UVS. *Space Biol. Med.*, **1**, 131–35 (1967)

116. Marshall, J. E., Brown, J. H. Visual-arousal interaction and specificity of nystagmic habituation. *Aerospace Med.*, **38**, 597–99 (1967)

117. Mertens, R. A., Collins, W. E. Unilateral caloric habituation of nystagmus in the cat: Effects of rotational and bilateral caloric responses. *Acta Oto-laryng.*, **64**, 781–97 (1967)

118. Miller, E. F., Jr., Fregly, A. R., Graybiel, A. *Visual horizontal perception in relation to otolith function, NAMI-989* (*Naval Aerospace Med. Inst.*, Pensacola, Fla., 1966)

119. Miller, E. F., Jr., Graybiel, A. Role of the otolith organs in the perception of horizontality. *Am. J. Psychol.*, **79**, 24–37 (1966)

120. Miller, E. F., Jr., Graybiel, A. Magnitude of gravitoinertial force, an independent variable in egocentric visual localization of the horizontal. *J. Exptl. Psychol.*, **71**, 452–60 (1966)

121. Miller, E. F., Jr., Graybiel, A. Effect of drugs on ocular counterrolling. In *Third Symposium on the Role of the Vestibular Organs in Space Exploration*, 341–49 (See Ref. 84)

122. Miller, E. F., Jr., Graybiel, A., Kellogg, R. S. Otolith organ activity within earth standard, one-half standard, and zero gravity environments. *Aerospace Med.*, **37**, 399–403 (1966)

123. Mishkin, S., Jones, G. M. Predominant direction of gaze during slow head rotation. *Aerospace Med.*, **37**, 897–900 (1966)

124. Money, K. E., Johnson, W. H., Corlett, B. M. Role of semicircular canals in positional alcohol nystagmus. *Am. J. Physiol.*, **208**, 1065–70 (1965)

125. Mygind, S. H. Physiological interpretation of the anatomy of the labyrinth. *Acta Oto-laryng.*, **59**, 264–74 (1965)

126. Nelson, J. G. Effect of water immersion and body position upon perception of the gravitational vertical. *Aerospace Med.*, **39**, 806–11 (1968)

127. Newsom, B. D., Brady, J. F. A comparison of performances involving head rotations about y and z cranial axes in a revolving space station simulator. *Aerospace Med.*, **37**, 1152–57 (1966)

128. Newsom, B. D., Brady, J. F., Goble, G. J. Equilibrium and walking changes observed at 5, 7½, 10 and 12 rpm in the revolving space station simulator. *Aerospace Med.*, **36**, 322–26 (1965)

129. Newsom, B. D., Brady, J. F., Shafer, W. A., French, R. S. Adaptation to prolonged exposures in the revolving space station simulator. *Aerospace Med.*, **37**, 778–83 (1966)

130. Nilsson, A., Henriksson, N. G. The oculogyral illusion—a form of rotation aftereffect—and its relation to the spiral aftereffect in repeated

trials. *Psychol. Res. Bull.*, **7,** 1–17 (1967)
131. Niven, J. I., Hixson, W. C., Correia, M. J. Ellicitation of horizontal nystagmus by periodic linear acceleration. *Acta Oto-laryng.*, **62,** 429–41 (1967)
132. O'Laughlin, T. W., Brady, J. F., Newsom, B. D. Reach effectiveness in a rotating environment. *Aerospace Med.*, **39,** 505–8 (1968)
133. Parker, D. E., Schöne, H. Inversion of the effect of increased gravity on the subjective vertical. *Naturwissenschaften*, **54,** 288–89 (1967)
134. Parsons, R. D. *Magnitude Estimates of the Oculogyral Illusion During and Following Angular Acceleration* (Master's thesis, San Jose State College, San Jose, Calif., 1968)
135. Pfaltz, C. R., Arx, S. von. Zur Wirkung wiederholter thermischer und rotatorischer Reize auf das normale vestibuläre Endorgan. *Acta Oto-laryng.*, **63,** 191–207 (1967)
136. Reason, J. T., Benson, A. J. Individual differences in the reported persistence of visual and labyrinthine after-sensations, and of exponentially decaying visual and auditory signals. *Brit. J. Psychol.*, **59,** 167–72 (1968)
137. Riccio, D. C., Igarashi, M., Eskin, A. Modification of vestibular sensitivity in the rat. *Ann. Otol. Rhinol. Laryng.*, **76,** 179–88 (1967)
138. Riccio, D. C., Thach, J. S. Rotation as an aversive stimulus for rats. *Psychon. Sci.*, **5,** 267–68 (1966)
139. Riccio, D. C., Thach, J. S. Response suppression produced by vestibular stimulation in the rat. *J. Exptl. Anal. Behav.*, **11,** 479–88 (1968)
140. Riccio, D. C., Urda, M., Thomas, D. R. Stimulus control in pigeons based on proprioceptive stimuli from floor inclination. *Science*, **153,** 434–35 (1966)
141. Roberts, T. D. M. *Neurophysiology of Postural Mechanisms* (Plenum, New York, 354 pp., 1967)
142. Sala, O. Some remarks on the vestibular efferent system. In *Structure and Function of Inhibitory Neuronal Mechanisms*, 169–79 (Euler, C. von, Skoglund, S., Söderberg, U., Eds., Pergamon, New York, 563 pp., 1968)
143. Schöne, H., de Haes, H. U. Perception of gravity-vertical as a function of head and trunk position. *Z. Vergleich. Physiol.*, **60,** 440–44 (1968)
144. Schöne, H., Mortag, H. G. Variation of the subjective vertical on the parallel swing at different body positions. *Psychol. Forsch.*, **32,** 124–34 (1968)
145. Schöne, H., Parker, D. E. Inversion of the effect of increased gravity on the subjective vertical. *Naturwissenschaften*, **54,** 288–89 (1967)
146. Schöne, H., Parker, D. E., Mortag, H. G. Subjective vertical as a function of body position and gravity magnitude. *Naturwissenschaften*, **54,** 288 (1967)
147. Sherrick, C. E. Somesthetic senses. *Ann. Rev. Psychol.*, **17,** 309–36 (1966)
148. Silverstein, H. Induced rotational nystagmus in normal infants. *J. Pediat.*, **67,** 432–37 (1965)
149. Spector, M., Ed. *Dizziness and Vertigo* (Grune & Stratton, New York, 299 pp., 1967)
150. Stone, R. W., Jr., Letko, W., Hook, W. R. Examination of a possible flight experiment to evaluate an onboard centrifuge as a therapeutic device. In *Second Symposium on the Role of the Vestibular Organs in Space Exploration*, 245–56 (See Ref. 17)
151. Thach, J. S., Graybiel, A. Behavioral responses of unrestrained normal and labyrinthectomized squirrel monkeys to repeated zero-gravity parabolic flights. *Aerospace Med.*, **39,** 734–38 (1968)
152. Thomas, D. R., Lyons, J. The interaction between sensory and tonic factors in the perception of the vertical in pigeons. *Percept. Psychophys.*, **1,** 93–95 (1966)
153. Thomas, D. R., Lyons, J. Visual field dependency in pigeons. *Anim. Behav.*, **16,** 213–18 (1968)
154. Thomas, D. R., Lyons, J., Freeman, F. The interaction between sensory and tonic factors in the perception of the vertical in pigeons: II. A replication via an alternative procedure. *Psychon. Sci.*, **4,** 395–96 (1966)
155. Tibbling, L., Henriksson, N. G. Effect of cigarette smoking on the vestibular nystagmus pattern. *Acta Oto-laryng.*, **65,** 518–26 (1968)

156. Torok, N. Nystagmus parameters of various rotatory stimuli. *Acta Oto-laryng.*, **62**, 109–17 (1966)
157. Valentinuzzi, M. An analysis of the mechanical forces in each semicircular canal of the cat under single and combined rotations. *Bull. Math. Biophys.*, **29**, 267–89 (1967)
158. Veenhof, V. B. On the influence of linear acceleration on optokinetic nystagmus. *Acta Oto-laryng.*, **60**, 339–46 (1965)
159. Voronin, G. V. Effect of an electrical stimulus on reaction of the human vestibular apparatus caused by acceleration. *Space Biol. Med.*, **1**, 142–52 (1967)
160. Wade, N. J. Visual orientation during and after lateral head, body, and trunk tilt. *Percept. Psychophys.*, **3**, 215–19 (1968)
161. Wade, N. J., Day, R. H. Tilt and centrifugation in changing the direction of body-force. *Am. J. Psychol.*, **80**, 637–39 (1967)
162. Wade, N. J., Day, R. H. Apparent head position as a basis for a visual after-effect of prolonged head tilt. *Percept. Psychophys.*, **3**, 324–26 (1968)
163. Wade, N. J., Day, R. H. Development and dissipation of a visual spatial after-effect from prolonged head tilt. *J. Exptl. Psychol.*, **76**, 439–43 (1968)
164. Weaver, R. S. Theoretical aspects of the role of angular acceleration in vestibular stimulation. *Acta Oto-laryng.*, Suppl. 205, 5–36 (1965)
165. Weissman, N. W. Response differentiation in slow rotation. In *Third Symposium on the Role of the Vestibular Organs in Space Exploration*, 59–62 (See Ref. 84)
166. Wendt, G. R. Vestibular functions. In *Handbook of Experimental Psychology*, 1191–1223 (Stevens, S. S., Ed., Wiley, New York, 1436 pp., 1951)
167. Wendt, G. R. Man in motion. In *Handbook of Physiology, section 4: Adaptation to the environment*, 999–1005 (Dill, D. B., Adolph, E. F., Wilber, C. G., Eds., Am. Physiol. Soc., Washington, D.C., 1056 pp., 1964)
168. Wersäll, J. Efferent innervation of the inner ear. In *Structure and Function of Inhibitory Neuronal Mechanisms*, 123–29 (See Ref. 142)
169. Wersäll, J., Flock, A. Functional anatomy of the vestibular and lateral line organs. In *Contributions to Sensory Physiology*, 39–61 (See Ref. 92)
170. Whiteside, T. C., Graybiel, A., Niven, J. I. Visual illusions of movement. *Brain*, **88**, 193–210 (1965)
171. Wolfe, J. W. Evidence for control of nystagmic habituation by folium-tuber vermis and fastigial nuclei. *Acta Oto-laryng.*, Suppl. 231, 1–48 (1968)
172. Wood, E. D., Graybiel, A., Kennedy, R. S. A comparison of effectiveness of some antimotion sickness drugs using recommended and larger than recommended doses as tested in the slow rotation room. *Aerospace Med.*, **37**, 259–62 (1966)
173. Young, L. R. Some effects of motion cues on manual tracking. *J. Spacecraft Rockets*, **4**, 1300–3 (1967)
174. Young, L. R., Meiry, J. L. A revised dynamic otolith model. *Aerospace Med.*, **39**, 606–8 (1968)
175. Yuganov, E. M., Gorschkov, A. I., Kasyan, I. I., Bryanov, I. I., Kolosov, I. A., Kopanev, V. I., Lebedev, V. I., Popov, N. I., Solodovnik, F. A. Vestibular reactions of cosmonauts during the flight in the "Voskhod" spaceship. *Aerospace Med.*, **37**, 691–94 (1966)

VISUAL SENSITIVITY

152

By Howard D. Baker and Barbara N. Baker

Department of Psychology and Institute of Molecular Biophysics
Florida State University, Tallahassee

General

Trends.—The period of time to be considered in this review includes the years 1966 through 1968. During this time there has been a shift in the techniques of research on visual sensitivity, toward less emphasis on purely psychophysical methods and toward more emphasis on biochemical techniques, while electrical methods have continued to be popular. There has been some change in theoretical emphasis as well. Photochemical theorizing has shown some resurgence, and is universally used to account for spectral luminosity. The neural nature of the eye remains the favored source for general sensitivity theory, however.

Nobel Prize.—The Nobel Prize for 1967 in medicine and physiology was given for work in vision, and was shared by H. K. Hartline, R. Granit, and G. Wald. Professor Wald has published his Nobel Prize lecture in the regular literature (164) and it is well worth the reading. He is selective in the research work he mentions, but he does recount the sources and highlights of his early important photochemical findings. Of special interest is his careful documentation of the places and persons that were important for the direction of his research. Wald stresses his recent efforts on color vision and color blindness more than one might expect, perhaps. The entire story is told with the grace and sense of conviction his readers have come to expect.

Textbook.—Probably the most significant visual text to appear in the review period is the translation of LeGrand's book entitled *Form and Space Vision* (116). It continues his earlier textbook on *Light, Colour and Vision* that was published in English in 1957. The new book contains so much material on visual adaptation and sensitivity that it must be included in this review. It is written with splendid competence and clarity, and is admirably complete on English and American research as well as European.

Adaptation

Mechanisms of adaptation.—The mechanism of light and dark adaptation continues to be a major concern. Dowling and his colleagues (70, 169) have emphasized the nonphotochemical machinery of rod dark adaptation. Using rat retinas, and comparing the rhodopsin regeneration in the dark with the electroretinogram (ERG) as a measure of sensitivity, they conclude that equilibrium sensitivity is largely unrelated to photochemical balance, but rather reflects neural feedback characteristics of the retina, as does the early part of dark adaptation. Photochemical regeneration supplies only the terminal improvement in dark adaptation curves. Dowling's theories are largely based on observations of synaptic associations in the retina by electron microscopy. Gouras disputes Dowling's conclusions because of his opinion that cones must be involved at the high intensities, but Dowling discounts the significance of cones in the rat retina (93).

Also from Dowling (68) is an attractive and clear review of the relationships between vitamin-A deficiencies and the loss of visual sensitivity; again, his criterion for visual sensitivity is the ERG. He has also considered the synaptic organization of the frog retina and compared it to that of some mammals, especially primates (71). The frog amacrine cell connections show greater complexity, and appear to carry functions associated in mammals with areas higher than the retina.

More recently, Frank & Dowling (86) have argued that scotopic visual sensitivity is not influenced by the presence of rhodopsin photoproducts after a bleach, because the b-wave of the ERG does not change during photoproduct dissipation in the dark. That would run counter to some older theories of dark adaptation, as well as questioning the conclusions of Donner and Reuter, below.

Reuter (144) and Donner & Reuter (66, 67) studied ganglion cell activity in the excised frog's eye under scotopic conditions and concluded that there are three distinguishable factors which separately influence dark adaptation: the intensity of any background light that may be present; the rate, per se, of regeneration of rhodopsin; and the amount of metarhodopsin II that remains. These factors were originally devised to account for rates of dark adaptation under conditions which alter the accumulation of rhodopsin and decomposition of metarhodopsin II in the dark, and they are supported by extensive calculations of quantum efficiencies, absorptions, and molecular changes. They end with an equation to describe the general behavior of the threshold which, surprisingly, omits rhodopsin concentration as a variable. It must be said that several assumed or selected quantities enter the calculations, and future experiments will have to show whether the theory will prove to be a pivotal contribution or a house of cards.

Baumann & Scheibner (14) present a rather different view of the importance of photochemistry in dark adaptation. Monitoring the activity of single units of the isolated frog retina, they observe that if less than 35 to 40 per cent of the pigment is bleached, duplex dark adaptation curves appear, and the subsequent luminosity curve of the unit is a typical rhodopsin curve. On the other hand, if more than that amount of pigment is bleached, then the dark adaptation curve is simplex, and the luminosity function turns out to be very narrow, rather like Granit's modulator curves. The result suggests that photochemical processes are dominant in setting the sensitivity level of the retina.

Easter's study of the electrical responses of the goldfish retina has been aimed largely at specifying the interrelations between adaptation variables and the effectiveness of light intensity in exciting spike activity in single ganglion cells of the retina (74–76). Perhaps his most interesting findings concern the disproportionately great additivity of stimulation on separate points within the receptive field of a unit (two equal but separate stimulations result in more than twice the effect), and the relative areas of the adaptation effects compared with summation effects due to stimulation (the adaptation area is much broader). Psychophysicists might also note his report that ". . . light intensity appears to be encoded as a power function of exponent less than one."

Brooks (32) has taken the approach of using gross electrodes implanted in the lateral geniculate to obtain electrical correlates of brightness discrimination. She finds that there is a general decrease in electrical activity with increase in adapting intensities; that brief test flashes yield a total on-off response, and that background lights depress the test-flash response.

Both slow potentials and spike potentials have been recorded from the honeybee drone eye, and F. Baumann (15) finds that they are similar to those of *Limulus* in appearance under conditions of both light and dark adaptation.

When the dark-adapted horseshoe crab eye is stimulated by very weak flashes of light, sharp discrete electrical pulses occur in the eye. These are thought to represent the response to single photons of light. Borsellino & Fuortes (26, 27) have applied stochastic ideas to the Hodgkin model of the *Limulus* eye, and report that they must include an amplification factor of 25 in the model to account for the behavior of the discrete pulses. This is a complex mathematical argument, and is one that the reviewer finds himself completely unable to judge.

Lateral effects in adaptation.—Alpern & Rushton (5) have devised a technique for measuring a kind of sensitivity of the eye that appears to be quite independent of the state of adaptation. The rod threshold for a test flash is raised by a surrounding flash to an amount which depends on the intensity of the contrast flash, but appears to be completely independent of the state of adaptation; the surround flash may even follow the test flash a bit in time and be fully effective. The efficacy of the contrast is itself reduced by light adaptation of its own area, however. Logic therefore demands that the new mechanism follow the adaptation site in the chain of visual information.

Stray light in the eye has always been a bane to experimenters and a convenient excuse for unexpected discrepancies in thresholds. Now Rushton & Gubisch (151) have developed a technique for determining the amount of stray light in an area of the eye. They show that stray light which bleaches the visual pigment to the same extent (measured by retinal densitometry) as does a uniform background will also yield the same dark adaptation curve as the background. So the effects of scattered light can be separated from those of lateral inhibition simply by observing the dark adaptation which follows exposure to stray light. A uniform background yielding the same adaptation curve will be exactly equal to the real stray light.

Related to the question of photoproducts and regeneration rates in dark adaptation is the question of the nature of "dark light," the hypothetical equivalent to a real adapting light that is assumed to be present during dark adaptation. Westheimer (172) has shown that the increase in the threshold of an area after bleaching (i.e., due to "dark light") does not inhibit the response to a real light in an adjacent area. There is no lateral inhibition from the bleached or "dark lit" area. Nor is the effectiveness of the supposed dark light in raising the threshold inhibited itself by surrounding lights, as is the case with real light. If "dark light" actually is a continuing signal from a bleached area, the signal is radically different from that due to real light.

The threshold is raised (or inhibited) by a surrounding adapting field, but as the surround becomes larger it becomes less efficient in raising the threshold. Apparently that is due to lateral inhibition of the field by itself, but it also could be due to changes in adaptation due to eye movements. Teller, Andrews & Barlow (159) show that the effect operates when the adapting field is presented as a stabilized image just as well (or better) than when presented normally. So light adaptation due to eye movements cannot be the basis of the effect.

Rods and cones in adaptation.—The rods and cones apparently share a common source of 11-*cis* retinal for regeneration of their visual pigment. From an ingenious series of experiments, Rushton (150) concludes that bleached cones will regenerate their pigment at the expense of the rods, because a delay occurs in the scotopic segment of the dark adaptation curve in cases when cones as well as rods have been bleached. His trick was to compare scotopic dark adaptation curves after bleaches by red and blue lights that were scotopic matches but had an unequal bleaching effect on the cones.

The three separate cone color mechanisms show the same independence in dark adaptation as Stiles found in his classical work on the difference threshold. DuCroz & Rushton (73) have demonstrated separate recovery processes for all three of the red, green, and blue mechanisms by bleaching with strong preadapting lights and by selecting appropriate wavelengths for bleaching and test lights.

When a white adapting field is first turned off, a rapid complex fluctuation of sensitivity occurs, and it has been proposed that this represents the interaction of the separate color mechanisms of the cones, each presumably having different time characteristics. Rinalducci (146) now has shown that the transient occurs with the same form in chromatic lights as in white lights, so the explanation is unlikely.

Biersdorf (22) has resolved the question of the rod basis of the ERG off effect by demonstrating that it has the luminosity and latency characteristics of rods at low intensity. Since K. Brown has related the off effect to the late receptor potential, Biersdorf's research seems to be directly related to that of Brown & Murakami, below.

It has been several years since the early and late receptor potentials were identified as discrete entities. Although most of the subsequent research has been aimed at the chemical and neural basis of the potentials (see the subsequent sections of this review), Brown & Murakami (43) have now identified a specific property of the late receptor potential which can be used to illuminate the old question of rod-cone interaction. The late receptor potential (LRP) decays at different rates for rods and cones when a stimulating light is cut off. The rod decay rate is slow, the cone decay rate is fast. After light adaptation the LRP is found to decay at a cone rate, and after dark adaptation, it decays at the rod rate. Brown & Murakami note that S-potentials follow the same rates, and suggest that they may represent the lateral inhibitory mechanism which inhibits the rod mechanism when the cones are dominant.

Gouras & Link (94) and Gouras (91, 92) have outlined some of the basics of rod-cone interaction from studies of ganglion cell activity in monkeys. They find that latency is completely determined by cones at high intensity and by rods at low intensities, with the result that the early-arriving cone signals cause refractoriness in the ganglion cells and interfere with excitation by the rods. Both rod and cone signals may go to the same ganglion cell in dark adaptation. In light adaptation only cone signals are transmitted. Gouras is unable to find any interaction at all in the b-wave of the electroretinogram.

A very useful and interesting article for anyone who requires a physical specification of photometric quantities, has come from Baumgardt & Scheibner (18). The authors establish the numerical relation between photopic and scotopic photometric systems, based on C.I.E. recommendations. They present in detail a method of driving the number of photons of 507 nm wavelength, per second per square degree of visual field, that correspond to one scotopic troland ($n = 4.47 \cdot 10^5$ quanta/sec/deg). They then generalize the procedure for any radiation distribution.

For the case of extreme luminances, Gaunt (87) has reviewed the physical possibilities inherent in floods of photons which saturate rods. His mathematical analysis of the results obtained by Rushton and by Aguilar and Stiles implies that the refractory period of the tissue is not prolonged by second hits.

Subjective relationships in dark adaptation.—The image in the eye of a grid pattern fades rapidly when stabilized, and ultimately vanishes even if the bars are rapidly alternated within the stabilized pattern. Whittle & Riggs (173) have measured the evoked electrical response in both the retina and the cortex while it fades, and find that there is no diminution of the evoked response at either locus, either during or after complete subjective fading. Apparently the locus of subjective suppression lies beyond the level at which the electrical effects are observed.

An interesting new adaptation after-effect has been reported by Anstis (6). Anstis showed his subjects a field which shifted in brightness in a temporal sawtooth pattern. After observing the fluctuating field for a while, his subjects subsequently see constant uniform fields as fluctuating in brightness but in phase opposite to that of the inducing light. Since each eye can adapt to a different temporal pattern simultaneously, the locus of the effect is placed in the retina.

Subjective scaling is the basis of a technique for measuring dark adaptation which should merit some sort of award for originality of treatment. Ekman, Hosman & Berglund (81) scaled the stimulus during dark adaptation as judged fractions of the perceived brightness of a fully dark-adapted standard. The results look rather like regular dark adaptation curves, but the authors conclude from curve-fitting procedures that the two processes it represents are very different from the usual rod-and-cone analysis. First, there is an early, slow process of increase in subjective brightness that gives way at about 7.6 min to a rapid increase, which continues to 18.6 min, when in turn the original slower process begins again.

Less original but equally courageous is a review by Stabell & Stabell (157) in which the authors note that color may be perceived well below the rod-cone break in dark adaptation, and are led to question the accepted correlation of color vision with cones. Their objection would attract more attention if the relative luminosities of the subject wavelengths were spelled out, and if attention were paid to the known complications of cone thresholds during dark adaptation (e.g., see DuCroz & Rushton, 73).

Connors (56) has made what must surely be the final study of the effect of red preadapting lights on subsequent dark adaptation. Up to 640 nm wavelength, longer wavelengths during preadaptation yield faster sensitivity returns, and beyond that wavelength there is little difference.

Lateral Effects

Békésy's model of lateral inhibition, which was so successful in describing Mach bands, has been extended to add another type of lateral inhibition called Hering inhibition (20). Both types appear when there is a discontinuity in luminance, but there are functional differences. Hering inhibition extends spatially over a broader area than does Mach inhibition. Mach inhibition is enhanced by flicker while Hering inhibition is not. Also, Mach inhibition increases with the size of the discontinuity, while Hering inhibition does not; Hering inhibition is all-or-none at an edge, and increases with an increase in the number of steps at the discontinuity.

Westheimer (171) has completed his earlier analysis of spatial interaction in the rods by showing similar mechanisms under photopic conditions. Like rods, cones show both excitatory and inhibitory lateral effects. The threshold for a small stimulus in the fovea is first increased by increasing the size of a surrounding field, but when it is made larger than about 5 min in diameter, threshold begins to decrease again. The result is explained as showing that a small excitation field, but a larger inhibition field, result from stimulation of a point on the retina; as the inhibiting field becomes larger, it begins to inhibit itself.

Westheimer's results were used by Luria (118) to explain why the acuity for a small target is most damaged by short sweeps of a moving masking light. Larger stimulations, he reasons, tend to inhibit themselves and so have less masking effect.

The original impetus for our present emphasis on lateral effects in vision derives from the work of Hartline and his co-workers on the horseshoe crab, *Limulus.* The work has reached a level of great sophistication, and its current status can be reviewed in reports by Ratliff, Hartline & Lange (143) and by Lange, Hartline & Ratliff (115). The work now includes such considerations as the facilitation of inhibition by other inhibition, overshoot effects due to reduction of inhibition, latency factors and self-inhibition. A mathematical model has been worked out and tested by new experiments.

Norton et al. (131) have classified the S-potential of the carp into three types on the basis of their waveform: negative monophasic, biphasic, and triphasic. Each of the types shows a receptive field very different from that of ganglion cells; in fact, they each use a large portion of the entire retina. For threshold, Ricco's law (area $\times$ intensity $=$ constant) holds over much of the retina for each type.

Michael's (123, 124) research is especially interesting for psychologists because he has studied the receptive fields of contrast sensitive units, directionally sensitive units, and opponent-color units all within the retina of one animal, the ground squirrel, whose only receptors are cones. The result is to pull together into a more coherent whole information from several important researches by earlier investigators on a variety of animals.

Something more than the loss of local retinal sensitivity is involved in adaptation to grating patterns. Sekular and his associates (109, 139) have found that subjects lose their sensitivity to a broad band of similar grating sizes, as well as to the identical size, after prolonged exposure. Their ability to discriminate single-bar patterns also is subsequently affected if the bar is oriented in the general direction of the grid.

Spectral Luminosity

Luminosity in humans.—Here is a novel way to measure luminosity. By maintaining a fixed (32 per cent) contrast between a heterochromatic stimulus pair, and noting the radiance required for detection of the difference, Burkhardt & Whittle (52) have constructed curves for spectral sensitivity for threshold or luminance match. The spectral contrast curve turns out to be narrower than the threshold curve, and the authors speculate that the difference may provide a new clue to the interactions between the specific color mechanisms. And indeed there are interactions. Guth (97) has demonstrated the failure at threshold luminances of Abney's Law (that the luminosities of different colored stimuli add simply). When different monochromatic lights are added to reach threshold, more must generally be added than their individual luminances would predict. Surprisingly, adding a second color to a color at threshold may even drive the first color below threshold, i.e., may inhibit the response to it.

Weale (168) has found by spectral reflectometry of the visual pigments that there are differences in spectral reflectance between small foveal areas and larger, but still rod-free, areas. He uses these reflectance differences to account for the greater red-sensitivity of the central fovea compared to that of other cone areas.

Both van Lith (163) and Granda & Biersdorf (96) have emphasized the similarity between the human luminosity function taken with the electroretinogram and the usual psychophysical luminosity function. With due allowances for reasonable systematic differences, so are the dark adaptation curves taken with the two methods similar. Van Lith even presents conversion factors to allow calculation of one curve from the other.

It is a question of long standing whether red light is seen by rods or by cones in complete dark adaptation. Baumgardt's theoretical answer (16), that red light is more likely to be seen by the red cones, is calculated from quantum fluxes and published curves of pigment densities in receptors.

If it can be obtained, J. L. Brown's technical report (34) on the spectral response of human vision at low luminances is a little gem. Brown collects data from a variety of experiments, published and unpublished, and discusses questions of luminosity and adaptation in a variety of visual tasks. His discussion of the relative contributions of rods and cones is of particular interest.

Luminosity in other species.—Although it is primarily a study of wavelength discrimination, the report by De Valois, Abramov & Jacobs (64) on the electrical response patterns of cells from the lateral geniculate nucleus of the macacque monkey yields an important luminosity curve. The spectral response of the "non-opponent" cells is a remarkably good fit to the C.I.E. luminosity curve for humans, and it underscores the utility of the animal for research to supplement human research.

The plaice fish is a more exotic case. Hammond (103) had analyzed the spectral response of cells in the tectum, at levels suprathreshold for the cones, and he finds the peak responses of the units to lie in four spectral ranges, blue, blue-green, green, and orange. No red-sensitive cells were found. These were on-off, center-surround types of cells; they surely represent some transformations from simple pigment curves, and may reflect inputs from twin cones which are common in plaice.

The distinction originally made between luminosity (L) potentials and depolarizing (S) potentials in the retina apparently must be modified. Incidental to their study of S-potentials, Naka & Rushton (128–130) have shown that the spectral response of L-potentials actually is modifed by chromatic adaptation. Their theoretical analysis of potential generation leads them to a procedure whereby they can plot the luminosity response of cones from the S-potentials. The technique is based on determinations of the reduction in sensitivity of the S-units at each wavelength when the whole eye is desensitized by background lights. For their experimental animal (the tench fish), the result gives a green cone with maximum response at 540 nm and a red cone whose maximum response is at 680 nm.

Even the common prawn has two receptors. Wald & Seldin (165) report ERG measurements to spectral lights on the prawn after differential adaptation to red and violet light. Two spectral response curves appear; one with maximum response at 540 nm, the other at 390 nm. These two pigments are likely to exist in separate systems, because the time constant of the response is different after the two conditions of adaptation color.

Murray (127) has shown that the photic response of the *Limulus* "lateral olfactory nerve" is based on the action of a photopigment. He dissected out the "olfactory" nerves and measured their light absorption with a microspectrophotometer. The result was a completely typical photopigment absorption spectrum with a maximum absorption at 529 nm.

Behavioral measurements of luminosity are still in use. The threshold response of the stickleback fish to constantly moving stripes under spectral illumination gave Cronly-Dillon & Sharma (59) the very interesting observation that the female luminosity curve varies with the season. For most of the year the female, and for all of the year the male, stickleback minnow shows a constant, double-peaked spectral luminosity curve of which the blue 505 nm peak is higher than the red 594 nm peak. During the breeding season, the female's luminosity curve changes. Her red peak becomes higher, and thus she presumably becomes better attuned to the red belly markings which the male shows at that time.

By teaching sooty mangabey monkeys to choose the one of a pair of lights that appeared to be flickering, then varying the radiance of the flickering light to locate a brightness threshold for seeing the flicker, Adams & Jones (3) have measured the luminosity curve for that monkey. A coarse flicker rate, perceptible at low radiances, yields a scotopic curve, while a fast rate, requiring high radiances, yields a photopic curve. The curves for the monkey are both somewhat narrower than the corresponding C.I.E. curves, but it appears to the reviewer that the human control curves taken by the apparatus are, too.

Subjective Brightness

Ekman's modification of Stevens' power function law is $R = c(S\text{-}a)^n$ in which R and S are, respectively, the perceptual and physical amounts, c and n are constants and a is an additive constant to make the equation general. Ekman & Gustafsson (80) have shown the function to be related to the detection threshold, and to be influenced by the nature of the stimulus and the conditions of measurement. They observe that the brightness function is nearly linear at low brightness levels. Ekman (79) has also reanalyzed some data by Raab to observe that it fits a simple logarithmic relationship between brightness and duration, like pain, loudness, and electrical stimulation. Baumgardt (17), in turn, has observed that Ekman's work contains an internal inconsistency that leads to a discrepancy in his calculations by a factor of 80. He suggests that this casts doubt on the utility of the work.

The question of how apparent brightness varies with area has been reinvestigated by Ogawa and associates (132), with special emphasis on stimuli which are well above threshold. Size has more effect on apparent brightness at low luminances than at high luminances. The authors relate the results of the current electrophysiological findings on inhibitory fields, but note that such perceptual variables as observation distance and visual angle affect the results as well as the purely physiological variable of inhibition.

Fechner's paradox lies in the observation that a dim light introduced into a previously closed eye makes a bright light viewed by the other eye look dimmer. The paradox has been explained on the one hand as representing an averaging of the output from each eye, and on the other hand as an averaging of the central response to each stimulation—a luminance-averaging explanation as opposed to a brightness-averaging explanation. Teller & Galanter (160) find that Fechner's paradox can be obtained when the apparent dimness of the inducing light is obtained by contrast effects or by light adaptation. They conclude that both contrast and adaptation are effects which occur at an earlier stage than Fechner averaging, which must therefore be a rather high-level central effect.

Vocal humming causes a vibration of the eye and produces a stroboscopic effect when dark bars are viewed under flickering light. Rushton (149) analyzes the circumstances, showing that the correct explanation is lateral vibration of the eye, and disposes of alternatives, in an exemplary demonstration of the scientific method. The problem may be a small one, but it is interesting and the report is most rewarding to read.

The Pupil

Everyone who works in human vision will want to read Westheimer's extremely useful discussion of the Maxwellian view (170). He discusses the troland unit, focus, field of view, and pupil size. He concludes with a theoretical consideration of the pupil and image transfer, which he relates to imaging by coherent light because Maxwellian view frequently approximates coherent illumination of the pupil.

Hornung (108) has made good measurements of the pupillary changes that occur after a step change in illumination. There is always a redilation after the contraction due to a luminance increase, although it may in turn be interrupted by a recontraction if the second luminance is high, and there is always a recontraction after dilation to a luminance decrease. He has also made an engineering analysis of the regulating mechanism of the pupil (107). Included is a new plot of retinal illuminance vs. luminance for the natural pupil. It should prove valuable whenever field and laboratory data have to be compared.

The Stiles-Crawford effect has always been associated with position of the beam through the pupil. Makous (119) has found that changing the incident angle of the beam on the pupil makes the field look brighter briefly, and the brightness decreases over about 40 sec. The new effect cannot be expained by cone angle, and Makous suggests it may indicate that the molecules within different cones are oriented differently.

Anatomy

The new anatomical research on the retina by Dowling & Boycott (72) and by Dowling (69, 71) marks a major change in attitude toward the retina. It is disclosed as the site of important mechanisms of adaptation and of lateral effects. The amacrine cell, previously considered so obscure that Polyak usually enclosed the name in quotation marks, now emerges as a major functional element. The locations of the synaptic vessicles in amacrine cell processes show that these cells must be intimately involved in the distribution of nervous activity in lateral patterns and in feedback loops. In the frog, which seems to have much of its perceptual organization performed in its retina, all information from the receptors appears to be processed in the amacrines before it even enters the optic nerve. In the primate, there are some connections directly from bipolars to ganglion cells.

The lateral geniculate connects serially to the Visual I area in the cat's cortex, but in addition there seems to be a parallel connection to Visual II. Berkley, Wolf & Glickstein (21) show that potentials with short latencies and high amplitudes are evoked from Visual II by pulses of light, and that they survive appropriate ablation of both areas 17 and contralateral 18, but are diminished by damage to the lateral geniculate.

Also in the cat, Sturr & Battersby (158) show that conditioning flashes can inhibit electrical responses in the cortex when they come from the eye opposite to the one receiving the test stimulus. The effect is less than if the same eye is used.

The Electroretinogram

A major analysis of the features of the ERG comes from K. Brown (35, 36). It starts with Granit's classical analysis and draws for the most part from a decade of Brown's own work. By electrode placement and selective circulation clamps, he identified the locus of the potential directly associated with stimulation in the receptors. He calls that the late receptor potential (42), and identifies it with the a-wave. The relations with the other less significant potentials are outlined. Brown & Murakami (43, 44) then show that the late receptor potential of cones decays rapidly, while that of the rods decays slowly. The basis of the rising phase of the d-wave is cone LRP decay, and the basis of the falling phase is decay of response from the inner nuclear layer.

Troelstra & Schweitzer (162) have taken a completely different theoretical approach. They have derived a mathematical equation relating the b-wave to the light stimulus as a function of time, based on the results from step-function and double-flash stimulus presentations. The equation is tested by a variety of predictions, with respectable success in experimentation, but physiological correlations are left to the future.

In electroretinography it is difficult to avoid the intrusion of rod responses when cone activity is the real object of study. Riggs and his group have been able to do this by using a stimulus pattern of rapidly alternating stripes of different wavelengths; the amplitude of the response depends upon the amount of wavelength difference between the stripes. The method yields photopic luminosity curves with the ERG which turn out to be very similar to psychophysical ones (113). When a matrix is constructed of the amplitude of response with each wavelength pair, the matrix is consonant with the idea of three color mechanisms whose response depends upon wavelength (145).

Buckser proposes that the a-wave includes a separate long-latency negative component. The conclusion is the culmination of studies on the recovery of the rat electroretinogram following brief strong bleaches (47–49) and on comparisons between the new negative component and the standard a- and b-waves as the parameters of wavelength, duration, and intensity of the stimulus are manipulated (50).

Evoked Potentials

Some progress has been made in sorting out the behavior of those potentials that are evoked from the visual cortex by a flash of light to the eyes, and that can be seen only in the summed responses of many trials. Dill, Vallecalle & Verzeano (65) have compared the neuronal discharge from multiple microelectrodes to the visual evoked response. They find that the neuronal discharge is greatest when the negative slope of the evoked response is greatest, and is least when the slope of the evoked response is most steeply positive. Neither stimulus intensity nor electrode depth alter the relationship.

Burkhardt & Riggs (51) show that a flickering monochromatic stimulus evokes much larger potential when the stimulus is superimposed on a background of a color different from itself. A different-colored background also shifts the phase of the response.

Perry & Copenhaver (141) have demonstrated that the evoked potential is largely a photopic phenomenon and is relatively unaffected by dark adaptation. Perry, Childers & McCoy (140) report that binocular responses are larger than monocular ones (by as much as half again as great) and that the manner of addition depends on the recording position; in fact, the "addition" varies from simple addition to a complete alteration of the shape of the curve.

A practical application for evoked potentials has been achieved by Beinhocker et al. (19). These authors show how the potentials can be used to obtain perimetric fields for clinical assessment of noncooperative cases.

Receptor Potentials

The electrical potentials which arise in the receptor layer of the retina have begun to yield to analysis during recent years. Brown & Wiesel (45, 46), using a recording intraretinal electrode and a reference electrode in the vitreous humor of the cat, were able to demonstrate a LERG—local electroretinogram. This method minimizes the recording of activity from distant sites and allows recording from a small retinal area around the electrode. Using this technique, the a-wave component was found to have maximal amplitude near the outer segment of the receptor.

Late receptor potential.—The development of the technique meant that by eliminating the components not associated with the receptors (b- and c-waves) it was possible to study the a-wave component in detail. By selectively clamping the retinal circulation in the monkey, Brown was able to abolish the b-wave of the inner nuclear layer and by light adaptation was able to eliminate the c-wave. The choroidal circulation was able to maintain the a-wave in good condition, and it was possible to isolate that component which gives rise to the leading edge of the a-wave. This response has a minimum latency of about 1.5 msec, and has been termed by Brown the late receptor potential. This late potential appears to be generated by changes in membrane potential (those resulting from ion movement) since it is reduced by excess extracellular $K+$ and lowered $Na+$ extracellularly (102). The response is also sensitive to anoxia, which is known to depolarize membranes.

Early receptor potential.—While investigating the effects of anoxia on the late receptor potential, a new potential was uncovered. This potential was not sensitive to anoxia (42). The new potential was called an early receptor potential (ERP). It was shown to have an extremely short latency. During 1964, R. A. Cone reported the identification of a biphasic early receptor potential in a number of animals (53). This response was a large corneal negative response preceded by a smaller corneal positive component. These two responses have been termed R 1 and R 2.

ERP and state of visual pigment.—Cone (53) and Pak & Cone (136) were able to demonstrate that the early receptor potential action spectrum in the rat closely corresponds to the absorption spectrum of rhodopsin. It was also shown that the amplitude of R 2 is directly proportional to the per cent of rhodopsin bleached by a short flash. This has also been demonstrated for the R 1 component. The latency of the initial positive phase, R 1, cannot be measured on a μsec scale (54), and the response reaches its peak in about 0.5 msec or less at room temperature. The negative phase, R 2, has a latency of less than 60 msec and reaches its peak in 1 to 2 msec. All this evidence points to the early receptor potential being generated in the outer segments of the receptor cell by some action on the visual pigment. In addition, the early receptor potential is unlike all other retinal potentials in that the time course of the response does not depend on the stimulus flash energy. Through the range of energy over which the early receptor potential can be observed, only the amplitude of the response varies and the time course of both R 1 and R 2 remains unchanged. This suggests that these potentials are algebraic sums of outputs of independent generators. Thus the early receptor potential does indeed appear to be an electrical potential mediated by molecular changes in the photosensitive material.

Arden, Ikeda & Siegel (9, 10) have demonstrated that the amplitude of the early receptor potential of dark-adapted albino rat eyes decreases with successive flashes but does not disappear. They were able to show that this is due to photoregeneration of pigment from photoproducts, viz. metarhodopsin I and metarhodopsin II. A very rapid negative wave was observed and called the "photoreversal potential." That the early receptor potential is closely tied not only to the photolysis of visual pigment but also to its orientation in the rod, and the subsequent dark production of intermediates, was also demonstrated by Cone & Brown (55), Cone (54) and Pak & Boes (135). Cone & Brown (55) found that the ERP is abolished by high temperature (58° C) and that this loss is associated with disorientation, but not thermal bleaching, of the pigment molecules in the disc membrane. Cone & Brown (55), by using essentially light-adapted retinae, found that responses of opposite polarity—a negative component followed by a positive component—can be shown for photolysis of metarhodopsin I and metarhdopsin II. Similar results were obtained by Pak & Boes (135).

Pak, Rozzi & Ebrey (138), in a study of the effect of chemical environment of the retina on the two components of the ERP, found that the negative component attains optimum amplitude near neutral pH and reversibly declines at both high and low pH. Additionally, the negative component is preferentially enhanced by certain ions, namely potassium, rubidium, and ammonium. At low temperature where only the positive component is observed, a low pH of 4 or less results in a striking enhancement of this component.

Attempts to identify the source of the ERP.—In order to investigate the properties and time relationships of the underlying generator mechanism of the ERP, Arden et al. (8) utilized a variety of reagents, including tissue fixatives. This work has led them to postulate that the positive component, R 1, is generated by the formation and decay of prelumirhodopsin. This disagrees with Cone, who has assigned the R 1 to the conversion of rhodopsin to metarhodopsin I. A later analysis of their work by Arden & Miller (11) suggests that R 2, the negative component, is not directly generated by rhodopsin but possibly develops in the surface membrane of the outer limb, as in invertebrates.

Hagins & McGaughty (99) observed fast photovoltages in the squid retina in response to short, intense flashes of light. The waveform depends on the relative amount of rhodopsin and light-absorbing photoproducts present during the flash. They also found a small, long-lasting, thermoelectric voltage which arises from the heating effect of absorbed light. When the thermal effect is corrected for, the interconversion of equal numbers of rhodopsin and acid-metarhodopsin molecules by the flash gives rise to a waveform whose time integral is zero. In another paper they found that, when a small region in the outer segment of squid photoreceptors fixed in glutaraldehyde is exposed to an intense flash, a brief pulse of membrane current flows locally (100). The passive spread of this current along the outer segments produces the photochemical components of the ERP. They found the source of the current to lie electrically in parallel with the cell membranes and perhaps to be located within them.

Intracellular recording in the retinular cells of the lateral eye of *Limulus* by Smith & Brown (154) showed a photoelectric potential with some of the characteristics of the ERP of vertebrate cells. Brown, Murray & Smith (33) determined the action spectra for the two components and found both to be that of a visual pigment with a λ max at 530 nm. They concluded that the photoelectric potential arises directly from the orderly array of pigment molecules which are an integral part of the photoreceptor cell membrane. A more recent paper by Smith, Stell & Brown (155) reports conductance changes associated with the *Limulus* receptor potential. This potential appears to be a consequence not of permeability changes in the membrane, but of alterations in a light-sensitive constant current generator. It is further suggested by Smith et al. (156) that the photoreceptor membranes in the *Limulus* possess an electrogenic sodium pump which contributes directly to the membrane potential and whose activity is altered by light. The light-induced changes in pump activity are considered to underlie the receptor potential. Thus, in the terminology normally applied to vertebrate receptor behavior, the early receptor potential reflects conformational changes in the pigment molecules which in some way lead to changes in membrane potentials thereby giving rise to the late receptor potential.

Goldstein (88), in an investigation of the early receptor potential in isolated frog retina, found that the potential recorded was generated by the cones; the spectral sensitivity of the response in the preparation peaks at about 560 to 590 nm. In experiments utilizing selective bleaching, he was further able to identify a pigment that contributes to the ERP of isolated frog retina which absorbed at shorter wavelength. This does not appear to be rhodopsin, however. Although the bleaching of rhodopsin causes an appreciable change in response waveform and the slope of the function of amplitude vs. intensity, it causes only small changes in the ERP action spectrum (89).

That the early receptor potential can be generated by light flashes of long duration (5 to 40 msec) and of intensity much lower than the short flashes normally used, was demonstrated by Fatechand (85) using the isolated frog retina. The characteristics of the responses appear to indicate a time integration of the evoked potentials and therefore support the view that there is an integrating circuit interposed between the ERP generator and the recording electrode.

Significance of the ERP.—Rapid biphasic responses to intense flashes similar to the ERP have been found in a number of pigmented tissues: guinea pig iris (7), frog skin (7), the leaf of the bean plant (77), and flame nettle (7). In a series of very detailed papers, Brown and co-workers (37–41, 57) have investigated a response of the pigment epithelium of the frog, and found it to be triphasic. Thus it would appear that the early receptor potential is not a unique property of visual pigments but an electrical expression of photochemical events and may not represent the excitation of rods per se.

Pak (134) has pointed out that vision is initiated by excitation of rhodopsin but not of its photoproducts. The ERP, on the other hand, has clearly been shown to have photoproduct responses which are simply rhodopsin responses of opposite polarity. Therefore, the ERP apparently lacks the asymmetry necessary for the generator potential of neural activity.

The question of its relationship to vision notwithstanding, the fact that the components of the ERP are so closely related to the state of the visual pigments makes this response an excellent probe for investigation of the pigments *in situ.* For example, Ebrey (78) has utilized the ERP responses of the albino rat retina to measure the half-lives of several intermediates in rhodopsin bleaching. The half-lives of metarhodopsin I, metarhodopsin II and P465 were determined at 37° C and found to be 40 μsec, 140 sec, and 1100 sec respectively.

Ionic mechanism of visual excitation.—An ionic mechanism for visual excitation received support from the work of Bonting and his colleagues. Using rhodopsin monolayers, Bonting & Bangham (25) found that illumination produces expansion of the layer. This they interpret to indicate penetration of the monolayer by retinal. Further, illumination of rod outer segments causes efflux of $K+$ ions and equivalent influx of $Na+$ ions. This effect can be duplicated qualitatively and quantitatively by addition of all-*trans* retinal in the absence of light. These results, along with the increased cation leakage caused by all-*trans* retinal in artificial membranes of phosphatidylethanolamine, are interpreted as suggesting that upon photolysis of rhodopsin, all-*trans* retinal is transferred from the protein to a Schiff base linkage with phosphatidylethanolamine. The resulting blockage of the amino group of the lipid would make the membrane more negatively charged and, therefore, more cation permeable. De Pont et al. (63) have now demonstrated Schiff base formation between retinal and phosphatidylethanolamine in monolayers. The efflux of $K+$ ions and influx of $Na+$ in isolated dark-adapted cattle outer segments in the presence of 11-*cis* or all-*trans* retinal was reinvestigated by Daemen & Bonting (60). They found that the aldehyde was necessary for the effect; retinol and retinoic acid had no significant effect on cation levels. This again supports the idea of Schiff base formation as an essential part of the process.

Photoreception

In the last two years, increasing interest has developed in the molecular aspects of vision. Biologist, biochemist, and biophysicist alike are bringing an increasing number of the tools of their disciplines to bear on this problem. Several excellent reviews of this area are available. Bridges discusses the biochemistry of visual processes in chapter II, *Comprehensive Biochemistry* (31), and Abrahamson & Ostroy have treated the photochemical and macromolecular aspects of vision in *Progress in Biophysics and Molecular Biology* (1). Weale (167) reviews the photochemistry of visual pigments, including fundus reflectometry and microspectrophotometry techniques. Additionally, Weale's article contains an interesting section on paired pigments and the possible role of ecology and/or chemistry in determining pigment distribution. Rosenberg (147), in another review article, discusses the more physical aspects of the visual process, with particular reference to the "photo-conduction theory." In an article for *Scientific American,* Hubbard & Kropf (111) develop the concept of molecular isomers and their photochemistry as they affect the visual process. Their article is written so that it should be of particular value to the nonchemist.

Mechanisms of bleaching.—Yoshizawa & Wald have investigated the reactions of iodopsin and isoiodopsin at −195° C (180). They conclude that the only action of light on iodopsin, as on the rod pigment rhodopsin, is to isomerize its chromophore from 11-*cis* to all-*trans*. An interesting difference between the cone pigment under investigation and the rod pigment previously studied is that production of prelumi-iodopsin at low temperature (−195° C) and subsequent warming (−78° C) causes thermal conversion back to iodopsin rather than to the lumi stage. In the rhodopsin system, prelumirhodopsin on warming produces lumirhodopsin, and no thermal back reaction to rhodopsin is observed.

The photoreaction of isorhodopsin at low temperatures was studied using flash photolysis by Pratt (142). This synthetic visual pigment, containing 9-*cis* retinal, was found to be converted to prelumirhodopsin, although less efficiently than is the natural 11-*cis* pigment rhodopsin.

The thermal decay of bovine lumirhodopsin was investigated by Erhardt et al. (82) using flash photolysis. No changes in pH or in titratable sulfhydryl groups accompany either the prelumirhodopsin to lumirhodopsin or lumirhodopsin to metarhodopsin I conversions. Analysis of the kinetics of the decay of lumirhodopsin to metarhodopsin I led the authors to suggest that three forms of lumirhodopsin produce three forms of metarhodopsin I by concurrent first-order reactions. They suggest that each rate may represent a different isomeric form of lumirhodopsin. The decay of metarhodopsin I was found to be equally complicated (133). Three forms of metarhodopsin I were found to decay by first-order, pH dependent processes to metarhodopsin II. Metarhodopsin II was observed to undergo conversion to metarhodopsin 465 (pigment 465), and the authors point out that this reaction is slow enough to be rate controlling at physiological temperatures. The Case-Western Reserve group feels that the 465 intermediate is an "on-line" component of the bleaching sequence. This is not the view of the Harvard group, which in 1963 (121) placed the 465 intermediate outside the normal bleaching pathway.

The problems encountered in the use of flash photolysis have been emphasized by Williams (176), who points out that the quantum efficiency of bleaching, defined as gamma, the ratio of the number of molecules bleached to the number of quanta absorbed, is a variable. He shows theoretically that gamma can vary from 0 to 1, on a relative scale, and that to obtain gamma = 1, very low light intensities must be employed. The variability of gamma is a function of quantal absorption by transient intermediates which leads to production of stable pigment. In another paper, Williams & Breil (178) have presented the first measurements on a rhodopsin system made during an intense electronic flash. Prior to this, flash photolysis studies were unable to observe the system during the period of light absorption due to blinding of the monitor photodetector. The technique utilized by Williams allows the evaluation of the photic and thermal components of metarhodopsin II production. The rate of production of this substance was studied, varying temperature, intensity, and extracting agent. The results of these experiments show that the rate of meta II production is photolimited at high temperature (37.5° C), while at 5° C the rate is thermolimited. Intermediate temperatures were either photo or thermolimited, depending on the extracting medium. A further consequence of the loss of thermal limitation at high temperature is that photoequilibria are established during the flash. When this occurs, additional quanta are not as effective in bleaching since they simply interconvert *cis* and *trans* isomers. Thus the quantum efficiency decreases. This was clearly demonstrated for digitonin extracts of frog rods at 37.5° C.

The photolysis of metarhodopsin II (λmax 380) by ultraviolet light was the subject of another paper by Williams (177). Metarhodopsin II, produced by irradiation of cattle rhodopsin at four temperatures between 5° C and 22° C, was found on light absorption to produce rhodopsin and P470 in the ratio of 1 : 3.5. The P470 was found to be produced at the rate of quantal input while the rhodopsin is produced slowly, several milliseconds after the flash. The latter was the first demonstration that a "dark" component of photoreversal exists.

Kropf (114) measured the photosensitivity of frog rhodopsin in the ultraviolet region corresponding to absorption by the protein, opsin. The wavelengths used were 280 nm and 254 nm. Irradiation with light of these wavelengths resulted in the *cis* to *trans* isomerization of the chromophore, and bleaching then occurred. Therefore, excitation energy, supplied by the ultraviolet photons, is transferred from the protein to the chromophore. The quantum efficiency for this ultraviolet bleaching was about 0.25, compared to 0.5 to 0.6 for light absorbed directly by the chromophore.

The rapid uptake of hydrogen ions by frog rod outer segments and rhodopsin solutions upon illumination has been reported by Falk & Fatt (84). The reaction shows the action spectrum for rhodopsin. In frog rods, one acid-binding group with a pH of about 7.9 is produced for each molecule of rhodopsin bleached. The authors suggest that the time course of the hydrogen-ion uptake in rhodopsin solutions reflects the kinetics of the conversion of meta I to meta II. Similarly, proton uptake in cattle rod outer segments is the subject of an article by McConnell et al. (122). They found that unbleached rhodopsin was necessary for the light-induced proton uptake. However, their results with Triton-dispersed outer segments do not support the view that the pH changes observed are attributable to the uptake of exactly one proton per molecule of pigment bleached.

Structure and Spectral Properties of Visual Pigments

The purification and amino acid composition of bovine rhodopsin has been reported by Shields et al. (153). Digitonin-extracted rod outer segments were analyzed for homogeneity by disc electrophoresis and were found to be essentially homogeneous. The amino acid composition of both bleached and reduced S-carboxymethylated derivative of rhodopsin were determined. The approximate molecular weight of the protein was 28,600. By extraction of cattle rod outer segments with cetyltrimethyammonium bromide (CTAB), Heller (104) prepared rhodopsin which on analysis was found to be a homogeneous glycoprotein. The spectrum of this material, λ max 500 nm, shows no beta peak and, as a complex with CTAB, has an extinction (500 nm) of 23,100 $\pm$ 800. This value is considerably lower than the ε_{500} of the rhodopsin-digitonin complex which has been determined as 40,600. Experiments by Heller (105) using gel-filtration showed an increase in Stokes radius of the protein on bleaching. Thus the native visual pigment has a compact configuration while light-exposed pigment shows an expanded configuration. Bownds (28) and Akhtar (4) have both reported that the sodium borohydride treatment of bleached cattle rhodopsin results in the irreversible binding of retinal to the ε amino group of a lysine in the protein, opsin. Heller (105), however, interprets his results on CTAB-extracted cattle rhodopsin to indicate a substituted aldimine bond as the linkage of 11-*cis* retinal and the lysine residue of the protein.

Yet another picture of the condensation of 11-*cis* retinal with the lipoprotein, opsin, has recently been presented by Abrahamson & Wiesenfeld (2). They have reported that in the native state, the 11-*cis* retinylidene chromophore is bound to the lipid, phoshatidylethanolamine, through a Schiff's base linkage which is probably protonated *in situ*. Although some inconsistencies remain in the matter of the site of retinal condensation, the last few years have seen some excellent work on the subject. It seems reasonable to suppose that a definitive answer to this question will not be long in coming.

A physical property of visual pigments which has been used as an indication of structure and stability is their behavior to elevated temperature. Hubbard (110) measured the thermal decomposition of rhodopsin, isorhodopsin, and opsin and concluded that the chromaphore lends thermal stability to the protein; the 11-*cis* isomer being more effective than the 9-*cis*. Bridges (29, 30) suggests that A_2-based pigments show decreased stability due to the additional double bond in the terminal ring of the chromophore. Williams & Milby (179) studied the thermal decomposition of some visual pigments in the temperature range 45 to 65° C. In most cases, A_2-based pigments were found to be less stable than A_1-based pigments, although this was not true in all cases. They also found that both A_1-based and A_2-based pigments are most stable near neutral pH. The earlier report of Lythgoe and Quilliam that added salt renders frog rhodopsin solutions more stable was confirmed for the frog pigment and a number of other pigments.

The structure of photoregenerated rhodopsin was investigated by Williams (175). He first demonstrated by use of optical rotatory dispersion techniques that a Cotton effect is generated in the visible region of the spectrum and attributed this to induced asymmetry in the 11-*cis* retinal. Using the same technique, he was able to show that the retinal of visual pigment generated by photolysis of metarhodopsin II—i.e., photoregenerated rhodopsin—exhibits as much induced asymmetry as the chromophore in native rhodopsin. Further evidence for the similarity of native and photoregenerated rhodopsin was provided by Baker & Williams (12). The thermal stabilities of the two types of rhodopsins were investigated and found to be the same. In addition, the thermal decomposition of P470 (also called P465), produced by photolysis of metarhodopsin II, was studied. It was found that P470 is thermally more stable than the meta II from which it is produced, but much more labile than rhodopsin. These results were interpreted as an indication that more chromophore-protein interaction exists in P470 than in meta II.

Another problem which has intrigued chemists for many years has received considerable attention recently. This is the problem of the substantial shift to longer wavelength which is observed when 11-*cis* retinal or 11-*cis* dehydroretinal is attached by a Schiff base linkage with an opsin. Related to this problem is the fact that all natural visual pigments so far investigated use either 11-*cis* retinal (A_1) or 11-*cis*-3,4-dehydroretinal (A_2) as a chromophore, yet the observed λ max values of these pigments vary from 450 nm to 620 nm. Several approaches to this question have been undertaken. Erickson & Blatz (83) used N-retinylidene-1-amino-2-propanol as a Schiff base analog of rhodopsin. Studies of the spectral properties of the model compound, both in 11-*cis* and all-*trans* configurations, in a number of different solvents have led the authors to suggest that the condensation of 11-*cis* retinal with opsin induces conformational changes within the lipoprotein. These changes confer the following properties to the visual pigment: (*a*) the C=N linkage is protected from hydrolysis; (*b*) an acid is in close proximity to the C=N, forming the immonium salt and causing an initial red shift in the λ max of the chromophore; (*c*) the chromophore is submerged into a hydrophobic region with a low dielectric constant, markedly shifting the λ max into the red but not significantly altering the band shape or molar absorptivity. The conclusion they draw is that the λ max of rhodopsin is dependent upon the dielectric constant of the local solvent environment about the protonated Schiff base and the association between the cation and its counterion. Blatz et al. (24), in a study of the carbonium ions of 11 retinal-related polyenes, conclude that the chromophore of visual pigments cannot be represented as a pure carbonium ion.

Model compounds have also been used by Rosenberg & Krigas (148) in attempting to account for the red-shift of visual pigments. They hypothesize that the λ max values in the protonated aromatic Schiff bases investigated are red-shifted as the positive charge on the nitrogen increases due to the inductive effects of substituents in the meta and parapositions. While their results do not rule out the side-chain interaction idea suggested previously by Dartnall, the authors feel that sufficient control of the λ max values of rhodopsins can be exerted by inductive or field effects on the positive charge on the $C = N^+$ nitrogen. The protonation of solutions of retinal with imines or secondary amine produces enamine salts which are comparable in structure to a retinylidene ammonium compound. Morton and Pitt suggested that it is a retinylidene ammonium structure which gives rise to N-retinylidene opsin in the bleaching sequence of visual pigments. Toth & Rosenberg (161) have investigated the nature of this reaction and the chemical properties of the resulting system. The extensive bathochromic shift, the ease of hydrolysis, the temperature dependence of stability, and the indicator-like properties of the model system are taken by the authors to indicate its possible relevance to the chemistry of visual pigments.

Two molecular orbital calculations have appeared which attempt to explain the spectra and isomerization behavior of rhodopsin. Inuzuka & Becker (112) and Wiesenfeld & Abrahamson (174) have made these calculations (on retinal) using similar methods and obtain comparable results. Wiesenfeld & Abrahamson (174) report the calculation as being consistent with the visual pigment model of a protonated Schiff base of retinal perturbed by a charged group in its environment.

During 1968, Blatz et al. (23) reported the synthesis of 5, 6-dihydroretinal, a new synthetic visual chromophore. This compound is the only polyene aldehyde other than the naturally occurring retinal and 3-dehydroretinal that has been found to combine with a visual protein. The visual pigment produced by condensation of (11-*cis*?) 5,6-dihydroretinal with cattle opsin has a λ max of 463 nm and was bleached by exposure to white light.

Visual pigment fluorescence has been measured by Guzzo & Pool (98). The fluorescence of rod outer segments and for rhodopsin in digitonin emits maximally between 575 to 600 nm. The observed quantum efficiency with 500 nm excitation is 0.005. The behavior of the emission reflects the known interconversion of rhodopsin to prelumirhodopsin at −196° C; that is, it is abolished when rhodopsin is converted to prelumirhodopsin and regenerated by irradiation of prelumirhodopsin thereby again producing rhodopsin. It, therefore, reflects a dissipative pathway from the excited state of rhodopsin.

Light-induced electron paramagnetic resonance signals were obtained from retinal, retinol, and rhodopsin by Grady & Borg (95). They accomplished this by using low temperature to "freeze in" the photoproducts. Several interesting results were obtained. The rhodopsin signal, unlike that of retinal or retinol, was only diminished on melting at about 0° C and persisted for several minutes before disappearing after the solution had been warmed to room temperature. The combination of the paramagnetic resonance and fluorescence data on retinal and retinol indicates a strong localization of excitation energy and of unpaired electron distribution in retinol, while retinal and rhodopsin show relative delocalization. Since this effect would enhance the photosensitivity of the compound, it perhaps suggests the selective advantage of retinal over retinol in the evolution of the chromophore of the visual pigments.

The visual pigments of the frog and the tadpole were examined by microspectrophotometry by Liebman & Entine (117). They found outer segments of five different morphologies, and five pigments were identified for both the frog and the tadpole. The wavenumber plots of the red rod pigments match published nomograms, but those of green rods, principal cones, accessory cones, and single cones do not. Dartnall (61), however, determined the spectra of the green rod pigments of three species of frogs using extraction techniques and found agreement with the nomogram. The green rod pigment is based on 11-*cis* retinal and has a λ max of 433 ± 2 nm. He found the overall retinal density ot the green-rod pigment to be about 9 per cent of that of rhodopsin. Since the green rods number 9 per cent of the red rods, the density at λ max in each dark-adapted receptor is approximately equal for the two pigments, namely 0.76.

The study of the light absorbing properties of porphyropsins, retinene$_2$ based visual pigments, was extended by Bridges (29). The chromophore of porphyropsin contains an extra double bond in the terminal ring. In earlier publications, Bridges (31), postulates that "the spectroscopic effect of this structural aberration is threefold, viz. (1) the photopigment absorption maximum or λ max, moves to longer wavelengths (bathochromic effect); (2) the extinction coefficient or λ max is reduced (hypochromic effect); (3) absorption on the blue side of the main band is increased (short wave effect.)" By analysis of difference spectra of hydroxylamine or sodium borohydride at a variety of pH values and the absorption spectrum of a porphyropsin extract which contained some impurities Bridges (29) has approximated the absorption spectrum of pure porphyropsin. An interesting investigation is reported by Schwanzara (152) in which the retinae of 59 species of freshwater fish were extracted and analyzed for pigment content. Visual pigments based on both 11-*cis* retinal and 11-*cis* 3,4 dehydroretinal were found to occur commonly among freshwater fish even in species which are neither migratory nor euryhaline. Schwanzara suggests from his evidence that the distribution of the visual pigments may be correlated with photic environment.

A nomogram for retinene$_2$-based pigments was prepared by Munz & Schwanzara (126). The nomogram was devised from the difference spectrum of the A_2 pigments of coho salmon. Since it was prepared from a difference spectrum, it is useful only in construction of difference spectra. Nevertheless, since the long-wavelength side of difference and absorption spectra coincide, its usefulness is extended.

The use of hydroxylamine in visual pigment spectrophotometry is commonplace. However, a careful study by Dartnall (62) of the photosensitivities of six A_1-based and five A_2-based pigments using the common frog pigment as an actinometer again emphasizes the importance of photoproduct removal by the use of hydroxylamine. In the presence of hydroxylamine, Dartnall found that all A_1-based pigments have nearly the same photosensitivity and all the A_2-based pigments have about 70 per cent of the A_1 value. When similar determinations are made in the absence of hydroxylamine, regeneration occurs and clear results are not obtained.

All visual pigments except for that of the honeybee are water-insoluble. At first, solubilizing of these proteins was done with bile salts, but more recently a number of ionic and non-ionic detergents have been utilized for this purpose. For example, Crescitelli (58) reports the extraction of frog rhodopsin with certain water-soluble, non-ionic, alkylphenol surfactants, commercially known as Triton. These pigment extracts can be analyzed spectrophotometrically with the same precision as the more commonly used digitonin extracts, with the exception of the far ultraviolet region. Triton itself absorbs in the region below 290 nm.

Visual Pigments *in situ*

In a study that may be related to thermal stability in an interesting way, Muntz & Northmore (125) report a behavioral experiment with turtles. In this work, increment thresholds were obtained at different levels of background illumination (I) with the animals maintained at different temperatures. When the value of I was low, the threshold was affected by temperature. They found that animals at 30° C were about 0.5 log units less sensitive than animals at 20° C. This suggests that the thresholds were limited by visual noise when the value of I was low and that the level of noise is dependent on temperature. Thus the level of background noise in the retina may be dependent on thermal breakdown of visual pigments as suggested by Barlow (13).

Pak & Helmrich (137) utilized the early receptor potential response of frozen or glutaraldehyde-fixed frog retina to examine the photodichroism of retinal receptors. The extent to which dichroism exist in a retina exposed to a linearly polarized flash was determined by comparison of the amplitudes of the R_1 responses elicited by two flashes linearly polarized parallel to each other with the amplitudes of the R_1 responses obtained using flashes linearly polarized perpendicular to each other. As has been found in other studies, using different techniques, the retinal receptors display no photodichroism. The authors point out, however, that since the Brownian motion in their preparation should be restricted, the lack of photodichroism cannot be attributed to molecular rotational movement. They suggest that short-range radiationless energy transfer offers a possible explanation for their observations.

A theoretical discussion of the possibility of "screening" effects in retinal receptors is given by Goldstein & Williams (90). The effective absorption spectra of rhodopsin in the presence of screening photopigments was calculated, and the spectral sensitivity resulting from such screening is discussed. The case of "self-screening" by a pigment in a given receptor is also considered.

Some interesting findings on the metabolism of retinal receptors have been reported by Young (181) and Young & Droz (182). Using quantitative electron microscope radioautography, they found that radioactive amino acids were incorporated in the disc membranes of rods of frog retina. The red-rods formed discs at the rate of 36 per day. In cones no neoformation of discs was observed and the radioactivity was diffusely distributed throughout the outer segments of the cones. In the rod receptors the radioactivity was found to move distally as a discrete band, indicating that discs are constantly being renewed. The most apical discs disappear and may be disposed of by the pigment epithelium cells whose processes envelop the outer segments. Hall, Bok & Bacharach (101) demonstrated that at least part of amino acid label is incorporated into rhodopsin in the rod disc of frog retinae. They isolated and purified rhodopsin from adult frogs injected with tritiated leucine and phenylalanine and recovered 65 per cent of the radioactivity extracted from the retinae of these frogs in the rhodopsin. Matsubara et al. (120) obtained similar results using C^{14} labeled methionine.

In a theoretical paper which collects and extends much of Rushton's earlier work on the kinetics of cone pigments *in situ,* measured by retinal densitometry, Henry & Rushton (106) reaffirm for cone pigments Rushton's equation for the relation between the fraction of pigment bleached and the intensity of the bleaching light. This paper additionally provides important information about pigment regeneration. The time-constant of regeneration is shown to be a function of the quantal flux. Recovery following a very strong 1 sec bleach was much faster than recovery following a strong 3½ min full bleach. The authors suggest that their results can be explained if there is a "local supply" of 11-*cis* retinal which is used up under the conditions of slow bleaching.

Also using fundus reflectometry, Weale (166) has measured density changes in the dark-adapted peripheral retina following the sequence of a short bleach (0.5 min), 0.5 min dark period, and another 0.5 min bleach. Analysis of the spectral shifts of difference spectra after each step in the sequence leads the author to propose a photosensitivity for the breakdown products of bleaching which is 1/130 the value of rhodopsin. After allowing for photoproducts, the λ max of the difference spectrum of rhodopsin was found to be 497 nm. Additionally, Weale finds that rhodopsin regenerates at half the rate previously noted for cone pigments.

ACKNOWLEDGMENT

The authors are grateful to Dr. A. M. Prestrude for bibliographic assistance, and to Prof. T. P. Williams and Dr. R. H. Johnson for a critical reading of portions of the manuscript. This report was prepared with the support of grants NB 07228-02 and 9RO1 EY-00479-03, both from the U.S.P.H.S.

LITERATURE CITED

1. Abrahamson, E. W., Ostroy, S. E. The photochemical and macromolecular aspects of vision. In *Progress in Biophysics and Molecular Biology,* **17,** 179–215 (Bulfer, J. A. V., Huxley, H. E., Eds., Pergamon Press, Oxford, 392 pp., 1967)
2. Abrahamson, E. W., Wiesenfeld, J. R. Paper presented at the 2nd Intern. Symp. on Biochemistry of the Eye, Nymegen, The Netherlands, 1968
3. Adams, C. K., Jones, A. E., Spectral sensitivity of the sooty mangabey. *Percept. Psychophys.,* **2,** 419–22 (1967)
4. Akhtar, M., Blosse, P. T., Dewhurst, P. B. Studies on vision. The nature of the retinal-opsin linkage. *Biochem. J.,* **110,** 693–702 (1968)
5. Alpern, M., Rushton, W. A. H. The nature of rise in threshold produced by contrast-flashes. *J. Physiol.,* **189,** 519–34 (1967)
6. Anstis, S. M. Visual adaptation to gradual change of intensity. *Science,* **155,** 710–12 (1967)
7. Arden, G. B., Bridges, C. D. B., Ikeda, H., Siegel, I. M. Rapid light-induced potentials common to plant and animal tissues. *Nature,* **212,** 1235–36 (1966)
8. Arden, G. B., Bridges, C. D. B., Ikeda, H., Siegel, I. M. Mode of generation of the early receptor potential. *Vision Res.,* **8,** 13–25 (1968)
9. Arden, G. B., Ikeda, H., Siegel, I. M. Effects of light-adaptation on the early receptor potential. *Vision Res.,* **6,** 357–71 (1966)
10. Arden, G. B., Ikeda, H., Siegel, I. M. New components of the mammalian receptor potential and their relation to visual photochemistry. *Ibid.,* 373–84
11. Arden, G. B., Miller, G. L. Generation of the vertebrate early receptor potential and its relation to rhodopsin. *Nature,* **218,** 646–49 (1968)
12. Baker, B. N., Williams, T. P. Thermal decomposition of rhodopsin, photoregenerated rhodopsin and P470. *Vision Res.,* **8,** 1467–69 (1968)
13. Barlow, H. B. Purkinje shift and retinal noise. *Nature,* **179,** 255–56 (1957)
14. Baumann, C., Scheibner, H. The dark adaptation of single units in the isolated frog retina following partial bleaching of rhodopsin. *Vision Res.,* **8,** 1127–39 (1968)
15. Baumann, F. Slow and spike potentials recorded from retinula cells of the honeybee drone in response to light. *J. Gen. Physiol.,* **52,** 855–75 (1968)
16. Baumgardt, E. Rhodopsine et sensibilité au rouge en vision scotopique. *C. R. Acad. Sci. (Paris),* **262,** 1874–77 (1966)
17. Baumgardt, E. On direct scaling methods. *Vision Res.,* **7,** 679–81 (1967)
18. Baumgardt, H., Scheibner, H. Sur l'emploi en optique physiologique des grandeurs scotopiques. *Vision Res.,* **7,** 59–63 (1967)
19. Beinhocker, G. D., Brooks, P. R., Anfenger, E., Copenhaver, R. M. Electroperimetry. *IEEE Trans. Biomed. Engin.,* **BME-13,** 11–18 (1966)
20. Békésy, G. Von. Mach- and Hering-type lateral inhibition in vision. *Vision Res.,* **8,** 1483–99 (1968)
21. Berkley, M., Wolf, E., Glickstein, M. Photic evoked potentials in the cat: evidence for a direct geniculate input to visual II. *Exptl. Neurol.,* **19,** 188–98 (1967)
22. Biersdorf, W. R. Rod and cone contributions to the off effect of the human ERG. *Invest. Ophthal.,* **7,** 371–77 (1968)
23. Blatz, P. E., Balasubramaniyan, P., Balasubramaniyan, V. Synthesis of all-trans-5-6-dihydroretinal, a new visual chromophore. *J. Am. Chem. Soc.* **90,** 3282 (1968)
24. Blatz, P. E., Pippert, D. L., Balasubramaniyan, V. Absorption maxima of cations related to retinal and their implication to mechanisms for bathochromic shift in visual pigment. *Photochem. Photobiol.,* **8,** 309–15 (1968)
25. Bonting, S. L., Bangham, A. D. On the biochemical mechanism of the visual process. *Exptl. Eye Res.,* **6,** 400–13 (1967)
26. Borsellino, A., Fuortes, M. G. F. Responses to single photons in

visual cells of *Limulus. J. Physiol.*, **196,** 507–39 (1968)

27. Borsellino, A., Fuortes, M. G. F. Interpretation of responses of visual cells of *Limulus. Proc. IEEE,* **56,** 1024–32 (1968)
28. Bownds, D. Site of attachment of retinal in rhodopsin. *Nature,* **216,** 1178 (1968)
29. Bridges, C. D. B. Spectroscopic properties of porphyropsins. *Vision Res.,* **7,** 349–70 (1967)
30. Bridges, C. D. B. Absorption properties, interconversions and environmental adaptation of pigments from fish photoreceptors. *Cold Spring Harbor Symp. Quant. Biol.,* **30,** 317–34 (1965)
31. Bridges, C. D. B. Biochemistry of visual processes, Chap. II, *Comprehensive Biochemistry,* **27** (Florkin, M., Stotz, E. H., Eds.) *Photobiology, Ionizing Radiations,* 31–78 (Elsevier, New York, 384 pp., 1967)
32. Brooks, B. Neurophysiological correlates of brightness discrimination in the lateral geniculate of the squirrel monkey. *Exptl. Brain Res.,* **2,** 1–17 (1966)
33. Brown, J. E., Murray, J. R., Smith, T. G. Photoelectric potential from photoreceptor cells in ventral eye of Limulus. *Science,* **158,** 665 (1967)
34. Brown, J. L. Sensitivity and spectral response of human vision at low luminances. *Tech. Rept., Dept. Psychol., Kansas State Univ.,* **2,** 1–10 (1966)
35. Brown, K. T. Analysis of the electroretinogram and the origins of its components. *Jap. J. Ophthal.,* **10,** 130–40 (1966)
36. Brown, K. T. The electroretinogram; its components and their origins. *Vision Res.,* **8,** 633–78 (1968)
37. Brown, K. T., Crawford, J. M. Intracellular recording of rapid light-evoked responses from pigment epithelium cells of the frog eye. *Physiologist,* **9,** 146 (1966)
38. Brown, K. T., Crawford, J. M. Intracellular recording of rapid light-evoked responses from pigment epithelium cells of the frog eye. *Vision Res.,* **7,** 149–63 (1967)
39. Brown, K. T., Crawford, J. M. Melanin and the rapid-light evoked responses from pigment epithelium cells of the frog eye. *Ibid.,* 165–78
40. Brown, K. T., Gage, P. W. An earlier phase of the light evoked electrical response from the pigment epithelium-choroid complex of the eye of the toad. *Nature,* **211,** 155–58 (1966)
41. Brown, K. T., Gage, P. W., Crawford, J. M. Ionic dependence of the third phase of the light-evoked response from amphibian pigment epithelium cells. *Vision Res.,* **8,** 369–82 (1968)
42. Brown, K. T., Murakami, M. A new receptor potential of the monkey retina with no detectable latency. *Nature,* **201,** 626–28 (1964)
43. Brown, K. T., Murakami, M. Delayed decay of the late receptor potential of monkey cones as a function of stimulus intensity. *Vision Res.,* **7,** 179–89 (1967)
44. Brown, K. T., Murakami, M. Rapid effects of light and dark adaptation upon the receptive field organization of S-potentials and late receptor potentials. *Ibid.,* **8,** 1145–71 (1968)
45. Brown, K. T., Wiesel, T. N. Intraretinal recording with micropipette electrodes in the intact cat eye. *J. Physiol.,* **149,** 537–62 (1959)
46. Brown, K. T., Wiesel, T. N. Localization of origins of electroretinogram components by intraretinal recording in the intact cat eye. *Ibid.,* **158,** 257–80 (1961)
47. Buckser, S. Inability of the electroretinogram to recover after a brief, high-intensity light stimulus. *Nature,* **210,** 425–26 (1966)
48. Buckser, S. Evaluation of several models treating recovery of ERG *a*-wave after light adaptation. *Curr. Mod. Biol.,* **1,** 285–90 (1967)
49. Buckser, S. The recovery of the albino rat electroretinogram after partial light adaptation. *Photochem. Photobiol.,* **6,** 73–82 (1967)
50. Buckser, S. Some properties of the electroretinogram long latency negative wave obtained below the b-wave threshold. *Comp. Biochem. Physiol.,* **24,** 487–500 (1968)
51. Burkhardt, D. A., Riggs, L. A. Modification of the human visual evoked potentials by monochromatic backgrounds. *Vision Res.,* **7,** 453–59 (1967)

52. Burkhardt, D. A., Whittle, P. Spectral-sensitivity functions for homochromatic-contrast detection. *J. Opt. Soc. Am.*, **57**, 416–20 (1967)
53. Cone, R. A. Early receptor potential of the vertebrate retina. *Nature*, **204**, 736–39 (1964)
54. Cone, R. A. Early receptor potential: photoreversible charge displacement in rhodopsin. *Science*, **155**, 1128 (1967)
55. Cone, R. A., Brown, P. K. Dependence of the early receptor potential on the orientation of rhodopsin. *Science*, **156**, 536 (1967)
56. Connors, M. M. Effect of wavelength and bandwidth of red light on recovery of dark-adaptation. *J. Opt. Soc. Am.*, **56**, 111–15 (1966)
57. Crawford, J. M., Cage, P. W., Brown, K. T. Rapid light-evoked potentials at extremes of pH from the frog's retina and pigment epithelium, and from a synthetic melanin. *Vision Res.*, **7**, 539–51 (1967)
58. Crescitelli, F. Extraction of visual pigments with certain alkye phenoxy polyethoxy ethanol surface-active agents. *Vision Res.*, **7**, 685–94 (1967)
59. Cronly-Dillon, J., Sharma, S. C. Effect of season and sex on the photopic spectral sensitivity of the three-spined stickleback. *J. Exptl. Biol.*, **49**, 679–87 (1968)
60. Daemen, F. J. M., Bonting, S. L. Biochemical aspects of the visual process III. Specificity of the retinaldehyde effect on cation movements in rod outer segments. *Biochem. Biophys. Acta*, **163**, 212–17 (1968)
61. Dartnall, H. J. A. The visual pigment of the green rods. *Vision Res.*, **7**, 1–16 (1967)
62. Dartnall, H. J. A. The photosensitivities of visual pigments in the presence of hydroxylamine. *Ibid.*, **8**, 333–39 (1968)
63. De Pont, J. J. H. H. M., Daemen, F. J. M., Bonting, S. L. Biochemical aspects of the visual process II. Schiff base formation in phosphatidylethanylamine monolayers upon penetration by retinaldehyde. *Biochem. Biophys. Acta*, **163**, 204–11 (1968)
64. De Valois, R. L., Abramov, I., Jacobs, G. H. Analysis of response patterns of LGN cells. *J. Opt. Soc. Am.*, **56**, 966–77 (1966)
65. Dill, R. C., Vallecalle, E., Verzeano, M. Evoked potentials neuronal activity and stimulus intensity in the visual system. *Physiol. Behav.*, **3**, 289–93 (1968)
66. Donner, K. O., Reuter, T. Dark adaptation processes in the rhodopsin rods of the frog's retina. *Vision Res.*, **7**, 17–41 (1967)
67. Donner, K. O., Reuter, T. Visual adaptation of the rhodopsin rods in the frog's retina. *J. Physiol.*, **199**, 59–87 (1968)
68. Dowling, J. E. Night blindness. *Sci. Am.*, **215**, 78–84 (1966)
69. Dowling, J. E. The organization of vertebrate visual receptors. In *Molecular Organization and Biological Function*, 186–210 (Allen, J. M., Ed., Harper & Row, New York, 243 pp., 1967)
70. Dowling, J. E. The site of visual adaptation. *Science*, **155**, 273–79 (1967)
71. Dowling, J. E. Synaptic organization of the frog retina; an electron microscopic analysis comparing the retinas of frogs and primates. *Proc. Roy. Soc. (B)*, **170**, 205–28 (1968)
72. Dowling, J. E., Boycott, B. B. Organization of the primate retina: electron microscopy. *Proc. Roy. Soc. (B)*, **166**, 80–111 (1967)
73. DuCroz, J. J., Rushton, W. A. H. The separation of cone mechanisms in dark adaptation. *J. Physiol.*, **183**, 481–96 (1966)
74. Easter, S. S. Excitation in the goldfish retina: evidence for a nonlinear intensity code. *J. Physiol.*, **195**, 253–71 (1968)
75. Easter, S. S. Adaptation in the goldfish retina. *Ibid.*, 273–81
76. Easter, S. S., MacNichol, E. F. Adaptation in the goldfish's retina. *Fed. Proc.*, **25** (1966)
77. Ebrey, T. G. Fast light-evoked potential from leaves. *Science*, **155**, 1556–57 (1967)
78. Ebrey, T. G. The thermal decay of the intermediates of rhodopsin *in situ*. *Vision Res.*, **8**, 965–82 (1968)
79. Ekman, G. Temporal integration of brightness. *Vision Res.*, **6**, 683–88 (1966)
80. Ekman, G., Gustafsson, U. Threshold values and the psycho-physical function in brightness vision. *Vision Res.*, **8**, 747–58 (1968)

81. Ekman, G., Hosman, J., Berglund, U. Perceived brightness as a function of duration of dark-adaptation. *Percep. Mot. Skills,* **23,** 931–43 (1966)

82. Erhardt, F., Ostroy, S. E., Abrahamson, E. W. Protein configuration changes in the photolysis of rhodopsin I. The thermal decay of cattle lumirhodopsin in vitro. *Biochem. Biophys. Acta,* **112,** 256–64 (1966)

83. Erickson, J. O., Blatz, P. E. N-retinylidene-1-amino-2-propanol; A schiff base analog for rhodopsin. *Vision Res.,* **8,** 1367–75 (1968)

84. Falk, G., Fatt, P. Rapid hydrogen ion uptake of rod outer segments and rhodopsin solution on illumination. *J. Physiol.,* **183,** 211–24 (1966)

85. Fatechand, R. Generation of the early receptor potential with long flashes. *Nature,* **219,** 390–92 (1968)

86. Frank, R. N., Dowling, J. E. Rhodopsin photoproducts: effects on electroretinogram sensitivity in isolated perfused rat retina. *Science,* **161,** 487–89 (1968)

87. Gaunt, P. The saturation of rod receptors. *Opt. Acta,* **15,** 287–93 (1968)

88. Goldstein, E. B. Early receptor potential of the isolated frog (Rana pipiens) retina. *Vision Res.,* **7,** 837–45 (1967)

89. Goldstein, E. B. Visual pigments and the early receptor potential of the isolated frog retina. *Ibid.,* **8,** 953–63 (1968)

90. Goldstein, E. B., Williams, T. P. Calculated effects of "screening pigments." *Vision Res.,* **6,** 39–50 (1966)

91. Gouras, P. Rod and cone independence in the electroretinogram of the dark-adapted monkey's perifovea. *J. Physiol.,* **187,** 455–64 (1966)

92. Gouras, P. The effects of light adaptation on rod and cone receptive field organization of monkey ganglion cells. *Ibid.,* **192,** 747–60 (1967)

93. Gouras, P. Visual adaptation: its mechanism. *Science,* **157,** 583–84 (1967)

94. Gouras, P., Link, K. Rod and cone interaction in dark-adapated monkey ganglion cells. *J. Physiol.,* **184,** 499–510 (1966)

95. Grady, F. J., Borg, D. C. Light-induced tree radicals of retinal, retinol and rhodopsin. *Biochemistry,* **7,** 675–82 (1968)

96. Granda, A. M., Biersdorf, W. R. The spectral sensitivity of the human electroretinogram during the temporal course of dark-adaptation. *Vision Res.,* **6,** 507–16 (1966)

97. Guth, S. L. Nonadditivity and inhibition among chromatic luminances at threshold. *Vision Res.,* **7,** 319–28 (1967)

98. Guzzo, A. V., Pool, G. L. Visual pigment fluorescence. *Science,* **159,** 312–14 (1968)

99. Hagins, W. A., McGaughty, R. E. Molecular and thermal origins of the fast photoelectric effects in the squid retina. *Science,* **157,** 813 (1967)

100. Hagins, W. A., McGaughty, R. E. Membrane origin of the fast photo voltage of squid retina. *Ibid.,* **159,** 213 (1968)

101. Hall, M. O., Bok, D., Bacharach, A. D. E. Visual pigment renewal in the mature frog retina. *Science,* **161,** 787–89 (1968)

102. Hamasaki, D. I. The effect of sodium concentration on the electroretinogram of the isolated frog retina. *J. Physiol.,* **167,** 156–68 (1963)

103. Hammond, P. Spectral properties of dark-adapted retinal ganglion cells in the plaice (Pleuronectes Platess, L.) *J. Physiol.,* **195,** 535–56 (1968)

104. Heller, J. Structure of visual pigments I. Purification, molecular weight and composition of bovine visual $pigment_{500}$. *Biochemistry,* **7,** 2906–13 (1968)

105. Heller, J. Structure of visual pigments. II. Binding of retinal and conformational changes on light exposure in bovine visual $pigment_{500}$. *Ibid.,* 2914–20

106. Henry, G. H., Rushton, W. A. H. Bleaching and regeneration of cone pigments in man. *Vision Res.,* **8,** 617–31 (1968)

107. Hornung, J. Über den statischen Regelfaktor der menschlichen Pupille. *Kybernetik,* **3,** 93–98 (1966)

108. Hornung, J. Pupillenbewegungen nach einem Sprung der Reizlichtintensität. *Pflügers Arch. Ges. Physiol.,* **296,** 39–48 (1967)

109. Houlihan, K., Sekuler, R. W. Contour interaction in visual masking.

J. Exptl. Psychol., **77,** 281–85 (1968)
110. Hubbard, R. The thermal stability of rhodopsin and opsin. *J. Gen. Physiol.,* **42,** 259–80 (1958)
111. Hubbard, R., Kropf, A. Molecular isomers in vision. *Sci. Am.,* **216,** 64–76 (1967)
112. Inuzuka, K., Becker, R. S. Mechanism of photoisomerization in the retinals and implications in rhodopsin. *Nature,* **219,** 383–85 (1968)
113. Johnson, E. P., Riggs, L. A., Schick, A. M. L. Photopic retinal potentials evoked by phase alternation of a barred pattern. *Clin. Electroretinography Suppl., Vision Res.,* 75–91 (1966)
114. Kropf, A. Intramolecular energy transfer in rhodopsin. *Vision Res.,* **7,** 811–18 (1967)
115. Lange, D., Hartline, H. K., Ratliff, F. Inhibitory interactions in the retina. *Ann. N.Y. Acad. Sci.,* **128,** 955 (1966)
116. LeGrand, Y., *Form and Space Vision* (Indiana Univ. Press, Bloomington, 367 pp., 1967)
117. Liebman, P. A., Entine, G. Visual pigments of frog and tadpole (Rana pipiens). *Vision Res.,* **8,** 761–77 (1968)
118. Luria, S. M. Effect of width of movement of a masking stimulus at constant target separation. *J. Opt. Soc. Am.,* **57,** 273–75 (1967)
119. Makous, W. L. A transient Stiles-Crawford effect. *Vision Res.,* **8,** 1271–84 (1968)
120. Matsubara, T., Miyata, M., Mizuno, K. Radiosotopic studies on renewal of opsin. *Vision Res.,* **8,** 1139–45 (1968)
121. Matthews, R. G., Hubbard, R., Brown, P. K., Wald, G. Tautomeric forms of metarhodopsin. *J. Gen. Physiol.,* **47,** 215–40 (1963)
122. McConnell, D. G., Rafferty, C. N., Dilley, R. A. The light-induced proton uptake in bovine retinal outer segment fragments. *J. Biol. Chem.,* **243,** 5820–26 (1968)
123. Michael, C. R. Receptive fields of directionally selective units in the optic nerve of the ground squirrel and receptive fields of opponent color units in the optic nerve of the ground squirrel. *Science,* **152,** 1092–97 (1966)
124. Michael, C. R. Receptive fields of single optic nerve fibers in a mammal with an all-cone retina I: Contrast-sensitive units II: Directional selective units III: Opponent color units. *J. Neurophysiol.,* **31,** 249–82 (1968)
125. Muntz, W. R. A., Northmore, D. P. M. Background light, temperature, and visual noise in the turtle. *Vision Res.,* **8,** 787–801 (1967)
126. Munz, F. W., Schwanzara, S. A. A nomogram for $retinene_2$ based visual pigments. *Vision Res.,* **7,** 111–20 (1967)
127. Murray, G. C. Intracellular absorption difference spectrum of Limulus extra-ocular photolabile pigment. *Science,* **154,** 1182–83 (1966)
128. Naka, K. I., Rushton, W. A. H. S-potentials from colour units in the retina of fish (Cyprinidae). *J. Physiol.,* **185,** 536–55 (1966)
129. Naka, K. I., Rushton, W. A. H. S-potentials from luminosity units in the retina of fish (Cyprinidae). *Ibid.,* 587–99
130. Naka, K. I., Rushton, W. A. H. The generation and spread of S-potentials in fish (Cyprinidae). *Ibid.,* **192,** 437–61 (1967)
131. Norton, A. L., Spekreijse, H., Wolbarsht, M. L., Wagner, H. G. Receptive field organization of the S-potential. *Science,* **160,** 1021–22 (1968)
132. Ogawa, T., Kozaki, T., Takano, Y., Okayma, K. Effect of area on apparent brightness. *Psychol. Lab. Rept.,* Keio Univ., Japan, **2,** 1–15 (1966)
133. Ostroy, S. E., Erhardt, F., Abrahamson, E. W. Protein configuration changes in the protolysis of rhodopsin II. The sequence of intermediates in thermal decay of cattle metarhodopsin in vitro. *Biochem. Biophys. Acta,* **112,** 265–77 (1966)
134. Pak, W. L. Rapid photoresponses in the retina and their relevance to vision research. *Photochem. Photobiol.,* **8,** 495–503 (1968)
135. Pak, W. L., Boes, R. J. Rhodopsin; responses from transient intermediates formed during its bleaching. *Science,* **155,** 1131–33 (1967)
136. Pak, W. L., Cone, R. A. Isolation and identification of the initial peak of the early receptor potential. *Nature,* **204,** 836 (1964)
137. Pak, W. L., Helmrich, H. G. Ab-

sence of photodichroism in retinal receptors. *Vision Res.,* **8,** 585–91 (1968)

138. Pak, W. L., Rozzi, V. P., Ebrey, T. G. Effect of changes in the chemical environment of the retina on the two components of the early receptor potential. *Nature,* **214,** 109–10 (1967)
139. Pantle, A., Sekuler, R. Size-detecting mechanisms in human vision. *Science,* **162,** 1146–48 (1968)
140. Perry, N. W., Childers, D. G., McCoy, J. G. Binocular addition of the visual evoked response at different cortical locations. *Vision Res.,* **8,** 567–73 (1968)
141. Perry, N. W., Copenhaver, R. M. Evoked retinal and occipital potentials during dark adaptation in man. *Clin. Electroretinography Suppl., Vision Res.,* 249–54 (1966)
142. Pratt, D. C. Photoreaction of isorhodopsin at low temperatures. *Photochem. Photobiol.,* **7,** 319–24 (1968)
143. Ratliff, F., Hartline, H. K., Lange, D. Dynamics of lateral inhibition in the compound eye of Limulus. In *The Functional Organization of the Compound Eye,* 399–450 (Bernhard, C. G., Ed., Pergamon Press, Oxford, 591 pp., 1966)
144. Reuter, T. The synthesis of photosensitive pigments in the rods of the frog's retina. *Vision Res.,* **6,** 15–38 (1966)
145. Riggs, L. A., Johnson, E. P., Schick, A. M. L. Electrical responses of the human eye to changes in wavelength of the stimulating light. *J. Opt. Soc. Am.,* **56,** 1621–27 (1966)
146. Rinalducci, E. J. Early dark adaptation as a function of wavelength and pre-adapting level. *J. Opt. Soc. Am.,* **57,** 1270–71 (1967)
147. Rosenberg, B. A physical approach to the visual receptor process. In *Advances in Radiation Biology,* 193–241 (Augenstein, L., Mason, R., Zelle, M., Eds., Academic Press, New York, **2,** **371** pp., 1966)
148. Rosenberg, B., Krigas, T. M. Spectral shifts in retinal Schiff base complexes. *Photochem. Photobiol.,* **6,** 769–73 (1967)
149. Rushton, W. A. H. Effect of humming on vision. *Nature,* **216,** 1173–75 (1967)
150. Rushton, W. A. H. Rod/cone rivalry in pigment regeneration. *J. Physiol.,* **198,** 219–36 (1968)
151. Rushton, W. A. H., Gubisch, R. W. Glare: its measurement by cone thresholds and by bleaching of cone pigments. *J. Opt. Soc. Am.,* **56,** 104–10 (1966)
152. Schwanzara, S. A. The visual pigments of freshwater fishes. *Vision Res.,* **7,** 121–48 (1967)
153. Shields, J. C., Dinovo, E. C., Henriksen, R. A., Kimbel, R. L., Jr., Miller, P. G. The purification and amino acid composition of bovine rhodopsin. *Biochem. Biophys. Acta,* **147,** 238–51 (1967)
154. Smith, T. G., Brown, J. E. A photoelectric potential in invertebrate cells. *Nature,* **212,** 1217–19 (1966)
155. Smith, T. G., Stell, W. K., Brown, J. E. Conductance changes associated with receptor potentials in Limulus photoreceptors. *Science,* **162,** 454–56 (1968)
156. Smith, T. G., Stell, W. K., Brown, J. E., Freeman, J. A., Murray, G. C. A role for the sodium pump in photoreception in Limulus. *Science,* **162,** 456–58 (1968)
157. Stabell, B., Stabell, U. Night vision as chromatic vision. *Scand. J. Psychol.,* **8,** 145–49 (1967)
158. Sturr, J. F., Battersby, W. S. Neural limitations of visual excitability. VIII: Binocular convergence in cat geniculate and cortex. *Vision Res.,* **6,** 401–18 (1966)
159. Teller, D. Y., Andrews, D. P., Barlow, H. B. Local adaptation in stabilized vision. *Vision Res.,* **6,** 701–6 (1966)
160. Teller, D. Y., Galanter, E. Brightness, luminances, and Fechner's paradox. *Percept. Psychophys.,* **2,** 297–300 (1967)
161. Toth, J., Rosenberg, B. Enamine salts of retinals with secondary amines. *Vision Res.,* **8,** 1471–82 (1968)
162. Troelstra, A., Schweitzer, N. M. J. Nonlinear analysis of electroretinographic B wave in man. *J. Neurophysiol.,* **31,** 558–606 (1968)
163. van Lith, G. H. M. Simultane Bestimmung der elektroretinographischen und sensorischen Reizschwelle. *Vision Res.,* **6,** 185–97 (1966)
164. Wald, G. The molecular basis of visual excitation. *Science,* **162,** 230–39 (1968)
165. Wald, G., Seldin, E. Spectral sen-

sitivity of the common prawn. *J. Gen. Physiol.*, **51**, 694–700 (1968)

166. Weale, R. A. On an early stage of rhodopsin regeneration in man. *Vision Res.*, **7**, 819–28 (1967)

167. Weale, R. A. Photochemistry and vision. In *Photophysiology*, **9**, 1–45 (Giese, A. C., Ed., Academic Press, New York, 373 pp. 1968)

168. Weale, R. A. Photochemistry of the human central fovea. *Nature*, **218**, 238–40 (1968)

169. Weinstein, G. W., Hobson, R. R., Dowling, J. E. Light and dark adaptation in the isolated rat retina. *Nature*, **215**, 134–38 (1967)

170. Westheimer, G. The Maxwellian view. *Vision Res.*, **6**, 669–82 (1966)

171. Westheimer, G. Spatial interaction in human cone vision. *J. Physiol.*, **190**, 139–54 (1967)

172. Westheimer, G. Bleached rhodopsin and retinal interaction. *Ibid.*, **195**, 95–105 (1968)

173. Whittle, P., Riggs, L. A. Human occipital and retinal potentials evoked by subjectively faded visual stimuli. *Vision Res.*, **7**, 441–51 (1967)

174. Wiesenfeld, J. R., Abrahamson, E. W. Visual pigments: their spectra and isomerizations. *Photochem. Photobiol.*, **8**, 487–93 (1968)

175. Williams, T. P. Induced asymmetry in the prosthetic group of rhodopsin. *Vision Res.*, **6**, 293–300 (1966)

176. Williams, T. P. Limitations on the use of the concept of quantum efficiency in rhodopsin bleaching. *Nature*, **209**, 1350–51 (1966)

177. Williams, T. P. Photolysis of metarhodopsin II. Rate of production of P 470 and rhodopsin. *Vision Res.*, **8**, 1457–66 (1968)

178. Williams, T. P., Breil, S. J. Kinetic measurements on rhodopsin solutions during intense flashes. *Vision Res.*, **8**, 777–86 (1968)

179. Williams, T. P., Milby, S. E. The thermal decomposition of some visual pigments. *Vision Res.*, **8**, 359–70 (1968)

180. Yoshizawa, T., Wald, G. Photochemistry of iodopsin. *Nature*, **214**, 566–71 (1967)

181. Young, R. W. The renewal of photoreceptor cell outer segments. *J. Cell. Biol.*, **33**, 61–68 (1967)

182. Young, R. W., Droz, B. The renewal of protein in retinal rods and cones. *J. Cell Biol.*, **39**, 169–84 (1968)

ATTENTION[1]

By John A. Swets
Bolt Beranek and Newman Inc., Cambridge, Massachusetts
and Alfred B. Kristofferson
McMaster University, Hamilton, Ontario

"The doctrine of attention is the nerve of the whole psychological system, and that as men judge of it, so shall they be judged before the general tribunal of psychology." That was Titchener (95) speaking, and leaving little doubt about the centrality of the concept of attention at the time that psychology was formed. Titchener spoke as a Structuralist. Though the Functionalists had a different view of the nature of attention, they agreed on the concept's importance. After the turn of the century, however, attention was almost totally ignored in psychology; it had little or no place in the behavioristic, gestalt, or psychoanalytic positions. Only in the 1950's was interest in the concept renewed. Work since has progressed enough to justify this first chapter on attention in the *Annual Review of Psychology*.

In stating the view of the Functionalists, William James could write that "Every one knows what attention is" (39), but it does not appear that simple to present-day reviewers. Moray (67) has listed six familiar categories of attention—mental concentration, vigilance, selective attention, search, activation, and set—and has suggested that Neisser's (72) recent treatment of analysis-by-synthesis may be a seventh. We focus here on two of these categories—as it happens, two that exhibit continuity with the earliest theoretical positions. The first is "selective attention," which is what the Functionalists thought attention was all about. The emphasis is on the process of the organism's choosing to notice a particular part of his environment. The second is "vigilance," or "sustained attention." The historical connection here is less direct, but the emphasis is on the result of the attentive process, or the "sensory clearness," that was stressed by the Structuralists.

Recent interest in these two aspects of attention was largely stimulated by work done in England, primarily at the Applied Psychology Research Unit in Cambridge. Broadbent's (2) and Cherry's (11) experiments inspired many others on selective attention to speech stimuli. Our review of this work takes its starting point in 1958 after the publication of Broad-

[1] Preparation of this review was supported by the Human Performance Branch of NASA-Ames Research Center under Contract No. NAS2–5108. Our search of the literature (concluded in March 1969) benefited from the advice of Joseph Markowitz, Neville Moray, and Charles S. Watson, and from the assistance of Belver C. Griffith, Philip J. Siegmann, and Kathleen Benson.

bent's book (3). Also under the heading of selective attention we consider simpler (e.g., sinusoidal) stimuli, which takes us back a few years before that. N. H. Mackworth (63) borrowed from Head (35) the term "vigilance" to describe his landmark experiments. For the most part we pick up this topic in 1963, after publication of the review by Frankmann & Adams (24) and the comprehensive symposium volume edited by Buckner & McGrath (10). We go back a few years before that to give full coverage to a related area of work, namely, "signal detection with undefined observation intervals"; the task so described merges with the classical vigilance task when the signal rate is low and the observation period is long.

An active area of research excluded from this review is that of "activation," or "neurophysiological correlates of attention." This work has recently been reviewed elsewhere [Hernández-Peón (36); Horn (37); Worden (109); Mostofsky (70)].

SELECTIVE ATTENTION

During the past 10 years the dominant approach to selective attention has been that concerned with speech stimuli in the Broadbent tradition. We review this approach first by presenting a précis of Broadbent's filter theory, an examination of subsequent experimental results, and an account of the five major, newer theories. Then several other classes of experiments are surveyed, mostly involving nonspeech stimuli. In conclusion, we offer a commentary on current theory and directions of research.

Speech Stimuli

Three classes of experiments belong under this heading, but the first of them, the "listen and answer" experiments which formed much of the base of Broadbent's theory, is covered in his book (3). The first experiments using the other two techniques, "split memory span" and "shadowing," also influenced filter theory in its original form, but there are many later studies using these methods and they are reviewed below.

Broadbent's filter theory.—Though this theory was based mainly upon experiments on selective listening to speech, it undoubtedly was strongly influenced by Broadbent's applications of it to vigilance, continuous work, conditioning and extinction, distraction, and other phenomena. The theory and these applications are described in his book.

Information enters the organism over many parallel sensory pathways, and the total quantity of this input usually exceeds the limited capacity of the single central channel (the "P-system"). To prevent overloading the P-system, a "filter" is posited that admits only part of the input at any one time. A part that can enter at one time is not defined in terms of rigidly-bounded sensory channels, and it is said that the contents of two input channels can pass the filter simultaneously if their total information does not exceed the capacity of the P-system. The functional boundaries of input channels are not defined further than this. But the identity of an input channel is said to be determined by a feature which all elements of a message have in common. Some possible features are physical ones such as frequency, intensity, spatial location, and sensory modality. The possibility of "nonphysical" features that can identify input channels is left open.

Inputs that are blocked by the filter at the time of their arrival may enter the P-system later because they remain in a short-term store for a matter of seconds. If the filter switches appropriately, the stored representation of an input will enter the P-system. Short-term storage, which is interposed between sensory input and the filter, may be refreshed by rehearsal via feedback from the output of the P-system into the short-term store. The theory has other structural components, but the ones mentioned are those relevant to selective attention.

The filter is biased toward input channels in which novel or intense events occur and toward the ear more than the eye. A formal principle is stated to this effect but no decision is reached as to whether a "favored" input attracts the filter, or whether the filter is merely more likely to remain on a channel containing, say, novelty once it has for other reasons zeroed in on it. The difference between these alternatives is important because it bears on the question of the extent to which inputs are processed prior to entering the P-system.

Broadbent also stresses the lability of the filter when he discusses distraction and vigilance. He does not expect the filter to remain locked on one input channel continuously for long periods of time.

Among the many important questions raised by this theory we single out these for emphasis: (*a*) Is information interpreted at all prior to the P-system? (*b*) What features of a message can serve to identify its channel? (*c*) Can the filter be locked on a particular channel, or away from a channel, for a long period of time? (*d*) Are the boundaries of input channels as flexibl as implied by filter theory? (*e*) What are the temporal characteristics of filter-switching between inputs? (*f*) Is the filter all-or-none or does it operate on some other principle?

Our survey will show that research since 1958 has not yet provided definitive answers to these and related questions.

Split-span experiments.—Six digits presented successively at the rate of two per second with each digit entering both ears can be reproduced without error 93 per cent of the time. However, if the six digits are presented as three pairs, with one member of a pair going into the right ear at the same time the other member enters the left ear, the percentage of correct reproductions drops to 65. The correct reproductions are almost always organized by ear of presentation rather than order of presentation; that is, the listener writes down all three from one ear and then all three from the other ear. If reproduction in order of presentation is required, the percentage correct drops to 20. Finally, in the last condition, if the rate of presenting the pairs is decreased to one pair every 2 sec, the percentage correct rises, but only to about 50 [Broadbent (2)]. In terms of filter theory, these results were taken to mean that the ears are separate channels with separate locations in short-term storage. At the moment of recall the contents of one location are read out before the contents of the other. And the grouping of responses thereby becomes a criterion for differentiating between sensory channels. Performance improves as presentation rate is slowed in the case where reproduction in order of presentation is demanded, because it becomes possible to switch the filter back and forth between channels during presentation. From this it was inferred that a double switch requires between 1 and 2 sec, although this interpretation fails to explain the still poor performance at the slowest rate or, for that matter, the partial success at the faster rate.

This interpretation was immediately challenged from two directions. Moray (66) repeated the experiment and showed, at the two-pairs-per-second rate, that if one member of a pair arrives 250 msec after the other member, rather than simultaneously with it, a high level of performance is achieved. This finding called into question Broadbent's interpretation in terms of filter-switching time. Gray & Wedderburn (27) showed that ear of arrival is only one possible cue for grouping by presenting, for example, "mice-5-cheese" to the left ear at the same time as "3-eat-4" to the right ear. This technique pits ear-of-arrival against meaning class (digits vs. words forming phrases) as bases for organizing output, and accuracy is impaired. However, while correct reproductions were sometimes organized by ear of arrival, they were often organized by meaning class. This phenomenon has been confirmed [Yntema & Trask (110); Broadbent & Gregory (7)].

In response to Moray, Broadbent & Gregory (4) presented two additional experiments. In the first, they confirmed Moray's result and also demonstrated that when the digit pairs are presented alternately to the two ears, recall is as accurate when the subject is instructed after stimulation as to whether he must recall in order of arrival or ear-by-ear as it is when the instruction is given before stimulation. In the second experiment, they presented the digits alternately to the eye and ear and found that instructions to recall all those to the ear before those to the eye produced greater accuracy than instructions to recall in order of arrival. They concluded that the two ears may or may not act as separate channels, and that with alternate presentation they may act as a single channel. As a result, when digits enter the two ears alternately, switching of the filter is not necessary. They claimed, however, on the basis of the second experiment, that this option is not open in the eye-ear case, even though they found that accuracy was as high when subjects were required to alternate in the second experiment as it was in the first experiment.

The effect demonstrated by Gray & Wedderburn was explored further by Broadbent & Gregory (7), who varied rate of presentation and found that accuracy improved markedly with slowing of rate when items were of two alternated classes. They eschewed the kind of interpretation they had directed at Moray and concluded instead that classes can act in a way similar to sensory channels, and that the results are due to the requirement that the filter switch between classes. In taking this tack they seemed to be influenced more by the literature that was accumulating on the shadowing technique, and by Treisman's (96) theoretical arguments, than by any requirement imposed by split-span results.

Sanders & Schroots (78, 79) reported results using mixed lists of digits and consonants presented all to one ear with different numbers of transitions between classes. From these results, which also include data from lists made up of other classes, they concluded that interpretations in terms of switching between classes are less satisfactory than interpretations that stress retrieval mechanisms. They pointed out that such a view makes it unnecessary to assume that classes act like sensory channels. Similar arguments had been advanced by others [Bryden (9); Yntema & Trask (110)]. We agree, and conclude that split-span experiments have not provided data that demand revisions in filter theory.

It would be of interest to know what happens when an experiment like that of Gray & Wedderburn is performed using the eye and ear as the two input channels.

Neisser (72) went even further in ascribing recall grouping to memory mechanisms and stated flatly that Broadbent was wrong in his first explanation of split-span. But Neisser did not seem to consider Broadbent & Gregory's explanation (4) of Moray's result. And Egeth (22), in his review of selective attention, excluded split-span experiments on the grounds that they are more germane to short-term memory.

An experiment by Savin (80) added yet another complication. He presented four digits in two pairs, the members of each pair being simultaneous and the second pair beginning one-half second after the onset of the first pair. All digits were spoken in the same voice and all were presented over one loudspeaker. When all four digits were reported correctly, the order of recall most likely by far was one from the first pair followed by one from the second pair followed by the second from the first pair. He concluded that there is a tendency in the auditory system to group successive rather than simultaneous items when there is no other basis for grouping. This principle does not explain earlier split-span results, but it does add to the general conclusion that we are a long way from an understanding of them.

Shadowing experiments.—If two streams of speech are presented simultaneously, one to each ear, a listener normally can separate them, following one and ignoring the other. With the shadowing technique, introduced by Cherry in 1953 (11), the listener is asked to follow one of the messages by repeating it as he receives it. Cherry described the phenomenon without presenting detailed data. He reported that the shadowed message can be repeated with great accuracy, although in monotone, and that the subject may have little idea of its content. The "rejected" message conveys little information. If the language of the rejected message is changed from English to German and back, the subject does not notice the change. But if the voice speaking the rejected message changes from a male to a female voice, the change is almost always noticed, and if the change is from voice to a pure tone it is always noticed. Speech in the rejected message is recognized as such but words are not identified. If the rejected message is identical to the shadowed message but lags behind it, the identity is noticed when the time lag is reduced to a few seconds.

Several years passed before the next relevant study, by Moray & Taylor in 1958 (69), showed that the number of errors made in shadowing is inversely related to the order of approximation to English of the shadowed message when the rejected message is normal English prose. They mentioned that two kinds of responding could be discerned, either continuous, in which there was no marked unevenness in the gaps between adjacent spoken words, or discontinuous, in which a group of words would be spoken followed by a silent period that spanned several words in the input message.

An influential article by Moray appeared the following year (65). In one experiment, the rejected message consisted of a short list of words repeated 35 times. In a recognition test begun 30 sec after shadowing ceased, he found no significant retention. In a separate experiment, brief instructions were given in the rejected ear during shadowing. Instructions that were immediately preceded by the subject's own name were "noticed" more often than were those unaccompanied by a name. Unfortunately, so many of the details that are needed to interpret these results were not included in the report that it is impossible to evaluate Moray's conclusions.

Two later experiments also investigated the effects of one's own name. One of these [Oswald, Taylor & Treisman (76)] showed enhanced responsiveness to one's own name during sleep, and the other [Howarth & Ellis (38)] found that one's own name has a higher probability of being recognized when embedded in noise than do other names. The latter authors concluded that Moray's finding does not require us to postulate a second pattern-analyzing mechanism.

Treisman (96) pursued the question of the role of context in shadowing. She interchanged ears during shadowing, switching the message that was being shadowed into the rejected ear at the same moment that the rejected message was switched to the accepted ear. This manipulation usually did not interfere with performance. On a small proportion of the trials, however, intrusions from the rejected ear were recorded. Intrusions were more likely to occur when the initially shadowed message was highly redundant than when it was a low-order approximation to English. When these errors in shadowing occurred, they were very transitory. Usually only one or two words from the rejected ear were spoken and then the subject reverted to shadowing the ear he had been instructed to shadow. In a control experiment, the initially shadowed message was replaced by another message in the same way as in the main experiment but it was not switched to the rejected ear. The rejected ear received an uninterrupted, irrelevant message throughout. This control established that the intrusions did come from the rejected ear. In the main experiment, intrusions were rare, amounting to about 6 per cent immediately following the interchanging of the ears and about 1 per cent at other times. These percentages are based upon the total number of words that intruded, so the proportion of trials on which the subjects switched ears in order to follow the context must have been even smaller. Treisman mentioned that many subjects made errors in shadowing immediately after the break in context even though they did not follow the context to the rejected ear.

Cherry (11) had found that it is very difficult to shadow one of two messages when both are presented to both ears. Treisman (98) explored this case in detail. She presented, for shadowing, passages from a novel read in a woman's voice, and she measured the extent of the interference produced by various kinds of rejected messages. When the rejected message was in a man's voice, the amount of interference was least. Much greater interference occurred when the rejected message was in the same woman's voice as the shadowed message, even when the rejected message was meaningless (reversed English). Similarity of meaning was influential: interference was greatest of all when the woman's voice read other passages from the same novel as the rejected message. When the rejected message was in another language but in the woman's voice, interference was great for subjects who were fluent in the second language and intermediate in amount for those who were unfamiliar with the language. She concluded that word class is not as effective a basis for filtering as are physical characteristics of the stimulus.

If the shadowed message and the rejected message are identical but the message entering one ear lags behind that entering the other ear, subjects spontaneously report the identity, provided the time lag is not too great. This phenomenon, another of Cherry's findings mentioned above, was also studied by Treisman (97). She found that identity is noticed when the rejected message leads as well as when it lags, but that the average delay is less in the former case. It does not seem to matter whether the two messages are in the same or different voices. But it does matter if one message is English and the other is "identical" but in French. In this case, the average delays are shorter and identity is often not reported at all; however, it often is reported. When two identical, irrelevant messages are presented to separate channels while the subject shadows a third message which is different, the identity between the two irrelevant messages is never reported.

In another important paper, Treisman (99) described effects of the rejected message or messages upon the accuracy of shadowing. Only one shadowing rate, 150 words per minute, was used. She found the prose message to be reproduced with 96 per cent of its words correct in the absence of any irrelevant message. When the irrelevant messages were present in channels defined by spatial localization or by voice, shadowing accuracy sometimes declined. When it did, omissions were the cause. Adding one irrelevant message in one separate channel did not reduce accuracy to a significant extent, although in all four such conditions accuracy was slightly less than 96 per cent. Adding two irrelevant message in two separate channels decreased accuracy substantially, although adding the two in a single separate channel reduced accuracy not at all. The content of the irrelevant messages was changed in several ways, and in no instance did this change influence shadowing accuracy.

Under other conditions, adding a single message in a nonshadowed channel disrupts shadowing performance to a great extent. In a study by Mowbray (71), the nonshadowed message was not a rejected message since the subjects were instructed to remember the infrequent words presented to the opposite ear by a different voice. They did remember a large proportion of them, unlike Moray's subjects mentioned above who received different instructions as well as a rejected message that was continuous. Mowbray was able to show that a target word in the second ear disrupted shadowing almost all of the time at the moment of its presentation, as well as slightly before and for some time after that moment.

Peterson & Kroener (77) also found that items in the nonshadowed ear, which were to be recalled immediately at the end of a short shadowing task, greatly disrupted shadowing. On trials on which no disruption could be detected, a significant proportion of the target items were recalled correctly at the short retention intervals that they used. But even when the target items occurred at the very end of the message and the retention interval was close to zero, only about half of the items were recalled. Norman (75) has recently reported a similar finding.

Lawson (47) measured reaction times to brief tone bursts presented to either the right or left ears, when a prose message in one ear was being shadowed and another passage of prose in the other ear was being rejected. Subjects responded to a tone in the left ear with their left hand and with their right hand to a tone in the right ear. Reaction times were unusually long, well over 50 msec, and did not depend upon whether the ear receiving the tone was being shadowed or rejected. Complicating to a greater degree the choice in the reaction-time task resulted in slower responding to tone bursts in the rejected ear compared to the shadowed ear.

In an experiment that superficially resembles Lawson's, Treisman & Geffen (103) obtained very different results. In addition to shadowing one of two dichotic messages, subjects were requested to make a secondary response of tapping whenever a target word occurred in either ear. Thus, when the target was presented to the shadowed ear, two responses were called for, tapping and repeating the target orally. But when the target entered the rejected ear, only tapping was required. They reasoned that if shadowing is a matter only of filtering out all responses other than the oral tracking response, then tapping should rarely occur to targets in either ear. But if the filtering is on the input side, tapping should occur to targets in the shadowed ear and not to those in the rejected ear. They obtained data that clearly favored the latter prediction. It is important to point out that, in contrast to Lawson's study, the targets here were words and they were spoken in the same voice as the rejected message. And we must comment that the particular response-selection theory that they reject is a strange one indeed, since it also predicts that shadowing one of two dichotic messages cannot be done. Further theoretical discussions of this paper appeared in the same journal [Deutsch, Deutsch & Lindsay (20); Treisman (101)].

The newer theories.—Anne Treisman (96) was the first to propose a systematic alternative to filter theory, although Moray (65) had already argued the need for alternatives. Treisman began with a simple modification of filter theory that has since developed into a much more elaborate theory. A complete statement of her theory is not available in any single source although two articles contain much of it (100, 102).

Because important words in the rejected message sometimes overcome the block imposed during shadowing, and because words from the rejected ear sometimes intrude when context is switched from the shadowed to the rejected message, Treisman concluded that the concept of a filter as an all-or-none block cannot be accepted. Other shadowing results later reinforced this contention. She proposed instead that filtering is a matter of attenuating signals rather than cutting them off entirely and that filtering is accomplished during, rather than before or after, recognition of the stimulus. Recognition occurs when a stimulus leads to the activation of an internal representation, referred to as a "dictionary unit" in early papers and as a "perceptual analyzer" more recently. Those corresponding to important stimuli require less information for their activation, and context and set can alter criteria temporarily. Thus, attenuation reduces input without completely excluding nonattended stimuli of special relevance.

Whether a message is attenuated depends upon the outcome of partial analysis of it. Recognition is hierarchical, a speech signal being analyzed first along physical dimensions, then phonemically, and eventually lexically. If it "fails a test" on a physical dimension, then it is attenuated for all higher analyses. The subject will be aware of its physical characteristics, which are unattenuated, but he may not extract its meaning. Selection is made among the responses of preperceptual analyzers.

It is not clear whether all unattended inputs are attenuated or whether some are blocked entirely. In early versions of the theory it seemed that all are attenuated. That was Broadbent's interpretation of it, and he seemed eager to accept that idea. Broadbent & Gregory (5) determined the detectability of a sinusoid in noise presented to one ear while the subject received a string of digits in the other ear. Comparing performance obtained when recall of the digits was required with that obtained when the digits could be ignored, they found a change in the sensitivity index d′ but none in the criterion index β. They argued that this result is consistent with Treisman's hypothesis and inconsistent with Broadbent's filter theory. We cannot understand why filter theory would predict no change in d′; it would seem to be necessary for it to do so, as Moray & O'Brien (68) have also pointed out. It would seem that the result obtained by Broadbent & Gregory is consistent with filter theory and, perhaps, inconsistent with Treisman's more recent formulation.

Treisman & Geffen (103), requiring identification of words, and Moray & O'Brien (68), requiring identification of letters, both also report a decrement in d′ and little change in β due to diversion of attention. Treisman & Geffen, in discussing Lawson's experiment described above, claim that meaningless signals should not be attenuated. Thus we are left with a discrepancy between the result of Broadbent & Gregory and the current form of Treisman's attenuation hypothesis.

For Treisman, selection is accomplished by the rejection of every irrelevant message, an active process that requires a partial analysis of every irrelevant message. Deutsch & Deutsch (19) proposed a theory in which one message is selected and all others are simply ignored. They insisted, however, that every stimulus is fully analyzed, to the point of recognition, before it is either accepted or ignored. This must be so because, they say, the most important stimulus is the one selected of all those present, and "importance to the organism" is a property of the internal representation of a stimulus. Hence, every stimulus excites its internal representation (i.e., is recognized) and the recognition response has an importance weighting. At any moment, the recognition response with the greatest importance weighting is selected for awareness, motor output, and memory storage.

The experiment conducted by Treisman & Geffen (103) was designed to differentiate between the two theories. It did not accomplish that [Deutsch, Deutsch & Lindsay (20)], but Treisman (101) had the last word, which included a brief description of a modified experiment.

Norman (73, 74) presented a theory of attention and memory that is very similar to, but more detailed than, the Deutschs' theory. It assumes full analysis of all inputs and the positive selection of the item having the largest combination of sensory activation and "pertinence." Neisser (72) presented attention as the result of "analysis-by-synthesis"—an active, reconstructive, general cognitive function.

Simple Stimuli

An experimental paradigm conceptually similar to the one used in the study of speech shadowing has been used to study the detection of pure tones. Tones as well as simple visual and cutaneous stimuli have been used in other types of signal detection experiments directed at the problem of selective attention.

Unexpected frequency.—Tanner & Norman (89) gave four unpracticed observers the task of detecting a 0.15-sec tone burst in a continuous background of white noise. On each trial the tone was presented in one chosen at random from four well-defined temporal intervals, and the proportion of correct choices, P(C), was taken as an index of sensitivity. Throughout several training sessions the tone was 1000 Hz. Then, without notice to the observers, the tone's frequency was changed to 1300 Hz, and presented with the same energy that had yielded P(C) = 0.65 for the 1000-Hz tone. For the next 50 trials, the observed P(C) for each observer was near 0.25, the value representing no sensitivity or chance success. The observers were then informed of the change and allowed to listen to 1300 Hz without noise. In subsequent trials with the 1300-Hz tone at the same energy, P(C) again approximated 0.65.

Karoly & Isaacson (42) presented to some 50 observers in classroom experiments an "expected frequency" of 1000 Hz and "unexpected frequencies" of 500 and 1500 Hz, also under the temporal forced-choice procedure. The unexpected frequencies were presented on infrequent trials chosen at random. The values of P(C) on trials containing unexpected frequencies were substantially lower than values of P(C) on trials containing the expected frequency, though on some trials the unexpected frequencies were presented at energies greater by several decibels. This probe-signal technique was recently developed further and used systematically by Greenberg & Larkin (32). Presenting as many as 14 different unexpected frequencies, they were able to determine quite reliably the observer's frequency response characteristic. Four experiments with a total of 16 observers showed that when the expected frequency (1000 or 1100 Hz) was correctly detected 75 to 90 per cent of the time, unexpected frequencies diverging by more than 150 to 200 Hz were detected with only chance accuracy.

Criticisms of these experimental procedures come readily. A deficiency intrinsic also to the selective-attention paradigm used in speech shadowing is that the observer is left unsettled if he finds he is being tested on other than what he was led to believe was his sole task. Although the observers in the experiments described were apparently unaware of the existence of the probe signals until they were told about them, another difficulty here is that one cannot confidently characterize the observer's conception of his task even before he learns of the subterfuge. Other procedures for use with simple signals, discussed shortly, were devised to avoid these criticisms.

Models of the selective process.—Earlier experiments, following the lead of Fletcher (23), had defined the concept of the "critical band" in audition, in large part by showing that components of the noise background outside a small region of frequencies about the signal do not contribute to masking of the signal [see, e.g., Scharf's review (82)]. The experiments just described were based on the further premise that a suppression of noise components outside the critical band would entail as well as suppression of signals outside the critical band. The basic difference between many experiments on the critical band and the ones discussed here is that the latter reflect the view that auditory frequency selectivity is substantially under the intelligent control of the observer—their focus is on attention rather than on the basilar membrane.

One simple filter model that emerged from detection studies postulates that the observer, in order to achieve a high degree of sensitivity, will attend at any point in time to a single (narrow) band of frequencies. According to this model, the observer changes the frequency location of his filter by sweeping it through intervening frequencies [Tanner & Norman (89)]. Another simple filter model assumes that the observer can attend at once to any number of selected frequency bands. Variants of the model assume different rules of combination of filter outputs, but in common they predict that sensitivity to a single tone will decrease as the number of bands attended to is increased [Tanner & Norman (89); Green (28); Creelman (16)]. We briefly summarize now the essential results of several experiments conducted in the framework of the "single-band" and "multiple-band" models. Some of the experiments in this series have been reviewed in more detail elsewhere [Swets (84); Green & Swets (31)].

Uncertain frequency.—In an often-used paradigm a brief tone is presented at either of two frequencies, both of them known to the observer, in one of the intervals of a temporal forced-choice trial. In the usual case the observer does not know which of the two frequencies will occur on a given trial. He has only to choose the interval that he believes to contain a tone; he is not asked to state which frequency was presented [Tanner & Norman (89); Tanner, Swets & Green (91); Veniar (105); Creelman (16)].

In all studies that have employed this procedure, the signal that is either of two known frequencies was found to be less detectable than a signal that is of a constant, known frequency throughout a group of trials. Several studies showed the detectability of the uncertain-frequency signal to decrease as the difference between the two frequencies is increased. Both results, as qualitatively stated, are consistent with both models. Under the single-band model, detection suffers whenever the observer is not tuned as precisely as possible to the frequency that is presented, and detection suffers maximally when the possible frequencies are so far apart that he cannot successively attend to both during the signal's duration. According to the multiple-band model, the two bands include more masking noise as they span a wider range of frequencies, up to the point where the bands do not overlap.

The multiple-band model predicts a smaller decrement from uncertainty, for large differences in frequency, than the single-band model. The difference between the predictions is not very great, however, and the weight of evidence on this score does not clearly favor either model. One possible reason for the ambiguity is a tendency for different observers to follow different strategies of listening. Observers have tended to match closely one or the other prediction, rather than fall in between, and cases have been noted of individual differences persisting in consistent fashion over different tasks. For example, in one group the observer most able at detecting single frequencies was least able at detecting a signal at either of two frequencies and at detecting a signal that was a band of noise. In another group the observer who suffered least from uncertain frequency was best at detecting signals composed of several frequencies [Swets (84)].

Another possible reason for the failure of existing data to distinguish between the two models was noted in a variation of the standard paradigm, which raised a question about the baseline used for the predicted decrement: detectability was found to be lower when the signal could be either of two frequencies even when the signal frequency on each trial was presented as a cue, in reduced noise, prior to the trial. The same study, we should add, showed that cueing after the observation but before the response was less effective than cueing prior to the observation [Swets & Sewall (86)].

A different analysis of data in this type of experiment favors the single-band model: in pairs of successive trials in which the frequency was the same on both trials, detectability on the second trial was greater if the response on the first had been correct; in pairs in which the frequency changed from the first to the second trial, detectability on the second trial was greater if the response on the first had been incorrect [Swets et al. (87)].

Sorkin, Pastore & Gilliom (83) reported recently an extension of the uncertain-frequency paradigm in which the presentation probabilities of the different frequencies were manipulated. They found 650, 750 and 850 Hz to be essentially equally detectable when they were equally probable, and 750 Hz to be consistently more detectable than the other two frequencies when it was four times more likely to occur. They argued that the effective listening band was constantly narrower in the latter condition; this interpretation was supported by the absence of significant trial-to-trial sequential dependencies.

Multicomponent signals.—In another experimental paradigm devised to study the detectability of signals outside a single critical band, signals are constructed by adding two or more sinusoids. We have indicated that the superiority of the multiple-band strategy over the single-band strategy may not be apparent to the observer when the signal is either of two frequencies —the decrement from uncertainty predicted by the multiple-band model is not much smaller, and, further, according to this model the observer loses information as to which of the two frequencies was present. It would seem, on the other hand, that the multiple-band strategy should appear superior to the observer when the signal is composed of two or more widely-separated frequencies. Not all of the evidence supports this view.

Gassler (26) presented signals composed of 1, 2, 3, . . . , *n* sinusoids spaced at intervals of 20 Hz. He found detectability to increase with the number of signal components, up to a point which he took to define the critical band. Beyond that point, additional components did not increase detectability. Marill (64) obtained results consistent with Gassler's: signals composed of two frequencies separated by approximately 50 Hz produced complete energy summation; when the frequency separation of two components was about 600 Hz, however, the pair of frequencies was no more detectable than the more detectable member of the pair. Both studies are consistent with the single-band model.

Green (28) obtained conflicting results which support the multiple-band model. He found that pairs of sinusoids separated as widely as 1500 Hz were more detectable than either member of the pair. These data are consistent with the earlier study by Schafer & Gales (81). Green, McKey & Licklider (30) added the 16 harmonics of 250 Hz, ranging up to 4000 Hz, and found almost exactly the 6 db improvement predicted by the multiple-band model. The reason for the contradictory results of the two sets of experiments has not yet become clear.

Predictions of the two models for the multicomponent-signal paradigm were investigated for sinusoidal signals to another sense modality by Franzén, Markowitz & Swets (25). In this experiment, brief vibratory signals, with all parameters fixed, were presented to the tips of the index or middle fingers or both. When only the index finger, or only the middle finger, or both fingers, were stimulated throughout a group of (forced-choice) trials, the single-band or single-channel model predicts the result. No spatial summation was evident; the sensitivity of the pair of fingers to two signals was no greater than that of the more sensitive single finger to one signal. When, however, the various kinds of trials were randomly mixed so that either or both fingers might be stimulated on any given trial, the sensitivity of the pair was greater than the sensitivity of either finger alone.
This result may be specific to dark flashes, and they may therefore be espe-
are present in both channels, the observer is always attending to a channel with a signal present; when a signal is present in only one channel, the observer will sometimes be attending to the wrong channel. Confirmation of this interpretation comes from the further result that the sensitivity of the pair when the types of trials were mixed was no greater than the sensitivity of the pair when the types of trials were grouped. Thus, the result of the second condition does not indicate summation as it might first appear to do, but rather a decrement due to uncertainty. The difference between the results of the two conditions points up the need to consider the knowledge the

observer has about the stimulus to be presented on any trial. This prescriptions seems obvious in a chapter on attention, but it has not always been heeded in sensory studies.

Kinchla (43) investigated the application of the two models to a visual detection experiment with multicomponent signals. Another of his papers (44) provides additional theoretical background. Two points of light separated by about 2.5 degrees of visual angle were viewed continuously against a dark background. On each trial in condition A the subject decided whether a "dark flash," a 15-msec dark interval, occurred. The dark flash occurred simultaneously in both, in either, or in neither of the two lights. In condition B, only one light was present, and the task was to decide whether a dark flash occurred in it. The major result is that there was no summation of the two dark flashes in condition A, that is, single and double flashes yielded essentially the same sensitivity.

The single-band model predicted the results within condition A, and predicted the results of condition A from condition B. An extension of the single-band model predicted the form of the trading relationship, or "attention operating characteristic," between the detection probabilities associated with the right and left flashes when presented alone, as the probability of attending to one light instead of the other was manipulated through instruction. A problem that plagues experiments of this kind, that of the control of eye position, does not seem important in this case, at least insofar as conclusions about the single-band model are concerned.

An interesting implication of these results is that sensory memory is ineffective under these conditions. If attention switches to one of the lights after the dark flash has occurred, no trace of the flash can then be retrieved. This result may be specific to dark flashes, and they may therefore be especially useful in the experimental analysis of attention. Still, neither was there any indication of sensory memory in the similar experiment using vibrotactile signals. It did not seem necessary in either study to consider the possibility of switching from one channel to another during the observation interval. We consider shortly the question of switching times and the relevant evidence obtained in experiments using simple signals.

Comment

One elementary question that must be answered by any theory of selective attention has to do with the fate of nonattended inputs. One possibility is that attention is all or none and nonattended inputs have no effects. Broadbent's original theory took this position. The more recent theories differ with Broadbent's theory on this point, basing their conclusions on the results of those shadowing experiments which seem to show that certain nonattended inputs sometimes do "get through." But the force of this argument depends upon a very strong assumption about the shadowing task, namely, that the act of shadowing locks attention on one channel continuously to the exclusion of all others and that the subject does not occasionally sample other inputs. The validity of this assumption is not defended in the literature, although Norman (74, p. 22) argues in favor of it, but only on subjective grounds.

Many investigators who use stimuli simpler than speech continue to entertain the all-or-none hypothesis, as we indicated in the preceding section. Another example is a study by Tulving & Lindsay (104), who presented evidence to show that simple visual and auditory stimuli simultaneously presented cannot be attended or responded to at the same time. Their experiments, however, led them to consider several possible interpretations, among them the hypothesis that attention is all or none. They pointed out that if it is all or none, they are compelled to conclude further that it can switch rapidly between channels.

The evidence against an all-or-none hypothesis does seem short of overwhelming. Broadbent's theory, together with his estimate of the time required to switch the filter from channel to channel (about 250 msec) (3), does not fare well in the face of the shadowing experiments. However, the same theory, with a much shorter switching time, is not ruled out. Broadbent's estimate of switching time was based on his split-span experiments and is open to question. Moray (67) has recently reviewed the evidence on switching time.

A theory of selective attention as an all-or-none gating of inputs has been proposed by Kristofferson (45, 46). It is similar to Broadbent's theory in assuming that inputs arriving in only one sensory channel can "enter the central processor" at any one time and that, as a result, an input that arrives in an unattended channel will be delayed by the amount of time required to switch attention. That delay is the "switching time." This view has led to experiments designed to measure switching time and to determine its distribution function. Pure tones and spots of light are the stimuli that have been used to measure switching times between the visual and auditory modalities. Two kinds of experiments have been done, both of them designed to isolate switching time from memory or response. In one, switching time is inferred from the change in discrimination reaction times produced by uncertainty as to which channel will contain the next signal. In the other, switching time is a major parameter determining the successiveness discrimination function, that is, the effect of the interval between two signals upon the probability of discriminating them from a simultaneous pair.

Both of these experiments indicate that switching time is much shorter than Broadbent had supposed, at least under ideal conditions. More specifically, the two methods both suggest that switching times are uniformly distributed over the interval between zero and about 50 msec.

In a 1967 paper, Moray & O'Brien (68) reported results from a selective listening experiment that led them to examine an all-or-none, switching model. The particular model that they chose to test accounts for their data qualitatively, but they concluded that it fails quantitatively. Nonetheless, in his forthcoming book, Moray (67) analyzes this kind of theory in some detail, even to the point of attempting to apply Kristofferson's theory to an analysis of the shadowing task.

Some quantitative experiments on selective attention as sensory input gating are being done. The gap between these and the speech experiments yawns wide indeed. Many important questions will have to be asked and answered before a rapprochement is achieved, but this process seems to be underway. It is a promising contact between quantitative psychophysics and cognitive psychology.

SUSTAINED ATTENTION

N. H. Mackworth reported several experiments on vigilance in a 1948 article (62), and these and several more in his 1950 book (63). In the original experiment, the subject watched a hand moving in jumps around a blank clock face; the hand moved in regular steps once each second and occasionally moved a double step. The subject was called upon to respond by pressing a key whenever a double step occurred. The major finding was an apparent large decline in performance as the watch progressed: the percentage of signals (double steps) correctly reported dropped substantially after only a half-hour of watching. The rapid deterioration of performance so indicated was striking because, after all, the subject's work load was very light.

Frankmann & Adams (24) have reviewed five theories of the performance decrement that were proposed in the following decade. Mackworth related the phenomenon to principles of classical conditioning, particularly to the principle of inhibition. Broadbent extended the analogy but related both vigilance and classical conditioning to attention. Deese offered expectancy as an explanatory construct: lower detection probabilities result from lower excitatory states of vigilance, which in large part result from decreasing expectations of signal occurrence. Scott considered Hebb's thesis that stimuli serve not only a cue function for goal responses, but also to arouse or activate the organism, and he related the loss of efficiency to the reduction in stimulus variation during a watch. Holland equated Skinnerian observing responses to sense receptor orientations, suggested a parallel between observing rate and detection probability, and assumed that signal detections reinforce observing responses.

Other tests besides the "jump-clock test" showed the sharp decrement in detection probability, including a "synthetic radar test," and a "listening test." Still other tests did not show a performance decrement. Notable in this category are tests with multiple stimulus sources, for example, the "20-dials test." In this case the subject was to react to an unusual reading on any of the monitored dials, and the signal remained visible until the reaction occurred. Response time was found to be as short at the end as at the beginning of the watch [Broadbent (3)]. As Frankmann & Adams have pointed out, the tests showing no decrement have received little study: "most investigators have chosen to use tasks where decrement is known to occur" (24, p. 265).

However that may be, several investigators have recently begun to question whether in fact a performance decrement occurs in any of the common vigilance tests. The question was prompted by the emergence of the theory of signal detectability and related evidence [Tanner & Swets (90); Swets (85); Green & Swets (31)], indicating that the proportion of signals detected is not a valid measure of signal detectability. This proportion was shown to reflect not only signal detectability or sensitivity, but also nonsensory factors that influence the subject's willingness to report a signal, that is to say, his decision or response criterion. Psychophysical experiments with well-marked times of possible signal occurrence and high signal rates showed that the proportion of false-alarm responses should also be considered if a relatively pure measure of sensitivity is desired. The detection-theory analysis, based on the theory of statistical decision, uses both proportions to derive independent measures of the subject's sensitivity and his decision criterion.

It thus became conceivable that in vigilance tests the probability of a false alarm declines over time along with the probability of a correct detection, in such a way as to indicate constant sensitivity but a progressively more conservative decision criterion. A progressively more conservative decision criterion would be expected to result from a decreasing expectation of signal occurrence. A decreasing expectation of signal occurrence would seem to follow naturally from the procedure often used in vigilance experiments, wherein untrained subjects are given brief practice with a high signal rate before the low rate of the experiment proper is introduced. In most instances the experiment proper has been confined to one or two sessions, probably not enough to yield a stable expectation.

The application of the detection-theory analysis to vigilance tests, however, is by no means straightforward. In tests in which the times of possible signal occurrence, that is, the "observation intervals," are not clearly marked for the observer, or in which a response interval is not defined for each observation interval, there is a problem about what to call any given response—is it a correct detection or a false alarm? The first investigators to attack this problem were Egan, Greenberg & Schulman (21). Their task had a high signal rate and a short observation period relative to the typical vigilance task. Broadbent & Gregory (6) and J. F. Mackworth & Taylor (61) first used the detection-theory measure of sensitivity in the context of the typical vigilance task.

In this section we consider first the methodological studies aimed at isolating sensitivity from the decision criterion when the observation intervals are not defined for the observer. We proceed to consider the studies which questioned the existence of a sensitivity decrement during vigilance. We can not review here the more than 100 empirical studies of task variables that have been reported in the last 5 years—variables such as work-rest cycle, intersignal interval, irrelevant stimulation, incentives, knowledge of results, drugs, age, and sex; no doubt a book will soon present such a review.

Detection with Undefined Observation Intervals

Estimation of hit and false-alarm probabilities.—The experiment conducted by Egan, Greenberg & Schulman (21) followed the vigilance paradigm, except that the mean time between signals was on the order of 10 sec, and the observation period, including brief "time outs," was less than 10 min. These investigators conceived their task as extracting from the available data—the time of occurrence of each signal and of each response—a quantity related to the probability of a correct detection (or "hit") and a quantity related to the probability of a false alarm. This they accomplished by cumulating rates of responding in two time intervals associated with each signal presentation, one interval immediately after the signal's occurrence and the other longer after the signal's occurrence but before the occurrence of the next signal.

They manipulated the observer's decision criterion by instructions to be "strict," "medium," or "lax," and observed appropriate changes in the rates of responding in the two intervals. They assumed, and verified, that the relationship between these two quantities, as the criterion varies, is described by a power function. A power function was known to describe reasonably well the empirical relationship of hit and false-alarm probabilities in experiments with clearly defined observation intervals, a relationship called the "receiver-operating-characteristic" (ROC) curve, or "iso-sensitivity" curve. It was therefore possible to convert rates of responding into the sensitivity index usually extracted from such asymmetric curves, namely d_e'. Values of this index obtained from the experiment with undefined observation intervals were linearly related to the signal-to-noise ratio E/N_0, as is the case in experiments with defined observation intervals.

Watson & Nichols (107) and Watson (106) have recently attempted to represent the hit and false-alarm probabilities by two quantities based on response latency rather than response rate. They obtained one distribution by measuring the latency of the first response following signals and a second distribution by measuring the corresponding latency after identically sampled instances of only the background noise. These two overlapping distributions of latencies were related to a criterion latency: any response less than this criterion was regarded as a positive response and any response greater than this criterion was regarded as a negative response. Any latency criterion thus produces a two-by-two matrix of frequencies, or probabilities, that can be converted to the sensitivity index d′ in the usual way, by means of published tables. The values of d′ obtained upon choosing a latency criterion for each observer to maximize d′ were the same as the values of d′ obtained from a defined-intervals procedure with a signal energy lower by one to two decibels; Egan et al. had estimated the difference between the two types of procedure to be of the same magnitude.

Thus, the work of Egan and his students demonstrated both that hit and false-alarm probabilities covary in the task with undefined intervals much as they do in the task with defined intervals, and that large changes in performance could be observed with no apparent change in sensitivity. The implications for the analysis of vigilance data were clear.

Examinations of signal-response time and inter-response time distributions.—Luce (53) has proposed a different way of separating sensitivity from response bias in experiments with undefined observation intervals. His method does not reduce the temporally continuous task to a series of discrete trials, and does not extract quantities related to the hit and false-alarm probabilities from the signal-response time distribution. Rather, this analysis ignores responses occurring shortly after other events, for example, occurrence of the signal, and concentrates mainly on the tails of certain latency distributions. Exponential parameters associated with the tails of the latency distributions are estimated, and from these estimates inferences are made about signal detectability. Luce's approach also differs from Egan's in being based on a simple threshold theory.

Green & Luce (29) tested empirically the analysis Luce proposed. Although they found the very simple, initial model inadequate to account for the data, the data were orderly and usefully analyzed in terms of several observable distributions of signal-response time and inter-response time. They believe that a detailed analysis will follow successfully from a few modifications of the experimental task and some slight changes in the general model. A continuation of the work, described to date only in an oral presentation [Luce & Green (54)], has yielded promising results.

Vigilance

Next let us review reports indicating that decrements in sensitivity do or do not occur during vigilance tasks. These will then bring us to a conclusion on this question.

Is there a sensitivity decrement? No.—Broadbent & Gregory (6) conducted an auditory vigilance test in which the signal was a tone burst, and a visual vigilance test in which the signal was an occasionally brighter flash of a light that flashed regularly. They assumed a duration of the subjective observation interval in order to permit calculation of the false-alarm proportion, and found the main effects in their experiment to be insensitive to the particular assumption used in the calculation. There were no statistically significant changes in the sensitivity index d′ from early to late portions of a watch. However, changes in the index of the decision criterion, denoted β, indicated a more cautious criterion at the end of the watch than at the beginning. In a later experiment, these investigators [Broadbent & Gregory

(8)] used again a flashing light as a background event; in this instance they facilitated calculation of the false-alarm proportion by presenting the background event at a low enough rate to permit defining a response interval for each such event. Again, as the watch progressed, they found no decrement in d′, and an increasingly conservative criterion. This effect was observed for both a high and a low rate of signal presentation. A difficulty of interpretation posed by both experiments is that while d′ did not decline during the watch, neither did the proportion of correct detections.

Loeb & Binford (49), using as a signal an increment in a train of pulses of broadband noise, found substantial decreases over time in both the proportion of false alarms and the proportion of correct detections. They chose not to calculate values of d′, but their use of a rating response permitted construction of ROC curves, which indicated a nearly constant sensitivity. A second experiment [Loeb et al. (51)] also showed significant declines in both hit and false-alarm proportions; in this instance values of d′ were calculated and found not to change. A third experiment was reported as showing a statistically significant decrement in d′ [Binford & Loeb (1)]. However, the change in d′ was only 2 to 4 per cent in three of four comparisons; in the fourth comparison, where the change was about 20 per cent, the initial value of d′ was too extreme (near 4.0) to be estimated with reasonable reliability. There was, moreover, in each case a substantial decline in false alarms as well as in hits.

Colquhoun & Baddeley (14) did not examine directly the question of a decrement in sensitivity over time, but they showed that manipulations of signal probability effected changes in the decision criterion while d′ remained constant. The salient result was that the criterion became more conservative when the signal rate was changed from a high to a low rate. They repeated the experiment with auditory instead of visual signals and found consistent results [Colquhoun & Baddeley (15)]. Colquhoun (12) found both d′ and the degree of caution to increase during a watch. In this experiment, as in the previous visual experiment, the signal was a slightly larger disc in a row of six discs. Colquhoun (13), in a test simulating auditory sonar detection, found that he could readily manipulate the decision criterion by simple instructions; he attributed a small decrement over time in the hit proportion to a shift in the criterion.

Jerison, Pickett & Stenson (41), with a signal corresponding to the deflection and return of a needle on a meter, found declines in the hit and false-alarm proportions but none in d′. Taylor (92) reanalyzed the data from a similar study by Wiener, Poock & Steele (108), and also found declines in hits and false alarms but none in d′. Tanner (88) and Watson (106) obtained this same result in auditory tasks. Lucas (52), using an auditory task, with subjects more trained and motivated than is typical in vigilance experiments, found hits, false alarms, and d′ to be constant through a watch.

Again, with a pure-tone signal in noise, Levine (48) found declines in hits and false alarms but constant d′. Levine, in addition, manipulated the costs to the subject of a miss and false alarm, and found changes in the criterion β that corresponded appropriately to changes in the pay-off matrix. Davenport, in both an auditory task (18) and a vibrotactile task (17), also found d′ invariant with time and with changes in the pay-off matrix, while the criterion β increased with time and with the cost of a false alarm.

Is there a sensitivity decrement? Yes.—Jane Mackworth, for a time, consistently found a decline in d′ in vigilance experiments. Her test was the "continuous-clock test": the signal consisted of a brief pause in the otherwise steady movement of a clock hand. The first experiment was reported by J. F. Mackworth & Taylor (61). Later experiments with the same test confirmed the result with variables such as true and false knowledge of results [Mackworth (56)], amphetamine [Mackworth (59)], and the decision interval [Mackworth (57)]. Mackworth (55) and Taylor (93) pointed out that the decline in d′ progressed linearly with the square root of the observing time.

Is there a sensitivity decrement? Yes and no.—J. F. Mackworth has recently reported two experiments that shed some light on the discrepancy between her earlier results and the results of the other investigators who used the d′ measure. Both experiments dealt with the "required rate of observing," which, of course, is very high in her continuous-clock test, and manipulable in tests that superpose a signal on a regularly occurring background event.

In the first of the experiments, the signal was a brighter flash on the left-hand one of two adjacent discs that flashed regularly. With a background flash rate of 200 per min, a decrement in d′ was observed. With a background flash rate of 40 per min, no such decrement was observed. In both instances a decrement in false alarms indicated a tightening decision criterion [Mackworth (58)]. The second experiment compared the continuous-clock test with the jump-clock test originally used by N. H. Mackworth. The former again showed significant decrements in d′, but the latter did not [Mackworth (60)].

More recently, Hatfield & Loeb (33), Hatfield & Soderquist (34), and Loeb & Binford (50) have pursued the idea that differences in the degree of "task coupling" may account for finding sensitivity decrements in some tests and not in others. A "loosely coupled" task permits the observer to do something equivalent to looking away from the display, whereas a "closely coupled" task does not. One might expect sensitivity decrements because of increasingly frequent lapses of attention in the former case, and only criterion changes in the latter case. This expectation is clearly fulfilled by Loeb & Binford's (50) experiment: a visual display yielded decrements over time in d′, more pronounced decrements the higher the required rate of observing, while an auditory display yielded constant d′ over time, for each of the observing rates examined; the index β increased over time, indicating a progressively more stringent decision criterion with both displays.

To summarize the vigilance research described in the foregoing sections, it appears that the question concerning the existence of a sensitivity decrement was well taken. Although certain vigilance tests were studied extensively because they seemed to show a sharp decline in sensitivity, most of them, including the original jump-clock test, do not show such a decline when the detection-theory analysis is used in an attempt to measure sensitivity independently of the decision criterion. These tests routinely show a decline in false alarms, consistent with a progressively more conservative decision criterion and a decreasing expectation of signal occurrence. We have no doubt, on the other hand, that tests can be found that will show a decrement of sensitivity. Present evidence suggests that visual tests requiring an exceptionally high rate of observing will consistently yield a performance decrement.

Interpretation of detection-theory measures.—A question has also arisen about what constitutes a legitimate interpretation of d′ and β, especially β, in the vigilance context—even when both the observation and response intervals are defined. One source of discomfiture is that values of these indices have been extreme in most of the vigilance experiments reported to date. Compounding the problem of extreme values is the fact that historically vigilance experiments have been confined to a few sessions with low data rates. (Some investigators, in fact, have made calculations based on arbitrarily chosen values of hit and false-alarm proportions near 1.0 and 0 for those observers who actually yielded values of 1.0 or 0.) A second cause for concern is that the assumptions underlying tabulated values of d′ and β are likely to be badly violated when the signal rate is low.

Jerison, Pickett & Stenson (41) attempted to account for the very high values of β they calculated by postulating three modes of observing—alert, blurred, and distracted—and by specifying the effects on d′ and β of various mixtures of these modes within a session. They acknowledged their quantitative theory to be speculative; other writers have termed it "complex" and "ingenuous." Jerison (40) has since reviewed his position that values of β obtained in vigilance experiments are psychologically unrealistic and should not be taken as indices of conservativeness.

Cautions that stem from the bases of detection theory about the interpretation of d′ and β were advanced by Taylor (94). In the theory, uncertainty on the part of the observer about physical parameters of the signal leads to asymmetric ROC curves; the symmetric ROC curves that underlie tabulated values of d′ and β are associated with a signal known exactly by the observer. Taylor pointed out that uncertainty about the signal is likely to be relatively great when the signal rate is low, and showed graphs illustrating the effects on d′ and β of asymmetry in the ROC curve. Values of β taken from published tables will almost always be substantially higher than the correct value, sometimes drastically so. Values of d′ will also tend to be high, but the absolute level of detectability is rarely very interesting in the vigilance situation, and these values may properly describe the experimental results. In any case, care is required, for spurious correlations between the two measures can result from asymmetric ROC curves.

Implications for future research.—This discussion suggests that it may be desirable to modify procedures typical of past vigilance experiments in the direction of more standard psychophysical experiments. The use of the measures d′ and β, or related measures, will require the use of somewhat weaker signals so that sensitivity is in a measurable range (in terms of d′, say, between 1.0 and 3.0). Using measures derived from detection theory will also require elicitation of higher false-alarm proportions (larger, say, than 0.02) so that they may be estimated more reliably. It is highly desirable to obtain a range of false-alarm proportions large enough to define an ROC curve. If the curve is as asymmetrical in typical vigilance tests as we expect it will be, then it will be necessary to use less biased variants of the measures d′ and β.

It is clearly important to continue trying to spell out what kinds of displays yield reduced sensitivity over time and what kinds of displays do not suffer with passing time. J. F. Mackworth and Loeb and Hatfield and associates are making progress, but the domain of displays is large, and parametric experiments seem to be necessary, so help from others will be required.

A major issue now is the clarification of what sorts of independent and dependent variables are critical. If certain kinds of displays yield a sensitivity decrement, and if these displays are not simply replaceable in all operational situations by displays that do not, then the traditional independent variables of vigilance studies, namely, physiological and environmental variables that affect alertness, continue to be of interest. It seems desirable in this case, however, to acknowledge the need to run practice sessions until the decision criterion stabilizes, so that the effects of the independent variables will not be confounded with effects of learning.

In vigilance tests resistant to a sensitivity decrement, apparently a larger set, examination of the familiar independent variables is of little import. The likelihood of a change in performance over time remains, however, in all of these tests—a criterion change—and it must be dealt with appropriately. For practical purposes, determinants of the decision criterion in vigilance should be studied with an eye toward controlling it. There is surely no point in allowing the criterion unnecessarily to change throughout a vigil. Thus, effort ought to be devoted to demonstrating techniques of instruction and training that will result in stable performance. Then a detection response, or the absence of a detection response, can have a constant significance, a significance not dependent on how far a given watch has progressed.

LITERATURE CITED

1. Binford, J. R., Loeb, M. Changes within and over repeated sessions in criterion and effective sensitivity in an auditory vigilance task. *J. Exptl. Psychol.,* **72,** 339–45 (1966)
2. Broadbent, D. E. The role of auditory localization in attention and memory span. *J. Exptl. Psychol.,* **47,** 191–96 (1954)
3. Broadbent, D. E. *Perception and Communication* (Pergamon Press, New York and London, 338 pp., 1958)
4. Broadbent, D. E., Gregory, M. On the recall of stimuli presented alternately to two sense organs. *Quart. J. Exptl. Psychol.,* **13,** 103–9 (1961)
5. Broadbent, D. E., Gregory, M. Division of attention and the decision theory of signal detection. *Proc. Roy. Soc.,* **158,** 222–31 (1963)
6. Broadbent, D. E., Gregory, M. Vigilance considered as a statistical decision. *Brit. J. Psychol.,* **54,** 309–23 (1963)
7. Broadbent, D. E., Gregory, M. Stimulus set and response set: The alternation of attention. *Quart. J. Exptl. Psychol.,* **16,** 309–18 (1964)
8. Broadbent, D. E., Gregory, M. Effects of noise and of signal rate upon vigilance analyzed by means of decision theory. *Hum. Factors,* **7,** 155–62 (1965)
9. Bryden, M. P. Order of report in dichotic listening. *Can. J. Psychol.,* **16,** 291–99 (1962)
10. Buckner, D. N., McGrath, J. J., Eds. *Vigilance: A Symposium* (McGraw-Hill, New York, 269 pp., 1963)
11. Cherry, E. C. Some experiments on the recognition of speech with one and two ears. *J. Acoust. Soc. Am.,* **25,** 975–79 (1953)
12. Colquhoun, W. P. Training for vigilance: A comparison of different techniques. *Hum. Factors,* **8,** 7–12 (1966)
13. Colquhoun, W. P. Sonar target detection as a decision process. *J. Appl. Psychol.,* **51,** 187–90 (1967)
14. Colquhoun, W. P., Baddeley, A. D. Role of pretest expectancy in vigilance decrement. *J. Exptl. Psychol.,* **68,** 156–60 (1964)
15. Colquhoun, W. P., Baddeley, A. D. Influence of signal probability during pretraining on vigilance decrement. *Ibid.,* **73,** 153–55 (1967)
16. Creelman, C. D. Detection of signals of uncertain frequency. *J. Acoust. Soc. Am.,* **32,** 805–10 (1960)
17. Davenport, W. G. Vibrotactile vigilance: the effects of costs and values on signals. *Percept. Psychophys.,* **5,** 25–28 (1969)
18. Davenport, W. G. Auditory vigilance: the effects of costs and values on signals. *Australian J. Psychol.,* **20,** 213–18 (1968)
19. Deutsch, J. A., Deutsch, D. Attention: Some theoretical considerations. *Psychol. Rev.,* **70,** 80–90 (1963)
20. Deutsch, J. A., Deutsch, D., Lindsay, P. H. Comments on "Selective attention: Perception or response" *Quart. J. Exptl. Psychol.,* **19,** 362–64 (1967)
21. Egan, J. P., Greenberg, G. Z., Schulman, A. I. Operating characteristics, signal detectability, and the method of free response. *J. Acoust. Soc. Am.,* **33,** 993–1007 (1961)
22. Egeth, H. Selective attention. *Psychol. Bull.,* **67,** 41–57 (1967)
23. Fletcher, H. Auditory patterns. *Rev. Mod. Phys.,* **12,** 47–65 (1940)
24. Frankmann, J. P., Adams, J. A. Theories of vigilance. *Psychol. Bull.,* **59,** 257–72 (1962)
25. Franzén, O., Markowitz, J., Swets, J. A. Spatially-limited attention to vibrotactile stimulation. *Percept. Psychophys.* (In press)
26. Gassler, G. Ueber die Hörschwelle für Schallereignisse mit Verschieden Breitem Frequenzspektrum. *Acustica,* **4,** 408–14 (1954)
27. Gray, J. A., Wedderburn, A. A. I. Grouping strategies with simultaneous stimuli. *Quart. J. Exptl. Psychol.,* **12,** 180–85 (1960)
28. Green, D. M. Detection of multiple component signals in noise. *J. Acoust. Soc. Am.,* **30,** 904–11 (1958)
29. Green, D. M., Luce, R. D. Detection of auditory signals presented at random times. *Percept. Psychophys.,* **2,** 441–50 (1967)
30. Green, D. M., McKey, M. J., Licklider, J. C. R. Detection of a

pulsed sinusoid in noise as a function of frequency. *J. Acoust. Soc. Am.,* **31,** 1446–52 (1959)

31. Green, D. M., Swets, J. A. *Signal Detection Theory and Psychophysics* (Wiley, New York, 445 pp., 1966)
32. Greenberg, G. Z., Larkin, W. D. Frequency-response characteristic of auditory observers detecting signals of a single frequency in noise : The probe-signal method. *J. Acoust. Soc. Am.,* **44,** 1513–23 (1968)
33. Hatfield, J. L., Loeb, M. Sense mode and coupling in a vigilance task. *Percept. Psychophys.,* **4,** 29–36 (1968)
34. Hatfield, J. L., Soderquist, D. R. Coupling effects and performance in vigilance tasks (In preparation)
35. Head, H. *Aphasia and Kindred Disorders of Speech* (MacMillan, New York, Vol. I, 549 pp.; Vol. II, 430 pp., 1926)
36. Hernández-Peón, R. Physiological mechanisms in attention. In *Frontiers in Physiological Psychology,* **I,** 121–47 (Russell, R. W., Ed., Academic Press, New York, 261 pp., 1966)
37. Horn, G. Physiological and psychological aspects of selective behavior. In *Advances in the Study of Behavior,* **I,** 155–215 (Lehrman, D. S., Hinde, R. A., Shaw, E., Eds., Academic Press, New York, 320 pp., 1965)
38. Howarth, C. I., Ellis, K. The relative intelligibility threshold for one's own name compared with other names. *Quart. J. Exptl. Psychol.,* **13,** 236–39 (1961)
39. James, W. Attention. In *Principles of Psychology,* 402–58 (Holt, New York, 703 pp., 1890); abridged version in *Attention,* 3–22 (Bakan, P., Ed., Van Nostrand, Princeton, New Jersey, 225 pp., 1966)
40. Jerison, J. J. Signal detection theory in the analysis of human vigilance. *Hum. Factors,* **9,** 285–88 (1967)
41. Jerison, J. J., Pickett, R. M., Stenson, H. H. The elicited observing rate and decision processes in vigilance. *Hum. Factors,* **7,** 107–28 (1965)
42. Karoly, A. J., Isaacson, R. L. *Scanning Mechanisms in Audition* (Presented at Michigan Acad. Sci., March 1956, Ann Arbor, Mich.)
43. Kinchla, R. A. *An Attention Operating Characteristic in Vision* (Tech. Rept. No. 29, Dept. Psychol., McMaster Univ., Hamilton, Ontario, 1969)
44. Kinchla, R. A. Temporal and channel uncertainty in detection: A multiple-observation analysis. *Percept. Psychophys.,* **5,** 129–36 1969)
45. Kristofferson, A. B. Attention and psychophysical time. *Acta Psychol.,* **27,** 93–100 (1967)
46. Kristofferson, A. B. Successiveness discrimination as a two-state, quantal process. *Science,* **158,** 1337–39 (1967)
47. Lawson, E. A. Decisions concerning the rejected channel. *Quart. J. Exptl. Psychol.,* **18,** 260–65 (1966)
48. Levine, J. M. The effects of values and costs on the detection and identification of signals in auditory vigilance. *Hum. Factors,* **8,** 525–37 (1966)
49. Loeb, M., Binford, J. R. Vigilance for auditory intensity changes as a function of preliminary feedback and confidence level. *Hum. Factors,* **6,** 445–58 (1964)
50. Loeb, M., Binford, J. R. Variation in performance on auditory and visual monitoring tasks as a function of signal and stimulus frequencies. *Percept. Psychophys.,* **4,** 361–67 (1968)
51. Loeb, M., Hawkes, G. R., Evans, W. O., Alluisi, E. A. The influence of *d*-amphetamine, benactyzine, and chlorpromazine on performance in an auditory vigilance task. *Psychon. Sci.,* **3,** 29–30 (1965)
52. Lucas, P. A. Human performance in low-signal-probability tasks. *J. Acoust. Soc. Am.,* **42,** 158–78 (1967)
53. Luce, R. D. A model for detection in temporally unstructured experiments with a Poisson distribution of signal presentations. *J. Math. Psychol.,* **3,** 48–64 (1966)
54. Luce, R. D., Green, D. M. Detection of signals with Poisson arrival time (abstract). *J. Acoust. Soc. Am.,* **45,** 327 (1969)
55. Mackworth, J. F. Performance decrement in vigilance, threshold, and high speed perceptual motor

tasks. *Can. J. Psychol.*, **18,** 209–23 (1964)

56. Mackworth, J. F. The effect of true and false knowledge of results on the detectability of signals in a vigilance task. *Ibid.*, 106–17
57. Mackworth, J. F. Decision interval and signal detectability in a vigilance task. *Ibid.*, **19,** 111–17 (1965)
58. Mackworth, J. F. Deterioration of signal detectability during a vigilance task as a function of background event rate. *Psychon. Sci.*, **3,** 421–22 (1965)
59. Mackworth, J. F. Effect of amphetamine on the detectability of signals in a vigilance task. *Can. J. Psychol.*, **19,** 104–10 (1965)
60. Mackworth, J. F. The effect of signal rate on performance in two kinds of vigilance task. *Hum. Factors*, **10,** 11–18 (1968)
61. Mackworth, J. F., Taylor, M. M. The d′ measure of signal detectability in vigilance-like situations. *Can. J. Psychol.*, **17,** 302–25 (1963)
62. Mackworth, N. H. The breakdown of vigilance during prolonged visual search. *Quart. J. Exptl. Psychol.*, **1,** 6–21 (1948)
63. Mackworth, N. H. *Researches on the Measurement of Human Performance* (Med. Res. Council Spec. Rept. Ser. No. 268, H. M. Stationery Off., London, 1950)
64. Marill, T. M. *Detection Theory and Pyschophysics* (Tech. Rept., No. 319, Res. Lab. Electron., M. I. T., Cambridge, Mass., 1956)
65. Moray, N. Attention in dichotic listening: Affective cues and the influence of instructions. *Quart. J. Exptl. Psychol.*, **11,** 56–60 (1959)
66. Moray, N. Broadbent's filter theory: Postulate H and the problem of switching time. *Ibid.*, **12,** 214–20 (1960)
67. Moray, N. *Attention: Selective Processes in Vision and Hearing* (Hutchinson, London, in press)
68. Moray, N., O'Brien, T. Signal detection theory applied to selective listening. *J. Acoust. Soc. Am.*, **42,** 765–72 (1967)
69. Moray, N., Taylor, A. The effect of redundancy in shadowing one of two dichotic messages. *Lang. Speech*, **1,** 102–9 (1959)
70. Mostofsky, D. I., Ed. *Attention: Contemporary Theory and Analysis* (Appleton-Century-Crofts, New York, in press)
71. Mowbray, G. H. Perception and retention of verbal information presented during auditory shadowing. *J. Acoust. Soc. Am.*, **36,** 1459–64 (1964)
72. Neisser, U. *Cognitive Psychology* Appleton-Century-Crofts, New York, 351 pp., 1967)
73. Norman, D. A. Toward a theory of memory and attention. *Psychol. Rev.*, **75,** 522–36 (1968)
74. Norman, D. A. *Memory and Attention* (Wiley, New York, 201 pp., 1969)
75. Norman, D. A. Memory while shadowing (In preparation)
76. Oswald, I., Taylor, A. M., Treisman, M. Discrimination responses to stimulation during human sleep. *Brain*, **83,** 440–53 (1960)
77. Peterson, L. R., Kroener, S. Dichotic stimulation and retention. *J. Exptl. Psychol.*, **68,** 125–30 (1964)
78. Sanders, A. F., Schroots, J. J. F. Cognitive categories and memory span: I. Shifting between categories. *Quart. J. Exptl. Psychol.*, **20,** 370–72 (1968)
79. Sanders, A. F., Schroots, J. J. F. Cognitive categories and memory span: II. The effect of temporal vs. categorical recall. *Ibid.*, 373–79
80. Savin, H. B. On the successive perception of simultaneous stimuli. *Percept. Psychophys.*, **2,** 479–82 (1967)
81. Schafer, T. H., Gales, R. S. Auditory masking of multiple tones by noise. *J. Acoust. Soc. Am.*, **21,** 392–98 (1949)
82. Scharf, B. Complex sounds and critical bands. *Psychol. Bull.*, **58,** 205–17 (1961)
83. Sorkin, R. D., Pastore, R. E., Gilliom, J. D. Signal probability and the listening band. *Percept. Psychophys.*, **4,** 10–12 (1968)
84. Swets, J. A. Central factors in auditory frequency selectivity. *Psychol. Bull.*, **60,** 429–40 (1963)
85. Swets, J. A., Ed. *Signal Detection and Recognition by Human Observers* (Wiley, New York, 702 pp., 1964)
86. Swets, J. A., Sewall, S. T. Stimulus vs. response uncertainty in recog-

nition. *J. Acoust. Soc. Am.,* **33,** 1586–92 (1961)

87. Swets, J. A., Shipley, E. F., McKey, M. J., Green, D. M. Multiple observations of signals in noise. *J. Acoust. Soc. Am.,* **31,** 514–21 (1959)
88. Tanner, W. P., Jr. *ROC Curves as Obtained from a "Vigilance" Experiment.* (Presented at Symposium on Signal Detection with an Undefined Observation Interval, 133rd Ann. Meeting Am. Assoc. Advan. Sci., Washington, D.C., December 1966)
89. Tanner, W. P., Jr., Norman, R. Z. The human use of information. II: Signal detection for the case of an unknown signal parameter. *Trans. IRE Prof. Group Inform. Theory, PGIT–4,* 222–27 (1954)
90. Tanner, W. P., Jr., Swets, J. A. A decision-making theory of visual detection. *Psychol. Rev.,* **61,** 401–9 (1954)
91. Tanner, W. P., Jr., Swets, J. A., Green, D. M. *Some General Properties of the Hearing Mechanism* (Tech. Rept. No. 30, Electron. Defense Group, Univ. Michigan, Ann Arbor, Mich., 1956)
92. Taylor, M. M. Detectability measures in vigilance: Comment on a paper by Wiener, Poock & Steele. *Percept. Mot. Skills,* **20,** 1217–21 (1965)
93. Taylor, M. M. The effect of the square root of time on continuing perceptual tasks. *Percept. Psychophys.,* **1,** 113–19 (1966)
94. Taylor, M. M. Detectability theory and the interpretation of vigilance data. *Acta Psychol.,* **27,** 390–99 (1967)
95. Titchener, E. B. Attention as sensory clearness. *Lectures on the Elementary Psychology of Feeling and Attention,* 171–206 (MacMillan, New York, 404 pp., 1908); abridged version in *Attention,* 23–34 (Bakan, P., Ed., Van Nostrand, Princeton, New Jersey, 225 pp., 1966)
96. Treisman, A. M. Contextual cues in selective listening. *Quart. J. Exptl. Psychol.,* **12,** 242–48 (1960)
97. Treisman, A. Monitoring and storage of irrelevant messages in selective attention. *J. Verbal Learn. Verbal Behav.,* **3,** 449–59 (1964)
98. Treisman, A. M. Verbal cues, language, and meaning in selective attention. *Am. J. Psychol.,* **77,** 206–19 (1964)
99. Treisman, A. M. The effect of irrelevant material on the efficiency of selective listening. *Ibid.,* 533–46
100. Treisman, A. Our limited attention. *Advan. Sci.,* **22,** 600–11 (1966)
101. Treisman, A. Reply to "Comments on 'Selective attention: Perception or response?'" *Quart. J. Exptl. Psychol.,* **19,** 364–67 (1967)
102. Treisman, A. Strategies and models of selective attention. *Psychol. Rev.,* **76,** 282–99 (1969)
103. Treisman, A., Geffen, G. Selective attention: Perception or response? *Quart. J. Exptl. Psychol.,* **19,** 1–17 (1967)
104. Tulving, E., Lindsay, P. H. Identification of simultaneously presented simple visual and auditory stimuli. *Acta Psychol.,* **27,** 101–9 (1967)
105. Veniar, F. A. Signal detection as a function of frequency ensemble, I. *J. Acoust. Soc. Am.,* **30,** 1020–24 (1958). Signal detection as a function of frequency ensemble, II. *Ibid.,* 1075–78
106. Watson, C. S. Towards a model of auditory signal detection without defined observation intervals. Presented at Symposium on Signal Detection with an Undefined Observation Interval (See Ref. 88)
107. Watson, C. S., Nichols, T. L. Replications and revisions of Egan's method of free response (abstract). *J. Acoust. Soc. Am.,* **36,** 1247 (1966)
108. Wiener, E. L., Poock, G. K., Steele, M. Effect of time-sharing on monitoring performance: Simple mental arithmetic as a loading task. *Percept. Mot. Skills,* **19,** 435–40 (1964)
109. Worden, F. G. Attention and auditory electrophysiology. In *Progress in Physiological Psychology,* **1,** 45–116 (Stellar, E., Sprague, J. M., Eds., Academic Press, New York, 285 pp., 1966)
110. Yntema, D. B., Trask, F. P. Recall as a search process. *J. Verbal Learn. Verbal Behav.,* **2,** 65–74 (1963)

INSTRUMENTAL LEARNING IN ANIMALS: PARAMETERS OF REINFORCEMENT[1,2] 154

By M. E. Bitterman
Bryn Mawr College, Bryn Mawr, Pennsylvania
and W. Michael Schoel
University of California, Davis, California

The first 10 volumes in this series have general chapters on learning, the most recent of which, by Kendler, was published in 1959. Since then, there has been no comprehensive review of the literature on animal learning, although parts of it have been touched upon under a variety of more specialized headings. Our purpose in this chapter is to summarize the work of the intervening years on the role of reinforcement in the instrumental learning of animals. Research on the process of classical conditioning is treated only insofar as it bears on the interpretation of the instrumental data, while research on larger problems of generalization, discrimination, and attention is reserved for subsequent consideration. Even so, the scope of the literature reviewed makes exhaustive citation impractical, and we must rely on representative studies to illustrate the principal findings.

An experiment on instrumental learning is one in which the occurrence of some event (reinforcement) is contingent upon the occurrence of some specified response (the instrumental response), and the effect of the contingency upon the occurrence of the response is measured. It is useful to distinguish two main categories of instrumental training: in the *Thorndikian* case, the instrumental response increases the probability of reinforcement; in the *avoidance* case, the instrumental response decreases the probability of

[1] This chapter covers the period from January 1959 through December 1968. It was written during the academic year 1968–69, while the senior author was visiting professor in the Department of Psychology at the University of California, Davis. Incidental costs were met by that department. The participation of the junior author was supported by Grant MH-02857 from the Public Health Service.

[2] The following abbreviations will be used in this chapter: A (alley); CER (conditioned emotional response); CR (conditioned response); CRF (continuous reinforcement); CS (conditioned stimulus); D (delayed reinforcement); FI (fixed interval schedule); FR (fixed ratio schedule); G (goalbox); ITR (intertrial reinforcement); N (nonreinforcement); PRE (partial reinforcement effect); R (reinforcement or response); R_F (unconditioned frustration response); r_F (anticipatory frustration response); R_G (unconditioned consummatory or goal response); r_G (anticipatory goal response); S (stimulus); s_F (feedback from the frustration response); s_G (feedback from the goal response); T-1 (unitary Thorndikian situation); T-2 (Thorndikian choice situation); VI (variable interval schedule).

reinforcement (67). The first main section of this chapter is devoted to Thorndikian training and the second, to avoidance training. The reinforcing events with which we are concerned also fall into two main categories: a *reward* is a reinforcement which increases the probability of the instrumental response in Thorndikian situations and decreases it in avoidance situations; a *punishment* is a reinforcement whose effects are directly opposite to those of reward.

While Kendler still could find good reason a decade ago to organize his chapter in terms of prevailing theoretical orientations, this one is more empirical in outline, because no substantial concern with systematic questions is evident in the period which it covers (68). The stimulus-response (S-R) language is the common language but there is little in the way of formal theory—only a loose collection of concepts, old and new, which are drawn upon as needed to deal with the data at hand. In the Thorndikian literature, which deals primarily with reward, the dominant approach is that of Spence, according to which instrumental habit strength is established by contiguity and activated both by drive and by the anticipatory goal response (r_G), a component of the unconditioned consummatory response to reward (R_G) which becomes connected to the sensory antecedents of the instrumental response. From this point of view, the role of reward in instrumental learning is simply to be anticipated. Instrumental performance also can be influenced by anticipatory frustration (r_F), a component of what is assumed to be an unconditioned emotional response to discrepancy between anticipated and actual reward (R_F). The effect of frustration is disruptive unless there has been opportunity for its sensory feedback (s_F) to become connected to the instrumental response, in which case the effect is facilitative (1). The avoidance literature is dominated by the early two-factor theory of Mowrer, according to which instrumental habit strength is established by the reduction of fear that has been conditioned to the sensory antecedents of the instrumental response. We shall have occasion to comment on the adequacy of these and other conceptions in the course of our review of the experimental results.

THORNDIKIAN EXPERIMENTS

Thorndikian situations fall into two main subcategories—unitary and choice (67). In unitary or T-1 situations, a single response is defined (such as running in a runway or pressing a lever) and the readiness with which it comes to expression is measured in terms of time or rate. In choice or T-2 situations, two or more responses are defined (such as turning right versus left at a maze junction or pressing the right versus the left lever in a two-lever apparatus) and choice among them is measured, although response times and rates may be measured as well. The experiments reviewed are grouped accordingly. We are careful, too, at each point to specify the subjects employed. While the most popular animal by far in experiments on instrumental learning still is the rat, increasing attention is being paid to submammalian forms, and evidence gradually is accumulating that the mechanisms of learning which operate in Thorndikian situations are not the same in all animals (65).

Hunger and Thirst

The motivating conditions most widely used in Thorndikian experiments continue to be hunger and thirst. Although some interest is evidenced in the finer points of drive manipulation (43, 182, 211, 345), most investigators are content with rather rough-and-ready procedures. Hunger more often is specified in terms of the number of hours since feeding than in terms of body weight. Thirst typically is specified in terms of the number of hours of deprivation or in terms of the amount of water given a deprived animal immediately prior to training.

When reward is appropriate, the rat's asymptotic performance in T-1 situations improves with drive level (176, 327, 476, 494, 519, 579, 583, 637, 674), and there is evidence that the improvement is not due entirely to the elimination of competing responses (159, 327, 493). The relationship for lever-pressing is less pronounced with continuous reinforcement (CRF) than with intermittent (152), and less pronounced with low fixed ratio (FR) than with high (463). Rate of pecking in pigeons increases with hunger (554), as does rate of lever-pressing in fish (219). Hunger and thirst also increase the rat's rate of lever-pressing for light-onset as reinforcement (589).

Rats (170, 176, 556, 674) and fish (374) show better performance in extinction when trained and extinguished under high as compared with low drive, although evidence of the opposite relationship appears (505). When training and extinction levels are unconfounded, a clear positive relationship between extinction performance and extinction drive is evident (161, 180, 219, 275, 476). There is some indication, too, of an effect of acquisition drive. Rats trained under high drive and extinguished under low drive are more resistant to extinction than rats both trained and extinguished under low drive, although stimulus generalization alone would tend to produce the opposite outcome (212, 596). The results for rats trained at one drive level and retrained at a second level also point to certain persisting effects of the original level (118, 123, 605, 675).

In T-2 situations, speed of response increases with drive, but the results for errors are inconsistent. A factorial experiment with rats in a T-maze shows no effect of acquisition drive, but better reversal performance with high drive in reversal (642). Errors in brightness discrimination often seem little affected by drive (346, 575), although a study of very young rats in a series of reversals suggests that performance may be impaired by very high drive (524). Spatial reversal studies with adult rats (223) and pigeons (265) also suggest that performance may be poor at high drive, especially when reward is small. Brightness discrimination in monkeys is unaffected by drive level, whether the task is easy or difficult (432); the performance of monkeys is better under high drive than under low in delayed response, but not in delayed alternation (268).

These experiments do not appreciably advance our understanding of the role of drive in Thorndikian situations. The familiar fact that performance in T-1 situations improves with the prevailing drive level is consistent both with the conception of drive as a general activator and with the conception of drive as a determinant of the incentive-value of the consequences of response, actual or anticipated. The evidence that training at one level may affect subsequent performance at another level certainly points to a process other than activation which remains to be analyzed experimentally. The inconsistent results on the effect of drive on performance in T-2 situations show how much still is to be done.

There is a continuing interest in the possibility that stimuli contiguous with hunger and thirst may acquire drive properties. Some experiments yield negative results (111, 462), while others yield positive results but lack essential controls (613, 667). The technique of inducing hunger by the injection of insulin shows some promise (31).

Amount of Reward

Food and drink continue to be the most widely used rewards in Thorndikian experiments. With solid food, amount of reward is specified either in terms of the time during which the animal is permitted to eat, or in terms of weight and number of pellets given. Apart from water, the most common liquid rewards are solutions of sucrose or saccharine, which are varied in volume and concentration. The many papers published in the past 10 years add substantially to our information about the role of amount of reward in Thorndikian experiments.

The asymptotic runway performance of deprived rats improves with amount of food, volume of water, and concentration of sucrose solutions available in the goalbox (101, 263, 327, 333, 337, 476, 519, 562, 637, 674). While ingestive load often produces an inverse relationship between rate of lever-pressing and amount of reward in CRF (115), intermittent schedules characteristically yield a direct relationship (48, 286, 418). Factorial studies of concentration and volume of sugar or saccharine solutions show that the rat's initial rate of lever-pressing in fixed interval schedules (FI) increases both with concentration and with volume, although there is a fall in rate within sessions which is particularly rapid for high concentration, large volume, and short FI (174–176). The monkey's rate of lever-pressing increases linearly with concentration in FI, but declines at high concentrations in CRF, especially when volume is large (538). The rat's rate of instrumental licking increases with concentration; the relationship of rate to volume is inverse in CRF, but direct in FR (293). In general, the sensory concomitants of concentration and volume seem to have facilitating effects on free-operant performance which may be offset by ingestive load and by satiation.

The mean force and variability in force exerted by rats on a lever are inversely related to amount of reward when the minimal force required for reward is 8 grams; the results are attributed to improved discrimination of the required force with larger reward (203). Like force, rate of lever-pressing can be learned as such when amount of reward is made dependent on rate; the adventitious reinforcement of alternative responses is involved to some extent in the maintenance of low rates by differential reinforcement (278, 349). Speed of response in the runway also can be controlled by making amount of reward contingent upon speed (371). Delay of reward is inversely related to speed in many T-1 situations, and it has been suggested that this relation may account for the fact that speed usually increases with amount of reward (368), but a critical experiment provides no confirmation (652).

Although T-1 performance in acquisition tends to improve with amount of reward, the opposite result often is obtained in extinction, either as a groups-effect or as a groups X trials interaction (14, 63, 620, 656). The conditions which produce an inverse relation between amount of reward and resistance to extinction are not well defined. Apart from consistency of reinforcement (620), a substantial level of drive seems to be required (392, 674), and a substantial number of training trials (282, 300, 471). Since the effect is found in spaced training (620), an interpretation in terms of stimulus generalization is ruled out. Two experiments with goldfish show a strong positive relation between amount of reward and resistance to extinction under conditions analogous to those which yield an inverse relation in rats (255, 261).

Studies of acquisition and reversal in T-2 situations indicate that the rat's preference for a rewarded as compared with an unrewarded response develops more rapidly with large reward than with small. Of five factorial experiments (281, 299, 323, 498, 645), four show fewer errors in acquisition with large reward, and all show fewer errors in reversal with large reward. The effect on reversal performance of amount of reward in the original training is significant in only one of the five experiments (large reward in acquisition tending to facilitate reversal), but there are some complex interactions between size of reward in acquisition and size of reward in reversal which remain to be analyzed. Two studies of choice in extinction (as opposed to reversal) fail, unfortunately, to throw much light on the matter (164, 629). Experiments with rats and pigeons show that the facilitating effects of large reward persist over a series of spatial reversals (223, 265). Brightness discrimination by rats also improves with amount of reward (629), but the discrimination of color and form by pigeons does not (60). The delayed-response performance of gibbons improves with the quality of reward (59).

Experiments with both alternatives rewarded provide further information about the role of reward in T-2 situations. The tendency of rats to repeat a forced choice when the two alternatives are rewarded equally increases with amount of reward (229). Where the two alternatives are unequally rewarded, the rate at which a preference for the larger reward develops increases with the difference in amount (73, 164, 283, 567), and the discrimination is better in massed than in spaced trials (124). A difference in visible amount produces a preference for the larger even when eating time is equated (206). Comparisons of fixed and variable amounts of the same mean value show no preference in rats (370) or pigeons (580) when both alternatives are consistently rewarded. Rats prefer two units of reward on 50 per cent of trials to one unit on 100 per cent of trials when the unit is small, but the opposite when the unit is large (483).

Experiments on the interaction of amount of reward with drive level often fail to give positive results even where the main effects of both variables are significant (476, 517, 519, 637), but there is considerable support for the commonsense notion that the reward-value of food and water depends upon prevailing levels of hunger and thirst. Interactive effects of amount of solid food, volume of water, and sucrose concentration with drive level appear in a variety of experiments on the acquisition and extinction of running and lever-pressing (171, 176, 327, 392, 530, 579, 674). Drive in acquisition and drive in extinction usually are confounded in these experiments, although there is fragmentary evidence that it may be useful to separate the two variables (392). Some results for hypothalamic stimulation and self-stimulation suggest that hunger and thirst give reward-value to food and water (178, 424, 425). The results of a more conventional deprivation experiment suggest the same conclusion (340).

The evidence permits two generalizations about amount of reward in Thorndikian situations which could not have been made with any confidence 10 years ago, although some fragmentary data already were available (497). The first is that resistance to extinction (in the rat, if not in the fish) varies inversely with amount of reward under a variety of conditions. The second is that amount of reward is an important variable in T-2 performance. Neither of these conclusions is incompatible with the view—which had already gained wide acceptance by 1960—that the growth of habit strength in Thorndikian situations is independent of amount of reward.

The extinction findings, reminiscent of Crespi's depression effect, seem rather to support that view. Like the depression effect, they are explained in terms of frustration. The larger the reward in training, the greater the r_G, the greater the frustration engendered by nonreward in extinction, and the greater the disruption of performance. The T-2 results are explained on the assumption that the difference in strength of the competing instrumental tendencies reflected in each choice is based on a difference in r_G rather than habit. There remains, however, the question of how the r_G selectively activates the rewarded response when the frequency of the two responses is equated by the use of forced trials. When the two responses are rewarded with equal frequency but with different amounts, we may ask also how the two r_Gs can be made concurrently, and by what process each r_G activates only one of the two responses.

Successive Contrast

The effect of a given amount of reward depends to a certain extent on previous experience with other amounts. The contrast which occurs when an animal is trained with one amount and then shifted to a different amount is called *successive,* while that which occurs when the animal encounters two amounts concurrently in the same series of training trials is called *simultaneous* (the word should not be taken literally). The effectiveness of one amount may be decreased by experience with a larger amount (negative contrast or depression), and it may be increased by experience with a smaller amount (positive contrast or elation).

Successive contrast typically is studied in T-1 situations. Two groups of animals are trained, each with a different amount of reward, for a certain number of trials, and then the amount given one group (experimental) is changed to the amount for the other (control). Negative contrast (poorer performance in a downshifted experimental group than in the control) is easy to demonstrate in rats when solid food is used (249, 258, 525, 574, 617), but, when concentration of sucrose is varied, there are more failures (264, 298, 301, 528) than successes (173, 618). Positive contrast is not found as often as negative (138, 525, 618), although it does occur (173, 302, 574). There is some indication that both effects tend to increase in magnitude with the number of preshift trials (18, 617). Both effects may occur without a contingency of preshift reward upon response, but more often they do not (301, 574). When rats are satiated in postshift trials, performance deteriorates both in downshifted and in upshifted groups (relative to their unshifted controls), but the change produced by downshifting occurs earlier (267).

A large and abrupt decrement in amount of reward produces more negative contrast than does a small decrement, while a large but gradual decrement (over a series of trials) produces only a gradual decline in performance from the experimental to the control level (258). Partial reinforcement in the preshift training either prevents or postpones negative contrast (430). Unreinforced trials given between preshift and postshift training do not prevent depression (574, 617), but the effect fails to appear if there is a long period without training just before or just after the first postshift trial (249). Very young rats fail to show elation or depression (525). Adult rats dosed with a barbiturate also fail to show elation or depression (302, 529). Furthermore, the performance of the downshifted animals remains at the preshift level, just as would be expected on the assumption that habit strength is a function of amount of reward, although there is an instance in the literature of persistently good performance in downshifted normal rats (non-contingently rewarded with sucrose prior to shift) which is not open to this interpretation (301). The results for undrugged goldfish are the same in all respects as those for tranquilized rats (378).

Successive contrast, both positive and negative, is found also in experiments with variables other than amount of reward. An increase in probability of reward produces elation in rats (359, 523), as does a decrease in delay of reward (551). An escape experiment with rise in water-temperature as reward shows depression but not elation (663), although an experiment with decrement in electric shock as reward shows neither (98). Pigeons reinforced with food on a variable interval (VI) schedule and punished with shock for each response show elation (relative to the unshocked control rate) when the shock no longer is given (22).

The concept of frustration produced by discrepancy between anticipated and actual reward plays a dominant role in contemporary accounts of successive contrast. The favored mechanism is the r_G, although it would be simpler for most purposes (especially when the data for aversive stimuli are considered) to assume that the sensory properties of reinforcement are anticipated as such. Evidence for positive contrast, which cannot be explained in terms of frustration, tends to be discounted. That positive contrast does in fact occur, albeit less dependably than negative, seems easier to understand, however, in terms of conventional psychophysics. The asymmetry of positive and negative effects may be nothing more than an artifact of measurement, since the baseline performance in these experiments typically is much closer to ceiling than floor, although frustration produced only by downshifting may play a contributory role. The greater difficulty of finding negative contrast with sweet tastes as compared with visually distinguishable amounts of solid food also may have a psychophysical explanation.

The phenomenon of successive contrast does suggest that reward is in some manner "learned about," but it does not rule out an effect on habit strength as well, although that possibility usually is dismissed for reasons of parsimony. The results for the fish in experiments on shift of reward and on resistance to extinction as a function of amount of reward are compatible with the S-R reinforcement principle. The results for fish, together with those for tranquilized rats, make it reasonable to speculate that the principle operates at both levels, but that its operation in rats is masked by an anticipatory mechanism not yet developed in fish.

Simultaneous Contrast

A familiar design for the study of simultaneous contrast is the T-1 amount-of-reward discrimination: animals are rewarded with a large amount of food for response to one stimulus and with a small amount of food for response to a different stimulus, while controls for negative contrast are rewarded with the small amount for response to both, and controls for positive contrast are rewarded with the large amount for response to both. Negative contrast is found more often than positive in runway experiments with rats (96, 383, 396, 488, 531). A variation of the design in which rats feed on sucrose of one concentration in the first part of each experimental session and then press a lever for sucrose of different concentration in the second part of the session yields both effects (485). A key-pecking experiment with pigeons shows stable negative contrast; the nature of the effect is highlighted by the fact that the rate of response to the small-reward color can be increased markedly by decreasing the amount of reward given for response to the large-reward color (114). Simultaneous contrast in amount of reward also is studied in T-2 situations (the alternative responses are rewarded with different amounts in the experimental group and with the same amount in the controls), although the sensitive measure is time rather than choice (time is measured on forced choices which are interspersed among free choices to equate experience with the two alternatives). Rats commonly show depression in these experiments (185, 567, 570); elation sometimes occurs (443) but often does not (283). An experiment with widely spaced trials shows a powerful elation effect which is evident as well in speed of response to the small-reward side (569).

A runway discrimination with a difference in delay rather than amount of reward produces depression but not elation in rats (49). Simultaneous contrast also is found in key-pecking experiments with pigeons when schedules providing different densities of reinforcement are used. The rate of response to a color reinforced on VI-3 min increases as the schedule of reinforcement for response to a second color changes from FR-75 to FR-150 and then to extinction (516). When response to one color is reinforced on some schedule and response to a second color is not reinforced at all, clear evidence of positive contrast is obtained, in that the rate of response to the reinforced color is much greater than when both are reinforced on the same schedule (81, 515). The effect is enhanced markedly, if temporarily, when response to the negative color postpones the appearance of the positive (80), although it does not seem to occur at all under conditions designed to prevent errors during the establishment of the discrimination (593). When two colors are reinforced on the same schedule and response to one of them also is punished, rate of response to the unpunished color is greater than when neither is punished (104). These effects have strong transient components which can be traced to immediately preceding conditions—there are transient increases in rate after exposure to higher-density schedules, and transient decreases in rate after lower-density schedules (154, 438, 457)—although there are strong stable components as well.

To account for the data on simultaneous contrast, it clearly is necessary to go beyond a simple frustrational interpretation. For one thing, positive effects are much too common to be ignored. For another, the negative effects are much too stable to be explained in terms of unrealized anticipations; every opportunity is provided in these experiments for the extinction of inappropriate r_Gs and of the consequent r_Fs. The data on transient as compared with stable effects define another dimension of the problem that remains to be analyzed.

Frustration

The frustrational interpretation of negative contrast is complicated by the fact that unrealized anticipation of reward sometimes appears to facilitate instrumental performance. The standard experiment is done with a double runway, the goalbox of the first (G_1) giving access to the alley of the second (A_2), but it may be done also with levers or pigeon-keys, techniques more appropriate to comparative experiments (187). The fact that the speed of rats in A_2 tends to be greater after nonreinforcement (N) than after reinforcement (R) in G_1 (the so-called *frustration effect*) is not in itself evidence of a facilitating effect of frustration (as once it was taken to be), because the effect of the presence or absence of food independently of the animal's anticipation of it must be controlled; but a number of experiments show that response in A_2 on N trials is more rapid in rats that are rewarded in G_1 on 50 per cent of trials than in rats that never are rewarded in G_1 (404, 619). The almost immediate appearance of the frustration effect in animals shifted from 0 to 50 per cent reinforcement in G_1 does, however, present some difficulty for frustration theory, since anticipation of reward is assumed to be a necessary condition of frustration (404). The magnitude of the frustration effect in animals shifted from 100 to 50 per cent reinforcement in G_1 increases with drive (413).

In an experiment with a triple runway, performance in A_3 shows no summation of the effects of nonreinforcement in G_1 and G_2, and no perseveration of the effect of nonreinforcement in G_1 after reinforcement in G_2 (272). In work with the double runway, there is interest also in the effect of amount of reward in G_1 on performance in A_2, and in the effect of incomplete reduction of reward in G_1, but an appropriate experiment is difficult to design (181, 339, 414, 429, 481); with different amounts of reward in G_1 and G_2, there may be some stable simultaneous contrast which obscures the effect of change in amount. It might be well, in fact, to consider the possibility that the frustration effect is to some extent at least a product of positive contrast based on difference in probability of reward. Support for this view is provided by the finding that response in A_2 on R trials is more rapid in rats that are rewarded in G_1 on 50 per cent of trials than in rats that always are rewarded in G_1 (166, 404).

When no reward ever is given in the first segment of a two-segment situation, an increase in the delay between segments sometimes increases speed of response in the second segment (149, 324), but that is not always the case (382, 661). Increased prereinforcement delay in G_1 slows response in A_2 (410), although an increase in delay coupled with a decrease in amount of reward in G_1 may facilitate performance in A_2 (411). A two-lever experiment with rats and monkeys shows a disappearance of the frustration effect when the time between the presentation of the levers (postreinforcement delay) is increased; the effect is due largely to an increase in the speed of response on R trials, which suggests a decline in postingestive inhibition rather than a decline in frustration (187).

Successive contrast in probability of reward is demonstrated in the double runway with one group shifted from 100 to 0 per cent reward in G_1, a control group never rewarded in G_1, and both always rewarded in G_2 (409). The shifted animals respond less rapidly in A_1 than do the controls, and somewhat less rapidly also in A_2. These results, like those obtained in the single runway, suggest that speed of response may be reduced rather than increased by frustration. At the same time, animals shifted from 100 to 50 per cent reward in G_1 respond more rapidly in A_1 than do the unrewarded controls and show the frustration effect in A_2. Stimuli associated with change from reward to nonreward, or with low probabilities of reward, certainly can be shown to acquire activating properties in rats and pigeons (23, 27, 622), but the conditions under which they may be expected to facilitate instrumental responding and the conditions under which they may be expected to disrupt it have not been fully specified.

Delay of Reward

Once held to be a factor in habit strength, delay of reward now is widely treated as an incentive variable (506). Like differences in amount of reward, differences in delay of reward are assumed to affect instrumental performance by way of the r_G. From this point of view, contiguity of reward with the instrumental response is important only insofar as it ensures contiguity of reward with the sensory antecedents of that response, and thus their connection to r_G. The results of some free-operant experiments on the discrimination of contingent from noncontingent reward by pigeons (13, 209), and on delay of secondary reward in rats (348) suggest, however, that delay of reward plays a role in the selection as well as in the activation of instrumental responses.

Evidence from a variety of sources is compatible with the view that delay of reward has an incentive function. The asymptotic performance of rats in a runway varies inversely with delay (505, 550), and an increase in delay after acquisition impairs runway performance (648, 661). Differences in delay may produce contrast effects, both simultaneous and successive (49, 551), and correlated delay of reward may be used to regulate speed of response in the runway (95). A very small amount of reward given immediately produces better performance in the runway than a large amount given after 15 sec, and at certain amount-delay combinations conflictful behavior in the animal becomes evident (381). The development of a preference for the larger of two amounts of reward in a choice situation may be offset by a difference in delay (185, 369). Two-key experiments with pigeons show a preference for short as compared with long delays which may be counteracted by a difference in density of reinforcement (156, 407). Trained in a Y-maze with a constant delay on one side and a variable delay of the same mean duration on the other, rats prefer the variable delay (370, 499). That the runway performance of rats is impaired by delay of reward as distinct from confinement in the delay box per se is demonstrated by an experiment with 50 per cent reinforcement and delay either on rewarded or on nonrewarded trials; performance is better with nonreward delay (643). Delay after reward (postreward confinement in the goalbox) also tends to impair instrumental performance (90, 431), but not as much as does delay of reward (369, 654).

There is some evidence that the rat's resistance to extinction in T-1 situations is increased by delay of reward in training (131, 403, 551, 607). The effect does not appear when training and extinction delays are confounded (505, 607), or when extinction delay is long (131, 550), perhaps because it is masked by an inverse relation between resistance to extinction and duration of confinement on extinction trials (131, 648). Postreward delay in training also tends to increase resistance to extinction (403, 431). A complete explanation of these results in terms of stimulus generalization is not possible for several reasons: One is that long delays in acquisition produce greater resistance than short delays when delay in extinction is short—the greater the difference between training and extinction conditions then, the greater is the resistance to extinction (131, 551, 607). A second is that the effect appears in widely spaced trials (551). If delay reduces the incentive value of reward, these results for delay may have the same explanation as the inverse relation between resistance to extinction and amount of reward. According to frustration theory, resistance to extinction should be particularly high after training with delayed reward, because the frustration produced by delay provides opportunity for the conditioning of r_F to sensory antecedents of the instrumental response and for the connection of s_F to that response.

Frequency of Reward

Although the deduction from Hull's concept of reactive inhibition—that the continued reinforcement of a response eventually will produce extinction—is without experimental verification (239), many investigators report that resistance to extinction is less after high than after intermediate frequencies of reinforcement (300, 460, 597, 623). The fact that this so-called *overlearning-extinction effect* is more likely to occur with large reward and spaced discrete trials (558) cannot, however, be explained in terms of reactive inhibition. There is, furthermore, some evidence that number of reinforcements rather than number of responses (typically confounded in these experiments) is the critical variable, and it has been suggested that the overlearning-extinction effect is an incentive phenomenon, the full force of which is masked by a positive relation between frequency of response and resistance to extinction (597).

The effect occurs quite dependably in experiments with spaced trials and large reward, although there is an occasional exception (285). In free-operant experiments with small reward, it occurs only under special conditions: with close spatial contiguity of response and reward (491), with discriminative training, which differentially increases resistance at low frequencies (192), and with punishment for response in extinction (88). A runway experiment with massed trials and small reward shows the effect only when a hurdle is placed in the runway (365). The frustration interpretation of the overlearning-extinction effect (more frequent reinforcement produces a greater r_G and greater frustration on extinction trials) is contradicted by the finding that the effect occurs with inconsistent reinforcement in training, although increased training with inconsistent reinforcement should afford increased opportunity for the connection of s_F to the instrumental response (623). Seemingly related to the overlearning-extinction effect is the finding that the difficulty of reversal in T-2 situations may be decreased by overtraining (558)—the so-called *overlearning-reversal effect*—a more complex phenomenon which is beyond the scope of this review.

Several other experiments are worthy of note under the heading of frequency: With reinforcement giving way to contiguity-frequency as the preferred explanation of instrumental habit strength, relative frequency of alternative responses in T-2 situations becomes an important variable, but available evidence on the interaction of drive level and relative frequency is inconsistent (346, 575). An interesting finding is that the resistance to extinction of rats subjected to a series of extinction sessions separated by retraining sessions soon becomes independent of the number of interpolated retraining trials, while the resistance of goldfish does not (260, 261). Here we have a further indication that the learning of the two animals may be differently affected by reward.

Probability of Reward

Information on the effects of partial or inconsistent reinforcement (0.5 still is the most widely studied probability) has increased substantially in the past 10 years (362). On early trials in T-1 situations, partially reinforced rats respond less rapidly after nonreinforcement (N) than after reinforcement (R), just as would be expected on the assumption that R strengthens the instrumental tendency and N weakens it (147, 402). Large reward strengthens the tendency more than small reward, and long confinement in the goalbox on N trials weakens it more than short confinement (78).

If the schedule of reinforcement is random (or quasi-random, e.g., Gellermann), the performance of partial animals may become equal to that of consistent animals as training continues, and differential response after R and N disappears (402). With further training, the performance of partial animals may exceed that of consistent animals (262, 363, 620), although with widely spaced trials superior performance in partial animals is found only when reward is large (620). Performance in a series of R trials is better after a series of partially reinforced trials, or after a series of N trials, than after a series of R trials (273, 523). Such results usually are attributed to the facilitating effect of frustration (1), but the interpretation is not entirely convincing. Superior performance on R trials after N trials which are not themselves preceded by R trials (523) cannot be explained in terms of frustration.

With massed trials and a regular schedule of partial reinforcement, such as RNRN or RNNRNN, discrimination of the schedule becomes evident as training continues (142). For example, when R and N are regularly alternated, rats soon come to respond less rapidly after R than after N (147). These patterning effects are enhanced by large reward (251) and diminished by spacing of trials (318). Although patterning has been reported in single alternation with an intertrial interval of one day (145), the reliability of the finding is in dispute (588). It is necessary in this kind of experiment to control for the possibility that the animals may be responding to stimuli produced by the reinforcement or nonreinforcement of their fellows (412).

The patterning which occurs in massed trials can be accounted for in terms of sensory carryover. In single alternation, for example, the animal is always reinforced for response to the after-effects of N and never reinforced for response to the after-effects of R. There is evidence that rats can discriminate, not only the after-effects of R and N, but also of amount of reward (132) and intertrial interval (91). Sensory carryover does not account for patterning in widely spaced trials, and the belief that such patterning occurs has prompted the claim that 'memories' or other mediating reactions may play the same role as sensory after-effects, but there has been no further attempt to specify the process (130, 145). Neither in its restricted nor in its broader form, however, can the after-effects theory account for the facilitation of performance by partial reinforcement, which fits frustration theory. There is evidence, in fact, that the facilitation does not occur in tranquilized rats (621). The patterning which undeniably occurs in massed trials points clearly, however, to the discrimination of after-effects.

The greater resistance to extinction produced by partial as compared with consistent reinforcement—the so-called *partial reinforcement effect* or PRE—usually is explained either in terms of after-effects or in terms of frustration. According to the after-effects interpretation, the lesser resistance of consistent animals is due to a generalization decrement: the consistent animals never are rewarded, as are the partials, for response to the after-effects of N, which both groups encounter in extinction. Since the PRE found in widely spaced trials (620) cannot be explained in terms of sensory carryover, the after-effects theorist must have recourse again to memories. According to frustration theory, the PRE—whether in massed or spaced trials—is due to the fact that in the partial animals, but not the consistent, the instrumental response is connected in training to s_F, a stimulus which both groups encounter in extinction (1).

There is no reason, of course, to think that the processes which account for the PRE in massed and spaced trials must be identical, and recent data suggest, in fact, that they are different. In massed trials, the PRE is found with small as well as with large reward; in spaced trials, it is found only with large reward and seems due entirely to the fact that the large reward sharply decreases resistance in the consistent animals (109, 568, 620). The possibility should be considered that the PRE with small reward is due to sensory carryover and therefore does not occur in spaced trials, while the PRE with large reward in spaced trials is due to negative contrast (frustration?). In massed trials with large reward, both mechanisms combine to produce a larger effect.

As may be deduced from after-effects theory, resistance to extinction increases with the number of transitions from N to R in the training schedule (134, 336, 577), while the effect of R-N transitions is relatively small (137, 578); but, as may be deduced from frustration theory, a partial schedule with only a single N-R transition may produce a substantial PRE, even when the interval between N and R is one day (306, 572). An experiment with one day between trials in which a single series of N trials followed by a single series of R trials yields a PRE presents serious difficulty for both theories (568). The fact that the PRE tends to increase with the number of consecutive N trials (N-length) in the partial schedule (148, 251, 254) fits both theories on the assumption that the effects of N are cumulative. The increase in the PRE with the total number of N trials and with the percentage of N trials in the partial schedule probably can be explained in terms of confounded increases in number of N-R transitions and in N-length (28, 148, 254, 336, 351, 577).

The PRE may be obtained after as few as five training trials, with large reward and an alternating partial schedule (2, 133, 136). This result is difficult to explain in terms of frustration theory, which requires sufficient opportunity, first for the conditioning of r_G, then for the conditioning of r_F, and finally for the connection of s_F to the instrumental response. In general, the PRE increases with the number of training trials when the partial schedule is random: in experiments with massed trials and small reward, there is a differential increase with training in the resistance of the partial animals (28, 284, 655), although with an effortful response resistance in partial animals may decrease with overtraining (672); with spaced trials and large reward, there is a differential decrease in the resistance of the consistent animals (623). Regular alternation of R and N produces more resistance than random partial reinforcement when the number of training trials is small (134), but less resistance when the number of training trials is large (139, 251). A large number of R trials given after training with partial or consistent reinforcement does not prevent the PRE (600).

Effects like those obtained with partial reinforcement also are obtained with long delay of reinforcement (D) substituted for N (the so-called *partial delay* procedure). Regular alternation of R and D produces patterning (651), a fact which must suggest to the after-effects theorist that the after-effects of D are distinguishable from those of R. With a small number of training trials, resistance to extinction is greater after single alternation of

R and D than after random partial delay (146), but with continued training patterning appears in the alternating group and its resistance becomes less than that of the random group (651). Transitions from D to R in training produce greater resistance than transitions from R to D (141, 647). Resistance increases also with the number of consecutive D trials in training (129), and there is some evidence that a single transition from D to R after a large number of consecutive D trials produces greater resistance than a larger number of transitions involving shorter runs of D trials (650). When an alternating schedule is used, patterning appears more readily with partial reinforcement than with partial delay, but resistance to extinction is greater after partial delay (122, 168), a fact which contradicts after-effects theory. When the schedule is random, N produces more resistance to extinction than D (140).

A special case of partial delay of reinforcement is partial reinforcement with an intertrial reinforcement or ITR after each N trial; it differs from partial delay only in that the animal is removed from the apparatus during the delay interval. Unfortunately, we find no direct comparison of the two procedures. With a small number of training trials in the runway, ITR eliminates the PRE if the box in which the reinforcement is given resembles the goalbox of the runway (143, 144), and if the interval between N and ITR is not very long (366); ITR after R as compared with N does not have this effect (135, 144). Random partial delay also fails to produce a PRE when the number of training trials is small (146). With a large number of training trials, neither ITR after N nor ITR after R prevents the PRE (75, 576).

When unrewarded placements in the goalbox of a runway are substituted for unrewarded runs, the PRE is not obtained (601), but partially reinforced placements, concurrent with or following consistently reinforced runs, do produce the PRE (227, 657). The effect seems, however, to depend on the manner of placement; it is said to occur only when the animal is put down in the goalbox a short distance away from the foodcup and required to run to it (610). The fact that the PRE occurs with nonrewarded placements which are not followed by R trials in the runway (610, 657) presents certain difficulties both for after-effects theory and for frustration, although the results which suggest the need for a run in the goalbox may, if substantiated, resolve these difficulties. An experiment on partially reinforced placement with satiated animals raises some questions which are worth exploring further (308).

Partial reinforcement may be regarded as a special case of training with different amounts of reinforcement, a procedure which seems to have similar effects. Rats trained in a runway with large and small rewards on alternate trials run faster after small reward than after large (132), and there is evidence that rate of lever-pressing is increased by variability in quality of reward (582). Rats trained in a runway with large and small rewards given in random sequence show greater resistance to extinction than do rats rewarded on every trial with the same (mean) amount (671), and similar results are obtained with instrumental licking (58, 292). Variability in kind of reward (668) and in drive level (646) during training increase resistance to extinction.

The PRE also is found in discriminative and choice situations. Rats trained in T-1 discriminations and then extinguished with the positive stimulus show more resistance than control animals trained only with the positive stimulus, or with both stimuli positive (192, 396). That the difference may be attributed to the partial reinforcement of response to irrelevant stimuli is suggested by the fact that the effect disappears with prolonged discriminative training (192). Resistance to extinction in T-2 situations (measured in terms of speed or choice) and difficulty of reversal (measured in terms of errors) are greater when the correct alternative is partially reinforced than when it is consistently reinforced; the effect is greater with large reward and with spaced trials (281, 477, 482, 660). Experiments on probability learning, in which animals of a variety of species are trained in T-2 situations with both alternatives inconsistently reinforced (65), are beyond the scope of this review.

Discriminative and choice situations also are used in attempts to demonstrate a within-subjects PRE: one alternative is consistently reinforced, the other partially reinforced, and resistance to extinction compared. The results of these experiments are conflicting. Some show the PRE (500, 573); others show no difference (502, 571), or a *reversed* PRE—greater resistance after consistent reinforcement (474, 475). The discrepancies perhaps can be explained on the assumption that the factors which make for the PRE are opposed in such experiments by generalization of the effects of partial reinforcement (501) and by preference for the consistently reinforced alternative (205). Superior performance in acquisition with partial as compared to consistent reinforcement also may be shown within subjects (3).

There remain to be cited under this heading a few other experiments with rats which have interesting implications for the major theories of the PRE. Partial reinforcement in the starting box of a runway produces greater resistance to extinction than consistent reinforcement or consistent nonreinforcement in the starting box, when all groups are trained with consistent reinforcement in the goalbox and extinguished without reward in either box (405). The resistance to extinction of consistently reinforced lever-pressing is greater in rats previously trained in a runway with partial as compared to consistent reinforcement (639). These results are more easily accounted for in terms of frustration than after-effects. The frustration theory is supported also by data on competing responses in the runway—the partial animals make more such responses early in training, but fewer later in training and in extinction (406)—and by the finding that the PRE increases with size of goalbox (329). A finding which contradicts frustration theory is that animals which are lever-trained with small reward after feeder-training with large reward learn more rapidly, but also extinguish more rapidly than animals feeder-trained with small reward (393). In this situation, then, training under conditions of frustration seems to decrease resistance to extinction.

All the data on partial reinforcement thus far considered are for the rat, but there are some data, too, for the submammalian vertebrates. With massed trials and small reward, the fish shows greater initial resistance to extinction after consistent than after partial reinforcement; in the course of subsequent extinctions separated by retraining sessions, the PRE appears, because the resistance of the consistent animals declines more rapidly than that of the partials, as might be expected in terms of sensory carryover (662). If instead of equating number of training trials (as typically is done in rat experiments), number of reinforcements is equated, the PRE appears in the first extinction, which suggests that the effect tends to be masked in equated trials by the greater number of reinforcements given the consistent animals (257). The PRE increases with N-length (257) and with amount of reward (255). When reward is large, the PRE appears even in equated trials; with increase in amount of reward, resistance increases in both groups, but more so in the partial (255). In massed training with small reward, the PRE also is produced by partial delay (252). In spaced training, however, the PRE fails to appear, even with large reward and equated reinforcements (252, 374). These results suggest that different mechanisms produce the PRE in massed and spaced trials, and that the mechanism which produces the spaced-trials effect in the rat does not operate in the fish. The suggestion that successive contrast is responsible for the spaced-trials effect in the rat is supported by the results of a Crespi experiment with the fish (378).

Work with young turtles shows the PRE in massed (450) but not in spaced trials (220). Pigeons show the PRE in massed trials, and the effect is markedly enhanced by large blocks of R trials after training with consistent and partial reinforcement (305). Where an alternating schedule does not produce patterning, resistance is no different after an alternating than after a Gellermann schedule, but greater in each case than after consistent reinforcement (526). Still longer runs of N trials increase resistance in massed (259) but not in spaced trials, although pigeons do show the PRE in spaced trials (526). Like rats, pigeons trained in a T-1 discrimination show greater resistance when extinguished with the positive stimulus than pigeons trained only with the positive stimulus (304).

Is there a PRE in classical conditioning? After-effects theory suggests that there should be. Frustration theory does not, because a PRE with food as US would require the uncomfortable assumption that s_G (the sensory feedback from r_G, which here is the CR) comes to elicit r_F, and that s_F then comes to elicit r_G, while a PRE with shock as US would require the equally uncomfortable assumption that the nonoccurrence of shock is frustrating. Experiments on salivary conditioning in dogs with food as US (532, 625) and on general-activity conditioning in pigeons with food as US (557) fail to show the PRE as a main effect, but only as a groups X trials interaction. The interaction is obtained also in an experiment on cardiac conditioning in dogs with shock as US, but only when reinforcements are equated (226). An experiment on eyelid conditioning in rabbits with air-puff as US shows no difference between partial and consistent groups (603). An equated-reinforcements experiment on general-activity conditioning with shock as US yields a reproducible PRE in African mouthbreeders but not in goldfish (53), although the interaction does appear occasionally in goldfish (57). The PRE also is reported in experiments on earthworms with vibration as US (670) and in planarians with shock as US (325).

In experiments with rats, the PRE fails to occur with shock as US when the startle response evoked by the CS is used as the index of conditioning, but it does occur when suppression of an on-going instrumental response is used as the index and the pairing takes place in the instrumental situation (105, 624). (It should be noted that the startle and suppression procedures differ in many respects other than in the measure of conditioning.) An experiment on conditioned suppression in goldfish fails to produce the PRE under circumstances like those in which it is found in rats (247). Rats also show the PRE when rewarding stimulation of the brain is used as US and conditioning subsequently is measured in terms of lever-pressing for the CS as (secondary) reward, the lever not having been present during the pairing (334).

Secondary Reward

Pairing a stimulus with reward may have several distinguishable effects. One is an increased preference for the stimulus. A monkey, rat, or chicken is more likely to choose (or less likely to leave) a stimulus which has been paired with reward than one which has not; the increase in preference varies with frequency of pairing, amount of reward, and drive level (421, 426, 428, 484, 513). These changes can be accounted for equally well in terms of a variety of associative mechanisms, r_G-conditioning among them, although there are some challenging problems. Perhaps the most serious of these is presented by the powerful effects which may be obtained even when a substantial interval of time separates the stimulus from the reward. For example, injections of thiamine given 30 min after thiamine-deficient rats have consumed flavored water increase their preference for the flavor (243). Analogous changes in preference obtained when rats with a dietary deficiency are given access to food which supplies the deficiency may be explained on the assumption that the animals are eating the food while its beneficial effects occur (527).

An old finding which seems readily explainable on the assumption that the preference for a stimulus is increased by pairing with reward is that discriminative learning under conditions of delayed reinforcement can be facilitated by pairing reward and nonreward with stimuli resembling the discriminanda. Recent experiments suggest, however, that the phenomenon is more complex. Rats trained in a brightness discrimination learn more rapidly when correct choice is rewarded in an endbox with the brightness of the positive stimulus, and incorrect choice leads to an endbox with the brightness of the negative stimulus, than when the opposite relation obtains, but the opposite relation does not prevent learning (248). With a delay of 10 sec after each choice, most rats fail to master the discrimination when both endboxes are of the same intermediate brightness, but they do learn when the opposite relation obtains (352). When pigeons are trained without delay of reward in a series of color discriminations, it makes no difference whether the aperture of the feeder is illuminated with the positive or the negative color, but performance is better in both cases than when the color associated with reward is different from either (253).

Another effect of pairing with reward is an increase in the activating properties of a stimulus. The activation may be quite general (375, 673) or rather specific: after a buzzer and food have been paired for one group of rats but presented in random order to a second group, and both groups then have been trained without the buzzer in a runway, sounding the buzzer on selected extinction trials facilitates performance in the first group but not in the second (395). Other experiments with rats show substantial transfer from Pavlovian training in which one stimulus is paired with food while a second is not, or in which the two stimuli are paired with different amounts of food, to Thorndikian training in which instrumental responding to the two stimuli is differentially reinforced (228, 609, 612). These results can be explained in terms of activation by the conditioned r_G.

To show that pairing with reward increases preference for a stimulus or increases its activating properties is not, however, to show that it has acquired rewarding properties in the usual meaning of the term, although the various changes may be correlated and have some common basis (408). The concept of secondary reward implies that a stimulus paired with reward will come in consequence to increase the probability of a response which produces it, or at least to retard the extinction of such a response (669). While there are many intuitively convincing demonstrations of secondary reward (321), experiments which meet all of the formal requirements are rare. A rather common error is to ignore the need for a control group which has equal but unpaired experience with the stimulus and the reward. Another common error is to use massed-trials or free-operant testing procedures which do not distinguish between the eliciting or activating properties of the stimulus and its rewarding properties. The distinction may be regarded as unimportant on the assumption that the function of primary reward itself is only to generate an activating r_G, but one should certainly like even so to know whether a stimulus in such an experiment affects the instrumental response as an antecedent (directly eliciting the response or an activating r_G) or as a consequent (eliciting an r_G that becomes connected by a process of higher-order conditioning to stimuli which do precede the instrumental response).

In practice, the effects attributable to secondary reward typically are small and transient, perhaps because primary reward cannot be presented during the test and whatever connection may be responsible for the effect therefore tends rapidly to extinguish. The possibility that more stable effects may be obtained by the use of partial reinforcement to increase resistance to extinction has been examined in experiments of four main types. In the first, the partial or consistent pairing of stimulus and reward in Stage I (with no response required of the animal) is followed in Stage II by instrumental training with the stimulus as reward. Two such experiments with rats show better performance after partial pairing than after consistent, although in one case the difference appears only with partial secondary reinforcement in Stage II (232, 334).

In an experiment of a second type, rats which are partially reinforced in Stage I for making some response in the presence of a stimulus, and then rewarded with that stimulus for making a different response in Stage II, show better performance in Stage II than do rats which are consistently rewarded in Stage I, whether partial or consistent secondary reinforcement is used in Stage II (184). In a third type of experiment, an instrumental response which produces a distinctive stimulus only when it produces reward is partially or consistently reinforced in Stage I—here the pairing of stimulus and reward is consistent for both groups. One such experiment, in which the response acquired in Stage I is extinguished in Stage II, shows greater resistance after partial reinforcement in Stage I, but no difference in the performance of animals which are secondarily reinforced in Stage II and those which are not (492). When rats are tested in Stage II with a pair of levers, one of which produces the stimulus, only those trained with partial reinforcement in Stage I develop a preference for the effective lever (16). In a single-group variant of the same design, one stimulus is paired with reward when the response is consistently reinforced in Stage I, while a second stimulus is paired with reward when the response is partially reinforced; in Stage II, the rats prefer the lever which produces the first stimulus to that which produces the second (17).

A fourth kind of experiment is like the third except that the stimulus is produced by each response in Stage I and so is inconsistently paired with reward when the instrumental response is partially reinforced—here consistency of pairing is confounded with consistency of reinforcement. Tested in Stage II with two levers of which only one produces the stimulus, rats show no preference for either, whether they have been partially or consistently reinforced in Stage I (15). Contradictory results are obtained in analogous experiments with rats which are partially or consistently reinforced for traversing a runway in Stage I, and then tested in a T-maze with turns leading either to the empty goalbox or to a neutral box: the partial animals develop a more persistent tendency than the consistent animals to turn in the direction of the goalbox (102, 330). That the difference is due to the inconsistent pairing of goalbox and reward in Stage I rather than to the partial reinforcement of running is suggested by the results of other experiments in which the partial animals find different goalboxes on reinforced and unreinforced trials: tested in the T-maze, the partial animals show no more stable preference for the turn leading to the rewarded goalbox than do the consistent animals (which have never before experienced the alternative box), except perhaps when the amount of primary reward is small (518, 520, 521). The most impressive evidence of secondary reward comes from an experiment of the fourth type, in which rats were partially rewarded with food in Stage I for traversing a runway, and then partially reinforced in Stage II with access to the runway (its goalbox now empty) for lever-pressing in the starting box (679). Attempts at replication fail, unfortunately, to produce comparable results (649).

There is continuing interest in a kind of experiment which often yields rssults opposite to those expected in terms of the concept of secondary reward. As has already been noted, rats which are partially reinforced in a runway with different goalboxes on R and N trials in Stage I develop a preference in Stage II for the turn in a T-maze leading to the R goalbox. These results follow from the concept of secondary reward. Rats which have the same training in Stage I, but in Stage II are extinguished in the runway, sometimes show greater resistance when the R goalbox is used than when the N goalbox is used (472), and the results of an analogous experiment with pigeons also are clearly those which the concept of secondary reward leads us to expect (259). More often, however, rats show greater resistance when the N stimulus alone is used in extinction, or when both N and R stimuli are used, than when the R stimulus alone is used (214, 217, 391, 638). Results of this sort do not, of course, contradict the principle of secondary reward, but only suggest that other mechanisms are strong enough to mask its operation. According to frustration theory, for example, an experiment on secondary reward inevitably must generate a good deal of R_F (97). Since the magnitude of R_F is proportional to the magnitude of r_G in the absence of primary reward, it is difficult, in fact, to understand in terms of frustration theory why evidence of secondary reward ever should be obtained. More in accord with the theory, perhaps, are the results of an experiment in which rats trained in a T-2 situation by the noncorrection method learn more rapidly when they are permitted after each incorrect choice to see the unobtainable reward and stimuli associated with that reward (29).

A variety of investigations bear on the relation between the informational and rewarding properties of stimuli. The claim has been made that a stimulus paired with reward itself becomes rewarding only if it gives information about impending reward, and support for the claim is provided by an experiment with rats which suggests that the second in a sequence of two stimuli preceding reward does not acquire rewarding properties unless the first stimulus occasionally occurs alone (210). Such results do not, of course, contradict the assumption that rewarding properties may be acquired by some process of conditioning, but go rather to the nature of the process. Similar experiments with pigeons show that the properties of the two stimuli in a sequence, and of both together, change as training continues: the second is most effective after a small number of pairings, the first after a larger number of pairings, and both together after a still larger number (602).

Other experiments demonstrate that stimuli which provide information about impending reward and nonreward are themselves more rewarding than stimuli which do not, quite apart from the nature of the events associated with them. When rats are trained in an E-maze with each turn leading, first to a delay box which is black on some trials and white on others, and then to a goalbox which has food on some trials but not on others, a preference develops for the side on which the color of the delay box is consistently related to the presence or absence of food in the goalbox, rather than for the side on which the relation is random (384, 440). To account for this preference in terms of secondary reward, it is necessary only to make the reasonable assumption that partial reinforcement with a stimulus which has been consistently paired with reward is more effective than consistent reinforcement with a stimulus which has been partially paired with reward (669). The results of analogous experiments with pigeons also have been taken to mean that information about impending reward and nonreward is itself rewarding (92, 277, 322), but they are not very difficult to deal with in associative terms.

The results of experiments on variation in drive have some relevance for the traditional r_G-conditioning interpretation of the effects of pairing a stimulus with reward. The fact that the rewarding properties acquired by goalbox stimuli during runway training (as measured in subsequent T-maze tests) increase with drive level (644) can be explained on the assumption that drive intensifies the consummatory response and so facilitates r_G-conditioning. Nor is any difficulty presented by the fact that a stimulus paired with water for hungry and thirsty rats will later facilitate the performance of an instrumental response which has been rewarded with food (295). It also is reported, however, that a stimulus paired with food when rats are only hungry will later, when the animals are only thirsty, facilitate the performance of an instrumental response previously established under conditions of thirst with water as reward (99). These results are difficult to explain in terms of r_G because it seems unreasonable to assume that a stimulus which has been paired with food elicits the r_G for food even when the food itself does not elicit the consummatory response. A recent experiment on conditioned licking with water as the US shows no response to the CS in rats which are not thirsty (193), and there are other data which suggest that a stimulus associated with food may be aversive to thirsty rats (489). That the r_Gs for food and water cannot be assumed to be incompatible, at least in rats which are both hungry and thirsty, is indicated by the finding that the activating properties of a stimulus paired with food on some trials and with water on others do not differ from those of a stimulus paired only with food (455).

The familar phenomenon of latent extinction—that rats which have been trained in a runway will extinguish more rapidly after unrewarded placements in the goalbox of the runway than after unrewarded placements in a dissimilar box—may be attributed to the extinction of r_G and the conditioning of r_F. The magnitude of the effect, measured in terms of the difference between the performance of the experimental group and that of the control, varies with the amount of training given in the first stage of the experiment, because resistance to extinction in the control group is a nonmonotonic function of frequency of reinforcement (165). Time between the unrewarded placements and the extinction trials also is an important variable (207, 208): the effect has a highly transient component which implicates, not r_G or r_F, but R_F. From the assumption that the function of r_G is to activate the instrumental response, it follows that unrewarded placements should be more effective when goalbox and alley are highly similar than when they are different, but the opposite, if anything, is the case (335).

The same assumption about the activating role of r_G is contradicted also by the results of analogous experiments on latent learning. Although the facilitating effect of rewarded goalbox placements should be greater when goalbox and runway are similar than when they are dissimilar, the opposite result is obtained; furthermore, where goalbox and runway are dissimilar, rewarded placements in a box like the goalbox give far better performance than rewarded placements in a box like the runway (256). Nor does runway-goalbox similarity facilitate performance in rewarded training trials (202). Other placement experiments in T-1 and T-2 situations give evidence of latent learning in rats which cannot be understood in terms of the generalization of r_G (35, 167, 347, 548). The most parsimonious interpretation of the placement results, as well as the results of experiments on sensory preconditioning (496, 539, 541, 604), and on irrelevant incentives (200, 338), is afforded by the S-S contiguity principle. The same principle also affords a reasonable alternative to the r_G interpretation of secondary reward and related phenomena.

The Relation Between Instrumental and Consummatory Responding

If the role of reward in Thorndikian situations is simply to produce a consummatory response of which some fraction becomes connected to sensory antecedents of the instrumental response and thus serves to activate that response, a rather close relation between instrumental and consummatory responding is to be expected. The S-R reinforcement principle also leads us to expect such a relation if the consummatory response is a measure of the magnitude of reward, or if (as some investigators in the past have been willing to assume) the consummatory response is in itself reinforcing. In recent years, the general principle has been proposed that the rate of occurrence of any response can be increased by rewarding it with the opportunity to make any other response having a higher rate of occurrence—the greater the rate of the second response, the greater the consequent increment in the rate of the first (494, 495). From this point of view (which has not found wide acceptance), there is no distinction between consummatory responses and other responses insofar as their reinforcing properties are concerned.

The relation between instrumental and consummatory responding does not, however, appear to be very close. The results for solid food are inconsistent. Rats given a shorter period of access to mash in the goalbox of a runway both eat and run more rapidly than do rats given a longer period of access to the mash (74), while rats given a quantity of dry food in several small pieces eat more rapidly but run less rapidly than do rats given the same quantity of food in a single large piece (240). Variation in the volume of a sucrose solution given in the goalbox, and variation in the size of the tube through which it is taken, produce marked differences in consummatory activity but not in running; the concentration of sucrose does, however, markedly affect running, a fact which suggests that taste rather than consummatory activity is determinative (333). Direct measures of consummatory licking in the goalbox show little relation to performance in the runway (337, 563, 661). Increases and decreases in concentration produce corresponding changes in running, although consummatory activity is disrupted by change in either direction (172). Runway performance increases with concentration of saccharine and with drive, while rate of licking in the goalbox increases with concentration and decreases with drive (562). The rate of lever-pressing for sucrose increases with drive, but the rate of consummatory licking is unaffected (170).

The results of experiments in which anticipatory goal responses are measured directly also fail to provide any substantial support for the theory that instrumental behavior is activated by such responses. Lever-pressing in rats (170) and key-pecking in pigeons (259) continue to appear in extinction after responses to the feeder have ceased; it would be unreasonable to assert that the manipulandum continues to elicit r_Gs after the feeder itself no longer does so. There is some correspondence in rats between lever-pressing for water and the conditioned licking of an implanted drinking tube, but there is as much evidence that pressing produces licking as there is that licking produces pressing (436). In dogs, there is some correspondence between lever-pressing for food and conditioned salivation (552), but it is far from complete. With a high FR, no salivation occurs early in a run of presses, and there is a seemingly independent adjustment of the two responses to the temporal cues provided by the schedule (328). When lever-pressing to one stimulus produces a second stimulus, which is followed after some delay by food, the animal presses only to the first stimulus and salivates only to the second (216).

The theory of the activation of instrumental performance by anticipatory goal responses implies that those responses fall into some special category with respect to the principles that govern either their acquisition or their activation. In order to avoid an infinite regress, it must be assumed at the very least that goal responses can be activated by drive alone. If different principles apply to them, some independent definition of goal responses as a class should be available. For many years, the idea has been considered that autonomic and skeletal responses are conditioned according to different principles—contiguity in the first case and reinforcement in the second, it usually has been assumed, although the reverse assumption also has been made. Consummatory responses are skeletal in great part, of course, but their activating components may be autonomic.

Recent reports suggest that Thorndikian procedures are effective for the control of autonomic as well as skeletal responses. While the fact that thirsty dogs can be trained to salivate for water as reward may perhaps be due to the acquisition of some mediating skeletal response (435), the instrumental training of intestinal and cardiac changes in curarized rats with brain stimulation as reward (434, 614) is rather convincing. These results do not, of course, demonstrate that the reinforcement principle applies to autonomic responses any more than analogous results for lever-pressing demonstrate that the reinforcement principle applies to skeletal responses. Some autonomic experiments like those which have been developed to deal with this question at the skeletal level would be useful. An interesting line of research already under way is on the instrumentalization of consummatory responses, such as licking. The results obtained may be compared with results for manipulative or locomotor responses in experiments of the same design (290, 291, 293, 618), and with results for the same consummatory responses in experiments on classical conditioning (193, 633).

Escape

In escape training, response in the presence of some stimulus is reinforced by the termination of that stimulus, or by a decrease in its intensity. A stimulus whose termination is rewarding may be described as aversive. The aversive stimulus most widely used in escape training is shock (too often specified in terms of voltage rather than current), but there also is some work on escape from cold and from noise. One difference between escape experiments and experiments in which animals are motivated by hunger or thirst is that escape trials usually begin with sharp increment in drive, since the aversive stimulus is itself the source of drive, but that is not necessarily the case; it is possible to reintroduce the aversive stimulus during the intertrial interval rather than at the start of the next trial. Another difference is that the aversive stimulus often elicits certain rather well-defined responses that may be incompatible with the response which the investigator has chosen to reward (85, 128, 461). In general, however, the results of escape experiments are rather similar to those which already have been considered.

The performance of rats trained to escape from shock by running (160, 611), lever-pressing (581, 658), or hurdle-jumping (54, 234) improves with the intensity of shock, although there is some indication that the latency of running (as distinct from the speed of running) may decline at very high intensities (611). With shock terminated by the instrumental response in each of these studies, drive (intensity of shock) and amount of reinforcement (decrement in intensity) are confounded, but an unconfounded study of escape from cold to warmer water gives a like result (666). An inverse relation between T-2 performance and intensity of shock is reported, but the conditions of the experiment are rather unusual (546). Work with irrelevant drive (unaffected by response) shows that it may either facilitate or impair performance: hunger facilitates escape from shock in rats (234), and shock before training facilitates escape from water (361), but shock during training impairs escape from noise (126). Summation of drives is demonstrated by an experiment in which the instrumental response terminates both noise and shock (126).

The performance of rats trained with shock improves as the decrement in the intensity of shock which follows the response becomes larger (98). When the response terminates the shock altogether, performance improves with the duration of the no-shock period (581). Running speed can be reduced by making termination of shock in the goalbox of a runway contingent upon slow running (94). When rats are trained in a runway to escape from cold to warmer water, their performance improves with the difference in temperature (663–666); contrary to the results of earlier experiments with shock, performance in experiments with cold water is determined by the absolute rather than the relative change in temperature (664, 666). As already has been noted, an experiment on shift in the amount of shock-reduction gives no evidence of successive contrast (98); a comparable experiment with cold water shows depression but not elation (663).

The performance of rats in experiments with shock and with noise is inversely related to the delay of reinforcement (86, 231); differences due to the intensity of shock are attentuated by increases in delay (54). Experiments with shock suggest that resistance to extinction after escape training is a simple growth function of the frequency of reinforcement (127, 388). With nonreinforcement defined as the nonoccurrence of shock, partial reinforcement impairs performance in acquisition but has little effect on resistance to extinction (233, 235). With nonreinforcement (more properly) defined as the nontermination of shock when the instrumental response is made, partial reinforcement impairs performance in acquisition and increases resistance to extinction (94).

There is somewhat more support in the recent literature than in the earlier literature (42) for the assumption that a stimulus associated with the termination of shock may acquire rewarding properties. Preference tests in which goalboxes into which rats previously have run to escape from shock are compared with neutral boxes give inconsistent results (350, 628); but there is evidence that rats will make a response which is rewarded only with a stimulus in the presence of which shock terminates (204), or a stimulus in the presence of which some other response has terminated shock (183), or a stimulus which has accompanied the termination of shock by some other response (326, 451).

The results of escape experiments are of interest because they serve to test the generality of theories developed to account for instrumental learning with food and water as reward. To the extent that the effects of reducing the intensity of shock are equivalent to those of presenting food, a theory of instrumental learning in which consummatory responding plays a central role would appear to be inadequate. It is conceivable, of course, that (despite the many similarities in the data) the mechanisms responsible for the rewarding effects of food-presentation and shock-termination are markedly different, but the most parsimonious assumption for the present seems to be the early assumption of Morgan and Thorndike that the two events are rewarding because they activate hedonic centers in the brain.

Punishment

A punishment may be defined as an event that decreases the probability of a response upon which its occurrence is contingent. Just as there are two sources of reward—the onset of certain stimuli and the offset of others—so there are two sources of punishment, reciprocally related to the sources of reward: when the onset of a stimulus is rewarding, its offset is punishing, and when the offset of a stimulus is rewarding, its onset is punishing. Examples of punishment by the offset of stimuli are to be found in the literature—instrumental responding in pigeons and monkeys can be reduced by the contingent withdrawal of stimuli associated with feeding or stimuli of more intrinsic interest (225, 417, 606)—but most of what we know about punishment comes from experiments with aversive stimuli, such as shock or noise, whose onset is punishing.

A common characteristic of these experiments is that the effect of punishment is pitted against the effect of reward. First a response is established with reward, and then punishment is added, although in some cases the response no longer is rewarded when punishment begins and the effect of the punishment on resistance to extinction is measured. The effect of punishment also is measured in terms of the rate of responding after the punishment has been discontinued. The results obtained in these experiments depend not only on the conditions of punishment, but also on the drive-reward conditions which tend to strengthen the punished response. The performance of a hungry pigeon working for food may not be affected at all by mild response-contingent shock, yet the animal will make some other response to prevent the punishment when given an opportunity to do so (24).

Increased hunger may offset increased intensity of punishment in pigeons rewarded with food (22, 26), although it does not speed the post-punishment recovery of response in rats (89). The results for amount of reward are unclear. One T-1 experiment with rats shows more suppression of performance by punishment when reward is small than when it is large (100); a second shows the opposite (224); a third shows facilitation of extinction by shock, but no interaction with amount of reward in acquisition (503). A fourth experiment shows that after rats have developed a preference for the turn in a T-maze leading to the larger of two rewards, and the preferred turn then is punished, the speed of reversal varies inversely with the difference between the two rewards (540). Increasing the number of rewarded training trials given rats prior to the introduction of punishment may under certain conditions increase the suppressing effect of punishment (315, 433); these results are reminiscent of the overlearning-extinction effect.

The way in which response is affected by punishment varies also with the schedule of reward. In FI, the pigeon's rate of response is reduced by shock, with little change in scalloping or in frequency of reward (25); in FR, the pause after reward is lengthened (21); if response is punished only when some schedule of reward is programmed, and not during extinction, performance may be better with mild punishment than without (289). Lever-pressing for food in rats is suppressed less by shock when food and shock occur together than when they are programmed independently on concurrent VIs (653). Rats trained in a T-maze prefer shock plus food to neither when the food is immediate, but not when the food is delayed (507).

Experiments with monkeys, rats, pigeons, and goldfish show that the suppressing effect of response-contingent shock is directly related to its intensity (22, 26, 83, 271, 315, 452, 659). In rats, the suppressing effect of shock increases with its duration (82, 89, 158). Both in rats and in goldfish, the effectiveness of punishment varies inversely with the interval between the response and the punishment (36, 86, 125, 452). Consistent punishment is more effective than intermittent (26, 368). Rats show more rapid recovery from the effects of consistent as compared with intermittent punishment after punishment has been discontinued (584)—an analogue of the PRE which merits further study—and more recovery after punishment on an FI as compared with a VI schedule (585). Experiments with rats suggest that the locus of shock is a variable of some importance (230, 279), perhaps because of the different responses elicited by shock at different points on the surface of the body. A stimulus which has been paired with shock may serve as punishment for monkeys, rats, and pigeons (270, 320, 542).

As training with combined reward and punishment continues, the suppressing effect of the punishment tends to diminish. Rate of response increases again in pigeons rewarded on interval-schedules (22, 24, 26), and the pause after reward in pigeons trained on ratio-schedules decreases (21). During periods of no training (466) or of training without punishment (22), susceptibility to punishment increases once more. The susceptibility of pigeons and rats to intense punishment is decreased by prior training with milder punishment (26, 316, 433, 595), and the susceptibility of rats to consistent punishment is reduced by prior training with intermittent punishment (32–34), although the punishing effect of shock often is increased by prior experience with noncontingent shock in another situation (342, 594, 630).

Apparently the animals can be trained to persist in the face of punishment as they can be trained to persist in the face of frequent nonreward. A relation between the effects of punishment and nonreward is suggested by the fact that training with partial as compared with consistent reward may increase resistance to punishment in the rat (113), while punishment of a rewarded response during acquisition may increase resistance to extinction (113, 222, 317, 368). The latter finding can, of course, be classified as a contrast effect. Other instances of contrast based on punishment already have been cited (22, 104).

In experiments with punishment, just as in experiments with reward, the occurrence of the reinforcement may be shown to have certain effects on instrumental performance which are independent of its contiguity with the instrumental response (157). For example, shocking a rat for entering a box may not reduce its tendency to enter the box any more than does shocking it in the box after it has been placed there (76). It is conceivable, certainly, that one factor in the suppression of punished behavior is the connection of its sensory antecedents to competing emotional or other responses elicited by the aversive stimulus. The results for delay of punishment as well as those obtained with the yoking procedure (288) suggest, however, that contiguity plays an important role in experiments with punishment as well as in experiments with reward. There is, in fact, no good reason now to assume that different learning mechanisms operate in the two kinds of experiment. Some principle of hedonic averaging such as is required by the results for amount, delay, and probability of reward can be applied also to the results for punishment. The problem common to both kinds of experiment is how the occurrence of a response is regulated by its hedonic consequences. The only alternative to an untruncated Law of Effect seems to be to begin with the even earlier assumption that the kinesthetic feedback from the response becomes associated with its consequences (68).

AVOIDANCE EXPERIMENTS

Research on avoidance is peculiarly restricted in scope. Almost all of the work has been done with unitary or A-1 situations, in which a single response is defined (such as running or lever-pressing) and the readiness with which it comes to expression is measured in terms of time or rate (67). Essentially nothing is known about the determinants of choice in avoidance situations, although A-2 experiments are perfectly feasible (303, 373) and their results would be of substantial theoretical interest. Furthermore, almost all of the work on avoidance has been done with aversive stimuli, although there is nothing in the concept of an avoidance experiment which makes that restriction either desirable or necessary (473, 553). A now-familiar procedure in discrete-trials Thorndikian experiments with nonretractable manipulanda is to prevent adventitious reward of intertrial responding (and thus reduce its incidence) by having each response in the interval between trials postpone the beginning of the next trial (67). The same strategy may be used to sharpen free-operant discrimination, response to the negative stimulus postponing the appearance of the positive (80). These are simply avoidance procedures with secondary rewards instead of aversive stimuli as reinforcements, although yoked control animals are necessary to show that their effectiveness is due to the avoidance contingency rather than to increased experience with the negative stimulus (309). There can be no doubt that such procedures merit careful study.

In the traditional avoidance experiment, a CS is followed by an aversive US, such as shock, whenever the animal fails to make some defined response to the CS. Pavlovian designations of the stimuli seem appropriate because the experiment begins as a Pavlovian experiment, the instrumental contingency having no effect until the first avoidance response is made. Through its pairing with the US, the CS is assumed to acquire aversive properties, much as a stimulus paired with food is assumed to acquire rewarding properties. In the popular terminology of Mowrer, *fear* is said to be conditioned to the CS. The fear is assumed to activate the animal, and its reduction is assumed to reward the avoidance response. From this point of view, an avoidance experiment is an escape experiment in which the aversive properties of the eliciting stimulus do not exist at the outset, but are established and maintained in the course of training.

The newer, free-operant procedure of Sidman—in which there is no exteroceptive CS, but a US scheduled by a timer which is reset by the avoidance response—may be analyzed in the same terms. Fear is assumed to be conditioned to a complex of stimuli which does not include traces of proprioceptive feedback from the avoidance response. Where the density of shock prior to response is high, the increase in probability of response may be attributed to the immediate decrease in density which it produces, without any recourse to the concept of fear (280), but such an explanation hardly is adequate to the results obtained with relatively long response-shock and shock-shock intervals. The good temporal discrimination shown by highly trained animals (10), and the facilitating effect on acquisition of adding auditory feedback to the naturally occurring proprioceptive feedback (84), fit the fear interpretation.

The Conditioning of Fear

To the extent that fear plays an important role in avoidance training, the study of fear-conditioning should contribute to our understanding of avoidance. During the past 10 years, the conditioning of fear has been analyzed primarily by two methods. In experiments on conditioned suppression (or the CER—which stands for conditioned emotional response), the aversive properties of a stimulus paired with shock are estimated from its disruptive effect on some ongoing instrumental or consummatory behavior. It should be noted that the CER experiment does not involve punishment, because the CS occurs independently of the response in terms of whose occurrence its effectiveness is measured. As usually is the case in experiments on punishment, however, the CS is pitted against the drive-reward variables which tend to maintain the response. Conditioned suppression develops less rapidly in rats trained with a more-preferred as compared with a less-preferred reward (246), and there is less suppression in pigeons rewarded on a VI-1 min as compared with a VI-4 min schedule (385). In experiments on secondary escape, which are perhaps more directly related than are CER experiments to avoidance training, the aversiveness of a stimulus previously paired with shock is measured in terms of the readiness of an animal to escape from it. Almost all of these experiments have been done with rats, and the results reported here are for rats unless other subjects are specified.

The course of fear-conditioning depends upon the nature of the CS. Speed of response in secondary escape is greater with bright than with dim light as the CS (197), and conditioned suppression is more rapid when loud rather than less-loud noise is used as the CS (314). While such results are to be expected in CER experiments, they are not necessarily to be expected either in secondary escape experiments or in traditional Pavlovian experiments (that is, experiments in which the index of conditioning is a reflexive response to the US), because an intense CS may itself reflexively elicit a response which competes with the response to be conditioned. An experiment on the pinna reflex of rabbits shows a positive relation between conditioning and the intensity of the CS (379), but an eyelid experiment with monkeys shows poorer conditioning with the more intense of two conditioned stimuli (445). In CER experiments, delayed conditioning (in which the CS remains on during the CS-US interval) is more effective than trace (314); the same result is obtained in traditional experiments on general-activity conditioning in goldfish (64), nictitating-membrane conditioning in rabbits (427), and salivary conditioning (with food) in dogs (215). Prior exposure to a stimulus reduces its effectiveness as a CS in CER experiments (153); the same result is obtained in traditional experiments on tail-movement conditioning in rats (155), leg-flexion conditioning in goats (380), and pinna-reflex conditioning in rabbits (379). Unfortunately, proper controls for stimulation per se are lacking.

Performance in secondary escape improves with the intensity of the shock used as US (77, 250, 587), even when experience with shock is equated by pairing the CS with one intensity and presenting the other alone (5). Shock of sudden onset is more effective than shock of gradual onset (238). The reluctance of an animal to enter a box in which it has been shocked provides a more sensitive measure of fear than the speed with which it leaves the box (77). Rats which have been conditioned when satiated for food and water escape more readily on test trials when they are hungry or thirsty than when they are satiated (364). In CER experiments, intense shock is a more effective US than less-intense shock (11), but discrimination is poorer because there is more generalization (20). Better conditioning with intense shock is found also in traditional experiments with general activity in goldfish (57) and with the nictitating-membrane response in rabbits (560). Second-order conditioning of fear is found in secondary escape (7, 398) as well as in CER (186) experiments. A stimulus which functions as a conditioned inhibitor in a CER experiment may be shown to have acquired rewarding properties (276). Instead of shock, withdrawal of the opportunity to work for food may be used as the US in CER training; a provocative finding is that this procedure produces suppression in rats (357), but acceleration of response in pigeons (356).

There is little concern in the period under review with the role of the CS-US interval in secondary escape and CER training. A CER experiment with pigeons shows decreasing suppression as the interval is increased from 100 to 300 sec (385). Neither kind of training yields evidence of backward conditioning in rats (310, 400). A CER experiment patterned after some of the informational studies of secondary reward suggests that redundancy is no bar to the conditioning of fear (19), and while there is no parallel secondary escape experiment, there is one in which the effects of pairing of stimuli with shock are tested by a punishment rather than an escape procedure; its results are easily understood in terms of conventional concepts of conditioning (542). Another CER experiment shows that the suppressive effect of the CS is a function, not simply of the probability of shock in its presence, but of the probability of shock in its presence relative to the probability of shock in its absence (510). This result should not be surprising, because the standard index of conditioned suppression—the *suppression ratio*—is a relative one; it measures change in the rate of response with the onset of the CS.

While good conditioned suppression is commonplace with CS-US intervals on the order of several minutes, the results for traditional Pavlovian experiments usually are quite different. The familiar textbook generalization that the optimal CS-US interval in classical conditioning is about half a second certainly is incorrect, but intervals of more than a few seconds do commonly retard or prevent acquisition. For the eyelid response of rabbits, the optimal interval is about 0.4 sec (236). For the nictitating-membrane response of rabbits, the optimal interval is about 0.25 sec (560, 615), and a shift to 1 sec produces a decrement in the performance of animals trained at 0.25 sec (358). Other responses conditioned simultaneously in the same animal show different optima—2.25 sec for heart rate, and 6.75 sec (the longest interval used in the experiment) for respiration (615). Another comparison of nictitating-membrane and cardiac conditioning in rabbits shows better conditioning at 0.3 sec than at 1 sec for the first response, and the opposite for the second (427). Conditioned flexion in monkeys is better at 2 sec than at 0.5 or 4 sec (459); in pigs, it is better at 1 to 2 sec early in training, but better at 4 to 8 sec later in training (458). An extensive study of general-activity conditioning in goldfish shows no acquisition at 0 sec, and progressively better conditioning as the interval increases to 0.8 sec (64). Over the range of 1 to 20 sec, there is no deterioration of performance, but only a consistent increase in the latency of response; tests with CS-duration greater than the CS-US interval show maximal activity in the 5-sec period just after the US normally would be presented in training. In pigeons, general-activity conditioning (with food as US) is better at 10 sec than at 1 sec (375).

Evidence of conditioning with CS-US intervals even longer than those which are common in CER experiments is obtained in experiments on aversions to food developed by association with X-irradiation, or with the ingestion or injection of toxic substances that produce gastric upset. In these experiments, aversions are produced in rats with intervals between food and toxin as long as 6 to 7 hr (242, 415, 512). The magnitude of the effect increases with the amount of irradiation (244, 512). When irradiation follows the ingestion of two foods, one novel and one familiar, it is the novel food which becomes aversive (514). An intriguing finding is that the visual and auditory correlates of feeding, but not the gustatory properties of the food, become aversive to rats when the US is shock, while the opposite is true when the US is one that produces gastric upset (245). A shock experiment with chickens also shows the development of an aversion to color rather than to taste (442). This should be a fruitful line of research on animal learning in the decade to come.

Avoidance Training

In avoidance as in secondary escape and CER training, the nature of the CS plays an important role. The acquisition of a wheel-turning response in rats—all the results reported here are for rats unless other subjects are specified—with tone as CS improves with the intensity of the tone, and acquisition is better with buzz than with tone (453). Although a buzzer even of moderate intensity is aversive independently of pairing with shock (454), it does not seem to matter in a buzz-tone discrimination which of the two stimuli is positive (677). Buzz is more effective than light in the shuttlebox (641), and more effective than white noise in lever-pressing (218). Noise is more effective than light, and both together are more effective than either alone early in training, although relative effectiveness changes with practice (61). Directionality also is important. With light as the CS, acquisition of lever-pressing is better when the lamps are mounted on the wall opposite the lever than on the wall with the lever (62). For cats (397), as well as for rats (641), performance in the shuttlebox is better when the animals are required to move away from the CS rather than toward it. The fact that performance in what is called one-way avoidance (with one of two compartments serving always as the starting point and the other always as the goal) is superior—at least early in training—to performance in the shuttlebox (598) may be due in large measure to conflict of cues in the shuttlebox. There is evidence that stimuli external to the apparatus as well as internal to the apparatus may be responsible for the difficulty (465). Several variations of the shuttlebox are designed to minimize the conflict while at the same time preserving the possibility of automation which it affords (41, 631)

As the fear interpretation leads us to expect, acquisition is better, and resistance to extinction is greater, when the avoidance response terminates the CS than when it does not (93, 190, 274, 319). A shuttlebox experiment with goldfish also shows less resistance to extinction when the CS is not terminated by the avoidance response (387). The magnitude of the effect varies with method; it is greater in the shuttlebox than in situations which require a manipulative response (441). The better acquisition produced by the delay procedure as compared with the trace procedure (70, 190) also can be explained by the fact that in the trace procedure the avoidance response does not terminate an exteroceptive CS. Trace performance can be markedly improved, as can delay performance with a nonterminated CS, by having the avoidance response produce an additional stimulus (84, 93, 190). Trace experiments on monkeys with deafferented limbs promise to provide some useful information on the role of feedback from the avoidance response, but as yet the proper controls are lacking (591, 592). In other experiments, the CS is terminated promptly by avoidance but not by escape, a procedure which results in poorer acquisition of avoidance (relative to the standard procedure) when the responses required for avoidance and for escape are the same (313), but better performance when they are different, perhaps because response-competition is minimized (69).

Although exteroceptive signaling is not an integral feature of Sidman training, a common procedure is to present some distinctive stimulus when the avoidance contingency is in effect and not during extinction. That such a stimulus becomes aversive for monkeys is shown by the fact that they will work to turn it off (555, 616). If a signal is presented in the last portion of each response-shock interval, the responding of rats (372), pigeons (266), and goldfish (51) tends to be confined largely to that portion of the interval —that is, the animals do not avoid the signal—presumably because the absence of the signal is not associated with shock.

It is interesting to note that a stimulus which has been paired with shock is not unqualifiedly aversive. For example, where shock is inevitable, rats prefer that it be preceded by a signal, perhaps because the signal permits them to make some preparatory response which minimizes the aversiveness of the shock (332, 367). Rats vocalize less to a shock preceded by a CS than to one which is not (30). Dogs prefer signaled to unsignaled electrical stimulation of the cortical motor area for leg-flexion; the disequilibrating effect of the stimulation apparently can be minimized by postural adjustment (626). Of some relevance here also may be the finding that a CS paired with acid delivered to the mouth of a dog does not come to elicit salivation unless the acid is permitted to reach the dog's stomach, although stimulation of the stomach is not necessary to produce the UR (169).

The relation of performance in the shuttlebox and in lever-pressing avoidance to the intensity of shock used as the US is nonmonotonic; although threshold values obviously must produce poor performance, the optimal intensities are relatively low, and further increases produce progressively poorer performance (188, 307, 447). Intense shock is particularly disruptive when the intertrial interval is short (343). After the acquisition of an avoidance response under conditions of mild shock, performance is not disrupted, but facilitated, by intense shock, and resistance to extinction is increased (87, 189). Only in one-way avoidance is there no evidence of poorer acquisition with intense shock (448, 599). All of these results are explained in terms of competing responses elicited by intense shock.

Perhaps for the same reason, acquisition in shuttling and lever-pressing avoidance is better with discontinuous (interrupted or pulsed) shock than with continuous shock (188, 446). A parametric study of lever-pressing shows better escape as well as better avoidance with shorter on-times and longer off-times (191). Even with discontinuous shock, however, the acquisition of lever-pressing is poor at high intensities (188). In Sidman avoidance, density of shock is an important variable. Rate of response varies inversely with shock-shock and response-shock intervals (162, 354, 355). Shuttlebox experiments with aversive stimuli other than shock give contrasting results: acquisition is poor with aversive brain stimulation (179), but good with compressed air, perhaps because of its directionality (504).

An avoidance experiment may or may not permit escape from the US when the animal fails to avoid. In the so-called *Warner* procedure, there is opportunity to escape from the US; in the *Hunter* procedure, the duration of the US (typically brief) is unaffected by the animal's response. A shuttlebox experiment with brief shock in the Hunter condition shows no marked difference between the two procedures for goldfish (52). A shuttlebox experiment on dogs shows better acquisition in Hunter with 5 sec of shock after each failure to avoid (151), and a shuttlebox experiment on rats shows greater resistance to extinction after Hunter training with 15 sec of shock for failure to avoid (394). In training by the Warner method, delayed termination of shock after the escape response impairs the acquisition of avoidance when the avoidance and escape responses are the same (9, 313), but the acquisition of avoidance is better with delayed than with immediate termination of shock after the escape response when the avoidance and escape responses are different (69). Several factors probably are at work in these experiments. Making escape difficult or impossible increases the aversiveness of the consequences of failure to avoid, but it also increases the likelihood that the animal will develop responses which compete with the avoidance response. Where escape and avoidance responses are the same, avoidance should be facilitated by Warner training if termination of shock in the presence of the CS connects the escape response to both stimuli. There even is some evidence that the CS may tend to evoke the US by generalization (561). There is evidence, too, that poor avoidance of the CS is correlated with poor escape from the US (117).

The CS-US interval plays an important role in avoidance training. A one-way experiment with rats (535) and a shuttlebox experiment with goldfish

(50) suggest that there is no acquisition when the CS-US interval is zero. Brief intervals do, however, produce good performance. A one-way experiment shows good avoidance in rats trained at a near-zero interval, much better than in rats trained at 10 sec (163). The shuttlebox performance of goldfish improves precipitously as the interval increases from 0 to 1.26 sec when opportunity for response is controlled by testing all groups at the same interval (20 sec), and then remains the same at least until 30 sec; when training and testing intervals are confounded, improvement is much more gradual (50). In general, the effects of CS-US interval on avoidance conditioning is goldfish are very much what we should expect from experiments on the classical conditioning of general activity in the same animals (66). Comparison of goldfish and mollies (which perform less well at longer intervals) shows that differences in avoidance training (52) may be predicted from differences in classical conditioning (331).

The shuttlebox performance of rats improves as the CS-US interval increases to about 10 sec, and then declines (70, 377). Lever-pressing performance in rats is better at 60 sec than at shorter intervals, and the performance of a group trained at intervals decreasing progressively from 60 to 5 sec is superior throughout to that of a group trained from the outset at 5 sec (478, 479). Cats in the shuttlebox show somewhat quicker learning at 20 sec than at shorter intervals (537). An interesting study of nictitating-membrane conditioning in rabbits shows better avoidance at 0.25 sec than at 1 sec, but a difference between experimental animals and their yoked controls only at the longer interval (294). It is regrettable that yoked groups are not used more often.

A common finding is that asymptotic avoidance latency varies with the CS-US interval. Both in rats and in goldfish, latency is shorter after training at 1 to 2 sec than at 0 sec (50, 535), which fits the assumption that there is no conditioning at 0 sec, but it increases progressively thereafter; in goldfish, the function is essentially linear at least to 60 sec (50). Both in rats and in goldfish, latency of avoidance in the shuttlebox is shorter after training with a varying CS-US interval than after training at a constant interval of the same mean value (52, 376), probably because almost all failures to avoid as training continues come at the shorter intervals. An unusual study of guinea pigs shows the acquisition of shuttling only with a varying CS-US interval (221).

Resistance to extinction is closely related to asymptotic avoidance latency and therefore to the CS-US interval. In rats, resistance is greater after training at 1.65 sec than at 0 sec (535), and greater after training at a variable than at a constant interval (376). A factorial study of resistance to extinction in goldfish shows an inverse relation with training interval over the range of 5 to 20 sec, as well as a direct relation with maximal CS-duration on extinction trials which probably is a function of increasing opportunity for response (50). In the course of extinction, latency of response increases progressively, and the greater resistance shown by animals with shorter initial latency may be due simply to the fact that they have a longer way to go.

Performance in avoidance training is a function also of the intertrial interval. For rats trained in the shuttlebox, performance is better in the 1 to 5 min range than at shorter or longer intervals (116, 360), and better (when training is relatively massed) with a constant than with a varying interval (360), although guinea pigs seem to learn only with a varying interval (221). The performance of fish in the shuttlebox is better at 5 min than at 30 sec (486). By contrast with their behavior in the shuttlebox, rats trained in lever-pressing avoidance do better at very short (0.2 sec) than at longer intervals (480). Rats trained in wheel-turning acquire the response rapidly—much of the behavior is due apparently to pseudo-conditioning—but then tend gradually to stop responding (177, 561); the decrement is much less marked with an intertrial interval of 1 min than of 2 min (8). There is not very much contemporary work on the intertrial interval in classical conditioning with which to compare these avoidance findings. An experiment on nictitating-membrane conditioning in rabbits shows more rapid acquisition at 111 sec than at 45 or 300 sec between trials (103), and there is evidence that some short-term process of consolidation may be at work in the interval (533). Another distributional variable to be considered is number of trials per session. For cats in the shuttlebox, 5 trials are better than 10 or 20 trials per session (536). For avoidance conditioning of the nictitating-membrane response in rabbits, acquisition is more rapid with 15 trials per session than with longer sessions (294).

Another significant variable in avoidance training is the interval between training sessions. The shuttlebox performance of rats in the second of two training sessions is a nonmonotonic function of the interval between sessions, declining over the first 1 to 6 hr, and then improving once more (119, 194, 311). The effect is obtained even when the CS-US interval in the first session is so brief that avoidance is impossible, although not when the two stimuli are unpaired, a finding which suggests that conditioned fear plays some role (119). Intertrial interval does not seem to be important (120). Ordinarily, little training is given in the first session; in one series of experiments, the effect appears only when the first session is terminated after the first avoidance, but not when training is carried to the criterion of two or three successive avoidances (6). An atypical experiment with running in an activity wheel as the response and extinction rather than retraining in the second session shows increasing performance (resistance) over a period of 48 hr, especially in groups with a great deal of overtraining (241).

One interpretation of the U-shaped intersession-interval function usually obtained in the shuttlebox is that conditioned fear first declines during the interval and then recovers, but the recovery is difficult to explain. Another possibility is that fear continues to increase in the interval (consolidation or incubation) and later declines. The second interpretation requires the further assumption that performance in the shuttlebox is disrupted by intense fear, at least in the early stages of training—an assumption which may not be too implausible in view of the data already reviewed on intensity of shock. Independent studies of fear provide some support for the incubation interpretation. The reluctance of rats to return to a place in which they have been shocked increases in the hours following the aversive experience (487, 522). Analogous results are obtained in a study of reversal in one-way avoidance: the performance of rats trained to go from *B* to *A* after previously having been trained to go from *A* to *B* declines in the first hour following the original training and then increases, just as would be expected on the assumption that fear of *A* first increases and then decreases with time (40). Two CER studies show increasing suppression by the CS in the first 4 hr after avoidance training (416, 590). Experiments of the secondary escape design show no substantial change in performance during the first 24-hr period between training and testing when the training and testing situations are identical, and a decline in performance thereafter, but performance improves with time during the first 24-hr period when the two situations are somewhat different (198, 399, 401). If this improvement is to be explained in terms of increasing fear, it must be assumed that the relation between intensity of fear and performance in a simple one-way locomotor situation is direct—an assumption consistent with the data on intensity of shock.

The Relation Between Fear and Avoidance

The most direct way to study the role of fear in avoidance is to make concurrent measurements of fear and instrumental responding in the same animals. The fear interpretation of avoidance does not, of course, require a high correlation between the measures; two animals may be equally fearful, yet behave differently as a consequence of different instrumental contingencies. For example, tests with the CS show no more suppression of food-rewarded lever-pressing in rats which have had avoidance training in the shuttlebox than in their yoked controls (107). As the fear interpretation suggests, however, rats which have been trained in the shuttlebox and then extinguished to different extents show corresponding differences in suppression tests with the CS—the further extinction is carried, the less the suppression (312). A related finding is that rats which have been extinguished after training in the shuttlebox show less leverpressing to turn off the CS than do unextinguished controls (608). The fear interpretation does not, however, lead us to expect that rats trained in the shuttlebox to a high criterion of performance will show less suppression than do rats trained to a moderate criterion (312). The explanation of this finding (which is of questionable statistical significance) may be that habit strength derived from frequency of response (or from frequency of fear-reduction) sustains avoidance despite the weakening of fear by nonreinforcement. For rats trained to press a panel for food and a lever to avoid signaled shock in the same situation, avoidance (pressing the lever) and suppression (not pressing the panel) are highly correlated, a result which is not very surprising because the two responses are incompatible (287).

In other experiments, the relation between heart rate and avoidance is studied on the assumption that heart rate provides a measure of fear. Dogs tested in the shuttlebox respond more promptly to a stimulus that has been paired with intense shock than to one that has been paired with milder shock, and they show greater cardiac acceleration to the first stimulus than to the second (150). Parallel results are not, however, obtained with differences in duration of shock—prompter response to the longer shock is not accompanied by greater cardiac acceleration (468). Dogs trained to avoid shock by pressing a lever continue to show a cardiac response to the CS long after the response is firmly established and no further shocks are received (566). When dogs are trained to discriminate between two stimuli, cardiac response to the negative continues after the skeletal response has disappeared; in extinction, too, cardiac response persists longer than skeletal (565).

When cats are trained to avoid shock by pressing a lever in response to one tone and rewarded with food for pressing another lever in response to a second tone, they show cardiac acceleration to the first tone but deceleration to the second (640); acceleration is not then just a general index of anticipation. A shuttlebox experiment with rats shows greater cardiac acceleration to the CS in an avoidance group than in a yoked control (437), and a lever-pressing experiment shows greater cardiac acceleration in rats which avoid successfully than in those which 'freeze' (386); the contribution of general activity to these differences is undetermined. The acceptability of heart rate as an index of the fear that is assumed to motivate avoidance is reduced by a recent finding that increase or decrease in heart rate in curarized rats may itself serve as the avoidance response (201). Vasomotor responses in rabbits do not, however, seem to be modifiable by avoidance training (237).

Another way to get at the role of fear in avoidance is to study the effect of Pavlovian training with an aversive US on subsequent performance in an avoidance situation. Many experiments provide clear evidence of positive transfer. The latency of avoidance in goldfish that are tested in a shuttlebox after they have been exposed to paired presentations of CS and brief shock while confined in one compartment of the apparatus increases with the CS-US interval; as in conventional avoidance training, a CS-US interval of 0 sec produces no better performance than does unpaired presentation of the stimuli (52). Dogs that are differentially conditioned while immobilized by curare and later tested in the shuttlebox respond more readily to the positive stimulus (the one previously paired with shock) than to the negative (353, 564); when one stimulus is paired with brief shock and a second stimulus is paired with longer shock in the Pavlovian stage, the dogs respond more promptly to the second stimulus in the avoidance stage (468).

There is evidence that the negative stimulus in differential Pavlovian fear conditioning, or a stimulus associated with a period of no shock under circumstances in which a rat or a dog often is shocked, is not merely neutral, but comes to serve as a "safety signal"—that is, to inhibit avoidance (121, 269, 508). A number of Pavlovian inhibitory phenomena can be demonstrated in the avoidance behavior of dogs. One is inhibition of delay: after training with a CS-US interval of 30 sec, the CS reduces avoidance in the seconds immediately following the onset of the CS and only later facilitates it (509). Another is conditioned inhibition: if CS_1 alone is paired with shock while CS_2 and CS_1 together are not, CS_1 comes to facilitate avoidance and CS_2 to inhibit it (511). If a single CS is presented alone on some trials and the shock alone on other trials in the Pavlovian phase of such an experiment, or if the CS immediately follows the shock (backward conditioning), the CS acquires inhibitory properties, but a stimulus whose occurrence is literally uncorrelated with that of the shock does not (444, 511). A stimulus which is followed by brief shock, but which persists for a time after the shock in the Pavlovian stage, elicits the avoidance response less effectively than one which terminates with the shock (467).

Clear evidence of transfer from Pavlovian to avoidance training comes also from a variety of experiments with rats in which shock is associated with presence in a discriminable locality. Again in these experiments, which are like many of the secondary-escape experiments except that avoidance rather than escape is measured, fear-inhibiting as well as fear-producing effects are obtained. Animals which are trained first to avoid shock in *A* by running to *B* and then reversed—that is, trained to avoid shock in *B* by running to *A*—learn more rapidly than do control animals if, before reversal, they are shocked in *B* or detained without shock in *A;* they learn less rapidly than do control animals if, before reversal, they are given further shock in *A* (37). Performance in one-way avoidance improves with the length of time which the animal is permitted to spend in the safe compartment (196). If the animal is permitted to spend more time without shock on one side of a shuttle-box than on the other, it runs less readily from the first side to the second than from the second to the first (635). The results of a placement experiment suggest that for a compartment to acquire fear-inhibiting properties active entrance to the compartment by the animal is not necessary (676). A stimulus which is produced by the avoidance response in training reduces the probability of avoidance when it is presented in advance of the response (634).

The transfer from Pavlovian to avoidance training may be negative. Pairing the CS with shock while a rat is confined in the apparatus without opportunity to escape or to avoid the shock produces poorer performance in subsequent avoidance training than presenting either the CS alone, the US alone, unpaired CS and US, or no stimuli at all in the first stage (449, 456, 636). A convenient explanation of negative transfer is that responses which compete with the avoidance response are connected to the CS in the Pavlovian training. Two experiments with cats give inconsistent results: one shows better (678) and the other poorer (547) avoidance after Pavlovian training in the first stage than after training to escape the US. Where the Pavlovian training is given outside the avoidance situation, rats perform better than control animals exposed to unpaired presentations or backward pairings of CS and US, or trained to escape from the US (559, 627).

Exposure to unsignaled inescapable shock outside the apparatus impairs the performance of dogs subsequently trained in the shuttlebox (469, 470, 545), but there is no impairment when the shock is given after the animals have had some avoidance training (545). The performance of dogs previously trained in Sidman avoidance is facilitated by inescapable shock (39). Unsignaled but escapable shock impairs the performance of rats trained in the shuttlebox (79), although the performance of rats in one-way avoidance is unaffected either by prior shock outside the apparatus or by nondifferential shock in the apparatus (199). It is not difficult after the fact to account for such results in terms of the combined effects of fear and competing responses, but a clear basis for the prediction of results has yet to be developed. In this connection, some studies of the effects of prior experience with unsignaled shock on the conditioning of fear are of interest. The results for CER are difficult to interpret because unsignaled shock lowers the baseline performance and therefore makes comparison difficult (106, 543). Experiments with rats show that the effectiveness of Pavlovian conditioning is reduced by prior shock in the same apparatus (586) but facilitated by prior shock in a different apparatus (4, 341).

According to the fear interpretation, extinction of avoidance should be facilitated by extinction of the fear evoked by the pattern of stimuli contiguous with shock in training. Preventing the avoidance response (whose occurrence changes that pattern) by the use of a barrier to confine the animal to one side of the shuttlebox during unreinforced presentations of the CS does not, however, stably depress the level of responding in tests made after removal of the barrier (56, 490, 632), perhaps because the barrier itself changes the pattern of stimulation; better results are obtained in a one-way apparatus (38). Another effective procedure may be to reduce the level of avoidance responding by the massing of extinction trials (464). Resistance to extinction is increased markedly by pairing shock with the stimuli that accompany spontaneous failure of avoidance (195); the fact that resistance in the second of two extinctions separated by retraining tends to be greater than resistance in the first extinction (71) may be explained in these terms. A period without shock in the shuttlebox before each of a series of training sessions impairs performance, although the effect does not seem due simply to extinction of fear elicited by the apparatus, because a like period of time in the shuttlebox after each training session does not produce impairment (344). Under certain conditions, resistance to extinction may be increased by making it impossible for the animal to avoid shock (108, 274). The extinction of one-way avoidance is facilitated by confining the animal in the starting compartment without shock, but impaired by shocking it during confinement (296).

Punishing the avoidance response first increases and then decreases the rate of responding in dogs and monkeys trained on a Sidman schedule (12, 72). Monkeys trained to avoid shock by pressing a lever show less resistance to extinction when they are punished during extinction than when they are not, although punishment during acquisition decreases the effectiveness of punishment during extinction (534). The resistance to extinction of rats trained in the shuttlebox is reduced by punishment either with the US or with the CS (213). The effectiveness of the punishment is decreased by delay (439). A one-way experiment with rats shows more rapid extinction with increasing intensity and duration of the shock used as punishment (544); a second experiment shows more rapid extinction in punished than in unpunished animals, but a positive relation between resistance to extinction and intensity of shock in the punished animals (297).

When rats are trained in a runway either to escape or to avoid shock, and then shocked in the runway (as distinct from the goalbox) during extinction, they run more rapidly and with few exceptions (420, 549) show much greater resistance than do rats which are not shocked during extinction (44, 389). This is the so-called *self-punitive* or *vicious-circle* phenomenon. The traditional explanation is that the shock reinforces the fear which motivates the response and its termination reinforces the response; given that the animal continues to run, the amount of shock it receives varies inversely with its speed.

The self-punitive effect is more marked when shock is given in the entire runway than when it is given only in one part of the runway (110, 112), and more marked when shock is given in the first part of the runway than in the last part (389, 420, 423). The fact that shock in the last part of the runway produces more rapid running in the first part shows that the more rapid running is not directly elicited by the shock (45, 112). The magnitude of the effect is largely independent of the probability of shock in acquisition, but is found with one exception (390) to increase with the proportion of shocked trials in extinction (55, 419). The magnitude of the effect also increases with the intensity of shock in extinction (46, 423), and there are some interesting cross-modal findings: buzzer in extinction after shock in training produces the effect, as does shock in extinction after buzzer in training, but buzzer in extinction after buzzer in training does not (422). The magnitude of the effect is greater after avoidance than after escape training (47, 55), and there is some evidence that it tends to decline with the number of training trials (112).

In general, then, the conditioned-fear interpretation still finds wide application to the facts of avoidance training, even if the rules for predicting instrumental behavior are in some cases unclear. The difficulties are reminiscent of some of those entailed in the r_G-conditioning interpretation of the Thorndikian results for food and water, although they do not seem to be as numerous, perhaps because the variety of experiments is not as great. It is interesting to compare the strengths and weaknesses of the two interpretations, developed independently and quite different in certain respects, yet strikingly similar in others. There can be little doubt that they will give way before long to a more general theory.

CONCLUDING REMARKS

That the time is ripe for a unified theory should be evident, and we hope that our summary of the more recent data which must be encompassed by such a theory will contribute to its development. There is no room in this chapter—already more than twice its anticipated length—for speculation about the form which the new theory might take. Nor is there room for any detailed commentary on the state of the literature reviewed—a strong and rewarding literature for the most part, but with substantial shortcomings. There still are many badly-designed experiments, prematurely-terminated experiments, and poorly-reported experiments (with essential procedural details skillfully hidden in the text or missing entirely, and original data so pooled or transformed as to be unrecognizable). We are particularly impressed with the need for a more efficient system of storing and retrieving information. It is encouraging to think that a reviewer of the literature of the next ten years, who will almost certainly have many more papers to consider, may nevertheless face an easier task.

LITERATURE CITED

1. Amsel, A. Partial reinforcement effects on vigor and persistence. In *The Psychology of Learning and Motivation,* 1–65 (Spence, K. W., Spence, J. T., Eds., Academic Press, New York, 381 pp., 1967)
2. Amsel, A., Hug, J. J., Surridge, C. T. Number of food pellets, goal approaches, and the partial reinforcement effect after minimal acquisition. *J. Exptl. Psychol.,* **77,** 530–34 (1968)
3. Amsel, A., MacKinnon, J. R., Rashotte, M. E., Surridge, C. T. Partial reinforcement (acquisition) effects within subjects. *J. Exptl. Anal. Behav.,* **7,** 135–38 (1964)
4. Anderson, D. C., Cole, J., McVaugh, W. Variations in unsignaled inescapable preshock as determinants of responses to punishment. *J. Comp. Physiol. Psychol.,* **65,** No. 3, Part 2, 1–17 (1968)
5. Anderson, D. C., Johnson, L. Conditioned fear as a function of US intensity under conditions of drive constancy. *Psychon. Sci.,* **5,** 443–44 (1966)
6. Anderson, D. C., Johnson, L., Schwendiman, G., Dunford, G. Retention of an incompletely learned avoidance response: Some problems with replication. *Psychon. Sci.,* **6,** 23–24 (1966)
7. Anderson, D. C., Plant, C., Johnson, D., Vandever, J. Second-order aversive classical conditioning. *Can. J. Psychol.,* **21,** 120–31 (1967)
8. Anderson, N. H., Nakamura, C. Y. Avoidance decrement in avoidance conditioning. *J. Comp. Psysiol. Psychol.,* **57,** 196–204 (1964)
9. Anderson, N. H., Rollins, H. A., Riskin, S. R. Effects of punishment on avoidance decrement. *J. Comp. Physiol. Psychol.,* **62,** 147–49 (1966)
10. Anger, D. The role of temporal discriminations in the reinforcement of Sidman avoidance behavior. *J. Exptl. Anal. Behav.,* **6,** 477-506 (1963)
11. Annau, Z., Kamin, L. J. The conditioned emotional response as a function of intensity of the US. *J. Comp. Physiol. Psychol.,* **54,** 428–32 (1961)
12. Appel, J. B. Some schedules involving aversive control. *J. Exptl. Anal. Behav.,* **3,** 349–59 (1960)
13. Appel, J. B., Hiss, R. H. The discrimination of contingent from noncontingent reinforcement. *J. Comp. Physiol. Psychol.,* **55,** 37–39 (1962)
14. Armus, H. L. Effect of magnitude of reinforcement on acquisition and extinction of a running response. *J. Exptl. Psychol.,* **58,** 61–63 (1959)
15. Armus, H. L., Devoy, W. E., Eisenberg, T. Effect of primary reinforcement strength with continuous secondary reinforcement during training. *Psychol. Rept.,* **11,** 203–8 (1962)
16. Armus, H. L., Garlich, M. M. Secondary reinforcement strength as a function of schedule of primary reinforcement. *J. Comp. Physiol. Psychol.,* **54,** 56–58 (1961)
17. Armus, H. L., Guinan, J. F., Crowell, R. A., Schroeder, S. R., Rudge, J. A., Comtois, D. R. Secondary reinforcement strength and primary reinforcement schedule: Single group technique. *J. Comp. Physiol. Psychol.,* **57,** 313–15 (1964)
18. Ashida, S., Birch, D. The effects of incentive shift as a function of training. *Psychon. Sci.,* **1,** 201–2 (1964)
19. Ayres, J. J. B. Conditioned suppression and the information hypothesis. *J. Comp. Physiol. Psychol.,* **62,** 21–25 (1966)
20. Ayres, J. J. B. Differentially conditioned suppression as a function of shock intensity and incentive. *J. Comp. Physiol. Psychol.,* **66,** 208–10 (1968)
21. Azrin, N. H. Punishment and recovery during fixed-ratio performance. *J. Exptl. Anal. Behav.,* **2,** 301–5 (1959)
22. Azrin, N. H. Effects of punishment intensity during variable-interval reinforcement. *Ibid.,* **3,** 123–42 (1960)
23. Azrin, N. H. Time-out from positive reinforcement. *Science,* **133,** 382–83 (1961)
24. Azrin, N. H., Hake, D. F., Holz, W. C. Motivational aspects of escape from punishment. *J. Exptl. Anal. Behav.,* **8,** 31–44 (1965)

25. Azrin, N. H., Holz, W. C. Punishment during fixed-interval reinforcement. *J. Exptl. Anal. Behav.*, **4**, 343–47 (1961)
26. Azrin, N. H., Holz, W. C., Hake, D. F. Fixed-ratio punishment. *J. Exptl. Anal. Behav.*, **6**, 141–48 (1963)
27. Azrin, N. H., Hutchinson, R. R., Hake, D. F. Extinction-induced aggression. *J. Exptl. Anal. Behav.*, **9**, 191–204 (1966)
28. Bacon, W. E. Partial-reinforcement extinction effect following different amounts of training. *J. Comp. Physiol. Psychol.*, **55**, 998–1003 (1962)
29. Baddeley, A. D. Enhanced learning of a position-habit with secondary reinforcement for the wrong response. *Amer. J. Psychol.*, **73**, 454–57 (1960)
30. Badia, P., Suter, S., Lewis, P. Rat vocalization to shock with and without a CS. *Psychon. Sci.*, **4**, 117–18 (1966)
31. Balagura, S. Conditioned glycemic responses in the control of food intake. *J. Comp. Physiol. Psychol.*, **65**, 30–32 (1968)
32. Banks, R. K. Persistence to continuous punishment following intermittent punishment training. *J. Exptl. Psychol.*, **71**, 373–77 (1966)
33. Banks, R. K. Persistence to continuous punishment and nonreward following training with intermittent punishment and nonreward. *Psychon. Sci.*, **5**, 105–6 (1966)
34. Banks, R. K. Intermittent punishment effect (IPE) sustained through changed stimulus conditions and through blocks of nonpunished trials. *J. Exptl. Psychol.*, **73**, 456–60 (1967)
35. Barch, A. M., Ratner, S. C., Morgan, R. F. Latent reacquisition and extinction. *Psychon. Sci.*, **3**, 495–96 (1965)
36. Baron, A. Delayed punishment of a runway response. *J. Comp. Physiol. Psychol.*, **60**, 131–34 (1965)
37. Baum, M. "Reversal learning" of an avoidance response as a function of prior fear conditioning and fear extinction. *Can. J. Psychol.*, **19**, 85–93 (1965)
38. Baum, M. Rapid extinction of an avoidance response following a period of response prevention in the avoidance apparatus. *Psychol. Rept.*, **18**, 59–64 (1966)
39. Baum, M. Perseveration of fear measured by changes in rate of avoidance responding in dogs. *Can. J. Psychol.*, **21**, 535–48 (1967)
40. Baum, M. Reversal learning of an avoidance response and the Kamin effect. *J. Comp. Physiol. Psychol.*, **60**, 495–97 (1968)
41. Baum, M., Bobrow, S. A. An automated analogue of the one-way Miller-type avoidance box. *Psychon. Sci.*, **5**, 361–62 (1966)
42. Beck, R. C. On secondary reinforcement and shock termination. *Psychol. Bull.*, **58**, 28–45 (1961)
43. Beck, R. C. The rat's adaptation to a 23.5-hour water-deprivation schedule. *J. Comp. Physiol. Psychol.*, **55**, 646–48 (1962)
44. Beecroft, R. S. Near-goal punishment of avoidance running. *Psychon. Sci.*, **8**, 109–10 (1967)
45. Beecroft, R. S., Bouska, S. A. Learning self-punitive running. *Psychon. Sci.*, **8**, 107–8 (1967)
46. Beecroft, R. S., Bouska, S. A., Fisher, B. G. Punishment intensity and self-punitive behavior. *Psychon. Sci.*, **8**, 351–52 (1967)
47. Beecroft, R. S., Brown, J. S. Punishment following escape and avoidance training. *Psychon. Sci.*, **8**, 349–50 (1967)
48. Beer, B., Trumble, G. Timing behavior as a function of amount of reinforcement. *Psychon. Sci.*, **2**, 71–72 (1965)
49. Beery, R. G. A negative contrast effect of reward delay in differential conditioning. *J. Exptl. Psychol.*, **77**, 429–34 (1968)
50. Behrend, E. R., Bitterman, M. E. Avoidance-conditioning in the goldfish: Exploratory studies of the CS-US interval. *Amer. J. Psychol.*, **75**, 18–34 (1962)
51. Behrend, E. R., Bitterman, M. E. Sidman avoidance in the fish. *J. Exptl. Anal. Behav.*, **6**, 47–52 (1963)
52. Behrend, E. R., Bitterman, M. E. Avoidance-conditioning in the fish: Further studies of the CS-US interval. *Amer. J. Psychol.*, **77**, 15–28 (1964)
53. Behrend, E. R., Bitterman, M. E. Partial reinforcement and classical conditioning in two species of fish. *Psychon. Sci.*, **11**, 167–68 (1968)

54. Bell, R. W., Noah, J. C., Davis, J. R., Jr. Interactive effects of shock intensity and delay of reinforcement on escape conditioning. *Psychon. Sci.*, **3**, 505–6 (1965)

55. Bender, L., Melvin, K. B. Self-punitive behavior: Effects of percentage of punishment on extinction of escape and avoidance responses. *Psychon. Sci.*, **9**, 573–74 (1967)

56. Benline, T. A., Simmel, E. C. Effects of blocking of the avoidance response on the elimination of the conditioned fear response. *Psychon. Sci.*, **8**, 357–58 (1967)

57. Berger, B. D., Yarczower, M., Bitterman, M. E. Effect of partial reinforcement on the extinction of a classically conditioned response in the goldfish. *J. Comp. Physiol. Psychol.*, **59**, 399–405 (1965)

58. Berkley, M. A. Discrimination of rewards as a function of contrast in reward stimuli. *J. Exptl. Psychol.*, **66**, 371–76 (1963)

59. Berkson, G. Food motivation and delayed response in gibbons. *J. Comp. Physiol. Psychol.*, **55**, 1040–43 (1962)

60. Biederman, G. B. Simultaneous discrimination: Parameters of reinforcement and ITI. *Psychon. Sci.*, **8**, 215–16 (1967)

61. Biederman, G. B. Discriminated avoidance conditioning: CS function during avoidance acquisition and maintenance. *Ibid.*, **10**, 23–24 (1968)

62. Biederman, G. B., D'Amato, M. R., Keller, D. M. Facilitation of discriminated avoidance learning by dissociation of CS and manipulandum. *Psychon. Sci.*, **1**, 229–30 (1964)

63. Birch, D., Valle, F. P. Resistance to extinction in the runway following a shift from small to large reward. *J. Comp. Physiol. Psychol.*, **63**, 50–53 (1967)

64. Bitterman, M. E. Classical conditioning in the goldfish as a function of the CS-US interval. *J. Comp. Physiol. Psychol.*, **58**, 359–66 (1964)

65. Bitterman, M. E. Phyletic differences in learning. *Amer. Psychologist*, **20**, 396–410 (1965)

66. Bitterman, M. E. The CS-US interval in classical and avoidance conditioning. In *Classical Conditioning: A Symposium*, Chap. 1, 1–19 (Prokasy, W. F., Ed., Appleton-Century-Crofts, New York, 421 pp., 1965)

67. Bitterman, M. E. Animal learning. In *Experimental Methods and Instrumentation in Psychology*, 451–84 (Sidowski, J., Ed., McGraw-Hill, New York, 803 pp., 1966)

68. Bitterman, M. E. Learning in animals. In *Contemporary Approaches to Psychology*, 140–79 (Helson, H., Bevan, W., Eds., Van Nostrand, New York, 596 pp., 1967)

69. Bixenstine, V. E., Barker, E. Further analysis of the determinants of avoidance behavior. *J. Comp. Physiol. Psychol.*, **58**, 339–43 (1964)

70. Black, A. H. The effects of CS-US interval on avoidance conditioning in the rat. *Can. J. Psychol.*, **17**, 174–82 (1963)

71. Black, A. H., Annau, Z. Time-out responding during avoidance conditioning and extinction in the rat. *Can. J. Psychol.*, **17**, 165–73 (1963)

72. Black, A. H., Morse, P. Avoidance learning in dogs without a warning stimulus. *J. Exptl. Anal. Behav.*, **4**, 17–23 (1961)

73. Black, R. W. Discrimination learning as a function of varying pairs of sucrose rewards. *J. Exptl. Psychol.*, **70**, 452–58 (1965)

74. Black, R. W., Elstad, P. Instrumental and consummatory behavior as a function of length of reward-period. *Psychon. Sci.*, **1**, 301–2 (1964)

75. Black, R. W., Spence, K. W. Effects of intertrial reinforcement of resistance to extinction following extended training. *J. Exptl. Psychol.*, **70**, 559–63 (1965)

76. Blanchard, R. J., Blanchard, D. C. Passive avoidance: A variety of fear conditioning? *Psychon. Sci.*, **13**, 17–18 (1968)

77. Blanchard, R. J., Blanchard, D. C. Escape and avoidance responses to a fear eliciting situation. *Ibid.*, 19–20

78. Bloom, J. M. Early acquisition responding on trials following different rewards and nonrewards. *Psychon. Sci.*, **7**, 37–38 (1967)

79. Bloom, J. M., Campbell, B. A. Effects of CS omission following avoid-

ance learning. *J. Exptl. Psychol.*, **72,** 36–39 (1966)

80. Bloomfield, T. M. Two types of behavioral contrast in discrimination learning. *J. Exptl. Anal. Behav.*, **9,** 155–61 (1966)
81. Bloomfield, T. M. Some temporal properties of behavioral contrast. *Ibid.*, **10,** 159–64 (1967)
82. Boe, E. E. Effect of punishment duration and intensity on the extinction of an instrumental response. *J. Exptl. Psychol.*, **72,** 125–31 (1966)
83. Boe, E. E., Church, R. M. Permanent effects of punishment during extinction. *J. Comp. Physiol. Psychol.*, **63,** 486–92 (1967)
84. Bolles, R. C., Popp, R. J., Jr. Parameters affecting the acquisition of Sidman avoidance. *J. Exptl. Anal. Behav.*, **7,** 315–21 (1964)
85. Bolles, R. C., Seelbach, S. E. Punishing and reinforcing effects of noise onset and termination for different responses. *J. Comp. Physiol. Psychol.*, **58,** 127–31 (1964)
86. Bolles, R. C., Warren, J. A., Jr. Effects of delay on the punishing and reinforcing effects of noise onset and termination. *J. Comp. Physiol. Psychol.*, **61,** 475–77 (1966)
87. Boren, J. J., Sidman, M., Herrnstein, R. J. Avoidance escape, and extinction as functions of shock intensity. *J. Comp. Physiol. Psychol.*, **52,** 420–25 (1959)
88. Born, D. G. Resistance of a free operant to extinction and suppression with punishment as a function of amount of training. *Psychon. Sci.*, **8,** 21–22 (1967)
89. Boroczi, G., Storms, L. H., Broen, W. E., Jr. Response suppression and recovery of responding at different deprivation levels as functions of intensity and duration of punishment. *J. Comp. Physiol. Psychol.*, **58,** 456–59 (1964)
90. Bowen, J. Effect of post-reward confinement on choice behavior. *Psychon. Sci.*, **6,** 131–32 (1966)
91. Bowen, J., Strickert, D. Discrimination learning as a function of internal stimuli. *Psychon. Sci.*, **5,** 297–98 (1966)
92. Bower, G., McLean, J., Meacham, J. Value of knowing when reinforcement is due. *J. Comp. Physiol. Psychol.*, **62,** 184–92 (1966)
93. Bower, G., Starr, R., Lazarovitz, L. Amount of response-produced change in the CS and avoidance learning. *J. Comp. Physiol. Psychol.*, **59,** 13–17 (1965)
94. Bower, G. H. Partial and correlated reward in escape learning. *J. Exptl. Psychol.*, **59,** 126–30 (1960)
95. Bower, G. H. Correlated delay of reinforcement. *J. Comp. Physiol. Psychol.*, **54,** 196–203 (1961)
96. Bower, G. H. A contrast effect in differential conditioning. *J. Exptl. Psychol.*, **62,** 196–99 (1961)
97. Bower, G. H. Secondary reinforcement and frustration. *Psychol. Rept.*, **12,** 359–62 (1963)
98. Bower, G. H., Fowler, H., Trapold, M. A. Escape learning as a function of amount of shock reduction. *J. Exptl. Psychol.*, **58,** 482–84 (1959)
99. Bower, G. H., Kaufman, R. Transfer across drives of the discriminative effect of a Pavlovian conditioned stimulus. *J. Exptl. Anal. Behav.*, **6,** 445–48 (1963)
100. Bower, G. H., Miller, N. E. Effects of amount of reward on strength of approach in an approach-avoidance conflict. *J. Comp. Physiol. Psychol.*, **53,** 59–62 (1960)
101. Bower, G. H., Trapold, M. A. Reward magnitude and learning in a single-presentation discrimination. *J. Comp. Physiol. Psychol.*, **52,** 727–29 (1959)
102. Boyle, R. E. Secondary reinforcement and a test of two reinforcement hypotheses concerning the PR effect. *J. Comp. Physiol. Psychol.*, **54,** 566–71 (1961)
103. Brelsford, J., Jr., Theios, J. Single session conditioning of the nictitating membrane in the rabbit: Effect of intertrial interval. *Psychon. Sci.*, **2,** 81–82 (1965)
104. Brethower, D. M., Reynolds, G. S. A facilitative effect of punishment on unpunished behavior. *J. Exptl. Anal. Behav.*, **5,** 191–99 (1962)
105. Brimer, C. J., Dockrill, F. J. Partial reinforcement and the CER. *Psychon. Sci.*, **5,** 185–86 (1966)
106. Brimer, C. J., Kamin, L. J. Disinhibition, habituation, sensitization, and the conditioned emotional response. *J. Comp. Physiol. Psychol.*, **56,** 508–16 (1963)
107. Brimer, C. J., Kamin, L. J. Fear of the CS in avoidance training and

fear from a sense of helplessness. *Can. J. Psychol.*, **17**, 188–93 (1963)

108. Brogden, W. J. General and local maintenance effects of adjacent classical trials during extinction of an avoidance CR. *J. Comp. Physiol. Psychol.*, **66**, 203–7 (1968)
109. Brooks, C. I., Dufort, R. H. Resistance to extinction as a function of amount of reinforcement and reinforcement schedule. *Psychon. Sci.*, **9**, 165–66 (1967)
110. Brown, J. S., Anderson, D. C., Chris, D., Weiss, C. G. Self-punitive behavior under conditions of massed practice. *J. Comp. Physiol. Psychol.*, **60**, 451–53 (1965)
111. Brown, J. S., Belloni, M. Performance as a function of deprivation time following periodic feeding in an isolated environment. *J. Comp. Physiol. Psychol.*, **56**, 105–10 (1963)
112. Brown, J. S., Martin, R. C., Morrow, M. W. Self-punitive behavior in the rat: Facilitative effects of punishment on resistance to extinction. *J. Comp. Physiol. Psychol.*, **57**, 127–33 (1964)
113. Brown, R. T., Wagner, A. R. Resistance to punishment and extinction following training with shock or nonreinforcement. *J. Exptl. Psychol.*, **68**, 503–7 (1964)
114. Brownlee, A., Bitterman, M. E. Differential reward conditioning in the pigeon. *Psychon. Sci.*, **12**, 345–46 (1968)
115. Brownstein, A. J. Predicting instrumental performance from the independent rates of contingent responses in a choice situation. *J. Exptl. Psychol.*, **63**, 29–31 (1962)
116. Brush, F. R. The effects of intertrial interval on avoidance learning in the rat. *J. Comp. Physiol. Psychol.*, **55**, 888–92 (1962)
117. Brush, F. R. On the differences between animals that learn and do not learn to avoid electric shock. *Psychon. Sci.*, **5**, 123–24 (1966)
118. Brush, F. R., Goodrich, K. P., Teghtsoonian, R., Eisman, E. H. Dependence of learning (habit) in the runway on deprivation under three levels of sucrose incentive. *Psychol. Rept.*, **12**, 375–84 (1963)
119. Brush, F. R., Myer, J. S., Palmer, M. E. Effects of kind of prior training and intersession interval upon subsequent avoidance learning. *J. Comp. Physiol. Psychol.*, **56**, 539–45 (1963)
120. Brush, F. R., Myer, J. S., Palmer, M. E. Joint effects of intertrial and intersession interval on avoidance learning. *Psychol. Rept.*, **14**, 31–37 (1964)
121. Bull, J. A., III, Overmier, J. B. Additive and subtractive properties of excitation and inhibition. *J. Comp. Physiol. Psychol.*, **66**, 511–14 (1968).
122. Burt, D. H., Wike, E. L. Effects of alternating partial reinforcement and alternating delay of reinforcement on a runway response. *Psychol. Rept.*, **13**, 439–42 (1963)
123. Butter, C. M., Campbell, B. A. Running speed as a function of successive reversals in hunger drive level. *J. Comp. Physiol. Psychol.*, **53**, 52–54 (1960)
124. Cakmak, M. B., Spear, N. E. Acquisition of discrimination between rewards. *Psychon. Sci.*, **7**, 97–98 (1967)
125. Camp, D. S., Raymond, G. A., Church, R. M. Temporal relationship between response and punishment. *J. Exptl. Psychol.*, **74**, 114–23 (1967)
126. Campbell, B. A. Interaction of aversive stimuli: Summation or inhibition. *J. Exptl. Psychol.*, **78**, 181–90 (1968)
127. Campbell, S. L. Resistance to extinction as a function of number of shock-termination reinforcements. *J. Comp. Physiol. Psychol.*, **52**, 754–58 (1959)
128. Campbell, S. L. Lever holding and behavior sequences in shock escape. *Ibid.*, **55**, 1047–53 (1962)
129. Capaldi, E. J. Sequential versus nonsequential variables in partial delay of reward. *J. Exptl. Psychol.*, **74**, 161–66 (1967)
130. Capaldi, E. J. A sequential hypothesis of instrumental learning. In *The Psychology of Learning and Motivation*, 67–156 (See Ref. 1)
131. Capaldi, E. J., Bowen, J. N. Delay of reward and goal box confinement time in extinction. *Psychon. Sci.*, **1**, 141–42 (1964)
132. Capaldi, E. J., Cogan, D. Magnitude of reward and differential stimulus consequences. *Psychol. Rept.*, **13**, 85–86 (1963)
133. Capaldi, E. J., Deutsch, E. A. Effects

of severely limited acquisition training and pretraining on the partial reinforcement effect. *Psychon. Sci.,* **9,** 171–72 (1967)

134. Capaldi, E. J., Hart, D. Influence of a small number of partial reinforcement training trials on resistance to extinction. *J. Exptl. Psychol.,* **64,** 166–71 (1962)

135. Capaldi, E. J., Hart, D., Stanley, L. R. Effect of intertrial reinforcement on the aftereffect of nonreinforcement and resistance to extinction. *J. Exptl. Psychol.,* **65,** 70-74 (1963)

136. Capaldi, E. J., Lanier, A. T., Godbout, R. C. Reward schedule effects following severely limited acquisition training. *J. Exptl. Psychol.,* **78,** 521–24 (1968)

137. Capaldi, E. J., Lynch, A. D. Magnitude of partial reward and resistance to extinction: Effect of N-R transitions. *J. Comp. Physiol. Psychol.,* **65,** 179–81 (1968)

138. Capaldi, E. J., Lynch, D. Repeated shifts in reward magnitude: Evidence in favor of an associational and absolute (noncontextual) interpretation. *J. Exptl. Psychol.,* **75,** 226–35 (1967)

139. Capaldi, E. J., Minkoff, R. Reward schedule effects at a relatively long intertrial interval. *Psychon. Sci.,* **9,** 169–70 (1967)

140. Capaldi, E. J., Olivier, W. P. Sequence of delayed reward and nonrewarded trials. *J. Exptl. Psychol.,* **72,** 307–10 (1966)

141. Capaldi, E. J., Poyner, H. Aftereffects and delay of reward. *J. Exptl. Psychol.,* **71,** 80–88 (1966)

142. Capaldi, E. J., Senko, M. G. Acquisition and transfer in partial reinforcement. *J. Exptl. Psychol.,* **63,** 155–59 (1962)

143. Capaldi, E. J., Spivey, J. E. Effect of goal-box similarity on the aftereffect of nonreinforcement and resistance to extinction. *J. Exptl. Psychol.,* **66,** 461–65 (1963)

144. Capaldi, E. J., Spivey, J. E. Intertrial reinforcement and aftereffects at 24-hour intervals. *Psychon. Sci.,* **1,** 181–82 (1964)

145. Capaldi, E. J., Spivey, J. E. Stimulus consequences of reinforcement and nonreinforcement: Stimulus traces or memory. *Ibid.,* 403–4

146. Capaldi, E. J., Spivey, J. E. Schedule of partial delay of reinforcement and resistance to extinction. *J. Comp. Physiol. Psychol.,* **60,** 274–76 (1965)

147. Capaldi, E. J., Stanley, L. R. Temporal properties of reinforcement aftereffects. *J. Exptl. Psychol.,* **65,** 169–75 (1963)

148. Capaldi, E. J., Stanley, L. R. Percentage of reward vs. *N*-length in the runway. *Psychon. Sci.,* **3,** 263–64 (1965)

149. Carlson, J. G. Effects of within-chain response delay upon postdelay operant performance. *Psychon. Sci.,* **11,** 309–10 (1968)

150. Carlson, N. J. Primary and secondary reward in traumatic avoidance learning. *J. Comp. Physiol. Psychol.,* **53,** 336–40 (1960)

151. Carlson, N. J., Black, A. H. Traumatic avoidance learning: The effect of preventing escape responses. *Can. J. Psychol.,* **14,** 21–28 (1960)

152. Carlton, P. L. The interacting effects of deprivation and reinforcement schedule. *J. Exptl. Anal. Behav.,* **4,** 379–81 (1961)

153. Carlton, P. L., Vogel, J. R. Habituation and conditioning. *J. Comp. Physiol. Psychol.,* **63,** 348–51 (1967)

154. Catania, A. C., Gill, C. A. Inhibition and behavioral contrast. *Psychon. Sci.,* **1,** 257–58 (1964)

155. Chacto, C., Lubow, R. E. Classical conditioning and latent inhibition in the white rat. *Psychon. Sci.,* **9,** 135–36 (1967)

156. Chung, S. H., Herrnstein, R. J. Choice and delay of reinforcement. *J. Exptl. Anal. Behav.,* **10,** 67–74 (1967)

157. Church, R. M. The varied effects of punishment on behavior. *Psychol. Rev.,* **70,** 369–402 (1963)

158. Church, R. M., Raymond, G. A., Beauchamp, R. D. Response suppression as a function of intensity and duration of a punishment. *J. Comp. Physiol. Psychol.,* **63,** 39–44 (1967)

159. Cicala, G. A. Running speed in rats as a function of drive level and presence or absence of competing response trials. *J. Exptl. Psychol.,* **62,** 329–34 (1961)

160. Cicala, G. A., Corey, J. R. Running speed in the rat as a function of shock level and competing re-

sponses. *J. Exptl. Psychol.*, **70,** 436–37 (1965)

161. Clark, F. C. Some quantitative properties of operant extinction data. *Psychol. Rept.*, **5,** 131–39 (1959)
162. Clark, F. C., Hull, L. D. Free operant avoidance as a function of the response-shock–shock-shock interval. *J. Exptl. Anal. Behav.*, **9,** 641–47 (1966)
163. Clark, R. A rapidly acquired avoidance response in rats. *Psychon. Sci.*, **6,** 11–12 (1966)
164. Clayton, K. N. T-maze learning as a joint function of the reward magnitudes for the alternatives. *J. Comp. Physiol. Psychol.*, **58,** 333–38 (1964)
165. Clifford, T. Extinction following continuous reward and latent extinction. *J. Exptl. Psychol.*, **68,** 456–65 (1964)
166. Clifford, T., Schindelheim, R. H. The frustration effect as a function of runway length. *Psychon. Sci.*, **10,** 109–10 (1968)
167. Clifton, C., Jr., Smith, K. H., Carlson, C. Identification of relevant intra-maze cues in latent learning. *Psychol. Rept.*, **14,** 967–74 (1964)
168. Cogan, D., Capaldi, E. J. Relative effects of delayed reinforcement and partial reinforcements on acquisition and extinction. *Psychol. Rept.*, **9,** 7–13 (1961)
169. Colavita, F. B. Dual function of the US in classical salivary conditioning. *J. Comp. Physiol. Psychol.*, **60,** 218–22 (1965)
170. Collier, G. Consummatory and instrumental responding as functions of deprivation. *J. Exptl. Psychol.*, **64,** 410–14 (1962)
171. Collier, G., Bolles, R. Hunger, thirst, and their interaction as determinants of sucrose consumption. *J. Comp. Physiol. Psychol.*, **66,** 633–41 (1968)
172. Collier, G., Knarr, F. A., Marx, M. H. Some relations between the intensive properties of the consummatory response and reinforcement. *J. Exptl. Psychol.*, **62,** 484–95 (1961)
173. Collier, G., Marx, M. H. Changes in performance as a function of shifts in the magnitude of reinforcement. *J. Exptl. Psychol.*, **57,** 305–9 (1959)
174. Collier, G., Myers, L. The loci of reinforcement. *J. Exptl. Psychol.*, **61,** 57–66 (1961)
175. Collier, G., Siskel, M., Jr. Performance as a joint function of amount of reinforcement and inter-reinforcement interval. *J. Exptl. Psychol.*, **57,** 115–20 (1959)
176. Collier, G., Willis, F. N. Deprivation and reinforcement. *J. Exptl. Psychol.*, **62,** 377–84 (1961)
177. Coons, E. E., Anderson, N. H., Myers, A. K. Disappearance of avoidance responding during continued training. *J. Comp. Physiol. Psychol.*, **53,** 290–92 (1960)
178. Coons, E. E., Cruce, J. A. F. Lateral hypothalamus: Food and current intensity in maintaining self-stimulation of hunger. *Science*, **159,** 1117–19 (1968)
179. Cox, V. C. Avoidance conditioning with central and peripheral aversive stimulation. *Can. J. Psychol.*, **21,** 425–35 (1967)
180. Crocetti, C. P. Drive level and response strength in the bar pressing apparatus. *Psychol. Rept.*, **10,** 563–75 (1962)
181. Daly, H. B. Excitatory and inhibitory effects of complete and incomplete reward reduction in the double runway. *J. Exptl. Psychol.*, **76,** 430–38 (1968)
182. Davenport, D. G., Goulet, L. R. Motivational artifact in standard food-deprivation schedules. *J. Comp. Physiol. Psychol.*, **57,** 237–40 (1964)
183. Davenport, D. G., Lerner, J. J. The cue in discriminated escape conditioning as a secondary positive reinforcer. *Psychon. Sci.*, **13,** 47–48 (1968)
184. Davenport, D. G., Sardello, R. J. Double intermittent reward scheduling and secondary reinforcer strength. *Psychon. Sci.*, **6,** 417–18 (1966)
185. Davenport, J. W. The interaction of magnitude and delay of reinforcement in spatial discrimination. *J. Comp. Physiol. Psychol.*, **55,** 267–73 (1962)
186. Davenport, J. W. Higher-order conditioning of fear (CER). *Psychon. Sci.*, **4,** 27–28 (1966)
187. Davenport, J. W., Flaherty, C. F., Dyrud, J. P. Temporal persistence of frustration effects in monkeys and rats. *Psychon. Sci.*, **6,** 411–12 (1966)

188. D'Amato, M. R., Fazzaro, J. Discriminated lever-press avoidance learning as a function of type and intensity of shock. *J. Comp. Physiol. Psychol.,* **61,** 313–15 (1966)
189. D'Amato, M. R., Fazzaro, J., Etkin, M. Discriminated bar-press avoidance maintenance and extinction in rats as a function of shock intensity. *J. Comp. Physiol. Psychol.,* **63,** 351–54 (1967)
190. D'Amato, M. R., Fazzaro, J., Etkin, M. Anticipatory responding and avoidance discrimination as factors in avoidance conditioning. *J. Exptl. Psychol.,* **77,** 41–47 (1968)
191. D'Amato, M. R., Keller, D., Biederman, G. Discriminated avoidance learning as a function of parameters of discontinuous shock. *J. Exptl. Psychol.,* **70,** 543–48 (1965)
192. D'Amato, M. R., Schiff, D., Jagoda, H. Resistance to extinction after varying amounts of discriminative or nondiscriminative instrumental training. *J. Exptl. Psychol.,* **64,** 526–32 (1962)
193. DeBold, R. C., Miller, N. E., Jensen, D. D. Effect of strength of drive determined by a new technique for appetitive classical conditioning of rats. *J. Comp. Physiol. Psychol.,* **59,** 102–8 (1965)
194. Denny, M. R., Ditchman, R. E. The locus of maximal "Kamin effect" in rats. *J. Comp. Physiol. Psychol.,* **55,** 1069–70 (1962)
195. Denny, M. R., Dmitruk, V. M. Effect of punishing a single failure to avoid. *J. Comp. Physiol. Psychol.,* **63,** 277–81 (1967)
196. Denny, M. R., Weisman, R. G. Avoidance behavior as a function of nonshock confinement. *J. Comp. Physiol. Psychol.,* **58,** 252–57 (1964)
197. Desiderato, O. Generalization of acquired fear as a function of CS intensity and number of acquisition trials. *J. Exptl. Psychol.,* **67,** 41–47 (1964)
198. Desiderato, O., Butler, B., Meyer, C. Changes in fear generalization gradients as a function of delayed testing. *J. Exptl. Psychol.,* **72,** 678–82 (1966)
199. de Toledo, L., Black, A. H. Effects of preshock on subsequent avoidance conditioning. *J. Comp. Physiol. Psychol.,* **63,** 493–99 (1967)
200. Deutsch, J. A. The Hull-Leeper drive discrimination situation—a control experiment. *Quart. J. Exptl. Psychol.,* **11,** 155–63 (1959)
201. DiCara, L. V., Miller, N. E. Changes in heart rate instrumentally learned by curarized rats as avoidance responses. *J. Comp. Physiol. Psychol.,* **65,** 8–12 (1968)
202. Di Lollo, V. Runway performance in relation to runway-goal-box similarity and changes in incentive amount. *J. Comp. Physiol. Psychol.,* **58,** 327–29 (1964)
203. Di Lollo, V., Ensminger, W. D., Notterman, J. M. Response force as a function of amount of reinforcement. *J. Exptl. Psychol.,* **70,** 27–31 (1965)
204. Dinsmoor, J. A., Clayton, M. H. A conditioned reinforcer maintained by temporal association with the termination of shock. *J. Exptl. Anal. Behav.,* **9,** 547–52 (1966)
205. Divak, M., Elliott, R. Effects in extinction, with and without free choice, of degree of experience with stimuli associated with both partial and continuous reinforcement. *Psychon. Sci.,* **7,** 255–56 (1967)
206. Dyal, J. A. Brightness and spatial discriminations based on perceived incentive magnitude. *J. Comp. Physiol. Psychol.,* **53,** 346–50 (1960)
207. Dyal, J. A. Latent extinction as a function of number and duration of pre-extinction exposures. *J. Exptl. Psychol.,* **63,** 98–104 (1962)
208. Dyal, J. A. Latent extinction as a function of placement-test interval and irrelevant drive. *Ibid.,* **68,** 486–91 (1964)
209. Edwards, D. D., West, J. R., Jackson, V. The role of contingencies in the control of behavior. *Psychon. Sci.,* **10,** 39–40 (1968)
210. Egger, M. D., Miller, N. E. When is a reward reinforcing?: An experimental study of the information hypothesis. *J. Comp. Physiol. Psychol.,* **56,** 132–37 (1963)
211. Eisman, E., Linton, M., Theios, J. The relationship between response strength and one parameter of hunger drive. *J. Comp. Physiol. Psychol.,* **53,** 359–63 (1960)
212. Eisman, E., Theios, J., Linton, M. Habit strength as a function of

drive in a bar-pressing situation. *Psychol. Rept.,* **9,** 583-90 (1961)

213. Eison, C. L., Sawrey, J. M. Extinction of avoidance behavior: CS presentations with and without punishment. *Psychon. Sci.,* **7,** 95–96 (1967)
214. Elam, C. B., Tyler, D. W. Secondary reinforcement in new learning-situations. *Amer. J. Psychol.,* **73,** 440–43 (1960)
215. Ellison, G. D. Differential salivary conditioning to traces. *J. Comp. Physiol. Psychol.,* **57,** 373–80 (1964)
216. Ellison, G. D., Konorski, J. Separation of the salivary and motor responses in instrumental conditioning. *Science,* **146,** 1071–72 (1964)
217. Elmes, D. G. The role of frustration in the extinction of a running response. *Psychon. Sci.,* **1,** 345–46 (1964)
218. Erickson, C. K. Facilitated responding in a discriminated lever press avoidance situation. *Psychon. Sci.,* **8,** 37–38 (1967)
219. Eskin, R. M., Bitterman, M. E. Fixed-interval and fixed-ratio performance in the fish as a function of prefeeding. *Amer. J. Psychol.,* **73,** 417–23 (1960)
220. Eskin, R. M., Bitterman, M. E. Partial reinforcement in the turtle. *Quart. J. Exptl. Psychol.,* **13,** 112–16 (1961)
221. Evonic, I. N., Brimer, C. J. Effect of variable temporal parameters in avoidance conditioning of the guinea pig. *J. Comp. Physiol. Psychol.,* **63,** 536–38 (1967)
222. Fallon, D. Resistance to extinction following learning with punishment of reinforced and nonreinforced licking. *J. Exptl. Psychol.,* **76,** 550–57 (1968)
223. Feldman, J. M. Successive discrimination reversal performance as a function of level of drive and incentive. *Psychon. Sci.,* **13,** 265–66 (1968)
224. Ferraro, D. P. Persistence to continuous punishment as a function of amount of reinforcement. *Psychon. Sci.,* **6,** 109–10 (1966)
225. Ferster, C. B., Appel, J. B. Punishment of sΔ responding in matching to sample by time out from positive reinforcement. *J. Exptl. Anal. Behav.,* **4,** 45–56 (1960)
226. Fitzgerald, R. D. Some effects of partial reinforcement with shock on classically conditioned heart-rate in dogs. *Amer. J. Psychol.,* **79,** 242–49 (1966)
227. Fitzgerald, R. D., Teyler, T. J. Extinction of a runway response following noncontingent partial reinforcement and nonreinforcement in the goal box. *J. Comp. Physiol. Psychol.,* **65,** 542–44 (1968)
228. Flaherty, C. F., Davenport, J. W. Noncontingent pretraining in instrumental discrimination between amounts of reinforcement. *J. Comp. Physiol. Psychol.,* **66,** 707–11 (1968)
229. Fowler, H., Blond, J., Dember, W. N. Alternation behavior and learning: The influence of reinforcement magnitude, number, and contingency. *J. Comp. Physiol. Psychol.,* **52,** 609–14 (1959)
230. Fowler, H., Miller, N. E. Facilitation and inhibition of runway performance by hind- and forepaw shock of various intensities. *J. Comp. Physiol. Psychol.,* **56,** 801–5 (1963)
231. Fowler, H., Trapold, M. A. Escape performance as a function of delay of reinforcement. *J. Exptl. Psychol.,* **63,** 464–67 (1962)
232. Fox, R. E., King, R. A. The effects of reinforcement scheduling on the strength of a secondary reinforcer. *J. Comp. Physiol. Psychol.,* **54,** 266–69 (1961)
233. Franchina, J. J. Effects of shock schedules on the acquisition and extinction of escape behavior. *Psychon. Sci.,* **4,** 277–78 (1966)
234. Franchina, J. J. Combined sources of motivation and escape responding. *Ibid.,* **6,** 221–22 (1966)
235. Franchina, J. J. Evaluation of zero transfer effects in escape training. *J. Comp. Physiol. Psychol.,* **66,** 769–73 (1968)
236. Frey, P. W., Ross, L. E. Classical conditioning of the rabbit eyelid response as a function of interstimulus interval. *J. Comp. Physiol. Psychol.,* **65,** 246–50 (1968)
237. Fromer, R. Conditioned vasomotor responses in the rabbit. *J. Comp. Physiol. Psychol.,* **56,** 1050–55 (1963)
238. Fromer, R., Berkowitz, L. Effect of sudden and gradual shock onset on the conditioned fear response. *J.*

Comp. Physiol. Psychol., **57,** 154–55 (1964)

239. Fuchs, S. S. An attempt to obtain inhibition with reinforcement. *J. Exptl. Psychol.*, **59,** 343–44 (1960)
240. Furchtgott, E., Wildasin, D. M. Incentive value and number of food units. *Psychon. Sci.*, **6,** 323–24 (1966)
241. Gabriel, M. Effects of intersession delay and training level on avoidance extinction and intertrial behavior. *J. Comp. Physiol. Psychol.*, **66,** 412–16 (1968)
242. Garcia, J., Ervin, F. R., Koelling, R. A. Learning with prolonged delay of reinforcement. *Psychon. Sci.*, **5,** 121–22 (1966)
243. Garcia, J., Ervin, F. R., Yorke, C. H., Koelling, R. A. Conditioning with delayed vitamin injections. *Science,* **155,** 716–18 (1967)
244. Garcia, J., Kimeldorf, D. J., Hunt, E. L. The use of ionizing radiation as a motivating stimulus. *Psychol. Rev.*, **68,** 383–95 (1961)
245. Garcia, J., Koelling, R. A. Relation of cue to consequence in avoidance learning. *Psychon. Sci.*, **4,** 123–24 (1966)
246. Geller, I. The acquisition and extinction of conditioned suppression as a function of the base-line reinforcer. *J. Exptl. Anal. Behav.*, **3,** 235–40 (1960)
247. Geller, I. Conditioned suppression in goldfish as a function of shock-reinforcement schedule. *Ibid.*, **7,** 345–49 (1964)
248. Gibson, A. R., Tighe, T. J. Discrimination learning with reversal of cues after choice. *J. Comp. Physiol. Psychol.*, **64,** 158–60 (1967)
249. Gleitman, H., Steinman, F. Depression effect as a function of retention interval before and after shift in reward magnitude. *J. Comp. Physiol. Psychol.*, **57,** 158–60 (1964)
250. Goldstein, M. L. Acquired drive strength as a joint function of shock intensity and number of acquisition trials. *J. Exptl. Psychol.*, **60,** 349–58 (1960)
251. Gonzalez, R. C., Bainbridge, P., Bitterman, M. E. Discrete-trials lever pressing in the rat as a function of pattern of reinforcement, effortfulness of response, and amount of reward. *J. Comp. Physiol. Psychol.*, **61,** 110–22 (1966)
252. Gonzalez, R. C., Behrend, E. R., Bitterman, M. E. Partial reinforcement in the fish: Experiments with spaced trials and partial delay. *Amer. J. Psychol.*, **78,** 198–207 (1965)
253. Gonzalez, R. C., Berger, B. D., Bitterman, M. E. A further comparison of key-pecking with an ingestive technique for the study of discriminative learning in pigeons. *Amer. J. Psychol.*, **79,** 217–225 (1966)
254. Gonzalez, R. C., Bitterman, M. E. Resistance to extinction in the rat as a function of percentage and distribution of reinforcement. *J. Comp. Physiol. Psychol.*, **58,** 258–63 (1964)
255. Gonzalez, R. C., Bitterman, M. E. Partial reinforcement effect in the goldfish as a function of amount of reward. *Ibid.*, **64,** 163–67 (1967)
256. Gonzalez, R. C., Diamond, L. A test of Spence's theory of incentive-motivation. *Amer. J. Psychol.*, **73,** 396–403 (1960)
257. Gonzalez, R. C., Eskin, R. M., Bitterman, M. E. Further experiments on partial reinforcement in the fish. *Amer. J. Psychol.*, **76,** 366–75 (1963)
258. Gonzalez, R. C., Gleitman, H., Bitterman, M. E. Some observations on the depression effect. *J. Comp. Physiol. Psychol.*, **55,** 578–81 (1962)
259. Gonzalez, R. C., Graf, V., Bitterman, M. E. Resistance to extinction in the pigeon as a function of secondary reinforcement and pattern of partial reinforcement. *Amer. J. Psychol.*, **78,** 278–84 (1965)
260. Gonzalez, R. C., Holmes, N. K., Bitterman, M. E. Asymptotic resistance to extinction in fish and rat as a function of interpolated retraining. *J. Comp. Physiol. Psychol.*, **63,** 342–44 (1967)
261. Gonzalez, R. C., Holmes, N. K., Bitterman, M. E. Resistance to extinction in the goldfish as a function of frequency and amount of reward. *Amer. J. Psychol.*, **80,** 269–75 (1967)
262. Goodrich, K. P. Performance in different segments of an instrumental response chain as a function of

reinforcement schedule. J. *Exptl. Psychol.*, **57**, 57–63 (1959)

263. Goodrich, K. P. Running speed and drinking rate as functions of sucrose concentration and amount of consummatory activity. *J. Comp. Physiol. Psychol.*, **53**, 245–50 (1960)
264. Goodrich, K. P., Zaretsky, H. Running speed as a function of concentration of sucrose incentive during pretraining. *Psychol. Rept.*, **11**, 463–68 (1962)
265. Gossette, R. L., Hood, P. The reversal index (RI) as a joint function of drive and incentive level. *Psychon. Sci.*, **8**, 217–18 (1967)
266. Graf, V., Bitterman, M. E. General activity as instrumental: Application to avoidance training. *J. Exptl. Anal. Behav.*, **6**, 301–5 (1963)
267. Gragg, L., Black, R. W. Runway performance following shifts in drive and reward magnitude. *Psychon. Sci.*, **8**, 177–78 (1967)
268. Gross, C. G. Effect of deprivation on delayed response and delayed alternation performance by normal and brain operated monkeys. *J. Comp. Physiol. Psychol.*, **56**, 48–51 (1963)
269. Grossen, N. E., Bolles, R. C. Effects of a classical conditioned 'fear signal' and 'safety signal' on nondiscriminated avoidance behavior. *Psychon. Sci.*, **11**, 321–22 (1968)
270. Hake, D. F., Azrin, N. H. Conditioned punishment. *J. Exptl. Anal. Behav.*, **8**, 279–93 (1965)
271. Hake, D. F., Azrin, N. H., Oxford, R. The effects of punishment intensity on squirrel monkeys. *Ibid.*, **10**, 95–107 (1967)
272. Hamm, H. D. Perseveration and summation of the frustration effect. *J. Exptl. Psychol.*, **73**, 196–203 (1967)
273. Harris, S. J., Smith, M. G., Weinstock, S. Effects of nonreinforcement on subsequent reinforced running behavior. *J. Exptl. Psychol.*, **64**, 388–92 (1962)
274. Hartley, D. L. Sources of reinforcement in learned avoidance. *J. Comp. Physiol. Psychol.*, **66**, 12–16 (1968)
275. Hatton, G. I. Drive shifts during extinction: Effects on extinction and spontaneous recovery of bar-pressing behavior. *J. Comp. Physiol. Psychol.*, **59**, 385–91 (1965)
276. Hendry, D. P. Conditioned inhibition of conditioned suppression. *Psychon. Sci.*, **9**, 261–62 (1967)
277. Hendry, D. P., Coulbourn, J. N. Reinforcing effect of an informative stimulus that is not a positive discriminative stimulus. *Psychon. Sci.*, **7**, 241–42 (1967)
278. Hendry, D. P., Van-Toller, C. Performance on a fixed-ratio schedule with correlated amount of reward. *J. Exptl. Anal. Behav.*, **7**, 207–9 (1964)
279. Hendry, D. P., Van-Toller, C. Fixed-ratio punishment with continuous reinforcement. *Ibid.*, 293–300
280. Herrnstein, R. J., Hineline, P. N. Negative reinforcement as shock-frequency reduction. *J. Exptl. Anal. Behav.*, **9**, 421–30 (1966)
281. Hill, W. F., Cotton, J. W., Clayton, K. N. Effect of reward magnitude, percentage of reinforcement, and training method on acquisition and reversal in a T maze. *J. Exptl. Psychol.*, **64**, 81–86 (1962)
282. Hill, W. F., Spear, N. E. Resistance to extinction as a joint function of reward magnitude and the spacing of extinction trials. *J. Exptl. Psychol.*, **64**, 636–39 (1962)
283. Hill, W. F., Spear, N. E. Choice between magnitudes of reward in a T maze. *J. Comp. Physiol. Psychol.*, **56**, 723–26 (1963)
284. Hill, W. F., Spear, N. E. Extinction in a runway as a function of acquisition level and reinforcement percentage. *J. Exptl. Psychol.*, **65**, 495–500 (1963)
285. Hill, W. F., Wallace, W. P. Reward magnitude and number of training trials as joint factors in extinction. *Psychon. Sci.*, **7**, 267–68 (1967)
286. Hodos, W., Kalman, G. Effects of increment size and reinforcer volume on progressive ratio performance. *J. Exptl. Anal. Behav.*, **6**, 387–92 (1963)
287. Hoffman, H. S., Fleshler, M. The course of emotionality in the development of avoidance. *J. Exptl. Psychol.*, **64**, 288–94 (1962)
288. Hoffman, H. S., Fleshler, M. Stimulus aspects of aversive controls: The effects of response contingent shock. *J. Exptl. Anal. Behav.*, **8**, 89–96 (1965)
289. Holz, W. C., Arzin, N. H. Inter-

actions between the discriminative and aversive properties of punishment. *J. Exptl. Anal. Behav.*, **5**, 229–34 (1962)

290. Hulse, S. H. Partial reinforcement, continuous reinforcement, and reinforcement shift effects. *J. Exptl. Psychol.*, **64**, 451–59 (1962)

291. Hulse, S. H. Licking behavior of rats in relation to saccharin concentration and shifts in fixed-ratio reinforcement. *J. Comp. Physiol. Psychol.*, **64**, 478–84 (1967)

292. Hulse, S. H., Firestone, R. J. Mean amount of reinforcement and instrumental response strength. *J. Exptl. Psychol.*, **67**, 417–22 (1964)

293. Hulse, S. H., Snyder, H. L., Bacon, W. E. Instrumental licking behavior as a function of schedule, volume, and concentration of a saccharine reinforcer. *J. Exptl. Psychol.*, **60**, 359–64 (1960)

294. Hupka, R. B., Massaro, D. W., Moore, J. W. Yoked comparisons of instrumental-avoidance and classical conditioning of the rabbit nictitating membrane response as a function of interstimulus interval and number of trials per day. *Psychon. Sci.*, **12**, 93–94 (1968)

295. Hyde, T., Trapold, M. A. Enhanced stimulus generalization of a food reinforced response to a CS for water. *Psychon. Sci.*, **9**, 513–14 (1967)

296. Hyson, S. P., Brookshire, K. H. Postacquisition exposure to inescapable shock and extinction of an avoidance response. *J. Comp. Physiol. Psychol.*, **66**, 6–11 (1968)

297. Imada, H. The effects of punishment on avoidance behavior. *Jap. Psychol. Res.*, **1**, 27–38 (1959)

298. Imada, H., Niihama, K. Running speed and "vigor" of consummatory behavior as functions of sucrose concentration and its shift. *Jap. Psychol. Res.*, **8**, 170–78 (1966)

299. Ison, J. R. Acquisition and reversal of a spatial response as a function of sucrose concentration. *J. Exptl. Psychol.*, **67**, 495–96 (1964)

300. Ison, J. R., Cook, P. E. Extinction performance as a function of incentive magnitude and number of acquisition trials. *Psychon. Sci.*, **1**, 245–46 (1964)

301. Ison, J. R., Glass, D. H. Long term consequences of differential reinforcement magnitudes. *J. Comp. Physiol. Psychol.*, **65**, 523–25 (1968)

302. Ison, J. R., Northman, J. Amobarbital sodium and instrumental performance changes following an increase in reward magnitude. *Psychon. Sci.*, **12**, 185–86 (1968)

303. Jacobs, B., Jr. Repeated acquisition and extinction of an instrumental avoidance response. *J. Comp. Physiol. Psychol.*, **56**, 1017–21 (1963)

304. Jenkins, H. M. The effect of discrimination training on extinction. *J. Exptl. Psychol.*, **61**, 111–21 (1961)

305. Jenkins, H. M. Resistance to extinction when partial reinforcement is followed by regular reinforcement. *Ibid.*, **64**, 441–50 (1962)

306. Jensen, G. D., Hill, W. F. Resistance to extinction when a single nonreinforced sequence is followed by immediate reinforcement or delayed reinforcement. *J. Exptl. Psychol.*, **75**, 396–99 (1967)

307. Johnson, J. L., Church, R. M. Effects of shock intensity on nondiscriminative avoidance learning of rats in a shuttlebox. *Psychon. Sci.*, **3**, 497–98 (1965)

308. Jones, E. C. Latent learning and the partial reinforcement effect. *Psychon Sci.*, **6**, 119–20 (1966)

309. Kamil, A. C., Davenport, J. W. The role of adventitious reinforcement in operant discrimination. *J. Exptl. Psychol.*, **76**, 609–17 (1968)

310. Kamin, L. J. Backward conditioning and the conditioned emotional response. *J. Comp. Physiol. Psychol.*, **56**, 517–19 (1963)

311. Kamin, L. J. Rentention of an incompletely learned avoidance response: Some further analyses. *Ibid.*, 713–18

312. Kamin, L. J., Brimer, C. J., Black, A. H. Conditioned suppression as a monitor of fear of the CS in the course of avoidance training. *J. Comp. Physiol. Psychol.*, **56**, 497–501 (1963)

313. Kamin, L. J., Campbell, D., Judd, R., Ryan, T., Walker, J. Two determinants of the emergence of anticipatory avoidance. *J. Comp. Physiol. Psychol.*, **52**, 202–5 (1959)

314. Kamin, L. J., Schaub, R. E. Effects of conditioned stimulus intensity on the conditioned emotional response. *J. Comp. Physiol. Psychol.*, **56**, 502–7 (1963)

315. Karsh, E. B. Effects of number of rewarded trials and intensity of punishment on running speed. *J. Comp. Physiol. Psychol.*, **55**, 44–51 (1962)

316. Karsh, E. B. Changes in intensity of punishment: Effect on runway behavior of rats. *Science*, **140**, 1084–85 (1963)

317. Karsh, E. B. Punishment: Effect on learning and resistance to extinction of discrete operant behavior. *Psychon. Sci.*, **1**, 139–40 (1964)

318. Katz, S., Woods, G. T., Carrithers, J. H. Reinforcement aftereffects and intertrial interval. *J. Exptl. Psychol.*, **72**, 624–26 (1966)

319. Katzev, R. Extinguishing avoidance responses as a function of delayed warning signal termination. *J. Exptl. Psychol.*, **75**, 339–44 (1967)

320. Kaye, H., Cox, J., Bosack, T., Anderson, K. Primary and secondary punishment of toe sucking in the infant rhesus monkey. *Psychon. Sci.*, **2**, 73–74 (1965)

321. Kelleher, R. T., Gollub, L. R. A review of positive conditioned reinforcement. *J. Exptl. Anal. Behav.*, **5**, 543–97 (1962)

322. Kelleher, R. T., Riddle, W. C., Cook, L. Observing responses in pigeons. *J. Exptl. Anal. Behav.*, **5**, 3–13 (1962)

323. Kendler, H. H., Kimm, J. Reversal learning as a function of the size of the reward during acquisition and reversal. *J. Exptl. Psychol.*, **73**, 66–71 (1967)

324. Kimmel, H. D., McGinnis, N. H. Frustration effect following changed S-R temporal relations. *Psychon. Sci.*, **5**, 333–34 (1966)

325. Kimmel, H. D., Yaremko, R. M. Effect of partial reinforcement on acquisition and extinction of classical conditioning in the planarian. *J. Comp. Physiol. Psychol.*, **61**, 299–301 (1966)

326. Kinsman, R. A., Bixenstine, V. E. Secondary reinforcement and shock termination. *J. Exptl. Psychol.*, **76**, 62–68 (1968)

327. Kintsch, W. Runway performance as a function of drive strength and magnitude of reinforcement. *J. Comp. Physiol. Psychol.*, **55**, 882–87 (1962)

328. Kintsch, W., Witte, R. S. Concurrent conditioning of bar press and salivation responses. *J. Comp. Physiol. Psychol.*, **55**, 963–68 (1962)

329. Kirkpatrick, D. R., Pavlik, W. B., Reynolds, W. F. Partial-reinforcement extinction effect as a function of size of goal box. *J. Exptl. Psychol.*, **68**, 515–16 (1964)

330. Klein, R. M. Intermittent primary reinforcement as a parameter of secondary reinforcement. *J. Exptl. Psychol.*, **58**, 423–27 (1959)

331. Klinman, C. S., Bitterman, M. E. Classical conditioning in the fish: The CS-US interval. *J. Comp. Physiol. Psychol.*, **56**, 578–83 (1963)

332. Knapp, R. K., Kause, R. H., Perkins, C. C., Jr. Immediate vs. delayed shock in T-maze performance. *J. Exptl. Psychol.*, **58**, 357–62 (1959)

333. Knarr, F. A., Collier, G. Taste and consummatory activity in amount and gradient of reinforcement functions. *J. Exptl. Psychol.*, **63**, 579–88 (1962)

334. Knott, P. D., Clayton, K. N. Durable secondary reinforcement using brain stimulation as the primary reinforcer. *J. Comp. Physiol. Psychol.*, **61**, 151–53 (1966)

335. Koppman, J. W., Grice, G. R. Goal-box and alley similarity in latent extinction. *J. Exptl. Psychol.*, **66**, 611–12 (1963)

336. Koteskey, R. L., Stettner, L. J. Role of nonreinforcement-reinforcement sequences in the partial-reinforcement effect. *J. Exptl. Psychol.*, **76**, 198–205 (1968)

337. Kraeling, D. Analysis of amount of reward as a variable in learning. *J. Comp. Physiol. Psychol.*, **54**, 560–65 (1961)

338. Krieckhaus, E. E., Wolf, G. Acquisition of sodium by rats: Interaction on innate mechanisms and latent learning. *J. Comp. Physiol. Psychol.*, **65**, 197–201 (1968)

339. Krippner, R. A., Endsley, R. C., Tacker, R. S. Magnitude of G_1 reward and the frustration effect in a between subjects design. *Psychon. Sci.*, **9**, 385–86 (1967)

340. Kurtz, K. H., Jarka, R. G. Position preference based on differential food privation. *J. Comp. Physiol. Psychol.*, **66**, 518–21 (1968)

341. Kurtz, K. H., Pearl, J. The effects of prior fear experiences on acquired-drive learning. *J. Comp. Physiol. Psychol.*, **53**, 201–6 (1960)

342. Kurtz, K. H., Walters, G. The effects of prior fear experiences on an approach-avoidance conflict. *J. Comp. Physiol. Psychol.*, **55,** 1075–78 (1962)

343. Kurtz, P. S., Shafer, J. N. The interaction of UCS intensity and intertrial interval in avoidance learning. *Psychon. Sci.*, **8,** 465–66 (1967)

344. Kurtz, P. S., Shafer, J. N., Hardesty, V. A. Adaptation to the conditioning chamber in multi-session avoidance learning. *Psychon. Sci.*, **6,** 225–26 (1966)

345. Kutscher, C. L. Adaptation to three types of water-deprivation schedules in the hooded rat. *Psychon. Sci.*, **6,** 37–38 (1966)

346. Lachman, R. The influence of thirst and schedules of reinforcement-nonreinforcement ratios upon brightness discrimination. *J. Exptl. Psychol.*, **62,** 80–87 (1961)

347. Lambert, K. A study of latent inference. *Can. J. Psychol.*, **14,** 45–50 (1960)

348. Landauer, T. K. Delay of an acquired reinforcer. *J. Comp. Physiol. Psychol.*, **58,** 374–79 (1964)

349. Laties, V. G., Weiss, B., Clark, R. L., Reynolds, M. D. Overt "mediating" behavior during temporally spaced responding. *J. Exptl. Anal. Behav.*, **8,** 107–16 (1965)

350. Lawler, E. E., III. Secondary reinforcement value of stimuli associated with shock reduction. *Quart. J. Exptl. Psychol.*, **17,** 57–62 (1965)

351. Lawrence, D. H., Festinger, L. *Deterrents and Reinforcement* (Stanford Univ. Press, Stanford, Calif., 179 pp., 1962)

352. Lawrence, D. H., Hommel, L. The influence of differential goal boxes on discrimination learning involving delay of reinforcement. *J. Comp. Physiol. Psychol.*, **54,** 552–55 (1961)

353. Leaf, R. C. Avoidance response evocation as a function of prior discriminative fear conditioning under curare. *J. Comp. Physiol. Psychol.*, **58,** 446–49 (1964)

354. Leaf, R. C. Acquisition of Sidman avoidance responding as a function of S-S interval. *Ibid.*, **59,** 298–300 (1965)

355. Leaf, R. C. Some effects of response consequences on Sidman avoidance acquisition, *Ibid.*, **61,** 217–20 (1966)

356. Leitenberg, H. Conditioned acceleration and conditioned suppression in pigeons. *J. Exptl. Anal. Behav.*, **9,** 205–12 (1966)

357. Leitenberg, H., Bertsch, G. J., Coughlin, R. C., Jr. "Time-out from positive reinforcement" as the UCS in a CER paradigm with rats. *Psychon. Sci.*, **13,** 3–4 (1968)

358. Leonard, D. W., Theios, J. Effect of CS-US interval shift on classical conditioning of the nictitating membrane in the rabbit. *J. Comp. Physiol. Psychol.*, **63,** 355–58 (1967)

359. Leung, C. M., Jensen, G. D. Shifts in percentage of reinforcement viewed as changes in incentive. *J. Exptl. Psychol.*, **76,** 291–96 (1968)

360. Levine, S., England, S. J. Temporal factors in avoidance learning. *J. Comp. Physiol. Psychol.*, **53,** 282–83 (1960)

361. Levine, S., Staats, S. R., Frommer, G. Drive summation in a water maze. *Psychol. Rept.*, **5,** 301–4 (1959)

362. Lewis, D. J. Partial reinforcement: A selective review of the literature since 1950. *Psychol. Bull.*, **57,** 1–28 (1960)

363. Lewis, D. J., Cotton, J. W. The effect of intertrial interval and number of acquisition trials with partial reinforcement on performance. *J. Comp. Physiol. Psychol.*, **52,** 598–601 (1959)

364. Ley, R. Effects of food and water deprivation on the performance of a response motivated by acquired fear. *J. Exptl. Psychol.*, **69,** 583–89 (1965)

365. Likely, D., Schnitzer, S. B. Dependence of the overtraining extinction effect on attention to runway cues. *Quart. J. Exptl. Psychol.*, **20,** 193–96 (1968)

366. Lobb, H., Runcie, D. Intertrial reinforcement as interference with consolidation. *Psychon. Sci.*, **9,** 25–26 (1967)

367. Lockard, J. S. Choice of a warning signal or no warning signal in an unavoidable shock situation. *J. Comp. Physiol. Psychol.*, **56,** 526–30 (1963)

368. Logan, F. A., *Incentive,* 1–285 (Yale Univ. Press, New Haven, 1960)

369. Logan, F. A. Decision making by rats: Delay versus amount of reward. *J. Comp. Physiol. Psychol.*, **59,** 1–12 (1965)
370. Logan, F. A. Decision making by rats: Uncertain outcome choices. *Ibid.*, 246–51
371. Logan, F. A. Continuously negatively correlated amount of reinforcement. *Ibid.*, **62,** 31–34 (1966)
372. Logan, F. A., Boice, R. Avoidance of a warning signal. *Psychon. Sci.*, **13,** 53–54 (1968)
373. Longo, N. Probability-learning and habit-reversal in the cockroach. *Amer. J. Psychol.*, **77,** 29–41 (1964)
374. Longo, N., Bitterman, M. E. The effect of partial reinforcement with spaced practice on resistance to extinction in the fish. *J. Comp. Physiol. Psychol.*, **53,** 169–72 (1960)
375. Longo, N., Klempay, S., Bitterman, M. E. Classical appetitive conditioning in the pigeon. *Psychon. Sci.*, **1,** 19–20 (1964)
376. Low, L. A., Low, H. I. Effects of variable versus fixed CS-US interval schedules upon avoidance responding. *J. Comp. Physiol. Psychol.*, **55,** 1054–58 (1962)
377. Low, L. A., Low, H. I. Effects of CS-US interval length upon avoidance responding. *Ibid.*, 1059–61
378. Lowes, G., Bitterman, M. E. Reward and learning in the goldfish. *Science*, **157,** 455–57 (1967)
379. Lubow, R. E., Markman, R. E., Allen, J. Latent inhibition and classical conditioning of the rabbit pinna response. *J. Comp. Physiol. Psychol.*, **66,** 688–94 (1968)
380. Lubow, R. E., Moore, A. U. Latent inhibition: The effect of nonreinforced preexposure to the conditional stimulus. *J. Comp. Physiol. Psychol.*, **52,** 415–19 (1959)
381. Ludvigson, H. W. Interaction of midchain detention and reward magnitude in instrumental conditioning. *J. Exptl. Psychol.*, **78,** 70–75 (1968)
382. Ludvigson, H. W., Caul, W. F., Korn, J. H., McHose, J. H. Development and attenuation of delay-engendered avoidance behavior. *J. Exptl. Psychol.*, **67,** 405–11 (1964)
383. Ludvigson, H. W., Gay, R. A. An investigation of conditions determining contrast effects in differential reward conditioning. *J. Exptl. Psychol.*, **75,** 37–42 (1967)
384. Lutz, R. E., Perkins, C. C., Jr. A time variable in the acquisition of observing responses. *J. Comp. Physiol. Psychol.*, **53,** 180–82 (1960)
385. Lyon, D. O. Frequency of reinforcement as a parameter of conditioned suppression. *J. Exptl. Anal. Behav.*, **6,** 95–98 (1963)
386. Malcuit, G., Ducharme, R., Belanger, D. Cardiac activity in rats during bar-press avoidance and "freezing" responses. *Psychol. Rept.*, **23,** 11–18 (1968)
387. Marsh, G., Paulson, N. The effect of partial reinforcement on extinction in avoidance conditioning. *Psychon. Sci.*, **12,** 39–40 (1968)
388. Martin, R. C. Resistance to extinction of an escape response as a function of the number of reinforcements. *Psychon. Sci.*, **4,** 275–76 (1966)
389. Martin, R. C., Melvin, K. B. Vicious circle behavior as a function of delay of punishment. *Psychon. Sci.*, **1,** 415–16 (1964)
390. Martin, R. C., Moon, T. L. Self-punitive behavior and periodic punishment. *Psychon. Sci.*, **10,** 245–46 (1968)
391. Marx, M. H. Resistance to extinction as a function of degree of reproduction of training conditions. *J. Exptl. Psychol.*, **59,** 337–42 (1960)
392. Marx, M. H. Interaction of drive and reward as a determiner of resistance to extinction. *J. Comp. Physiol. Psychol.*, **64,** 488–89 (1967)
393. Marx, M. H. The frustration-suppression effect: A replication with variation in amount of prior magazine training. *Ibid.*, **66,** 231–33 (1968)
394. Marx, M. H., Hellwig, L. R. Acquisition and extinction of avoidance conditioning without escape responses. *J. Comp. Physiol. Psychol.*, **58,** 451–52 (1964)
395. Marx, M. H., Murphy, W. W. Resistance to extinction as a function of the presentation of a motivating cue in the startbox. *J. Comp. Physiol. Psychol.*, **54,** 207–10 (1961)
396. MacKinnon, J. R. Interactive effects of the two rewards in a differential magnitude of reward discrimina-

tion. *J. Exptl. Psychol.*, **75**, 329–38 (1967)

397. McAdam, D. Effects of positional relations between subject, CS, and US on shuttlebox avoidance learning in cats. *J. Comp. Physiol. Psychol.*, **58**, 302–4 (1964)
398. McAllister, D. E., McAllister, W. R. Second-order conditioning of fear. *Psychon. Sci.*, **1**, 383–84 (1964)
399. McAllister, D. E., McAllister, W. R. Forgetting of acquired fear. *J. Comp. Physiol. Psychol.*, **65**, 352–55 (1968)
400. McAllister, W. R., McAllister, D. E. Role of the CS and of apparatus cues in the measurement of acquired fear. *Psychol. Rept.*, **11**, 749–56 (1962)
401. McAllister, W. R., McAllister, D. E. Increase over time in the stimulus generalization of acquired fear. *J. Exptl. Psychol.*, **65**, 576–82 (1963)
402. McCain, G. Performance after reinforcement and nonreinforcement in a partial reinforcement situation. *Psychol. Rept.*, **19**, 402 (1966)
403. McCain, G., Bowen, J. Pre- and postreinforcement delay with a small number of acquisition trials. *Psychon. Sci.*, **7**, 121–22 (1967)
404. McCain, G., McVean, G. Effects of prior reinforcement or nonreinforcement on later performance in a double alley. *J. Exptl. Psychol.*, **73**, 620–27 (1967)
405. McCain, G., Power, R. Extinction as a function of reinforcement conditions in the start box. *Psychon. Sci.*, **5**, 193–94 (1966)
406. McCoy, D. F., Marx, M. H. Competing responses and the partial-reinforcement effect. *J. Exptl. Psychol.*, **70**, 352–56 (1965)
407. McDiarmid, C. G., Rilling, M. E. Reinforcement delay and reinforcement rate as determinants of schedule preference. *Psychon. Sci.*, **2**, 195–96 (1965)
408. McGuigan, F. J., Equen, B., Stellings, J. Evocation and learning tests for secondary reinforcement. *Amer. J. Psychol.*, **78**, 307–8 (1965)
409. McHose, J. H. Effect of continued nonreinforcement on the frustration effect. *J. Exptl. Psychol.*, **65**, 444–50 (1963)
410. McHose, J. H. Incentive reduction: Delay increase and subsequent responding. *Psychon. Sci.*, **5**, 213–14 (1966)
411. McHose, J. H. Incentive reduction: Simultaneous delay increase and magnitude reduction and subsequent responding. *Ibid.*, 215–16
412. McHose, J. H., Jacoby, L. L., Meyer, P. A. Extinction as a function of number of reinforced trials and squad composition. *Psychon. Sci.*, **9**, 401–2 (1967)
413. McHose, J. H., Ludvigson, H. W. Frustration effect as a function of drive. *Psychol. Rept.*, **14**, 371–74 (1964)
414. McHose, J. H., Ludvigson, H. W. Role of reward magnitude and incomplete reduction of reward magnitude in the frustration effect. *J. Exptl. Psychol.*, **70**, 490–95 (1965)
415. McLaurin, W. A. Postirradiation saccharin avoidance in rats as a function of the interval between ingestion and exposure. *J. Comp. Physiol. Psychol.*, **57**, 316–17 (1964)
416. McMichael, J. S. Incubation of anxiety and instrumental behavior. *J. Comp. Physiol. Psychol.*, **61**, 208–11 (1966)
417. McMillan, D. E. A comparison of the punishing effects of response-produced shock and response-produced time out. *J. Exptl. Anal. Behav.*, **10**, 439–49 (1967)
418. Meltzer, D., Brahlek, J. A. Quantity of reinforcement and fixed-interval performance. *Psychon. Sci.*, **12**, 207–8 (1968)
419. Melvin, K. B. Escape learning and "vicious-circle" behavior as a function of percentage of reinforcement. *J. Comp. Physiol. Psychol.*, **58**, 248–51 (1964)
420. Melvin, K. B., Athey, G. I., Heasley, F. H. Effects of duration and delay of shock on self-punitive behavior in the rat. *Psychol. Rept.*, **17**, 107–12 (1965)
421. Melvin, K. B., Brown, J. S. Neutralization of an aversive light stimulus as a function of number of paired presentations with food. *J. Comp. Physiol. Psychol.*, **58**, 350–53 (1964)
422. Melvin, K. B., Martin, R. C. Facilitative effects of two modes of punishment on resistance to extinction. *J. Comp. Physiol. Psychol.*, **62**, 491–94 (1966)
423. Melvin, K. B., Stenmark, D. E.

Facilitative effects of punishment on establishment of a fear motivated response. *J. Comp. Physiol. Psychol.,* **65,** 517–19 (1968)

424. Mendelson, J. Role of hunger in T-maze learning for food by rats. *J. Comp. Physiol. Psychol.,* **62,** 341–49 (1966)
425. Mendelson, J. Lateral hypothalamic stimulation in satiated rats: The rewarding effects of self-induced drinking. *Science,* **157,** 1077–79 (1967)
426. Menzel, E. W., Draper, W. A. Primate selection of food by size: Visible versus invisible rewards. *J. Comp. Physiol. Psychol.,* **59,** 231–39 (1965)
427. Meridith, A. L., Schneiderman, N. Heart rate and nictitating membrane classical discrimination conditioning in rabbits under delay versus trace procedures. *Psychon. Sci.,* **9,** 139–40 (1967)
428. Meyer, D. R., LoPopolo, M. H., Singh, D. Learning and transfer in the monkey as a function of differential levels of incentive. *J. Exptl. Psychol.,* **72,** 284–86 (1966)
429. Meyer, P. A., McHose, J. H. Facilitative effects of reward increase: An apparent "elation effect." *Psychon. Sci.,* **13,** 165–66 (1968)
430. Mikulka, P. J., Lehr, R., Pavlik, W. B. Effect of reinforcement schedules on reward shifts. *J. Exptl. Psychol.,* **74,** 57–61 (1967)
431. Mikulka, P. J., Vogel, J. R., Spear, N. E. Postconsummatory delay and goal box confinement. *Psychon. Sci.,* **9,** 381–82 (1967)
432. Miles, R. C. Discrimination in the squirrel monkey as a function of deprivation and problem difficulty. *J. Exptl. Psychol.,* **57,** 15–19 (1959)
433. Miller, N. E. Learning resistance to pain and fear: Effects of overlearning, exposure, and rewarded exposure in context. *J. Exptl. Psychol.,* **60,** 137–45 (1960)
434. Miller, N. E., Banuazizi, A. Instrumental learning by curarized rats of a specific visceral response, intestinal or cardiac. *J. Comp. Physiol. Psychol.,* **65,** 1–7 (1968)
435. Miller, N. E., Carmona, A. Modification of a visceral response, salivation in thirsty dogs, by instrumental training with water reward. *J. Comp. Physiol. Psychol.,* **63,** 1–6 (1967)
436. Miller, N. E., DeBold, R. C. Classically conditioned tongue-licking and operant bar pressing recorded simultaneously in the rat. *J. Comp. Physiol. Psychol.,* **59,** 109–11 (1965)
437. Miller, R. E., Banks, J. H., Jr., Caul, W. F. Cardiac conditioned responses in avoidance and yoked-control rats. *Psychon. Sci.,* **9,** 581–82 (1967)
438. Mintz, D. E., Mourer, D. J., Gofseyeff, M. Sequential effects in fixed-ratio postreinforcement pause duration. *Psychon. Sci.,* **9,** 387–88 (1967)
439. Misanin, J. R., Campbell, B. A., Smith, N. F. Duration of punishment and the delay of punishment gradient. *Can. J. Psychol.,* **20,** 407–12 (1966)
440. Mitchell, K. M., Perkins, N. P., Perkins, C. C., Jr. Conditions affecting acquisition of observing responses in the absence of differential reward. *J. Comp. Physiol. Psychol.,* **60,** 435–37 (1965)
441. Mogenson, G. J., Mullin, A. D., Clark, E. A. Effects of delayed secondary reinforcement and response requirements on avoidance learning. *Can. J. Psychol.,* **19,** 61–73 (1965)
442. Moore, M. J., Capretta, P. J. Changes in colored or flavored food preferences in chickens as a function of shock. *Psychon. Sci.,* **12,** 195–96 (1968)
443. Morrison, J. H., Porter, J. J. Magnitude of reward in selective learning. *Psychon. Sci.,* **3,** 531–32 (1965)
444. Moscovitch, A., LoLordo, V. M. Role of safety in the Pavlovian backward fear conditioning procedure. *J. Comp. Physiol. Psychol.,* **66,** 673–78 (1968)
445. Mourant, R. R., Pennypacker, H. S. The effects of CS intensity upon learning and performance of the conditioned eyelid response in monkeys. *Psychon. Sci.,* **12,** 81–82 (1968)
446. Moyer, K. E., Chapman, J. A. Effect of continuous vs. discontinuous shock on shuttle box avoidance in the rat. *Psychon. Sci.,* **4,** 197–98 (1966)
447. Moyer, K. E., Korn, J. H. Effect of UCS intensity on the acquisition and extinction of an avoidance

response. *J. Exptl. Psychol.*, **67**, 352–59 (1964)

448. Moyer, K. E., Korn, J. H. Effect of UCS intensity on the acquisition and extinction of a one-way avoidance response. *Psychon. Sci.*, **4**, 121–22 (1966)

449. Mullin, A. D., Mogenson, G. J. Effects of fear conditioning on avoidance learning. *Psychol. Rept.*, **13**, 707–10 (1963)

450. Murillo, N. R., Diercks, J. K., Capaldi, E. J. Performance of the turtle, Pseudemys scripta troostii, in a partial-reinforcement situation. *J. Comp. Physiol. Psychol.*, **54**, 204–6 (1961)

451. Murray, A. K., Strandberg, J. M. Development of a conditioned positive reinforcer through removal of an aversive stimulus. *J. Comp. Physiol. Psychol.*, **60**, 281–83 (1965)

452. Myer, J. S., Ricci, D. Delay of punishment gradients for the goldfish. *J. Comp. Physiol. Psychol.*, **66**, 417–21 (1968)

453. Myers, A. K. Effects of CS intensity and quality in avoidance conditioning. *J. Comp. Physiol. Psychol.*, **55**, 57–61 (1962)

454. Myers, A. K. Instrumental escape conditioning to a low-intensity noise by rats. *Ibid.*, **60**, 82–87 (1965)

455. Myers, W. A., Trapold, M. A. Two failures to demonstrate superiority of a generalized secondary reinforcer. *Psychon. Sci.*, **5**, 321–22 (1966)

456. Nakamura, C. Y., Anderson, N. H. Test of a CER interpretation of the avoidance decrement phenomenon. *J. Comp. Physiol. Psychol.*, **66**, 759–63 (1968)

457. Nevin, J. A., Shettleworth, S. J. An analysis of contrast effects in multiple schedules. *J. Exptl. Anal. Behav.*, **9**, 305–15 (1966)

458. Noble, M., Adams, C. K. Conditioning in pigs as a function of the interval between CS and US. *J. Comp. Physiol. Psychol.*, **56**, 215–19 (1963)

459. Noble, M., Harding, G. E. Conditioning in rhesus monkeys as a function of the interval between CS and US. *J. Comp. Physiol. Psychol.*, **56**, 220–24 (1963)

460. North, A. J., Stimmel, D. T. Extinction of an instrumental response following a large number of reinforcements. *Psychol. Rept.*, **6**, 227–34 (1960)

461. Norton, R., Daley, M. F. The effects of bar-holding training and rapid ratio shaping of fixed-ratio escape responding. *Psychon. Sci.*, **11**, 165–66 (1968)

462. Novin, D., Miller, N. E. Failure to condition thirst induced by feeding dry food to hungry rats. *J. Comp. Physiol. Psychol.*, **55**, 373–74 (1962)

463. O'Kelly, L. I., Crow, L. T., Tapp, J. T., Hatton, G. I. Water regulation in the rat: Drive intensity and fixed ratio responding. *J. Comp. Physiol. Psychol.*, **61**, 194–97 (1966)

464. Oler, I. D., Baum, M. Facilitated extinction of an avoidance response through shortening of the inter-trial interval. *Psychon. Sci.*, **11**, 323–24 (1968)

465. Olton, D. S., Isaacson, R. L. Importance of spatial location in active avoidance tasks. *J. Comp. Physiol. Psychol.*, **65**, 535–39 (1968)

466. Orme-Johnson, D. Response suppression as a function of a vacation from punishment. *Psychon. Sci.* **8**, 277–78 (1967)

467. Overmier, J. B. Differential transfer of control of avoidance responses as a function of UCS duration. *Psychon. Sci.*, **5**, 25–26 (1966)

468. Overmier, J. B. Instrumental and cardiac indices of Pavlovian fear conditioning as a function of US duration. *J. Comp. Physiol. Psychol.*, **62**, 15–20 (1966)

469. Overmier, J. B. Interference with avoidance behavior: Failure to avoid traumatic shock. *J. Exptl. Psychol.*, **78**, 340–43 (1968)

470. Overmier, J. B., Seligman, M. E. P. Effects of inescapable shock upon subsequent escape and avoidance responding. *J. Comp. Physiol. Psychol.*, **63**, 28–33 (1967)

471. Padilla, A. M. A few acquisition trials: Effects of magnitude and percent of reward. *Psychon. Sci.*, **9**, 241–42 (1967)

472. Paige, A. B., McNamara, H. J. Secondary reinforcement and the discrimination hypothesis: The role of discrimination. *Psychol. Rept.*, **13**, 679–86 (1963)

473. Patten, R. L., Rudy, J. W. The Sheffield omission training procedure applied to the conditioning of

the licking response in rats. *Psychon. Sci.,* **8,** 463–64 (1967)

474. Pavlik, W. B., Carlton, P. L. A reversed partial-reinforcement effect. *J. Exptl. Psychol.,* **70,** 417–23 (1965)
475. Pavlik, W. B., Carlton, P. L., Lehr, R., Hendrickson, C. A reversed PRE. *J. Exptl. Psychol.,* **75,** 274–76 (1967)
476. Pavlik, W. B., Reynolds, W. F. Effects of deprivation schedule and reward magnitude on acquisition and extinction performance. *J. Comp. Physiol. Psychol.,* **56,** 452–55 (1963)
477. Pavlik, W. B., Reynolds, W. F. Conventional and reversed partial reinforcement effects in selective learning. *Psychon. Sci.,* **1,** 155–56 (1964)
478. Pearl, J., Edwards, R. E. Delayed avoidance conditioning: Warning stimulus (CS) duration. *Psychol. Rept.,* **11,** 375–80 (1962)
479. Pearl, J., Edwards, R. E. CS-US interval in the trace conditioning of an avoidance response. *Ibid.,* **13,** 43–45 (1963)
480. Pearl, J., Fitzgerald, J. J. Better discriminated bar-press avoidance at short intertrial intervals. *Psychon. Sci.,* **4,** 41–42 (1966)
481. Peckham, R. H., Amsel, A. Within-subject demonstration of a relationship between frustration and magnitude of reward in a differential magnitude of reward discrimination. *J. Exptl. Psychol.,* **73,** 187–95 (1967)
482. Pennes, E. S., Ison, J. R. Effects of partial reinforcement on discrimination learning and subsequent reversal or extinction. *J. Exptl. Psychol.,* **74,** 219–24 (1967)
483. Perkins, C. C., Jr., Levis, J. C., Sulzbacher, S., Berger, D. F. The discrepancy between mean reward and mean reinforcement. *Psychon. Sci.,* **3,** 539–40 (1965)
484. Pick, H. L., Jr., Kare, M. R. The effect of artificial cues on the measurement of taste preference in the chicken. *J. Comp. Physiol. Psychol.,* **55,** 342–45 (1962)
485. Pieper, W. A., Marx, M. H. Effects of within-session incentive contrast on instrumental acquisition and performance. *J. Exptl. Psychol.,* **65,** 568–71 (1963)
486. Pinckney, G. A. Intertrial interval shift and avoidance behavior in fish. *Psychon. Sci.,* **8,** 353–54 (1967)
487. Pinel, J. P. J., Cooper, R. M. Incubation and its implications for the interpretation of the ECS gradient effect. *Psychon. Sci.,* **6,** 123–24 (1966)
488. Platt, J. R., Gay, R. A. Differential magnitude of reward conditioning as a function of predifferential reward magnitude. *J. Exptl. Psychol.,* **77,** 393–96 (1968)
489. Pliskoff, S., Tolliver, G. Water-deprivation-produced sign reversal of a conditioned reinforcer based upon dry food. *J. Exptl. Anal. Behav.,* **3,** 323–29 (1960)
490. Polin, A. T. The effects of flooding and physical suppression as extinction techniques on an anxiety motivated response. *J. Psychol.,* **47,** 235–45 (1959)
491. Porter, J. J. Reinforcement locus and and free-operant extinction. *Psychon. Sci.,* **9,** 593–94 (1967)
492. Porter, J. J., Kopp, R. Extinction of a discrete-trial bar-press as a function of percentage reinforcement, reinforcement cue, and manipulandum condition. *Psychol. Rept.,* **21,** 385–92 (1967)
493. Porter, J. J., Madison, H. L., Senkowski, P. C. Runway performance and competing responses as functions of drive level and method of drive measurement. *J. Exptl. Psychol.,* **78,** 281–84 (1968)
494. Premack, D. Predicting instrumental performance from the independent rate of the contingent response. *J. Exptl. Psychol.,* **61,** 163–71 (1961)
495. Premack, D., Schaeffer, R. W., Hundt, A. Reinforcement of drinking by running: Effect of fixed ratio and reinforcement time. *J. Exptl. Anal. Behav.,* **7,** 91–96 (1964)
496. Prewitt, E. P. Number of preconditioning trials in sensory preconditioning using CER training. *J. Comp. Physiol. Psychol.,* **64,** 360–62 (1967)
497. Pubols, B. H., Jr. Incentive magnitude, learning, and performance in animals. *Psychol. Bull.,* **57,** 89–115 (1960)
498. Pubols, B. H., Jr. The acquisition and reversal of a position habit as a function of incentive magnitude. *J. Comp. Physiol. Psychol.,* **54,** 94–97 (1961)

499. Pubols, B. H., Jr. Constant versus variable delay of reinforcement. *Ibid.,* **55,** 52–56 (1962)
500. Rashotte, M. E. Resistance to extinction of the continuously rewarded response in within-subject partial-reinforcement experiments. *J. Exptl. Psychol.,* **76,** 206–14 (1968)
501. Rashotte, M. E., Amsel, A. Transfer of slow-response rituals to extinction of a continuously rewarded response. *J. Comp. Physiol. Psychol.,* **66,** 432–43 (1968)
502. Rashotte, M. E., Amsel, A. The generalized PRE: Within-*S* PRF and CRF training in different runways, at different times of day, by different experimenters. *Psychon. Sci.,* **11,** 315–16 (1968)
503. Ratliff, R. G., Koplin, S. T., Clayton, K. N. Runway extinction with and without shock as a function of acquisition reward magnitude. *Can. J. Psychol.,* **22,** 79–84 (1968)
504. Ray, A. J., Jr. Non-incremental shuttle-avoidance acquisition to pressurized air US. *Psychon. Sci.,* **5,** 433–34 (1966)
505. Renner, K. E. Influence of deprivation and availability of goal box cues on the temporal gradient of reinforcement. *J. Comp. Physiol. Psychol.,* **56,** 101–4 (1963)
506. Renner, K. E. Delay of reinforcement: A historical review. *Psychol. Bull.,* **61,** 341–61 (1964)
507. Renner, K. E. Temporal integration: Amount of reward and relative utility of immediate and delayed outcomes. *J. Comp. Physiol. Psychol.,* **65,** 182–86 (1968)
508. Rescorla, R. A. Predictability and number of pairings in Pavlovian fear conditioning. *Psychon. Sci.,* **4,** 383–84 (1966)
509. Rescorla, R. A. Inhibition of delay in Pavlovian fear conditioning *J. Comp. Physiol. Psychol.,* **64,** 114–20 (1967)
510. Rescorla, R. A. Probability of shock in the presence and absence of CS in fear conditioning. *Ibid.,* **66,** 1–5 (1968)
511. Rescorla, R. A., LoLordo, V. M. Inhibition of avoidance behavior. *J. Comp. Physiol. Psychol.,* **59,** 406–12 (1965)
512. Revusky, S. H. Aversion to sucrose produced by contingent X-irradiation: Temporal and dosage parameters. *J. Comp. Physiol. Psychol.,* **65,** 17–22 (1968)
513. Revusky, S. H. Effects of thirst level during consumption of flavored water on subsequent preference. *Ibid.,* **66,** 777–79 (1968)
514. Revusky, S. H., Bedarf, E. W. Association of illness with prior ingestion of novel foods. *Science,* **155,** 219–20 (1967)
515. Reynolds, G. S. Behavioral contrast. *J. Exptl. Anal. Behav.,* **4,** 57–71 (1961)
516. Reynolds, G. S. Relativity of response rate and reinforcement frequency in a multiple schedule. *Ibid.,* 179–84
517. Reynolds, W. F., Anderson, J. E. Choice behavior in a T maze as a function of deprivation period and magnitude of reward. *Psychol. Rept.,* **8,** 131–34 (1961)
518. Reynolds, W. F., Anderson, J. E., Besch, N. F. Secondary reinforcement effects as a function of method of testing. *J. Exptl. Psychol.,* **66,** 53–56 (1963)
519. Reynolds, W. F., Pavlik, W. B. Running speed as a function of deprivation period and reward magnitude. *J. Comp. Physiol. Psychol.,* **53,** 615–18 (1960)
520. Reynolds, W. F., Pavlik, W. B., Goldstein, E. Secondary reinforcement effects as a function of reward magnitude training methods. *Psychol. Rept.,* **15,** 7–10 (1964)
521. Reynolds, W. F., Pavlik, W. B., Schwartz, M. M., Besch, N. F. Maze learning by secondary reinforcement without discrimination training. *Psychol. Rept.,* **12,** 775–81 (1963)
522. Riddell, W. I., Herman, T. Incubation in one-trial passive avoidance learning: A cautionary note. *Psychon. Sci.,* **12,** 335–36 (1968)
523. Robbins, D., Chait, H., Weinstock, S. Effects of nonreinforcement on running behavior during acquisition, extinction, and reacquisition. *J. Comp. Physiol. Psychol.,* **66,** 699–706 (1968)
524. Roberts, W. A. Learning and motivation in the immature rat. *Amer. J. Psychol.,* **79,** 3–23 (1966)
525. Roberts, W. A. The effects of shifts in magnitude of reward on runway performance in immature and adult rats. *Psychon. Sci.,* **5,** 37–38 (1966)
526. Roberts, W. A., Bullock, D. H., Bitterman, M. E. Resistance to extinction in the pigeon after parti-

ally reinforced instrumental training under discrete-trials conditions. *Amer. J. Psychol.*, **76,** 353–65 (1963)
527. Rodgers, W., Rozin, P. Novel food preferences in thiamine-deficient rats. *J. Comp. Physiol. Psychol.*, **61,** 1–4 (1966)
528. Rosen, A. J. Incentive-shift performance as a function of magnitude and number of sucrose rewards. *J. Comp. Physiol. Psychol.*, **62,** 487–90 (1966)
529. Rosen, A. J., Glass, D. H., Ison, J. R. Amobarbital sodium and instrumental performance changes following reward reduction. *Psychon. Sci.*, **9,** 129–30 (1967)
530. Rosen, A. J., Jacobs, M. Sucrose incentive shifts in the Skinner box with thirsty rats. *Psychon. Sci.*, **13,** 175–76 (1968)
531. Rossman, B. B., Homzie, M. J. Contrast effects in instrumental differential conditioning with a nonnutritive liquid reinforcement. *Psychon. Sci.*, **9,** 173–74 (1967)
532. Sadler, E. W. A within- and between-subjects comparison of partial reinforcement in classical salivary conditioning. *J. Comp. Physiol. Psychol.*, **66,** 695–98 (1968)
533. Salafia, W. R., Papsdorf, J. D. The effects of ITI interpolated stimuli and CS intensity on classical conditioning of the nictitating membrane response of the rabbit. *Psychon. Sci.*, **13,** 187–88 (1968)
534. Sandler, J., Davidson, R. S., Greene, W. E., Holzschuh, R. D. Effects of punishment intensity on instrumental avoidance behavior. *J. Comp. Physiol. Psychol.*, **61,** 212–16 (1966)
535. Santos, J. F. The influence of amount and kind of training on the acquisition and extinction of escape and avoidance response. *J. Comp. Physiol. Psychol.*, **53,** 284–89 (1960)
536. Scharlock, D. P., Yarmat, A. J. Avoidance learning as a function of trials per training session in normal and brain operated cats. *J. Comp. Physiol. Psychol.*, **55,** 455–57 (1962)
537. Schrier, A. M. Effects of CS-US interval on avoidance conditioning of cats. *J. Genet. Psychol.*, **98,** 203–10 (1961)
538. Schrier, A. M. Response rates of monkeys (Macaca Mulatta) under varying conditions of sucrose reinforcement. *J. Comp. Physiol. Psychol.*, **59,** 378–84 (1965)
539. Schuckman, H., Battersby, W. S. Frequency specific mechanisms in learning. I. Occipital activity during sensory preconditioning. *Electroencephalog. Clin. Neurophysiol.*, **18,** 45–55 (1965)
540. Sears, D. O. Punishment and choice in the rat. *J. Comp. Physiol. Psychol.*, **57,** 297–99 (1964)
541. Seidel, R. J. A review of sensory preconditioning. *Psychol. Bull.*, **56,** 58–73 (1959)
542. Seligman, M. E. P. CS redundancy and secondary punishment. *J. Exptl. Psychol.*, **72,** 546–50 (1966)
543. Seligman, M. E. P. Chronic fear produced by unpredictable electric shock. *J. Comp. Physiol. Psychol.*, **66,** 402–11 (1968)
544. Seligman, M. E. P., Campbell, B. A. Effect of intensity and duration of punishment on extinction of an avoidance response. *J. Comp. Physiol. Psychol.*, **59,** 295–97 (1965)
545. Seligman, M. E. P., Maier, S. F. Failure to escape traumatic shock. *J. Exptl. Psychol.*, **74,** 1–9 (1967)
546. Senf, G. M. Effects of hunger versus shock on spatial learning in the rat. *J. Comp. Physiol. Psychol.*, **65,** 140–44 (1968)
547. Seward, J. P., Humphrey, G. L. Avoidance learning as a function of pretraining in the cat. *J. Comp. Physiol. Psychol.*, **63,** 338–41 (1967)
548. Seward, J. P., Jones, R. B., Summers, S. A further test of "reasoning" in rats. *Amer. J. Psychol.*, **73,** 290–93 (1960)
549. Seward, J. P., King, R. M., Chow, T., Shiflett, S. C. Persistance of punished escape responses. *J. Comp. Physiol. Psychol.*, **60,** 265–68 (1965)
550. Sgro, J. A., Dyal, J. A., Anastasio, E. J. Effects of constant delay of reinforcement on acquisition asymptote and resistance to extinction. *J. Exptl. Psychol.*, **73,** 634–36 (1967)
551. Sgro, J. A., Weinstock, S. Effects of delay on subsequent running under immediate reinforcement. *J. Exptl. Psychol.*, **66,** 260–63 (1963)
552. Shapiro, M. M. Temporal relationship between salivation and lever pressing with differential reinforce-

ment of low rates. *J. Comp. Physiol. Psychol.,* **55,** 567–71 (1962)

553. Sheffield, F. D. Relation between classical conditioning and instrumental learning. In *Classical Conditioning: A Symposium,* Chap. 15, 302–22 (See Ref. 66)
554. Shull, R. L., Brownstein, A. J. Effects of prefeeding in a fixed-interval reinforcement schedule. *Psychon. Sci.,* **11,** 89–90 (1968)
555. Sidman, M. Time out from avoidance as a reinforcer: A study of response interaction. *J. Exptl. Anal. Behav.,* **5,** 423–34 (1962)
556. Singh, D. Resistance to extinction as a function of differential levels of drive and effortfulness of response. *Psychol. Rept.,* **21,** 189–93 (1967)
557. Slivka, R. M., Bitterman, M. E. Classical appetitive conditioning in the pigeon: Partial reinforcement. *Psychon. Sci.,* **4,** 181–82 (1966)
558. Sperling, S. E. Reversal learning and resistance to extinction: A review of the rat literature. *Psychol. Bull.,* **63,** 281–97 (1965)
559. Slotnick, B. M. Effects of fear conditioning on the subsequent acquisition of an avoidance response. *Psychon. Sci.,* **13,** 159–60 (1968)
560. Smith, M. C. CS-US interval and US intensity in classical conditioning of the rabbit's nictitating membrane response. *J. Comp. Physiol. Psychol.,* **66,** 679–87 (1968)
561. Smith, O. A., Jr., McFarland, W. L., Taylor, E. Performance in a shock-avoidance conditioning situation interpreted as pseudo-conditioning. *J. Comp. Physiol. Psychol.,* **54,** 154–57 (1961)
562. Snyder, H. L. Saccharine concentration and deprivation as determinants of instrumental and consummatory response strengths. *J. Exptl. Psychol.,* **63,** 610–15 (1962)
563. Snyder, H. L., Hulse, S. H. Effect of volume of reinforcement and number of consummatory responses on licking and running behavior. *J. Exptl. Psychol.,* **61,** 474–79 (1961)
564. Solomon, R. L., Turner, L. H. Discriminative classical conditioning in dogs paralyzed by curare can later control discriminative avoidance responses in the normal state. *Psychol. Rev.,* **69,** 202–19 (1962)
565. Soltysik, S. Studies on the avoidance conditioning. II. Differentiation and extinction of avoidance reflexes. *Acta Biol. Exp., Warsaw,* **20,** 171–82 (1960)
566. Soltysik, S., Kowalska, M. Studies on the avoidance conditioning. I. Relations between cardiac (Type I) and motor (Type II) effects in the avoidance reflex. *Acta Biol. Exp., Warsaw,* **20,** 157–70 (1960)
567. Spear, N. E., Hill, W. F. Adjustment to new reward: Simultaneous- and successive-contrast effects. *J. Exptl. Psychol.,* **70,** 510–19 (1965)
568. Spear, N. E., Hill, W. F., O'Sullivan, D. J. Acquisition and extinction after initial trials without reward. *J. Exptl. Psychol.,* **69,** 25–29 (1965)
569. Spear, N. E., Pavlik, W. B. Percentage of reinforcement and reward magnitude effects in a T maze: Between and within subjects. *J. Exptl. Psychol.,* **71,** 521–28 (1966)
570. Spear, N. E., Spitzner, J. H. Simultaneous and successive contrast effects of reward magnitude in selective learning. *Psychol. Monogr.,* **80,** No. 10, 1–31 (1966)
571. Spear, N. E., Spitzner, J. H. PRE in a T-maze brightness discrimination within and between subjects. *J. Exptl. Psychol.,* **73,** 320–22 (1967)
572. Spear, N. E., Spitzner, J. H. Effect of initial nonrewarded trials. Factors responsible for increased resistance to extinction. *Ibid.,* **74,** 525–37 (1967)
573. Spear, N. E., Spitzner, J. H. PRE within *S*s: Conventional effect on differential speeds, reverse effect on choices. *Psychon. Sci.,* **7,** 99–100 (1967)
574. Spear, N. E., Spitzner, J. H. Residual effects of reinforcer magnitude. *J. Exptl. Psychol.,* **77,** 135–49 (1968)
575. Spence, K. W., Goodrich, K. P., Ross, L. E. Performance in differential conditioning and discrimination learning as a function of hunger and relative response frequency. *J. Exptl. Psychol.,* **58,** 8–16 (1959)
576. Spence, K. W., Platt, J. R., Matsumoto, R. Intertrial reinforcement and the partial reinforcement effect as a function of number of training trials. *Psychon. Sci.,* **3,** 205–6 (1965)
577. Spivey, J. E. Resistance to extinction as a function of number of N-R transitions and percentage of re-

inforcement. *J. Exptl. Psychol.*, **75,** 43–48 (1967)

578. Spivey, J. E., Hess, D. T., Black, D. Influence of partial reinforcement pattern and intertrial reinforcement on extinction performance following abbreviated training. *Psychon. Sci.*, **10,** 377–78 (1968)
579. Stabler, J. R. Performance in instrumental conditioning as a joint function of time of deprivation and sucrose concentration. *J. Exptl. Psychol.*, **63,** 248–53 (1962)
580. Staddon, J. E. R., Innis, N. K. Preference for fixed vs. variable amounts of reward. *Psychon. Sci.*, **4,** 193–94 (1966)
581. Stavely, H. E., Jr. Effect of escape duration and shock intensity on the acquisition and extinction of an escape response. *J. Exptl. Psychol.*, **72,** 698–703 (1966)
582. Steinman, W. M. Response rate and varied reinforcement: Reinforcers of different strengths. *Psychon. Sci.*, **10,** 37–38 (1968)
583. Stricker, E. M., Miller, N. E. Thirst measured by licking reinforced on interval schedules: Effects of prewatering and of bacterial endotoxin. *J. Comp. Physiol. Psychol.*, **59,** 112–15 (1965)
584. Storms, L. H., Boroczi, G. Effectiveness of fixed ratio punishment and durability of its effects. *Psychon. Sci.*, **5,** 447–48 (1966)
585. Storms, L. H., Boroczi, G., Brown, W. E., Jr. Recovery from punishment of bar pressing maintained on fixed and variable interval reward schedules. *Psychon. Sci.*, **3,** 289–90 (1965)
586. Strouthes, A. Desensitization and fear conditioning. *Psychol. Rept.*, **17,** 787–90 (1965)
587. Strouthes, A., Hamilton, H. C. UCS intensity and number of CS-UCS pairings as determiners of conditioned fear R. *Psychol. Rept.*, **15,** 707–14 (1964)
588. Surridge, C. T., Amsel, A. Confinement duration on rewarded and nonrewarded trials and patterning at 24-hour ITI. *Psychon. Sci.*, **10,** 107–8 (1968)
589. Tapp, J. T., Mathewson, D. M., Jarrett, P. The effects of terminal food and water deprivation on the reinforcing properties of light-onset. *Psychon. Sci.*, **13,** 9–10 (1968)
590. Tarpy, R. M. Incubation of anxiety as measured by response suppression. *Psychon. Sci.*, **4,** 189–90 (1966)
591. Taub, E., Bacon, R. C., Berman, A. J. Acquisition of a trace-conditioned avoidance response after deafferentation of the responding limb. *J. Comp. Physiol. Psychol.*, **59,** 275–79 (1965)
592. Taub, E., Teodoru, D., Ellman, S. J., Bloom, R. F., Berman, A. J. Deafferentation in monkeys: Extinction of avoidance responses, discrimination and discrimination reversal. *Psychon. Sci.*, **4,** 323–24 (1966)
593. Terrace, H. S. Discrimination learning with and without "errors." *J. Exptl. Anal. Behav.*, **6,** 1–27 (1963)
594. Terris, W., Wechkin, S. Approach-avoidance conflict behavior as a function of prior experiences with mild or intense electric shock. *Psychon. Sci.*, **7,** 39–40 (1967)
595. Terris, W., Wechkin, S. Learning to resist the effects of punishment. *Ibid.*, 169–70
596. Theios, J. Drive stimulus generalization increments. *J. Comp. Physiol. Psychol.*, **56,** 691–95 (1963)
597. Theios, J., Brelsford, J. Overlearning-extinction effect as an incentive phenomenon. *J. Exptl. Psychol.*, **67,** 463–67 (1964)
598. Theios, J., Dunaway, J. E. One-way versus shuttle avoidance conditioning. *Psychon. Sci.*, **1,** 251–52 (1964)
599. Theios, J., Lynch, A. D., Lowe, W. F., Jr. Differential effects of shock intensity on one-way and shuttle avoidance conditioning. *J. Exptl. Psychol.*, **72,** 294–99 (1966)
600. Theios, J., McGinnis, R. W. Partial reinforcement before and after continuous reinforcement. *J. Exptl. Psychol.*, **73,** 479–481 (1967)
601. Theios, J., Polson, P. Instrumental and goal responses in non-response partial reinforcement. *J. Comp. Physiol. Psychol.*, **55,** 987–91 (1962)
602. Thomas, D. R., Berman, D. L., Serednesky, G. E. Information value and stimulus configuring as factors in conditioned reinforcement. *J. Exptl. Psychol.*, **76,** 181–89 (1968)
603. Thomas, E., Wagner, A. R. Partial reinforcement of the classically

conditioned eyelid response in the rabbit. *J. Comp. Physiol. Psychol.*, **58**, 157–58 (1964)

604. Thompson, R. F., Dramer, R. F. Role of association cortex in sensory preconditioning. *J. Comp. Physiol. Psychol.*, **60**, 186–91 (1965)
605. Timberlake, W. Straight alley acquisition drive and ad lib test performance. *Psychon. Sci.*, **9**, 585–86 (1967)
606. Tolman, C. W., Mueller, M. R. Laboratory control of toe-sucking in a young rhesus monkey by two kinds of punishment. *J. Exptl. Anal. Behav.*, **7**, 323–25 (1964)
607. Tombaugh, T. N. Resistance to extinction as a function of the interaction between training and extinction delays. *Psychol. Rept.*, **19**, 791–98 (1966)
608. Trapold, M. A., Blehert, S. R., Sturm, T. A failure to find a response persisting in the apparent absence of motivation. *J. Exptl. Psychol.*, **69**, 538–40 (1965)
609. Trapold, M. A., Carlson, J. G. Proximity of manipulandum and food-cup as a determinant of the generalized S^D effect. *Psychon. Sci.*, **2**, 327–28 (1965)
610. Trapold, M. A., Doren, D. G. Effect of noncontingent partial reinforcement on the resistance to extinction of a runway response. *J. Exptl. Psychol.*, **71**, 429–31 (1966)
611. Trapold, M. A., Fowler, H. Instrumental escape performance as a function of the intensity of noxious stimulation. *J. Exptl. Psychol.*, **60**, 323–26 (1960)
612. Trapold, M. A., Lawton, G. W., Dick, R. A., Gross, D. M. Transfer of training from differential classical to differential instrumental conditioning. *J. Exptl. Psychol.*, **76**, 568–73 (1968)
613. Trost, R. C., Homzie, M. J. A further investigation of conditioned hunger. *Psychon. Sci.*, **5**, 355–56 (1966)
614. Trowill, J. A. Instrumental conditioning of the heart rate in the curarized rat. *J. Comp. Physiol.* Psychol., **63**, 7–11 (1967)
615. Vandercar, D. H., Schneiderman, N. Interstimulus interval functions in different response systems during classical discrimination conditioning of rabbits. *Psychon. Sci.*, **9**, 9–10 (1967)
616. Verhave, T. The functional properties of a time out from an avoidance schedule. *J. Exptl. Anal. Behav.*, **5**, 391–422 (1962)
617. Vogel, J. R., Mikulka, P. J., Spear, N. E. Effect of interpolated extinction and level of training on the "depression effect." *J. Exptl. Psychol.*, **72**, 51–60 (1966)
618. Vogel, J. R., Mikulka, P. J., Spear, N. E. Effects of shifts in sucrose and saccharine concentrations on licking behavior in the rat. *J. Comp. Physiol. Psychol.*, **66**, 661–66 (1968)
619. Wagner, A. R. The role of reinforcement and nonreinforcement in an "apparent frustration effect." *J. Exptl. Psychol.*, **57**, 130–36 (1959)
620. Wagner, A. R. Effects of amount and percentage of reinforcement and number of acquisition trials on conditioning and extinction. *Ibid.*, **62**, 234–42 (1961)
621. Wagner, A. R. Sodium amytal and partially reinforced runway performance. *Ibid.*, **65**, 474–77 (1963)
622. Wagner, A. R. Conditioned frustration as a learned drive. *Ibid.*, **66**, 142–48 (1963)
623. Wagner, A. R. Overtraining and frustration. *Psychol. Rept.*, **13**, 717–18 (1963)
624. Wagner, A. R., Siegel, L. S., Fein, G. G. Extinction of conditioned fear as a function of percentage of reinforcement. *J. Comp. Physiol. Psychol.*, **63**, 160–64 (1967)
625. Wagner, A. R., Siegel, S., Thomas, E., Ellison, G. D. Reinforcement history and the extinction of a conditioned salivary response. *J. Comp. Physiol. Psychol.*, **58**, 354–58 (1964)
626. Wagner, A. R., Thomas, E., Norton, T. Conditioning with electrical stimulation of motor cortex: Evidence of a possible source of motivation. *J. Comp. Physiol. Psychol.*, **64**, 191–99 (1967)
627. Wagner, M. K. Restriction of the unconditioned response and its effect upon the learning of an instrumental avoidance response. *Psychol. Rept.*, **15**, 803–6 (1964)
628. Wahlsten, D., Cole, M., Fantino, E. Is a stimulus associated with the escape from shock a positive or negative reinforcer? Study II. *Psychon. Sci.*, **8**, 285–86 (1967)
629. Waller, T. G. Effects of magnitude of reward in spatial and brightness

discrimination tasks. *J. Comp. Physiol. Psychol.*, **66**, 122–27 (1968)

630. Walters, G. C. Frequency and intensity of pre-shock experiences as determinants of fearfulness in an approach-avoidance conflict. *Can. J. Psychol.*, **17**, 412–19 (1963)

631. Wedeking, P. W. Rat avoidance behavior in a dual, one-way shuttle apparatus. *Psychon. Sci.*, **8**, 33–34 (1967)

632. Weinberger, N. M. Effect of detainment on extinction of avoidance responses. *J. Comp. Physiol. Psychol.*, **60**, 135–39 (1965)

633. Weisman, R. G. Experimental comparison of classical and instrumental appetitive conditioning. *Amer. J. Psychol.*, **78**, 423–31 (1965)

634. Weisman, R. G., Denny, M. R., Platt, S. A., Zerbolio, D. J., Jr. Facilitation of extinction by a stimulus associated with long nonshock confinement periods. *J. Comp. Physiol. Psychol.*, **62**, 26–30 (1966)

635. Weisman, R. G., Denny, M. R., Zerbolio, D. J., Jr. Discrimination based on differential nonshock confinement in a shuttle box. *J. Comp. Physiol. Psychol.*, **63**, 34–38 (1967)

636. Weiss, J. M., Krieckhaus, E. E., Conte, R. Effects of fear conditioning on subsequent avoidance behavior and movement. *J. Comp. Physiol. Psychol.*, **65**, 413–21 (1968)

637. Weiss, R. F. Deprivation and reward magnitude effects on speed throughout the goal gradient. *J. Exptl. Psychol.*, **60**, 384–90 (1960)

638. Weiss, S. J., Lawson, R. Secondary reinforcement as a suppressor of rate of responding in the free operant situation. *J. Comp. Physiol. Psychol.*, **55**, 1016–19 (1962)

639. Wenrich, W. W., Eckman, G. E., Moore, M. J., Houston, D. F. A trans-response effect of partial reinforcement. *Psychon. Sci.*, **9**, 247–48 (1967)

640. Wenzel, B. M. Changes in heart rate associated with responses based on positive and negative reinforcement. *J. Comp. Physiol. Psychol.*, **54**, 638–44 (1961)

641. Whittleton, J. C., Kostanek, D. J., Sawrey, J. M. CS directionality and intensity in avoidance learning and extinction. *Psychon. Sci.*, **3**, 415–16 (1965)

642. Wike, E. L., Blocher, O., Knowles, J. M. Effects on drive level and turning preference on selective learning and habit reversal. *J. Comp. Physiol. Psychol.*, **56**, 696–99 (1963)

643. Wike, E. L., Cour, C. A., Sheldon, S. S. Delay of reward as a secondary reinforcer. *Psychon. Sci.*, **9**, 377–78 (1967)

644. Wike, E. L., Farrow, B. J. The effects of drive intensity on secondary reinforcement. *J. Comp. Physiol. Psychol.*, **55**, 1020–23 (1962)

645. Wike, E. L., Farrow, B. J. The effects of magnitude of water reward on selective learning and habit reversal. *Ibid.*, 1024–28

646. Wike, E. L., Kintsch, W., Gutekunst, R. The effects of variable drive, reward, and response upon instrumental performance. *J. Comp. Physiol. Psychol.*, **52**, 403–7 (1959)

647. Wike, E. L., Kintsch, W., Gutekunst, R. Patterning effects in partially delayed reinforcement. *Ibid.*, 411–14

648. Wike, E. L., McWilliams, J., Cooley, J. D. Delay patterns, delay-box confinement, and instrumental performance. *Psychol. Rept.*, **21**, 873–78 (1967)

649. Wike, E. L., Platt, J. R., Knowles, J. M. The reward value of getting out of a starting box: Further extensions of Zimmerman's work. *Psychol. Rec.*, **12**, 397–400 (1962)

650. Wike, E. L., Platt, J. R., Parker, L. Patterns of delayed reinforcement and resistance to extinction. *Psychon. Sci.*, **3**, 13–14 (1965)

651. Wike, E. L., Platt, J. R., Wicker, A., Tesar, V. Effects of random vs. alternating delay of reinforcement in training upon extinction performance. *Psychol. Rept.*, **14**, 826 (1964)

652. Williams, D. R. Relation between response amplitude and reinforcement. *J. Exptl. Psychol.*, **71**, 634–41 (1966)

653. Williams, D. R., Barry, H., III. Counter conditioning in an operant conflict situation. *J. Comp. Physiol. Psychol.*, **61**, 154–56 (1966)

654. Williams, R. L. Response strength as a function of pre- and post-reward delay and physical confinement. *J. Exptl. Psychol.*, **74**, 420–24 (1967)

655. Wilson, J. J. Level of training and goal-box movements as parameters of the partial reinforcement effect. *J. Comp. Physiol. Psychol.*, **57**, 211–13 (1964)
656. Wilton, R. N. Extinction of a running response as a function of reinforcement magnitude. *Quart. J. Exptl. Psychol.*, **18**, 228–35 (1966)
657. Wilton, R. N. Extinction of a runway response following runway or goal box partial reinforcement. *Ibid.*, **19**, 162–65 (1967)
658. Winograd, E. Escape behavior under different fixed ratios and shock intensities. *J. Exptl. Anal. Behav.*, **8**, 117–24 (1965)
659. Wischner, G. J., Fowler, H., Kushnick, S. A. The effect of strength of punishment for "correct" and "incorrect" responses on performance. *J. Exptl. Psychol.*, **65**, 131–38 (1963)
660. Wise, L. M. Supplementary report: The Weinstock partial reinforcement effect and habit reversal. *J. Exptl. Psychol.*, **64**, 647–48 (1962)
661. Wist, E. R. Amount, delay, and position of delay of reinforcement as parameters of runway performance. *J. Exptl. Psychol.*, **63**, 160–66 (1962)
662. Wodinsky, J., Bitterman, M. E. Partial reinforcement in the fish. *Amer. J. Psychol.*, **72**, 184–99 (1959)
663. Woods, P. J. Performance changes in escape conditioning following shifts in the magnitude of reinforcement. *J. Exptl. Psychol.*, **75**, 487–91 (1967)
664. Woods, P. J., Davidson, E. H., Peters, R. J., Jr. Instrumental escape conditioning in a water tank: Effects of variations in drive stimulus intensity and reinforcement magnitude. *J. Comp. Physiol. Psychol.*, **57**, 466–70 (1964)
665. Woods, P. J., Feldman, G. B. Combination of magnitude and delay of reinforcement in instrumental escape conditioning. *J. Comp. Physiol. Psychol.*, **62**, 149–51 (1966)
666. Woods, P. J., Holland, C. H. Instrumental escape conditioning in a water tank: Effects of constant reinforcement at different levels of drive stimulus intensity. *J. Comp. Physiol. Psychol.*, **62**, 403–8 (1966)
667. Wright, J. H. Test for a learned drive based on the hunger drive. *J. Exptl. Psychol.*, **70**, 580–84 (1965)
668. Wunderlich, R. A. Strength of a generalized conditioned reinforcer as a function of variability of reward. *J. Exptl. Psychol.*, **62**, 409–15 (1961)
669. Wyckoff, L. B. Toward a quantitative theory of secondary reinforcement. *Psychol. Rev.*, **66**, 68–78 (1959)
670. Wyers, E. J., Peeke, H. V. S., Herz, M. J. Partial reinforcement and resistance to extinction in the earthworm. *J. Comp. Physiol. Psychol.*, **57**, 113–116 (1964)
671. Yamaguchi, H. G. The effect of continuous, partial, and varied magnitude reinforcement on acquisition and extinction. *J. Exptl. Psychol.*, **61**, 319–21 (1961)
672. Young, A. G. Resistance to extinction as a function of number of nonreinforced trials and effortfulness of response. *J. Exptl. Psychol.*, **72**, 610–13 (1966)
673. Zamble, E. Classical conditioning of excitement anticipatory to food reward. *J. Comp. Physiol. Psychol.*, **63**, 526–29 (1967)
674. Zaretsky, H. H. Runway performance during extinction as a function of drive and incentive. *J. Comp. Physiol. Psychol.*, **60**, 463–64 (1965)
675. Zaretsky, H. H. Learning and performance in the runway as a function of the shift in drive and incentive. *Ibid.*, **62**, 218–21 (1966)
676. Zerbolio, D. J., Jr. Escape and approach responses in avoidance learning. *Can. J. Psychol.*, **22**, 60–71 (1968)
677. Zerbolio, D. J., Jr., Reynierse, J. H. Discriminated learning and reversal in the wheel-turn avoidance situation. *Can. J. Psychol.*, **21**, 185–95 (1967)
678. Zielinski, K., Soltysik, S. The effect of pretraining on the acquisition and extinction of avoidance reflex. *Acta Biol. Exp., Warsaw*, **24**, 73–87 (1964)
679. Zimmerman, D. W. Sustained performance in rats based on secondary reinforcement. *J. Comp. Physiol. Psychol.*, **52**, 353–58 (1959)

MEMORY AND VERBAL LEARNING[1]

By Endel Tulving and Stephen A. Madigan
University of Toronto, Toronto, Canada

The domain of psychological research known today under the bifurcated title of verbal learning and memory has suffered through a long and dull history. Ever since Aristotle, some 2300 years ago, popularized the notion that we remember things by virtue of their contiguity, similarity, and contrast, and ever since Ebbinghaus, less than 100 years ago, experimentally proved that Aristotle's claims about the importance of contiguity were not entirely unfounded, psychological study of how people learn and remember things has kept countless thinkers, scholars, researchers, teachers, and students gainfully occupied without yielding any dramatic new insights into the workings of the human mind.

Many inventions and discoveries in other fields of human intellectual endeavor would bewilder and baffle Aristotle, but the most spectacular or counter-intuitive finding from psychological studies of memory would cause him to raise his eyebrows only for an instant. At the time when man has walked on the moon, is busily transplanting vital organs from one living body into another, and has acquired the power to blow himself off the face of the earth by the push of a button, he still thinks about his own memory processes in terms readily translatable into ancient Greek.

Fortunately, all this will be changed in the not too distant future. Gordon Rattray Taylor, in his widely read book, *Biological Time Bomb* (158a), has predicted that selective erasure of memories will become possible soon, perhaps by 1975, and that the skills required for transmission of memories will take only a little longer to develop, being available perhaps by 2000. Unfortunately for the psychologists interested in problems of verbal learning and memory—and reading between Mr. Taylor's lines—these great changes that would truly amaze Aristotle will be effected without their help or contribution. Once man achieves the control over erasure and transmission of memory by means of biological and chemical methods, psychologists armed with memory drums, *F* tables, and even on-line computers will have become superfluous in the same sense as philosophers became superfluous with the advancement of modern science: they will be permitted to talk—about memory, if they wish—but nobody will take them seriously.

[1] This chapter covers the period from approximately 350 B.C. to 1969 A.D., with a strong emphasis on the literature published between January 1967 and March 1969. The writing of the chapter would have been impossible without the support from the National Research Council of Canada under Grant APA 39, and it was aided by the National Science Foundation Grant GB 3710.

The knowledge that we are rapidly approaching the twilight of the era of psychological study of memory—again if we believe Mr. Taylor—imparts to us a calm feeling of detachment and serenity as we contemplate the state of the art in verbal learning and memory at the end of the seventh decade of the twentieth century. It also relieves us of some anxiety about displaying our ignorance and biases to the public—ignorance reflected in our failure to appreciate the profound significance of many things our wiser colleagues do in their laboratories, and biases that are too many to enumerate. If we are all out of business in another few decades, our being utterly wrong does not matter. Besides, an excellent source of objective information about who did what, and what he thought he found, is available in the form of *Psychological Abstracts*.

Verbal Learning and Memory: Some General Impressions

Research in verbal learning and memory has as its goal the understanding of how human beings retain and use information about symbolically representable events and objects, as well as information about relations among them. Symbolically representable events and objects that have most frequently been used in research to date—although they need not be—are verbal items: letters, letter combinations, digits, numbers, words, sentences, and the like. The perceived relations—as they necessarily must be—are spatial-temporal: an event, a verbal item to be remembered, occurs simultaneously with, appears next to, or is preceded or followed by some other discretely specifiable aspect of the perceived environment. It is also possible to specify the co-occurrence of an item with some other item in terms of other characteristics of the time span in which the items occur.

Why the split title when we refer to the field of research directed at the goal just stated? The reasons are primarily historical and therefore not really determinable. But some purely descriptive comments may help the reader to prepare himself for the somewhat schizophrenic state of affairs discussed under the general title of the present chapter.

If a chapter such as this one had been written between 1885 and 1930, it would have been entitled "Memory," because the expression "verbal learning" did not come into use until the late 1920s. As far as we know, the first time it occurred in the title of a paper was in 1929 (158). The imaginary early chapter entitled "Memory" would have contained mostly information about research that today would be labeled "verbal learning." Between 1940 and 1955 the same chapter in the *Annual Review* would have been entitled "Verbal Learning," and the term "memory" would not have occurred anywhere in it.

In the first full-fledged review of "verbal learning and memory" in the *Annual Review*, Keppel (82) devoted seven pages to the "memory" part of the bipartite field. Research concerned with memory storage and that relevant to theories of forgetting was discussed in this section. The rest of Keppel's chapter, and hence presumably identifiable with the first part of the bipartite title, was concerned with matters classified under associative repertoire, acquisition, response learning, associative learning, and different topics of transfer.

Our impression of the relation between verbal learning and memory can be summarized in the following set of propositions: (*a*) Two different subcultures—verbal learning and memory—are clearly identifiable in the broad field with which this chapter is concerned. (*b*) The two subcultures share a common goal, but they talk different languages, ask different questions, use different methods, and have sworn allegiance to different pretheoretical assumptions. (*c*) Members of the two subcultures can be readily recognized in terms of kinds of things they write on the pages of learned journals, although not in terms of things they say to each other in face-to-face situations. (*d*) The members of each of the two subcultures—we will refer to them as students of verbal learning and students of memory—can again be divided into two categories depending upon their reactions to the other subculture. They either tend to mind their own business and consequently are completely oblivious of what the other subculture does, or they spend their waking hours plotting and executing forays into the other's territory.

Let us next consider the two subcultures in greater detail.

Research in verbal learning.—Students of verbal learning talk the stimulus-response language. For them, research in verbal learning has to do with acquisition and retention of verbal responses to stimuli. Acquisition is frequently equated with "attachment of responses to stimuli," and forgetting is frequently referred to as the "loss of response availability." Acquisition of responses reflects the strengthening of associations between the responses and the stimuli to which the responses are "attached." The response can be "made," in the course of acquisition or at the time of a subsequent retention test, as long as the strength of the association exceeds a hypothetical evocation threshold.

Forgetting is conceptualized as the consequence of weakening of associations, but recall failure may also reflect competition of responses attached to one and the same stimulus. Weakening of associations, frequently referred to as "extinction" or "unlearning," can be brought about by various experimental manipulations, or it may occur "normally," outside the laboratory.

The emphasis on stimulus-response connections in verbal learning dictates a concern with explicit specification of stimuli. Use of experimental paradigms in which the stimuli could be specified at least nominally—serial anticipation and paired-associate methods—and, more recently, the search for functional stimuli in paradigms such as serial learning and free recall, reflect this concern.

Subjects in verbal learning experiments usually learn lists of materials under carefully paced conditions and over several trials. A strong motor element is thus involved in their performance. It is frequently possible for the subject to "know" the material and still fail to get credit for his performance in which he has to make the responses at a rapid pace. For instance, even though a person can write the letters of the alphabet in their reverse order, he may require many trials to "learn" a serial "list" consisting of all the letters of the alphabet in reverse order if he is tested under the typical 2-sec rate. Finally, students of verbal learning frequently derive both experimental and theoretical inspiration from the classical conditioning paradigm.

Research in memory.—Students of memory are concerned with the study of storage and retrieval of item and order information. Item information has been stored and retrieved if the subject can (*a*) recall that item *i* occurred in a specified set of previously presented items, or (*b*) can identify a test item as being identical with one that was presented earlier. Storage and retrieval of order information implies the subject's ability to reconstruct from memory a smaller or larger segment of an ordered set of items presented on an earlier occasion. Many experimental situations require the subject's use of both item and order information.

Students of memory get their experimental and theoretical ideas from watching electronic computers. Consequently, they talk the information-processing language. When a subject sees an object or a picture, or hears an isolated item or a sentence, appropriate information is entered into his memory store. Frequently a distinction is drawn between at least two kinds of memory stores—short-term and long-term—with the information being "transferred" from either store to the other. Stored material can be "utilized" by the subject in recall or recognition tasks. Utilization of stored information, or retrieval, is often likened to a search and decision process. Forgetting occurs when retrieval is unsuccessful, either as a consequence of some loss or deterioration of the stored information, or because of the failure to "find" the desired information in the store.

Students of memory are more eclectic than students of verbal learning in their choice of methods and experimental paradigms. They are quite willing to use traditional list-learning tasks, but they are equally happy to study the performance of subjects in tasks in which students of verbal learning would have difficulty specifying the stimulus to which the response is attached, such as free recall and recognition memory.

If students of verbal learning are preoccupied with time—temporal contiguity between stimulus and response is regarded as the most important necessary condition for the development of an association—then students of memory are preoccupied with space: information is placed or laid down in the memory store or stores, it can be transferred from one store to another, and retrieval in a search through the store. The division between space-oriented and time-oriented individuals is not new to psychology: only 20 years ago place-learning organisms, guided by cognitive maps in their head, successfully negotiated obstacle courses to food at Berkeley, while their response-learning counterparts, propelled by habits and drives, performed similar feats at Yale. No wonder then that the label of "cognitive psychologist" is frequently applied to a student of memory, while the equally complimentary term "behaviorist" is often used to describe a student of verbal learning.

In this chapter, we will speak both stimulus-response and information-processing languages, depending upon the type of work we happen to be describing. We would like to refrain from using the cumbersome label of "verbal learning and memory," but we know of no ready substitute free from undesirable connotations. Our own preferred name for the field of research covered by this chapter is "ecphoric[2] processes," to parallel terms such as "sensory processes," "perceptual processes," and "cognitive processes." We will try out the reaction to this new term in the present chapter. Whenever the term occurs in what follows, the traditionalist can avoid a feeling of discomfort by substituting "verbal learning and memory" for it.

Some general impressions.—In the course of preparation for this chapter, we selected a sample of 540 publications—slightly less than one half of all relevant publications that appeared during the main time-period under review here—and independently rated each paper in terms of its "contribution to knowledge." We agreed to a remarkable extent in classifying all papers into three categories. The first, containing approximately two thirds of all papers, could be labeled "utterly inconsequential." The primary function these papers serve is giving something to do to people who count papers instead of reading them. Future research and understanding of verbal learning and memory would not be affected at all if none of the papers in this category had seen the light of day.

The second category, containing approximately one quarter of all the papers in our test sample, fell into the "run-of-the-mill" category. These represent technically competent variations on well-known themes. Their main purpose lies in providing redundancy and assurance to those readers whose faith in the orderliness of nature with respect to ecphoric processes needs strengthening. Like the papers in the first category, these articles also do not add anything really new to knowledge, and they, too, will have fallen into oblivion 10 years from now.

Many papers in the first two categories simply demonstrate again something that is already well known. Many others offer one or more of the following conclusions: (*a*) variable X has an effect on variable Y; (*b*) the findings do not appear to be entirely inconsistent with the ABC theory; (*c*) the findings suggest a need for revising the ABC theory (although no inkling is provided as to how); (*d*) processes under study are extremely complex and cannot be readily understood; (*e*) the experiment clearly demonstrates the need for further research on this problem; (*f*) the experiment shows that the method used is useful for doing experiments of this type;

[2] According to the dictionary, "ecphory" means "activation of a latent engram." We suggest using the term in a broader sense on the tacit assumption that the understanding of the activation of the latent engram also requires the understanding of the characteristics and origin of the engram.

(*g*) the results do not support the hypothesis, but the experiment now appears to be an inadequate test of it. Apart from providing dull reading, papers with such conclusions share another feature: they contain an implicit promise of more along the same lines in the future. They make one wish that at least some writers, faced with the decision of whether to publish or perish, should have seriously considered the latter alternative.

The third category of papers in our sample, comprising less than 10 per cent of the total, was classified as "worthwhile," including a small group of real gems. The papers in this category carry the burden of continuous progress in our field, by clarifying existing problems, opening up new areas of investigation, and providing titillating glimpses into the unknown. In most cases, the contribution that each particular paper makes is of necessity most modest. Nevertheless, the papers in this category unmistakably stand out from the large mass of other publications.

A phenomenon that should prove to be of great interest to future historians of verbal learning and memory is one that we would like to call—with a nod of acknowledgment to Gordon Allport—the functional autonomy of methods: yesterday's methods have become today's objects of study. Early investigators used serial anticipation and paired-associate list-learning methods to study acquisition and retention of associations; for a long time now the study of serial and paired-associate learning for their own sake has been proceeding apace (9, 185). More recent instances of canonization of method show new areas of research growing up around verbal discrimination (about which we will have more to say later), Peterson and Peterson's short-term "distractor" technique, Sternberg's method of studying errorless retrieval (156), and the like. We wish that someone wiser than we would explain the functional autonomy of methods to us.

Without saying why, we will assume that the function of experiments is to allow the construction, elaboration, modification, and overthrow of theories. By this criterion, too, much of the current research into ecphoric processes fails to make any contribution. Very few new theoretical ideas are being distilled from a flood of data. Existing theoretical notions are hardly ever modified or abandoned. Whenever the results of an experiment clearly do not support the hypothesis derived from a theory, the last thing the typical experimenter does is to question the theory. He usually finds good reasons why the theory should emerge unscathed from contact with the data.

Association, Redintegration, and Organization

Association.—The concept of association is almost as important to a student of verbal learning as the concept of cell is to a biologist, molecule to a chemist, and atom to a nuclear physicist, but despite its much greater age, its usefulness has not yet been universally acknowledged. It has aided the thinking of many at the same time that it has confused some, and it has been both used and abused more often than any other concept we know.

In a scholarly and timely review of the concept, Postman (133) has gone a long way towards clarifying some of the misunderstandings. He distinguishes among different senses of "association" and points out that in most of these senses association represents a disposition or capacity. To say that an association exists between A and B does not mean that whenever A occurs B will follow. It only means that B will follow A if some other conditions are met. "In any given situation the probability of a particular response will be a function not only of associative strength but also of the conditions of performance" (133, p. 556).

So far so good. But difficulties arise in the specification of these "conditions of performance." Under "performance variables," Postman includes a consideration of differences between intentional and incidental learning, the effects of instructions on learning, and preference effects in acquisition. But these factors are clearly concerned with initial acquisition and hence must have relevance primarily for associative factors. Other matters Postman considers—transfer and retention tests—also fail to clarify the nature and role of nonassociative "performance" variables. These tests do tell us something about what the subject has learned, but they do not tell us what else, beside an intact association, is required for successful performance of a learned act. The vase on the mantel—an example Postman uses—has the capacity to fall if touched by the wind. What are the events that combine with the capacity of A to evoke B to actually produce B? The associative framework of learning and memory will not come of age until it comes fully to grips with this problem.

Contextual associations.—Of all the different "kinds" of associations discussed by Postman, the contextual association enjoys the greatest popularity with students of verbal learning today. It is an old concept, although its name is relatively new. It usually refers to the association between a response—corresponding to a given item in the list—and the general environmental stimuli in presence of which the response is learned and recalled.

The increasing fondness with which the concept of contextual association is regarded by students of verbal learning is attributable to several factors.

First, it represents "one half" of the two-stage theory of paired-associate learning (167) that continues to guide a lot of thinking. Second, it has permitted the inclusion of free-recall phenomena, previously a source of embarrassment to the associative tradition, within the associative framework (133, 134, 147, 148). Third, the concept of contextual association has played an important role in explanations of unlearning in retroaction paradigms (81, 101). Fourth, the concept can be invoked to explain certain phenomena in recognition memory, such as the identification as "old" of words associated with study-list items (186). Finally, accrual of frequency units to items in the course of acquisition of verbal discrimination tasks (59) represents a quantal analogue of the development of contextual associations and promises to bring about a true marriage of the associative view of learning and recognition memory.

We have no objection to the concept of contextual association as a descriptive term, but we doubt its theoretical usefulness. Contextual association is simply a shorthand expression for the fact that the subject can recall individual items or small subsets of items from larger sets in absence of any specific experimentally manipulated retrieval cues. It explains such recall behavior in the same sense as the soporific quality of sleeping pills explains the effectiveness of these pills in inducing sleep.

Redintegration.—Association is the relation between two parts which, by virtue of their relation, constitute a whole; redintegration, on the other hand, refers to the relation between a whole and any one of its constituent parts. The term "redintegration" was introduced by William Hamilton (68), who used it as a name for his 'supreme principle of association,' according to which "thoughts or mental activities, having once formed part of the same total thought or mental activity, tend ever after immediately to suggest each other" (68, p. 436). The principle of redintegration thus was an early alternative to the conception of thought and memory as a chain of ideas.

The concept has recently been resurrected by Horowitz & Prytulak (74) to explain certain memory phenomena which cannot be accounted for by traditional principles of association. Horowitz & Prytulak define redintegrative memory in terms of a high conditional probability of recall of a "whole unit" given that a part of the unit has been recalled. They also introduce and illustrate the "principle of redintegrative power": the part of a unit that is best remembered in free recall is also the best cue for eliciting the whole unit. It remains to be seen whether the surplus meaning the concept of redintegration possesses over and above its basic definition as a strong association between a part and a whole will provide any fresh insights into the nature of memory and learning, but the effort is certainly worthwhile.

Organization.—Organization was just a synonym for association in McGeoch's (100) evaluation, but McGeoch was a temperate man. Many contemporary students of ecphoric processes are willing to die defending the proposition that organization, as a concept in psychological study of memory, has no more in common with association than a nobleman has with a beggar.

Mandler is the chief proponent of the position that phenomena of memory cannot be understood without recourse to the concept of organization, a concept that is very different from that of association. He has recently written extensively on the subject (92–95). Mandler's basic position is that organization is a necessary condition for memory.

What is organization and why is it such an indispensable concept in the study of memory? Mandler defines organization explicitly in several places, both generally, following Garner's (61) definition of structure, and more specifically, when referring to organization of words in lists to be learned. These words, he says, are organized "when the functional aspects of a word, specifically its meaning, depend at least in part on the set of words of which it is a member, and the relation of the members of the set to each other" (95 p. 102). Organization can take several forms: a set of words can be organized hierarchically, categorically (in unordered sets), or serially (in ordered sets). According to the definition of organization, the meaning of a word depends at least partly upon its position in the hierarchy, in the category, or in the series.

The evidence Mandler presents in support of his theoretical position comes mostly from experiments in which free recall of words is shown to be a linear function of the number of subject-determined categories into which words are sorted prior to their recall. In these experiments, the correlation between number of words recalled and number of sorting trials taken by the subject, and hence amount of exposure to the words to be recalled, is essentially zero. Thus the conclusion follows that the classification of words into groups on the basis of their meaning is a sufficient condition for recall above the limits set by immediate memory, while repetition—strengthening of contextual associations—is not a necessary condition. The same principle is also neatly demonstrated in another experiment: subjects who were simply asked to categorize a set of words into a convenient number of categories, in absence of any instructions to memorize the words, recalled as many words as did subjects who were explicitly instructed to commit all items to memory (92).

Mandler views the effect of organization on memory in terms of the format of storage of to-be-remembered materials—multiple hierarchies, subjectively determined categories, or series. Recent experiments by Bower and his associates (17) have complemented this view by emphasizing retrieval processes. Bower et al. had subjects learn sets of words presented for study either in familiar or randomly arranged hierarchies. The results were dramatic: in one experiment, after a single trial, subjects recalled 73 words out of 112 when the words were presented in hierarchical organizations, but only 21 words out of 112 when the same words were presented in random sets. Bower et al. concluded that hierarchical organization was used by subjects as a retrieval plan for cuing recall.

Both association and organization refer to relations between and among verbal units. The associative relation has its origin in the spatial-temporal proximity of the associated items, while organization is based on the intrinsic characteristics of organized items. Association has a single property—strength—while organization has many facets. Whether we need one set of laws governing the learning and recall of associated items and another set to handle memory of organized items remains an interesting and important question. Available evidence, although scant and indirect (149, 161), suggests the answer to the question is affirmative.

Acquisition and Storage

We discuss six topics under the general heading of acquisition and storage: repetition and memory, learning of paired associates, memory and mental imagery, memory for serial order, verbal discrimination, and sensory modalities and memory. Research that can be fitted into these rubrics is concerned primarily with the "what" and "how" of establishment of associations, or placement of mnemonic information into the store.

Repetition and memory.—Rather simple and straightforward classical frequency theories have held for a long time that repeated presentations of nominally identical test items result in the strengthening of the trace of that item, or strengthening of the association of that item with some general contextual features present during all presentations. Alternative views are (*a*) that each occurrence of a test item creates an independent trace, and (*b*) that each repetition creates many replicas of the trace.

This distinction between strengthening of a single trace versus multiplexing a trace as a consequence of presentation of a nominally identical event is an old one. Ward (171), for instance, referred to it as the functional vs. atomistic view. The functional view held that repetition produces further growth or some other such change in the old trace, while according to the atomistic view, each repeated event calls into being a new trace, thus resulting in a large number of traces "qualitatively alike but numerically distinct."

The stimulus-response theory of acquisition ascribes a mechanical "stamping-in" function to repetition, and sometimes assumes a continuity of repetition and "reinforcement" effects (1). Such a point of view encounters difficulty when confronted with the results from experiments such as that of Glanzer & Meinzer (65): overt repetition of items in free recall added less to the memory store by way of information capable of supporting recall than did "silent rehearsal." Such data suggest that a normal subject does not use processing time for mechanical repetition, and that repetition per se is not a sufficient condition for trace strengthening (cf. also 52).

Other data suggest the need for a much finer-grained analysis of repetition effects than that offered by the classical trace-strengthening view. Melton (104) has found the effect of repeated presentation of items in single-trial free recall to depend critically on the interval between repetitions: recall increases as the interval between two occurrences of a repeated item increases. Melton has suggested that at least a part of this distribution phenomenon is attributable to differences in contextual encoding of two nominally identical items.

Melton's distribution effect, replicated by Glanzer (62), is fascinating because of the apparent paradox it demonstrates: as the repetition interval increases, it becomes less likely that the subject will recognize the second presentation of an item as being a repetition; yet recall of repeated items is better as the interval is greater. The paradox is the same as the one posed by Peterson (126) for the short-term recall of paired-associates (cf. 87).

The intriguing nature of Melton's data is enhanced by Waugh's (172,

173) repeated failure to find any trace of the distribution effect, and by Underwood's failure to find an interval effect beyond a difference between massed and distributed presentations (159). The discrepancy between Melton and Glanzer on the one hand and Waugh and Underwood on the other may be attributable, at least in part, to differences in input modalities: the former two investigators presented their material visually and the latter two auditorily. But even if this hypothesis turns out to be tenable, it would only deepen the mystery of the Melton effect by an order of magnitude.

The more experiments are done on repetition effects, the more modifications must be added to the classical trace or association strengthening view. Bower & Lesgold (19) have replicated and clarified the finding that the inclusion of previously learned items in free-recall lists retards the acquisition of these lists, in comparison to control conditions in which subjects learned lists composed of new "weak" or "unlearned" items, and similar findings have been reported by others (121a, 182).

The negative transfer effects found in these experiments point to the importance of meaningful specific interitem associations, or subjective organization, in free-recall learning. They also should dampen the enthusiasm of those who believe in the importance of contextual associations in learning tasks such as serial learning and free recall. It is rather difficult to see why contextual associations count so little in learning of second lists in these transfer studies. Items in the first list should be reasonably strongly associated with the context when the subject starts learning the second list. Yet they end up being recalled less readily than items the subject has not seen before the second list.

All current theories and almost all extant data tell us that the best way to learn verbal material beyond the immediate memory span is to allow its repetition—exactly the same item presented trial after trial. It is therefore interesting to note conditions under which something other than straight repetition might lead to superior retention. The two relevant papers are by Bevan and his associates (13, 14).

In one experiment (13), subjects were tested for free recall of lists varying in the similarity of successive presentations of to-be-remembered material. For example, a list might contain four presentations of one member of a conceptual category, or one presentation of each of four different members of that category. Recall of categories improved as more "variation" in category instances was provided. In another study (14), the same kind of effect occurred when cues for to-be-remembered items were changed from one presentation to the next instead of being simply repeated.

These data illustrate one of the problems in studying repetition effects within lists (62, 172), and raise some interesting questions. With free recall tests, there is no way of knowing which of two or more presentations of an item is being recalled. This problem does not arise in the context of a trace-strengthening theory, but if we assume that two temporally distinct presentations of one item constitute two different "events," and produce similar but not identical traces, the problem becomes meaningful and its implications quite exciting.

A new method of investigating repetition effects in typical list-learning experiments was described by Jung (77). His subjects learned paired-associate lists, starting with a single item and seeing one additional new item on each successive "mini-trial." This method, for which we would like to suggest the simple name of "adit method," is being adopted in different versions. We can distinguish between "redundant" and "nonredundant" adit methods. In the former, on successive mini-trials the input from the preceding trial is repeated along with the added item, while in the latter, the subject is given just a single item on each mini-trial, with instructions to "carry" the rest of the set in memory and to reproduce the whole set on each mini-trial.

Mandler & Dean (96) have used both versions of the adit method for fine-grained analyses of recall in tasks requiring "seriation" and free recall. These experiments have shown no consistent difference in the acquisition of lists depending upon whether traditional or adit methods were used. Since the subject spends very much less time examining the input under the adit conditions, the finding of no difference constitutes a departure from the total-time hypothesis which has been shown to hold under many conditions (46).

Dalrymple-Alford (52) compared subjects' immediate memory spans for digits obtained by means of the classical method with those obtained under the nonredundant adit method. Digits were presented visually at the rate of one per second, and subjects' verbal recall was paced at the same rate. Two methods yielded identical measures of memory span. Apparently, repeated reproduction of systematically increasing parts of the span series under the adit conditions are totally ineffective in producing learning that would enable the subject to recall more material than he could after a single presentation of the whole series.

Repetition seems to be effective, however, under conditions investigated by Buschke & Hinrichs (35). These investigators used the redundant adit method in presenting to their subjects series of numbers selected from the set of 1 to 20. Numbers were presented auditorily at the rate of one per second, and subjects' recall was obtained under different recall instructions. Recall was higher when the subject recalled the items in the ascending natural serial order (given the input of 12, 8, 17, 2, recall in the order of 2, 8, 12 and 17) than in the order in which the items were presented, despite the fact that in the former case a continuous rearrangement of items in the store would appear to be necessary, while in the latter case it is not. This latter finding is consistent with the format of what Buschke has called a "marker" storage system (33, 34).

The reasons for the apparent discrepancy between the Dalrymple-Alford findings on the one hand, and those of Buschke & Hinrichs on the other, with respect to the effect of repetition or rehearsal, are not clear. The two experiments differed from one another in many ways. Could it be that the difference is related to inputs in different sensory modalities?

Learning of paired associates.—No reviewer can possibly ignore research in paired-associate learning primarily because of its great quantity in the contemporary literature. Why does the enthusiasm for it continue unabated?

It is possible to identify at least four different uses to which the paired-associates method has been put. First, it has been regarded as a close facsimile of conditioning procedures, and used to extend animal behavior principles to "complex" learning tasks. Second, it has served as a type of cued recall test, one of many different ways of indicating to a subject which item he is to attempt to recall. Third, it has been the main tool for investigating the interference theory of forgetting, that is, a means and not an end. Fourth, paired-associates learning has become a topic of study in its own right, that is, an end and not a means.

This fourth category finds its most vocal advocate in Battig (9). He views paired-associate learning as a very complex task requiring multiprocess models to explain it, and quite unlike a simple stimulus-response situation as it was previously thought to be. It is in fact so complex that what is needed to advance our understanding of it is, according to Battig, a gigantic factorial experiment, "involving the simultaneous orthogonal manipulation of all known task and procedural variables known or suspected to have any effect whatever within any kind of PA learning task" (9, p. 167). Battig adds that this would probably require the "cooperation of a large number of PA researchers," although he has taken a modest step in this direction on his own (10). We hope that when the day of the ICBM (Intercontinental Battig Method) arrives, we shall be able to fill one of the cells.

Battig's hopes for the future define one kind of theory about paired-associates phenomena. Presumably, once his giant factorial is done (and replicated ?), one would have a listing of all the effects of all the variables. This would then tell us everything about paired-associate learning and would thus obviate the need for a theory, at least until such time as someone thought up a new variable.

Until such time that a complete table of facts about paired-associate learning becomes available, we have to manage with old-fashioned theorizing. The theoretical light that has guided a good deal of experimental work was provided by Underwood & Schulz in 1960 (167). By far the most impressive thing about their two-stage theory is its longevity. After 10 years of steady use, it shows absolutely no signs of wear and tear, and it looks as if it is going to be around in the same form for a long time to come.

The theory as stated makes some interesting predictions. The one we like is a straightforward deduction from the basic principles: given that paired-associate learning is a matter of establishing response availability and specific intrapair associations, if responses are fully available and the strength of associations between each stimulus and its corresponding response is the maximum possible, the list requires no learning, or should be learned in one trial at the most.

A list consisting of, say, 24 common nouns as stimulus terms, each accompanied by the same noun, either in the singular or plural form, as the response member would constitute such a list. We can call it the A-A list. All response terms would be readily available if subjects were informed about the construction of the list, and an association between two identical words is presumably stronger than any other association. The singular-plural wrinkle is introduced in order to convert the task from a reading task into one requiring the learning of specific associations, as in any other paired-associate list.

We suspect the list cannot be learned too readily, even though the two-stage theory as it is known today says it can. We also suspect that the list of this kind would be learned in the all-or-none fashion. Analysis of the data in the way suggested by Bower & Trabasso (20) should prove that. Although the issue of all-or-none vs. the incremental learning of association was successfully pronounced dead by Restle (139), it may be worth reviving for the purpose of the demonstration that a list entailing highly available responses and extremely strong intrapair associations is learned in the all-or-none fashion.

A major step in the conceptual analysis of classical paired-associate phenomena has been provided by Martin (99). His is the most important theoretical statement in the area since Underwood & Schulz's two-stage model.

The central concept of Martin's thesis is "encoding variability": a nominal (experimenter-defined) stimulus may evoke a different perceptual "encoding" response from the subject on each of its successive appearances. In simple paired-associate learning tasks, subjects must recognize each stimulus term as "old" before they can respond to it. Martin's (98) and Bernbach's (12) experiments have made it quite clear that the recall of the response term is no better than chance if the subject fails to recognize the stimulus as an "old" item.

Success or failure of recognition of the stimulus term as "old" at the time of the attempted recall of its corresponding response term, according to the theory, depends upon the similarity of the encoding responses made to the stimulus term on the test trial and on the original learning trial. Since the associative bond supporting the response recall is built up between the encoded version of the stimulus and the response term, the subject's failure to encode the stimulus term identically on study and recall trials leads to the consequence that the associative bond, even if intact, cannot be activated.

The power of the encoding variability hypothesis can be seen in Martin's account of the role of stimulus meaningfulness (*m*) in paired-associate learning and transfer. For example, the hypothesis predicts that while List 1 learning may be slower for low *m* stimuli than for high *m* stimuli, transfer to an A-Br list will be positive for low *m*, negative for high *m*. This follows from the theory since low *m* stimuli can be encoded differently during List 2 learning, while high *m* material cannot. Thus, encoding variability effectively reduces interlist similarity for low-*m* stimuli.

Most paired-associate work continues to be done in the context of multi-trial situations, and most theory is couched in learning terms. Despite the early start made by Calkins in 1896 (36), followed a little later by Murdock (110), little attention has been paid to short-term processes inherent in any trial-by-trial procedure. The subject always knows the pair he has just seen, if the pair is composed of two well-integrated items, but the pair is quickly "forgotten" as other pairs are presented and recalled (3). The effect of repetition, therefore, can be viewed as the production of increasing resistance to forgetting by individual pairs (11). Increasing resistance to forgetting and strengthening of associations may turn out to be nothing more than two different ways of talking about the same process, but different labels frequently suggest different further thoughts, and in that sense one name may be better than another.

An experiment by Bregman (21) on massed and distributed practice in paired-associate learning illustrates some of the differences between short-term memory and traditional methods and analyses. Bregman defined massing and distribution of practice in terms of interitem intervals, rather than in terms of interlist intervals. The conclusions he reached were the exact opposite to those accepted earlier in traditional experiments: distributed practice facilitated retention, not acquisition. In addition, the effects Bregman obtained were large ones, in contrast with some of the tiny differences that usually result from massing and distribution in list-learning experiments (160).

Paired-associate research has been dominated by stimulus-response concepts since its early days. It is high time, therefore, that someone posed the question about the function of stimulus terms in paired-associate tasks. What exactly do stimulus terms do in such tasks?

Plainly, stimulus terms are not necessary to produce response recall. The fact that subjects store information about stimulus items and can recall them (53, 168), the fact that free recall tests or MMFR (modified method of free recall) tests may reveal only the smallest of differences in amount recalled (83), and the fact that either item in a pair can function as a cue for recall of the other (90), make it clear that the labels "stimulus" and "response" have been somewhat inappropriate. They are replete with surplus meaning, and have apparently escaped the notice of the soul-searching that Postman (133) says is a mark of the associationist's use of theoretical terms.

Memory and mental imagery.—The use of mental imagery as a mnemonic device is an ancient and venerable practice, but it failed to interest the followers of Ebbinghaus. In 1963, Noble (119) suggested that the claims of professional mnemonists be subjected to impartial scientific evaluation, presumably by the hard-nosed, no-nonsense techniques of rote learning research. We can report that this evaluation is under way, and it is indicating that the efficacy of imagery in memorization does not always vanish in the laboratory.

Modern researchers have approached the study of imagery and memory in two ways. The first revolves around the use of to-be-remembered materials that are presumed to differ in their ease of representation as visual images. Paivio (122), in an extensive research program, has found that pictures of objects are more readily recalled than their labels, and that concrete words are superior to abstract words in almost any task: paired-associate learning, free recall, serial recall (123), and recognition. In addition, the rated concreteness or imagery value of words appears to be a much better predictor of paired-associate learning than other more traditional measures of word attributes such as meaningfulness and frequency (124).

The second approach has been taken through the use of instructions: subjects coached in the use of special imagery techniques can perform at levels that are stunning in comparison to those common to rote learning situations. The effects of imagery instructions such as those reported by Bugelski (32) and Bower et al. (18) qualify as something more than amusing demonstrations of a mnemonic device. Imagery recommends itself as an extremely powerful means of producing strong associations without the use of laborious trial-by-trial procedures or norms of pre-experimental relatedness.

The study of imagery and memory has just begun, and consequently, there has been little by way of explanation of why imagery "works." Paivio (122) suggested that independent verbal and visual "codes" could be stored for certain kinds of materials (concrete words and pictures) while only verbal codes could be employed for abstract words. This position identifies imagery effects with amount of information stored, and agrees with the interesting hypothesis that verbal and visual components of a trace can be forgotten independently (7). The basis of imagery effects may lie in the "distinctiveness" of information stored as images (90), but this hypothesis offers little by way of explanation for an effect that appears in so many different kinds of tasks.

The revival of interest in imagery and the dividends it is paying in imaginative experiments such as those by Brooks (27) and Huttenlocher (76) may indicate the end of dominance of the field of verbal learning and memory by theories concerned exclusively with verbal associative processes. Just 10 years ago, Bousfield (15) could say that the concept of word meaning made sense only if it referred to verbal associations, and many were apparently willing to agree. Unobservable verbal processes were acceptable in this formulation; they were called "mediators." Unobservable visual images at that time were, of course, nonexistent and therefore could not be investigated.

The main problem facing imagery research now is to provide some integration of the data with memory theory in general. To say that some material is remembered because some images are remembered, or because natural language mediators are remembered (1), is to say nothing about the workings of memory.

Memory for serial order.—The acquisition and retention of information about the temporal and serial order of items in memory tasks continue to be heavily researched topics. Major interest focuses on three areas: identification of the effective stimulus for recall of individual elements of a series; explanation of the serial position effect; and short-term retention of order information.

Both the stimulus-response chaining and position-learning hypotheses and their various combinations, have continued to inspire experimenters (185). Some rather peculiar approaches have been taken to demonstrate the superiority of one theoretical position over the others. Foremost among these we find transfer tests—serial to paired-associate learning, as well as vice versa. The rationale of these tests has been discussed by Postman (133). But whatever the reasons for the use of such tests as measures of cue functions in serial learning, whatever the apparent degree of clarity of predictions—e.g., formation of item-to-item associations producing positive transfer—we think that attempts to understand serial learning by studying a subject's subsequent performance on another task which is itself not understood will only serve to confuse the issues further.

If transfer tests do not tell us what the functional stimulus is in serial learning, is it possible that some other method will? Woodward & Murdock (183) showed their subjects a list of 10 words and then probed for the recall of a specific word by giving as the retrieval cue (*a*) the immediately preceding word, (*b*) the ordinal number of the position of the target word, or (*c*) both of these cues (double cue). They concluded, on basis of their data, that sequential and positional cues "may be equally effective" in serial learning.

The most interesting finding, however, of the Woodward & Murdock studies, in our opinion, was the failure of the double cues to yield any higher recall than single cues. The lack of additivity of cues means that the immediately preceding word and the position of an item represent completely redundant information to the subject and that the contrast between them is meaningless.

Nothing is as futile, even silly, in our opinion, as the search for the stimulus in serial or any other type of learning. One can think of scores of queries or "stimuli" that would produce various proportions of correct responses in different retention tests of a series of items (22). We can call all these queries "functional stimuli" and thereby express the realization that the human mind is an extremely fine and powerful information processing device. This insight, however, requires no experimental evidence; Aristotle was well aware of it.

At this point we cannot resist the temptation to concur in Cofer's judgment (42) about the snail's pace of progress in our field. In 1912, Franz

Nagel (116) reported some observations relevant to the question of sequential associations. A single well-trained subject learned series of 12 nonsense syllables. After reaching the criterion of one perfect recitation on a given series, the subject was given 24 overlearning trials for the same series, and then tested by means of the sequential probe method (Trefferversuche). The subject was explicitly instructed to refrain from thinking about the whole series, and to produce the desired syllable solely "out of" the probe syllable. The probability of correct responses, over six such series, was 0.30. This and similar findings should have led investigators to be wary of (*a*) the proposition that one item is a stimulus for the recall of the next item in a series, (b) the usefulness of the sequential probe method for the purpose of testing the hypothesis, or (*c*) both the hypothesis and the method. The hypothesis and the method, however, are still being put together by indomitable students of verbal learning and memory more than 50 years later.

A refreshingly novel approach to the problem of "the stimulus" in serial learning has been taken by Voss (169, 170). His experimental findings have revealed the inadequacy of both chaining and position theories, and his methodological innovations promise to give new life to research in serial learning.

The serial position curve.—The difference in recall at the ends and middle of a list maintains its reputation as the Chinese puzzle of verbal learning. Despite a great deal of imagination shown in applying the word-magic treatment to the phenomenon, frequently under the guise of "theory," many still believe that our understanding of the phenomenon has advanced little since Ebbinghaus first described it.

We do not understand why serial position effect is frequently investigated in multitrial experiments. The largest difference between recall of items from the ends and from the middle of a serially ordered collection occurs on the first trial, thus clearly suggesting that the explanation for the phenomenon must be sought in the psychological events occurring on such a single trial, rather than in the processes underlying acquisition of the list over multiple trials.

The fact that serial position effects are obtained on a single trial, with fast input rates (183), and in general show marked similarities to curves produced by tachistoscopic presentation (69), suggests that it may be worth-while to consider the effects as a perceptual-memory phenomenon rather than a learning phenomenon. Morin et al. (108) found serial position effects for latencies of responding in a task in which the subjects "scanned" the memory trace of a serially presented set of four digits—a situation involving the barest minimum by way of "learning."

The similarity of one "serial position curve" to another, of course, is no guarantee that both are consequences of one and the same set of underlying processes. Serial position curves in a task requiring recall of a briefly flashed series of items, for instance, need not be produced by the same factors as those responsible for the serial position curve demonstrated in an interesting experiment by Slamecka (151). In Slamecka's study the effect was produced by output order rather than by input order: the first and last items recalled showed fewest errors, and their point of presentation did not matter. At least in some situations (47), the output order seems to be determined independently of the organization of the items in the store, reflecting characteristics of output processes as such. On the other hand, serial position curves can be demonstrated under conditions where the subject's retention of the material is tested by the recognition method (41), thus clearly implicating the properties of the stored information.

It is clear, to use the most popular phrase in the field of verbal learning and memory, that further research is needed on this problem.

A spate of studies concerned with order information in short-term memory has recently appeared. We would classify many of them as studies in perceptual-motor learning, to the probable consternation of their authors. The most conspicuous example is provided by studies that investigate the effect of acoustic and visual similarity of items on their ordered recall (72, 88). The effects of acoustic similarity, of interest to students of memory since Conrad's (44) influential paper, are thought to be relevant to the continuity-discontinuity problem: are the laws governing short-term memory the same as, or different from, those that describe long-term memory?

To the extent that experimental data generated in these short-term perceptual-motor experiments can be variably interpreted, thus creating "theoretical" issues, they may turn out to have some usefulness. The problem of whether acoustic similarity has its effects via audition or kinaesthesia (72, 88, 115, 177), for instance, appears to be one of those local skirmishes that will provide some excitement to the participants, even if it is not going to teach us much about basic issues in memory.

Verbal discrimination learning.—A special type of recognition memory task that has become increasingly popular over the past few years and has all the earmarks of a new "hot" area of research in verbal learning is verbal discrimination. Pairs of items are presented to the subject, one pair at a time; the subject pays attention or responds to both members of the pair, and then is told that one of the two items is "right." After all pairs of a list have been presented, subsequent trials follow the typical anticipation procedure: a pair of items is presented, the subject says which item was "right" and then receives informative feedback from the experimenter. Many variations on this general paradigm are possible.

The verbal discrimination paradigm has been around for some time. It was initially used as a method or technique for a variety of purposes. Recently, the means has become the end: the method for studying other phenomena was elevated to the status of something to be studied in its own right. An important impetus for this development was provided by the Frequency Theory of verbal-discrimination learning by Ekstrand, Wallace & Underwood (59).

The Frequency Theory of verbal discrimination is wrong, in the same sense that all extant theories in our field are wrong: ten years from now, or a hundred years, or a thousand years, students of memory will look at it in the same way as we regard the attempts of the ancient Greeks to explain the composition of the universe in terms of four basic elements. But at the present time, the Frequency Theory must be counted among the few genuine theories we have. It does explain data from a number of experiments, it does make specific predictions about outcomes of as yet undone experiments, it does deal with important fundamental processes in learning and memory, and it is specific enough so that it is capable of being proved wrong. Because of these outstanding characteristics that distinguish it from many other collections of speculations referred to as "theories," we predict that it will receive a lot of attention, will generate a lot of research, and will be hotly debated at least over the foreseeable future.

The basic propositions of the Frequency Theory are simple enough: (*a*) in the course of trial-by-trial events, each item in the list acquires a certain number of "frequency units"; (*b*) frequency units are added to each item when (i) it is perceived in the study phase of the trial, (ii) when it is pronounced in anticipation of the feedback, (iii) when it is rehearsed after the feedback, and (iv) when some other item that elicits the item in question as implicit association occurs in the list and is perceived, pronounced, or rehearsed; (*c*) the subject discriminates between "right" and "wrong" items in a given pair on the basis of their respective frequency units.

A number of predictions and postdictions fall neatly out of the small set of basic assumptions of the Frequency Theory:

1. When some items occur as members of two different pairs in the same list, the list can be learned faster if the repeated items are all "right" than if they are all "wrong." If a repeated item is correct in one pair and incorrect in the other pair, learning is most difficult. This prediction has clearly been confirmed (59). The findings are particularly interesting in that from the point of view of common sense, subjects should have no greater difficulty learning to say "wrong" to repeated items than they should in learning to say "right" to each repeated item. Thus, the prediction and related findings are counter-intuitive. It makes this type of research interesting and greatly limits the number of alternative applicable explanations.

2. If a high frequency associate of a "right" item appears in the list as the "right " item in another pair, discrimination learning of both is facilitated; if it occurs as the "wrong" item of the other pair, learning of both pairs suffers interference. Experimental evidence in support of these predictions has been described by Ekstrand, Wallace & Underwood (59).

3. Pronunciation of "right" items facilitates discrimination, while pronunciation of "wrong" items interferes with it. The first half of the prediction has been demonstrated as an empirical fact by Carmean & Weir (37) in an experiment designed independently, and submitted for publication prior to the appearance, of the Frequency Theory. Other evidence relevant to this prediction has been reported by Kausler & Sardello (80) and by Un-

derwood & Freund (164). The sheer magnitude of some of the effects of pronunciation should delight those researchers who want to work with large effects.

4. Verbal discrimination performance is facilitated if "right" items have acquired frequency units prior to the experimental task proper, and retarded if frequency of "wrong" items has been built up prior to the task. Prior frequency of "right" and "wrong" items can be manipulated in another verbal discrimination task or in the context of another paradigm such as free recall. In either case, the effect of the manipulation is exactly what the Frequency Theory predicts (164, 165).

Some findings slightly embarrassing to the theory, however, should be mentioned.

First, in transfer experiments in which incorrect items initially start with a larger number of frequency units than correct items—having accumulated them in a previous task—the performance curve should drop to chance level at the point where frequency units for the two classes of items are balanced in the transfer task. This should be observable at least in the learning curves for the transfer list of individual subjects, but it is not (164, 165).

Second, according to the original version of the Frequency Theory, subjects should not be able to master a double-function discrimination list: a list in which each item serves as a correct item in one pair and as an incorrect item in another pair. While learning of such a double function discrimination list is very difficult and proceeds extremely slowly, subjects do learn under these conditions (79). As long as one assumes that frequency units accrue to a word regardless of its context (that is, the other member of the pair), a mechanism other than frequency discrimination must be postulated to account for such discrimination of double function lists, however slow such learning is.

Third, the Frequency Theory has difficulty with data showing transfer effects for sets of "right" and "wrong" responses (125).

These kinds of findings may imply that mechanisms other than frequency discrimination of nominal list items may be involved, or they may mean that the theory is incomplete or inadequate. But it is safe to predict that as long as no alternative theory is developed to account for verbal discrimination phenomena, the Frequency Theory will rule supreme, accounting for most of the findings, running into difficulty with some data, and in general keeping a large number of researchers fully occupied.

Ekstrand, Wallace & Underwood (59) have pointed out that any alternative theory will above all have to be able to handle the critical finding of the large difference in learning of lists with repeated items which are both "right" or which are both "wrong," a finding which we discussed above. The next few years should show whether any theorist dares to pick up the gauntlet.

Sensory modalities and memory.—Early students of memory were quite aware of the possibly important influences exerted by sensory modality in which material was presented upon recall. They also knew that these comparisons would be inconclusive owing to the lack of experimental control over the subject's handling of the material. McGeoch pointed out that a subject "may straightaway translate material presented to one sense organ into terms of other modalities . . . The receptor is the starting point of the practiced response, but it is by no means its sole determiner" (100, p. 169).

McGeoch examined the available evidence and concluded that differences between modalities are usually small and irregular in direction, and that the sensory character of the material is one of the "unimportant determiners" of rate of learning. Such a pronouncement by the master must have discouraged his disciples and their descendants from showing any interest in possible differences in retention and recall of visually and auditorily presented materials. For a long time, college sophomores serving time in verbal learning laboratories were exposed to the material to be learned in whatever modality happened to be more convenient to the experimenter.

Thus it has come to pass that the variable of input modality has been largely ignored in recent and contemporary theoretical conceptions of learning and memory. Theories postulate a sensory buffer or a perceptual store through which incoming material passes into the short-term memory (6, 50), but once the relevant information is safely inside, its origin in the eyes or in the ears is assumed to make no difference in what happens to it thereafter. Nevertheless, several reliable observations have recently alerted psychologists to the importance of the distinction between auditory and visual inputs, and a small but growing body of knowledge now exists about modality effects in short-term and "very short-term" memory.

A series of experiments by Murdock (111–113) has demonstrated pervasive modality effects in a variety of short-term memory tasks. Auditory presentation produces performance superior to visual presentation for paired-associate and serial recall, recognition, and single-trial free recall. Some of the differences are enormous. In one experiment (111) involving serial recall of mixed modality lists, probing for an item presented auditorily with another auditory item yielded recall four times as high as did any other combination of probe and target modality.

Serial position analyses suggest that the auditory superiority tends to be limited to the last few items in a list—the last two or three pairs in paired-associate lists (111) or the last six or seven items in free recall. Serial recall with the probe technique has sometimes shown auditory superiority over all serial positions (111). Auditory presentation results in higher recall even if to-be-remembered items are spoken by spatially distributed speakers, when there is no systematic relation between speaker location and temporal order of presentation, and when the probe is the spatial location of the speaker (113). Thus the superiority of auditory presentation is not necessarily related to the fact that the auditory modality is temporally distributed.

If one assumes, as Murdock (112) has done, that recognition tests obviate the need for the "search" phase of retrieval, then the superior recall of auditory material in tests of recognition of order and list membership implicates storage differences as the locus of the modality effect. These recognition data are of additional interest in that they indicate that auditory and visual inputs are equally well encoded or registered: modality had no effect on recognition of the last three items in a list. A similar lack of differences can be found for the last pair in paired-associate recall as well.

Auditory inputs seem more resistant to output interference than do visual inputs. The marked recency effect in digit-span tests under conditions when the subject pronounces visually presented items during input all but disappears under conditions of no pronunciation (45). This pronounced-visual-input task has also been shown to produce an instance of visual superiority: Ellis (60) found that recall from the last few positions in a list was superior when subjects read items aloud during presentation, but inferior to "silent" conditions when probes were for items in earlier parts of lists.

The disappearance or reversal in direction of modality effects when recall is from secondary memory constitutes a stumbling block for a number of possible explanations of modality effects. If auditory presentation is more effective than visual presentation because the short-term store holds only auditory information, or because auditory presentation ensures entry into a short-term processing buffer (23), then there should be modality differences in secondary memory as well. In a task such as single-trial free recall, all items "pass through" the short-term store, and if they reside in that store longer when presentation is auditory, or if the rehearsal buffer is more capacious for auditory inputs, then more information should be transferred to the long-term store for auditory items.

The notion that short-term memory might be an "acoustic store" has received quite an airing in recent work. While theorists are willing to entertain the possibility that initial storage of information can be either auditory, visual, or both, it has become most fashionable to assume that "the next level of processing"—in short-term memory proper—is exclusively auditory in nature.

Sperling was first to advocate the view that visual input is translated into an auditory analogue (154, 155). The idea received a great boost from observations that short-term memory for a series of acoustically similar items was impaired when compared with acoustically dissimilar items, regardless of whether the input modality was auditory or visual (72, 114).

Since students of memory are as quick on the draw when it comes to generalizing the findings as are any other psychologists, no one has worried too much about the boundary conditions under which this type of apparent translation takes place, and consequently it is very easy to talk oneself into believing that the initial encoding of verbal input is always auditory. The natural thing to do next is to analyze the auditory mode of presentation of material into finer components, such as acoustic and articulatory features (72, 177), and to extend the translation one more step. Despite this peculiar type of reductionism, we know that much of the mnemonic information human beings possess must be stored in some form analogous to visual images. Recognition of faces and familiar scenes proceeds without any apparent verbal mediation (51, 73, 145), and the storage of spatial information in short-term memory tasks (107, 142) could not possibly be handled by synesthesia alone. More generally, we fail to appreciate the logic—or perhaps intuition—involved in equating experimentally demonstrable modality effects with the properties of stored information.

Very little has been said or done about the modality effects in terms of the characteristics of auditory and visual signals per se, or about non-memorial aspects of processing of the two kinds of information. An outstanding exception is Savin's (143) examination of processing simultaneous auditory stimuli. We like this study because it is one that should have been done by those concerned with sensory channels and attention very soon after Broadbent's book (26) appeared, but was apparently overlooked. What Savin found was that the tendency to report one message and then the other has nothing particularly to do with sensory channels and attention-switching; he obtained the "channel-by-channel" reporting of simultaneous inputs when there was no channel distinction possible. His conclusion may prove to be important for modality effects in memory: the auditory system groups successive rather than simultaneous stimuli.

Why have we devoted so much space to the modality effects? The main reason is that they necessitate the rethinking of many problems and the rewriting of many theories. Auditory and visual information may be processed quite differently, and some phenomena may be entirely peculiar to one or the other modality. Understanding these differences seems to be a partial prerequisite to understanding human memory.

Storage and Retrieval

In the same way as storage of presented information depends on factors other than those prevailing at the time of the acquisition, retrieval of information from the memory store depends on things other than the contents of the store. In this section we will consider matters that are at least to some extent relevant to the interrelation between storage and retrieval, or to the ecphoric processes proper.

In order to understand retrieval processes, some basic principles must first be accepted. One of the most important of these was formulated by St. Augustine more than 1500 years ago: we cannot seek in our memory for anything of which we have no sort of recollection; by seeking something in our memory, "we declare, by that very act, that we have not altogether forgotten it; we still hold of it, as it were, a part, and by this part, which we hold, we seek that which we do not hold" (68, p. 442). Another principle, also known to the scholars of antiquity, says that the failure of retrieval does not necessarily imply the lack of appropriate information in the memory store.

Both principles are being continually overlooked by some researchers and theorists. A naive observer of the contemporary scene might assume that 1500 years is long enough to try to figure out exactly what it is that one has not forgotten about some previous experience, such as a word or some other verbal item in a memory task, and exactly what are the characteristics of the "part which we hold and by which we seek that which we do not hold." The successful evasion of these apparently fundamental problems by students of memory and verbal learning must be considered a ringing testimony to their ingenuity.

Part of the blame for this peculiar state of affairs must be laid to the chaining notion of associations. Associationistic pretheoretical assumptions preclude raising questions about recall mechanisms: after all, is it not a self-evident truth that recall is a function of a stimulus with which the response to be recalled is associated?

The changing conceptions of memory have not remedied the shortcoming. Instead of taking the knowledge of the "part which we hold and by which we seek that which we do not hold" for granted, as the traditional associationists do, most students of memory simply ignore the necessity of postulating such a "part." Instead, retrieval is thought of as consisting of two basic subprocesses, search and decision. A search and scanning process somehow finds access to stored information of all kinds, and a decision mechanism compares some property of the "found" information, such as its "familiarity" or its "list tag," with a hypothetical entity called the "criterion." Depending upon the results of such a comparison, the information is used to produce a corresponding response or is rejected, whereupon the search process continues until the desired information is found and identified as such, or when it grinds to a halt for as yet unknown reasons.

Despite the rather discouraging picture reflected by the inadequate handling of retrieval processes, some research seems to be gradually zeroing in on relevant issues. The impetus for it has come from the study of phenomena conveniently subsumed under the category of "coding processes."

Coding of individual items.—Underwood & Erlebacher define coding as "the changes, transformations, additions, subtractions, adumbrations, and so on which occur to and between verbal units as presented and which are, we assume, reflected in what is stored as memory" (162, p. 1). The definition is quite broad, and a reader who fixates too long on "subtractions" may become confused, but it is obviously better than no attempt at definition at all, a practice that characterizes the work of many authors who otherwise use the term. Underwood & Erlebacher's definition implies that a difference may exist between a physical stimulus presented to the subject for memorization and the trace, engram, information, or association that is laid down in the memory store. Differential covert responses that subjects are assumed to make to verbal items, implicit associative responses, mediating responses, and other like terms are synonyms for "coding operations."

Two different types of coding must be distinguished. We will refer to these as substitution and elaboration coding. Substitution coding refers to the replacement of the input stimulus by another symbol, the code, together with a general "decoding" rule—general in the sense that it might apply to many other symbols as well. The encoded version of the stimulus and the decoding rule are completely sufficient for the reproduction of the original stimulus. Translation of octal into binary digits, the unitization of "dits" and "dahs" of a telegraphic message into letters, words, or even longer phrases, and various mnemonic systems specifying a fixed correspondence between digits and letters represent examples of coding operations in which the to-be-remembered stimulus is completely redundant with its substitute code. Replacement of anagrams on the study sheet with their word-solutions in memory also qualifies as an instance of substitution coding, although the success of such coding in facilitating the performance on the memory task depends on how well various decoding rules are remembered (162).

Elaboration coding refers to the storage of additional nonredundant information with the verbal unit to be remembered. Such auxiliary information, if present at the time of attempted retrieval, may facilitate the reproduction of the verbal item to be remembered, but its exact copy in absence of original encoding is not sufficient for such production. Nor is it usually possible to state a general rule which permits the decoding of the coded information into the originally presented stimulus. Elaboration coding thus differs from substitution coding in important ways.

When subjects remember the serial position of an item in the free-recall task (187), when they use initial letters of words to retrieve these words (58), when their behavior at the time of recall suggests that implicit associative responses were elicited by input items at the time of presentation (67), or when the subject remembers that a word such as CLEVER was paired with a trigram VEC in the paired-associate list, to give but a few examples of an infinitely large number of possibilities, we have evidence for elaboration coding.

Wickens (178) has summarized many experiments that have convincingly demonstrated the complexity and variety of coding operations that take place in apparently straightforward memory tasks. In these experiments, subjects are first tested with a series of trigrams from some single class of materials, under the conditions of the short-term memory distracter task originally used by the Petersons. Investigators partial to the interference theory assume that over successive tests proactive inhibition is "built up," since recall of trigrams drops over the first few trials before reaching a stable asymptote. If on a given trial the type of material is changed, recall of this new "class" of material abruptly rises. This finding is referred to as "release from proactive inhibition."

The class changes sufficient for the production of the "release" effect are many and varied. They include changes of conceptual category, connotative meaning, input modality, physical characteristics of items, mode of presentation, and the like. As yet, no theory can predict what kind of changes will produce release, or how much release. Grammatical class change, for instance, is ineffective (179) while changes in word length do produce the release effect (178). Data of this kind, as Wickens points out, make it quite clear that in many short-term memory tasks subjects store much more information about verbal materials than is apparent in standard methods of assessment, and that they do so quickly and efficiently without any prodding by the experimenter.

Temporal coding.—Almost any experiment in verbal learning and memory requires the presentation of a series of events distributed over some temporal interval. Given the complex nature of coding operations indicated by many studies, it would be most surprising if coding of items to be remembered did not include information about the temporal date of the occurrence of an item. Storage of information about this "temporal" date—or the "time tag" of an item (184)—is referred to as temporal coding .We devote a separate short section to it since we believe that understanding of temporal coding processes is an extremely important step towards understanding of memory.

Research on temporal coding is just beginning. The first experiments are understandably directed at the question of whether such temporal coding in fact occurs. In search of the answer to this question, Peterson (127, 129), Hinrichs & Buschke (71), Morton (109), and Lockhart (89) have studied judgments of recency by forced-choice and absolute judgment procedures. In these experiments, the subject is shown a series of items (words, pictures, numbers) and at given points in the presentation sequence is required to estimate how recently a particular item occurred in the preceding series, or to choose the more recent of two previously shown items.

What is the mechanism of recency judgments of this type? The only serious explanation offered so far is the "strength hypothesis": recency of an item is judged on the basis of its trace strength (109, 129). In our opinion, the strength hypothesis is a product of desperation. It is entirely possible that in absence of any other relevant information the subject may, correctly or incorrectly, reason that of the two items the one appearing more familiar may look so because it occurred more recently, but this does not mean that the subject has no access to more direct information about the temporal code of an item in many other situations.

We suggest the following simple experiment to those who believe in the strength hypothesis. Present to the subject a series of items, one of which is the subject's own name or some other very conspicuous item. Test many subjects for recall of all the items from such series. All subjects will remember seeing their own name. Hence, the trace strength of the name must be very high, possibly higher than that of any other item. Then ask the subjects to estimate the recency of various items, including the name. If the subjects say that the name was the last item in the series, please write to us, and to *Science* or *Nature*. If the subjects are reasonably accurate in their recency judgments about the name, do some more thinking about the strength hypothesis.

We have not done such an experiment nor do we plan to: the outcome appears to be too obvious. Other variations on this theme may be more interesting. Memory for the temporal order of two highly conspicuous adjacent or closely separated items—say the subject's own name and that of his or her sweetheart—might be investigated with profit.

There are additional difficulties with the strength hypothesis, some of which may stem from the lack of clarity of the trace strength notion itself. For example, the flat portion of the serial position curve in single-trial free recall can in some sense be taken as indicative of equal trace strength for all items in these positions. According to the simple strength hypothesis, the subject should not be able to discriminate the temporal recency of these items, but we already know that discrimination of recency varies positively with the intraserial distance between the two items (71, 184).

Temporal coding appears to be relevant to the question of how subjects keep apart successive lists of similar items. Winograd (180, 181) has suggested that the list differentiation process might proceed through the storage of "time tags along with relevant item information." This interpretation of list discrimination is a step in the development of an explanation of the processes described—and only described—by the "selector mechanism" (167) and the classical concept of list discrimination.

Bower (16) has suggested that "time tags" allow a subject to select only the most recently presented items from a crowded store of items otherwise tagged as having been presented in the context of the experiment. Temporal coding and temporal distinctiveness have also been invoked to account for the reduction in proactive inhibition with spaced acquisition trials on the interfering material (163), and the notion may be useful in understanding the dissipation of proactive inhibition with increasing intertrial intervals in short-term memory tasks (91).

Zimmerman & Underwood (187) found that subjects could recall temporal features of input in free recall even when they were not specifically instructed to do so. Subjects instructed to remember temporal information in the experiment recalled as many items as those instructed to remember items only. This finding suggests that temporal information about items is processed without any apparent "cost" to the system: a temporal code about each item is part and parcel of what the subject stores about the material to be remembered even under instructions to process only item information.

The issue of temporal coding is closely related to the whole question of memory for serial order. Tasks requiring subjects to make recency judgments about items appear to be the short-term discrete analogues of the much-neglected method of reconstruction. Bryden (31) has proposed a model of serial recall which is independent of item-to-item associations and according to which recall is guided solely by stored temporal information about items. There is also an obvious relationship between absolute judgments of recency (127) and the "reverse probe" technique (5): given an item from a short series, the subject must indicate its serial position.

Systematic study of temporal coding in all its aspects and in its relation to many problems of memory deserves much more emphasis than it has received so far. At the present time, experimental studies are hard to find in the literature, theoretical concepts are still ingenuous, and the whole approach to the issue is characterized by hesitation and reluctance. It is as if no one knew exactly what to do next. And yet, as shown by Peterson (127) among others, the literature on verbal learning and memory is replete with case histories demonstrating the profound importance that temporal discrimination and temporal coding of events and their order plays in determining subjects' performance in retention and forgetting of verbal material.

Cued and noncued recall.—The Latin-speaking sage who first proposed that *"ex nihilo nihil fit"* probably made the observation when pondering about retrieval processes. He must have realized, as did St. Augustine much later, that if a person is not, in some as yet unspecified sense, "aware" of certain characteristics of an event or item stored earlier, he possibly could not retrieve that item from the store. These characteristics, when present in the subject's active memory at the time of attempted retrieval, constitute the retrieval cues.

All retrieval of information from the memory store is cued. The distinction between cued and noncued recall (8, 48, 56, 57, 75, 78), strictly speaking, refers to the specificity of cues that are present at the time of attempted retrieval, unless the terms are used to describe experimental operations. Free recall, for instance, can be thought of as "noncued." But this usage of the term only illustrates our present ignorance as to what constitute the cues for retrieval in this situation. Luckily for the experimenter, the subject usually understands what the experimenter wants him to do when he is told to recall the words from the "most recent" or "the first" list.

Effectiveness of retrieval cues.—While there are many questions one can pose about retrieval processes, one which deserves highest priority at the present time, in our opinion, has to do with the effectiveness of retrieval cues. One need not do any experiments to know that (*a*) many kinds of cues are effective in getting the subject to recall the desired item or items, and (*b*) that large variations exist in the effectiveness of different kinds of retrieval cues. Exactly what determines the effectiveness of retrieval cues?

One thing with which few theorists would probably disagree is the belief that efficiency of retrieval cues depends strongly upon the nature of coding operations that have taken place at the time of the storage of the material to be remembered. A necessary condition of the effectiveness of a retrieval cue seems to be the correspondence between it and some part of the auxiliary information stored with the stimulus item. Another factor determining the efficiency of a retrieval cue is the number of items for which it serves as the cue (57). A third variable shown to be highly relevant is the strength of the pre-experimental association between the cue and the stored item (8). But apart from these rather obvious facts, relatively little is known about the conditions determining the nature and efficiency of retrieval cues.

Slamecka seems to be the only theorist so far who believes that retrieval processes are at least partially independent of the format of stored information. On the basis of an experiment showing that part of a free-recall list does not facilitate the recall of the other part—reminiscent of a similar finding under somewhat different conditions by Brown (28)—Slamecka proposed a dual-component hypothesis according to which "perception of the general list structure forms the basis for a retrieval plan which then operates upon the independently stored traces" (152, p. 504). This notion appears implausible to us, for reasons into which we cannot go in this chapter, but it does represent a novel way of thinking about the relation between storage and retrieval.

Temporal coding in retrieval.—An extremely important question, in our opinion, concerns the role that temporal coding plays in effecting retrieval. Intuitively it is obvious that availability of information about the temporal date of the occurrence of an item is an absolutely necessary condition for the recall or recognition of the item as a member of a particular collection of other items, but few experiments have been directed at this question. Brelsford, Freund & Rundus (24) had subjects both judge the recency of items and recall them in a continuous short-term memory task with paired associates. They found that the accuracy of recency judgment was highly contingent upon correct responding on probe recall tests. Even when a tested item was well within the range of the typical recency effect, judgment of temporal position was quite inaccurate if the subject could not respond correctly on that paired-associate test.

Because of the correlational nature of these data it is difficult to interpret them, but an obvious possibility is that recall of a pair of items in this situation is mediated by reasonably precise and readily accessible temporal codes of both stimulus and response members of a pair, rather than, or in addition to, being determined by a "direct association" between the two.

Recognition memory.—An upsurge of interest in recognition memory, apparent in recent literature, serves as yet another symptom of changing times. The pretheoretical assumptions underlying the stimulus-response associative approach to problems of verbal learning always made those who followed those assumptions wary when they were faced with phenomena of recognition memory. Nothing is more admirable, from a mechanistic point of view, than a stimulus eliciting an associated response. But a subject who observes a test item in a recognition memory task and tells the experimenter that he "remembers" seeing that item in the earlier study list, that the test item "looks familiar," or that he is quite "confident" that the stimulus is an "old" one, even if he communicates these messages to the experimenter by pushing a lifeless button, conjures up images of introspecting homunculi sitting in the middle of the head, deeply absorbed in thought. Under the circumstances, by far the best action indicated was to steer clear of recognition memory, and a study of the literature over the past few decades proves that this is exactly what students of verbal learning did.

Now it appears that recognition memory is here to stay. To those who despair of the limited capacity shown in some tests of memory, studies in recognition memory offer the solace of impressive levels of performance. Shepard's (145) subjects looked through a series of approximately 600 stimuli—words, sentences, or pictures—and correctly recognized "old" stimuli 90, 88, or 98 per cent of the time, for the three classes of stimuli respectively.

To those who just do not have the heart to administer 120 paired-associate trials to their subjects (66), or who otherwise hesitate to bore them to tears with rote learning of nonsense syllables, recognition memory experiments also offer a way out. One can do these experiments with pictures as items to be remembered, and one can even blur them or turn them upside down. This sounds like fun! But such experiments also provide instructive data. For instance, degradation does not seem to affect recognizability of pictures too much if it occurs at both the input and test, but degradation at only one point does lead to impairment in performance (51).

Students of memory who are on the lookout for interesting puzzles find them in recognition memory. Two perennials remain as mysterious as ever: first, why does recognition performance deteriorate with the increase in the proportion of "lures," that is "new" items (30, 84, 150); and second, why are unfamiliar or less frequently occurring verbal items recognized more easily than familiar or frequently occurring items (2, 144, 145)? Although it is possible to treat the first finding as a self-evident truth not requiring any explanation, the challenge of explaining the phenomenon by relating it to other known facts about memory remains. The second finding is also successfully resisting attempts at its conceptual clarification.

A new puzzle for those who have already tried the other ones is to figure out whether "organization" of the learning material has an effect on recognition memory or not. Everyone agrees that appropriate organization facilitates recall, but its role in recognition performance is unclear. Some investigators find that organization does not affect recognition (18, 85), while others find that it does (17, 97). Mandler et al. (97) have proposed the notion of a "postrecognition retrieval check" to account for their finding of the correlation between degree of categorization of material and recognition performance. The notion sounds intriguing, but since we do not understand it, we prefer to classify Mandler et al. as part of the puzzle.

Measurement of retention by recognition procedures provides interesting insights into the format of storage of materials such as connected discourse. Experiments show that subjects have excellent memory for the meaning of sentences, and rather poor memory for the exact lexical units and their grammatical arrangement (131, 141). When words are presented to the subjects one at a time, however, subjects are no more seduced by synonym lures than they are by unrelated distractors (97). This finding suggests a rather fine discrimination of meaning.

Signal detection analysis.—Recognition memory also provides good research opportunities for those students who like exotic quantitative techniques that work in other fields. We refer here to the new fad of the signal detection analysis. The theory of signal detection, in our opinion, will rank with the invention of the memory drum and the paired-associate list-learning method in changing the course of history in our field. Whether the change will be for good or for bad remains to be seen. We think it will have some meritorious effects: it will stifle wild fantasy, put a clamp on silly speculation, and keep many people from raising new and therefore irrelevant questions about recognition memory. It is so much easier to explain experimental data by talking about differences in sensitivity, criterion, or both, than to admit the existence of naughty problems!

Given the choice—and we are afraid that we will have none—we would take information about hits and false alarms any day in preference to ROC (Receiver Operating Characteristic) or MOC (Memory Operating Characteristic) curves with slopes of less than unity (2, 55, 144, 176, 186). To the extent that the slopes of ROC curves depart from unity, measures of sensitivity and criterion are not independent. Lack of independence between the two measures removes the only possible reason for using signal detection measures. What is wrong with forced-choice methods?

The section on recognition memory would be incomplete without mentioning an extremely interesting finding reported by Cofer et al. (43). Cofer and his associates showed their subjects nouns in presence or absence of adjectival modifiers and tested subjects' recognition memory for the nouns (Exp. VII). Recognition was considerably higher for the "nouns alone" than for the "modified nouns" condition. To us this finding signals the importance of retrieval problems in recognition memory: available information is not automatically accessible when an "old" test item is presented.

When Memory Fails

When a person recalls or recognizes something now, but does not on a subsequent occasion, forgetting is said to have occurred. Understanding of the mechanisms and processes underlying forgetting in its infinitely many forms ranks among the major objectives of students of ecphoric processes. In the following short section that we can devote to the topic, we will concentrate on theoretical problems and issues.

Forgetting in short-term memory.—Most current models of short-term memory postulate two separate storage mechanisms, a short-term store and a long-term store (6, 63, 140, 174). The two-store notions usually hold that (*a*) all the material presented under typical conditions enters the short-term store, and (*b*) some of this material is transferred into the long-term store (6, 174). This means that some items accessible in the short-term store now cannot be recalled later. What do contemporary thinkers say about this type of forgetting?

The most popular position at the present time appears to be what George Miller called the "leaky bucket" hypothesis: as items enter the short-term store, a point is reached at which old items "leak out" as fast as new ones are put in, or existing memory traces fade away as fast as new ones are created (106). The modern versions of this hypothesis are couched in more "scientific" terms, but the basic conception is the same. The short-term store is assumed to have a limited capacity for holding information, and once that capacity is reached, further incoming items displace those currently in the short-term store according to some probabilistic schedule.

Research concerned with the properties of such a displacement mechanism has barely begun. It has been known for a few years that some 15 to 30 sec of interpolated "neutral" activity, such as counting numbers backwards, "empties" the short-term store (63, 135). Results of recent research by Glanzer et al. (64) now permit the short-term store to be "emptied" of all the material contained in it in two seconds flat. We leave it as an exercise to the reader to figure out how this could be done. If he fails he can consult the interesting paper by Glanzer et al.

If the interpolated material contains items already in the short-term store, it produces less displacement than does material completely different from that in the store (175). This finding implies, if one believes in the existence of the short-term store, a comparison of the incoming information with that contained in the short-term store prior to the placement of the incoming information into the store. Depending upon the outcome of this comparison, redundant information is not entered into the store or is entered into the same "slot" in which its copies already exist.

Most theorists agree on the nature of the mechanisms that save the material in the short-term store from being "lost" or forgotten: transfer of information from the short-term store into the long-term store is a consequence of an active process called "rehearsal" (6, 174). Some rather ingenious techniques have been used by investigators such as Peterson (128), Rabbitt (138), and Crowder (49) in support of the reality of rehearsal-like processes responsible for converting information in the short-term store into a more permanent trace. The next important step to be taken should be the working out of the characteristics and properties of the rehearsal process. To say that rehearsal provides a vehicle for the transfer of information from short-term into long-term memory defines an interesting problem, but obviously does not solve it.

Decay theory.—The attempts to revive the ancient notion of decay of memory traces and to make use of it in contemporary theoretical thinking about forgetting seem to have run out of steam. The British psychologists who advocated the decay notion—Broadbent, Brown, and Conrad—have not had much to add to their earlier writings, and American psychologists who briefly flirted with the notion have given it up, unless one identifies displacement with decay. Most experts, however, think of displacement as more akin to interference than to decay (174).

Some remnants of decay theory of forgetting, however, are found in various disguises in theoretical accounts of recognition memory. Theorists such as Bower (17), Kintsch (85), and Murdock (112) all assume that recognition tests eliminate the problem of accessibility of stored traces: the test stimulus somehow automatically—presumably because it is nominally equivalent with an earlier item—provides access to the stored trace. Given this assumption, forgetting in recognition memory, that is failure to recognize an "old" test item as "old," must be attributable to some kind of deterioration or modification of the stored trace.

In our opinion, the advantages of the postulation of "automatic access" to the stored trace in recognition memory tasks are the same as the advantages of theft over honest toil, to borrow an analogy from Bertrand Russell as quoted by Stevens (157, p. 14). We can only ascribe the automatic access assumption to the corrupting influence or abuse of the theory of signal detection, and hope that the record will soon be set straight.

Interference theory.—At a major verbal learning conference held in 1959 (40), attended by a dozen or so most prominent investigators, Postman began his review of the state of affairs with respect to interference theory by stating that, "Interference theory occupies an unchallenged position as the major significant analysis of the process of forgetting" (132, p. 152). Now, barely 10 years later, the theory lies in a state of ferment if not chaos.

The analysis and description of events bridging Postman's optimistic assessment of the health of the theory in 1959 and the present confusion would make for fascinating reading to anyone who has a bit of the sociologist of science in him. Those who are impatient with the slow pace at which our knowledge of the phenomena of memory expands would also find food for thought from a close study of the recent history of the interference theory. The extinction-recovery version of the interference theory (81, 101, 132, 166) that indeed ruled the domain of the study of forgetting without challenge since its inception in 1940 (105) has for all practical intents and purposes been relegated to the attic full of past curiosities.

The handwriting had been on the wall for some time. The Underwood-Postman theory of extra-experimental forgetting (166) had run into great resistance from the data. Theoretical expectations about laboratory-produced retroactive and proactive interference also rather regularly came out second best. While some of the loyal adherents of the theory either tried to explain away the discrepancies between the data and theory, or to patch up the theory by adding little bits and pieces where needed, "neutral" observers had felt for some time that the demise of the theory was simply a matter of time.

The historic moment came when Postman delivered his vice-presidential address to a symposium at the meeting of the American Association for the

Advancement of Science in New York, on the last day of 1967. The substance of his comments was subsequently published in two papers of Postman co-authored by Stark & Fraser (137) and Stark (136). Those who are familiar with the interference theory and who read and study these two papers in detail will realize what an impact the two papers will have on future experimentation and theorizing.

Knowing full well that any summary of the rather unsettled state of affairs can only distort and confuse the picture even further, we offer what we understand to be the situation now. Unlearning is still a major concept in the theory but it has changed its character drastically. Rather than referring to the extinction of both specific (stimulus-term and response-term) and general (experimental context and specific response terms) associations, it is now envisaged as a kind of suppression of the whole first-list repertoire of responses in the course of second-list learning. During learning of the first list, the subject limits his response selection to those occurring in that list. When he comes to learn the second list containing different responses, new "criteria of selective arousal" must be established. These criteria require the suppression of the first-list repertoire. When the subject is asked, immediately after learning the second list, to recall the first list, the selector mechanism cannot shift back to the criteria used during first-list acquisition because of its "inertia." With passage of time, however, the set to give second-list responses dissipates, resulting in the lifting of the suppression of the first-list responses and consequent observable "spontaneous recovery."

This formulation by Postman and his associates does not represent a new theory, but rather only some initial guidelines for the development of a new theory. But even in its tentative form, it is radically different from the old theory. The emphasis on response repertoires—rather than on specific associations—the central position of the concept of the selector mechanism, the postulated relation between the scanning process and criteria of selection, and the elevation of the concept of "generalized response competition" (118) to a position of dominance have drastically changed the nature of the theory.

It is far too early to tell exactly what is going to happen next. In the present confusion it is difficult to see the forest for the trees. We suspect it will be several years before the new theory will acquire clearly identifiable properties and characteristics. In the meantime, interference phenomena will become fair game for heretics such as Slamecka (153), who has raised some interesting questions of fundamental importance about some of the laboratory rituals developed over the years, such as the use of multiple lists, in studying retroactive and proactive phenomena.

The current revolution in the domain of interference theory contains two important lessons to be heeded by all researchers and theorists. First, the fact that the theory was found wanting testifies to its truly singular position in our field. Very few collections of speculations politely referred to as theories have been specified precisely enough so that they could be proved wrong. The specificity of the extinction-recovery version of the interference theory was its major strength. By all means, let us have more theories that can be proved wrong. Therein lies our only hope for progress.

The second lesson to be learned from the story of interference theory is a bit more embarrassing. Why did it take so long for the theory to be found out? At the same conference in 1959 at which Postman declared the interference theory to occupy "an unchallenged position," Melton (102) explicitly and in no uncertain terms pointed to two kinds of critical evidence necessary for the acceptance of the unlearning of specific associations as the major mechanism of interference. First, Melton wanted to have evidence about the correlation between the unavailability of specific first-list pairs following second-list learning and frequency of nonreinforced intrusions of the same specific responses during the second-list learning. Secondly, he wanted to have evidence that in a situation in which an A-B list is followed by learning of A-C and C-D pairs in a mixed list, items given the A-C treatment in the interpolated list would be significantly less available in the retention test than the items not represented in the interpolated list.

Why was the evidence Melton wanted in 1959 not produced in 1960 or 1961? Ceraso (38, 39) did report experiments of this kind in 1964 and 1968, with results largely at variance with those expected on the basis of the notion of unlearning of specific A-B associations, but for reasons beyond our ken, nobody apparently paid much attention to them.

Melton made some other rather interesting observations at the 1959 conference. When Postman discussed the notion of generalized response competition that now has assumed central importance in the "new look" of the interference theory, Melton said that there seemed to be a "strong commonality" between the finding of unlearning of the first list in absence of any specific formal or meaningful similarity to the second list on the one hand, and "the problems of mental set and shift" on the other hand. Melton may have seen more than 10 years into the future when he added that "an independently useful contribution to the science of memory phenomena will come from systematic pursuit of the concept of generalized response interference with this commonality in mind" (102, p. 186).

Trace-dependent and cue-dependent forgetting.—The currently popular conceptualizations of the forgetting process, be they interference, displacement, or decay, completely ignore and have nothing to say about a very common type of forgetting: the information sought for is available in the memory store, but is inaccessible at a given time because of inadequate retrieval cues. If a subject cannot recall a particular item in the absence of specific retrieval cues, but can do so if the experimenter gives him a part of the missing information (8, 48, 56), the apparent forgetting under the noncued recall conditions cannot be attributed to unlearning, displacement, or decay of the association or trace, nor to competition, but must be understood in terms of the presence or absence of appropriate retrieval cues.

It would be useful, therefore, to draw a distinction between trace-dependent and cue-dependent forgetting, and to evaluate extant theories of forgetting in the light of the distinction. Trace-dependent forgetting is a function of processes that have been described in the past by terms such as unlearning, displacement, and decay. Cue-dependent forgetting is attributable to the changes in the quantity and quality of retrieval cues between two retention tests separated in time. This distinction is an old one (100, 103), and in our opinion it is high time that investigators and theorists start paying attention to its implications.

Forgetting in most situations probably represents some combination of changes in the nature of stored information with a retention interval and the lack of appropriate retrieval cues that otherwise would provide access to the information. An important experimental task is to work out the relative contribution of these two sources of forgetting in any given task. This whole approach might be useful also for testing the most fundamental assumption underlying interference theory, namely that the retroactive and proactive designs used in the laboratory merely accelerate the rate of forgetting that would "normally" occur outside the laboratory (81, 132). We may find that retroaction designs produce a different kind of forgetting altogether, different in the sense that the contribution from the two sources—changed memory traces and changed retrieval cues—differs from that characterizing forgetting outside the laboratory.

Theories of Memory

Among the important events that took place during the period under review was the emergence of attempts at the construction of "comprehensive" theories of memory. The precursor of these theories was Broadbent's (26) sketch of a memory system composed of a short-term store, a limited capacity channel, and a "store of conditional probabilities of past events." It has taken 10 years since this modest beginning for the first relatively full-fledged conceptual account of human memory to appear (6).

Despite the frequent claims to the contrary, researchers in verbal learning never shunned theory completely. There was a brief period in the 1950s when analysis of variance tables in the Results sections were accompanied by explanations in the Discussion sections as to the reasons for using one or another error term, as there are papers today in which the Discussion sections are empty, but by and large researchers in verbal learning have been as much concerned with the deeper meaning of their findings as have been psychologists in other fields. The earlier attempts to make more general sense out of experimental findings produced theories concerned with specific phenomena: serial position curve, reminiscence, paired-associate learning, transfer, retroactive inhibition, intralist similarity, distributed practice, and the like. A general theory of verbal learning, however, was never attempted.

Students of memory, on the other hand, have shown no inhibitions against grandiose speculation under the guise of general theories of memory. A variety of more or less general and more or less ambitious theories have already made their appearance (6, 146, 155, 174), and at the time of this writing several additional ones are in press. A book edited by Norman and entitled *Models of Memory* (121) contains chapters by Norman & Rumelhart, Shiffrin, Bernbach, Morton, Kintsch, and Wickelgren, each of which strikes out in the direction of a comprehensive theory of memory.

To this list we must also add theoretical papers by Bower (16), Crowder & Morton (50), Mandler (92), Neisser (117), and Norman (120). All these papers—in Neisser's case the final chapter of his book—deal with theoretical issues of memory, although they do not aspire to the status of a complete system like the papers in the previous category.

Most of the "comprehensive" conceptual schemes have been proposed by psychologists who would not mind being called mathematical modelers. Most distinguish between a general theoretical framework and specific models that relate the general framework to experimental facts. Many, but not all, represent what we will refer to as "boxes-in-the-head" type of theory of memory: the memory system is thought of as consisting of several different storage "compartments," with mnemonic information being transferred from one compartment to another.

The number of similar but different theories seems to be multiplying at an accelerated rate, and they all vie for the attention of potential adherents. In our more pessimistic moments we have visions of hundreds of different theories of memory, say around 1975, being subjected to factor analysis and discriminated from one another in terms of weights on different major factors.

Because of limitations of space, we can say only a few things about what we believe to be the most ambitious and most highly developed theory, namely that proposed by Atkinson & Shiffrin.

Atkinson and Shiffrin theory.—The theory of Atkinson & Shiffrin (6, but see also 4, 5, 23, 25, 146) in many ways represents the distilled wisdom of many contemporary thinkers who have been imprinted on the electronic computer. It is the most enterprising, comprehensive, and detailed account of human memory seen from the information processing point of view.

The structure of memory is held to consist of three major components: the sensory register, the short-term store, and the long-term store. Incoming sensory information enters the sensory register, is "lost" from it or transferred into short-term store, from which it is also either "lost" or transferred (copied) into the long-term store. The description of such a structure consists of the specification of the characteristics and capabilities of different components of the system as well as the specification of the nature of the mechanisms underlying the loss of information from various components and their transfer from one part of the system to another. It is complemented by a description of "control processes," flexible aspects of the system controlled by the subject.

In most verbal learning and memory experiments, the sensory buffer can be ignored, since all incoming information in typical experiments readily reaches the short-term store. An item such as a number-letter pair that enters the short-term store can always be recalled if it is tested immediately after its presentation, but it decays in a few seconds unless it is placed into the "rehearsal buffer" which constitutes the essential part of the short-term store. An item in the buffer is transferred from the buffer into the long-term store with a probability that is proportional to the length of its stay in the buffer, and it is displaced from the buffer by other incoming items also on a probabilistic basis.

The long-term store serves primarily two functions: it is used to identify stimuli in the sensory buffer so that meaningful representations of these stimuli can be entered into the short-term store, and it serves as a storage "space" for information copied into it from the short-term store.

An item can always be recalled from the short-term store as long as it stays in the rehearsal buffer. The success of retrieval of items from the long-term store depends upon the efficacy of the "search process" which is made along some dimension or on the basis of some available cues. Atkinson & Shiffrin have little to say about retrieval—although it is said to be the "crux" of the theory—other than to offer names for some putative components of retrieval: search, recovery, and response generation.

The fate of the information copied into the long-term store from the short-term store depends upon the mechanisms responsible for transfer. Some information can enter the long-term store as a consequence of rehearsal of that information in the buffer. In that case the information transferred into the long-term store "would be in a relatively weak state and easily subject to interference" (6, p. 150). Alternatively, rehearsal operations may be replaced with various "coding operations which will increase the strength of the stored information" (6, p. 115). A coding process is thought of as a "select alteration and/or addition to the information in the short-term store as the result of a search of the long-term store" (6, p. 115).

Atkinson & Shiffrin's theoretical framework for human memory is, as they themselves put it, "extremely general." As such it can be easily criticized on many counts, as can any other theory that has ever existed in psychology. We would like to express our dissatisfaction with only three matters:

1. Some fits between "observed and theoretical probabilities," e.g., Figures 14 and 20 in (6), in our humble opinion, at best oversimplify and at worst distort the facts. These figures are useful only for some kinds of didactic purposes.

2. We do not understand how data such as those described for Experiment IV in the Spences' book (6, p. 153 ff) and in the paper by Brelsford & Atkinson (23) can possibly be reconciled with the theory. These experiments show that overt rehearsal of items prolongs their residence in the buffer, without having any effect on the transfer of relevant information into the long-term store. These findings, we feel, rather than supporting the

theory, represent strong evidence not only against Atkinson & Shiffrin's theory, but any other "boxes-in-the-head" theory that postulates transfer of information into the long-term store through the short-term store.

3. We are worried about the bent arrows in Atkinson & Shiffrin's Figures 1 and 2 in (6). These bent arrows labeled "lost" illustrate the fact that, according to the theory, information decays from the sensory register, short-term store, and perhaps even the long-term store. We are worried because we would like to know what happens to an item "knocked out" of the short-term store. Where does "lost" information go? The arrows point to the left-hand bottom corner of the printed page, but that does not help us very much. We also feel that the whole notion of items being "lost" violates the first law of thermodynamics. We rather like the idea—expressed by Herbart over 100 years ago—that information in any store remains there, in one form or another, and sometimes simply cannot be used for the desired purposes. We can only hope that the mystery of the downward pointing arrows in the system will be cleared up eventually. Our own recommended remedy is simply to erase the "lost" arrow pointing from the short-term store into the void—this has been done in (146)—and presume that all information in short-term store is transferred into the long-term store—but this has not yet been done. Changing the name of the short-term store to something like active memory, operational memory (130), or even consciousness might also constitute a modest improvement.

The theory seems to be undergoing rapid changes. One of the problems that the readers may have in the future is to keep up with all of them. For instance, in one place (6) loss of information from the long-term store is postulated and one parameter of the model is provided to describe it, but in another place (146) the notion of decay from long-term store is abandoned, and failure of retrieval is attributed entirely to the failure of the search mechanism, that is, to the inaccessibility of the stored information.

Despite these and some other minor blemishes, Atkinson & Shiffrin's theory can be set as a paragon to all researchers. Its virtues easily outweigh its deficiences. It genuinely and explicitly attempts to come to grips with, or at least say something about, most of the important aspects of human memory. It generates some interesting implications for experimental results from the continuous paired-associate tasks, it has varied success with other paradigms, and it is comprehensive—at least in comparison with other existing theories. It may turn out to be somewhat more intractable *vis-à-vis* phenomena shaped by the orienting attitudes of traditional work in verbal learning—transfer, mediation, and interference effects in list-learning experiments—but, one might argue, the extremely complex tasks generating these phenomena should not be investigated anyhow before we have developed a modicum of understanding of simpler tasks.

Conclusion

We mentioned at the outset that nothing very much has changed over the past hundred years in the understanding of how people learn and remember things. Anyone disputing this assertion is either not familiar with the history of our field, confuses new labels for phenomena with understanding of these phenomena, or is fixated on minor details while we are talking about the general picture. We have hundreds and thousands of little facts, we can make quantitative instead of qualitative statements, we can talk about all kinds of fine details in experimental data and characteristics of underlying processes—but the broad picture we have of human memory in 1970 does not differ from that in 1870. We know of no compelling reason why a chapter like this, discussing the kind of research we have discussed, could not have been written a hundred years ago; but it was not.

What is the solution to the problem of lack of genuine progress in understanding memory? It is not for us to say, because we do not know. But one possibility does suggest itself: why not start looking for ways of experimentally studying, and incorporating into theories and models of memory, one of the truly unique characteristics of human memory: its knowledge of its own knowledge. No extant conceptualization, be it based on stimulus-response associations or an information processing paradigm, makes provisions for the fact that the human memory system cannot only produce a learned response to an appropriate stimulus or retrieve a stored image, but it can also rather accurately estimate the likelihood of its success in doing it (29, 70).

Hart (70) has reported some experimental data in support of the reality of what he calls the memory-monitoring process and has thus pointed the way to the study of the most important and the least understood aspect of human memory. We cannot help but feel that if there is ever going to be a genuine breakthrough in the psychological study of memory, one that would save the students of ecphoric processes from the fate we talked about at the beginning of this chapter, it will, among other things, relate the knowledge stored in an individual's memory to his knowledge of that knowledge.

LITERATURE CITED

1. Adams, J. A. *Human Memory* (McGraw-Hill, New York, 326 pp., 1967)
2. Allen, L. R., Garton, R. F. The influence of word-knowledge on the word-frequency effect in recognition memory. *Psychon. Sci.,* **10,** 401–2 (1968)
3. Arbuckle, T. Y. Differential retention of individual paired associates within an RTT "learning" trial. *J. Exptl. Psychol.,* **74,** 443–51 (1967)
4. Atkinson, R. C., Brelsford, J. W., Shiffrin, R. M. Multiprocess models for memory with applications to a continuous presentation task. *J. Math. Psychol.,* **4,** 277–300 (1967)
5. Atkinson, R. C., Hansen, D. N., Bernbach, H. A. Short-term memory with young children. *Psychon. Sci.,* **1,** 255–56 (1964)
6. Atkinson, R. C., Shiffrin, R. M. Human memory: A proposed system and its control processes. In *The Psychology of Learning and Motivation,* Vol. 2, 89–195 (Spence, K. W., Spenee, J. T., Eds., Academic Press, New York, 249 pp., 1968)
7. Bahrick, H. P. Discriminative and associative aspects of pictorial paired associate learning: Acquisition and retention. *J. Exptl. Psychol.,* **80,** 113–19 (1969)
8. Bahrick, H. P. Measurement of memory by prompted recall. *Ibid.,* **79,** 213–19 (1969)
9. Battig, W. F. Paired-associate learning. In *Verbal Behavior and General Behavior Theory,* 146–71 (See Ref. 54)
10. Battig, W. F., Berry, J. K. Effects of number and similarity of pre-training alternatives on paired-associate performance on pre-trained and new items under correction and non-correction procedures. *J. Exptl. Psychol.,* **72,** 722–30 (1966)
11. Bernbach, H. A. A forgetting model for paired-associate learning. *J. Math. Psychol.,* **2,** 128–44 (1965)
12. Bernbach, H. A. Stimulus learning and recognition in paired-associate learning. *J. Exptl. Psychol.,* **75,** 513–19 (1967)
13. Bevan, W., Dukes, W. F., Avant, L. The effect of variation in specific stimuli on memory for their superordinates. *Am. J. Psychol.,* **79,** 250–57 (1966)
14. Bevan, W., Dukes, W. F. Stimulus-variation and recall: The role of belongingness. *Ibid.,* **80,** 309–12 (1967)
15. Bousfield, W. A. The problem of meaning in verbal learning. In *Verbal Learning and Verbal Behavior,* 81–91 (Cofer, C. N., Ed., McGraw-Hill, New York, 241 pp., 1961)
16. Bower, G. A multicomponent theory of the memory trace. In *The Psychology of Learning and Motivation,* Vol. 1, 229–325 (Spence, K. W., Spence, J. T., Eds., Academic Press, New York, 381 pp., 1967)
17. Bower, G., Clark, M. C., Lesgold, A. M., Winzenz, D. Hierarchical retrieval schemes in recall of categorized word lists. *J. Verbal Learn. Verbal Behav.,* **8,** 323–43 (1969)
18. Bower, G., Lesgold, A. M., Tieman, D. Grouping operations in free recall. *Ibid.,* 481–93
19. Bower, G., Lesgold, A. M. Organization as a determinant of part-to-whole transfer in free recall. *Ibid.,* 501–6
20. Bower, G., Trabasso, T. Reversals prior to solution in concept identification. *J. Exptl. Psychol.,* **66,** 409–18 (1963)
21. Bregman, A. S. Distribution of practice and between-trials interference. *Can. J. Psychol.,* **21,** 1–14 (1967)
22. Bregman, A. S. Forgetting curves with semantic, phonetic, graphic, and contiguity cues. *J. Exptl. Psychol.,* **78,** 539–46 (1968)
23. Brelsford, J. W., Jr., Atkinson, R. C. Recall of paired-associates as a function of overt and covert rehearsal procedures. *J. Verbal Learn. Verbal Behav.,* **7,** 730–36 (1968)
24. Brelsford, J. W., Jr., Freund, R., Rundus, D. Recency judgments in short-term memory tasks. *Psychon. Sci.,* **8,** 247–48 (1967)
25. Brelsford, J. W., Jr., Shiffrin, R. M., Atkinson, R. C. Multiple reinforce-

ment effects in short-term memory. *Brit. J. Math. Statist. Psychol.*, **21**, 1–19 (1968)
26. Broadbent, D. E. *Perception and Communication* (Pergamon, London, 1958)
27. Brooks, L. R. Spatial and verbal components of the act of recall. *Can. J. Psychol.*, **22**, 349–68 (1968)
28. Brown, J. Reciprocal facilitation and impairment of free recall. *Psychon. Sci.*, **10**, 41–42 (1968)
29. Brown, R., McNeill, D. The "tip of the tongue" phenomenon. *J. Verbal Learn. Verbal Behav.*, **5**, 325–37 (1967)
30. Bruce, D., Cofer, C. N. An examination of recognition and free recall as measures of acquisition and long-term retention. *J. Exptl. Psychol.*, **75**, 283–89 (1967)
31. Bryden, M. P. A model for the sequential organization of behavior. *Can. J. Psychol.*, **21**, 37–55 (1967)
32. Bugelski, B. R. Images as mediators in one-trial paired-associate learning. II: Self-timing in successive lists. *J. Exptl. Psychol.*, **77**, 328–34 (1968)
33. Buschke, H. Two kinds of short-term storage. *Psychon. Sci.*, **8**, 419–20 (1967)
34. Buschke, H. Perceiving and encoding two kinds of item-information. *Percept. Psychophys.*, **3**, 331–36 (1968)
35. Buschke, H., Hinrichs, J. V. Controlled rehearsal and recall order in serial list retention. *J. Exptl. Psychol.*, **78**, 502–9 (1968)
36. Calkins, M. W. Association. *Psychol. Rev.*, **3**, 32–49 (1896)
37. Carmean, S. L., Weir, M. W. Effects of verbalization on discrimination learning and retention. *J. Verbal Learn. Verbal Behav.*, **6**, 545–50 (1967)
38. Ceraso, J. Specific interference in retroactive inhibition. *J. Psychol.*, **58**, 65–77 (1964)
39. Ceraso, J., Tendler, M. Pair vs. list interference. *Am. J. Psychol.*, **81**, 47–52 (1968)
40. Cofer, C. N., Ed. *Verbal Learning and Verbal Behavior* (See Ref. 15)
41. Cofer, C. N. Does conceptual organization influence the amount retained in immediate free recall? In *Concepts and the Structure of Memory*, 181–225 (See Ref. 86)
42. Cofer, C. N. Problems, issues, implications. In *Verbal Behavior and General Behavior Theory*, 522–37 (See Ref. 54)
43. Cofer, C. N., Segal, E., Stein, J., Walker, H. Studies on free recall of nouns following presentation under adjectival modification. *J. Exptl. Psychol.*, **79**, 254–64 (1969)
44. Conrad, R. Acoustic confusions in immediate memory. *Brit. J. Psychol.*, **55**, 75–84 (1964)
45. Conrad, R., Hull, A. J. Input modality and the serial position curve in short-term memory. *Psychon. Sci.*, **10**, 135–36 (1968)
46. Cooper, E. H., Pantle, A. J. The total-time hypothesis in verbal learning. *Psychol. Bull.*, **68**, 221–34 (1967)
47. Corballis, M. C. Serial order in recognition and recall. *J. Exptl. Psychol.*, **74**, 99–105 (1967)
48. Crouse, J. H. Storage and retrieval of words in free-recall learning. *J. Educ. Psychol.*, **59**, 449–51 (1968)
49. Crowder, R. G. Short-term memory for words with a perceptual-motor interpolated activity. *J. Verbal Learn. Verbal Behav.*, **6**, 753–61 (1967)
50. Crowder, R. G., Morton, J. Precategorical acoustic storage (PAS). *Percept. Psychophys.* (In press)
51. Dallett, K., Wilcox, S. G., D'Andrea, L. Picture memory experiments. *J. Exptl. Psychol.*, **76**, 312–20 (1968)
52. Dalrymple-Alford, E. C. Repetition and immediate memory. *Brit. J. Psychol.*, **58**, 63–67 (1967)
53. DiVesta, F. J., Ingersoll, G. M. Influence of pronounceability, articulation, and test mode on paired-associate learning by the study-recall procedure. *J. Exptl. Psychol.*, **79**, 104–8 (1969)
54. Dixon, T. R., Horton, D. L., Eds. *Verbal Behavior and General Behavior Theory* (Prentice-Hall, Englewood Cliffs, N.J., 1968)
55. Donaldson, W., Murdock, B. B., Jr. Criterion change in continuous recognition memory. *J. Exptl. Psychol.*, **76**, 325–30 (1968)
56. Dong, T., Kintsch, W. Subjective retrieval cues in free recall. *J. Verbal Learn. Verbal Behav.*, **7**, 813–16 (1968)

57. Earhard, M. Cued recall and free recall as a function of the number of items per cue. *J. Verbal Learn. Verbal Behav.,* **6,** 257–63 (1967)
58. Earhard, M. The facilitation of memorization by alphabetic instructions. *Can. J. Psychol.* **21,** 15–24 (1967)
59. Ekstrand, B. R., Wallace, W. P., Underwood, B. J. A frequency theory of verbal-discrimination learning. *Psychol. Rev.,* **73,** 566–78 (1966)
60. Ellis, N. R. Evidence for two storage processes in short-term memory. *J. Exptl. Psychol.,* **80,** 390–91 (1969)
61. Garner, W. R. *Uncertainty and Structure as Psychological Concepts* (Wiley, New York, 396 pp., 1962)
62. Glanzer, M. Distance between related words in free recall: Trace of the STS. *J. Verbal Learn. Verbal Behav.,* **8,** 105–11 (1969)
63. Glanzer, M., Cunitz, A. R. Two storage mechanisms in free recall. *J. Verbal Learn. Verbal Behav.,* **5,** 351–60 (1966)
64. Glanzer, M., Gianutsos, R., Dubin, S. The removal of items from short-term storage. *J. Verbal Learn. Verbal Behav.,* **8,** 435–47 (1969)
65. Glanzer, M., Meinzer, A. The effects of intralist activity on free recall. *J. Verbal Learn. Verbal Behav.,* **6,** 928–35 (1967)
66. Goss, A. E., Cobb, N. J. Formation, maintenance, generalization, and retention of response hierarchies: The role of meaningfulness of response members. *J. Exptl. Psychol.,* **74,** 272–81 (1967)
67. Hall, J., Sekuler, R., Cushman, W. Effects of IAR occurrence during learning on response time during subsequent recognition. *J. Exptl. Psychol.,* **79,** 39–42 (1969)
68. Hamilton, W. *Lectures on Metaphysics and Logic,* Vol. I (Gould & Lincoln, Boston, 718 pp., 1859)
69. Harcum, E. R. Parallel functions of serial learning and tachistoscopic pattern perception. *Psychol. Rev.,* **74,** 51–62 (1967)
70. Hart, J. T. Memory and the memory-monitoring process. *J. Verbal Learn. Verbal Behav.,* **6,** 685–91 (1967)
71. Hinrichs, J. V., Buschke, H. Judgment of recency under steady-state conditions. *J. Exptl. Psychol.,* **78,** 574–79 (1968)
72. Hintzman, D. L. Articulatory coding in short-term memory. *J. Verbal Learn. Verbal Behav.,* **6,** 312–16 (1967)
73. Hochberg, J., Galper, R. E. Recognition of faces: 1. An exploratory study. *Psychon. Sci.,* **9,** 619–20 (1967)
74. Horowitz, L. M., Prytulak, L. S. Redintegrative memory. *Psychol. Rev.,* **76,** 519–32 (1969)
75. Howe, M. J. A. Verbal context as a retrieval cue in long-term memory for words. *Psychon. Sci.,* **9,** 453–54 (1967)
76. Huttenlocher, J. Constructing spatial images: A strategy in reasoning. *Psychol. Rev.,* **75,** 550–60 (1968)
77. Jung, J. A cumulative method of paired-associate and serial learning. *J. Verbal Learn. Verbal Behav.,* **3,** 290–99 (1964)
78. Jung, J. Cued versus non-cued incidental recall of successive word associations. *Can. J. Psychol.,* **21,** 196–203 (1967)
79. Kausler, D. H., Boka, J. A. Effects of double functioning on verbal-discrimination learning. *J. Exptl. Psychol.,* **76,** 558–67 (1968)
80. Kausler, D. H., Sardello, R. J. Item recall in verbal discrimination learning as related to pronunciation and degree of practice. *Psychon. Sci.,* **7,** 285–86 (1967)
81. Keppel, G. Retroactive and proactive inhibition. In *Verbal Behavior and General Behavior Theory,* 172–213 (See Ref. 54)
82. Keppel, G. Verbal learning and memory. *Ann. Rev. Psychol.,* **19,** 169–202 (1968)
83. Keppel, G., Postman, L., Zavortink, B. Response availability in free and modified free recall for two transfer paradigms. *J. Verbal Learn. Verbal Behav.,* **6,** 654–60 (1967)
84. Kintsch, W. An experimental analysis of single stimulus tests and multiple-choice tests of recognition memory. *J. Exptl. Psychol.,* **76,** 1–6 (1968)
85. Kintsch, W. Recognition and free recall of organized lists. *Ibid.,* **78,** 481–87 (1968)
86. Kleinmuntz, B., Ed. *Concepts and the Structure of Memory* (Wiley, New York, 286 pp., 1967)
87. Landauer, T. K., Eldridge, L.

Effects of tests without feedback and presentation-test interval in paired-associate learning. *J. Exptl. Psychol.,* **75,** 290–98 (1967)

88. Levy, B. A., Murdock, B. B., Jr. The effects of delayed auditory feedback and intralist similarity in short-term memory. *J. Verbal Learn. Verbal Behav.,* **7,** 887–94 (1968)
89. Lockhart, R. S. Recency discrimination predicted from absolute lag judgments. *Percept. Psychophys.,* **6,** 42–44 (1969)
90. Lockhart, R. S. Retrieval asymmetry in the recall of adjectives and nouns. *J. Exptl. Psychol.,* **79,** 12–17 (1969)
91. Loess, H., Waugh, N. C. Short-term memory and intertrial interval. *J. Verbal Learn. Verbal Behav.,* **6,** 455–60 (1967)
92. Mandler, G. Organization and memory. In *The Psychology of Learning and Motivation,* Vol. 1, 327–72 (See Ref. 16)
93. Mandler, G. Verbal learning. In *New Directions in Psychology,* Vol. III, 1–50 (Newcomb, T. M., Ed., Holt, Rinehart & Winston, New York, 289 pp., 1967)
94. Mandler, G. Association and organization: Facts, fancies, and theories. In *Verbal Behavior and General Behavior Theory,* 109–19 (See Ref. 54)
95. Mandler, G. Words, lists, and categories: An experimental view of organized memory. In *Studies in Thought and Language* (Cowan, J. L., Ed., Univ. Arizona Press, Tucson, 1969)
96. Mandler, G., Dean, P. J. Seriation: The development of serial order in free recall. *J. Exptl. Psychol.,* **81,** 207–15 (1969)
97. Mandler, G., Pearlstone, Z., Koopmans, H. S. Effects of organization and semantic similarity on recall and recognition. *J. Verbal Learn. Verbal Behav.,* **8,** 410–23 (1969)
98. Martin, E. Relation between stimulus recognition and paired-associate learning. *J. Exptl. Psychol.,* **74,** 500–5 (1967)
99. Martin, E. Stimulus meaningfulness and paired-associate transfer: An encoding variability hypothesis. *Psychol. Rev.,* **75,** 421–41 (1968)
100. McGeoch, J. A. *The Psychology of Human Learning* (Longman's, New York, 633 pp., 1942)
101. McGovern, J. B. Extinction of associations in four transfer paradigms. *Psychol. Monogr.,* **78**(16), 21 pp. (1964)
102. Melton, A. W. Comments on Professor Postman's paper. In *Verbal Learning and Verbal Behavior,* 179–96 (See Ref. 15)
103. Melton, A. W. Implications of short-term memory for a general theory of memory. *J. Verbal Learn. Verbal Behav.,* **2,** 1–21 (1963)
104. Melton, A. W. Repetition and retrieval from memory. *Science,* **158,** 532 (1967)
105. Melton, A. W., Irwin, J. McQ. The influence of degree of interpolated learning on retroactive inhibition and the overt transfer of specific responses. *Am. J. Psychol.,* **53,** 173–203 (1940)
106. Miller, G. A. Human memory and the storage of information. *IRE Trans. Inform. Theory,* **IT–2,** 129–37 (1956)
107. Monty, R. A. Spatial encoding strategies in sequential short-term memory. *J. Exptl. Psychol.,* **77,** 506–8 (1968)
108. Morin, R. E., DeRosa, D. V., Stultz, V. Recognition memory and reaction time. *Acta Psychol.,* **27,** 298–305 (1967)
109. Morton, J. Repeated items and decay in memory. *Psychon. Sci.,* **10,** 219–20 (1968)
110. Murdock, B. B., Jr. Short-term memory and paired-associate learning. *J. Verbal Learn. Verbal Behav.,* **2,** 320–28 (1963)
111. Murdock, B. B., Jr. Auditory and visual stores in short-term memory. *Acta Psychol.,* **27,** 316–24 (1967)
112. Murdock, B. B., Jr. Modality effects in short-term memory: Storage or retrieval? *J. Exptl. Psychol.,* **77,** 79–86 (1968)
113. Murdock, B. B., Jr. Where or when: Modality effects as a function of temporal and spatial distribution of information. *J. Verbal Learn. Verbal Behav.,* **8,** 378–83 (1969)
114. Murray, D. J. The role of speech responses in short-term memory. *Can. J. Psychol.,* **21,** 263–76 (1967)
115. Murray, D. J. Articulation and acoustic confusability in short-

term memory. *J. Exptl. Psychol.*, **78**, 679–84 (1968)

116. Nagel, F. Experimentelle Untersuchungen über Grundfragen der Assoziationslehre. *Arch. Ges. Psychol.*, **23**, 156–253 (1912)

117. Neisser, U. *Cognitive Psychology* (Appleton-Century-Crofts, New York, 351 pp., 1967)

118. Newton, J. M., Wickens, D. D. Retroactive inhibition as a function of the temporal position of interpolated learning. *J. Exptl. Psychol.*, **51**, 149–54 (1956)

119. Noble, C. E. Meaningfulness and familiarity. In *Verbal Behavior and Learning: Problems and Processes*, 76–119 (Cofer, C. N., Musgrave, B. S., Eds., McGraw-Hill, New York, 397 pp. 1963)

120. Norman, D. A. Toward a theory of memory and attention. *Psychol. Rev.*, **75**, 522–36 (1968)

121. Norman, D. A. *Models of Memory* (Academic Press, New York, 1970)

121a. Novinski, L. Part-whole and whole-part free recall learning. *J. Verbal Learn. Verbal Behav.*, **8**, 152–54 (1969)

122. Paivio, A. Mental imagery in associative learning and memory. *Psychol. Rev.*, **76**, 241–63 (1969)

123. Paivio, A., Yuille, J. C., Rogers, T. B. Noun imagery and meaningfulness in free and serial recall. *J. Exptl. Psychol.*, **79**, 509–14 (1969)

124. Paivio, A., Yuille, J. C., Smythe, P. C. Stimulus and response abstractness, imagery and meaningfulness, and reported mediators in paired-associate learning. *Can. J. Psychol.*, **20**, 362–77 (1966)

125. Paul, C., Callahan, C., Mereness, M., Wilhelm, K. Transfer-activated response sets: Effect of overtraining and percentage of items shifted on a verbal discrimination shift. *J. Exptl. Psychol.*, **78**, 488–93 (1968)

126. Peterson, L. R. Associative memory over brief intervals of time. *J. Verbal Learn. Verbal Behav.*, **2**, 102–6 (1963)

127. Peterson, L. R. Search and judgment in memory. In *Concepts and the Structure of Memory*, 153–180 (See Ref. 86)

128. Peterson, L. R. Concurrent verbal activity. *Psychol. Rev.*, **76**, 376–86 (1969)

129. Peterson, L. R., Johnson, S. T., Coatrey, R. The effect of repeated occurrences on judgments of recency. *J. Verbal Learn. Verbal Behav.*, **8**, 591–96 (1969)

130. Posner, M. I. Short-term memory systems in human information processing. *Acta Psychol.*, **27**, 267–84 (1967)

131. Pompi, K. F., Lachman, R. Surrogate processes in the short-term retention of connected discourse. *J. Exptl. Psychol.*, **75**, 143–50 (1967)

132. Postman, L. The present status of interference theory. In *Verbal Learning and Verbal Behavior*, 152–79 (See Ref. 15)

133. Postman, L. Association and performance in the analysis of verbal learning. In *Verbal Behavior and General Behavior Theory*, 551–71 (see Ref. 54)

134. Postman, L., Keppel, G. Retroactive inhibition in free recall. *J. Exptl. Psychol.*, **74**, 203–11 (1967)

135. Postman, L., Phillips, L. W. Short-term temporal changes in free recall. *Quart. J. Exptl. Psychol.*, **17**, 132–38 (1965)

136. Postman, L., Stark, K. Role of response availability in transfer and interference. *J. Exptl. Psychol.*, **79**, 168-77 (1969)

137. Postman, L., Stark, K., Fraser, J. Temporal changes in interference. *J. Verbal Learn. Verbal Behav.*, **7**, 672–94 (1968)

138. Rabbitt, P. M. A. Channel-capacity, intelligibility and immediate memory. *Quart. J. Exptl. Psychol.*, **20**, 241–48 (1968)

139. Restle, F. Significance of all-or-none learning. *Psychol. Bull.*, **64**, 313–25 (1965)

140. Roberts, W. A. An analysis of multitrial free recall learning with input-order held constant. *J. Psychol.*, **68**, 227–42 (1968)

141. Sachs, J. S. Recognition memory for syntactic and semantic aspects of connected discourse. *Percept. Psychophys.*, **2**, 437–42 (1967)

142. Sanders, A. F. Short-term memory for spatial positions. *Psychologie*, **23**, 1–15 (1968)

143. Savin, H. B. On the successive perception of simultaneous stimuli. *Percept. Psychophys.*, **2**, 479–82 (1967)

144. Schulman, A. I. Word length and rarity in recognition memory. *Psychon. Sci.*, **9**, 211–12 (1967)
145. Shepard, R. N. Recognition memory for words, sentences, and pictures. *J. Verbal Learn. Verbal Behav.*, **6**, 156–63 (1967)
146. Shiffrin, R. M., Atkinson, R. C. Storage and retrieval processes in long-term memory. *Psychol. Rev.*, **76**, 179–93 (1969)
147. Shuell, T. J. Retroactive inhibition in free-recall learning of categorized lists. *J. Verbal Learn. Verbal Behav.*, **7**, 797–805 (1968)
148. Shuell, T. J., Keppel, G. Retroactive inhibition as a function of learning method. *J. Exptl. Psychol.*, **75**, 457–63 (1967)
149. Slamecka, N. J. Differentiation versus unlearning of verbal associations. *J. Exptl. Psychol.*, **71**, 822–28 (1966)
150. Slamecka, N. J. Recall and recognition in list-discrimination tasks as a function of the number of alternatives. *Ibid.*, **74**, 187–92 (1967)
151. Slamecka, N. J. Serial learning and order information. *Ibid.*, 62–66
152. Slamecka, N. J. An examination of trace storage in free recall. *Ibid.*, **76**, 504–13 (1968)
153. Slamecka, N. J. A temporal interpretation of some recall phenomena. *Psychol. Rev.*, **76**, 492–503 (1969)
154. Sperling, G. A model for visual memory tasks. *Human Factors*, **5**, 19–31 (1963)
155. Sperling, G. Successive approximations to a model for short-term memory. *Acta Psychol.*, **27**, 285–92 (1967)
156. Sternberg, S. High-speed scanning in human memory. *Science*, **153**, 652–54 (1966)
157. Stevens, S. S. Mathematics, measurement, and psychophysics. In *Handbook of Experimental Psychology*, Chap. 1, 1–49 (Stevens, S. S., Ed., Wiley, New York, 1436 pp., 1951)
158. Stoddard, G. D. An experiment in verbal learning. *J. Educ. Psychol.*, **20**, 452–57 (1929)
158a. Taylor, G. R. In *Biological Time Bomb* (Thames & Hudson, London, 240 pp., 1968)
159. Underwood, B. J. Some correlates of item repetition in free-recall learning. *J. Verbal Learn. Verbal Behav.*, **8**, 83–94 (1969)
160. Underwood, B. J., Ekstrand, B. R. Effect of distributed practice on paired-associate learning. *J. Exptl. Psychol. Monogr. Suppl.*, **73** (4, part 2), 21 pp. (1967)
161. Underwood, B. J., Ekstrand, B. R. Linguistic associations and retention. *J. Verbal Learn. Verbal Behav.*, **7**, 162–71 (1968)
162. Underwood, B. J., Erlebacher, A. H. Studies of coding in verbal learning. *Psychol. Monogr.*, **79**(13), 25 pp. (1965)
163. Underwood, B. J., Freund, J. S. Effect of temporal separation of two tasks on proactive inhibition. *J. Exptl. Psychol.*, **78**, 50–54 (1968)
164. Underwood, B. J., Freund, J. S. Two tests of a theory of verbal discrimination learning. *Can. J. Psychol.*, **22**, 96–104 (1968)
165. Underwood, B. J., Jesse, F., Ekstrand, B. R. Knowledge of rights and wrongs in verbal-discrimination learning. *J. Verbal Learn. Verbal Behav.*, **3**, 183–86 (1964)
166. Underwood, B. J., Postman, L. Extraexperimental sources of interference in forgetting. *Psychol. Rev.*, **67**, 73–95 (1960)
167. Underwood, B. J., Schulz, R. W. *Meaningfulness and Verbal Learning* (Lippincott, Philadelphia, 430 pp., 1960)
168. Voss, J. F. Intralist interference in associative learning. *J. Verbal Learn. Verbal Behav.*, **6**, 773–79 (1967)
169. Voss, J. F. Serial acquisition as a function of number of successively occurring list items. *J. Exptl. Psychol.*, **78**, 456–62 (1968)
170. Voss, J. F. Serial acquisition as a function of stage of learning. *Ibid.*, **79**, 220–25 (1969)
171. Ward, J. Assimilation and association. *Mind*, **2**, 347–62 (1893)
172. Waugh, N. C. Immediate memory as a function of repetition. *J. Verbal Learn. Verbal Behav.*, **2**, 107–12 (1963)
173. Waugh, N. C. Presentation time and free recall. *J. Exptl. Psychol.*, **73**, 39–44 (1967)
174. Waugh, N. C., Norman, D. A. Primary memory. *Psychol. Rev.*, **72**, 89–104 (1965)
175. Waugh, N. C., Norman, D. A. The measure of interference in primary

memory. *J. Verbal Learn. Verbal Behav.,* **7,** 617–26 (1968)

176. Wickelgren, W. A. Exponential decay and independence from irrelevant associations in short-term recognition memory for serial order. *J. Exptl. Psychol.,* **73,** 165–71 (1967)

177. Wickelgren, W. A. Auditory or articulatory coding in verbal short-term memory. *Psychol. Rev.,* **76,** 232–35 (1969)

178. Wickens, D. D. Encoding categories of words: An empirical approach to meaning. *Psychol. Rev.* (In press)

179. Wickens, D. D., Clark, S. E., Hill, F. A., Wittlinger, R. P. Investigation of grammatical class as an encoding category in short-term memory. *J. Exptl. Psychol.,* **78,** 599–604 (1968)

180. Winograd, E. List differentiation as a function of frequency and retention interval. *J. Exptl. Psychol. Monogr. Suppl.,* **72** (2, part 2), 18 pp. (1968)

181. Winograd, E. Retention of list differentiation and word frequency. *J. Verbal Learn. Verbal Behav.,* **7,** 859–63 (1968)

182. Wood, G. Higher order memory units and free recall learning. *J. Exptl. Psychol.,* **80,** 286–88 (1969)

183. Woodward, A., Jr., Murdock, B. B., Jr. Positional and sequential probes in serial learning. *Can. J. Psychol.,* **22,** 131–38 (1968)

184. Yntema, D. B., Trask, F. P. Recall as a search process. *J. Verbal Learn. Verbal Behav.,* **2,** 65–74 (1963)

185. Young, R. K. Serial learning. In *Verbal Behavior and General Behavior Theory,* 121–48 (See Ref. 54)

186. Young, R. K., Saegert, J., Linsley, D. Retention as a function of meaningfulness. *J. Exptl. Psychol.,* **78,** 89–94 (1968)

187. Zimmerman, J., Underwood, B. J. Ordinal position knowledge within and across lists as a function of instructions in free-recall learning. *J. Gen. Psychol.,* **79,** 301–7 (1968)

DERIVED MOTIVES 156

By Mortimer H. Appley
University of Massachusetts, Amherst, Massachusetts

"Of the many intervening variables that psychologists use," wrote Chaplin in his recent *Dictionary of Psychology* (43), "the concept of motive (or motivation) is among the most controversial and least satisfactory" (p. 304). And this assessment is supported, to a greater or lesser extent, by the several major books on the subject which have appeared in the past half-dozen years [e.g., Atkinson (11), Bolles (32), Cofer & Appley (44), Haber (77), and Madsen (109)]. But in defense of the area, it must be recognized that motivational concepts are devised to account for or deal with the most subtle, complex, and difficult to isolate of all psychological processes. No easy or direct measurement of motivation is possible, and the inference must be made from behavior change. Such inferences are in turn subject to confounding by large numbers of simultaneously operative variables. Not the least of the problems arises from the fact that presumed motivational changes are of necessity accompanied by cue or stimulus changes, and the effects of the two classes of events often defy separate analysis (cf. 38).

Over the years, a number of explanatory constructs, variables, and mechanisms have been proposed that seemed to give promise of providing means of organizing or classifying motivational phenomena, only to be found wanting on more penetrating examination. (The paths of science are strewn with discarded concepts!) Some of the main organizing ideas have fallen into disuse or died, only to rise again, like the fabled Egyptian phoenix, albeit in sometimes considerably modified form. *Instinct* is such a case (16, 44, 88, 171). *Drive* may be another (41, 44, 109, 156). Now the concept of *motive* itself may be under attack (27, 32), while at the same time it is undergoing series of refinements and transformations which will likely assure its survival.

We have given reasons elsewhere for the belief that motive-like constructs are necessary in order to account for the invigoration of behavior (44), while at the same time recognizing the limitations with which particular (e.g., directional) conceptions of motive are burdened. Whether this assessment was correct or not remains to be determined.

An additional reason for believing that motivational ideas will remain important to psychological theorizing is their embeddedness in the conceptualization of other areas of psychology. Thus, for example, in the 1969 volume of *Annual Review of Psychology,* in addition to the chapter on "Basic Drives" [Campbell & Misanin (41)], at least three other sections include considerations of motivational explanatory constructs as integral to their subjects of study. Flavell & Hill (69), writing on "Developmental Psychology," consider such topics as effects of social deprivation, satiation and reinforcement, achievement motivation, environmental factors influencing selective attending, and social determinants of aggression and altruism. Adelson (2), in a review of "Personality," deals with self-esteem and self-acceptance, achievement, anxiety, stress, defense, aggression, and cognitive dissonance. And Sears & Abeles (158), under "Attitudes and Opinions," discuss dissonance and consistency, attribution, fear arousal, and balance theory. One can reasonably assume that this current volume will likewise include considerations of motivational concepts and variables in several of its chapters (which is as it should be, in our view).

Recent volumes of the *Nebraska Symposium on Motivation* (e.g., 100) and recent general collections, symposia, and theoretical treatments in developmental, personality, and social psychology also show this interlocking of motivational ideas and the larger theoretical development of these other fields (e.g., 1, 15, 66, 86, 110).

It could be claimed, of course, that such dependence on motivational constructs is keeping other areas from developing their own theoretical bases and thus retarding conceptual growth in psychology. However, there seems little doubt that such concepts are used only because they appear to be of value in explicating phenomena in these areas [cf. Berger & Lambert (21)] and may indeed be integral to the theoretical structure of these fields.

In addition, the refinement and development of the motivational concepts themselves in the contexts of their applications has been worthwhile regardless of their utility to the fields in which they are applied [e.g., witness the continuing evolution of concepts of anxiety (62, 127, 151, 165) and of achievement motivation (12, 30, 83, 178) in the crucibles of personality and social psychological research].

The only cautionary note that must be sounded in regard to the considerations above is the concern that motivational concepts developed in particular contexts not become more uniquely situation-specific than is absolutely necessary, lest their general theoretical value be lost. This is no more than the counterface to the concern that theoretical conceptions be sufficiently anchored in manipulable variables to be able to be applied or tested in specifiable settings.

Derived Motives vs. Secondary Motivational Systems

The decision of the Editorial Committee of the *Annual Review of Psychology* to divide the treatment of motivation by alternate yearly coverage of "basic drives" (e.g., 41) and "derived motives" (this review) seemed eminently reasonable when this assignment was accepted, but became less and less so as it was undertaken. For one thing, as has already been suggested, many of the topics which might properly have been included in a review such as this were found to be appropriately (and competently) treated in reviews of areas other than motivation.

Of equal or greater importance, however, is the fairly clear implication of the term "derived motives" that these are particular, self-contained, unidimensional, motivational categories in the tradition of instincts or drives although somehow acquired, learned, secondary, or derived. Avoiding use of the word "drive" (more traditionally applied to "basic" or biological system deficits and their motivational effects) does little to disengage the derived motives notion from implied attachment (assumedly via some form of learning or association) to either specific conditions of need, deprivation, or distress, on the one hand, or specific rewards on the other. Brown & Farber (38) chose the phrase "secondary motivational systems" in preference to "learned drives" for these and other reasons in their excellent "first" review of this area, and we would agree that their term avoids many problems in which the carryover of drive-motive language can embroil us. However, it is possible that current theoretical developments may have made even their phrase obsolete in that *all* motivational processes may have *both* "primary" and "secondary" determinants. Thus the present need may be to reconceptualize motivational processes as involving an interlocking of innate and acquired (or unlearned and learned) aspects in such a way as to render meaningless the kinds of distinctions made so much of in an earlier period (44, 82).

In the sections which follow, we shall examine certain of the major current developments that appear to be moving toward such an interactive conceptualization.

The Decline of Drive

The drive concept, whether based on a drive-stimulus or hydraulic model, has been a mainstay of motivation theory ever since Woodworth (184) introduced the term half a century ago. Its centrality to Freudian theory and to Hullian theory served to protect it despite periodic strong challenges to its validity [e.g., Seward (159, 160), Sheffield (161), Young (187)]. Adherents of the two theoretical positions continue to use the drive concept, though occasionally modifying its scope or meaning (78, 109). The cumulative weight of evidence as to its shortcomings, however, has been felt for some time both within the ranks of the psychoanalysts (63, 89, 141) and among the Hullian theorists (36, 122–124, 164).

By 1964, Cofer & Appley (44), after extensively reviewing the research literature, assessed the drive concept as being not only "without utility" but actually "a liability" in preventing investigators from arriving at new formulations. Bolles (32), in a separate analysis, summarized the case against drive by noting that ". . . we have failed to find that D [drive] and H [habit] are independent, that the stimulus concomitants of drive have any real existence, that drive reduction constitutes reinforcement, that different sources of drive are motivationally equivalent, or that there are consistent individual differences in drive strength . . ." (p. 329). He concludes that ". . . *the worst failure of the drive concept continues to be that it does not help us to explain behavior*" (p. 329, italics added).

The evidence on which these views are based has been well developed in the two sources cited and will not be recapitulated here. It seems convincing enough to suggest that the drive concept, insofar as it refers to a deprivation-based drive-stimulus or "push" model of motivation, ought finally to be retired to make way, as Bolles has put it, for "younger, more vigorous, more capable concepts [to] take over" (p. 330).

Alternatives to Drive

There are perhaps three main (though by no means mutually exclusive) groups of concepts which have been proposed as possible alternatives to drive. These are *arousal, incentive,* and *reinforcement.* All three seem capable of dealing with the effects of conditions of bodily need (privation, deprivation) on behavior, but none assigns the central importance to vegetative processes they held in drive theory (cf. 32, 38, 103, 104). At the same time, these alternative concepts seem more able than classical drive theory to account for behavior invigoration and persistence in the absence of readily identifiable deprivation operations (26, 44), and thus to "explain" a much wider range of human motivating conditions without the addition of untenable assumptions.

Each of the alternative concepts will be discussed briefly below.

Arousal theory.—Campbell & Misanin (41) have called activation and arousal "two intertwined and currently interchangeable concepts" (p. 68). In fact, these are only two of a family of overlapping concepts, including emotionality, energization, energy mobilization, excitation, generalized drive, invigoration, and tension, among others, which date back at least as far as the drive concept (57, 58, 147). But except for the continued efforts of a few investigators such as Darrow (49), Duffy (54, 55, 57), and Freeman (72, 73), these concepts had little general acceptance as compared with drive theory. In the 1950s, however, and increasingly since, considerable attention has been given to them, largely because of the reawakened interest in neuropsychology resulting from Hebb's work (80, 81) and in psychophysiology and neurophysiology, stimulated by Lindsley (101, 102), Lacey (94, 95), Duffy (55, 56), and Malmo (111, 112), among others.

Although there are somewhat varying emphases in the different activation and arousal theories, the general conception can be understood by examining Malmo's views, which we will do briefly here.

Malmo (113), in his "neuropsychological" or later "multifactor" (117) theory of activation, describes a continuum of neural excitation extending from comatose states or deep sleep at the low end to states of high excitement (though not necessarily high overt activity) at the other. This activation continuum forms a "tonic" background for organized neural activity. "According to this theory there is an optimal amount of this background activity for best supporting the organized activity. Below and above this optimal amount . . . the efficiency of the organized activity is relatively impaired" (117, p. 288). Thus, although the arousal continuum is depicted as unidimensional, its relation to behavioral efficiency is not. The inverted U-shaped curve (81) is said to best describe the course of performance in relation to arousal level. Malmo (113) points out that the determination of low, moderate, and high activation levels is intra-subject and intra-task rather than absolute, and thus "optimal" levels for different tasks may be expected to differ.

Arousal level at any time is "the product of an interaction between internal conditions such as hunger or thirst, and external cues" (113, p. 385). Unlike its function in drive theory, however, the effect of deprivation in Malmo's concept of arousal is not translated directly into motor activity but remains as a latent, "sensitizing" factor to be activated only in the presence of environmental stimulating conditions. As a consequence, level of motivation (arousal) cannot be inferred from knowledge of antecedent (deprivation) conditions alone but must be measured contemporaneously.

Following the lead of Hebb (81) and Lindsley (101, 102), Malmo (113) considered the most likely mechanism of activation mediation to be through the ascending reticular activating system (ARAS). Stimulation of the ARAS would increase cortical bombardment from that system and combine with direct stimulation of the cortex to produce vigorous responding. An insufficiency of such "tonic" stimulation would lead to low levels of performance, an excess to disruption of sequential activity and similar low levels of efficiency (hence the inverted U-shaped curve).

Malmo (113) recognized the many technical difficulties associated with use of EEG desynchronization as a measure of activation and in using "peripheral indicants" (heart rate, respiration, palmar conductance, muscle tension, etc.) when correlations among these indicants were questionable and measurement problems severe. He nevertheless argued that "physiological measures show a sufficiently high intra-individual concordance for quantifying this (activation) dimension" (p. 378). Lacey's (96) criticisms and his own further research (114–116) have subsequently led Malmo to alter some of his views (117).

In what can only be described as a brilliant *tour de force,* Lacey (96) has convincingly argued that electrocortical, autonomic, and behavioral arousal are "*different forms* of arousal, each complex in itself . . . [and] that one cannot easily use one form of arousal as a highly valid index of another" (pp. 15–16, italics in original). He suggests that the assumed commonality of arousal systems has been a result of the artifactual use of limited, usually aversive, intensive arousal manipulations which produce similar responses in the various systems (but not because the systems are part of a communal activation process). Citing work from his own laboratory and elsewhere, Lacey challenges not only the unidimensionality of activation processes but also the assumption [Hebb (81), Malmo (113)] that activation is a reflection of behavior intensity only and not direction. Here Lacey refers to the situation-specific patterning of somatic responses (*situational stereotypy*) [Lacey et al. (97); Obrist (130)], observing that ". . . different somatic processes have different roles to play in the execution of different kinds of behavior and different interactions with other concurrent responses, and hence appear in different amounts and temporal evolution, depending on the requirements of the *intended* interaction between the organism and its environment" (96, p. 25, italics added). This point is illustrated by examples of *directional fractionation* in which heart rate *deceleration* and restraint in systolic blood pressure increase were predictably observed (contrary to what a general arousal theory might expect) in situations calling for attentive observing of the external environment, while situations requiring concentration ("environmental rejection") produced opposite results.

Malmo & Bélanger (117) find themselves in agreement with Lacey on a number of his criticisms of arousal theory. Malmo (116) had already accepted two major modifications of his earlier position: first, based on the findings of Feldman & Waller (67), cited by Lacey, Malmo acknowledged that the (posterior) hypothalamus might be equally as important as the midbrain reticular formation in mediating arousal phenomena; and second, on the basis of his own experiment in which he found that performance impairment resulting from "divided set" instructions was not reflected in any of eleven psychophysiological measures, and similar findings of Elliott (61), he accepted that there were clear limitations on "generalizations concerning relations between physiological activation and performance" (16, p. 189). Malmo & Bélanger (117) deny that they consider activation "as a parasympathetic-sympathetic dimension" and emphasize that "recorded autonomic changes are interpreted as merely imperfect indicators of the primary central nervous system events" (p. 307).

In reply to Lacey, Malmo [see Lacey (96, p. 19); Malmo & Bélanger (117)], suggests that differences in interpretation may have arisen from use of different reference data. He points out that whereas Lacey and his associates had studied relatively brief, dynamic responses, it was the *long-term* changes in *level* of activity which alone could index activation level. He further notes, in the same exchange, that while quantitative changes in individual measures may not be correlated, "significantly concordant change in the *direction* of *group* means (associated with situation change) is the sufficient evidence for change in 'level of activation'" (117 p. 306, italics in original). Finally, Malmo & Bélanger (117) make a major concession on the basis of evidence of dissociation in their own work—Malmo's study of divided set (116) and the demonstration by Bélanger (19) and his student (59) of meprobamate-induced effect on performance but not on heart rate. They accept that performance is multiply determined, and that behavior changes of a "cognitive" kind may be mediated chiefly by changes within the "cue system" independently of the "arousal system."

There can be little doubt, as Campbell & Misanin (41) have so succinctly put it, that "the elegant simplicity" of general activation theory has disappeared. Nevertheless, there appears to be sufficient integrity remaining to consider activation or arousal as a viable alternative conception to drive.

Ax (13) and Berlyne (26) both draw the analogy between general arousal and Spearman's general factor of intelligence, suggesting the usefulness of a component or factor analysis of arousal. One possible bi-polar factor, according to Berlyne (26), is pleasantness-unpleasantness. A second might be derived from Lacey's observations (96) and those of Graham & Clifton (75) that cardiac deceleration occurs in external attending or orientation while acceleration is typically observed in attention withdrawal or defensive reactions. Berlyne doesn't label this possible factor, but one could think of receptiveness-rejection as a pair of dimension names. Additional components may well be determined if this approach is seriously pursued, which it should be.

Berlyne (26) reviews an impressively wide range of arousal and learning studies to show, among other things, (*a*) the dependence of reinforcement effects on changes in arousal level; (*b*) the likelihood that arousal *increase,* rather than arousal- or drive-*reduction,* is necessary for learning; (*c*) the probability that reciprocally interacting central "reward" and "aversion" systems [Grastyan et al. (76)]—as well as a possible third, "aversion-reducing" system—"are brought into play by different magnitudes of arousal increment" (p. 86); and (*d*) that the posited reward system mediates positive feedback, is related to positive affect, and is somehow related to the orientation reaction, while the proposed aversion system mediates negative feedback, is related to negative affect, and is associated with both defensive reactions and possible inhibition of the reward system. He further offers some suggestions [after Schönpflug (155)] that would explain the inverted U-curve relating arousal to performance in terms of the interaction of reward and aversion systems having different and varying arousal thresholds [see Epstein (62) below].

Berlyne's proposals significantly advance arousal theory toward the desired specificity that will permit testing and sharpening. Unfortunately, many of the studies he cites in support of his views use the kinds of indices of arousal which Lacey (96) has so tellingly questioned. Nevertheless, Berlyne's contribution is an important one and should stimulate considerable further work.

Arousal theory, as has been noted earlier, has the advantage of not being tied to survival needs, and can thus more readily incorporate affective (81, 101, 153) and collative (22–25) variables as well as those deriving from biogenic disturbances. Miller's "go mechanism" (124), Cofer & Appley's "sensitization-invigoration (SIM)" and "anticipation-invigoration (AIM)" mechanisms (44), Sheffield's "drive induction" theory (161), and Hunt's "incongruity" concept (91), among many others, draw upon an arousal principle, although in each case the theory goes beyond the general conceptions here described. It seems clear at this writing that the arousal concept, despite the criticisms its early presentations have (justly) sustained, has become central to motivation theory.

Incentive theories.—Incentive motivation refers to the energizing effect on behavior of the anticipation of (reinforcing) events (32). Whereas drive (D) is anchored in antecedent events, is presumed to be present at the onset of a behavior sequence, and is said to "push" the organism, incentive is anchored, in a sense, in postcedent events (through their anticipations), may or may not be present at the onset of a behavior sequence, and is described as a "pull" theory. Incentive may be no more than a learned form of drive (36), a parallel and supplementary source of motivation (164), or a replacement for drive as the primary source of behavior energization (128).

Wants, wishes, purpose, desire, interest, and similar terms referring to incentive-like concepts have appeared in the psychological literature over the years (168, 170, 172). Nevertheless, little attention was paid to integrating such concepts into a comprehensive behavior theory or to finding possible mechanisms through which the anticipatory motivational function might be expected to operate.

Hull-Spence stimulus-response (S-R) theory has, since the early 1950s (90, 163, 164), included an incentive motivational concept (K), along with drive (D), as its two major motivational elements. In this theory, D and K are given equal weight in combining with habit (${}_{S}H_{R}$) to determine excitatory potential. K was introduced to identify the motivational increment posited as a consequence of anticipatory goal reactions (r_gs), and the anticipatory responses and their response-produced stimuli (r_g-s_gs) were presumed to provide the underlying mechanism for K. Whereas Hull held that D and K should be combined multiplicatively in the facilitation of performance, Spence argued for additive combination. This question and its implications continue to be matters of theoretical interest and dispute (31, 60, 71, 104).

Incentive motivation (K) has proved useful to S-R theory in permitting interpretation of motivational effects not attributable to D (e.g., effects of reward magnitude on response vigor). But, as Brown & Farber (38) and Logan (104) have shown, the identification of K with the r_g-s_g mechanism (i.e., fractional anticipatory goal responses and the stimuli they produce) may have been a serious mistake. In the Hull-Spence formulation, D, K, and ${}_{S}H_{R}$ are presumably independent variables, D being a motivational factor determined by deprivation or noxious stimulation, K a learned motivational factor derived from anticipatory reactions, and ${}_{S}H_{R}$ an associative factor with no motivational component. Yet, as Brown & Farber point out, K depends on the strength of habits underlying r_g-s_g connections, on the one hand, and on the other, since drive level affects response vigor, D also indirectly determines the magnitude of K (27, 31, 38, 104).

Brown & Farber (38) raise the more fundamental question of whether the r_g-s_g-K mechanism has motivational properties at all. They point out, as does Bolles (32), that stimuli associated with satisfactions ought to be tranquilizing rather than energizing, and they cite studies showing that stimuli previously associated with reward—and thus presumed capable of arousing K and thus invigorating behavior—either failed to augment or actually depressed startle-response amplitude (9, 10, 173). Brown & Farber conclude that "responses anticipatory of attractive events do not qualify as secondary motivational systems" (38, p. 114). Alternatively, they suggest that the apparent motivating effect of such responses might be attributable to their capacity to arouse frustration (see below) or to associative rather than motivational factors.

Logan (104) has independently raised similar doubts about the usefulness of the r_g-s_g mechanism in mediating incentive motivation. Having previously accepted it (103), he has now come to the view that "incentive motivation [*sINr*] is a fundamental process like habit (i.e., it is not mediated) . . ." (pp. 8–9). He reports a series of well-controlled choice experiments with rats in which he sought to determine if the rate at which *sINr* changes with experience is modifiable. Negative findings lead him to conclude that "the rate of change in incentive motivation is an invariant state parameter of the subject and is not significantly affected by prior reinforcement history" (p. 28).

Marx (118) proposes a "response-activation hypothesis" which also rejects r_g-s_g (along with other specific mediating mechanisms). He argues that activation is response-specific, in contrast to the generalized character of the activation or incentive effect assumed for r_g [Spence (164)], and further, that the response nature of the r_g-s_g mechanism places an unnecessary limitation on the functioning of a motivational variable.

Both the evidence and arguments against response mediation of incentive motivational effects now seem rather convincing (see also 27, 32, 124, 126, 146, 162, 183). On the other hand, there would appear to be ample reason to accept the notion of incentive motivation itself (cf. 27, 28, 32, 44) as different from drive (whatever that is!) and as deriving somehow from the anticipation of (and/or commerce with) a goal object or state. However, the case for the generality vs. response- or situation-specificity of incentive motivation has not yet been convincingly made, nor has a clear explanation of how incentives operate yet been given.

The evidence regarding generality vs. specificity of incentive motivational effects should, of course, be directly relevant to the resolution of the mechanism question. If the effect of incentive motivation is to create a general arousal state which can affect the vigor of any response, an undifferentiated (probably central) activation mechanism is the most likely candidate (e.g., 27, 81, 124). On the other hand, response-specific (118), stimulus-response-specific (104), or situation-specific (96) activation may require postulation of a series of different (possibly peripheral) arousal processes linked innately or through learning to the presence of particular conditions of deprivation, stimulation, or response.

Weinrich et al. (182) and Bacon & Bindra (14) have shown that incentive motivation generated in the training of one instrumental response or under one set of drive-reinforcement conditions could affect performance of a different response or under different drive-reinforcement conditions (including a shift from thirst-water to shock-avoidance). Bindra (27) concludes from these studies that ". . . it seems reasonable to assume that an incentive-motivational stimulus creates a central state with widespread influences" (p. 11). In what appears to be a significant attempt at integration, he presents a "neuropsychological model of motivational effects," positing hypothetical positive and negative incentive-motivational states, which are capable of energizing either environmentally oriented (exploratory) or aversive (withdrawal) response tendencies, respectively (29). While Bindra seems to emphasize the role of incentive-motivational stimuli, a more pervading (if not independent) role in his model is actually assigned to "the presence of appropriate drive." Drive manipulations seem to affect the level of motor readiness (arousal), to influence selective attention, to activate neural consummatory-activation sites, and indirectly, to determine the induction of the incentive motivational state. Nevertheless, he holds that drive is incapable of facilitating instrumental responses in the absence of incentive stimulation.

In a later paper (28) Bindra spells out more clearly the importance of the interaction between the *central* consequences of prevailing physiological or organismic state and environmental incentive stimuli (including emotional stimuli). The concatenation of neural events apparently both energizes and directs the subsequent behavior pattern. Like Mowrer (128), Bindra attributes response determination to motivational factors. For Mowrer, however, it is sensory feedback from emotional states—fear, hope, relief, and disappointment—that determines approach or avoidance behaviors. For Bindra, conditioned or remote incentive stimuli, facilitated by the dually influenced "central motive state," induce the appropriate approach or avoidance patterns [cf. Schneirla (154)].

Bindra's two provocative theoretical papers (27, 28) contain more than can be described here. While avoiding very specific "neurologizing," he nevertheless gives emphasis to central factors in association with incentive stimuli in determining both behavior energization and direction.

Trowill, Panksepp & Gandelman (174), in a timely and useful review, propose that electrical stimulation of the brain (ESB) be used to elucidate the mechanisms of drive (deprivation)—incentive interaction. They point out the possibility of ESB experimentation providing conditions paralleling those arising out of deprivation but with opportunity for much greater control and precision (e.g., 132) and without the complications of the "side-effects" associated with natural deprivation-consummatory sequences (e.g., satiation effects). In their "incentive model of rewarding brain stimulation," Trowill and his students propose that "ESB has the same properties as other rewards and . . . its motivational properties are inherent in its reinforcement properties in the form of incentive motivation, rather than in the induction of drive energization" (174, p. 264).

The very brief reviews given here of developments in arousal and incentive theory, give clear evidence of two highly positive trends: a greater willingness to discard hypotheses and concepts in the face of new evidence (one need only mention the "latent learning" controversy to remember when this was not the case), and a significant convergence of behavioral, physiological, and neuropsychological approaches to the explication of motivational phenomena (e.g., 117, 149, 150, 174, 175).

One line of investigation of incentive motivation that may have been unduly neglected of late has been the study of hedonic processes on which P. T. Young has based his theory of "affective arousal" (186–190). According to Young, the attractiveness (incentive or arousal value) of goal objects is determined by their pleasantness or unpleasantness (palatability) on the basis of sensory feedback from intercourse with them. Such hedonic information is then processed centrally (in the limbic system and related structures) where it is interacted with by such "cerebral dispositions" as attitudes, habits, expectancies, etc., developed on the basis of earlier hedonic experiences (189). Homeostatic needs may increase acceptability of needed substances (although the mechanism is as yet unclear), but well-established habits may override such needs.

Young has long argued for a "directing, regulating, evaluating," as well as an energizing role for motivation, and rejects a general arousal principle because it is "one-dimensional." He also faults arousal theory for neglecting to give sufficient recognition to inhibitory functions. Perhaps the "new look" in motivational psychology introduced by brain stimulation and brain-behavior studies will revive interest in studies of pleasantness-unpleasantness and lead to a continuation of Young's work, now that he has retired. The possibilities of such an approach have by no means been exhausted.

Incentive continues to be (or, with the attack on r_g-s_g, has become) a concept in search of a mechanism. That it is functionally different from drive seems clear enough (27, 32), but whether it is more than an arousal process resulting from learning or an associative process resulting from arousal is not yet clear.

Cofer & Appley (44) have proposed two interacting concepts which attempt to bridge the drive-arousal-incentive gap. They suggest that an *anticipation-invigoration mechanism* (AIM) and a *sensitization-invigoration mechanism* (SIM) could, in combination, account for behavior energization (invigoration). The AIM concept is proposed to deal with the pervading *fact* of anticipation (or expectancy, appetite, preference, or incentive). It is seen as "dependent on the stimuli which have regularly antedated or accompanied consummatory behavior" (including any deriving from the depriva tion state). These stimuli, according to Cofer & Appley, "may have a double function: they come through learning to evoke anticipations (and thus arousal) and they serve (after learning) as cues for responses" (44, p. 822). These authors distinguish their use of stimulation in an energizing role from Neal Miller's similar use of stimuli for drive-plus-cue function in that in the Cofer-Appley concept "stimulus intensity is not critical to the evocation of anticipations." The proposed AIM is *not* identified with r_g, though this is indicated as an example. It is suggested that anticipations "may be central as well as peripheral in origin" (44, p. 821).

The parallel SIM concept is proposed to deal with those instances in which learning is apparently unnecessary for motivated behavior to occur. Following Beach's (17) sexual arousal model, Cofer & Appley argue for a sensitization (or readiness) factor—probably hormonal, probably innate (though modifiable)—which accounts for (selective) arousal in the presence of appropriate environmental stimuli. The dual invigoration concepts are examined in relation to a wide range of motivational phenomena and motivation theories and found by these authors to be reasonable fits. They are offered as an "interpretive reconceptualization" of the facts of motivation. Cofer & Appley consider the *directional* component of behavior to be essentially nonmotivational, incidentally, though emphasizing the interaction of motivational, learning and nonpsychological factors in behavior determination.

Reinforcement theories of motivation.—According to Bolles (32), "whatever can be said in the language of motivation can be said as well in the language of reinforcement" (p. 439). Thus, he claims, (*a*) asking "what motivates behavior" can be translated to "what reinforces it" without loss; (*b*) energization is found in instrumental and consummatory behavior, viz., where reinforcement occurs; (*c*) incentive motivation and secondary reinforcement "appear in many cases to be conceptually equivalent and empirically indistinguishable"; and (*d*) the "surplus meaning" attached to motivation theories adds nothing to their ability to account for behavior that is not included in reinforcement theory.

In attempting to explain energization (the core motivational concept) in nonmotivational terms, Bolles suggests several alternatives: stimulus change (e.g., 64, 65); innate incentive response energization mechanisms (88); and the differential reinforcement of more rapid (vigorous) responding (103).

The *elicitation hypothesis* (51, 52, 107, 108) offers a reinforcement explanation of instrumental approach and withdrawal tendencies in terms of the selective conditioning of (innate or previously learned) cues that elicit such tendencies (e.g., sight or smell of food). Premack's *response-probability hypothesis* (138–140) suggests that responses of low probability which are followed by (reinforced by) responses of higher probability of occurrence will subsequently have a greater response probability. While Premack acknowledges the influence of "nonreinforcement" variables (e.g., response periodicity, novelty or stimulus change), his explanation is a parsimonious statement of the reinforcement view [Bolles (32)] and could account for differential (or graded) instrumental response vigor on the basis of the probabilistic certainty of the reinforcing event.

Perkins (134, 135) has recently elaborated his differential reinforcement theory. The key concept in this view is the transmission of differential *attractiveness* from a reinforcement situation to antecedent stimulus situations. Following Thorndike's original law of effect (169), Perkins proposes to account for *both* increments and decrements in response tendencies. "Positive reinforcers both reinforce antecedent responses and transmit 'secondary reinforcement properties' to antecedent stimuli; negative reinforcers both weaken antecedent response tendencies and transmit 'anxiety,' 'fear,' or aversiveness to antecedent stimuli" (135, p. 162). He identifies his analysis as an elaboration of Mowrer's (128) theory and is able to incorporate Premack's (138–140) response probability hypothesis as an instance of the transmission of attractiveness.

Classically conditioned responses are seen by Perkins as being preparatory responses (PRs) (136; see also 34, 145) which "increase the characteristic attractiveness of the stimulus situation at the time of US [unconditioned stimulus] presentation" (135, p. 164). He sees the demonstrations by Neal Miller and his associates (125) of the acquisition of instrumental visceral and glandular responses as further evidence of a preparatory response explanation of classical conditioning and as supportive of his reinforcement analysis.

The similarity of Perkins' (135) differential reinforcement concepts to decision theory and utility theory is noted by him (and this emphasis is itself worth some differential reinforcement). Here again, the possible confluence of several lines of investigation is to be applauded. If, in addition, a greater commonality of language among investigators could be made more attractive, we should see significantly greater progress in our search for an understanding of behavior.

That reinforcement theories are relevant to the explication of motivational phenomena is obvious. But whether such theories can be "made isomorphic" with theories of motivation is unclear. The prediction that behavior will be more highly energized in one situation than in another, or that it may take the form of approach patterns in one case or of avoidance patterns in others can probably be made by application of reinforcement concepts. But our curiosity impels us to ask how reinforcement works and, for this reviewer, at least, the answer seems still to require the positing of some form of motivational (invigoration or energization) mechanism operating antecedent to the initiation of behavior and its subsequent reinforcement in order to "explain" the motivational effect of reinforcement. At the moment, arousal and/or incentive-like models are more likely to provide the answers, though these may turn out to be dependent on reinforcement or to operate only conjointly with acquired associative tendencies or with innate factors or both. As they say in the experimental research literature: "Further research is needed. . . ."

Motivating Effects of Nonreward

Amsel's laboratory continues to be highly productive of experiments seeking to clarify and extend the concept of frustrative nonreward (3–7). This concept was developed by Amsel when he was at the University of Iowa and, like a similar proposal there by Brown & Farber (37), is an elaboration of Hull-Spence S-R theory, extending the idea of the r_g-s_g mechanism to deal with the effects of nonreward.

In brief, Amsel's frustration theory posits that when previously acquired anticipatory goal responses (r_gs) are evoked in the absence of reward (i.e., where reward had previously been given), a primary response (R_f) occurs. In a manner analogous to the development of the incentive mechanism (r_g-s_g) for rewarded trials, a conditioned anticipatory frustration response (r_F) develops in nonreward trials, producing its own stimuli (s_F), and the "competing" anticipatory response moves back in time so as to occur with and affect the instrumental (approach) response. R_f is aversive, as is its anticipatory form, r_F. In the reference experiment (6) for this theory, a long runway was used with goal boxes midway and at the end. The first goal box provided the reward-nonreward experiences. As the theory predicted, the running speed *to* this goal box (i.e., the frustrated response) was reduced, presumably as a result of the competing approach-avoidance tendencies mediated by the two anticipatory responses (r_g and r_F); while running speed in the alley following this goal box (the frustration-motivated response) was increased. This latter phenomenon, attributed to the motivational consequences of the R_F generated in the goal box as a result of nonreward, has been labeled the *frustration effect* (*FE*).

The theory of frustrative nonreward has generated a large amount of research, particularly on problems of intermittent reinforcement and discrimination learning, and is seen to have potentially wide applicability (98). Recent studies of punishment (179, 180) have suggested important similarities in the effects of nonreward and punishment on instrumental behavior. And the relevance of theoretical explanations of frustrative nonreward to the study of fear and other aversive conditions is also evident (37, 38, 180).

In the ongoing series of studies which Amsel and his students are carrying out on within-subject partial reinforcement-continuous reinforcement (PRF-CRF) differences (4, 5, 7), a theoretical distinction is made between processes affecting responses during behavior acquisition and extinction. Response speed differences *during acquisition* are attributed to a motivational intensity or vigor factor, reflecting an underlying "excitement" level resulting from frustrative nonreward. Differences in response speed in extinction, however, are attributed to a nonmotivational persistence dimension, assumed to be determined by an associative mechanism (4). (Since only the former are considered motivational, we shall here ignore the work on extinction effects).

The studies reported use a segmented runway which allows running speed measures to be taken for five successive segments from start to goal box. In results on acquisition comparisons (PRF vs. CRF) using separate groups for each condition, Amsel and his associates found more vigorous responding (i.e., faster running) in the goal region throughout training under continuous reward (as compared with a partially rewarded group). In within-subject comparisons (representing successive discrimination or "differential reward training"), on the other hand, more vigorous responding occurs to the partial stimulus, as compared to the continuous, in the goal region early in training and less vigorous responding later in training. Further, in comparison of differential percentage (and probably of differential magnitude) of reward in within-subject studies, performance is found to be more vigorous in the *middle* of the runway to the stimulus signaling the less frequent (or the lesser) reward. Amsel (4) describes these findings as "paradoxical" and explains them only by invoking a rather involved set of theoretical assumptions. These include the positing of different strengths for r_F and r_g early and late in training. He notes that both anticipatory responses are generated in the goal area at first and then move backward. In the beginning they are both weak and can be expected only to contribute to K (general arousal) in the early stages of their development. Only later, as they are strengthened by successive trials and generate sufficient stimuli, would they come under the directional control of their respective stimuli (i.e., s_g and s_F). As r_g develops first, approach tendencies occur early and are supplemented by the r_F augmentation of K. By further positing K and s_g and s_F thresholds and different generalization gradients (that for r_F is steeper), Amsel believes that the reported findings can be rationalized.

Although Amsel (4) attributed acquisition effects to motivational factors and extinction differences to associative determinants, it is clear that he has had to invoke associative factors in explaining the observed differences in acquisition of responses to partial and continuous stimuli. It is equally likely that explication of persistence differences in extinction will require the mutual involvement of motivational and associative variables.

Logan (104) and Hill (87) have independently indicated the need for extension of the theoretical structure of the frustrative nonreward concept in at least one important way. Since frustration is said to occur only while the expectation of reward exists (i.e., during differential reward training), they are concerned to explain the level and persistence of incentive during extinction (Logan) and the maintenance (and cross-situation effectiveness) of the frustration-induced aversiveness of a stimulus after training (Hill). Amsel has, of course, denied the necessity of a motivational explanation of extinction effects, but has in fact probably provided the beginning of an answer to these (and some additional questions raised by Hill) in the theoretical extension briefly described above. The current research in which he and his students are heavily involved should further clarify these particular points. But we may expect additional pressure on Amsel (and on others who have found this construct useful) to continue the conceptual as well as the empirical development of frustration theory as it gains wider application.

What will likely compel reconceptualization, however, is the commitment Amsel has so explicitly made to the r_g-s_g model as the basis for his theorizing (4, p. 9). In light of the serious criticism which has been leveled at the use of this response concept as a mediating mechanism (e.g., 38, p. 118), it seems likely that Amsel will want to examine alternative conceptual schemata.

Stimulus-Change as Motivation

For approximately two decades, experimental evidence has been accumulating to the effect that certain stimulus attributes, apparently independently of any known deprivation operation or internal deficit state, were capable of motivating certain kinds of (approach) behavior (22, 70). Research in this area in the 1950s and early 1960s was largely directed toward demonstrations of the existence of curiosity and nondeprivation-instigated exploratory behavior, and the motivational characteristics of such stimulus attributes as complexity, asymmetry, incongruity, relative novelty and unfamiliarity, ambiguity, surprisingness, etc. (22, 24–26, 70, 71).

Only in the past few years have significant attempts been made to build comprehensive motivation models that integrate the established findings from this area into the main body of motivation theory (see 44). One reason for the slow acceptance of work on stimulus-change as motivation was the dominance of deprivation-based drive explanations in motivation and learning theory in this period. Early curiosity and stimulus-change theories sought accommodation to a drive interpretation by positing the existence of curiosity drives, manipulatory drives, boredom drives, etc. (22, 39, 79). It was partly through the inability of the drive concept (or unwillingness of drive theorists) to handle such apparently nondeficit-based types of motivation that alternative models began to receive attention. (One might facetiously suggest that curiosity killed the concept, though as we earlier hinted, the concept has more than one life!)

Alternation behavior.—Two opposing (though complementary) theoretical explanations have been offered for the observation that animals in mazes or other choice situations display spontaneous alternation behavior, i.e., other things being equal, they choose an alley different from the one previously entered. The two types of explanation have been nicely described by Walker (181) as "titillation" and "tedium" theories. "Titillation" theories seek explanations of exploratory and alternation behavior in terms of characteristics of the stimulus situations which are approached; "tedium" theories are cast in terms of either some form of response inhibition or decrement or of adaptation to or satiation with the stimulus situation previously experienced (71, 131, 181). O'Connell (131) has critically compared the assumptions underlying the several theories contributing to the two positions. He concluded that tedium or satiation theories are less parsimonious than titillation or curiosity theories. The prediction of moving *away from* (or lessening of activity in connection with) experienced stimuli, readily made by tedium theories, must be supplemented to account for movement *toward* novel stimulus situations, whereas explanations that satisfactorily deal with the latter (i.e., titillation theories) can more readily incorporate the former.

Fowler (71) takes some exception to O'Connell's conclusion, noting the possibility of unchanging stimulation producing a "boredom drive" (129) reducible by sensory variation, freedom of action, etc. In defending a possible drive interpretation of curiosity, Fowler rejects the suggestion that "attractiveness" might explain not only curiosity but the eliciting of eating and drinking as well, on the basis that "animals that have not recently been deprived of food and water typically do not eat and drink" (71, p. 197). Unfortunately, Fowler ignores the literature on appetite, palatability, and other nondeprivational determinants of eating and drinking (cf. 44, 190), which weaken his arguments.

Drive and incentive theory of stimulus-change motivation.—Fowler's (71) paper offers an interesting reconceptualization of both drive and incentive theory in an attempt to incorporate the findings of stimulus-change motivation into an extended stimulus-response position. He describes the results of a series of experiments conducted in his laboratory over the past several years, designed to provide a neat test of the separate contributions of pre- and post-behavior determinants of response vigor. He studied running speed in rats, using a straight runway with start and goal boxes at the ends. By counterbalancing of stimulus components and length of exposure in both start and goal boxes, Fowler was able to show that speed of response in the runway was influenced by both start box ("drive" condition) manipulations and goal box (incentive or reinforcement condition) manipulations. Fowler than varied the conditions of brightness during rearing and of maintenance over the experimental period. Findings from this study enabled him to implicate *recency,* or temporal proximity, as well as similarity-difference and duration of exposure of pre-exploratory stimulus conditions, as factors affecting vigor of performance instrumental to stimulus-change.

In a tightly argued "formalization" of his drive and incentive-motivational interpretation of stimulus-change phenomena, including his own experimental findings, Fowler draws heavily on the Hull-Spence concepts of D and K and the familiar anticipatory response mechanism (r_g-s_g). The application of this model to exploration is considerably less complex than Amsel's use of it for frustration (4), since Fowler can identify a positive "consummatory" response to change (R_C), whereas Amsel had to posit an aversive and conflicting frustration response (R_F). Fowler's concept of R_C is described as including such elements as "orienting to, observing, and perceptually attending to the change [as evidenced in such responses as] . . . dilation of the pupil, photochemical activity, an opening of the eye, specific head-turning and general movements toward the source of stimulation, a rise in general muscle tonus, and so forth" (71, p. 210). The anticipatory form of R_c, namely r_c, like any other r_g, can subserve the incentive motivational function for stimulus-change situations, thus providing a means for otherwise satiated organisms to become curious.

Fowler (71) pursues the argument (see also 31, 60, 164, and earlier discussion above) that empirical determinants of D (e.g., exposure time, number of trials) necessarily act upon both R_c and its conditioned anticipatory form r_c, thus affecting the motivational value of K. In this way he is able to make a case for the additive (if not independent) effects of D and K on the vigor of the instrumental response. The rationale offered by Fowler can be reviewed instructively in the context of criticisms earlier noted of the r_g-s_g mechanism and of the drive concept.

In arriving at the "new look" in drive theory, Fowler is critical of some of the assumptions of arousal theory alternatives (68, 81, 99, 113). He points out that their "optimal level" concept, allowing for the reinforcing effects of both increase and decrease in arousal, requires either an initially low level of activation as instigation for exploring novel environments or an already high level of arousal (which in novelty exploration would presumably be followed by an even higher level), neither of which would appear a reasonable basis for instigating instrumental stimulus-change behavior.

Fowler's "new look" calls for a relatively minor modification in the definition of drive (71, p. 218) which he feels, however, would allow drive theory to handle stimulus-change situations. He suggests that the defining condition of drive strength be enlarged to incorporate *stimulus duration* as well as *stimulus intensity*. Reinforcement would thus also become a function of reduction of either the intensity or the duration of stimulation, or both. These changes leave inviolate the stimulus intensity reduction aspects of reinforcement. By allowing stimulus *duration* reduction to provide an alternate means of reinforcement, Fowler is enabled to deal with stimulus-change conditions involving "(*a*) the imposition of new and different stimulus elements, (*b*) the removal of 'familiar' stimulus elements, and/or (*c*) *an increment or decrement in the intensity of the new or prevailing stimulation*" (71, p. 218, italics added). Accepting further the previously established limitation on the range of stimulus intensity which can be reinforcing without inducing competing responses [cf. Brown (35)], Fowler is able to see an accommodation of the modified drive theory with adaptation-level theory [Helson (84)] and to the "optimal levels" concept of arousal theory.

Fowler suggests a final important accommodation to arousal theory [see Berlyne (67); and earlier discussion] in allowing that "the anticipatory occurrence of the consummatory reaction to change (r_c) will comprise *both peripheral and central (arousal) components*, the latter presumably reflecting a neurophysiological mechanism by which the incentive-motivational construct K exerts its intensifying action on performance" (71, pp. *220–221*, italics added). If drive theorists are willing to accept Fowler's modifications, there would be little serious difference between changed drive theory and changing arousal theory.

Arousal and reinforcement.—Berlyne's important *Nebraska Symposium* paper (26) on "arousal and reinforcement" has been referred to earlier. He reviews and updates some of his own concepts in light of the current findings of his laboratory and in the context of some 400 other papers to which he refers (including a number of Russian and European papers, some as yet untranslated). Berlyne examines the similarities between arousal and three aspects of the drive concept: 1. as a nonspecific energizing agent which strengthens (indiscriminately) any responses evoked or instigated; 2. as a collection of specific drives, each attached to a specific class of behavior; and 3. in regard to its intimate connection with reward (via drive reduction). Agreeing with the first of these descriptions (nonspecific energizing agent), he rejects the second and third conceptions as requiring an inordinate number of specific drives (and attendant physiological and neural centers) to correspond with the many subtle differences in stimulus events which could be energizing, on the one hand, and capable of independent satiation, on the other. (Yet these points are partially contradicted by concessions later in his paper, as noted below.)

After reviewing the evidence for alternative possibilities, Berlyne concludes that a general arousal concept *is* viable [despite Lacey's (96) criticism, noted earlier] if one allows that learning (or innate inhibitory factors) may modify arousal in certain systems and certain situations. However, he considers general arousal, like general intelligence (see earlier discussion), to need supplementation by many other factors (e.g., pleasantness-unpleasantness) in determining behavior.

The paper, though not a complete restatement of Berlyne's theoretical position, is an excellent review of his current conceptions. Some of his conclusions which have bearing on concepts discussed throughout the present review are as follows: 1. There are three kinds of determinants of arousal: (*a*) *psychophysical,* which "depend on amplitude or frequency of some energy transformation"; *(b) ecological,* "correlated with specific threats and specific gratifications"; and *(c) collative,* which "involve conflict between incompatible response tendencies . . . depend on distributions of information [in the stimulus field, and] . . . generally induce some subjective uncertainty" (26. pp. 18–20). 2. ". . . high levels of arousal are aversive and . . . drops from them to more moderate levels are rewarding. These drops may well go together with increases in external stimulation, e.g., when fear or subjective uncertainty is relieved" (p. 30). 3. ". . . reinforcement, and in particular reward, can result in some circumstances from an increase in arousal regardless of whether it is soon followed by a decrease" (p. 30). [This represents a modification of earlier views (22) in which *boredom* and *arousal jag* mechanisms had been proposed.] 4. "All in all, the experimental findings . . . suggest that Sheffield (161) may have been right in pointing to drive induction, rather than drive reduction, as the condition responsible for the reinforcing power of positive rewards like food" (p. 44). Berlyne agrees with Sheffield that vigorous consummatory responses "are indicants of intense drive or excitement." However, he feels that Sheffield has assigned too much significance to such overt responses. "If an increase in drive or arousal is the basis of reward," suggests Berlyne, "evocation of a consummatory response is probably a sufficient rather than a necessary condition for it. The central processes on which reinforcement depends can evidently come from external stimulus conditions and from such events as direct introduction of food into the stomach without specific consummatory activity" (p. 44). Following Olds (133) and others, Berlyne accepts that there are separate reward and aversion systems associated with orientation (approach) and defensive (withdrawal) reactions, respectively. He summarizes his views of how the arousal mechanism works as follows:

> Both systems are, we assume, activated by external stimuli, internal stimuli, or chemical agents that raise arousal. The threshold of the aversion system is higher than that of the reward system, so that moderate increases in arousal mobilize the reward system, while more intense increases in arousal cause the aversion system to become active and exert an inhibitory influence on the reward system. The degree of arousal potential [inherent in the characteristics of the stimulus] that causes the aversion threshold to be crossed seems to vary with the subject's arousal level, going down when arousal is abnormally high (26, p. 87).

This paper contains much more of interest and value than can be conveyed here, and in any case it has been referred to earlier in this review and elsewhere (8). Berlyne's position seems to be moving closer to both information theory and aesthetics.

Adaptation level vs. affective arousal.—Helson's adaptation level (AL) theory (84, 85) is not particularly a theory of motivation, but it has relevance to motivational phenomena as it has to most other psychological processes. It is mentioned here briefly to note the disagreement between Helson's views and those of McClelland et al. (120) regarding affectively toned stimuli. McClelland et al. had posited that affect should be a monotonic function of stimulus intensity, a contention which Helson has recently made clear he does not accept:

> . . . affectively toned stimuli above AL are pleasant (unpleasant), and those below are unpleasant (pleasant), the intensity of affect being a function of distance from the indifference or neutral point. We also assume that motivating power is a function of intensity of affect. Needless to say, affect is not a monotonic function of intensity of stimulation as emphasized in the McClelland-Clark butterfly theory. However, this does not preclude a monotonic ordering of stimuli according to their affective value on a bipolar continuum ranging from extremely unpleasant through indifference to extremely pleasant (85, p. 144).

Verinis, Brandsma & Cofer (176) have now reported a series of experiments designed to test McClelland's hypothesis. They gave college students a set of four successive procedures: 1. a series of questionnaires which manipulated information confirming or disconfirming expectations, obtaining ratings of pleasures and motivation as a result of information return; 2. a series of tasks of graded difficulty to perform, followed by choices of which to continue; 3. a repeat of the first condition but with high interest materials; and 4. a highly ego-involving "aptitude test" situation. In all situations, ratings were obtained to measure the effects of confirmation and disconfirmation of expectancies on affect and motivation. Their findings were that (*a*) direction of discrepancy, rather than magnitude, determined whether affect (and motivation) would be positive or negative; (*b*) most pleasant reactions appeared for large (positive) discrepancies; and (*c*) only in task preference for moderately as compared to very or slightly easy tasks was there part of a "butterfly effect." The authors conclude that little support is given to McClelland's hypothesis but that most of the results are consistent with AL theory expectations.

Fear and Anxiety as Derived Motives

There are at least two major literatures in psychology dealing with acquired fear and anxiety: the one deriving from experimental (largely animal) studies of aversive conditioning (largely with shock), and the other deriving from clinical and personality (largely human) research. Points of contact between the two are limited, although tenuous bridges have been extended from time to time (e.g., 53, 127, 128, 166, 167). Continuity with the previous review of this topic (38) and with the preceding sections of this review is best achieved by dealing with the first of these literatures, assuming that other chapters will be responsible for the second. However, it has seemed the better part of wisdom to treat both, albeit briefly, in the hope that by doing so we can contribute somewhat to the bridge we hope to see some day between them.

Emotional conditioning in animals.—Brown & Farber (38) have shown that conditioned fear meets their criteria (reinforcement, punishment, energization) as a bona fide "secondary motivational system" and we shall not re-review their evidence or arguments. Beecroft (18) provides an overview of some 200 or so papers on subprimate aversive behavior to shock stimulation. He identifies and discusses four types of aversive (or emotional) conditioning: *fear* (neutral stimulus becomes aversive), *escape* (response terminating aversive stimulus is learned), *punishment* (organism learns to refrain from response which produces aversive stimulus), and *avoidance* (organism learns response which prevents an aversive stimulus).

Studies of fear learning demonstrate its acquisition by using the acquired aversive conditioned stimulus (CS) either in a new learning situation or to produce conditioned suppression of ongoing rewarding responding (the conditioned emotional response, or CER), both of which seem to involve the same fear concept (18). Beecroft approaches cautiously the question of whether or not fear learning is an instance of Pavlovian or classical conditioning, as Mowrer (128) and other two-process learning theorists have maintained (cf. 145). After weighing the evidence, he concludes that it probably is. The following points of similarity are noted: "(1) conditioning is rapid; (2) extinction is slow; (3) conditioning depends importantly upon UCS intensity; (4) CS functions are similar; (5) partial reinforcement retards acquisition" (18, p. 52). Two differences lie in (*a*) a lesser continuity in both acquisition and extinction of the fear response than would be expected of a classical conditioning process, and (*b*) the much longer CS-UCS intervals possible for fear learning than have been found effective in classical conditioning.

That fear conditioning is the basic underlying process in punishment and avoidance learning seems likely, even though the precise nature of the mediation remains unclear. Its function in escape learning acquisition is not so evident, however, since the UCS is ever present. D'Amato (47) has called attention to the occurrence of anticipatory responses in avoidance settings even in the absence of avoidance contingencies and, although he doesn't suggest it, these might evidence a role for fear. That it is present can in any case be inferred from observation of emotionality and of freezing to the CS, and from the fact of resistance to extinction of escape responses. The demonstration that fear can be conditioned to apparatus cues (cf. 50, 119) would also implicate an acquired fear mechanism in the retention of escape learning.

LoLordo and Rescorla (105, 106, 142–144) have reported an interesting series of studies on inhibitory processes in fear conditioning in dogs. Their research was conceived in the framework of two-process theory (both were students of Richard Solomon) and designed to support and extend this position. The reasoning behind the studies was that if conditioned fear can be established by excitatory Pavlovian procedures, it should likewise be able to be inhibited by appropriate Pavlovian conditioning. The general experimental procedure employed was a shock-avoidance shuttle box in which dogs were trained on a Sidman avoidance schedule. After initial avoidance training had begun, a series of Pavlovian conditioning sessions, employing tones as CSs, were introduced and alternated with further sessions of avoidance training. The avoidance response was used to index fear.

In a first series of three experiments (144), they were able to demonstrate both conditioned inhibition and discrimination learning in confirmation of their hypotheses. The attempt to extend similar logic to include the "protection of the fear-eliciting capacity of a stimulus from extinction" by pairing it with a previously conditioned inhibitor during extinction was unsuccessful, however (106). In two further studies using the same approach, Rescorla (142, 143) was able to demonstrate nicely the phenomenon of inhibition of delay for fear conditioning (142) and to show "the operation of an underlying Pavlovian timing mechanism in Sidman avoidance behavior" (143, p. 59). In this last study, a CS was paired with different parts of the response-shock interval, following Konorski's (93) suggestion that feedback from the avoidance response is inhibitory as a result of being paired with UCS termination. The paired CSs were subsequently demonstrated to have either excitatory or inhibitory effects on responding, as hypothesized, depending on where in the interval they had been introduced (143).

LoLordo (105), in an experimental arrangement somewhat different from that of the other studies cited, was able to confirm the findings of shock-avoidance response enhancement or depression as a result of classical conditioning of a neutral stimulus paired with shock. Pairing of the CS with a loud noise as UCS was also reported to enhance shock-avoidance responding, although response decrement was not obtained with a negative discriminant stimulus in the noise UCS part of the study. Pavlovian extinction inhibition was likewise not found. These authors interpret the findings of their studies as generally supportive of two-process learning theory, which they are. But it is clear that all of the predictions the theory would have expected to be confirmed were not.

Benline & Simmel (20) tested some predictions from two-process theories by training rats in an avoidance shuttle box and then blocking any CRs for 0, 40, 80, or 160 trials following training but prior to extinction. They expected fear to become extinguished and thus subsequent regular extinction trials to show a deficit. Their results showed only temporary suppression in blocked groups, however, thus only weakly supporting their fear-extinction hypothesis.

D'Amato [D'Amato, Fazzaro & Etkin (48)] continues to question two-process explanations of avoidance conditioning, pointing to alternate possibilities of interpretations of the same experimental findings. In a neatly designed set of experiments, D'Amato, Fazzaro & Etkin (48) tested the possibility that CS termination on CR trials in avoidance learning facilitated such responses as a function of the *cue* value of the removal of the CS rather than its role in fear reduction, as posited by two-process theory. They were able to demonstrate significant improvement in learning, in both delayed and trace conditioning paradigms, as a consequence of the use of discriminative cues introduced at the occurrence of the CR. The distinctive cues (light or noise) were given on avoidance trials only and were thus not associated with either shock onset or shock offset (48, p. 42). Since the fear reduction idea is central to the two-process position, some accommodation seems called for. A reinterpretation in terms of some kind of uncertainty or confirmation hypothesis might be possible and would not be inconsistent with some of the arousal notions discussed earlier.

The parameters of fear learning and other aversive conditioning situations are sufficiently complex so as to continue to absorb much of the energy of investigators in this field in their unraveling. Study after study (cf. 18,

38) presents findings of often quite subtle effects on acquisition, extinction, long-term retention, generalization, "incubation," etc. These in turn are attributed to sometimes subtle variations in such factors as the length and temporal patterning of CS, UCS, CS-UCS intervals, intertrial intervals, and intersession intervals; the number of pretraining, training or extinction trials; CS or UCS intensity; delay vs. trace conditioning paradigms; similarities and differences in pretraining, training, extinction, and even post-extinction environments; or combinations or permutations of same. (And these omit any parallel physiological, psychophysical and neuropsychological manipulations that are rapidly becoming part of the scene!) Such studies are necessary, of course, if the issues in question are to be resolved. And the experiments generated are often ingeniously designed and carefully executed. One only regrets that they seem to advance our knowledge of relevant variables (whichever these are) less rapidly than could be desired.

Anxiety and arousal in man.—Attention should be drawn to an interesting set of formal proposals by Epstein (62), which he offers "toward a unified theory of anxiety." Reviewed favorably and in some detail last year under the personality topic (2), Epstein's paper is one of many in the burgeoning annual *Progress in. . . .* series and may not be read as widely as it should. It is as much a theory of arousal as of anxiety and draws on a wide range of both clinical and psychophysiological sources, as well as on Epstein's interesting studies (with Fenz) of sport parachutists.

The theory has many features in common with other arousal positions: two-factor (anxiety-inhibition), inverted U-shaped arousal function, generalization gradients of different steepness for excitation and inhibition, etc. A number of differences, however, and an elaborate set of postulates plus a single, unifying, general Law of Excitatory Modulation proposed as underlying the functioning of all excitatory-inhibitory systems, make the theory unique enough to warrant study.

Anxiety and derived human motives.—The expanding literature of experimental studies of motivation in animals is like a small brook in comparison to the flood of articles and books on human motivation. For anxiety alone, Spielberger (165) reports some 3500 items since 1950 and shows an exponential growth curve (p. 6) for the number appearing each year. In confirmation, Adelson (2) notes that anxiety was the "most popular topic" in the field of personality research last year.

One reason for the relative frequency of references to anxiety is the increasing use being made of the concept as a relevant variable in a wide range of studies, from achievement motivation (12) and fear of failure (30) through interpersonal attraction (40, 185), conformity (121), approval need (46, 148), and cognitive control (137, 191).

While there is still little agreement as to what anxiety scales really measure [Cattell & Scheier (42) had reported more than 120 such scales in existence close to a decade ago], there is common agreement that anxiety is a formidable energizer, functioning to instigate or release avoidant behavior (and thus confounding measurement of other motives). Common to many concepts of anxiety, as defined by their measures, are the bipolar factors of *defensiveness* and *emotionality* (2, 74). The validity (as well as circularity) of this finding is amply demonstrated in many studies of conformity, need for approval, and fear of failure, where characteristics of "high defensiveness" and "vulnerable self-esteem" are reported (30, 46).

Methodological problems continue to plague investigators in this area, though they are of a different kind than those cited for animal experimenters above. Adelson (2) has more than adequately reviewed these difficulties, and they will not be re-examined here. It is encouraging to note, however, the evidently increasing awareness of and sensitivity to problems of sampling subjects, situations, and variables. Variables intrinsic to the design of motivation measures have come under closer scrutiny, as well. Thus greater attention is directed to distinguishing task from dispositional arousal traits (157), for example, and to the need to identify "false negative" (defensive denial) responding to anxiety and other "threatening" questionnaires (cf. 33) Crowne & Marlowe (46) were obliged to invoke a concept of "defensiveness and vulnerable self-esteem" to account for certain paradoxical results in their assessment of the approval motive. And the problem of "defenses" was raised as well by Zimbardo (191). After obtaining data demonstrating the efficiency of cognitive control over motivational state (in a lowering of physiological, behavioral, and subjective arousal indices), he questions "whether dissonance reduction has in fact led to a real reduction of the original drive," or if he has uncovered "the first stage in a process of active denial of the motivation which eventually leads to a functional reduction of the drive" (191, p. 921). The function of defenses in the elaboration of inappropriate emotional response to a hostility-provoking situation is also evident in a study by Conn & Crowne (45), based on the model of the Schachter-Singer (152) experiments.

Achievement Motivation vs. Fear of Failure

The most active area of research in the field of derived motives remains that of achievement and fear of failure motivation. Research and current theorizing are summarized in three relatively recent books: Atkinson & Feather's *A Theory of Achievement Motivation* (12), Heckhausen's *The Anatomy of Achievement Motivation* (83), and Birney, Burdick & Teevan's *Fear of Failure* (30). The conceptualizing of the three differ, but their methodologies and approach are similar.

The Atkinson-Feather theoretical model uses the Spence-Brown formulation which assigns energizing properties to drive and directing properties to habit. The term *tendency* (T) has replaced the term motivation (11) in referring to the product of motive, expectancy, and incentive, although no change in meaning is implied. Tendency to achieve success is indicated by the formula $T_s = P_s \times (M_s \times I_s)$, where P_s is the strength of expectancy (*subjective probability*) that success will be the consequence of a particular activity, *Ms* is the motive to succeed, and I_s is the *incentive value* of success at that activity. The incentive value (I_s) is proportionate to the difficulty of a given task ($I_s = 1 - P_s$), and M (motivation) and I (incentive) may be conceived as equivalent to the subjective value of success. Since $I_s = 1 - P_s$ and I and M combine multiplicatively, differences in T_s that are attributable to M_s will be large only when P_s is near 0.50.

This formulation (with assumptions spelled out more fully) provides the theoretical justification for a new method of measuring the strength of the achievement motive. A set of inverted-U curves can be projected by plotting M_s as a function of T_s and P_s (with the steepness rising with value of M_s). Failure to find the normally expected superiority in performance of persons high in achievement need (nAch) may now be understood as a function of a task which is either too difficult or too easy.

Atkinson & Feather treat a posited *tendency to avoid failure* (T_{-f}) in a parallel manner ($T_{-f} = M_{AF} \times P_f \times I_f$), where M_{AF} is the motive to avoid failure, etc. It is maintained that in the case of achievement-oriented activity, anxiety about failure is associated with the tendency to inhibit a particular activity. Thus, what an individual in whom M_{AF} is greater than M_s does (in an achieving context) may be construed as avoidant or defensive behavior. In the Atkinson-Feather view, anxiety is symptomatic, not causal.

Birney, Burdick & Teevan (30) are critical of the Atkinson-Feather failure avoidance model on a number of grounds. They consider variations in *incentive* (I_s or I_f) more critical than M_s or M_f in predicting behavior in particular contexts. "A person with a high Fear of Failure score can be placed in game settings, examinations, and championship contests, and there is no doubt his resultant motivation will vary, but it is the situational index related to Incentive that gives us our estimates of variation, not changes in his Fear of Failure score" (30, p. 179). After studying achievement and failure avoidance motivation for a number of years, Birney, Burdick & Teevan conclude that the two are probably independent personality dimensions.

Heckhausen's (83) work on achievement and fear of failure motivation has been done in Germany, and provides an interesting opportunity for cross-cultural comparisons.

The search for developmental origins of achievement, fear of failure, approval, and other "needs" is evident in current research (cf. 177, 178). Within the achievement motivation domain, theoretical formulations have reached a high level of sophistication, but the problems of measurement have trailed far behind. Klinger (92) summarizes the problem: "Insofar as TATnAch has been found systematically related to a number of other organismic variables, its unrelatedness to self-descriptive achievement measures and to performance scores poses a serious puzzle of construct validity" (p. 158).

Concluding Comments

No attempt was made to "cover the field" since there was obviously too much to cover. Our choice then was either to restrict the field more narrowly or to sample. We chose the latter. In doing so we made some difficult choices and left out subareas of interest and reasonable activity. (Some areas were undoubtedly left out as a function of ignorance, as well.) What we hope was conveyed in this review is the sense of movement and change that is going on in relation to theory and research on derived motives and some suggestions as to its vitality.

There would appear to be an abundance of excellent "mini-theories," but there hasn't been a book with the impact of Hebb's *Organization of Behavior* (80) in 20 years. There are many "mini-languages" as well, but as yet no common one. Convergence and accommodation are clearly in evidence. Perhaps the time for integration across conceptual barriers and across the animal-human literature gap is finally upon us.

We conclude where we began. "Of the many intervening variables that psychologists use, the concept of motive (motivation) is among the most controversial and least satisfactory" (43, p. 304); but certainly among the most invigorating!

LITERATURE CITED

1. Abelson, R. P., Aronson, E., McGuire, W. J., Newcomb, T. M., Rosenberg, M. J., Tannenbaum, P. H., Eds. *Theories of Cognitive Consistency: A Sourcebook* (Rand McNally, Chicago, 1968)
2. Adelson, J. Personality. *Ann. Rev. Psychol.,* **20,** 217–52 (1969)
3. Amsel, A. The role of frustrative nonreward in noncontinuous reward situations. *Psychol. Bull.,* **55,** 102–19 (1958)
4. Amsel, A. Partial reinforcement effects on vigor and persistence. In *The Psychology of Learning and Motivation: Advances in Research and Theory,* **1,** 1–65 (Spence, K. W., Spence, J. T., Eds., Academic Press, New York, 1967)
5. Amsel, A., Rashotte, M. E., MacKinnon, J. R. Partial reinforcement effects within-subject and between-subjects. *Psychol. Monogr.,* **79,** No. 20 (1966)
6. Amsel, A., Roussel, J. Motivational properties of frustration: I. Effect on a running response of the addition of frustration to the motivational complex. *J. Exptl. Psychol.,* **43,** 363–68 (1952)
7. Amsel, A., Ward, J. S. Frustration and persistence: Resistance to discrimination following prior experience with the discriminanda. *Psychol. Monogr.,* **79,** No. 4 (1965)
8. Appley, M. H. Review. *Nebraska Symposium on Motivation, 1967. Am. Scientist,* **56,** 303–4A (1968)
9. Armus, H. L., Carlson, K. R., Guinan, J. F., Crowell, R. A. Effect of a secondary reinforcement stimulus on the auditory response. *Psychol. Rept.,* **14,** 535–40 (1964)
10. Armus, H. L., Sniadowski-Dolinsky, D. Startle decrement and secondary reinforcement stimulation. *Psychon. Sci.,* **4,** 175–76 (1966)
11. Atkinson, J. W. *An Introduction to Motivation* (Van Nostrand, Princeton, N.J., 335 pp., 1964)
12. Atkinson, J. W., Feather, N. T., Eds. *A Theory of Achievement Motivation* (Wiley, New York, 392 pp., 1966)
13. Ax, A. F. Invited commentary. In *Psychological Stress: Issues in Research,* 37–39 (Appley, M. H., Trumbull, R., Eds., Appleton-Century-Crofts, New York, 471 pp., 1967)
14. Bacon, W. E., Bindra, D. The generality of the incentive-motivational effects of classically conditioned stimuli in instrumental learning. *Acta Biol. Exptl. (Warsaw),* **27,** 185–97 (1967)
15. Baldwin, A. L. *Theories of Child Development* (Wiley, New York, 618 pp., 1967)
16. Beach, F. A. The descent of instinct. *Psychol. Rev.,* **62,** 401–10 (1955)
17. Beach, F. A. Characteristics of masculine sex drive. In *Nebraska Symposium on Motivation, 1956,* 1–32 (Jones, M. R., Ed., Univ. Nebraska Press, Lincoln)
18. Beecroft, R. S. Emotional conditioning. *Psychon. Monogr. Suppl.,* **2,** 45–72 (1967)
19. Bélanger, D. *Studies on the Relation Between Motivation, Activation and Behavior* (Presented to Can. Psychol. Assoc., Montreal, 1961)
20. Benline, T. A., Simmel, E. C. Effects of blocking of the avoidance response on the elimination of the conditioned fear response. *Psychon. Sci.,* **18,** 357–58 (1967)
21. Berger, S. M., Lambert, W. W. Stimulus-response theory in contemporary social psychology. In *Handbook of Social Psychology,* Rev. Ed., **2,** Chap. 2, 81–178 (Lindzey, G., Aronson, E., Eds., Addison-Wesley, Reading, Mass., 1968)
22. Berlyne, D. E. *Conflict, Arousal and Curiosity* (McGraw-Hill, New York, 1960)
23. Berlyne, D. E. Conflict and the orientation reaction. *J. Exptl. Psychol.,* **62,** 476–83 (1961)
24. Berlyne, D. E. Motivation problems raised by exploratory and epistemic behavior. In *Psychology—A Study of a Science,* **5,** 284–364 (Koch, S., Ed., McGraw-Hill, New York, 1963)
25. Berlyne, D. E. Curiosity and exploration. *Science,* **153,** 25–33 (1966)
26. Berlyne, D. E. Arousal and reinforcement. In *Nebraska Symposium on Motivation, 1967,* 1–110 (See Ref. 100)
27. Bindra, D. Neuropsychological interpretation of the effects of drive and incentive-motivation on general

activity and instrumental behavior. *Psychol. Rev.,* **75,** 1–22 (1968)

28. Bindra, D. The interrelated mechanisms of reinforcement and motivation, and the nature of their influence on response. In *Nebraska Symposium on Motivation, 1969* (Levine, D., Ed., Univ. Nebraska Press, Lincoln, in press)
29. Bindra, D., Palfai, T. Nature of positive and negative incentive-motivational effects on general activity. *J. Comp. Physiol. Psychol.,* **63,** 288–97 (1967)
30. Birney, R. C., Burdick, H., Teevan, R. C. *Fear of Failure* (Van Nostrand-Reinhold, New York, 280 pp., 1969)
31. Black, R. W. On the combination of drive and incentive motivation. *Psychol. Rev.,* **72,** 310–17 (1965)
32. Bolles, R. C. *Theory of Motivation* Harper & Row, New York, 546 pp., 1967)
33. Boor, M., Schill, T. Digit symbol performance of subjects varying in anxiety and defensiveness. *J. Consult. Psychol.,* **31,** 600–3 (1967)
34. Bower, G., McLean, J., Meacham, J. Value of knowing when reinforcement is due. *J. Comp. Physiol. Psychol.,* **62,** 184–92 (1966)
35. Brown, J. S. Principles of intrapersonal conflict. *J. Confl. Resol.,* **1,** 135–54 (1957)
36. Brown, J. S. *The Motivation of Behavior* (McGraw-Hill, New York, 1961)
37. Brown, J. S., Farber, I. E. Emotions conceptualized as intervening variables—with suggestions toward a theory of frustration. *Psychol. Bull.,* **48,** 465–95 (1951)
38. Brown, J. S., Farber, I. E. Secondary motivational systems. *Ann. Rev. Psychol.,* **19,** 99–134 (1968)
39. Butler, R. A. Incentive conditions which influence visual exploration. *J. Exptl. Psychol.,* **48,** 19–23 (1954)
40. Byrne, D., Clore, G. L., Jr. Effectance arousal and attraction. *J. Pers. Soc. Psychol.,* **6,** 1–18 (1967)
41. Campbell, B. A., Misanin, J. R. Basic drives. *Ann. Rev. Psychol.,* **20,** 57–84 (1969)
42. Cattell, R. B., Scheier, I. H. *The Meaning and Measurement of Neuroticism and Anxiety* (Ronald Press, New York, 1961)
43. Chaplin, J. P. *Dictionary of Psychology* (Dell Publ., New York, 537 pp., 1968)
44. Cofer, C. N., Appley, M. H. *Motivation: Theory and Research* (Wiley, New York, 958 pp., 1964)
45. Conn, L. K., Crowne, D. P. Instigation to aggression, emotional arousal and defensive emulation. *J. Pers.,* **32,** 163–79 (1964)
46. Crowne, D. P., Marlowe, D. *The Approval Motive* (Wiley, New York, 1964)
47. D'Amato, M. R. Role of anticipatory responses in avoidance conditioning: An important control. *Psychon. Sci.,* **8,** 191–92 (1967)
48. D'Amato, M. R., Fazzaro, J., Etkin, M. Anticipatory responding and avoidance discrimination as factors in avoidance conditioning. *J. Exptl. Psychol.,* **77,** 41–47 (1968)
49. Darrow, C. W. The galvanic skin reflex (sweating) and blood-pressure as preparatory and facilitative functions. *Psychol. Bull.,* **33,** 73–94 (1936)
50. DeBold, R. C. Stimulus control of acquired fear and instrumental behavior. *Psychon. Sci.,* **5,** 439–40 (1966)
51. Denny, M. R., Adelman, H. M. Elicitation theory: I. An analysis of two typical learning situations. *Psychol. Rev.,* **62,** 290–96 (1955)
52. Denny, M. R., Martindale, R. L. The effect of the initial reinforcement on response tendency. *J. Exptl. Psychol.,* **52,** 95–100 (1956)
53. Dollard, J., Miller, N. E. *Personality and Psychotherapy: An Analysis in Terms of Learning, Thinking and Culture* (McGraw-Hill, New York, 1950)
54. Duffy, E. Emotion: An example of the need for reorientation in psychology. *Psychol. Rev.,* **41,** 184–98 (1934)
55. Duffy, E. The concept of energy mobilization. *Ibid.,* **58,** 30–40 (1951)
56. Duffy, E. The psychological significance of the concept of "arousal" or "activation." *Ibid.,* **64,** 265–75 (1957)
57. Duffy, E. *Activation and Behavior* (Wiley, New York, 1962)
58. Duffy, E. The nature and development of the concept of activation. In *Current Research in Motivation,* 278–81 (See Ref. 77)
59. Dufresne, C. Influence de la priva-

tion de nourriture sur le rythme cardiaque et l'activité instrumentale. (Master's thesis, Université de Montreal, 1961)

60. Dyal, J. A. "On the combination of drive and incentive motivation:" A critical comment. *Psychol. Rept.,* **20,** 543–50 (1967)

61. Elliott, R. Physiological activity and performance: A comparison of kindergarten children with young adults. *Psychol. Monogr.,* **78,** 10 (1964)

62. Epstein, S. Toward a unified theory of anxiety. In *Prog. Exptl. Personality Res.,* **4,** 1–89

63. Erikson, E. H. Identity and the life cycle: Selected papers. *Psychol. Issues,* **1,** No. 1 (1959)

64. Estes, W. K. Growth and function of mathematical models for learning. In *Current Trends in Psychological Theory,* 134–51 (Univ. Pittsburgh Press, Pittsburgh, Pa., 1961)

65. Estes, W. K. Learning theory. *Ann. Rev. Psychol.,* **13,** 107–44 (1962)

66. Feldman, S., Ed. *Cognitive Consistency: Motivational Antecedents and Behavioral Consequences* (Academic Press, New York, 1966)

67. Feldman, S. M., Waller, H. J. Dissociation of electrocortical activation and behavioral arousal. *Nature,* **196,** 1320–22 (1962)

68. Fiske, D. W., Maddi, S. R. A conceptual framework. In *Functions of Varied Experience,* 11–56 (Fiske, D. W., Maddi, S. R., Eds., Dorsey Press, Homewood, Ill., 1961)

69. Flavell, J. H., Hill, J. P. Developmental psychology. *Ann. Rev. Psychol.,* **20,** 1–56 (1969)

70. Fowler, H. *Curiosity and Exploratory Behavior* (Macmillan, New York, 1965)

71. Fowler, H. Satiation and curiosity: Constructs for a drive and incentive-motivational theory of exploration. In *The Psychology of Learning and Motivation: Advances in Research and Theory,* **1,** 157–227 (See Ref. 4)

72. Freeman, G. L. The optimal muscular tensions for various performances. *Am. J. Psychol.,* **51,** 146–50 (1938)

73. Freeman, G. L. *The Energetics of Human Behavior* (Cornell Univ. Press, Ithaca, N.Y., 1948)

74. Golin, S., Herron, E. W., Lakota, R., Reineck, L. Factor analytic study of the manifest anxiety, extraversion, and repression-sensitization scales. *J. Consult. Psychol.,* **31,** 564–69 (1967)

75. Graham, F. K., Clifton, R. K. Heart-rate change as a component of the orienting response. *Psychol. Bull.,* **65,** 305–20 (1966)

76. Grastyan, E., Karmos, G., Vereczkey, L., Kellenyi, L. The hippocampal electrical correlates of the homeostatic regulation of motivation. *Elecroenceph. Clin. Neurophysiol.,* **21,** 34–53 (1966)

77. Haber, R. N., Ed. *Current Research in Motivation* (Holt, Rinehart & Winston, New York, 800 pp., 1966)

78. Hall, C. S., Lindzey, G. *Theories of Personality* (Wiley, New York, 1957)

79. Harlow, H. F. Motivation as a factor in the acquisition of new responses. In *Current Theory and Research in Motivation,* 24–49 (Brown, J. S., Harlow, H. F., Postman, L. J., Nowlis, V., Newcomb, T. M., Mowrer, O. H., Univ. Nebraska Press, Lincoln, 1953)

80. Hebb, D. O. *The Organization of Behavior* (Wiley, New York, 1949)

81. Hebb, D. O. Drives and the C.N.S. (Conceptual nervous system). *Psychol. Rev.,* **62,** 243–54 (1955)

82. Hebb, D. O. *A Textbook of Psychology,* 2nd ed. (W. B. Saunders, Philadelphia, 353 pp., 1966)

83. Heckhausen, H. *The Anatomy of Achievement Motivation* (Academic Press, New York, 215 pp., 1967)

84. Helson, H. *Adaptation-Level Theory: An Experimental and Systematic Approach to Behavior* (Harper, New York, 1964)

85. Helson, H. Some problems in motivation from the point of view of the theory of Adaptation Level. In *Nebraska Symposium on Motivation, 1966,* 137–82 (Levine, D., Ed., Univ. Nebraska Press, Lincoln)

86. Hill, J. P. *Minnesota Symposia on Child Psychology, I* (Univ. Minnesota Press, Minneapolis, 239 pp., 1967)

87. Hill, W. F. An attempted clarifica-

tion of frustration theory. *Psychol. Rev.*, **75**, 173–76 (1968)

88. Hinde, R. A. *Animal Behavior* (McGraw-Hill, New York, 1966)
89. Holt, R. R. Recent developments in psychoanalytic ego psychology and their implications for diagnostic testing. *J. Project. Tech.*, **24**, 254–66 (1960)
90. Hull, C. L. *A Behavior System* (Yale Univ. Press, New Haven, Conn., 1952)
91. Hunt, J. McV. Motivation inherent in information processing and action. In *Cognitive Factors in Motivation and Social Organization*, 35–94 (Harvey, O. J., Ed., Ronald Press, New York, 1963)
92. Klinger, E. Short-term stability and concurrent validity of TAT need scores; achievement, affiliation and hostile press. *Proc. 76th Ann. Conv., Am. Psychol. Assoc., 1968*, 157–58
93. Konorski, J. *Conditioned Reflexes and Neuron Organization* (Cambridge Univ. Press, London, 1948)
94. Lacey, J. I. Individual differences in somatic response patterns. *J. Comp. Physiol. Psychol.*, **43**, 338–50 (1950)
95. Lacey, J. I. The evaluation of autonomic responses: Toward a general solution. *Ann. N.Y. Acad. Sci.*, **67**, 123–64 (1956)
96. Lacey, J. I. Somatic response patterning and stress: Some revisions of activation theory. In *Psychological Stress: Issues in Research*, 14–42 (See Ref. 13)
97. Lacey, J. I., Kagan, J., Lacey, B. C., Moss, H. A. The visceral level: Situational determinants and behavioral correlates of autonomic response patterns. In *Expression of the Emotions in Man*, 161–96 (Knapp, P. H., Ed., Intern. Univ. Press, New York, 1963)
98. Lawson, R. *Frustration* (MacMillan, New York, 192 pp., 1965)
99. Leuba, C. Toward some integration of learning theories: The concept of optimal stimulation. *Psychol. Rept.*, **1**, 27–33 (1955)
100. Levine, D., Ed. *Nebraska Symposium on Motivation, 1967* (Univ. Nebraska Press, Lincoln, 335 pp.)
101. Lindsley, D. B. Emotion. In *Handbook of Experimental Psychology*, 473–516 (Stevens, S. S., Ed., Wiley, New York, 1951)
102. Lindsley, D. B. Psychophysiology and motivation. In *Nebraska Symposium on Motivation, 1957*, 44–105 (Jones, M. R., Ed., Univ. Nebraska Press, Lincoln)
103. Logan, F. A., Ed. *Incentive* (Yale Univ. Press, New Haven, Conn., 1960)
104. Logan, F. A. Incentive theory and changes in reward. In *The Psychology of Learning and Motivation: Advances in Research and Theory*, **2**, 1–30 (Spence, K. W., Spence, J. T., Eds., Academic Press, New York, 1968)
105. LoLordo, V. M. Similarity of conditioned fear responses based upon different aversive events. *J. Comp. Physiol. Psychol.*, **64**, 154–58 (1967)
106. LoLordo, V. M., Rescorla, R. A. Protection of the fear-eliciting capacity of a stimulus from extinction. *Acta Biol. Explt. (Warsaw)*, **26**, 251–58 (1966)
107. Maatsch, J. L. Reinforcement and extinction phenomena. *Psychol. Rev.*, **61**, 111–18 (1954)
108. Maatsch, J. L. Learning and fixation after a single shock trial. *J. Comp. Physiol. Psychol.*, **52**, 408–10 (1959)
109. Madsen, K. B. *Theories of Motivation*, 4th ed. (Kent State Univ. Press, Kent, Ohio, 365 pp., 1968)
110. Maher, B. A., Ed. *Prog. Exptl. Personality Res.*, **4** (1967)
111. Malmo, R. B. Anxiety and behavioral arousal. *Psychol. Rev.*, **64**, 276–87 (1957)
112. Malmo, R. B., Measurement of drive: An unsolved problem. In *Nebraska Symposium on Motivation, 1958*, 229–65 (Jones, M. R., Ed., Univ. Nebraska Press, Lincoln)
113. Malmo, R. B. Activation: A neuropsychological dimension. *Psychol. Rev.*, **66**, 367–86 (1959)
114. Malmo, R. B. On central and autonomic nervous system mechanisms in conditioning, learning, and performance. *Can. J. Psychol.*, **17**, 1–36 (1963)
115. Malmo, R. B. Physiological gradients and behavior. *Psychol. Bull.*, **64**, 225–34 (1965)
116. Malmo, R. B. Cognitive factors in impairment: A neuropsychological study of divided set. *J. Exptl. Psychol.*, **71**, 184–89 (1966)
117. Malmo, R. B., Bélanger, D. Related

physiological and behavioral changes: What are their determinants? In *Sleep and Altered States of Consciousness,* Assoc. Res. Nerv. Ment. Dis., **45,** Chap. 14, 228–318 (Williams & Wilkins, Baltimore, Md., 1967)

118. Marx, M. H. The activation of habits. *Psychol. Rept.,* **19,** 527–50, Monogr. Suppl. 4–V19 (1966)
119. McAllister, W. R., McAllister, D. E. Variables influencing the conditioning and measurement of acquired fear. In *Classical Conditioning* (Prokasy, W. F., Ed., Appleton-Century-Crofts, New York, 1965)
120. McClelland, D. C., Atkinson, J. W., Clark, R. A., Lowell, E. L. *The Achievement Motive* (Appleton-Century-Crofts, New York, 1953)
121. McGhee, P. E., Teevan, R. C. Conformity behavior and need for affiliation. *J. Soc. Psychol.,* **72,** 117–21 (1967)
122. Miller, N. E. Liberalization of basic S-R concepts: Extensions to conflict behavior, motivation, and social learning. In *Psychology—A Study of a Science,* **2,** Study I, 196–292 (Koch, S., Ed., McGraw-Hill, New York, 1959)
123. Miller, N. E. Analytic studies of drive and reward. *Am. Psychologist,* **16,** 739–54 (1961)
124. Miller, N. E. Some reflections on the law of effect produce a new alternative to drive reduction. In *Nebraska Symposium on Motivation, 1963,* 65–112 (Jones, M. R., Ed., Univ. Nebraska Press, Lincoln)
125. Miller, N. E., Learning of visceral and glandular responses. *Science,* **163,** 434–45 (1969)
126. Miller, N. E., DeBold, R. C. Classically conditioned tongue-licking and operant bar pressing recorded simultaneously in the rat. *J. Comp. Physiol. Psychol.,* **59,** 100–11 (1965)
127. Mowrer, O. H. *Learning Theory and Personality Dynamics: Selected Papers* (Ronald Press, New York, 1950)
128. Mowrer, O. H. *Learning Theory and Behavior* (Wiley, New York, 1960)
129. Myers, A. K., Miller, N. E. Failure to find a learned drive based on hunger; evidence for learning motivated by "exploration." *J. Comp. Physiol. Psychol.,* **47,** 428–36 (1954)
130. Obrist, P. A. Cardiovascular differentiation of sensory stimuli. *Psychosomat. Med.,* **25,** 450–59 (1963)
131. O'Connell, R. H. Trials with tedium and titillation. *Psychol. Bull.,* **63,** 170–79 (1965)
132. Olds, J. Self-stimulation experiments and differential reward systems. In *Reticular Formation of the Brain,* 671–87 (Jaspers, H. H., Knighton, L. D., Noshay, W. C., Costello, R. T., Eds., Little, Brown, Boston, 1958)
133. Olds, J., Olds, M. E. Drives, rewards and the brain. In *New Directions in Psychology II,* 329–410 (Baron, F., Dement, W. C., Edwards, W., Lindman, H., Phillips, D., Olds, J., Olds, M. E., Holt, Rinehart & Winston, 1965)
134. Perkins, C. C., Jr. A conceptual scheme for studies of stimulus generalization. In *Stimulus Generalization* (Mostofsky, D. I., Ed., Stanford Univ. Press, Stanford, Calif., 1965)
135. Perkins, C. C., Jr. An analysis of the concept of reinforcement. *Psychol. Rev.,* **75,** 155–72 (1968)
136. Perkins, C. C., Jr., Seymann, R. G., Levis, D. J., Spencer, H. R., Jr. Factors affecting preference for signal-shock over shock-signal. *J. Exptl. Psychol.,* **72,** 190–96 (1966)
137. Pillard, R. C., Atkinson, K. W., Fisher, S. The effect of different preparations on film-induced anxiety. *Psychol. Rec.,* **17,** 35–41 (1967)
138. Premack, D. Predicting instrumental performance from the independent rate of the contingent response. *J. Exptl. Psychol.,* **61,** 163–71 (1961)
139. Premack, D. Reversibility of the reinforcement relation. *Science,* **136,** 255–57 (1962)
140. Premack, D. Reinforcement theory. In *Nebraska Symposium on Motivation, 1965,* 123–88 (Levine, D., Ed., Univ. Nebraska Press, Lincoln)
141. Rapaport, D. On the psychoanalytic theory of motivation. In *Nebraska Symposium on Motivation, 1960,* 173–247 (Jones, M. R., Ed., Univ. Nebraska Press, Lincoln)
142. Rescorla, R. A. Inhibition of delay

in Pavlovian fear conditioning. *J. Comp. Physiol. Psychol.,* **64,** 114–20 (1967)
143. Rescorla, R. A. Pavlovian conditioned fear in Sidman avoidance learning. *Ibid.,* **65,** 55–60 (1968)
144. Rescorla, R. A., LoLordo, V. M. Inhibition of avoidance behavior. *J. Comp. Physiol. Psychol.,* **59,** 406–12 (1965)
145. Rescorla, R. A., Solomon, R. L. Two-process learning theory: Relationships between Pavlovian conditioning and instrumental learning. *Psychol. Rev.,* **74,** 151–82 (1967)
146. Roberts, W. W., Carey, R. J. Rewarding effect on performance of gnawing aroused by hypothalamic stimulation in the rat. *J. Comp. Physiol. Psychol.,* **59,** 317–24 (1965)
147. Robinson, E. S. Work of the integrated organism. In *Handbook of General Experimental Psychology,* 571–650 (Murchison, C., Ed., Clark Univ. Press, Worcester, Mass., 1934)
148. Rosenfeld, J. M. Some perceptual and cognitive correlates of strong approval motivation. *J. Consult. Psychol.,* **31,** 507–12 (1967)
149. Rosenzweig, M. R. Environmental complexity, cerebral change, and behavior. *Am. Psychologist,* **21,** 321–32 (1966)
150. Routtenberg, A. The two-arousal hypothesis: Reticular formation and limbic system. *Psychol. Rev.,* **75,** 51–80 (1968)
151. Schachter, S. *The Psychology of Affiliation* (Stanford Univ. Press, Stanford, Cal., 141 pp., 1959)
152. Schachter, S., Singer, J. E. Cognitive, social and physiological determinants of emotional state. *Psychol. Rev.,* **69,** 379–99 (1962)
153. Schosberg, H. Three dimensions of emotion. *Psychol. Rev.,* **61,** 81–88 (1954)
154. Schneirla, T. C. An evolutionary and developmental theory of biphasic processes underlying approach and withdrawal. In *Nebraska Symposium on Motivation, 1959,* 1–42 (Jones, M. R., Ed., Univ. Nebraska Press, Lincoln)
155. Schönpflug, W. Paarlernen, Behaltensdauer und Aktivierung. *Psychol. Forsch.,* **29,** 132–48 (1966) (cited by Berlyne, 1967)
156. Scott, J. P. The development of social motivation. In *Nebraska Symposium on Motivation, 1967,* 111–32 (**See** Ref. 100)
157. Sears, D. O. Social anxiety, opinion structure and opinion change. *J. Pers. Soc. Psychol.,* **7,** 142–51 (1967)
158. Sears, D. O., Abeles, R. P. Attitudes and opinions. *Ann. Rev. Psychol.,* **20,** 253–88 (1969)
159. Seward, J. P. Introduction to a theory of motivation in learning. *Psychol. Rev.,* **59,** 405–13 (1952)
160. Seward, J. P. Drive, incentive and reinforcement. *Ibid.,* **63,** 195–203 (1956)
161. Sheffield, F. D. A drive-induction theory of reinforcement. In *Current Research in Motivation,* 99–122 (See Ref. 77)
162. Solomon, R. L., Turner, L. H. Discriminative classical conditioning in dogs paralyzed by curare can later control discriminative avoidance responses in the normal state. *Psychol. Rev.,* **69,** 202–19 (1962)
163. Spence, K. W. Theoretical interpretations of learning. In *Comparative Psychology,* 3rd ed., 239–91 (Stone, C. P., Ed., Prentice-Hall, New York, 1951)
164. Spence, K. W. *Behavior Theory and Conditioning* (Yale Univ. Press, New Haven, Conn., 1956)
165. Spielberger, C. D., Ed., *Anxiety and Behavior* (Academic Press, New York, 1966)
166. Taylor, J. A. Drive theory and manifest anxiety. *Psychol. Bull.,* **53,** 303–20 (1956)
167. Taylor, J. A., Spence, K. W. Conditioning level in behavior disorders. *J. Abnorm. Soc. Psychol.,* **49,** 497–502 (1954)
168. Thomas, W. I. *The Unadjusted Girl* (Little, Brown, Boston, Mass., 1923)
169. Thorndike, E. L. *Animal Intelligence* (MacMillan, New York, 1911)
170. Thorndike, E. L. *The Psychology of Wants, Interests and Attitudes* (Appleton-Century, New York, 1935)
171. Thorpe, W. H. *Learning and Instinct in Animals* (Harvard Univ. Press, Cambridge, Mass., 1956)
172. Tolman, E. C. *Purposive Behavior in Animals and Men* (Appleton-Century, New York, 1932)

173. Trapold, M. A. The effect of incentive motivation on an unrelated reflex response. *J. Comp. Physiol. Psychol.,* **55,** 1034–39 (1962)
174. Trowill, J. A., Panksepp, J., Gandelman, R. An incentive model of rewarding brain stimulation. *Psychol. Rev.,* **76,** 264–81 (1969)
175. Valenstein, E. S. The anatomical locus of reinforcement. In *Progress in Physiological Psychology,* 149–90 (Stellar, E., Sprague, J. M., Eds., Academic Press, New York, 1966)
176. Verinis, J. S., Brandsma, J. M., Cofer, C. N. Discrepancy from expectation in relation to affect and motivation: Tests of McClelland's hypothesis. *J. Pers. Soc. Psychol.,* **9,** 47–58 (1968)
177. Veroff, J. Theoretical background for studying the origins of human motivational systems. *Merrill Palmer Quart.,* **11,** 3–18 (1965)
178. Veroff, J. Report from achievement motivation. In *Explorations in Human Potentialities,* Chap. 26 (Otto, H. A., Ed., Thomas, Springfield, Ill., 1966)
179. Vogel-Sprott, M., Thurston, E. Resistance to punishment and subsequent extinction of a response as a function of its reward history. *Psychol. Rept.,* **22,** 631–37 (1968)
180. Wagner, A. R. Frustration and punishment. In *Current Research in Motivation,* 229–39 (See Ref. 77)
181. Walker, E. L. Curiosity: Tedium or titillation? (Presented at Eastern Psychol. Assoc. Conv., Atlantic City, April, 1959)
182. Weinrich, W. W., Cahoon, D. D., Ambrose, G., Laplace, R. Secondary stimulus control of a "new" operant incompatible with "running to the food magazine." *Psychon. Sci.,* **5,** 189–90 (1966)
183. Williams, D. R. Classical conditioning and incentive motivation. In *Classical Conditioning: A Symposium,* 340–57 (Prokasy, W. F., Ed., Appleton-Century-Crofts, New York, 1965)
184. Woodworth, R. S. *Dynamic Psychology* (Columbia Univ. Press, New York, 1918)
185. Worchel, P., Schuster, S. Attraction as a function of the drive state. *J. Exptl. Res. Personality,* **1,** 277–81 (1966)
186. Young, P. T. The role of hedonic processes in motivation. In *Nebraska Symposium on Motivation, 1955,* 193–238 (Jones, M. R., Ed., Univ. Nebraska Press, Lincoln)
187. Young, P. T. *Motivation and Emotion* (Wiley, New York, 1961)
188. Young, P. T. Hedonic organization and regulation of behavior. *Psychol. Rev.,* **73,** 59–86 (1966)
189. Young, P. T. Affective arousal: Some implications. *Am. Psychologist,* **22,** 32–40 (1967)
190. Young, P. T. Palatability: The hedonic response to foodstuffs. In *Handbook of Physiology.* Sec. 6. *Alimentary Canal,* **1,** 353–66 (Code, C. F., et al., Eds., Williams & Wilkins, Baltimore, Md., 1967)
191. Zimbardo, P. G. The cognitive control of motivation. *Trans. N.Y. Acad. Sci.,* Series II, **28,** 902–22 (1966)

PSYCHOLOGY OF MEN AT WORK

By John R. Hinrichs
International Business Machines Corporation
White Plains, New York

As industrial psychology moves from the 1960's into the 70's, our review of the research literature for the last two years suggests that the field still suffers from the lingering aspects of a long-standing malaise: a plethora of data and a paucity of generalizable research insights and theory. While the symptoms definitely appear less acute than a decade ago, and there are some encouraging signs of outright therapy, the problems are quite pervasive. Despite the fact that our journals are burgeoning, our graduate schools crowded, and our users and sponsors increasingly receptive to our wares, too much of today's research continues to address problems of limited relevance to either the key issues of our times or the advancement of knowledge, to be *ad hoc* rather than integrative, and to use questionable or at least untested metrics.

Perhaps as John Darley suggested (40) there is really very little new in the field that cannot be found somewhere in the literature of the last 50 years. But we would prefer not to think so. And this in-depth excursion into the literature has served at least to raise our hopes. For there are some significant innovative trends—some new concepts, ideas, and viewpoints—and some of these are quite exciting.

But probably more significant than any specific new developments in theory and research is an almost universal recognition that our old and traditional and comfortable models are no longer adequate. The classical concern of industrial psychology has been one of predicting or explaining some aspect of "what makes Sammy work." Our models have been causal: independent variables leading to behaviors; predictors to criteria. Such a traditional view of the world makes possible a nice, neat, comfortable sorting out of cause and effect. Oh for the good old days!

Any attempt today to categorize research and thinking in the field has to view the world of men at work within a systems framework. Cause can just as easily be viewed as effect, effect as cause, and both interact within a dynamic ongoing system linked together in largely unclear relationships about which our models and model builders are making only very primitive explanatory efforts.

Perhaps the significant point is that the field has at least come to recognize that "a pretzel-shaped universe requires pretzel-shaped hypotheses" [Fiedler (56, p. 14)] and that it is premature to expect all of the convolutions of these explanations to have been clarified.

But current research is making a stab at it. Within the last two years we have had studies that have viewed job satisfaction, for example, in the classical sense as an independent variable in explaining behavior; studies that have evaluated job satisfaction as a dependent variable [Locke (128)]; and studies which looked at the extent to which the effects occur in both directions [Lawler(114)]. Similarly, there have been studies which investigated job satisfaction as a moderator variable in the relationship between individual difference measurements and performance [Dawis et al. (42)]; and other studies which attempted to moderate the relationship between job satisfaction and performance with individual difference measures [Korman (110)]. And the same line of analysis can be found in research in the area of leadership [Lowin & Craig (138)]. We have learned to live with the fact that searching for the cause and the effect in understanding the role of man at work is like searching for the Holy Grail—and it is not terribly challenging to boot.

Previous reviews in this biennial series [Smith & Cranny (173), Porter (157), Sells (169), Dunnette (48)] have all called for a melding of traditional industrial/differential psychology and the newer concerns of organizational social psychology. Universally, these reviewers have contended that such factors cannot be considered in isolation and that our area of concern must be man in interaction with his working environment in an effort to explicate all of the factors which impact this relationship. The point was expressed most tangibly in the change of title for the review chapter in 1968 —from "Personnel Management" to "The Psychology of Men at Work"—a more appropriate title which has been maintained this year. And the point has been reiterated by comments such as those by Bass (17).

At the outset of the decade of the 70's, the field has matured to the point where it should not be necessary to repeat this exhortation. We have to concern ourselves simultaneously with both individual variables and environmental variables to advance the state of the art. And much of current research does just that, though traditional modes of thinking have a way of persisting long past their point of effective utility, and *the* predictor or *the* criterion model is still applied in many studies.

However, even in the field of classical personnel selection—not included in this review—there has been a clear trend toward broader horizons. Selection research is increasingly being built upon the recognition of the systems nature of organizational effectiveness and the interaction between individual and organizational variables. The current concern with dynamic and multifaceted criteria, the search for individual and organizational moderators in the prediction statement, and the use of simulations of organizational behavior as selection methodologies as advocated by Wernimont & Campbell (187) and as central to the industrial assessment center technique as pioneered at AT&T (28, 71, 72), suggests that the new viewpoint of organizazational behavior advocated in past reviews has had its impact on the classical concerns of industrial psychologists—the selection and placement functions. It would seem time to re-emphasize this important subfield of selection and placement and tie it firmly into the growing organizational orientation of industrial psychology. How, who, and when new manpower inputs enter the system is a vital component of our understanding of organization behavior.

As a generalization, the research of the last two years still is not fully adequate for understanding the systems nature of man at work. For one thing, with but only a handful of exceptions, today's research ignores the crucial dimension of time which, as MacKinney (139) pointed out, is a key variable for the development of theory and understanding. We need more longitudinal rather than cross-sectional research. The key problems impacting our industrial society today are all dynamic and can only be adequately researched through longitudinal designs: factors such as changing value systems regarding work and leisure, the impact of technology on tasks, the obsolescence of skills, changing patterns of occupational mobility, and so forth. Methodologies for dealing with longitudinal data are appearing somewhat more frequently in the literature—cross-lagged or dynamic correlational analysis, three-mode factor analysis, multivariate covariance analyses, and so forth. We need to see more use of these tools; perhaps industrial psychology should shuck off some of its complacency and borrow more from allied disciplines rather than attempting to reinvent the wheel. The field of economics is a pertinent example, and we have been slow to learn from economists concerned with time series and the causal analysis of correlational data [Rozelle & Campbell (164)].

Probably one reason why there has been so little longitudinal research in the past is that so little industrial research which is done by in-house researchers is published. For the university-based researcher, the premium is on getting in, collecting data, getting out, and publishing. Too often there is no continuity, no follow-through, no integration into a total research program to uncover the key linkages in the behavioral system. And it is significant that the most useful longitudinal studies are the ones where an in-house research staff has existed to nurture and care for the long-term research program, such as the research at AT&T [Hall & Nougaim (79)]. We would expect future reviews in this series to reflect some significant changes, based upon longitudinal research currently under way and cooperative research programs which have been set up between a number of university centers and industrial organizations. There is need for more of this joint industry and academic effort.

There is also a clear need for more comparability in the variables which are utilized across studies and less reliance upon attitudinal or behavior scales with often untested or dubious reliability and certainly with dubious validity to the constructs being measured. The research literature of the last two years suggests some trend toward the recurrent use of standardized measures such as the Job Description Index, Porter's Need Deficiency Methodology, or the Least Preferred Co-worker measure, but too often the variables employed in research are *ad hoc*. There have been several laudable attempts to specify the key variables required for understanding the parameters of the man at work system [Inkson, Payne & Pugh (98), Wofford (191)], but it remains to be seen how adequate these efforts are.

In organizing this review, we have taken the position outlined by Pervin (156), that performance and satisfaction result from the interaction of individual and environmental factors. The first part of the review covers studies which concentrate primarily on significant aspects of the job content and context—the tangible world external to the psychological characteristics of the individual. Within this framework, we include studies dealing with task characteristics, studies dealing with the structural and interpersonal work environment, the reward system as it is structured to impact behavior, and research covering "situational' factors associated with the working environment, including studies of leadership and communications.

The second section of the review deals with research which concentrates primarily on individual characteristics—psychological attributes which the individual brings to the job or which develop as a result of his exposure to the work role. We include here research dealing with ability and personality factors (other than selection research) and evaluations of the motivational characteristics of people at work including studies of needs, goals, expectancies, and the burgeoning literature dealing with job attitudes and satisfactions.

Clearly this type of sorting out is not a clear-cut process. As we have pointed out, some of the better research straddles both areas. But there is a trend toward more specific identification of the variables when their interrelationships are evaluated, and most of the studies can be categorized within the basic framework we have elected to use.

The final section of the review covers a number of specifically personnel-oriented areas, such as studies dealing with training, turnover, labor relations, and research methodology.

JOB CONTENT AND CONTEXT

Task Characteristics

Job description and analysis.—During the period of the review, there were several studies dealing with various aspects of job description and analysis. Two articles were published from the continuing program of research in this area under the direction of McCormick. McCormick, Cunningham & Gordon (141) reported on a replicated factorial study to identify the major dimensions among jobs. While they recognized that the specific dimensions which emerged from their analysis do not exhaust the total domain of human work, their research does demonstrate that it should be possible to develop a meaningful and comprehensive taxonomy of jobs.

An article by McCormick, Cunningham & Thornton (142) evaluated the relationship between ratings of job attributes and job analysis data from the U. S. Employment Service and suggested that it is possible to rate individual components of jobs in terms of the human attributes required. The approach is seen as eventually having utility for the development of synthetic validation systems.

In a related study, Allen (6) found that typical verbs used in job descriptions were multidimensional rather than falling along a single continuum between the poles of worker versus job orientation. He suggested that job analysis should be based upon actual observed job behaviors rather than oriented to job elements in the abstract.

Landy & Elbert (113) found that different approaches to scaling paired comparison job classification data yielded three different orderings of the weights for the various job elements. Their study suggested that different scaling assumptions and practices applied in the job analysis system may eventually be translated as inequities in the job classification and compensation system actually used in an organization.

Atchison & French [12) compared three different methods of establishing pay differentials for scientists and engineers in two government installations. They found the traditional classification method of job evaluation and the time span of discretion method to produce quite comparable positioning of jobs, while the maturity curve approach produced somewhat different results. All three methods were seen as resulting in fair payment by subjects in the study.

This whole area of job analysis and description has probably not received enough attention in the past. It has just not had the glamour of other areas. But because of its central role in determining equity within an organization's classification and compensation structure—an area on which the majority of current research on compensation focuses, as will be outlined below—there is a need for additional involvement by industrial psychologists in this important "nuts and bolts" aspect of the field.

Some new analytical methodologies are beginning to be used in job analysis. Carr (36) described a computer based method for evaluating the technical, organizational, and communicational dimensions of jobs. The procedure has been given the acronym of the "Samoa" system (Systematic Approach to Multidimensional Occupational Analysis).

A number of different methodologies have been utilized for studying tasks by sampling job behaviors. Stewart (177) reported on an analysis of the allocation of time among a management group based upon data collected by diaries maintained for a four-week period. Nelson & Bartley (153) administered questionnaires twice a day, collecting data relevant to each hour of the day regarding feelings of boredom and fatigue on the job. Lawler, Porter & Tennenbaum (122) used a modified form of work sampling to obtain self-recorded reactions by managers to interaction and communication episodes. Managers were asked to complete the data collection form following each "behavioral episode" that occurred during the work day, defined as "any situation that has an integrity of its own." Carroll & Taylor (37) reported data collected by a self-observational central signaling method of work sampling (flicking the overhead lights as a cue for self-recording of behavioral data.)

There is a need for increasing emphasis on the description and measurement of on-the-job behavior within field settings. Without a better understanding of the nature of tasks, we will be missing an important component in understanding the total system of organizational behavior. The true work sampling methodology utilizing random observations of behavior appears to have the most promise for providing reliable and valid information, particularly for managerial and professional levels.

Goal specificity.—In a very prolific program of research, Locke and his associates have continued to report on some convincing research suggesting that goals or performance intentions which are consciously set are the primary direct correlates of performance in a variety of laboratory tasks. They have repeatedly found that specifically set hard goals result in higher performance than do very general and unspecific goals of "do your best" (30). It has been demonstrated that performance goals which are set serve not only to energize behavior and induce higher levels of performance, but to do so selectively and to energize behavior only along dimensions specifically covered within the goal framework (130).

This program of research has also investigated the validity of Parkinson's law (work expands so as to fill the time available for its completion) (31). The Parkinson's effect was found to occur in two experiments, though the phenomenon was mediated by performance related to set goals.

A particularly interesting group of experiments in this series demonstrated that goals or intentions serve as critical mediators of the relationship between monetary incentives and performance. While monetary incentive levels were related to performance, when levels of goals or intentions were controlled or partialed out, there remained no incentive effect of money on behavior (133).

Several studies in this series have concentrated on the effects of knowledge of results as opposed to the effects of goal setting on performance (127, 131, 132). These replicated studies rather convincingly suggest, at least within the framework of the simple addition tasks utilized in the laboratory, that knowledge of results versus no knowledge of results is not related to differences in performance. Rather, differences in the difficulty level of the goals which are set is significantly related to performance. The implication is that the facilitating effects usually atrributed to knowledge of results in many studies in actuality are probably due to motivational differences produced by the setting of performance goals. Locke, Cartledge & Koeppel (134) have presented a comprehensive review of the literature dealing with knowledge of results as it relates to the goal setting phenomenon.

In a related study, Korman (109) found that goal difficulty significantly moderated the realtionship between self-esteem and performance in a creative thinking task. Under hard goals, high self-esteem subjects produced more than did low self-esteem subjects. There were no differences under conditions of easy goals.

Locke (129) has presented a comprehensive summary of much of his research along with other research dealing with goal setting. While there can be little doubt that conscious goals and intentions are extremely important mediators in the relationship between behavior and monetary incentives, knowledge of results, time limits, and probably other factors as well, there is need for more research before this can be generalized to the work setting. It is also impossible to make inferences about the effects of conscious goals on long-term behavior. The research has utilized relatively clear-cut and short-term laboratory tasks; will similar results carry through in the complex behaviors required in organizations? Perhaps it will be possible to carry this line of research forward into field settings, for example, assessing the interactions between incentives and quotas in determining the performance of salesmen, or looking at the relationships between the setting of work goals and participation in decision making in determining productivity and satisfactions. We anticipate increasingly useful outcomes from this important program of research.

Task performance as an independent variable.—Traditional studies in industrial psychology have usually looked upon task performance, and productivity specifically, as a dependent variable—an outcome of such independent variables as job satisfaction, incentives, rewards, or managerial style. More recently there has been a continuing trend, as suggested in the last review by Smith & Cranny (173), toward recognition of the important role played by task performance per se as an independent variable. Several studies [Feather (55), Zander, Forward & Albert (193)] reported data showing that successful performance is associated with continuing success, and failure tends to be associated with continuing failure, presumably through impact on level of confidence or expectations. Longitudinal data collected at AT&T [Hall & Nougaim (79)] found a similar effect with regard to career development and suggested the emergence of a success syndrome early in a manager's career which tends to lead to an upward spiral of success. Lawler & Porter (121) presented a model and some supportive data from a population of managers suggesting that performance is more apt to influence satisfaction through a linkage with rewards than for the causal relationship to operate in the traditionally assumed direction.

Goodman & Baloff (64) provided a theoretical analysis and some data from an experiment illustrating the differential effects of task experience on attitudes. Locke (128), in a laboratory study, showed that success is related to satisfaction in terms of congruence between expectations and outcomes. This is an important distinction, injecting the concept of goal attainment into the dynamics of attitude formation. Korman (110) reported on several studies showing the relationship between success or failure and satisfaction to be moderated by an individual's degree of self-esteem (as measured by the Self-Assurance scale of the Ghiselli Self-Description Inventory).

Thus, data from a number of different frameworks have emphasized the importance of task characteristics as causal variables influencing subsequent task performance and satisfactions. The increasing emphasis on an understanding of the dynamics of task structure and the relationships between tasks and other aspects of organizational behaviors is a welcome trend which we hope to see more of in future research.

Job enlargement.—There has been an increasing emphasis in the management literature on the concept of job enlargement, and, happily, some increased concern with testing these concepts in the psychological literature. Shepard (171) presented data showing that the degree of task specialization and job satisfaction were negatively correlated and suggesting that automation—at least in terms of automation of process technology within an oil refinery—actually entails job enlargement and relatively higher levels of job satisfaction. Sexton (170), on the other hand, found a positive correlation between the degree of job structure and job satisfaction among assembly line workers. Alderfer (3) found that degree of job complexity was positively correlated with satisfaction with use of skills and abilities, but was negatively related to satisfaction with respect from superiors, and was unrelated to satisfaction with pay.

Hulin & Blood (94) attempted to explain many of the discrepant findings in job enlargement research. Their review of the literature concluded that broadly based cultural factors significantly moderate workers' affective response to tasks, and specifically to job enlargement. While job enlargement—or the increasingly *au courant* term "job enrichment"—is seen more and more as the direction in which organizations should go in providing motivation in the work place [for example, Herzberg (83)]. Blood & Hulin cautioned against universal application of the concept. Their review, substantiated by some research (25), suggested that alienation from middle-class values characteristic of blue-collar workers in urban locations results in a negative correlation between job complexity and satisfaction. For "non-alienated" workers (white-collar workers and blue-collar workers from essentially rural locations) the relationship is held to be positive.

We need more detailed study of the concept of job enlargement, both in the laboratory, such as that by Maher (140) which systematically varied content and discretionary aspects of a task, as well as field studies which attempt to control more systematically the factors impacting the relationships among task structure, productivity, and satisfactions.

The Occupational Role

A number of studies have attempted to describe various aspects of perceived occupational roles. Several studies contrasted role perceptions within military and civilian settings (88, 147). Barnett (14) studied the properties of the role set within engineering positions, and two studies have been specific to management and executive roles (74, 103). Slobin, Miller & Porter (172) made inferences regarding role relationships within a business setting as a result of analysis of the interrelationships and form of address among employees at four organizational levels.

While these studies describing the role characteristics of various jobs are of interest in their own right, there is a real need to go beyond mere description in this research. What are the behavioral or organizational effectiveness correlates of discrepant or congruent or ambiguous role perceptions within organizational settings? How do role perceptions develop and how may they be modified when they become inappropriate or inaccurate for particular structural or technical or interpersonal environments? What are the common elements of role perceptions, and which are unique across occupations and environments? What are the relationships between individual difference variables and role set variables? A study by Katzell et al. (103) attempted to evaluate many of these questions, but the data are not conclusive.

Leadership

The most significant contribution in the area of leadership during the period of this review was the publication of Fiedler's book (56) describing his contingency model of leadership and reporting on an impressive 15-year program of research leading up to the development of the model and its validation. Though the model and most of the research have been reported previously, it is good to see the book which draws together the material into a comprehensive presentation.

The model essentially says that leader effectiveness (defined as group performance effectiveness) is a result of the individual leader's style, operationalized and measured along the dimension of task-orientation versus relationship-orientation by the Least Preferred Co-worker (LPC) measure—interacting with specific situations—ordered in terms of their degree of favorability for the leader. Leadership situations are categorized within an eight-celled matrix defined by dimensions of degree of affective leader-member relationships, task structure, and position power of the leader. Tests of the model suggest a curvilinear relationship, with groups managed by low LPC leaders (high task-orientation) exhibiting highest performance under very favorable or very unfavorable leadership situations, and high LPC (relationship-oriented) leadership most effective in situations of intermediate favorability.

Hunt (96) reported on a direct test of the model utilizing data collected within five very different sets of work groups. Within these settings, while the model was essentially supported, the degree of affective leader-member relationship was the primary dimension in determining the favorability of the situation, with the degree of task structure and power position apparently having little relationship to group effectiveness.

Gruenfeld & Arbuthnot (75) reported on a factor analysis of the LPC measure and concluded that LPC is multidimensional. They found significant correlations between a "competence" subscale of the LPC and measures of psychological differentiation, but no relationships for three other subscales.

Nealey & Fiedler (151) reviewed the literature dealing with differences between levels of management in the correlates of leadership effectiveness.

They concluded that this is a severely under-researched area with important implications for managerial selection, placement, and development. A study by Nealey & Blood (150) demonstrated sharp differences in LPC between first and second level high performance supervisors within a psychiatric nursing situation. This is a line of research which needs to be extended into industrial and business organizations.

Other research in leadership showed that many of the key elements have not been tied down. Korman, in a review of the literature regarding the prediction of effective leadership, concluded that "little has been learned from selection research which can contribute to a theory of leadership behavior" (107, p. 319). He suggested that a change in the orientation of predictive research is necessary and that there should be more emphasis on informed judgments in the development and weighting of both predictors and criteria, citing the apparent success of management assessment center methodologies.

Lowin (137), in an excellent review of the literature on participative decision making, suggested that research does not at all conclusively demonstrate the effectiveness of participation. He feels that future research should focus on identifying more of the mediating and environmental variables rather than trying directly to prove or disprove the participative decision-making hypothesis.

Two studies by Dubno (47) evaluated the interactions of leader personality, task conditions, and task instructions with essentially ambiguous results, concluding that the interaction of task variables with situational variables must be more fully explicated—precisely the road down which Fiedler's comprehensive research has moved.

Rowland & Scott (163), following a review of leadership research and an analysis of a broad array of variables collected within a government facility, arrived at a similar conclusion. One of their specific findings was that the Consideration scale of the Leader Opinion Questionnaire (LOQ) was uncorrelated with work group satisfaction or with performance.

Graham (70) also studied the relationship between LOQ and performance and found that it was significantly moderated by LPC. While on the average groups of high versus low LPC managers did not differ on mean Consideration scores, there was significantly greater variance in Consideration scores among low LPC managers than among high LPC managers. The inference is that low LPC managers, in comparison with high LPC managers are more selectively considerate; i.e., they differentially apply consideration behavior in congruence with the needs of their individual subordinates. There were no differences in the rated performance effectiveness of low versus high LPC leaders. Correlational analysis suggested that self-reports of leader behavior (LOQ) interacts with self-reports of leader style (LPC) in determining leader effectiveness.

A study by Rubin & Goldman (165) within a different context presents an interesting parallel. They related the openness of the manager-member communications and performance differentiation behavior to leader effectiveness. Differentiators (assumed to be analogous to low LPC leaders) appeared to be most effective in a situation of high openness of communications. Presumably the manager who differentiates "is one who is predisposed to treating his subordinates as individuals. Given a climate of open communication, such a manager can function effectively in a wide range of situations with subordinates having a variety of needs" (165, p. 153).

A study by Andrews & Farris (8) in a NASA research center, in addition to an extensive analysis of supervisory correlates of innovation, found interesting moderators in the relationship between the degree of freedom provided for subordinates to "explore, discuss, and challenge ideas on their own." Provision of freedom was positively correlated with innovation where the leader was rated as low on task functions, low on administrative functions, or low on human relations. Andrews & Farris suggested that within the research environment, "provision of freedom was a substitute for skillful leadership"! (8, p. 507). Similarly, for supervisors rated high on sensitivity to differences between people, there was a negative correlation between administrative behavior (effectiveness at planning and scheduling) and group innovation, while there was a positive correlation for supervisors rated low on sensitivity to differences. Their discussion of these results suggested a concern with the direction of causality in leader behavior, and Andrews & Farris speculated that the effective leader is one adept at shaping his own behavior in response to the behavior of his subordinates, while the ineffective leader fails to do so. The previously cited laboratory study by Lowin & Craig (138) demonstrated the extent to which subordinate behavior can differentially affect leader behavior.

The resurgence of interest in research on leadership provides an interesting microcosm to the development of the total field of industrial psychology. During and following World War II, the research emphasis was largely trait oriented. By the 1950's, the dominant conclusion was the one emerging from the Ohio State studies that effective leadership was situation specific. The search for leadership traits was in large measure abandoned except for the development of such measures as the LOQ, intended to measure leadership behavior, and the development of such heuristic devices as the "Management Grid."

Meanwhile, the research evidence in the intervening years on the effectiveness of the LOQ has been disappointing at best [Korman (106)]. What has been lacking has been a systematic approach for operationalizing situation specific characteristics as they interact with leader style. Current research, most significantly that of Fiedler and his associates, has begun now to tackle these questions, and we are seeing a renewed intensification of the search for the correlates of effective leadership. It is a healthy example of the process by which our field, and any field of science, progresses, not as a steady process but in stages and spurts. We may expect to see the seminal effect of Fiedler's work reflected in the literature covered in future *Annual Reviews.*

Communications

Several studies have evaluated various aspects of communications. Gerstberger & Allen (61), in studying the significant factors in the utilization of technical information within a research and development laboratory, found that convenience was the primary factor influencing an engineer's choice of an information source. It was also found that any specific communications channel was perceived as being increasingly accessible the more an engineer had experience in using it. The implications for the communication of technical information are that engineering organizations must make information sources more readily available, rather than concentrating primarily on improving quality.

Lawler, Porter & Tennenbaum (122) studied patterns of interactions within a management hierarchy and found that managers are more favorable to self-initiated interactions and that they evaluated interactions with their superiors more highly than interactions with their subordinates. The implications of these patterns for the breakdown of communications within organizations are clear. Bass (19), utilizing a simulated group discussion situation, investigated some of the implications for group consensus and satisfaction as a result of the extent to which the group leader communicated his opinions.

Bassett & Meyer (20), in studying the process of communicating performance appraisal information, evaluated employee and manager reactions to performance review sessions where the employee himself prepared his own performance rating, as opposed to traditional review situations based upon manager ratings. They reported less employee defensiveness, higher management satisfaction, and higher employee satisfaction for the review situation utilizing self-ratings. Employees who expressed high need for independence were especially more favorable and more satisfied with the self-review procedure.

Rewards Systems

Research dealing with reward systems has focused largely on pay, and a majority of this work still revolves around equity theory. There have been several direct attempts (1, 59, 65, 115, 118, 120) at replicating various aspects of equity theory research findings as outlined by Adams (2).

Weick & Nesset (185) evaluated most of the significant possible combinations of compensation inequity by having subjects express their degree of comfort with a series of forced choice fictitious work situations. The study demonstrated the potential complexity of any equity comparison—inputs versus outcomes for Person, for Other, and for Person in relationship with Other—and demonstrated that in most situations absolute balance is impossible to attain. Weick & Nesset concluded that "if situations of equity are pulled apart in terms of the elements . . . , significant variation occurs in each of these components, consequently all of them need to be considered when statements are made regarding the induction and reduction of inequity" (185, p. 416).

Lawler (116) reviewed many of the equity studies in his discussion of the four aspects of inequity usually dealt with in research in this area (underpayment versus overpayment in both hourly and piecework conditions). He suggested that under the hourly situation, traditional "expectancy" theory (motivation may be represented as some function of expectancy times valence) is adequate to explain the results of most studies. Under piece rate situations, Lawler found some support for the predictions of equity theory but also some support for expectancy theory. Longer-term studies of piecework compensation suggest that the impact of equity considerations may be somewhat transitory. Lawler concluded that perhaps there is a need to tie together these two theoretical approaches in compensation research, suggesting that a fruitful approach may be to study the extent to which feelings of equity impact the valence of rewards.

If one hopes to draw inferences from equity research for application in the industrial setting, the major problems are these: most of the research is based upon small samples; nonindustrial populations have usually been employed; the tasks (most frequently interviewing) usually have a built-in negative correlation between productivity and quality; the experiments have been of a short time duration; and often the effectiveness of the induction of feelings of overpayment has not been clear cut. It would seem appropriate to begin to move the framework for equity research from the laboratory to field settings.

Several compensation studies were found which were not carried out within the traditional framework of the experimental studies testing equity theory. Klein & Maher (105) evaluated differences in expectations and satisfactions regarding outcomes for groups of college educated versus noncollege managers. College educated managers had higher expectations of contributing to the company (inputs, in equity terms) and higher salary expectations than noncollege managers. They also exhibited higher dissatisfaction with salary (outcomes) than noncollege managers, even though in fact their earnings were greater. Dissatisfaction with salary did not generalize to other areas of satisfactions.

Nealey & Goodale (152) evaluated paired-comparison preferences among six different time-off and vacation options and one pay option for a group of 197 blue-collar workers. On the average, additional time-off options were chosen more frequently than additional pay, and foremen were able to predict the overall preferences of the workers with high accuracy. Because of differential preferences for various subgroups based on sex, age, and marital status, Nealey & Goodale suggested some degree of "cafeteria style" individual choice in wage and benefit selection.

Beer and Gery (22) assessed employee preferences among four different hypothetical pay systems encompassing varying mixes of automatic versus merit compensation. They also evaluated the motivational correlates of different choices. Lawler & Levin (119) compared preferences for various compensation components for union officers, rank and file, and officers' estimates of rank and file preferences. They found high agreement among these preferences.

Haire, Ghiselli & Gordon (78) reported on comprehensive analyses of 25 years of compensation data for three samples of managers. By evaluating means and standard deviations of pay and pay increases over time, and the correlations between pay and raises, they were able to draw some extensive conclusions regarding the operation of reward systems and the probable psychological implications in terms of expectations and equity evaluations for these managers. They presented a model based on statistics generated from these longitudinal salary data regarding the areas of leverage which salary administrators may apply in setting compensation policy.

Bass (16) simulated salary administration actions for engineers utilizing his Exercise Compensation. His study emphasized the subjectivity of much salary action and the extent to which recommendations of compensation decisions are impacted by intelligence and personal values of the recommender.

Zedeck & Smith (194) used the psychophysical method of limits to determine the threshold of equitable compensation in terms of actual dollar amounts for several groups in a university setting. The methodological implications of this study are probably more important than the substantive findings and may provide a vehicle for study of the equity phenomenon within field settings, as well as a more concrete basis for identifying individuals falling in underpayment versus overpayment inequity conditions.

INDIVIDUAL CHARACTERISTICS

Among research which concentrated primarily on individual characteristics as they relate to outcomes at work—characteristics which we have defined as both those attributes which the individual brings to the job or which develop as a result of his exposure to the work role—by far the bulk of the literature deals with job satisfaction and what might rather loosely be subsumed under the heading of motivation. The extent to which the merging of individual differences psychology and organizational psychology has not been fully consumated is reflected by the relatively few studies dealing with ability and personality factors. However, some trends are evident.

Ability and Personality Factors

Most of the research dealing with ability and personality correlates of performance falls within the domain of testing and selection research recently summarized by Owens & Jewell (154). Korman (107) provided a comprehensive review of much of this research in the managerial area. He generally concluded that very little utility has been demonstrated for cognitive ability tests or for personality and interest inventories for the prediction of managerial potential.

Berdie (23), in an interesting analysis of variability and performance from repeated testing on six different perceptual and motor tasks utilizing 20 different forms of each test, found large individual differences in variability of performance. Such intraindividual variability was not unique to a single task but was correlated between several but not all of the tasks. There was no explication of what this variability might be related to, but it might represent an important psychological variable. One could well visualize utilizing some measure of intraindividual variability as a moderator within a range of selection and assessment situations or learning environments.

Bass (18) presented a comprehensive review of research experience utilizing the Orientation Inventory. The Inventory was designed to assess attitudes toward various aspects of social situations, yielding scales measuring an individual's self-orientation, interaction-orientation, and task-orientation. Bass concluded that the scales were useful for increasing understanding of performance in a variety of social settings, though greater retest reliability would have been desirable.

Several studies have evaulated the work relevant aspects of the personality variable of self-evaluation or self-esteem. Korman (108) found that need satisfaction was significantly related to overall satisfaction for high self-esteem individuals but not for low. This parallels his finding cited earlier (110) of a significant correlation between task success and liking of the task for high self-esteem individuals but not for low. Utilizing a different measure, Lefkowitz (123) reported data on factors associated with self-esteem among a blue-collar industrial population and some suggestive data regarding changes in self-esteem following job change (job "bumping" due to union contractural seniority provisions). However, because of a low response rate and a suggestion of bias in the response, his results must be viewed cautiously. The concept of self-esteem is important and deserves further research to evaluate the impact of various managerial actions and organizational variables on the self-concept and the significance of these for work satisfactions and performance.

Two studies attempted to look directly at the interaction between ability and motivation in determining performance. Ghiselli (62) found that scores on motivational scales from his Self-Description Inventory could be used to moderate the relationship between trait scores derived from the same instrument and managerial success. All four motivational scales moderated the relationship between self-assurance and success, with significantly stronger relationships for those high on job security and power motives as well as for those low on financial rewards and self-actualization motives. These two sets of motives were seen as qualitatively different, and Ghiselli suggested that self-assurance might be a significant correlate of a manager's success "only when his goals are selfish (security, power) and are not an expression of his individuality (rewards, self-actualization)" (62, p. 483). This presents an interesting parallel to the findings regarding the moderating effects of self-esteem (utilizing this same Self-Assurance scale from the Self-Description Inventory) in job satisfaction reported by Korman (108, 110). Perhaps concern with job satisfaction and task liking may be interpreted within this same framework of the gratification of "selfish goals."

Galbraith & Cummings (60) attempted to test Vroom's (182) suggestion that performance is a multiplicative function of motivation and ability. They operationalized motivation as a function of valences of job outcomes (money, fringe benefits, promotion, managerial supportiveness, and group acceptance) and the perceived instrumentality of performance for each factor. Ability was operationalized as time on the job. Their analysis suggested that ability (tenure) does interact multiplicatively with motivation in determining the relationship with performance, but the data are far from clear cut. Galbraith & Cummings point to problems of restricted variance in their measures, but it is also clear that any model such as this suffers very severely from the multiplicative effects of error variance. Also, more appropriate measures of ability would have been desirable. But their study illustrates the type of comprehensive model testing that is needed and which should be attempted within more heterogeneous samples with more reliable measures.

Motivational Factors

Indicative of recent trends in the field over the period of the review has been the considerable interest in motivational factors in an effort to explain behavioral outcomes at work—performance, turnover, and job satisfaction. Most studies have been concerned with concepts of needs, expectancies, and satisfactions, usually relying on survey data of some form as a base for analysis.

Several studies have employed less survey-oriented approaches to the study of motivations in work settings. Baruch (15) utilized TAT (Thematic Apperception Test) measures of need achievement in studying the correlates of women's participation in the labor market. She found a temporal cycle of need achievement for college educated women associated with age and family status, and suggested that this related to and perhaps was antecedant to seeking paid employment. Mukherjee (148, 149) presented data collected in India on a forced choice scale designed to measure achievement values and found that achievement motivation was related to productivity (publication rates) among a group of scientists.

Ghiselli (63) reported on the development of four motivational scales for his 64-item forced choice adjective check list, the Self Description Inventory. The scales covered job security, financial rewards, power, and self-actualization. Across a number of organizations, Ghiselli found self-actualization scores to be positively related to managerial job success indices, and motivation by job security and financial rewards negatively related.

Cummings & ElSalmi (39) reviewed the literature dealing with research on managerial motivation and pointed to two strands of research: the need hierarchy approach and the motivator-hygiene concept. They concluded that "a theory of managerial motivation that is unified, definitive, and univeral does not yet exist" (39, p. 140) and called for more research covering a greater range of organizational and psychological variables, with greater control over the effects of independent variables. One cannot argue with this for the field in general, but it does seem spurious to apply such research to managers alone. Managerial status is only one variable in the determination of the setting for man at work and not a very definitive one in isolation. There seems little reason to assume that we have controlled any significant variance by lumping foremen on production lines, project managers of R & D groups, sales managers, and vice presidents of finance. While we may obtain some control by studying homogeneous groups of "scientists" or of "salesmen," it would seem unlikely that there is much hope for developing a comprehensive "theory" specific to manageral motivation which is not generalizable to work in general. An approach that fails to control for differences in work groups by lumping them together, or does control by studying a single group in isolation, goes only part way toward filling the broader need for understanding the world of work motivation.

Needs, goals, and expectancies.—Three studies were built explicitly around Maslow's need hierarchy concept and measures of need satisfaction. Beer (21) reported data for clerical employees (mainly female), El-Salmi & Cummings (53) for managers, and Johnson & Marcrum (100) for career army officers. These studies serve largely a descriptive and normative function and illustrate the problems in generalizing about needs and need satisfactions. Interactions in these studies resulted from such situational factors as job complexity, job level, organizational size, or line versus staff job assignment.

Graen, Dawis & Weiss (68) attempted to identify through obverse correlational analysis clusters of individuals falling into need types or patterns. Comparing the first clear-cut cluster with all others in their sample, they found differing patterns of relationships between need strengths and need satisfactions. For this population of research and development scientists, the patterning was seen as roughly analogous to those holding to a company or organization orientation versus those with a profession orientation (or at least those not exhibiting an organization orientation). Their study suggested that needs may fall into typologies and that efforts to identify typologies as psychological variables may be fruitful. Most current emphasis has been on organizational correlates of needs, and it might be worthwhile to draw more on personality theory and research methodology and investigate individual differences in need patterns.

Paine, Deutsch & Smith (155) investigated the family background correlates of various work values among a university population. While their results are modest, this is a line of research which could be usefully expanded into industry. Research into the developmental aspects of work values and needs could have important ramifications for manpower selection and placement and for effective utilization of manpower.

Ritti (160) contrasted the work goals of engineers and scientists and concluded that they are basically different and that these differences are brought to the laboratory by the individual rather than being inculcated as part of his experience in the laboratory environment. The goals of scientists were seen as largely the traditional academic goals of publication of results and professional autonomy, while for engineers the goals were more in line with those of the organization and centered around advancement and a voice in decision making. Efforts to increase the professional aspects of engineering positions in organizations were seen as not resonating with the dominant goals of engineers and as not being motivationally effective.

Hackman & Porter (77) investigated the interaction effects of expectancies and valence as predictors of how hard an individual would work on a job (effort) for groups of telephone service representatives. This predictor correlated .40 with a composite criterion of effectiveness, and a multiplicative function was seen as the most appropriate predictor. Such an approach was seen as useful in operational settings in order to specify and measure both valence and expectancies as an evaluation of motivational climate within organizations.

Lawler (114) analyzed longitudinal data among managers dealing with the relationship between expectancies of reward and job performance. Cross-lagged correlations between expectancy attitudes and job performance were evaluated in order to assess the direction of causality, and the results were seen as suggesting that expectancy attitudes were more apt to lead to job performance than the other direction of causality. While Rozelle & Campbell may contend that "to an economist, claims of novelty for the device of lagging cross-sectional correlations would probably seem spurious" (164, p. 74), they are relatively novel within the psychological literature, particularly in the literature dealing with industrial motivation. With more longitudinal research being undertaken, we will need more careful sorting out of cause and effect. The cross-lagged correlational approach may be a very useful analytical methodology.

Job attitudes.—As was the case at the time of the last *Annual Review* chapter (173), over the last two years there has been a considerable amount of attention to studies and reviews designed to prove or disprove or clarify or amplify or modify the two-factor theory of job satisfaction. Hopefully, the polemics on this issue have just about burned themselves out with the publication of the review by Whitsett & Winslow (188) defending motivator-hygiene theory and criticizing studies which purport to refute it; the review by House & Wigdor (91), independently prepared, suggesting that the two-factor theory oversimplifies the dynamics of job satisfaction; the rebuttal by Winslow & Whitsett (190); and the reply to the rebuttal by House &

Wigdor (92). While such interchanges can sometimes be entertaining, one might hope that the effort expended on such questions will be redirected toward a fresh attempt at understanding the dynamics of job satisfaction and motivation at work. Several other reviews and summaries of research dealing with the two-factor theory were presented (39, 86).

Most of the articles describing research designed to test directly the two-factor proposition (67, 69, 86, 95, 126, 174) concluded that more complex models are required to explain industrial motivation. Other studies of job satisfaction not designed directly to test the model but which were discussed within that framework came to comparable conclusions (112, 124, 162, 186, 192).

Perhaps the most telling and persistent criticisms of the research supportive of the two-factor concept is concerned with possible biases in the data because of the story telling or critical instant methodology. Comprehensive reviews of the controversy do suggest that the theory is to at least some extent method bound, and several recent studies suggest how it is possible for bias to arise in data collected within this framework. Meltzer & Ludwig (144, 145) found that a work motivated group—a group of individuals who cited work as one of the outstanding pleasant experiences of their lifetime in response to an open-ended question—differed significantly on a number of personality type variables (memory optimism, autonomy, interpersonal competence) from a matched group of nonwork oriented workers. The work motivated group was also rated more adequate at work. These findings suggest the possibility of influence of personality makeup on responses within the story telling framework. Gottlieb, Wiener & Mehrabian (66) found that there was less immediacy in verbalizations regarding failure as opposed to success experiences. This suggests that there is a tendency for people to associate things remote from them (job context) with failure (dissatisfaction) and things close to them (content) with success (satisfaction), a tendency which could certainly have an impact on the data collected by the critical incident methodlogy.

There has been only a limited amount of research on job attitudes—with the exception of some of the studies reported above on needs, goals, etc., which deal also with job attitudes—which has not been related to the motivator-hygiene concept. An exception is the book by Porter & Lawler (158) which goes well beyond merely presenting data on job attitudes of managers and also presents a model tying together rewards, role perceptions, need fulfillment, satisfaction, and job performance. This is an important contribution, pointing out some of the complexities involved in understanding job attitudes. Their model is succinctly explained in an article in *Harvard Business Review* (159) in which they contend that satisfaction results from rewards for performance and that organizations should monitor the effectiveness of their motivational system by evaluating this linkage. Rather than assess morale (satisfaction) directly, Porter & Lawler suggest than an organization should monitor the correlation between satisfaction and performance as it changes over time. Where this correlation is high, the motivational climate may be taken as favorable, and effective goal-path linkages are visible in the organization. Where low, goal-paths presumably would be blocked and the environment could be taken to be motivationally frustrating.

Hinrichs (84) reported on a factorial study of job attitude data for five different industrial white-collar populations (male nonexempt, male exempt, male managers, female nonexempt and female exempt). He found generally comparable components of job attitudes within each population. However, the various attitude dimensions appeared to be differentially important in explaining an overall measure of job satisfaction, with satisfaction regarding the work itself less correlated with overall satisfaction for managers than for other groups, evaluation of the company in general less important for females than for males, and ratings of job security more important for exempt females than for the other groups. Satisfaction with pay was about equally correlated with overall satisfaction for all five of the groups.

Scott (168) reported on research utilizing factor analysis of semantic differential measures of "morale," evaluating concepts of opportunities for growth, job, supervisor, top management, company benefits, fellow workers, pay, and working conditions. He concluded that morale is multidimensional with components of general affective tone, activation (including vigor and emotionality), and cognitive components of self-perception and evaluation. This is an interesting analysis of the intraindividual dimensions of morale which enter into the evaluation of any of the separate job components.

In recent years, research on satisfaction and motivation variables has tended to dominate the literature of industrial psychology. Studies of job satisfaction and morale utilizing *ad hoc* measurements, loosely conceptualized surveys of motivation concentrating on goals and needs, or fishing expeditions to define the behavioral correlates of various opinion measures have been prominent in almost every recent issue of our journals. The dominant organizing theme in the past, to the extent that there has been one, has been the two-factor controversy. There can be little doubt that Herzberg's motivator-hygiene concept has played a lasting and important role in providing at least some degree of order out of chaos. But it is clearly time to move ahead. We have gained valuable insights from two-factor research, but we need to know more.

Recently, more comprehensive models have been developed. Research should now focus on testing these models. We need to include a broader array of measures, to insure some degree of control over organizational variables, and to deal with the links between goals (valences), expectancies, abilities, and rewards within a systems (time dimensioned) framework. We also need more concern with measurement and the development of comparable measures across studies to deal with these variables.

For a start, at least, we need more consistently to relate our attitudinal and motivational measures to the kinds of variables which have been looked upon traditionally as output measures (productivity, turnover, absenteeism). Too much current research fails to evaluate even these linkages.

SPECIFIC PERSONNEL MANAGEMENT TOPICS

There are a number of areas not clearly related to our previous discussion of environmental and individual factors impacting effectiveness or attitudes but which are significant aspects of the psychology of man at work. We have elected to deal with them as a sort of potpourri in this final section.

Several books pertinent to the total field were published, in addition to the more specialized volumes discussed already. Two significant revised editions appeared. Fleishman's (57) comprehensive text has been updated and expanded after seven years. It continues as one of the best selections of readings covering most of the gamut of industrial psychology. Blum & Naylor (27) published a thoroughly updated and comprehensive new edition of Blum's Text on *Industrial Psychology and Its Social Foundations.* The emphasis on treating the different areas of industrial psychology within a framework of current theoretical developments makes this one of the more up-to-date texts in the field.

Several texts dealing with personnel administration in general may be of some interest to psychologists. Two new books were published—a paperback by Calhoon (33) and a text by McFarland (143). Strauss & Sayles published a revision of their popular personnel text (178). And during the period of the review there was a spate of new and revised books within the broader framework of organizational behavior (13, 41, 80, 81, 97, 184).

Industrial Training

Most of the literature in the training area focused on management development and training. The proceedings of an Executive Study Conference (54) and a book by House (90) provided an overview of the current state of the field of management development. House (89) also discussed why there are often problems "back at the work place" following much leadership training for managers.

The area of laboratory or sensitivity training received considerable emphasis. An extensive review by Campbell & Dunnette (35) covered research evaluating the effectiveness of laboratory education. Their review also included an excellent discussion of the nature of the T-group method, the assumptions on which it is based, and problems associated with it. They concluded that the weight of the evaluative research—which has probably been more concerned with sensitivity training than with any other area of management development—does tend to indicate that exposure to the T-group experience results in considerable changes in behavior for many individuals. However, they pointed out that it is not clear what the implications are for the increased effectiveness of individuals within their work roles at home in the organization. The review concluded with an outline of research approaches needed to more fully clarify the utility of the T-group technique.

This article, in conjunction with the interchange between Dunnette & Campbell and Argyris (9, 10, 49, 50), will provide the reader with as complete an overview of research to evaluate the T-group method and of the controversy surrounding the technique as can be found anywhere. Currently, the *Journal of Applied Behavioral Science* is publishing most of the information dealing with organizational development, including laboratory training. [Significant articles are (32), (51), (181)].

Friedlander (58) evaluated changes in attitudes with regard to six dimensions of group functions for four work groups within a government facility following participation in an organizational training laboratory, versus eight groups which did not participate in training. On a comparison of pre- and post-attitude measures, the training groups increased significantly in feelings of competence, in group effectiveness, and in personal involvement. There were no changes in attitudes regarding chairman approachability, intragroup trust, or the evaluation of group meetings. Friedlander emphasized the importance of this type of training for a total intact group, and the study suggested that, in all probability, attitudes and behaviors are differentially affected by this type of training.

Deep, Bass & Vaughan (43) compared performance in a business game of groups which had previously been together in a "quasi T-group experience" versus groups composed of individuals who had not been associated with one another during their T-group experience. Generally, the intact groups did less well in the business game, suggesting that the high degree of openness and interpersonal familiarity characteristic of the group with common T-group experience were dysfunctional to performance on many of the financial objectives of the business game.

Blake & Mouton (24) published another book describing aspects of their managerial grid training procedure. Brolly (29) presented a rather complete description of the grid training process. As yet, research on the effectiveness of grid training is not at all conclusive.

In the training literature not necessarily specific to management, Smith (176) provided an annotated bibliography for the period 1950 through 1965 regarding significant aspects involved in the design of instructional systems.

Elbing (52) studied the relationship of attitudes prior to training with acceptance and attitude change as a result of role playing. He found that subjects whose attitudes were congruent with the role which they were asked to play reacted most favorably to the technique, but did not reflect greater acceptance or openness for the opposing point of view. Those placed in roles at variance with their prior attitude had significantly larger attitude change toward acceptance of the opposing point of view. Elbing concluded that for role playing to achieve the most broadening of acceptance of opposing points of view, individuals should be put into roles with which they originally disagree.

Chaney & Teel (38) reported a very significant improvement in performance through use of training and visual aids to correct deficiencies in an inspection task. Unfortunately, no data on the long-term stability of these very sizeable performance changes were presented.

Two studies were related to adult training or retraining. Rubin & Morgan (166) assessed attitudes of engineers toward continuing technical education through an evaluation of resumes reflecting different levels of graduate education. Higher levels of educational attainment were evaluated more favorably than mere completion of a single course. Continuing education seemed to be seen as more related to advancement in management than to technical needs for this group of engineers. Dodd (44) described a program of adult retraining within the steel industry in Great Britain.

Employment of Minority Groups

The equitable employment of minority group members within business and industry is today widely recognized as one of the most pressing problems facing our society, and the last several *Annual Review* chapters have deplored the lack of research attention by psychologists to this issue. Yet we must conclude that still only a very minimum of research is being published which can help to provide better understandings in this critical area.

There seems to be growing concern in the area of selection, no doubt forced by Title 7 of the Civil Rights Act and the necessity to abide by EEOC guidelines. This is an example of how necessity can be the mother of invention—or at least of research, when the law is involved. A detailed review of selection studies falls outside the domain of this chapter, though reference will be made to one significant book in the area (104).

Several reports on the results of the effectiveness of training programs for minority group employees (for example, 87, 101) were presented. We may hope to begin to see more of this research reported within the psychological journals with adequate research designs and controls.

One study reported on job satisfaction data for Negro versus white workers [Bloom & Barry (26)]. However, due to a low rate of questionnaire response and insufficient presentation of data, we are unable to draw any clear conclusion regarding differences between the groups. Bloom & Barry suggested that the two-factor theory is too simple to explain the concepts of job satisfaction and dissatisfaction for Negro blue-collar employees.

A significant monograph was published by Dreger & Miller (46) reviewing comparative psychological studies of Negroes and whites between 1959 and 1965. This is an updating of a similar monograph published in 1960. They concluded that it would be seriously misleading to generalize by race to "*the* American Negro" or "*the* American White," but that complex and multiple interactions among individual and environmental variables must be accounted for in any comparative research.

Assessment

There were a number of significant contributions in the area of manpower assessment for evaluation, promotion, and placement purposes (other than for initial selection). Jackson & Messick (99) published a comprehensive book of readings covering the gamut of the assessment process. This is a must for anyone engaged in this activity. Two reports on conferences specific to management evaluation and assessment were published (135, 189).

Staff members of the Life Insurance Agency Management Association prepared a description of the career analysis procedure in use in the life insurance industry (125). The procedure is designed to assess the career path an agent should follow (either into management or career selling) "and to develop specific, individualized, training programs and supervision for the candidate" (p. 9). The initial hurdle is a reasonably firm placement instrument, and those indicated for management are then considered further through a number of other screens for promotion and development. Comprehensive training of interviewers and evaluators are included in the process. This is a useful description of an operational multifaceted career development program.

Thornton (180) evaluated the relationship between self-ratings and ratings by superiors for a group of executives. The two sets of ratings were found to be quite dissimilar, with self-ratings more favorable, especially for executives who were judged least promotable. Data presented by Lawler (117) also showed little agreement between self-ratings and either superior or subordinate ratings, though superior and subordinate ratings themselves exhibited considerable convergent and discriminate validity.

There has been considerable emphasis on the use of various situational approaches to the assessment of managerial potential. Three reports appeared on additional analyses of aspects of the AT&T formal management assessments center procedures. These analyses showed that data obtained from interviews [Grant & Bray (71)] and from projective techniques [Grant, Katkovsky & Bray (72)] do contribute to staff assessments of management potential and also relate to subsequent progress in the organization. Bray & Campbell (28) reported on a successful experience in utilizing the assessment center methodology among newly hired salesmen in the Bell System.

Hardesty & Jones (82) discussed a similar assessment center carried out at a Midwestern oil company and presented data showing those variables which discriminated managers judged high in potential from those judged low. Lowe-Holmes & Brocklesby (136) discussed factor analysis of managerial assessment data in Great Britain, including background information, test data, and interview data, and concluded that a single overall factor was most important in the promotional decision and that the major emphasis was on the evaluation of negative elements.

There is clearly a need for better procedures for the evaluation of management potential. Much of this research is going to have to be specific to individual orgnaizations. The prospects for validating situational exercises and multiple assessment procedures within specific organizations appear promising, probably in large measure because of the common elements within both the assessment and the criterion measures judgmentally weighted by individuals knowledgeable about the milieu of managerial success within a specific organization. When members of the organization serve both as assessors (observers in assessment situations) and as managers of the organization's promotion and management advancement systems, we may expect reasonably strong predictor-criterion relationships.

The trend toward situational exercises in management assessment suggests the need for development of more comprehensive job samples and points to the possible use of these as criteria in themselves against which possibly initial selection instruments may be validated. In the area of ratings, certainly multiple raters—superior, peer, subordinate, and self-ratings as outlined by Lawler (117)—should be attempted more frequently to provide better understanding of the nature of assessments and a richer array of measures both for research and for personnel action.

Turnover

This important aspect of organizational success has received relatively limited attention in the recent literature. Schuh (167) reviewed the literature on the prediction of turnover. He found that intelligence, aptitude, and personality tests were not consistently related to turnover. There were some indications that interest inventories were often related to turnover, and the best prediction came from scaled biographical data blanks and job satisfaction data. He suggested that in the selection situation, weighted application blanks must be re-keyed and cross-validated regularly.

Ronan (161) reported on a study of the reasons given for termination in a large manufacturing concern and found major differences for employees in different functions or with differing lengths of service. Pay and job security were the most frequently cited reasons for leaving. Downs (45) evaluated turnover rates versus age at time of hiring in two public service organizations in Great Britain. She concluded that there was higher turnover among older than younger recruits during the first few months of employment, but a higher rate of turnover for younger than older recruits after the passage of the first six months or so.

Hulin (93) reported on the results of a program designed specifically to increase job satisfaction and reduce turnover among a large group of female office workers in Montreal. The program focused on increasing the effectiveness of salary administration practices, facilitating interdepartmental transfers, and encouragement of changes in job content. Over a two-year period, there were significant increases in satisfaction scores as measured by the Job Description Index, especially in the areas of pay and promotion which were most heavily emphasized in the programs, and a significant decline in the turnover rate. The study suggested that high turnover may be directly controllable or at least reducible by a concerted program of administrative action.

There is a surprising lack of comprehensive research on turnover in view of the obvious costs to industry, especially among executive and professional employees. Research to tie down systematically more of the individual difference factors and environmental moderators explaining turnover variance could be quite useful both to organizations to reduce their manpower costs and to individuals to reduce the disruption often associated with job changes. The research data suggest that it may be easier to find the correlates of turnover than of productivity, perhaps because of the perfect reliability of the dependent variable and freedom from many of the criterion problems associated with research into the correlates of performance. It may be that because of the sensitive nature of turnover information, more research is being done in this important area than gets into the psychological literature. Perhaps some form of clearinghouse of turnover information with built-in assurances for adequate confidentiality for individual organizations is needed for us to compile the data base to adequately understand this important organizational behavior.

Safety and Accidents

There is a disturbing lack of attention to the area of safety and accident prevention in the applied psychological literature. Greenshields & Platt (73) reported on a carefully constructed job sample of automobile driving behavior over a 17-mile route, which was reasonably successful in categorizing high-accident drivers, high-violation drivers, and beginning drivers. Considering the chance factors involved in violation and accident data the authors felt that their job sample procedure showed considerable promise for identifying probable driver effectiveness.

Kunce (111) reported on the relationship between an accident proneness score derived from the Strong Vocational Interest Blank and accident data for a number of populations. The Accident Proneness index was the difference between standard scores on two Strong Vocational Interest Blank scales —"adventuresome" (the aviator scale) and "cautiousness" (the banker scale). For an industrial population, the score correlated 0.28 with accident rate.

Labor Relations

A study by Ash (11) among 43 companies showed that labor relations activities (contract negotiations, contract interpretation, and grievance administration) were among the most frequently occurring industrial relations activities. With the exception of grievance administration, labor relations were also among the most highly centralized activities. Yet despite this pervasive role which they seem to play in setting the environment for man at work in organizations, very little psychological research is devoted to the dynamics of labor relations.

Sulkin & Pranis (179) compared a group of grievants within a heavy machinery company with a group of nongrievants. They found that grievants tended to have higher education, to be more active in their union, to have higher tardiness records, and to be paid less.

There were two studies dealing with attitudes in labor-management relations. Zweig (195) reported on the development of a scale for measuring partisanship in labor management issues. However, the scale exhibited somewhat low reliability, and there was no evidence of behavioral validation of it. Alsikafi et al. (7) reported on the development of a Guttman-type scale for measuring the attitudes of managers toward labor unions. In comparing data collected in five Southern corporations with data from a contemporary Gallup poll, they suggested that the level of favorability in the South regarding labor unions is about comparable to national trends.

Research Methods and Techniques

Several methodological articles appeared. Gullahorn (76) presented a comprehensive monograph comparing various multivariate approaches to the analysis of survey data. Campbell & O'Connell (34) evaluated the method factors which occur in factor analysis of multitrait multimethod matrices. They suggested that the inflation of intertrait *r*'s because of common variance due to a single method or common time of data collection may make suspect many typical factor analyses of individual differences data.

Alderfer (5) utilized the multitrait multimethod technique for comparing questionnaire and interview data dealing with satisfaction and desire or personal goals in an industrial population. In addition to demonstrating reasonably high convergent and discriminant validity for satisfaction measures and relatively low validity for desire measures, his results suggested that the interview and questionnaire techniques can lead to quite comparable results. In a follow-up article, Alderfer (4) compared questionnaire responses for a group of employees who were interviewed prior to filling out an attitude questionnaire with responses of a group who completed the questionnaire without a preceding interview. He found significantly less satisfaction by peers in a group which had the initial interview than for the noninterviewed group. There were no differences on scales for satisfaction with pay, with use of skills and ability, or (contrary to his hypothesis) satisfaction with superiors. Alderfer suggested a continuum of threat associated with the method of data collection in survey research which largely related to the degree of intimacy of the data being solicited.

Hinrichs & Gatewood (85) found greater favorability, primarily in attitudes dealing with the company in general, for a group which completed an opinion questionnaire in group sessions at the place of work versus employees surveyed at home by mail. Presumably implicit threat in the at-company administration condition inflated the favorability of attitudes. There were no differences in data collected by the traditional method of responding within the questionnaire booklet itself versus the use of answer sheets for direct machine processing of the data.

Mikes & Hulin (146) found that an index made up of satisfaction measures multiplied by importance measures was less strongly correlated with a criterion of turnover than were satisfaction measures alone. They concluded that the unreliability of both measures is multiplied, and they made a rather strong case against using satisfaction X importance measures in attitude research.

Several reports of behavioral simulations hopefully may be a forerunner of more research emphasis in this area. Vroom & MacCrimmon (183) discussed how the career movements of managers and professionals within organizations may be described by a Markov chain model. Kaczka & Kirk (102) reported on an effort to develop a computer model to investigate a set of hypotheses concerning the effects of managerial climate on organizational performance. The results tended to support their hypotheses, but even more importantly, they demonstrated the feasibility of computer simulation of behavioral systems. Smith (175) reported on the development of a model to simulate the decision processes involved in personnel selection and reported a 94% level of agreement between human decisions regarding ultimate employment recommendations and decisions arrived at under the model.

While these are relatively primitive efforts in model building and simulation, we will probably see more of this type of work in the not too distant future. Hopefully, such efforts will contribute to a broader understanding of the key factors impacting the psychology of man at work.

OVERVIEW

Most of our qualitative concerns with the contemporary scene in industrial psychology have already been expressed in the introduction to this chapter. Our excursion through the literature should have helped to clarify our contention that applied psychological research needs to deal with a broader set of variables pertinent to man at work, that more standardization of variables in needed, complex interactions need to be assessed more adequately, and that a longitudinal orientation should be applied increasingly to research in the field.

These are methodological criticisms. Our feeling, however, is that methodological advances are taking place with an increasing rapidity that will overcome many of these problems. These revolve mainly around a rapidly expanding capability for economical and convenient broad scale data retention, access, and manipulation. We are in a period of rapid change in this area.

More disturbing, however, is the conclusion we must reach concerning the content of much current research in industrial psychology. The questions raised by prior reviews are still appropriate: Why is it that so little of today's applied psychological research is addressed to the more pressing issues of our times, when clearly there is a broad array of such issues which are having or will have a pervasive impact on the world of man at work? Does the balance of research effort devoted to evaluating T-group training versus the number of studies devoted to understanding the key issues in the training of minority employees, for example, mirror the balance of priority which society in general would probably place on these two areas? How appropriate is the volume of research on managerial motivations versus the number of studies focusing on the motives of college students or new entrants to the work force? Does this reflect the best balance to help us to understand what the impact of changing personal and social value systems will be on industrial organizations of the future? In terms of priorities, does the amount of effort devoted to compensation equity experiments or management style offset an almost complete inattention to the need for understanding the impact of automation on an increasing range of white-collar and clerical tasks? What are the ramifications of new information technology on our traditional concerns of selection, motivation, training, and job satisfaction?

In light of the continuing parade of time-worn themes and over-researched topics in many of our journals, an outside observer migh question—as has been done in the past—is industrial psychology bankrupt? It's a good valid question! Our answer is based partly on the research of the last two years, and partly on hope: industrial psychology is not bankrupt; some strong positive trends are evident, as pointed out throughout the chapter; we have every confidence that future reviews will reflect increasing relevance of applied psychological research to the pressing issues of our society; all that is needed is some refocusing of attention and a sense of commitment.

LITERATURE CITED

1. Adams, J. S. Effects of overpayment: two comments on Lawler's paper. *J. Pers. Soc. Psychol.*, **10**, 315–16 (1968)
2. Adams, J. S. Inequity in social exchange. In *Advances in Experimental Social Psychology*, **2**, 267–99 (Berkowitz, L., Ed., Academic Press, New York, 348 pp., 1965)
3. Alderfer, C. P. An organizational syndrome. *Admin. Sci. Quart.*, **12**, 440–60 (1967)
4. Alderfer, C. P. Comparison of questionnaire responses with and without preceding interviews. *J. Appl. Psychol.*, **52**, 335–40 (1968)
5. Alderfer, C. P. Convergent and discriminant validation of satisfaction and desire measures by interviews and questionnaires. *Ibid.*, **51**, 509–20 (1967)
6. Allen, J. C. Multidimensional analysis of worker-oriented and job-oriented verbs. *J. Appl. Psychol.*, **53**, 73–79 (1969)
7. Alsikafi, M., Jokinen, W. J., Spray, S. L., Tracy, G. S. Managerial attitudes toward labor unions in

a southern city. *J. Appl. Psychol.,* **52,** 447–53 (1968)

8. Andrews, F. M., Farris, G. F. Supervisory practices and innovation in scientific teams. *Personnel Psychol.,* **20,** 497–515 (1967)
9. Argyris, C. A rejoinder to Dunnette and Campbell. *Indust. Relat.,* **8,** 45 (1968)
10. Argyris, C. Issues in evaluating laboratory education. *Ibid.,* 28–40
11. Ash, P. Measurement of industrial relations activities. *J. Appl. Psychol.,* **51,** 387–92 (1967)
12. Atchison, T., French, W. Pay systems for scientists and engineers. *Indust. Relat.,* **7,** 44–56 (1967)
13. Athos, A. G., Coffey, R. E. *Behavior in Organizations: A Multidimensional View* (Prentice Hall, Englewood Cliffs, N. J., 549 pp., 1968)
14. Barnett, A. N. A factor analytic study of the properties of the engineer's role set. *Multivar. Behav. Res.,* **3,** 47–59 (1968)
15. Baruch, R. The achievement motive in women: Implications for career development. *J. Pers. Soc. Psychol.,* **5,** 260–67 (1967)
16. Bass, B. M. Ability, values, and concepts of equitable salary increases in exercise compensation., *J. Appl. Psychol.,* **52,** 299–303 (1968)
17. Bass, B. M. Interface between personnel and organizational psychology. *Ibid.,* 81–88
18. Bass, B. M. Social behavior and the orientation inventory: a review. *Psychol. Bull.,* **68,** 260–92 (1967)
19. Bass, B. M. Some effects on a group of whether and when the head reveals his opinion. *Organ. Behav. Hum. Perform.,* **2,** 375–82 (1967)
20. Bassett, G. A., Meyer, H. H. Performance appraisal based on self-review. *Personnel Psychol.,* **21,** 421–30 (1968)
21. Beer, M. Needs and need satisfaction among clerical workers in complex and routine jobs. *Personnel Psychol.,* **21,** 209–22 (1968)
22. Beer, M., Gery, G. J. Pay system preferences and their correlates. *Proc. 76th Ann. Conv. Am. Psychol. Assoc.,* 569–70 (Am. Psychol. Assoc., Washington, D.C., 758 pp., 1968)
23. Berdie, R. F. Consistency and generalizability of intraindividual variability. *J. Appl. Psychol.,* **53,** 35–41 (1969)
24. Blake, R., Mouton, J. S. *Corporate Excellence Through Grid Organization Development* (Gulf Publ. Co., Houston, 374 pp., 1968)
25. Blood, M. R., Hulin, C. L. Alienation, environmental characteristics and worker responses. *J. Appl. Psychol.,* **51,** 284–90 (1967)
26. Bloom, R., Barry, J. R. Determinants of work attitudes among Negroes. *J. Appl. Psychol.,* **51,** 291–94 (1967)
27. Blum, M., Naylor, J. C. *Industrial Psychology: Its Theoretical and Social Foundations,* revised ed. (Harper, New York, 633 pp., 1968)
28. Bray, D. W., Campbell, R. J. Selection of salesmen by means of an assessment center. *J. Appl. Psychol.,* **52,** 36–41 (1968)
29. Brolly, M. The managerial grid. *Occup. Psychol.,* **41,** 231–37 (1967)
30. Bryan, J. F., Locke, E. A. Goal setting as a means of increasing motivation. *J. Appl. Psychol.,* **51,** 274–77 (1967)
31. Bryan, J. F., Locke, E. A. Parkinson's law as a goal-setting phenomenon. *Organ. Behav. Hum. Perform.,* **2,** 258–75 (1967)
32. Bunker, D. R., Knowles, E. S. Comparison of behavioral changes resulting from human relations training laboratories of different length. *J. Appl. Behav. Sci.,* **3,** 505–23 (1967)
33. Calhoon, R. P. *Personnel Management and Supervision* (Appleton-Century-Crofts, New York, 423 pp., 1967)
34. Campbell D. T. O'Connell, E. J. Methods factors in multitrait multimethod matrices: multiplicative rather than additive? *Multivar. Behav. Res.,* **2,** 409–26 (1967)
35. Campbell, J. P., Dunnette, M. D. Effectiveness of T-group experiences in managerial training and development. *Psychol. Bull.,* **70,** 73–104 (1968)
36. Carr, M. J. Technical, organizational, and communicational dimensions in modeling for job analysis. *IEEE Trans. Engin. Mgmt.,* **15,** 94–99 (1968)
37. Carroll, S. J., Jr., Taylor, W. H., Jr. A study of the validity of a self-observational central signaling method of work sampling. *Personnel Psychol.,* **21,** 359–64 (1968)

38. Chaney, F. B., Teel, K. S. Improving inspector performance through training and visual aids. *J. Appl. sychol.*, **51**, 311–15 (1967)
39. Cummings, L. L., ElSalmi, A. M. Empirical research on the bases and correlates of managerial motivation: a review of the literature. *Psychol. Bull.*, **70**, 127–44 (1968)
40. Darley, J. G. 1917: A journal is born. *J. Appl. Psychol.*, **52**, 1–9 (1968)
41. Davis, K. *Human Relations at Work: The Dynamics of Organizational Behavior*, 3rd Ed. (McGraw-Hill, New York, 559 pp., 1967)
42. Dawis, R. V., Weiss, D. J., Lofquist, L. H., Betz, E. Satisfaction as a moderator in the prediction of satisfactoriness. *Proc. 75th Ann. Conv. Am. Psychol. Assoc.*, 269–70 (Am. Psychol. Assoc., Washington, D.C., 383 pp., 1967)
43. Deep, S. D., Bass, B. M., Vaughan, J. A. Some effects on business gaming of previous quasi-T group affiliations. *J. Appl. Psychol.*, **51**, 426–31 (1967)
44. Dodd, B. A study in adult retraining: The gas man. *Occup. Psychol.*, **41**, 143–53 (1967)
45. Downs, S. Labor turnover in two public service organizations. *Occup. Psychol.*, **41**, 137–42 (1967)
46. Dreger, R. M., Miller, K. S. Comparative psychological studies of Negroes and whites in the United States: 1959–1965. *Psychol. Bull., Monogr. Suppl.*, **70**, No. 3, pt. 2, 58 pp. (1968)
47. Dubno, P. Group congruency patterns and leadership characteristics. *Personnel Psychol.*, **21**, 335–44 (1968)
48. Dunnette, M. D. Personnel Management. *Ann. Rev. Psychol.*, **13**, 285–314 (1962)
49. Dunnette, M. D., Campbell, J. P. A response to Argyris. *Indust. Relat.*, **8**, 41–44 (1968)
50. Dunnette, M. D., Campbell, J. P. Laboratory education: Impact on people and organizations. *Ibid.*, 1–27
51. Eisenstadt, J. W. An investigation of factors which influence response to laboratory training. *J. Appl. Behav. Sci.*, **3**, 575–78 (1967)
52. Elbing, A. O., Jr. The influence of prior attitudes on role playing results. *Personnel Psychol.*, **20**, 309–21 (1967)
53. ElSalmi, A. M., Cummings, L. L. Managers' perceptions of needs and need satisfactions as a function of interactions among organization variables. *Personnel Psychol.*, **21**, 465–77 (1968)
54. The Executive Study Conference. *Management, Education and Development* (Educ. Testing Serv., Princeton, N.J., 150 pp., 1968)
55. Feather, N. T. Change in confidence following success or failure as a predictor of subsequent performance. *J. Pers. Soc. Psychol.*, **9**, 38–46 (1968)
56. Fiedler, F. E. *A Theory of Leadership Effectiveness* (McGraw-Hill, New York, 310 pp., 1967)
57. Fleishman, E. A. *Studies in personnel and Industrial Psychology*, revised ed. (Dorsey Press, Homewood, Ill., 835 pp., 1967)
58. Friedlander, F. The impact of organizational training laboratories upon the effectiveness and interaction of ongoing work groups. *Personnel Psychol.*, **20**, 289–307 (1967)
59. Friedman, A., Goodman, P. Wage inequity, self-qualifications, and productivity. *Organ. Behav. Hum. Perform.*, **2**, 406–17 (1967)
60. Galbraith, J., Cummings, L. L. An empirical investigation of the motivational determinants of task performance: Interactive effects between instrumentality—valence and motivation—ability. *Organ. Behav. Hum. Perform.*, **2**, 237–57 (1967)
61. Gerstberger, P. G., Allen, T. J. Criteria used by research and development engineers in the selection of an information source. *J. Appl. Psychol.*, **52**, 272–79 (1968)
62. Ghiselli, E. E. Interaction of traits and motivational factors in the determination of the success of managers. *J. Appl. Psychol.*, **52**, 480–83 (1968)
63. Ghiselli, E. E. Some motivational factors in the success of managers. *Personnel Psychol.*, **21**, 431–40 (1968)
64. Goodman, P., Baloff, N. Task experience and attitudes towards decision making. *Organ. Behav. Hum. Perform.*, **3**, 202–16 (1968)
65. Goodman, P., Friedman, A. An examination of the effect of wage inequity in the hourly condition. *Organ. Behav. Hum. Perform.*, **3**, 340–52 (1968)

66. Gottlieb, R., Wiener, M., Mehrabian, A. Immediacy, discomfort-relief quotient and content in verbalizations about positive and negative experiences. *J. Pers. Soc. Psychol.*, **7**, 266–74 (1967)

67. Graen, G. B. Testing traditional and two-factor hypotheses concerning job satisfaction. *J. Appl. Psychol.*, **52**, 366–71 (1968)

68. Graen, G. B., Dawis, R. V., Weiss, D. J. Need type and job satisfaction among industrial scientists. *J. Appl. Psychol.*, **52**, 286–89 (1968)

69. Graen, G. B., Hulin, C. L. Addendum to "an empirical investigation of two implications of the two-factor theory of job satisfaction." *J. Psychol.*, **52**, 341–42 (1968)

70. Graham, W. K. Description of leader behavior and evaluation of leaders as a function of LPC. *Personnel Psychol.*, **21**, 457–64 (1968)

71. Grant, D. L., Bray, D. W. Contributions of the interview to assessment of management potential. *J. Appl. Psychol.*, **53**, 24–34 (1969)

72. Grant, D. L., Katkovsky, W., Bray, D. W. Contributions of projective techniques to assessment of management potential. *J. Appl. Psychol.*, **51**, 226–32 (1967)

73. Greenshields, B. D., Platt, F. N. Development of a method of predicting high accident and high violation drivers. *J. Appl. Psychol.*, **51**, 205–10 (1967)

74. Gregson, R. A. M., Jamieson, B. D. A psychometric exploration of some attitudes to the managerial role. *Occup. Psychol.*, **42**, 167–80 (1968)

75. Gruenfeld, L., Arbuthnot, J. Field independence, achievement values, and the evaluation of a competency related dimension of the Least Preferred Co-worker (LPC) measure. *Percept. Mot. Skills*, **27**, 991–1002 (1968)

76. Gullahorn, J. E. Multivariate approaches in survey data processing: comparisons of factor, cluster, and Guttman analyses and of multiple regression and canonical correlation methods. *Multivar. Behav. Res. Monogr.*, 67–71, 73 pp. (1967)

77. Hackman, J. R., Porter, L. W. Expectancy theory predictions of work effectiveness. *Organ. Behav. Hum. Perform.*, **3**, 417–26 (1968)

78. Haire, M., Ghiselli, E. E., Gordon, M. E. A psychological study of pay. *J. Appl. Psychol. Monogr.*, **51**, No. 4, pt. 2, 24 pp. (1967)

79. Hall, D. T., Nougaim, K. E. An examination of Maslow's need hierarchy in an organizational setting. *Organ. Behav. Hum. Perform.*, **3**, 12–35 (1968)

80. Hampton, D. R., Summer, C. E., Webber, R. A. *Organizational Behavior and the Practice of Management* (Scott Foresman Co., Glenview, Ill., 758 pp., 1968)

81. Haney, W. V. *Communication and Organizational Behavior: Text and Cases*, revised ed. (Irwin, Inc., Homewood, Ill., 533 pp., 1967)

82. Hardesty, D. L., Jones, W. S. Characteristics of judged high-potential management personnel—the operations of an industrial assessment center. *Personnel Psychol.*, **21**, 85–98 (1968)

83. Herzberg, F. One more time: how do you motivate employees? *Harv. Bus. Rev.*, **46**, 53–62 (1968)

84. Hinrichs, J. R. A replicated study of job satisfaction dimensions. *Personnel Psychol.*, **21**, 479–503 (1968)

85. Hinrichs, J. R., Gatewood, R. D. Differences in opinion survey response patterns as a function of different methods of survey administration. *J. Appl. Psychol.*, **51**, 497–502 (1967)

86. Hinton, B. L. An empirical investigation of the Herzberg methodology and two-factor theory. *Organ. Behav. Hum. Perform.*, **3**, 286–309 (1968)

87. Hodgson, J. D., Brenner, M. H. Successful experience: Training hard-core unemployed. *Harv. Bus. Rev.*, **46**, 148–56 (1968)

88. Holloman, C. R. The perceived leadership role of military and civilian supervisors in a military setting. *Personnel Psychol.*, **20**, 199–210 (1967)

89. House, R. J. Leadership training: Some dysfunctional consequences. *Admin. Sci. Quart.*, **12**, 556–71 (1968)

90. House, R. J. *Management Development: Design, Evaluation, and Implementation* (Bur. Indust. Relat., Grad. Sch. Bus. Admin., Univ. Michigan, Ann Arbor, 138 pp., 1967)

91. House, R. J., Wigdor, L. A. Herzberg's dual-factor theory of job satisfaction and motivation: a review of the evidence and a criticism. *Personnel Psychol.,* **20,** 369–89 (1967)

92. House, R. J., Wigdor, L. A. Reply to Winslow and Whitsett. *Ibid.,* **21,** 58–62 (1968)

93. Hulin, C. L. Effects of changes in job satisfaction levels on employee turnover. *J. Appl. Psychol.,* **52,** 122–26 (1968)

94. Hulin, C. L., Blood, M. R. Job enlargement, individual differences, and worker responses. *Psychol. Bull.,* **69,** 41–55 (1968)

95. Hulin, C. L., Smith, P. A. An empirical investigation of two implications of the two-factor theory of job satisfaction. *J. Appl. Psychol.,* **51,** 396–402 (1967)

96. Hunt, J. G. Fiedler's leadership contingency model: An empirical test in three organizations. *Organ. Behav. Hum. Perform.,* **3,** 290–308 (1967)

97. Hutchinson, J. G. *Organizations: Theory and Classical Concepts* (Holt, Rinehart & Winston, New York, 178 pp., 1967)

98. Inkson, K., Payne, R., Pugh, D. Extending the occupational environment: The measurement of organizations. *Occup. Psychol.,* **41,** 33–47 (1967)

99. Jackson, D. N., Messick, S., Eds. *Problems in Human Assessment* (McGraw-Hill, New York, 873 pp., 1967)

100. Johnson, P. V., Marcrum, R. H. Perceived deficiencies in individual need fulfillment of career army officers. *J. Appl. Psychol.,* **52,** 457–561 (1968)

101. Jones, J. J., Jr. Hard-core unemployables: A good investment. *Personnel Admin.,* **31,** 30–35 (1968)

102. Kaczka, E. E., Kirk, R. V. Managerial climate, work groups, and organizational performance. *Admin. Sci. Quart.,* **12,** 253–72 (1967)

103. Katzell, R. A., Barrett, R. S., Vann, D. H., Hogan, J. M. Organizational correlates of executive roles. *J. Appl. Psychol.,* **52,** 22–28 (1968)

104. Kirkpatrick, J. J., Ewen, R. B., Barrett, R. S., Katzell, R. A. *Testing and Fair Employment; Fairness and Validity of Personnel Tests for Different Ethnic Groups* (New York Univ. Press, New York, 145 pp., 1968)

105. Klein, S. M., Maher, J. R. Education level, attitudes, and future expectations among first level management. *Personnel Psychol.,* **21,** 43–53 (1968)

106. Korman, A. K. "Consideration," "Initiating structure," and organizational criteria—a review. *Personnel Psychol.,* **19,** 349–61 (1966)

107. Korman, A. K. The prediction of managerial performance: A review. *Ibid.,* **21,** 295–322 (1968)

108. Korman, A. K. Relevance of personal need satisfaction for overall satisfaction as a function of self-esteem. *J. Appl. Psychol.,* **51,** 533–38 (1967)

109. Korman, A. K. Self-esteem, social influence, and task performance: Some tests of a theory. *Proc. 76th Ann. Conv. Am. Psychol. Assoc.,* 567–68 (See Ref. 22)

110. Korman, A. K. Task success, task popularity, and self-esteem as influences on task liking. *J. Appl. Psychol.,* **52,** 484–90 (1968)

111. Kunce, J. T. Vocational interests and accident proneness. *J. Appl. Psychol.* **51,** 223–25 (1967)

112. Lahiri, D. K., Srivastva, S. Determinants of satisfaction in middle management personnel. *J. Appl. Psychol.,* **51,** 254–65 (1967)

113. Landy, F. J., Elbert, A. J. Scaling assumptions underlying weighting in job classification systems. *J. Appl. Psychol.,* **51,** 442–43 (1967)

114. Lawler, E. E., III. A correlational-causal analysis of the relationship between expectancy attitudes and job performance. *J. Appl. Psychol.,* **52,** 462–68 (1968)

115. Lawler, E. E., III. Effects of hourly overpayment on productivity and work quality. *J. Pers. Soc. Psychol.,* **10,** 306–14 (1968)

116. Lawler, E. E., III. Equity theory as a predictor of productivity and work quality. *Psychol. Bull.,* **70,** 596–610 (1968)

117. Lawler, E. E., III. The multitrait-multirater approach to measuring managerial job performance. *J. Appl. Psychol.,* **51,** 369–81 (1967)

118. Lawler, E. E., III, Koplin, C. A., Young, T. F., Fadem, J. A. Inequity reduction over time in

an induced overpayment situation. *Organ. Behav. Hum. Perform.*, **3**, 253–68 (1968)

119. Lawler, E. E., III, Levin, E. Union officers' perceptions of members' pay preferences. *Indust. Labor Relat. Rev.*, **21**, 509–17 (1968)

120. Lawler, E. E., III, O'Gara, P. W. Effects of inequity produced by underpayment on work output, work quality, and attitudes toward the work. *J. Appl. Psychol.*, **51**, 403–10 (1967)

121. Lawler, E. E., III, Porter, L. W. The effect of performance on job satisfaction. *Indust. Relat.*, **7**, 20–28 (1967)

122. Lawler, E. E., III, Porter, L. W., Tennenbaum, A. Managers' attitudes toward interaction episodes. *J. Appl. Psychol.*, **52**, 432–39 (1968)

123. Lefkowitz, J. Self-esteem of industrial workers. *J. Appl. Psychol.*, **51**, 521–28 (1967)

124. Levine, E. L., Weitz, J. Job satisfaction among graduate students: Intrinsic versus extrinsic variables. *J. Appl. Psychol.*, **52**, 263–71 (1968)

125. Life Insurance Agency Management Assoc. Career guidance in the life insurance industry. *Personnel Psychol.*, **21**, 1–21 (1968)

126. Lindsay, C. A., Marks, E., Gorlow, L. The Herzberg theory: a critique and reformulation. *J. Appl. Psychol.*, **51**, 330–39 (1967)

127. Locke, E. A. Motivational effects of knowledge of results: Knowledge or goal setting? *J. Appl. Psychol.*, **51**, 324–29 (1967)

128. Locke, E. A. Relationship of success and expectation to affect on goal-seeking tasks. *J. Pers. Soc. Psychol.*, **7**, 125–34 (1967)

129. Locke, E. A. Toward a theory of task motivation and incentives. *Organ. Behav. Hum. Perform.*, **3**, 157–89 (1968)

130. Locke, E. A., Bryan, J. The directing function of goals in task performance. *Organ. Behav. Hum. Perform.*, **4**, 35–42 (1969)

131. Locke, E. A., Bryan, J. F. Goal-setting as a determinant of the effect of knowledge of score on performance. *Am. J. Psychol.*, **81**, 398–406 (1968)

132. Locke, E. A., Bryan, J. F. Knowledge of score and goal level as determinants of work rate. *J. Appl. Psychol.*, **53**, 59–65 (1969)

133. Locke, E. A., Bryan, J. F., Kendall, L. M. Goals and intentions as mediators of the effects of monetary incentives on behavior. *J. Appl. Psychol.*, **52**, 104–21 (1968)

134. Locke, E. A., Cartledge, N., Koeppel, J. Motivational effects of knowledge of results: A goal-setting phenomenon? *Psychol. Bull.*, **70**, 474–85 (1968)

135. Lopez, F. M., Jr. (Chairman) Theories and problems in the evaluation of executive performance. *Proc. Exec. Study Conf.*, May 24–25, 1966 (Educ. Testing Serv., Princeton, N.J., 126 pp., 1967)

136. Lowe-Holmes, A. R., Brocklesby, I. A factor analytic study of selection decision making. *Occup. Psychol.*, **42**, 85–88 (1968)

137. Lowin, A. Participative decision making: A model, literature critique, and prescriptions for research. *Organ. Behav. Hum. Perform.*, **3**, 68–106 (1968)

138. Lowin, A., Craig, J. R. The influence of level of performance on managerial style: An experimental object-lesson in the ambiguity of correlational data. *Organ. Behav. Hum. Perform.*, **3**, 440–58 (1968)

139. MacKinney, A. C. The assessment of performance change: An inductive example. *Organ. Behav. Hum. Perform.*, **2**, 56–72 (1967)

140. Maher, J. *Stimulus Variability as a Factor in Performance and Job Satisfaction* (Doctoral thesis, Columbia Univ., New York, 1968)

141. McCormick, E. J., Cunningham, J. W., Gordon, G. G. Job dimensions based on factorial analyses of worker-oriented job variables. *Personnel Psychol.*, **20**, 417–30 (1967)

142. McCormick, E. J., Cunningham, J. W., Thornton, G. C. The prediction of job requirements by a structured job analysis procedure. *Personnel Psychol.*, **20**, 431–40 (1967)

143. McFarland, D. E. *Personnel Management: Theory and Practice* (Macmillan, New York, 694 pp., 1968)

144. Meltzer, H., Ludwig, D. Memory dynamics and work motivation. *J. Appl. Psychol.*, **52**, 184–87 (1968)

145. Meltzer, H., Ludwig, D. Relation-

ship of memory optimism to work competency and personality variables. *Ibid.*, 423–28

146. Mikes, P. S., Hulin, C. L. Use of importance as a weighting component of job satisfaction. *J. Appl. Psychol.*, **52**, 394–98 (1968)
147. Mitchell, V. F., Porter, L. W. Comparative managerial role perceptions in military and business hierarchies. *J. Appl. Psychol.*, **51**, 449–52 (1967)
148. Mukherjee, B. N. Achievement values and scientific productivity. *J. Appl. Psychol.*, **52**, 145–47 (1968)
149. Mukherjee, B. N. Achievement values, social desirability, and endorsement of trait names on the Berdie check list. *Ibid.*, 127–32
150. Nealey, S. M., Blood, M. R. Leadership performance of nursing supervisors at two organizational levels. *J. Appl. Psychol.*, **52**, 414–22 (1968)
151. Nealey, S. M., Fiedler, F. E. Leadership functions of middle managers. *Psychol. Bull.*, **70**, 313–29 (1968)
152. Nealey, S. M., Goodale, J. G. Worker preferences among time off benefits and pay. *J. Appl. Psychol.*, **51**, 357–61 (1967)
153. Nelson, T. M., Bartley, S. H. The pattern of personal response arising during the office work day. *Occup. Psychol.*, **42**, 77–83 (1968)
154. Owens, W. A., Jewell, D. O. Personnel Selection. *Ann. Rev. Psychol.*, **20**, 419–46 (1969)
155. Paine, F. T., Deutsch, D. R., Smith, R. A. Relationship between family backgrounds and work values. *J. Appl. Psychol.*, **51**, 320–23 (1967)
156. Pervin, L. A. Performance and satisfaction as a function of individual-environment fit. *Psychol. Bull.*, **69**, 56–68 (1968)
157. Porter, L. W. Personnel Management. *Ann. Rev. Psychol.*, **17**, 395–422 (1966)
158. Porter, L. W., Lawler, E. E., III. *Managerial Attitudes and Performance* (Irwin, Homewood, Ill., 217 pp., 1968)
159. Porter, L. W., Lawler, E. E., III. What job attitudes tell about motivaion. *Harv. Bus. Rev.*, **46**, 118–26 (1968)
160. Ritti, R. R. Work goals of scientists and engineers. *Indust. Relat.*, **7**, 118–31 (1968)
161. Ronan, W. W. A study of and some concepts concerning labor turnover. *Occup. Psychol.*, **41**, 193–202 (1967)
162. Rothe, H. F. Attitudes of various groups of employees toward job and company. *Personnel Psychol.*, **21**, 515–22 (1968)
163. Rowland, K. M., Scott, W. E., Jr. Psychological attributes of effective leadership in a formal organization. *Personnel Psychol.*, **21**, 365–77 (1968)
164. Rozelle, R. M., Campbell, D. T. More plausible rival hypothesis in the cross-lagged panel correlation technique. *Psychol. Bull.*, **71**, 74–80 (1968)
165. Rubin, I. M., Goldman, M. An open system model of leadership performance. *Organ. Behav. Hum. Perform.*, **3**, 143–56 (1968)
166. Rubin, I. M., Morgan, H. G. A projective study of attitudes toward continuing education. *J. Appl. Psychol.*, **51**, 453–60 (1967)
167. Schuh, A. J. The predictability of employee tenure: A review of the literature. *Personnel Psychol.*, **20**, 133–52 (1967)
168. Scott, W. E., Jr. The development of semantic differential scales as measures of "morale." *Personnel Psychol.*, **20**, 179–98 (1967)
169. Sells, S. B. Personnel management. *Ann. Rev. Psychol.*, **15**, 399–420 (1964)
170. Sexton, W. P. Organization and individual needs: A conflict? *Personnel J.*, **46**, 337–43 (1967)
171. Shepard, J. M. Functional specialization and work attitudes. *Indust. Relat.*, **8**, 185–94 (1967)
172. Slobin, D. I., Miller, S. H., Porter, L. W. Forms of address and social relations in a business organization. *J. Pers. Soc. Psychol.*, **8**, 289–93 (1968)
173. Smith, P. C., Cranny, C. J. Psychology of men at work. *Ann. Rev. Psychol.*, **19**, 467–96 (1968)
174. Smith, P. E. *An Empirical Analysis of Employee Attitudes: The Two-Factor Theory Versus the Traditional Theory of Job Satisfaction* (Doctoral thesis, Columbia Univ., New York, 1968)
175. Smith, R. D. Heuristic simulation of psychological decision processes. *J. Appl. Psychol.*, **52**, 325–30 (1968)
176. Smith, R. G., Jr. An annotated bibli-

ography on the design of instructional systems. *HumRRO Tech. Rept.*, 67–5, 132 pp. (1967)

177. Stewart, R. *Managers and Their Jobs; A Study of the Similarities and Differences in the Ways Managers Spend Their Time* (Macmillan, London, 186 pp., 1967)
178. Strauss, G., Sayles, L. R. *Personnel: The Human Problems of Management,* 2nd ed. (Prentice Hall, Englewood Cliffs, N.J., 756 pp., 1967)
179. Sulkin, H. A., Pranis, R. W. Comparison of grievants with nongrievants in a heavy machinery company. *Personnel Psychol.,* **20,** 111–19 (1967)
180. Thornton, G. C. The relationship between supervisory- and self-appraisals of executive performance. *Personnel Psychol.,* **21,** 441–55 (1968)
181. Valiquet, M. I. Individual change in a management development program. *J. Appl. Behav. Sci.,* **4,** 313–25 (1968)
182. Vroom, V. H. *Work And Motivation* (Wiley, New York, 331 pp., 1964)
183. Vroom, V. H., MacCrimmon, K. R. Toward a stochastic model of managerial careers. *Admin. Sci. Quart.,* **13,** 26–46 (1968)
184. Wadia, M. S. *Management And The Behavioral Sciences: Text And Readings* (Allyn & Bacon, Boston, 543 pp., 1968)
185. Weick, K. E., Nesset, B. Preferences among forms of equity. *Organ. Behav. Hum. Perform.,* **3,** 400–16 (1968)
186. Weissenberg, P., Gruenfeld, L. W. Relationship between job satisfaction and job involvement. *J. Appl. Psychol.,* **52,** 469–73 (1968)
187. Wernimont, P. F., Campbell, J. P. Signs, samples, and criteria. *J. Appl. Psychol.,* **52,** 372–76 (1968)
188. Whitsett, D. A., Winslow, E. K. An analysis of studies critical of the motivator-hygiene theory. *Personnel Psychol.,* **20,** 391–415 (1967)
189. Wickert, F. R., McFarland, D. E., Eds. *Measuring Executive Effectiveness* (Appleton-Century-Crofts, New York, 242 pp., 1967)
190. Winslow, E. K., Whitsett, D. A. Dual-factor theory: A reply to House and Wigdor. *Personnel Psychol.,* **21,** 55–58 (1968)
191. Wofford, J. C. Behavior styles and performance effectiveness. *Personnel Psychol.,* **20,** 461–95 (1967)
192. Wolf, M. G. The relationship of content and context factors to attitudes toward company and job. *Personnel Psychol.,* **20,** 121–32 (1967)
193. Zander, A., Forward, J., Albert, R. Adaptation of board members to repeated failure or success in their organization. *Organ. Behav. Hum. Perform.,* **4,** 56–76 (1969)
194. Zedeck, S., Smith, P. C. A psychophysical determination of equitable payment: A methodological study. *J. Appl. Psychol.,* **52,** 343–47 (1968)
195. Zweig, J. P. A compound-attitude scaling technique for the measurement of partisanship in labor-management issues. *J. Appl. Psychol.,* **51,** 382–86 (1967)

BRAIN FUNCTIONS[1] 158

By Burton S. Rosner[2]
Department of Psychiatry, University of Pennsylvania, and Philadelphia General Hospital, Philadelphia, Pennsylvania

Observations on recovery of function after brain injury carry important scientific and clinical implications. Theories about the neural mechanisms of psychological processes must confront the facts of functional elasticity of the nervous system. Clinically, the design of rational therapies for neurologically injured patients requires knowledge of the determinants of recovery. These considerations have motivated the present review of recent findings on variables which control restitution of function after damage to the central nervous system.

Many of the studies cited here originally pursued quite different sorts of questions. I therefore beg forebearance from any authors whose results suddenly appear in unexpected contexts. I also must note the similar spirit but distinct content of this chapter compared to its predecessor by Rosenzweig & Leiman (160). Their review is a valuable companion piece to mine.

REDUNDANT REPRESENTATION AND MULTIPLE CONTROL

There are two obvious and related devices for achieving recovery of function in the mammalian brain with its numerous anatomical and physiological specializations. The first one is redundant representation of a psychological capacity within a specialized center or region. For example, a local region of a sensory surface such as skin (140) or retina (92) projects to many neurons at any particular stage of the relevant afferent pathway. Loss of some of these neurons leaves others at the same level that still can process signals from the local peripheral region. The second device for obtaining recovery of function is to place a given psychological capacity under multiple control by several centers. The centers may be bilaterally paired or may lie at different levels of the nervous system. Each center may exert direct influence on a final common pathway, or some centers may modulate the operation of others, or both. "Series-parallel" arrangements like these

[1] Preparation of this review was aided by a grant from the Foundations Fund for Research in Psychiatry and by Career Development Award K-3-MH-23,691 from the National Institute of Mental Health. I am indebted to Dr. Philip Teitelbaum and Mrs. Sandra Norman for carefully reading and commenting on earlier versions of this chapter.

[2] Present address: Department of Psychology, University of Pennsylvania, Philadelphia, Pennsylvania.

can assume many forms, with various configurations and degrees of coupling between constituent centers.

Many configurations of multiple control would allow centers that remain intact after brain injury to compensate for damage to others. Compensation could occur through either of two mechanisms which I shall designate "re-establishment" and "reorganization." Re-establishment means that interrelated neural centers which are partly or wholly intact after a lesion recover from shock and gradually resume their normal mode of functioning. Redundant representation within a damaged center would favor a successful outcome of recovery by re-establishment. Reorganization means that neural centers related to an injured one assume the activities of the latter. The concepts of re-establishment and reorganization are theoretical polar extremes. Actual cases of recovery may involve both mechanisms in varying degrees.

The concept of multiple control is hardly new. Almost a century ago, Hughlings Jackson (97) recognized "rerepresentations" of a function in successively higher and phylogenetically younger levels of the nervous system. He held that the higher representations were more complex, more voluntary, and less organized. His observations of behaviors which survive cerebral maladies convinced him that higher centers also inhibit lower centers. After shock had subsided, the lower centers would yield some functioning, albeit of a more automatic, stereotyped, and "primitive" sort. These views account for many clinical observations of "release" phenomena in such diverse disorders as epilepsy and aphasia. Recent data, however, also draw attention to the possible play of descending facilitation as well as descending inhibition in neural systems that embody redundancy and multiple control.

Sensory Processing

Vision.—Let us begin with a striking case of redundancy. Galambos and his co-workers (47, 147) found that bilateral transection of up to 98.5 per cent of the optic tracts did not abolish brightness and pattern discriminations in cats. Lesions that spared less than 1 per cent of the optic tracts blocked pattern discrimination. In line with these psychological findings, destruction of less than 85 to 90 per cent of the tracts did not affect evoked responses at visual cortex to flashes (46). Chow (28) carried matters a step further. He destroyed 85 per cent of the optic tracts and removed enough visual cortex to cause 85 per cent degeneration of the lateral geniculate bodies. His cats still retained preoperatively learned brightness and pattern habits. Although 90 per cent loss of the tracts and geniculates prevented retention of both types of habits, the animals gradually relearned them.

Complementing this remarkable redundancy are distinct sets of cerebral cortical areas which control different aspects of vision. In the rat, either anterior or posterior cortex alone can sustain learning or relearning of a brightness discrimination (90). Only posterior cortex, however, mediates learning or relearning of pattern discriminations. After combined frontal and lateral occipital damage, monkeys lose flicker discrimination partially or completely. Ablating either region separately has no effect (194). In contrast, cortical arrangements for multiple control of primate pattern vision seem somewhat different. Although inferotemporal lesions do not lessen flicker discrimination, they do attenuate pattern discrimination. Furthermore, while preoccipital cortical damage causes a much smaller deficit in pattern discrimination than does temporal injury, combined preoccipital and inferotemporal ablations profoundly retard differential responses to pattern (42). Multiple control of pattern vision through an extrastriate region even occurs in an insectivore, the hedgehog (74), and in a primitive primate, the tree shrew (183, 184). For both of these exotic species, striate cortex lesions had mild to negligible effects on pattern discriminations. Additional removal of an immediately adjacent belt of extrastriate cortex seriously disrupted the discriminations. Thus, the earliest representatives of the primate line seem to have multiple cortical control of pattern vision.

Interhemispheric communication provides another device for multiple cortical control of vision. Sperry's celebrated "split-brain" monkeys showed no interocular transfer of color or brightness discriminations (76, 77). Interocular transfer failed in chimpanzees with transections limited to the chiasm, the callosal splenium, and the anterior commissure (8). In several subsimian species, however, partial or complete section of forebrain commissures did not prevent interhemispheric transmission of certain visual information, especially brightness (6, 50, 158). Some amusing demonstrations of the power of commissural communication have appeared recently. Split-brain monkeys can handle more information than normals when the stimuli fall on different hemiretinae (57). Similarly, human patients with callosal sections did two simultaneous visual discriminations as easily as they performed a single one (55). Each task utilized a single hemiretina and a single hand. Normal subjects responded much more slowly on the double simultaneous test than on single discriminations. Finally, Butler (20) taught pattern differentiations to one eye of chiasm-sectioned monkeys and then split the forebrain commissures. Interocular transfer promptly occurred after he had primed the test eye by training the animal on an old or on a new discrimination.

Thompson (200) has offered a theory to account for the better interocular transfer of brightness than of pattern discrimination in split-brain animals. He contends that a cortico-pretectal-mesencephalic-hypothalamic system mediates brightness appreciation, while pattern perception depends on a cortico-tegmental tract. Lack of commissural fibers between the paired red nuclei, which are the termini of the cortico-tegmental system, prevents pattern transfer in split-brain animals. Commissural fibers between pretectal centers, however, mediate brightness transfer in such preparations. Some recent data agree with Thompson's theory. Horel (89) found that lesions of the pretectum or ventral lateral geniculate necessitated relearning of a brightness habit by rats that had originally acquired the habit after striate cortical lesions. Serial tectal then striate lesions in cats produced less retention of a brightness discrimination than did striate lesions alone (44). Serial lesions of the superior colliculi and posterior two-thirds of cortex permitted relearning of a brightness differentiation after each ablation (209). Neither the order of the lesions nor atropinization of the pupils influenced final level of performance. The investigators suggested that the pretectum facilitates acquisition of a brightness habit. Finally, Myers (141) reported that collicular lesions had little effect on pattern discriminations, although tegmental lesions produced deficits.

Other experiments, however, have revealed an apparent role for the optic tectum itself in pattern vision. Sprague & Meikle (191) found homonymous field defects and oculomotor disruption after damage to one superior colliculus. Injury to both colliculi produced initial blindness and permanent defects in visual following. Pasik et al. (149), however, reported no oculomotor dysfunction after bilateral collicular ablation. Their lesions may not have invaded the tectospinal tract, which Sprague & Meikle found to control oculomotor activity. In any case, the data show that tectal damage ultimately permits some visual function.

Sprague's (190) demonstration of cortico-collicular integration suggests a powerful role for the tectum in normal vision. Unilateral removal of posterior cortex produced the usual homonymous hemianopsia in cats. Ablation of the contralateral superior colliculus or section of the commissure of the superior colliculi diminished the deficit! Sprague argues that each visual cortex sends descending facilitating impulses to the homolateral colliculus; the colliculi in turn inhibit each other. Normal collicular mediation of vision requires a proper balance between facilitation and inhibition. Unilateral ablation of cortical visual areas upsets the balance for the homolateral colliculus. Subsequent removal of the contralateral colliculus tends to restore the balance. The functionally balanced colliculus seems to possess almost as good visual capacities as do visual cortical regions in the absence of the colliculus. Anatomical (48) and electrophysiological (100) data on descending cortical projections to the tectum support Sprague's analysis. Schwartz & Cheney (170) reported findings, however, which suggest tectal inhibition of the thalmo-cortical visual system. They found that damage to striate cortex, lateral geniculate, or other adjacent thalamic nuclei decreased critical fusion frequency in cats. In contrast, tectal lesions increased critical fusion frequency.

Besides thalamic and mesencephalic structures, other subcortical regions may exercise conjoint control over visually guided habits. Meyer et al. (135) observed that combined lesions of septum and visual cortex interfered more with retention of a brightness discrimination than did either lesion alone. The effect of the septal injury did not seem to be primarily motivational. Lesions of the tail of the caudate nucleus, to which inferotemporal cortex projects, produced loss of visual discriminations in monkey (36). In this latter instance, caudate and inferotemporal cortex seem to work together.

Analysis of visuomotor coordination also reveals the operation of multiple control at several levels. Gazzaniga (49) trained split-brain monkeys on a form discrimination habit involving one eye and a response by the homolateral hand. The animals could transfer the response to the opposite hand. Unlike normals, however, the operated animals could not make a contralateral-to-homolateral transfer of response. Nevertheless, these data and Hamilton's (75) show that split-brain animals can use either eye with either hand. Thus, either the two hands are represented in each half of the brain, or else the brain stem integrates eye-hand coordination.

A recent study contradicts the latter interpretation. Gazzaniga (51) bisected the forebrains of monkeys. He then found no further deleterious effects upon homolateral eye-hand coordination after frontoparietal lesions or after division of midbrain, brainstem, or cerebellum. Removal of sensorimotor cortex from the contralateral hemisphere, however, disrupted homolateral coordination. Gazzaniga concluded that proprioceptive stimuli from movements of eyes, head, and neck mediate performance of homolateral tasks in split-brain preparations. In a different approach to visuomotor coordination, Bossom (11) studied adaptation in monkeys to the apparent visual displacements produced by their wearing prisms. He found that frontal lobectomy or lesions of caudate nucleus retarded the animal's adjustment.

In summary, the initial stages of the visual system show considerable redundancy for pattern and brightness perception. Multiple control over visual functioning and visuomotor coordination resides in extrastriate cortex, in interhemispheric mechanisms, and in interlocking sets of centers in the mesencephalon, diencephalon, and basal ganglia. Thompson's (200) theory further suggests that somewhat different combinations of centers partipate in mediating different aspects of vision. Available data lead us to ask whether more widely distributed neural regions underlie the easier habit of brightness discrimination than support the harder one of pattern discrimination. Wider distribution of multiple control for some visual habits might explain their easier acquisition by a normal animal and their better retention after injury. Extent of "rerepresentation," to use Jackson's term, might relate directly to rate of normal acquisition and to rate of recovery of a given visual habit. Symmes (194), however, found a wider cortical involvement in flicker discriminations than in pattern discriminations, even though his normal monkeys took longer to master the flicker task. Thus, variables besides difficulty of a task may correlate with the distribution of its neural control and with its rate of recovery after a given lesion. Relations between ease of learning, rate of recovery, and extent of neural representation remain unclear.

Somesthesis and hearing.—As one might expect, multiple control occurs in other sensory modalities. Norrsell (145) trained dogs to make a conditioned response with a forelimb to a tactile stimulus exciting a hindlimb. Cutting either the dorsal columns or the spino-cervical tract yielded at most a transient disturbance of the habit. Transecting both pathways, however, badly impaired the conditioned response. Even after this lesion, some somesthetic function remained in the form of conditioned responses to electrocutaneous stimulation with sinusoidal current. In a related study, Diamond et al. (35) trained cats to avoid shock when a tactile stimulus to a hindlimb changed to alternating stimulation of hindlimb and forelimb. After bilateral ablation of cerebral somatic areas I and II, the animals had to relearn the habit. Subsequent transection of the dorsal columns necessitated a second relearning of the avoidance task.

Interhemispheric mechanisms operate in somesthesis and hearing as well as in vision. Norrsell (146) conditioned cats to make a pedal-pushing response with a foreleg to a tactile conditioned stimulus on the contralateral hindlimb. Removal of cerebral somatic cortex to which the hindleg projects produced a transient loss of the habit. Subsequent ablation of somatic cortical areas I and II homolateral to that hindleg yielded a larger transient depression of the conditioned response. Neither lesion disturbed the motor act itself. Gazzaniga et al. (52) originally reported that split-brain patients generally could not perform a response with one hand to cutaneous stimulation of the opposite side of the body. The exceptions involved stimuli to the face or to the top or back of the head. Homolateral representation of the face in cerebral somatic area I, however, does not include the top and back of the head and thus cannot explain all of the exceptions.

Heene (84) reported on a patient with transection of the anterior and middle parts of the callosum who could not transfer tactile discriminations across the midline. The patient could transfer visual discriminations between hemiretinae. This case agrees with the data of Gazzaniga et al. Together with the findings of Black & Myers (8), it also implies that separate parts of the callosum transfer information for different modalities. More recent results, however, indicate that conjoint but differential transmission of somesthetic information occurs over several commissural systems. Lee-Teng & Sperry (127) found that section of callosum and of anterior and hippocampal commissures permitted slow postoperative recovery of a bimanual size discrimination. Bimanual matching to sample never returned.

Possible evidence of interhemispheric transmission of auditory information after complete splitting of the forebrain was found by Mosidze & Sheresheva (139). A conditioned response by one limb to stimulation of the homolateral ear did not generalize promptly to stimulation of the opposite ear. Normal animals immediately made this generalization. After homolateral training, however, operated animals quickly learned the conditioned response to contralateral acoustic stimuli. The savings might indicate interhemispheric transfer of acoustic information through midbrain connections. The result also might simply reflect bilateral ascending projection of each ear.

"Complex" Behavior

Language.—Patients with commissurotomies have provided new insights into the balance between cerebral dominance and multiple control in language functions. Gazzaniga et al. (53) initially reported that patients succeeded in tasks involving speech and writing if and only if the relevant cues went to the left hemisphere. Further study showed that both hemispheres could comprehend speech (56, 189), although the right hemisphere was less versatile. The right hemisphere also proved capable of very simple expressive speech and of some reading and reasoning. Butler & Norrsell (21) carefully investigated reading and speaking by the right hemisphere of a 15-year-old boy who 3 years previously had undergone transection of the anterior commissure and corpus callosum. The patient could read and pronounce words presented to the left visual field. He responded more rapidly, however, to printed material in the right visual field. Thus, the right hemisphere has some limited or sluggish influence over various linguistic activities which are under major control by the left hemisphere.

Delayed response and habit suppression.—Psychologists have continued to probe deficiencies in delayed response and delayed alternation after lesions to lateral frontal cortex. Teuber & Proctor (198) searched for but did not find poor delayed responding in human frontal patients. Later, Chorover & Cole (27) did show that patients with frontal or nonfrontal cerebral lesions performed poorly on a 10-sec delayed alternation. The frontal patients were worse than nonfrontals but not significantly so. These observations suggest that somewhat different neural systems control delayed response and delayed alternation. Teuber & Proctor obtained other and more interesting results. Patients with frontal damage did poorly on the Aubert task. This test requires setting a line to the vertical without visual cues while the body is tilted. Diseases of the basal ganglia which produced Parkinsonism also caused poor performance on the Aubert task. The hint of a relationship between frontal cortex and basal ganglia grew firmer when a lesion of the putamen in a monkey disrupted delayed responding.

Attention to this possible relationship came to concentrate on the caudate nucleus with very rewarding results. Divac et al. (36) and Johnson et al. (101) showed a beautiful linkage between cortical projections to different regions of the caudate and the diverse behavioral effects of lesions in those regions. The dorsolateral frontal cortex projects to anterodorsal caudate. Lesions in either locus produced losses in delayed alternation. Gross (69) had found earlier that the region of sulcus principalis was the frontal cortical focus for delayed response and delayed alternation. Johnson et al. reported that the sulcus principalis area projects to an even wider area of the rostral and dorsal caudate than does other dorsal frontal cortex. In contrast to dorsal frontal cortex, lateral orbital areas project to the ventrolateral caudate. Damage to either structure retarded reversals of visual discriminations. Orbitofrontal areas also project to the septum. Lesions in this region or in ventrolateral caudate increased resistance to extinction of bar-pressing on a variable interval schedule (22). Finally, as mentioned earlier, removing the tail of the caudate or ablating inferotemporal cortex interfered with visual discrimination.

In brief, the sulcus principalis area works conjointly with rostral and dorsal caudate, lateral orbital cortex works conjointly with ventrolateral caudate, and inferotemporal cortex works with the tail of the caudate. Thus, different cortical sectors in primates collaborate with different parts of the caudate nucleus. The one puzzling exception is posteroventral caudate, which receives no cortical projections in primates. Lesions in this part of the caudate disturbed delayed alternation. Divac et al. do point out, however, that frontal cortex in cat does send fibers to posteroventral caudate.

Further evidence of a relationship of cortex and caudate appears in subprimate species. Nielson & Davis (144) trained cats to make a conditioned leg flexion response to avoid shock. The conditioned stimuli were electrical shocks to various subcortical regions. Removal of precruciate and postcruciate cortex raised the threshold for conditioned stimuli to the basal ganglia and to diffuse midbrain and thalamic systems. No rise in threshold occurred in thalamic relay nuclei or the basal forebrain. In the rat, Mikulas & Isaacson (138) showed that lesions of the caudate eliminated performance of delayed responses. Gross et al. (71) found that damage to anterior cortex, caudate, hippocampus, or dorsomedial thalamus deterred postoperative acquisition or retention of a two-bar alternation habit. Lesions of posterior cortex did not. Schmaltz & Isaacson (165), however, have reported a case of nonparallelism between caudate and anterior cortex in rat. Caudate lesions before or after frontal lesions always produced a transient loss of bar-pressing on a DRL-20 schedule. Initial frontal lesions had no effect; nor did frontal ablation reinstitute any disruption after recovery from damage to caudate.

Motor Systems

Pyramidal tract section.—A new outburst of studies on the pyramidal tract has radically altered our view of its function. Tower's (206) old data had indicated that section of a pyramid produced profound paralysis and flaccidity. Thus, the tract appeared to be the first segment of the final common pathway for motor control. This classical outlook has now been shattered. In a 70-year-old patient with hemiballismus, Bucy and his colleagues (17) divided the right cerebral peduncle. A temporary flaccid hemiplegia ensued and then gradually vanished. Before his death 30 months postoperatively, the patient showed no spasticity. This accords with Tower's observations. But the patient showed only an unexpectedly mild left hemiparesis. Post-mortem examination of the brain revealed loss of all Betz cells and sparing of a mere handful of pyramidal fibers arising from parietal lobe.

Numerous experiments on animals have confirmed and extended these findings. Destruction of up to 60 per cent of either or both pyramidal tracts in cat merely increased the latency of a conditioned response (122). The animals walked, ate, and maintained themselves normally. Total unilateral pyramidotomy diminished contralateral flexor activity and disorganized various placing responses (121). Both symptoms improved markedly within a month postoperatively. Damage to the medial lemniscus did not affect flexor reflexes, although it blocked tactile placing. Voneida (213) reported that unilateral or bilateral section of pyramidal tract still permitted relearning of a conditioned leg flexion. Complete bilateral sections may have retarded relearning somewhat more than unilateral sections. Partial peduncular section in monkeys produced little paresis but did reduce voluntary movement (214). Destruction of parietospinal fibers which facilitate posterior horn cells in the cord, however, may have altered voluntary motion.

A study of bilateral section of cerebral peduncles in monkey reinforces these findings. Bucy et al. (18) found that animals who underwent this operation ultimately fed themselves, walked, climbed, and recovered general motor competence. The subjects only lost some speed and strength of distal movements. The second stage of a bilateral peduncular section added to the deficit due to the first stage itself. This result implies bilateral parallel control of motor function by the pyramidal tract and may account partly for the bilateral motor control seen in split-brain subjects (54, 56, 132). Finally, Bucy and his colleagues observed the severe motor disturbances reported by Tower only when the intended peduncular lesions invaded mesencephalic areas adjacent to the tracts. The work of Lawrence & Kuypers (123–125) described below accounts for this result.

Experimental analyses of effects of damage to descending motor pathways have explored several factors which contribute to the remarkable restitution of function after pyramidal tract lesions. Laursen & Wiesendanger (122) found that partial unilateral pyramidotomy did not ultimately affect bar-pressing rate on a fixed-ratio schedule. Reinforcement occurred only during a discriminative stimulus. The contralateral paw performed the response in an apparently normal fashion. Pyramidotomy, however, increased the latency to the first response following onset of the stimulus. Although differential reinforcement of shorter latencies speeded up this initial response in normal animals, it could not decrease initial latencies in the operates. Thus, reinforcement directed against a specific pyramidal symptom proved futile.

Górska and co-workers have studied the effects of pyramidotomy on performance of instrumental responses based on different classes of "reflexes." Unilateral or bilateral sections of the medullary pyramids in cats did not block conditioning or reconditioning of such responses as placing a paw on a food tray, pressing a horizontal button, or pressing a vertical button (62). The animals had trouble using the vertical button and generally seemed to lack some coordination and skill.

In contrast to these results on the three conditioned "manipulatory reflexes," unilateral or bilateral pyramidotomy noticeably disturbed conditioned responses based on cleaning the anal skin, rubbing a cheek, or scratching (63). The animals lost and then slowly and imperfectly relearned the conditioned responses based on scratching or cleaning. Conditioned responses founded on rubbing a cheek were neither learned nor relearned postoperatively. The investigators suggested that pyramidotomy eliminates descending facilitatory impulses destined for the spinal cord. This raises the threshold for rubbing the cheek and impairs production and coordination of instrumental behavior organized around unconditioned reflexive acts.

The distinction between "manipulatory reflexes" and "unconditioned reactions" is not, however, all that evident. True, the former require shaping in the experimental situation while the latter do not. But raising a paw and putting it on an object involves an "unconditioned reaction." The fragility of the distinction shows itself in a newer study by Górska on dogs (61). As long as reinforcing shocks occurred over the muscles used, pyramidotomized dogs could learn or relearn conditioned avoidance responses based on placing the paw, flexing a rear leg, or rubbing a cheek. Once again, speed and amplitude of response decreased postoperatively. These results suggest that parameters of reinforcement rather than class of original unconditioned reaction are the important determinants of instrumental learning after damage to pyramidal tract.

Lawrence & Kuypers (123–125) have analyzed the sources of multiple control that sustain recovery from pyramidotomy. They observed the behavioral effects of various lesions below the diencephalon. The results permitted them to distinguish three descending efferent pathways which play upon motor systems in the spinal cord. Two pathways run through the tegmentum. The lateral one originates in the red nucleus, passes through the lateral funiculus, and ends on lateral and dorsal spinal interneurons which control movements of the limbs. The ventromedial system originates from the medullary and pontine reticular formation, the interstitial nucleus of Cajal, and the vestibular nuclei. It traverses the ventral funiculus to reach ventral and medial spinal interneurons which ultimately command the axial musculature. Transection of the lateral path impoverished distal movements. Cutting the medial path produced loss of proximal movements.

The pyramidal system is superimposed on the two tegmental pathways and ends on the same spinal interneurons which they influence. Pyramidal projections, unlike the endings of the tegmental pathways, also directly engage motoneurons. After a pyramidotomy which does not invade the tegmentum, the two tegmental pathways suffice to restore coordinated movement. The pyramidal system normally facilitates the action of these pathways. It thereby guarantees more speed, more agility, and independent fractionation of finger movements. Loss of both the corticospinal and rubrospinal systems impairs independent motions of the distal parts of limbs and of the hand and foot. This combined lesion also impedes flexion of an extended limb. Damage to both the medial tegmental and the pyramidal pathways produces a bias towards flexion and limits motion of the trunk and proximal extremities. The lateral and medial tegmental systems thus are critical for distal movements and locomotion respectively. The pyramidal path works in conjunction with both tegmental systems and also provides fine fractionation of movements.

Descending tegmental pathways apparently support recovery from pyramidal damage. Although further study of recovery from tegmental lesions is necessary to define the independent capacities of the pyramidal system, the latter in turn can buttress recuperation from cerebellar dyskinesia. Growdon et al. (73) analyzed the effects of damage to the dentate nucleus and nucleus interpositus. When the animal tried to correct an erroneous movement of the ipsilateral limb, tremor and ataxia resulted. This disorder abated somewhat with time. Lesions in the pyramids or in motor tracts of the cord reinstituted the dyskinesia in an exaggerated form.

Thompson & Spencer (202) have summarized phenomena associated with habituation of the flexor reflex in spinal cats. The reflex declines during slowly repeated stimulation. It then shows some psychologically interesting properties, such as generalization of habituation and spontaneous recovery. The corticospinal system may influence temporal modulation of flexion reflexes, since frontal cortical lesions 7 days before spinal transection in rats diminished habituation (67). This finding suggests that pyramidal projections maintain normal flexor excitability. Loss of habituation also indicates decrease of a descending trophic influence on the cord.

Finally, results from split-brain monkeys and patients suggest that bilateral cerebral mechanisms for multiple control of motion may aid compensation for unilateral lesions in motor pathways. Gazzaniga et al. (54) found evidence for homolateral as well as contralateral cerebral motor mechanisms. The homolateral system affords poorer performance of fine distal movements. Considering the results on pyramidotomy, this fact suggests a weak homolateral pyramidal projection which gross dissection of the brain confirms. A spectacular experiment by Mark & Sperry (132) yields further insight into the significance of bilateral representation of the motor apparatus. Sectioning of the callosal or tectal commissures had little effect on performance of a bimanual task by monkeys. Splitting both bundles created a marked deterioration of bimanual responding, if the task was not under visual control. Introduction of visual cues promptly restored preoperative performance. After several months, performance without visual guidance returned to normal. Subsequent bisection of the cerebellum then had no effect on bimanual coordination.

Feeding

The "lateral hypothalamic syndrome" (197) is now a famous case of recovery of function. After damage to the lateral hypothalamus, rats traverse a series of stages of recuperation. They first require tube feeding; some days later they will eat chocolate; and then they accept successively less palatable foods. The animals eventually maintain themselves, although they display various deficiencies of regulation. A unilateral lesion can produce some of these effects; subsequent lesions on the other side produce more severe deficits (59).

Teitelbaum & Cytawa (196) used spreading cortical depression to trace some of the processes underlying recovery in the lateral hypothalamic rat. They induced bilateral spreading depression by application of 25 per cent potassium chloride to the dura overlying cerebral cortex. Spreading depression stops normal animals from eating and drinking, and recovery takes some 6 to 8 hours. In compensated lateral hypothalamic animals, bilateral spreading depression sometimes produced reenactment of the whole sequence of recovery from the original lesions. The animals took days to pass from aphagia and adipsia back to the final, stable state of finicky eating and prandial drinking. These results suggest cortical participation in normal control of eating and drinking and in recovery from lateral hypothalamic lesions. Spreading depression may have produced a recurrence of shock to the already damaged system of centers which regulate feeding and drinking in the lesioned animal.

Repetition of this experiment by Balińska et al. (3), however, produced some different results. Their animals that underwent spreading depression from 25 per cent KCl 3 weeks after completion of recovery did not regress, unlike those which Teitelbaum & Cytawa had observed. Balińska et al. obtained a short-lived recrudescence of the lateral syndrome in this group with cortical spreading depression induced by only 1 per cent KCl. Thalamic spreading depression gave the same effect. In newly compensated lateral hypothalamic animals, however, cortical depression induced by 25 per cent KCl caused a full-blown return of aphagia and adipsia. Recovery required some days. The sources of the discrepancies between results of Balińska et al. and those of Teitelbaum & Cytawa are not evident from their reports.

Cortical spreading depression clearly institutes transient aphagia and adipsia in normal animals. Why does this happen? One possible explanation appears in papers by Donoso (37) and Donoso & Stefano (39). These investigators found that about 10 min of cortical spreading depression reduced hypothalamic norepinephrine. Mesencephalic norepinephrine rose, while cortical and pontine levels remained steady. During this time, plasma concentrations of steroids and catechol amines also were stable. The neurochemical effects thus were not local responses to systemic outpourings from the adrenals. These findings suggest that hypothalamic loss of norepinephrine could underlie the transient aphagia and adipsia which accompany cortical spreading depression. Hypothalamic norepinephrine started increasing after spreading depression ended and may even have overshot normal levels at a later time.

Any sustained effects of spreading depression after recovery from lateral hypothalamic damage might reflect the limited capacity of lesioned animals to regulate synthesis of hypothalamic norepinephrine. Therefore, α-methyl-*p*-tyrosine (188) or disulfiram (60), which selectively block manufacture of norepinephrine in the brain, should induce a prolonged return bout of aphagia and adipsia in recovered lateral hypothalamic animals. Grossman's (72) results increase the attractiveness of the norepinephrine hypothesis: applications of adrenergic agents to hypothalamus produced eating but not drinking. Cholinergic compounds yielded drinking but not eating. The beauty of hypotheses is often skin deep, however, and this one has its hidden complexities. Spreading "cortical" depression produces widespread effects on the normal electrophysiology of various subcortical areas (e.g., 217). Thus, the effects on hypothalamus may be direct, indirect, or a mixture of both.

Besides cortical regions that work concurrently with lateral hypothalamus, other portions of the brain influence feeding. Probably the best known is the ventral medial nucleus of the hypothalamus, whose destruction causes hyperphagia (15). This nucleus and lateral hypothalamus seem mutually inhibitory. Amygdaloid lesions also produce hyperphagia (64) and potentiate the effect of ventromedial hypothalamic lesions which already have caused overeating (128). Regulation of feeding thus expresses the net action of two opposed systems, each of which embodies multiple control by various neural loci. Damage to one system releases the other; recovery seems to involve gradual re-establishment of influence by the remaining partners in the lesioned system.

Septal Emotionality

"Septal emotionality" designates the increased touchiness and irritability which immediately follow septal lesions in the rat. The qualifying phrase, "in the rat," is important, since septal emotionality may be specific to one or a few species. Septal lesions do not cause emotionality in the golden hamster (185) or in the squirrel monkey (19). Furthermore, septal emotionality in the rat gradually disappears over a period of several weeks. Recent studies indicate the importance of cerebral cortical mechanisms for this process of compensation.

Cytawa & Teitelbaum (34) investigated the effects of spreading cortical depression on animals which had overcome septal emotionality. Spreading depression rearoused septal emotionality, just as it had recreated aphagia and adipsia in lateral hypothalamic animals. The septal animals took about 10 days after cortical spreading depression to regain their placidity. Similar effects of a second episode of spreading depression required about 4 days to disappear. (Cytawa & Teitelbaum also demonstrated analogous phenomena in rats which had lost and then regained temperature regulation after anterior hypothalamic damage.) A series of papers by the Meyers and their students further pinpoints the role of cortex in recovery from septal emotionality. Yutzey et al. (222, 223) and Clark et al. (30) showed that rats with combined septal and cortical lesions lost their emotionality more slowly than did animals with septal lesions alone. Cortical damage by itself did not produce heightened irritability. Size of cortical lesion seemed to be the crucial variable in slowing the disappearance of septal emotionality. Anterior, posterior, lateral, or medial lesions all had the same effect. Even more strikingly, unilateral removal of 80 to 90 per cent of cortex of one hemisphere was as effective as bilaterally ablating the anterior or posterior halves of cortex.

These observations support the idea of multiple neocortical and septal modulation of emotional reactivity in the rat. An additional source of conjoint control may lie in the amygdala. Kleiner et al. (111) found that simultaneous septal and amygdaloid lesions produced more emotionality on the first postoperative testing day than did either lesion alone. Curiously, however, Schwartzbaum & Gray (174) report that subsequent amygdaloid lesions reversed the freezing in an open field test and the hyper-reactivity due to previous septal damage alone. Further study of septal-amygdaloid governance of emotionality clearly is needed.

Hierarchial Organization and Recovery

Redundant representation and multiple control are principles which underlie the organization of neural mechanisms of behavior. Thus, a particular behavior or class of behaviors engages many neurons with similar properties in a given center and also calls into play several different centers. These centers differ in phylogenetic and ontogenetic history. Hughlings Jackson held that "higher" (more recently evolved) centers inhibit "lower" (older) ones. Available data now suggest additional sets of arrangements. Higher centers frequently facilitate lower ones. Inhibition may occur between centers of the same evolutionary status. Bilaterally paired higher centers also may mutually facilitate each other in the production of behavior.

The tightness of descending coupling seems to vary from one function to another. Cortical activity, for example, appears necessary for tectal mediation of vision and helpful but not essential for most aspects of movement. Speed of recovery of these functions after cortical lesions varies inversely with degree of descending influence. Similarly, recovery from damage in a lower center seems to be a joint function of the size of the injury and of the obligatory routing of descending impulses through the center. A larger lesion or restricted channeling of descending influences onto the center tend to prevent restitution of function after damage to it.

Each neural center interlocked in a system of multiple control is not necessarily equal in weight to its collaborators. Thus, the system may not show "equipotentiality." Furthermore, we do not know whether all parts of a system must act in concert or whether temporal distribution of activity obeys other laws. "Mass action" therefore may or may not prevail.

What is the biological point to this hierarchical organization of the brain with descending facilitation and inhibition? Such an organization is unlikely to have evolved due to its selective advantage for a species against brain injury. The rate of insult to the nervous system simply does not seem that high in nature. The advantage of hierarchical organization lies in quite another direction. As Jackson first realized, it provides greater complexity and reduced stereotypy of behavior. Members of a species thereby gain the flexibility to conquer differing and constantly changing environmental challenges. The evolution of neural capacity for variability entails addition of new structures together with expansion of old ones. This creates hierarchical organization and multiple control as well as redundant representation. A secondary consequence of these developments is protection for the organism against effects of brain damage.

PREINJURY INFLUENCES ON RECOVERY

The ultimate psychological outcomes of brain damage evidently depend on the locus and extent of injury and on compensation through redundant representation and multiple control. Other factors, however, also participate in fixing the pace and scope of recovery. Among them are general experience before injury, training on specific tasks, age at time of injury, and genetic constitution. As the next sections will show, uneven amounts of data have accumulated recently on these four topics, but it is clear that the fourth is not being investigated sufficiently.

General Experience Before Injury

Two popular methods are available to manipulate general properties of long-term experience: "environmental enrichment" by addition of numerous and diverse stimuli, and visual deprivation. These methods are applicable to infant animals. Rosenzweig & Leiman (160) have reviewed studies of anatomical and physiological effects due to continual exposure to these "radical environments," as I shall dub them. For readers unfamiliar with this material, I shall quickly sketch some general background by touching on a few selected recent studies.

Hubel (91) recently summarized his work with Wiesel on physiological effects of visual deprivation. Visual cortical neurons in neonatal and normally reared cats often receive binocular inputs. Hubel & Wiesel raised kittens from infancy with the eyelids of one eye sutured closed. These animals lost the powerful binocular inputs to cortical cells. The eyes deprived of normal stimulation excited relatively few neurons. Suturing the eyelids closed on one side in adult, normally reared animals did not have any effect on cortical neuronal responses some weeks later. Thus, early visual deprivation can lead to degeneration of the physiological organization of visual cortex. Anatomical changes detectable at the level of light microscopy also may occur. Among other investigators, Fifková (43) and Globus & Scheibel (58) have studied direct anatomical effects of visual deprivation. In rats that underwent monocular eyelid suturing at 14 or 15 days of age, Fifková saw a reduced volume of contralateral visual cortex and lateral geniculate 8 weeks later. The superior colliculus and optic tract seemed intact. Globus & Scheibel studied Golgi-stained visual cortex from dark-reared rabbits. They reported more variation than is normal in length of dendrites of stellate cells. They also observed deformed spines on the central parts of apical dendrites of pyramidal cells.

Adding to as well as subtracting from the environment seems to alter the nervous system. Heron & Anchel (86) raised rats in an environment containing continuous 5/sec clicks and flashes. The animals subsequently showed more electrocortical spindling without stimulation than did normal controls. More importantly, however, the experimental rats gave 5/sec waves instead of the normal 7/sec ones in the spindles. One week's exposure to a normal environment abolished the electrocortical peculiarities of the experimental animals. Adults exposed to the 5/sec environmental rhythm developed more corticographic spindle bursts than normals but retained the basic 7/sec waves. On the anatomical side, Rosenzweig (159) has summarized studies showing that cortical glia cells proliferate in infant or adult rats exposed for weeks to a complex environment. Similarly, Holloway (88) reported that dendrites in visual cortex of rats exposed to a complex environment may branch more than those of rats raised in isolated cages.

Generally, the physiological effects of radical environments are more impressive in reliability and magnitude than are the reported neuroanatomical changes. The anatomical measures used have been relatively gross or else have approached the limits of resolution of light microscopy. Furthermore, the measures sometimes are hard to interpret biologically. Low power electron microscopy may provide more telling indices of structural effects arising from prolonged exposure to radical environments.

The available data on physiological effects of radical environments clearly raise the question of whether general level of experience influences reactions to subsequent brain lesions. Hughes (93) reported an affirmative answer. Lesions in neocortex, posteroventral hippocampus, or anterodorsal hippocampus produced increasing deficits in that order on the Hebb-Williams maze among normally reared subjects. Environmental enrichment during rearing decreased these deficits to the point where cortically lesioned animals were as capable as sham-operated controls. Preoperative environmental restriction magnified the sizes of the losses. Schwartz (171) found a similar beneficial effect of environmental enrichment on Hebb-Williams maze performance by rats that received cortical lesions in infancy. A possible general environmental effect appeared in Ursin's (210) experiments on effects of bilateral amygdaloid lesions on flight and defense reactions. The lesions abolished the responses in wild but not in tame cats. (This result might also reflect genetic differences, however.) Finally, Pickens & Kelley (151) observed no effects of dark-rearing on hemispheric independence in cats subjected to forebrain division in adulthood.

Preinjury Training

The scattered studies of the impact of radical environments on recovery from brain lesions open up a new problem. They suggest that quality and quantity of preinjury experience can help to determine restoration of function. More limited experiments on the effects of specific types or amounts of preoperative training reinforce this suggestion. Cianci et al. (29) and Pinsker & French (152) found that sulcus principalis lesions did not disrupt a preoperatively learned indirect delayed response. The indirect delayed response involves marking each baitable food cup with a different visual stimulus pattern. In addition, Pinsker & French found that longer delays or changes in the marking stimuli had no effect. Substituting an opaque screen for the usual transparent one during the delay interval did upset postoperative performance. This suggests that the animals oriented towards highly differentiable visual cues. Cianci et al., however, showed that animals trained preoperatively on indirect delayed response transferred quite nicely after operation to the classical direct delayed response. Animals without preoperative indirect training did not pass the direct test postoperatively.

Fried & Goddard (45) found another type of effect of preoperative training. Rats were first trained to run a straight alley for reward. They next received punishment during running on some trials but not on others. This intermittent punishment initially lengthens running times. The animals adapt to further irregular punishment by apparently losing their fear and decreasing their running times. Hippocampal lesions after the early stages of intermittent punishment, when fear seemed highest, did not affect postoperative learning of passive avoidance to continuous shock in the alley. In contrast, lesions before training or after diminution of fear in later stages of intermittent punishment did interfere with acquisition of passive avoidance. Thus, hippocampal lesions left active fear intact but hindered initial formation or reinstatement of fear.

Increased preoperative training on a specific task generally favors postoperative retention on performance. Worthington & Isaac (221) formed an avoidance response in rats to a conditioned stimulus of increased light intensity. Occipital lesions were less debilitating for the habit in overtrained than in nonovertrained animals. A similar effect of overtraining occurred in animals taught an avoidance habit under unilateral cortical spreading depression. Escape or avoidance overtraining facilitated performance in tests with the opposite hemisphere depressed (119). Bignami et al. (7) reported that frontal lesions decreased retention of active and passive avoidance after overtraining of rats in a situation requiring both kinds of avoidance. Nonovertrained rats performed even worse postoperatively on the passive avoidance part but retained the active avoidance quite well. Amygdaloid lesions caused rats trained to criterion to lose an active two-way avoidance habit; overtrained animals suffered no loss (199). Lukaszewska & Thompson (130) reported that fivefold preoperative overtraining on a pattern discrimination dramatically increased postoperative savings after pretectal lesions. In fact, the overtrained pattern task was relearned as efficiently as was a preoperatively acquired standard brightness discrimination.

Developmental Status

A mere trickle of results obtained before 1960 suggested that a given brain lesion in an infant or immature animal has far less deleterious effects than an equally large lesion in an adult. This trickle has recently swollen to a modest stream. The results continue to flow in the original direction.

Perceptual processes.—Tucker et al. (208) ablated striate cortex bilaterally in cats 2 to 60 days old and in 8-month-old controls. The controls were impaired compared to normal animals in learning discriminations of brightness and flash frequency. The early operates learned both tasks at normal rates in adulthood. Their lateral geniculates contained more small pockets of intact nerve cells than did those of the adult operates. Nonetheless, resections of striate cortex were more complete in the early operates, who also showed few visual evoked potentials in the ectosylvian area. Koroleva (116) removed occipital lobes from baboons of different ages. All animals formed a positive conditioned reaction to a light. Those lesioned at maturity could not develop a brightness discrimination, while those lesioned at 2 to 12 weeks of age slowly acquired this habit. A monkey some 20 weeks old subjected to bilateral removal of striate cortex later discriminated different fluxes, different contour lengths, and stationary from moving objects (215). A study on cats that underwent removals of visual cortex before 10 days of age turned up no apparent deficits (219). Visual placing, navigation through the environment, and pattern discrimination were intact. As in the study by Tucker et al., the lateral geniculates were heavily but not completely degenerated. Adult animals that sustained smaller lesions, however, could not form a pattern discrimination. Finally, Scharlock et al. (162) found that adult cats permanently lost an auditory tone duration discrimination after extensive ectosylvian and insulotemporal cortical removals. Similar lesions in infant animals still allowed acquisition of a duration discrimination (163).

Complex functions.—A virtual axiom among physiological psychologists is that delayed response and delayed alternation performances depend on the integrity of frontal cortex. Studies of frontal lesions made in infancy have undermined this view. Harlow et al. (78) produced bilateral prefrontal lesions in monkeys of 5 and 150 days of age. The animals performed quite normally at older ages on discrimination learning set, oddity learning set, the pattern strings test, the Hamilton search test—and delayed response. Furthermore, they were not hyperactive. Delayed response and color discrimination were normal in Tucker & Kling's (207) early frontal operates. Adult frontal operates failed on delayed response. Neither group, however, could do a 5-sec delayed alternation. Kling & Tucker (115) added caudatal to frontal lesions in infant monkeys. The animals showed diminished growth and survival, poor motor function, seizures, and subnormal performance on both delayed response and delayed alternation. Orbitofrontal lesions in neonatal or adult cats (204) did not produce poorer overall performance of a three-way delayed response to an acoustic stimulus. Both groups of operated animals, however, showed a pattern of errors different from that displayed by normals. Taken together, these various studies indicate that early frontal lesions produce fewer symptoms than late ones but still disrupt certain aspects of performance.

Raisler & Harlow (154) investigated the effects of parieto-temporo-occipital lesions made in monkeys at about 110, 350, and 880 days of age. As many other investigators had observed, the third group of animals which received lesions in preadolescence performed poorly on various visual discrimination and learning set tasks. Delayed response was intact. The two groups of young operates performed normally on all problems, except for marginal deficiencies in forming learning sets to color or form. Green & Levinthal (66) tested the effects of subcallosal lesions in juvenile and adult rats on "hypothesis" behavior. Both groups chose less efficient paths than normal controls. The adult operates were abnormally active but the juvenile operates were not.

Age at time of brain injury seems to affect the integrity of complex functions in man. An older report by Nathan & Smith (143) indicated that normal functioning could occur even with congenital absence of certain central structures: In a 34-year-old patient who died of an abdominal malignancy, autopsy revealed apparent congenital absence of the hippocampal fimbria, the fornix, septum pellucidum, and mass intermedia thalami. The hippocampus and hippocampal and dentate gyri were small. Nonetheless, the patient had always displayed an "easygoing" personality and at least normal intelligence. In fact, he had led his class in school! Griffith & Davidson (68) found that 5 of 12 patients who had undergone hemispherectomies in childhood for intractable seizures apparently improved their IQs. More remarkably, a majority of the 8 patients who had removals on the left side regained speech or developed it *de novo*. This observation accords with a study by Branch et al. (12) who used intracarotid injection of sodium amytal to determine lateralization of speech. Only 22 per cent of patients with signs of early injury to the left hemisphere showed localization of speech there. Sixty-four per cent of the patients without such signs displayed left hemispheric control of speech. Finally, Sperry (189) mentions that patients with forbrain commissurotomies can relearn performance of some tasks requiring cross-integration. This is more characteristic of patients who undergo surgery at younger ages. The effect of age also may account partly for Butler & Norrsell's (21) report of right hemispheric control of vocalization in a youngster with section of forebrain commissures.

Emotional responses.—Age at time of lesion also modulates affective changes due to subcortical ablations. Green (65) demonstrated heightened emotionality and activity in an open field test in rats that received ventromedial hypothalamic damage postpubertally. The animals also were poor in passive but not in active avoidance. None of the changes appeared in rats lesioned before puberty. Kling and his co-workers have tracked some developmental aspects of amygdaloid functioning. The hypothalamus matures before the amygdala in the capacity to produce defensive and aggressive behavior upon stimulation through implanted intracranial electrodes (113). Bilateral amygdaloid lesions in cats less than 75 days old produced no hyperphagia, slowing of avoidance learning, or orality (112). Similar lesions in adults made the animals hyperphagic and inefficient in avoidance learning. The general development of the early operates was normal.

Kling & Green (114) amygdalectomized infant monkeys and did not obtain the tameness, orality, hypermetamorphosis, and hypersexuality seen after similar lesions in adults. Maternal deprivation caused the usual fear and withdrawal responses in the infant operates. Adult animals amygdalectomized after maternal deprivation lost their fear and withdrawal. Lesions in juvenile animals had an intermediate effect.

Genetic Factors

Far too few studies have explored this potentially important determinant of recovery of function. Those available provide a mere whisper of a hint. As mentioned previously, rats develop emotionality after septal lesions but hamsters (185) and squirrel monkeys (19) do not. An interesting study points up possible differences between strains of rats in recovery from brain lesions. Posterior cortical lesions in albino rats caused slower relearning of a black-white discrimination than in hooded rats. Anterior lesions produced a smaller loss of the habit but no differences between strains (134).

Developmentally Preferred Modes of Neural Organization

Normal development of the nervous system establishes redundant representation and multiple control. Genetic and experiential factors, including early nutrition (4), jointly determine the results of this process. Genetic aberrations or severe environmental constraints lead to abnormal neural development and altered psychological capacities. Early congenital, traumatic, or other injury to the brain also impedes normal development. The evidence just reviewed, however, indicates that the growing nervous system compensates for damage by following other but less preferred developmental paths which utilize intact tissue. This response is not available in adulthood. By then, the organism has achieved the normally preferred modes of neural organization. Early lesions thus permit compensation for brain injury by reorganization of systems of multiple control. Recovery after lesions in adult animals may rely increasingly on re-establishment of previously developed modes of control. The ratio of importance of reorganization to that of re-establishment in recovery may decline as age at time of brain injury increases.

Experimental data on effects of brain damage in infancy may help explain the pediatric neurologist's frequent surprise at the extensive brain injury in a child who shows relatively few symptoms and signs. The data also suggest that children diagnosed as cases of "minimal cerebral dysfunction"

(82) may actually have considerable structural damage to the brain. These children show combinations of learning disabilities and retardation of motor development without specific neurologic signs. Werry, however, (218) has described some of the weaknesses of the diagnosis.

TYPE AND TEMPORAL SPREAD OF LESION

Recovery of function may depend in part on certain properties of the lesion itself. Neurologists and neurosurgeons have long recognized the different effects of irritative as against purely destructive aspects of injury. Physiological psychologists have long known that multi-stage ablations tend to produce more recovery than equal single stage ablations There are recent experiments on both of these problems.

"Irritative" Lesions

Brobeck et al. (15) made electrolytic lesions for their famous demonstration that destruction of the ventromedial nucleus of hypothalamus creates hyperphagia. The obvious interpretation of this classical finding ran into some recent criticism from Reynolds (156). According to this investigator, non-irritative radio-frequency lesions of ventromedial nucleus did not produce hyperphagia. Radio-frequency lesions in lateral hypothalamus, however, caused the full-blown syndrome of aphagia and adipsia. Reynolds concluded that electrolytic damage to the ventromedial nucleus produced irritative effects on the lateral hypothalamic "feeding" center, driving the animal to overeat. This argument attacks the appropriateness of considering the ventromedial nucleus a "satiety center."

Both Hoebel (87) and Pool (153), however, have reported results that contradict Reynold's findings. Hoebel found obesity after ventromedial radio-frequency lesions. Pool obtained the same effect with suction lesions, although he reported that his animals seemed less excitable than controls receiving electrolytic lesions. Furthermore, radio-frequency lesions of ventromedial hypothalamus acutely increased lateral hypothalamic self-stimulation which previous feeding had depressed (87). Reynolds (157) also reported no difference between effects of radio-frequency and electrolytic lesions of the septum. Douglas & Isaacson (40) recorded opposite effects of aspiration and electrolytic lesions of hippocampus on running in an activity wheel. The two kinds of lesions had qualitatively similar effects on alternation and exploratory behavior. In brief, available evidence suggests only modest differences, at the most, between the effects of electrolytic as against other types of lesions.

Single-stage Versus Multi-stage Ablations

The typical finding of less disability after multi-stage than after single-stage lesions has materialized several more times. Braun (13) reported that anterior and then posterior decortication permitted some recovery of visual placing in rats. One-stage ablation of almost all cortex prevented any recovery, unless the animals received extensive practice. Similarly, successive bilateral removals of lateral, suprasylvian, and ectosylvian areas in cat necessitated retraining of a preoperatively learned light-dark discrimination after each lesion (2). Ultimately, relearning was still possible without the posterior two-thirds of cortex. Petrinovich & Bliss (150) gave an impressive demonstration of interaction between experience and temporally distributed lesions. Bilateral occipital cortical lesions produced the usual loss of a previously learned brightness discrimination in rats. Two-stage lesions yielded the same loss, if animals stayed in total darkness between lesions. Animals kept in home cages between successive lesions showed no loss of the discrimination.

Two-stage bilateral lesions of the tegmentum dorsal to the red nucleus yielded less aphagia than one-stage injury (10). A similar differential effect on aphagia and adipsia occurred with two-stage lesions of midbrain reticular formation (106). Capps & Stockwell (24), however, found no differential effect of these lesions on habituation of the startle response. Finally, Kleiner et al. (111) and Lewińska (128) reported asymmetrical order effects with temporally distributed lesions. Lewińska found that amygdaloid lesions potentiated hyperphagia established by prior ventromedial hypothalamic damage; hypothalamic lesions abolished the hyperphagia due to amygdaloid damage and sometimes even led to hypophagia. Similarly, Kleiner et al. observed that amygdaloid and then septal lesions caused more emotionality than ablations in the opposite order.

In short, multi-stage lesions and perhaps their clinical counterpart, progressive neurological disease, produce less net disability than a single, equal insult. Experience between successive lesions may help to promote better compensation or may even be prerequisite for it. Finally, the overall shock from successive lesions also may be smaller than from a single large injury.

POSTINJURY DETERMINANTS OF RECOVERY

Recovery of function is sensitive to influences from several classes of conditions prevailing after brain damage. These factors include pharmacological agents, motivational status, distraction and novel stimuli, parameters of postinjury training, and time allowed for recovery. Apparent loss of function on a specific test may change as these factors vary.

Pharmacological Influences

Several investigators have uncovered beneficial effects of amphetamine on postoperative behavior. Krieckhaus (118) found that mammillothalamic tractotomy interfered with a preoperatively learned avoidance habit in a shuttle box. *d*-Amphetamine reversed both the increased freezing and decreased avoidance in lesioned animals. Freezing declined first. Withdrawal of the drug reinstated the symptoms. Krieckhaus also pointed out that amphetamine facilitates avoidance learning in recalcitrant normal animals. The drug also decreased loss of escape and avoidance behavior after injury to the parafascicular area of thalamus (26) or after combined lesions to this region and to mesencephalic periventricular tissue (25). Interestingly, Vanderwolf (212) reported that electroconvulsive shock facilitated avoidance learning after medial thalamic lesions which otherwise would have prevented acquisition. The facilitation may have reflected diminished freezing. Electroconvulsive shock had no influence on avoidance learning in normal animals.

The effects of amphetamine on avoidance habits after various subcortical lesions apparently reflects decreased freezing. Braun et al. (14), however, found that the drug facilitated relearning of an aversively controlled black-white discrimination after removal of visual cortex. Amphetamine did not influence original learning after visual decortication. Except for animals receiving small doses, retention without the drug was intact after relearning under the drug. The authors suggested that amphetamine counteracts the lesion's interference with access to an old engram. In line with this argument, amphetamine did not noticeably hasten recovery of visual placing after large cortical lesions (13). Amphetamine also can be harmful after brain injury. Cole (31) reported that the agent produced increased suppression of eating but no effect on activity in animals with anterior hypothalamic lesions.

A few scattered studies have examined other pharmacological compounds. Although scopolamine normally increases activity, it had no effect on the lethargy due to bilateral cortical spreading depression (136). Strychnine after each run in a Lashley III maze did not help animals with hippocampal lesions improve their poor acquisition (192). A nice positive effect balances these negative findings. Meprobamate did not affect activity but did improve delayed responses in monkeys with frontal lesions (216). Taken altogether, the available data on effects of drugs on recovery after brain damage are just sufficient to be tantalizing. More systematic experimentation is needed.

"Chemical diaschisis."—Some recent data suggest one possible mode of action of drugs in promoting recovery of function. Lesions in one part of the brain may alter the neurochemistry of distant areas. Drugs might reverse these effects. Donoso (38) found that it took 20 days for hippocampal lesions to reduce hypothalamic norepinephrine. Thalamic lesions had a smaller effect and limited cortical lesions had none. Heller et al. (85) turned up a similar remote effect of lesions placed in the medial forebrain bundle. Thirty to 60 days postoperatively, serotonin (5-hydroxytryptamine) had declined in the telencephalon; so had the enzyme 5-hydroxytryptophan decarboxylase, which converts 5-hydroxytryptophan to serotonin. A behavioral parallel appeared in a study by Harvey & Lints (80). They found that lesions in medial forebrain bundle caused a slow decline in thresholds of

jumping in response to electric shock. The authors interpret this as a possible case of denervation hypersensitivity in the central nervous system.

Finally, Hatton's (83) results also may reflect a slow buildup of a "chemical diaschisis," as I shall label these remote neurochemical changes. He found that lesions of the interpeduncular nucleus decreased retention of an avoidance habit on the seventh but not on the first postoperative day. It did not matter whether the lesion invaded the ventral tegmental decussation. Lesions which did, however, immediately upset a brightness discrimination.

These examples of chemical diaschisis may also relate to the problem of "shock." A new lesion seems to exert widespread disorganizing effects on the brain. Some of these general disturbances may be due to edema or temporary evolution of irritative processes. Others, however, may represent remote chemical disturbances. Recovery from shock would occur as these various pathological changes subsided.

Motivational Changes and Arousal

Motivational changes such as aphagia, hypersexuality, or low arousability may follow various lesions to the central nervous system. Performances based on reinforcements coupled to the affected motivational system may suffer. Even fairly subtle motivational changes may disrupt complex behavior. Manipulation of motivational parameters by altering deprivation or arousal may then restore or improve performance.

A nice instance of the influence of motivation on apparent recovery of function comes from studies on disruption of DRL performance in rats after septal lesions. Ellen et al. (41) reported that these lesions decreased inter-response times on a DRL schedule with food reinforcement. Kaplan (103) found a similar effect with septal stimulation. Kasper showed that septal stimulation reduced passive avoidance (104) and slowed reversal of a position habit (105) when water was the positive reinforcer. All of these deficits might indicate that septal tissue controls inhibition of prepotent responses. Harvey & Hunt (79), however, exposed septally damaged animals and normals to fixed interval or continuous reinforcement with water for bar-pressing. The operates drank more and responded faster. The lesioned animals also did poorly on a DRL schedule. Preloading them with water before testing reinstated normal DRL performance. Harvey et al. (81) went on to show that septal lesions interfered with acquisition or retention of a conditioned emotional response or of discriminated punishment. Increasing the shock intensity for lesioned animals or increasing the thirst of controls abolished the differences. Thus, manipulating motivation in several ways could wipe out apparent deficits due to septal lesions. It should be noted, however, that Kasper (105) found no effect of septal stimulation on drinking. The effects of septal lesions thus may be more complicated than the results of Harvey and his co-workers imply. Furthermore, their results do not explain why septal lesions disrupt DRL performance for food.

Other manipulable motivational effects have appeared in studies on hippocampal lesions in rats. Large lesions produced poor passive avoidance when shock conflicted with access to food or water; small hippocampal lesions reduced passive avoidance of a locus which previously had yielded food reinforcement only; and parietal cortical lesions reduced passive avoidance tested against water reinforcement only (182). Kamback (102) reported that hippocampal damage decreased habituation of bar-pressing for onset of light only when the animals were hungry. This effect is reminiscent of the well-known clinical exacerbation of neurological symptoms by arousal. For example, Marsden & Owen (133) found that mental arithmetic or injection of 1-adrenalin or insulin stirred up Parkinsonian tremor. Propranolol, a β-adrenergic blocking agent, reversed the effect of adrenalin and of insulin hypoglycemia. It did not attentuate the effects of mental arithmetic.

Exploration and Distraction

Brain injury may disrupt normal control over reactions to novel stimuli. As a secondary consequence of this impairment, performance on a variety of tasks may deteriorate. Under these conditions, direct attempts to restore function by specific training may prove fruitless. An example of secondary disruption of behavior due to impaired reaction to novelty appears in Slotnick's (179) study. Female rats subjected to prior cingulate lesions did poorly in retrieving and nursing their young. Repeated testing, however, produced gradual improvement. Retesting at this point in a strange, bright cage revived the deficits. Kimble et al. (109) reported that hippocampal but not cortical lesions increased exploratory activity and disrupted maternal behavior. Other experiments also point to altered exploratory functioning after hippocampal injury. This lesion, unlike cortical damage, produces more exploration of a maze along with less latent learning (107), less habituation to "interesting" stimuli (126), but reduced distractibility to novel stimuli in a runway (155). Evidently, deficits due to hippocampal damage may reflect altered responses to novelty. A stable environment may maximize restoration of performance.

Other evidence indicates that cerebral cortex modulates reactions to novelty. Nadel (142) found that bilateral spreading cortical depression reduced habituation of exploration between but not within sessions, despite the animal's lowered activity. Squire (186), however, reported that habituation which developed during depression of one hemisphere transferred during testing with depression of the other hemisphere. Discrete inferotemporal or frontal lesions in monkeys disturbed visual exploration (129). Animals with inferotemporal damage made fewer and less prolonged viewing responses than normals. Frontal animals only shortened the viewing time per response. Amygdalectomy had other effects, producing more but briefer responses (173) and disturbing the usual intersession adaptation to visual reinforcement (172).

Shortened durations of exploratory responses after temporal lobe injury recall a report by Hutt et al. (95). They found "short time" exploratory sampling of the environment by children with gross lesions of the upper central nervous system. All of these data suggest that helping the return of visual performance after brain injury may demand presenting stimuli so as to match an impaired scanning mechanism.

Generalization Decrement and Recovery

Several experiments with cortical spreading depression (166, 169) led Schneider (167) to a new view of its mechanism of action on retention. Performance generally decreases when unilateral spreading depression is switched to the opposite hemisphere after avoidance training. Previous interpretations of this phenomenon have emphasized the concept of the memory trace. The "trace" presumably formed in the initially undepressed hemisphere becomes less available during testing with that hemisphere depressed. Schneider suggested that the ensuing loss of performance is actually a case of failure of stimulus generalization. The animal's perceived world undergoes a marked change when depression is switched between hemispheres. Performance changes thus would reflect a failure of stimulus generalization. Furthermore, generalization would account for complete transfer which occurs with the opposite hemisphere depressed after only one trial without any depression at all (e.g., 5). Schneider proposed that altered sensory feedback due to disruption of motor patterns may create the different stimulus situations which arise when different hemispheres are depressed. Naturally, a theory this simple could not help but evoke a critical response (187) and a counter-response (168).

Whatever its merits in explaining the effects of spreading depression, Schneider's idea may have some bearing on processes underlying recovery from brain injury. Damage to the nervous system can alter an organism's perceptions of the world. Preinjury habits thus might remain intact but seem less strong due to changes in perceived stimuli. Recovery would involve training of old responses to new apparent stimulus constellations. Although generalization decrement and its elimination are hardly sufficient to explain all recovery, they may play some role in early stages of restitution of function. For example, this idea might help account for the larger deficits which follow one-stage lesions. These ablations might produce considerable and sudden perceptual changes compared with milder effects of two-stage lesions.

Parameters of Postinjury Training

Restoration of behavior after brain damage depends partly on the properties of postinjury training. Several parameters which control the quality, amount, or rate of occurrence of experience after injury influence the ultimate level of performance. I shall classify these parameters roughly under training procedures, overtraining, and rate of training.

Training procedures.—Numerous subtle variations in training procedures influence postoperative performance. Some variations seem psychologically sensible, while others are apparently arbitrary. The following summary of some recent studies unfortunately assumes certain qualities of a catalogue. This circumstance frankly mirrors the lack of any compelling theoretical analyses of the results. A similar aura of groping inevitably surrounds clinical attempts at retraining of function.

Creel & Sheridan (33) studied monocular training and interocular transfer of a horizontal-vertical discrimination in albino rats with unilateral striate lesions. Normal animals transferred this discrimination incompletely between eyes. Lesioned animals could not learn with the contralateral eye unless the ipsilateral one learned first. Attempts to train the contralateral eye first interfered with later ipsilateral monocular training. The animal probably first experienced a sequence of irregular reinforcements during the unprofitable original contralateral training. This would have slowed down learning with ipsilateral vision. A more startling result on interocular transfer comes from Sechzer's (176) work on split-brain cats. Sperry's laboratory originally reported no interocular transfer of a pattern discrimination in such animals. Sechzer found that aversive control of the discrimination produced transfer where positive reinforcement did not. Another effective change in training procedures appears in Vanderwolf's (211) study of impaired avoidance behavior following lesions of mediodorsal thalamus. Letting the animals explore a different novel environment just before testing reduced the deficit.

Certain behavioral changes following septal lesions respond to environmental manipulation. Ahmad & Harvey (1) found that septal injury increased shock-elicited attack but not threat behavior in rats. Housing the operated animals individually maintained this symptom for 45 days. Placing the animals with cagemates for 17 days eliminated the increased aggression. Septal emotionality also proved sensitive to environmental variables. Handling septal animals postoperatively hastened the decline of hyper-reactivity; merely shaking their cages had less effect (177). These two procedures also reduced emotionality in normal rats. Another septal stigmatum, poor performance on a DRL schedule, did not occur in animals trained preoperatively on continuous reinforcement and introduced gradually to DRL postoperatively. Operates performed poorly if subjected to the usual abrupt introduction of training on a DRL schedule with a long interval (23). These three different instances of the sensitivity of septal dysfunctions to environmental variables may depend partly on re-establishment of cortical control over the appropriate behaviors.

Deficits due to hippocampal lesions also respond to parameters of training. Long exposure to continuous reinforcement after operation reduced the efficiency of performance on a subsequent DRL schedule (164). In another study, exposure to the CS alone for 60 preliminary trials interfered with acquisition or retention of a one-way avoidance response after hippocampectomy. Normal and cortically lesioned controls did not show this effect (148). Curiously, the hippocampal lesions facilitated performance in a two-way active avoidance test. Lash (120) found that increased response discriminability produced more alternation and thus faster acquisition of a T-maze after hippocampal or cortical damage.

Stimulus conditions in the test situation itself affect postinjury performance. Variations in apparatus and stimuli reinstituted delayed alternation in monkeys during electrical stimulation of sulcus principalis (70). Scharlock & Miller (161) reported that cats with bilateral auditory cortex lesions performed a frequency discrimination in a shuttlebox only when the negative stimulus lasted more than 1 sec. Cats with mammillothalamic tract lesions showed better retention of a preoperatively learned two-way avoidance when the conditioned stimulus was well localized (117). Finally, guide lights at the choice points helped rats with bilateral caudate lesions learn a spatial alternation but did not facilitate their subsequent learning of a position habit (137). Normal animals learned the spatial alternation more slowly when the guide lights were present.

Amount of training.—Extent of postinjury training can promote or interfere with expression of normal behavior. Sheridan (178) showed that callosal transection suppressed interocular transfer of brightness or of pattern discrimination in albino rats. Overtraining of the discrimination on the acquisition eye, however, increased the interocular transfer. Passive avoidance presents a case of deficit due to overtraining. Hippocampal lesions interfered with acquisition of passive avoidance following punishment of a well-trained, rewarded response (96, 108, 193). Less training of the rewarded habit promoted formation of a passive avoidance reaction at a normal rate. Rats with cortical lesions, however, did not have difficulty in acquiring passive avoidance of an overtrained response. Striatal lesions (110) or septal damage (175) also blocked formation of a passive avoidance of a well-established response. In the septal animals, increasing the intensity of the punishing shock did not accelerate the slow acquisition.

Intertrial interval.—Rate of training can sometimes help or hinder postoperative performance. Thompson et al. (201) made lesions in dorsal hippocampus, mammillary bodies, or mammillothalamic tracts in rats. They next taught the animals to avoid shock in a T-maze. Reversal of this habit was faster with a 30-sec than with a 30-min intertrial interval. Control rats reversed even more rapidly than operates at the short interval. Other studies on hippocampal lesions, however, have shown little or no effect of intertrial interval on acquisition or extinction of a complex maze habit (99, 131) or of a runway response (98). Effects of cortical dysfunction do seem sensitive to intertrial interval. Avoidance learning during bilateral spreading depression improved as trials were distributed (203). Longer intertrial intervals also helped dogs with prefrontal dorsal or lateral lesions to inhibit responses to a negative stimulus during differential conditioning with positive reinforcement (16). Animals with medial or basal frontal lesions still failed to inhibit unreinforced behavior at the longer intertrial intervals. Finally, a variable schedule of intertrial intervals made the task still harder for dogs with medial lesions (195).

Multiple control and flexibility.—The data on effects of parameters of postinjury training on recovery of function are spotty and sometimes seem inconsistent. No truly signficant generalizations about optimal conditions of training currently are possible. Nevertheless, available results suggest that brain damage makes the organism less capable of learning under a variety of conditions. Reduced behavioral variability again appears as a consequence of injury to neural systems which exert multiple control over behavior. The rules which determine losses in this higher-order adaptability after a given lesion are unknown. This is doubly unfortunate, since rational treatment of the effects of brain injury ultimately requires knowledge of those rules.

Time Needed for Recovery

It is banal to point out that recovery from brain injury is a process requiring time. Re-establishment or reorganization of neural function proceeds with all deliberate speed. A nontrivial question, however, concerns the time required for recovery from neurological insult. A few clinical reports show how long that time may be. Smith (180) and Smith & Burkland (181) described a patient who underwent left hemispherectomy. Before death about 7 months later, the patient had developed some expressive and even more receptive linguistic function. Blakemore and Falconer (9) reported much longer recovery after left temporal lobectomy. Defects persisted for 4 to 5 years in IQ and in recall or recognition of verbal paired associates. These defects virtually disappeared, however, after 5 years. Patients with right temporal lobectomies did not show similar long-term recovery.

Similar findings have emerged from a few animal experiments. Cowey (32) found that visual field defects in monkeys with striate cortex lesions slowly improved over months of repeated testing. After a lesion, thresholds for lights in various areas of the visual fields were grossly elevated but gradually fell somewhat. An animal first retested two and a half years postoperatively showed the same slow improvement with testing. Even more impressive is the slow return of discrimination of movement, detection of dim flashes, and reactions to stationary objects many months after removal of striate cortex (94). In another species, the rat, Tkhu (205) reported changes over 2 months in learning of instrumental conditioned responses after cortical lesions. Woods (220) found recovery over months in hopping, righting, and locomotion in decerebrated rats. Finally, we may recall the slow recovery over weeks or months from lateral hypothalamic damage in rats (197).

These limited results give a rough impression of the rate at which recovery can proceed. The time needed for recovery of a class of behaviors after a given lesion in a certain species increases with the difficulty or complexity of behavior, the degree of involvement of relevant tissue, and perhaps with the life span of the species. Indeed, available data suggest that recovery may take as long as about one-tenth of the life span for different species. Interestingly, this may represent the fraction of the life span needed for postnatal development of preferred modes of multiple control and redundant representation. The argument then suggests that reorganization, which is akin to the unfolding of a preferred mode of control, may even participate in recovery from brain injury in adulthood.

LITERATURE CITED

1. Ahmad, S. S., Harvey, J. A. Long-term effects of septal lesions and social experience on shock-elicited fighting in rats. *J. Comp. Physiol. Psychol.*, **66**, 596–602 (1968)
2. Baden, J. P., Urbaitis, J. C., Meikle, T. H., Jr. Effects of serial bilateral neocortical ablations on a visual discrimination by cats. *Exptl. Neurol.*, **13**, 233–51 (1965)
3. Balińska, H., Burešová, O., Fifková, E. The influence of cortical and thalamic spreading depression on feeding behavior of rats with lateral hypothalamic lesions. *Acta Biol. Exptl.*, **27**, 355–63 (1967)
4. Barnes, R. H. Experimental animal approaches to the study of early malnutrition and mental development. *Federation Proc.*, **26**, 144–47 (1967)
5. Beach, F. A., III. Spreading depression and interhemispheric transfer of an avoidance response. *Psychon. Sci.*, **5**, 9–10 (1966)
6. Bianki, V. L., Morozova, N. P. Visual discrimination of size and shape after section of the corpus callosum in rats. *Federation Proc. Transl. Suppl.*, **24**, T773–76 (1965)
7. Bignami, G., Carro-Ciampi, G., Albert, M. Effects of frontal lesions on "go-no go" avoidance behavior in normal and scopolamine-treated rats. *Physiol. Behav.*, **3**, 487–93 (1968)
8. Black, P., Myers, R. E. Visual function of the forebrain commissures in the chimpanzee. *Science*, **146**, 799–800 (1964)
9. Blakemore, C. B., Falconer, M. A. Long-term effects of anterior temporal lobectomy on certain cognitive functions. *J. Neurol. Neurosurg. Psychiat.*, **30**, 364–67 (1967)
10. Blatt, B., Lyon, M. The interrelationship of forebrain and midbrain structures involved in feeding behavior. *Acta Neurol. Scand.*, **44**, 576–95 (1968)
11. Bossom, J. The effect of brain lesions on prism-adaptation in monkey. *Psychon. Sci.*, **2**, 45–46 (1965)
12. Branch, C., Milner, B., Rasmussen, T. Intracortical sodium amytal for the lateralization of cerebral speech dominance. *J. Neurosurg.*, **21**, 399–405 (1964)
13. Braun, J. J. The neocortex and visual placing in rats. *Brain Res.*, **1**, 381–94 (1966)
14. Braun, J. J., Meyer, P. M., Meyer, D. R. Sparing of a brightness habit in rats following visual decortication. *J. Comp. Physiol. Psychol.*, **61**, 79–82 (1966)
15. Brobeck, J. R., Tepperman, J., Long, C. N. H. Experimental hypothalamic hyperphagia in the albino rat. *Yale J. Biol. Med.*, **15**, 831–53 (1943)
16. Brutkowski, S., Dabrowska, J. Prefrontal cortex control of differentiation behavior in dogs. *Acta Biol. Exptl.*, **26**, 425–39 (1966)
17. Bucy, P. C., Keplinger, J. E., Siqueira, E. B. Destruction of the "pyramidal tract" in man. *J. Neurosurg.*, **21**, 385–98 (1964)
18. Bucy, P. C., Ladpli, R., Ehrlich, A. Destruction of the pyramidal tract in the monkey. The effects of bilateral section of the cerebral peduncles. *J. Neurosurg.*, **25**, 1–23 (1966)
19. Buddington, R. W., King, F. A., Roberts, L. Emotionality and conditioned avoidance responding in the squirrel monkey following septal injury. *Psychon. Sci.*, **8**, 195–96 (1967)
20. Butler, C. R. A memory-record for visual discrimination habits produced in both cerebral hemispheres when only one hemisphere has received direct visual information. *Brain Res.*, **10**, 152–67 (1968)
21. Butler, S. R., Norrsell, U. Vocalization possibly initiated by the minor hemisphere. *Nature*, **220**, 793–94 (1968)
22. Butters, N., Rosvold, H. E. Effect of caudate and septal nuclei lesions on resistance to extinction and delayed-alternation. *J. Comp. Physiol. Psychol.*, **65**, 397–403 (1968)
23. Caplan, M., Stamm, J. DRL acquisition in rats with septal lesions. *Psychon. Sci.*, **8**, 5–6 (1967)
24. Capps, M. J., Stockwell, C .W. Lesions in the midbrain reticular formation and the startle response in rats. *Physiol. Behav.*, **3**, 661–65 (1968)
25. Cardo, B., Faure, A. Influence de lésions combinées thalamiques et

mésencéphaliques, sur le conditionnement d'évitement chez le rat. *Compt. Rend. Soc. Biol. (Paris),* **160,** 77–82 (1966)
26. Cardo, B., Valade, F. Rôle du noyau thalamique parafasciculaire dans la conservation d'un conditionnement d'évitement chez le rat. *Compt. Rend. Acad. Sci. (Paris),* **261,** 1399–1402 (1965)
27. Chorover, S. L., Cole, M. Delayed alternation performance in patients with cerebral lesions. *Neuropsychologica,* **4,** 1–7 (1966)
28. Chow, K. L. Visual discriminations after extensive ablation of optic tract and visual cortex in cats. *Brain Res.,* **9,** 363–66 (1968)
29. Cianci, N., Black, P., Spyropoulos, P., Maser, J. Differential recovery of delayed response function following prefrontal ablation. *Exptl. Neurol.,* **17,** 381–88 (1967)
30. Clark, S. M., Meyer, P. M., Meyer, D. R., Yutzey, D. A. Emotionality changes following septal and neocortical ablations in the albino rat. *Psychon. Sci.,* **8,** 125–26 (1967)
31. Cole, S. O. Increased suppression of food intake by amphetamine in rats with anterior hypothalamic lesions. *J. Comp. Physiol. Psychol.,* **6,** 302–5 (1966)
32. Cowey, A. Perimetric studies of field defects in monkeys after cortical and retinal ablations. *Quart. J. Exptl. Psychol.,* **19,** 232–45 (1967)
33. Creel, D. J., Sheridan, C. L. Monocular acquisition and interocular transfer in albino rats with unilateral striate ablations. *Psychon. Sci.,* **6,** 89–90 (1966)
34. Cytawa, J., Teitelbaum, P. Spreading depression and recovery of subcortical functions. *Acta Biol. Exptl.,* **27,** 345–53 (1967)
35. Diamond, I. T., Randall, W., Springer, L. Tactual localization in cats deprived of cortical areas SI and SII and the dorsal columns. *Psychon. Sci.,* **1,** 261–62 (1964)
36. Divac, I., Rosvold, H. E., Szwarcbart, M. K. Behavioral effects of selective ablation of the caudate nucleus. *J. Comp. Physiol. Psychol.,* **63,** 184–90 (1967)
37. Donoso, A. O. Cortical "spreading depression" and hypothalamic noradrenaline. *Acta Physiol. Latinoam.,* **14,** 399–400 (1964)
38. Donoso, A. O. Effect of brain lesions on hypothalamic noradrenaline in rats. *Experientia,* **22,** 191 (1966)
39. Donoso, A. O., Stefano, F. J. E. Cerebral changes in the noradrenaline content during cortical spreading depression in the rat. *Acta Physiol. Latinoam.,* **16,**, 22–25 (1966)
40. Douglas, R. J., Isaacson, R. L. Hippocampal lesions and activity. *Psychon. Sci.,* **1,** 187–88 (1964)
41. Ellen, P., Wilson, A. S., Powell, E. W. Septal inhibition and timing behavior in the rat. *Exptl. Neurol.,* **10,** 120–32 (1964)
42. Ettlinger, G., Iwai, E., Mishkin, M., Rosvold, H. E. Visual discrimination in the monkey following serial ablation of inferotemporal and preoccipital cortex. *J. Comp. Physiol. Psychol.,* **65,** 110–17 (1968)
43. Fifková, E. The effect of unilateral visual deprivation on optic centers. *Brain Res.,* **6,** 763–66 (1967)
44. Fischman, M. W., Meikle, T. H., Jr. Visual intensity discrimination in cats after serial tectal and cortical lesions. *J. Comp. Physiol. Psychol.,* **59,** 193–201 (1965)
45. Fried, P. A., Goddard, G. V. The effects of hippocampal lesions at different stages of conflict in the rat. *Physiol. Behav.,* **2,** 325–30 (1967)
46. Frommer, G. P., Galambos, R., Norton, T. T. Visual evoked responses in cats with optic tract lesions. *Exptl. Neurol.,* **21,** 346–63 (1968)
47. Galambos, R., Norton, T. T., Frommer, G. P. Optic tract lesions sparing pattern vision in cats. *Exptl. Neurol.,* **18,** 8–25 (1967)
48. Garey, L. J., Jones, E. G., Powell, T. P. S. Interrelationships of striate and extrastriate cortex with the primary relay sites of the visual pathway. *J. Neurol. Neurosurg. Psychiat.,* **31,** 135–57 (1968)
49. Gazzaniga, M. S. Cerebral mechanisms involved in ipsilateral eye-hand use in split-brain monkeys. *Exptl. Neurol.,* **10,** 148–55 (1964)
50. Gazzaniga, M. S. Interhemispheric cuing systems remaining after section of neocortical commissures in monkeys. *Ibid.,* **16,** 28–35 (1966)
51. Gazzaniga, M. S. Visuomotor integration in split-brain monkeys with

other cerebral lesions. *Ibid.*, 289–98

52. Gazzaniga, M. S., Bogen, J. E., Sperry, R. W. Laterality effects in somesthesis following cerebral commissurotomy in man. *Neuropsychologica*, **1**, 209–15 (1963)
53. Gazzaniga, M. S., Bogen, J. E., Sperry, R. W. Observations on visual perception after disconnexion of the cerebral hemispheres in man. *Brain*, **88**, 221–36 (1965)
54. Gazzaniga, M. S., Bogen, J. E., Sperry, R. W. Dyspraxia following division of the cerebral commissures. *Arch. Neurol.*, **16**, 606–12 (1967)
55. Gazzaniga, M. S., Sperry, R. W. Simultaneous double discrimination response following brain bisection. *Psychon. Sci.*, **4**, 261–62 (1966)
56. Gazzaniga, M. S., Sperry, R. W. Language after section of the cerebral commissures. *Brain*, **90**, 131–48 (1967)
57. Gazzaniga, M. S., Young, E. D. Effects of commissurotomy on the processing of increasing visual information. *Exptl. Brain Res.*, **3**, 368–71 (1967)
58. Globus, A., Scheibel, A. B. The effect of visual deprivation on cortical neurons: a Golgi study. *Exptl. Neurol.*, **19**, 331–45 (1967)
59. Gold, R. M. Aphagia and adipsia produced by unilateral hypothalamic lesions in rats. *Am. J. Physiol.*, **211**, 1274–76 (1966)
60. Goldstein, M., Anagnoste, B., Lauber, E., McKereghan, M. R. Inhibition of dopamine-β-hydroxylase by disulfiram. *Life Sci.*, **3**, 763–67 (1964)
61. Górska, T. Instrumental conditioned reflexes after pyramidotomy in dogs. *Acta Biol. Exptl.*, **27**, 103–21 (1967)
62. Górska, T., Jankowska, E., Mossakowski, M. Effects of pyramidotomy on instrumental conditioned reflexes in cats. I. Manipulatory reflexes. *Acta Biol. Exptl.*, **26**, 441–50 (1966)
63. Górska, T., Jankowska, E., Mossakowski, M. Effects of pyramidotomy on instrumental conditioned reflexes in cats. II. Reflexes derived from unconditioned reactions. *Ibid.*, 451–62
64. Green, J. D., Clemente, C. D., deGroot, J. Rhinecephalic lesions and behavior in cats. *J. Comp. Neurol.*, **108**, 505–45 (1957)
65. Green, P. C. Effects of early vs. late lesions on cognitive-affective behavior in rats: VMH. *Psychon. Sci.*, **7**, 11–12 (1967)
66. Green, P. C., Levinthal, C. F. Effects of subcallosal lesions on "hypothesis" behavior in rats. *Psychon. Sci.*, **7**, 113–14 (1967)
67. Griffin, J. P., Pearson, J. A. Habituation of the flexor reflex in spinal rats, and in rats with frontal cortex lesions followed by spinal transection. *Brain Res.*, **6**, 777–80 (1967)
68. Griffith, H., Davidson, M. Long-term changes in intellect and behavior after hemispherectomy. *J. Neurol. Neurosurg. Psychiat.*, **29**, 571–76 (1966)
69. Gross, C. G. A comparison of the effects of partial and total lateral frontal lesions on test performance by monkeys. *J. Comp. Physiol.* Psychol., **56**, 41–47 (1963)
70. Gross, C. G. Aspects of the delayed alternation deficit produced by electrical stimulation in monkeys. *Psychon. Sci.*, **3**, 501–2 (1965)
71. Gross, C. G., Chorover, S. L., Cohen, S. M. Caudate, cortical, hippocampal, and dorsal thalamic lesions in rats: alternation and Hebb-Williams maze performance. *Neuropsychologica*, **3**, 53–68 (1965)
72. Grossman, S. P. Direct adrenergic and cholinergic stimulation of hypothalamic mechanisms. *Am. J. Physiol.*, **202**, 872–82 (1962)
73. Growdon, J. H., Chambers, W. W., Liu, C. N. An experimental study of cerebellar dyskinesia in the rhesus monkey. *Brain*, **90**, 603–32 (1967)
74. Hall, W. C., Diamond, I. T. Organization and function of the visual cortex in hedgehog: II. An ablation study of pattern discrimination. *Brain Behav. Evol.*, **1**, 215–43 (1968)
75. Hamilton, C. R. Effects of brain bisection on eye-hand coordination in monkeys wearing prisms. *J. Comp. Physiol. Psychol.*, **64**, 434–43 (1967)
76. Hamilton, C. R., Gazzaniga, M. S. Lateralization of learning of color

and brightness discriminations following brain bisection. *Nature,* **201,** 220 (1964)

77. Hamilton, C. R., Hillyard, S. A., Sperry, R. W. Interhemispheric comparison of color in split-brain monkeys. *Exptl. Neurol.,* **21,** 486–94 (1968)
78. Harlow, H. F., Akert, K., Schiltz, K. A. The effects of bilateral prefrontal lesions on learned behavior of neonatal, infant, and preadolescent monkeys. In *The Frontal Granular Cortex and Behavior,* Chap. 7, 126–48 (Warren, J. M., Akert, K., Eds., McGraw-Hill, New York, 492 pp., 1964)
79. Harvey, J. A., Hunt, H. F. Effect of septal lesions on thirst in the rat as indicated by water consumption and operant responding for water reward. *J. Comp. Physiol. Psychol.,* **59,** 49–56 (1965)
80. Harvey, J. A., Lints, C. E. Lesions in the medial forebrain bundle: delayed effects on sensitivity to electric shock. *Science,* **148,** 250–52 (1965)
81. Harvey, J. A., Lints, C. E., Jacobsen, L. E., Hunt, H. F. Effects of lesions in the septal area on conditioned fear and discriminated instrumental punishment in the rat. *J. Comp. Physiol. Psychol.,* **59,** 37–48 (1965)
82. Hatton, D. A. The child with minimal cerebral dysfunction. *Develpm. Med. Child Neurol.,* **8,** 71–78 (1966)
83. Hatton, G. I. Retention of discrimination and avoidance habits following lesions in the interpeduncular nucleus. *J. Comp. Physiol. Psychol.,* **59,** 331–34 (1965)
84. Heene, R. Klinsche Untersuchungen bei Defekten des Corpus Callosum. *Deutsch. Z. Klin. Nervenheilk.,* **188,** 62–69 (1966)
85. Heller, A., Seider, L. S., Procher, W., Moore, R. Y. 5-Hydroxytryptophan decarboxylase in the rat brain: effect of hypothalamic lesions. *Science,* **147,** 887–88 (1965)
86. Heron, W., Anchel, H. Synchronous sensory bombardment of young rats: effects on the electroencephalogram. *Science,* **145,** 946–47 (1964)
87. Hoebel, B. G. Hypothalamic lesions by electrocauterization: disinhibition of feeding and self-stimulation. *Science,* **149,** 452–53 (1965)
88. Holloway, R. L., Jr. Dendritic branching: some preliminary results of training and complexity in rat visual cortex. *Brain Res.,* **2,** 393–96 (1966)
89. Horel, J. A. Effects of subcortical lesions on brightness discrimination acquired by rats without visual cortex. *J. Comp. Physiol. Psychol.,* **65,** 103–9 (1968)
90. Horel, J. A., Bettinger, L. A., Royce, G. J., Meyer, D. R. Role of neocortex in the learning and relearning of two visual habits by the rat. *J. Comp. Physiol. Psychol.,* **81,** 66–78 (1966)
91. Hubel, D. H. Effects of distortion of sensory input on the visual system of kittens. *Physiologist,* **10,** 17–45 (1967)
92. Hubel, D. H., Wiesel, T. N. Receptive fields of single neurons in the cat's striate cortex. *J. Physiol.,* **148,** 574–91 (1959)
93. Hughes, K. R. Dorsal and ventral hippocampus lesions and maze learning: influence of preoperative environment. *Can. J. Psychol.,* **19,** 325–32 (1965)
94. Humphrey, N. K., Weiskrantz, L. Vision in monkeys after removal of the striate cortex. *Nature,* **215,** 595–97 (1967)
95. Hutt, C., Hutt, S. J. Ounsted, C. The behavior of children with and without upper CNS lesions. *Behavior,* **24,** 246–68 (1965)
96. Isaacson, R. L., Olton, D. S., Bauer, B., Swart, P. The effect of training trials on passive avoidance deficits in the hippocampectomized rat. *Psychon. Sci.,* **5,** 419–20 (1966)
97. Jackson, J. H. Evolution and dissolution of the nervous system. In *Selected Writings of John Hughlings Jackson,* **2,** 45–75 (Taylor, J., Ed., Staples Press, London, 510 pp., 1958)
98. Jarrard, L. E., Isaacson, R. L., Wickelgren, W. O. Effects of hippocampal ablation and intertrial interval on runway acquisition and extinction. *J. Comp. Physiol. Psychol.,* **57,** 442–44 (1964)

99. Jarrard, L. E., Lewis, T. C. Effects of hippocampal ablation and intertrial interval on acquisition and extinction in a complex maze. *Am. J. Psychol.*, **80,** 66–72 (1967)
100. Jassik-Gerschenfeld, D., Ascher, P., Guevara, J. A. Influence of the geniculo-cortical system on visual responses of the superior colliculus. *Arch. Ital. Biol.*, **104,** 30–49 (1966)
101. Johnson, T. N., Rosvold, H. E., Mishkin, M. Projections from behaviorally-defined sectors of the prefrontal cortex to the basal ganglia, septum, and diencephalon of the monkey. *Exptl. Neurol.*, **21,** 20–34 (1968)
102. Kamback, M. Effect of hippocampal lesions and food deprivation on response for stimulus change. *J. Comp. Physiol. Psychol.*, **63,** 231–35 (1967)
103. Kaplan, J. Temporal discrimination in rats during continuous brain stimulation. *Psychon. Sci.*, **2,** 255–56 (1965)
104. Kasper, P. Attenuation of passive avoidance by continuous septal stimulation. *Psychon. Sci.*, **1,** 219–20 (1964)
105. Kasper, P. Disruption of position habit reversal by septal stimulation. *Ibid.*, **3,** 111–12 (1965)
106. Kesner, R. P., Fiedler, P., Thomas, G. J. Function of the midbrain reticular formation in regulating level of activity and learning in rats. *J. Comp. Physiol. Psychol.*, 452–57 (1967)
107. Kimble, D. P., Greene, E. G. Absence of latent learning in rats with hippocampal lesions. *Psychon. Sci.*, **11,** 99–100 (1968)
108. Kimble, D. P., Kirkby, R. J., Stein, D. G. Response perseveration interpretation of passive avoidance deficits in hippocampectomized rats. *J. Comp. Physiol. Psychol.*, **61,** 141–43 (1966)
109. Kimble, D. P., Rogers, L., Hendrickson, C. W. Hippocampal lesions disrupt maternal, not sexual, behavior in the albino rat. *J. Comp. Physiol. Psychol.*, **63,** 401–7 (1967)
110. Kirkby, R. J., Kimble, D. P. Avoidance and escape behavior following striatal lesions in the rat. *Exptl. Neurol.*, **20,** 215–27 (1968)
111. Kleiner, F. B., Meyer, P. M., Meyer, D. R. Effects of simultaneous septal and amygdaloid lesions upon emotionality and retention of a black-white discrimination. *Brain Res.*, **5,** 459–68 (1967)
112. Kling, A. Behavioral and somatic development following lesions of the amygdala in the cat. *J. Psychiat. Res.*, **3,** 263–73 (1965)
113. Kling, A., Coustan, D. Electrical stimulation of the amygdala and hypothalamus in the kitten. *Exptl. Neurol.*, **10,** 81–89 (1964)
114. Kling, A., Green, P. C. Effects of neonatal amygdalectomy in the maternally reared and maternally deprived macaque. *Nature,* **213,** 742–43 (1967)
115. Kling, A., Tucker, T. J. Effects of combined lesions of frontal granular cortex and caudate nucleus in the neonatal monkey. *Brain Res.*, **6,** 428–39 (1967)
116. Koroleva, L. V. Conditioned reflexes to photic stimuli in baboons after removal of occipital lobes at various ages. *Federation Proc. Transl. Suppl.*, **23,** T1117–21 (1964)
117. Krieckhaus, E. E. Decrements in avoidance behavior following mammillothalamic tractotomy in cats. *J. Neurophysiol.*, **27,** 753–67 (1964)
118. Krieckhaus, E. E. Decrements in avoidance behavior following mammillothalamic tractotomy in rats and subsequent recovery with *d*-amphetamine. *J. Comp. Physiol. Psychol.*, **60,** 31–35 (1965)
119. Kukleta, M. The use of unilateral cortical spreading depression in the study of subcortical storage of memory traces in rats. *Physiol. Behav.* **2,** 301–4 (1967)
120. Lash, L. Response discriminability and the hippocampus. *J. Comp. Physiol. Psychol.*, **57,** 251–256 (1964)
121. Laursen, A. M., Wiesendanger, M. Motor deficits after transsection of a bulbar pyramid in the cat. *Acta Physiol. Scand.*, **68,** 118–26 (1966)
122. Laursen, A. M., Wiesendanger, M. The effect of pyramidal lesions on response latency in cats. *Brain Res.*, **5,** 207–20 (1967)
123. Lawrence, D. G., Kuypers, H. G. J. M. Pyramidal and non-pyra-

midal pathways in monkeys: anatomical and functional correlation. *Science,* **148,** 973–75 (1965)

124. Lawrence, D. G., Kuypers, H. G. J. M. The functional organization of the motor system in the monkey. I. The effects of bilateral pyramidal lesions. *Brain,* **91,** 1–14 (1968)
125. Lawrence, D. G., Kuypers, H. G. J. M. The functional organization of the motor system in the monkey. II. The effects of lesions of the descending brain-stem pathways. *Ibid.,* 15–36
126. Leaton, R. N. Exploratory behavior in rats with hippocampal lesions. *J. Comp. Physiol. Psychol.,* **59,** 325–30 (1965)
127. Lee-Teng, E., Sperry, R. W. Intermanual stereognostic size discrimination in split-brain monkeys. *J. Comp. Physiol. Psychol.,* **62,** 84–89 (1966)
128. Lewińska, M. K. Ventromedial hypothalamus: participation in control of food intake and functional connections with ventral amygdala. *Acta Biol. Exptl.,* **27,** 297–302 (1967)
129. Lindsley, D. F., Weiskrantz, L., Mingay, R. Differentiation of frontal, inferotemporal and normal monkeys in a visual exploratory situation. *Anim. Behav.,* **12,** 525–30 (1964)
130. Lukaszewska, I., Thompson, R. Retention of an overtrained pattern discrimination following pretectal lesions in rats. *Psychon. Sci.,* **8,** 121–22 (1967)
131. Madsen, M. C., Kimble, D. P. The maze behavior of hippocampectomized rats under massed and distributed trials. *Psychon. Sci.,* **3,** 193–94 (1965)
132. Mark, R. F., Sperry, R. W. Bimanual coordination in monkeys. *Exptl. Neurol.,* **21,** 92–104 (1968)
133. Marsden, C. D., Owen, D. A. L. Mechanisms underlying emotional variation in parkinsonian tremor. *Neurology,* **17,** 711–15 (1967)
134. Meyer, D. R., Yutzey, D. A., Meyer, P. M. Effects of neocortical ablations on relearning of a black-white discrimination habit by two strains of rats. *J. Comp. Physiol. Psychol.,* **61,** 83–86 (1966)
135. Meyer, P. M., Yutzey, D. A., Dalby, D. A., Meyer, D. R. Effects of simultaneous septal-visual, septal-anterior and anterior-posterior lesions upon relearning a black-white discrimination. *Brain Res.,* **8,** 281–90 (1968)
136. Meyers, B., Stern, W. C. Effect of bilateral spreading depression and scopolamine on motor activity in rats. *Psychol. Rept.,* **18,** 267–70 (1966)
137. Mikulas, W. L. Effects of lights at the choice points on spatial alternation and position learning by normal rats and rats with bilateral lesions of the caudate nucleus. *Psychon. Sci.,* **5,** 275–76 (1966)
138. Mikulas, W. L., Isaacson, R. L. Impairment and perseveration in delayed tasks due to bilateral lesions of the caudate nucleus in rats. *Psychon. Sci.,* **3,** 485–86 (1965)
139. Mosidze, V. M., Sheresheva, N. B. Interhemispheric relations in split-brain dogs. *Federation Proc. Transl. Suppl.,* **25,** T924–26 (1966)
140. Mountcastle, V. B., Powell, T. P. S. Neural mechanisms subserving cutaneous sensibility, with special reference to the role of afferent inhibition in sensory perception and discrimination. *Bull. Johns Hopkins Hosp.,* **105,** 201–32 (1959)
141. Myers, R. E. Visual deficits after lesions of brain stem tegmentum in cats. *Arch. Neurol.,* **11,** 73–90 (1964)
142. Nadel, L. Cortical spreading depression and habituation. *Psychon. Sci.,* **5,** 119–20 (1966)
143. Nathan, P. W., Smith, M. C. Normal mentality associated with a maldeveloped "rhinencephalon." *J. Neurol. Neurosurg. Psychiat.,* **13,** 191–97 (1950)
144. Nielson, H. C., Davis, K. B. Effect of frontal ablation upon conditioned responses. *J. Comp. Physiol. Psychol.,* **61,** 380–87 (1966)
145. Norrsell, U. The spinal afferent pathways of conditioned reflexes to cutaneous stimuli in the dog. *Exptl. Brain Res.,* **2,** 269–82 (1966)
146. Norrsell, U. A conditioned reflex study of sensory defects caused by cortical somatosensory ablations. *Physiol. Behav.,* **2,** 73–81 (1967)

147. Norton, T. T., Galambos, R., Frommer, G. P. Optic tract lesions destroying pattern vision in cats. *Exptl. Neurol.,* **18,** 26–37 (1967)
148. Olton, D. S., Isaacson, R. L. Hippocampal lesions and active avoidance. *Physiol. Behav.,* **3,** 719–24 (1968)
149. Pasik, T., Pasik, P., Bender, M. B. The superior colliculi and eye movements. *Arch. Neurol.,* **15,** 420–36 (1966)
150. Petrinovich, L., Bliss, D. Retention of a learned brightness discrimination following ablations of the occipital cortex in the rat. *J. Comp. Physiol. Psychol.,* **61,** 136–38 (1966)
151. Pickens, R. W., Kelley, R. L. Visual discrimination learning by the visually-naive split-brain cat. *Psychon. Sci.,* **7,** 305–6 (1967)
152. Pinsker, H. M., French, G. M. Indirect delayed reactions under various testing conditions in normal and midlateral frontal monkeys. *Neuropsychologica,* **5,** 13–24 (1967)
153. Pool, R. Suction lesions and hypothalamic hyperphagia. *Am. J. Physiol.,* **213,** 31–35 (1967)
154. Raisler, R. L., Harlow, H. F. Learned behavior following lesions of posterior association cortex in infant, immature, and preadolescent monkeys. *J. Comp. Physiol. Psychol.,* **60,** 167–74 (1965)
155. Raphelson, A. C., Isaacson, R. L., Douglas, R. J. The effect of distracting stimuli on the runway performance of limbic damaged rats. *Psychon. Sci.,* **3,** 483–84 (1965)
156. Reynolds, R. W. An irritative hypothesis concerning the hypothalamic regulation of food intake. *Psychol. Rev.,* **72,** 105–16 (1965)
157. Reynolds, R. W. Equivalence of radio frequency and electrolytic lesions in producing septal rage. *Psychon. Sci.,* **2,** 35–36 (1965)
158. Robinson, J. S., Voneida, T. J. Central cross-integration of visual inputs presented simultaneously to the separate eyes. *J. Comp. Physiol. Psychol.,* **57,** 22–28 (1964)
159. Rosenzweig, M. R. Environmental complexity, cerebral change, and behavior. *Am. Psychologist,* **21,** 321–32 (1966)
160. Rosenzweig, M. R., Leiman, A. L. Brain functions. *Ann. Rev. Psychol.,* **19,** 55–98 (1968)
161. Scharlock, D. P., Miller, M. H. Negative stimulus duration as a factor in frequency discrimination by cats lacking auditory cortex. *Percept. Mot. Skills,* **18,** 9–10 (1964)
162. Scharlock, D. P., Neff, W. D., Strominger, N. L. Discrimination of tone duration after bilateral ablation of cortical auditory areas. *J. Neurophysiol.,* **28,** 673–81 (1965)
163. Scharlock, D. P., Tucker, T. J., Strominger, N. L. Auditory discrimination by the cat after neonatal ablation of temporal cortex. *Science,* **141,** 1197–98 (1963)
164. Schmaltz, L. W., Isaacson, R. L. The effects of preliminary training conditions upon DRL performance in the hippocampectomized rat. *Physiol. Behav.,* **1,** 175–82 (1966)
165. Schmaltz, L. W., Isaacson, R. L. Effects of caudate and frontal lesions on retention and relearning of a DRL schedule. *J. Comp. Physiol. Psychol.,* **65,** 343–48 (1968)
166. Schneider, A. M. Retention under spreading depression: a generalization-decrement phenomenon. *J. Comp. Physiol. Psychol.,* **62,** 317–19 (1966)
167. Schneider, A. M. Control of memory by spreading cortical depression: a case for stimulus control. *Psychol. Rev.,* **74,** 201–15 (1967)
168. Schneider, A. M. Stimulus control and spreading cortical depression: some problems reconsidered. *Ibid.,* **75,** 353-58 (1968)
169. Schneider, A. M., Hamburg, M. Interhemispheric transfer with spreading depression: a memory transfer or stimulus generalization phenomenon? *J. Comp. Physiol. Psychol.,* **62,** 133–36 (1966)
170. Schwartz, A. S., Cheney, C. Neural mechanisms involved in the critical flicker frequency of cats. *Brain Res.,* **1,** 369–80 (1966)
171. Schwartz, S. Effect of neonatal cortical lesions and early environmental factors on adult rat be-

havior. *J. Comp. Physiol. Psychol.*, **57**, 72–77 (1964)

172. Schwartzbaum, J. S. Visually reinforced behavior following ablation of amygdaloid complex in monkeys. *J. Comp. Physiol. Psychol.*, **57**, 340–47 (1964)
173. Schwartzbaum, J. S., Bowman, R. E., Holdstock, L. Visual exploration in the monkey following ablation of the amygdaloid complex. *J. Comp. Physiol. Psychol.*, **57**, 453–56 (1964)
174. Schwartzbaum, J. S., Gray, P. E. Interacting behavioral effects of septal and amygdaloid lesions in the rat. *J. Comp. Physiol. Psychol.*, **61**, 59–65 (1966)
175. Schwartzbaum, J. S., Spieth, T. M. Analysis of the response-inhibition concept of septal functions in "passive-avoidance" behavior. *Psychon. Sci.*, **1**, 145–46 (1964)
176. Sechzer, J. A. Successful interocular transfer of pattern discrimination in "split-brain" cats with shock-avoidance motivation. *J. Comp. Physiol. Psychol.*, **58**, 76–83 (1963)
177. Seggie, J. Effect of somatosensory stimulation on affective behavior of septal rats. *J. Comp. Physiol. Psychol.*, **66**, 820–22 (1968)
178. Sheridan, C. L. Interocular transfer of brightness and pattern discrimination in normal and corpus callosum-sectioned rats. *J. Comp. Physiol. Psychol.*, **59**, 292–94 (1965)
179. Slotnick, B. M. Disturbances of maternal behavior in the rat following lesions of the cingulate cortex. *Behavior*, **29**, 204–36 (1967)
180. Smith, A. Speech and other functions after left (dominant) hemispherectomy. *J. Neurol. Neurosurg. Psychiat.*, **29**, 467–71 (1966)
181. Smith, A., Burkland, C. W. Dominant hemispherectomy: preliminary report on neuropsychological sequelae. *Science*, **153**, 1280–82 (1966)
182. Snyder, D. R., Isaacson, R. L. Effects of large and small bilateral hippocampal lesions on two types of passive-avoidance responses. *Psychol. Rept.*, **16**, 1277–90 (1965)
183. Snyder, M., Diamond, I. T. The organization and function of the visual cortex in the tree shrew. *Brain Behav. Evol.*, **1**, 244–88 (1968)
184. Snyder, M., Hall, W. C., Diamond, I. T. Vision in tree shrews (*Tupia glis*) after removal of striate cortex. *Psychon. Sci.*, **6**, 243–44 (1966)
185. Sodetz, F. J., Matalka, E. S., Bunnell, B. N. Septal ablation and affective behavior in the golden hamster. *Psychon. Sci.*, **7**, 189–90 (1967)
186. Squire, L. R. Transfer of habituation using spreading depression. *Psychon. Sci.*, **5**, 261–62 (1966)
187. Squire, L. R., Liss, P. H. Control of memory by spreading cortical depression: a critique of stimulus control. *Psychol. Rev.*, **75**, 347–52 (1968)
188. Spector, S., Sjoerdsma, A., Udenfriend, S. Blockade of endogenous norepinephrine synthesis by α-methyl-tyrosine, an inhibitor of tyrosine hydroxylase. *J. Pharmacol. Exptl. Ther.*, **147**, 86–95 (1965)
189. Sperry, R. W. Mental unity following surgical disconnection of the cerebral hemispheres. *Harvey Lectures*, Series 62, 293–323 (1966–1967)
190. Sprague, J. M. Interaction of cortex and superior colliculus in mediation of visually guided behavior in the cat. *Science*, **153**, 1544–47 (1966)
191. Sprague, J. M., Meikle, T. H., Jr. The role of the superior colliculus in visually guided behavior. *Exptl. Neurol.*, **11**, 115–46 (1965)
192. Stein, D. G., Kimble, D. P. Effects of hippocampal lesions and post-trial strychnine administration on maze behavior in the rat. *J. Comp. Physiol. Psychol.*, **62**, 243–49 (1966)
193. Stein, D. G., Kirkby, R. J. The effects of training on passive avoidance deficits in rats with hippocampal lesions: a reply to Isaacson, Olton, Bauer, and Swart. *Psychon. Sci.*, **7**, 7–8 (1967)
194. Symmes, D. Flicker discrimination by brain-damaged monkeys. *J. Comp. Physiol. Psychol.*, **60**, 470–73 (1965)
195. Szwejkowska, G. The effect of prefrontal lesions on instrumental

conditioned alternation reflexes in dogs. *Acta Biol. Exptl.*, **25**, 379–86 (1965)

196. Teitelbaum, P., Cytawa, J. Spreading depression and recovery from lateral hypothalamic damage. *Science*, **147**, 61–63 (1965)

197. Teitelbaum, P., Epstein, A. N. The lateral hypothalamic syndrome: recovery of feeding and drinking after lateral hypothalamic lesions. *Psychol. Rev.*, **69**, 74–90 (1962)

198. Teuber, H. L., Proctor, F. Some effects of basal ganglia lesions in subhuman primates and man. *Neuropsychologica*, **2**, 85–93 (1964)

199. Thatcher, R. W., Kimble, D. P. Effect of amygdaloid lesions on retention of an avoidance response in overtrained and nonovertrained rats. *Psychon. Sci.*, **6**, 9–10 (1966)

200. Thompson, R. Centrencephalic theory and interhemispheric transfer of visual habits. *Psychol. Rev.*, **72**, 385–98 (1965)

201. Thompson, R., Langer, S. K., Rich, I. Lesions of the limbic system and short-term memory in albino rats. *Brain*, **87**, 537–42 (1964)

202. Thompson, R. F., Spencer, W. A. Habituation: a model phenomenon for the study of neuronal substrates of behavior. *Psychol. Rev.*, **73**, 16–43 (1966)

203. Thompson, R. W. Effect of intertrial interval on avoidance learning in rats trained under bilateral spreading depression. *Psychol. Rept.*, **16**, 472–74 (1965)

204. Thompson, V. E. Neonatal orbitofrontal lobectomies and delayed response behavior in cats. *Physiol. Behav.*, **3**, 631–35 (1968)

205. Tkhu, D. Localization of functions in rat cerebral cortex: 3. Optic and acoustic CRs following early extirpation of temporal and occipital lobes. *Federation Proc. Transl. Suppl.*, **23**, T1142-44 (1964)

206. Tower, S. S. The pyramidal tract. In *The Precentral Motor Cortex*, Chap. 6, 149–72 (Bucy, P. C., Ed., Univ. Illinois Press, Urbana, Ill., 605 pp., 1944)

207. Tucker, T. J., Kling, A. Differential effects of early and late lesions of frontal granular cortex in the monkey. *Brain Res.*, **5**, 377–89 (1967)

208. Tucker, T. J., Kling, A., Scharlock, D. P. Sparing of photic frequency and brightness discriminations after striatectomy in neonatal cats. *J. Neurophysiol.*, **31**, 818–32 (1968)

209. Urbaitis, J. C., Meikle, T. H., Jr. Relearning a dark-light discrimination by cats after cortical and collicular lesions. *Exptl. Neurol.*, **20**, 295–311 (1968)

210. Ursin, H. The effect of amygdaloid lesions on flight and defense behavior in cats. *Exptl. Neurol.*, **11**, 61–79 (1965)

211. Vanderwolf, C. H. Warm-up effects in the avoidance performance of rats with medial thalamic lesions. *Anim. Behav.*, **14**, 425–29 (1966)

212. Vanderwolf, C. H. Recovery from large medial thalamic lesions as a result of electroconvulsive therapy. *J. Neurol. Neurosurg. Psychiat.*, **31**, 67–72 (1968)

213. Voneida, T. J. The effect of pyramidal lesions on the performance of a conditioned avoidance response in cats. *Exptl. Neurol.*, **19**, 483–93 (1967)

214. Walker, A. E., Richter, H. Section of the cerebral peduncle in the monkey. *Arch. Neurol.*, **14**, 231–40 (1966)

215. Weiskrantz, L. Contour discrimination in a young monkey with striate cortex ablation. *Neuropsychologica*, **1**, 145–64 (1963)

216. Weiskrantz, L., Gross, C. G., Baltzer, V. The beneficial effects of meprobamate on delayed response performance in the frontal monkey. *Quart. J. Exptl. Psychol.*, **17**, 118–24 (1965)

217. Weiss, T., Roldán, E., Bohdanecky, Z., Fifková, E. Electroencephalographic signs of anesthesia and sleep during neocortical spreading depression in rats. *Electroenceph. Clin. Neurophysiol.*, **16**, 429–37 (1964)

218. Werry, J. S. Studies on the hyperactive child. IV. An empirical analysis of the minimal brain dysfunction syndrome. *Arch. Gen. Psychiat.*, **19**, 9–16 (1968)

219. Wetzel, A. B., Thompson, V. E., Horel, J. A., Meyer, P. M. Some

consequences of perinatal lesions of the visual cortex in the cat. *Psychon. Sci.*, **3**, 381–82 (1965)

220. Woods, J. W. Behavior of chronic decerebrate rats. *J. Neurophysiol.*, **27**, 635–44 (1964)

221. Worthington, C. S., Isaac, W. Occipital ablation and retention of a visual conditioned avoidance response in the rat. *Psychon. Sci.*, **8**, 289–90 (1967)

222. Yutzey, D. A., Meyer, D. R., Meyer, P. M. Effects of simultaneous septal and neo- of limbic-cortical lesions upon emotionality in the rat. *Brain Res.*, **5**, 452–58 (1967)

223. Yutzey, D. A., Meyer, P. M., Meyer, D. R. Emotionality changes following septal and neocortical ablations in rats. *J. Comp. Physiol. Psychol.*, **58**, 463–65 (1964)

PSYCHOPHARMACOLOGY[1]

159

By R. Kumar,[2] I. P. Stolerman,[3] and Hannah Steinberg
Department of Pharmacology, University College, London

INTRODUCTION

This review of psychopharmacology[4] is the third to appear in the series: our predecessors (234, 242) critically appraised contemporary trends and developments in the subject, and this will also be our main aim. We shall refer whenever possible to the many excellent general and specialised reviews that have appeared recently, and so increase reference material and at the same time restore any imbalance due to our intentionally restricted treatment of the literature. Our main concern is with preclinical studies, and particularly with the ways in which drugs can modify animal behaviour. At the outset we shall consider methods for analysing effects of drugs on some drive states, e.g. hunger and thirst, fear, exploratory drive, and then the concept of drugs as reinforcers with particular reference to dependence. Subsequent sections will deal with some effects of drugs on learning and memory, methods of testing for new drugs, and of relating their effects to differences among individuals.

If we appear to reiterate methodological principles that are well known to psychologists, this is because they are only gradually being applied to the study of drugs. The multiple effects of drugs and the complexities of drug-behaviour interactions mitigate strongly against a simple interpretive approach. Within a given context it is possible to define predominant effects of drugs, either by reference to a step-by-step analytical research programme [e.g. Miller (188)], or by extracting a consensus from the available literature. The former is always preferable but still unfortunately rare, and one is all too often forced upon the latter.

One of us (268) has described progress in psychopharmacology as a process of successive approximations, with continuous reappraisal and modification of the two tools of research, drugs and behaviour. The past few years, on the whole, have been a time for consolidation, of refinement of existing methods, rather than a time when major new drugs appeared or when im-

[1] We thank Dr. Daphné Joyce, Dr. M. Lader, and Professor H. McIlwain for discussion. The preparation of this manuscript was supported by grant No. MH-03313 from the National Institute of Mental Health, U. S. Public Health Service.

[2] Beit Memorial Research Fellow.

[3] Supported by a Medical Research Council grant.

[4] Additional discussion on psychopharmacology also appears in the chapter entitled "Brain Functions" in this volume; see the section "Pharmacological influences," p. 576.

portant new techniques for testing their actions on behaviour were devised. Lasagna's (161) general observation that "the history of therapeutic discoveries is in large measure a tribute to chance, the prepared mind and serendipity," still applies forcefully to psychopharmacology, where chlorpromazine, iproniazid, imipramine, and meprobamate are examples of drugs whose main uses were found to be outside their original applications (135).

In spite of the relative sophistication of electrophysiological, biochemical, and pharmacological techniques, the eventual value of a particular manipulation or treatment is ultimately judged in behavioural terms, animal or human. One school of thought has emphasized the importance of overt patterns of behaviour as critical determinants of the effects of drugs (59, 72, 95), and an extreme view is that of Dews (71): "Motivation, emotion, learning and other factors that people have considered targets of selective drug action all seemed to be overshadowed in importance as determinants of drug action by the pattern of manifest behaviour." Gollub & Brady (95) questioned the efficacy of

> psychopharmacological approaches which emphasize a search for drugs expected to have selective effects upon such inadequately specified processes as 'fear', 'anxiety', 'conflict' and the like. To the extent that such terms fail to specify operationally unified behavioural processes and depend for definition upon a broad range of environmental and physiological measurement conditions, no simple psychopharmacological relationships are likely to be found.

Weiskrantz (303) has pointed to the fictional "pure behavioural task," and to this one may add that multiple sites and types of pharmacological action characterise "pure" compounds. Thus, even when precise schedules of reinforcement have been specified, should "simple" relationships ever be expected? Minimising the importance of phenomena because they are poorly specified is just as likely to lead to erroneous conclusions as overemphasizing them.

HUNGER AND THIRST

The amounts of food and water consumed are not always reliable indices of hunger and thirst. In a well-known series of experiments, Miller and his co-workers have shown that the results obtained from measures of consummatory and instrumental behaviour can conflict, and that conclusions based on a single measure may therefore be misleading (185, 186). The amount of food eaten might more precisely be regarded as an index of the onset of satiety rather than of the initial degree of hunger (272).

The problems associated with alternative methods of measuring hunger and thirst to some extent counterbalance the advantages. Methods based on the amount of bitter substance, usually quinine, which animals tolerate in their diet (186), are obviously dependent on normal sensory functioning. On the other hand, the rate of emission of operant responses for food rewards

(284) appears to be reliable as an index of hunger only if it is assumed that drugs neither modify the retrieval of recently learned information nor interfere with the execution of complex chains of motor responses. Russell (243) has said:

> Even in the simple test situations involved in the studies of drinking behaviour . . . instrumental components were involved: each subject went through a preliminary training period during which he learned, under conditions of water deficit, to approach the drinking tube where water was available . . . we have been observing a surprising array of individual differences among subjects even in what would appear to be the very restricted response of licking the drinking tube.

With food consumption, which is almost as robust and as easily measured as drinking, conflicting results are obtained in different laboratories, suggesting that precise control of relevant variables is as important as in other areas of psychopharmacology. Usually, among the uncontrolled variables are palatability of the food and its nutritional value, both of which are important determinants of the amount of food eaten following treatments such as lesions or electrical stimulation of some regions of the brain (63, 283, 285), and they may be equally important in relation to effects of drugs.

Although many techniques have been developed for measuring consummatory behaviour of laboratory animals, evaluations of their validity are rarely published. "Drinkometers" are an exception; the results of several studies suggest that lapping rates (124) are valuable as an index of thirst induced by deprivation (145, 278). Such methods have been usefully applied to study effects of drugs, e.g. the thirst induced by intracerebral application of carbachol (79, 223). "Eatometers" have been described (78, 262), but like some types of drinkometer (144), they measure contact with food or its container rather than the amount actually consumed. Animals can find a multitude of ways to defeat the experimenter's ingenuity [see the photograph of a rat having "breakfast in bed" (6)].

Very elaborate equipment has been developed to provide a continuous record of the weights of food and water removed from containers by animals (261, 302), but the complication and expense are considerable. A particular advantage of automated measuring equipment is that the time course of action of a drug can be studied very easily. This is sometimes essential, as drugs can have biphasic effects and the total consumption over a long period may hardly change. For example, chlorpromazine can depress the food intake of rats in the 2 hour period beginning 30 minutes after injection, but intake subsequently rises above that of controls, so that the total consumed in 24 hours actually increases (275).

An interesting point arising from Miller's work is that a drug that alters a drive level may itself function as a reinforcer (186). For example, would hunger increase the rate at which animals self-administer a drug with anorectic properties? An analogous situation was one in which rats that were subjected to stress increased their rate of responding for intravenous injections of amylobarbitone (65); this was taken as evidence for a fear-reducing action. The relationship between such experiments and those generally considered to be more directly relevant to drug dependence may be more than merely fortuitous.

Of the psychoactive drugs that have been shown to increase eating and drinking, the most prominent have been those with anti-anxiety actions. Chlordiazepoxide and meprobamate increase eating (7, 177, 206, 225, 263); barbiturates appear more effective in stimulating water intake (246), although phenobarbitone also increases food consumption (263). Some experiments suggest that as well as consuming more, the animals will work harder for food or water rewards (7, 110, 231, 247), but more systematic studies using a variety of test situations are needed to establish the generality of the findings, as there are negative reports, e.g. (10). The significance of increased eating in relation to anti-anxiety actions has not been evaluated, but it has been suggested that such effects could be used empirically in screening tests (109), and could conceivably have some face validity in the sense that there is some evidence that eating reduces anxiety and emotionality (193, 200, 273, 293). Margules & Stein (172, 266) have suggested that the increases in food intake are a consequence of a more general disinhibitory action, and they are developing a neuropsychological hypothesis involving the limbic system.

When acetylcholine, carbachol, noradrenaline, and most other directly acting adrenergic and cholinergic drugs are injected systemically, penetration into areas of the brain other than the hypothalamus is minimal (301). Russell (242) has discussed some of the early results obtained with direct intracerebral injection of drugs. More recent experiments have tended to confirm the early evidence that local applications of potential transmitter substances, both cholinergic and adrenergic, can elicit and enhance various patterns of behaviour. There have been several demonstrations (81, 100, 101, 147, 191) that applications of suitable doses of noradrenaline and carbachol to appropriate regions of the brains of rats elicit eating and drinking respectively, and that responses learned to relieve hunger and thirst elicited in this way appear to transfer when the motivation is induced by deprivation. Such transfer would only be expected if the internal stimuli associated with normal hunger or thirst were similar to those produced by intracerebral injections.

Artefacts due to the method of drug application and to the lesions produced by the cannulae may lead to false conclusions. Some of these problems have been discussed (102, 304), but such difficulties need not prevent investigators from using these techniques unless clear evidence appears which refutes their validity. Extensive control tests and experiments with pharmacological antagonists (102, 189, 267) have suggested that interpretations in terms of specific actions at postsynaptic sites (possibly mimicking the action of endogenous amines) were plausible. Because exogenous amines can modify the functioning of a system, it does not mean that the same or even similar endogenous substances are certainly responsible for activation of eating or drinking due to deprivation, but only that such a hypothesis may help. Even now, many years after the pioneer experiments (81, 100), localised central release of a cholinergic substance as a result of thirst remains to be demonstrated.

With the Gaddum "push-pull" cannula (85, 266), perfusates can be extracted from small areas of brain tissue; this would greatly advance research on the interdependence of the various regions involved in regulating hunger and thirst, and might also indicate whether there are areas in which the application of carbachol elicits drinking but which are not normally involved in a cholinergic thirst system. Recent evidence (243) suggests that normal thirst is associated with increased electrical activity in the regions previously shown to be responsive to carbachol. It appears that more specific control of localized neural activity can be achieved by chemical than by electrical stimulation, but Valenstein (294) has questioned the idea that eating and drinking are elicited by activation of specific neural circuits underlying hunger and thirst. When eating, drinking, and gnawing were recorded, it was found (295) that electrical stimluation in the hypothalamus elicited any one of these three kinds of behaviour depending on which goal object was present in the cage. Although neuropharmacological studies (37) suggest that the responses of individual neurones to endogenous active substances are complex, it seems valuable to investigate further the relations between unit activity and behaviour (e.g., 151a).

FEAR

Drugs that can be shown to diminish fear in animals are clearly of interest from the therapeutic point of view. The question is often raised as to whether it is not better to limit oneself to a simple description of the animals' behaviour and not assign to them qualities of subjective experience (13, 49, 50). Nevertheless, fear is a convenient shorthand term (188), a theoretical construct with as much predictive value as hunger or thirst, and is it anything other than that in man (269, 279)? The danger arises when fear is loosely assumed to be a critical motivational variable simply because the behavioural manipulations include punishment. For example, complex animal models mimicking neurotic states have been only moderately successful, either in furthering the understanding of anxiety or in terms of predictive validity for man (40, 130, 241).

The study of emotional states associated with stress is greatly simplified if the problem can be reduced to its bare essentials. The only homology required is that unpleasant stimuli produce an identifiable emotional reaction in the subject, man or rat. The structure of learned or unlearned behaviour that derives from this must inevitably differ across species, but if a drug is found to diminish fear reliably in the laboratory rat, the hypothesis that it has comparable effects in man can be tested with some confidence. Various emotional responses have been fully discussed elsewhere (104, 303); they may not only mediate changes in ongoing behaviour, but some, e.g. "freezing," can also interfere with the behaviour being tested.

A large part of the psychopharmacological literature consists of studies on the acquisition, performance, or extinction of punished behaviour. In many cases the discovery of the effects of drugs on the relevant motivational state is not the main purpose of the work, which may be concerned with obtaining profiles of action; for example, a modified Sidman avoidance schedule has been used (34, 89) to compare various phenothiazines, reserpine, imipramine, chlordiazepoxide, amphetamine, scopolamine, and benactyzine. Using a similar method, Smythies et al. (259) have extended the work to mescaline and related drugs. In this as in other experiments involving analysis and comparison of different facets of behaviour during the same test, it is difficult to be certain about the interdependence of the variables being measured.

Barry & Buckley (8) have recommended the use of techniques that produce simple and readily understandable results and have commented: "the preclinical tests should measure simple, prototype components of the naturalistic situation." Conditioned suppression tests are frequently used as a way of demonstrating that a drug has predominantly fear-reducing actions, rather than effects on concurrent behaviour maintained by food or water rewards. Weiskrantz (303) has raised some problems about interpretations of conditioned suppression data, e.g. the possibility that incompatible responses are conditioned to the CS and the likelihood of interactions between base-line and suppressed response rates. In addition, comparisons between experiments are made very difficult if among other things the base-line schedules differ greatly.

There are both practical and theoretical objections to using active avoidance as a means of testing for effects of drugs on fear. Two-factor theories of avoidance behaviour [e.g. (230)], relying as they do on the premise that the conditioned stimulus becomes aversive by contiguity with punishment, cannot easily account for avoidance in which explicit warning signals are absent (121, 255). However, as Herrnstein (120) observes: "to show that the Pavlovian component of two-factor theory is not necessary is not to prove that it is not significant in procedures where the CS is unquestionably present."

How far the performance of well-established active avoidance responses remains under the control of central mechanisms involved in punishment is also a matter of controversy. Behavioural indices of fear, while prominent during early stages of learning, diminish with repeated testing (142, 202), and it is well known that conditioned active avoidance behaviour extinguishes with great difficulty when punishment is withheld. Neurophysiological formulations have been put forward (203, 265) suggesting that a shift occurs between central mechanisms involved in rewarded and punished behaviour and that eventually avoidance behaviour comes under the control of the former. In his review, Herz (123) concluded that while tests involving active avoidance were empirically valuable in determining profiles of action for drugs, assumptions about fear reducing actions were of doubtful validity. If studies with drugs are restricted to the acquisition phases of conditioned avoidance behaviour, possible effects of the drugs on learning may, of course, confound the results. It is of interest that barbiturates can facilitate shuttle-box avoidance responding during the acquisition phase (141), possibly by reducing "freezing" due to excessive fear, but they do not improve established performance levels (123, 175).

Phenothiazines.—Controversies about possible fear-reducing actions of chlorpromazine illustrate the difficulties met by experimenters. The drug retards the acquisition of both rewarded and punished behaviour (56, 75, 114). It also impairs the established performance of both types of behaviour, and the amount of training and the difficulty of the task can be critical determinants of the effects of the drug (75, 227, 257). One-way avoidance is on the whole less affected than shuttle-box avoidance or lever-pressing to avoid shocks (8). The presence of warning signals reduces the magnitude of the effects of the drug on avoidance responding (52, 201), and an important factor is the interval between the onset of the signal and the arrival of shock. A report that the drug produced deficits in response initiation (221) was countered by Low et al. (168), who found that with longer intervals impairments in responding were greater.

Suggestions that the drug may intensify "freezing" and crouching (8, 164) are not supported by the finding that it slightly counteracted conditioned immobility when movements were punished with shocks (24). There is disagreement about the drug's effects on conditioned emotional responses (70, 129), and results from conditioned suppression studies are also equivocal. While some attenuation of suppression has been demonstrated (5, 119), other experiments have indicated a lack of effect (56, 150, 165). The majority of reports on conflict procedures also indicate a failure of phenothiazines to depress the avoidance component of such tests (91, 105, 195). When positive findings were obtained (12, 99), the procedures included certain important modifications, e.g. omission of inevitable response-contingent punishment during the conflict signal.

Following early demonstrations that chlorpromazine "selectively" attenuated avoidance rather than escape responding (60, 64), several confirmatory experiments were reported (see reviews 8, 58, 59, 96, 123). However, an experiment by Barry & Miller (10) suggested that this effect was a function of differences in the intensity of the drive in the escape and avoidance tests. Reports that extinction of conditioned fear was facilitated (2, 67, 134) were not confirmed by a well-controlled study (197) which suggested that the drug did not affect extinction processes when the exposure to the CS was held constant.

Attempts to compare results are complicated by important procedural differences in the various supporting and contradictory experiments. Often only single dose levels of chlorpromazine ranging up to 10 mg/kg have been tested, and, for example, intervals between intraperitoneal administration of the drug and the start of testing have varied between 15 and 150 minutes.

Nevertheless, most of the clinical and experimental evidence is against the hypothesis that chlorpromazine and related drugs reduce fear and anxiety. Interpretations in terms of impairment of arousal and responsiveness to external stimuli [see (192) for a recent review] appear to provide the most satisfactory framework for elucidating the effects of the drug.

Benzodiazepines.—Drugs such as chlordiazepoxide, diazepam, and oxazepam seem to have a different spectrum of effects. In their recent review of the behavioural effects of these drugs, Randall & Schallek (224) comment:

> No consistent mechanism of action can be discerned in the variety of complex types of behaviour affected by the anti-anxiety drugs in various tests. All the anti-anxiety drugs are anti-convulsants and muscle relaxants, 'tame,' or reduce fighting in aggressive animals and increase the amount of food eaten by deprived animals.

In the context of tests of conflict behaviour, they add that "these drugs may specifically attenuate passive avoidance behaviour (learning not to respond)."

In small or moderate doses, chlordiazepoxide can impair the acquisition of escape responses (55); however, performance during acquisition of active shuttle-box avoidance is either unaffected (140) or facilitated (245), although the latter finding does not necessarily represent effects on learning. Chlordiazepoxide increases suppressed responding (56, 165), and similar effects have been found with chlordiazepoxide or oxazepam in conflict procedures when both positive and negative reinforcement are contingent on an operant response (7, 80, 90, 92, 118, 173, 194). Margules & Stein (172) propose a general disinhibitory action on suppressed behaviour. Olds (204) has suggested that chlordiazepoxide and diazepam affect posterior hypothalamic reward pathways, as they produce marked increases in responding for electrical stimulation of those areas. In rats, acquisition of responding for stimulation of lateral hypothalamic areas was not facilitated by chlordiazepoxide, although increased responding in extinction was observed (87). Relationships between the actions of these drugs and reward and punishment systems in the brain have been described and summarised recently (172, 266). The hypothesis (266) that these drugs act on "a final common pathway for the suppression of behaviour" is controversial and will undoubtedly stimulate further experiments.

Barbiturates.—The studies on the possible fear-reducing effects of barbiturates undertaken by N. E. Miller and his colleagues illustrate the importance of an approach in depth to a particular problem. Several behavioural techniques used by these workers gave results supporting the view that barbiturates do reduce fear (188, 190). Perhaps the most direct approach was that of Davis & Miller (65). They found, however, that after some days the rate of responding for intravenous injections of amylobarbitone by stressed rats dropped to the base-line level; these findings have now been confirmed (64a).

Amphetamines.—The facilitating effect of dexamphetamine on active avoidance has been demonstrated both in lever-press and locomotor test situations (22, 116, 153, 228, 248). This has been attributed to a "lytic" effect of the drug on freezing responses. Increased responding in "time-out" periods and increased inter-trial hurdle crossing are also typical of the effects of the drug (8, 213, 305). Krieckhaus (152) demonstrated that lesions of the mamillothalamic tract resulted in deficits in the performance of shuttle-box avoidance responding, and related this to an increased tendency to freeze. Dexamphetamine markedly reduced the freezing and this resulted in improved shock avoidance (153).

In other experiments where fear-reducing drugs have been observed to facilitate the acquisition of active avoidance responding, the authors have commented on the tendency for these drugs to reduce freezing, e.g. chlordiazepoxide (244), and to increase inter-trial activity, e.g. amylobarbitone (141). This mechanism of action can be contrasted with that of dexamphetamine, which can augment conditioned emotional responses (38), and this should in turn produce increased freezing. Two apparently different effects of dexamphetamine have been identified in a passive avoidance test; the drug maintained high levels of fear by retarding its extinction and simultaneously increased activity in "safe" areas of the test environment (156). Related work has been directed at manipulating and measuring levels of brain catecholamines and correlating these with changes in performance of active avoidance (84, 111, 112), and such research should help to define the mechanisms of action of amphetamine (93, 133), and to clarify the role of adrenergic pathways in reward and punishment systems in the brain (266).

Cholinergic systems.—Drugs with direct actions on cholinergic function have been intensively studied, and there are several recent reviews of the experimental literature and current theory (45, 46, 166, 205, 304). While the effects of anti-cholinergic drugs have frequently been tested on punished behaviour, there does not seem to be any clear evidence that they affect fear (297). Experiments involving localised electrical and chemical stimulation of specific areas of the brain (103, 106, 107, 171, 233, 251, 266), with simultaneous behavioural and electrophysiological recording, may provide ways in which the multiple behavioural effects of drugs may be understood in terms of differential central actions.

EXPLORATORY BEHAVIOUR

The analysis of exploratory behaviour in terms of drives has been fully discussed recently (82, 83, 108). We shall limit our review of the psychopharmacological literature to problems of interpreting drug-induced changes in the organisation of responses of exploring animals. Exploration implies that the subjects are responding to, and registering information about, the environment in which they have been placed. Support for this assumption may be derived from a variety of sources—e.g. spontaneous alternation, instrumental responding for stimulus change or complexity, or changes in behaviour on repeated exposures to test environment—but probably the firmest evidence comes from demonstrations of latent learning (149, 157, 286).

In many experiments, the subjects, usually rats or mice, are placed in novel environments and various aspects of their behaviour are recorded; these include walking, rearing, grooming, sniffing, and freezing (28). Most attention is given to locomotion, but since "perambulation serves a variety of functions at different times" (19), the effects of a drug on walking and rearing should be related to some other non-locomotor measure of exploration (108, 157). Since the contributions of various motivational variables—e.g. curiosity or exploratory drive, fear of novelty, general arousal level—can only be inferred from behavioural output of one form or another, when drugs are tested one is attempting to solve simultaneous equations with too many unknowns. Comparisons between different aspects of behaviour in the same and in different test situations are therefore desirable.

When such comparisons are attempted for amphetamines, the results appear to be complex and often discrepant. Locomotor activity is somewhat increased (155, 156, 235), although in certain conditions reductions have been reported with comparable doses (277). Large doses result in reductions of locomotor activity, but increased repetitive movements such as "head-shaking" also occur. Various types of repetitive "stereotyped" behaviour have been reported in social situations (51) or when rats are tested alone with doses larger than those which increase locomotor activity (226). Increased responding for environmental changes (148) may be related to base-line "arousal" levels (20). Wimer & Fuller (312) analysed the effects of several doses of dexamphetamine on mice in three experiments and found that the drug could increase, decrease, or have no effect on open-field activity, lever-pressing for light onset, and response to environmental change, respectively. Small doses of dexamphetamine reduce the frequency with which mice dip their heads into holes, while larger doses increase this form of exploratory activity (31). On the whole, there appears to be a close similarity between results from this type of test in mice (36) and experiments with rats in Y-mazes (235). In a recent experiment, where an investigative response and locomotor activity were recorded simultaneously, it was found that dexamphetamine reduced investigation but increased locomotion (157). This supports other evidence (312) that the increased activity often obtained with amphetamines is not a function of increased exploration, which is, if anything, reduced.

Small doses of drugs such as amylobarbitone can also increase activity, and it has been suggested that this may be related to reduced fear (235), although it is possible that the effects on activity and fear are independent of each other (156). Activity early in a Y-maze trial is also increased by small doses of chlordiazepoxide, but may be succeeded by almost complete immobility (236); chlorpromazine, on the other hand, consistently diminishes the amount of locomotor activity (174).

Resemblances between human and animal responses to amphetamine-barbiturate combinations illustrate the possibility of systematic analyses across species. Various combinations of these drugs were tested, and some of them produced increments in activity in rats far greater than might have been expected by simple addition of the effects of the two components (235). Similar combinations had been in clinical use for some time. When studied in human subjects under laboratory conditions, these also were found to have rather special properties (73). These analyses have been extended to amphetamine-chlordiazepoxide combinations (236), and again very marked potentiations in activity levels of rats have been observed. Preliminary data (21) suggest that the effects in man also differ from those produced by amphetamine and chlordiazepoxide separately. Amphetamine-barbiturate combinations have been found to facilitate performance during the acquisition of a lever-pressing task for water rewards (138) and to improve learning in a T-maze for water rewards (Porsolt, personal communication); rates of self-stimulation of the brain are also increased in rats treated with certain combinations (62). These experiments raise problems both for pharmacologists and behavioural scientists, since it has not yet been established at what levels the interactions between these drugs are occurring (44, 183, 239, 300).

One feature of tests of activity is their extreme sensitivity to previous experience. A single exposure to the test situation has been shown to modify the responses of both drugged and undrugged rats up to 13 weeks later (239). Other work has shown that various environmental (69, 233, 237) and pharmacological (117) treatments during infancy and early life can markedly influence subsequent behaviour, including reactions to drugs.

DRUGS AS REINFORCERS

Apart from modifying reinforced behaviour, drugs can themselves act as reinforcers. Early demonstrations of physical dependence on morphine in animals (e.g. 282), and the pioneer work of Spragg (264) which showed that monkeys displayed morphine-seeking behaviour, were followed by a series of studies by Nichols and his collaborators showing that physically dependent rats could learn to self-administer morphine both by the intraperitoneal route (115) and by drinking solutions of the drug (198, 199). They regarded this as an indication that escape from withdrawal symptoms served as a reinforcing event, and further experiments provided more convincing evidence for an operant conditioning model; rats and monkeys could be induced to press levers and thus to administer morphine to themselves via indwelling venous catheters (290, 299, 315). It has also been shown that it is possible to condition symptoms of morphine withdrawal (94, 310), and one can therefore suggest that animals may learn to avoid withdrawal symptoms much as they learn to avoid electric shocks. However, readdiction did not occur more rapidly in an environment in which rats had previously been withdrawn, but was facilitated if the environment was the same as that in which they had originally been addicted (288).

Until quite recently, it was implied in the literature that animals would only self-administer morphine after they had been made physically dependent by a course of premedication consisting of repeated injections of the drug. Several groups of investigators have now reported that premedication is unnecessary: a proportion of monkeys and rats will press levers to obtain intravenous injections of morphine even if they have not previously been given the drug (68, 289). The initial doses are obtained by "accidental" responses made during exploration of the test chamber. Rats can also be persuaded to select a solution of morphine in preference to water; in such experiments the initial doses are obtained in the course of repeatedly relieving thirst when only morphine solution is available (158). In addition to normal thirst, other methods to induce animals to drink solutions of drugs are schedule-induced polydipsia (184, 250) and forced drinking to obtain food (113, 216).

There is little agreement about the precise nature of the operant conditioning model of drug-dependence. In contrast to the escape model (198, 199), Thompson (289) has suggested that morphine can serve as a positive reinforcer, somewhat analogous to food. As well as restoring homeostasis, food might be consumed on account of its taste and because it might reduce the effects of environmental stress (193, 200, 273, 293). Drugs might be self-administered both for the novelty of the sensations which they produce and for the sensations themselves—for example, "euphoria" and the "high" produced by heroin. It has been reported that small doses of morphine that do not appear to produce physical dependence in monkeys can function as reinforcers (249). Beach (16) has interpreted results obtained in a discriminated learning experiment as evidence for a "euphoriant" action of morphine in rats. Relief of stress by amylobarbitone (65) and by alcohol (47, 176) may facilitate the development of dependence on them, and a similar action may be involved in dependence on morphine. However, there has been a report that electric shocks do not increase the rate of self-administration of morphine by monkeys (249).

Self-administration by animals of drugs which do not produce physiological signs of withdrawal, e.g. amphetamine and cocaine (219, 220), suggests that an escape-training model (198, 199), if appropriate at all, is not generally applicable. Such behaviour, which apparently develops spontaneously without the need for deliberately introduced stress or other predisposing factors, has been called "psychogenic" dependence (68). This descriptive term poses more questions than it answers; what psychic functions are being rewarded by a group of drugs so disparate as to include barbiturates, alcohol, amphetamines, cocaine, and morphine?

The analogy between the rewarding properties of food and the actions of drugs as unconditioned positive reinforcers (287) also has its limitations, since in the case of hunger and thirst it has been suggested that there are mechanisms which actively inhibit eating and drinking when enough food and water have been ingested, even before complete absorption from the alimentary canal and restoration of homeostasis have occurred (4, 104). The limiting factors for self-administration of drugs have not been clearly defined. In some cases animals can limit their intake (159, 289); but monkeys can self-administer very large amounts of drugs such as alcohol, barbiturates, cocaine, and morphine (68), which may then interfere with regulation of the intake of the drugs and eventually lead to intermittent or continuous intoxication and gross debility. It is difficult to see how doses of drugs that induce such extreme states continue to have rewarding properties.

The ability of certain drugs to induce powerful drives and the development of drug-centered behaviour seem to be exceptions to the aphorism that drugs do not put anything new into behaviour, but only alter ongoing processes (146).

LEARNING AND MEMORY

Pretrial Administration of Drugs

The learning of new responses is sensitive to so many factors that, unless experiments incorporate really adequate controls, changes in performance induced by drugs during acquisition are not valid as evidence that learning has been affected. Indeed, because of their very sensitivity to so many treatments, it has even been suggested that tests involving acquisition rather than the performance of well-established responses may be valuable in screening programmes (252). If the effects of a drug on any of the stages of learning (i.e. registration, retention, and retrieval) are being assessed, experimental designs should take into account some of the more important confounding variables, e.g. effects on sensory function, on effector mechanisms, on motivation, and the possibility of dissociation of learning between drug and non-drug states. The relationships between these and central learning processes, and also among themselves, are not likely to be simple, as is evident from recent reviews (180, 212).

Many drugs with widely differing pharmacological actions can increase spontaneous activity, e.g. amylobarbitone (235), chlordiazepoxide (174), amphetamine (72), and magnesium pemoline (15, 32, 260, 304a); it is therefore necessary to ensure that the apparent facilitation of learning is not just a more sophisticated means of demonstrating an effect on activity. Deficits in performance may be due to ataxia, and a method has been developed for assessing this quantitatively (235).

Artefacts due to activity are minimised if the accuracy rather than the rate of performance is measured (180)—for example, the number of correct entries in a T-maze as compared with running speed. This approach has been used to study anti-depressant drugs (163), pentylenetetrazol (76, 128), amphetamine (229), amylobarbitone (48), and atropine (308, 309). However, discrimination learning experiments are critically dependent on normal sensory functioning. Another refinement is the use of latent learning designs (30, 307) which control for effects of drugs on specific drives and reinforcement mechanisms.

Miller (187) and Kimble (149) have advocated the use of experiments with factorial designs; these have the advantage that measures of the rate or speed of performance can be used without inevitably confounding effects on learning with those on activity. The inclusion of measures of accuracy in addition to measures of response rate would be a further advantage.

In factorial studies of acquisition, half of the subjects are trained under the drug and half under a placebo; for the subsequent and crucial testing phase, the drug treatments are reversed in half of the subjects in each training group. The effects of the drug can thus be compared during learning (training phase) and after learning (testing phase). When the results suggest that performance is determined by the drug actually given during testing, regardless of whether training was under a placebo or the drug, they can be interpreted as evidence for an action either on the recall phase of learning or on the effector system, which can be analysed further.

The design tests for effects on learning by examining the extent to which the changes during training persist and modify performance during subsequent testing. An apparent "permanent" or "learning" effect could come about because the drug had really modified associative processes (encoding or consolidation), or because there continue to be present an effective amount of the drug, an active metabolite, or other biochemical changes. The distinction between effects on learning and these possibilities can be attempted either by means of post-trial injections (11, 245), or by varying the interval between training and testing. Experimenters in the field of learning have been increasingly using one-trial avoidance situations which have the advantage that problems arising from tolerance or accumulation are greatly reduced; if present and uncontrolled, such effects can invalidate interpretations of factorial experiments. However, the demonstration of an action of a drug specifically on the acquisition phase by means of a factorial design does not exclude motivational or sensory effects. Some of the methods for analysing motivational changes were considered earlier in this article, and the problems of analysing sensory effects have been considered elsewhere (43, 122, 303).

One of the most intractable problems in the analysis of the effects of drugs on learning, and indeed on other variables contributing to performance, is the role to be assigned to nonspecific arousal (294). Some investigators have related attention and arousal mainly to perceptual function (192, 296), while others emphasize its motivating properties (104). Indeed, at one time or another, arousal has been conceived as modifying sensory input, associative processes, motivation (particularly fear), and motor activities.

State-dependent learning.—Responses that have been learned under one drug state sometimes fail to appear if the drug state of the animal is changed on a subsequent occasion. In such cases the learning is said to be state-dependent, and failure of the learning to transfer from one state to another is described as dissociation. The practical importance of this is that adaptive learning may dissociate and thus may contribute to the relapses that often occur when drug therapy is stopped (139, 190, 208).

The interaction term in the factorial design already discussed is a measure of the effect of changing the drug state between training and testing, and is therefore a direct measure of the amount of dissociation. In spite of several reminders (105, 187, 212), many experiments apparently concerned with dissociation have not incorporated complete factorial designs, and as a result, dissociation has often been confounded with other effects of drugs on performance. However, even factorial designs are not completely satisfactory; e.g. interpretations of interactions are usually dependent on the assumption that measurement is on an interval scale (105, 314).

There are no clear criteria for predicting which drugs and types of learning will produce state-dependence. It is not surprising, therefore, that the proposed mechanisms behind this phenomenon are tentative and controversial. Bindra (23) has reviewed work where decrements in performance were consequent on stimulus changes, and it is possible that a change in the drug state may result in alterations of the stimuli associated with the environment, both external and internal. Dissociation, however, has not been demonstrated with drugs that have only peripheral actions (29, 66, 88), and this is inconsistent with "stimulus change" theories.

Overton (209, 210, 212) has presented evidence to support the view that stimulus changes due to drugs are not sufficient to account for dissociation of learning. Whereas rats could discriminate fairly easily between certain drug states (e.g. pentobarbitone and placebo) because they could serve as cues for differential escape responses, changes such as muscle flaccidity with gallamine, autonomic blockade (with tetraethylammonium), hunger and thirst, alterations in noise levels, light intensity and shock level were far poorer ways of producing differential responding in the same shock escape situation. Rats could also discriminate between the nondrug state and drugs such as alcohol, urethane, and meprobamate (210). The drugs, however, seemed to be exerting some common depressant effect since they could be substituted for each other. It was necessary to use extremely large doses, in some cases just subanaesthetic, to produce discrimination. Atropine and scopolamine and benactyzine could also be discriminated from saline as well as from the group of drugs with depressant effects, and this led Overton to suggest that state-dependence did not occur on a single continuum. In a three-choice maze, rats were able to learn correct escape responses with any one of three drug states as the appropriate cue, i.e. phenobarbitone, atropine, and saline (211). Imipramine, physostigmine, bemegride, and chlorpromazine all produced very slow acquisition of differential responding (210). Stewart (274) has, however, obtained good response control with several phenothiazines (which were mutually interchangeable). It would be extremely interesting to know why good response control occurs with some drugs and not with others.

Bindra & Reichert (27) were unable to confirm the findings of Overton (209) that a discriminated escape response could be state-dependent, but reversal learning was facilitated if it took place under a drug state different from the one present during initial training (27). The authors commented that their rats were less affected by pentobarbitone than those of Overton; in another study (26), they gave phenobarbitone to rats in an avoidance test and found that response choice did not dissociate but that response initiation did. In addition, habituation of exploratory activity also dissociated between phenobarbitone and saline states (27), although not between an amphetamine-amylobarbitone mixture and saline (238). It appears, therefore, that different components in learning situations are not equally likely to dissociate.

Other interesting findings may eventually clarify the picture, e.g. the extinction of conditioned immobility under phenobarbitone appears to be state-dependent, whereas acquisition does not (25). Further analysis is necessary of the tasks and doses of drugs where other discrepant results are reported, e.g. chlordiazepoxide (55, 140, 245), barbiturates (9, 27, 209), chlorpromazine (56, 128, 208, 274). Recently, Osborn et al. (207) have attempted to produce state-dependent learning in man using high doses of thiopentone, but in contrast to some studies in rats, responses transferred between drug and nondrug states.

Overton (212) has discussed the question of asymmetrical dissociation, that is, the possibility that the size of decrements due to state change are dependent on the direction of change. It has been noted (212, 244) that although the "stimulus change" model predicts symmetrical dissociation, the response decrement is usually greater when the change is from drug to nondrug than when it is from nondrug to drug. Overton (212) cites several studies which suggest that asymmetrical dissociation may be occurring, but such effects can easily be confounded with factors such as tolerance, or actions of the drug on acquisition and performance, even if a factorial design is used.

Post-trial Administration of Drugs

The technique of post-trial administration of drugs is particularly suitable for studying effects on memory mechanisms; provided the drug is completely eliminated between trials, only those dependent variables which are concerned with memory will remain. There are, however, certain limitations since drugs may differ both in terms of the delay before onset and the duration of action (178). These factors are of great importance in the light of some studies on the duration of the labile phase of memory (53, 54, 214), and thus apparent differences between drug effects could partly be due to different time courses of action.

Improved consolidation has been reported with post-trial administration of a number of drugs on a variety of tasks. For example, strychnine has improved maze responding for food rewards (182), delayed-alternation responding for water rewards (218), complex discriminated escape learning (127), and conditioned avoidance by mice in a shuttle-box (35).

Both sex and strain differences have been observed with the facilitating effects of strychnine on memory and learning (97, 181). Females were superior to males, and maze-bright rats were superior to maze-dull animals. Kato et al. (143) have shown that the metabolism of strychnine differs in male and female rats and that this difference is also a function of age. McGaugh et al. (182) found that as the intervals between learning trials and post-trial injections of strychnine were increased, a strain difference appeared. The maze-bright strain, which continued to show facilitation at longer intervals, was also found to be more resistant to the amnesic effects of electroconvulsive shock (291).

Petrinovich (217) has suggested that failures to demonstrate facilitation with post-trial strychnine (167, 222) might be due to strain differences in susceptibility to the drug, and he warned that "it is essential to determine the dose-response relations for the particular task the animal is performing." Recent data reported by McGaugh (178) illustrate how misleading results could have been obtained had only a single dose-level been used. Full dose-response information is also needed for comparisons between different test situations, since the shapes of the dose-response curves may be different for different tests and, indeed, for the same test if carried out in varying circumstances (180).

The finding (61) that a single injection of strychnine given up to three days before testing improved the performance of rats poses difficulties; apart from being inconsistent with an earlier study (182), such a residual effect would convert all the post-trial experiments using intertrial intervals of less than three days into pretrial administration to some extent. Greenough & McGaugh (97), however, were not able to demonstrate this type of residual effect.

Facilitation of retention has been demonstrated with post-trial administration of a number of other drugs, e.g. picrotoxin, pentylenetetrazol, diphenyldiazadamantanol, amphetamine, and eserine, and the literature has been fully reviewed recently (178, 180, 306). In selected strains of mice, post-trial administration of ether has also been shown to improve retention (313), a possible mechanism being stimulation of transmitter activity (311). In human subjects, Steinberg & Summerfield (270) found that administration of 30% nitrous oxide after learning improved retention, and they suggested that interference with consolidation had been minimised (136). In most experiments, depressant drugs—e.g., barbiturates (215, 271), ether (1, 215), and nitrous oxide (35)—have been found to impair memory. With ether, and probably with other drugs, the depth and length of anaesthesia and the ambient temperature appear to be critical (3, 179). Retrograde amnesia has also been demonstrated with post-trial carbon dioxide administration

(214, 280), and with bis-trifluoroethyl-ether given up to 4 hours after passive avoidance learning (3).

Most of the drugs which facilitate retention are in some sense central stimulants, although they have different neuropharmacological actions. The neuronal mechanisms involved in the early labile phase of memory storage remain unidentified. McGaugh (178) has shown that under rather precisely defined conditions strychnine can attenuate the effects of electroconvulsive shock. Studies with topical application of drugs to the cortex [e.g. (74)] and to other structures may prove helpful in understanding how such drugs interact with neuronal mechanisms of memory. The physiological and biochemical processes involved in information storage are being intensively studied, and there are a number of recent reviews of the subject (33, 39, 86, 104, 137, 178, 232, 233). The search for the engram has provided an interface for several disciplines with exciting and often controversial results. Different forms of behaviour under different drives may or may not share common processes of encoding and consolidation. The mechanisms of "reading out" of complex memories in response to specific external and internal stimuli is a closely related problem (243) which will tax the ingenuity of research workers for some time to come.

TESTING OF NEW DRUGS

In a discussion of screening methods, Irwin (131) said that there was "no consensus on the over-riding value of any particular methodological approach and little agreement on what constitutes appropriate preclinical information for reasonably predicting drug effects in man." The development of new drugs is heavily dependent on the tests utilized at the initial screening stage; usually these involve assessing the "spontaneous" activity of animals, either by observation or by automatic recording. Available methods have been reviewed by Kinnard & Watzman (151), who concluded that although the precise procedures and conditions were critically important in determining the results, such tests were among the least standardized of all aspects of screening programmes.

The practical advantages of automated equipment are offset by the inherent limitations of the apparatus used. Since the term "activity" does not refer to a unitary variable (57, 98), the type of activity elicited and the results obtained depend largely on the method of measurement. Tapp et al. (281) found that the scores obtained from several types of automated equipment were not correlated, and the effects of drugs have been shown to depend on the precise components of activity measured by any single apparatus (154, 155, 240). Photocell activity cages are widely used, but until recently little information was available about the kinds of behaviour actually picked up, or on the extent to which observation and automatic recording correlated. In undrugged rats the frequency of walking and rearing, recorded visually, correlated with photocell counts; the agreement broke down when dexamphetamine was tested, but remained high with amylobarbitone

(154). It seems, therefore, that detailed observation is essential, either alone or in association with automated techniques. Irwin (132) has described a procedure based on observation and handling; a comprehensive assessment of the behavioural, neurological, and autonomic states of mice appears possible, and so distinctions can be made between the main classes of psychoactive drugs.

Ethological techniques are also of great value since they allow observation of relatively unrestrained behaviour. With skilled observation, the occurrence and incidence of many different types of social interactions can be recorded. Changes in patterns of behaviour may not only be empirically sensitive indices of the effects of drugs, but may also provide a coherent framework for the analysis of such effects (14, 50, 51, 256).

Further analyses of the behavioural actions of drugs selected by the initial screen are of necessity based on largely empirical procedures. The aetiology of mental illnesses is poorly understood, and animal models of pathological human behaviour ought to be viewed critically. Shepherd et al. (254) are perhaps unduly pessimistic in commenting: "None of the animal models of aberrant behaviour is satisfactory. No anatomical, biochemical, physiological or behavioural 'lesion' is homologous to any mental illness in man." Nevertheless, the substances which are self-administered by rats and monkeys are on the whole only those associated with dependence in man (68). This is valuable, indeed essential, evidence for the validity and relevance of animal studies to a clinical problem in man. While animal models of conflict behaviour and experimental neuroses have superficial resemblances to human states, there would seem to be homologous physiological and behavioural mechanisms underlying learned fear reactions. In the case of depressive illnesses and some psychotic states, psychopharmacologists are, however, forced into using empirical tests, such as the reversal of "depression" produced by tetrabenazine, or into comparing profiles of action of chemically similar compounds. The risk taken with such methods, as has often been pointed out, is that useful drugs without these specific properties may well be lost.

A potentially valuable approach is to test combinations of known drugs. In this way it is sometimes possible to obtain patterns of effects different from those of the constituents (73, 235, 236). However, drug-interactions which appear as unwanted side effects naturally attract more attention. Macgregor (169), at a symposium on drug-interaction, stated that: "Undoubtedly the most important fields where drug-interactions may be of greatest inconvenience and danger are in the realm of psychopharmacology and cardiovascular physiology." Shepherd (253) surveyed investigations on interactions between centrally acting drugs and commented on how few studies had used well-established pharmacological and psychological techniques under laboratory conditions, and on the even fewer studies [e.g. (73) (235)] where analogous investigations were performed on human and animal subjects. Clinically, mixtures of different psychoactive drugs are often used.

INDIVIDUAL REACTIONS TO DRUGS

In both clinical and experimental situations, it is generally recognised that the response to a dose of a drug is not the same in all the individuals who receive it. Several questions immediately arise. Are certain individuals particularly susceptible to effects of drugs in general or only to certain classes of drugs? Are subjects who are sensitive to one effect of a drug also very responsive if different kinds of behaviour are tested? Can we predict individual differences in response and modify them if necessary?

Two types of approach have usually been applied to individual differences. One approach is to form groups of subjects that differ with regard to some parameter, either by selective breeding (41, 125) or by some experimental treatment (238) with which a drug might interact. It is assumed that any differences in drug responses between the groups are related to the individual differences in a more homogenous population. This approach can have the advantage of maximising the differences in terms of predetermined variables; for example, increments in performance with amphetamines may most readily be shown when the base line of responding is low (72). Mixtures of amphetamine and amylobarbitone may greatly increase the locomotor activity of naive rats in a Y-maze, but they are ineffective when given to "experienced" rats that have been repeatedly exposed to the maze (268). Chlorpromazine impairs lever-pressing for water rewards most markedly when the base line of responding is high (170). However, when the baseline rate (and of course the schedule of reinforcement) is held constant, it can be shown that chlorpromazine produces a greater depression of recently learned responses than of well-established behaviour (227, 258).

The alternative approach is to work with a specified strain of animals, and to assess the responses to drugs of the individuals within it (276). These responses are then correlated with various predrug measures of behaviour or of physiology. This retrospective analysis is intended to isolate the factors that give the most precise prediction of drug effects. This is the most direct method for the study of individual differences, but it has the disadvantage that it is necessary to administer the drug several times in order to estimate the reproducibility of individual responses. Apart from being tedious, this introduces complications due to tolerance and other persistent effects of treatment with drugs. It has been shown that in certain situations a single experience can modify subsequent reactions to drugs for prolonged periods (238, 239). Patients are rarely pharmacologically naive, and this raises a potential problem both for clinical evaluation and for preclinical screening.

Some drug effects are robust and, provided that the doses are suitably adjusted, will manifest themselves irrespective of the differences between subjects, e.g. the hypnotic action of barbiturates. Others [e.g., facilitation of performance by amphetamines (72, 162)] will appear only if certain combinations of factors are present in the test situation. Often there may be apparently discrepant results that can only be resolved by systematic analysis.

Such research could proceed from the demonstrations that many individual differences can be accounted for by variations in the absorption, distribution, and metabolism of drugs; measurements of the plasma levels of drugs often correlate much more highly with pharmacological and behavioural effects than do the injected doses (42). For example, the higher toxicity of morphine in young rats does not appear to be related to changes in sensitivity of the brain, but rather to changes in the distribution of morphine with age (160). Similarly, reduced sensitivity in recent years of a strain of Sprague-Dawley rats to hexobarbitone and desipramine can be attributed to increasingly rapid metabolism (42). Consequently, it seems almost essential to include measurements of the plasma levels of drugs if meaningful interpretations of experiments on individual differences are to be made.

Greater control of such factors ought to enable one to make more effective use of available drugs. For example, the excretion, and hence the potency and duration of action of amphetamine, is correlated with, and may be controlled by, the pH of the urine (18). Acidifying the urine by including ammonium chloride in the diet enhances amphetamine excretion and greatly reduces variability. Evidence of the importance of this for experiments with animals can be adduced from a demonstration (298) that rats on a high protein diet (which would acidify the urine) were less sensitive to dexamphetamine as measured by activity in a Y-maze, although other interpretations are not excluded. It appears that excretion of methadone (17) and of the anti-depressant tranylcypromine (292) is also related to urinary pH, and the results of further investigations, particularly into behavioural correlates, will be very interesting. However, individual variations in response to drugs can only partly be accounted for in such terms (126, 196).

In man, personality factors, both normal and pathological, are obvious major determinants of effects of psychoactive drugs, and this fundamental type of drug-behaviour interaction has recently been discussed in some detail (77, 254, 316, 317). Attempts to discern related predisposing factors in animals (41, 77, 178, 233) are of the greatest importance. Comparisons between subjects differing, for example, in terms of "maze-brightness" or "emotionality" have already been discussed. Ideally, whenever drugs are tested in animals, factors such as these should be taken into account; certain drugs may shift different members of a group of subjects in opposite directions and yet leave the mean response unchanged (77, 235).

CONCLUSIONS

It is inevitable, and indeed productive, that the rapid growth of psychopharmacology should be accompanied by controversies about both mechanisms of action of drugs and central processes mediating behaviour. Whole areas of the subject are in a state of flux; but perhaps 10 years from now, with the knowledge gained from new methods and better drugs, our present speculations about the physiology and biochemistry of learning and memory and of other aspects of behaviour will have been replaced by a more coherent framework. Meanwhile, a growing number of drugs can be used with reasonable confidence to manipulate the behaviour of animals and men, Among the advances to be hoped for, one might select both a much fuller understanding of individual differences in reactions to drugs and more success in the identification of drugs with narrowly specific actions. Much more also needs to be known about how patterns of responding change with repeated administration of drugs, and about long-term effects of drugs generally.

From the practical point of view, the demands made on psychopharmacology show every sign of multiplying; aside from the very real and vital contribution to the treatment of mental illness, there is an immediate need for more concrete information about the dangers and, dare one say it, the advantages to be derived from drugs in social use. Future generations of drugs will undoubtedly raise ethical problems far more profound than those already under discussion.

LITERATURE CITED

1. Abt, J. P., Essman, W. B., Jarvik, M. E. Ether induced retrograde amnesia for one-trial conditioning in mice. *Science,* **133,** 1477–78 (1961)
2. Ader, R., Clink, D. W. Effects of chlorpromazine on the acquisition and extinction of an avoidance response in the rat. *J. Pharmacol. Exptl. Therap.,* **121,** 144–48 (1957)
3. Alpern, H. P., Kimble, D. P. Retrograde amnesic effects of diethyl ether and bis(trifluorethyl) ether. *J. Comp. Physiol. Psychol.,* **63,** 168–71 (1967)
4. Andersson, B. The physiology of thirst. *Progress in Physiological Psychology,* **1,** 191–207 (Stellar, E., Sprague, J. M., Eds., Academic Press, New York, 1966)
5. Appel, J. B. Drugs, shock intensity and the CER. *Psychopharmacologia,* **4,** 148–53 (1963)
6. Azrin, N. H., Holz, W. C. Punishment. *Operant Behaviour: Areas of Research and Application,* 380–447 (Honig, W. K., Ed., Appleton-Century-Crofts, New York, 1966)
7. Bainbridge, J. G. The effect of psychotropic drugs on food reinforced behaviour and on food consumption. *Psychopharmacologia,* **12,** 204–13 (1968)
8. Barry, H. III, Buckley, J. P. Drug effects on animal performance and the stress syndrome. *J. Pharm. Sci.,* **55,** 1159–83 (1966)
9. Barry, H. III, Etheredge, E. E., Miller, N. E. Counterconditioning and extinction of fear fail to transfer from amobarbital to nondrug state. *Psychopharmacologia,* **8,** 150–56 (1965)
10. Barry, H. III, Miller, N. E. Comparison of drug effects on approach, avoidance and escape motivation. *J. Comp. Physiol. Psychol.,* **59,** 18–24 (1965)
11. Barry, H. III, Miller, N. E., Tidd, G. E. Control for stimulus change while testing effects of amobarbital on conflict. *J. Comp. Physiol. Psychol.,* **55,** 1071–74 (1962)
12. Barry, H. III, Wagner, S. A., Miller, N. E. Effects of several drugs on performance in an approach-avoidance conflict. *Psychol. Rept.,* **12,** 215–21 (1963)
13. Barton, R. *The Scientific Basis of Drug Therapy in Psychiatry,* 50 (Marks, J., Pare, C. M. B., Eds., Pergamon, Oxford, 1965)
14. Bateson, P. P. G. Ethological methods of observing behaviour. *Analysis of Behavioural Change,* 389–99 (Weiskrantz, L., Ed., Harper & Row, New York, 1968)
15. Beach, G., Kimble, D. P. Activity and responsivity in rats after magnesium pemoline injections. *Science,* **155,** 698–701 (1967)
16. Beach, H. D. Morphine addiction in rats. *Can. J. Psychol.,* **11,** 104–12 (1957)
17. Beckett, A. H. Distribution and metabolism in man of some narcotic analgesics and some amphetamines. *Scientific Basis of Drug Dependence,* 129–48 (Steinberg, H., Ed., Churchill, London, 1969)

18. Beckett, A. H., Rowland, M. Urinary excretion kinetics of methylamphetamine in man. *J. Pharm. Pharmacol.*, **17**, 109–14S (1965)
19. Berlyne, D. E. *Conflict, Arousal and Curiosity* (McGraw-Hill, New York, 1960)
20. Berlyne, D. E., Koenig, I. D. V., Hirota, T. Novelty, arousal and the reinforcement of diversive exploration in the rat. *J. Comp. Physiol. Psychol.*, **62**, 222–26 (1966)
21. Besser, G. M., Steinberg, H. L'intéraction du chlordiazépoxide et du dexamphétamine chez l'homme. *Thérapie*, **22**, 977–90 (1967)
22. Bignami, G., Robustelli, F., Janku, I., Bovet, D. Action de l'amphétamine et de quelques agents psychotropes sur l'acquisition d'un conditionnement de fuite et d'évitement chez des rats selectionnés en fonction du niveau particulièrement bas de leurs performances. *Compt. Rend. Acad. Sci. Paris*, **260**, 4273–78 (1965)
23. Bindra, D. Stimulus change, reactions to novelty and response decrement. *Psychol. Rev.*, **66**, 96–103 (1959)
24. Bindra, D., Anchel, H. Immobility as an avoidance response, and its disruption by drugs. *J. Exptl. Anal. Behav.*, **6**, 213–18 (1963)
25. Bindra, D., Nyman, K., Wise, J. Barbiturate-induced dissociation of acquisition and extinction: role of movement-initiation processes. *J. Comp. Physiol. Psychol.*, **60**, 223–28 (1965)
26. Bindra, D., Reichert, H. Dissociation of movement initiation without dissociation of response choice. *Psychon. Sci.*, **4**, 95–96 (1966)
27. Bindra, D., Reichert, H. The nature of dissociation: effects of transitions between normal and barbiturate-induced states on reversal learning and habituation. *Psychopharmacologia*, **10**, 330–44 (1967)
28. Bindra, D., Spinner, N. Response to different degrees of novelty: the incidence of various activities. *J. Exptl. Anal. Behav.*, **1**, 341–50 (1958)
29. Black, A. H., Carlson, N. J., Solomon, R. L. Exploratory studies of the conditioning of autonomic responses in curarized dogs. *Psychol. Monogr.*, **76**, No. 29 (1962)
30. Bloch, S., Silva, A. Factors involved in the acquisition of a maze habit, analysed by means of tranquilizing and sedative drugs. *J. Comp. Physiol. Psychol.*, **52**, 550–54 (1959)
31. Boissier, J-R., Simon, P. Dissociation de deux composantes dans le comportement d'investigation de la souris. *Arch. Intern. Pharmacodyn.*, **147**, 372–87 (1964)
32. Boitano, J. J., Boitano, J. C. Magnesium pemoline: enhancement of spontaneous motor activity. *Psychon. Sci.*, **9**, 295–96 (1967)
33. Booth, D. A. Vertebrate brain ribonucleic acids and memory retention. *Psychol. Bull.*, **68**, 149–77 (1967)
34. Bovet, D., Gatti, G. L. Pharmacology of instrumental avoidance conditioning. *Pharmacology of Conditioning, Learning and Retention*, 75–89 (Mikhelson, M.Ya., Longo, V. G., Votava, Z., Eds., Pergamon, Oxford, 1965)
35. Bovet, D., McGaugh, J. L., Oliverio, A. Effects of post trial administration of drugs on avoidance learning of mice. *Life Sci.*, **5**, 1309–15 (1966)
36. Bradley, D. W. M., Joyce, D., Murphy, E. H., Nash, B. M., Porsolt, R. D., Summerfield, A., Twyman, W. A. Amphetamine-barbiturate mixture: effects on the behaviour of mice. *Nature*, **220**, 187–88 (1968)
37. Bradley, P. B., Wolstencroft, J. H. Actions of drugs on single neurones in the brain-stem. *Brit. Med. Bull.*, **21**, 15–18 (1965)
38. Brady, J. V. Assessment of drug effects on emotional behavior. *Science*, **123**, 1033–34 (1956)
39. Briggs, M. H., Kitto, G. B. The molecular basis of memory and learning. *Psychol. Rev.*, **69**, 537–41 (1962)
40. Broadhurst, P. L. Abnormal animal behaviour. *Handbook of Abnormal Psychology*, 726–63 (Eysenck, H. J., Ed., Pitman, London, 1961)
41. Broadhurst, P. L. The biometrical analysis of behavioural inheritance. *Sci. Prog. (Oxford)*, **55**, 123–39 (1967)
42. Brodie, B. B. Idiosyncrasy and intolerance. *Drug Responses in Man*, 188–213 (Wolstenholme, G., Porter, R., Eds., Churchill, London, 1967)
43. Brown, H. Behavioural studies of animal vision and drug action.

Intern. Rev. Neurobiol., **10,** 277–322 (1967)

44. Burgen, A. S. V. The pharmacological basis of drug interactions in the nervous system. *Neuropsychopharmacology*, 459–63 (Brill, H., Cole, J. O., Deniker, P., Hippius, H., Bradley, P. B., Eds., Excerpta Med. Found., Amsterdam, 1967)
45. Carlton, P. L. Cholinergic mechanisms in the control of behaviour by the brain. *Psychol. Rev.*, **70,** 19–39 (1963)
46. Carlton, P. L. Cholinergic mechanisms and the control of behaviour. *Psychopharmacology: A Review of Progress 1957–1967*, 125–38 (Efron, D. H., Cole, J. O., Levine, J., Wittenborn, J. R., Eds., U. S. Public Health Serv. Publ. No. 1836, 1968)
47. Casey, A. The effect of stress on the consumption of alcohol and reserpine. *Quart. J. Stud. Alcohol*, **21,** 208–16 (1960)
48. Caul, W. F. Effects of amobarbital on discrimination acquisition and reversal. *Psychopharmacologia*, **11,** 414–21 (1967)
49. Chance, M. R. A. *Animal Behaviour and Drug Action*, Discussion, 19 (Steinberg, H., de Reuck, A. V. S., Knight, J., Eds., Churchill, London, 1964)
50. Chance, M. R. A. Ethology and psychopharmacology. *Psychopharmacology: Dimensions and Perspectives*, 283–318 (Joyce, C. R. B., Ed., Tavistock, London, 1968)
51. Chance, M. R. A., Silverman, A. P. The structure of social behaviour and drug action. *Animal Behaviour and Drug Action*, 65–79 (See Ref. 49)
52. Chipman, H. L. The differential effects of conditioned stimulus intensity and chlorpromazine on avoidance. *Psychon. Sci.*, **6,** 413–14 (1966)
53. Chorover, S. L., Schiller, P. H. Short-term retrograde amnesia in rats. *J. Comp. Physiol. Psychol.*, **59,** 73–78 (1965)
54. Chorover, S. L., Schiller, P. H. Reexamination of prolonged retrograde amnesia in one-trial learning. *Ibid.*, **61,** 34–41 (1966)
55. Cicala, G. A., Hartley, D. L. Effects of chlordiazepoxide on the acquisition and performance of a conditioned escape response in rats. *Psychol. Rec.*, **15,** 435–40 (1965)
56. Cicala, G. A., Hartley, D. L. Drugs and the learning and performance of fear. *J. Comp. Physiol. Psychol.*, **64,** 175–78 (1967)
57. Cofer, C. N., Appley, M. H. Activity and exploration. *Motivation: Theory and Research*, 269–301 (Wiley, New York, 1964)
58. Cook, L., Catania, A. C. Effects of drugs on avoidance and escape behaviour. *Federation Proc.*, **23,** 818–35 (1964)
59. Cook, L., Kelleher, R. T. Effects of drugs on behaviour. *Ann. Rev. Pharmacol.*, **3,** 205–22 (1963)
60. Cook, L., Weidley, E. Behavioural effects of some psychopharmacological agents. *Ann. N.Y. Acad. Sci.*, **66,** 740–52 (1957)
61. Cooper, R. M., Krass, M. Strychnine: duration of the effects on maze learning. *Psychopharmacologia*, **4,** 472–75 (1963)
62. Cooper, S. J., Joyce, D., Summerfield, A. Self-stimulation of the brain after administration of an amphetamine-barbiturate mixture. *Brit. J. Pharmacol.*, **36,** 192–93P (1969)
63. Corbit, J. D., Stellar, E. Palatability, food intake and obesity in normal and hyperphagic rats. *J. Comp. Physiol. Psychol.*, **58,** 63–67 (1964)
64. Courvoisier, S., Fournel, J., Ducrot, R., Kolsky, M., Koetschet, P. Propriétés pharmacodynamiques du chlorhydrate de chloro-3 (diméthylamino-3′propyl)—10 phénothiazine (4,560 R.P.). *Arch. Intern. Pharmacodyn.*, **92,** 305–61 (1953)

64a. Davis, J. D., Lulenski, G. C., Miller, N. E. Comparative studies of barbiturate self-administration. *Int. J. Addictions*, **3,** 207–14 (1968)

65. Davis, J. D., Miller, N. E. Fear and pain: their effect on self-injection of amobarbital sodium by rats. *Science*, **141,** 1286–87 (1963)
66. Davis, W. M., Babbini, M. Decamethonium and the conditioned avoidance response. *Psychopharmacologia*, **11,** 372–75 (1967)
67. Davis, W. M., Capehart, J., Lewellin, W. L. Mediated acquisition of a fear-motivated response and inhibitory effects of chlorpromazine. *Psychopharmacologia*, **2,** 268–76 (1961)

68. Deneau, G. A. Psychogenic dependence in monkeys. *Scientific Basis of Drug Dependence,* 199–208 (Steinberg, H., Ed., Churchill, London, 1969)
69. Denenberg, V. H. Stimulation in infancy, emotional reactivity and exploratory behaviour. *Neurophysiology and Emotion,* 161–90 (Glass, D. C., Ed., Rockefeller Univ. Press and Russell Sage Found., 1967)
70. Denenberg, V. H., Ross, S., Ellsworth, J. Effects of chlorpromazine on acquisition and extinction of a conditioned response in mice. *Psychopharmacologia,* **1,** 59–64 (1959)
71. Dews, P. B. Conditioned behaviour as substratum for behavioural effects of drugs. *Psychiatric Drugs,* 22–31 (Solomon, P., Ed., Grune & Stratton, New York/London, 1966)
72. Dews, P. B., Morse, W. H. Behavioural pharmacology. *Ann. Rev. Pharmacol.,* **1,** 145–74 (1961)
73. Dickins, D. W., Lader, M. H., Steinberg, H. Differential effects of two amphetamine-barbiturate mixtures in man. *Brit. J. Pharmacol.,* **24,** 14–23 (1965)
74. Doolittle, J. H., Thompson, C. W. Retroactive effects of topical applications of potassium chloride, pentylenetetrazol, and strychnine on the acquisition of a maze habit in rats. *Psychon. Sci.,* **5,** 265–66 (1966)
75. Doty, L. A., Doty, B. A. Chlorpromazine-produced response decrements as a function of problem difficulty level. *J. Comp. Physiol. Psychol.,* **56,** 740–45 (1963)
76. Elliott, R., Schneiderman, N. Pentylenetetrazol: facilitation of classical discrimination conditioning in rabbits. *Psychopharmacologia,* **12,** 133–41 (1968)
77. Eysenck, H. J. Personality and experimental psychology. *Bull. Brit. Psychol. Soc.,* **19,** 1–28 (1966)
78. Fallon, D. Eatometer: a device for continuous recording of free feeding behaviour. *Science,* **148,** 977–78 (1965)
79. Feider, A. Feedback control of carbachol-induced drinking. *J. Comp. Physiol. Psychol.,* **64,** 336–38 (1967)
80. Feldman, R. S., Green, K. F. Effects of chlordiazepoxide on fixated behaviour in squirrel monkeys. *J. Psychopharmacol.,* **1,** 37–45 (1966)
81. Fisher, A. E., Coury, J. N. Cholinergic tracing of a central neural circuit underlying the thirst drive. *Science,* **138,** 691–93 (1962)
82. Fowler, H. *Curiosity and Exploratory Behavior* (Macmillan, New York, 1965)
83. Fowler, H. Satiation and curiosity: constructs for a drive and incentive motivational theory of exploration. *The Psychology of Learning and Motivation. Advances in Research and Theory,* **1,** 157–227 (Spence, K. W., Spence, J. T., Eds., Academic Press, New York, 1967)
84. Fuxe, K., Hanson, L. C. F. Central catecholamine neurons and conditioned avoidance behaviour. *Psychopharmacologia,* **11,** 439–47 (1967)
85. Gaddum, J. H. Push-pull cannulae. *J. Physiol.,* **555,** 1P (1961)
86. Gaito, J., Zavala, A. Neurochemistry and learning. *Psychol. Bull.,* **61,** 45–62 (1964)
87. Gandelman, R., Trowill, J. Effects of chlordiazepoxide on ESB-reinforced behaviour and subsequent extinction. *J. Comp. Physiol. Psychol.,* **66,** 753–55 (1968)
88. Gardner, L., McCollough, C. A reinvestigation of the dissociative effects of curareform drugs. *Am. Psychologist,* **17,** 398 (1962)
89. Gatti, G. L., Bovet, D. Analysis of the action of psychotropic drugs in 'lever pressing avoidance' conditioning. *Psychopharmacological Methods,* 50–57 (Votava, Z., Horvath, M., Vinar, O., Eds., Pergamon, Oxford, 1963)
90. Geller, I. Relative potencies of benzodiazepines as measured by their effects on conflict behaviour. *Arch. Intern. Pharmacodyn.,* **149,** 243–47 (1964)
91. Geller, I., Seifter, J. The effects of meprobamate, barbiturates, *d*-amphetamine and promazine on experimentally induced conflict in the rat. *Psychopharmacologia,* **1,** 482–92 (1960)
92. Geller, I., Kulak, J. T., Jr., Seifter, J. The effects of chlordiazepoxide and chlorpromazine on a punishment discrimination. *Psychopharmacologia,* **3,** 374–85 (1962)

93. Glowinski, J., Baldessarini, R. J. Metabolism of norepinephrine in the central nervous system. *Pharmacol. Rev.*, **18,** 1201–38 (1966)
94. Goldberg, S. R., Schuster, C. R. Conditioned suppression by a stimulus associated with nalorphine in morphine-dependent monkeys. *J. Exptl. Anal. Behav.*, **10,** 235–42 (1967)
95. Gollub, L. R., Brady, J. V. Behavioural pharmacology. *Ann. Rev. Pharmacol.*, **5,** 235–62 (1965)
96. Gordon, M. Phenothiazines. *Psychopharmacological Agents,* **2,** 1–198 (Gordon, M., Ed., Academic Press, London, 1967)
97. Greenough, W. T., McGaugh, J. L. The effect of strychnine sulphate on learning as a function of time of administration. *Psychopharmacologia,* **8,** 290–94 (1965)
98. Gross, C. G. General activity. *Analysis of Behavioural Change,* 91–106 (See Ref. 14)
99. Grossman, S. P. Effects of chlorpromazine and perphenazine on bar pressing performance in approach-avoidance conflict. *J. Comp. Physiol. Psychol.*, **54,** 517–21 (1961)
100. Grossman, S. P. Direct adrenergic and cholinergic stimulation of hypothalamic mechanisms. *Am. J. Physiol.*, **202,** 872–82 (1962)
101. Grossman, S. P. Effects of adrenergic and cholinergic blocking agents on hypothalamic mechanisms. *Ibid.*, 1230–36
102. Grossman, S. P. Behavioural effects of direct chemical stimulation of central nervous system structures. *Intern. J. Neuropharmacol.*, **3,** 45–58 (1964)
103. Grossman, S. P. Acquisition and performance of avoidance responses during chemical stimulation of the mid-brain reticular formation. *J. Comp. Physiol. Psychol.*, **61,** 42–49 (1966)
104. Grossman, S. P. *A Textbook of Physiological Psychology* (Wiley, New York, 1967)
105. Grossman, S. P., Miller, N. E. Control for stimulus-change in the evaluation of alcohol and chlorpromazine as fear-reducing drugs. *Psychopharmacologia,* **2,** 342–51 (1961)
106. Grossman, S. P., Peters, R. H. Acquisition of appetitive and avoidance habits following atropine-induced blocking of the thalamic reticular formation. *J. Comp. Physiol. Psychol.*, **61,** 325–32 (1966)
107. Grossman, S. P., Peters, R. H., Freedman, P. E., Willer, H. I. Behavioural effects of cholinergic stimulation of the thalamic reticular formation. *J. Comp. Physiol. Psychol.*, **59,** 57–65 (1965)
108. Halliday, M. S. Exploratory behaviour. *Analysis of Behavioural Change,* 107–26 (See Ref. 14)
109. Hanson, H. M., Stone, C. A. Animal techniques for evaluating anti-anxiety drugs. *Animal and Clinical Pharmacologic Techniques in Drug Evaluation,* 317–24 (Nodine, J. H., Siegler, P. E., Eds., Yearbook Publ., Chicago, 1964)
110. Hanson, H. M., Witoslawski, J. J., Campbell, E. H. Drug effects in squirrel monkeys trained on a multiple schedule with a punishment contingency. *J. Exptl. Anal. Behav.*, **10,** 565–69 (1967)
111. Hanson, L. C. F. The disruption of conditioned avoidance response following selective depletion of brain catechol amines. *Psychopharmacologia,* **8,** 100–10 (1965)
112. Hanson, L. C. F. Evidence that the central action of (+)-amphetamine is mediated via catecholamines. *Ibid.*, **10,** 289–97 (1967)
113. Harris, R. T., Claghorn, J. L., Schoolar, J. C. Self-administration of minor tranquilizers as a function of conditioning. *Psychopharmacologia,* **13,** 81–88 (1968)
114. Hartlage, L. C. Effects of chlorpromazine on learning. *Psychol. Bull.*, **64,** 235–45 (1965)
115. Headlee, C. P., Coppock, H. W., Nichols, J. R. Apparatus and technique involved in a laboratory method of detecting the addictiveness of drugs. *J. Am. Pharm. Assoc.*, **44,** 229–31 (1955)
116. Hearst, E., Whalen, R. E. Facilitating effects of *d*-amphetamine on discriminated-avoidance performance. *J. Comp. Physiol. Psychol.*, **56,** 124–28 (1963)
117. Heimstra, N. W., Sallee, S. J. Effects of early drug treatment on adult dominance behaviour in rats. *Psychopharmacologia,* **8,** 235–40 (1965)
118. Heise, G. A. Mode of action of anti-anxiety compounds. *The Scientific*

Basis of Drug Therapy in Psychiatry, 165–76 (See Ref. 13)

119. Heistad, G. T. Effects of chlorpromazine and electro-convulsive shock on a conditioned emotional response. *J. Comp. Physiol. Psychol.,* **51,** 209–12 (1958)
120. Herrnstein, R. J. Method and theory in the study of avoidance. *Psychol. Rev.,* **76,** 46–69 (1969)
121. Herrnstein, R. J., Hineline, P. N. Negative reinforcement as shock-frequency reduction. *J. Exptl. Anal. Behav.,* **9,** 421–30 (1966)
122. Herxheimer, A., Ed. *Drugs and Sensory Functions* (Churchill, London, 1968)
123. Herz, A. Drugs and the conditioned avoidance response. *Intern. Rev. Neurobiol.,* **2,** 229–77 (1960)
124. Hill, J. H., Stellar, E. An electronic drinkometer. *Science,* **114,** 43–44 (1951)
125. Holland, H. C., Gupta, B. D. The effects of different doses of methylpentynol on escape avoidance conditioning in two strains of rats selectively bred for high and low 'emotionality.' *Psychopharmacologia,* **9,** 419–25 (1966)
126. Hollister, L. E. *Drug Responses in Man,* Discussion, 173 (See Ref. 42)
127. Hudspeth, W. J. Strychnine: its facilitating effect on the solution of a simple oddity problem by the rat. *Science,* **145,** 1331–33 (1964)
128. Hunt, E., Krivanek, J. The effects of pentylenetetrazol and methylphenoxypropane on discrimination learning. *Psychopharmacologia,* **9,** 1–16 (1966)
129. Hunt, H. F. Some effects of drugs on classical (type S) conditioning. *Ann. N.Y. Acad. Sci.,* **65,** 258–67 (1956)
130. Hunt, H. F. Methods for studying the behavioural effects of drugs. *Ann. Rev. Pharmacol.,* **1,** 125–44 (1961)
131. Irwin, S. Considerations for the preclinical evaluation of new psychiatric drugs: a case study with phenothiazine-like tranquilisers. *Psychopharmacologia,* **9,** 259–87 (1966)
132. Irwin, S. Comprehensive observational assessment: 1a. A systematic quantitative procedure for assessing the behavioral and physiologic state of the mouse. *Ibid.,* **13,** 222–57 (1968)
133. Iversen, L. L. The catecholamines. *Nature,* **214,** 8–14 (1967)
134. Iwahara, S., Iwasaki, T., Hasegawa, Y. Effects of chlorpromazine and homofenazine upon a passive avoidance response in rats. *Psychopharmacologia,* **13,** 320–31 (1968)
135. Jarvik, M. E. Drugs used in the treatment of psychiatric disorders. *The Pharmacological Basis of Therapeutics,* 159–214 (Goodman, L. S., Gilman, A., Eds., Macmillan, New York, 1965)
136. Jenkins, J. G., Dallenbach, K. M. Oblivescence during sleep and waking. *Am. J. Psychol.,* **35,** 605–12 (1924)
137. John, E. R. *Mechanisms of Memory* (Academic Press, New York/London, 1967)
138. Joyce, D., Summerfield, A. Amphetamine-barbiturate mixtures and the early conditioning of behaviour. *Proc. Intern. Pharmacol. Congr., 3rd, U.S.A., 1966*
139. Kamano, D. K. Selective review of effects of discontinuation of drug treatment: some implications and problems. *Psychol. Rept.,* **19,** 743–49 (1966)
140. Kamano, D. K., Arp, D. J. Effects of chlordiazepoxide (Librium) on the acquisition and extinction of avoidance responses. *Psychopharmacologia,* **6,** 112–19 (1964)
141. Kamano, D. K., Martin, L. K., Powell, B. J. Avoidance response acquisition and amobarbital dosage levels. *Psychopharmacologia,* **8,** 319–23 (1966)
142. Kamin, L. J., Brimer, C. J., Black, A. H. Conditioned suppression as a monitor of fear of the CS in the course of avoidance training. *J. Comp. Physiol. Psychol.,* **56,** 497–501 (1963)
143. Kato, R., Chiesara, E., Frontino, G. Influence of sex difference on the pharmacological action and metabolism of some drugs. *Biochem. Pharmacol.,* **11,** 221–27 (1962)
144. Kavanau, J. L. Precise monitoring of drinking behavior in small mammals. *J. Mammalogy,* **43,** 345–51 (1962)
145. Keehn, J. D., Arnold, E. M. M. Licking rates of albino rats. *Science,* **132,** 739–41 (1960)

146. Kety, S. S. Chemical boundaries of psychopharmacology. *Control of the Mind,* 79–91 (Farber, S. M., Wilson, R. H. L., Eds., McGraw-Hill, New York, 1961)
147. Khavari, K. A., Russell, R. W. Acquisition, retention and extinction under conditions of water deprivation and of central cholinergic stimulation. *J. Comp. Physiol. Psychol.,* **61,** 339–45 (1966)
148. Kiernan, C. C. Modification of the effects of amphetamine sulphate by past experience in the hooded rat. *Psychopharmacologia,* **8,** 23–31 (1965)
149. Kimble, G. A. *Conditioning and Learning. Hilgard and Marquis* (Appleton-Century-Crofts, New York, 1961)
150. Kinnard, W. J., Aceto, M. D. G., Buckley, J. P. The effects of certain psychotropic agents on the conditioned emotional response behaviour pattern of the albino rat. *Psychopharmacologia,* **3,** 227–30 (1962)
151. Kinnard, W. J., Watzman, N. Techniques utilised in the evaluation of psychotropic drugs on animal activity. *J. Pharm. Sci.,* **55,** 995–1012 (1966)
151a. Komisaruk, B. R., Olds, J. Neuronal correlates of behavior in freely moving rats. *Science,* **161,** 810–13 (1968)
152. Krieckhaus, E. E. Decrements in avoidance behaviour following mamillothalamic tractotomy in rats and subsequent recovery with *d*-amphetamine. *J. Comp. Physiol. Psychol.,* **60,** 31–35 (1965)
153. Krieckhaus, E. E., Miller, N. E., Zimmerman, P. Reduction of freezing behaviour and improvement of shock avoidance by *d*-amphetamine. *J. Comp. Physiol. Psychol.,* **60,** 36–40 (1965)
154. Krsiak, M., Steinberg, H., Stolerman, I. P. Discrepancies in results obtained with activity cages and by observation. *Brit. J. Pharmacol.,* **34,** 684P (1968)
155. Krsiak, M., Steinberg, H., Stolerman, I. P. Efficacy of a photocell activity cage for assessing effects of drugs. (To be published)
156. Kumar, R. Psychoactive drugs, exploratory activity and fear. *Nature,* **218,** 665–67 (1968)
157. Kumar, R. Exploration and latent learning: effects of dexamphetamine on components of exploratory behaviour in rats. *Psychopharmacologia* (At press)
158. Kumar, R., Steinberg, H., Stolerman, I. P. Inducing a preference for morphine in rats without premedication. *Nature,* **218,** 564–65 (1968)
159. Kumar, R., Steinberg. H., Stolerman, I. P. How rats can become dependent on morphine in the course of relieving another need. *Scientific Basis of Drug Dependence,* 209–20 (See Ref. 68)
160. Kupferberg, H. J., Way, E. L. Pharmacological basis for the increased sensitivity of the newborn rat to morphine. *J. Pharmacol. Exptl. Ther.,* **141,** 105–12 (1963)
161. Lasagna, L. On evaluating drug therapy: the nature of the evidence. *Drugs in Our Society,* 91–105 (Johns Hopkins Press, Baltimore, 1964)
162. Laties, V. G., Weiss, B. Performance enhancement by the amphetamines: a new appraisal. *Neuropsychopharmacology,* 800–8 (See Ref. 44)
163. Latz, A., Bain, G. T., Goldman, M., Kornetsky, C. Maze learning after the administration of antidepressant drugs. *J. Pharmacol. Exptl. Ther.,* **156,** 76–84 (1967)
164. Latz, A., Bain, G. T., Kornetsky, C. Attenuated effect of chlorpromazine on conditioned avoidance as a function of rapid acquisition. *Psychopharmacologia,* **14,** 23–32 (1969)
165. Lauener, H. Conditioned suppression in rats and the effect of pharmacological agents thereon. *Psychopharmacologia,* **4,** 311–25 (1963)
166. Longo, V. G. Behavioural and electroencephalographic effects of atropine and related compounds. *Pharmacol. Rev.,* **18,** 965–96 (1966)
167. Loutitt, R. T. Central nervous system stimulants and maze learning in rats. *Psychol. Rec.,* **15,** 97–102 (1965)
168. Low, L. A., Eliasson, M., Kornetsky, C. Effect of chlorpromazine on avoidance acquisition as a function of CS-US interval length. *Psychopharmacologia,* **10,** 148–54 (1966)
169. Macgregor, A. G. Review of points at which drugs can interact. *Proc. Roy. Soc. Med.,* **58,** 943–46 (1965)

170. Manocha, S. N. Performance level and drug effects. *Psychopharmacologia,* **12,** 123–26 (1968)
171. Margules, D. L. Noradrenergic basis of inhibition between reward and punishment in the amygdala. *J. Comp. Physiol. Psychol.,* **66,** 329–34 (1968)
172. Margules, D. L., Stein, L. Neuroleptics vs. tranquilisers: evidence from animal behaviour studies of mode and site of action. *Neuropsychopharmacology,* 108–20 (See Ref. 44)
173. Margules, D. L., Stein, L. Increase of "anti-anxiety activity" and tolerance of behavioural depression during chronic administration of oxazepam. *Psychopharmacologia,* **13,** 74–80 (1968)
174. Marriott, A. S., Spencer, P. S. J. Effects of centrally acting drugs on exploratory behaviour in rats. *Brit. J. Pharmacol.,* **25,** 432–41 (1965)
175. Martin, L. K., Powell, B. J., Kamano, D. K. Effect of amobarbital administered at various stages of avoidance response acquisition. *Psychol. Rept.,* **19,** 12–14 (1966)
176. Masserman, J. H. Alcohol and other drugs as preventives of experimental trauma. *Quart. J. Stud. Alcohol,* **20,** 464–66 (1959)
177. McDonald, D. G., Stern, J. A., Hahn, W. W. Behavioural, dietary, and autonomic effects of chlordiazepoxide in the rat. *Dis. Nerv. Syst.,* **24,** 95–103 (1963)
178. McGaugh, J. L. Drug facilitation of memory and learning. *Psychopharmacology: A Review of Progress 1957–1967,* 891–904 (See Ref. 46)
179. McGaugh, J. L., Alpern, H. P. Effects of electroshock on memory: amnesia without convulsions. *Science,* **152,** 665–66 (1966)
180. McGaugh, J. L., Petrinovich, L. F. Effects of drugs on learning and memory. *Intern. Rev. Neurobiol.,* **8,** 139–96 (1965)
181. McGaugh, J. L., Thomson, C. W. Facilitation of simultaneous discrimination learning with strychnine sulphate. *Psychopharmacologia,* **3,** 166–72 (1962)
182. McGaugh, J. L., Thomson, C. W., Westbrook, W. H., Hudspeth, W. J. A. A further study of learning facilitation with strychnine sulphate. *Psychopharmacologia,* **3,** 352–60 (1962)
183. McIlwain, H. Metabolic approach to interpreting animal exploratory activity. *Nature,* **220,** 889–90 (1968)
184. Meisch, R. A., Pickens, R. A new technique for oral self-administration of drugs by animals (At press)
185. Miller, N. E. Shortcomings of food consumption as a measure of hunger; results from other behavioural techniques. *Ann. N.Y. Acad. Sci.,* **63,** 141–43 (1955)
186. Miller, N. E. Effects of drugs on motivation: the value of using a variety of measures. *Ibid.,* **65,** 318–33 (1956)
187. Miller, N. E. Objective techniques for studying motivational effects of drugs on animals. *Psychotropic Drugs,* 83–102 (Garratini, S., Ghetti, V., Eds., Elsevier, Amsterdam, 1957)
188. Miller, N. E. The analysis of motivational effects illustrated by experiments on amylobarbitone sodium. *Animal Behaviour and Drug Action,* 1–18 (See Ref. 49)
189. Miller, N. E. Chemical coding of behavior in the brain. *Science,* **148,** 328–38 (1965)
190. Miller, N. E. Some animal experiments pertinent to the problem of combining psychotherapy with drug therapy. *Compr. Psychiat.,* **7,** 1–12 (1966)
191. Miller, N. E., Gottesman, K. S., Emery, N. Dose response to carbachol and norepinephrine in rat hypothalamus. *Am. J. Physiol.,* **206,** 1384–88 (1964)
192. Mirsky, A. F., Kornetsky, C. The effects of centrally-acting drugs on attention. *Psychopharmacology: A Review of Progress 1957–1967,* 91–104 (See Ref. 46)
193. Mirsky, A. F., Rosvold, H. E. The effect of electroconvulsive shock on food intake and hunger drive in the rat. *J. Comp. Physiol. Psychol.,* **46,** 153–57 (1953)
194. Morrison, C. F. The effects of nicotine on punished behaviour. *Psychopharmacologia,* **14,** 221–32 (1969)
195. Morse, W. H. Effect of amobarbital and chlorpromazine on punished behavior in the pigeon. *Psychopharmacologia,* **6,** 286–94 (1964)

196. Munkelt, P., Lienert, G. A. Blutalkoholspiegel und psychophysische Konstitution. *Arzneimittel-Forsch.* **14,** 573–75 (1964)
197. Nelson, F. Effects of chlorpromazine on fear extinction. *J. Comp. Physiol. Psychol.,* **64,** 496–98 (1967)
198. Nichols, J. R., Davis, W. M. Drug addiction II: variation of addiction. *J. Am. Pharm. Assoc.,* **48,** 259–62 (1959)
199. Nichols, J. R., Headlee, C. P., Coppock, H. W. Drug addiction I: addiction by escape training. *J. Am. Pharm. Assoc.,* **45,** 788–91 (1956)
200. Nicholson, W. M. Emotional factors in obesity. *Am. J. Med. Sci.,* **211,** 443–47 (1946)
201. Nielsen, I. M., Neuhold, K. The comparative pharmacology and toxicology of chlorprothixene and chlorpromazine. *Acta Pharmacol. Toxicol.,* **15,** 335–55 (1959)
202. Nieschulz, O., Hoffmann, I., Popendiker, K. Pharmakologische Untersuchungen über N-Methyl-piperazinyl-N[1]-propyl-phenothiazin. *Arzneimittel-Forsch.,* **8,** 199–210 (1958)
203. Olds, J. Hypothalamic substrates of reward. *Physiol. Rev.,* **42,** 554–604 (1962)
204. Olds, M. E. Facilitatory action of diazepam and chlordiazepoxide on hypothalamic reward behaviour. *J. Comp. Physiol. Psychol.,* **62,** 136–40 (1966)
205. Oliverio, A. Neurohumoral systems and learning. *Psychopharmacology: A Review of Progress 1957–1967,* 867–78 (See Ref. 46)
206. Opitz, K., Akinlaja, A. Zur Beeinflussung der Nahrungsaufnahme durch Psychopharmaka. *Psychopharmacologia,* **9,** 307–19 (1966)
207. Osborn, A. G., Bunker, P. J., Cooper, L. M., Frank, G. S., Hilgard, E. R. Effects of thiopental sedation on learning and memory. *Science,* **157,** 574–76 (1967)
208. Otis, L. S. Dissociation and recovery of a response learned under the influence of chlorpromazine or saline. *Science,* **143,** 1347–48 (1964)
209. Overton, D. A. State-dependent or "dissociated" learning produced with pentobarbital. *J. Comp. Physiol. Psychol.,* **57,** 3–12 (1964)
210. Overton, D. A. State-dependent learning produced by depressant and atropine-like drugs. *Psychopharmacologia,* **10,** 6–31 (1966)
211. Overton, D. A. Differential responding in a three choice maze controlled by three drug states. *Ibid.,* **11,** 376–78 (1967)
212. Overton, D. A. Dissociated learning in drug states (state-dependent learning). *Psychopharmacology: A Review of Progress 1957–1967,* 918–30 (See Ref. 46)
213. Owen, J. E., Jr. Psychopharmacological studies of some 1-(chlorophenyl)-2-aminopropanes II. *J. Pharm. Sci.,* **52,** 684–88 (1963)
214. Paolino, R. M., Quartermain, D., Miller, N. E. Different temporal gradients of retrograde amnesia produced by CO_2 anaesthesia and ECS. *J. Comp. Physiol. Psychol.,* **62,** 270–74 (1966)
215. Pearlman, C. A., Jr., Sharpless, S. K., Jarvik, M. E. Retrograde amnesia produced by anesthetic and convulsant agents. *J. Comp. Physiol. Psychol.,* **54,** 109–12 (1961)
216. Persensky, J. J., Senter, R. J., Jones, R. B. Induced alcohol consumption through positive reinforcement. *Psychon. Sci.,* **11,** 109–10 (1968)
217. Petrinovich, L. Drug facilitation of learning: strain differences. *Psychopharmacologia,* **10,** 375–78 (1967)
218. Petrinovich, L., Bradford, D., McGaugh, J. L. Drug facilitation of memory in rats. *Psychon. Sci.,* **2,** 191–92 (1965)
219. Pickens, R., Harris, W. C. Self-administration of *d*-amphetamine by rats. *Psychopharmacologia,* **12,** 158–63 (1968)
220. Pickens, R., Thompson, T. Cocaine-reinforced behaviour in rats; effects of reinforcement magnitude and fixed-ratio size. *J. Pharmacol. Exptl. Ther.,* **161,** 122–29 (1968)
221. Posluns, D. An analysis of chlorpromazine-induced suppression of the avoidance response. *Psychopharmacologia,* **3,** 361–73 (1962)
222. Prien, R. F., Wayner, M. J., Jr., Kahan, S. Lack of facilitation in maze learning by picrotoxin and strychnine sulphate. *Am. J. Physiol.,* **204,** 488–92 (1963)
223. Quartermain, D., Miller, N. E. Sensory feedback in time-response of drinking elicited by carbachol in preoptic area of the rat. *J. Comp.*

Physiol. Psychol., **62,** 350–53 (1966)

224. Randall, L. O., Schallek, W. Pharmacological activity of certain benzodiazepines. *Psychopharmacology: A Review of Progress 1957–1967,* 153–84 (See Ref. 46)
225. Randall, L. O., Schallek, W., Heise, G. A., Keith, E. F., Bagdon, R. E. The psychosedative properties of methaminodiazepoxide. *J. Pharmacol. Exptl. Ther.,* **129,** 163–71 (1960)
226. Randrup, A., Munkvad, I., Udsen, P. Adrenergic mechanisms and amphetamine induced abnormal behaviour. *Acta Pharmacol. (Kobenhavn),* **20,** 145–57 (1963)
227. Ray, O. S., Bivens, L. W. Performance as a function of drug, dose, and level of training. *Psychopharmacologia,* **10,** 103–9 (1966)
228. Rech, R. H. Amphetamine effects on poor performance of rats in a shuttle-box. *Psychopharmacologia,* **9,** 110–17 (1966)
229. Rensch, R., Rahmann, H. Einfluss des Pervitins auf das Gedächtnis von Goldhamstern. *Pfluegers Arch. Ges. Physiol.,* **271,** 693–704 (1960)
230. Rescorla, R. A., Solomon, R. L. Two-process learning theory: relationships between Pavlovian conditioning and instrumental learning. *Psychol. Rev.,* **74,** 151–82 (1967)
231. Richelle, M., Djahanguiri, B. Effet d'un traitement prolongé au chlordiazépoxide sur un conditionnement temporel chez le rat. *Psychopharmacologia,* **5,** 106–14 (1964)
232. Richter, D., Ed. *Aspects of Learning and Memory* (Heinemann, London, 1966)
233. Rosenzweig, M. R., Leiman, A. L. Brain functions. *Ann. Rev. Psychol.,* **19,** 55–98 (1968)
234. Ross, S., Cole, J. O. Psychopharmacology. *Ann. Rev. Psychol.,* **11,** 415–38 (1960)
235. Rushton, R., Steinberg, H. Mutual potentiation of amphetamine and amylobarbitone measured by activity in rats. *Brit. J. Pharmacol.,* **21,** 295–305 (1963)
236. Rushton, R., Steinberg, H. Combined effects of chlordiazepoxide and dexamphetamine on activity of rats in an unfamiliar environment. *Nature,* **211,** 1312–13 (1966)
237. Rushton, R., Steinberg, H. Reactions to drugs influenced by early experience. *Anim. Behav.,* **14,** 585–86 (1966)
238. Rushton, R., Steinberg, H., Tinson, C. Effects of a single experience on subsequent reactions to drugs. *Brit. J. Pharmacol.,* **20,** 99–105 (1963)
239. Rushton, R., Steinberg, H., Tomkiewicz, M. Equivalence and persistence of the effects of psychoactive drugs and past experience. *Nature,* **220,** 885–89 (1968)
240. Rushton, R., Steinberg, H., Tomkiewicz, M. Manipulating activities of rats by giving amphetamine alone and in combination with other drugs (To be published)
241. Russell, R. W. The comparative study of "conflict" and "experimental neurosis." *Brit. J. Psychol.,* **41,** 95–108 (1950)
242. Russell, R. W. Psychopharmacology. *Ann. Rev. Psychol.,* **15,** 87–114 (1964)
243. Russell, R. W. Biochemical substrates of behavior. *Frontiers in Physiological Psychology,* 185–245 (Russell, R. W., Ed., Academic Press, New York, 1966)
244. Sachs, E. Dissociation of learning in rats and its similarities to dissociative states in man. *Comparative Psychopathology,* 249–304 (Zubin, J., Hunt, H., Eds., Grune & Stratton, New York, 1967)
245. Sachs, E., Weingarten, M., Klein, N. W., Jr. Effects of chlordiazepoxide on the acquisition of avoidance learning and its transfer to the normal state and other drug conditions. *Psychopharmacologia,* **9,** 17–30 (1966)
246. Schmidt, H. Variation in water ingestion; the response to barbiturates. *Progr. Brain Res.,* **16,** 263–84 (1965)
247. Schmidt, H., Stewart, A. L. Acute effects of phenobarbital upon a locomotor response. *Physiol. Behav.,* **2,** 403–7 (1967)
248. Schuster, C. R., Dockens, W. S., Woods, J. H. Behavioral variables affecting the development of amphetamine tolerance. *Psychopharmacologia,* **9,** 170–82 (1966)
249. Schuster, C. R., Villarreal, J. E. The experimental analysis of opioid dependence. *Psychopharmacology: A Review of Progress 1957–1967,* 811–28 (See Ref. 46)
250. Senter, R. J., Sinclair, J. D. Self-

maintenance of intoxication in the rat: a modified replication. *Psychon. Sci.*, **9**, 291–92 (1967)

251. Sepinwall, J. Cholinergic stimulation of the brain and avoidance behaviour. *Psychon. Sci.*, **5**, 93–94 (1966)
252. Sheldon, M. H. Learning. *Analysis of Behavioural Change*, 127–57 (See Ref. 14)
253. Shepherd, M. Interaction between centrally acting drugs in man: some general considerations. *Proc. Roy. Soc. Med.*, **582**, 964–67 (1965)
254. Shepherd, M., Lader, M., Rodnight, R. *Clinical Psychopharmacology* (English Univ. Press, London, 1968)
255. Sidman, M. Avoidance conditioning with brief shock and no exteroceptive warning signal. *Science*, **118**, 157–58 (1953)
256. Silverman, A. P. Ethological and statistical analysis of drug effects on the social behaviour of laboratory rats. *Brit. J. Pharmacol.*, **24**, 579–90 (1965)
257. Singh, S. D. Habit strength and drug effects. *J. Comp. Physiol. Psychol.*, **58**, 468–69 (1964)
258. Singh, S. D., Manocha, S. N. The interaction of drug effects with drive level and habit strength. *Psychopharmacologia*, **9**, 205–9 (1966)
259. Smythies, J. R., Bradley, R. J., Johnston, V. S., Benington, F., Morin, R. D., Clarke, L. C. Structure-activity relationship studies on mescaline. III. The influence of the methoxy groups. *Psychopharmacologia*, **10**, 379–87 (1967)
260. Soumireu-Mourat, B., Cardo, B. Activity and learning in rats after magnesium pemoline. *Psychopharmacologia*, **12**, 258–62 (1968)
261. Spengler, J. Beeinflussung des Nahrungs-und Trinkverhaltens von Ratten durch getrenntes Futter- und Wasserangebot sowie durch Pharmaka. *Arch. Exptl. Pathol. Pharmakol.*, **238**, 312–19 (1960)
262. Spengler, J., Waser, P. Ein Apparat zur Messung des Futterverzehrs und zur Registrierung des Fressverhaltens von Ratten. *Helv. Physiol. Pharmacol. Acta*, **15**, 444–49 (1957)
263. Spengler, J., Waser, P. Der Einfluss verschiedener Pharmaka auf den Futterkonsum von Albino-Ratten im akuten Versuch. *Arch. Exptl. Pathol. Pharmakol.*, **237**, 171–85 (1959)
264. Spragg, S. D. S. Morphine addiction in chimpanzees. *Comparative Psychology Monographs XV*, 79–132 (Johns Hopkins Press, Baltimore, 1940)
265. Stein, L. Facilitation of avoidance behavior by positive brain stimulation. *J. Comp. Physiol. Psychol.*, **60**, 9–19 (1965)
266. Stein, L. Chemistry of reward and punishment. *Psychopharmacology: A Review of Progress 1957–1967*, 105–23 (See Ref. 46)
267. Stein, L., Seifter, J. Muscarinic synapses in the hypothalamus. *Am. J. Physiol.*, **202**, 751–56 (1962)
268. Steinberg, H. Drugs and animal behaviour. *Brit. Med. Bull.*, **20**, 75–80 (1964)
269. Steinberg, H. Methods of assessment of psychological effects of drugs in animals. *The Scientific Basis of Drug Therapy in Psychiatry*, 25–38, 51 (See Ref. 13)
270. Steinberg, H., Summerfield, A. Reducing interference in forgetting. *Quart. J. Exptl. Psychol.*, **9**, 146–54 (1957)
271. Steinberg, H., Tomkiewicz, M. Drugs and memory. *Psychopharmacology: A Review of Progress 1957–1967*, 879–84 (See Ref. 46)
272. Steiner, J. Positive reinforcement. *Analysis of Behavioural Change*, 4–18. (See Ref. 14)
273. Sterritt, G. M. Inhibition and facilitation of eating by electric shock. *J. Comp. Physiol. Psychol.*, **55**, 226–29 (1962)
274. Stewart, J. Differential responses based on the physiological consequences of pharmacological agents. *Psychopharmacologia*, **3**, 132–38 (1962)
275. Stolerman, I. P. Factors determining the effect of chlorpromazine on the food intake of rats. *Nature*, **215**, 1518–19 (1967)
276. Stone, G. C. Effects of drugs on nondiscriminated avoidance behavior. *Psychopharmacologia*, **6**, 245–55 (1964)
277. Stretch, R. Effects of amphetamine and pentobarbitone on exploratory behaviour in rats. *Nature*, **199**, 787–89 (1963)

278. Stricker, E. M., Miller, N. E. Thirst measured by licking reinforced on interval schedules; effects of pre-watering and of bacterial endotoxin. *J. Comp. Physiol. Psychol.*, **59**, 112–15 (1965)

279. Summerfield, A. *The Scientific Basis of Drug Therapy in Psychiatry*, 52. (See Ref. 13)

280. Taber, R. I., Banuazizi, A. Co_2-induced retrograde amnesia in a one-trial learning situation. *Psychopharmacologia*, **9**, 382–91 (1966)

281. Tapp, J.T., Zimmerman, R. S., D'encarnacao, P. S. Intercorrelational analysis of some common measures of rat activity. *Psychol. Rept.*, **23**, 1047–50 (1968)

282. Tatum, A. L., Seevers, M. H., Collins, K. H. Morphine addiction and its physiological interpretation based on experimental evidences. *J. Pharmacol. Exptl. Ther.*, **36**, 447–75 (1929)

283. Teitelbaum, P. Sensory control of hypothalamic hyperphagia. *J. Comp. Physiol. Psychol.*, **48**, 156–63 (1955)

284. Teitelbaum, P. The use of operant methods in the assessment of motivational states. *Operant Behavior: Areas of Research and Application*, 565–608 (See Ref. 6)

285. Teitelbaum, P., Epstein, A. N. The lateral hypothalamic syndrome: recovery of feeding and drinking after lateral hypothalamic lesions. *Psychol. Rev.*, **69**, 74–90 (1962)

286. Thistlethwaite, D. A critical review of latent learning and related experiments. *Psychol. Bull.*, **48**, 97–129 (1951)

287. Thompson, T. Drugs as reinforcers; experimental addiction. *Intern. J. Addictions*, **3**, 199–206 (1968)

288. Thompson, T., Ostlund, W., Jr. Susceptibility to readdiction as a function of the addiction and withdrawal environments. *J. Comp. Physiol. Psychol.*, **60**, 388–92 (1965)

289. Thompson, T., Pickens, R. Drug self-administration and conditioning. *Scientific Basis of Drug Dependence*, 177–98 (See Ref. 68)

290. Thompson, T., Schuster, C. R. Morphine self-administration, food-reinforced and avoidance behaviors in rhesus monkeys. *Psychopharmacologia*, **5**, 87–94 (1964)

291. Thomson, C. W., McGaugh, J. L., Smith, C. E., Hudspeth, W. J., Westbrook, W. H. Strain differences in the retroactive effects of electroconvulsive shock on maze learning. *Can. J. Psychol.*, **15**, 69–74 (1961)

292. Turner, P., Young, J. H., Paterson, J. Influence of urinary pH on the excretion of tranylcypromine sulphate. *Nature*, **215**, 881–82 (1967)

293. Ullman, A. D. The experimental production and analysis of a "compulsive eating symptom" in rats. *J. Comp. Physiol. Psychol.*, **44**, 575–81 (1951)

294. Valenstein, E. S. Biology of drives. *Neurosciences Res. Prog. Bull.*, **6**, 1–111 (1968)

295. Valenstein, E. S., Cox, V. C., Kakolewski, J. W. Modification of motivated behavior elicited by electrical stimulation of the hypothalamus. *Science*, **159**, 1119–21 (1968)

296. Venables, P. H. Input dysfunction in schizophrenia. *Progr. Exptl. Personality Res.*, **1**, 1–47 (1964)

297. Vogel, J. R., Hughes, R. A., Carlton, P. L. Scopolamine, atropine and conditioned fear. *Psychopharmacologia*, **10**, 409–16 (1967)

298. Watson, R. H. J. Modification of the effects of drugs on behaviour by the nutritional state. *Animal Behaviour and Drug Action*, 249–56 (See Ref. 49)

299. Weeks, J. R. Experimental morphine addiction; method for automatic intravenous injections in unrestrained rats. *Science*, **138**, 143–44 (1962)

300. Weijnen, J. A. W. M. Effects of amphetamine-amylobarbitone mixtures on ambulation of rats in the Y-maze. *Eur. J. Pharmacol.*, **5**, 180–84 (1969)

301. Weil-Malherbe, H. The passage of catechol amines through the blood-brain barrier. *Adrenergic Mechanisms*, 421–23 (Vane, J. R., Ed., Churchill, London, 1960)

302. Weihe, Von W. H., Bolliger, W. Apparat zur fortlaufenden Messung der Futter-und Wasseraufnahme und der Laufaktivität der Ratte. *Z. Versuchstierk.*, **5**, 38–45 (1964)

303. Weiskrantz, L., Ed. *Analysis of Behavioural Change* (See Ref. 14)

304. Weiss, B., Heller, A. Methodological problems in evaluating the role of

cholinergic mechanisms in behaviour. *Federation Proc.*, **28**, 135–46 (1969)

304a. Weiss, B., Laties, V. G. Behavioral pharmacology and toxicology. *Ann. Rev. Pharmacol.*, **9**, 297–326 (1969)

305. Weissman, A. Correlation between baseline nondiscriminated avoidance behavior in rats and amphetamine-induced stimulation. *Psychopharmacologia*, **4**, 294–97 (1963)

306. Weissman, A. Drugs and retrograde amnesia. *Intern. Rev. Neurobiol.*, **10**, 167–98 (1967)

307. Westbrook, W. H., McGaugh, J. L. Drug facilitation of latent learning. *Psychopharmacologia*, **5**, 440–46 (1964)

308. Whitehouse, J. M. Effects of atropine on discrimination learning in the rat. *J. Comp. Physiol. Psychol.*, **57**, 13–15 (1964)

309. Whitehouse, J. M. Cholinergic mechanisms in discrimination learning as a function of stimuli. *Ibid.*, **63**, 448–51 (1967)

310. Wikler, A., Pescor, F. T. Classical conditioning of a morphine abstinence phenomenon, reinforcement of opioid-drinking behavior and "relapse" in morphine-addicted rats. *Psychopharmacologia*, **10**, 255–84 (1967)

311. Wimer, R. E. Bases of a facilitative effect upon retention resulting from post-trial etherization. *J. Comp. Physiol. Psychol.*, **65**, 340–42 (1968)

312. Wimer, R. E., Fuller, J. L. Effects of *d*-amphetamine sulphate on three exploratory behaviours. *Can. J. Psychol.*, **19**, 94–103 (1965)

313. Wimer, R., Symington, L., Farmer, H., Schwartzkroin, P. Differences in memory processes between inbred mouse strains C57 BL/6J and DBA/2J. *J. Comp. Physiol. Psychol.*, **65**, 126–31 (1968)

314. Winer, B. J. *Statistical Principles in Experimental Design* (McGraw-Hill, London, 1962)

315. Yanagita, T., Deneau, G. A., Seevers, M. H. Evaluation of pharmacologic agents in the monkey by long term intravenous self or pro grammed administration. *Proc. Intern. Cong. Physiol. Sci., 23rd, Tokyo (1965)*, 453–57 (Excerpta Med. Intern. Congr. Ser. No. 87)

316. Zubin, J. Classification of the behavior disorders. *Ann. Rev. Psychol.*, **18**, 373–406 (1967)

317. Zubin, J., Katz, M. M. Psychopharmacology and personality. *Personality Change*, 367–95 (Worchel, P., Byrne, D. E., Eds., Wiley, New York, 1964)

AUTHOR INDEX

C

G

I

J

Y

SUBJECT INDEX

CUMULATIVE INDEXES

VOLUMES 17-21

INDEX OF CONTRIBUTING AUTHORS

INDEX OF CHAPTER TITLES

VOLUMES 17 -21